1996 SUPPLEMENT
to
THE TOOLS AND TECHNIQUES
OF ESTATE PLANNING
Tenth Edition

COVERING THE SMALL BUSINESS JOB PROTECTION ACT (SBJPA '96), AND THE HEALTH INSURANCE PORTABILITY AND ACCOUNTABILITY ACT (HIPAA '96)

CHAPTER 2, CHARITABLE CONTRIBUTIONS

Page 22

The special rule allowing donors who make contributions of qualified appreciated stock to deduct the full fair market value of the stock has been renewed. The rule expired on December 31, 1994 but has been extended for contributions made after June 30, 1996 and through May 31, 1997. Deductions for contributions made after December 31, 1994 and through June 30, 1996 were limited to the donor's adjusted basis. IRC Sec. 107(e)(5(D). SBJPA '96.

CHAPTER 8, EMPLOYEE DEATH BENEFIT EXCLUSION

The employee death benefit exclusion has been repealed for decedents dying after August 20, 1996. IRC Sec. 101(b). SBJPA '96, Sec. 1402(a).

CHAPTER 9, EMPLOYEE STOCK OWNERSHIP PLAN

Page 73, top of right column

The provision allowing lending institutions to exclude from tax 50% of interest income from ESOP securities acquisition loans has been repealed. The repeal takes effect for loans made after the date of enactment (i.e., August 20, 1996); however, exceptions are provided for certain financings of ESOP securities acquisition loans, and for loans made pursuant to a binding written contract in effect before June 10, 1996. IRC Sec. 133. SBJPA '96, Sec. 1602.

Page 77, top of right column

Beginning after 1996, S corporation stock may be held by an "electing small business trust." This may permit planning similar to that applicable to ESOPs and stock bonus plans. However, a tax exempt qualified plan trust is not eligible to be an electing small business trust. IRC Secs. 1361(c), 1361(e). SBJPA '96, Sec. 1302.

CHAPTER 13, FREEZING TECHNIQUES— CORPORATIONS AND PARTNERSHIPS

Pages 110-113

A number of statutory changes have been made to Code section 2701, all effective as if included in OBRA '90. Thus, the changes are retroactive to transfers after October 8, 1990. SBJPA '96, Sec. 1702(i).

Section 2701 has been amended to exclude from its coverage distribution rights with respect to qualified payments where there is no liquidation, put, call, or conversion right with respect to the distribution right. IRC Sec. 2701(a)(3)(C). SBJPA '96, Sec. 1702(f)(1)(A).

Section 2701 has been amended to state that, in the case of partnerships, regulations may provide that the term junior equity interest includes a partnership interest whose rights as to income *or* principal are junior to the rights of all other equity interests. IRC Sec. 2701(a)(4)(B)(i). SBJPA '96, Sec. 1702(f)(2).

Section 2701 has been modified to provide that distribution rights do not include a right to distributions with respect to any interest if such right is junior to the rights of the transferred interest. Previously, the exception applied to junior equity interests. IRC Sec. 2701(c)(1)(B)(i). SBJPA '96, Sec. 1702(f)(4).

For purposes of determining control of a corporation or partnership under Section 2701, the term "applicable family member" has been changed to include any lineal descendant of any parent of the transferor or the transferor's spouse. IRC Sec. 2701(b)(2)(C). SBJPA '96, Sec. 1702(f)(3)(A).

Section 2701 now provides that, with respect to the transferor, an otherwise qualified payment is to be treated as such unless the transferor elects otherwise. With respect to applicable family members, an otherwise qualified payment is not to be treated as such unless the applicable family member so elects. IRC Sec. 2701(c)(3)(C)(i). SBJPA '96, Sec. 1702(f)(5)(A).

Section 2701 now provides that a transferor or an applicable family member can elect to treat any distribution right as a qualified payment. IRC Sec. 2701(c)(3)(C)(ii). SBJPA '96, Sec. 1702(f)(5)(B).

Section 2701 has been amended to clarify that in the case of a transfer of an applicable retained interest from an applicable family member to the transferor, Section 2701 continues to apply as long as the transferor holds the interest. IRC Sec. 2701(d)(4)(C). SBJPA '96, Sec. 1702(f)(9).

Section 2701 has been amended to provide that adjustments to be made when property subject to Section 2701 is later transferred or included in the gross estate also include adjustments for any additional tax due to recapture of cumulative but unpaid distributions. IRC Sec. 2701(e)(6). SBJPA '96, Sec. 1702(f)(10).

CHAPTER 18, INDIVIDUAL RETIREMENT PLANS (AND SEPS)

Page 165, et. seq.

Effective for tax years beginning after 1996, non-working spouses are permitted to deduct up to $2,000 per year in contributions to an individual retirement arrangement, the same as their working counterparts. Previously, the maximum annual deductible contribution available to a married couple was $2,250 where one spouse had no compensation or elected to be treated as having no compensation; the combined limit for both spouses under the new provision is $4,000. IRC Sec. 219(c). SBJPA '96, Sec. 1427(a).

Page 167, second full paragraph

The 15% excess distribution penalty (but not the penalty on excess accumulations in deceased participant's estates) is suspended for years beginning after December 31, 1996 and before January 1, 2000. Distributions during this period are deemed to be made first from non-grandfathered amounts. IRC Sec. 4980A. SBJPA '96, Sec. 1452(b).

Page 169, right column, last paragraph of answer to first question

New salary reduction SEPs may not be adopted after December 31, 1996; however, existing arrangements established before 1997 may continue. IRC Sec. 408(k)(6). SBJPA '96, Sec. 1421(c).

Page 171, right column, add new question

Question—What is a SIMPLE plan?

Answer—The new law provides for plans referred to as "savings incentive match plans for employees" (SIMPLE) with the following major features:

- the plans are available only to employers with 100 or fewer employees (only employees with at least $5000 in compensation for the prior year are counted) during any 2 preceding years

- the plans are available only to employers who do not sponsor another qualified plan, 403(b) plan, or SEP

- contributions can be made to each employee's IRA or to a 401(k) account for the employee. In effect, there are thus two types of SIMPLE plans—those that include the 401(k) requirements, and those funded through IRAs.

- employees who earned at least $5000 from the employer in the preceding 2 years, and are reasonably expected to earn at least $5000 in the current year, can contribute (through salary reductions) up to $6,000 (indexed) annually

- the plans require an employer contribution equal t either

  a) a dollar for dollar matching contribution of up 3% of the employee's compensation (the emplo can elect a lower percentage, not less than 1%, not more than 2 out of any 5 years), or

  b) a nonelective contribution of 2% of compensati for all eligible employees earning at least $5,0((whether or not they elect salary reductions)

The new SIMPLE plans are somewhat simpler to administer and explain than the SARSEPs available under prior law, and SIMPLE plans are available to a broader range of employers (up to 100 employees instead of 25). However, the benefits to employees are potentially somewhat lower than from SARSEPs because of the $6,000 limitation (the 1996 SARSEP limitation was $9,500). Also, from the employer viewpoint, contributions to a SIMPLE are less flexible than for SARSEPs. IRC Sec. 408(p). SBJPA '96, Sec. 1421(a).

CHAPTER 21, LIFE INSURANCE

Accelerated Death Benefits

Generally, the new legislation states that any amount received under a life insurance contract on the life of a terminally ill insured or a chronically ill insured will be treated as an amount paid by reason of the death of the insured. Section 101(a) of the Code states that amounts received under a life insurance contract by reason of the death of the insured are not includable in gross income.

However, amounts paid to a chronically ill individual are subject to the same limitations that apply to long-term care benefits added to the Code in section 7702B(d). Generally, this is a $175 per day limitation. Accelerated death benefits paid to terminally ill individuals are not subject to this limit.

There are several special rules that apply to chronically ill insureds. Generally, the tax treatment outlined above will not apply to any payment received for any period unless such payment is for costs incurred by the payee (who has not been compensated by insurance or otherwise) for qualified long-term care services provided to the insured for the period. Additionally, the terms of the contract under which such payments are made must comply with the requirements of newly-added Code section 7702B plus several other requirements.

A terminally ill individual is a person who has been certified by a physician as having an illness or physical condition which can reasonably be expected to result in death within 24 months following the certification. A chronically ill individual is a person who is not terminally ill and who has been certified as being unable to perform, without substantial assistance, at least two activities of daily living (ADLs) for at least 90 days or a person with a similar level of disability. Further, a person may be considered chronically ill if he requires substantial supervision to protect himself from threats to his health and safety due to severe cognitive impairment and this condition has been certified by a health care practitioner within the previous 12 months.

There is one exception to this general rule of non-includability for accelerated death benefits. The rules outlined above do not apply to any amount paid to any taxpayer other than the insured if the taxpayer has an insurable interest in the life of the insured because the insured is a director, officer or employee of the taxpayer or if the insured is financially interested in any trade or business of the taxpayer.

These provisions are effective for amounts received after December 31, 1996. HIPAA '96, Sec. 331.

Company Owned Life Insurance

After TRA '86, a taxpayer could deduct policy loan interest on a policy covering the life of an officer or employee or an individual who was financially interested in the taxpayer's trade or business to the extent that the indebtedness did not exceed $50,000. The new legislation has eliminated the exception for debt less than $50,000, making nondeductibility the rule for policy loan interest on company-owned policies. The legislation did add another, even more limited, exception which states that the general nondeductibility rule does not apply to policy loan interest paid on policies insuring a "key person" up to $50,000 of indebtedness. A key person is an officer or 20 percent owner of the taxpayer. The number of persons who may be treated as key persons is limited to the greater of: (1) five persons; or (2) the lesser of five percent of the total officers and employees or 20 individuals. In effect, no more than 20 persons may be treated as key persons.

Additionally, the Code now imposes an interest rate cap for interest paid or accrued after December 31, 1995. Interest in excess of that which would have been paid had the "applicable rate of interest" been used cannot be deducted. The applicable rate of interest is that rate described in Moody's Corporate Bond Yield Average – Monthly Average Corporates as published by Moody's Investors Service. The Code section also specifies a manner in which to determine the applicable rate of interest for pre-1986 contracts.

Generally this provision is applicable to interest paid or accrued after October 13, 1995, but there are several transitional provisions. For indebtedness incurred before January 1, 1996 or indebtedness incurred before January 1, 1997 on contracts entered into in 1994 or 1995, these rules do not apply to qualified interest paid or accrued after October 13, 1995 and before January 1, 1999. There are several requirements for interest paid during this period to be considered qualified interest eligible for the transitional treatment. First, for interest paid or accrued after December 31, 1995, the indebtedness must not be with respect to more than 20,000 insured persons and it must use the lesser of the following rates: (1) the rate of interest stated in the contact as in effect on October 13, 1995; or (2) the applicable percentage of the interest rate as described by Moody's. The applicable percentage is 100 percent in 1996, 90 percent in 1997, and 80 percent in 1998. Generally, these rules, other than the interest rate cap, do not apply to policies issued before June 20, 1986.

The new provisions create a spread of income rule that may ease the transition out of company-owned life insurance policies with loans for some taxpayers. Any amount received from a policy subject to Code section 264(a)(4) upon the complete surrender, redemption or maturity of the policy during 1996, 1997 or 1998 or in full discharge during these years of the obligation under the policy which is in the nature of a refund of the consideration paid for the policy will be includable in gross income ratably over the four year period beginning with the taxable year such amount would have been included in income but for this rule. HIPAA '96, Sec. 501.

CHAPTER 28, PROFIT SHARING/PENSION PLAN

Page 243, right column, item 8

Distributions from qualified plans no longer have to begin by April 1 of the year following the year in which the participant attains age 70½, if the participant continues to work for the employer and is not a more than 5% owner. Instead, such distributions may be deferred until April 1 of the year following retirement. Note that this provision is not available to an owner of more than 5 percent of the business, as defined in the top-heavy rules, nor to IRA owners. This provision is effective for years beginning after December 31, 1996. IRC Sec. 401(a)(9). SBJPA '96, Sec. 1404.

Page 245, left column, second paragraph after "Eligibility" heading

The 50 employee/40% test has been modified. Beginning after 1996, it applies only to defined benefit plans and, as modified, states that a defined benefit plan must cover the lesser of (1) 50 employees of the employer, or (2) the greater of (a) 40% of all employees of the employer, or (b) 2 employees (or, if there is only 1 employee, that employee). IRC Sec. 401(a)(26). SBJPA '96, Sec. 1432(a).

Page 246, right column, beginning at "Combination Defined Benefit and Defined Contribution Plans"

The combined limits described under this heading is repealed effective after 1999. IRC Sec. 415(e). SBJPA '96, Sec. 1452(a).

Page 251, left column, item 3, part b

Five-year averaging is repealed for taxable years beginning after 1999. For taxpayers who attained age 50 before January 1, 1986, 10-year averaging will continue to be available as under prior law. IRC Secs. 402(d), 402(e)(4). SBJPA '96, Sec. 1401.

Page 252, left column, item 5

Effective for annuity starting dates that are later than November 18, 1996, the exclusion ratio method of recovering basis from annuity payments under a qualified plan or 403(b) plan is not generally available.

There is now a single method of recovering basis, similar to the safe harbor method referenced in footnote 63, but with the following table superseding the table contained therein (IRC Sec. 72(d). SBJPA '96, Sec. 1403.):

Age on annuity starting date	Number of anticipated payments
Not more than 55	360
More than 55 but not more than 60	310
More than 60 but not more than 65	260
More than 65 but not more than 70	210
More than 70	160

Page 252, left column, item 7

The 15% excess distribution penalty (but not the penalty on excess accumulations in deceased participant's estates) is suspended for years beginning after December 31, 1996 and before January 1, 2000. Distributions during this period are deemed to be made first from non-grandfathered amounts. This suspension is intended to provide interim relief until the repeal of the "combined plan formula" takes effect (as described above under page 246). Note also that 5-year averaging continues to be available during this suspension period. IRC Sec. 4980A. SBJPA '96, Sec. 1452(b).

Page 259, left column, answer to first question

The ADP tests have been revised to make them easier to administer. First, for years beginning after 1996, deferral percentages for nonhighly compensated employees are based on the preceding rather than the current year. IRC Sec. 401(k)(3)(A)(ii). SBJPA '96, Sec. 1433(c)(1). Also, beginning after 1998, an alternative ADP test has been added. Under this test, the nondiscrimination requirements are satisfied if the employer (a) satisfies a matching contribution requirement for nonhighly compensated employees (100 percent of the employee contribution up to 3 percent of compensation, plus 50 percent from 3 to 5 percent) and certain design requirements, or (b) the employer makes a nonelective (nonmatching) contribution for all eligible nonhighly compensated employees equal to at least 3 percent of compensation. IRC Sec. 401(k)(12). SBJPA '96, Sec. 1433(a).

SIMPLE 401(k) plans are subject to somewhat different design requirements. See the description above under page 171 for details. IRC Sec. 408(p). SBJPA '96, Sec. 1421(a).

CHAPTER 29, S CORPORATION

Pages 270-271

The legislation made several changes concerning the restrictive rules of S corporation formation. The following changes are effective for tax years beginning after December 31, 1996:

1. The number of permitted S corporation shareholders is increased from 35 to 75. IRC Sec. 1361(b)(1)(A). SBJPA '96, Sec. 1301.

2. The legislation creates "electing small business trust" as trusts, which along with qualified subchapter S trusts (QSSTs), are permitted as S corporation shareholders. An electing small business trust is one in which all of the beneficiaries are individuals or estates eligible to hold S corporation stock. However, charitable organizations are permitted to hold contingent remainder interests. An interest in an electing small business trust may not be obtained by "purchase." This means that it must be acquired by gift, bequest, or other means. A small business trust must "elect" to be treated as an electing small business trust. Neither a QSST nor a trust that is exempt from income tax is permitted to make this election. IRC Secs. 1361(c)(2)(A), 1361(c)(2)(B), 1361(e). SJPA '96, Sec. 1302.

3. A trust, all of which is treated as owned by the trust grantor or a beneficiary who is a citizen or resident of the United States (a "grantor" trust), is a permitted S corporation shareholder. IRC Sec. 1362 (c)(2)(A)(i). Under the legislation, a trust which is classified as a grantor trust, above, immediately before the death of the deemed owner and which continues in existence after such death, will be permitted to hold S corporation stock for two years instead of 60 days, which was the case under prior law. The two-year period begins on the day of the deemed owner's death. IRC Sec. 1361(c)(2)(A)(ii). SBJPA '96, Sec. 1303(1). The legislation also extends to two years the 60-day period for a trust with respect to stock transferred to it pursuant to the terms of a will. In this instance, the two-year period begins on the day on which such stock is transferred to the trust. IRC Sec. 1361(c)(2)(A)(iii). SBJPA '96, Sec. 1301(2).

4. An S corporation may now be a member of an affiliated group. That is, it may own 80 percent or more of the stock of a C corporation. IRC Sec. 1361(b)(2). SBJPA '96, Sec. 1308. To this end, the Code now contains provisions regarding the treatment of wholly owned subsidiaries. IRC Sec. 1361(b)(3). SBJPA '96, Sec. 1308.

5. An S corporation is also allowed to own a "qualified subchapter S subsidiary." A qualified subchapter S subsidiary is a domestic corporation that is not an ineligible corporation if (a) 100 percent of the stock of the subsidiary were held by its S corporation parent and (b) for which the parent elects to treat as a qualified subchapter S subsidiary. IRC Sec. 1361(b)(3)(B). SBJPA '96, Sec. 1308.

6. A financial institution is permitted as an S corporation unless it uses a reserve method of accounting for bad debts. IRC Sec. 1361(b)(2)(A). SBJPA '96, Sec. 1315.

Page 273

The legislation also provides added relief for inadvertent terminations and invalid elections. An S corporation is required to strictly follow the S election requirements. Failure to strictly follow these requirements could result in either an invalid S election or a termination of S status if the error occurred after the election was in effect. The Service is permitted certain discretion and may waive the effect of an "inadvertent" termination. Under the SBJPA '96, this discretion is extended to allow the Service to waive the effect of an invalid election caused by an inadvertent failure to qualify as a small business corporation or to obtain the required shareholder consents, or both. The SBJPA '96 also provides that the Service may treat a late election as timely if it determines that there was reasonable cause for the late election and steps were taken within a reasonable time after the discovery of the circumstances surrounding the inadvertent termination in order to correct same. IRC Sec. 1362(f). SBJPA '96, Sec. 1305(a).

CHAPTER 33, SURVIVOR'S INCOME BENEFIT PLAN

Page 296

The $5,000 employee death benefit exclusion has been repealed for decedents dying after August 20, 1996. IRC Sec. 101(b). SBJPA '96, Sec. 1402(a).

10th Edition

The Tools & Techniques of
Estate Planning

Stephan R. Leimberg, Jerry A. Kasner, Stephen N. Kandell,
Ralph Gano Miller, Morey S. Rosenbloom, Herbert L. Levy

Library of Congress Catalog Card Number: 95-74592

ISBN 0-87218-147-2

published by

NULAW SERVICES

a department of

THE NATIONAL UNDERWRITER COMPANY

Copyright © 1977, 1979, 1980, 1982, 1983, 1985,
1987, 1989, 1990, 1992, 1995
The National Underwriter Company
505 Gest Street
Cincinnati, Ohio 45203

Tenth Edition

Printed in the United States of America

DEDICATION

To our parents and our children
and others
whom we love,
who have taught us —
and from whom
we will learn so much more.
And to our friend and co-author,
Herbert L. Levy,
whom we deeply miss.

ABOUT THE AUTHORS

Stephan R. Leimburg

Stephan R. Leimberg designed the format for and is the principal author of this text and the entire *Tools and Techniques* Series. He has served as a full time member of the faculty of The American College since 1971 and is currently Professor of Taxation and Estate Planning. He has been granted the B.A. degree by Temple University, a J.D. by the Temple University School of Law, and holds the CLU designation. Mr. Leimberg is a Lecturer in Law in the Tax Masters of Temple University School of Law.

Professor Leimberg is on the Board of Advisors of the Bureau of National Affairs—Tax Management—Financial Planning, and Commerce Clearing House's Financial and Estate Planning Advisory Board. He was the co-chairman, with Sidney Kess, of the National Conference on Financial Planning and has served on the Personal Financial Planning Risk Management Task Force of the AICPA.

Mr. Leimberg is the editor and publisher of *Think About It*, a monthly newsletter on income, estate, and gift taxes relating to insurance, business and estate planning, published by many associations of life underwriters, CLU chapters, and insurance companies, *Golden Bullets*, a monthly client oriented newsletter on estate and business planning, and 11 client oriented brochures on estate, financial, and business succession planning.

Professor Leimberg has been a main platform speaker at the Million Dollar Round Table annual meeting, the Top of the Table, and at AALU. He has appeared before numerous estate planning councils, life underwriters associations, life insurance companies, and CPA societies. He has also addressed the International Association of Financial Planners, the state bars of Texas, Wisconsin and Oklahoma, the Pennsylvania Bar Institute Basic Legal Practice Course, numerous CPA societies, and has been a featured speaker at three workshops of the National Aeronautics and Space Administration. He appeared as an expert witness on IRAs before a subcommittee of the House Ways and Means Committee of the United States House of Representatives, and has conducted a series of courses on financial planning.

Professor Leimberg has also spoken at the N.Y.U. Tax Institute, the Southern California Tax and Estate Planning Forum, the Notre Dame Law School Estate Planning Institute, the Duke University Estate Planning Conference, and at the annual meeting of the National Association of Estate Planning Councils.

Leimberg has served on the Board of Directors of the Philadelphia CLU chapter, the Philadelphia Estate Planning Council, and was a director of the Delaware Valley Chapter of the International Association for Financial Planning, Inc. He has been awarded the "Planner of the Year" by the Montgomery County Estate Planning Council, the "President's Cup" by the Philadelphia Association of Life Underwriters, and has twice been named as Boris Todorovitch Lecturer by the New York Society of CLUs and ChFCs.

Jerry A. Kasner

Jerry A. Kasner is a Professor of Law at Santa Clara University. He has also been an Adjunct Professor of Law in the Graduate Tax Program at the University of San Diego and a Lecturer in the Graduate Estate Planning Program at the University of Miami (Florida). Professor Kasner is an attorney and a Certified Public Accountant in California. He is an Academic Fellow in the American College of Trusts and Estate Counsel. He is also presently acting as a consultant to the California Law Revision Commission.

Professor Kasner is the author of *Post Mortem Estate Planning* and the co-author of *After Death Tax Planning*. His articles have appeared in *Journal of Taxation, Taxation for Accountants, Community Property Journal, The Practical*

Lawyer, Tax Ideas, Phi-Net, and various other publications. He has also written course materials for the AICPA, California Continuing Education of the Bar, California Society of CPAs, and the College for Financial Planning.

He has appeared at numerous conferences for legal, accounting and other estate planning professionals throughout the country, including the New York University Tax Institute, the University of Miami Estate Planning Institute, the Southern California Tax and Estate Planning Forum, the Notre Dame Estate Planning Institute, AICPA Estate and Financial Planning Conferences, American College/CCH Financial Planning Conferences, *Trusts and Estates* Estate Planning Conference, and the IAFP Annual Conference.

About the Authors

Stephen N. Kandell

Stephen N. Kandell is a CLU (1973) and the Director of Estate and Business Analysis for Consolidated Brokerage Services, Inc., West Conshohocken, PA. He attended City College of New York (B.B.A. 1964) and completed his legal training at New York University School of Law (J.D. 1967 and LL.M. 1968). Mr. Kandell has written several articles in the estate planning field and has lectured before various groups on estate planning and taxation.

Ralph Gano Miller

Ralph Gano Miller is a member of the California Bar and a cum laude graduate of Stanford University with a BA and Masters Degree in Business Administration. He is a summa cum laude graduate of the University of San Diego Law School.

Mr. Miller is a CPA and author of numerous law review and journal articles on various estate planning tools and techniques. He is the author of the estate planning Primer and co-authored the Tax Planning Handbook for Educators on income tax, as well as the Handbook of Estate Planning. He is the designer of ViewPlan's Estate Forecast Model software, and currently edits ViewPlan's quarterly newsletter, the ViewPlanner. He has served as a member of the Board of Regents of the University of San Diego Law School, and as a professor of federal income taxation and gift and estate taxation at the California Western Law School.

He was a founding member of the Independent Board of Trustees of the California Western University Law School. He was an instructor of the Advanced Estate Planning Course of the CLU program for many years and has spoken at many tax institutes, including the New York University and University of Southern California Tax Institutes.

He is a member of the American Bar Association Sections on Taxation and Real Property, Probate and Trust Law and served as Chairman of the Administrative Law Section.

Mr. Miller has served as Chairman, Section of Taxation, of the San Diego County Bar Association's Section on Taxation and Real Property, Probate and Trust Law. He served as President of the Southern California Estate Planning Council.

He is past Chairman of the Taxation Advisory Commission, Board of Legal Specialization for the State Bar of California, and is a certified specialist in tax law in California. He also served as a member of the Board of Legal Specialization.

Mr. Miller is the Chairman of Miller, Ewald & Monson, a Professional Law Corporation in San Diego, California.

Morey S. Rosenbloom

Morey S. Rosenbloom is a principal in CMS Companies, a Philadelphia based personal investment banking firm. Prior to his joining CMS, Mr. Rosenbloom was a partner in the Philadelphia law firm of Blank, Rome, Comisky & McCauley. He graduated from Temple University School of Law and served as a legal assistant to the then Chief Justice, John C. Bell, of the Supreme Court of the commonwealth of Pennsylvania.

Mr. Rosenbloom is an adjunct professor of law at the Law School at Temple University and has been an instructor of the American College Advanced Estate Planning Course. He has served as the Chairman of the Real Property, Probate and Trust Law Section of the Pennsylvania Bar Association.

He has lectured at numerous seminars on the topic of estate and business planning to various legal, banking, insurance and estate planning groups throughout the country.

Mr. Rosenbloom has co-authored many publications and articles, including *Practical Will Drafting, Computing The Federal Estate Tax, The Wait and See Buy-Sell, and Funding Corporate Buy-Sell Agreements With Life Insurance.*

Herbert L Levy

Herbert L. Levy was, before his death in December, 1982, in the private practice of law in Allentown, Pa. He graduated from City University of New York (B.S. in accounting, 1964), St. John's University School of Law (J.D. 1966) and New York University School of Law (LL.M. in taxation, 1967) where he served as Tax Editor of the N.Y.U. *Tax Law Review*.

He was co-author of *Introduction to Estates and Trusts Practice in the Commonwealth of Pennsylvania* (7 editions).

Mr. Levy instructed the American College's Advanced Estate Planning Course and was a frequent lecturer on estate planning and taxation.

ACKNOWLEDGMENTS

We wish to thank attorney Charles K. Plotnik for his chapters on selection of an executor, trustee, and attorney and a probate primer for the could be executor.

NumberCruncher software illustrations throughout the book are courtesy of Leimberg and LeClair, Inc. (610-527-5216). The Estate Forecast Model software illustrations are courtesy of ViewPlan, Inc., P.O. Box 80788, San Diego, CA, 92138 (800-826-2127).

Special thanks to William J. Wagner, J.D., LL.M., CLU, of the National Underwriter staff who was the major technical editor of this 10th edition. Bill, along with the following staff, does much more than merely "polish up" a fine job; he and his associates proof voluminous copy, meticulously check each point for accuracy, and assure an up-to-the-last-minute update before *Tools and Techniques* goes to press. Thank you, Deborah A. Miner, J.D., CLU, ChFC; William W. Thomas, III, J.D., CLU; Darlene K. Chandler, J.D., CLU, ChFC; April A. Caudill, J.D., CLU, ChFC; Peter A. Fossett, J.D., CLU, ChFC; Kimberely J. Adams, J.D; Scott W. Baker, J.D.; for your help.

Most importantly, the authors would like to acknowledge you, our loyal readers, who have kept *Tools and Techniques* one of the most widely read professional books on estate planning ever. Many of you have had every one of the previous nine editions on your shelves. To you, and to those of you for whom the 10th is the first, we want you to know how very much we appreciate your trust.

PREFACE TO THE TENTH EDITION

Ten editions of a book, any book, is a major accomplishment. The popularity and endurance of this and the other TOOLS AND TECHNIQUES books lies in several areas: First, our readers are busy. They want concise information. Second, they want information presented objectively. Third, they want to be able to compare that information (i.e., a given tool or technique) with other information. Fourth, they want accurate information. Finally, they want to know the tools that will help them help others in a cost-efficient highly practical manner.

All five of these characteristics must be practiced by the readers of this book. You must provide clients with concise information because they are busier than ever before. They want to know the pros - and the cons - of any suggestion you provide. They want to know of any alternatives to those concepts you have given them - and why you have selected one course of action over another. Of course, they want you to get it right the first time. Your ideas must be practical and able to be implemented in a cost efficient manner.

Your role continues to be to absorb and understand highly complex information consisting of both tax and nontax law, and select between or create the proper mix among the various tools and techniques to put a workable plan into effect. But more than ever, it is your ability to understand the client and convey your ultimate suggestions in relatively simple terms that will make the difference.

Yet another dimension to the entire estate planning process is ethics. It is important for you to distinguish between a strictly legalistic view of ethics and ethics as a higher standard, an acknowledgement of your own personal responsibility to your clients. In other words the standards to which you hold yourself as a member of the estate planning team must rise much higher than the mere avoidance of legal violations or the appearance of a conflict of interest. You must decide - as you practice day by day - to root out the cause of misconduct, to use your moral imagination, to consider the moral legitimacy of your choices, and strive for far more than moral mediocrity.

A strong part of your professional ethical mandate is to continually acquire new knowledge to assist clients in making decisions. A portion of your ethical responsibility to gain new knowledge was met when your purchased and as you read this book. But now you have many ethical decisions to make concerning how to apply that new knowledge. You can not ethically advise a client on estate planning matters by refusing to consider what you have learned in your CFP, CLU, ChFC, law school, or CPA studies.

My co-authors and I urge you to continue to use all the resources at your command to gain knowledge. But with your knowledge - gain both wisdom - and the core of ethical strength to apply that information to properly and compassionately help others not only as an "expert" but also as a caring human being.

We hope you will read our many new chapters - and review those that have changed since the publication of the 9th Edition. My co-authors and I hope the 10th Edition of TOOLS AND TECHNIQUES OF ESTATE PLANNING provides you with the "instant answers" resource it was meant to be.

Stephan R. Leimberg

INTRODUCTION AND BIBLIOGRAPHY

Estate planning is a fascinating subject. No two problems are ever quite the same and no perfect answers or well-established rules exist to solve problems. Estate planning is not merely planning to save or reduce taxes during lifetime or at death; it is far more complex because a person and his or her relationship with property and other people is involved.

There is no easy way to learn estate planning. The field is vast, increasingly complex, and covers not only income, estate, and gift tax law but involves many facets of corporate, probate, estate, trust, and securities law as well.

The essential concern is to ascertain all the facts, whether they may seem material or relevant at the time. From those facts you must then recognize and clearly state the problems. Then the real challenge begins: finding or creating the appropriate solutions.

A good library of up-to-date texts, tapes and articles is essential. The following is a list of some of the books and information sources we have found useful: (It is extremely important to check with the publisher to see if the version you are purchasing or using is the most recent version and if it encompasses all of the major tax law changes.)

Bittker and Eustice, *Federal Income Taxation of Corporations and Shareholders*, (Student Edition), Warren, Gorham and Lamont

Bureau of National Affairs, *Tax Management Income, Estates, Gifts and Trusts Portfolios*

Bureau of National Affairs, *Tax Management Financial Planning Service*

Casner, *Estate Planning*, Little, Brown and Co.

Commerce Clearing House, Inc., *Federal Tax Articles*

Commerce Clearing House, Inc., *Financial and Estate Planning Reporter*

Commerce Clearing House, Inc., *Inheritance Estate and Gift Tax Reporter*

Ferguson, Freeland and Stephens, *Federal Income Taxation and Estates and Beneficiaries*, Little, Brown and Co.

Harris, *Handling Federal Estate and Gift Taxes*, Bancroft Whitney

Helfert, *Techniques of Financial Analysis*, Dow, Jones, Irwin, Inc.

Hendrickson, *Interstate and International Estate Planning*, Practicing Law Institute

Herz and Baller, *Business Acquisitions: Planning and Practice*, Practicing Law Institute

Kahn and Colson, *Federal Taxation of Estates and Trusts*, ALI-ABA

Leimberg, *The Cutting Edge*, Leimberg Assoc.

Leimberg, Kazenbloom and Yohlin, *The Corporate Buy-Sell Handbook*, Dearborn Financial Press

Leimberg, Satinsky, Ivers, Krader, and Parker, *The Federal Income Tax Law*, Warren, Gorham, and Lamont

Mertens, *Law of Federal Gift and Estate Taxation*, Lofit Publications, Inc.

Mertens, *Law of Federal Income Taxation*, Callahan and Co.

Nossaman and Wyatt, *Trust Administration and Taxation*, Matthew Bender and Co.

Prentice-Hall, *Tax Ideas*

Rabkin and Johnson, *Current Legal Forms With Tax Analysis*, Matthew Bender and Co.

Rabkin and Johnson, *Federal Income Gift and Estate Taxation*, Matthew Bender and Co.

Sellin, *New York University Institute on Federal Taxation*, Matthew Bender and Co.

Stephens, Maxfield and Lind, *Federal Estate and Gift Taxation*, Warren, Gorham and Lamont

Tax Facts 1 and 2, The National Underwriter Company

Warren and Surrey, *Federal Estate and Gift Taxation*, Foundation Press

Weisz, *Supertrust III*

Zaritsky, *Structuring Buy-Sell Agreements*, Warren, Gorham and Lamont

Zaritsky, *Tax Planning for Family Wealth Transfers*, Warren, Gorham and Lamont

We highly recommend tax services such as Prentice-Hall, Research Institute of America, and Commerce Clearing House. These services are most useful. The Advanced Sales Reference Service, published by The National Underwriter Company, has a strong following within the life insurance industry. Additionally, journals such as the *Journal of Taxation, Tax Law Review, Taxes, Taxation for Lawyers, Estate Planning, Taxation for Accountants, Trusts and Estates, Financial Planning Magazine, The Practical Lawyer*, and *The CLU Journal* are highly useful.

One of the best tools for "Keeping Current" is a quarterly cassette service of the same name available from the American Society of Chartered Life Underwriters.

A service that specializes in the taxation and uses of life insurance in business and estate planning is *Think About It*, a monthly newsletter used extensively by life underwriters associations and insurance companies throughout the country.

Keep in mind that TOOLS AND TECHNIQUES is a survey text. It is not meant to be a detailed examination of any one particular area. We have tried to design the text to give you enough familiarity with an area so that when doing research, you will have an initial understanding of that area.

Because no single text can replace broad, substantive courses in estate and gift taxation planning coupled with a case study approach, we strongly recommend the two-part Masters-level Advanced Estate Planning Course of The American College and the Advanced Estate Planning courses of the College For Financial Planning. Helpful background and supplementary technical reading may be found in the *Advanced Sales Reference Service*, referred to earlier. References to "ASRS" appearing immediately above "Footnote References" at the ends of chapters are to this service.

PRINCIPLES OF COMMUNITY PROPERTY LAW

Arizona, California, Idaho, Louisiana, Nevada, New Mexico, Texas, Washington, and Wisconsin all use some form of the community property system in establishing the legal relationship between a husband and wife. The general theory is that the husband and wife form a partnership and that property acquired during marriage by the labor and skill of either belongs to both. Community property laws originate from the community property system of Spain, transplanted in turn to Mexico and California.

Community property laws have significant effects on the legal relationships between spouses who reside or formerly resided in one of the eight community property states. To help illustrate those effects, sections have been added to various chapters discussing community property implications and issues relating to the chapter's subject matter.

In many respects, the laws of the community property states are different. Focus will be placed on California's community property laws. Thus, *while general principles should be noted, the community property laws of a particular state should be reviewed before relying on any discussion.*

California law generally defines community property to be all real property situated in California and all personal property wherever situated acquired during marriage, other than separate property, by a married person while domiciled in California. The husband and wife have equal interests in all community property.

California law generally defines separate property as (1) property owned by either spouse before marriage, (2) property acquired after marriage by gift, devise, bequest or descent, (3) in certain respects, the rents, issues and profits of separate property and (4) property acquired during marriage with the proceeds of separate property. Separate property is owned solely by the spouse who originally acquired it.

California law provides, however, that if the spouses separate, their respective earnings and profits accruing after the date of separation are their separate property. Thus, it is not an absolute rule that earnings during marriage in California are community property. The spouses may also alter the normal community property rules by agreement.

Many married couples move into California, having accumulated property in separate property states. In these situations, some of the property may be characterized under California law as quasi-community property.

Quasi-community property is all real or personal property, wherever situated, which would have been community property if the spouses had acquired the property while living in California. Quasi-community property is treated as separate property of the acquiring spouse for all purposes other than division on divorce or upon the death of the acquiring spouse. In the event of divorce or the death of the acquiring spouse, quasi-community property is treated similarly to community property (except that only real property situated in California is treated as quasi-community property in the event of a division on death of the acquiring spouse). As quasi-community property rights apply only to division on divorce or upon the death of the acquiring spouse, the property will retain its separate property character if the non-acquiring spouse dies first.

Courts in several community property states, especially California, have also found that non-married couples can expressly or impliedly agree to apply community property principles to earnings and accumulations during their relationship. In some cases, one "partner" has proven such an agreement over the denial of the other. Although the non-married couple may feel uncomfortable discussing property rights, in many situations major problems could be avoided by an appropriate agreement.

CONTENTS

Contents

Appendix A

Appendix B

Appendix C

Appendix D

Appendix E

BUY-SELL (BUSINESS CONTINUATION) AGREEMENT

WHAT IS IT?

A business continuation agreement is an arrangement for the disposition of a business interest in the event of the owner's death, disability, retirement, or upon withdrawal from the business at some earlier time. Business continuation agreements can take a number of forms:

(1) an agreement between the business itself and the individual owners (either a corporate stock redemption agreement or partnership liquidation agreement), frequently called an "entity" plan;

(2) an agreement between the individual owners (a cross-purchase or "criss-cross" agreement);

(3) an agreement between the individual owners and key person, family member, or outside individual (a "third-party" business buy-out agreement); or

(4) a combination of the foregoing.

In the case of corporations, the most common types of business continuation agreements are stock redemption plans (often called stock retirement plans), or shareholder cross-purchase plans. The distinguishing feature of the redemption agreement is that the corporation itself agrees to purchase (redeem) the stock of the withdrawing or deceased shareholder. In a cross-purchase plan the individuals agree between or among themselves to purchase the interest of a withdrawing or deceased shareholder.

In the case of a partnership, an agreement similar to the corporate stock redemption plan is the partnership liquidation agreement, where the partnership in effect purchases the interest of the deceased or withdrawing shareholder by distributing assets in liquidation of his or her interest or the partners agree to a cross-purchase similar to the corporate cross-purchase plan.

WHEN IS THE USE OF SUCH A DEVICE INDICATED?

1. When a guaranteed market must be created for the sale of a business interest in the event of death, disability, or retirement.

2. When it is necessary or desirable to "peg" the value of the business for federal and state death tax purposes.

3. When a shareholder or partner would be unable or unwilling to continue running the business with the family of a deceased co-owner.

4. When the business involves a high amount of financial risk for the family of a deceased owner and it is desirable to convert the business interest into cash at his or her death.

5. When it is necessary or desirable to prevent all or part of the business from falling into the hands of "outsiders."

    This could include a buyout of an owner's interest in the event of a divorce, disability, or insolvency, if there is a danger a business interest would be transferred to a former spouse or creditors.

6. Where it is desirable to lend certainty to the disposition of a family closely-held business. Rather than relying on will provisions of a parent to transfer the business interest, a binding buy-sell agreement between parent and child could be used. However, under Section 2703 of the Internal Revenue Code, this has become exceedingly difficult.

WHAT ARE THE REQUIREMENTS?

A written agreement is drawn stating the purchase price, terms, and funding arrangements. The agreement obligates the retiring or disabled owner or owner's estate to sell the business either (a) to the business itself, (b) to the surviving owner(s), or (c) to a third party nonowner. Occasionally the agreement combines the types of obligations. For example, the agreement may give the other owners the option to purchase the stock or partnership interest, but provide that if they fail to exercise that option, the interest must be redeemed or liquidated by the corporation or partnership. Conversely, the agreement may provide that if the entity cannot purchase the interest, the remaining owners have either an obligation or option to do so. Such agreements must be carefully drafted to avoid a situation in which the entity discharges an obligation of the other owners to purchase the interest, which could have adverse tax consequences to the other owners. For example, if the shareholders under the agreement are obligated to buy the stock of a deceased shareholder, and the corporation redeems the stock, the amount of the obligation of which the remaining shareholders are relieved could be considered a taxable dividend to them.

The buy-sell agreement specifies the event triggering the respective obligations. Generally that event is death, disability, or retirement of the owner. However, as already indicated, it could include divorce or insolvency, and could also include such events as loss of a professional license by an owner or conviction of an owner of a crime. Valuation may be based on several factors, including book value, asset value, formula value, or some agreed amount.

"Funding" pertains to how the promises under the agreement will be financed. Generally, in a redemption or liquidation agreement, the business will purchase, own, and be the beneficiary of life and disability income insurance on each person who owns an interest in the business.

In the case of a cross-purchase agreement, the prospective buyer (each business associate) purchases, owns, and is beneficiary of a life and disability income insurance policy on his or her co-owners.

HOW IT IS DONE — AN EXAMPLE

Stock Redemption Plan

Herb and Steve are equal stockholders in a business valued at $500,000. The business purchases $250,000 of life insurance and a policy providing $2,500 a month of disability insurance on both men.

At Herb's death, his stock passes to his estate. The life insurance proceeds on Herb's life are paid to the business. Then the business pays the cash proceeds to Herb's estate according to the agreement. In return for the cash, Herb's executor transfers the stock to the business. Steve, therefore, ends up with ownership of all the outstanding voting stock (the stock owned by the business itself is not entitled to vote).

Under the buy-sell agreement, should Herb become totally disabled prior to retirement, he would receive his full salary for one year. At the end of a year of total disability, Herb's interest would be sold to the business. The business would pay at least $25,000 (10 percent of $250,000) as a down payment to Herb. The business would also issue Herb a 10-year note (secured by his stock which is placed in an escrow account) for the remaining value of the stock, $225,000. The business would pay 9 percent interest on the note (assuming 9% is the safe harbor rate needed to avoid the unstated interest rules of

Code section 483). Thus, Herb would receive approximately $2,500 a month for 120 months. In order to help pay off the note, the business would receive $2,500 a month of disability income insurance proceeds from a policy owned by and made payable to the business.

In the event Herb retired, he would sell his stock to the business. The business would pay Herb at least $25,000 (10 percent of $250,000) as a down payment, plus it would give Herb a 10-year note (secured by his stock) for the remaining $225,000. The business would also pay Herb 9 percent interest. Herb, therefore, would receive about $2,500 a month for 120 months. The cash value of the life insurance policy on Herb's life could be used to help finance the down payment. One limiting factor, in general, is that in many states, the corporation can redeem its stock only to the extent it has earned surplus.

Cross-Purchase Agreement

Assume Herb and Steve are equal stockholders in a business valued at $500,000. Herb purchases a $250,000 life insurance policy and a $2,500 a month disability income policy on Steve's life. Steve purchases policies in an equal amount on Herb's life.

Assuming Herb dies first, his stock passes to his estate. The insurance proceeds on Herb's life are paid directly to Steve. Steve then pays cash to Herb's estate according to the cross-purchase agreement. In return for the cash, Herb's executor transfers stock to Steve. Therefore, Steve becomes the sole owner of the corporation.

In the event of Herb's disability, he receives his full salary for one year assuming he is totally disabled. At that time, Herb must sell his business interest to Steve. Steve will pay at least $25,000 (10 percent) down payment to Herb. Steve will also give Herb a 10-year note (secured by his stock) for the balance upon which he will pay 9 percent interest. This will provide approximately $2,500 a month for 120 months. During this time, Steve will be receiving $2,500 a month of income from a disability income insurance policy purchased on Herb's life which can be used to pay off the note.

At Herb's retirement, Herb will sell his stock to Steve. Steve will pay at least $50,000 (10 percent) down payment to Herb. Steve will also give Herb a 10-year note (secured by his stock) for the $225,000 balance. Interest at 9 percent will be paid so that Herb will receive about $2,500 a month for 120 months. Steve can use the cash value of the policy he owns on Herb's life to provide the down payment.

WHAT ARE THE TAX IMPLICATIONS?

Stock Redemption Agreements

1. Assuming the corporation is owner and beneficiary of the policy(ies), the value of the insurance on the decedent's life will not be includable (as insurance proceeds per se) in his gross estate for federal estate tax purposes. However, the insurance proceeds will be considered in valuing the decedent's interest in the business unless there is a valid agreement fixing the price for federal estate tax purposes and the proceeds are excluded from the purchase price under the terms of the agreement.[1]

    The agreement will generally establish the value of the business for federal estate tax purposes if: (1) the estate is obligated to sell at the decedent-shareholder's death, or the estate is obligated to offer the decedent's shares at his or her death at the agreement price; (2) the agreement prohibits the shareholder from disposing of his interest during his lifetime without first offering it to the corporation at no more than the contract price; (3) the price was fair and adequate at the time the agreement was made and resulted from a bona fide arms-length transaction; and (4) the price must be fixed by the terms of the agreement, or the agreement must contain a formula or method for determining price.[2] Where the shareholders or partners are related, or the "natural objects of the bounty" of each other, there are additional requirements, discussed later under the heading "Family Business Enterprises."

2. Life insurance or disability income premiums used to fund the agreement are not deductible by the corporation.[3] On the other hand, death proceeds (or disability income proceeds) will be received by the corporation income tax free.[4] (But see discussion later on alternative minimum tax). Premiums paid by the corporation will not be taxable income to its shareholders.

3. The biggest potential problem in a corporate stock redemption agreement is the possibility that the redemption will be treated as a dividend distribution. The Internal Revenue Code states the general rule that distributions of money or property in redemption of stock by a corporation will be treated as a dividend (subject to ordinary income taxation to the extent of the corporation's earnings and profits) unless the distribution or redemption meets certain exceptions to the general rule. The most common exception is that a redemption of all of a shareholder's stock (a complete termination of his interest) will not be treated as a dividend.

    For example, Herb and Steve, unrelated parties, own stock in a closely held corporation. Herb dies and his stock passes to his estate. The corporation redeems all of Herb's stock from his estate. The result is a total redemption. The distribution will not be subjected to dividend treatment because Herb's estate has given up all control, share of future profits, and share of future assets in the event of a sale or liquidation of the corporation, i.e., Herb's estate has completely terminated its interest.

The favorable tax treatment can be complicated or even thwarted by what is known as "constructive ownership" (attribution) rules.[5] Essentially, the basic constructive ownership rules work as follows:

a. The "estate/beneficiary" attribution rule. Under this rule, stock owned by a beneficiary of an estate is considered constructively (treated for tax purposes as if it were actually) owned by the estate.[6] A redemption of all the stock actually owned by the estate (without a simultaneous redemption of stock owned by a beneficiary) may be considered a partial redemption and may be taxable to the estate as a dividend. The estate is still considered a stockholder because it is deemed to own stock actually owned by the beneficiary.

    For example, Herb and Steve are father and son. Herb owns 75 percent of the stock while Steve owns the remaining 25 percent. Steve is a beneficiary under Herb's will. If the corporation redeems only Herb's stock from his executor, the entire amount paid by the corporation for the stock may be treated and taxed as a dividend (to the extent of corporate earnings and profits) because the redemption is *deemed* to be of less than all the stock owned directly or indirectly by the estate. After the redemption, the estate is considered to own *all* the outstanding shares of the corporation because Steve's stock is attributed to (deemed to be owned by) Herb's estate.

    In other words, Herb's estate constructively owns the shares actually owned by Herb's son. (It may be possible to avoid the estate/beneficiary attribution rule by "eliminating the beneficiary." If, before the redemption takes place, the son has received all the property to which he is entitled from the estate, no longer has a claim against the estate, and no liabilities of the estate can be assessed against him as a beneficiary, his stock will not be attributed to the estate because he will no longer be considered a beneficiary.)

b. The "family/trust/corporation" attribution rule. Under this rule, an individual is considered to own the stock owned directly or indirectly by or for his or her spouse, children, grandchildren, and parents. Stock owned by certain other parties and entities is also attributed to and from each party or entity in determining whether all the stock has been redeemed.[7] These other parties include:

(i) With certain exceptions, a trust and its beneficiaries.

(ii) A partnership and its partners.

(iii) A corporation and over 50% shareholders.

There is also the possibility of an incomplete termination as a result of stock being attributed from a close family member to an estate beneficiary and in turn through the estate beneficiary to the estate.

For example, Herb owns 1,000 shares in a closely held corporation. His son, Steve, owns the remaining 500 shares. Herb's widow is the sole beneficiary under Herb's will. Even if the corporation immediately redeems Herb's entire 1,000 shares at his death, the redemption will be treated as less than a complete redemption and therefore may become subject to dividend treatment because Steve's 500 shares are attributed to (treated as if owned by) his mother under the family attribution rules. Then the shares she is deemed to own are in turn considered to be owned by Herb's estate under the estate/beneficiary attribution rules. So even after all the shares Herb actually owned are purchased by the corporation from Herb's estate, his estate is still constructive owner of all the outstanding stock of the corporation. Steve's shares are traced to his mother and from her to Herb's estate.

There is an exception to the family attribution rule. Under certain circumstances, it may be possible to "waive" the family attribution rule (but not the estate or entity rules) and therefore break the "chain" between family members. This "10-year waiver rule" works as follows: In essence, the family attribution rules will not apply if, immediately following the redemption, the stockholder whose stock is redeemed has no interest in the corporation (except as creditor) and agrees not to acquire an interest for 10 years following the redemption, other than by bequest or inheritance.[8]

One of the difficulties of implementing a redemption of a family member coupled with a waiver of family attribution is the unwillingness of a key person, often a founder of the business, to completely disassociate from it. The cases are clear that he or she cannot function in any capacity (other than creditor), even as a consultant.

In the example discussed above, Herb's executor would sell Herb's stock to the corporation. Herb's widow would notify the IRS of her election to waive attribution between her son, Steve, and herself. Because she doesn't own any stock personally and because she has "waived" her right to receive any stock except by bequest or inheritance, when the corporation redeems the stock held by the estate's executor, there is no attribution from Steve to her and then from her to the estate. Therefore, the redemption results in a complete termination of the estate's interest. The proceeds of the redemption, therefore, are not subject to dividend treatment.

Entities such as a corporation, trust, or estate may waive the constructive ownership and break the fictional ownership linkage from a family member who actually owns stock to a beneficiary who does not (but is deemed to own it). The individual who is deemed to own stock must join in the waiver. After the redemption, neither the entity nor the beneficiary may hold an interest in the corporation. They must agree not to acquire such an interest for at least 10 years. They must also agree to notify the IRS if they do acquire such an interest. There is joint and several liability in the event either the entity or the waiving family members acquires a prohibited interest within the 10-year period. The statute of limitations remains open during that time for the IRS to levy on any deficiency.

It is important to note that an entity may break the fictional linkage only between family members; it may not waive "entity" attribution, the constructive ownership between a beneficiary and an entity. For example, assume 30 percent of the stock of a corporation is owned by a trust. Its beneficiaries, Michael, David, and Danny Green, own no stock personally. Debbie Green, the trust beneficiaries' mother, owns 52 percent of the corporation's stock. The remaining stock is held by unrelated employees of the corporation.

Assume the trust sells all of its stock back to the corporation. The redemption is still not complete because the trust's beneficiaries, Michael, David, and Danny, are deemed to own stock owned by their mother through the "family" attribution rule. The stock they are deemed to own is then attributed from them to the trust through the entity attribution rule. So the redemption of stock from the trust would be less than complete. But if the trust and all three brothers waive attribution and break the link connecting the mother's stock to the sons, the redemption would be complete. But what if one or more of the sons actually owned stock in the corporation? In that case the trust could break the link from Debbie Green to her children (the family attribution) but not the link between the children and itself (the entity attribution).

4. A purchase (either through stock redemption or cross-purchase) of a decedent-shareholder's interest generally means that the estate of a decedent will not realize any taxable gain for income tax purposes. The stock purchased from the estate obtains a "stepped-up basis," i.e., a new "cost" in the executor's hands equal to its value for federal estate tax purposes.[9] Because the purchaser generally pays a price equal to the value of the stock at the applicable federal estate tax valuation date, there would not be any gain realized by the estate; the amount paid for the stock equalled the basis of the stock in the hands of the executor.

For example, on January 1, 1980, Herb and Steve, who are unrelated, each invested $50,000 in a corporation that is worth $500,000 ($250,000 each) at Herb's death. If the corporation paid Herb's estate $250,000 in complete redemption of his stock, there would be no income tax consequences to his estate because the estate's basis in the stock is "stepped up" from $50,000 to $250,000 (the value for death tax purposes) and this was the amount received by the estate under the redemption. The "amount realized" ($250,000) by the estate did not exceed the estate's basis ($250,000) and so there is no taxable gain.

But note, the surviving shareholder (Steve) does not receive an increase in basis for income tax purposes since the corporation is redeeming Herb's stock. In a cross purchase arrangement, if Steve had purchased Herb's stock from his estate, Steve would receive an increase in basis by the amount of the price paid.

5. Congress was concerned corporations would be able to report large profits for financial accounting purposes but report little profit (and therefore pay little or no tax) for income tax purposes. So it imposed a revenue raising measure called the corporate alternative minimum tax (AMT). This is based on a variety of adjustments to the taxable income of the corporation to arrive at an amount defined as "alternative minimum taxable income" (AMTI).[10]

For tax years beginning after 1989, roughly speaking, "C" (regular) corporations must pay AMT at a 20 percent rate on an amount equal to 75 percent of the excess of certain earnings and profits (technically called "adjusted current earnings," or "ACE") over alternative minimum taxable income.

Here's a simplified example of how it works with respect to

A. Death Benefits from corporate owned life insurance:

Step 1:	State the total death benefit	$_____
Step 2:	State the cash value	$_____
Step 3:	Subtract to find the Net Amount at Risk	$_____
Step 4:	Multiply Step 3 Result by	.75
	Amount Taxable	$_____
Step 5:	Multiply by AMT rate	.20
	Alternative Minimum Tax	$_____

For instance, if your client's C corporation receives $1,200,000 of (otherwise income tax free) life insurance proceeds at the death of its key man, assuming the cash surrender value of the policy was $200,000 the day before the key person's death, the net amount at risk would be $1,000,000. Because only 75 percent is taxable, $750,000 (.75 x $1,000,000) would be exposed to tax at a 20 percent rate. This means the net alternative minimum tax is $150,000 (.20 x $750,000).

You can compute the amount necessary before the AMT to net your "target amount" by multiplying the target amount by 118%. For example, suppose your client's target amount is $1,000,000. To net this much after any possible AMT, your client should purchase $1,180,000 ($1,000,000 x 118%). Using the five step formula above, out of $1,180,000, $885,000 would be subject to the AMT. The AMT, at a 20 percent rate, would be $177,000. The net result, $1,003,000 is just slightly more than the $1,000,000 target amount. (To be precise, multiply your target amount by 117.7%).

It is important to understand that the AMT is truly an alternative tax, not an additional tax. Once the total AMT is computed, as in the above example, that amount is compared to the "regular" tax on the corporate income for the year in question. The alternative amount is paid only if it is higher than the regular tax.

Keep in mind that payments of AMT are more like prepayments of a future tax than a separate tax; what a corporation pays as an AMT can be used in future tax years as a dollar for dollar reduction (credit) against the corporation's regular income tax liability (but not below the alternative minimum tax in any given year).

B. Cash Values

The inside buildup on a corporate owned life insurance policy is included in adjusted current earnings (ACE). Therefore, to the extent the policy cash value increase exceeds the premium paid in a given year, exposure to the AMT goes up.

C. Premiums

A deduction for AMT purposes is allowed for the portion of any premium that is attributable to insurance coverage. Therefore, to the extent the premium paid is greater in a given year than the policy's cash value increase, exposure to the AMT goes down.

The bottom line is no surprise: both (otherwise income tax free) death benefits and the (otherwise income tax free) inside buildup in a life insurance contract are includable in the amount upon which the corporate AMT is based.

So what should you advise clients?

First, tell them that the corporation needs the insurance, "BUY IT! Buy enough — after the AMT — to meet the need!" There is no question that even considering a "worst case" scenario, there is no more cost effective means of creating surplus to protect both the corporation and its creditors in the event of a key employee's death than corporate owned life insurance. Likewise, in most cases nonqualified deferred compensation and corporate debt reduction should be funded with corporate owned insurance "grossed up" enough to net the target amount.

Second, where it is possible and appropriate in the opinion of the firm's advisers to purchase necessary life insurance outside the corporation, do so. Other factors being equal, buy-sell agreements should be set up on a cross purchase basis.

Third, remember that this tax does not impact S corporations, regulated investment companies, real estate investment trusts, or real estate mortgage investment conduits.

Fourth, no AMT is imposed until the corporate exemption of $40,000 is used up. (This exemption is reduced by 25% of the amount by which alternative minimum taxable income exceeds $150,000, but not less than zero). Therefore, small amounts of tax preference in a given year will typically have no effect.

Cross-Purchase Agreements

1. The value of life insurance owned on a decedent-shareholder's life by a surviving co-shareholder will not be included in the decedent's estate for federal estate tax purposes. This is because the decedent-shareholder has no incidents of ownership in the policy his co-shareholder owns. However, the value of life insurance the decedent owned at the time of death on the lives of co-shareholders will be includable.[11] (Generally, this is equivalent to the policy's interpolated terminal reserve plus unearned premiums.)

As with the stock redemption agreement a properly drawn cross-purchase agreement will, generally, be effective in establishing the value of the business for federal estate tax purposes providing: (1) the estate is obligated to sell at the decedent-shareholder's death, or the estate is obligated to offer the decedent's shares at his or her death at the agreement price (2) there is a lifetime "first offer" provision prohibiting a shareholder from disposing of his or her stock interest without first offering it to the other shareholders at no more than the contract price, (3) the price was fair and adequate when made and resulted from a bona fide arm's length transaction, and (4) the price is fixed by the terms of the agreement or the agreement contains a formula or method for determining the price. (Where there are family members involved see discussion below on Family Business Enterprises).

2. Life insurance or disability income premiums paid to fund the agreement are not deductible by the co-shareholders. The death proceeds or disability benefits will be received by the respective co-shareholders income tax free.

3. There is no possibility under a cross-purchase agreement that "redemptions" will be treated as dividends and no potential attribution problems because there are no redemptions; there should be no transaction between the corporation and its shareholders in a cross-purchase agreement. By definition, in a cross-purchase plan the entire transaction is between the co-shareholders.

4. As is the case with a stock redemption, if the price paid for the stock is more than its basis (cost) in the selling shareholder's hands, the difference is taxable at ordinary income rates despite the fact that the asset sold is a capital asset.

5. Under a cross-purchase agreement, the surviving shareholder has the advantage of increasing his basis in the company for income tax purposes by the amount of money paid for the stock. This is not available under a stock redemption. This will result in a reduced gain, in the event of a subsequent lifetime sale, to the surviving shareholders.

6. Where more than one shareholder is involved, the implications of the transfer for value rule, see Question below, must be analyzed if there are life insurance policies that could be transferred among the shareholders or from the corporation to the shareholders.

Business Continuation Plans for S Corporations

Where the entity or cross-purchase plan is structured for a corporation electing to be taxed under subchapter S of the Internal Revenue Code, there are additional issues that must be considered. The tax characteristics of S corporations are discussed in Chapter 25.

Most practitioners favor the cross-purchase plan for an S corporation. There is some concern that a stock redemption plan under which the corporation will purchase stock of shareholders would create a second class of stock, which would disqualify the corporation for the S election. However, rulings and regulations indicate the IRS will not take this position. More practical reasons for preferring the cross-purchase plan include the fact that any life insurance owned by the corporation to fund a stock redemption agreement is really paid for with shareholder dollars, because the dollars used to pay premiums are dollars taxed to the shareholders. Also, the impact of the life insurance premiums and proceeds on the income tax basis of the shareholders' stock is unclear. If the S corporation has corporate earnings and profits accumulated before the S election is made, the insurance may affect the amount the corporation can distribute to shareholders without dividend consequences. The impact of life insurance on S corporation shareholders is discussed further in Chapter 25.

On the other hand, life insurance in an S corporation does not trigger alternative minimum tax problems. A stock redemption would decrease any earnings and profits of the S corporation which could someday give rise to dividends. And because most S corporations have little or no earnings and profits, all the complex dividend issues under the redemption-family attribution rules are generally not an issue, because a redemption cannot create a taxable dividend if there are no earnings and profits.

In structuring a buy-sell agreement for an S corporation, note that corporate profit and loss is allocated on a daily basis to all shareholders, including a deceased shareholder, to the date of death, or a selling shareholder to date of sale. An election can be made to actually close the tax year on the date of death or sale and allocate income or loss between two tax years. The agreement should spell out which approach is to be used. Remember that a shareholder's pro rata share of corporate profit or loss will increase or decrease the income tax basis of his or her stock, which would have an impact on the gain or loss realized on the sale.

One of the purposes of a buy-sell agreement in an S corporation is to prevent the stock from falling into the hands of a disqualifying shareholder, such as a trust which cannot hold S stock or a nonresident alien. The agreement should be structured so that the sale is complete before any such disqualifying transfer is made.

Business Continuation Plans for Partnerships

Partnership buyouts present several different problems and solutions. Unlike a corporation, if more than 50% of the total partnership capital *and* profits are sold within a 12-month period, the partnership is dissolved under Code section 708. However, the regulations under Section 708 indicate that if the interest of a partner is liquidated rather than sold, there is no dissolution even if that interest exceeds 50%. If the buyout does terminate the partnership, it is treated as having made a pro rata liquidating distribution of all of its assets to the partners, which are then recontributed to the partnership. Both are generally tax free.

If a partnership buy-sell agreement involves the sale of a partnership interest to other partners (or even a third person, such as an employee), any gain or loss realized by the selling partner is treated as a gain from sale or exchange of a capital asset, except to the extent it is attributable to so-called "hot assets" as defined in Code section 741 (generally, unrealized receivables and substantially appreciated inventory). Note that in the case of a sale of a deceased partner's interest, the stepped-up basis at death will eliminate most of this gain, except that attributable to items of income in respect of a decedent owned by the partnership. The purchaser acquires the cost basis in the partnership interest under Code section 742, and in addition, may seek to adjust the basis of the partnership assets to reflect the purchase price under Code sections 743(b) and 754.

Consideration should always be given to the use of a liquidation plan that meets the requirements of Code section 736, so that part of the payment can take the form of a tax-deductible guaranteed payment that can be spread over a period of several years. Under that section, payments in *complete* liquidation of a retiring or deceased partner's interest are broken into two categories, 736(b) payments and 736(a) payments.

Section 736(b) payments are those made in exchange for a deceased partner's interest in partnership property, including goodwill if specified as such in the agreement, and will result in taxable gain to the selling partner only if cash received, including relief from liabilities, exceeds the basis of the partner's interest in the partnership.

Section 736(a) payments made to successors of a deceased partner are classified as guaranteed payments, or represent an interest in future partnership income. Either way, they are tax-deductible to the partnership and taxable income to the recipient. Payments for receivables are always characterized as 736(a) payments. Payments for goodwill can be 736(a) payments unless the partnership agreement specifies they are for goodwill.

In summary, liquidation plans prevent termination of the partnership because the over 50% sale rule will not apply, so long as there are at least two partners remaining after liquidation is complete. Part of the liquidation payment can be made tax deductible to the remaining partners, and payments for goodwill can specifically be made tax deductible by bringing them under Code section 736(a).

However, the use of guaranteed payments under Section 736(a) has been severely curtailed in the case of partnership agreements entered into on or after January 5, 1993. Section 736(b) has been amended to provide that payments for unrealized receivables and goodwill of the partnership cannot be characterized as guaranteed payments under Section 736(a) unless capital is NOT a material income producing factor for the partnership, and the partner who is retiring or deceased is (or was) a general partner. This will not apply to partners retiring under an agreement which was binding on the parties on January 4, 1993. This change effectively limits the use of Section 736(a) guaranteed payments to service partnerships, such as professional practices.

If life insurance is used to provide funding in the case of the liquidation plan, the insurance is owned by the partnership and used to make liquidation payments. The IRS could argue that each partner has incidents of ownership in the policy on his or her life because of his management rights as partner. However, the IRS has taken this position only where the insurance proceeds were payable outside the partnership.[12]

Note that the receipt of the insurance proceeds increases the income tax basis of the partnership interests of all partners, including the interest owned by the decedent. It may be possible to change this by a provision in the partnership agreement.

Where insurance on the life of each partner is owned by other partners under a cross-purchase plan, the policies can be transferred between the partnership and partners without fear of the transfer for value rule under Code section 101(a)(2)(B). Cross ownership should not be the basis for an IRS claim that each partner has incidents of ownership in the policy on his or her life owned by the other partner by reason of the agreement.[13]

Family Business Enterprises

Code section 2703, applicable to options or agreements created or "substantially modified" after October 8, 1990, raises a host of additional problems in planning business continuation agreements for family businesses. It provides that any restrictions that result from options or agreements permitting *any* person to acquire any property at less than fair market value, or any such restriction on the right to sell or use the property, are disregarded in valuing that property. However, there is an exception for options, agreements, etc., that meet the following three tests:

- They are bona fide business arrangements;

- They are not devices to transfer property to the decedent's family or the natural objects of the decedent's bounty for less than full and adequate consideration; and

- The terms are comparable to similar arrangements entered into by persons in arm's length transactions.

While the first two requirements are not really new, the third requirement, establishing that the terms of the agreement are comparable to others entered into by unrelated persons, is very difficult to meet in most planning situations. Such agreements simply do not exist, or if they do, they are not available for comparison. Both the congressional committee reports and the regulations under Code section 2703 indicate that there are four factors in such agreements:

- the present fair market value of the property or business,

- its expected value at the date of exercise of rights under the agreement,

- adequacy of any consideration offered for the option or agreement, and

- the expected terms of the agreement.

According to the congressional committee reports, the third test is not met simply by showing isolated comparables but requires a demonstration of the general practices of unrelated parties. Expert testimony would be evidence of such practice. In unusual cases where comparables are difficult to find because the taxpayer owns a unique business, the taxpayer can use comparables from other businesses.

The Senate report also emphasizes that the law does not alter other preexisting requirements for buy-sell agreements, such as a requirement of lifetime restrictions if the agreement is to be binding at death.

According to the regulations, the restrictive agreement will meet the requirements of the statute to control valuation if it is a binding agreement and if more than 50% of the value of the property or business is owned by persons who are not family members (or natural objects of the transferor's bounty).

However, the use of the term "natural objects of the transferor's bounty" means that the provisions of Section 2703 may apply even where the shareholders are unrelated. The final regulations do not say this, but they do say that members of the family include persons described in Code section 2701, covered in Chapter 13, and other persons who are natural objects of the transferor's bounty. The preamble to the final regulations also states that natural objects of bounty may include persons not "related by blood or marriage."

Similar arrangements among unrelated parties in the same business are generally comparable, if they consider the term of the agreement, present and anticipated fair market value of the property, and adequacy of consideration. General business practice of unrelated parties is comparable, but again, isolated comparables are insufficient, and if two or more valuation methods are generally used, the fact that the agreement falls within one of them is not sufficient. It is important to note that the requirement of finding comparable buy-sell agreements, which is very difficult in most cases, appears to have been replaced in the regulations by a requirement of proof that unrelated persons dealing at arm's length would have entered into the same agreement. Thus, in setting the terms of a business continuation agreement where family members are involved, remember to consider the four key factors — present and anticipated future value of the business, the expected term of the agreement, and consideration. Obtain evidence and expert opinions to establish that the terms and conditions of this buy-sell agreement would be acceptable to unrelated persons. Under no circumstances set arbitrary prices or values, such as, for example, a price based on the face value of the life insurance, and consider a provision for periodic review and adjustment of the price, or a formula.

If a business continuation agreement was in place before the effective date of Code section 2703, it is not covered unless it is "substantially modified" thereafter. The following are not substantial modifications:

- a modification required by the instrument,

- a discretionary modification containing a right or restriction that does not change the right or restriction, or results in only a de minimis change,

- a modification of a capitalization rate tied to a market rate, or

- a modification to a price that more adequately reflects fair market value.

The following are considered substantial modifications:

- failure to update an agreement that by its terms requires periodic updating, and

- the addition of a family member to the agreement, unless mandated by the terms of the agreement, or unless the new family member is assigned to a generation no lower than that of existing parties to the agreement (generation assignment is determined under the generation-skipping rules, discussed in Chapter 12).

IMPLICATIONS AND ISSUES IN COMMUNITY PROPERTY STATES

Several problems can arise in connection with buy-sell agreements as a result of community property rights. If all or part of the stock is subject to a buy-sell agreement, careful planning is required (1) to protect against the risk that the shareholder's spouse may predecease the seller and leave the spouse's community property interest in the stock to third parties, (2) to protect against attachment by creditors of the shareholder's spouse, and (3) to protect the agreement from attachment by the stockholder's spouse if the spouse survives the stockholder and seeks to claim his or her community property interest in the stock free of the agreement. If all or part of the stockholder's interest is quasi-community property, care should be taken to protect against the spouse's claim, if he or she survives the stockholder, that he or she is entitled to a community property interest in the stock free of the agreement. Appropriate written consents should be obtained in the above situations.

The impact of divorce in a community property state must be considered. If a spouse who is not active in the business should receive stock in the closely held corporation, or a partnership interest, as part of the property settlement, this may not be covered by the buy-sell agreement.

Consideration should be given to making provisions in the buy-sell agreement for such an eventuality. One solution is to grant the remaining shareholders or partners, particularly the other spouse in the divorce action, a right to purchase the interest of the soon-to-be ex-spouse. Alternatively, the corporation or partnership could have at least an option to purchase the interest. If the spouses are all made parties to such an agreement, great care must be taken to assure these provisions are fair, or else they may be unenforceable.

It is important to determine the nature of the interest held by the stockholder, not only for purposes of determining whether consents need to be obtained and wills reviewed, but also to evaluate the tax consequences. If all of the stock is community property, the community property interest of the stockholder's spouse will be included in the spouse's estate if he or she predeceases the stockholder, and will be excluded from the stockholder's estate if the stockholder dies first. If all of the stock is the separate property of the stockholder, it will be included in the stockholder's estate only (unless he or she passes the stock to the spouse and then dies). If all of the stock is quasi-community property, the stockholder's spouse will have no interest if he or she dies first, and the full value of the stock will be in the stockholder's estate for federal estate tax purposes.

The basis of property acquired from a decedent is subject to a peculiar set of rules.

Generally, the basis of property acquired from a decedent is the fair market value of the property at the date of the decedent's death. Revenue Code Section 1014 defines which property is deemed "acquired from a decedent" and therefore subject to these special basis rules. Generally, Section 1014 applies to all property includable in the gross estate.

The surviving spouse is deemed to have acquired her one-half share of the community property from the decedent spouse. This gives the surviving spouse a new basis even though her one-half of the community property was not included or taxed in the decedent spouse's estate. The new basis for the surviving spouse's one-half will therefore be equal to the fair market value of the property at date of death. This rule operates, however, only if the decedent's one-half is fully included in the gross estate.[14] If the property's fair market value is greater than its adjusted income tax basis, the basis will receive a "step-up" free of either estate or income taxes. If the fair market value is less than the adjusted basis, the new basis will actually be a "step-down."

This "step-up" or "step-down" in basis for both spouses' halves of the community property does not apply to property held as joint tenancy or tenancy in common property. Even though the original nature of the property was community property (e.g., a spouse's earnings in a community property state), taking the title as joint tenants or tenants in common will change its nature so that it no longer has the attributes of community property. However, in most states with community property laws, it is possible to re-establish the property as community property by an agreement between the spouses without actually changing the recorded title to the property. As of January 1, 1985, some states, such as California, require such agreements to be in writing.

The ability of the surviving spouse to sell immediately the entire community interest of corporate stock, either under a buy-sell contract to other shareholders or to redeem some or all of it within the scope of Section 303 (avoiding dividend treatment), can often be the most significant estate planning step taken by husband and wife shareholders in community property states!

Problems can occur when attempting to determine whether stock held by a married person in a community property state is community property. A portion of the stock can be separate property and a portion community property. A common example is a man who owns a business prior to marriage.

Let us examine the setting in which this issue frequently arises. Assume that Mr. Jones owns all of the stock in Jones Manufacturing Company, Inc. The company was incorporated prior to his marriage to Mrs. Jones. At the time of the marriage, the company was worth $100,000. However, during the marriage the value of the company appreciates rapidly. If Mr. Jones dies, will the stock in the company, or, in the alternative, the appreciation in value of the stock, be deemed his separate property or will it be community property?

Court decisions characterizing appreciation in closely-held businesses arise in only three settings: (1) a claim by a creditor that the business should be made available for the payment of a debt, (2) divorce and the division of property pursuant to divorce, and (3) the death of one of the spouses.

Most states use some form of an "apportionment rule" to characterize the increase in value of closely-held business interests during marriage which were originally held as a spouse's separate property. Under the apportionment rule, if one of the spouses invests separate property in a business and conducts that business during the marriage, the resulting projects or increases in value of the business will be apportioned or allocated between the community estate and the spouse's separate estate according to the amount attributable to the spouse's personal efforts on the one hand (inuring to the benefit of the community), and to the capital improvement on the other (inuring to the benefit of the spouse's separate estate).

The possibility of creating such a community property interest in a corporation originally held as the separate property of one spouse can be determined only by a court in the absence of a written agreement. Thus, it is advisable for the spouses to agree, in writing, on the nature of their interests and the proportion of community and separate property.

There are other possible combinations of interest such as combinations of community property and quasi-community property or combinations of separate property and quasi-community property or combinations of all three types of property. In any event, the exact nature of stock ownership and their respective proportions should be identified and agreed upon in writing. In many situations it may be advisable to incorporate the property agreement into the buy-sell agreement.

QUESTIONS AND ANSWERS

Question — Under what situations would a business buy-out by a third party be indicated?

Answer — There are certain situations in which an owner of a business interest is either unwilling or unable to enter into a conventional stock redemption or cross-purchase agreement. Usually, such a business owner will have problems as estate liquidity, lack of management skills or interest by members of his or her family, or desires the value of the business to be "pegged" for federal estate tax purposes.

A typical example is where an individual has a wife and three children, only one of whom he desires or expects to be able to take over the business. He would like to treat his children as equally as possible. One way he could do this is by entering into a buy-sell agreement with the one child he expects to take over the business. That child will take over the business through the buy-sell agreement. The funds paid by that child to the decedent's executor in return for the business interest could provide the client's widow and remaining children with cash for their living needs and estate settlement costs.

Question — What are some of the various methods of establishing the purchase price of a business?

Answer — The purchase price to be paid for the stock of a shareholder may be set by a variety of methods. One method is to provide for the exact purchase price in advance with the further provision that the parties may change the price at any time upon mutual agreement.

Another method of fixing the price is to use book value based on the company's financial statements.

A third method of valuation is a formula approach. Formula valuation methods are often used to take into account net profits and, to some degree, goodwill. An example would be straight capitalization of the average net profits of the business at a definite rate. For instance, as the illustration below shows, at a 12 percent rate, a business producing average net after-tax profits of $100,000 would be worth about $833,333 using this approach ($100,000 divided by .12). A 50 percent interest in such a business would be worth $416,667, half of $833,333. Combinations of these three methods can also be used. (See Chapter 36 on Valuation Planning.)

CAPITALIZATION OF INCOME

INPUT: CAPITALIZATION RATE 0.120
INPUT: ADJUSTED EARNINGS $100,000

EXPECTED RATE OF RETURN	VALUE OF ASSET OR BUSINESS
0.08	$1,250,000
0.09	$1,111,111
0.10	$1,000,000
0.11	$909,091
0.12	$833,333
0.13	$769,231
0.14	$714,286
0.15	$666,667
0.16	$625,000
0.17	$588,235

Question — What can be done if one of the persons involved in a business continuation agreement is uninsurable?

Answer — Life insurance may be used for the insurable stockholders, and for the uninsurable stockholders, a sinking fund method should be used to at least accumulate enough money for a down payment. Often an amount equivalent to the appropriate insurance premium on the uninsurable's life (given his or her age) is deposited into some type of segregated reserve account. Such an account might be invested in bonds, mutual funds, fixed or variable annuity, or merely left in a savings account until the death of the uninsurable.

Typically, the agreement will provide that installment payments covering the remainder of the purchase price can be spread over a relatively long period of time.

Several life insurance companies are offering guaranteed issue type contracts even on those stockholder-employees previously thought to be uninsurable as long as the stockholder-employee is actively at work full time. One type of policy provides that if a death occurs during a certain initial period of time, e.g. 3 years, only premiums paid plus interest are payable as a death benefit. After the initial period the full death benefit is payable. A second type policy provides for a graded death benefit, i.e., one that increases over a period of time to the full death benefit.

Question — Will an agreement giving a surviving stockholder or the corporation an *option* to buy the deceased shareholder's stock usually fix the value of a business interest for federal estate tax purposes?

Answer — Yes, if there is a "first offer" provision and the price was fair and adequate when made. (A "first offer" provision requires the selling shareholder [or his or her executor] to offer the interest to the specified purchaser at an agreed upon price [fixed or set by formula] both during lifetime and after death before offering it to others.) Although the estate must be either obligated to sell at death or obligated to offer at death at the agreement price, the survivor(s) or the corporation need not be obligated to buy. An option in their hands would be sufficient. However, agreements involving substantially only family members may be determined not to be made at arm's length and therefore not effective in pegging the value for federal estate tax purposes. (See discussion above — Family Business Enterprises).

Question — Assume that there are three stockholders of a corporation and all stockholders have entered into a cross-purchase agreement. One of the stockholders dies and the other two stockholders purchase the decedent's stock using the life insurance proceeds under which the decedent was the insured and the remaining two stockholders were the policyowners and beneficiaries.

The decedent's personal representative now owns an insurance policy on the life of each of the surviving shareholders. They purchase their respective policies from the personal representative. Are there any potential tax problems?

Answer — No. This situation brings into play the "transfer-for-value" rule. This tax trap creates an exception to the general rule that the proceeds of an insurance policy are not subject to federal income tax.

The transfer-for-value rule provides that if insurance policies are transferred for value (no gift has taken place but a consideration has been given for such transfer) then the owner-beneficiary of that policy will have taxable income when the insured dies. The difference between the proceeds of the policy and the sum of (a) the value paid and (b) the premiums paid by the new owner-beneficiary will be taxable as ordinary income.

There are exceptions to the transfer-for-value rule where the transfer for value is made

(1) to the insured (as is the case here),

(2) to a corporation in which the insured is an officer or stockholder,

(3) to a partner of the insured,

(4) to a partnership in which the insured is a partner,

(5) where the new owner's basis (cost) is determined in whole or in part by reference to the transferor's basis, or

(6) where a transfer of a policy or an interest in a policy is made between spouses or between spouses incident to a divorce. For instance, if a divorce decree requires one spouse to transfer a policy to another, the transfer will be considered a nontaxable event which results in a carryover basis in the policy and avoids the transfer-for-value tax trap.

Question — Assume that there is a stock redemption agreement funded by life insurance. The amount of the life insurance on the date of the death of one of the stockholders exceeds the corporate obligation under the redemption agreement. Are there any tax consequences?

Answer — The proceeds of corporate-owned life insurance will not generally be taxable to the corporation when it receives the same (except for potential exposure to a corporate level alternative minimum tax). However, the earnings and profits of the corporation will be increased by the amount of the proceeds and then reduced when a portion of the proceeds is used to redeem the shares of stock.

If the entire amount of the proceeds has not been used to redeem a decedent-shareholder's interest, there will be a permanent increase in corporate earnings and profits, which means that there should be additional dollars available for the payment of dividends; because of this, the potential exists for imposition of the accumulated earnings tax penalty, as well as dividend treatment on any distribution made by the corporation to its shareholders.

Question — Assume that the parties enter into either a redemption agreement or a cross-purchase agreement. Should anything be done to protect their rights with respect to a possible transfer to third parties?

Answer — The stock certificates owned by the parties to either the redemption agreement or the cross-purchase agreement should bear a legend indicating a restriction on the ability to transfer those shares of stock as a result of the redemption or cross-purchase agreement.

Question — Why is a cross-purchase plan often preferred over a stock redemption arrangement?

Answer — Where a corporation purchases the stock of a withdrawing, disabled, or deceased stockholder, the surviving shareholders cannot increase their basis (cost for purposes of determining gain) by the amount paid. For example, assume Steve, Roberta, and Lee each own an interest in the SRL Corporation worth $100,000. Each invested $10,000 in 1977 when the corporation was formed. If Lee dies and the corporation (pursuant to a fully funded buy-sell agreement) pays his executor $100,000 for his stock, Steve's basis and Roberta's basis remain at $10,000. But if Steve and Roberta had been the purchasers and had each *personally* paid $50,000 to Lee's executor, their individual basis would have increased by that $50,000 amount. The distinction is important because, in this simplified example, the taxable gain on a future sale of Steve's stock or Roberta's stock could be as much as $50,000 less using a cross-purchase arrangement.

It is important to recognize, however, that this does not mean a cross-purchase plan will always be better than a stock redemption. In some cases a stock redemption will be preferred:

(1) The basis increase may be higher when a stock redemption is used if

    (a) surviving shareholders intend to retain the stock they own until death, and

    (b) there is high appreciation in the value of the stock.

(2) Shareholders will often prefer, for both psychological and cash flow reasons, that corporate dollars be used to pay premiums.

(3) Premium payments by a corporation may be indicated when the corporation is in a lower income tax bracket than the individual shareholders.

(4) Where there are more than 3 shareholders involved, administrative inconvenience and cost generally make corporate-owned life insurance preferable over the multiplicity of policies required in a cross-purchase arrangement. For example, if there were 5 shareholders, 20 separate policies would be required. (The formula for determining the number of policies is N x (N - 1) with N being the number of shareholders.)

Other factors to consider in deciding between a cross-purchase and stock redemption include:

(1) possibility of dividend treatment because of constructive ownership (attribution) rules in family-owned corporations;

(2) state law restrictions on a corporation's right to purchase its own stock in the absence of sufficient surplus;

(3) transfer-for-value problems at the death of a shareholder if estate-owned policies are transferred to individuals other than the insureds;

(4) stock ownership desired after the purchase occurs;

(5) premium outlay differences due to differences in age and ownership interests between shareholders;

(6) possible alternative minimum tax problems where life insurance is used to fund a stock redemption.

Question — Is there a solution to the dilemma of the cross-purchase vs. stock redemption decision?

Answer — One technique that may avoid or minimize problems inherent in a buy-sell of either the cross-purchase or the stock redemption type is the "Wait and See" (also known as the "option") approach.

Under a "Wait and See" type agreement, the estate of a deceased shareholder is bound to sell at an agreed-upon price or according to a predetermined formula, but the parties *wait* a specified length of time after the death of a shareholder to *see* if — and to what extent — a cross-purchase or stock redemption or combination (perhaps even coordinated with a Section 303 stock redemption) should be used.

The suggested method is for the corporation to have a first option to purchase any or all of a deceased shareholder's interest. Surviving shareholders have a secondary option to purchase any or all stock remaining. If, at this point, some stock still remains in the executor's hands, the corporation is *required* to purchase the entire balance.

Life insurance could be purchased by the corporation, by the surviving shareholders, or by both. (The corporation might, for example, purchase permanent life insurance while the shareholders might purchase term insurance.) If the corporation is owner and beneficiary of the insurance it can apply proceeds directly to the extent a stock redemption is indicated or make loans to the extent necessary to shareholders who will be purchasing stock on an individual basis. If life insurance is owned by and payable to shareholders on an individual basis, they could apply proceeds directly to the extent a cross-purchase is indicated or make loans or capital contributions to the corporation to enable it to effect a stock redemption.

The "Wait and See" approach provides an infinite variety of options and a maximum in planning flexibility.

Question — If a cross-purchase agreement funded with life insurance is changed to a stock redemption agreement, and the insurance that was owned by the individuals on each other is transferred to the corporation, will there be any income tax consequences as relates to the insurance?

Answer — No. Changing insurance from a cross-purchase agreement to a stock redemption agreement will not violate the transfer-for-value rule, because policies can be transferred from a stockholder to a corporation of which the insured is a stockholder. This will qualify as an exception to the transfer-for-value rule. Note, however, that the reverse, i.e., change from a stock redemption to a cross-purchase, will be a violation of the transfer-for-value rule if insurance is transferred from the corporation to a stockholder other than the insured.

Question — Can a buy-sell agreement "peg" the value of a business interest for federal gift tax purposes?

Answer — Although an agreement will probably not be controlling for federal gift tax purposes, it should carry strong evidentiary weight as to the business value and will be considered along with other relevant factors. An agreement will probably be successful in establishing value if:

(1) the price (or formula) is reasonable at the time the agreement is signed.

(2) the agreement is negotiated by parties knowledgeable of relevant facts and at arms-length.

(3) the price (or formula) agreed upon is as binding during lifetime as at death, i.e., the lifetime price permitted can't be higher than the sale price at a shareholder's death.

(4) the price is fixed by the terms of the agreement or the agreement contains a formula or method for determining price.

Where family members own at least 50% of the business, additional requirements will probably apply. See discussion above — Family Business Enterprises.

Question — What is the advantage of using a trustee in a buy-sell agreement?

Answer — Potential difficulty can be avoided through use of a trustee in carrying out the terms of the agreement. Prior to death of one of the parties to the agreement there are many duties to be performed. The trustee can obtain the premiums on insurance used to fund the agreement from the appropriate parties and can pay the premiums when they become due. The trustee can also serve as custodian of the policies subject to the agreement.

After death of a party to the agreement, the trustee will receive proceeds of the insurance on the life of the deceased business owner. The trustee can then act as a disinterested middleman in paying the purchase price for the decedent's business interest to the legal representative of the decedent's estate and in transferring the business interest to the purchaser.

Note that although the law is not entirely clear, the use of a trustee will probably not eliminate a transfer for value problem as to life insurance acquired by the trustee. For example, assume a corporation has three equal shareholders who enter into a cross-purchase plan. A trustee is named to act under the agreement and purchases insurance on all three shareholders to fund the agreement. After the death of the first shareholder, the agreement continues for the remaining two shareholders. Many authorities believe that the shift of economic interests in the insurance policies on the remaining shareholders will constitute a transfer for value.

Question — Is it possible to be certain the price established in a business continuation agreement involving family members will establish the estate tax value of the interest of a deceased partner or shareholder?

Answer — Maybe. "Pegging" values in a family buy-sell agreement has become more difficult since the adoption of Code section 2703. Because related persons are by definition not dealing at arm's length in establishing the terms and price of their business continuation agreement, the price may not determine value for tax purposes unless it can be shown the terms and price of the agreement could have been obtained in a fair bargain among unrelated parties in the same business dealing with each other at arms length.[15] This standard, which is from the regulations, appears to be more demanding than the one Congress intended, which mandates a showing that the agreement could have been obtained in a hypothetical arms length agreement.[16]

Careful planning, however, should increase the likelihood that the agreement will be able to "peg" values. Using a formula approach, rather than a stated dollar value, has a better chance of accomplishing this goal.

Question — Four shareholders in a closely held corporation want to enter into a cross purchase plan to acquire the stock of a deceased shareholder, fully funded with life insurance. You have explained to them the problems that will occur upon the death of any shareholder under the transfer for value rule if economic interests in the insurance policies on the remaining shareholders are shifted so that the agreement may remain in effect. Can you offer any solutions to this problem?

Answer — Other than canceling existing policies and acquiring new ones, there appear to be two other techniques to deal with this problem. The first is to have all of the remaining shareholders transfer their interests in policies on the other shareholder to the corporation, and substitute a stock redemption plan for the cross purchase plan. Since they are all shareholders in the corporation, the transfer of the policies to it is not a transfer for value.

Another solution, which has been the subject of a series of private letter rulings, is to consider the establishment of a partnership among all of the shareholders. As discussed in the text, transfers of policies among partners are not subject to the transfer for value rule. Frequently the shareholders are involved in other business or investment activities, such as the ownership of property leased to the corporation, which could be the basis for the formation of a partnership. One private letter ruling held that the mere ownership of the life insurance policies would be a sufficient business or investment activity to justify formation of a partnership. However, cautious practitioners are not relying on this ruling, and advise the parties that they should carry out some other business or investment activity in such a partnership to assure its validity.

Question — Are the costs involved in a stock redemption deductible to the corporation?

Answer — No. Tax law prohibits a deduction for the costs involved in a stock redemption.[17] This prohibition applies even if it is necessary to save the corporation's business life. The purchase of a corporation's own stock is a capital transaction and no deduction is allowed for either the purchase price or the expenses associated with the purchase.

ASRS, Secs. 40 - 43.

Footnote References

Buy-Sell (Business Continuation) Agreement

1. Reg. §20.2031-2(f).
2. Reg. §20.2031-2(h); *May v. McGowan*, 194 F.2d 396 (2d Cir. 1952); *Comm. v. Child's Est.*, 147 F.2d 368 (3rd Cir. 1945), *rev'd on other grounds* 223 F2d 218 (3rd Cir. 1955); *Est. of Mitchell*, 37 BTA 1 (1938). See also Rev. Rul. 59-60, 1959-1 CB 237.
3. IRC Sec. 264(a)(1).
4. IRC Sec. 101(a)(1).
5. IRC Secs. 302(c)(1), 318.
6. IRC Sec. 318(a)(3).
7. IRC Secs. 318(a)(1), 318(a)(2).
8. IRC Sec. 302(c)(2).
9. IRC Sec. 1014.
10. IRC Secs. 55, 56
11. IRC Sec. 2033.
12. Rev. Rul. 83-147, 1983-2 CB 158.
13. See *Est. of Infante*, TC Memo 1970-206.
14. IRC Sec. 1014(b)(6).
15. Reg. §25.2703-1(b)(4).
16. *Explanation of Revenue Provisions for Inclusion in Fiscal Year 1991 Budget Reconciliation Package as Approved by Committee 10/13/90*, Senate Finance Committee, 101st Cong., 2nd Sess., 136 Cong. Rec. S 15679, S 15683.
17. IRC Sec. 162(k).

Chapter 2

CHARITABLE CONTRIBUTIONS

WHAT IS IT?

A charitable contribution is a gratuitous transfer of property to charitable, religious, scientific, educational, and other specified organizations. If the donee of the gift falls within categories designated by the law, a charitable deduction may be taken for income, gift, or estate tax purposes.

Charitable contributions have tax value, therefore, because they result in a current income tax deduction, may reduce federal estate taxes, and can be made free of gift tax. From the charity's point of view, charitable contributions are also tax favored; the charity itself pays no tax upon the receipt of either a lifetime gift or a bequest and, generally, no income tax is paid by the qualified charity on income earned by the charity on donated property.

WHEN IS THE USE OF SUCH A DEVICE INDICATED?

1. When the donor wishes, for nontax reasons, to benefit the charity.

2. When the donor wishes to reduce income or estate taxes by taking advantage of the deductions allowed for such gifts.

3. When the donor would like to achieve both motives described above.

WHAT ARE THE REQUIREMENTS?

1. Charitable contributions are deductible only if they are made to organizations which are "qualified." Examples of "qualified" organizations include nonprofit schools and hospitals, churches and synagogues, the United Fund, Community Chest, YMCA, YMHA, The American Red Cross, the Boy Scouts, Campfire Girls, and the Heart Association.

   A donee will be considered qualified only if it meets three conditions: (a) it must be operated exclusively for religious, charitable, scientific, literary, or educational purposes; or to foster national or international amateur sports competition or to prevent cruelty to children or animals; (b) no part of the organization's earnings can benefit any private shareholder or similar individual; (c) the organization cannot be one disqualified for tax exemption because it attempts to influence legislation or participates in, publishes or distributes statements for, or intervenes in, any political campaign on behalf of any candidate seeking public office. The Internal Revenue Service publishes a list of qualified charities in IRS Publication 78.

   It is important to note that the statutory descriptions of qualified charities for federal income tax purposes are not exactly the same as the descriptions of qualified charities for federal estate or gift tax purposes. One basic distinction is that for income tax purposes the donee must be a domestic organization whereas the donee for estate tax charitable deduction purposes can be a foreign or a domestic charity. (Be certain to check the rules under all applicable Code sections.) Generally, the income tax deduction is available for contributions to churches, educational organizations, hospitals and medical research organizations, governmental units, and various other organizations and support organizations described in Code section 170(b). The client or practitioner should ascertain whether a potential donee is qualified under the Code. If it is not listed in IRS Publication 78, it is wise to request a copy of a determination letter from the IRS indicating that the charity does or does not qualify.

2. The second requirement necessary for a charitable contribution deduction is that property must be the subject of the gift. Therefore, the value of a taxpayer's time or services, even if contributed to a qualified charity, is not deductible. For example, if a carpenter spent 10 hours building chairs for his church, he could not deduct his normal hourly wage as a charitable contribution. However, he could deduct the cost of materials he purchased and used in producing the finished product.

   A taxpayer who donates the use of his property to a charity has not made a contribution of property. So the rent-free use of an office or even an office building will not be considered a charitable contribution any more than a contribution of personal services.

3. A third requirement for a charitable contribution deduction is that there must in fact be a contribution to the

charity in excess of value received by the donor. In some cases the donor will receive a benefit in conjunction with his charitable gift. Such a contribution is deductible only to the extent that the value of the contributed property exceeds any consideration or benefit to the donor. For example, the individual might donate cash to a charity. The charity in turn might pay the donor (and perhaps his survivors) an annuity income for life. Only the difference between the contribution made and the value of the annuity would be deductible.

4. The fourth requirement that must be met for a deduction to be allowed is that the gift to charity must actually be paid in cash or other property before the close of the tax year in question. Typically, therefore, even an accrual basis taxpayer must actually pay cash or contribute other property before the close of the tax year in order to receive a deduction.

5. A charitable contribution at death will be deductible regardless of whether it is made by will, by the terms of a life insurance policy, or by gift during the decedent's lifetime in such a manner that the gift will be includable in his gross estate. But the transfer must be made by the decedent, as distinguished from a transfer made by his estate or beneficiaries, in order to be deductible. Therefore, a deduction would not be allowed for a bequest to charity if the bequest requires the approval of a third party.

6. Where the lifetime transfer or bequest to charity is a gift of a "partial interest" (i.e., where the gift will be split between noncharitable and charitable beneficiaries), strict rules apply. Generally, if a charity's interest in the transfer of property is a remainder interest (the charity receives what remains after the noncharitable income beneficiaries have received income for a specified time), a transfer in trust will qualify only if it is an annuity trust, unitrust, or a pooled income fund. These terms are defined and described in Chapter 3.

7. A qualified appraisal must accompany a tax return showing donations of property valued at over $5,000. Who can be an appraiser? You are qualified to be an appraiser for tax purposes only if (1) you hold yourself out to the public as an appraiser, (2) you are qualified to appraise the particular type of property in question, and (3) you understand that an overstatement of value may lead to the imposition of penalties. The appraisal may not be made by the donor, the organization receiving the contribution, any person from whom the property was acquired, or certain related individuals or entities. Generally, a separate appraisal must be made for each item of property unless similar items are donated in the same year. Partner-

ships donating property valued at over $5,000 must provide a copy of the appraisal to every partner who receives a proportionate share of the deduction.

In addition, in the case of charitable contributions of art valued at more than $20,000, it is necessary to furnish a signed appraisal to support the deduction with the tax return. The IRS may also require a color photograph.

While the appraisal requirement does not apply to gifts of publicly traded securities, it does to nonpublicly traded securities worth more than $10,000. Note there are severe penalties for undervaluation of charitable gifts.

In the case of all contributions, including cash, a charitable deduction is not allowed for any contribution of $250 or more unless the donor obtains written acknowledgement which includes (1) the amount of money or description of the property contributed, and (2) whether the organization gave any goods or services to the taxpayer in return for the contribution. Starting in 1994, cancelled checks are no longer sufficient in such cases.

All donors must keep cancelled checks, a receipt, or other reliable written records. These documents must show the name of the donee, the date of the contribution, and the amount of the gift. The safest approach is to make the records at the same time you make the gift and have the recipient charity sign a receipt.

HOW IT IS DONE — AN EXAMPLE

A gift to charity is probably one of the simplest estate planning techniques. During lifetime, such a gift can be accomplished merely by writing a check, assigning stock, transferring life insurance policies, signing a deed to real estate, or conveying property to charity in any other normal outright manner. Likewise, at death, gifts to charity can be made by will, by life insurance contract, by employee benefit contract (the death benefits from a pension plan can be paid to charity), or by trust.

WHAT ARE THE TAX IMPLICATIONS?

1. A charitable contribution to a qualified charity reduces current income taxes (assuming the donor itemizes deductions). Since the top marginal income tax bracket is currently 39.6 percent, the income tax savings to an individual making a gift to charity will generally be

greater than previously when the top marginal rate was lower (i.e. 31%).

2. No federal gift tax is payable on a gift to a qualified charity regardless of the size of the gift.

3. Gifts to qualified charities can reduce the federal estate tax, with the amount of the deduction limited only by the value of the gift (i.e., the donor's entire estate can be left to charity and a deduction will be allowed for the entire gift).

4. The charity itself will pay no tax upon the receipt of either a lifetime gift or a bequest.

5. Generally, no income tax will be payable by a qualified charity on income earned by donated property.

6. If an otherwise deductible charitable contribution to a college or university entitles the donor to purchase tickets for athletic events, 80% of the contribution will be deductible.

7. For federal income tax purposes, there are percentage limitations on the amount that can be claimed as a charitable contribution deduction; these depend on, among other things, the type of property transferred. (The percentage limitations are discussed, below, in the Questions and Answers section, and are also displayed in Figure 2.1.)

For tax purposes, potential charitable donees will be classified either as a private foundation or a public charity. The percentage limitations discussed below are those generally applicable to publicly charities. There are stricter limitations on deductions for contributions to most private foundations.

Any organization which is classified as a charity under IRC Sec. 501(c)(3) is deemed a private foundation unless it is a church, educational organization with a regular curriculum, faculty, and student body; a hospital, a government unit, and certain other publicly supported institutions or support organizations.

In view of the importance of the charitable contribution deduction and the limitations, it is important for the advisor to determine not only whether or not the charitable recipient is a qualified charity, but also whether or not it is a private foundation, and if so, what type of private foundation.

ISSUES AND IMPLICATIONS IN COMMUNITY PROPERTY STATES

Because of the equal ownership aspect of community property as between a husband and wife, care must be exercised in the creation of a charitable trust that benefits both parties, since taxable transfers may occur.

For example, if community property is used to fund a trust which benefits only one of the spouses, there has been a gift by the other spouse. Conversely, if the separate property of one of the spouses is used to fund a trust which provides for a lifetime benefit for both spouses, there is a recognized gift to the non-contributing spouse. After 1981, the availability of the unlimited marital deduction for federal gift tax purposes eliminates the prior concerns as to federal gift tax. (See Chapter 37.) However, many states do have some form of gift tax and only some have an unlimited gift tax marital deduction. Therefore, state gift tax can still be a problem in these circumstances. If community property is used to fund a trust that provides a lifetime benefit for both spouses, there will be no gift tax consequences.

It is possible for community property to be "split," creating separate interests for each spouse, which could then be used to fund separate charitable trusts, each involving life interests of only the spouse making the gift. Or, one spouse can make a gift with her half of the "split" funds, and the other can use the funds for his own purposes or to pay their joint income tax liability. In order for community property to be "split," an agreement between the parties must be made to that effect. A "split" is essentially a transmutation of community property to separate property, and, since January 1, 1985, such transmutations in some states, such as California, must be in writing.

Under the community property laws in many states, a valid contribution of community property cannot be made to a charity by one spouse without the consent of the other spouse. This consent should be obtained before the close of the tax year for which his deduction will be claimed; otherwise the IRS may argue the contribution was not complete and is not deductible.

Generally, the same income, estate and gift tax advantages which are available for gifts of separate property will be available in situations where community property is the subject of a charitable contribution.

QUESTIONS AND ANSWERS

Question — How do you calculate the after-tax-savings cost of a charitable contribution?

Answer — The tax savings and after-tax cost can be found as follows:

Tax Savings = Amount of deductible gift x Effective tax bracket

For example, a $2,000 gift by a 39.6 percent taxpayer equals $792 in tax savings. Stated another way, the out-of-pocket cost of the gift equals:

Amount contributed — Tax savings

For instance, the $2,000 gift above less the $792 in tax savings equals the out-of-pocket cost of the gift, $1,208.

Question — How do you determine the amount of an income tax charitable deduction?

Answer — The amount of a charitable contribution deduction that will be allowed for income tax purposes depends on the five following factors, which will be discussed in detail below:

1. *The type of property given away.*

    (a) rent-free occupancy

    (b) cash

    (c) long-term capital gain property

    (d) ordinary income property

    (e) tangible personal property where the use of that property by the donee is related to the exempt functions of the donee; and tangible personal property where the use of that property is unrelated to the exempt purposes of the donee

    (f) future interests in property

(These various types of property will be discussed in detail in the following question.)

2. *The identity of the donee.* Generally, contributions to publicly supported domestic organizations—so-called public charities—are more favorably treated than contributions to foreign organizations or to most private foundations. Cash contributions to public charities, for example, are fully deductible up to 50 percent of a donor's contribution base (adjusted gross income computed without regard to any net operating loss carryback to the taxable year). The deduction for an individual's contributions to most nonpublic (private) charities, regardless of the type of property given away, is limited to the lesser of (a) 30 percent of the taxpayer's contribution base, or (b) 50 percent of his contribution base minus the amount of charitable contribution deductions allowed for contributions to the public-type charities.[1] For example, if a wealthy individual donates property worth 40 percent of his contribution base (A.G.I.) to a public charity such as the Boy Scouts, his contributions to "30 percent charities" (private charities) are deductible only up to 10 percent of his contribution base.[2] Donations to individuals or to foreign charities (except where allowed by treaty) are not deductible. The limit for gifts of capital gain property to private foundations is the lesser of 20 percent or the unused portion of the 30 percent.

3. *The identity of the contributor.* Individuals are limited to specified percentages of their contribution base. An individual must itemize deductions in order to claim a charitable contribution deduction. A corporation is limited to a deduction based on a percentage of its taxable income.[3]

4. *The amount of property given away.* Both individuals and corporations can carry over excess contributions—contributions above their deductible limit—for up to 5 years.[4]

5. *The place where the contribution is to be used.* As mentioned above, gifts made to United States charities are treated more favorably than gifts to most foreign charities.

Question — How does the type of property interest given to charity affect the income tax limit on deductions and what is the effect of a contribution of a partial interest in property to charity?

Answer — Generally, a charitable contribution of less than a donor's entire interest in property is not deductible. Gifts of a partial interest in property are deductible only in four very narrowly defined situations:

1. The first is a gift of an undivided portion of the donor's entire interest.[5] For example, if Jesse Verr, a successful businessman, gave his original Ramlo sculpture to the Philadelphia Museum of Art, but agreed with the museum that he could keep it as long as he or his wife lived, no current deduction would be allowed. However, if Jesse gave an undivided one-half interest in the sculpture, that is, if he gave the museum an immediate, absolute, and complete right of ownership (for display purposes or otherwise) for one-half of each year, he would likely be successful in obtaining a current deduction.[6]

2. The second situation involves a gift of a remainder interest in a personal residence or farm.[7] If Robin Lynn Kay gives a qualified organization her home or farm with the stipulation that she may live there for life, she may take a current income tax deduction for the value of the future gift. This assumes, of course, that the gift is irrevocable.

3. The third circumstance in which a charitable contribution of less than the donor's entire interest could generate a deduction is where the donor makes a gift to a qualified charitable organization of a remainder interest in real property granted solely for conservation purposes.[8]

4. Finally, a gift of a partial interest would be deductible if transferred in trust. This exception allows a charitable deduction for transfers of property in trust even if less than the taxpayer's entire interest is transferred. The deduction is allowed to the same extent that a deduction would be allowed had the same property been transferred directly to the charitable organization rather than in trust.

The chart at Figure 2.1 and the discussion that follows illustrate how each type of property influences the limit on the deduction for an individual who itemizes deductions.

(A) Rent-Free Occupancy

Contributions of a mere right to use property (such as a rent-free lease to the Boy Scouts) are not deductible.[9] This is the situation because, to be deductible, contributions must be made in cash or other property. The mere right to use property is considered neither cash nor other property. The IRS considers a contribution of the right to use property as a contribution of less than the donor's entire interest in the property.

(B) Cash

Where the property is cash (as in a gift of any other type of property), it is necessary to ask, "Who is the donee?" If the donee is a publicly supported charity, the deduction ceiling (column 3) is 50 percent of the individual taxpayer's contribution base (generally, adjusted gross income).[10] A corporation's deduction is limited to 10 percent of its taxable income (with certain adjustments).[11] Regardless of the type of property gifted, a corporation can always take a current deduction of 10 percent of its taxable income (column 4). Likewise, regardless of the identity of the donee, a corporation may carry over excess contributions for up to five years (column 6).

Contributions by individuals to "public" charities in excess of the deductible limit for the taxable year may also be carried over (column 5) for a period of up to five years.[12] In other words, excess contributions are not wasted and can be used as itemized deductions in future years. For example, if Scott Jeffries contributed $20,000 in cash to a synagogue, but his adjusted gross income was only $36,000, he could currently deduct only 50 percent of his adjusted gross income, $18,000. He could, however, carry over the $2,000 excess ($20,000 contribution minus $18,000) to the following year (a five-year carryover is also provided for excess contributions to private foundations).

A full deduction, up to the percentage limitation of 50 percent of contribution base for individuals who itemize deductions (or 10 percent of taxable income for corporations) is allowed for gifts of cash (column 7).[13]

(C) Long-Term Capital Gain Property

The Tax Reform Act of 1986 retained the technical distinction between capital gains and ordinary income. The maximum non-corporate rate on capital gains is 28%. This distinction remains important for charitable gift purposes.

Long-term capital gain property is property which would have produced a long-term capital gain on the date of the gift had it been sold rather than donated to charity. Long-term capital gain property can be divided into two types:

The first type would consist of intangible personal property and all real property. A gift of Xerox stock purchased 11 years ago at $100 a share, now worth $400 a share, would be considered intangible personal long-term capital gain property. Appreciated land held the requisite "long-term" period would be an example of real property properly classified as long-term capital gain property.

The second type of long-term capital gain property is tangible personal property such as a car, a painting, sculpture, an antique, or jewelry. Tangible personal property will be discussed in *Section E*.

Where intangible long-term capital gain property, such as stock held for the requisite period, is given to a "public" donee (column 2), an individual's deduction may not exceed 30 percent of his adjusted gross income (column 3).[14] If his gift exceeds this percentage limitation, he may carry over the disallowed portion of the deduction for up to five succeeding years (column 5). The

Figure 2.1

CHARITABLE CONTRIBUTION DEDUCTION LIMITATIONS						
		PERCENTAGE LIMITATION				
		INDIVIDUAL AS DONOR	*CORP. AS DONOR*			
Type of Property N(1)	*Donee†* (2)	*Adjusted Gross Income*** (3)	*Taxable Income* (4)	*Individual Carryover* (5)	*Corporation Carryover* (6)	*TAX TREATMENT* (7)
(A) Rent-Free Occupancy or Services	—	—	—	—	—	No Deduction
(B) Cash	Public	50%	10%	5 yrs.	5 yrs.	Full Deduction
(C) Long-Term Capital Gain Property (except for tangible personal property)	Public	30%*	10%	5 yrs.	5 yrs.	Full Deduction for Fair Market Value
(D) Ordinary Income Property	Public	50%	10%	5 yrs.	5 yrs.	Deduction Limited to Basis††
(E) Tangible Personal Property (L.T.C.G. Property)						
(1) Use-Related	Public	30%*	10%	5 yrs.	5 yrs.	Full Deduction for Fair Market Value
(2) Use-Unrelated to Exempt Purposes of Donee	Public	50%	10%	5 yrs.	5 yrs.	Deduction Limited to Adjusted Basis
(F) Future Interests in Property*						

* See detailed discussion in text.

* * With certain adjustments.

† Regardless of the type of property given, the deduction for an individual's contributions to private charities is limited to the lesser of (a) 30 percent of the taxpayer's "contribution base" (roughly the same as adjusted gross income) or (b) 50 percent of the contribution base less any charitable contribution deduction allowed for contributions to public-type charities.

†† There is an important exception. The deduction for corporate donors (other than S corporations) has a higher limit, basis plus one-half of appreciation in value, where the property is to be used by the donee solely for the care of the ill, the needy, or infants. (See the text below.)

full fair market value of the gift is deductible (column 7).[15]

For example, suppose Nick Catrini donates stock worth $25,000 to the United Fund. The stock cost him $12,000 when he purchased it four years ago. If his adjusted gross income is $50,000, his maximum deduction for the contribution is $15,000 (30 percent of $50,000). He will be able to carry over the $10,000 balance and apply that as a 30%-type deduction against future years' income.

The deduction for contributions of long-term capital gain property is doubly advantageous. First, a person saves the taxes on his potential profit; in the above example, Nick saves the tax on a $13,000 long-term capital gain. Second, he gets a deduction for the full fair market value of the gift. Here it will be $25,000.

Contributions of certain publicly trade stock to private foundations do not share the same advantages as similar gifts to public charities. Prior to 1995, a gift of publicly traded stock, which, if sold, would result in a long-term capital gain, made to a private foundation was deductible at its fair market value provided that the amount of stock did not exceed 10% in value of all the outstanding stock of the corporation. For tax years after 1994, the deduction is limited to the donor's adjusted basis in the stock.[16]

There is an election the taxpayer may want to make in certain situations. The 30 percent limit can be increased to 50 percent if the donor is willing to reduce the value of his gift by his potential gain.[17] The election can be extremely important for a taxpayer whose income fluctuates widely from year to year. It is of particular value when the amount of appreciation is small. For example, the value of a gift of long-term capital gain property with a basis of $980 and a fair market value of $1,000 would be reduced by only $20. In this way, the taxpayer could qualify for the higher 50 percent limitation at the expense of losing only a very small portion of his deduction.

(D) Ordinary Income Property

"Ordinary income property" is an asset that would have generated ordinary income (rather than capital gain) on the date of contribution had it been sold at its fair market value rather than contributed.[18] Ordinary income property includes (a) capital assets held less than the requisite long-term period at the time contributed; (b) Section 306 stock (stock acquired in a nontaxable corporate transaction which is treated as ordinary income if sold); (c) works of art, books, letters, and musical compositions, but only if given by the person who created or prepared them or for whom they were prepared; and (d) a taxpayer's stock in trade and inventory (which would result in ordinary income if sold).[19]

Ordinary income property given to a public charity (column 2) by an individual is deductible subject to a 50 percent of contribution base ceiling. However, generally a taxpayer's deduction is limited to his basis (cost) for the property (column 7).[20] For example, if a famous painter donated one of his paintings worth $25,000 to an art museum, his deduction would be limited to his cost for producing the painting. This means that only the cost for canvas, paint, etc., would be deductible. No deduction would be allowed for the value of his time and talent.

A similar situation occurs where Tony Molino owned his National Motors stock for 4 months. (A sale would have resulted in short-term capital gain.) He purchased the stock at a cost of $12,000 and gave it to The American College when it was worth $25,000. Only his cost (basis) is deductible. Therefore, since the property is considered ordinary income property, he will be limited to a charitable deduction of $12,000 even though the property had a fair market value of $25,000 at the time of the gift.

An exception to this rule is provided for ordinary income property, such as inventory, given by a corporation to a public charity or private operating foundation for use in its exempt purpose for care of the ill, the needy, or infants (for example, a contribution of medical supplies to the Red Cross).[21] In situations where this requirement can be met, the allowable deduction for contributions of appreciated ordinary income property is limited to (a) the donor's basis plus (b) one-half the potential gain in the property (but in no event can this deduction exceed twice the basis).[22]

Assume a pharmaceutical corporation donates $11,000 worth of medicine (inventory) to a charity that performs services for ill and infirm individuals. If the basis to the corporation was $5,000, it may deduct $8,000: its $5,000 basis plus one-half the $6,000 potential gain.

Gifts of substantially appreciated ordinary income property should be avoided if possible. Capital assets should be held for the requisite long-term period if that will make it long-term capital gain property (deductible at full fair market value) or left to charity by will so that a full estate tax deduction can be obtained. Alternatively, ordinary income property could be left to the donor's children by will. The stepped-up basis they receive in the property after the donor's death will enable them to obtain a larger income tax deduction if they give the property to charity.

(E) Tangible Personal Property

Tangible personal property (which would have produced capital gain if sold) includes cars, jewelry, sculpture, art works, books, etc., but only if created or produced by persons other than the donor.[23] With respect to this type of property, a distinction must be made between (a) gifts that will be used by the donee charity in such a manner that the use of the gift is related to the exempt purposes of the donee and (b) gifts that will not be used by the charity in a manner related to the exempt purposes of the donee.

An example might be the contribution of a stamp collection to an educational institution. If the stamp collection is placed in the donee organization's library for display and study by students, the use of the donated property is related to the educational purposes constituting the basis of the charitable organization's tax exemption. However, if the stamps were sold, even if the proceeds were used by the organization for educational purposes, the use of the property is an unrelated use.

Jeff Green has $10,000 of adjusted gross income. He contributes a collection of whaling harpoons to the Cape May County Historical Museum for display purposes. The collection cost him $2,000, but on the date of contribution it was worth $10,000. The type of property contributed is tangible personal property. The donee is a public charity and the gift is use related to the exempt purposes of the Museum. Therefore, for the year of contribution, he can deduct up to 30 percent of his contribution base (A.G.I.), $10,000. This figure is $3,000. In addition, because the full $10,000 contribution is deductible, he will be able to carry over the remaining $7,000 for up to five years (subject to the 30 percent rule each year).

If the gift is use unrelated (i.e., made to a donee whose direct use of the asset is unrelated to the charitable function of the donee) the deductible amount is limited to the donor's basis in the property. This is true for corporations as well as individuals.[24]

(F) Future Interests in Property

A "future interest" is any interest or right that will vest in possession or enjoyment at some time in the future. The term "future interest" includes situations where a donor purports to give tangible personal property to a charitable organization but has made a written or oral agreement with the organization reserving to a noncharitable beneficiary (himself or a member of his immediate family) the right to use, possess, or enjoy the property. For example, suppose Robin Lynn donates a genuine Meccariello photograph to an art museum but arranges with the museum to keep the photograph in her home as long as she lives. The museum has a future interest in the photograph.

One of the basic general rules governing charitable deductions is that contributions must (a) actually be paid, (b) be paid in cash or other property, and (c) be paid before the close of the tax year. Furthermore, generally no deductions are allowed for an outright contribution of less than the donor's entire interest in property.

Since the benefit to the museum—and consequently to the public—was deferred in the gift of the Meccariello photograph, no current tax deduction would be allowed. The implication is that a deduction will not be allowed until the charity receives actual possession or enjoyment of the work of art. The gift of tangible personal property must be complete in the sense that all interest and rights to the possession and enjoyment of the property must vest in the charity. This means that a transfer of a future interest in property to a charity is not deductible until all intervening interests in and rights to possession held by the donor or certain related persons or organizations have expired or unless the gift is in the form of a future interest in trust which meets the requirements discussed in Chapter 3.

Charitable remainder interests are a form of future interest in which an income interest is either retained by the donor or is given by the donor to another person. At the death of the income beneficiary, the principal goes to a designated charity. An example would be a gift to X for life where the remainder (the principal at the death of X) goes to charity (the "remainderman") upon the death of X (the income beneficiary). A gift "to X for life, remainder to The American College" would be considered a gift of a future interest to The American College. Charitable remainder trusts are discussed in more depth in Chapter 3.

Question — Why are stocks and bonds often used for charitable gifts?

Answer — Securities such as listed stocks, mutual funds, or bonds are often selected as the subject of a charitable gift because:

(a) they are transferable with minimal cost or delay;

(b) as mentioned above, appreciated securities can often be transferred without causing the donor to realize gain on the appreciation and still yield a current deduction measured by the fair market value of the gift;

(c) securities selling below their cost should be sold and the net proceeds donated (this sale-gift procedure can lower the donor's tax);

(d) the donor's spendable income is often increased rather than decreased by the contribution;

(e) a lifetime gift removes appreciating property from an individual's estate and may lower death taxes and administration expenses.

Question — What is a bargain sale and how is it used for charitable purposes?

Answer — The bargain sale is a device used to minimize the out-of-pocket cost of a charitable gift. Prior to the Tax Reform Act of 1969, an individual could sell appreciated property to a charity at his cost. The donor would receive back an amount equal to his investment. In addition, he would obtain a charitable deduction for the appreciation in the property with no tax on his portion.

Under current law, the taxpayer may have to recognize a taxable gain on the bargain sale because he must allocate his cost basis between the part of the property he sold to the charity and the part he donated.[25] This means the donor pays tax on his pro rata share of the appreciation.

For example, suppose a donor sells property he has owned for several years to his favorite charity. At the date of the sale it was worth $10,000. The sale price is the same as his cost, $4,000. The gift amounts to 6/10 (60 percent) of the property, so he is deemed to have given the charity 60 percent of his $4,000 cost basis, $2,400. This leaves him only the difference, $1,600 of cost, to apply against the $4,000 he received. His long-term capital gain is therefore $2,400.

The $6,000 gift ($10,000 - $4,000) saves him $2,376 in taxes if he is in a 39.6 percent marginal tax bracket. He also has recovered his $4,000 investment, so his total "recovery" is $6,376. Since the maximum long-term capital gain rate is 28%, his tax will be 28 percent of $2,400, or $672. The net return is $5,704 ($6,376 - $672), and the charity is enriched by $6,000.

Question — How can gifts of closely held stock be used to generate a charitable contribution deduction?

Answer — Several court decisions have opened the door to a relatively new charitable contribution deduction tool: the use of closely held stock. The idea is to enable the owner of a closely held corporation to siphon funds from his business free of income tax by making a charitable contribution of his personally owned stock followed by an unrelated redemption of that stock by the corporation.[26] If used properly, the technique may eliminate or reduce the threat of an accumulated earnings tax problem, generate a current income tax deduction for the donor (at no loss of control), and provide cash for the donor's favorite charity with no out-of-pocket outlay.

It works like this. First, the stockholder donates some of his stock to the charitable organization. He receives a charitable deduction measured by the present value of the stock contributed. Then the corporation redeems the stock from the charity. (Had the corporation redeemed the stock directly from the donor, dividend treatment would probably have resulted.)

One use of this device involved a closely held corporation whose controlling shareholder gave a school about 200 shares of his corporation's stock each year. He took an annual deduction for the present value of the gifts, about $25,000.

The terms of the gift provided that the university could not dispose of the shares without first offering them to the corporation at their book value. The corporation was not required to purchase the stock but did have 60 days in which to purchase any stock offered to it.

Within a year or two after the shares were received by the school, they were offered to the corporation which always purchased them. The proceeds of these redemptions were then invested by the school.

It appears that the key elements in the success of this device are that the gifts were, in fact, complete and irrevocable and that there was no formal or informal agreement that the university would offer the stock for redemption or that it would be redeemed. This avoided the obvious attack that the redemptions from the charity were in essence redemptions from the donor and should have been taxed as ordinary income to him.[27]

Retention of substantial rights in the stock given to charity, such as voting rights, will result in disallowance of the deduction because the entire interest in the property is not transferred.[28]

Question — Why is life insurance a good way to make charitable contributions?

Answer — Life insurance, like any other property, can be, and often is, the subject of a gift. In fact, life insurance is a favored means of making charitable contributions for a number of reasons.

First, the death benefit going to charity is guaranteed as long as premiums are paid. This means that the charity will receive an amount which is fixed in value and not subject to the potential downside risks of securities.

Second, life insurance provides an "amplified" gift that can be purchased on the installment plan. Through a relatively small annual cost (premium), a large benefit can be provided for the charity. A large gift can be made without impairing or diluting the control of a family business interest or other investments. Assets earmarked for the donor-insured's family can thus be kept intact.

Third, life insurance is a self-completing gift. If the donor lives, cash values, which can be used by the charity currently, grow constantly from year to year. If the donor becomes disabled, the policy will remain in full force if the policy contains a waiver-of-premium feature, guaranteeing both the ultimate death benefit to the charity as well as the same cash values and dividend build-up that would have been earned had the insured not become disabled. Even if death occurs after only one deposit, the charity is assured of its full gift.

Fourth, the death proceeds can be received by the designated charity free of federal income and estate taxes, probate and administrative costs and delays, brokerage fees, or other transfer costs. Thus, the charity, in fact, receives "one hundred cent" dollars. This prompt cash payment should be compared with the payment of a gift to the selected charity under the terms of an individual's will. In that case, probate delays of up to several years are not uncommon.

Fifth, because of the contractual nature of the life insurance policy, large gifts to charity are not subject to attack by disgruntled heirs. Life insurance proceeds also do not run afoul of the so-called mortmain statutes which prohibit or limit gifts made within a short time of death.

Finally, a substantial gift may be made with no attending publicity. Since the life insurance proceeds paid to charity can be arranged so that they will not be part of the decedent's probate estate, the proceeds can be paid confidentially. Of course, publicity may be given if desired.

Warning: In Private Letter Ruling 9110016, the Service denied a charitable deduction for premiums paid on a life insurance policy assigned to a charity on the grounds that since the charity had no insurable interest (under New York law) in the insured, payment of the proceeds to the charity could violate state law. If so, it was determined that the proceeds would be included in the insured's estate and, thus, subject to federal estate tax. Subsequent to the Service's treatment of the matter, New York amended its insurable interest statute to give charities an insurable interest in donors' lives. The Service responded to New York's amendment by issuing Letter Ruling 9147040, which revoked Letter Ruling 9110016. Most states now have insurable interest statutes giving charities an insurable interest in the lives of their contributors. Some states require the charity to be the owner and irrevocable beneficiary while others allow the insured to be the initial owner if a subsequent transfer to the charity is made.

Question — How is the gift of a life insurance policy valued?

Answer — Since the bundle of rights in a life insurance policy can be considered equivalent to property, a gift of a life insurance policy is valued according to the same general tax rules as any other gift of property.

If a life insurance policy were sold at a gain, the gain would be taxed at ordinary income rates; therefore, a gift of life insurance is a gift of ordinary income property. Assuming the value of the policy (interpolated terminal reserve plus unearned premium on the date of the sale) exceeds the policyholder's net premium payments, the deduction for a gift of a policy is generally limited to the policyholder's basis (cost), in other words, his net premium payments.

For example, suppose an individual assigns a policy on his life to the College for Financial Planning. His charitable contribution deduction is limited to his basis (i.e., his cost in the contract or the value of the policy, if lower). If he paid net premiums of $15,000 but the policy had a value of $18,000, his charitable contribution deduction would be limited to $15,000.

If there would have been no gain upon a sale of the policy, the value of the donated policy would have been equal to its replacement cost at the date of the gift. In other words, if the total net premiums paid exceed the value of the policy when the individual assigns it (i.e., the policy

would not give rise to a gain if sold), the deduction would be limited to its replacement cost.

The amount of the deduction is dependent on the replacement cost of the policy. This differs depending on whether the policy in question is (1) a single premium or paid-up policy, (2) a premium-paying policy, or (3) a newly issued policy. The insurance company in question will generally calculate the exact value on IRS Form 712 upon request.

The replacement cost of a single premium or paid-up policy is the single premium the same insurer would charge for a policy of the same amount at the insured's attained age (increased by the value of any dividend credits and reduced by the amount of any loans outstanding).

The replacement cost of a premium-paying policy is the policy's interpolated terminal reserve plus any unearned premium at the date of the gift (again, taking into consideration any dividend credits and outstanding loans).

The replacement cost of a newly issued policy is the gross premium paid by the insured.

A gift of a life insurance policy to charity must, of course, satisfy local requisites of a valid gift. In most states, this means that the donor must have intended to make a present gift of the policy and that he delivered it, actually or constructively, to the charitable donee. An absolute assignment is the clearest way of effectuating the transfer.

Question — Is it possible to obtain a charitable deduction for premium payments if a charity owns a life insurance policy on the donor's life?

Answer — Premium payments are considered gifts of cash and are, therefore, fully and currently deductible as charitable contributions if the charity owns the policy outright.

The donor should send his check directly to the charity and have it pay the premium to the life insurance company in order to insure the most favorable tax results. The canceled check will serve as proof of (1) the fact that a gift was made to the charity, (2) the date the gift was made, and (3) the amount of the gift. It will also assure the donor of a full deduction up to 50 percent of his adjusted gross income.

When an "indirect" gift is made to a charity, the annual deduction limit is lowered to 30 percent of the taxpayer's income. A gift in trust is one such example. Another example of an indirect gift is where premiums on a policy owned by a charity are remitted directly to the life insurance company instead of to the charity itself.

If the gift to the charity exceeds $250, a statement will be required from the charitable organization showing the amount of money contributed and whether the charity gave any goods or services in return for the contribution.

Question — Is it possible to use life insurance in a way that "balloons" or "swells" the marital deduction?

Answer — Some authorities believe that it is possible for a policy owner to obtain both an immediate income tax deduction and an estate tax advantage through the gift of a life insurance policy to charity. During his life, the policyholder gives a policy on his life to a charity. He transfers all but one of the incidents of ownership to the charitable organization. Thus, the charity would receive the right to surrender the policy, the right to borrow the cash value, etc.[29]

A gift of property (the rights in the policy) is made which gives rise to a current income tax deduction for the fair market value of the policy—the same value that the policy would have for gift tax purposes. The former policyowner may or may not decide to continue to pay premiums on the policy. If he does, in essence he is making additional gifts each year to the charity as the premium is paid.

At his death, because of his retained incident of ownership, the death proceeds should be included in his gross estate. Since the proceeds will be paid to the charity, they will be deducted under Code section 2055, resulting in a wash. However, if the marital deduction is based on the value of the gross estate (less debts, funeral expenses and administration expenses), the inclusion of the death proceeds should increase the maximum marital deduction by half the amount of the death proceeds. Many estates will continue to use the prior marital deduction limitation of one-half the adjusted gross estate, and will not use the unlimited marital deduction.

The following example illustrates how a larger gross estate could mean a lower federal estate tax. This is the estate tax picture of an individual before using the life insurance gift technique. Assume the marital deduction provided in the will is limited to one-half the adjusted gross estate.

Gross Estate		$1,500,000
Less deductions:		
Administration fees		
Funeral costs, debts		50,000
Adjusted Gross Estate		$1,450,000
Less deductions:		
Marital deduction	$725,000	
Charitable bequest	0	
Total Deductions		$725,000
Taxable Estate (Tentative Tax Base)		$725,000
Federal Estate Tax		
(after unified credit)		$ 46,250

Now assume the estate owner, using the same marital deduction formula, purchases a $100,000 whole life policy on his own life and names a qualified charity as owner-beneficiary. Certain ownership rights in the policy are restricted so that the insured must consent to their exercise. (This retained power is discussed in footnote 29.) His new federal estate tax computation would look like this:

Gross Estate		$1,600,000
Less deductions:		
Administrative fees		
Funeral costs, debts		50,000
Adjusted Gross Estate		$1,550,000
Less deductions:		
Marital deduction	775,000	
Charitable bequest	100,000	
Total Deductions		$875,000
Taxable Estate (Tentative Tax Base)		$675,000
Federal Estate Tax		
(after unified credit)		$ 27,750

By increasing the gross estate by $100,000, the estate owner decreases his estate tax by $18,500 ($46,250 - $27,750). This is because in the example given, the marital deduction is based on the adjusted gross estate, which is calculated before the deduction for the charitable bequest is taken.

The significance of this technique is diminished to the extent that an individual wishes to avail himself of the unlimited marital deduction permitted by ERTA '81. If such individual uses an unlimited marital deduction, he would not have any federal estate tax at his death. Thus, from an estate tax point of view the technique of "swelling" the marital deduction will not achieve any tax savings and will be of no significance unless a formula type marital deduction clause is used which is based on a percentage of the adjusted gross estate.

Another way to "balloon" the estate tax marital deduction might be to establish a charitable trust. The donor will name himself trustee and the trust instrument will give the trustee broad discretion in the selection of the specific qualified charity or charities to be benefited. The trust would be named owner and beneficiary of the insurance proceeds, but the death proceeds should be includable in the gross estate of the donor. This is because he has retained the power, during his lifetime, to affect the beneficial interests of the trust beneficiaries in the life insurance proceeds.

The estate owner (given the same numerical facts and the same marital deduction formula as in the prior illustration) should also realize an income tax benefit during his lifetime. He can deduct the amount of the premium from his gross income within the allowable percentage limits. If it is assumed that net premiums were $3,000 a year and that the estate owner died after 20 years, his total premium outlay would have been $60,000. If he was in the 39.6 percent income tax bracket, his income tax savings would have been $23,760 over the 20 years. Stated another way, he contributed $100,000 to charity at an after-tax cost of $17,740 ($60,000 premium outlay minus (a) $18,500 estate tax savings and (b) $23,760 income tax savings).[30]

Question — How could life insurance enable a charity to convince a donor to make an immediate gift of land or other property?

Answer — Life insurance can serve as a means of enabling a donor to make a large current gift. For example, an individual is 50 years old, is a widower, and has three children. His gross estate is about $1 million. One of his assets is a parcel of land with a basis and fair market value of about $200,000. He wants to perpetuate the memory of his late wife through a memorial scholarship fund, but at the same time he does not want to deprive his children of a significant part of his estate.

He can satisfy his overall objective through an immediate gift coupled with the purchase of life insurance to replace the gifted property. Assuming his income is taxed at a marginal rate of 39.6 percent, the arrangement would work like this:

He would contribute the $200,000 parcel of land to his favorite charity immediately. Since the gift is an outright contribution, it will be currently deductible up to 30 percent of his adjusted gross income. (If his income is not high enough to allow him to deduct the entire $200,000 in one year, he could carry over the excess and deduct it against his next 5 years' income.) The $200,000 charitable contribution would result in $79,200 of tax savings, since he is in a 39.6 percent income tax bracket. He can take this $79,200 that otherwise would have been used to

pay taxes and instead make annual gifts of up to $10,000 each to his children. They in turn could purchase a policy on his life and name themselves as owners and beneficiaries.

The chart at Figure 2.2 compares a charitable bequest of the $200,000 parcel of land by will to an immediate lifetime charitable gift of the property coupled with the purchase of life insurance to replace the gifted land. Although the federal estate tax is the same in either situation, the heirs receive $100,000 more by the lifetime gift/insurance purchase technique. Assume death occurs in 1995.

The premium on a $100,000 whole life policy for a male age 50 is only about $3,000 a year; so it will take almost 26 years before the premiums even equal his $79,200 tax savings. The charity has the ownership of the land immediately, and he has provided his children with everything they would have received even if he made no gift. In fact, properly arranged, the policy proceeds will be received free of income, estate tax, inheritance tax, and probate cost. Thus, his children could be in better financial condition than if he had waited to make the gift.

Question — Can a donor obtain a charitable deduction if he splits policy cash values or death benefits between a charity and a family member?

Answer — A life insurance policy can be split into two parts, the protection element and the policy cash value. The protection element, often called the net amount at risk, is the difference between the face amount of the policy and its cash (surrender) value. By splitting the proceeds of a policy between a donor's family and a charity, a donor can provide additional protection for the benefit of his family and at the same time make a meaningful gift to charity.

Note that if a donor attempts to "split dollar" the charitable gift (i.e., to name his personal beneficiary as the recipient of the policy's pure death benefit (the amount at risk) but making the charity owner of the cash value) the Service will claim that this is a gift of a "partial interest" in property and will disallow a deduction for the amount of the increase in cash surrender value of the insurance policy attributable to the taxpayer's annual payment of premium.[31] The same principle applies where the donor retains an interest in the policy cash value but assigns an interest in the "amount at risk" portion to the charity. The problem is caused by Code section 170, which provides that a charitable deduction is not allowed for contributions to charity "of less than the taxpayer's entire interest in the property."

Figure 2.8

	BEQUEST OF PROPERTY BY WILL	LIFETIME GIFT OF PROPERTY			BEQUEST OF PROPERTY BY WILL	LIFETIME GIFT OF PROPERTY
Gross Estate	$1,000,000	$800,000		Gross Estate	$1,000,000	$800,000
		less		Estate Tax (after unified credit)	75,000	less 75,000
Charitable Bequest by Will	200,000	0			925,000	725,000
Taxable Estate (Tentative Tax Base)	$ 800,000	$800,000		Charitable Bequest by Will	200,000	less 0
					725,000	725,000
						plus
				New Life Insurance	0	100,000
				Passing to Heirs	725,000	825,000
				Advantage of Lifetime Gift	$100,000	

A gift of the cash value is considered a gift of less than the entire interest in the property regardless of whether the donor retains the right to designate the beneficiary of the risk portion or irrevocably designates the beneficiary before making the gift.[32] Furthermore, if the gift is considered "less than the policyowner's entire interest," disallowance of the gift tax deduction will cause a gift of the policy cash value to be a taxable transfer.[33]

Question — Can group term life insurance be used for charitable contributions?

Answer — Currently, employees must include the cost of group term life insurance coverage over $50,000 in their taxable income. The tax on this economic benefit must be paid with after-tax dollars, which has the effect of reducing the spendable income of the employee.

However, by naming a charity as the beneficiary of group insurance coverage over $50,000, the employee can provide for a gift to charity and at the same time avoid the tax on the economic benefit.

For example, a 63-year-old executive who is taxed at a marginal rate of 39.6 percent who had $140,000 of coverage would save 39.6% of $105.30 per month ($1,263.60 annually), or $500.39 annually. The advantage of this technique was significantly enhanced by the introduction of higher group term rates for individuals over age 65 who receive group term insurance on or after January, 1989.

Question — What are some other ways a life insurance policy can be used to generate income or capital for a charity?

Answer — There are a number of additional ways life insurance may be utilized for charitable purposes. Some potential donors are not in a position to turn over to a charity an entire portfolio of life insurance or even a single policy. It is still possible to provide protection for their families and at the same time make periodic cash donations. Annual policy dividends can be paid directly to a specific charity.

The donor could retain control over the disposition of the policy proceeds and the charity's interest in the policy would be limited to the right to receive annual cash dividends. The donation could be for a specified period only, for example, 5, 10, or 15 years. It could be on an unlimited basis but with the insured-owner reserving the right to revoke at anytime. Alternatively, the gift could be made without limitation. As the dividends are paid, they could be taken as deductions.

Alternatively, the dividends from the existing policy could be used to purchase a new policy. The charity, instead of receiving the dividend itself, would be named owner and beneficiary of the policy purchased by the dividend (and perhaps an additional cash donation). The charitable contribution would equal the premium paid.

For example, Scott Kay is a 26-year-old attorney who is married and has one child. On his 21st birthday his father purchased a $50,000 whole life policy for him, which Scott now owns.

Scott would like to make annual contributions to the long-term library building program of his law school but does not feel his income will support additional contributions. He could use the current dividend on his $50,000 policy—which is now in excess of $150 per year—and use that dividend to purchase a policy to be owned by the law school. He could buy over $5,000 of life insurance that would guarantee the law school a gift whether he lived, died, or (assuming he purchased a waiver-of-premium feature) became disabled.

Sometimes an individual will want to make a charitable contribution at death but is concerned with his family's needs. He could name the charity as the revocable beneficiary of a policy on his life so that any time before his death he could change the beneficiary designation to his wife and children. Although he would not qualify for a current income tax deduction, at his death, when the proceeds were paid to the charity, the increase in the marital deduction due to the inclusion of the policy proceeds in his estate—coupled with the charitable deduction—would result in an overall lower estate tax burden assuming the marital deduction is based on a percentage of the adjusted gross estate. Alternatively, a donor could name the charity as contingent or second contingent beneficiary under life insurance protecting his dependents. In this way insurance can serve a dual purpose—it is primarily for the protection of an individual's family but also is a means for providing a potential gift to a charity if conditions should warrant it.

Question — How are charitable deductions valued?

Answer — If a charitable (income, estate or gift tax) deduction is allowed with respect to a significant part of the property transferred, a client can elect to (a) value the property using the Section 7520 valuation table interest rate for the month in which the valuation date falls, or (b) value interests in the property by reference to the Section 7520 valuation table interest rate in effect for either of the two months preceding the valuation date. (Valuation tables, other than those used for unitrusts, are reproduced in Appendix D. Unitrust factors can be obtained from IRS Publication 1458.)

ASRS, Secs. 53, ¶¶9.1, 20.5(h); 54, ¶¶31, 44.5(d); 55, ¶¶46, 57.10; and 49, ¶¶400.6(c), 400.12(d).

Footnote References

Charitable Contributions

1.   IRC Secs. 170(b)(1)(B), 170(b)(1)(E), 170(c).
2.   Reg. §1.170A-8(f).
3.   IRC Secs. 170(b)(2), 170(d)(2)(A), 170(a)(2), Reg. §1.170A-11.
4.   IRC Secs. 170(b)(1)(B), 170(d)(1)(A), 170(d)(2).
5.   IRC Sec. 170(f)(3)(B). *See also,* Rev. Rul. 58-260, 1958-1 CB 126; Reg. §1.170A-7(a).
6.   Reg. §1.170A-7(b)(1).
7.   IRC Sec. 170(f)(3)(B)(i).
8.   IRC Secs. 170(f)(3)(B)(iii), 170(h); Reg. §1.170A-7(b)(5).
9.   IRC Sec. 170(f)(3)(A); Reg. §1.170A-7(a).
10. IRC Sec. 170(b)(1)(A).
11. IRC Secs. 170(b)(2), 170(d)(2).
12. IRC Secs. 170(d)(1), 170(b)(1)(B), 170(b)(1)(D)(ii); Reg. §1.170A-10(a).
13. IRC Secs. 170(b)(1), 170(d)(1)(A), 170(b)(2), 170(d)(2)(A), 170(a)(2); Regs. §§1.170A-8(b), 1.170A-11.
14. IRC Sec. 170(b)(1)(C)(i).
15. IRC Secs. 170(b)(1)(C)(ii), 170(e)(1).
16. IRC Section 170(e). Note that IRC Section 170(e)(5) concerning contributions of certain publicly traded stock to private foundations shall not apply to contributions made after December 31, 1994.
17. IRC Secs. 170(b)(1)(C)(iii), 170(e)(1)(B); Regs. §§1.170A-8(b), 1.170A-8(d)(2).
18. IRC Sec. 170(e).
19. IRC Sec. 1221.
20. IRC Sec. 170(e)(1)(A); Sen. Rep. P.L. 91-171 (12060).
21. IRC Sec. 170(e)(3); Tax Reform Act of 1976, Title XXI, Sec. 2135.
22. Joint Committee on Taxation, General Explanation of Tax Reform Act of 1976, *reprinted in* 1976-3 CB (Vol. 2) 1; IRC Sec. 170(e)(3)(B).
23. IRC Sec. 170(e)(1)(B)(i); Reg.§1.170A-4.
24. IRC Sec. 170(e)(1)(B)(i). See Cong. Record, 12-23-69.
25. Reg. §1.1011-2.
26. Note that the basic planning principle in these cases (i.e., that the redemption by a corporation of closely held stock from a charity will not be considered a dividend to the individual who donated the stock to the charity in the absence of a prearranged plan) is still useful. *Grove v. Comm.,* 490 F.2d 241 (2nd Cir. 1973); *Dewitt v. U.S.,* 503 F.2d 1406 (Ct. Cl. 1974); *Carrington v. Comm.,* 476 F.2d 704 (5th Cir. 1973). Although both *Grove* and *Carrington* were decided after 1969, they were decided on the basis of pre-1969 Tax Reform Act law. This is why the retention of a life income by the donor did not cause a loss of the charitable deduction. But under present law, a retention of the life income produced by the donated stock or by the proceeds of a sale of such stock would make the contribution a gift of "less than the donor's entire interest in the contributed property." Such a gift would not qualify for a charitable deduction. See Letter Ruling 8123069 where the Service held that appreciated securities used for the redemption of all stock held by the charity would not cause dividend consequences.
27. *Palmer v. Comm.,* 62 TC 684 (1974), *aff'd on other grounds,* 523 F.2d 1308 (8th Cir. 1975), *acq.* 1978-1 CB 2. *See also* TAM 8623007, reaching the same conclusion as *Palmer* on "materially identical" facts. *But see* TAM 8552009, where controlling shareholders, H and W, gave nonvoting common stock shares in a family corporation to a qualified charitable trust. The shares were subject to a stock restriction agreement that would not allow the trust to sell the stock to anyone outside the stockholder group without first offering it to the corporation and the other authorized shareholders at a value contained in the agreement. The donors claimed a fair market value for the stock on their income tax return for the year of the gift of $18 million, and later had the corporation redeem the stock from the trust for the same amount. The IRS refused to apply the rationale of the *Palmer* case, above, claiming that the fair market value of the stock at the time of the gift was $32 million and at the time of the redemption was $36 million, and that the gift and the redemption were part of the taxpayers' plan to use the trust as a conduit to make a gift to the remaining stockholders, their descendants, by

increasing the value of their descendants' shares and correspondingly decreasing the value of H's and W's shares. The Service characterized the transaction as a redemption by the corporation from H and W of all the ostensibly donated stock, followed by a gift of the proceeds to their descendants.

28. Rev. Rul. 81-282, 1981-2 CB 78.

29. One possible flaw in this argument is that the IRS could insist that the taxpayer is giving less than his entire interest in the property. Success with this argument could cause forfeiture of the income tax deduction. Furthermore, the gift tax deductions for charitable contributions could be disallowed. In Revenue Ruling 76-200, 1976-1 CB 308, the Service said that where an insured assigns (even irrevocably) the cash surrender value of a policy to a charity but retains the right to name or change the beneficiary of proceeds in excess of the cash value and assign the balance of the proceeds in excess of the charity's right to the cash value, he has given less than his entire interest (and not an undivided portion of his entire interest). The gift tax deduction was disallowed.

30. The probability of success of this concept was reinforced by Revenue Ruling 72-552, 1972-2 CB 43, which stated that the value of inter vivos transfers to a charitable corporation would be includable in the estate of the donor who, as president of the corporation, retained power over the disposition of its funds. The ruling also held that the value was includable in determining the marital deduction allowable and qualified as a charitable deduction. The Section 2036 control retained was the right to select the charitable beneficiaries who would receive the funds of the charitable corporation. By inference, the retention by the policy-owner-donor of the right to choose between two charitable beneficiaries or the right to consent to any change in beneficiary should qualify as an "incident of ownership" under IRC Section 2042 and have the same effect as that discussed in Rev. Rul. 72-552.

Some courts have held that the mere right to change the time or manner of payment of proceeds to the beneficiary (as by electing, changing, or revoking settlement options) is a taxable incident of ownership. *Est. of Lumpkin, Jr. v. Comm.*, 474 F.2d 1092 (5th Cir. 1973). *See also Eleanor M. Schwager,* 64 TC 781 (1975), which held that the right to require written consent to a beneficiary change is an incident of ownership.

31. IRC Sec. 170(f)(3).

32. Rev. Rul. 76-143, 1976-1 CB 63. *See also* Rev. Rul. 76-1, 1976-1 CB 57, which disallowed a deduction for a gift to charity of the annuity portion of a split-life contract.

33. Rev. Rul. 76-200, 1976-1 CB 308.

Chapter 3

CHARITABLE SPLIT INTEREST TRUSTS

WHAT IS IT?

With the exception of a pooled income fund, and wealth replacement trust, discussed below, this section deals with charitable split trusts which have both charitable and noncharitable beneficiaries.

A distinction must be made between trusts established solely for the benefit of charity (deductible without meeting the requirements below) and trusts which have both charitable and noncharitable beneficiaries. Deductions for contributions to this second type of trust are measured by the present value of the ultimate gift to charity. If the charity receives annuity or unitrust payments for a specified term and then the corpus goes to the donor's family or some other noncharitable beneficiary, the trust is referred to as a charitable lead trust (discussed in more detail below.) But if noncharitable beneficiaries receive annuity or unitrust payments for a specified period (e.g., "for 10 years" or "for life") and afterwards the charity receives the remaining corpus, the trust is called a charitable remainder trust.

Gifts of a remainder interest in trust generally are deductible only if made in one of three ways: (1) a "fixed annuity" trust, (2) a "unitrust," or (3) a "pooled income fund."[1]

These three permissible forms of trust are an outgrowth of congressional concern over potential abuses of gifts of a remainder interest in trust to charity. For example, suppose Mr. and Mrs. W were a financially secure but childless couple. Mr. W might leave his property to his wife in trust. Mrs. W, according to the terms of the trust, would receive the income for life if she survived her husband. At her death, the principal in the trust would pass to a designated charity. Mr. W would take a current charitable contribution deduction for the present value of the gift which the charity would receive at the death of the income beneficiary. To counteract inflation and provide for contingencies, a clause might be inserted in the trust agreement authorizing an invasion of principal for Mrs. W's benefit.

The potential for abuse was that the principal in the trust was often invested in securities that produced an extremely high income but at the cost of a correspondingly high risk. This situation naturally worked to the detriment of the charitable remainderman. In addition, the ability of the trustee to make substantial invasions of the principal of the trust further increased the likelihood that little, if any, of the original contribution would be received by the charity. The result was a decrease in the value of the charity's remainder interest.

For these reasons, rules were designed to prevent a taxpayer from receiving a current charitable contribution deduction for a gift to charity of a remainder interest in trust which may be substantially in excess of the amount the charity may ultimately receive (because the assumptions used in calculating the value of the remainder interest had little relation to the actual investment policies of the trust).

Pursuant to these rules, deductions are basically limited to situations where the trust specifies (a) a fixed annual *amount* which is to be paid to the noncharitable income beneficiary (an annuity trust), or (b) the amount the income beneficiary will receive in terms of a *fixed percentage* of the value of the trust assets ascertained each year (a unitrust), or (c) that property contributed by a number of donors is commingled with property transferred by other donors and each beneficiary of an income interest will receive income determined by the rate of return earned by the trust for such year (a pooled income fund).[2]

A charitable lead annuity or unitrust, which is essentially the reverse of the remainder trust, provides that a fixed annual payment, either in the form of an annuity or a unitrust percentage, is made to one or more qualified charities during the term of the trust. At the end of that term, the property is normally transferred either to the donor or members of the donor's family.[3]

A "wealth replacement trust," discussed below, is often used in conjunction with a charitable remainder trust to replace the loss of value to the family of the donor of the trust assets passing to a charitable remainder trust.

WHEN IS THE USE OF SUCH A DEVICE INDICATED?

A primary function of the charitable split interest trust is to provide either a present (remainder) or future (lead) economic benefit to the donor or other members of the family, or both, with a present or future transfer to charity which qualifies for income, estate, and gift tax charitable deductions. Refer to the extended discussion of these deductions in Chapter 2.

However, in the case of charitable remainder trusts, particularly the charitable remainder unitrust, a primary motivation for the use of the trust is for the transfer of substantially appreciated property by the donor, which will then be sold by the trust, a entity exempt from federal income tax. The trustee will then reinvest the proceeds of the sale to generate a high income yield. The retained annuity or unitrust interest of the donor, and/or the family of the donor, will be based on the pretax value of the property transferred to the trust. In other words, the donor can receive payments on the entire value of the fund, with no reduction for tax on the built-in gain on the transferred assets.

A principal drawback to this plan is the loss of the value of the trust assets to the family of the donor. This in turn leads to the concept of the wealth replacement trust, generally an irrevocable life insurance trust. The idea is that the additional income stream to the donor which results from the use of this device can be used to pay premiums on life insurance on the donor held in such a trust, which ultimately is distributed to the family to replace the "wealth," i.e., the value of the assets in the charitable remainder trust.

WHAT ARE THE REQUIREMENTS?

A charitable remainder annuity trust is a trust designed to permit payment of a fixed amount annually to a noncharitable beneficiary with the remainder going to charity.[4]

The donor transfers money or securities to a trust which pays him a fixed dollar amount each year for life. If the income of the trust is insufficient to meet the required annual payment, the difference is paid from capital gains or principal. If the income is greater than the amount required in any given year, the excess is reinvested in trust. The income tax deduction is computed in the year funds are irrevocably placed in trust and is measured by the present value of the charity's right to receive the trust assets at the death of the income beneficiary.

In order to qualify for income (and estate and gift) tax deductions, the charitable remainder annuity trust must meet a number of tests.[5] The primary requirements are these:

1. A fixed amount or fixed percentage of the initial value of the trust must be payable to the noncharitable beneficiary.

2. This annuity must be not less than an amount equal to 5 percent of the initial fair market value of all the property transferred in trust.

3. The specified amount must be paid at least annually to the beneficiary out of income and/or principal.

4. The trust must be irrevocable and not subject to a power by either the donor, the trustee, or the beneficiary to invade, alter, or amend the trust.

5. The trust must be for the benefit of a named individual or individuals who must be living at the time of the transfer in trust and their interests must be for a life estate or a term of years not exceeding 20 years.

6. The entire remainder must go to charity.

If all the necessary tests are met, the donor of a charitable remainder annuity trust will be entitled to an income tax deduction limited to the value of the remainder interest.

A charitable remainder unitrust, like a charitable remainder annuity trust, is basically designed to permit payment of a periodic sum to a noncharitable beneficiary with a remainder to charity.[6] The key distinction is in how the periodic sum is computed.

It works like this: The donor would irrevocably transfer money or securities to a trustee. In return, the trustee would pay the donor (or other beneficiary) a unitrust amount from the property for life. The donor could also provide that if he predeceased his spouse, she in turn would receive a unitrust amount from the donated property for life. The donor would receive payments based on a fixed percentage of the fair market value of the assets placed in trust. The assets would be revalued each year.

In order to qualify for income (and estate and gift) tax deductions, the structure of a charitable remainder unitrust must conform to guidelines set forth in the Code.[7] These include:

1. A fixed percentage of the net fair market value of the principal, as revalued annually, must be payable to the noncharitable beneficiary.

2. The percentage payable must be not less than 5 percent of the annual value.

3. The unitrust may provide that the noncharitable beneficiary can receive the lesser of (a) the specified fixed percentage or (b) the trust income for the year, plus any excess trust income to the extent of any deficiency in the prior years by reason of the distribution being limited to the amount of trust income in such years.

4. The noncharitable income beneficiaries must be living at the time of transfer in trust, and their interests must be for a term of years not exceeding 20 years, or a life estate.

5. The entire remainder must go to charity.

The tax deductions allowed are the same as in the case of a charitable remainder annuity trust.

The deduction is allowed in the year funds are irrevocably placed in trust. The deduction is measured by the present value at the date of the gift of the charity's right to eventually receive the unitrust's assets.

The IRS has stated that it will challenge the use of charitable remainder unitrusts to convert appreciated assets into cash while avoiding a substantial portion of the tax on the gain. In the transactions in question, appreciated assets are transferred to a short-term charitable remainder unitrust that has a high percentage unitrust amount.[8]

A pooled income fund is a trust generally created and maintained by a public charity rather than a private donor, which meets the requirements explained below.

The basic requirements are these:

1. The donor must contribute an irrevocable, vested remainder interest to the charitable organization which maintains it.

2. The property transferred by each donor must be commingled with the property transferred by other donors.

3. The fund cannot invest in tax-exempt securities.

4. No donor or income beneficiary can be a trustee.

5. The donor must retain (for himself or one or more named income beneficiaries) a life income interest.

6. Each income beneficiary must be entitled to and receive a pro rata share of the income (annually) based upon the rate of return earned by the fund.

If these tests are met, the donor will generally be entitled to an income, and gift or estate tax deduction.[9]

As stated above, a charitable lead trust is essentially the reverse of a charitable remainder trust. It is an income tax device that will enable a taxpayer to reduce the tax burden of an unusually high income year. If certain requirements are met, he will be allowed a current deduction for the value of the annuity or unitrust interest he gives to a charity in trust with the remainder going to a noncharitable beneficiary (or a reversion in the donor). The cost of the large current deduction is that the donor is taxed on the trust income each year under the "grantor trust" provisions of the Code. This means that the grantor *must* be treated as the owner of such interest under Code section 671 in order to obtain a current income tax deduction. Also, the charity must receive either a guaranteed annuity or a fixed percentage of the annual net fair market value of the trust assets.[10]

If for some reason the taxpayer is no longer taxed on the yearly income of the trust, there will be a partial recapture of the previously allowed deduction which must be reported by the taxpayer as income in that year. For example, if the individual contributes the income for five years but dies within three years of this contribution, recapture would be triggered. His income for the year of his death would have to include a recaptured portion of the excess deduction that he took at the time the trust was established.[10]

The charitable lead trust works like this: The donor transfers income-producing property to a trust. The trust in turn will provide the charity with a guaranteed annuity or annual payments equal to a fixed percentage of the fair market value of the trust property as annually recomputed. At the end of the specified period, the property would be returned to the donor (or go to a noncharitable beneficiary of the donor's choice).

As long as the donor has a reversionary interest in the income or the principal of the trust that is greater than 5%, or is otherwise considered the owner of the income or principal under the grantor trust rules of the Code, he can take an immediate deduction at the inception of the trust. The deduction is based on the present value of the charity's future rights to annuity or unitrust payments.

A lead trust structured in such a way ensures that the income from the securities held in trust, while payable to the charity, is includable in the donor's income. The donor does not receive an income tax charitable contributions deduction each year of the trust for the income payable to the charity, but he does receive a charitable contributions deduction in the year the trust is funded for the present value of the payments the charity is to receive over the ensuing ten years. He would not receive this deduction unless he were considered owner of the annuity or unitrust amount, as described in section 170(f)(2)(B) of the Code.

QUESTIONS AND ANSWERS

Question — What factors should be examined in deciding between an annuity trust and a unitrust?

Answer — The choice between an annuity trust and a unitrust involves a number of considerations. An annuity trust is indicated where simplicity in administration is desired since there is no need for an annual revaluation. (At least 5 percent of the initial fair market value of the trust property must be distributed in the case of an annuity trust, while if a unitrust is used, there must be a distribution of at least 5 percent of the trust's fair market value as redetermined each year.) Furthermore, depending on payout rate, and age of the annuitant, the annuity trust may yield a larger charitable contribution deduction (see example in footnote 13). Generally, if the payout is greater than the current valuation table interest rate, the unitrust will produce a larger value for the remainder interest than the annuity trust.

There are, however, a number of disadvantages of an annuity trust when compared with a unitrust. First, inflation may cause a fixed annuity to lose some of its value. Of course, the unitrust may, under adverse circumstances, also fail the income beneficiary. If investment results are poor, the life income beneficiary may experience an absolute loss of income. This will result in both an inflation loss and a diminution of the dollar amount of his annual payment. On the other hand, if the trustee of the unitrust is skillful, he may be able to enhance the value of the principal fund and consequently the dollar amount of the annual payment.

A second disadvantage is caused by regulations which provide that the governing instrument in the case of an annuity trust must prohibit any additional contributions from being made.[12] This is probably to confine the trust to a single valuation date. It therefore becomes impossible to pour over future testamentary bequests into the trust or to have other grantors make inter vivos additions to the already created trust rather than having to set up new

trusts for the same purpose. Conversely, regulations specifically permit additional contributions to unitrusts if the governing instruments contain provisions regarding the effect of such an addition upon valuation and the unitrust amount payable.[13] If trust income is less than the required percentage payment in a unitrust, the liquidity problem could be avoided if the noncharitable beneficiary is willing to forgive all or a part of any particular year's payment, an act tantamount to a contribution to the trust.

A third disadvantage of an annuity trust is that the specified annuity must be paid each year regardless of whether there is sufficient trust income. If the corpus of the trust were real property, such as an apartment house, and if rents were to fall below the specified annuity plus expenses, the trustee would have to borrow against the property or sell it to make the required payments. However, a unitrust, if the trust instrument so provides, can limit its payout to the income beneficiary to the actual trust income. In later years, if trust income exceeds the percentage regularly distributable, the deficiency could be made up by excess distributions. This is referred to as a "net income with makeup unitrust."

Question — A client is considering transferring $100,000 to a trust which will pay him $5,000 a year for life, with a remainder to charity. How will his charitable contribution be determined?

Answer — His deduction would depend on his age at his nearest birthday. As Figure 3.1 illustrates (arbitrarily assuming a 10% interest rate), a 55-year-old donor would receive a $58,725 deduction. A 65-year-old would receive a $64,393 deduction for the same contribution.[14]

Figure 3.1

CHARITABLE REMAINDER ANNUITY TRUST — ONE LIFE*	
Table Rate	10.0%
Fair Market Value of Trust	$100,000.00
Rate of Annuity	0.05000
Payment Periods in Year	1
Payments Made at End of Period	
Age of Person Whose Life Determines the Term of the Trust	55 Years
Amount of Annuity	$5,000.00
Annual Percentage Payout	5.000%
Annuity Factor	8.2550
Payout Frequency Factor	1.0000
Present Value of Annuity	$41,275.00
Charitable Remainder = FMV of Trust Less PV of Annuity	$58,725.00
Charitable Deduction for Remainder Interest	$58,725.00
Donor's Deduction as Percentage of Amount Transferred	58.725%

*Courtesy NumberCruncher Software

The Tools and Techniques of Estate Planning

Figure 3.2

CHARITABLE REMAINDER UNITRUST — ONE LIFE*	
Table Rate	10.0%
Fair Market Value of Trust	$250,000.00
Rate of Annuity	0.09000
Payment Periods in Year	4
Number of Months Valuation Date Precedes First Payout	3
Age of Person Whose Life Determines the Term of the Trust	67
Payout Sequence Factor	0.942505
Adjusted Payout Rate	8.483%
Interpolation: Factor at 8.4% at Age 67	0.338760
Factor at 8.6% at Age 67	0.331640
Difference	0.007120
(8.483% - 8.4%) / 0.2% = X / 0.00712; therefore X = 0.002950	
Factor at 8.4% at Age 67 Less X = Interpolated Factor	
Interpolated Single Life Factor = 0.338760 - 0.002950	0.335810
Present Value of Remainder Interest = $250,000.00 x 0.335810	$83,952.50
Donor's Deduction $83,952.50	
Donor's Deduction as Percentage of Amount Transferred	33.581%

*Courtesy NumberCruncher Software

Question — Assuming the same facts, how would the result be different if the client were to transfer $100,000 to a charitable remainder unitrust, retaining an annual payment equal to 5% of the value of the trust each year?

Answer — The donor would receive $5,000 the first year. If the value of the trust had increased to $120,000 a year later, the donor would receive 5 percent, $6,000, and so on each year. If the income of the unitrust were insuffi-

cient in a given year to pay the stated percentage, capital gains or principal could be used to make up the deficit (but they need not be so used).

Question — A 67 year old donor places $250,000 in a charitable remainder unitrust, retaining a payment equal to 9% of the annual value of the trust, payments to be made quarterly. What is the total income tax deduction available to the donor?

Figure 3.3

ESTATE TAX SAVINGS USING A CHARITABLE REMAINDER TRUST (assume death occurs in 1990)		
	Without Charitable Trust	*With Charitable Trust*
Adjusted Gross Estate	$1,000,000	$1,000,000
Charitable Contribution		100,000
Taxable Estate (Tentative Tax Base)	$1,000,000	$ 900,000
Estate Tax Before Unified Credit	$ 345,800	$ 306,800
Unified Credit	192,800	192,800
Estate Tax after Unified Credit	$ 153,000	$ 114,000
Net Cost of $100,000 Charitable Contribution Is $61,000 ($100,000 - $39,000)		$39,000 Estate Tax Savings

Figure 3.4

INCREASE IN INCOME USING CHARITABLE REMAINDER TRUST (assume death occurs in 1990)	Estate Going Outright to Brother	Charitable Trust with Income to Brother
Adjusted Gross Estate	$1,000,000	$1,000,000
Less Charitable Deduction	0	320,000
Taxable Estate (Tentative Tax Base)	1,000,000	680,000
Federal Estate Tax (F.E.T. Less Credit)	153,000	29,600
Capital Remaining to Produce Income for Brother	847,000	970,400
Income Produced at 10%	84,700	97,040

$12,340
Increase in Annual Income

Answer — Assuming the use of a 10% interest rate, the donor's deduction would be $83,952. The computation is illustrated in Figure 3.2.

Question — How can a charitable remainder trust be used to generate estate tax savings?

Answer — The estate tax deduction created by the use of a qualified charitable remainder trust is measured by the value of the remainder interest that will pass to charity, using the same tables applied in connection with trusts created during life.

Figure 3.3 shows the federal estate tax savings possible through an inter vivos charitable remainder trust. The "without charitable trust" column shows the results for a widow who makes no provisions for a charitable remainder trust (or outright donation). In this situation her taxable estate is $1,000,000. If the same individual created a charitable remainder trust, her taxable estate would be reduced considerably. In addition, a current income tax deduction would have been obtained for the value of the remainder interest of the property donated.

Question — Can a charitable remainder trust be used to increase the income of a life beneficiary?

Answer — The charitable remainder trust (either annuity or unitrust) can be used to provide income for members of the donor's family in lieu of, or in addition to, the donor. For example, assume Mrs. W is a widow with no children or other close relatives except for her 50-year-old brother. Her estate is worth $1,000,000 after taking into consideration estimated debts and administration expenses. She has been debating whether to leave her estate outright to her brother or provide in her will that it pass to a charitable remainder trust for her late husband's law school with income reserved for her brother's life.

Should Mrs. W die, the remainder gift to the law school—taking into consideration her brother's age—would be worth about 32 percent of the $1,000,000, or $320,000. Figure 3.4 illustrates that the charitable trust will generate $12,340 a year in additional lifetime income for her brother. Furthermore, note that over $123,000 which would otherwise have been paid in estate taxes is instead given to the law school.

Figure 3.5

POOLED INCOME FUND	LIFE OF ONE BENEFICIARY
Amount Transferred in Trust	$100,000
Fund's Yearly Rate of Return	10.00
Factor From Table S	.32937
Donor's Deduction	$32,937
Deduction as a Percentage of Amount Transferred	32.9

Question — Your client, who is 68 years of age, has been approached by her alma mater with a request that she make a sizeable contribution. She would like to transfer $100,000 to the university, but believes she will need the income generated by that amount to live on the rest of her life. The university maintains a pooled income fund that is producing an annual return of 10%. What would be her total charitable deduction?

Answer — As illustrated in Figure 3.5, your client would be able to deduct $32,937.

Question — your client is a physician with a large annual income from her practice. She has reached the maximum limits on her qualified retirement plan, and is seeking a method to invest in such a way that she can accumulate funds tax free for her retirement. Could a charitable remainder trust be of any use?

Answer — The client may want to consider what is sometimes called the net income charitable remainder unitrust. As noted in the text, this is a trust in which the annual payment is the LESSER of the fixed unitrust percentage or the actual income generated by the trust.

An optional provision in such a trust is called the "make up" provision. Under it, if the actual unitrust payment in any year based on the income is less than the unitrust percentage, the net difference is carried over to later years, and in any subsequent year in which the net income exceeds the unitrust percentage, the amount carried over can be paid, so long as the total does not exceed the actual income.

Assume the physician in this example contributes $20,000 per year to such a trust, and the trustee invests in maximum growth, minimum income investments. Assume the unitrust percentage is 6%, and the actual income is in the range of 2 to 3%. The trustee would distribute only the actual income for the next several years, during which the donor will build up a substantial carryover credit. When the physician is ready to retire, the trustee changes the investments to maximum growth, and is now able to pay the entire amount of income to the donor because of the make-up provision. This plan functions much the same as a deferred annuity.

Again, life insurance may be a key element in such a plan. It will function as a wealth replacement vehicle in the manner just described. It can also be used as a hedge against premature death of the client. In other words, since the purpose of this technique is to provide for retirement, there will be a substantial economic loss if the client dies before retirement or early into retirement.

Question — If an appreciated asset is transferred to a charitable remainder trust, does the donor, the income beneficiary, or the charity pay an income tax, or capital gains tax if that asset is sold by the trust and the proceeds are reinvested?

Answer — None of the parties to a charitable remainder trust would have any income tax liability on the sale, since charitable remainder trusts are exempt from income tax, except in years when they have unrelated business income. Therefore, a charitable remainder trust can accumulate free of income or capital gains tax, any income in excess of that needed to satisfy non-charitable beneficiaries' income obligations.

This fact would also allow the donor to receive a greater income than he otherwise would be able to, since if he sold the asset without transferring it to the trust, he would have income or capital gains taxes to pay.

Question — How can a charitable lead trust be used for estate tax savings?

Answer — A charitable lead trust can be used for purposes of estate tax savings. As explained above, property is placed in the trust. A fixed amount of the income it produces is paid annually to a charity for a specified period of time (this is the "front-end" or "lead" period). At the end of that time, full ownership of the property and the income it produces passes to noncharitable beneficiaries such as the children or grandchildren of the trust's grantor.

When property is placed in the trust by bequest, an estate tax deduction is allowed for the actuarial value of the front-end annuity interest. As illustrated in Figure ?.6, a $510,816 estate tax deduction would be allowed (arbitrarily assuming a 10% interest rate) if a client left a $1,000,000 bequest in trust to pay $60,000 a year to The American College for 20 years. Stated another way, the deduction could wipe out 51 percent of the estate tax liability on trust property; but then—in the 21st year—the property would go intact to the donor's family. And, by properly combining the annuity payout level and the duration of the annuity period, it might be possible to eliminate an even greater amount of estate tax! For example, an annuity payout of 9 percent of the trust's original corpus for 20 years would result in a deduction of $766,224 (arbitrarily assuming a 10% interest rate). Furthermore, those same remainder beneficiaries can be named as trustees and therefore control the property they someday will own.

Figure 3.6

CHARITABLE LEAD TRUST — FOR TERM CERTAIN*	
Table Rate	10.0%
Fair Market Value of Trust	$1,000,000.00
Rate of Annuity	0.06000
Payment Periods in Year	1
Payments Made at End of Period	
Payment Years	20
Amount of Annuity	$60,000.00
Annual Percentage Payout	6.000%
Annuity Factor	8.5136
Payout Frequency Factor	1.0000
Present Value of Annuity = Annual Payout times Factors	$510,816.00
Remainder Interest = FMV of Trust Less PV of Annuity	$489,184.00
Charitable Deduction for Annuity Interest	$510,816.00
Deduction as Percentage of Amount Transferred	51.08%
*Courtesy NumberCruncher Software	

Question — What is a wealth replacement trust?

Answer — A wealth replacement trust, (sometimes called an asset replacement trust), is an irrevocable life insurance trust, which is put into place in conjunction with a charitable remainder trust, to replace the assets the heirs of the donor of a charitable remainder trust would be losing by the assets passing to the charity after the non-charitable income beneficiaries' death.

For example, assume a client, who is in a 55% federal estate tax bracket, transfers $1,000,000 worth of appreciated stock to a charitable remainder annuity trust, retaining a 6% annuity trust for himself. After his death, the assets pass to a charity of his choice. Had he not created the trust, his heirs would have inherited $450,000 ($550,000 would have been the federal estate tax). Therefore, to replace the amount his heirs would have been disinherited by, he created an irrevocable life insurance trust, which can purchase insurance on his life.

Since the client receives immediate tax benefits upon establishing a charitable remainder trust (through an income tax distribution), and since the client would have an increased cash flow with the trust (since the trust paid no income tax on the sale of the assets, which could be reinvested at a potentially higher yield), the funding for the premium can, in many cases, be achieved between the tax savings and the increased cash flow without any additional outlays by the client.

Question — Your client has a sizeable block of stock in a company which he started and has taken public. He is now able to sell that stock. However, it has an income tax basis of $100,000, and a current market value of $1,100,000. Assuming he is in the 35% income tax bracket, how might he use the wealth replacement trust concept? Assume a 10% investment return.

Answer — Under current capital gain rates, the client would pay federal income tax of $280,000 and be left with $820,000. If that amount is reinvested at 10%, he will have an annual yield of $82,000. Assume instead he transfers the stock to a charitable remainder annuity trust, in which he retains a 10% annual annuity. The trustee sells the stock, pays no income tax, and pays your client an annual annuity of $110,000 per year for life, This is $28,000 per year more than if the client had simply sold the stock and reinvested the proceeds.

However, the client's family will lose a potential inheritance of $1,000,000, plus the future growth in that investment, but less the federal and state death taxes that would have to be paid on that amount. If we assume, based on the client's life expectancy and an anticipated growth rate of the property that the investment would double in value by the time the client dies, his net loss of wealth is two times ($820,000) or $1,640,000 less federal estate tax (assume 55%) or $738,000.

If the client is insurable, the client can replace this lost wealth by purchase of approximately $738,000 in life insurance, which is either owned directly by his potential heirs or by an irrevocable trust for their benefit. If the annual premiums for such insurance are less than $28,000, the transaction produces a net economic savings to the client.

Footnote References

Charitable Split Interest Trusts

1. IRC Secs. 170(f)(2)(A), 664(d). But see discussion of gifts of a partial interest in Chapter 2 for an exception.
2. IRC Secs. 170(f)(2)(A).
3. IRC Secs. 170(f)(2)(B).
4. IRC Secs. 664(d)(1), 2055(e)(3); Reg. §20.2055-2(a).
5. IRC Secs. 170(f)(2)(A), 664(d)(1).
6. IRC Sec. 664(d)(2).
7. IRC Sec. 664(d)(2).
8. Notice 94-78, 1994-32 IRB 15.
9. IRC Sec. 642(c)(5). To calculate the deduction for a contribution to a pooled income fund: (1) Take the highest rate of return for the previous 3 years, (2) Look to Valuation Table S in Appendix D for that rate, (3) Find proper age of donor, (4) Proceed to column 4 to find appropriate remainder factor, and (5) Multiply factor by amount contributed to obtain deduction.
10. Reg. §1.170A-6(c).
11. Reg. §1.170A-6(c)(4).
12. Reg. §1.664-2(b).
13. Reg. §1.664-3(b).
14. The computation of these amounts and all like amounts referred to hereafter involve the following steps:

    For both annuity trust and unitrust computations, age is determined as of the individual's nearest birthday. Regs. §§20.2031-7A(d)(1)(ii), 1.664-4(e)(5).

In the case of an annuity trust, go to Valuation Table S (reproduced in Appendix D) to determine the value of an annuity at the given age. Arbitrarily assuming an interest rate of 10%, in the case of a person age 55 this is 8.2550. If the principal sum is $100,000 and the payout is 5 percent, the annuity will be for $5,000; and $5,000 x 8.2550 = $41,275, the value of the annuity. The value of the remainder is $100,000 (the principal sum) minus the value of the annuity: ($100,000 - $41,275) = $58,725.

In the case of the unitrust, go to IRS Publication 1458, Table U(1). The value of a remainder interest after a 5 percent unitrust payout at age 55 is .34404. This factor applied to the principal sum of $100,000 is $34,404; the deduction allowed. (The actual payout rate may require adjustment under Table F, also found in Publication 1458, to reflect the number of months by which the valuation date precedes the first payment.)

It is interesting to note that the value of a charitable remainder interest of a residence in the hands of a noncharitable tenant may be greater for gift tax than for income tax purposes because no deduction for depreciation is required for gift tax purposes. Rev. Rul. 76-473, 1976-2 CB 306. For relevant decisions regarding the federal estate tax deduction for charitable remainders, see Rev. Rul. 76-543, 1976-2 CB 287, as amplified by Rev. Rul. 77-169, 1977-1 CB 286 and distinguished by Rev. Rul. 83-158, 1983-2 CB 159; Rev. Rul. 76-544, 1976-2 CB 288; Rev. Rul. 76-545, 1976-2 CB 289, as clarified by Rev. Rul. 82-97, 1982-1 CB 194; Rev. Rul. 76-546, 1976-2 CB 290.

Chapter 4

DEFERRED COMPENSATION (NONQUALIFIED)

WHAT IS IT?

Nonqualified deferred compensation is an arrangement whereby an employer promises to pay an employee in the future for services rendered currently. The plan is generally set up to provide for the employee's salary to be continued over a period of years after retirement or other termination of employment.

These payments are referred to as "deferred" compensation because they represent compensation earned currently but which will not be paid until a future date or event. The term "nonqualified" refers to the fact that the plan does not attempt to meet the stringent coverage and contribution requirements necessary to obtain government approval for qualified pension/profit-sharing tax treatment.

WHEN IS THE USE OF SUCH A DEVICE INDICATED?

1. When a business does not have a government approved ("qualified") retirement plan to offer key employees and would like to provide those key employees with retirement benefits.

2. Where a business has a qualified retirement plan, but would like to provide additional retirement benefits for certain key people over and above those permissible under a qualified plan.

3. Where a highly paid employee or executive would like to defer the taxation on income from peak earning years to a future date when he might be in a lower income tax bracket (usually at retirement).

4. When an executive or other highly paid individual would like to use his employer to, in effect, provide a forced savings program for him and to use such a savings program as a retirement plan.

5. With the 1993 changes in individual and corporate income tax rates, deferred compensation will be more attractive. Since corporate rates at the top brackets will be lower than individual rates at the top bracket, the deferral of both income to the employee and the deduc-

tion to the employer will make more sense. Also, continuing limitations on the maximum benefits under qualified plans will stimulate the use of nonqualified plans.

WHAT ARE THE REQUIREMENTS?

1. In order to successfully defer income tax, an agreement should contain a contingency that may cause the employee to forfeit rights to future payments. As long as an employee's rights are forfeitable, there can be no constructive receipt of income under the agreement.[1]

2. Even if an employee's rights are nonforfeitable, he will not be deemed to have constructive receipt of income if the agreement is entered into before the employee earns the compensation in question and the employer's promise to pay is not secured in any way. This means that the agreement cannot be formally funded (no interest in a trust or escrow fund or in a specific asset can be given to the employee without causing the money to be immediately taxable).[2]

However, it is permissible for a corporation to finance its obligation under the agreement by purchasing a life insurance contract, annuities, mutual funds, securities, or a combination of these investment media, without adverse tax consequences to the employee. The assets that will be used to finance the employer's obligation to the employee must remain the unrestricted property of the corporation (subject to the claims of the corporation's creditors). The employee must be given no interest or specific rights in the monies the corporation sets aside to meet its obligation under the agreement.[3]

The Internal Revenue Service has permitted the establishment of so-called "Rabbi Trusts" in conjunction with certain plans of deferred compensation. These trusts enable an employer to transfer funds to an irrevocable grantor trust that satisfies certain criteria (including the requirement that the trust assets remain subject to the claims of the employer's general creditors in the event of insolvency).[4] Although such a trust can provide some protection from loss of benefits (for example, in the event of a hostile takeover), its real benefit is more psychological, since in the event of employer insolvency or bankruptcy the assets held in trust must be available to the employer's general creditors.[5] (This topic is covered in more detail in *Tools and Techniques of Employee Benefits and Retirement Planning*.)

HOW IT IS DONE — AN EXAMPLE

The selected employee enters into an employment contract with his employer. The contract stipulates that specific payments will be made to the employee or the employee's beneficiaries in the event of death, disability, or retirement. This creates a direct enforceable obligation; the employer must provide the agreed upon benefits. In return for this promise, the selected employee agrees to continue in the service of the company.

The agreement sometimes will obligate the employee to (1) refrain from engaging in any competitive business after retirement, and (2) remain available for consultation purposes after retirement.

Often, the employer will purchase life insurance (alone or in combination with other savings vehicles, such as a fixed or variable annuity or a mutual fund) to provide the required benefits. The business will apply for and own the policy (or other security) on the life of the employee. The business will pay the premiums and be named the policy beneficiary. The business will completely control and own the policy (as well as any other asset used to finance the employer's obligation under the agreement).

The purpose of the life insurance policy is to provide funds necessary to pay retirement benefits called for under the contract. Policy cash values can be used for this purpose. Alternatively, the policy can be held by the corporation until the employee's death, and the employee can be paid the agreed upon deferred compensation out of other corporate assets. Should the employee die prior to retirement, the life insurance will be received by the corporation and then can be used to provide death benefit payments to the employee's family.

Assume the Krauss Corporation is in a 34 percent federal income tax bracket. The corporation enters into a nonqualified deferred compensation agreement with its president, Robert P. Krauss, who is 45 years old. Krauss agrees to defer a $5,000 a year salary increase. Instead of receiving the $5,000 salary increase currently, the after-tax cost of this raise ($3,300) is applied on Krauss' behalf as the annual premium for a life insurance policy on his life.

The Krauss Corporation then agrees to provide retirement and death benefits as follows: (1) If Krauss dies before retirement, $5,000 a year will be paid to his widow for a period equal to the number of years he was covered under the plan. (2) If he remains with the corporation until retirement at age 65, he will receive $10,000 a year for 10 years, in addition to any other fringe benefits to which he may be entitled.

Because the Krauss Corporation is in a 34 percent marginal tax bracket (plus state income taxes), each $1,000 of benefit payments made to its president (or his widow) would actually cost only $660. Retirement benefits could be paid out of current earnings and the corporation could continue the insurance policy in force until the tax-free death proceeds are received. Alternatively, the cash values of the policy could be used to finance the corporation's obligation under the contract.

Assume for this example that a premium of $3,300 would purchase approximately $75,000 of life insurance (life paid up at age 65) for a male age 45. If Krauss died at age 50 after five years' premium payments, the corporation would receive $75,000 of tax free policy proceeds[6] (in addition to dividends and perhaps interest); it would have paid $16,500 in premiums; it is obligated to pay a total of $25,000 ($5,000 a year for five years) to Bob's widow, but its after-tax cost for making such payments is only $16,500 (66% x $25,000). This results in a net gain to the corporation of approximately $42,000 ($75,000 insurance proceeds less $16,500 of premiums and less $16,500 of after-tax cost of such payments).

If Bob Krauss' death occurs at age 75, the corporation receives over $122,000 in death proceeds and dividends; it has paid $66,000 in premiums; it has made lifetime payments of $100,000 ($10,000 a year for 10 years) so its net after-tax-deduction cost for those deferred compensation payments has been $66,000 ($100,000 minus $100,000 x 34 percent tax) and its total cost to provide the promised benefits is approximately $10,000 ($122,000 insurance proceeds minus $66,000 premiums, minus $66,000 cost of deferred compensation payments).

WHAT ARE THE TAX IMPLICATIONS?

The Employer's Tax Position

1. Premiums paid by the employer are not tax deductible. The life insurance policy is considered an asset of the employer and is, therefore, carried on the books of the employer as such. Therefore, no tax deduction is allowed for payment of the premiums.[7] (No current deduction is allowed for any other informal funding vehicle as well.)

2. When the executive reaches retirement age, the employer, as owner of the policy, may choose one of the settlement options available under the policy to fulfill its

obligation under the plan. In this case, a portion of each installment payment received by the employer would be taxable under the annuity rules.[8] However, if the policy is surrendered and a lump sum payment is received, that portion which exceeds the employer's cost (the net premiums the employer has paid) is treated as ordinary income.[9]

3. At the employee's death, the entire policy proceeds receivable by the employer are generally income tax free.[10] (See paragraph 5 of "What Are The Tax Implications?" in Chapter 1 for possible alternative minimum tax on proceeds received by a regular C corporation.) If the employee dies before retirement, these proceeds can be used to pay his or her family the agreed upon benefits. If the employee lives beyond retirement and begins to receive deferred compensation, the employer, rather than surrendering the policy at this time, may choose to make benefit payments out of current or accumulated earnings. Therefore, the employer can continue the policy in force until the employee dies. At that time, the death proceeds would be received by the corporation on an income tax free basis.

4. When the benefits are paid by the employer under the deferred compensation plan, either to the employee (after retiring) or to his or her family (on death before retirement), payments by the corporation are deductible assuming that benefits constitute reasonable additional compensation.[11]

5. For payments made to an employee under a nonqualified deferred compensation program for services performed after 1983, the deferred amounts will be subject to social security tax in the year services are performed unless they are subject to a substantial risk of forfeiture, in which case the deferred amounts will be subject to social security tax when the substantial risk of forfeiture disappears.[12]

Before the Omnibus Budget Reconciliation Act of 1993 (OBRA '93) eliminated the taxable wage base cap for the Medicare hospital insurance (HI) portion of the social security tax, this did not present much of a problem. In most instances, it was employees who earned in excess of the social security taxable wage base who elected to defer compensation, and they were not be affected by the provision in the prior paragraph unless the deferred amount was forfeitable when earned and subject to social security tax in a later period when their earnings had dropped below the taxable wage base. But because OBRA '93 eliminated the taxable wage base cap for the HI portion of the social security tax (subjecting all wages to the HI portion of the tax), nonqualified deferred compensation taken into account as wages for social security tax

purposes in 1994 or later calendar years will be taxed under at least the HI portion of the social security tax.[13] (In 1995, the HI tax rate is 1.45% for the employer and the same rate for the employee.) Whether such nonqualified deferred compensation will also be taxed under the old age, survivors, and disability insurance (OASDI) portion of the social security tax will depend upon whether or not the participant's other earnings for the year at issue equal or exceed that year's OASDI taxable wage base.

The Employee's Tax Position

1. During employment, the employee is not taxed on amounts set aside by the employer to meet its financial obligation. Therefore, if a life insurance policy is purchased on the life of the employee, assuming it is part of the general assets of the employer and is not specifically earmarked for the purpose of carrying out the liabilities under the deferred compensation agreement, premiums paid by the employer will not be taxable to the employee.[14] This same principle applies to a purchase by the employer of an annuity, mutual fund or other savings vehicle to finance its obligation.

2. Benefits received from the deferred compensation plan by the employee (or his family) are taxable at ordinary income rates as received; however, the tax liability may be reduced because benefit payments typically commence at retirement. Yet, while some individuals will be in a lower income tax bracket at retirement, others will not be. Under federal tax law changes in 1993, there are effectively five individual income tax brackets for tax years beginning in 1995. In the case of married individuals filing joint returns, these will be as follows:

Taxable Income	Tax
Not over $39,000	15%
Over $39,000, but not over $94,250	$5,850 plus 28% of the excess over $39,000
Over $94,250, but not over $143,600	$21,320 plus 31% of the excess over $94,250
Over $143,600, but no over $256,500	$36,618.50 plus 36% of the excess over $143,600
Over $256,500	$77,262.50 plus 39.6% of the excess over $256,500

Long-term capital gains are taxed at a rate not higher than 28%.

3. If the employee dies prior to retirement, the first $5,000 of benefits paid to his widow may be excludable from income as an employee's death benefit.[15] (Death benefits under this type of agreement qualify only if the employee's rights to living benefits at the time of death are forfeitable.)

4. The commuted value of benefit payments will be included in the employee's gross estate for federal estate tax purposes. Therefore, the present value of the future income promised to the employee's spouse will be taxable in the employee's estate.[16] This is "income in respect of a decedent" (Section 691 Income) and an income tax deduction will be allowed to the recipient of such income for the additional federal estate tax attributable to the inclusion of the deferred compensation.[17]

   But because of the unlimited federal estate tax marital deduction, if the death benefit is payable to the employee's surviving spouse in a qualifying manner, no estate tax will be incurred when the employee dies. (Therefore, no deduction for income in respect of a decedent will be allowed.)

5. As pointed out in paragraph 5 of "The Employer's Tax Position," above, deferred amounts attributable to services performed after 1983 are generally considered wages for social security tax purposes in the year services are performed or, if later, when they are no longer subject to a substantial risk of forfeiture.[18] Because all wages are now subject to the HI portion of the social security tax, nonqualified deferred compensation counted as wages in 1994 or later calendar years will be taxed under at least the HI portion of the social security tax.[19] (In 1995, the HI tax rate is 1.45% for the employee and the same rate for the employer.) Whether nonqualified deferred compensation counted as wages in 1994 or later calendar years will also be taxed under the OASDI portion of the social security tax will depend upon whether or not the participant's other earnings for the year at issue equal or exceed that year's OASDI taxable wage base.

IMPLICATIONS AND ISSUES IN COMMUNITY PROPERTY STATES

As stated previously (see general discussion in Introduction), the earnings of a resident husband or wife are generally treated as community property in the nine community property states. This can cause some problems in the context of nonqualified deferred compensation. A spouse may enter into a deferred compensation arrangement with his or her employer. The deferred amount would be community property if paid currently. If the spouses obtain a divorce or one of the spouses dies, it may be necessary to determine the present value of the deferred amount in order to divide the community assets.

Whether, as regards forfeitable nonqualified deferred compensation rights, there is "property" subject to division in divorce or at death is a preliminary problem, although not one of as much importance now as it was previously under the former reasoning that only "vested" rights could be "property" subject to division. Under the extreme view, there was "property" only if the rights had fully matured and payments were either being presently received or there was a nonforfeitable right to immediate payment. The generally accepted current analysis establishes that there is "property" subject to division even though there is no certainty that compensation will ever be received.

A useful classification of nonqualified deferred compensation rights and pension rights has been suggested: (1) "vested and matured"—a nonforfeitable right to immediate payment; (2) "vested and unmatured"—a nonforfeitable right to payment at some future time, even though the right might terminate on a participant's death prior to retirement; (3) "contingent"—a nonvested accrued right and the contractual right to continue in the plan with, probably, a reasonable expectation of acquiring vested benefits within a relatively short time; and (4) "mere expectancy."

While forfeitable deferred compensation has been treated as a "mere expectancy" and thus of no value in a division of community property, at least one community property state, California, has abandoned this approach in the context of deferred compensation. California courts hold that the present value of deferred compensation can be determined. The fact that the deferred compensation obligation is unsecured and not formally funded would be a significant factor in reducing value. If the benefits are forfeitable, additional reductions in value are appropriate. In many circumstances, it may be appropriate to order a division of deferred compensation as it is paid, rather than requiring a current division. Thus, the spouse who did not earn the deferred compensation may not be paid. He or she presumably would receive a greater amount if the deferred benefit was actually paid (as opposed to 50 percent of a current value discounted for risk factors).

Another aspect commented on elsewhere in *Tools and Techniques,* which also relates to all community property planning, is the danger of signing a so-called "community property agreement," which makes all property owned by both spouses the community property of both of them. For example, assume Dr. Lee Stein, an employee who worked for a national corporation while he was a resident of a separate property state, accrued a substantial deferred compensation benefit. If Lee then moves to a community property state, the deferred compensation benefit already accrued is still his separate property (specifically, "quasi-community property"); if he then signs an agreement making all property of his wife, Rhonda, and himself community property, he will be making a taxable gift to Rhonda. Because of the nature of the gift, it may be that even the $10,000 annual gift tax exclusion will not be available (since the wife may not be able to dispose of her newly received interest). On the other hand, the transfer should qualify for the unlimited marital deduction; however, the long range tax implications of that deduction should be fully understood (see Chapter 37). Moreover, state gift tax laws should still be considered.

Therefore, one should be very careful in entering into such agreements without receiving competent advice from an attorney knowledgeable in both property law and taxation.

QUESTIONS AND ANSWERS

Question — Can a nonqualified deferred compensation plan provide a disability benefit?

Answer — Yes. A plan may be set up to include a disability benefit. There are several ways of providing disability benefits: (1) A disability income policy can be purchased along with the other assets used to finance the employer's obligation under the plan. (2) A disability waiver of premium benefit attached to the life insurance policy will enable the company to cover its liability in the event the employee becomes totally disabled. (3) A combination of these methods can be used. The second approach works like this:

Assuming Bob Krauss, in the example above, became disabled, the money normally set aside for premium payments ($3,300 a year) would not have to be paid since premiums would be waived. The Krauss Corporation would have $5,000 to pay out to the employee since his salary continuation payments by the corporation would be deductible.

Generally, wage continuation payments and disability retirement income payments are fully includable in an employee's gross income. However, under Code section 22, an employee who is under the age of 65, is retired on disability, and is considered totally and permanently disabled may be entitled to a tax credit for disability retirement income.

Question — What effect does ERISA (the Employee Retirement Income Security Act of 1974) have on unfunded nonqualified deferred compensation plans?

Answer — Very little, if the plans fit into certain "safe harbors." For example, unfunded plans maintained primarily for the purpose of providing deferred compensation for a select group of management or highly compensated employees are exempt from almost all ERISA requirements. They are subject to easily complied with reporting requirements, and are subject to administrative and enforcement provisions — including the obligation to provide a claims procedure. (To the extent such a deferred compensation plan is also considered an employee welfare benefit plan for ERISA purposes, it may also be subject to at least some fiduciary responsibility requirements, although this is not clear.) Thus, such plans are not subject to ERISA requirements as to participation, vesting, nondiscrimination, minimum funding, and (at least to the extent they are not employee welfare benefit plans) fiduciary responsibility rules.[20]

The employer can comply with the reporting requirement by (1) filing within 120 days of the adoption of the plan a simple written statement (a letter will do) with the Secretary of Labor including the employer's name and address, the employer's IRS identification number, a declaration that the employer maintains a plan primarily for the purpose of providing deferred compensation to a select group of management or highly compensated employees, and a statement of the number of such plans and the number of employees in each plan, and (2) providing plan documents upon request to the Secretary of Labor.

Question — What is the earliest date the corporation can take a deduction for unfunded deferred compensation payments?

Answer — Generally, a corporation cannot take a deduction until it actually makes payments to the employee (or a deceased employee's beneficiary), regardless of whether the corporation is on a cash or accrual basis of accounting.[21]

Question — Can directors' fees be deferred through an unfunded deferred compensation agreement?

Answer — Yes. Individual nonqualified deferred compensation agreements can be made with independent contractors, directors, and even employees of other business organizations. Also, tax-exempt organizations can establish nonqualified deferred compensation plans.[22]

Question — If a corporation finances its obligation under a deferred compensation agreement with corporate owned annuity contracts, are there any current adverse tax consequences to the employee or to the employer-corporation?

Answer — There are no current tax consequences to the employee so long as the annuity remains the asset of the corporation and the employee has no interest in the annuity. However, for contributions made after February 28, 1986 to annuity contracts held by a "nonnatural person," such as a corporation, "the income on the contract" for the tax year of the policyholder is generally treated as ordinary income received by the contract owner for that year.[23]

Question — What is a secular trust?

Answer — A secular trust is an irrevocable trust used to formally fund and protect nonqualified deferred compensation. Funds placed in a secular trust are not subject to the claims of the employer's creditors. Thus, a secular trust can protect deferred compensation from an employer's bankruptcy or insolvency.

There are two principal types of secular trust: employer-funded trusts and employee-funded trusts. The employer can make contributions to an employee-funded trust, but the arrangement is structured in such a way that the employee is considered to have constructively received the amounts before they are given to the trust.

Generally, use of a secular trust causes immediate or accelerated taxation to the employee and provides an immediate or accelerated deduction to the employer.[24] Employers may "gross up" participants to help them pay their taxes.

The secular trust became popular in the years after the Tax Reform Act of 1986 (TRA '86), when the top corporate income tax rate bracket (34% before OBRA '93) was higher than the top individual income tax rate bracket and the top individual rate bracket was relatively low (28% after TRA '86, 31% after the Omnibus Budget Reconciliation Act of 1990). However, the imposition in OBRA '93 of brackets of 36% and 39.6% marginal rates on individuals will curtail the use of this device, since most employees who are candidates for this planning are in their highest income tax brackets while employed, and will be in lower brackets when deferred benefits are received.

Question — What is the impact of deferred compensation plans that provide an employee can make a "phantom" investment of the deferred amounts, or will be credited with interest on the deferred amounts?

Answer — Such arrangements are often considered as a hedge against inflation or to offset the erosion in the value of the deferred benefit equal to a fixed dollar amount payable at the end of several years. Both plans present problems. If the employee is permitted to make a hypothetical invest-

ment of the funds, the employer will be put to the cost of record keeping for hypothetical gains, losses, dividends, etc., and will be faced with a problem of accounting for the actual cost of the benefit.[25]

The use of hypothetical interest is more feasible. It could be based on something like a cost of living adjustment, or an average rate of inflation, such as 4%. It seems clear such interest or other adjustment should be treated as part of the total deferred compensation, with no deduction to the employer or taxation to the employee until paid or made available to the employee.[26]

Question — Where an employer has entered into a deferred compensation plan that provides for accrual of additional benefits based on the passage of time, could these additional amounts be deducted by the employer before they are paid or made available to the employee on the theory they are interest?

Answer — The answer is apparently no, since the 9th Circuit Court of Appeals recently reversed a 1993 decision allowing such an interest deduction and now holds there is no deduction for such amounts until such amounts are includable in employee income.[27]

ASRS, Sec. 64

Footnote References

Deferred Compensation (Nonqualified)

1. See Regs. §§1.451-1, 1.451-2.
2. See Rev. Rul. 60-31, 1960-1 CB 174, as modified by Rev. Rul. 70-435, 1970-2 CB 100. See also Let. Rul. 8439012, where under an executive's deferred compensation plan his compensation was placed in a trusteed bank account, but his rights were only those of an unsecured general creditor of the company. No income was recognized by the executive as a result of the company's placing the money in the trust account. See also *Oates v. Comm.*, 18 TC 570, *aff'd*, 207 F.2d 711 (7th Cir. 1953), *acq.*, 1960-1 CB 5.
3. See, e.g., Rev. Rul. 72-25, 1972-1 CB 127; Rev. Rul. 68-99, 1968-1 CB 193.
4. See Rev. Proc. 92-64, 1992-2 CB 422, including model form of the trust. Also see Rev. Proc. 92-65, 1992-2 CB 428.
5. See, e.g., *Goodman v. Resolution Trust Corp.*, 7 F.3d 1123 (4th Cir. 1993).
6. See paragraph 5 of "What Are The Tax Implications?" in Chapter 1 for possible alternative minimum tax on proceeds received by a regular C corporation.
7. IRC Sec. 264(a)(1).
8. See generally IRC Sec. 72.
9. IRC Sec. 72(e); Reg. §1.72-11(d)(1).
10. IRC Sec. 101(a)(1).
11. See IRC Secs. 404(a)(5), 162(a)(1), 212. Note that publicly held corporations generally cannot deduct compensation in excess of $1

million per tax year to certain top level executives. See IRC Sec. 162(m).

12. IRC Sec. 3121(v)(2). See also Notice 94-96, 1994-46 IRB 10.

13. See IRC Sec. 3121(a)(1); the Omnibus Budget Reconciliation Act of 1993 (OBRA '93), Sec. 13207(a), deleting IRC Sec. 3121(x); OBRA '93, Sec. 13207(e).

14. Rev. Rul. 68-99, 1968-1 CB 193. See also Rev. Rul. 72-25, 1972-1 CB 127 (annuity contracts).

15. See IRC Sec. 101(b).

16. IRC Sec. 2039(a); *Goodman v. Granger*, 243 F.2d 264 (3rd Cir. 1957), *cert. denied*, 355 U.S. 835 (1957).

17. IRC Sec. 691(c). The income tax deduction for the additional federal estate tax generated by the inclusion of the IRD is as follows:

	Federal estate tax payable (with net 691 income included in the gross estate
Minus	
	Federal estate tax payable (with no 691 income included in gross estate)
Equals	
	Portion of Federal Estate Tax attributable to 691 items

Note the planning implication of this computation: To the extent no estate tax is generated by IRD, no income tax deduction will be allowed. So if deferred compensation payments are made to a surviving spouse (or to a marital trust on her behalf), to the extent they qualify for the marital deduction, the 691 income tax deduction is lost.

18. See note 12, above. Self-employeds pay social security taxes through self-employment (SECA) taxes rather than through FICA taxes. Nonqualified deferred compensation of self-employeds is usually counted for SECA purposes when it is includable in income for income tax purposes. See IRC Sec. 1402(a); Reg. §1.1402(a)-1(c). (As with the FICA tax, there is no wage base cap for the hospital insurance portion of the SECA tax after 1993. See IRC Sec. 1402(b)(1); OBRA '93, Sec. 13207(b)(2), deleting IRC Sec. 1402(k); OBRA '93, Sec. 13207(e).) So, deferred compensation of self-employeds is generally counted for SECA purposes when paid (or constructively received, if earlier). As an exception to this rule, corporate directors who deferred receipt of fees for services performed in tax years beginning on or after January 1, 1988, but before 1991 were required to include the deferred fees for SECA purposes in the year(s) in which the services were performed. IRC Sec. 1402(a), as amended by the Omnibus Budget Reconciliation Act of 1987 (OBRA '87), Sec. 9022(b), and the Omnibus Budget Reconciliation Act of 1990 (OBRA '90), Sec. 5123(a); see also Let. Rul. 8819012.

19. See note 13, above.

20. See ERISA Secs. 201(1), 201(2), 301(a)(1), 301(a)(3), 401(a)(1), 503, 4021(a), 4021(b)(6); Labor Regs. §§2520.104-23, 2520.104-24, 2560.503-1(a), 2560.503-1(b).

21. See IRC Secs. 404(a)(5), 404(d). The weight of authority even holds that an accrual basis taxpayer cannot take a current deduction for amounts credited as "interest" on unfunded deferred compensation; the deduction for such amounts must be postponed until such amounts are includable in employee income. See the final two Questions and Answers in this chapter and the authorities cited in notes 26 and 27.

22. See generally IRC Sec. 457.

23. IRC Sec. 72(u).

24. The full picture of the taxation of employees participating in secular trusts is much more complex than this. For the rules applicable to participants in employer-funded secular trusts, see IRC Sec. 402(b); Regs. §§1.402(b)-1(a), 1.402(b)-1(b); Let. Ruls. 9502030, 9417013, 9302017, 9212024, 9212019, 9207010, 9206009. For the rules applicable to employees participating in employee-funded secular trusts, see Let. Ruls. 9450004, 9437011, 9337016, 9328007, 9322011, 9316018, 9316008, 9235044, 9031031, 8843021, 8841023. For more on the employer's deduction in the context of an employer-funded secular trust, see Reg. §1.404(a)-12(b)(1); Let. Ruls. 9502030, 9417013, 9302017, 9212024, 9212019, 9207010, 9206009. For more on the employer's deduction in the context of an employee-funded secular trust, see Let. Ruls. 9450004, 9437011, 9337016, 9328007, 9322011, 9316018, 9316008, 9235044, 9031031, 8843021, 8841023.

25. The ground rules governing employee direction of investments in nonqualified deferred compensation plans are not entirely clear. To avoid accelerated taxation, plans probably should not allow employees to control the actual investment of funds. In other words, plans allowing employee input into the actual investment of funds probably should provide that the asset holder (for example, the employer, or the trustee of a rabbi trust) need not follow the employee's wishes. Whether plans that allow participants to select hypothetical investments also should provide that the employee's investment wishes need not be followed is not clear. See generally Let. Ruls. 9517019, 9505012, 9504007, 9452035, 9332038, 9122019, 8952037, 8903088, 8834015, 8804057, 8804023, 8648011, 8607022, 8507028; Tax Mgmt. (BNA), U.S. Income Series, Portfolio #385-3rd (Deferred Compensation Arrangements), V.D.1; AALU *Washington Report*, Bulletins Nos. 94-107 (12/19/94) and 94-46 (5/13/94).

Plans allowing employee input into the actual investment of funds may also want to limit the employee's investment choices to broad categories of investments (such as stocks, bonds, or money market instruments) rather than allowing the employee to choose more specific investments. Compare Rev. Rul. 82-54, 1982-1 CB 11 (annuity policyholders who could direct investment of annuity fund among several mutual funds representing different, broad investment strategies would not control individual investment decisions and for tax purposes would not be considered to own the mutual fund shares). Whether plans permitting employees to select hypothetical investments should similarly limit choices is not clear.

26. See *Albertson's, Inc. v. Comm.*, 95 TC 415 (1990) (divided court) ("interest" credited on unfunded deferred compensation is really additional deferred compensation that cannot be deducted until includable in employee income), *aff'd on other grounds*, 42 F.3d 537, 94-2 USTC ¶50,619 (9th Cir. 1994); TAM 8619006 (same); see also Notice 94-38, 1994-1 CB 350 (amounts credited as interest on unfunded deferred compensation are deductible when includable in employee income); Let. Rul. 9201019 (amounts credited as interest on unfunded deferred compensation are includable in employee income when paid or made available).

27. *Albertson's, Inc. v. Comm.*, 42 F.3d 537, 94-2 USTC ¶50,619 (9th Cir. 1994), *vacating in part* 12 F.3d 1529 (9th Cir. 1993), *aff'g in part* 95 TC 415 (1990) (divided court), *en banc rehearing denied*, ___ F.3d ___, *petition for cert. filed* (May 1, 1995); see also Notice 94-38, 1994-1 CB 350; Let. Rul. 9201019; TAM 8619006.

Chapter 5

DISCLAIMERS

WHAT IS IT?

A disclaimer (or renunciation) is an unqualified refusal by a potential beneficiary to accept benefits given through a testamentary or lifetime transfer of property. Most often a disclaimer refers to the refusal by a potential beneficiary to accept a bequest under the terms of a will or trust.

For federal tax purposes, the disclaimant is regarded as never having received the property (that is, for tax purposes it's as if he predeceased the transferor). As a result of this consequence, no transfer is considered to have been made *by the disclaimant* for federal gift, estate, or generation-skipping transfer tax purposes.[1]

However, it is possible for a disclaimer to create a generation-skipping transfer (GST) *by someone other than the disclaimant*. This result can occur because under GST tax law a "direct skip" transfer (i.e., a transfer to or for an individual two or more generations younger than the transferor) is a GST subject to the GST tax (if it is also subject to federal estate or gift tax).[2] The first example below will illustrate how a disclaimer can create such a GST.

The requirements of federal law will apply, for federal estate, gift, and generation-skipping transfer tax purposes even if local law does not characterize the refusal as a disclaimer. For these federal tax purposes, the time limits prescribed for a qualified disclaimer should also supersede any time period prescribed by local law. To be fully effective for both state and federal purposes, the disclaimer must also comply with the applicable state law, and may have to meet separate rules for state gift or state death taxes.

However, even though a disclaimer that meets the federal requirements does not also have to meet the state requirements, the effect of the disclaimer must be that the disclaimant must not receive the property or accept benefits from the property, which must pass to some other person, or the surviving spouse. The result is that for a disclaimer to be recognized, it must shift the property rights under state law as well as federal law. In other words, if the disclaimer has no effect under state law, and the disclaimant is treated as the owner of the property, the disclaimer is also ineffective for federal purposes.

WHEN IS THE USE OF SUCH A DEVICE INDICATED?

1. When an individual with children and a large estate in his own right is left a bequest by another individual and this bequest would compound his potential estate tax problem, a disclaimer may be an appropriate estate planning tool. He may wish to disclaim the bequest in favor of the next recipients under the will or trust, very often his children. By making the disclaimer, the disclaimed property will not be included in the parent's estate at his death.

2. Where an individual who is in a high income tax bracket is left a bequest "if he is living otherwise to his children" (who are in lower income tax brackets), a disclaimer can shift the income taxation to the children's lower brackets (assuming they are age 14 or older) if they are the next recipients of the gift under the will or trust.

3. Where an individual wishes to make a tax free gift to the person who would be the next recipient under the will or trust, he can disclaim the property.

4. When property is left to a spouse who doesn't need or want it, she could disclaim the portion she doesn't want and avoid a needless double taxation.

5. As a corollary to the last situation, where the value of the property left to the spouse creates a marital deduction which reduces the decedent's taxable estate below the amount offset by the decedent's unified credit, a disclaimer by the surviving spouse can be used to increase the decedent's estate to an amount which will be fully offset by the unified credit, and keep the property out of the estate of the surviving spouse. Refer to the extended discussion in Chapter 37.

6. Where the bequest to the surviving spouse is not sufficient to take advantage of the optimum marital deduction, a disclaimer by other beneficiaries in favor of the surviving spouse may be used to qualify a transfer for the marital deduction. Refer to the discussion of marital deduction planning in Chapter 37.

7. Where there is a trust with an interest passing to charity which does not meet the requirements for a charitable

deduction discussed in Chapter 3, a disclaimer by other beneficiaries may be used to qualify the trust interest for the deduction.

WHAT ARE THE REQUIREMENTS?[3]

1. There must be an irrevocable and unqualified refusal to accept an interest in property.

2. The refusal must be in writing.

3. The writing must be received by the transferor, his legal representative, or the holder of legal title to the property.

4. The refusal must be received no later than nine months after the day on which the transfer creating the interest is made or, if later, nine months after the day on which the donee or beneficiary attains the age of 21.

5. The disclaimer must be made prior to acceptance of the interest or any of its benefits.

6. The interest must pass either to the spouse of the decedent or to a person other than the disclaimant without any direction on the part of the disclaimant. (A valid disclaimer by a surviving spouse may be made even though the interest passes to a trust in which she has an income interest.)

7. The interest disclaimed should be an entire interest, but can be an undivided fractional part of the proposed gift.

8. As a corollary to the last situation, where the potential disclaimant is entitled to receive an annuity or unitrust payment from a charitable remainder trust, discussed in Chapter 3, and does not need the payment, a disclaimer of that interest will allow the transferor a 100% charitable deduction instead of a deduction limited to the value of the charitable remainder.

9. The beneficiary of a gift or bequest who is insolvent or in bankruptcy may disclaim the gift or bequest to avoid claims of creditors. However, local law must be consulted to assure this will be effective.

HOW IT IS DONE — EXAMPLES

1. Doug Koch, a wealthy client, has four children. An aunt of his just died and, under the terms of her will, named Mr. Koch as recipient of her entire estate if he is alive. If he is deceased when she dies, Mr. Koch's four children are named equally as contingent heirs. Mr. Koch has ad-

equate assets and income to live comfortably, and does not need additional property to compound his already high potential estate tax. By filing in writing an effective "qualified disclaimer" within nine months of his aunt's death, Mr. Koch will be deemed to have predeceased his aunt for both federal gift and estate tax purposes and his interest in her estate would be distributed to his children under the terms of her will without any federal gift, estate, or GST tax liability to him.

However, if Doug had consulted his estate planner before taking action, the planner might have brought about Doug's reconsideration of his proposed disclaimer by an explanation along these lines: The Code says that if Doug makes a qualified disclaimer, then for federal transfer tax purposes, his interest in his aunt's estate will be treated as if the interest had never been distributed to him. That means her estate will be distributed to whomever local law says will take upon Doug's disclaimer. *If the distributees are Doug's children (or others in their generation or younger), Doug's disclaimer will have created a direct skip transfer(s) from his aunt to his children.* The transfer(s) may or may not attract the GST tax, depending upon how much property is involved and on the extent to which the aunt's $1,000,000 GST exemption is allocated to the transfer(s). If the aunt's estate is in the 55% federal estate tax bracket, the estate tax and the GST tax combined could virtually confiscate the property otherwise going to Doug's children.

2. Mr. Ed Radosh specifically leaves $100,000 to his son with a gift over to his favorite charity if his son disclaims. His son can decide after his father's death whether to accept the bequest and donate the bequest to charity if he wishes and receive an income tax deduction or if it would be more beneficial to disclaim the property in favor of the charity and have the estate receive the charitable deduction.

3. Mr. Jules Einhorn thought that at his death his wife would have ample funds and his son very little. Therefore, he left most of his property to his son with a contingent gift to his wife in the event his son predeceased him. At the time of Mr. Einhorn's death the son was financially well off, but the mother was in dire financial straits. By disclaiming his share and permitting the wife to take, the son not only allowed a better distribution of assets but also may have qualified Mr. Einhorn's estate for a marital deduction due to the transfer of the assets to the surviving spouse. This could result in a substantial saving on federal estate taxes. She could then make gift tax-free transfers to her son using the annual gift tax exclusion and the unified credit.

4. The combined estates of Mr. and Mrs. Smith are worth approximately $500,000. They each intend to leave their

share of the estate to the other, or if both are deceased, in trust for their minor children. Since the total value of their estates is less than $600,000, there is no estate tax consequence. However, the estate has a substantial growth potential.

The Smiths should consider the use of a disclaimer trust. This is a trust inserted in the will which will only function in the event the surviving spouse (or his or her estate representative) disclaims the bequest under the will. The trust may be for the benefit of the spouse and the children, or the children only. If, at the death of the first spouse, the combined estates of the deceased and surviving spouses would exceed the unified credit equivalent, presently $600,000, then the surviving spouse can disclaim into the trust to take advantage of all or part of the unified credit of the estate of the deceased spouse. When the surviving spouse dies, the trust will bypass his or her taxable estate.

WHAT ARE THE TAX IMPLICATIONS?

1. A disclaimer of a property interest or a power is not treated as a gift for gift tax purposes.[4]

2. A disclaimed interest in property is not considered to be a transfer by a disclaimant/decedent for estate tax purposes and will not be included in his estate at death as a transfer with a retained life estate.[5]

3. If property is disclaimed by a person in favor of a surviving spouse or charity, the marital or charitable deduction will be permitted provided the property would otherwise qualify for these deductions.[6]

4. Any income received on disclaimed property will be chargeable to the person in whose favor the property was disclaimed.

IMPLICATIONS AND ISSUES IN COMMUNITY PROPERTY STATES

Please refer to the background information on Community Property contained in the Introduction. A qualified disclaimer is taken into account for purposes of the marital deduction. In either a separate property or a community property state, a disclaimer can be expected initially to qualify the estate for the marital deduction or to increase or decrease the deduction if the surviving spouse gains or loses because of the disclaimer.

The availability of the unlimited marital deduction, which applies to both separate and community property, alleviates

concerns for future planning in this area. However, different rules apply to the disposition of separate and community property by Will in community property states and therefore it is still important to carefully characterize all of the property interests held by a decedent and his or her spouse to determine if under community property rules a disclaimer is desired or required.

Where the entire community property is subjected to probate (both the decedent's one-half interest and the surviving spouse's one-half interest) upon the death of only one spouse, the surviving spouse should exercise caution to disclaim only the community property interest of the decedent. A disclaimer of both halves would probably result in a taxable gift to the individual who takes as the result of the disclaimers. As mentioned in the Introduction, several types of problems can arise when attempting to determine whether specific property is to be characterized as community, quasi-community or separate.

QUESTIONS AND ANSWERS

Question — Can a beneficiary of a life insurance policy disclaim his interest in the proceeds?

Answer — Yes, such an interest may be disclaimed within nine months of the decedent's death. However, if the beneficiary was an irrevocable beneficiary, the disclaimer most likely must be made within nine months of the beneficiary designation.

Question — Can an interest in jointly held property be disclaimed?

Answer — Yes, if made within nine months of the creation of the gift and before any of the property or its benefits have been accepted by the disclaimant. However, with respect to a disclaimer of joint property which passes by right of survivorship, the nine month period starts with the date of death of the first joint tenant if both tenants could have partitioned the property under state law while both tenants were living.[7]

Question — Can an individual after attaining age 21 disclaim property if he has received an interest in the property during his minority?

Answer — The law indicates that an individual can make a "qualified disclaimer" after attaining age 21, if the disclaimer is made within nine months after reaching age 21 and if the other requirements of the law are met. However, the law does not allow a "qualified disclaimer" if benefits have been received from the property prior to the disclaimer.

A beneficiary who is under 21 years of age has until 9 months after his 21st birthday in which to make a qualified disclaimer of his interest in property. Any actions taken with regard to an interest in property by a beneficiary or a custodian prior to the beneficiary's 21st birthday will not be an acceptance by the beneficiary of the interest. For example, a minor who receives dividends on stock prior to the age of 21 will not be deemed to have made an acceptance, assuming he did not accept dividends after attaining age 21. This rule holds even with respect to a gift under the Uniform Gifts to Minors Act or the Uniform Transfers to Minors Act where under the Act custodianship ends and the property is delivered to the donee when he attains age 18.[8]

Question — If a testator dies leaving a trust with income payable to his wife for her lifetime and remainder payable to his children, can the children disclaim their remainder interest after their mother's death?

Answer — Not unless the mother died within nine months of the testator since the disclaimer must be made within nine months of the testator's death since this is when the gift was complete. The children would have to disclaim within this period or, if later, within 9 months of the date the child reaches age 21. Note that the answer here is the same even if the children must survive their mother to receive the bequest.

Question — Is a disclaimer valid where a surviving spouse refuses to accept all or a portion of an interest in property passing from a decedent, and, as a result of that refusal, the property passes to a trust in which that spouse has an income interest [such as the typical family (nonmarital "B") trust]?

Answer — A disclaimer will be valid where a spouse refuses an interest in property even if, as a result of that disclaimer, he or she receives an income interest (as long as that income interest does not result from the surviving spouse's direction). Also, the spouse must not have the power after the disclaimer, as trustee or otherwise, to direct the distribution of the trust assets to other beneficiaries.

This "Blank Check" postmortem marital deduction planning tool means an estate owner doesn't have to decide how much of his estate should go to a surviving spouse by will. His will can allow that decision to be made by the survivor when more facts are known. All the estate owner's property could be left to the surviving spouse

with a provision that any part of the bequest which is disclaimed will be placed in the nonmarital ("by pass") trust. This planning may—in some cases—be preferable to a specific marital formula bequest.

Question — What are some of the other things one considers about the use of a disclaimer?

Answer — Some of the factors to be considered are:

1. If a disclaiming beneficiary is indebted to the estate, the instrument should specify whether the debt may be set off against the alternative takers (who might be the disclaimant's children).[9]

2. A disclaimer of a power may extinguish it; hence, it may be desirable to designate an alternative donee of the power.[10]

3. A disclaimer of a legacy may result in the disclaimed legacy passing to the disclaimant's issue under an anti-lapse statute.[11]

4. A disclaimer could cause a premature "closing" of a class of beneficiaries.[12]

5. It is generally desirable to express a partial disclaimer in the form of a fraction or percentage. A partial disclaimer may be valid only if it represents an "undivided portion of an interest."[13] However, the disclaimer regulations do permit a beneficiary to disclaim specific assets in a trust, if as a result of that disclaimer, the assets in question will be allocated to another trust or to beneficiaries other than the trust.

6. To guard against the possibility that the disclaimed property may not pass to someone other than the disclaimant (unless it is to a surviving spouse), an alternative taker should be provided for. Further, the statutory schedule may not coincide with the settlor's intent.

7. The instrument should indicate whether a disclaimer accelerates future interests.[14]

Question — What is the effect of a disclaimer if federal requirements are met but state disclaimer laws are not?

Answer — State law is important because it governs property rights, and how and under what conditions and to whom property will pass. It is possible that a person could make a valid disclaimer under Federal Law—say within the nine month statutory period—which would not meet a shorter period required for an effective disclaimer of property rights under state law. Federal law provides that the disclaimer can be effective if the property passes as the result of the disclaimer to the party who would have received it if the disclaimer had been effective under state law.

Question — What is the problem, if any, in disclaiming life insurance proceeds?

Answer — If a life insurance policy names a spouse but no secondary beneficiary, a disclaimer could result in the policy proceeds falling into the estate of the insured. This would expose the proceeds to creditors, additional probate fees, will provisions, and in many states unnecessary estate inheritance taxes. If the disclaiming spouse is the beneficiary under the will, a further renunciation would be necessary because the insurance proceeds would fall into the probate estate because of the first disclaimer. Planners should examine beneficiary designations and coordinate life insurance (or pension plan) proceeds so that a single renunciation will accomplish the intended objectives.

Question — Is it possible to disclaim some but not all of a beneficiary's interest in a trust?

Answer — It is possible to disclaim separately different income or corpus interests in a trust, and it is permissible to disclaim a specific dollar amount of a gift or inheritance. Certain disclaimers will be effective for federal estate and gift tax purposes even if not recognized under local law (provided that, under local law the interest is transferred to another person as the result of attempting the disclaimer without any direction on the part of the disclaimant.)

Mandatory actions by the disclaimant that are required under local law merely to divest ownership of the property in the disclaimant and vest it in another person will not disqualify the disclaimer. In the case of a beneficiary of an interest in property who is under 21 years of age, any actions taken with regard to the interest by the beneficiary or a custodian prior to the beneficiary's 21st birthday will not be considered an acceptance of the interest by the beneficiary. In case of disclaimers of less than an entire interest, each interest or power with respect to property that is separately created by the transferor is generally treated as a separate interest. This means that a client can make a qualified disclaimer of one interest in corpus while retaining another interest.

Question — Assume the surviving spouse is entitled to survivor's benefits under a qualified pension or profit sharing plan. Can he disclaim all or any part of those benefits?

Answer — The IRS has recently ruled that such disclaimers are effective. This planning device can be extremely important in view of the requirements that such plans provide survivor annuities, discussed in Chapter 28. Where the retirement plan benefit is most of the value in the estate, the mandatory payment to a surviving spouse may deprive the decedent's estate of the full value of the unified credit. A disclaimer can be used to shift at least part of the benefit away from the surviving spouse to take full advantage of the decedent's credit, and keep that part of the benefit out of the estate of the surviving spouse.

Question — Can the trustee of a trust disclaim powers held as a trustee, such as the power to make distributions to the trustee as a beneficiary?

Answer — Although the cases and rulings are not entirely clear on this issue, the cautious answer is that a qualified disclaimer can be made only by the beneficiary or donee, not the trustee. For example, if the trustee has the power to make distributions to himself or herself and wants to avoid the tax consequences of such a power, the trustee should disclaim the right to *receive* the distributions, not the right to make them. The trustee would then be disclaiming as a beneficiary, not as a trustee.

ASRS, Secs. 54, ¶44.3(m); 55, ¶57.5(f).

Footnote References

Disclaimers

1. IRC Sec. 2518(a).
2. IRC Secs. 2612(c), 2613(a).
3. IRC Sec. 2518(b).
4. IRC Sec. 2518(a).
5. See *Brown v. Routzahn*, 63 F.2d 914 (6th Cir.) Cert. denied 290 U.S. 641 (1933).
6. IRC Secs. 2056(d)(2), 2055(a).
7. *MacDonald v. Comm.*, 88-2 USTC ¶13,778 (8th Cir. 1988), acq. AOD 1990-06.
8. Reg. §25.2518-2(d)(3), (4), Example (11).
9. *Matter of Colacci*, 549 P.2d 1096 (Colo. App. 1976).
10. Schwartz, "Effective Use of Disclaimers," 19 B.C. Law Rev. 551 (1978).
11. *Brannan v. Ely*, 157 Md. 100, 145 Atl. 361 (1929); *Thompson v. Thornton*, 197 Mass. 273, 83 N.E. 880 (1908).
12. See Schwartz, *Future Interests & Estate Planning*, §11.4 (Supp. 1978).
13. Schwartz, "Effective Use of Disclaimers," 19 B.C. Law Rev. 551, 567, 573 (1978).
14. Schwartz, *Future Interests & Estate Planning*, §§11.5-11.9 (Supp. 1978).

Chapter 6

DURABLE POWER OF ATTORNEY

WHAT IS IT?

A Power of Attorney is a written document which enables an individual, the "principal," to designate another person or persons as his "attorney-in-fact," that is, to act on the principal's behalf. The scope of the power can be severely limited ("only to pay my utility bills") or quite broad ("all the legal powers I myself have, including but not limited to the following —").

A "Durable" Power of Attorney is a Power of Attorney which is not terminated by subsequent disability or incapacity of the principal. At this date, all states have recognized some form of Durable Power of Attorney. The vast majority of such states have either enacted in total the Durable Power of Attorney provisions of the Uniform Probate Code (U.P.C.) or have drafted their own statutes in conformity with the provisions of the U.P.C.

The definition of a Durable Power of Attorney, according to the Uniform Probate Code, is:

"A durable power of attorney is a power of attorney by which a principal designates another his attorney in fact in writing and the writing contains the words 'This power of attorney shall not be affected by subsequent disability or incapacity of the principal, or lapse of time,' or 'This power of attorney shall become effective upon the disability or incapacity of the principal,' or similar words showing the intent of the principal that the authority conferred shall be exercisable notwithstanding the principal's subsequent disability or incapacity, and, unless it states a time of termination, notwithstanding the lapse of time since the execution of the instrument."

WHEN IS THE USE OF SUCH A DEVICE INDICATED?

1. When the principal is elderly and there is a significant chance that he will become senile. The use of a broadly drawn Durable Power of Attorney may negate the necessity of petitioning the local court for appointment of a guardian or conservator to handle the principal's assets.

2. When an individual is suffering from a physical disability or illness, the effect of which could lead to a permanent or long term incapacity.

3. In all situations where an individual desires to provide for the continuity of the management of his or her assets in the event he or she is unable to manage such assets for either a short or long duration of time because of physical or mental incapacity. The Durable Power of Attorney permits the individual, when competent, to make a determination of who will handle his or her affairs.

4. As a temporary and expedient substitute for a living revocable trust. The trust device is more burdensome and possibly much more costly than the Durable Power of Attorney.

5. As an addition to the revocable living trust, to provide flexibility.

6. To avoid the necessity of legal proceedings to establish a legal guardianship or conservatorship for an individual who may face short or long term incapacity.

WHAT ARE THE REQUIREMENTS?

1. The principal (the one giving the Power) must be of legal age and competent at the time the Power is given.

2. The attorney in fact (the one receiving the Power) must be of legal age at the time the Power is exercised.

3. The Power of Attorney must include the words "this Power of Attorney shall not be affected by subsequent disability or incapacity of the principal" or "this Power of Attorney shall become effective upon the disability or incapacity of the principal" or similar words showing the principal's intent that the authority conferred shall be exercisable regardless of whether or not he or she subsequently becomes disabled or incapacitated.

HOW IS IT DONE?

Assume your client, Joe Mozino, a widower, is on his deathbed on December 28. He could make annual exclusion gifts for this year and if he's alive four days later on January 1 he could make another round of gifts. None of these gifts would be includable in his estate for federal estate tax purposes.

The problem is, he may be mentally competent to act—and physically able—on the 28th of December. But if he becomes either physically or mentally incompetent after that date, the estate tax savings he is legally entitled to will be lost unless someone is entitled by state law to act (specifically to make gifts) on his behalf. Joe could name his son, Andrew, his attorney-in-fact and give him the power (in addition to other powers) to make gifts on his behalf. Andrew could draw checks on Joe's account to each of the donees (just as if Joe drew the checks).

An example of a broadly drawn Durable Power of Attorney appears at Figure 6.1.

WHAT ARE THE TAX IMPLICATIONS?

The holder of the Durable Power of Attorney, if the Power is broadly drawn, can be given: (1) the right to execute on behalf of the principal all tax returns including income and gift tax returns; (2) the power to make gifts on behalf of the principal (thereby possibly reducing the principal's estate for Federal Estate Tax purposes) and (3) the right to elect to treat gifts made by the competent spouse as split between the competent spouse and the incompetent principal for federal gift tax purposes. Other nontax powers which can be given under a power of attorney include the right to buy or sell real estate, the right to invest in stocks, bonds or other securities, or the right to sue on behalf of the principal.

"Flower Bonds" are government obligations issued by the U.S. Treasury which can generally be purchased at a discount and can be redeemed at par value to pay federal estate taxes if owned by an individual at his death and includable in his estate. ("Flower bonds" are discussed in depth in Chapter 12.)

Due to the relatively low interest rate payable on flower bonds, they are often not purchased until a very short time before death. The Treasury has taken the position that flower bonds purchased pursuant to a Power of Attorney at a time when the principal was incompetent were not purchased by the decedent.[1] The courts in the State of New York have rejected the Treasury position on the basis that under New York law the transaction was only voidable and not void.[2] A *Durable* Power of Attorney which specifically authorizes the purchase of flower bonds should be beyond Treasury attack in all jurisdictions that recognize such Powers.

ISSUES AND IMPLICATIONS IN COMMUNITY PROPERTY STATES

Because community property is owned equally by both husband and wife, many transactions require the signature of both spouses in order to be effective. Particularly in situations where the couple has a community property proprietorship business, the incapacity of one spouse could seriously affect the stability and viability of the business.

Incapacity of one spouse could also prevent the sale of securities or the sale of or even borrowing against real or other property. Because of presumptions of community property status in many instances, title companies and others concerned with the completeness of title transfer usually require the signature (personally or by exercise of a power of attorney) of both spouses even though the property is in the name of only one spouse.

In many cases, a wife will give a power of attorney to her husband if he is the primary manager of the property for the sake of convenience of management. However, consideration should also be given to providing a method of dealing with both halves of the property if either the husband or the wife should suffer any incapacity.

It should be noted that while all states authorize some form of durable power, not all states have adopted the Uniform Durable Power of Attorney provisions.

Some community property states, such as California, provide that if one spouse is legally incompetent, the other spouse will succeed to management of the community property, with court approval required for some transactions. If the attorney-in-fact is not the spouse, there could be serious conflicts between the competent spouse and the attorney-in-fact pertaining to management and investment of community property.

QUESTIONS AND ANSWERS

Question — How broad can a Durable Power of Attorney be written?

Answer — The extent of the powers conferred by the principal upon the attorney-in-fact are limited only by the desires of the principal. The example of a broad general Power of Attorney shown in Figure 6.1 is an attempt by a principal to confer upon the "attorney-in-fact" the right to act to the same extent the principal could have acted if the principal were present and able to act.

Question — What is the duration of a Durable Power of Attorney?

Answer — The Durable Power of Attorney, once properly executed, continues until revoked by the principal or until it terminates by its terms on the death of the principal.

Figure 6.1

POWER OF ATTORNEY

KNOW ALL MEN BY THESE PRESENTS, that I, Brett A. Rosenbloom, of Delaware County, Pennsylvania, hereby revoke any general power of attorney that I have heretofore given to any person, and by these Presents do constitute, make and appoint my brother, Eric J. Rosenbloom, of Delaware County, Pennsylvania, my true and lawful attorney.

1. To ask, demand, sue for, recover and receive all sums of money, debts, goods, merchandise, chattels, effects and things of whatsoever nature or description which are now or hereafter shall be or become owing, due, payable, or belonging to me in or by any right whatsoever, and upon receipt thereof, to make, sign, execute and deliver such receipts, releases or other discharges for the same, respectively, as he shall think fit.

2. To deposit any moneys which may come into his hands as such attorney with any bank or bankers, either in my or his own name, and any of such money or any other money to which I am entitled which now is or shall be so deposited to withdraw as he shall think fit; to sign mutual savings bank and federal savings and loan association withdrawal orders; to sign and endorse checks payable to my order and to draw, accept, make, endorse, discount, or otherwise deal with any bills of exchange, checks, promissory notes or other commercial or mercantile instruments; to borrow any sum or sums of money on such terms and with such security as he may think fit and for that purpose to execute all notes or other instruments which may be necessary or proper; and to have access to any and all safe deposit boxes registered in my name.

3. To sell, assign, transfer and dispose of any and all stocks, bonds (including U.S. Savings Bonds), loans, mortgages or other securities registered in my name; and to collect and receipt for all interest and dividends due and payable to me.

4. To invest in my name in any stock, shares, bonds (including U.S. Treasury Bonds referred to as "flower bonds"), securities or other property, real or personal, as to vary such investments as he, in his sole discretion, may deem best; and to vote at meetings of shareholders or other meetings of any corporation or company and to execute any proxies or other instruments in connection therewith.

5. To enter into and upon my real estate, and to let, manage, and improve the same or any part thereof, and to repair or otherwise improve or alter, and to insure any buildings thereon; to sell, either at public or private sale or exchange any part or parts of my real estate or personal property for such consideration and upon such terms as he shall think fit, and to execute and deliver good and sufficient deeds or other instruments for the conveyance or transfer of the same, with such covenants of warranty or otherwise as he shall see fit, and to give good and effectual receipts for all or any part of the purchase price or other consideration; and to mortgage my real estate and in connection therewith to execute bonds and warrants and all other necessary instruments and documents.

6. To contract with any person for leasing for such periods, at such rents and subject to such conditions as he shall see fit, all or any of my said real estate; to give notice to quit to any tenant or occupier thereof; and to receive and recover from all tenants and occupiers thereof or of any part thereof all rents, arrears of rent, and sums of money which now are or shall hereafter become due and payable in respect thereof; and also on non-payment thereof or of any part thereof to take all necessary or proper means and proceedings for determining the tenancy or occupation of such tenants or occupiers, and for ejecting the tenants or occupiers and recovering the possession thereof.

Figure 6.1 continued

7. To commence, prosecute, discontinue or defend all actions or other legal proceedings pertaining to me or my estate or any part thereof; to settle, compromise, or submit to arbitration any debt, demand or other right or matter due me or concerning my estate as he, in his sole discretion, shall deem best and for such purpose to execute and deliver such releases, discharges or other instruments as he may deem necessary and advisable; and to satisfy mortgages, including the execution of a good and sufficient release, or other discharge of such mortgage.

8. To execute, acknowledge and file all Federal, State and Local tax returns of every kind and nature, including without limitation, income, gift and property tax returns.

9. To engage, employ and dismiss any agents, clerks, servants or other persons as he, in his sole discretion, shall deem necessary and advisable.

10. To convey and transfer any of my property to trustees who shall hold the same for my benefit and/or the benefit of my children and other members of my immediate family upon such trust terms and conditions as to my attorney shall deem desirable.

11. To make gifts to my wife and/or issue upon such terms and conditions as he in his discretion shall determine.

12. In general, to do all other acts, deeds and matters whatsoever in or about my estate, property and affairs as fully and effectually to all intents and purposes as I could do in my own proper person if personally present, giving to my said attorney power to make and substitute under him an attorney or attorneys for all the purposes herein described, hereby ratifying and confirming all that the said attorney or substitute or substitutes shall do therein by virtue of these Presents.

13. In addition to the powers and discretion herein specially given and conferred upon my attorney, and notwithstanding any usage or custom to the contrary, to have the full power, right and authority to do, perform and to cause to be done and performed all such acts, deeds and matters in connection with my property and estate as he, in his sole discretion, shall deem reasonable , necessary and proper, as fully, effectually and absolutely as if he were the absolute owner and possessor thereof.

14. In the event of my disability or incompetency, from whatever cause, this power of attorney shall not thereby be revoked.

IN WITNESS WHEREOF, I have hereunto set my hand and seal this   day of

          , 19   .

_____(SEAL)

BRETT A. ROSENBLOOM

STATE OF PENNSYLVANIA:

                    ss.

COUNTY OF DELAWARE

Before me, the undersigned, a Notary Public within and for the County of Delaware, Commonwealth of Pennsylvania, personally appeared Brett A. Rosenbloom, known to me to be the person whose name is subscribed to the within instrument, and acknowledged that he executed the same for the purposes therein contained.

IN WITNESS WHEREOF, I have hereunto set my hand and official seal this   day of

          , 19   .

_____

Notary Public

However, as a practical matter, many insurance companies and financial institutions attempt not to recognize any Power of Attorney which has been executed more than six months before the date it is presented for use. The obvious purpose of this "rule of convenience" is to make certain that the Power of Attorney is still in full force and effect.

However, the six month rule suggested above should not be applicable to a Durable Power of Attorney. The Durable Power of Attorney by its very nature is designed to cover the situation where the principal becomes incompetent. If, in fact, the principal is incompetent, it would be impossible for the attorney to obtain a freshly dated Power of Attorney.

Question — Can there be more than one attorney-in-fact under a Durable Power of Attorney?

Answer — Yes; however, caution must be taken in drafting the Power of Attorney. If the Power of Attorney merely names John Doe and Mary Roe as the holders of the Power, then both must act together in order for the Power to be operable. If, however, the Power is in favor of, "John Doe *or* Mary Roe, either of them to act in place of the principal," then each person can act independently.

Furthermore, the Power of Attorney can provide for successor "attorneys-in-fact" in the event of the primary attorney's death or inability to serve.

Question — Does a Power of Attorney terminate upon disability?

Answer — A Power of Attorney which is not a "Durable Power of Attorney" terminates upon disability. However, actions taken by the attorney-in-fact when he or she is unaware of the principal's disability are binding upon the principal.

A Durable Power of Attorney by its very definition survives and continues and is not affected by subsequent disability or incapacity of the principal.

Question — Does the death of the principal terminate a Durable Power of Attorney?

Answer — Yes. The death of the principal terminates a Power of Attorney whether or not it is durable. However, as in the case of a Power of Attorney which is not durable, the Durable Power of Attorney permits the attorney-in-fact who has no notice of the death of his principal to continue to act according to and under the Power until the attorney-in-fact learns of the death of the principal.

Question — What is the relationship between the "attorney-in-fact" under a Durable Power of Attorney and a court appointed guardian for the incompetent?

Answer — The Durable Power of Attorney continues in operation after the appointment of a guardian for the incompetent. However, the guardian of the incompetent appointed by the Court has the same rights as the principal and can terminate the Durable Power of Attorney on behalf of his ward, the incompetent.

Question — What is a "springing" power of attorney?

Answer — Four-fifths of the states recognize a particular form of durable power of attorney known as the springing power. The typical durable power of attorney takes effect upon execution. Clients who are reluctant to grant another person wide powers to act at a time when the principal is capable of acting may prefer to use a springing power. A springing power does not become effective until the occurrence of a specified event such as physical or mental incapacity or disappearance.

Some states define the contingencies under which the springing power becomes effective by statute, while other states require that the contingencies be specified in the instrument. All states require that the instrument name the person or persons who are to determine whether the contingency has occurred. For instance, if the contingency is incapacity, a doctor or group of doctors should be named to make such a determination. The attorney-in-fact may be the person making the determination. Obviously, alternate individuals should be named in case the person originally named is no longer able to make such a determination.

As with all tools and techniques, there are costs and downsides. The major drawback of a springing power is the potential difficulty in determining whether the contingency has occurred. There may be family disputes over whether a disability has in fact triggered the springing power. This puts a premium on clear and precise language in the instrument defining the contingency and creating an objective mechanism for determining whether it has actually occurred. An even greater potential problem is the reluctance on the part of banks, hospitals, and other organizations to accept a document granting broad powers over property if that document was executed a number of years prior to the date when it "springs." Financial institutions quite often raise the problem of "staleness," even though there is nothing in state law suggesting that the mere passage of time dates a power. For this reason, all powers of attorney should be revised every three years or less.

Question — What is a durable power of attorney for health care?

Answer — A durable power of attorney for health care is a document in which the principal confers upon the attorney in fact the power to make health care decisions for the principal in the event the principal is not legally competent. The extent of the permissible powers varies according to state law. In general, the principal authorizes the attorney-in-fact to consent to medical treatment, including surgical procedures. One of the most important and controversial aspects of this document is the extent to which it authorizes the attorney-in-fact to terminate treatment or even terminate life support where the principal is terminally ill or is in what is called "a persistent vegetative state," meaning the principal is in a permanent coma and the best medical opinion is that he or she will never recover.

In some states, the durable power of attorney for health care is a separate legal document, and requires more formality in execution than the durable power for management of property requires. In other states, the two powers are combined in a single document.

Question — Can the attorney-in-fact make gifts on behalf of the principal?

Answer — This is the one area involving the use of durable powers that has resulted in the most tax controversy. In the usual situation, the principal is elderly and/or seriously ill, and is not legally competent. The attorney-in-fact proposes to make a series of gifts that fall within the $10,000 annual exclusion discussed in Chapter 3 to reduce the principal's taxable estate. The IRS has successfully argued that unless gift giving is clearly authorized in the power of attorney itself, or under state law pertaining to the durable powers, the gifts are incomplete for federal tax purposes and still included in the taxable estate of the principal.[3]

Note that if the durable power of attorney is drafted to permit the attorney-in-fact to make gifts, consideration should be given to whether or not the power holder can make gifts to himself or herself. Bear in mind that the attorney-in-fact is often a close family member. If that person can make gifts to himself or herself, this power could be deemed a general power of appointment for federal tax purposes, and the failure to exercise the power could be a taxable gift.

Question — Does the attorney-in-fact under the durable power assume the same legal liabilities and responsibilities as a trustee?

Answer — The law in this area is unclear, but it is safe to assume the attorney in fact assumes at least some of the potential liability and duties of a trustee. This includes possible claims the attorney in fact made imprudent investments, or failed to protect the best interests of the principal. A person who is being considered for such an appointment should be fully informed of his or her potential liabilities.

Footnote References

Durable Power of Attorney

1. See, Treasury Form PD 1782, Application for Redemption at Par of United States Treasury Bonds Eligible for Payment of Federal Estate Tax; Treas. Reg. §306.28(G).
2. *Est. of Watson v. Simon*, 442 F. Supp. 1000 (D.C.N.Y. 1977), rev. on jurisdictional grounds.
3. *Est. of Casey v. Comm.*, 91-2 USTC ¶60,091 (4th Cir. 1991); TAMs 9347003, 9342003.

Chapter 7

ELDERLY AND DISABLED (PLANNING FOR)

WHAT IS IT?

Planning for the elderly and disabled focuses on clients or their dependents who, by reason of age or disability, or both, require specific health care and financial planning. Several other chapters in this book deal with aspects of this area of planning. For example, durable powers of attorney and durable powers of attorney for health care, discussed in Chapter 6, are particularly important for persons who fall within these definitions. So are revocable trusts, discussed in Chapter 38, which are often used for management of the assets of persons who are unable to manage their own affairs.

Unlike many other tools and techniques discussed in this book, the practice in this area requires the practitioner to deal with a variety of person problems and decisions of the client or dependent. These range from health care decisions to who will care for these persons if they are unable to care for themselves, and even where they will live.

WHEN IS THE USE OF SUCH A DEVICE INDICATED?

This planning should always be undertaken where, by reason of age or health, there is a real possibility the individual will become mentally or physically incapacitated with age or deteriorating health. In many cases, the need for this planning will be be speculative, as most elderly and disabled persons are able to function without special assistance.

However, this chapter also covers the problems of medical care for clients who are not disabled in the sense they have suffered no loss of their capacity to manage their own affairs and make their own decisions. It also discusses the problems of support for persons who are unable to support themselves.

WHAT ARE THE REQUIREMENTS?

The planning scenarios for elderly and disabled persons include the following:

1. Provision for management of the financial affairs of the client or dependent in the event they are unable to do so themselves. This employs such techniques as durable powers of attorney, revocable living trusts, and nomina-

tions of persons the individual would want to serve as a guardian or conservator in the event he needs someone to manage his affairs.

2. Providing for support of individuals who, due to age and/or health, are no longer self supporting and have not accumulated sufficient assets to provide for their cost of living.

3. Planning for long term health care, including possible institutional care.

4. Protecting property from claims of the state or federal government for reimbursement of health care costs.

WHAT ARE THE TAX IMPLICATIONS?

Planning in this area is not particularly tax driven. However, there are some special tax benefits available to the elderly which should not be overlooked. While income and self employment taxes are not dependent upon age, persons over 65 and those who are blind are entitled to an increase in their standard deduction in filing their income tax returns.[1] Widows and widowers may use joint income tax returns for two years following the death of the spouse.[2] Taxpayers who are supporting dependent family members may be entitled to additional dependency exemptions on their income tax returns. These include parents and grandparents, among others.[3] There is a dependent care credit available for certain employment related expenses.[4]

Taxpayers over 55 who sell their personal residences are entitled to a one time exclusion of up to $125,000 of the gain realized on the sale.[5]

IMPLICATIONS AND ISSUES IN COMMUNITY PROPERTY STATES

As a general rule, each spouse has a legal duty to support the other spouse, and both community and separate property can be reached to provide for such support. In addition, community assets can be reached to pay the debts and obligations of either spouse incurred during marriage.

If one spouse becomes incompetent, the law may vary on the right of the other spouse to manage community assets. The other spouse may be able to take over complete management, or may in some circumstances be required to share management with a guardian or conservator for the incompetent spouse.

QUESTIONS AND ANSWERS

Question — What federal programs are available to assist in providing health care for the elderly and disabled?

Answer — Government assistance programs include the following:

1. Social security disability benefits where an individual is unable to engage in gainful employment by reason of medically established mental or physical impairment. This impairment must be expected to last until death, or continuously over a period of at least 12 months.

2. Supplemental security income, often called SSA, which provides for needy persons who are elderly, blind, or otherwise disabled.

3. Medicare, which provides medical benefits on the basis of the age of the person, without regard to need.

4. Medicaid, which provides medical assistance regardless of age to the needy.

Question — In general, what are the eligibility requirements for Medicare?

Answer — Taxpayers who are 65 and eligible for social security, or who are 65 and whose spouses are eligible for social security, are eligible for Medicare. Part A of Medicare provides hospital insurance at no cost except for deductible and coinsurance amounts which must be paid by the patient. Part A also provides limited coverage for care in a skilled nursing facility, a hospice, or post-hospital home health services. Part B of Medicare primarily covers physician's services, and is voluntary. Premiums are required under Part B. Certain individuals over 65 who are not covered by Part A may elect voluntary coverage by paying premiums if they are enrolled in Part B. Certain disabled persons under 65 can also be eligible for Medicare benefits.

Question — What is medigap insurance?

Answer — "Medigap" is a generic name for health insurance which covers some or all of the expenses not covered by either Part A or Part B of Medicare.

Question — What is Medicaid?

Answer — Medicaid is a joint federal and state program which provides assistance for health care to certain aged, disabled, or blind individuals. The intent is to provide help to needy individuals. In some cases, this is integrated with the requirements for supplemental security income (SSI) mentioned above. Many states impose an income cap based on SSI requirements. The tests here are largely dependent on state law. There are also special requirements for nursing home benefits.

Question — For purposes of Medicaid, what are "resources," and how do they affect eligibility?

Answer — Resources refer to assets owned by an individual or available to an individual. If these exceed a certain dollar value, that individual will be ineligible for various benefits, particularly nursing home care. These generally include assets owned by the spouse of the individual. In addition, the income of the individual and spouse are also available resources.

Question — Does the individual's personal residence count as an asset for purposes of Medicaid eligibility?

Answer — This depends on state law. For example, in California, the residence is exempt even if the individual is in a nursing home six months or less, because the individual is presumed to intend to return to it.

Question — Can individuals transfer assets so that they will not be counted as resources for purposes of Medicaid?

Answer — Congress has imposed and continues to impost strict limits on transfers of assets to achieve Medicaid eligibility. For example, the value of any transfer of assets within 36 months before the individual makes an application for Medicaid will be considered an available resource.[6] The penalties are in the form of denial of Medicaid benefits for a period of months depending on the value of the property transferred. There are exceptions, including one for transfers to children who are "caretakers" for their parent. There are other exceptions for transfers to spouses, minor children, trusts for disabled children, etc. Check the law for the effective dates of this look-back period.

In general, for assets transferred to trusts, the look-back period is 60 months from the date the individual makes a Medicaid application or the date the individual enters a nursing home. Assets transferred to trusts within 60 months prior to these dates are considered an available resource.[7] This includes trusts, other than trusts created by will, created by the individual, his spouse, and certain third persons, such as conservators and trustees. The purpose for which the trust was created is not relevant.

Assets in a revocable trust are presumed available resources, regardless of when the trust was created. Further, if any assets are transferred from the revocable trust to another individual within the 60-month period, that is also a transfer subject to the 60-month look-back period. Note that if the individual who created the trust personally removes the assets and personally transfers them by gift, the 36-month rather than the 60-month look-back period will apply.

Assets in an irrevocable trust are also deemed to be available resources if payment could be made to the individual from the trust. There are various exemptions, and the statutes are confusing as to the extent of availability. However, it appears the 60-month rather than the 36-month look-back period applies in this situation.

Question — May an individual or his spouse waive or forfeit pension rights to become eligible for Medicaid?

Answer — No. Any waiver of pension income, inheritances, or damage claims, as in personal injury suits, is ineffective.

Question — Will amounts paid to family members who are furnishing personal care for an individual be counted as resources?

Answer — While reasonable payments for personal care are not viewed as gifts for Medicaid purposes, payment for past services are viewed with suspicion.

Question — If an individual transfers property by gift, but retains a life estate, what amount will be treated as an available resource?

Answer — According to the federal government, the actuarial value of the life estate, based on the life expectancy of the individual, is subtracted from the value of the property, and the remainder is considered the gift of an available resource.[8]

Question — If an individual purchases a life annuity, will that be subject to the look back gift rules?

Answer — If the annuity is "actuarially sound," based on the life expectancy of the individual, it will not be deemed a partial gift.

Question — Will the transfer of a personal residence to either a revocable or irrevocable trust trigger the look-back rules?

Answer — No. Since the personal residence is an excluded asset under the Medicaid rules, the transfer is not subject to the rule. However, the federal government takes the position[9] that it is a resource. As noted above, the personal residence is often an exempt asset.

Question — Three adult children are contributing equally to the support of their elderly parent. May any of them claim her as a dependent?

Answer — Since no child is furnishing over one half of the parent's support, none of them can claim her as a dependent unless they sign a multiple support agreement. Essentially, this is an agreement that one of the children will claim the mother as a dependent, and the others will not.

Question — When one spouse is in a nursing home, to what extent are the assets of the other spouse protected from claims for reimbursement for public assistance or counted as available resources of the institutionalized spouse?

Answer — The law permits the other spouse, who is called the "community" spouse, to retain assets of a certain value. The amount varies from state to state. In this regard, revocable trusts, discussed in Chapter 38, may cause substantial problems. If the trust language permits the use of trust assets for the support of the institutionalized spouse, the trust will be considered an available resource. Further, the community spouse may not be able to claim any exemption for the trust assets since they are not in his name. The revocable trust should contain specific language dealing with these issues.

Question — What is a special needs trust?

Answer — A special needs trust is one established by clients who have children who are under a disability and are receiving supplemental social security (SSI) benefits, or other forms of state or federal assistance. They are intended to permit the parents to furnish some economic benefits to their children without disqualifying them for public assistance. The device may also be used to provide for elderly persons who are disabled, such as parent.

The purpose of the special needs trust is to permit payments by the trustee to cover needs of the disabled person which do not affect his eligibility for public assistance. The special needs trust should not be geared to the basics, such as food, clothing, shelter, and in particular, medical care.

The guidelines for what assets may be considered available resources to the disabled person are found in the Program Operational Manual, commonly referred to as POM, which is used by government representatives. If the assets in the trust are available for the basic needs of the disabled person, they may result in denial of public assistance, or the appropriate government agency may even seek to compel reimbursement of public assistance payments from the trust assets.

On the other hand, property held in such a trust does not count as a resource of the disabled person if access to the trust assets is restricted. In general, such trusts should follow a discretionary or protective trust format used for asset protection, but must be even more restrictive. For example, if the trust provided that the trustee could use trust assets only for the "support" of the disabled person, it would count as an available resource.

Such trusts should specifically provide that the trustee may not make any payments which cover items provided by public assistance programs. The trust must be irrevocable and an independent trustee is preferred. It may be part of the basic estate plan of the parents, either in a will or living trust which takes effect at death. While the trust could be created irrevocably while the parents are alive, this is generally discouraged. It may have gift tax consequences, and government officials must be informed whenever the disabled person becomes the beneficiary of an irrevocable trust.

To guard against attacks from the providers of public assistance, these trusts may provide for contingent ben-eficiaries, such as other children, who could become the exclusive beneficiaries of the trust if such an attack is launched. The trust may also have a destruct clause, providing that if the providers do attempt to reach it, or use it to disqualify the disabled person, it will terminate and be distributed entirely to contingent beneficiaries, such as the other children.

Question — Can a client who wishes to qualify for Medicaid create a form of special needs trust for his own benefit?

Answer — Both state and federal law provide that if the individual or spouse transfers assets to an irrevocable trust for the benefit of the individual, all of its assets are deemed available resources.[10] However, this will not apply to trusts created by third persons, such as children, which should be structured as special needs trusts.

Footnote References

Elderly and Disabled (Planning for)

1. IRC Sec. 63.
2. IRC Sec. 2.
3. IRC Sec. 151, 152.
4. IRC Sec. 21.
5. IRC Sec. 121.
6. 42 USC Sec. 1396p(c)(1)(B)(i).
7. Id.
8. Transmittal No. 64, State Medicaid Manual, November, 1994.
9. Id.
10. 42 USC Sec. 1396A(k).

Chapter 8

EMPLOYEE DEATH BENEFIT EXCLUSION

WHAT IS IT?

The Internal Revenue Code allows the estate or other beneficiary of an employee to receive up to $5,000 from the decedent's employer free from income tax. This exclusion applies to the beneficiary of any employee of a corporation, a sole proprietorship, or a partnership.

The income tax exclusion is available regardless of whether the benefit is paid voluntarily or under contract, whether paid directly or to a trust, and whether paid in a lump sum or in installments. The exclusion will be allowed regardless of whether the benefit is paid to a former or to an active employee.

WHEN IS THE USE OF SUCH A DEVICE INDICATED?

1. When an employer desires to reward key officers or long service employees by providing an income tax free fringe benefit.

2. When an employee-stockholder wishes to provide a fringe benefit that will be income tax free to his or her spouse or other beneficiary.

3. When an employee needs additional financial security to provide for his or her family upon death.

WHAT ARE THE REQUIREMENTS?

1. The $5,000 exclusion is not available when an employee has a nonforfeitable right to receive that amount while living. (An exception is made for total distributions made within one taxable year of the recipient under a qualified pension or profit-sharing plan or under some tax-deferred annuity plans.)[1]

2. The $5,000 exclusion is not available for payments under a joint and survivor annuity where the annuity starting date occurs (annuity payments have begun) before the death of the employee.[2]

3. The $5,000 exclusion is not available with respect to interest payments on amounts held by an employer under an agreement to pay interest.[3]

4. The $5,000 exclusion is not available for payments with respect to self-employed individuals except for distributions from a qualified retirement plan made by reason of the employee's death.[4]

HOW IT IS DONE — AN EXAMPLE

Generally, an employer will select one or more key officers, long service employees, or even himself (assuming he is an employee). The business will agree to pay that employee's widow or family a certain amount in the event the employee dies while employed. The employer can provide this benefit entirely on a selective basis and thus can pick and choose the executives, supervisors, or other employees to be covered.

WHAT ARE THE TAX IMPLICATIONS?

1. When benefits are paid out to the widow or family of the deceased employee, those benefits, assuming they are reasonable, will be deductible as a business expense.[5]

2. The first $5,000 paid by (or on behalf of) an employer as a death benefit will be income tax free to the employee's estate or beneficiary.[6]

3. Amounts paid by an employer in excess of $5,000 will usually be taxable as ordinary income since such payments will generally be considered additional compensation for past services rendered by the employee (even if the employer uses tax-free life insurance proceeds to fund the benefit). However, in the case of a purely voluntary payment by an employer, there are some cases in which the amounts in excess of $5,000 have been considered as tax-exempt gifts.[7]

HOW CAN LIFE INSURANCE ENHANCE THIS TOOL?

In many instances, an employer may use a life insurance policy to fund its promise. The corporation would insure the employee and own, pay premiums on, and be named beneficiary of the policy. The policy cash values would grow tax free and are considered a corporate asset.

At the employee's death, the employer would receive the policy proceeds. Once the employer receives the insurance proceeds, it would then pay the promised amount to the beneficiary of the employee. Assuming the payments were reasonable, they would be deductible by the corporation as a business expense. (Amounts in excess of $5,000 will not be deductible if such amounts are considered gifts.)

Premiums for the insurance purchased to fund the agreement are not deductible by the employer.[8] The death proceeds, when received by the employer, will be income tax free.[9]

IMPLICATIONS AND ISSUES IN COMMUNITY PROPERTY STATES

As stated previously in this chapter, the $5,000 employee's death benefit exclusion is not available when the benefit is nonforfeitable (other than lump sum distributions from a qualified pension or profit sharing plan or some tax deferred annuity plans). If the spouse is the beneficiary of the death benefit, no community property issues would arise. Problems could arise, however, if the spouse were not the beneficiary of the death benefit and did not consent to the designation of beneficiary. A spouse usually cannot be deprived of community property rights without giving consent. The major question then becomes whether the death benefit is community property. The other possible question is whether the Employee Retirement Income Security Act (ERISA) will preempt state law, a possibility that is discounted by many estate planners in this particular situation.

IRS regulations specify that the $5,000 exclusion does not apply to amounts constituting income payable during the employee's life as compensation for services, such as bonuses or uncollected salary, or other amounts which the employee possessed a nonforfeitable right to receive while living (other than distributions from qualified plans).

The rules relating to distributions from qualified plans, which have been previously discussed, will apply to determine whether a benefit payable from a qualified plan is community property.

If, however, the death benefit subject to the $5,000 exclusion is not paid from a qualified plan, difficult issues arise. Where an employer voluntarily makes payment to the survivor of an employee, the payment would not be community property. The employee would have had no property interest or contractual right before his death. In some cases, however, courts have found an implied agreement on the part of the employer to pay the death benefit. Thus, the lack of an express agreement to pay death benefits is not alone sufficient to support a claim that the employer's payment of the death benefit was intended as a gift.

In the absence of a gift, it is likely that the death benefit will be found to be community property. California courts have held that accidental death benefits paid by an employer are community property.

If the death benefit is community property, only one-half of the death benefit would be includable in the employee's gross estate.

QUESTIONS AND ANSWERS

Question — Is the $5,000 exclusion available if the payment is made in installments?

Answer — Generally, the $5,000 exclusion is available whether amounts were paid in a lump sum or in installments.[10] If the death benefit is paid in installments, the $5,000 exclusion will be treated as part or all of the cost basis of the employee. Under the annuity rules, an exclusion ratio is determined. Basically, a fraction is established. The employee's "investment in the contract" is divided by the "expected return" under the contract. The resulting quotient is the percentage of each payment which may be excluded from gross income. In this case, the surviving spouse or other beneficiary would use $5,000 (or the amount the employer paid if less) as his or her cost or investment in the contract. The expected return would be the total amount estimated to be received under the contract.

Question — Will a deduction be allowed for amounts paid by an employer in excess of $5,000?

Answer — The Internal Revenue Service will examine the specific situation. If facts indicate that the payment was purely a gift or was made to disguise a dividend, the deduction will be denied. For example, if the widow of the employee is a controlling stockholder, the Internal Revenue Service could claim payments are in essence constructive dividends. This would make the entire death benefit, including the first $5,000, taxable to the widow and nondeductible by the corporation.[11]

Question — What are the estate tax ramifications of a voluntary death benefit paid by the employer to the survivor or other beneficiary of a deceased employee?

Answer — Where an employer voluntarily makes payments to the survivor of an employee, there will be no inclusion of those amounts in the employee's estate;[12] however, benefits provided will be includable in the employee's estate if, at the time of his death, the employee was, in fact, receiving, or had an enforceable right to receive, lifetime benefits under a contract or plan.

All rights and benefits which the employee had by reason of his employment (except rights under a qualified pension or profit-sharing plan) are treated as one contract or plan in determining whether the employee had an enforceable right to lifetime payments. Therefore, inclusion of death payments cannot be avoided by providing lifetime benefits under one arrangement and death benefits under another plan.[13]

Even if the employer promised only a pure death benefit and made no promises to pay income during the lifetime of the employee, amounts paid to his widow or other beneficiaries will still be includable in his estate if the employee retained, at the time of his death, power to alter, amend, revoke, or terminate the agreement or change the beneficiary.[14]

Question — If an employee works for two or more employers, can the employee's survivors take two or more $5,000 exclusions?

Answer — No. Each employee is allowed only one $5,000 exclusion regardless of the number of employers or beneficiaries or plans involved.

Question — Can an employer provide a death benefit to more than one beneficiary?

Answer — Yes, but the $5,000 exclusion would have to be divided among the beneficiaries. The apportionment ratio would be:

$$\$5,000 \times \frac{\text{Beneficiary's portion of death benefit}}{\text{Total death benefit payable}}$$

For example, Allan Gart, the president of the Allover Travel Company, died recently. Pursuant to an agreement with Allan, Allover Travel Company pays a total of $20,000 to various members of his family—$10,000 is paid to Allan's widow, $4,000 to Allan's son, and $6,000 to his daughter. These were the only taxable employer-produced death benefits received by Allan's family. The firm was under no obligation to provide Allan with retirement or disability benefits. Figure 8.1 shows Allan's widow received $10,000 out of the $20,000 total death benefit. So she is entitled to exclude an amount equal to

$^1/_2$ of the $5,000 exclusion, $2,500. Allan's son received $4,000 out of the $20,000 total, $^1/_5$ of the total. Therefore, he is entitled to $^1/_5$ of the $5,000 exclusion, $1,000. Allan's daughter is allowed to take the remaining portion of the exclusion ($5,000 - $3,500), $1,500.

Question — Will payments made under the pre-retirement death benefit provisions of a nonqualified deferred compensation program be eligible for the $5,000 exclusion?

Answer — The $5,000 death benefit exclusion can be used against a variety of death benefits, including a death benefit made under a deferred compensation plan for key executives. With some exceptions (as previously noted), the executive must not have had a nonforfeitable right to such amounts while he was alive.

ASRS, Secs. 53, ¶20.4(g); 59, ¶930.3; 61, ¶230; 64, ¶420.6(d).

Footnote References

Employee Death Benefit Exclusion

1. IRC Sec. 101(b)(2).
2. Reg. §1.101-2(b)(2).
3. IRC Sec. 101(c); Reg. §1.101-3(a).
4. IRC Sec. 101(b)(3).
5. See *Rubber Assoc., Inc.*, 335 F.2d 75 (6th Cir. 1964); *Fifth Ave. Coach Lines Inc.*, 31 TC 1080 (1958).
6. IRC Sec. 101(b)(2).
7. The courts, following the rules laid down by the Supreme Court in *Comm. v. Duberstein*, 363 US 278 (1960) are divided as to whether the payments are tax free gifts or taxable compensation. Each case is decided on its facts. See *Flarsheim v. U.S.*, 156 F.2d 105 (8th Cir. 1946); *Simpson v. U.S.*, 261 F.2d 497 (7th Cir. 1958).
8. IRC Sec. 264(a)(1).
9. IRC Sec. 101(a).
10. Reg. §1.101-2(a)(1).
11. See *Lengsfield v. Comm.*, 241 F.2d 508 (5th Cir. 1957); *Schner-Block Co., Inc. v. Comm.*, 329 F.2d 875 (2nd Cir. 1964) aff'g TC Memo 1963-166.
12. *Est. of Barr*, 40 TC 227 (1963) acq. in result only, 1978-1 CB 1; *Est. of Albright*, 42 TC 642 (1964).
13. Reg. §20.2039-1(b)(2)(Ex. 6).
14. IRC Secs. 2036, 2038.

Figure 8.1

COMPUTING THE EMPLOYEE DEATH BENEFIT EXCLUSION				
INPUT:	**REMAINING EXCLUSION**	**$5,000**	**AMOUNT EXCLUDIBLE**	**AMOUNT INCLUDIBLE**
Input:	Payment to Beneficiary 1	$10,000	$2,500	$7,500
Input:	Payment to Beneficiary 2	$4,000	$1,000	$3,000
Input:	Payment to Beneficiary 3	$6,000	$1,500	$4,500
Input:	Payment to Beneficiary 4	$0	$0	$0
Input:	Payment to Beneficiary 5	$0	$0	$0
	Total Death Benefit Payable	$20,000	$5,000	$15,000

Chapter 9

EMPLOYEE STOCK OWNERSHIP PLAN

WHAT IS IT?

An employee stock ownership plan, commonly referred to as an ESOP (the ESOP plan trust is usually called an employee stock ownership trust or ESOT), is technically considered a stock bonus plan and the trust may qualify as a tax-exempt employee trust.[1]

Stock bonus plans are one of the oldest forms of deferred compensation recognized by the Internal Revenue Service. These plans are established by employers to provide benefits similar to those of a profit sharing plan. Benefits may be distributable in the form of the employer's stock.

There are significant advantages to both the employer and the employee which can be derived from the stock bonus plan and, as a result, a significant increase in the use of such plans has occurred in recent years. Favorable tax treatment has made ESOPs even more attractive for many employers; however changes to federal law in 1989 did reduce some of the tax incentives for employers to establish such plans.

WHEN IS THE USE OF SUCH A DEVICE INDICATED?

1. When a shareholder who is a substantial owner of a closely-held business would like to shift his investment, on a tax-deferred basis, into publicly traded securities. Tax-free rollover of the proceeds received from the sale of a business to an ESOP may be available if the proceeds are invested in another business; this rollover provision is intended to encourage employee stock ownership (see discussion of mechanics under "What Are the Tax Implications," infra).

2. When an employer would like to obtain an income tax deduction with little or no cash outlay. A current deduction is allowed for both employer contributions of cash and for contributions of stock (including stock of the employer company) or other property contributed to the ESOP.[2] A contribution of an employer's stock generates a deduction equal to its fair market value. The sizable deduction reduces cash flow out of the corporation in profit years and in loss years a carry-back is created which might result in a tax refund to the corporation.[3]

3. When an employer wants to create a market for its stock. An ESOP may be able to purchase treasury stock or authorized but unissued stock as well as stock owned by individual shareholders without causing a loss of corporate control by majority shareholders. (But note that if a defined contribution plan—other than a profit sharing plan—is established by an employer whose stock is not readily tradable on an established market and employer stock comprises more than 10 percent of the plan's assets, participating employees must be entitled to exercise voting rights of stock allocated to their account on certain major corporate matters.)

4. When a corporation faces an accumulated earnings threat. An ESOP can be used to take cash out of a corporation and thus reduce the potential for an accumulated earnings tax problem. The reduction in taxable income of the corporation due to deductible contributions lessens the pressure on a corporation to pay dividends which are taxable at ordinary income rates to the recipient and nondeductible by the corporation.

5. When an employer is seeking a way to motivate and compensate long service employees. Since the ultimate value of an employee's ESOP interest is directly related to the value of the employee's stock, increased productivity and corporate growth become an employee concern. ESOPs also provide a means for employees (including shareholder-employees) to supplement social security as well as other corporate-provided retirement benefits.

6. When shareholders with large amounts of corporate stock in their estate want liquidity, the stock may be sold to the ESOP in exchange for cash, thus providing the liquidity to pay taxes and other debts. Prior to 1990, there was an estate tax deduction allowed up to $750,000 for half of the value of stock sold to an ESOP.[4]

7. When a corporation desires to have payment of premiums for life insurance on key employees made from deductible contributions. In appropriate cases, life insurance payments on key employees, who are also shareholders, may be shifted to the ESOP from the corporation, and these premium payments, which are otherwise not deductible to the corporation, effectively become deductible contributions to the ESOP. The insurance policy is an investment of the ESOP and may be the source of liquidity to buy the shareholder's stock at his death.

8. When an employer is seeking a means for financing corporate growth through the use of untaxed dollars. By

selling rather than contributing stock to the ESOP, an employer can obtain a large amount of cash. Conversely, if the corporation had borrowed cash from a bank to finance corporate expansion, only interest payments on the loan would be deductible. The principal would have to be repaid with "expensive" (nondeductible) dollars. On the other hand, the corporation will get a deduction for the dollars it then contributes to the ESOP. The ESOP receives these free of tax and uses them (without reduction for income taxes) to repay the bank loan.

WHAT ARE THE REQUIREMENTS?

1. ESOPs meeting certain requirements may distribute benefits in the form of employer stock *or* cash. Participants must be given the right to receive employer stock if they so desire, unless the employer's charter or by-laws restrict the ownership of substantially all outstanding employer stock to employees and/or the ESOP. If ownership is so restricted, a participant need not be given the right to receive employer stock. The participant must then be given the right to receive his benefit in cash. If employer stock is distributed, participants must be given a "put" option for a limited time which allows them to force the employer to purchase the stock at its fair market value.[5] The put option requirement does not apply to a bank which maintains an ESOP if the bank is prohibited by law from redeeming or buying its own stock and participants are given the right to receive their benefits in cash. It appears that an ESOP with no cash distribution option (which would not be typical) is required to give a put option to participants only with respect to employer stock acquired by the plan after December 31, 1979 or acquired with proceeds of a loan obtained from or guaranteed by a disqualified person (unless the stock is readily tradable on an established securities market).

2. The plan must meet requirements pertaining to coverage, nondiscrimination in contributions, nondiscrimination in benefits, nonforfeitable rights on termination, rules regarding forfeitures, and rules relative to the source of contributions.[6] IRS regulations do not allow an ESOP to be integrated with social security contributions.[7] Certain ESOPs in existence on November 1, 1977, with social security integration provisions were "grandfathered" and may be able to continue to use those provisions. As is the case for all qualified retirement plans, an ESOP must be in writing.[8]

3. The trust must be for the exclusive benefit of the employees or their beneficiaries (e.g., the ESOP is not meant as a means of bailing out financially troubled employers).[9]

4. The trust must be a United States trust and not a foreign trust.

5. The cost of employer stock purchased by the trustee must not exceed its fair market value. An independent appraisal is required for all ESOP security transactions.[10]

6. Participants must be entitled to vote employer stock which has been allocated to their accounts if the stock is registered under the Securities Exchange Act of 1934. If the employer's stock is not readily tradable on an established market and more than 10 percent of the plan's assets are invested in employer stock, the plan must give participants voting rights on major corporate issues (generally those involving the approval or disapproval of any corporate merger or consolidation, recapitalization, reclassification, liquidation, dissolution, sale of substantially all assets of a trade or business, or similar transactions) on employer stock acquired after December 31, 1979.[11]

7. Participants who have completed 10 years of participation in the ESOP must be given the opportunity to diversify 25 percent of their account balances at age 55 and an additional 25 percent at age 60. This applies only to stock acquired after December 31, 1986.[12]

8. With respect to distributions attributable to stock acquired after December 31, 1986, the plan must provide that, if the participant elects (and if required spousal consent is properly given), the distribution of a participant's account balance will commence within one year after the plan year (1) in which he separates from service by reason of attainment of normal retirement age, disability, or death, or (2) which is the fifth plan year following the plan year in which he otherwise separates from service.[13]

9. The plan must insure that, in the case of certain "qualified sales" (after October 22, 1986) of employer securities by a participant (under Code section 1042) or executor (under former Code section 2057) to the ESOP, no portion of the assets of the plan attributable to the securities purchased by the plan may accrue or be allocated during the nonallocation period for the benefit of (1) the taxpayer who made the election under Section 1042 (or the decedent whose executor made the election under former Section 2057), (2) any individual who is a member of the family (brother, sister, spouse, ancestor, lineal descendant) of the taxpayer or decedent, or (3) any person who owns, or is considered as owning under the attribution rules of Section 318(a), more than 25% (by number or value) of any class of outstanding stock of the employer or any corporation which is a member of the same controlled group of corporations as is the employer.[14]

HOW IT IS DONE — EXAMPLES

A corporate client has been consistently earning $200,000 per year. The corporation has no pension or profit-sharing plan. The employees are eager to see some type of deferred compensation program instituted. Because of an expansion program, the corporation periodically is in a cash-poor position. The schedule below shows the amount of the increase in corporate working capital by comparing an ESOP with a profit-sharing plan and no deferred compensation plan.

From the comparison, it is clear that establishing an ESOP gives the greatest increase in working capital.

A corporate client needs a new building which will cost approximately $250,000. The only available loans require an amortization of the $250,000 at the rate of $50,000 per year for five years plus interest on the unpaid balance. Using the schedule set forth below, if the corporation established a profit-sharing plan, only $66,000 would be left after taxes on $200,000 of earnings in order to amortize the principal debt and pay the interest. Clearly this would not be enough money. If the corporation had no plan, sufficient monies would be available to amortize the debt and pay the interest although the net worth increase after such payments would be rather small. If an ESOP were established, the ESOP could borrow the $250,000 from the bank (the loan may have to be guaranteed by the corporation) and the ESOP would immediately purchase $250,000 of capital stock from the corporation. The corporation's net working capital would be immediately increased by $250,000. The corporation would then make contributions to the ESOP on an annual basis and the ESOP would repay the bank.

	No Plan	Profit Sharing Plan	ESOP
Earnings Before Tax	$200,000	$200,000	$200,000
Contributions (15% x $600,000 of compensation eligible for coverage)	0	90,000	90,000
Taxable Income	$200,000	$110,000	$110,000
Tax (assume combined federal and state bracket is 40%)	80,000	44,000	44,000
Net Earnings After Taxes	$120,000	$ 66,000	$ 66,000
Net Worth Increase: Net Earnings After Taxes	$120,000	$ 66,000	$ 66,000
Cash from Sale of Capital Stock to ESOP	0	0	90,000
Increase in Working Capital	$120,000	$ 66,000	$156,000

One-half of the interest received by a lender on loans for an ESOP to purchase stock or to refinance stock purchases is exempt from income tax if certain conditions are met.[15] This exemption can make such acquisition and refinance loans easier to obtain and less expensive.

A third example for the use of the ESOP is a situation where a majority of the stock of a close corporation is owned by one individual, and his wife and/or children own the balance of the stock. The stock represents a part of the individual's estate, but not "more than 35 percent of his adjusted gross estate" and therefore not enough to qualify for a redemption under section 303 of the Internal Revenue Code. Additionally, the spouse and/or the children, also shareholders, are beneficiaries of the estate and therefore a redemption of the stock by the corporation would constitute a dividend to the estate (by reason of the attribution rules of section 318 of the Code). Also consider that the corporation may not have sufficient funds to redeem all the shares of stock and certainly any partial redemption would also constitute a dividend.

Creation of the ESOP would establish an entity that could purchase all or any portion of the stock owned by the estate and not create dividend consequences to the estate. Such a purchase would indirectly give rise to a deduction for the corporation, a deduction it could not take if the purchase had been made directly from the estate. Although such a transaction has been given approval by the Internal Revenue Service in at least one private letter ruling, it is advisable to obtain a favorable ruling in advance of the sale.

The Internal Revenue Service has stringent requirements that must be met for an advance ruling. These requirements are updated annually.[16]

A fourth example of the use of an ESOP involves the conversion of premiums on nondeductible key individual life insurance into a tax deduction. Assume that a corporation is owned by two or more stockholders equally and the stockholders desire to have a buy-sell agreement (either an entity or cross purchase type) funded by life insurance so that on the death of any one stockholder there will be sufficient monies to purchase or redeem the shares of stock of the decedent and permit the company to continue in business. Payment of the life insurance premiums are normally nondeductible.

If, however, the company established an ESOP and the investment committee directed the ESOP to purchase key individual insurance on the lives of all of the stockholders, then upon the death of any stockholder, the trust being the beneficiary of the life insurance policy, would be entitled to the proceeds and would then be able to use the proceeds and negotiate with the personal representative of the deceased stockholder for the purchase of the shares of stock at the then fair market value of those shares on the date of the decedent's death. Consideration must be given to the possibility that the ESOP would not be able to acquire the stock, which then would leave the life insurance proceeds in the plan. An alternative may be to have the corporation continue to own the policies and contribute enough stock to the plan each year to offset the insurance premium tax cost.

Final regulations prohibit an ESOP from buying life insurance with the proceeds of a loan obtained from or guaranteed by a disqualified person. In addition, a leveraged ESOP must not obligate itself to purchase stock at an indefinite future time (although it can be given an option to acquire stock).[17]

WHAT ARE THE TAX IMPLICATIONS?

A corporation is allowed a deduction for contributions made to the ESOP even if it had no profits during the year the contribution was made.[18] The excess deduction might therefore generate a net operating loss carryback with a resulting tax refund.

An employer can generally deduct a contribution to a single ESOP of up to 15 percent of the total compensation paid to all participants in the plan. If the employer deducts less than 15 percent of covered compensation, the difference between the amount which was actually contributed and the amount which could have been deducted may not be carried forward and used to increase the deduction limit in future years.[19]

An employer can combine an ESOP of the stock bonus type with a money purchase pension plan (which need not, but can, be an ESOP) to increase its annual deduction to 25 percent of plan participants' compensation.[20]

Special deduction rules apply to plans which have incurred debt to purchase employer stock. An employer may contribute as much as 25 percent of covered compensation to a single ESOP where the contributions are applied to make principal payments on the loan. Additional unlimited deductions are allowed for employer contributions used to pay interest on the loan.[21] Limitations on allocations to employee accounts which apply if more than one-third of contributions are allocated to certain key employees may limit the availability of these special deduction limits in some circumstances.[22]

The employer does not have to make the contribution to the ESOP in stock of the employer. The contribution may be made in cash, any other property, or employer stock. However, a contribution of property may involve a prohibited transaction or other problems which should be carefully examined. Any one of the three contribution media, alone or in combination with the others, will create a deduction to the corporation equal to the cash and the fair market value of the assets being transferred.

If the corporation transfers assets to the ESOP that have appreciated in value, the gain will constitute income to the corporation.[23] For example, if the corporation bought stock which grew from $3 to $8 a share, a contribution of that stock would result in a $5 per share gain. This is true on the transfer of all property with the exception of cash and stock of the employer.

The corporation is allowed a special corporate deduction for cash dividends paid with respect to stock held on the dividend record date by an ESOP, provided the dividends (a) are paid directly in cash to participants or their beneficiaries, or (b) are paid indirectly to them through the plan within 90 days after the close of the plan year, or (c) are used to make payments on a loan incurred to purchase qualifying employer securities.[24] For shares acquired by an ESOP after August 4, 1989, a deduction is allowed under (c) only if the dividends are paid on shares purchased with the loan proceeds.

Code section 1042 provides a major income tax break on sales of stock to an ESOP. Under this section recognition of gain may be deferred on certain sales of closely held stock to an ESOP if (1) the sale would qualify for long term capital gain treatment, (2) after the sale the ESOP owns 30 percent of the total value of the employer securities, (3) within a 15-month period (beginning 3 months prior to the day of sale) "qualified replacement securities" are purchased, *and* (4) for sales after July 10, 1989, the taxpayer held the shares for 3 years or longer. "Qualified replacement security" generally means stock or bonds issued by a domestic corporation which, for the taxable year of issuance, does not have passive investment income of more than 25 percent of gross receipts. If the cost of the replacement securities is less than the amount of the deferred gain, the difference is currently taxable.

Although it is possible for a shareholder to obtain beneficial nonrecognition of gain on the sale of stock to an ESOP under Code section 1042, there is a pitfall to avoid. With respect to sales of securities after October 22, 1986, if there is a prohibited accrual or allocation (see paragraph (9) under "What are the Requirements," above), a penalty tax equal to 50% of the amount of the prohibited accrual or allocation will be levied against the employer sponsoring the plan.[25] In addition, the amount of any prohibited accrual or allocation will be treated as if distributed to the individual involved and taxed as such.[26] Up to 5% of the securities purchased by the ESOP in the Section 1042 or former Section 2057 transaction can be allocated to the benefit of lineal descendants of the seller without creating any adverse tax consequences.[27]

Employer contributions are not currently taxable to participating employees. ESOP trust assets grow tax free, even if an employee's rights become nonforfeitable. An employee pays no tax until a distribution is made to him (see the discussion of the tax treatment of distributions in Chapter 28).

IMPLICATIONS AND ISSUES IN COMMUNITY PROPERTY STATES

Benefits from qualified plans (pension/profit sharing plans, HR-10 plans and ESOPs) and IRAs are generally held to be community property to the extent contributions are made by or on behalf of a married employee who is a resident of one of the community property states (enumerated in the discussion of community property in the "Introduction") during the period of employment.

This rule, while relatively simple to state, can present significant problems when applied to specific situations. The major areas of difficulty are divorce and death of an employee.

There was a question after the enactment of the Employee Retirement Income Security Act of 1974 (ERISA) as to whether community property laws continued to apply to qualified plan benefits. Some argued that ERISA "preempted" state community property laws. Others argued that award of a part of an employee's qualified plan benefits to his spouse was an assignment or alienation of benefits prohibited by ERISA. If the courts had followed these arguments, spouses in community property states would no longer be entitled to the 50 percent of qualified plan benefits which they had prior to ERISA. Most courts faced with the issue have determined that ERISA does not supersede state community property laws.

A spouse's community property interest in his spouse's qualified plan benefits is included in his gross estate if he or she predeceased the spouse with the qualified plan benefits. Estate taxes are imposed even though the surviving spouse may have no immediate access to the benefit to provide funds to pay the tax. Unfortunate situations also arise where the appraised "value" of the deceased spouse's community property interest is much greater than the benefit actually received from the plan; for example, when the surviving spouse is less than 100 percent vested and terminates employment soon after his spouse's death. However, most such benefits go to the surviving spouse and thus are eligible for the marital deduction and no federal death tax is due.

However, if any employee with qualified plan benefits predeceases his spouse, and benefits are paid to a beneficiary other than the surviving spouse, the surviving spouse may be treated as making a gift of 50 percent of the benefits payable to other beneficiaries (to the extent the benefits were community property). Thus, it may be found that the surviving spouse

has made a taxable gift where the participant has directed both community property interests in the benefit to other beneficiaries. However, with the significant rights given to non-participant spouses by the Retirement Equity Act of 1984, it became difficult to have significant plan proceeds distributed without the spouse's permission. Such accidental and unintended taxable gifts can be a problem for persons not aware of the possible trap.

A question arises as to whether a spouse's consent to the designation of a trust as a beneficiary of the employee's plan benefits is a transfer with a retained life estate under Section 2038 of the Internal Revenue Code. If the spouse is a lifetime beneficiary of the trust, care must be exercised to minimize the possibility that the IRS will claim that the spouse's community property share of plan benefits remaining in the trust is subject to federal estate tax at the spouse's death.

The community property states have adopted varying positions to deal with the problem of valuing qualified plan benefits for purposes of division in a divorce. Prior to 1976, for example, California courts divided only *vested* qualified plan benefits, holding that non-vested benefits were "mere expectancies." However, a 1976 decision of the California Supreme Court overruled that position and held that *non-vested* qualified plan benefits were community property assets subject to division in a divorce proceeding. The benefits can be valued using actuarial methods. The court, recognizing that unfairness may result if the benefit does not actually "vest," stated that it may be appropriate in certain situations to divide benefit payments as they are received (rather than fixing a lump sum value at the time of the divorce). Thus, each spouse would share the risk that the full benefit would fail to fully vest.

QUESTIONS AND ANSWERS

Question — What are some concerns associated with an ESOP?

Answer — One concern relates to the need for annual revaluation. If the employer's stock is not readily tradable on an established market, an independent appraisal is necessary annually to establish the value of the stock for contribution purposes (if the corporation contributes its stock) or for purposes of determining a proper purchase price (if the ESOP purchases stock from the corporation or from any third party stockholder). This valuation is always subject to scrutiny by the Internal Revenue Service and the Department of Labor.

Question — If there are no stock purchases or stock contributions during the year, is an annual appraisal still necessary?

Answer — An annual appraisal is probably still necessary in order to meet the reporting requirements established by ERISA with respect to the current value of the plan assets and the ERISA requirement that the value of a participant's account be determined annually. This information would have to be submitted to the Labor Department, and current value probably could not be determined without such an appraisal. If there is a purchase of employer stock by the ESOP trust, the value of the stock must be ascertained at the time of purchase. If an ESOP were to pay a price greater than the fair market value of the employer's stock, the investment would be considered improper and might result in a disqualification of the plan.

Question — Are there any provisions of ERISA that do not apply to an ESOP?

Answer — ERISA treats the ESOP as an individual account plan. An individual account plan escapes that part of the ERISA reporting provisions that requires a statement of an actuary and is also exempt from paying plan termination insurance premiums to the Pension Benefit Guaranty Corporation.

Question — Can an ESOP allow voluntary nondeductible employee contributions?

Answer — Voluntary nondeductible contributions can be made to an ESOP, as well as to qualified pension, profit-sharing, or stock bonus plans. These contributions will be deemed annual additions for maximum contribution purposes and thus, will have the impact of reducing the maximum employer contribution. The contributions will also have to pass a special nondiscrimination test.[28]

Provisions allowing voluntary nondeductible contributions to an ESOP should be approached with caution. Voluntary contributions to an ESOP should not be invested in employer stock unless the employer has complied with applicable federal and state securities requirements.

Question — What is the tax treatment of a distribution of employer stock to a plan participant?

Answer — If employer stock is paid to a plan participant in a lump-sum distribution (as that term is defined in the Internal Revenue Code), any unrealized appreciation on that stock which is not attributable to deductible employee voluntary contributions will not be taxed to the participant until the participant sells the stock.[29]

This unrealized appreciation will be treated as long-term capital gain when the stock is sold. Any appreciation after distribution will be treated as long- or short-term capital gain depending on whether the participant has held the stock for the requisite holding period following the date of distribution. The cash portion and that portion of the lump-sum distribution which is an amount equal to the employer contributions used to purchase stock may, under some circumstances, be taxed to the participant at the time of distribution, subject to a 15 percent excise tax on distributions over $150,000.[30] This excise tax can be avoided by spreading out distribution payments. (See the discussion of the excess distribution and excess accumulation taxes in Chapter 28.)

For example, if the individual receives an ESOP distribution of $30,000 cash and employer stock worth $100,000 on the distribution date and if the employer had contributed an amount equal to $75,000 which was used to purchase that stock, then the $25,000 gain will not be taxed to the participant until the securities are sold. But at the date of distribution, the $105,000 will be taxed under the lump-sum distribution rules in effect at the time of distribution.

Amounts attributable to deductible employee contributions are not considered part of a lump sum distribution and are taxed as ordinary income on receipt; any net unrealized appreciation on employer securities attributable to deductible employee contributions is taxed upon distribution of the securities, whether or not they are sold.[31]

If the participant or beneficiary of a participant does not take a lump-sum distribution of the cash or employer securities but instead receives the employer securities over a period in excess of one taxable year of the recipient (or beneficiary), the entire amount attributable to the employer contribution, deductible employee contributions, and any subsequent appreciation on employer stock will be taxed at the ordinary income rate in effect at the time of distribution.[32]

If the employee has made any nondeductible contributions to the ESOP, any unrealized appreciation in the employer stock which is attributable to such contributions will escape taxation until the participant sells the securities. At that time, the gain will be taxed.[33]

Question — A participant in an ESOP retires. He receives a distribution of employer stock. Is he under any obligation to sell the stock to the ESOP?

Answer — It seems clear that no prearranged enforceable agreement can exist between the participants of the plan and the ESOP requiring that the participants, upon receipt of the stock distribution from the ESOP, sell those securities back to the ESOP. (ESOPs are allowed by law in order to encourage employers to place capital stock in the hands of employees. An agreement binding the employee to sell the stock back defeats this intent.) Regulations specifically prohibit a "call" option on employer stock acquired with the proceeds of a loan obtained from or guaranteed by a disqualified person.[34]

The IRS has permitted an ESOP to retain a "right of first refusal" on employer stock which is not publicly traded. In other words, if the participant wants to sell the employer stock distributed to him to a third party, he must first offer it to the employer or the ESOP.[35]

It is possible to have a large number of stockholders with minimal interests in a company as a result of employer-stock distributions from the ESOP. All of these "small" stockholders are entitled to certain information and have certain rights under ERISA, state corporate laws, and state and federal securities laws. This factor can be a deterrent to establishing ESOPs.

Question — Can an ESOP purchase life insurance on the life of a key employee of the corporation?

Answer — The ESOP can purchase life insurance, commonly referred to as "key person" life insurance, on the life of an important employee of the corporation. The ESOP can use monies contributed to it by the corporation to pay the premiums, provided, however, that the amount of dollars used for the purchase of such insurance are limited to ensure that the ESOP meets the requirements of investing primarily in qualifying employer securities. On the death of the insured, the ESOP would be the beneficiary of the life insurance and could then use the proceeds for the purchase of shares of stock from the insured, thereby providing a market for the insured's stock as well as liquidity in the insured's estate.

Question — Can an ESOP purchase life insurance and make the proceeds payable to the beneficiaries of employees participating in the ESOP?

Answer — An ESOP may provide life insurance for its participants so long as the insurance is deemed "incidental." The plan will generally meet this requirement if the premiums for any participant do not exceed 25% of the amount allocated to his or her ESOP account.

Question — If a shareholder makes a sale of "qualified securities" to the ESOP, can the replacement securities be transferred to a revocable trust or other form of grantor trust?

Answer — The IRS has ruled that such a transfer will not result in a recapture of the gain rolled over, and that any purchases of stock by the trust will be deemed purchases by the grantor.[36]

Question — Assume that there is only one key person in a corporation and that key person owns 100 percent of the stock of the corporation. Is an ESOP an appropriate estate planning tool to use if there is no one in management who wishes to, or who is capable of continuing the business?

Answer — The ESOP sometimes does not present an appropriate estate planning tool in this situation because the obligation to continue the business would be on the trustee of the ESOP. It can be very difficult to find a trustee willing to take the responsibility for operating the business. However, this problem can be avoided by finding another company (possibly a competitor) or person who will want to acquire the corporation at the stockholder's death.

Question — Can an ESOP be used to purchase the majority of the stock of a corporation from present owners?

Answer — There is no problem with a transfer of ownership from present stockholders to employees through an ESOP purchase of the present owners' stock.

Question — A man entitled to $50,000 from an ESOP dies having designated his adult son as the beneficiary of his plan benefits. Assume the funds are community property. The wife did not consent to the beneficiary designation. Can the wife be deprived of her 50 percent share of the pension benefits by her husband's action? If she did consent, has she made a taxable gift to her son of $25,000?

Answer — In most community property states, the wife cannot be deprived of her community property interest by her husband's unilateral action of naming their son as the sole beneficiary. Thus, she is entitled to $25,000 from the plan. If the plan has already paid the funds to the son, the plan could be liable to the wife. Thus, it is important for plans to verify the existence or nonexistence of community property rights before distributing benefits. If the wife consented to the designation of the son as beneficiary, however, she would have no claim. It may be found that the surviving spouse has made a taxable gift to the son. Additional restrictions are imposed on a married participant's ability to name a beneficiary for plan death benefits other than the surviving spouse. Generally, unless the ESOP designates the surviving spouse as the sole beneficiary, a qualified plan is now required to pay plan benefits in the form of a "Qualified Pre-retirement Survivor Annuity" for participants who die prior to reaching retirement age and in the form of a "Qualified Joint and Survivor Annuity" for married participants who die after reaching retirement age (see Chapter 28).

Question — Does an employer contribution in excess of 25 percent of covered compensation to pay interest on a loan obtained by an ESOP to buy employer stock exceed the annual additions limit?

Answer — Employer contributions applied to pay loan interest, and forfeitures of fully leveraged (loaned) employer stock owned by the ESOP are disregarded for purposes of the 25 percent/$30,000 annual additions limit to a participant's account in the ESOP which would otherwise apply. However, this rule applies only if deductible contributions allocated to "highly compensated employees" (as defined in Code section 414(q) — see Chapter 28), are not more than one-third of the total contributions.[37]

Question — What types of employer stock qualify as "employer securities" for purposes of an ESOP?

Answer — An ESOP must be designed to invest primarily in "employer securities." Shares of common stock of an employer which are readily tradable on an established securities market are "employer securities." If the employer has no stock which is publicly traded, "employer securities" are shares of common stock issued by the employer with a combination of voting power and dividend rights equal or greater than the classes of common stock of the employer with the greatest voting power and dividend rights. Noncallable preferred stock can be "employer securities" if the preferred stock is convertible at any time into common stock meeting the above requirements, and the conversion price is reasonable.[38]

Question — Are pre-age 59½ distributions from ESOPs assessed a 10 percent excise tax?

Answer — Yes. A pre-age 59½ distribution from an ESOP was exempt from the early distribution excise tax if (1) the distribution occurred prior to 1990; (2) the distribution was attributable to assets invested in employer stock for the 5-year period preceding the year of distribution; and (3) the ESOP requirements were met with respect to such stock during the 5 year period.[39] Some legislators have proposed reinstating the ESOP exception to the early withdrawal penalty, since current law requires an ESOP to distribute benefits to terminated employees without regard to age. Some have argued that it is improper to subject a mandatory distribution to a penalty tax.

Question — Can an S corporation implement an ESOP?

Answer — No. Only certain types of trusts may hold stock in an S corporation, and employee stock ownership trusts are not among them.[40] Legislation has been proposed which would allow an S corporation to implement an ESOP. The proposal would impose a corporate level tax on the income attributable to an ESOP to preserve revenue neutrality or generate a modest revenue gain.

Question — In general, does an ESOP provide much in the way of tax benefits?

Answer — Yes. ESOPs are presently one of the most effective tax minimization techniques available under the Internal Revenue Code! The arguments of former Senator Russell Long still prevail to the effect that employers should be given significant tax incentives to persuade them to make their employees owners of the business.

ASRS, Sec. 59, ¶270.1.

Footnote References

Employee Stock Ownership Plan

1. IRC Secs. 401, 4975(e)(7); ERISA Secs. 407(d)(1), (5) and (6) and 408(e).
2. IRC Secs. 404(a)(3), 404(a)(9).
3. IRC Sec. 172.
4. IRC Sec. 2057, prior to repeal by OBRA '89, Sec. 7304(a)(1). The U.S. Supreme Court has held that a retroactive amendment to IRC Sec. 2057 limiting the sales of stock to situations where the decedent owned the stock at death was effective. *U.S. v. Carlton*, 114 S.Ct. 2018 (1994).
5. IRC Secs. 4975(e)(7), 409(h)(1)(B).
6. See, generally, IRC Sec. 401(a).
7. Reg. §1.401(l)-1(a)(4).
8. ERISA Sec. 402(a)(1).
9. IRC Sec. 401(a).
10. ERISA Sec. 408(e); IRC Sec. 401(a)(28)(C).
11. IRC Sec. 401(a)(22).
12. IRC Sec. 401(a)(28)(B).
13. IRC Sec. 409(o).
14. IRC. Sec. 409(n).
15. IRC Sec. 133.
16. See Rev. Proc. 95-6, 1995-1 IRB 153, for the 1995 version.
17. Regs. §§54.4975-7, 54.4975-11.
18. Reg. §1.401-1(b)(iii).
19. IRC Sec. 404(a)(3)(A). Unused pre-1987 contribution carryforwards may still be used.

20. IRC Sec. 404(a)(7).
21. IRC Sec. 404(a)(9).
22. IRC Sec. 415(c)(6).
23. Rev. Rul. 73-345, 1973-2 CB 11.
24. IRC Sec. 404(k).
25. IRC Sec. 4979A.
26. IRC Sec. 409(n)(2).
27. IRC Sec. 409(n)(3)(A).
28. IRC Sec. 401(m).
29. IRC Sec. 402(e)(4)(B) (formerly Sec. 402(e)(4)(J)), redesignated by P.L. 102-318, Sec. 521(a), effective for distributions after December 31, 1992.
30. IRC Sec. 4980A.
31. IRC Sec. 402(e)(4)(A) (formerly Sec. 402(a)(1)), redesignated by P.L. 102-318, Sec. 521(a), effective for distributions after December 31, 1992.
32. Ibid.
33. Ibid.
34. Reg. §54.4975-7(b)(4).
35. Reg. §54.4975-7(b)(9).
36. Let. Rul. 9141046.
37. IRC Sec. 415(c)(6).
38. IRC Secs. 4975(e)(8), 409(l).
39. IRC Sec. 72(t)(2)(C), prior to amendment by TAMRA '88, Sec. 1011A(c).
40. IRC Secs. 1361(c)(2), 1361(d).

Chapter 10

EXTENSIONS OF TIME TO PAY FEDERAL ESTATE TAX

WHAT IS IT?

Generally, the federal estate tax is payable in full within nine months of the date of death.[1] The Internal Revenue Code does provide relief under certain circumstances by allowing an executor to pay the federal estate taxes attributable to the decedent's business over a period of years.

Under Code §6166 the executor in his discretion may elect to pay the federal estate tax (and generation-skipping transfer tax) attributable to the decedent's interest in a closely held business in installments over a period of up to 14 years. During the first four years the executor pays only interest on the unpaid tax. Then, in equal annual increments over as many as ten additional years, the executor pays off the principal of the unpaid tax (together with interest on the unpaid balance).

Code §6166 permits a four year deferral of tax followed by a maximum ten year payout of the tax. Roughly speaking, interest is payable at 4 percent on the tax generated by the first $1,000,000 of business value and at the "going rate" on the balance. The "going rate" charged by the IRS varies quarterly.

Section 6166 is available for any estate that qualifies under the rules of the Internal Revenue Code, regardless of the position of the local District Director of the Internal Revenue Service. However, if the estate does not qualify for the §6166 extension, it still may be possible to obtain some extension under an alternative Section 6161, which is discretionary with the District Director.

Under §6161, the District Director may extend the period for payment of tax for a period up to ten years beyond the due date of the estate tax return if he finds that there is "reasonable cause" to grant such an extension.

Under §6159, the Secretary may permit the installment payment of taxes where the Secretary believes it will facilitate payment of such taxes.

WHEN IS THE USE OF SUCH A DEVICE INDICATED?

1. When the estate has insufficient liquidity to pay the estate taxes when due without selling assets at a substantial loss.

2. Where the estate can earn a greater after-tax rate of return than it spends in interest for the deferral privilege.

3. Where future profits or cash flow from the decedent's business can be used to pay all or part of the deferred tax.

WHAT ARE THE REQUIREMENTS?

A. §6159

Section 6159 provides that the Secretary is authorized to enter into written agreements with taxpayers to pay taxes in installments where the Secretary determines that such an agreement will facilitate payment of such taxes. Such an agreement may be modified or terminated by the Secretary if (1) information provided by the taxpayer was inaccurate or incomplete, (2) the Secretary believes that collection of such tax is in jeopardy, (3) the Secretary determines that the financial condition of the taxpayer has changed (in which case 30 days notice to the taxpayer is required, including the reason for such change), (4) the taxpayer fails to make a timely installment payment (or to timely pay any other tax), or (5) the taxpayer fails to provide a financial update as requested by the Secretary.

B. §6161

1. A district director may extend the time for payment of the tax shown on the return for a period of up to ten years beyond the due date of the return, upon a showing of "reasonable cause" for the granting of the extension.

2. "Reasonable cause" for the extension is not expressly defined. Each case is examined on an independent factual basis. However, there are certain guidelines used to establish the presence of reasonable cause. These include: (a) inability to marshal assets to pay the estate tax when otherwise due; (b) an estate comprised in substantial part of assets consisting of rights to receive payments in the future, with the estate having insufficient present cash to pay the estate tax and an inability to borrow against these assets except on unreasonable terms; (c) the assets cannot be collected without litigation; or, (d) there are not sufficient funds available, after the exercise of due diligence, with which to pay the tax in a timely fashion.

C. §6166

1. The gross estate must include an interest classified as a "closely held" business, the value of which *exceeds* 35 percent of the adjusted gross estate. In the case of an estate in which the decedent made a gift of property within three years of death, the estate is treated as meeting the more than 35% requirement only if the estate meets such requirement both with and without the application of the three-year inclusion rule of Code section 2035 (see Appendix C, Computing the Federal Estate Tax).[2]

2. Aggregation of various business interests of the decedent is allowed for purposes of meeting the percentage requirement, provided the decedent owned at least 20 percent of the total value of each, and each activity otherwise qualifies as a closely held trade or business.

3. The amount of federal estate or generation-skipping transfer tax which may be deferred, i.e., paid in installments, is only that amount of value attributable to the value of the closely held trade or business. The balance of the estate tax or GST tax must be paid at the regular payment date.

4. If the estate qualifies under section 6166 and an election is made, the first installment of principal is due not later than five years and nine months from the date of death. Each succeeding installment is to be paid within one year after the previous installment.

   The maximum number of principal installments which may be paid under this provision is ten, thus allowing for payment over a 14-year period (four years interest only, up to 10 more years principal and interest).

   During the 4-year period immediately following death, interest only payments are to be made, with interest being at a beneficial 4 percent rate in relation to the first $1,000,000 value of the closely held business (roughly translated into approximately $345,800 of tax). But this 4 percent amount is reduced by the available credit, as shown in Figure 10.1. The practical result in many estates is that only $153,000 in federal estate tax can be deferred at the 4% interest rate.

5. To qualify as an interest in a "closely held" business, the interest can be in a sole proprietorship, a partnership, or a corporation. A partnership interest will qualify if 20 percent or more of the total capital interest in the partnership is included in the gross estate, or if the partnership has 15 or fewer partners. Stock in a corporation qualifies if 20 percent or more in value of the voting stock is included in determining the gross estate of the decedent, or the corporation has 15 or fewer shareholders.

For purposes of the "15 or fewer owners" test, a partnership interest or corporate stock held by another partnership or corporation or by an estate or trust will be treated as if owned proportionately by shareholders, partners, or beneficiaries (the rule applies in the case of trusts only if a beneficiary has a present interest). A partnership interest or stock held by a member of the decedent's family is considered to be owned by the decedent for purposes of the "15 or fewer owners" test. (But if this attribution is necessary to qualify for §6166, the 4 year deferral of tax and the special 4 percent interest rates are forfeited.)

6. In addition, as interpreted by the Service, the definition of a "trade or business" is not as broad in scope as under many other provisions of the Internal Revenue Code. The business must be "actively" carried on and require a "management" function, rather than being of a nature where the taxpayer merely supervises his investment (such as an apartment house), and the investment is the actual capital producing factor.[3]

7. Only *active* business assets are considered for purposes of the "more than 35 percent of adjusted gross estate" test. Only active business assets can be considered in determining the value of the business interest that qualifies for the deferral. This "active asset" rule which denies installment payment for passive assets applies to all corporations and partnerships. (It does not apply, however, for purposes of determining whether or not an acceleration of the tax will be required.)

HOW IT IS DONE—AN EXAMPLE OF §6166

Dr. Andrea Apter died at a time when the value of her closely held business, a computer center, was $600,000. Her gross estate was $1,000,000. Administrative costs, debts, and expenses totalled $200,000. Federal estate taxes totalled $75,000. The computation to test qualification is directly below. The computation of the §6166 deferral limitation is at Figure 10.1.

Section 6166 (up to 14 year) Installment Payout:
(1) Estate Tax Value of closely held business included in gross estate $600,000
(2) Adjusted Gross Estate $800,000
(3) 35 percent of Adjusted Gross Estate $280,000

If Line 1 exceeds Line 3, the executor can elect to pay that portion of estate taxes attributable to the inclusion of the farm or other closely held business in installments over up to 14 years (first 4 years, no tax due, only interest—up to next 10 years equal annual installments of tax and declining interest on unpaid balance).

Two or more businesses may be aggregated if the decedent held 20 percent or more interest in each such business.

In this example, the decedent's estate could utilize a Section 6166 installment payout. The deferral amount would be computed according to the following formula: (Assume the net estate and GST tax payable after credits is $75,000.)

Computing §6166 Deferral Limitation:

$$\text{Net F.E.T. and G.S.T.T. Payable (after credits)} \times \frac{\text{Value of Includible Closely Held Business Interest}}{\text{Adjusted Gross Estate}}$$

$$\$75,000 \times \frac{\$600,000}{800,000} = \$56,250$$

Therefore, $18,750 of tax ($75,000-$56,250) must be paid immediately.

The figures that follow illustrate how expensive the installment payout can be. The first set of figures (Figure 10.1) follows the Dr. Andrea Apter example and assumes the estate is in a 31% income tax bracket.

The second set (Figure 10.2) shows the cost and cash flow for a widower with a $3,000,000 estate and a $2,000,000 business, Sections 2053 and 2054 deductions of $500,000, and an estate income tax bracket of 31 percent. The interest on amounts of unpaid tax in excess of the 4 percent amount are taxed at an assumed 10 percent.

The figures are courtesy of NumberCruncher software.

WHAT ARE THE TAX IMPLICATIONS?

1. Interest is payable on the tax which is not paid by the due date of the return.[4] Under Code section 6166, a special 4 percent interest rate is allowed. This rate is limited to the estate tax attributable to the first $1,000,000 of farm or other closely held business property ($345,800 of tax).[5] (However, as is obvious from Figure 10.1, that $345,800 amount, when reduced by the unified credit as required, amounts to only $153,000.) Amounts of estate tax attributable to value in excess of the $1,000,000 amount bear interest at the regular rate for interest on deferred payments.

    Interest rates on the unpaid balance of the tax in excess of the "4 percent" portion are redetermined quarterly so as to be three percentage points over the short-term federal rate. The interest owed is compounded daily. This can make the use of Section 6166 extremely expensive.

2. The interest charged for the deferred tax is a deductible administration expense for estate tax purposes (which reduces the gross estate, thereby reducing the estate tax payable—and also makes it easier to qualify under the percentage requirements).[6] Alternatively, the interest paid each year can be deducted by the executor as an income tax deduction on the estate's income tax return.

IMPLICATIONS AND ISSUES IN COMMUNITY PROPERTY STATES

In general, for purposes of the definition of an interest in a closely held trade or business under §6166, in regard to the 15 owner test of the allowable number of shareholders or partners, the husband and wife are treated as one partner or shareholder if the interest is owned as community property. This also applies if the form of ownership is as joint tenants, tenants by the entirety, or tenants in common.

QUESTIONS AND ANSWERS

Question — Is a bond required of the executor?

Answer — The IRS can, if it deems necessary, require the executor to post a bond for the payment of the tax. The amount is up to twice the amount of the tax for which an extension is granted. The executor is also liable—personally—for payment of the tax. He can only be discharged if (a) he pays the tax due or (b) furnishes a bond or security for unpaid (but not yet due) taxes.

Question — Is there an alternative to the requirement that the executor post bond?

Answer — The executor can make an election—under Section 6166—to accept an IRS lien in lieu of the executor's personal liability or bond.[7]

The requirements of the lien (which serves to discharge the executor from personal liability and eliminate the requirement of a bond) are:

(1) The executor—and all parties who have an interest in the property subject to the lien—must file an agreement consenting to the lien.

Figure 10.1

SECTION 6166 INSTALLMENT PAYOUTS OF ESTATE TAX	
YEAR OF DEATH	1992
ESTATE'S INCOME TAX BRACKET	0.31
PROFIT MARGIN OF BUSINESS	0.10
NON-4% INTEREST RATE	0.10
GROSS ESTATE	$1,000,000
ADMINISTRATIVE EXPENSE	$200,000
VALUE OF BUSINESS	$600,000
NET FEDERAL ESTATE TAX	$75,000
ADJUSTED GROSS ESTATE	$800,000
35% OF ADJUSTED GROSS ESTATE ESTATE QUALIFIES	$280,000
AMOUNT THAT CAN BE DEFERRED	$56,250
TAX THAT MUST BE PAID NOW	$18,750
TAX ON ONE MILLION	$345,800
UNIFIED CREDIT	$192,800
4 PERCENT AMOUNT	$56,250
AMOUNT TAXED AT "GOING RATE"	$0

(2) A person must be designated as agent for the persons who consented to the lien and the estate's beneficiaries.[8]

(3) The Service may require additional lien property if the value of the original property is—or falls below—the total of (a) unpaid taxes and (b) aggregate interest owed.

Question — Once the installment payout period begins, can the IRS terminate it?

Answer — The deferred tax is accelerated (i.e., becomes due immediately) in three situations:

(1) when all or a significant portion of the business is disposed of or liquidated;

(2) interest or installment payments are not made within 6 months of due date; or

(3) if the estate has undistributed net income (there may be an acceleration to that extent).

Question — Why shouldn't an advisor suggest that a client use a Section 6166 installment payout as an alternative to life insurance?

Answer — First, Section 6166 cannot be relied upon. The mathematical percentage test may be failed or the firm may be considered an asset holding company rather than a trade or business.

Second, Section 6166 does not "create" assets—the right to make installment payments merely postpones the

Figure 10.1 continued

	SECTION 6166 PAYMENT SCHEDULE					
Yr	Principal 4%	Interest 4%	Principal 10%	Interest 10%	Total Interest	Total Payment
1	$56,250	$2,295	$0	$0	$2,295	$2,295
2	$56,250	$2,295	$0	$0	$2,295	$2,295
3	$56,250	$2,295	$0	$0	$2,295	$2,295
4	$56,250	$2,295	$0	$0	$2,295	$2,295
5	$50,625	$2,295	$0	$0	$2,295	$7,920
6	$45,000	$2,066	$0	$0	$2,066	$7,691
7	$39,375	$1,836	$0	$0	$1,836	$7,461
8	$33,750	$1,607	$0	$0	$1,607	$7,232
9	$28,125	$1,377	$0	$0	$1,377	$7,002
10	$22,500	$1,148	$0	$0	$1,148	$6,773
11	$16,875	$918	$0	$0	$918	$6,543
12	$11,250	$689	$0	$0	$689	$6,314
13	$5,625	$459	$0	$0	$459	$6,084
14	$0	$230	$0	$0	$230	$5,855
Totals:		$21,805		$0	$21,805	$78,055

necessity of paying a certain portion of the total estate tax. Interest *added* to the tax increases the total cost substantially.

Where will the money to pay both tax and interest come from? If it comes from the business, it probably will be in the form of a dividend. In any event, *the dollars to make the deferred payments have to come from somewhere—and they will be after-tax (expensive) dollars.* (See Figure 10.1.)

Third, only a portion of the Federal taxes can be deferred in most cases.

Where will the executor find the cash to pay

(a) administrative expenses?

(b) debts?

(c) remaining portion of Federal estate taxes?

(d) state death taxes?

(e) income taxes?

(f) pecuniary bequests?

Fourth, with certain exceptions, successors in interest cannot dispose of the business—or a major portion of it— without triggering an acceleration ("pay it now").

Figure 10.1 continued

SECTION 6166 SUMMARY	
TOTAL TAX PRINCIPAL OVER TERM	$56,250
ESTATE INCOME TAX BRACKET	0.31
NET COST OF INTEREST	$15,045
COST OF PRINCIPAL	$56,250
TOTAL COST	$71,295
SALES NEEDED TO NET ONE CENT	$0.10
SALES TO PAY TOTAL COST	$712,950

Fifth, the executor may remain personally liable for unpaid taxes during the entire deferral period (or the successors-in-interest have to tie their hands with a special tax lien to assure the IRS that payment will be made).

Sixth, final distribution to beneficiaries may be delayed over an extended period of time. Most beneficiaries will not want to wait for 14 years to receive their full share of the inheritance.

Seventh, since all beneficiaries must sign the elective agreement to discharge the executor from personal liability, guardians may have to be appointed for minors and otherwise incompetent beneficiaries. Such guardians may refuse to sign such an exoneration.

Question — Is there any danger of losing the right to have an extension of time if the estate, as it appears on the estate tax return as filed, qualifies for an extension?

Answer — Yes. The values of the various assets in the estate can be changed upon audit by IRS. It is the ultimately determined values that will control. It is possible that the estate will not meet the Section 6166 requirements after the IRS increases the value of assets other than the decedent's business.

Question — How is the election made under §6166?

Answer — Notice of election under §6166 must be filed on or before the due date (including any extensions) of the U.S. Estate Tax Return[9] (Form 706). No special form of notice is required and a letter addressed to the IRS setting forth

the identity of the taxpayer, the amount of tax to be deferred, the identity of the closely held business and the computation of qualification under the applicable section will suffice.

Question — What if, based upon the value set forth on the U.S. Estate Tax Return, the decedent's interest in the closely held business does not qualify under §6166, but it is possible that after examination by the IRS such interest will qualify?

Answer — If the estate does not qualify for a payout of federal estate taxes on the values returned or if the estate does qualify, but no tax is due on the values returned, the executor can file a "protective election." The "protective election" would set forth the information required under Revenue Ruling 74-499.

Question — In determining the "at least 20 percent" requirement of §6166 for the aggregation of two or more closely held businesses, or whether 20 percent or more of the value of a closely held business is included in the gross estate, can the executor elect to have interests of family members considered as owned by the decedents?

Answer — Yes. The interest of family members can, if elected by the executors, be considered as owned by the decedent in determining the "at least 20 percent" requirements for qualification under §6166.[10] This election is applicable only to a capital interest in a partnership and to stock which is "not readily tradable." If this election is made by the Executor, the five year deferral provision of §6166 is not available and the payout must be spread over a period

Figure 10.2

SECTION 6166 INSTALLMENT PAYOUTS OF ESTATE TAX	
YEAR OF DEATH	1992
ESTATE'S INCOME TAX BRACKET	0.31
PROFIT MARGIN OF BUSINESS	0.10
NON-4% INTEREST RATE	0.10
GROSS ESTATE	$3,000,000
ADMINISTRATIVE EXPENSE	$500,000
VALUE OF BUSINESS	$2,000,000
NET FEDERAL ESTATE TAX	$833,000
ADJUSTED GROSS ESTATE	$2,500,000
35% OF ADJUSTED GROSS ESTATE ESTATE QUALIFIES	$875,000
AMOUNT THAT CAN BE DEFERRED	$666,400
TAX THAT MUST BE PAID NOW	$166,600
TAX ON ONE MILLION	$345,800
UNIFIED CREDIT	$192,800
4 PERCENT AMOUNT	$153,000
AMOUNT TAXED AT "GOING RATE"	$513,400

not to exceed ten years. In addition, the interest rate charged on the payout is at the "going rate" (the 4 percent special rate is not available).

Question — Can holding company stock qualify for installment payout of estate taxes under Section 6166?

Answer — "Yes, but." Only the portion of stock of a holding company that directly or indirectly owns stock in a closely held active trade or business (so called "business company") will be treated as stock in the active company and may therefore qualify. To qualify, the "15 or fewer shareholders" or the "20 percent or more" test and the "more than 35 percent" test must be met.

The ability to payout federal estate taxes attributable to holding company stock may come at a significant cost.

The executor must agree to forego both the deferral of principal payments and the special four percent interest rate. This adds to the cost of the payout in two important ways: first, the time value of money works against the estate since much more money (the principal of the unpaid estate tax) must be paid much more quickly. Second, the "going" rate is substantially above the special four percent rate, it compounds daily making the true cost higher than it appears, and it is applied to a much larger base.

Question — Can rental activities ever be classified as active businesses to meet the requirements of Code section 6166?

Answer — Although the estate will face an uphill battle on this issue, the IRS has ruled that the decedent's rental activi-

Figure 10.2 continued

	SECTION 6166 PAYMENT SCHEDULE					
Yr	Principal 4%	Interest 4%	Principal 10%	Interest 10%	Total Interest	Total Payment
1	$153,000	$6,244	$513,400	$53,987	$60,231	$60,231
2	$153,000	$6,244	$513,400	$53,987	$60,231	$60,231
3	$153,000	$6,244	$513,400	$53,987	$60,231	$60,231
4	$153,000	$6,244	$513,400	$53,987	$60,231	$60,231
5	$137,700	$6,244	$462,060	$53,987	$60,231	$126,871
6	$122,400	$5,619	$410,720	$48,588	$54,207	$120,847
7	$107,100	$4,995	$359,380	$43,189	$48,184	$114,824
8	$91,800	$4,371	$308,040	$37,791	$42,162	$108,802
9	$76,500	$3,746	$256,700	$32,392	$36,138	$102,778
10	$61,200	$3,122	$205,360	$26,993	$30,115	$96,755
11	$45,900	$2,497	$154,020	$21,595	$24,092	$90,732
12	$30,600	$1,873	$102,680	$16,196	$18,069	$84,709
13	$15,300	$1,249	$51,340	$10,797	$12,046	$78,686
14	$0	$624	$0	$5,399	$6,023	$72,663
Totals:		$59,316		$512,875	$572,191	$1,238,591

ties may be classified as closely held businesses for purposes of Code section 6166. These rulings only apply where the decedent took an active role in managing the rental properties, and generally involve such activities as negotiating leases, supervising repairs and maintenance, and dealing directly with tenants.

ASRS, Sec. 54, §44.7.

Footnote References

Deferred Payment of Federal Estate Taxes

1. IRC Secs. 6151(a), 6075(a).
2. IRC Sec. 2035(d)(4).
3. Reg. §20.6166-2(c); Rev. Rul. 75-365, 1975-2 CB 471; Rev. Rul. 75-366, 1975-2 CB 472; Rev. Rul. 75-367, 1975-2 CB 472.
4. IRC Secs. 6601(a), 6621.
5. IRC Sec. 6601(j).
6. *Est. of Charles A. Bahr, Sr.*, 68 TC 74 (1977); acq. Rev. Rul. 78-125, 1978-2 CB 149.
7. IRC Sec. 6324A.
8. IRC Sec. 6324A(c).
9. Rev. Rul. 74-499, 1974-2 CB 397.
10. IRC Secs. 6166(b)(1)(B)(i), 6166(b)(7), 6166(b)(8), 6166(b)(9), 6166(g)(1), 6166(g)(2).

Figure 10.2 continued

SECTION 6166 SUMMARY	
TOTAL TAX PRINCIPAL OVER TERM	$666,400
ESTATE INCOME TAX BRACKET	0.31
NET COST OF INTEREST	$394,812
COST OF PRINCIPAL	$666,400
TOTAL COST	$1,061,212
SALES NEEDED TO NET ONE CENT	$0.10
SALES TO PAY TOTAL COST	$10,612,120

Chapter 11

FAMILY LIMITED PARTNERSHIPS

WHAT IS IT?

A family partnership is a partnership that exists between members of a family (defined for income tax purposes as including only an individual's spouse, ancestors, lineal descendants, and any trusts established primarily for the benefit of such persons).[1] If a partnership among family members is a genuine partnership, it will be treated tax wise the same as any other partnership and the same rules will apply.

The family partnership is a technique frequently used as a means of shifting the income tax burden from parents to children or other family members. However, the benefit of income shifting to children under age 14 has been substantially eliminated. For children under age 14, unearned income in excess of $1,200 (as indexed for 1994) generally will be taxed at the parent's top marginal rate under the "Kiddie Tax" rules.

Although family partnerships have sometimes been attacked by the IRS as being mere tax avoidance schemes that should not be recognized for tax purposes, if the rules for establishing and operating such partnerships are carefully followed the IRS will recognize the validity of this income shifting device.[2]

Two major forms of family partnerships commonly used are the general partnership and the limited partnership.

The general partnership is an entity under which all partners have a voice in management (by percentage vote) but are personally liable for all of the debts and other liabilities of the general partnership. This very negative aspect often makes the general partnership entity unsuitable for family wealth preservation and has prompted the use of the limited partnership for the majority of family activities for which a partnership is appropriate.

One benefit of a general partnership is that, in some circumstances, the partners may share in the losses generated by the partnership for income tax purposes. This is much more difficult for limited partners due to the relatively recent passage of various "anti-tax shelter" laws which restrict the sharing of losses among partners in limited partnerships.

A family limited partnership (FLP) is a statutory limited liability entity created under state law. Family limited partnerships are so named because ownership of partnership interests typically is limited to members of the same family unit. Since the limited partnership form is most frequently used for the majority of family activities, this chapter will deal mainly with that form of doing business or holding assets.

Ownership rights in the FLP are governed by state law as modified by the FLP agreement. Most states have adopted the Uniform Limited Partnership Act (ULPA) or some modified version thereof. Although there may be slight differences in the statutory partnership rules from one state to another, there generally is a high degree of uniformity among the states.

Upon formation, family members contribute property in return for an ownership interest in the capital and profits of the FLP. The partners designate a general partner (or general partners) who will be given management responsibility and who will assume personal liability for debts and other liabilities which are not satisfied from the assets of the FLP. Conversely, in return for giving up their rights of management and control over the assets of the FLP, the personal liability of the limited partners generally is limited to the amount of capital which they contribute.

Although an underlying purpose of most FLPs is to manage family assets and to plan for the transfer of such assets from parents to children, many parents are not willing to part with control over their assets when the FLP is created. In some cases the parents simply desire to continue managing their property and in other cases the children lack the maturity or business skills required to manage the assets. In the latter case, an FLP usually provides the parents with the time and opportunity to educate their children about managing their assets.

Although a thorough understanding of partnership law is essential to preparing an effective limited partnership agreement, the concepts underlying FLPs are not difficult to comprehend and an FLP can be easily integrated into an estate plan.

WHEN IS THE USE OF SUCH A DEVICE INDICATED?

Family limited partnerships are often used to fractionalize the ownership of business assets or real estate to take advantage of valuation discounts (see Chapters 25 and 42) which significantly reduce transfer taxes. In most cases, an FLP will be used to facilitate the gifting of limited partner interests from parents to children and other family members without divesting control from the parents. In other cases, an FLP will be used to ensure continuous ownership of assets within the family unit for several generations.

Until most recently, FLPs were used primarily as a means of (1) shifting the income tax burden from parents to children or other family members or (2) to "freeze" the value of assets by shifting future growth in various assets to other family members. Although these uses have been somewhat curtailed by the passage of the Kiddie Tax and the enactment of Code section 2701, the many other benefits provided by the FLP have made it a valuable tool in developing a comprehensive estate plan.

With greater frequency, many practitioners are coming to recognize the many tax and non-tax benefits that an FLP can provide. An FLP would be an appropriate device in the following circumstances:

1. To reduce the value of an estate for transfer tax (e.g. estate, gift and generation skipping) purposes.

   Because control of the assets of an FLP is centralized in the general partner(s), a limited partner often experiences an immediate decrease in the value of his interest compared to the value of the property contributed to the FLP. This decrease in value results because of the lack of control and marketability which accompany ownership of a limited partnership interest and the inherent inability to access the capital and profits of the FLP.

   It is well accepted that value often appears and disappears in an FLP. Value can appear in the form of a control premium which attaches to the right to manage assets or to liquidate assets into cash. Value can also disappear due to the giving up of management rights and exchange of assets in return for an unmarketable security interest.

   Past cases demonstrate that the value of FLP interests typically will be reduced by valuation discounts falling in the 30% to 35% range. Under these circumstances, a married couple with a taxable estate of $2,000,000 could use an FLP to reduce the value of their estate to a point where little or no estate tax is owed.

2. When it is desired to shift the income tax burden from a parent who is in a high income tax bracket to a child or other relative who is in a lower income tax bracket, thus providing intra-family income splitting and tax saving.

   Use of an FLP can permit parents to shift income to their children to be taxed at the child's lower income tax bracket, thereby increasing cash flow. Although the gradual narrowing of the federal income tax rate brackets for individuals (once as high as 70%, now at 39.6%) and enactment of the Kiddie Tax has reduced the effects of income shifting, substantial income tax savings can still be achieved in the majority of cases. (Example 1 at the end of this chapter presents an illustration of the income shifting context in the case of a family business.)

3. Where it is desirable to conduct a family business in a form other than a sole proprietorship or in a corporate form.

   In selecting a choice of business entity, the use of a corporation may cause tax problems that would not exist if the business were instead operated as an FLP. For example, subchapter C corporations are subject to personal holding company, accumulated earnings and unreasonable compensation problems, while subchapter S corporations are restricted as to who and how many persons may be shareholders. Similarly, placing a sole proprietorship business into trust may result in the trust being taxable by the IRS as a corporation, usually a very bad result. Family limited partnerships generally offer flexibility in income taxation compared to these other forms of doing business. (A summary of some of the differences in these business entity forms is provided at the end of this chapter).

4. Where a parent desires to maintain control over assets which will be transferred to younger generations through gifts of limited partner interests.

   One of the major benefits of an FLP is the ability to retain control over assets without having to own a majority of the interests of the FLP. This permits parents to transfer their assets to an FLP and then gift or sell a majority interest (50% or more) to the children while retaining control over the assets. Such control can be achieved by retaining as little as a 1% general partner interest in the FLP. Although the children may hold a majority interest in the FLP, the control over the assets remains in the hands of the general partner.

   Use of an FLP can also permit the parents to implement a succession plan for the ownership, management and control of assets so that undesired beneficiaries do not gain access to the assets.

5. Where it is desirable to protect assets from creditors of the partners.

   If a family member is in a high risk profession, such as a doctor or engineer who is vulnerable to lawsuits, an FLP may be effective to shield personal assets by placing them in the hands of other family members, away from the reach of future creditors. In most cases, a judgment creditor will be unable to attach partnership assets to satisfy a debt of an individual partner.

However, although the asset protection features of an FLP (discussed below) may discourage a creditor from aggressively seeking satisfaction of the debt from the partnership assets, the use of an FLP as an asset protection device may also prevent the assets from being reached by the partner since a judgment creditor has the right to attach the partner's interest in the FLP or attach any assets that are distributed by the FLP to the partner. This characteristic may cause a stalemate between the partner and creditor and encourage settlement of the debt at an amount which is favorable to both parties.

Protecting assets may also present a number of ethical issues for the practitioner since certain transfers can be attacked as fraudulent conveyances. For these reasons, extreme care and consideration should accompany the use of an FLP for any such purpose.

6. When retention of ownership of assets within the family unit is desired.

By including in the FLP agreement a right of first refusal for transfers of partnership interests, the partners can virtually guaranty that outside persons will not acquire ownership interests in the FLP. Also, by limiting the rights of a transferee partner to that of an "assignee" (who lacks voting rights) the ability of a partner to sell his or her interest is likely to be severely impaired, thereby achieving the intended goal of maintaining immediate family ownership.

7. Where a parent desires to protect assets, which are to be transferred to younger generations, from being dissipated through mismanagement or divorce.

A parent who makes gifts of property to his children runs the risk that the child will cause the gift to be unwisely managed or lost to a spouse or creditor. These pitfalls can be avoided by placing the assets into an FLP instead and transferring a limited partner interest to the child. In this case, the parent may retain control over the assets until the child is mature and has achieved sufficient financial acumen to manage the property.

Similarly, because a divorce action can result in the court awarding the spouse a share of the limited partner interest, it may be worthwhile for the parent to transfer the interest to the child in trust to be held for the child's lifetime, thereby defeating the rights of the spouse.

8. Where flexibility in setting the rules for managing property is desired.

Unlike an irrevocable trust, an FLP can be amended by vote of a given percentage of partnership interests. This results in a parent being able to easily change the governing rules which apply to the partnership if the parent maintains the necessary percentage ownership interest to amend the agreement.

9. To simplify ownership of assets.

Use of an FLP may allow for cost savings through consolidation of ownership into one entity. Such consolidation may result in diversification of money managers and reduced investment adviser fees. By pooling family assets, the FLP may obtain advantages in terms of diversification and size of investment which cannot be achieved individually by the partners.

Further, by giving the general partner discretion to reinvest partnership profits over the long-term, the FLP can carry out an investment strategy which focuses on long-term benefits to the partners. In situations where generation skipping trusts are used to hold FLP interests during the lifetime of a beneficiary, the death of the beneficiary will not pose a threat to the continued operation of the FLP since estate tax will not be due (to the extent the assets and estate tax "skip" the child).

10. To ease the distribution of assets at death among family members without having to remove the assets from the partnership.

Upon the death of a parent, assets may remain in the partnership and only partnership interests transferred to the heirs (to the extent permitted under the Limited Partnership Agreement) thereby enabling the partnership operations to remain intact.

11. To avoid out of state probate costs.

Since FLP interests are personal property, they should not be included for probate purposes in those states in which the partnership owns property. Such interests are subject to probate only in the domiciled state of the partner.

12. To discourage family members from fighting over FLP assets and to provide a forum for the resolution of disputes among family members when such disputes arise.

Unlike trusts, an FLP agreement may require binding arbitration of disputes among the partners for all issues relating to partnership assets. Further, the FLP agreement may be drafted so that the losing partner must pay the court fees of the prevailing party, thereby reducing the likelihood and cost of litigation among the partners.

WHAT ARE THE REQUIREMENTS?

Because state law governs the formation of partnerships, it is necessary to refer to the applicable law of the state in which the partnership is formed to determine the various procedural aspects of forming a partnership. In general, the following requirements will have to be met in order to create a partnership that will be respected for both state law and tax purposes.

1. A written agreement setting forth the rights and duties of the partners. If no written agreement exists, the terms of the partnership may be difficult to prove if claimed to be different than under applicable state law.

2. Filing a certificate of limited partnership and fictitious business name statement and obtaining all necessary business licenses and registrations.

3. Obtaining a separate tax identification number for the partnership.

4. Transferring title of all contributed assets into the name of the partnership and opening new accounts in the name of the partnership.

5. Amending contracts to show the partnership as the real party in interest (e.g., adding the partnership as an additional insured on liability insurance policies).

6. Avoiding commingling of partnership assets with those assets of the individual partners or using partnership assets for personal business of the partners.

7. Filing annual state and federal income tax returns and allocating partnership income to the partners.

PROVIDING MANAGEMENT AND CONTROL

Control over assets contributed to an FLP is achieved by retaining ownership of the general partner interest (or the managing partner interest in cases where the FLP has multiple general partners). In most instances, the most important decision to be made in creating an FLP is who to name as the general partners since they will exercise exclusive control over the partnership business operations and determine if, when, and how much of the partnership income is to be distributed to the partners.

For estate planning purposes, it may be advisable for the partners to implement a succession plan for management. This may be achieved by designating a non-managing general partner who will succeed in the duties of management and control upon vacancy of the general partner's interest.

For most FLPs, possible general partners include one or both parents, either individually or as trustee of a family living trust, subchapter S corporations controlled by one or more persons, mature and financially experienced children or grandchildren (individually or using trusts for their benefit). It is not recommended that children be given management powers over their parents' assets unless the parents expressly desire to relinquish control and the child has sufficient experience and maturity in managing property.

Even though much of the value of the FLP may be gifted away by transferring limited partner interests to the children, the general partners maintain control of the assets in the FLP even though they retain only a small percentage ownership interest. For this reason, many practitioners recommend use of an FLP for parents who desire to maintain control of their assets while having transferred away most of the assets' economic benefits.

The general partner should have the necessary willingness, knowledge and experience to do the following:

1. Manage and invest partnership assets.

2. Make decisions as to distributions of partnership income and/or assets.

3. File income tax returns on behalf of the partnership and understand income tax law.

4. Furnish annual partnership income tax information (Schedule K-1) to the partners.

5. Make necessary filings with the Secretary of State.

6. Give or withhold consent to transfers of partnership interests and amendment of the FLP agreement.

ENSURING FAMILY OWNERSHIP

Continuous family ownership of the FLP is guaranteed by restricting each partner's ability to sell or otherwise transfer his or her interest to non-family members. Because most FLPs are used by parents to transfer partnership interests to their children at reduced transfer tax values, the existence of rights of first refusal, buy-sell provisions, or other restrictions on transfer are of paramount concern and require considerable attention. However, much care must be exercised in drafting the partnership agreement in order to avoid the transfer tax pitfalls of Chapter 14 of the Code (see Chapter 42).

In almost all instances, the FLP agreement should prohibit the partners from selling or transferring their interests in a manner which is disruptive to the continuation of the family asset arrangement plan or disruptive to family harmony. To achieve this result, the FLP agreement typically will provide the partners a right of first refusal to deal with a circumstance where another partner wishes to sell his or her interest to a non-family member. In such cases, the non-selling partners will usually have the right to purchase the interest of the selling partner for cash or with an unsecured long-term promissory note which bears an interest rate favorable to the buyer (but note that the restriction should not constitute "financial detriment" to any donee partner and such restriction should also satisfy the requirements of Code sections 2703 and 2704). Only if the non-selling partners fail to exercise their purchase rights may the interest then be sold to the non-family member.

If the family members do not wish for the new partner to possess any voting rights, then the agreement should permit them to treat the new partner as a mere assignee who is only entitled to receive income distributions and a proportionate share of partnership income, expenses, deductions and credits. This mechanism provides the family members with protection from the influence of undesired active partners, enhances continued family ownership and does not disrupt good asset management.

REDUCING TRANSFER TAXES

For individuals having substantial wealth, another important benefit of implementing an FLP is the reduction of values for transfer tax purposes.

As a general rule, the value of an FLP interest is worth less than direct ownership of the same percentage interest in the underlying assets of the FLP. Put another way, the sum of all of the FLP interests combined does not equal the sum of the assets themselves. This is because ownership of a limited partner interest in an FLP does not convey any rights of management or control over the underlying assets and the FLP agreement prohibits the partners from freely transferring their interests to non-family members. Accordingly, transfer tax values are reduced by the application of discounts (determined by appraisal) to reflect these restrictions.

Because FLPs may be used to transfer partnership interests to lower generation family members, reduced transfer tax values allow for (1) shifting a greater amount of partnership interests by percentage from parents to subsequent genera-

tions and (2) lower overall estate tax liability on those interests at death retained by a deceased partner. For the majority of FLPs, combined discounts in the range of 25% to 35% are typically achieved.

Despite the reduction in value of FLP interests, the real income production and growth potential of the FLP's assets remain available to the partners since control remains within the family unit.

SECURING VALUATION DISCOUNTS

A *discount for lack of control* is routinely applied in establishing estate and gift tax values of minority limited partner interests (see Chapter 42 for a detailed discussion of discounts to FLP interests). This discount reflects the inability of a limited partner to control the operations of the FLP and to invest its assets in a manner which is of the greatest benefit to the limited partner.

Because management and investment decisions (including the decision as to when to distribute partnership income) are outside the control and influence of the limited partners, the value of a limited partner's interest is reduced to reflect such lack of control. Typical discounts for lack of control (minority interest) generally range between 20% and 30%.

A *discount for lack of marketability* is also applied to the value of privately-held limited partnership interests which do not offer a readily available market for trading. Such a discount reflects the fact that a partner who contributes assets to an FLP in return for a limited partnership interest generally will have difficulty in finding a buyer (if one exists).

Factors which typically influence the amount of the discount for lack of marketability include the nature of the FLP's asset mix (e.g. real property, securities, equipment, etc.), the availability and accuracy of information relating to the FLP and its owners, the existence of transfer restrictions against ownership interests, the willingness of the partners to accept new partners, whether income is currently being distributed to the partners and the expected date on which capital contributions will be returned to the partners.

Whereas an understood purpose of most family limited partnerships is to maintain ownership of assets for the benefit of members of one or more selected families, marketability outside the family group is generally disfavored.

The inclusion of rights of first refusal and other transfer restrictions in the FLP agreement will also reduce the marketability of an FLP interest for transfer tax valuation purposes (provided that the requirements of Code section 2703 are satisfied) further reducing values for estate tax and gift tax purposes. Based upon the number and severity of the transfer restrictions and the factors stated above, lack of marketability discounts may reach as high as 30% or more.

Additionally, in determining the value of an interest in an FLP, consideration should always be given as to whether the interest can be liquidated through the enforcement of withdrawal rights. If the partnership agreement or state law does not confer upon the limited partner any right to withdraw capital, then the interest may remain in the partnership until expiration of the partnership term (often 35-50 years in length) or longer if the partners elect to amend the partnership and continue its term. In such case, the limited partner's interest is said to be "locked-in" to maintaining his investment in the partnership and a *lock-in discount* is appropriate.

In determining whether a lock-in discount is applicable, Section 2704(b) must be reviewed. This section is discussed in greater detail in Chapter 42.

PROTECTING ASSETS

Family limited partnerships provide a limited degree of asset protection to the partners since assets of the FLP generally cannot be attached to satisfy personal debts of the partners. Under the Uniform Limited Partnership Act, the remedy of a personal creditor is to obtain a "charging order" from a court against the interest of the limited partner. The charging order entitles the creditor to receive the distributions which would normally be paid to the limited partner until the debt is fully paid.

A charging order does not give the creditor any voting rights in FLP matters and the creditor cannot be assured that the general partner will elect to pay out the FLP income to the partners. Furthermore, the IRS in Rev. Rul. 77-137 has indicated that even though the general partner does not pay out any income to the creditor and other partners, the responsibility for paying the income tax attributable to the attached limited partner's interest will fall upon the creditor.[3]

Notwithstanding the negative aspects of a charging order, a debtor partner is not necessarily guaranteed access to FLP assets if the judgment creditor is insistent upon collecting its debt. The judgment creditor may quietly wait for the partnership to distribute assets to the debtor partner in hope of attaching the assets immediately after distribution. For this reason, the use of an FLP by itself as an asset protection device is not a guaranteed means of avoiding creditor liability.

Additionally, in view of the surge in popularity of the use of FLPs and the emphasis placed on their asset protection features, it is possible that future courts may be reluctant to continue such asset protection for partnerships in which substantially all of the interests are owned by one person or family, or the assets of the partnership are mainly liquid in nature (e.g., marketable securities, cash, etc.).

INCOME TAX ASPECTS

Section 704(e) of the Code was enacted to prevent taxpayers from using family partnerships as a means of splitting family income and circumventing the progressive tax rate structure of the federal income tax. In order for a family partnership to be recognized for income tax purposes, the following three factors must be satisfied:

(a) Capital must be a material income producing factor. This means that the FLP's business must require substantial inventories or substantial investment in plant, machinery or other equipment, as contrasted with a personal service corporation.[4]

(b) A donee or purchaser of a capital interest in a partnership is not recognized as a partner unless such interest is acquired in a bona fide transaction, not a mere sham for tax avoidance or evasion purposes, and the donee or purchaser is the "real owner" of such interest.[5]

(c) Reasonable compensation must be paid to a donor partner for services rendered to the partnership and the share of income attributable to a donee partner's interest cannot be proportionately greater than his share attributable to his capital.[6]

The validity of an FLP for income tax purposes is dependent upon the a donee partner's "owning" a capital interest. The Code does not define exactly what constitutes "ownership" of a capital interest. However, the regulations state that a transferee of a partnership interest must be the "real owner" of the capital interest and have dominion and control over that interest.

As provided in the IRS regulations, there are four types of retained controls (i.e., powers retained by a donor of an FLP) that are of particular importance in showing that a donee lacks true ownership of his interest. If the donee is not the real owner of his capital interest, then the income attributable to the capital interest will be taxable to the donor. These controls include:

(a) The donor's retaining control of the distribution of income or restricting the amount of such distributions.

(b) The donor's limiting the right of a donee partner to dispose of his interest without financial detriment.

(c) The donor's retaining control of assets which are essential to the partnership business.

(d) The donor's retaining management powers which are inconsistent with normal partnership relations.[7]

The cases that have discussed whether a donee is a real owner stress the importance of receiving current distributions of income.[8]

Because partnership agreements frequently limit the ability of a partner to transfer or liquidate his interest, it is important that the partner be able to dispose of the interest "without financial detriment." This test is aimed at determining whether the partner has control over the current benefits of the interest. The term "financial detriment" is interpreted as requiring that the partner be able to realize the fair market value of the interest. Thus, the regulations indicate that a partnership agreement that requires a partner first offer his interest to the partnership (or partners) at the same price as that of any bona fide offer from an outside party will not be considered as imposing a financial detriment upon the interest of a donee partner.

The regulations under Section 704(e) allow a donor to retain management or voting control over a family partnership if the retention is of a manner which is common in ordinary business relationships.[9] However, the donor's retention of control is directly related to the donee's ability to dispose of the interest without financial detriment. Generally, the donee will not be deemed to possess this right unless he is both independent of the donor and has sufficient maturity and understanding of his rights to exercise them. Thus, FLP interests which are transferred to minors should be held either by a guardian or in trust.

In addition to these direct controls, an examination of several indirect controls may determine if a donee partner is a real owner of his capital interest. As provided in the regulations, the following factors are to be examined:

(a) Whether the donee participates in the management of the business.

(b) Whether there have been income distributions to the donee partner.

(c) Whether the donee partner is held out to the public as a partner.

(d) Whether the partnership has complied with local laws regarding use of fictitious names and other business registration statutes.

(e) Control of business bank accounts.

(f) Whether the donee's rights in distributions of partnership property and profits have been recognized.

(g) Whether the donee's interest is recognized in insurance policies, leases, and other business contracts and in litigation affecting business.

(h) The existence of written agreements, records, memoranda, which establish the partnership and partners' rights.

(i) Whether the partnership has filed income tax returns.[10]

Assuming that a family partnership satisfies the above requirements of Section 704(e), a number of valuable income tax benefits may be provided to the partners. Among these benefits are the following:

1. Pass through of items of income, expense, credit and deduction to the partners.

2. Achieving a "step-up" in income tax basis in FLP assets for interests received from a deceased partner (or upon purchase by a new partner) if an election is made by the general partner under Code section 754.

3. Withdrawal of assets without recognition of taxable gain (unlike corporate ownership).

4. Income shifting to family members.

5. No income tax gain on contribution of assets to the FLP or upon dissolution of the FLP in most cases.

These income tax benefits make FLPs extremely attractive in planning for income tax responsibilities of the partners. If properly structured, the FLP will not increase income taxes and may even reduce income taxes in some cases.

Other tax implications exist in operating an FLP. In general, the following rules will apply:

1. A reasonable allocation of partnership income must be made to any donor partner (which includes a parent who has sold a partnership interest to a family member) to recognize the value of his services to the FLP in order for the family partnership rules of Section 704(e) to be satisfied.

   Where interests of family members are acquired by gift and/or intra-family sale, a mandatory allocation of the FLP's profits in proportion to capital contributed, after due allowance has been made for the donor's services, must be made. For example, assume father and son are each 50% partners in an FLP that has a net income of $100,000. Father is paid $20,000 as reasonable compensation for his services. The remaining $80,000 would be taxed $40,000 each to father and son. This would be in addition to the father's reporting $20,000 of income for his services to the FLP.

If a contributing partner acquires capital from an independent source and not by an intra-family gift or purchase, the mandatory allocations described above will not apply and profit and loss may be allocated in a different manner.

2. Unless found by the IRS to be taxable as a corporation, the partnership itself does not pay federal income taxes since it is a passthrough entity.

However, a federal income tax return (Form 1065) must be filed showing each partner's allocable share of income, expenses, deductions and credits. Each partner must pay income taxes based upon his or her share of partnership income.

3. Generally, no gain or loss is realized when property is contributed to the FLP.

However, Section 721 should be examined in order to ensure that the FLP is not classified as an "investment company" which would cause income tax on gains to be owed due to the formation of the partnership. The rules for determining whether an FLP is an investment company are the same rules found under Code section 351. Under these rules, an investment company exists if 80% or more of the entity's capital is comprised of marketable securities and diversification of assets among the partners has occurred. In making contributions to an FLP, the basis of the FLP in the contributed assets is the same basis the property had in the hands of the contributing partners.

4. Gifts of FLP interests are subject to gift tax and will likely raise questions concerning the value of the transferred interest.

The regulations state that the same principles which apply in valuing stock in corporations apply to valuing interests in an FLP. The fair market value at the date of gift will be the value for gift tax purposes.[11]

IMPLICATIONS AND ISSUES IN COMMUNITY PROPERTY STATES

In Arizona, California, Nevada, New Mexico, and Washington, the income from separate property of one spouse is separate property income. In Texas, Louisiana, Idaho and

Wisconsin, the income from the separate property of one spouse is community property income. It is in the former group of states where the FLP may require extra vigilance if it is owned prior to marriage, is given or inherited, or is separate property of a spouse for whatever reason. In these instances, it is necessary to make a distinction between the earnings of the manager (which is probably community property) and the income received from ownership of the partnership interest (which is separate property).

Using the separate property income from the FLP to purchase items that are taken in the names of both spouses creates a taxable gift (with the exception of real property taken as joint tenants). Thus, if the partner-spouse receives $80,000 income from an FLP that was owned prior to marriage, over and above his wages from the FLP, and if he uses the $80,000 to buy stock in both his and his spouse's names, he will have made a gift of $40,000 taxable to the spouse. For transfers after 1981, this does not create a federal gift tax problem because of the unlimited marital deduction that applies to both separate property and community property (see Chapter 37). Depending upon state gift tax law, however, it may still create a gift tax problem.

Another frequently encountered problem in an FLP in community property states is the failure to designate in the agreement whether the FLP interest is separate property or community property. This failure is a great source of comfort and fees to litigation attorneys in divorce proceedings. This is rather important in view of the high rate of divorce over the past ten years.

DETRIMENTS

As exists with the formation of any entity, use of an FLP also has some detriments. For example, the following issues will generally be encountered:

1. The FLP will have to pay applicable minimum franchise tax fees in most states in which it does business (currently $800 annually in California).

2. The FLP must file annual income tax returns and keep separate accounting records.

3. In states with restrictions on real property tax increases, great care should be taken in contributing real property to the FLP and in transferring partnership interests so that the property tax assessment on the property is not adversely changed.

4. The cost of formation and transferring title of assets into the FLP.

For the most part, the detriments which accompany the use of an FLP are heavily outweighed by its benefits and the decision to implement an FLP should not be materially affected by these issues.

COMPARING FLPs WITH OTHER BUSINESS ENTITIES

The differences between FLPs and other business entities can be significant in determining which entity would best suit a particular business need. Figure 11.1 below provides a brief review of the differences between FLPs, C corporations, S corporations and limited liability companies. More detailed explanations concerning these different types of business entities are discussed elsewhere in this book. (See Chapter 17 on Incorporation, Chapter 22 on Limited Liability Companies, Chapter 29 on S Corporations.)

HOW IS IT DONE — EXAMPLES

1. Mark Ciarelli, a successful businessman, is married and has two adult children, Irv and Eric. He presently is the sole owner of an unincorporated manufacturing business (Pierz Enterprises) in which both personal services and capital are material income producing factors. The net profits from the business for last year were approximately $200,000 before Mark's salary. Mark files a joint return with his wife, Judy. His wife and children do not have an income of their own. Mark pays himself a salary of $1,000 per week. The net profit of the business after

salary was actually $148,000. Because Mark is unincorporated, both the $52,000 salary and the $148,000 net profit are taxable to him.

Mark can minimize his income tax burden by "splitting" the income with his children through an FLP. He could transfer a 30% interest in the business assets directly to Irv and Eric with each child receiving a 15% interest. If Irv and Eric were minors, these interests could be placed in trust for their benefit. A gift tax return would be filed and gift tax paid to the extent that Mark's (and Judy's) $600,000 unified transfer credit has been used up. An FLP agreement could be drafted and Irv and Eric could transfer their 15% interests to the FLP. Mark could continue to run the business and would have to pay himself a salary of $52,000 per year. However, the balance of the FLP income would be divided 70% to Mark, 15% to Irv and 15% to Eric.

This planning would cause Mark to receive $103,600 in addition to his salary and Irv and Eric would each receive $22,200 of annual income. These amounts would be taxable to each partner. The net result is that Mark will have shifted $44,400 of income each year to his children. This income will be taxed at the children's lower income tax brackets (if they are over the age of 14), thus generating an immediate income tax saving. Further, if the business continues to grow, 30% of the future appreciation will accrue to Irv and Eric and not to Mark, thereby reducing Mark's estate.

Figure 11.1

	S Corp.	C Corp.	FLP	LLC
Limited Liability	All Owners	All Owners	Limited Partners	All Owners
Income Tax Levels	Single	Double	Single	Single
Capital Ownership Restrictions	Yes	No	No	No
Limits on Classes of Capital	Yes	No	No	No
Basis Adjustments	Outside Only	Outside Only	Outside and Inside	Outside and Inside
All Members Vote	Yes	Yes	No	Yes
Election Required	Yes	No	No	No
Distributions on Liquidation Taxable	Yes	Yes	No	No

2. John and Robin Scott are each age 70. They have four children and six grandchildren and their estate consists of the following assets held in their family living trust:

Asset	Value
Marketable Securities	$1,500,000
Apartment Complex	$1,000,000
Other Real Estate	$1,500,000
Residence	$ 500,000
Total	$4,500,000

During the year, John and Robin meet with their attorney and agree to implement an FLP to maintain ownership of their property in the family. The securities, apartment and other real estate (but not the residence) are contributed to an FLP, constituting a total value of partnership assets of $4,000,000.

In return for their capital contributions, Mr. and Mrs. Scott each receive a 1% general partner interest and the Scott Family Trust receives a 98% limited partner interest. The FLP agreement gives the general partners the discretion to accumulate partnership income for future business needs and restricts the partners' ability to transfer their interests to persons outside the Scott family.

At the end of the year, the Scotts implement a gifting program in which they each transfer a 6.25% limited partner interest to each of their four children, thereby transferring away a total of 50% of the partnership and $2,000,000 of the underlying asset value. An appraiser is hired to determine the value of the gifted limited partner interests and concludes that a combined 40% discount for lack of control, lack of marketability and lock-in status is appropriate for the limited partner gifts.

After applying this discount to the proportionate value of FLP assets, Mr. and Mrs. Scott were found to have each gifted limited partner interests worth $150,000 to each child for a total gift by each of $600,000. Because the Unified Transfer Credit of each of them is fully intact, no cash payment of gift tax is required. At the end of the year, ownership of the Scott FLP is as follows:

	General Partner	Limited Partner
John Scott	1.00%	0.00%
Robin Scott	1.00%	0.00%
Scott Family Trust	0.00%	48.00%
Child No. 1	0.00%	12.50%
Child No. 2	0.00%	12.50%
Child No. 3	0.00%	12.50%
Child No. 4	0.00%	12.50%
Totals	2.00%	98.00%

In the next year and each year thereafter, the Scotts make annual gifts of limited partner interests worth $10,000 to each of the four children and six grandchildren. The same 40% discount to value is applied to the gifts. During the next ten years, the assets in Scott FLP grow at a 5% annual rate. During this period, Mr. and Mrs. Scott continue to make annual exclusion gifts of $10,000 to the children and grandchildren and significantly reduce their ownership interests in the FLP while remaining in control as the general partners.

At the end of the tenth year, John is struck with a sudden illness and dies. At that time, the underlying value of the FLP assets is $6,205,313 and ownership is as follows:

	General Partner	Limited Partner
John Scott	1.00%	0.00%
Robin Scott	1.00%	0.00%
Scott Family Trust	0.00%	18.40%
Child No. 1	0.00%	15.46%
Child No. 2	0.00%	15.46%
Child No. 3	0.00%	15.46%
Child No. 4	0.00%	15.46%
Grandchild No. 1	0.00%	2.96%
Grandchild No. 2	0.00%	2.96%
Grandchild No. 3	0.00%	2.96%
Grandchild No. 4	0.00%	2.96%
Grandchild No. 5	0.00%	2.96%
Grandchild No. 6	0.00%	2.96%
Totals	2.00%	98.00%

In determining the value of the FLP interests includible in John's estate, a 25% discount was applied to the general partner interest and a 40% discount was applied to the limited partner interest on the estate tax return. As shown on the return, the estate tax value of Mr. Scott's interest in the FLP after adding back his $600,000 in gifts in prior years is as follows:

	Value
General Partner (1.00%)	$ 46,540
Limited Partner (9.20%)	$342,237
Total	$388,777
Prior Taxable Gifts	$600,000
Total Gifts and Interests	$988,777

Had the Scotts chosen not to form their FLP and if no discounts to value were applied on the estate tax return, the value of John's one-half interest in the apartments, real estate and marketable securities would have been $3,102,657 at his death. However, by implementing a gifting program using an FLP, his taxable estate was reduced by $2,123,188 and $1,167,753 in estate tax was saved.

QUESTIONS AND ANSWERS

Question — Can a minor hold a partnership interest directly?

Answer — Yes. A minor will be recognized as a bona fide partner if it is determined that he is competent to manage his own property and to participate in the FLP activities. This requires that the minor possess sufficient maturity and experience to assume dominion and control over the interest transferred to him. Ordinarily, however, a minor will not be deemed to possess the requisite maturity and experience. Therefore, as a practical matter, an FLP interest should not be transferred directly to a minor.

If a minor's interest is transferred to a fiduciary, such as a court-appointed guardian whose conduct is subject to judicial supervision, the minor will be recognized as a partner. Similarly, if an FLP interest is transferred in trust for the benefit of a minor to an independent trustee, this will also permit the minor to own an interest in the FLP.

Question — Parent and child create an FLP to hold and operate a farm. The parent transfers interests in the farm partnership by gift to the children, who are limited partners. The parent is the sole general partner, lives in a farm house on the property, operates the farm, and takes most of the partnership profits as salary. Is this a valid FLP for estate tax purposes?

Answer — The IRS will likely assert that the parent has retained the enjoyment of the entire farm for his or her life and seek to include 100% of the value of the farm in the parent's taxable estate under Section 2036(a). The IRS reached this conclusion in Let. Rul. 7824005, where the parent lived on the property and received income in the form of salary although she did not manage the property. Compare Let. Rul. 9131006 where the FLP was recognized although the parent retained a great deal of control over it.

It is recommended that a person who uses assets of the FLP for non-business purposes should enter into a lease agreement and pay a reasonable market rent for the used property. The payment of rent is consistent with the FLP's business purpose of owning assets for the purpose of making a profit. A failure to pay reasonable rental rates could be construed as a retention of the enjoyment of FLP assets and create adverse estate tax results.

Question — Do gifts of interests in an FLP qualify for the $10,000 annual gift tax exclusion?

Answer — The IRS has ruled that such gifts do qualify where there is no substantial restriction under the FLP agreement on the rights of the donee partners to dispose of their interests in the FLP. Note that if the partnership agreement attempts to prohibit assignment, there will be a problem.

Question — When a partner dies, is there any change in the income tax basis of partnership assets?

Answer — Generally, under Section 1014, the income tax basis of a decedent's assets is adjusted to the value of such assets for federal estate tax purposes, typically their fair market value as of the date of death. Where the estate owns an FLP interest, this basis adjustment will apply to the basis of the FLP interest. Also, if the general partner makes a timely election under Section 754, the basis of the assets owned by the FLP will be adjusted to reflect the date of death values according to Section 743(b). If assets have appreciated in value, this adjustment will be advantageous only to the interest of the deceased partner who will receive a date of death basis in the FLP assets.

Question — What are some helpful hints for operating an FLP?

Answer — Helpful hints include:

1. There should be a written FLP agreement setting forth the rights of the partners.

2. Accurate business records should be kept.

3. The donor (general partner) should receive reasonable compensation for his services.

4. Distributions to the donee partners should not be used to discharge parental support obligations.

5. If minors are partners and their interests are held in trust, the trustee should be an independent trustee and not subject to the direct or indirect control of the donor.

6. Assets should be transferred into the name of the partnership.

Question — Can a family partnership be funded solely by contributing marketable securities?

Answer — To date, family partnerships holding such assets have not been invalidated. Section 7701(a)(2) defines a partnership as including a "syndicate, group, pool, joint venture, or other unincorporated organization, through or by means of which any business, financial operation, or venture is carried on, and which is not, within the meaning of this title, a trust or estate or a corporation." Those practitioners who advocate the creation of family partnerships solely to hold marketable securities often point to this statute as partial authority for their position. However, the recent attempt of the Service in promulgating Reg. §1.704-2 and retraction of Examples (5) and (6) (the latter of which was to be used to attack certain "paper shuffling" partnerships) suggests that the Service may attack such entities in the future. Where the transferred assets include large amounts of publicly traded securities, watch out for the investment company rules, discussed above, which could result in gain or loss on the transfer.

Question — Under what circumstances can the IRS tax a family partnership as a corporation?

Answer — The Service may treat a family partnership as an association taxable as a corporation if three or more of the following characteristics are determined to exist in the partnership.

1. Centralized management;

2. Free transferability of interests;

3. Continuity of life; and

4. Limited liability.

The drafter of the partnership agreement should be careful in assuring that the partnership lacks at least two of the above characteristics. For FLPs, the agreement is usually drafted so that free transferability of interests and continuity of life are lacking.

Question — What are guaranteed payments and are they significant in the family limited partnership?

Answer — Guaranteed payments are payments for services or the use of capital, often made to senior partners, under Code section 707(c). If these are determined without regard to partnership income, they will be treated as payments to unrelated persons, which will generally be taxable income to the recipient and deductible by the partnership if they are reasonable, ordinary and necessary. They provide a method of making cash flow available to senior family members on a tax deductible basis. Note, however, they may be subject to self-employment tax.

Question — What action should be taken in structuring a family limited partnership to avoid the special valuation rules of Code section 2701?

Answer — Gifts of interest in a family limited partnership may have to be valued under the artificial valuation rules of Section 2701, which are discussed in Chapter 42. Section

2701 will apply if the senior family members retain interests that are defined as "applicable retained interests." These partnership interests resemble preferred stock in that they confer preferential distribution rights, or have a fixed liquidation value.

A so-called "vertical slice" in the entity is not covered by this section. For example, if the transferor, each family member, and each applicable family member hold substantially the same interest before and after the transfer, Section 2701 does not apply. Similarly, it does not apply if the interests transferred are of the same class proportionately as the interests retained. Differences only in voting rights, or in the case of partnerships, differences in management and liability, are generally considered proportionate.

The key to avoiding Section 2701 is to structure the partnership so that each partner will share proportionately in capital, income, losses and distributions. For examples, see Let. Ruls. 9427023 and 9451050.

Question — Are there any problems in transferring stock in a closely held corporation to a family limited partnership?

Answer — If voting stock in a controlled corporation as defined in Section 2036(b) is transferred to a family partnership and the transferor votes the stock as a general partner, this would appear to be an indirect retained voting power over the stock, resulting in its inclusion in the transferor's taxable estate. It would be better to limit transfers of stock to nonvoting shares. Note that control under this statute is broadly defined, and includes any corporation in which the transferor and family members own a 20% interest.

Question — Can life insurance be transferred to a family limited partnership?

Answer — The family partnership may be an excellent vehicle for holding life insurance, functioning in a manner similar to an irrevocable insurance trust as discussed in Chapter 36. However, if the only function of the partnership is to hold life insurance policies, there are serious questions. Under both general legal principles and tax law, a valid partnership is supposed to engage in some business or financial activity. At least one private letter ruling has held that ownership of life insurance with investment characteristics is sufficient.[12] However, caution indicates the partnership should be engaged in some other business or investment activity in addition to holding life insurance.

ASRS, Sec. 42.

Footnote References

Family Partnerships

1. IRC Sec. 704(e)(3).
2. Effective May 12, 1994, Reg. §1.704-2 sets forth three additional requirements in order for a family partnership to be acknowledged for income tax purposes. Although the Service's attempt at applying the scope of the new regulation to estate, gift and generation skipping taxes failed in this instance, it is likely that the Service will continue to look for ways to challenge family partnerships which substantially reduce transfer taxes.
3. Rev. Rul. 77-137, 1977-1 C.B. 178.
4. IRC Sec. 704(e)(1).
5. Reg. §1.704-1(e)(1)(iii).
6. IRC Sec. 704(e)(2).
7. Reg. §1.704-1(e)(2)(ii)(a)-(d).
8. See, e.g. *Payton v. U.S.*, 425 F.2d 1324 (5th Cir. 1970); *Kuney v. U.S.*, 448 F.2d 22 (9th Cir. 1971).
9. See Reg. §1.704-1(e)(2)(ii).
10. See Reg. §1.704-1(e)(2)(vi)(a)-(f).
11. See Reg. §§25.2512-2, 25.2512-3. See also Rev. Rul. 59-60, 1959-1 C.B. 237.
12. Let. Rul. 9309021

Chapter 12

FLOWER BONDS

WHAT IS IT?

Certain United States Treasury obligations (which are traditionally traded at a discount) owned by a decedent at death can be redeemed at par value (plus accrued interest) in payment of federal estate taxes. Although these bonds (often called "flower bonds" because of the engraving of flowers on their reverse side and because they "blossom" at death) can no longer be purchased directly from the federal government, they can be obtained through stock brokers and bank trust departments.

Because these bonds pay interest in the 3 to 4% range, they can typically be purchased at a substantial discount. As interest rates on alternative government bonds rise, these discounts tend to increase. Discounts exceeding 20 percent were not uncommon.

Flower bonds can be used at par value to pay federal estate taxes. The difference between par value and the purchase price provides a way to pay federal estate taxes at a "discount."

WHEN IS THE USE OF SUCH A DEVICE INDICATED?

1. These treasury bonds are useful in any situation in which the client would like to pay federal estate taxes at a discount.

2. This type of treasury bond is a good way to provide needed liquidity in an estate that otherwise is relatively illiquid. (It may be advantageous for an individual to use relatively nonmarketable securities as collateral for a loan and use the borrowed cash to purchase the bonds, rather than to sell securities to purchase the flower bonds.)

3. Flower bonds are a possible alternative to life insurance where the decedent would be highly "rated" for life insurance purposes or is uninsurable. Flower bonds can be obtained even if the decedent is critically ill.

WHAT ARE THE REQUIREMENTS?

1. The bonds must be purchased during the lifetime of the decedent.

2. These bonds must be owned by the decedent at his death.[1] However, the bonds may be held in a grantor-type trust, as opposed to being in the decedent's individual name, as long as the trust contains a direction to the trustee to use the bonds for payment of estate taxes.

In any case, the bonds must have been purchased by the decedent or at his direction. If the bonds are purchased by someone for the decedent, pursuant to a power of attorney given by the decedent, the power of attorney must have been effective under state law on the date of purchase. (See Chapter 6—Durable Power of Attorney.)

HOW IT IS DONE — AN EXAMPLE

Assume that: (1) a federal estate tax of $200,000 will be due; (2) that the estate is approximately in the 37 percent federal estate tax bracket; (3) John Donne, age 60, a widower, is in a 31 percent federal income tax bracket; and (4) Mr. Donne is quite ill and possibly has terminal cancer (therefore, obtaining life insurance on the client's life is out of the question).

Mr. Donne contacts the local office of a nearby trust company. Assume he selects three and one-half percent 1998 series bonds issued October 3, 1960. This bond is due November 5, 1998. Assume the price quoted for the series is $73.26 ($732.60 cost to purchase a $1,000 par value flower bond). This means that for a purchase price of $146,520 ($73.26 x 2,000 or $732.60 x 200), Mr. Donne's estate can obtain enough bonds to pay $200,000 in federal estate taxes.

The gain (or increased liquidity) thus appears to be $53,480 ($200,000 - $146,520). However, the gain must be reduced by the additional estate taxes generated by the inclusion of the flower bonds in the gross estate at par.[2] The estate tax of 37 percent will reduce the $53,480 gain by $19,788. Therefore, the actual cost of the flower bonds is the purchase price ($146,520) plus the $19,788 federal estate tax on the difference between the purchase price and $200,000 par value.

The following additional example will help illustrate that the true advantage of flower bonds may be less than it appears.

Raymond Fry, an 80-year-old bachelor, has assets worth over $5 million that consist entirely of listed stocks. Although he is not well physically, his mind is alert. His only heir is his grandnephew, Pete Summers. Pete has told his granduncle that certain United States Treasury bonds (often referred to as "flower bonds") could save federal estate taxes. Certain flower bonds with a $1,000 maturity value were selling for $850. Pete suggested that his uncle sell enough of his stock portfolio to purchase flower bonds with a total par value of $1 million. Raymond's marginal estate tax rate is 55 percent. His marginal capital gain income tax rate is 28 percent. Assume enough stock to net $850,000 were sold. If the proceeds from the sale, net of any commissions and fees, were $950,000, of which $357,143 were gain, Raymond would have a tax payable of $100,000 ($357,143 x .28). The current yield of flower bonds is 3 percent. See Figure 12.1.

You should consider that the current yield on the bond during the individual's lifetime will not be anywhere near comparable to the yield on an alternative investment of the same amount of money. However, this will be of little importance if the client is seriously ill or perhaps only a few hours away from death.

It is important to note that the difference between purchase price of the bonds and par value might increase not only the federal estate taxes but also the administration expenses of the estate. Of course, additional taxes would be involved if liquidation of other investments were required in order to raise the cash needed to purchase the flower bonds. But, in spite of these factors, buying bonds below par to pay federal estate taxes should be considered in appropriate cases.

WHAT ARE THE TAX IMPLICATIONS?

The tax implications have been discussed above and, as stated, such treasury bonds are redeemable at par (plus accrued interest) only for the purpose of applying the proceeds in payment of the federal estate tax. The essential flaw is that to the extent that these bonds can be used to pay the federal estate tax at par, they must be valued in the estate at not less than par, *whether or not the bonds actually are redeemed to pay the estate tax.*[3] Bonds held in excess of the amount of the estate tax are includable at the market price plus accrued interest.

These obligations are no longer issued by the treasury since the 1971 repeal of Code Section 6312, but millions of dollars of bonds issued before March 3, 1971, are still available.

IMPLICATIONS AND ISSUES IN COMMUNITY PROPERTY STATES

Since one of the primary requirements for use of flower bonds to pay estate taxes is their ownership by the decedent, purchase of the bonds with community funds would necessitate buying twice the amount of bonds needed to pay the tax, in order to have a sufficient amount in the decedent's ownership.

One way to avoid this (where the individual does not have separate funds available for this purpose, and where the estate

Figure 12.1

FLOWER BONDS — AN ANALYSIS OF THEIR UTILITY		
INPUT: MARGINAL ESTATE TAX RATE		0.55
INPUT: MARGINAL INCOME TAX RATE		0.28
INPUT: TAX COST IF ASSETS MUST BE SOLD TO PURCHASE FLOWER BONDS		$ 100,000
INPUT: PAR VALUE OF FLOWER BONDS		$1,000,000
INPUT: MARKET VALUE OF FLOWER BONDS		$ 850,000
GROSS INCREASE IN ESTATE ASSETS		$ 150,000
Less tax on sale of assets to purchase flower bonds		$ 100,000
NET INCREASE IN ESTATE ASSETS		$ 50,000
GROSS INCREASE IN LIQUIDITY VIA FLOWER BONDS		$ 150,000
Less —		
tax on sale of assets to buy bonds	$100,000	
increase in federal estate tax	27,500	$ 127,500
NET INCREASE IN ESTATE ASSETS (OR LIQUIDITY)		$ 22,500

plan anticipates that federal tax will be paid by design at the death of the first spouse to die) is to effect a "split" of community property, whereby an amount equal to the cost of the bonds is allocated to the spouse and placed in a bank account or other investment as the spouse's sole and separate property, and the other half of the split funds placed in the ill spouse's sole name, in a traceable fashion, and thereafter used to purchase the flower bonds in the ill spouse's sole name. In order to effect a "split," some states, such as California, require the "split" agreement to be in writing.

Where cash must be borrowed to purchase the bonds, the loan amount, and the obligation to repay, should clearly be documented as being entirely the decedent's.

QUESTIONS AND ANSWERS

Question — How distant a maturity date may be obtained?

Answer — Three and one-half percent bonds are available with a maturity date of November 15, 1998. Information on the only bonds still available follows:

Series	Dated	Due
3¹/₂%, 1998	October 3, 1960	November 5, 1998

A current list of eligible bond issues may be obtained from any Federal Reserve Bank or from the Bureau of Public Debt, Division of Loans & Currency, Treasury Dept., Washington, D.C.

Question — Suppose an executor had the right to use all of the estate's flower bonds to pay estate taxes but chose to use only some of them for that purpose and retained the balance. How would the remaining bonds be taxed?

Answer — Where all the bonds could have been used to pay federal estate taxes, their value is par value regardless of whether or not they were actually used for estate tax payment purposes.

Question — What if the estate owned more bonds than were needed to pay the federal estate taxes, so that after paying the taxes the estate still had bonds which were unredeemed. How would these bonds be valued in the estate?

Answer — Those bonds in excess of the amount that could be redeemed at par for estate tax purposes would be valued at fair market value.[4]

Question — What does the executor do if the par value of the bonds is greater than the amount necessary to pay the estate tax due?

Answer — The executor can exchange the bond for others of smaller value. For example, if a $10,000 treasury bond was submitted in payment of a federal estate tax liability of $9,500 and the lowest denomination in which such bonds are issued is $500, the bond would be redeemed to the extent of $9,500 par value. It would then be applied toward the payment of the federal estate tax liability and the government would reissue a $500 denomination bond for the portion of the bond that could not be applied to the payment of the tax.

Question — How and where are the bonds submitted for payment of the taxes?

Answer — Flower bonds are not accepted directly by the IRS in payment of the federal estate tax. Instead, the bonds, together with a certified copy of the decedent's death certificate, are submitted to any Federal Reserve Bank or branch, to the Bureau of the Public Debt, Division of Loans and Currency, Washington, D.C. 20226, or to the Office of the Treasurer of the U.S., Securities Division, Washington, D.C., 20220. They should be submitted well in advance (at least a month) of the date specified for redemption. The form that should be used is number PD1782, *Application for Redemption at Par of United States Treasury Bonds Eligible for Payment of Federal Estate Tax.* These forms can be obtained from any Federal Reserve Bank or branch.

Question — What if the federal estate tax was paid in cash, but the flower bonds were later discovered; can the flower bonds still be used?

Answer — If flower bonds are available for payment of the tax, they can be substituted, as long as the substitution occurs before the distribution of the estate or within two years of the date the tax is paid (whichever occurs earlier).

Question — Can flower bonds be purchased with borrowed funds?

Answer — Yes. Also, the interest expense incurred to finance the purchase of flower bonds may be deductible for income tax purposes. (However, where the client also holds substantial amounts of tax-exempt bonds, it is likely that the Internal Revenue Service will attempt to disallow the interest deduction.)

Question — Can an executor purchase flower bonds and use them to pay the federal estate tax?

Answer — The bonds can only be redeemed at par to pay federal estate taxes if the decedent owned the bonds at the date of death.

Question — How are flower bonds taxed for state inheritance or estate tax purposes?

Answer — There is no uniform rule for valuing flower bonds for state death tax purposes. Some states, such as Illinois and Montana, value the bonds at fair market value. Other states, such as New York and California, value flower bonds at par. Valuing these bonds at par for state purposes reduces their tax savings potential.

Question — Compared to life insurance as a means of paying death costs at a "discount," what are the disadvantages of flower bonds?

Answer — There are a number of reasons flower bonds should be considered only as a last resort alternative to life insurance

(1) To obtain the discount, the bonds must be owned at death. This means the bonds must be includable in the estate.

A great deal of the advantage of the discount is given up because such bonds are includable in the gross estate—not at the discount price, but at their (higher) par value—to the extent that they are or can be used to pay estate taxes. Estate taxes must be paid on "phantom assets"; i.e., the tax must be paid on a greater amount of property than the decedent actually had the day before he bought the bonds (and unlike life insurance, there's no way to assign the bonds out of his estate and still obtain the discount).

A 1978 case involved a situation where an executor used some flower bonds to pay taxes and, thinking he had paid the entire estate tax due, sold the others at the (low) market price. The IRS later assessed a deficiency and included the bonds at par (rather than at their much lower market price) in the decedent's estate. The IRS argued (successfully) that since the

bonds *were* available to pay estate taxes when the return was filed they should be includable at par value. In other words, it doesn't matter that the bonds were not actually used to pay the federal estate tax; if they could have been used they must be included at their par value even if the bonds were sold before the deficiency was assessed.[5] Also, heirs could sue the executor since bonds that could have been used to pay the estate tax at a discount were sold prematurely.

(2) Life insurance is usually not subject to probate; flower bonds usually are.

(3) Life insurance purchased while an individual is in good health results in a "deeper" discount—possibly as much as a 97 percent discount.

(4) Life insurance can be state inheritance tax free; flower bonds can't.

(5) Life insurance can be used to pay state inheritance taxes *and* all other probate and death-related costs; flower bonds can be used at par only to pay federal estate tax costs.

ASRS, Sec. 51.

Footnote References

Flower Bonds

1. See Treasury Dept., Circular No. 300, 4th Rev. Section 306.28(b), 38 F.R. 7083.
2. Rev. Rul. 156, 1953-2 CB 253.
3. Rev. Rul. 156, 1953-2 CB 253; *Bankers Tr. Co., Exr. v. U.S.*, 284 F.2d 537 (2nd Cir. 1960), rev'g. 178 F. Supp. 267 (D.C.N.Y.).
4. Rev. Proc. 69-18, 1969-2 CB 300; Rev. Rul. 69-489, 1969-2 CB 172.
5. *Est. of Simmie v. Comm.*, 69 TC 890 (1978).

Chapter 13

FREEZING TECHNIQUES — CORPORATIONS AND PARTNERSHIPS

WHAT IS IT?

In the most fundamental sense, an estate freeze is any planning device where the owner of property attempts to freeze the present value of his estate and shift the future growth to successors, generally the next generation. It may also involve the retention of some form of income stream or cash flow from the property.

This definition of an estate freeze is so broad it includes a variety of techniques, including installment sales of property (see Chapter 19), a variety of gift planning techniques (see Chapter 15), and buy-sell agreements (see Chapter 1). As generally used, the term has been more limited to cover structuring of family businesses and investments in such a way that the original owners retain much of the present value and control, and some source of revenue, while the growth is shifted. The usual vehicle is the family partnership or corporation.

In the case of the family corporation, the senior generation typically retains control through the use of voting preferred stock which has a fixed liquidation value, usually par value. Either by forming a new corporation or recapitalizing an existing one, one or more classes of common stock are created, which may be nonvoting or at least have limited voting rights. All or part of this common stock is sold or given to the next generation.

The counterpart in the case of the partnership is the formation or restructuring of an existing partnership in such a way that the senior family members retain partnership interests which control the management of the business or investments, from which they receive preferred profit distributions, but which have a fixed liquidation value. Thus, the retained partnership interests resemble preferred stock in a corporation. The remaining partnership interests may then, like the common stock in the case of a corporation, be sold or given to the next generation.

WHEN IS THE USE OF SUCH A DEVICE INDICATED?

Where a family business is involved, the freeze has been an important planning tool to assure retention of the enterprise in the family at minimum tax cost. The same may apply to family investments, particularly real estate. It will only be used where there is a desire to perpetuate the business or investment in the family.

WHAT ARE THE REQUIREMENTS?

As discussed above, a business entity, either a corporation or a partnership, must be created or altered to structure this form of a freeze. The retained stock or partnership interests of the senior generation must have a limited liquidation value, since that is what makes it impossible for the value of those interests to grow. The retention of preferred dividends or profit distributions is not essential, but adds to the value of the retained interest, which in turn reduces the value of the interests transferred to the next generation. Since the transfer of interests may and probably will have gift tax implications, the value of the retained interests is very important.

HOW IT IS DONE — AN EXAMPLE

Client owns 100 percent of the common stock in Acme corporation, a manufacturing concern. It has been valued at $1,000,000. He wants to bring his two children into the business, give them an incentive to work there by giving them an equity stake in the enterprise, and minimize his own gift and estate taxes.

Client recapitalizes the corporation with $1,000,000 par value preferred stock with an 8 percent cumulative preferred dividend and common stock. The preferred stock is voting, and in the event of corporate liquidation, the preferred shareholders can receive only par value for it. The common stock is then transferred by gift or sale to the children.

WHAT ARE THE TAX IMPLICATIONS?

1. Code section 2701, titled "Special valuation rules in case of transfers of certain interests in corporations or partnerships" (applicable to transactions entered into after October 8, 1990), focuses on the valuation of retained senior interests in such entities in determining the extent of

taxable gifts of other junior interests in the same entity. It also deals with the transfer tax treatment of the retained interests, and how those retained interests will be valued for subsequent transfers during life or at death.

2. Also to be considered in this area is Code section 2704, providing in general that most lapsing restrictions on transferred interests in businesses created after October 8, 1990 will be ignored in valuing the interest for transfer tax purposes, or the lapse itself will trigger a transfer tax. This involves situations in which restrictions are imposed on the value of retained stock or partnership interests, which depress the value of those interests. After the owner dies, these restrictions either lapse or can be readily removed by family members.

Section 2701

How Retained Interests Are Valued for Gift Tax Purposes

For the purposes of determining whether or not the transfer of interests in partnerships or corporations to family members are gifts, and the value of the gifts, any retained interest in the partnership or corporation must be valued under Section 2701, unless it falls within an exception. The assumption under the statute is that the value of the residual interests transferred to "family members," in this case corporate stock or partnership interests, will be valued by subtracting from the total value of the entire corporation or partnership the value of any retained interests which have preferred rights, adjusted to reflect the proportionate interest of the transferor in the business entity. For purposes of Section 2701, "family members" are the transferor's spouse, lineal descendant of the transferor or spouse, and the spouse of any descendant.[1] Covered transfers include contributions to capital, redemptions, and other changes in capital structure, as well as any transfer that increases the property owned by or the value of the applicable retained interest (defined below) of the transferor or applicable family member, including transfers to a start up entity.[2] A sale is covered by these valuation rules if there is an applicable retained interest (e.g., the sale of common stock in the entity for its full fair market value where the transferor retains preferred stock).[3]

Example. Transferor owns 100% of the common stock of a corporation worth $1,000,000. He recapitalizes, taking voting preferred stock with a par value of $1,000,000, paying a cumulative preferred dividend of 8%, and made a gift of the nonvoting common stock to his children. The gift is valued at $1,000,000 less the value of the preferred stock.

According to Section 2701(b), what is valued under the statute is an "applicable retained interest," which is:

1. A "distribution right," if immediately after the transfer the transferor and "applicable family members" "control" the entity; or

2. Liquidation, put, call, or conversion rights.

A distribution right is defined as a right to distributions from a corporation with respect to its stock or a partnership with respect to a partnership interest, except:

1. Rights in connection with "junior equity interests," defined as common stock or partnership interests under which rights to income and capital are junior to all other equity interests.[4]

2. "Liquidation, put, call, or conversion rights," defined as any such right, or similar right, which affects the value of the transferred interest.[5] However, the term does not include any right which must be exercised at a specific time at a specific amount.

3. Rights to guaranteed payments from a partnership defined in Code section 707(c), which are certain payments determined without regard to partnership income.[6]

"Control" means at least a 50 percent interest in a corporation by vote or value of the corporate stock, or at least 50 percent of the capital or profits in a partnership, or the holding of any partnership interest as a general partner. Control includes interests held by "applicable family members." It also includes attribution through entities and interests held by brothers or sisters or lineal descendants of an individual.[7]

An "applicable family member" means the transferor's spouse, ancestor of the transferor or transferor's spouse, or the spouse of an ancestor.[8]

According to the regulations, applicable retained interests include extraordinary payment rights and distribution rights in a controlled entity.[9] As noted, guaranteed payments from a partnership covered by Code section 707(c), and possibly other rights to distributions under Code section 707, are excluded from Section 2701. Also excluded from this definition are any right to distributions of the same class as the transferred interests.

Extraordinary payment rights are retained put, call, conversion rights, and a right to compel liquidation, or similar rights.[10] A right falls within this definition only if it affects the value of the transferred interest.

Certain rights, such as the right to mandatory payments fixed as to time and amount are neither extraordinary payment rights nor distribution rights.[11] Thus, mandatory redemption rights (e.g., a requirement that preferred stock be redeemed at a fixed price at a time certain) are not covered. A right to participate in a liquidation is not covered unless the transferor, family members, and applicable family members can compel liquidation. Non-lapsing conversion rights in a corporation (i.e., the right to convert an equity interest into a fixed percentage of shares of the transferred interest except for nonlapsing differences in voting rights) are not covered.[12] Similar rights in a partnership are also not covered (e.g., where all rights in partnership interests are the same except for nonlapsing differences in management rights and limitation of liability).

If the transferor retains both a qualified payment right and an extraordinary right, the value of all rights is determined by assuming the extraordinary right is exercised in such a way as to produce the lowest possible valuation.[13] The special valuation rules do not apply to the transfer of any interest for which market quotations are readily available on the date of transfer from an established securities market,[14] and the following retained interests are specifically excluded from these special valuation rules:

1. An interest which can be valued on an established securities market.

2. An interest which is of the same class as the transferred interest.

3. An interest which is proportionately the same as the transferred interest, except for nonlapsing differences in voting rights or in the case of a partnership, nonlapsing differences in management and limitations on liability unless the transferor or applicable family member can alter the liability of the transferee.

The valuation of the applicable retained interest is zero, except to the extent it consists of the right to receive a "qualified payment."[15] Qualified payments are any periodic dividend on cumulative preferred stock, any comparable payment from a partnership interest, or any other payment where an irrevocable election is made to treat other payments, such as noncumulative preferred dividends, as qualified payments. Further, an irrevocable election can be made out of qualified payment status, in which case the distribution right will apparently be valued at zero. The right to a qualified payment is to be valued at fair market value (i.e., what a willing buyer would pay a willing seller for it).

The rules of Section 2701 are complex. Possibly the following summary of how the section works will be helpful:

Section 2701 applies to an interest in a corporation or partnership transferred to a family member where the transferor or "applicable family member" retains a certain interest in the enterprise classified as an "applicable retained interest." If the section applies, the gift resulting from the transfer is determined by subtracting from the value of the entire entity the value of any interests senior to those transferred.

The applicable retained interest consists of the following:

1. An "extraordinary payment right" (i.e., a discretionary liquidation, put, call, conversion, or similar right, valued at zero).

2. A distribution right, also valued at zero unless it is a "qualified payment" right.

3. A qualified payment right, generally a fixed-rate cumulative payment, or a payment which the transferor elects to treat as such a payment, valued as if the rights valued at zero do not exist, but otherwise without regard to Section 2701.

If an extraordinary payment right is held in conjunction with a qualified payment right, the rights are valued on the assumption they will be exercised in such a way as to produce the lowest possible value.

The Minimum Value Rule

Since the value of the gift under the above rules is determined by subtracting the value of the retained qualified payment from the value of the entire entity, it is possible the result could be a small amount where the value of the qualified payment is large. However, regardless of the results of the subtraction method, the minimum value that can be assigned to the transfer of a junior equity interest is 10 percent of the total value of all equity interests in the partnership or corporation, plus the total indebtedness of the entity to the transferor, or applicable family member.[16]

Transfer Taxation of Cumulative Unpaid Distributions

If the corporation or partnership fails to make the required cumulative distributions, or noncumulative distributions the transferor has elected to treat as cumulative distributions, then upon the occurrence of a "taxable event," the taxable gifts or estate of the transferor will be increased by the value of such unpaid distributions. This value will be determined on the assumption all payments are made when due, then compounded as if reinvested at the same discount rate used in valuing the retained interest, less actual distributions paid, based on the date actually paid, but with a 4 year grace period for late payment. However, the total amount subject to tax cannot exceed the transferor's proportionate interest in the excess value of all junior interests in the entity at the applicable date of the taxable event over the value of all such transfers at the original date of transfer. In other words, the additional amount subject to federal transfer tax is limited to the actual growth in the enterprise that was shifted.

A taxable event is the death of the transferor if the applicable retained interest is included in his or her estate, or the transfer of such applicable retained interest. Also, the transferor can elect to treat late payment as a taxable event.[17]

Where the transfer is to a spouse and is not taxable because of the marital deduction or because the transfer was for full and adequate consideration, the above rules will not apply, but the spouse will inherit the tax consequences on a subsequent taxable event.[18] Applicable family members other than the transferor are subject to the same taxable event rule with respect to their retained interests, and if the applicable retained interest is transferred to an applicable family member, such applicable family member is subject to the same rules as to distributions accumulating after the transfer.[19]

Qualified payments can be made in the form of debt instruments if they are for not more than 4 years and compound interest at a rate no less than the appropriate discount rate payable from the due date of the payment.[20]

It is important to note that the value of the unpaid distribution is added to the taxable estate or taxable gifts of the transferor along with the value of the retained corporate stock or partnership interest. According to the regulations, the amount subject to transfer tax will be reduced by any amount subject to transfer tax with respect to the same rights to prevent double taxation.

Value of the Retained Frozen Interests
for Purposes of Subsequent Transfers

Section 2701 only deals with the value of the retained interest for purposes of valuation of a transferred interest at the time of the transfer of the transferred interest. Apparently, the retained preferred stock or partnership interests would be valued under normal rules for purposes of any subsequent transfers. This means any retained put, call, conversion or liquidation rights valued at zero under Section 2701 will subsequently be valued when the retained interest is transferred. The result is clearly double taxation, since an interest that was valued at zero when retained is subsequently valued at fair market value when the transferor dies or transfers the

retained interest. To avoid this result, there is an adjustment to the decedent's adjusted taxable gifts by reducing them to reflect the amount by which decedent's taxable gifts were increased due to Section 2701 over the increase in the estate or adjusted taxable gifts attributable to inclusion of the applicable retained interest in the estate. The adjustment may also be available to the transferor's spouse.[21]

Is the Freeze a Viable Planning Alternative?

Although a corporate or partnership freeze through the use of common and preferred stock or partnership interests is now available, many commentators believe it has less utility than in the past. In order to avoid a zero valuation for retained interests, it will be necessary to make distributions with respect to the retained interests. The double tax on corporate distributions (once at the corporate level and once at the shareholder level), which generally cannot be avoided, will be a 63.156% maximum. The income tax will be paid now, while the estate tax is deferred, often until the death of a surviving spouse. Note that the use of the freeze eliminates qualification for the S election, since preferred stock is involved. However, if the entity is a partnership, particularly one with a good cash flow, the freeze may make a great deal more sense — the effective federal income tax rate is decreased to 39.6% maximum.

If the qualified payments are not made, the resulting inclusion of accumulated distributions in the transferor's taxable gifts or estate could easily exceed the value of the retained interest for federal gift tax purposes.

Example. Assume the applicable discount rate is 10%, and the retained dividend is 8%. Based on the assumption that the present value of the annual dividend is its fair market value, as required by the regulations, the value of the retained interest is 80% of the value of the transferred property. Thus, if the business is valued at $1,000,000, the retained interest is valued at $800,000, the gift at $200,000.

However, if the dividends are not paid for 10 years, and the grace period does not apply, the amount of the cumulative unpaid distributions subject to federal gift or estate tax under Section 2701(d)(1) would be approximately $1,275,000.

Note: In the above example, the amount included in the taxable transfers of the transferor cannot exceed the actual growth in the business.

If the freeze is contemplated, can the amount of the taxable transfer be reduced by discounts? The Congressional Committee Reports acknowledge that all existing discounts are preserved, which means it is possible to argue that the value of the transferred interest for federal gift tax purposes must be reduced to reflect discounts for minority interests, lack of marketability, etc. The regulations under Section 2701 recognize the existence of such discounts, and set forth a four step method to value the taxable gift, taking into account such discounts, as follows:

1. Determine the fair market value all family-held interests in the entity.

2. Subtract all senior equity interests held by the family other than applicable retained interests held by the transferor or applicable family members, with a pro-rata adjustment for any control premium, followed by the subtraction of the value of all applicable retained interests held by the transferor and applicable family members.

3. Allocate the remaining value among the transferred interests and any other family-held junior (or subordinate) interests.

4. Reduce value for consideration received, and for any minority or similar discounts (presumably including a discount for lack of marketability), determined by subtracting the fair market value of the family-held interests (determined as if voting rights were held by one person who had no other interest in the entity other than the family-held interests of the same class) from the value of the transferred interest determined without regard to Section 2701.

Note that if the transfer is to a grantor retained interest trust (i.e., a GRAT or GRUT, see Chapter 35), any reduction in the value of the transfer under Code section 2702 will also be subtracted to determine the net taxable gift.

Alternatives to the Freeze

If the transferor retains common stock or partnership interests, and transfers the preferred interests, Section 2701 does not apply. This is sometimes called a "reverse" freeze. When the transferor dies, the value of the common stock will reflect growth, but should be substantially discounted in value because of the burden of the preferred stock with its prior claim to dividends and liquidation proceeds.

Consider the use of a variety of other techniques to freeze growth. This includes installment sales of business interests to family members (see Chapter 19), use of the private annuity (see Chapter 27), and premortem stock redemptions or part-nership liquidations of interests of senior family members, giving them a cash flow and transferring the growth in the value of the enterprise to the next generation. Under some circumstances, if the transferor receives a debt instrument issued by a family partnership or corporation, the IRS may seek to treat it as retained preferred stock. See Example 1, Senate Committee Report (OBRA '90), referring to "convertible debt" and treating it as retained preferred stock.

Section 2704

Section 2704 deals with the transfer tax consequences of lapsing rights, and provides that property in general will be valued without regard to lapsing restrictions. As a result, the lapse of a voting or liquidation right in a family controlled corporation will have transfer tax consequences.

Example. If parent and child control a corporation, and parent's stock has a voting right which lapses at parent's death, parent's stock is valued for federal estate tax purposes as if that right were nonlapsing. See Example 6, Conference Report (OBRA '90).

Section 2704 applies if the individual holding such right and members of the family control the corporation, as control is defined in Section 2701(b)(2). However, in this case, "family member" includes the spouse of the individual, ancestors and lineal descendants of the individual or spouse, brothers and sisters of the individual, and spouses of any of them.[22]

Under the regulations, the taxable transfer is measured by the reduction in value of all interests in the entity owned by the holder immediately before the lapse unless attributable to other causes. The lapse of the right is deemed to be a transfer subject to transfer tax, at date of lapse, based on the difference between the value of all interests in the entity held by the individual before the lapse and after the lapse.[23] This provision is so broad that any shift of equity or growth could be deemed a lapse, and any contingency which results in lapse of payment, voting, or other rights could have transfer tax consequences.

A voting right is defined as the right to vote on any matter, and in the case of a partnership, includes the rights of management held by general partners.[24] A liquidation right is the right to compel the entity to acquire all or a portion of the holder's interest, including a right arises solely by reason of the fact the holder owns sufficient voting rights to compel liquidation.[25]

A lapse occurs whenever a presently exercisable right is restricted or eliminated. However, a transfer with respect to a liquidation right is not a lapse of a liquidation right unless the transfer eliminates the right of that individual to compel liquidation of an interest other than the interest conferring the power.

Example. D, who owns 84% of the voting common stock of corporation, gives 14% each to three children. Even though this reduces D's voting rights to 42%, and D loses control, this is not a lapse covered by the statute.

Example. Assume D is both the general and a limited partner in a family partnership. As general partner, D can compel liquidation. If D transfers her general partnership interest, she can no longer compel liquidation, but since the successor general partner has the same voting rights, there is no lapse as to D's rights as a general partner. However, there is a lapse as to D's rights as a limited partner, since D has lost the power to compel liquidation of the limited partnership interest, which was an interest other than the interest conferring the power.

A lapse of rights in a retained interest valued under Section 2701 is not subject to Section 2704.[26] Nor is the inability of the family to liquidate after the transfer where the holder could have liquidated before the transfer.[27] If the lapsed right may be restored upon the occurrence of a future event not within the control of the family, there is no lapse so long as the right could be restored.[28]

A voting or liquidation right may arise by state law, corporate charter or bylaws, an agreement, or in any other manner. Similarly, a lapse may occur by reason of state law, corporate charter or by-laws, agreement, or any other means. However, if the lapse is caused only by a change in state law, it is not subject to Section 2704.[29]

In addition, an "applicable restriction," which is any restriction which effectively limits the ability of the corporation or partnership to liquidate, is to be disregarded if the transferor and family members control the entity, and the restriction either lapses after the transfer or can be removed by the transferor or family members, individually or collectively.[30] However, the term does not include a commercially reasonable restriction imposed in connection with financing if furnished as either a debt or equity contribution by an unrelated person (as defined by Code section 267(b), excluding banks as defined by Code section 581) for trade or business operations.[31]

An "applicable restriction" is a limitation on liquidation of an entity that is more restrictive than state law. It is only a restriction if it will either lapse or can be removed by the transferor, transferor's estate, or members of the family. Any buy-sell agreement, option, or restriction covered by Section 2703 (see Chapter 1), is not subject to Section 2704.[32]

Example. D owns all of the preferred stock of corporation, and can compel liquidation after 10 years. All common stock is owned by children. If D transfers the preferred stock to the children, it is valued without regard to the restriction on liquidation (i.e., as if the right to compel liquidation was immediately exercisable).

IMPLICATIONS AND ISSUES IN COMMUNITY PROPERTY STATES

In a community property state, the business or investment assets may be co-owned by both husband and wife as community property. If so, both must participate in the transaction, and the preferred stock or partnership interests will be held by them as community property. If the common stock or partnership interests are transferred to the children by gift, they may be separate property of the children, depending on state law. However, it is possible the spouses of the children will obtain a community interest in the transferred property; particularly, if they purchase the stock, its status as community or separate property will depend on what assets they use to pay for it.

QUESTIONS AND ANSWERS

Question — Client owns 100% of the common stock of X Corporation, which has been valued at $1,000,000. It has been suggested that he recapitalize the corporation to create voting preferred stock with a par and liquidation value of $1,000,000, and a noncumulative preferred dividend of 8% per annum, and nonvoting nopar common stock. He would then transfer the common stock to his children. What are the gift tax consequences?

Answer — Under Section 2701, unless an election is made, the gift will be $1,000,000. The transaction falls within Section 2701, assuming none of the interests involved have a readily ascertainable market value. The common stock is being transferred to "family members," children of the transferor. The transferor has an "applicable retained interest," the preferred stock. It consists of a "distribution right," i.e., the right to the preferred dividend, and a "liquidation right." Under Section 2701, the liquidation right is valued at zero. The distribution right is also valued at zero unless it is a "qualified payment." Since a qualified payment is the right to a fixed cumulative preferred dividend, this dividend is not a qualified payment. As a result, under the "subtraction" method required by Section 2701, the gift is the entire value of the enterprise, $1,000,000, less the value of the applicable retained interest, zero.

However, the transferor could elect to treat the noncumulative dividend as if it were cumulative. If so, it is a qualified payment and can be valued and subtracted from the value of the enterprise to determine the taxable gift.

The regulations indicate the qualified payment is to be valued under general valuation principals, that is, at fair market value.

Question—In 1991, parent transferred undivided interests in the family farm, which was worth $1,000,000, to her children, and simultaneously, parent and children formed a family partnership into which they transferred their respective interests in the property. Parent, who was the general partner, received a capital interest of $1,000,000, and is entitled to an annual distribution of partnership profits of up to $80,000 before any profits are distributed to children. This right to distributions is cumulative, and if not made in one year, carries over to the next. If the partnership liquidates, the parent will receive the first $1,000,000 in liquidation proceeds, and any additional proceeds will be distributed to the children. The children receive limited partnership interests and are entitled to share in any partnership profits and liquidation proceeds not distributed to the parent.

Ten years later, parent dies. No partnership distributions were ever made to parent. Under the terms of the decedent's will, her partnership interest, and all rights to distributions, passes to her surviving spouse outright. The farm was worth $1,500,000 at date of death. What are the estate tax consequences?

Answer — The initial formation of the partnership was covered by Section 2701, and the gift tax on the transfers of interests in the farm to the children would be computed by subtracting from the value of the farm in 1991 the value of the right to partnership distributions, which would be "qualified payments."

However, since the qualified payments were never made, they constitute "cumulative unpaid distributions" under the statute. When a "taxable event" occurs, in this case the death of the parent, the value of those unpaid distributions is subject to the applicable federal transfer tax, in this case the federal estate tax. However, since the right to the payments passes to the surviving spouse, the tax will be deferred until the surviving spouse either dies or otherwise transfers the interest.

Note several other points. The maximum amount that could have been taxed in the estate would have been the total growth of the enterprise, $500,000. Also, since there is a four year grace period during which qualified payments can be made to avoid the transfer tax at death, the full unpaid amount may not be subject to tax. When the partnership was formed, parent could have elected to value the qualified payment at zero and pay gift tax on the full value of the farm, $1,000,000. If she had done so,

there would be no additional tax on the cumulative unpaid amounts.

Also note that the decedent's estate would in any case include the value of her capital interest in the partnership, arguably worth at least $1,000,000, and her right to unpaid distributions, since those are valuable property rights owned by her estate. The regulations indicate there will be no double tax on the unpaid distributions.

Question — A family corporation is owned equally by two shareholders, parent and child. In 1991, the corporation is recapitalized, with parent and child each receiving voting preferred stock with a fixed liquidation value and a cumulative preferred dividend, and the child also receiving nonvoting common stock. The child then makes a gift of the nonvoting common stock to grandchild. Assume the preferred stock issued to the parent was equal to the full value of his interest in the corporation. What are the potential transfer tax consequences, if any, to the parent?

Answer—The parent did not make a taxable transfer when the corporation was recapitalized, since he received full value for his interest in the business and made no gift to the grandchild. However, since parent is an "applicable family member," he or his estate may be vulnerable to a later transfer tax.

In computing the taxable gift to grandchild under the subtraction method, the child may subtract from the value of the corporation the right to all "qualified payments," in this case, the right to cumulative preferred dividends held by both the parent and child. If this is done, the parent is subject to the rules for transfer tax on cumulative unpaid distributions, i.e., if the corporation does not pay the dividends, there will be a gift or estate tax to parent on a lifetime or deathtime transfer of his preferred stock. As a result, even though the parent was not even a party to the taxable gift, he or his estate can incur a substantial transfer tax liability.

Note that the parent can avoid this result if he elects not to have his right to the preferred dividend treated as a qualified payment. If he does so, the child cannot subtract its value for gift tax purposes, and there would be no later transfer tax to the parent under the cumulative unpaid distribution rules.

Question — Client proposes to form a family partnership to operate a business enterprise. He will retain a general partnership interest and a limited partnership interest, and sell limited partnership interests to his children for their full value. All partners will participate proportionately in partnership profits and the proceeds of liquidation. Will either Section 2701 or 2704 apply to him?

Answer — Since the facts indicate all partners will share proportionately in both profits and growth, the gift tax consequences of this transactions are not subject to the provisions of Section 2701. As a result, since client sold interests to his children for their full value, there are no gift tax consequences. Note that limitations affecting liability and management do not bring the transaction under Section 2701, unless there is a provision for lapse of voting rights and management rights, or the transferor or applicable family member can alter the liability of the transferee partners. Such was not the case here.

However, if client dies or transfers his general partnership interest, he loses the power to compel liquidation of the partnership. Under Section 2704, this would be treated as a lapse of his power to compel liquidation of his limited partnership interest, subject to gift tax if he makes a lifetime transfer of his general partnership interest, or estate tax on his death.

Footnote References

Freezing Techniques

1. IRC Sec. 2701(e)(1).
2. Reg. §25.2701-1(b)(2).
3. Reg. §25.2701-1(b)(1).
4. IRC Sec. 2701(a)(4)(B)(i).
5. IRC Sec. 2701(c)(2).
6. IRC Sec. 2701(c)(1)(B).
7. IRC Secs. 2701(b)(2), 2701(e)(3).
8. IRC Sec. 2701(e)(2).
9. Reg. §25.2701-2(b)(1).
10. Reg. §25.2702-2(b)(2).
11. Reg. §25.2702-1(b)(4).
12. IRC Sec. 2701(c)(2)(C).
13. Reg. §25.2701-2(a)(3).
14. IRC Sec. 2701(a)(1).
15. IRC Sec. 2701(a)(3)(A).
16. IRC Sec. 2701(a)(4).
17. IRC Sec. 2701(d).
18. IRC Sec. 2701(d)(3)(B).
19. IRC Sec. 2701(d)(4).
20. Reg. §25.2701-4(c)(5).
21. Reg. §25.2701-5.
22. IRC Sec. 2704(c).
23. Reg. §25.2704-1(d).
24. Reg. §25.2704-1(a)(2)(iv).
25. Reg. §25.2704-1(a)(2)(v).
26. Reg. §25.2704-1(c)(2)(ii).
27. Reg. §25.2704-1(c)(2)(i).
28. Reg. §25.2704-1(a)(3).
29. Reg. §§25.2704-1(c)(2)(i)(B); 25.2704-1(c)(2)(iii).
30. IRC Sec. 2704(b).
31. Reg. §25.2704-2(b).
32. Reg. §25.2704-2(b).

Chapter 14

GENERATION-SKIPPING TRANSFERS

WHAT IS IT?

A generation-skipping transfer (GST) is any transfer of property by gift or at death, to any person who, under federal tax law, is assigned to a generation that is two or more generations below that of the transferor (i.e., one or more generations below the transferor is skipped). In the case of family members, this means, for example, that transferor's grandchildren and great nieces and nephews would be assigned two generations below the transferor. Such persons who are two or more generations below that of the transferor are defined as skip persons.

WHEN IS THE USE OF SUCH A DEVICE INDICATED?

The generation-skipping transfer was traditionally used as a device to save federal gift and estate tax by keeping property out of the taxable estates of the members of the intermediate generation. The beneficiary could be trustee, have all the income, invade the principal for needs and control the distribution of the property as long as the beneficiary did not have a general power of appointment (i.e., the power to appoint the property to the beneficiary or the beneficiary's estate, or creditors of either). Now the generation-skipping transfer tax considerations of such transfers must also be considered.

There are three levels where generation-skipping transfer techniques are useful. First, where a client stands to inherit a substantial estate from a parent and already has a substantial estate of his own, a generation-skipping trust would be set up for the parent's property for the benefit of the client. A generation-skipping trust would allow the client-beneficiary the use and enjoyment of the inherited property, together with protection against creditors, divorce courts or bankruptcy. The amount subject to the $1 million GST exemption will also be excluded from the beneficiary's already substantial estate. Although the client's parent may pay gift or estate tax, the client does not pay estate tax or GST tax on the exempt inherited property at death. Furthermore, no estate tax or GST tax is paid by the client's children or future issue depending on the term allowed for the trust.

Secondly, a generation-skipping trust may be used where parents wish to minimize transfer taxes in a child's estate but

still give the child the use and benefit of the property, or where the parents wish to protect the property from a spendthrift child, or from being subject to loss through a child's divorce or bankruptcy. In these situations, a generation-skipping trust would be set up to provide income to the child for life, but with the principal being preserved for subsequent distribution to grandchildren. The trust can continue through the grandchildren's lives (and for great-grandchildren as well), avoiding transfer tax in each generation, subject only to the limitation on the maximum life of a trust under state law. In the case of many estates, however, the generation skip occurs as a result of the death of a member of the intermediate generation before such member receives full ownership of the gift or inheritance, as when a trust is provided for a child until he attains age 30, and that child dies before attaining age 30 leaving grandchildren surviving.

Thirdly, a client may wish to make direct transfers to a grandchild or other skip person for the beneficiary's education, support or enjoyment, or in order to avoid tax in the estate of the intervening generation. Gifts that immediately benefit grandchildren will generally be subject to the GST tax unless they qualify for the $1,000,000 per donor generation-skipping exemption or the $10,000 per donor per donee annual exclusion.

WHAT ARE THE REQUIREMENTS?

There is no special form of generation-skipping transfer. It could simply be a gift or bequest to a skip person, or the establishment of a trust in which distributions will or may be made to a skip person. All that is really required to trigger the device is any gift or transfer of property at death which will or may benefit a skip person.

HOW IT IS DONE — AN EXAMPLE

An intervivos trust is usually used to establish the method of trust distribution's during life as well as to avoid probate of trust assets at death. In many cases, the trust is created as a receptacle for lifetime gifts and to receive assets at the death of the donors. The trust instrument would provide for the creation of two separate trusts. An amount equal to the child's share of the donor's $1 million GST tax exemption would be allocated to one trust (the exempt trust). The other trust would be the nonexempt trust for GST purposes. For optimal results, planners prefer to fund the exempt trust with assets with the greatest growth potential. This concept allows the maximum amount of assets to pass to future generations without transfer tax because once the exemption is allocated to the trust, the growth is also exempt.

When a trust is created to receive both current gifts and assets from the donors' estates, a limited power of appointment is often given to some nonbeneficiary (sometimes called a "trust protector") to be able to alter the trust to deal with changes in tax law or other circumstances.

The exempt and nonexempt trusts are established so that they have GST tax inclusion ratios of zero and one respectively (i.e., no trust is partially exempt and partially nonexempt). When the exempt trust is established with an inclusion ration of zero, that trust maintains its 100% immunity from GST tax as long as there are no later additions of nonexempt property.

In a family intervivos trust with distributions to the survivor's trust, a bypass trust and a QTIP trust, assuming that the donors have made no taxable lifetime gifts, the person making the allocation would typically make an allocation of the GST tax exemption of the first trustor to die to the bypass trust using up $600,000 of the exemption. If the remaining assets exceed $400,000, the trust instrument would instruct the executor to split the QTIP into two separate trusts. $400,000 would be placed in an exempt QTIP trust, to which the remaining $400,000 of GST exemption would be allocated. The rest of the assets would go to the other separate QTIP trust and would be fully nonexempt. On the federal estate tax return, the executor would make a "reverse QTIP election," so that the $400,000 of property in the exempt QTIP would be treated as passing from the first spouse to die for purposes of the GST tax.) Use of the reverse QTIP election, permits the full use of the $1 million exemption of the first donor spouse to die without incurring any gift or estate tax at the first death.

The trust instrument would also instruct the trustee to make any distributions of principal to the surviving spouse first from the nonexempt trust. This is because there is no GST tax on distributions to nonskip persons such as spouses. In addition the trustee would also be instructed to pay any taxes attributable to the QTIP trusts first from the nonexempt QTIP, upon the death of the surviving trustor. When the surviving spouse dies, that spouse's executor would allocate the spouse's $1 million exemption to other trust property that was not already exempt under the first spouse's exemption.

Many practitioners advise clients to pay estate tax on $400,000 of assets at the first death, eliminating the need for separate accounting and income tax returns for two separate QTIP trusts for the lifetime of the surviving spouse.

After the death of both donors, the exempt bypass and QTIP trusts, together with up to $1,000,000 of assets from the surviving spouse (to which that spouse's GST exemption would be allocated) could be held in trust for the children for their lives, and then held in trust for the grandchildren, and then held for the great grandchildren, subject to the rule against perpetuities. There would be no tax imposed (either estate tax or GST tax) at the death of each successive generation.

The provisions of the trust for the children would provide that the trust for their benefit be divided/maintained in exempt and nonexempt trusts for GST purposes. The children are typically given the income from both the exempt and nonexempt trusts. The children are also usually given a nongeneral power of appointment over the assets of the exempt trust.

The nongeneral power of appointment allows the children the flexibility to appoint the principal of the trust in different proportions either to whomever they like or sometimes only to a specified class of beneficiaries, usually their own children or perhaps a life estate to their spouse. Since the power is not a general power of appointment, the property is not included in their estates. In addition, since the original donor's GST tax exemption was allocated to the exempt trust, when the trust passes to the grandchildren or their issue (all classified as skip persons), it is exempt from generation-skipping tax. Thus, the exempt trust passes from the parents, through the children's generation, to future generations free from estate and GST tax.

The trust instrument typically grants the children a general power of appointment over the principal of the nonexempt trust so that the nonexempt trust will be purposely included in their estate for estate tax purposes. This avoids the GST tax that would otherwise be imposed at the maximum estate tax rate (because the nonexempt trust will pass to skip persons). By having the property included in the child's estate for estate tax purposes, it is possible to take advantage of the child's $600,000 unified transfer credit and graduated tax rates. The nonexempt trust can also be drafted to allow the child to make gifts to his or her issue (or others) under the $10,000 annual gift tax exclusion.

The same exempt/nonexempt structure would continue to apply to the trusts as they pass to the grantor's grandchildren, great-grandchildren and so on, the object being to preserve the exempt trust from transfer tax at each generation level.

WHAT ARE THE TAX IMPLICATIONS?

Generation-Skipping Transfer Tax

General Rules

A flat rate tax equal to the highest gift and estate tax bracket (currently 55 percent) is imposed on every generation-skipping transfer.[1] Essentially the generation-skipping transfer tax (GSTT) will affect transfers to grandchildren or others in the grandchildren's or younger generations. The tax applies to outright transfers and to transfers in trust or arrangements having substantially the same effect as a trust, such as transfers involving life estates and remainders, estates for years, and insurance and annuity contracts.[2]

Every individual is allowed to make aggregate transfers of up to $1 million either during lifetime or at death, that will be wholly exempt from the GST tax.[3]

Essentially the GST tax rate is equal to the maximum gift and estate tax rate at the time a *taxable distribution, taxable termination*, or *direct skip* is made.[4] Technically, the *applicable rate* is the maximum federal estate tax rate multiplied by a fraction that the Code calls an *inclusion ratio*. This inclusion ratio is described below.

The *taxable amount*, which is the amount multiplied by the applicable rate mentioned in the preceding paragraph, depends on whether the transfer is considered a taxable distribution, a taxable termination, or a direct skip.

Generation Assignment

For GST purposes, all persons are assigned to a generation. In the case of related persons, this is done by reference to the ancestral chain relating back to grandparents of the transferor, except that spouses of the transferor or a descendent are always assigned to the same generation as the transferor or descendant. Unrelated persons are assigned to the transferor's generation if such person is not more than 12½ years younger than the transferor, otherwise unrelated persons are assigned to succeeding generations on the basis of 25 years for each generation (i.e., first younger generation — 12½ to 37½ years younger than transferor). Where the transferee is an entity (i.e., estate, trust, partnership, or corporation), individuals who own beneficial interests in the entity are assigned to generations.[5]

Where persons are initially assigned to generations under the rules just discussed, it is possible that subsequent events will result in generation reassignment. For example, upon a taxable transfer to succeeding generations of skip persons, such as grandchildren and great-grandchildren, each transfer is subject to tax, but upon each successive transfer, the transferor is assigned to one lower generation. This is to prevent the imposition of the GST tax twice on transfers to persons in the same generation.[6]

In the case of direct skips only (defined below), if a grandchild's parent who is a lineal descendant of the transferor or transferor's spouse is deceased, the grandchild and all succeeding generations move up one generation.[7]

Skip Persons

A person assigned two or more generations below the transferor is a "skip person." A trust may be a skip person if all beneficiaries holding interests in the trust are skip persons, or no person holds an interest in the trust, but no distributions could be made to "nonskip persons." If a trust is a skip person, its beneficiaries are not assigned to a generation.[8]

Solely for GSTT purposes, a person holds an "interest" in a trust or trust equivalent if he or she is entitled to receive current nondiscretionary distributions of income or corpus, or is a permissible current recipient of income or corpus and is not a qualified charity.[9]

Taxable Distribution

A taxable distribution is any distribution of income or corpus from a trust to a skip person that is not otherwise subject to estate or gift tax.[10] For instance, a distribution from a trust to a grandson of the grantor would be to a skip person. Likewise, if a mother creates a trust providing distributions of income or principal to her daughter or granddaughter at the discretion of the trustee, a distribution from that trust to the granddaughter is a taxable distribution. A distribution from one trust to a second trust would be considered a transfer to a skip person if all interests in the second trust were held by skip persons.

The taxable amount in the case of a taxable distribution is the net value of the property received by the distributee less any consideration he paid. In other words, the taxable amount is what the distributee received, reduced by (1) any expenses incurred by him in connection with the determination, collection, or refund of the GST tax, and (2) any consideration paid for the distribution. The transferee is obligated to pay the GST tax in a taxable distribution. If the trust itself pays the tax for the transferees, the payment will be treated as an additional taxable distribution.[11]

The tax levied upon a taxable distribution is *tax inclusive*. That means the amount subject to tax includes (1) the property *and* (2) the GST tax itself.

Example. If a trustee makes a taxable distribution of $10,000 of trust income to a grandchild, the tax would be $5,500 (if paid by the grandchild). The grandchild will net only $4,500.

Taxable Termination

A taxable termination is essentially the termination by death, lapse of time, release of a power, or otherwise of an interest in property held in a trust resulting in skip persons holding all the interests in the trust. For instance, if Alan leaves a life income to his son, Sam, with a remainder to his granddaughter, Gina, the son's death terminates his life interest in trust property and it then passes to Gina, a skip person. A taxable termination occurs on the date of the son's death. A taxable termination cannot occur as long as at least one nonskip person has a present interest in the property. However, nominal interests are disregarded in determining whether a person has an interest in a trust if a significant purpose for their creation is to postpone or avoid a GST tax.[12] Furthermore, there is no taxable termination if an estate or gift tax is imposed on the nonskip individual (the son in this example) at termination.

The taxable amount in the case of a taxable termination is the value of all property involved less (1) a deduction for any expenses, debts, and taxes (other than the GST tax) generated by the property, and (2) any consideration paid by the transferee. If one or more taxable terminations with respect to the same trust occur at the same time as a result of the death of an individual, the executor may elect to value all the taxable termination property under federal estate tax alternate valuation rules. The trustee (broadly defined to mean the person in actual or constructive possession of the GST property) is responsible for the payment of the tax in a taxable termination.

The tax payable upon a taxable termination is *tax inclusive*. The tax is imposed as if a transfer were made one generation down and at that individual's death the tax was levied. The transfer is tax inclusive because, as with the taxable distribution, the property subject to the transfer includes the generation-skipping tax itself.

Example: Assume $1 million is placed into an irrevocable trust for the benefit of the grantor's daughter for life with remainder to his granddaughter. At the daughter's death in 1992, a taxable termination occurs. Assume no exemptions are claimed. The tax is 55 percent of $1 million, or $550,000. It must be paid out of property

passing to the granddaughter. Therefore, the granddaughter nets only $450,000.

Direct Skips

A direct skip is a transfer subject to an estate or gift tax made to a skip person.

A gift from an individual to his grandchild is a direct skip. A direct skip can also occur when an individual makes a transfer to a trust if all the beneficiaries of the trust are skip persons. Therefore, an individual who creates an irrevocable trust for the benefit of his grandchildren would be making a direct skip upon funding the trust.

In the case of a transfer to grandchildren (of the grantor, the grantor's spouse, or the grantor's former spouse), a person will not be considered a skip person if, at the time of the transfer, his parent (the grantor's child or the grantor's spouse's or former spouse's child) is dead. Instead of treating that person as a grandchild, that person will be treated as a child. His children (the grantor's great grandchildren) will then be treated as if they were the grantor's grandchildren.

The taxable amount in the case of a direct skip is the value of the property or interest in property (including the current right to receive income or corpus or power of appointment) received by the transferee, reduced by any consideration paid by the transferee. The transferor (the decedent in the case of a death time transfer or the donor in the case of a lifetime transfer) is responsible for payment of the GST tax in the case of a direct skip.

The tax in a direct skip is *tax exclusive*. In other words, the tax is paid by the transferor or the estate and the taxable amount does not include the amount of generation-skipping tax. Here the tax is similar to that which would have applied had the transfer been made to a member of the skipped generation who then immediately used the property (net of the transfer tax) to make a second gift to the ultimate recipient (typically the grantor's grandchild) and to pay the gift tax. Note that the amount of the gift tax is not included in the taxable value of the gift. Therefore, the tax can be no higher than the gift tax that would have been paid by the intervening generation level (the grantor's son or daughter in most cases) had that individual been in the top gift tax bracket and made a gift to the skip beneficiary.

Example: A grandfather makes a lifetime gift of $1 million to his granddaughter in 1992. Assume no exemptions are claimed. The grandparent must pay a generation-skipping tax of $550,000. But the tax is paid, not out of the gift, but out of additional assets of the grandparent. The grandchild will therefore net the full $1 million.

Exemptions and Exclusions

An important exemption is the $1 million per donor/decedent exemption from the GST tax. For a married couple, each spouse has a $1 million exemption. A gift subject to the GST tax which is "split" by the spouses will be treated as having been made half by each spouse, and each spouse can use some (or all) of his or her $1 million exemption to avoid the GST tax.[13]

Certain transfers are excluded from the definition of the term generation-skipping transfer. Transfers excluded from the definition include

- certain transfers that, if made by gift, would qualify as gift tax free under the Code provisions as direct payments made for the donee's educational or medical expenses.[14]

- transfers that pass gift tax free under the annual exclusion rules. Transfers in trust will not qualify for this exemption unless (1) no portion of the trust's income or principal can be distributed to or used for the benefit of anyone other than the grandchild as long as the grandchild is alive, and (2) if the grandchild dies prior to the termination of the trust, the assets of the trust must be includable in the grandchild's estate.[15]

- certain transfers that have already been subjected to the GST tax in which the transferee was in the same or lower generation as the present transferee.[16]

Unless the governing instrument directs otherwise (by specific reference to the GST tax), the GST tax is charged to the property constituting the transfer.[17]

Property subject to the GST tax must be valued as of the time of the generation-skipping transfer. However, where the tax involves a direct skip (for example, from grandparent to grandchild), if the property is included in the transferor's estate, its value for GST tax purposes is the same as its value for federal estate tax purposes, including elections for the alternate valuation date or special-use valuation.

Computing the Tax

A $1 million exemption is allowed in computing the tax actually payable. Because married individuals making a lifetime transfer can elect to treat the transfer as if made one-half by each, the $1 million exemption can be doubled to $2

million. To understand how this exemption works and how the tax is actually calculated, it is first necessary to examine the "inclusion ratio."

The inclusion ratio procedure is in two parts. Compute the *applicable fraction* as follows:

1. State the portion of the $1 million GST tax exclusion allocated to the trust or direct skip (every individual is allowed a GST tax exemption of $1 million). This exemption may be allocated by that individual (or the executor) among any property that is transferred. If this allocation is not made on or before the estate tax return is due, it will be made automatically under statutory provisions. Once made, the allocation is irrevocable. $_____

2. (a) State the value of the property transferred to the trust (or involved in the direct skip). $_____

   (b) State the total of any federal estate or state death tax actually recovered from the trust attributable to such property. $_____

   (c) State the amount of any charitable deduction allowed under estate or gift tax law with respect to the property. $_____

   (d) Add (b) and (c). $_____

3. Subtract (d) from (a). $_____

4. Divide the line 1 exemption by line 3. This is the "applicable fraction." $_____

Once you have computed the applicable fraction, you then find the inclusion ratio. The inclusion ratio is 1 minus the applicable fraction (line 4).

An exception to the above computation is for a charitable lead annuity trust. The computation for transfers to such a trust after October 13, 1987 is as follows:

$$\frac{\text{GST exclusion allocated to the transfer, increased by the interest rate used in computing the lead interest for the number of years of the term}}{\text{Actual value of property after the lead interest terminates}}$$

If you allocate GST exclusion equal to the remainder interest and if the trust performs as expected by the government valuation tables, your fraction would be $^1/_1$. However, it is obviously impossible to know in advance how the trust will perform, so allocation of the GST for a charitable lead annuity trust is a guessing game.

After computing the inclusion ratio, you then multiply that number by the maximum federal estate tax rate to arrive at the applicable rate.

The total GST tax due is determined by multiplying the taxable amount by the applicable rate.[18] (See Figure 14.1.)

A credit for state death taxes will be allowed against the GST tax if the transfer (other than a direct skip) occurs at the same time and as a result of an individual's death. The credit is the lower of (a) the amount of any GST tax actually paid to a state under its laws or (b) 5 percent of the GST tax payable to the federal government.

The worksheet at Figure 14.2, illustrates the entire process for a transfer other than a charitable lead annuity trust.

Figure 14.3 shows the impact of the GST tax when the taxable event occurs, not at the time assets are placed into the trust, but at a later date (20 years in this example).

Liability for Payment of GST Tax

If the transfer is a taxable distribution, the GST tax is on the amount received by the transferee, less expenses relating to the determination of the GST tax, and the transferee pays it. If the transfer is a taxable termination or partial termination, the GST tax is on the value of the property in which the interest terminates, less expenses "attributable" to the property, and the trustee pays it. In the case of direct skips (other than a direct skip from a trust), the GST tax is on the value of the property received, and the transferor pays it.[19]

Special Provisions

There are special provisions for the following:

- QTIP property (see below)

Figure 14.1

		COMPUTING THE GENERATION SKIPPING TRANSFER TAX A SIMPLIFIED WORKSHEET	
Step 1	List	Value of property transferred	$4,000,000
Step 2	List	Exemption allocated to transfer	$1,000,000
Step 3	List	State & fed tx paid on transfer	$600,000
Step 4	List	Gift or estate tax charitable deductions allowed on transfer	$0
Step 5	Add	Steps 3 and 4	$600,000
Step 6	Subtract	Step 5 from Step 1	$3,400,000
Step 7	Divide	Step 2 by Step 6	
		This is the "applicable fraction"	0.2941
Step 8	Subtract	Step 7 from one (1)	
		This is the "inclusion ratio"	0.7059
Step 9	Multiply	Step 8 by 55%	0.3882
		This is the "Applicable rate"	
Step 10		Assuming no growth, the GST tax is:	$1,552,941

This computation assumes:
(A) Transfer of $4,000,000
(B) Federal and state death taxes of $600,000
(C) No charitable deductions
(D) Use of full $1,000,000 exemption.

Illustration Courtesy of NumberCruncher Software.

Figure 14.2

		GENERATION SKIPPING TRANSFER TAX SIMPLIFIED WORKSHEET	
Step 1	List	Value of property transferred	_____
Step 2	List	Exemption allocated to transfer	_____
Step 3	List	State & fed tx paid on transfer	_____
Step 4	List	Gift or estate tax charitable deductions allowed on transfer	_____
Step 5	Add	Steps 3 and 4	_____
Step 6	Subtract	Step 5 from Step 1	_____
Step 7	Divide	Step 2 by Step 6 This is the "applicable fraction"	_____
Step 8	Subtract	Step 7 from one (1) This is the "inclusion ratio"	_____
Step 9	Multiply	Step 8 by 55% This is the "applicable rate"	_____
Step 10	Multiply	Step 1 by Step 9	$_____

Courtesy of Leimberg and LeClair, Inc.

- taxation of multiple skips

- basis adjustments (In general, basis is increased by an amount equal to the portion of the GST tax actually imposed which is attributable to the appreciation of the property transferred.[20])

- disclaimers (A disclaimer that results in property passing to a person at least two generations below that of the original transferor will result in a GST tax. For instance, assume a daughter disclaimed a bequest from her mother.

As a result of that disclaimer, certain property passes to the mother's granddaughter. The GST tax would be imposed on the transfer — in addition to the federal estate tax.)

- administration

- return requirements (The GST tax return must be filed by the person liable for the payment of the generation-skipping tax. In the case of a direct skip other than a direct skip from a trust, the return must be filed on or before the

Figure 14.3

	PROJECTING THE ULTIMATE GST TAX		
Less	Initial value of assets		$4,000,000
Equals	Federal and state death taxes		$600,000
	Net value of assets		$3,400,000
Input:	Assumed growth rate (net after tax)	.06	
Input:	Years until taxable event	20	

		Future Value	GST Tax
At	.040	$7,449,819	$2,892,020
At	.050	$9,021,212	$3,502,034
At	.060	$10,904,261	$4,233,034
At	.070	$13,156,927	$5,107,519
At	.080	$15,847,254	$6,151,904

Courtesy of NumberCruncher Software.

The Tools and Techniques of Estate Planning

due date of the applicable gift or estate tax return. In other cases, the GST tax return must be filed on or before the 15th day of the 4th month after the close of the taxable year in which the transfer occurs.)

Multiple-trust skips are taxed more than once. But if a direct skip is directly to a great grandchild, two taxes are not imposed.

Section 303 can be used to make protected redemptions of stock to pay a GST tax.

Code Section 6166, which allows for installment payments of federal estate tax, allows deferral of the tax generated under a GST because of direct skips resulting at death.

Planning for GST Tax

The generation-skipping tax may be imposed *in addition to* any estate or gift tax that may also be due because of the transfer. It appears that in many cases the total cost of making a property transfer can exceed the value of the gift.

Example 1. Assume a grandfather in a 55 percent gift tax bracket makes a gift in 1992. Assume the value of his gift is $2 million, and it is made to a trust for his grandchild. Assume he doesn't allocate any of his $1 million generation-skipping transfer tax exemption to the gift (or has already used the exemption). The generation-skipping transfer tax is $1,100,000 ($2,000,000 x .55). For gift tax purposes, the amount of the gift to the grandson is $2,000,000. The gift tax on the total deemed gift is $1,100,000 ($2,000,000 x .55). The total tax therefore is $2,200,000, which exceeds the value of the gift actually made.

Example 2. Assume a father in a 55 percent federal estate tax bracket establishes a testamentary trust that provides, "to my son for life, then to my grandson." Assume he has already used his $1 million exemption. He leaves $5 million, and the federal estate tax is $2,750,000 ($5,000,000 x .55). That leaves $2,250,000 to provide income for his son. Assume that during the son's lifetime there is no appreciation in the trust. At the son's death, a generation-skipping transfer tax is levied at 55 percent and amounts to $1,347,000 ($2,250,000 x .55). The total tax on the $5 million is therefore $4,097,000 ($2,750,000 plus $1,347,000).

Trust distributions will be subjected to the tax regardless of whether they are made from income or from corpus. Recipients of income subject to the GST tax may take an income tax deduction (similar to the IRD deduction under Code Section 691) for the GST tax imposed on the distribution.

Allocation of the $1 Million GST Exemption

Given the severity of the GST tax, probably the most important planning decision is how to allocate the $1 million exemption.

When all or a portion of a person's $1 million exemption is allocated to a GST in computing the applicable fraction, this has the effect of exempting from the GST tax all future appreciation on the property designated to be exempt. For example, assume a divorced man transfers $1 million in trust for his children and grandchildren. To eliminate the GST tax he allocates his entire $1 million exemption to the trust and avoids any GST tax. All the property in that trust will always be exempt from the GST tax no matter how much it appreciates. (If asset values are rapidly increasing, the more quickly the allocation is made, the better.) But if the individual had allocated only half of his exemption, one-half of all future distributions from the trust to his grandchildren would be subject to the tax as taxable distributions, and one-half of the value of the assets remaining in the trust would be subject to the GST tax when his children die (as taxable terminations). When selecting assets that will be protected by the $1 million exclusion, assets most likely to appreciate should be used. This is because once assets are protected by the exemption, any growth in the value of the assets is beyond the scope of the GST tax. Therefore, it would make great sense to include life insurance on the grantor's life among these assets.

Allocations of the exemption must be made on a timely filed estate tax return. Once made, the election is irrevocable. In addition, proposed regulations now specifically permit allocations of the exemption by formula without requiring taxpayers to specify a dollar amount on the estate tax return.[21]

In addition, a transferor can also make an allocation of the exemption on a gift tax return. Where a transferor makes one or more direct skips during his life, the exemption is automatically allocated to those transfers unless the transferor elects otherwise. When a transferor makes a transfer during his life that is not a direct skip, the exemption is not automatically allocated. The exemption may be allocated at any time on or before the due date of the estate tax return.[22]

As a general rule, the allocation of the exemption will be based on the fair market value of the property on the effective date of allocation. The effective date of allocation for direct skips during the transferor's lifetime is the date of transfer. Where a timely filed gift tax return is filed, the effective date of allocation even for skips other than direct skips is the date of transfer as to which the Form 709 relates. Where late allocations are made during life, the transferor may, solely for purposes of determining the fair market value, elect to treat the allocation as having been made on the first day of the month during which the late allocation is made. However, such an election is not effective with respect to life insurance.[23] Where property is held in trust, the allocation must be made to the entire trust, rather than to specific trust assets.[24]

Where some GST tax exemption is allocated to gifts to pay premiums through an irrevocable life insurance trust, some practitioners suggest deliberately filing "late" so that the allocation will apply to the then reduced value of the policy rather than to the full amount of the premium. Obviously, this involves the risk of the insured dying and requiring the exemption to be allocated on the basis of the face amount of its policy.

As discussed above, taxable distributions and taxable terminations are *tax inclusive* whereas direct skips are *tax exclusive*. Since the government takes less from the donor where the transfer is tax exclusive (direct skip) an allocation to direct skips tends to be wasteful. Therefore in order to maximize the use of one's GST tax exemption it is preferable to allocate it whenever possible to what otherwise would be to taxable distributions and taxable terminations.

Where the executor or other person making the allocation fails to allocate the exemption, it is allocated automatically according to a statutory formula. The statute allocates any unused exemption first to direct skips on a pro rata basis, and then to any trusts from which a taxable distribution or termination could occur after the transferor's death.[25] Thus, the statutory order of allocation tends to be nonoptimal.

Split-gifts and the Reverse QTIP Election

If husband and wife elect to split a gift pursuant to Code section 2513; each is deemed transferor as to one-half.[26] Since each spouse has a $1 million exemption to allocate, this can be extremely important in planning transfers that could be subject to the tax.

Where one spouse makes a gift to the other, either during lifetime or at death, in a form which qualifies for the marital deduction, there is a danger that all or part of the available $1 million exemption of the transferor spouse will be lost. For example, if husband dies and leaves his entire estate in excess of the amount necessary to offset his available unified credit to his wife, this will leave a taxable estate of no more than $600,000 (see Chapter 37). Since his estate can shelter up to $1 million from GST tax, the result is a loss of up to $400,000 of that exemption.

However, where the transfer is in the form of a QTIP trust, even though the transferor spouse or estate claims the full marital deduction, an election can be made solely for GST purposes to treat the QTIP property as if no QTIP election was made at the date of gift or death.[27]

Example. Husband dies, and his total estate is valued at $1 million. His estate plan creates a $400,000 QTIP trust for his wife and a $600,000 credit shelter or bypass trust for his family (see Chapter 37). His executor can elect to apply $600,000 of decedent's $1,000,000 GST exemption to the bypass trust, and by making the "reverse" QTIP election, can apply the remaining $400,000 to the QTIP trust, even though the full marital deduction is claimed for it. The result is that all of husband's estate is completely sheltered from GST tax.

This is an "all or nothing election," i.e., the election to treat the property as if no QTIP election has been made must apply to all qualifying property in the trust. If the total value of the QTIP trust may exceed the available GST exemption, the will or trust should provide for division of the single QTIP trust into two trusts to take advantage of the reverse election.

Example. Wife's taxable estate is valued at $2 million. Her estate plan creates three trusts — a bypass trust of $600,000 to offset the unified credit, one QTIP trust equal in value to any unused GST exemption not otherwise applied by her executor, and a second QTIP trust for the balance of her estate. Assuming the executor applies $600,000 of the $1 million GST exemption to the bypass trust, the first QTIP trust can be established with a value of $400,000, and the remaining GST exemption will be applied to it. This will leave a second QTIP trust of $1 million, which may be subject to GST tax on subsequent distributions or termination. (Of course, the husband could allocate his $1 million GSTT exemption against the second QTIP trust.)

Grantor Retained Income, Annuity, and Unitrust

The GST tax may have an impact on transfers of remainder interests in property where the transferor retains the income, use of, or payment from a trust for a term of years. The subject of grantor retained income trusts, annuity trusts, and unitrusts is covered in Chapter 35. The issue here is the GST tax consequences of such trusts where the remainder interests pass to skip persons.

It is possible to make such a transfer that is complete for gift tax purposes, but which may be includable in the transferor's taxable estate. The question is whether for GST purposes the transfer is made at the date or transfer or the date of death of the transferor. The grantor retained income trust, or now grantor retained annuity trust or grantor retained unitrust is a perfect example.

Example. A transferred $500,000 to an irrevocable trust which provided he would receive $60,000 per year for 10 years, remainder to his grandchildren, and allocated enough of his $1 million GST remainder interest. At his death 8 years later, the trust was worth $1,500,000. Apparently it would all be exempt from GST tax even though at least part of it is includable in A's taxable estate under Code Section 2036.

To eliminate this possibility, the GST rules postpone allocation of the exemption until there is an actual GST transfer, or the transferor dies, or the property would no longer be included in his estate.[28] The law provides that where transferred property would be includable in the transferor's taxable estate under any statute other than Code Section 2035 if the transferor were to die immediately after the transfer, allocation of his $1 million exemption will be postponed during the "estate tax inclusion period," which runs until the earlier of (1) the date the property would no longer be included in the taxable estate, (2) the date there is an actual generation-skipping transfer, or (3) if neither event occurs during the transferor's lifetime, the death of the transferor. If the transfer is a direct skip, allocation is deemed to occur at the end of the estate tax inclusion period. The postponement period is only for purposes of determining the inclusion ratio, and should not affect other exemptions and exclusions, such as the exclusion for direct skips to grandchildren whose parent who is a lineal descendant of the transferor who was alive when the transfer was made but dies before the end of the inclusion period.

Multi-Generational Planning

If the taxable transfer is to succeeding generations of skip persons (i.e., grandchildren and great-grandchildren), each transfer is subject to tax. Upon each successive taxable transfer, the transferor is assigned to one lower generation.[29] However, a transfer to a person more than two generations below the transferor is subject to only one GST tax. This may lead to the establishment of multi-generational trusts which permit distributions at least two generations below the transferor. In the case of older clients, direct skip transfers assigned at least two generations below the transferor should be considered. Compare the result where a trust provides for distributions to children for life, then grandchildren for life, remainder to great-grandchildren. There will be three taxable events — when the trust is created (estate or gift tax), when child dies, (taxable termination), and when the last surviving grandchild dies (taxable termination). Allowing distributions directly to great-grandchildren while child is still alive eliminates one level of tax. Also, direct transfers to grandchildren after child is dead eliminates one level of tax, since the grandchildren move up a generation.

Another approach to multi-generational planning is the establishment of a "dynastic" trust to take advantage of the $1,000,000 GST exemption each for client and spouse that is intended to continue through succeeding generations as long as the law will permit. The actual distribution of these trust assets will be postponed as long as possible, to avoid estate tax as long as possible. Such trusts could last many years, limited only by a legal limitation called the rule against perpetuities, which prohibits the establishment of trusts which last indefinitely. For example, if a trust with a present value of $2,000,000 will continue in existence at least 75 years, and grows at an annual rate of only 4%, it will increase to over $37,000,000. This kind of planning may appeal to clients who have a tradition of preserving wealth in a family through succeeding generations.

Example. Tom and Pam Monson have an estate of $2,600,000 and plan to use life insurance and leveraging to maximize the utilization of their GST tax exemptions for the benefit of their five children and their issue. The transferors make annual gifts to the trust to pay the life insurance premiums. Those annual gifts are exempt from gift tax under the annual exclusion. In addition, the transferors allocate GST exemption to the annual gifts. The premiums are $25,000 per year for 16 years, for a total of $400,000 of premium (assume $200,000 given by each spouse). The insurance is the "survivorship" type which only pays when the survivor dies.

In this situation, although only $400,000 of GST exemption was allocated to the life insurance trust premiums, all of the $1,000,000 of insurance proceeds paid at the second spouse's death will be sheltered from generation-skipping transfer tax.

At Tom's prior death, his estate is divided $600,000 to the bypass trust and $700,000 to the QTIP trust. The QTIP trust is split into $200,000 exempt and $500,000 nonexempt QTIP trusts. Tom's executor allocates $600,000 of his GST exemption to the bypass trust and $200,000 under a reverse QTIP election to the $200,000 QTIP exempt trust.

Pam's executor, at her death, allocates her remaining $800,000 GST exemption to the generation-skipping gift trust for the children into which Tom's $600,000 bypass trust and $200,000 exempt QTIP trust both flow. That trust holds the $1,000,000 life insurance policy. The end result, as shown on Figure 14.4, is that $2,600,000 ends up being exempt from GST tax instead of just $2,000,000 because of the leveraging of life insurance, even assuming a zero growth rate. If the assets in Tom's bypass and exempt QTIP trusts grow in value in the period between Tom's death and Pam's death, the amounts going to the

GST tax exempt trust for the children would be even greater. Furthermore, as the trust continues down to lower generations, assets in the trust avoiding GST and estate tax may compound even further.

Planning to Pay Estate Tax Rather than GST Tax

Almost the reverse of multi-generational planning is planning transfers to trigger federal estate tax in the estates of each succeeding generation. Any transfer from a trust other than a direct skip which is subject to estate or gift tax with respect to a person in the first generation below the grantor is exempt from GST tax. In many situations, since the GST tax is computed at the highest possible federal estate tax rate, it would be preferable to allow the property to pass through the taxable estates of children to grandchildren, since the federal estate tax imposed on the property cannot exceed the GST tax, and in many cases, will be substantially less. This could be accomplished by giving children a general power of appointment over the trust, at least up to the amount needed to put the child in the highest estate tax bracket. While this may result in tax saving, there is always a danger the children will exercise the power and cause the property to pass to someone other than the grandchildren. A possible solution is to give the child only the power to appoint to creditors of his estate, which is a general power of appointment.

Exclusion for Nontaxable Gifts

Gifts which are not taxable by reason of the $10,000 annual exclusion are also exempt from GST tax under most circumstances. The inclusion ratio for nontaxable gifts is zero. This includes gifts not subject to tax under Code Section 2503(b) and 2503(e), and by inference, 2503(c). However, in the case of transfers after March 31, 1988, only nontaxable gifts which are direct skips would have a zero inclusion ratio. In addition, nontaxable gifts to trusts would not have a zero inclusion unless:

1. No portion of the trust could be distributed to a person other than a single beneficiary, and

2. If that beneficiary dies before the trust terminates, the trust assets will be included in his estate.

Figure 14.4

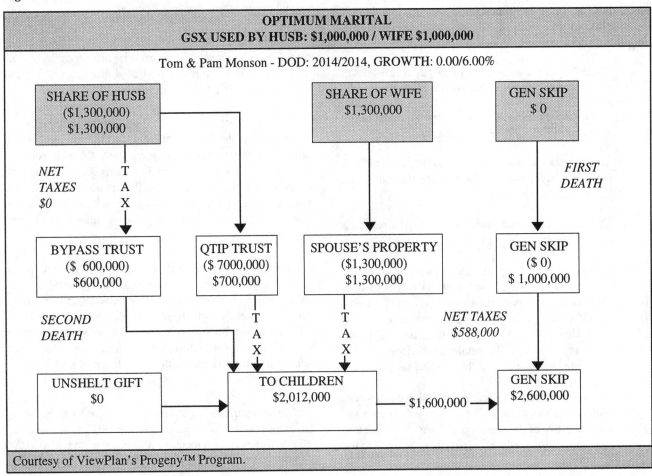

Courtesy of ViewPlan's Progeny™ Program.

It appears that the intent of the limitation for trusts is to eliminate the exclusion of nontaxable gifts to beneficiaries other than skip persons, such as a life income interest to a child. However, the new language is much more limiting, since a trust could only qualify if it has a single beneficiary who is a skip person, or separate shares where each beneficiary is a skip person. What is not clear is the impact on transfers to trusts where beneficiaries who are skip persons have a Crummey invasion power (see Chapters 15 and 36). If the transfer is to the trust, it would not qualify for the exclusion if the trust had beneficiaries who were not skip persons, or the trust was discretionary, or it has multiple beneficiaries. This will have a tremendous impact on irrevocable life insurance trusts where various beneficiaries, including grandchildren or other skip persons, have Crummey withdrawal powers. Premium payments after the effective date of the new law covered by such invasion powers would not be subject to gift tax, but taxable distributions or terminations could trigger GST tax.

To Skip or Not to Skip?

Where there is intentional planning to skip generations, the GST tax cost must be compared to the estate or gift tax cost of transferring the property to the first generation (children) who would then transfer to the second generation (grandchildren). Relative tax cost on a tax inclusive basis should be considered. Assuming a 55% transfer tax rate:

1. Since the gift tax is exclusive of the gift, a 55% gift tax rate amounts to a tax inclusive rate of 35.5%.

2. The estate tax inclusive rate is 55%, since the tax is included in the tax base, i.e., the taxable estate.

3. The GST tax on taxable distributions and terminations is tax inclusive, since it is imposed on the transferee, and the tax inclusive rate is 55%.

4. The GST tax on direct skips is tax exclusive, resulting in a 35.5% tax inclusive rate.

5. However, the GST tax on lifetime gifts is also considered to be a taxable gift, and a gift tax will be paid on the GST tax. Similarly, if a direct skip is made at death, the GST tax will have to be paid from assets which were also subject to the federal estate tax. If the applicable rates of gift or estate tax are 55%, the total tax could exceed 100% of the value of the gift.

6. On the other hand, if a lifetime direct skip gift is made, both the gift tax and GST tax paid will reduce the taxable estate of the donor (in the case of the gift tax, assuming he or she lives at least three years after the transfer).

Other Planning Considerations

As a general rule, the GST tax applies to transfers after October 22, 1986. However, lifetime transfers that were made after September 25, 1985 and were subject to gift tax are also subject to the GST tax. GST tax does not apply to any transfer from a trust that was irrevocable on September 25, 1985, so long as no additions are made after that date. Even if a trust is grandfathered for GST purposes, the trust may become tainted to the extent that there are either actual or constructive additions.

A constructive addition will occur where a general power of appointment is exercised or released, or lapses over a portion of the grandfathered trust. However a constructive addition will not occur where a nongeneral power of appointment is exercised if the exercise will not postpone or suspend the vesting, absolute ownership or power of alienation of the interest for a period longer than allowed by the rule against perpetuities from the date of the creation of the trust. However, the exercise of a power of appointment that validly postpones or suspends the vesting, absolute ownership or power of alienation of an interest in property for a term of years that will not exceed 90 years (measured from the date of creation of the trust) is not considered an exercise that will extend beyond the perpetuities period.[30]

These rules create the opportunity to change the distribution of grandfathered trusts via exercise of nongeneral powers of appointment without adversely affecting its grandfathered (exempt from GST tax) status.

Since irrevocable trusts created before September 26, 1985, are completely exempt from the GST tax system (but only to the extent no additions are made to the trust from that date), it is important not to taint such trusts by adding new property to them. Not only would this create a tax where none existed, but it would also create an administrative nightmare tracking and allocating pre- and post- September 26 assets and appreciation.

Whenever possible, transfer assets from a super rich spouse to a less wealthy spouse. This is because the $1 million exemption is not freely transferable between spouses. But a transfer to a less wealthy spouse doubles the advantage of the $1 million exemption since both spouses can take advantage of it. This is similar to the rationale for making transfers to a spouse in order to achieve the full benefit of both spouses' unified credits.

Greater emphasis should now be placed on protecting irrevocable life insurance trusts from the GST tax by advising clients to consider allocating a portion of the $1,000,000 exemption to each transfer made to the trust. Keep in mind that the use of a portion of the $1,000,000 exemption to shield, say, twenty $50,000 annual premiums protects not only that $1,000,000, but also the future trust corpus generated by the policy proceeds created by those premium payments. Leveraging the $1,000,000 exemption this way (for as long as this technique lasts) may be the single most effective long run means of keeping wealth within the family.

ISSUES AND IMPLICATIONS IN COMMUNITY PROPERTY STATES

Where community property is involved, gift splitting by husbands and wives may not be necessary, nor may it be necessary for one spouse to consider a transfer to the other so that both may use their full $2,000,000 GST exemption. So long as there is at least $2,000,000 in community assets, the full exemptions will be available.

QUESTIONS AND ANSWERS

Question — The will of a client provides for a family trust which authorizes the trustee to make distributions from the trust to the spouse, children, and grandchildren of client. On the death of the spouse, the trust will be distributed to the then surviving children. However, if no children then survive, the share of such a deceased child will pass to his or her issue. Under what circumstances will trust distributions be subject to GST tax?

Answer — Distributions of trust income or principal to the spouse and children will not be subject to GST tax. The spouse is assigned to the same generation as the client, and the children to the first generation below. Thus none of these beneficiaries are skip persons. However, any income or principal distributions to grandchildren will be subject to GST tax, since they are skip persons.

When the spouse dies, distributions of shares of the trust to children will not be subject to GST tax, since the children are not skip persons. However, any distribution of a share of the trust to the issue of a deceased child of the client will be a taxable termination subject to GST tax, since they are skip persons.

Question — Client's will directs that his estate be distributed to a trust which will be divided into separate shares, one for each of his children living at his death, and one for the issue of any child who predeceased the client. Under what circumstances will distributions from this trust be subject to GST tax?

Answer — Under the GST rules, separate shares in a single trust are treated as separate trusts. Distributions to chil-

dren from the trusts created for them are not subject to GST tax, since they are not skip persons. Distributions from the shares set aside for the issue of a child who predeceased the client are also not subject to GST tax. The reason is that the sole beneficiaries of such a share, which is treated as a separate trust, would be skip persons (i.e., grandchildren of the client). When all of the beneficiaries of a trust are skip persons, the trust itself is a skip person. Thus the transfer to the trust is a direct skip. However, the law also provides that when a transfer is a direct skip, but the skip persons are grandchildren of the transferor whose parents have predeceased, those grandchildren move up a generation. As a result, it appears they are no longer skip persons, and distributions to them should not trigger a GST tax.

Question — Under the terms of an irrevocable trust, Trustee is directed to accumulate income until beneficiary attains age 21, and cannot make corpus distributions to beneficiary until that time. For GST purposes, does the beneficiary have an "interest" in the trust?

Answer — Beneficiary has no interest in the trust until attaining age 21. This is because he is not entitled to receive any present distributions of trust income or principal. If he or she is the only beneficiary, there is no person with an interest in the trust. It appears there could be no taxable termination until the beneficiary attains age 21.

Question — Transferor creates a trust providing for an annuity payable to his granddaughter for life, remainder to charity. Assume this is a qualified charitable remainder trust (see Chapter 3). Who is treated as having an interest in the trust?

Answer — Both the granddaughter and the charity have interests in the trust, and the future interest of the charity becomes a present interest for GST tax purposes. This is a special rule which only applies to charities. The transfer to the trust cannot be a direct skip since the charity, which is assigned to the transferor's generation, has an interest. However, distributions to the granddaughter will be taxable distributions to a skip person.

Question — A family trust created under a will is a pot trust for lineal descendants, which will terminate and be distributed to then living lineal descendants when the youngest grandchild attains age 65. Assuming all children of the testator die before the youngest grandchild attains age 65, what are the GST tax consequences?

Answer — Upon the death of the last child, there is a taxable termination, since the only remaining beneficiaries of the trust, grandchildren and possibly their descendants, are skip persons. At this time, the grandchildren will be reassigned to their parent's generation, so that subsequent distributions to them will not be taxed again. But distributions to their descendants will be subject to GST tax.

Question — At date of death, the estate value of assets in decedent's estate is $2 million. The will provides that the executor is to allocate $1 million in assets to a trust based on date of death value. However, the actual value of the assets transferred to the trust at date of allocation has increased from $1 million to $1.3 million. For purposes of computing the exclusion ratio, is the denominator of the fraction $1,000,000 or $1,300,000?

Answer — The denominator of the fraction is the pecuniary amount ($1 million in this example) only if the pecuniary payment of property must be satisfied on a basis that fairly reflects net appreciation or depreciation (between the valuation date and the date of distribution) in all of the assets from which the distribution could have been made. Otherwise the denominator of the fraction would have to be the date of distribution value ($1.3 million in this example).[31]

Question — Transferor conveyed property worth $500,000 to a generation-skipping trust in 1987 and allocated $300,000 of her exemption to it. In 1990, when that property was worth $700,000, she transferred $100,000 cash to the trust, and claimed a $100,000 exemption. What is the inclusion ratio?

Answer — The inclusion ratio is 1 minus

$$\frac{\$100,000 + 60\% \ (700,000) = \$520,000}{\$100,000 + \$700,000 = \$800,000}$$

The 60% represents the nontax portion of the trust before the second transfer, $300,000/$500,000.[32]

Question — Where a preexisting life insurance trust is grandfathered as a pre- September 25, 1985 trust, can gifts to cover premium payments continue without the trust being subject to GST tax?

Answer — No, additional transfers to pay life insurance premiums would be considered additions to the trust. The additions to the trust will result in inclusion of part of the trust for GST tax purposes unless the lifetime exemption is allocated to cover the portion of the trust which is not grandfathered.

Footnote References

Generation-Skipping Transfers

1.   IRC Secs. 2601, 2602. The GST tax rate is not affected by the gift and estate tax 5 percent surcharge on transfers from $10,000,000 to $21,040,000 (the GST tax has no unified credit or lower tax brackets to phase out).
2.   IRC Sec. 2652(b).
3.   IRC Sec. 2631.
4.   IRC Sec. 2641.
5.   IRC Sec. 2651.
6.   IRC Sec. 2653(a).
7.   IRC Sec. 2612(c)(2).
8.   IRC Sec. 2613.
9.   IRC Sec. 2652(c).
10. IRC Sec. 2612(b).
11. IRC Secs. 2622, 2623.
12. IRC Sec. 2652(c)(2); Prop. Reg. §26.2612-1(e)(2)(ii).
13. IRC Sec. 2652(a)(2).
14. IRC Sec. 2611(b).
15. IRC Sec. 2642(c).
16. IRC Sec. 2611(b).
17. IRC Sec. 2603(b).
18. IRC Sec. 2641, 2642.
19. IRC Sec. 2603.
20. IRC Sec. 2654(a).
21. Prop. Reg. §26.2632-1(d).
22. IRC Sec. 2632.
23. Prop. Reg. §26.2642-2(a)(2).
24. Prop. Reg. §26.2632-1.
25. IRC Sec. 2632(c).
26. IRC Sec. 2652(a)(2).
27. IRC Sec. 2652(a)(3).
28. IRC Sec. 2642(f).
29. IRC Sec. 2653(a).
30. Prop. Reg. §26.2652-1(a)(4).
31. Prop. Reg. §26.2642-2(b).
32. IRC Sec. 2642(d).

Chapter 15

GIFTS

WHAT IS IT?

For gift tax purposes a gift can be broadly defined to include a sale, exchange, or other transfer of property from one person (the donor) to another (the donee) without adequate and full consideration in money or money's worth.

In addition to an outright transfer, gifts can take other forms. For example, the forgiveness of a debt, foregone interest on an intra-family interest-free or below market loan, the assignment of the benefits of an insurance policy, or the transfer of property to a trust can also be considered gifts.[1] Gifts are a major estate planning tool because of their potential for income as well as estate tax savings and for their nontax advantages.

The gift tax computation itself is explained in detail in Appendix C.

WHEN IS THE USE OF SUCH A DEVICE INDICATED?

1. When the donor has an asset which is likely to appreciate in value over a period of time and would like to save estate taxes on the potential growth.

2. When a donor would like to see the donee (an individual, charity, or other organization) benefited by a gift during the donor's life for nontax motives.

3. When the donor would like to reduce probate costs and estate administration expenses, and protect family members from the claims of the client's creditors.

4. When giving away assets other than closely held stock will make it easier to qualify for a Section 303 redemption of stock, a Section 6166 installment payout of taxes attributable to a closely held business interest, and a Section 2032A special use valuation for certain real property used for farming or closely held business purposes. (This technique works only if the gift is made more than 3 years prior to death.)

5. When the estate owner desires to maximize the marital deduction provisions of the federal estate and gift tax law.

He could give his spouse an unlimited amount of property during his lifetime and pay no federal gift tax because of the 100% gift tax marital deduction. It is important to consider any state gift tax laws as well as the federal gift tax.

6. By giving income-producing property, the donor may be able to remove the income it produces from his income tax bracket and subject it to the lower income tax bracket of a donee. A high bracket property owner may make a gift to reduce federal income tax from a bracket as high as 39.6% to a bracket as low as 15%.[2]

All *net unearned income* of a child who has not attained age 14 before the close of the taxable year and who has at least one parent alive at the close of the taxable year will be taxed to the child, but not at the child's tax bracket. This applies to *all* net unearned income; the *source* of the assets creating the income, the *date* the income-producing property was transferred, or the *identity* of the transferor is *irrelevant*.

The tax payable by the under age 14 child on net unearned income is essentially the additional amount of tax the parent would have had to pay if the net unearned income of the child were included in the parent's taxable income.

If parents have two or more children with unearned income to be taxed at the parent's marginal tax rate, all of the children's applicable unearned income will be added together and the tax calculated. The tax is then allocated to each child based on the child's pro rata share of unearned income.

This "kiddie tax" is calculated in three stages (numbers are as indexed for 1995):

(1) There will be no tax on the first $650 of unearned income because of the child's standard deduction. (The standard deduction offsets *un*earned income first, up to $650. Any remaining standard deduction is then available to offset earned income.)

(2) The next $650 of unearned income will be taxed to the child at the child's bracket.

(3) Unearned income in excess of the first $1,300 will be taxed to the child at the appropriate parent's rate.

A dependent child under age 14 with $1,300 of unearned income is taxed as follows:

Unearned income	$1,300
Standard deduction	- 650
Net unearned income	$ 650
Taxed at child's rate	x 15%
Tax	$ 97.50

Therefore, even for children under age 14, there is still some income shifting possible.

For children age 14 or older, unearned income will be taxed to the child at his own tax bracket.

As Figure 15.1 shows, income shifting can be very successful, where a child is age 14 or older.

WHAT ARE THE REQUIREMENTS?

1. There must be a gratuitous transfer or delivery of property.[3]

2. The property which is the subject of the gift must be accepted by the donee.[4] (Of course, when the property is of benefit to the donee, acceptance is seldom an issue.)

3. The gratuitous transfer must divest the donor of control, dominion, and title over the subject matter of the gift.[5]

HOW IT IS DONE — AN EXAMPLE

1. Caroline O'Gara is age 55, married, and owns $20,000 of dividend-paying stock. The stock yields $1,000 annually. Caroline is presently in a 28 percent federal income tax bracket. On the advice of her lawyer, she gives the $20,000 of stock to her 15 year old son, James. This will have the result of shifting the income tax liability from Caroline, who would have netted only $720 ($1,000 - $280) from the $1,000 dividends (28 percent x $1,000), to James, who will net $947.50 from the dividends ($1,000 - $52.50), a saving of $227.50 yearly. [James is in a 15 percent federal income tax bracket and is entitled to a $650 standard deduction, so a 15% rate is applied only to the taxable $350.]

2. Gerald Carter owns an asset which is worth $100,000 today. It is anticipated that the asset will appreciate at the rate of 10 percent per year, i.e., in 10 years it will be worth approximately $260,000. If the property is given away now, the gift tax is computed on the $100,000 (less the annual exclusion if allowable). If the asset is not given away and it becomes part of the estate (ten years from today), the estate tax is computed on approximately $260,000. Thus, a gift made currently removes future appreciation from the estate.

WHAT ARE THE TAX IMPLICATIONS?

1. A gift will remove future appreciation in the property's value from an individual's estate.

Figure 15.1

POST TRA '86 INCOME SHIFTING — CHILD 14 OR OVER

INPUT:	AMOUNT OF INVESTMENT	$ 20,000
INPUT:	RATE OF RETURN ON INVESTMENT	0.100
INPUT:	YEARS INVESTMENT LASTS	21
INPUT:	PARENT'S COMBINED (FEDERAL AND STATE) TAX BRACKET	0.40
INPUT:	CHILD'S COMBINED (FEDERAL AND STATE) TAX BRACKET	0.20
INPUT:	TRUST'S COMBINED (FEDERAL AND STATE) TAX BRACKET	0.20

		PARENT	CHILD
INTEREST INCOME		$2,000	$2,000
TAX		$800	$400
AFTER-TAX INCOME		$1,200	$1,600
ANNUAL ADVANTAGE			$400
TOTAL SAVINGS OVER	21 YEARS		$28,161
TOTAL SAVINGS OVER	26 YEARS		$48,040
TOTAL SAVINGS OVER	31 YEARS		$80,055

2. Gift tax may have to be paid if the value of the gift exceeds the annual exclusion and if the tax exceeds the unified credit available to the donor.[6] (The credits and exemption equivalents are shown below in the Questions and Answers.) If an individual is married and his spouse consents to "split" the gift, the donor spouse will have the $10,000 annual exclusion as well as the unified credit of his spouse in addition to his own.[7] A married individual can give sizable gifts to a spouse with little or no gift tax liability through the gift tax marital deduction discussed below. See QUESTIONS AND ANSWERS concerning the phase-out of the unified credit and graduated tax brackets for large gifts.

3. Dividend or other income generated by the property given will be taxed to the donee rather than the donor (see the discussion above at 6 under the heading "WHEN IS THE USE OF SUCH A DEVICE INDICATED").

4. The gift tax subtracted from the tentative tax in the estate tax computation is the tax that would have been payable on such gifts if the tax rate schedule as in effect at decedent's death had been in effect at the time such gifts were made. The top gift and estate tax rate is 55 percent. Note also that certain ultra large gift or estate tax transfers result in a 5 percent surtax on the portion of the transfer. See table in Appendix D.

It is apparent, then, that the estate of a donor who makes gifts in any of the phase-in years in excess of the dollar amount where that year's top rate begins and then dies in a later calendar year will probably pay a larger estate tax than if the gift had not been made. The change in the estate tax computation, then, amounts to a disincentive for wealthy donors to make such gifts during the top tax rate phase-in years.[8]

The tax implications also include state gift tax where applicable, which in many instances can be greater than the federal gift tax, because of the large credit and exemptions currently available under federal gift tax law.

IMPLICATIONS AND ISSUES IN COMMUNITY PROPERTY STATES

All community property states have adopted statutes which to some degree and by different methods grant equal powers of management and control of community property to each spouse. In many states one spouse cannot make a gift of community property without the prior written consent of the other spouse. If one spouse makes a gift of community property to a third person without the consent of the other spouse, the gift is ordinarily avoidable rather than void.

The gift can be avoided only at the request of the "injured" spouse. The amount of the gift which can be declared void and brought back to the community estate is generally dependent upon whether the community circumstance is still in existence. If the spouses are still married, the entire gift is returned to the community estate. However, if the community has been terminated (e.g., divorce, death), the "injured" spouse has the right to recapture only one-half of the gift. The other half is allowed to remain with the donee. Therefore, it is advisable to obtain both spouses' consent prior to the gift transfer.

In general, gifts of community property have the same benefits as gifts of separate property where the gift is to a third party. However, since each spouse actually "owns" his or her one-half interest in the property, there is no need to "split" the gift. This provides an advantage for persons with community property since each has property and each can give $10,000 without filing a gift tax return.

As to gifts between spouses, a marital deduction is available for the entire amount of the gift, where one spouse gives his or her community interest in property to the other.

"Accidental gifts" (that is, taxable gifts which were not intended to be events subject to tax) can be created by transfers of title. This is particularly true in community property states where a husband and wife have acquired property in a common law state and then moved to a community property state. An example would be where a husband and wife who have acquired assets by the husband's earnings in a common law state sell their home and other real property and move to a community property state, where they invest their cash in securities in joint tenancy or community property title. The parties have always considered their property as "belonging to both of them" and frequently do not understand that purchasing joint tenancy securities resulted in a gift of one-half the value from the husband to the wife. While the unlimited marital deduction avoids federal gift tax on such transfers, there may be state gift taxes to consider. In addition, any pre-1982 transfers may have caused taxable gifts under the pre-Economic Recovery Tax Act (ERTA) rules (which did tax interspousal transfers), and interest and penalties may well apply to those gifts. Without having filed a gift tax return for the year in question, the statute of limitations does not run and the taxes, interest and penalty must still be faced.

Many states do not impose a gift tax where real property (as opposed to securities or other types of property) is placed in joint tenancy between a husband and wife, unless the spouses elect to have the transfer treated as a gift. However, the separate nature of the property still remains, and if the title is later changed to community property or tenancy in common, or if the property is sold and a mortgage or trust deed is taken back "as joint tenants," a gift will be triggered! This is a real

Gifts

danger-area for persons moving to a community property state with assets earned by one of the spouses.

In addition, some states (Texas, Louisiana, Idaho) consider the income from assets with a separate property nature to be community property. Others (Arizona, California, Nevada, New Mexico, Washington) consider such income to be the separate property of the spouse who actually "owns" the property. Thus, in the latter group of states, income which comes from an asset which one spouse had before marriage or was given to or inherited by the spouse during marriage is the separate property of that spouse.

It is important to maintain in separate accounts the proceeds of sale of one's separate property and any separate property income. Commingling these funds can transmute them into community property of both spouses and can result in a gift, an act which may result in state gift tax being imposed even though no gift was intended, by using those commingled funds to buy something in co-ownership between the spouses.

Aside from any gift tax aspects, with the increasing frequency of divorce, it may be important for ownership reasons to be able to trace separate and community property.

QUESTIONS AND ANSWERS

Question — What annual gift tax exclusions are available to a donor?

Answer — A donor can make, gift tax free, up to $10,000 worth of gifts (other than "future interest" gifts) to any number of persons or parties each year.[9] The total maximum excludable amount is determined by multiplying the number of persons (or organizations) to whom gifts are made by $10,000.

If the donor is married and his or her spouse consents (by signing the donor's gift tax return) to "splitting" the gift, each spouse is deemed to have given half the gift— even though one spouse in actuality made the entire gift. This has the effect of raising the per donee exclusion to $20,000 per year.

An annual exclusion is allowed only for "present interest" gifts and is denied for "future interest" gifts.[10]

A present interest gift is one in which the donee's possession or enjoyment begins at the instant the gift is made. A future interest is any interest which the donee's use, possession, or enjoyment will not begin until some period of time after the gift is made. In a nutshell, if there is any delay, no matter how short, or any possibility, no

matter how remote, that the donee's legal right to use, possession, or enjoyment will not begin at the moment the gift is made, the annual exclusion is denied.

Future interests (which do not qualify for the annual exclusion) include:

(1) reversions,

(2) remainders,

(3) any other delayed interest.

A single transfer may actually be two gifts and for tax purposes have to be split into two parts. One may be a present interest that qualifies for the annual exclusion. The other gift may be a future interest that will not qualify for the annual exclusion. For instance, assume a donor put $100,000 into a trust which provided that "all the income is to go annually to my son for ten years and one day. The remainder is to go to my daughter at the end of that time."

The first gift, the income to the son, would be a present interest. That's because at the moment of the gift the son has the immediate right to the income stream for 10 years and a day. The present value of that right, according to government valuation tables and arbitrarily assuming a 10 percent interest rate, approximately $62,000, would be the gift. If the donor was married and his spouse consented to splitting the gift, the two annual exclusions would total $20,000, so only $42,000 would be taxable.

The second gift, the daughter's right to the capital at the end of ten years and a day, would be a future interest because her right to possession would be delayed. No annual exclusion would be allowed on that portion (worth approximately $38,000).

Question — What are in summary the requirements for the gift tax annual exclusion?

Answer — The rules regarding the annual exclusion can be summarized as follows:

(1) A gift in trust is a gift to a trust's beneficiaries for purposes of determining how many annual exclusions may be allowed.

(2) The value of an income interest in a trust qualifies for the annual exclusion if the trustee is required to distribute the income annually or more frequently—even if the value of the remainder interest does not qualify.

(3) The gift of an interest that is contingent upon survivorship is a gift of a future interest. For instance,

134

The Tools and Techniques of Estate Planning

a gift, "to my son for life, then to my daughter for life, then to my brother if he survives me" is really three gifts. The first gift (to the son) is a present interest if the trustee is given no right to accumulate income and all income must be paid at least annually. The other two gifts (to the daughter and brother) are future interest gifts.

(4) A gift is a future interest gift if the donee's enjoyment depends on the exercise of a trustee's discretion. So if a trustee has the right to accumulate income, the gift is a future interest even if the trustee never exercises the right. The nature of the gift (present or future) is ascertained as of the moment of the transfer and is not determined by what the trustee actually does.

(5) A gift must have an ascertainable value to qualify for the exclusion. If the donor or anyone can divert the income from the beneficiary or it is not reasonably possible at the time of the gift to value it, the exclusion may be denied.

Question — Just how valuable is the annual exclusion—and how is it computed?

Answer— The annual exclusion can be an extremely effective income, estate, and generation-skipping transfer tax saving device.

The illustration at Figure 15.2 multiplies the number of donees by the amount of the annual exclusion available for each and then multiplies that amount by the donor's life expectancy according to the government's table in the regulations. This result is then multiplied by the federal estate tax bracket that you have projected the donor will be in at death. The result is the potential federal estate tax savings if none of the annual gifts are invested by the donees.

The illustration then assumes the donees do invest the annual gifts at the specified rate of return (be conservative since this is an after-tax figure). The final result is the potential estate tax savings—the amount that might have gone to the federal government—if no gifts were made.

Question — What is the unified credit against the gift tax?

Answer — The law provides a single tax credit called the "unified" credit, which is a dollar-for-dollar reduction of any gift or estate tax due. The credit was roughly equivalent to an exemption of $175,625 in 1981, scaling up to $600,000 in 1987, and later years.

	Credit	Exemption Equivalent
1977	$30,000 [11]	$120,667
1978	34,000	134,000
1979	38,000	147,333
1980	42,500	161,563
1981	47,000	175,625
1982	62,800	225,000
1983	79,300	275,000
1984	96,300	325,000
1985	121,800	400,000
1986	155,800	500,000
1987	192,800	600,000

For example, assume Robin Scott and her husband make a $600,000 gift in 1994 to their son. The computation for *each* spouse would be as follows:

Gift (split under section 2513)	$300,000
Annual Exclusion	10,000
Net Gift	290,000
Tax on Net Gift	84,400
Unified Credit	192,800
Net Tax Due	$ 0

To the extent the credit is used during lifetime it will have the effect of reducing the credit available against the estate tax. Thus, for estate tax purposes there will be only a $108,400 ($192,800 - $84,400) credit left for each spouse after 1994 (see Appendix C, Estate Tax Computation, for details).

Question — What is a "split gift"?

Answer — When a husband or wife makes a gift to a third person, it may be treated as having been made one-half by the husband and one-half by the wife. This is true even though only one spouse actually makes the gift providing the other spouse consents to the gift.[12]

This would cause the gift tax rate to be lower since the unified rates are progressive. For example: A present interest gift of $110,000 (taxable gift of $100,000) made by a single individual would result in a gift tax of $23,800, whereas the same $110,000 gift made by a husband and his consenting wife to a third party (such as a child) would result in each being considered to have made a $45,000 taxable gift and the gift tax would be $9,400 each ($18,800 for both). The savings would be $5,000. (These examples ignore the unified credit and assume no prior taxable gifts.) A gift tax return must be filed in order to be able to split the gift. Only individuals married to each other can consent to split a gift.

It should be noted that gifts by a husband and wife of community property are *not* eligible for any gift splitting.

Figure 15.2

ESTATE TAX OR GST TAX ADVANTAGE OF THE GIFT TAX ANNUAL EXCLUSION*

DONOR'S AGE 40
DONEES' ANNUAL AFTER-TAX RETURN ON GIFTS 4.00%
AMOUNT OF UNUSED ANNUAL EXCLUSION $20,000
NUMBER OF DONEES 5
DONOR'S LIFE EXPECTANCY (YEARS) 42.5
TOTAL AMOUNT OF GIFTS $4,250,000
DONOR'S PROJECTED ESTATE TAX BRACKET 55.00%
POTENTIAL ESTATE TAX SAVINGS $2,337,500
PROJECTED VALUE OF GIFTS AT LIFE EXPECTANCY $10,739,053
POTENTIAL ESTATE TAX SAVINGS IF ANNUAL GIFTS
      INVESTED BY DONEES AT COMPOUND INTEREST $5,906,479

Illustration courtesy of NumberCruncher Software

Question — What is the gift tax marital deduction?

Answer — In computing the amount of a taxable gift, a deduction is allowed for a gift made by a husband to his wife or vice versa. This deduction is unlimited, so one spouse could conceivably give an entire estate to the other spouse without adverse gift tax consequences.

To qualify for this deduction, the donee-spouse must be given the property outright or must have at least the right to the income from the property and a general power of appointment (essentially the right to say "who gets it") over the principal.[13] (Certain so called "Qualified terminable interest" type property which gives the spouse only a life income may also qualify. This planning technique is discussed more thoroughly in the chapter on marital deduction trusts.)

Question — What is the gift tax based on?

Answer — The gift tax is based on the fair market value of the property transferred.[14]

Question — How is a life insurance policy valued for gift tax purposes?

Answer — If a policy is transferred as a gift immediately after purchase, its value for gift tax purposes is the gross premium paid by the donor.

If a person makes a gift of a previously purchased policy, and the policy is a single-premium or paid-up policy, its gift value is the single premium which the issuing company would charge currently for a compa-rable contract of equal face value on the life of a person who is the insured's age at the time of the gift.

If the gift is of a policy on which further premium payments are payable, its value is the "interpolated terminal reserve" (roughly equivalent to the cash value) and the value of any unearned portion of the last premium.[15] A gift of group term life is measured by the value of the unearned premium at the date of the transfer, so the ideal time to make an assignment of group term life is immediately before the next premium is due.

If the insured is now uninsurable, the value of the policy may be much more than the interpolated terminal reserve value, depending on health circumstances.

Question — Who must file a gift tax return and when must it be filed?

Answer — The donor must file a gift tax return on or before April 15th following the close of the calendar year in which a gift was made exceeding the annual exclusion or a split gift elected. (An extension of time to file the income tax return automatically extends the time for filing gift tax returns.)

Rules for filing of state gift tax returns vary with the different states.

Question — When is the best time to make a gift?

Answer — Like the answer to the question "When is the best time to plant an oak tree?" the answer to this question is, "twenty years ago." The next best time is right now! The $10,000 per donee annual exclusion ($20,000 when a spouse consents) discussed above is noncumulative; either use it or lose it!

Generally, stocks and other assets which fluctuate widely in value should be given away when the market value for that asset is as low as possible.

However, in any decision making as to the giving of property, the financial security of the donor, both current and long-term, should be very carefully considered.

Question — What is the best type of property to give away?

Answer — That depends on the circumstances and objectives of the parties. Income-producing property can be good property to give away if the donor is in a higher income tax bracket than the donee. However, the Tax Reform Act of 1986 has somewhat curtailed this income shifting device. See the discussion under the heading "WHEN IS THE USE OF SUCH A DEVICE INDICATED?" at number 6.

Property which is likely to grow substantially in value (such as, life insurance, common stock, antiques and art, or real estate) is also prime property for giving since future appreciation can be removed from the estate and the gift can be made when the gift tax values (and therefore gift tax transfer costs) are lowest.

Property which has already appreciated should be given away if a sale of such property is contemplated and the donee is in a lower income tax bracket than the donor. Property with relatively low gift tax value and high estate tax value (such as life insurance) makes an excellent gift.

Generally, it is not a good idea to give away "loss property" (property which, if sold, would result in a loss) since the donee cannot use the donor's loss. The donor should sell that property, take the deduction for the loss himself, and give away the cash proceeds.

Although stock in a closely held corporation is often thought of as an ideal asset for gift purposes, care must be taken so that not too much stock is given away. The retention of too little closely held stock might cause an estate to fail the various percentage tests which may qualify it for preferential treatment, e.g., Section 303 redemptions and Section 6166 installment payments of the federal estate tax. (See Chapters 10 and 31.)

Another type of property which might be given is property owned by the donor in a state other than his own state of residence, in order to avoid facing an ancillary probate at the time of the donor's death.

Be sure to consider the age, maturity, and experience of the donee in selecting the gift.

Question — Are there certain types of property which should not be given away?

Answer — It is extremely important to focus on the circumstances of the parties (particularly your client) before making a gift. Do not give away any asset if it will reduce the client's standard of living or financially (or psychologically) endanger his "comfort level." Particularly focus on the impact of the gift on the client's income and capital needs (both present and anticipated) as well as on the client's need for liquidity.

Be aware of the effect of gifts of stock or business or farm interests on qualification for favorable tax law breaks under Code sections 303 (partial stock redemptions to pay death taxes — see Chapter 31), 2032A (special use valuation of closely held business and farm real property — see Chapter 42), and 6166 (extension of time to pay federal estate tax attributable to closely held business interest — see Chapter 10).

Perhaps more important than "what" to give is "how." Outright gifts should be made only after a great deal of consideration. A trust or custodial account or some other form of property management arrangement is appropriate where:

(1) the beneficiary is unwilling or unable to invest, manage, or handle the responsibility of the gift;

(2) the beneficiaries are minors or are adults who lack the emotional or intellectual maturity, physical capacity, or technical training to handle large sums of money or securities;

(3) the donor does not want to significantly reduce the beneficiary's financial dependence on the donor;

(4) the property does not lend itself to fragmentation but the donor desires to spread beneficial ownership among a large number of people (for instance, real estate

The Tools and Techniques of Estate Planning

may be more valuable in some instances if it is not subdivided);

(5) the donor wants to limit the class of beneficiaries and prevent the donee from transferring the property to persons outside the donor's family;

(6) the donor wants to treat children or other relatives equally. A donor may own several parcels of property of equal value. If he gives each to different beneficiaries, one may go up and the other may go down in value. But if they are all placed into one trust and each beneficiary is given an equal share, they will all be treated equally.

It is often recommended that small outright gifts be made over a period of time to allow beneficiaries to handle money and other assets under the guidance of the donor. Then larger amounts can be placed into trust — again during the donor's lifetime so that the donor can watch how the trustee invests and manages the property. Lifetime gifts give the donor the opportunity to see how both the trustee and the beneficiaries handle assets and make investments. The donor can then make adjustments to his will and other estate planning vehicles accordingly.

Question — How does the donee of property compute gain or loss on that property if it is subsequently sold?

Answer — Where property is received by gift, the donee is generally required to take over the donor's basis in the property (this is often called a substituted or "carryover" basis).

In addition to that, carryover basis is allowed for the federal gift tax attributable to the appreciation element of the gift. The formula for computing this is:

$$\text{Gift Tax} \quad \times \quad \frac{\text{Net Amount of Appreciation}}{\text{Value of Gift}}$$

For instance, assume property worth $100,000 was given to a donee. The donor's basis was $40,000. Gift tax paid on the gift was $18,000. The donee's basis, as shown in the computer printout below, is $50,800 [$40,000 + (60,000/100,000 x $18,000)].

COMPUTING BASIS OF GIFT PROPERTY

INPUT:	F.M.V. OF PROPERTY AT TIME OF GIFT	$100,000
INPUT:	DONOR'S BASIS (COST) FOR GIFT...............................	$40,000
	NET APPRECIATION IN VALUE OF GIFT	$60,000
INPUT:	GIFT TAX PAID	$18,000
	DONEE'S BASIS	$50,800

If the donee sells property at a gain, he must pay income tax on such gain.

For purposes of determining loss, the donee's basis is the lesser of (a) the donor's basis, or (b) the fair market value of the property at the time of the gift.

Question — What is a "net gift" and what are its tax implications?

Answer — A net gift is a gift of property subject to some obligation or encumbrance. Typically, a net gift results when the donee agrees, as a condition of the gift, to pay gift taxes on the transfer. The "debt" or obligation against the property may exist before the transfer or arise at the time of the gift.

Netting the gift can be an attractive means of transferring property when a donor does not have cash on hand (and does not want to sell other property to raise cash) to pay gift taxes. A net gift is also useful when a donor wants to limit the extent of the gift to its net value.

For gift tax purposes, the gross amount of the gift is reduced by the amount of the gift tax the donee must pay. In other words, the amount of the gift tax which the donee pays reduces the value of the gift and gift tax is computed on the value of the remaining (net) amount. This means that the actual gift tax liability is lowered since the gift taxes paid reduce the value of the taxable gift.

The value of the "net gift" is measured by the fair market value of the property passing from the donor less the amount of any gift tax paid by the donee. In computing the donee's gift tax liability, you must use the donor's unified credit.

The formula used to compute the donee's tax is: Tentative tax ÷ (1.00 + donor's estate tax bracket).

For instance, assume a retired, 66 year old, single donor living almost entirely from the income of $4,000,000 worth of tax-free municipal bonds, who made no prior gifts, made a gift of property worth $1,010,000. The gift was made to his niece on the condition that she pay the federal gift tax. The tentative tax on a gift of $1,000,000 ($1,010,000 minus $10,000 annual exclusion) is $153,000 ($345,800 less a $192,800 unified credit). But the gift tax actually payable (see calculation below) is $110,072.

TRUE TAX ON A NET GIFT*

INPUT:	YEAR OF GIFT	1995
INPUT:	TAXABLE GIFT	$1,000,000
	GIFT TAX ON GIFT	$345,800
	UNIFIED CREDIT	- $192,800
	TENTATIVE TAX	$153,000

TRUE TAX ON NET GIFT EQUALS:

$$\frac{\text{TENTATIVE TAX}}{(1.00 + \text{RATE OF TAX})} .. \qquad \$110,072$$

*Courtesy of NumberCruncher Software

Note that the formula is not applicable if the gift is split between the donor and spouse, each of whom is in a different gift tax bracket because either or both have made prior taxable gifts. Quite often, however, you can determine the correct tax bracket by inspection and adjusting for the bracket differential by computing the tentative tax in the correct lower bracket. In other situations you'll have to make trial computations using first the bracket indicated by the tentative taxable gift and then later using the next lower bracket.

If you have difficulty with making the computation, state your facts in a letter to the Commissioner of Internal Revenue (Actuarial Department), Washington, D.C.

For estate tax purposes, only the net amount of the gift will be considered in the estate tax computation as an adjusted taxable gift. The gift tax paid by the donee can be credited against the donor's estate taxes.

A net gift is treated for income tax purposes as a part sale/part gift transaction to the extent the donor is relieved from paying the gift tax liability. To the extent the donor is relieved of such liability he or she realizes an immediate economic benefit which is taxable.[16] Specifically, net gifts (made after March 4, 1981) will result in income tax to the donor to the extent the gift tax paid by the donee exceeds the donor's basis in the property.

Question — Can gifts made to a dying spouse cut estate taxes and boost up the basis of appreciated property?

Answer — The so-called "reverse gift" technique is still an appealing strategy where one spouse possesses most of the family wealth and the less affluent spouse is about to die. The wealthier spouse makes a gift of low basis assets to the dying spouse. This inclusion steps up the basis of the property and better utilizes the dying spouse's unified credit.

Note that if a decedent acquires appreciated property by gift within one year of decedent's death and that property passes directly or indirectly to the donor (or donor's spouse) from the decedent, the basis of such property is not stepped up. It remains the basis in the hands of the decedent immediately before the decedent's death.[17] But the technique will work if the decedent lives more than one year after the transfer or the property passes from the decedent to a child or some person other than the donor or the donor's spouse.

Question — What is the Crummey technique?

Answer — Typically, a gift in trust does not become immediately available to or enjoyable by beneficiaries; it is therefore a gift of a "future" rather than a "present" interest. Only present interest gifts qualify for the $10,000 annual exclusion allowed by the gift tax law.

Crummey (a case decided by the 9th Circuit in 1968) involved an irrevocable life insurance trust in which the beneficiaries were given the right to *demand*—each year— the lesser of (a) $4,000 or (b) the amount of the donor's transfer (usually an amount approximating the life insurance premiums necessary) to the trust. It was held that the beneficiaries' legal right to immediate use and enjoyment of the contributions to the trust made the transfers present interest gifts which qualified for the annual gift tax exclusion. (Most authorities feel that the trust should include a provision giving each beneficiary the right to demand the lesser of $5,000 or the amount of cash transferred to the trust.)

This technique is an important estate planning tool for four reasons:

First, it enables a donor to transfer money into a trust (to enable the trustee to pay life insurance premiums) gift tax free.

Second, the donor's potential estate tax is reduced by eliminating from the estate tax base the entire amount excluded under the $10,000 annual exclusion.

Third, the technique is an ideal method of saving gift tax on gifts in trust to minors and works even if

(a) the minor beneficiary's right to demand immediate distribution of the contributed corpus is specified to be within a limited period of time, such as the calendar year of the gift to the trust,

(b) the beneficiary in fact does not withdraw the amount contributed to the trust and loses the right to withdraw it after the end of the year in which the gift is made,

(c) the minor beneficiary doesn't have a formal guardian.

Fourth, a gift in trust that qualifies for the annual exclusion by reason of a Crummey withdrawal power will also be shielded from the generation-skipping transfer tax if such power holder is given a separate share of the trust.

The effectiveness of the Crummey gift technique and the rules regarding its use will be subject to "clarification" by case law and Revenue Rulings. One such clarification relates to the donee having a reasonable period of time in which to exercise the power to withdraw the funds and sufficient notice of the existence of the creation of the power. These refinements can be dealt with by providing a reasonable period of time for exercise of the power to withdraw (e.g., 30 days) and actual notice to the donee or his or her actual guardian or legal guardian. The restriction imposed by these rules is that the trust should be created (or subsequent gifts made to it) no later than November or perhaps very early December, but not in the last few days of December.

The Crummey trust gift technique has become a very important aspect of estate planning (see chapter 36).

Question — Does the purchase of property in joint names create a taxable gift?

Answer — It depends on the type of property and also the parties involved. Generally, when property is purchased with the funds of one party and the property is titled jointly, a completed gift is made. The most notable exceptions to this are the titling of property jointly between husband and wife (which because of the unlimited marital deduction is not a taxable event), and titling of joint bank accounts and United States Savings Bonds.

In the case of a joint bank account or United States Savings Bonds, a completed gift does not occur until the noncontributing joint owner draws upon the bank account or surrenders part of the bond for cash.[18]

Question — What techniques remain available to shift wealth and income to children to save taxes?

Answer — There are still many ways to shift both wealth and income and save taxes.

(1) Give a Series EE U.S. Savings Bond that will not mature until after the donee-child is age 14. No tax will be payable until the bond is redeemed. At that time the gain will be taxed at the child's relatively lower tax bracket. A child who already owns Series EE bonds and is reporting each year's interest accrual as income may elect to change to deferred reporting. However, once an election is made to change from annual reporting it may not be revoked for 5 years.

(2) Give growth stocks (or growth stock mutual funds) which pay little or no current dividends. The child will therefore pay no tax currently and can hold the stock until reaching age 14. Upon a sale the child will be taxed at the child's bracket.

(3) Give *deep discount* tax-free municipal bonds that mature on or after the child's 14th birthday. The bond interest will be tax free to the child and the discount (face less cost basis) will be taxed to the child at the child's bracket when the bond is redeemed at maturity.

(4) Employ your children. Pay them a reasonable salary for work they actually perform. Remember that the standard deduction for children is the greater of (a) $650 or (b) *earned* income up to $3,900. [Numbers are as indexed for 1995.] Regardless of how much is paid to the child, the business will have a deduction at its tax bracket, and the amount will be taxable to the child at the child's bracket. Furthermore, the child could establish an IRA to shelter income further.

(5) Consider the multiple advantages of a *term of years* charitable remainder trust for children over age 14 — so the income will be taxed to the child, but the grantor will receive an immediate income tax deduction.

(6) In making gifts to children consider support obligation cases such as *Braun*[19] and *Sutliff*[20]. Parents who can with ease meet the support needs of even an adult college-age child may be considered obligated to provide support. If UGMA (Uniform Gifts to Minors Act) or UTMA (Uniform Transfers to Minors Act) custodial funds or Section 2503(c) trust funds are used to send a child to college, will the parent be taxed? Worse yet, do these cases mean that the custodian or the trustee violates a fiduciary duty by using such funds to pay for a college education when it's the parent's duty (thus making such

funds unavailable for the very purpose for which they were intended)?

Assuming the support problems addressed above are not applicable, judicious use of a 2503(c) trust (but not a UGMA or UTMA account) will allow significant income shifting. The trust can accumulate income while the beneficiary is under age 14 and avoid the kiddie tax. Although only the first $1,550 of that income is taxed at the 15 percent rate, it may not be necessary to fund the trust with property generating more than $1,550 of income. This is so because the 2503(c) trust is designed to make distributions of principal and income to meet its funding objectives.

(7) Emphasis should now be placed on *convertible planning*—the use of a *value shift* followed at the appropriate time by an *income shift*. For example, a GRAT (Grantor Retained Annuity Trust—see chapter 35) retains for a trust grantor the right to a fixed annuity for a specified number of years. At the end of that time all income and principal will go to the grantor's child (who by then will be 14 or older). None of the principal or appreciation will be in the grantor's estate if the grantor survives the trust term. (Consider a saving clause that terminates the trust in favor of the grantor if tax law is changed to provide that a completed gift does not occur until the donor's interest is terminated.)

(8) Life insurance and annuity policies that stay within statutory guidelines (ask for written guarantee from home office) of life insurance should be particularly attractive assuming *loading* costs are relatively low and/or backended. This includes universal, variable, and traditional whole life of the single-, annual-, and limited-payment types. In the case of the SPWL (Single Premium Whole Life) the entire single premium paid at purchase starts earning the declared interest rate immediately. The cost of insurance and expenses is recovered by the insurer from the difference between the declared interest rate and the rate the insurer actually earns. If the policy is surrendered, any unrecovered expenses are deducted from the policy's cash values. The owner can obtain cash values at any time by (1) surrender (gain over cost is taxable) or (2) loan (loan interest is probably nondeductible). Interest is charged at about the same rate credited on borrowed sums and is free of current tax. Earnings compound free of current taxation. Unlike tax-free municipal bonds there is no market risk and SPWL is highly liquid. A parent can purchase the product on his own life, which makes college education for the children more likely, and the parent does not have to give up control or make a gift. If the policy is a modified endowment contract, there could be adverse income taxes on both policy surrenders and policy loans.

(9) Concentrate on gift and estate tax saving devices such as the annual exclusion. Parents should consider giving $10,000 to $20,000 a year of non-income-producing assets to a minor's trust or custodial account; the assets could be converted into income-producing assets slowly after the child turns age 14. The fund can be self-liquidating and exhaust itself by the time the child finishes college/graduate school.

(10) If the parent's return shows a loss, will the child's return be affected by it? (The Code is silent.)

(11) The custodial parent is often the mother, who may have less income (and therefore be in a lower tax bracket) than the father. But what about the logistics of tax return disclosure where the father is filing returns and paying tax for the children? (Suppose he doesn't want her to know how much he has put aside for the kids, and she doesn't want to reveal her income or her new husband's income. Furthermore, the filing father cannot prepare the children's returns until the mother prepares her returns.) What about multiple children from multiple marriages? Split custody?

Techniques for funding a child's education are covered in greater detail in our book, *The Tools and Techniques of Financial Planning*.

Question — Are all gifts, regardless of amount, entitled to the unified credit and the benefit of the graduated gift tax rates?

Answer — No. For gifts made after December 31, 1987, the benefit of the graduated estate and gift tax rates and the benefit of the unified credit will be phased out for large gifts (see rate tables in Appendix D).

This is accomplished by increasing the gift tax by an additional 5% for taxable amounts exceeding $10,000,000 up to $21,040,000. The additional 5% is imposed until the benefits of the graduated rates and the unified credit are recaptured.[21] The benefits of the graduated rates and the unified credit are, however, fully available for taxable transfers of less than $10,000,000.

Gifts made before January 1, 1988 are counted in determining the amount of the unified credit subject to the phase-out. Thus, even if a gift of $600,000 were made before January 1, 1988, it would be subject to the full 5% rate adjustment on transfers after 1987.

Question — What is a "qualified transfer"? Is it a taxable gift?

Answer — A qualified transfer means any amount paid on behalf of an individual:

(1) as tuition to an educational institution, or

(2) to any person who provides medical care with respect to such individual as payment for such medical care.[22]

A qualified transfer is not considered a gift for gift tax purposes and no gift tax return is required for these transfers.

Question — When a gift is made to a trust, how do you figure how many annual exclusions are available if the gifts are present interest gifts?

Answer — If a gift is made in trust, the donee is considered to be each beneficiary of the trust and not the trust itself. Therefore, there are as many annual exclusions as there are present interest beneficiaries. For example, Gary DeVicci creates an irrevocable trust for his three minor children. Each child is given an annual non-cumulative demand right to withdraw his or her pro-rata share of any contribution to the trust not to exceed $5,000. Gary contributes $15,000 to the trust. He is considered to have made a $5,000 present interest gift to each of his three children.

ASRS, Secs. 51 and 55.

Footnote References

Gifts

1. Reg. §25.2511-1(a); IRC Sec. 7872(f)(3).
2. IRC Sec. 1.
3. Reg. §25.2511-1(c).
4. Reg. §25.2511-1(c).
5. Reg. §25.2511-2(b).
6. IRC Sec. 2503(b).
7. IRC Sec. 2513.
8. See Greenberger, "New Method of Computing Taxes May Weaken ERTA Relief," *Tr. & Est.*, Nov. 1981, p. 28.
9. IRC Sec. 2503(b).
10. Reg. §25.2503-3.
11. For gift tax purposes, only $6,000 of the unified credit could be applied to gifts made after December 31, 1976 and before July 1, 1977. IRC Sec. 2505.
12. Reg. §25.2513-1.
13. IRC Sec. 2523.
14. IRC Sec. 2512; Reg. §25.2512-1.
15. Reg. §25.2512-6.
16. See Rev. Rul. 75-12, 1975-1 CB 310 for examples of how to compute the net gift. *Diedrich, et. al. v. Comm.*, 82-1 USTC §9419, 50 AFTR2d 82-5054 (S.Ct., 1982), aff'g 643 F.2d 499, 81-1 USTC §9249, 47 AFTR2d 81-977 (8th Cir. 1981), rev'g TC Memo 1979-441.
17. IRC Sec. 1014(e).
18. Reg. §25.2511-1(b)(4).
19. *Frederick C. Braun, Jr. v. Comm.*, TC Memo 1984-285.
20. *Sutliff v. Sutliff*, 489 A.2d 764 (Pa. Super. Ct. 1985).
21. IRC Sec. 2001(c)(3).
22. IRC Sec. 2503(e).

Figure 15.3

UNIFIED RATE SCHEDULE FOR ESTATE AND GIFT TAXES	
If the amount with respect to which the tentative tax to be computed is	**The tentative tax is:**
Not over $10,000	18% of such amount.
Over $10,000 but not over $20,000	$1,800 plus 20% of the excess of such amount over $10,000.
Over $20,000 but not over $40,000	$3,800 plus 22% of the excess of such amount over $20,000.
Over $40,000 but not over $60,000	$8,200 plus 24% of the excess of such amount over $40,000.
Over $60,000 but not over $80,000	$13,000 plus 26% of the excess of such amount over $60,000.
Over $80,000 but not over $100,000	$18,200 plus 28% of the excess of such amount over $80,000.
Over $100,000 but not over $150,000	$23,800 plus 30% of the excess of such amount over $100,000.
Over $150,000 but not over $250,000	$38,800 plus 32% of the excess of such amount over $150,000.
Over $250,000 but not over $500,000	$70,800 plus 34% of the excess of such amount over $250,000.
Over $500,000 but not over $750,000	$155,800 plus 37% of the excess of such amount over $500,000.
Over $750,000 but not over $1,000,000	$248,300 plus 39% of the excess of such amount over $750,000.
Over $1,000,000 but not over $1,250,000	$345,800 plus 41% of the excess of such amount over $1,000,000.
Over $1,250,000 but not over $1,500,000	$448,300 plus 43% of the excess of such amount over $1,250,000.
Over $1,500,000 but not over $2,000,000	$555,800 plus 45% of the excess of such amount over $1,500,000.
Over $2,000,000 but not over $2,500,000	$780,800 plus 49% of the excess of such amount over $2,000,000.
Over $2,500,000 but not over $3,000,000	$1,025,800 plus 53% of the excess of such amount over $2,500,000.
Over $3,000,000	$1,290,800 plus 55% of the excess of such amount over $3,000,000.

There is a 5 percent additional tax for amounts which exceed $10,000,000, but do not exceed $21,040,000.

Figure 15.4

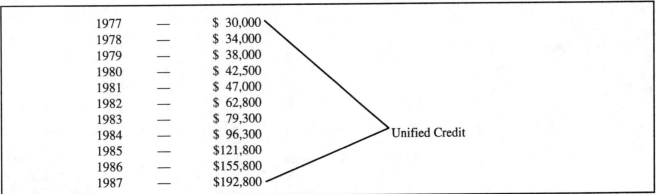

1977	—	$ 30,000
1978	—	$ 34,000
1979	—	$ 38,000
1980	—	$ 42,500
1981	—	$ 47,000
1982	—	$ 62,800
1983	—	$ 79,300
1984	—	$ 96,300
1985	—	$121,800
1986	—	$155,800
1987	—	$192,800

Unified Credit

HR-10 (KEOGH) RETIREMENT PLAN
FOR THE SELF-EMPLOYED

WHAT IS IT?

Under an HR-10 (Keogh) plan, a self-employed individual (this term includes a sole proprietor and partners owning 10 percent or more of an interest in a partnership) is allowed to take a tax deduction for money he sets aside to provide for retirement. The HR-10 plan is also a means of providing retirement security for employees working for the self-employed individual.

WHEN IS THE USE OF SUCH A DEVICE INDICATED?

1. When there is a desire on the part of the self-employed to provide personal retirement funds.

2. When there is a desire on the part of the self-employed to provide financial security for the retirement of his or her employees.

3. When the self-employed individual would like to defer tax on otherwise currently taxable income.

WHAT ARE THE REQUIREMENTS?

1. HR-10 eligibility rules are the same as those for corporate plans. Full time employees who are below age 21 or who have less than one year of service may be excluded from coverage. However, a plan may require two years of service if there is 100 percent immediate vesting for each participant. A year of service generally means a 12-month period during which the employee has worked at least 1,000 hours.[1]

   Likewise, an HR-10 plan must meet the minimum participation, coverage and nondiscrimination rules applicable to corporate qualified plans.[2] See the discussion in Chapter 28 under "Eligibility."

2. HR-10 plans must meet the minimum vesting standards applicable to regular corporate plans. Vesting refers to the nonforfeitability of employer contributions for covered employees. Full vesting is required after 5 years or after 7 years under an accelerated graduated vesting schedule.[3]

3. An HR-10 plan must be in writing.[4] The plan can be described in an individually drafted trust instrument or in a master or prototype plan. A "master plan" refers to a standardized form of plan, with or without a trust, administered by an insurance company or bank acting as the funding medium for purposes of providing benefits on a standardized basis. In a master plan, the sponsoring organization both funds the benefits and administers the plan.

   A "prototype plan" refers to a standardized form of plan which is made available by the sponsoring organization for use without change by a self-employed individual who wishes to adopt such a plan. A prototype plan will not be administered by the sponsoring organization. The employer (the self-employed individual) administers the plan. Internal Revenue Service approval of the plan is generally sought by the sponsoring organization.

   An HR-10 plan is not required to have an institutional trustee, such as a bank or insured credit union. Thus, the owner-employee maintaining the plan can be the trustee.

4. In addition to the creation of a written instrument, the owner-employee must make a contribution in order to bring the plan into being.

In addition to the above requirements, there are a number of others that an HR-10 plan must meet in order to be "qualified" under section 401(a) of the Internal Revenue Code. The advantages of being "qualified" are many, including a current deduction for contributions to the plan and deferred taxation of benefits until distribution.

HOW IT IS DONE — AN EXAMPLE

Your client, Marvin Gimpel, is a druggist. He has four full-time employees. Marvin's earned income is $80,000 a year. All his employees have more than one year of service and have attained age 21. Two of his assistants earn $20,000 each, and two other clerks earn $10,000 a year each, a total of $60,000.

Marvin establishes an HR-10 plan. The plan calls for contributions of 10 percent of his earned income to be used to provide a pension for him and contributions of 10 percent of each employee's earnings to provide for their retirements. Since his employees' total salary was $60,000, he would contribute 10 percent of the $60,000 of salary paid to his employees.

Marvin could deduct this entire amount. After making the contribution, however, his own earned income drops to $74,000 ($80,000 minus his $6,000 contribution). However, his earned income would drop further because it is computed after taking into account amounts contributed by the self-employed individual to the HR-10 plan for himself, as well as for his common law employees.[5] Thus, a formula is needed to determine how much he can contribute on his behalf, since one cannot know what the contribution will be until after one knows how much the earned income is for the self-employed individual, and one does not know what the earned income is until one knows what the contribution will be. This calculation is further complicated by the deduction for one-half of the self-employment tax permitted for self-employed individuals.[6] Both calculations are explained at the question and answer on "earned income," below.

WHAT ARE THE TAX IMPLICATIONS?

1. Contributions made on behalf of an owner-employee to an HR-10 plan are deductible from gross income on the owner-employee's federal income tax return.[7] Although substantial parity has been established between HR-10 plans and corporate qualified plans for federal tax purposes, some states may still allow a lower deduction for contributions to an HR-10 plan.

2. The deductible deposits made by an employer are not currently taxable either to the employer himself or to a participating employee. No tax will be paid until benefits are actually received.[8]

3. Income earned by assets in the plan accumulates tax free.[9]

4. A lump-sum distribution receives basically the same tax treatment that a similar distribution would receive from a corporate pension plan.[10]

5. For years commencing after December 31, 1984, the entire estate tax exclusion has been repealed, so that plan benefits are subject to estate tax like any other asset.[11]

    The Tax Reform Act of 1984 contained a provision which permitted individuals who were both in pay status and had made an irrevocable election as to the form of benefit distribution to continue to have the benefit of the estate tax exclusion (the unlimited exclusion for participants in pay status prior to January 1, 1983, or the $100,000

exclusion for participants in pay status prior to January 1, 1985). The Tax Reform Act of 1986 somewhat liberalized the grandfathering provisions by providing that the participant no longer needs to have been in pay status as of the applicable date. The participant needs only to have separated from service prior to the applicable date and not to have made any change in the form of benefit to be paid.

6. The maximum contribution to a defined contribution plan on behalf of a self-employed individual is limited to the lesser of (a) 25 percent of earned income or (b) $30,000. The $30,000 limit is frozen until the defined benefit pension plan limit reaches $120,000, at which time the limit will be one-fourth of the then defined benefit limit.[12] The 25 percent/$30,000 limit does not apply to defined benefit HR-10 plans. Contributions to defined benefit plans are based on actuarial calculations designed to accumulate a reserve large enough to pay the retirement benefits promised by the plan. A defined benefit HR-10 plan based on retirement at Social Security retirement age can be funded to provide an annual retirement benefit of the lesser of 100 percent of the participant's average compensation for his highest paid three years of participation or $90,000.[13] The $90,000 limit is indexed for increases in the cost-of-living ($120,000 for 1995).[14] If retirement benefits are to commence prior to normal retirement age for receiving full Social Security benefits, the limit is reduced.[15]

7. An owner-employee may make nondeductible voluntary contributions (like a common law employee), in addition to his deductible contribution. All such contributions are counted for purposes of the annual additions limitation and must conform to the special nondiscrimination test provided in Code section 401(m).

8. The deductible limits on contributions to HR-10 plans depend on the type of plan. In the case of profit sharing plans, the amount that is deductible cannot exceed 15% of total compensation of plan participants (earned income in the case of the self-employed individual).[16] In the case of a defined benefit plan, the amount that is deductible is limited to the amount actuarially determined to be necessary to pay for the benefits promised.[17] In no event, however, can amounts in excess of the Section 415 limits (discussed in paragraph 6, above) be deducted.[18]

9. There is a 10 percent annual nondeductible excise tax on "excess" contributions (i.e., contributions above the deductible limits mentioned above) made to the plan until the excess is eliminated.[19]

10. A 10 percent penalty tax is imposed on distributions before the participant attains age 59½, with certain

exceptions (death, divorce, disability, payments made over the participant's life starting from separation from service, and medical expenses).[20]

11. See Chapter 28 for a discussion of the excise tax imposed on excess distributions and accumulations in an HR-10 plan.

IMPLICATIONS AND ISSUES IN COMMUNITY PROPERTY STATES

The benefit accumulated in an HR-10 plan for an employee who was married during his participation in the plan while a resident of a community property state belongs equally to the employee and his or her spouse. The employee and spouse can, however, change the normal effect of community property laws by an agreement, such as a pre-nuptial agreement, to the effect that all earnings of the individual will be community property but that contributions to a qualified retirement plan for the employee's benefit will be solely the employee's property. However, the Retirement Equity Act of 1984 limits the ability of a married participant to solely retain plan benefits without the consent of the participant's spouse (see Chapter 28).

One frequent issue concerns individuals moving from common law to community property states. For instance, assume a married employee was a resident of a non-community property state for ten years. He and his wife then moved to California where they resided for five years. Contributions were made to an HR-10 plan each year on his behalf throughout the fifteen-year period. What is the status of ownership of benefits accumulated in the plan over the fifteen-year period? The answer is that a portion of the benefits will be community property. Depending on the circumstances, a court may determine the community property portion on the basis of the "contributions made" or the "time" method.

The "contributions made" method would divide the benefits in the proportion of contributions made after moving to the community property state, plus earnings, to the total amount in the plan. The "time" method would divide benefits on the basis of proportionate years of participation in the plan; i.e., one-third of the benefits would be community property.

Each method has advantages and disadvantages. If annual contributions for the employee were greater in the years in which he lived in a community property state, the "time" method would cause more of the benefits to be separate property than the "contributions made" method. Other methods of dividing community property HR-10 benefits could be used where appropriate.

The non-community property portion of the HR-10 benefit would be the separate property of the employee. In the event of a divorce or the death of the employee, California law provides that certain separate property of the employee will be treated as community property for purposes of division on divorce or the employee's death. This separate property is referred to as quasi-community property. Generally, quasi-community property is personal property, wherever situated, and real property situated in California, which would have been community property had the owner acquired it in California. For all purposes other than division on divorce or the employee's death, the benefits remain the employee's separate property. Thus, if the employee's wife predeceases him, her estate will not have any rights to any part of the separate property portion of the HR-10 benefits.

QUESTIONS AND ANSWERS

Question — What is meant by the term "earned income"?

Answer — Earned income is, generally, net earnings derived from a self-employed individual's business as a result of personal efforts or personal service rendered as distinguished from investment income. Therefore, inactive owners, such as limited partners, whose income is derived solely from an investment made in the partnership, have no earned income from the firm.

Generally the entire net earnings received by a self-employed individual who is an attorney, an accountant, a physician, or other professional is considered as earned income. However, for purposes of determining earned income, net earnings must be adjusted. Adjusted net earnings means gross earnings less all allowable business deductions, allowable deductions under Code sections 62 and 404 pertaining to contributions to a qualified plan, and the deduction for one-half of the self-employed individual's self-employment tax.[21] The allowable deductions for HR-10 contributions include not only the deductions for common law employees but deductions for self-employed individuals as well.

It appears that if deductions for self-employed individuals must be taken into account before determining such self-employed individual's "earned income," an unknown situation presents itself. One cannot determine a self-employed individual's earned income until the allowable contribution for him is known. The allowable contribution cannot be determined until his earned income is known. In some cases an interdependent variable formula will be needed to determine the proper deductible contribution. Added to this complexity is the fact that the IRS has ruled that self-employment tax must be computed and the deduction for one-half of the self-employment tax must be taken before determining the HR-10 contribution.[22]

Self-employment tax is determined by subtracting 7.65% from the self-employed individual's net earnings. In 1995, net earnings up to $61,200 are subject to 12.4% OASDI tax and all net earnings are subject to 2.9% for hospital insurance tax. One-half of the self-employment tax is then subtracted from net earnings (i.e., 6.2% OASDI and 1.45% HI). The resulting figure is the base amount used to determine the self-employed individual's HR-10 contribution.[23]

Determining the HR-10 contribution is relatively simple when there are no employees. For example, if the self-employed individual's net earnings (after deducting one-half of self-employment tax) are $60,000, multiply that amount by 20 percent to obtain the maximum contribution allowable on his behalf. The figure arrived at is $12,000. That is the same figure computed by multiplying his $48,000 earned income ($60,000 - $12,000) by 25 percent.

Calculating the self-employed individual's maximum contribution is not difficult even if there are employees. For instance, assume a payroll of $10,000 for other employees. If that amount is multiplied by 25 percent, a $2,500 contribution must be made on behalf of those employees. This drops the $60,000 base for determining the self-employed individual's contribution in the example above down to $57,500. If $57,500 is then multiplied by 20 percent, a contribution of $11,500 is arrived at. This is the same as if his earned income of $46,000 ($57,500 - $11,500) was multiplied by 25%.

Question — Can an individual who is a full-time corporate employee but who conducts independent consulting work or "moonlights" and receives fees make contributions based on self-employment income?

Answer — Yes. For example, Sel Horvitz, a practicing attorney who teaches three days a week at a local law school and who is participating in the school's tax deferred annuity plan, can still set up an HR-10 plan for himself based on the income earned in private practice. However, there are overall "all plans" limits which may not be exceeded. Sel can also contribute to an IRA up to a maximum of $2,000 or 100% of his compensation, whichever is lower. However, a tax deduction for his IRA contributions will be permitted only if his income falls within the limits discussed in Chapter 18.[24] Tax deferred compounding of IRA contributions still occurs, even if the contribution to the IRA is not deductible.[25]

Question — Under what circumstances can benefits be paid from an HR-10 plan?

Answer — A 10 percent nondeductible tax penalty is imposed on all distributions before the participant attains age 59½, with certain exceptions (death, divorce, disability, payments made over the participant's life starting from separation from service, and medical expenses).[26]

Special 5-year forward averaging[27] using single current rates, or 10-year forward averaging[28] using the 1986 income tax rates if the participant reached age 50 by January 1, 1986, is available for "lump-sum distributions." A distribution will be considered to be made in a "lump-sum" if (a) it is made within one taxable year of the recipient, (b) it consists of the balance of the employee's account, and (c) it occurs under one of the following circumstances:

1. On account of the death of an employee or self-employed person.

2. After the disability of a self-employed person.

3. After a self-employed individual or any other employee attains age 59½ (even if employment has not yet terminated).[29]

In addition, an HR-10 plan, as well as all corporate qualified plans, generally must begin distributing benefits by April 1 of the year following the year the employee attains age 70½. However, employees who are not 5-percent-owners and who attained age 70½ before 1988 need not begin distributions until April 1 of the year following the year they retire, if that is later.[30] The distribution date may also be postponed beyond age 70½ for participants who made elections prior to January 1, 1984 to postpone distributions under TEFRA Section 242(b). (See Chapter 28 for other distribution requirements.)

Question — How may contributions be invested?

Answer — HR-10 plan funds can be invested in life insurance contracts (subject to limitations), mutual funds, variable annuities, government bonds, savings accounts, securities, real estate, etc., or a combination of these funding media.

Question — Can pre-retirement death benefits be provided under an HR-10 plan?

Answer — Yes. Immediate and substantial death benefits can be made available through life insurance to beneficiaries of the self-employed individual and other plan participants. These benefits will be received income tax free and can be coordinated with the personal life insurance programs of the participants. (Note, however, that the cash value portion of the death benefit will be subject to income tax.)[31]

Question — If life insurance is used in a plan and paid for by employer contributions to the plan, is any of the premium taxable to the employee?

Answer — The cost of pure insurance is taxable as a current economic benefit. For common law employees the amount the covered person must include is based on government tables.[32] The cost of insurance for a self-employed person is not a deductible contribution. (Pure insurance is the difference between the face amount of the policy, i.e., the death benefit, and the policy's cash value.)[33]

For example, if a $1,000 premium is paid for an ordinary life insurance policy and $150 of the premium represents the cost of pure life insurance, an employee is taxed currently on $150, and a self-employed individual cannot deduct the $150.

Any deductible employee contributions which are applied toward the purchase of life insurance will be treated as a distribution in the year so applied.[34]

Question — Many HR-10 plans are "defined contribution plans," i.e., the pension benefit at retirement will be whatever a specified contribution, plus appreciation on the contributions, will earn. Are there other types of plans?

Answer — Yes. There are two general types of plans: (1) A defined contribution (profit-sharing) plan, as described above, can be used. Contributions in this case would be based on a formula that is applied to the earned income (the profits) of the self-employed individual. (2) A defined benefit plan can also be devised. Under a defined benefit plan, a predetermined annual retirement benefit is funded on an annual basis. A defined benefit formula may have some advantages for the self-employed person over a defined contribution formula. For one, contributions can exceed the 25 percent/$30,000 limits. Second, the proportionate contribution for other employees may be lower than in a defined contribution plan, especially if the other employees are younger than the self-employed person.

Question — In an HR-10 plan, may employees below a certain age be excluded from coverage?

Answer — Yes, an HR-10 plan may require the same eligibility requirements as a corporate qualified plan (see "Eligibility," Chapter 28, infra).

Question — What must a sole proprietor or partnership do to set up an HR-10 plan?

Answer — To set up an HR-10 plan, a plan that meets the applicable requirements for tax qualification must be executed on or before the last day of the proprietor's or partnership's tax year. Employees must be informed in writing of the plan and contributions must be made within the period required for filing the sole proprietor's or partnership's income tax return (including extensions).

Question — If a self-employed individual contributes less than the maximum allowed in any one year, can he make up the excess in the next tax year?

Answer — Generally, no. Contributions to an HR-10 plan for self-employed individuals are allowed only on a year-to-year basis. The law has no carryover provisions for self-employed individuals. If the amount contributed in a given year was less than the amount allowable, the self-employed individual cannot make it up and contribute more than the limit in the following year.[35]

Question — Can an excess contribution be made to an HR-10 plan without penalty?

Answer — No. Contributions exceeding the deductible limit are subject to a 10 percent annual nondeductible excise tax until the excess is eliminated.[36]

Question — Can a loan be made from an HR-10 plan to an employee without its being treated as a taxable distribution?

Answer — Yes, but only for persons who are not self-employed individuals. Within certain limits a loan from an HR-10 plan (made after August 13, 1982), which must be repaid within 5 years will not be considered a taxable distribution if it does not exceed the lesser of $50,000 or one-half of the employee's nonforfeitable accrued benefit under the plan. (A loan of up to $10,000 is allowed, even though more than half the employee's accrued benefit.) For loans made after December 31, 1986, the $50,000 limit is reduced by the highest outstanding loan balance during the prior 12-month period.[37] This effectively prohibits "rollovers" of loans in excess of $25,000.

The loan should bear a reasonable rate of interest, be adequately secured, provide a reasonable repayment schedule, and be made available on a basis which does not discriminate in favor of employees who are highly-paid.

Note, the 5-year repayment rule does not apply to loans used for residential mortgages.[38] A loan in excess of these prescribed limits would be treated as a taxable distribution.

Generally, loans to "owner-employees" are prohibited transactions and should not be made.[39] The availability of loans to owners is one of the advantages of a corporate plan.

Question — What is a "top heavy" HR-10 plan? Of what significance is the term?

Answer — Any plan is a "top heavy" plan if as of the determination date (generally, the last day of the preceding plan year or last day of a new plan's first year) the present value of the aggregate accrued benefits of "key employees" in a defined benefit plan or the account balances of "key employees" in a defined contribution plan exceed 60 percent of the aggregate accrued benefits or account balances of all employees.[40] Under this definition most HR-10 plans will be considered "top heavy".

A key employee is any employee-participant who, at any time during the plan year or in the 4 preceding plan years, is (or was) an officer earning more than 50% of the Section 415 dollar limit, an employee owning one of the ten largest interests in the employer, a more than 5 percent owner, or a more than 1 percent owner earning more than $150,000 a year.[41]

If a plan is considered "top heavy" certain additional requirements must be met. These include:

(1) Rapid Vesting—A top heavy plan must provide for vesting under one of two alternative schedules. One schedule that provides any employee with 3 years of service must be 100 percent vested. The other alternative provides a 6 year graduated schedule beginning after 2 years of service.

(2) Minimum non-integrated contribution or benefit for non-key employees—For a defined contribution plan, the employer generally must contribute for a non-key employee an amount equal to at least 3 percent of that participant's compensation. However, if the key employee uses a percentage for himself which is lower, that percentage may be used.

For a defined benefit plan, the benefit for a non-key employee which must be accrued is at least 2 percent of the employee's average annual compensation multiplied by the employee's years of ser-

vice with the employer in which a top heavy plan year ends. The minimum benefit, however, need not exceed 20 percent of such annual compensation. Years of service before January 1, 1984 need not be counted.

(3) Aggregate limit on benefits and contributions for key employees in a defined benefit and a defined contribution plan—If an employee participates in both types of plans, both of which are top heavy, the sum of the "defined benefit plan fraction" (a fraction based on the portion of the maximum permitted limit for a defined benefit plan the participant has used) and the "defined contribution plan fraction" (a fraction based on the portion of the maximum permitted limit for a defined contribution plan the participant has used) for any year may not exceed 1.0.

The vesting, minimum benefits and limits on compensation requirements do not apply to any employee who is represented by a collective bargaining unit where evidence exists that retirement benefits were the subject of good faith bargaining.

Question — Can plans covering self-employed individuals be integrated with Social Security?

Answer — Yes, an HR-10 plan may be integrated under the same rules that apply to corporate plans. (The current terminology refers to "permitted disparity" instead of integration.) For example, in the case of defined contribution plans, the contribution rate (%) that applies to compensation above the taxable wage base may not exceed the contribution rate (%) that applies to compensation below the taxable wage base by more than the *lesser of* (1) the rate applied to compensation below the wage base or (2) 5.7% points (or, if greater, the rate of social security tax attributable to old-age insurance).[42] For example, if the plan provides for contributions of 10 percent of pay in excess of the wage base, it would be properly integrated if it provided for contributions of at least 5 percent on pay below the wage base.

Question — Are Keogh plans subject to the survivor annuity rules under the Retirement Equity Act of 1984?

Answer — Yes; the survivor annuity requirements apply to any defined benefit or defined contribution plan, which would include an HR-10 plan. This means that in the event a married owner-employee retires, the retirement income must be in the form of a qualified joint and survivor annuity. If the owner-employee dies leaving a surviving spouse, there must be a qualified survivor annuity for the surviving spouse. This requirement may be waived; see the discussion in Chapter 28.

ASRS, Sec. 51, Sec. 60.

Footnote References

HR-10

1. IRC Sec. 410(a).
2. IRC Secs. 401(a)(4), 410(b), 401(a)(26).
3. IRC Sec. 411(a)(2).
4. ERISA Sec. 402(a)(1).
5. IRC Sec. 401(c)(2)(A).
6. IRC Sec. 164(f).
7. IRC Sec. 62(a)(6). Contributions on behalf of common law employees are deductible under Sec. 404(a).
8. IRC Sec. 402(a); Reg. §1.402(a)-1(a)(1)(i).
9. IRC Sec. 501(a).
10. IRC Sec. 402(d).
11. IRC Sec. 2039, as amended by TRA '84, Sec. 525.
12. IRC Sec. 415(c)(1)(A).
13. IRC Sec. 415(b).
14. IRC Sec. 415(d).
15. IRC Sec. 415(b)(2)(C).
16. IRC Sec. 404(a)(3)(A).
17. IRC Sec. 404(a)(1)(A).
18. IRC Sec. 404(j).
19. IRC Sec. 4972.
20. IRC Sec. 72(t).
21. IRC Sec. 401(c)(2)(A).
22. GCM 39807.
23. See IRS Pub. 560, "Retirement Plans for the Self-Employed."
24. IRC Sec. 219(g).
25. IRC Sec. 408(o).
26. IRC Sec. 72(t).
27. IRC Sec. 402(d)(1).
28. TRA '86, Secs. 1122(h)(3), 1122(h)(5).
29. IRC Sec. 402(d)(4)(A).
30. IRC Sec. 401(a)(9)(C). A special transition rule applied to certain employees who turned age 70$\frac{1}{2}$ in 1988. See Notice 89-42, 1989-1 CB 683.
31. IRC Sec. 72(m)(3)(C).
32. Regs. §§1.402(a)-1(a)(3); 1.72-16.
33. IRC Sec. 404(e).
34. IRC Sec. 72(o)(3).
35. IRC Sec. 404(a)(3)(A).
36. IRC Sec. 4972.
37. IRC Sec. 72(p)(2)(A).
38. IRC Sec. 72(p)(2)(B).
39. IRC Sec. 4975(d)(1). The Department of Labor may grant an administrative exemption for a loan to an owner-employee. ERISA Sec. 408(d).
40. IRC Sec. 416(g).
41. IRC Sec. 416(i).
42. IRC Sec. 401(l).

Chapter 17

INCORPORATION

Note: This discussion deals with the general treatment of corporations. In the case of corporations which have elected special status under Subchapter S, different rules may apply. (See Chapter 29).

WHAT IS IT?

There is no formal definition of a corporation under the tax law, as neither the Code nor the regulations expressly define the term. Local law does not control for tax purposes. Under the Code, an organization generally will be taxed as a corporation if it has a preponderance of the following elements: (1) associates, (2) limited liability, (3) free transferability of interests, (4) centralized management, (5) continuity of life, and (6) an objective to carry on business and divide the gains therefrom.[1] These terms are explained in the paragraphs that follow.

A corporation must generally have *associates* because it is an inanimate entity that can act only through its board of directors, officers, or agents. These individuals must be bound together for common objectives. However, "one man" corporations may still be recognized as corporations for purposes of federal tax law, provided that the requisite formalities are complied with. Generally, the primary purposes of their association will be the operation of a business for profit.

Limited liability is possessed by an organization that can answer negatively to the question, "Could a creditor of the organization proceed against the individual owners personally in an attempt to satisfy an obligation incurred by the organization?" This is one of the best-known reasons for choosing the corporate form.

If the formalities of corporate procedure are followed, then the corporation is really operating as a business and financial unit entirely separate from its shareholders for tax and most legal purposes. Shareholders will ordinarily not be personally liable for the corporation's debts or other liabilities. (As a practical matter, principal shareholders of small corporations will often be required to cosign a note or give a personal guarantee for the corporation and, therefore, become personally liable for loans to the corporation by banks or other lending institutions. Generally, however, the most a shareholder can lose is his investment in the business.)[2]

Free transferability of interest generally means that a member of a corporation can transfer his interest in the profits, assets, and control of the business freely and without restraint. If each member, without the consent of the other members of the organization, can transfer his entire interest to a person who is not a member, there is "free transferability of interest." It is permissible, however, to impose reasonable restrictions on shareholders to preserve the nature of close corporate membership. These restrictions are often contained in "buy-sell" agreements and facilitate family estate planning with respect to a business interest.[3]

The characteristic of *centralized management* poses the question, "Is the operating authority concentrated in one man or a relatively small class within the group as opposed to the sharing of management decisions commonly found in partnerships?" If any person or group of persons (which does not include all of the members) has continuing, exclusive authority to make the decisions necessary to the management and daily operation of the business, there is centralized management.

The group in which that authority is legally vested is called the board of directors. The board of directors uses its best judgment and independent discretion to determine and execute corporate policies. Although these persons are in fact elected by the shareholders and removable by them for cause (and possibly without cause), the directors are not agents of the shareholders. They are fiduciaries whose duties primarily run to the corporation itself.

It is the board of directors, not the shareholders, who make policy decisions with respect to the products, services, prices, and wages of the company. Likewise, even in the smallest corporation, legally speaking, it is the board of directors that has the right to select, supervise, and remove officers and other personnel. For example, the board of directors, and not the shareholders, fixes compensation and decides on the installation and benefit levels of pension and profit sharing plans, as well as other employee benefits. In short, the supervision and vigilance for the welfare of the entire corporate enterprise is vested in the hands of a very select group.[4]

Continuity of life means that death, disability, incapacity, addition of a new member, or withdrawal of an old member will not cause legal dissolution of the business. If the effect of

The Tools and Techniques of Estate Planning

the death of a member of the firm is the automatic death of the business, a vital element of corporate status is lacking. A corporation is the only form of business enterprise which — theoretically at least — has the advantage of perpetual existence. For example, even the death of a 100 percent stockholder would not cause the legal termination of the business. Practically, speaking, however, without successor management, such a corporation will "die" as quickly as a sole proprietorship. (Some states impose limitations on corporate duration although most jurisdictions allow a corporation to select any period of time desirable.)[5]

WHEN IS THE USE OF SUCH A DEVICE INDICATED?

1. When the individual owners desire limited liability, a corporation and not its individual shareholders is responsible for corporate obligations.

2. When the individual owners desire a relatively simple and inexpensive means of transferring ownership, it is relatively easy to provide for a new owner's entrance and an existing owner's exit merely by endorsing shares of stock. This is especially important in making gifts to minors.

3. When the individual owners desire to take advantage of the wide range of fringe benefits that the corporation can provide. These benefits are, within limits, tax deductible by the corporation and generally not currently taxable to the employee — including shareholder-employees. These fringe benefits may include:

   • pension/profit-sharing plans,

   • group life insurance,

   • group health insurance,

   • disability income coverage,

   • medical reimbursement plans,

   • cafeteria plans, and

   • auto and travel costs.

4. When other tax-oriented advantages are desired. For instance, assuming a corporation does not have to pay out substantial dividends, the overall tax result may be lower federal income taxes than if the enterprise were run in the form of a sole proprietorship or partnership. It might be easiest to illustrate this point by comparing partnership

with corporate tax treatment. If a partnership were formed, owners would be taxed on all the income earned as partners — even if they did not actually withdraw all partnership earnings from the firm. However, as stockholder-employees, they would be taxed only on salaries (assuming no dividend had to be paid). A lower federal income tax under the corporate form may result because a new tax-paying entity, the corporation, has been created.

Because the corporation's tax rate may be lower than the individual's tax rate, this income splitting can yield a lower overall current tax. This is especially true on the first $50,000 of corporate income, which is taxed at only a 15% rate. However, as a result of the Tax Reform Act of 1986, the maximum corporate rate is greater than the maximum individual rate. Additionally, it may be more expensive tax wise to be a corporation when it comes down to selling the business. Under the new rules, there may be two taxes as a result of a corporate sale of assets (followed by liquidation) instead of one tax when the seller is a proprietorship or partnership. Thus, if the corporation has assets that are likely to appreciate, the income-splitting benefit may be more than offset by the additional taxes.

The rates on corporate taxable income (1995 Corporate Tax Table), including worksheets for computing the tax, are shown below:

1995 CORPORATE TAX TABLE

Taxable Income	Base Amount	Base Tax Owed	% on Excess
0	50,000	0	0.15
50,001	75,000	7,500	0.25
75,001	100,000	13,750	0.34
100,001	335,000	22,250	0.39
335,001	....	113,900	0.34

CORPORATE TAX CALCULATING WORKSHEET

		Example
Step 1:	List Taxable Income	$200,000
Step 2:	List Base Tax	22,250
Step 3:	Compute "Excess" Over Base Amount	$100,000
Step 4:	List % on "Excess"	.39
Step 5:	Multiply Step 3 x Step 4	39,000
Step 6:	Total Steps 2 and 5	61,250

Figure 17.1 compares the tax payable by various entities on $100,000 of taxable income.

Figure 17.1

TAX COMPARISON — 1995					
	INPUT: TAX. INCOME	TAX	NET INCOME	MARGINAL RATE	OVERALL RATE
CORPORATE*	$100,000	$22,250	$77,750	34	22
PERSONAL SERVICE CORPORATION	$100,000	$35,000	$85,000	35	35
JOINT	$100,000	$35,000	$76,897	31	23
SINGLE	$100,000	$28,103	$73,732	31	26
SEPARATE	$100,000	$28,268	$71,539	36	28
HEAD/HOUSEHOLD	$100,000	$24,515	$75,485	31	25
TRUST/ESTATE	$100,000	$38,732	$61,268	39.6	39
*Not a personal service corporation					

Note that personal service corporations are taxed at a flat rate of 35 percent. The term "qualified personal service corporation" means one in which (a) substantially all of the activities involve the performance of services in the fields of health, law, engineering, architecture, accounting, actuarial science, performing arts, or consulting, and (b) substantially all of the stock of which is held by employees or by their estates.

A corporation can generally declare and pay dividends — as well as salaries — in such a manner as to avoid a "bunching" of income in those years when personal income is highest. On the other hand, if the business were established in the partnership form, the owners would have little control over the receipt and taxation of income. This ability to "time" income is important because, if income can be timed, the ultimate taxes payable can be lowered.

5. When the estate owner wants to entice family members into the business by giving them a stake in the business without giving them control.

6. When privacy is desired. The transfer of stock in a closely held corporation is not generally a matter of public record. This makes it possible to shield family financial affairs from public scrutiny.

7. When continuity of operation is important. A corporation may, within limits, legally continue its business with little or no hindrance from the probate court. This makes it possible for corporate officers to make major decisions regarding property that the client has contributed to the corporation without the necessity or delay of the judicial process, and with little or no publicity.

8. When gift tax savings are desired. The transfer of a minority interest in a closely held business may result in

a discounted value for gift tax purposes. In other words, transfers of property (via its stock "wrapper") can sometimes be made at discounted values for gift tax purposes.

9. When estate tax savings are desired. Transfers of stock reduce the donor's estate by (1) shifting appreciation in value from donor to donee and (2) shifting income on stock (dividends) to the donee. The stock that is ultimately included in the donor's estate may itself be a minority interest and may therefore (or because of lack of marketability) be valued at a discount.

Disadvantages of the Corporate Form

1. There are a number of additional expenses associated with forming and maintaining a corporation (e.g., attorney fees, accounting fees, corporate supplies, state incorporation fees, and the ongoing expenses of maintaining the corporate form).

2. Since the passage of the 1986 Tax Reform Act, the maximum tax rate at the corporate level is higher than the maximum tax rate at the individual level. Thus, for businesses with substantial taxable income, incorporating may increase income taxes. (For a form of corporation that can take advantage of the lower individual rates, see Chapter 29, S Corporation.)

3. While some types of income passed through to shareholders are taxed only once (e.g., salaries), dividends are subject to both corporate and shareholder levels of tax.

4. One of the most dramatic disadvantages created by the Tax Reform Act of 1986 was the repeal of the *General Utilities* doctrine. The *General Utilities* doctrine allowed a corporation to avoid recognizing a gain upon a liquida-

tion or sale (followed by a liquidation) of the business. There was generally only one tax at the shareholder level (except for certain recaptures, receivables, etc.).

For example, under the prior rules, if a shareholder invested $10,000 in a corporation and the corporation invested the cash in a piece of land that was worth $100,000 after 10 years, upon liquidation the corporation would give the land to the shareholder, and the shareholder would receive a $100,000 value in exchange for turning in the stock that cost him $10,000. This would result in a $90,000 capital gain. The corporation generally would not recognize any gain and was not taxed on any excess of value over the cost the corporation had in the land.

Under the 1986 Act abolishing the doctrine, upon liquidation, the corporation would be treated as having "sold" the corporate assets and would be taxed on the excess value of the assets over the corporation's basis in the assets. If the corporation had only a $10,000 income tax basis in the land and the land was worth $100,000, then the corporation would first have to recognize a $90,000 gain. Whatever was left after the corporation paid the tax would come out to the shareholder in the liquidation and the shareholder would then be taxed on that receipt, resulting in two taxes to pay.

5. Corporations demand a more complex organizational structure and may have to contend with additional complex issues (e.g., personal holding company tax, accumulated earnings tax, dividend treatment, and collapsible corporation rules).

6. Personal service corporations are taxed at a flat rate of 35 percent from the very first dollar. This 35 percent tax eliminates the benefit of the "run up the brackets" for doctors, lawyers, accountants, architects, and other professionals who practice in the corporate form. If the corporation "zeroes out" its taxable income through reasonable salary payments to employee shareholders, there will be no taxable income upon which the IRS can impose the 35 percent tax. But this makes it more likely that the IRS will soon try to disallow deductions for salary payments in a professional service corporation under the "reasonableness" test. In other words, the IRS has a strong incentive to claim that payments made as compensation should be recharacterized as nondeductible dividends to shareholder employees. If the IRS is successful with such an attack, the corporation will then be taxed at 35 percent — and then the same dollars will again be taxed to the shareholders upon receipt. One way out of the 35 percent tax trap is to elect S corporation treatment.

HOW IT IS DONE — AN EXAMPLE

Stevens, Roberts, and Lee are engineers who feel they can develop a relatively inexpensive process for manufacturing an aircraft safety component that is in great demand for new jet airliners.

Stevens is a sole proprietor currently engaged in producing aircraft parts. Roberts, a young man who has a post-graduate degree in business administration and an undergraduate degree in engineering, has worked for Stevens for a number of years. He first started as an engineer and almost by accident moved into the firm's sales division. Robert's sales efforts have been so successful that Stevens would like to offer him an interest in a new business venture.

Lee is slightly older than Stevens or Roberts. He is a well-known and highly respected authority in the area of aircraft safety parts. He does quite a bit of consulting work for both government and private enterprise. He met Stevens and Roberts on such a consulting project, and the three men have become good friends. Lee is quite wealthy, and he is interested in keeping both his money and his mind at work.

All three men have something to contribute to a corporation. In return they will want to participate in the control and profits of the business while it is running, or in a distribution of the assets of the business if the corporation's life ends. In other words, they will expect "shares" of the corporation. Assume Stevens will contribute his business (his sole proprietorship). Lee will contribute cash or securities. Roberts wants to contribute his services and a small amount of cash in return for his stock.

Assuming this were the case, here is what might happen: If Lee decides that his contribution to the capital of the corporation will be cash, the stock he receives will normally have a value at the time of the exchange equal to the cash. For example, if he transfers $10,000 of cash to the corporation, he will ordinarily receive back stock with a fair market value of $10,000. Because the value of the stock he receives is no more or less than the value of the cash he transfers to the corporation, he realized neither a gain nor a loss. If he later sells his stock, the cash he paid will determine the basis of his stock. If he realizes $21,000 on the sale of the stock, his gain would be $11,000, the difference between his basis for the stock ($10,000) and the amount he realizes on the sale ($21,000).

Absent provisions in the tax law to the contrary, if any of the three contributed appreciated property to the corporation in return for its stock, a taxable gain would result. But there is an important exception to that general rule.

The exception was designed to encourage the formation of a new corporation. It enables a taxpayer to transfer appreciated property, or even a going business, into a new corporation without the transferor recognizing income on the appreciation at the very time when his other expenses — the expenses involved in the organization and operation of the corporation — are the highest. The exception provides that even if the transferor "realizes" a gain when he transfers appreciated property to his new corporation, he does not have to "recognize" gain for tax purposes.[6]

This exception is conditioned on meeting certain basic requirements. It basically states that where a person or persons transfer *property* to a corporation (a) solely in exchange for the corporation's own stock, and (b) the transferor(s) control the corporation immediately after the transfer, no gain will be recognized on the appreciated business or securities contributed to the new corporation. Control generally means ownership of 80 percent or more of the corporation's stock.[7]

For incorporations prior to October 2, 1989, "securities," which could include long term notes, could also be received in exchange for appreciated assets without the recognition of gain. OBRA '89 narrowed this exemption solely to the receipt of stock by treating as "boot" any securities received. This results in the recognition of gain to the extent of the lesser of the amount of gain inherent in the assets transferred or the amount of "boot" received.

The tax free exchange for stock is similar to the theory making a like-kind exchange tax free. The transferor who receives stock in exchange for his property has really maintained an interest in the original property. It has merely changed form and now has the physical identity of "stock." This "continuity of interest" concept is a key to nonrecognition of the gain on the appreciated property transferred. [It is important to recognize, however, that for the purposes of corporate law, a shareholder has an undivided interest (shared with all other shareholders) in all corporate property, but that his rights in any specific corporate property (even though originally transferred by him to the corporation in a tax-free exchange) are extremely limited.]

For example, suppose Stevens, who is now operating as a sole proprietor, decides to transfer his going business to the new corporation. If his basis for the sole proprietorship is $10,000, and the fair market value of his business is $50,000 at the time he transfers it to the new corporation, he would probably receive $50,000 worth of stock.

Under the general rule for taxing sales and exchanges, he would realize a $40,000 gain. However, the nonrecognition provision provides that because he received only stock and through that stock controlled the corporation (just as he previously controlled his sole proprietorship), what has happened is really only a substitution of stock certificates for his former physical possession of the property.

This rule is logical because to realize gain there must be a taxable event which usually occurs in the form of a sale, exchange, or other disposition of property. Although technically there may be a sale (a transfer of property in return for money or a promise to pay money) or exchange (a transfer of property in return for other property or services), there has been no exchange in substance. Stevens, in the example, has not disposed of his property. He has merely received certificates that evidence that he changed the form of ownership in the original property. This would apply no matter how many people transfer property to the corporation. As long as it was done collectively, if the taxpayers transferring property to the corporation still have both (a) control and (b) interest in the property they originally owned, they would not have to recognize any gain on receipt of the new corporation's stock. Thus, Stevens would not have to recognize the $40,000 gain until and unless he later sells his stock.

Under the assumed facts, if Roberts were to receive stock in the new corporation in exchange for his services, the value of the stock would be currently taxable to him, as stock issued for services is not considered as issued for "property." If Roberts' stock was issued solely for services, it will not be counted in determining whether the transferors of property control the corporation after the exchange.

In addition, if the property that is contributed is subject to liabilities in excess of basis, gain will be recognized to the extent of such excess.

IMPLICATIONS AND ISSUES IN COMMUNITY PROPERTY STATES

Stock purchased by an investor in a corporation will take on the character of the assets used to purchase the stock. Thus, if an individual transfers $1,000 to a corporation in return for stock and that $1,000 consists of community property earnings, the stock itself will be community property. Of course, this result could be altered by a written agreement between the spouse and the investor to treat the stock as property other than community property, or by titling the stock in some other fashion, e.g., as joint tenancy or as the separate property of one spouse.

Upon divorce or death of the stockholder, the community property interest of the spouse will become important. It will be necessary to determine what portion of the stock is community property. As discussed in Chapter 1, a common problem is the situation where a person owned all or most of the stock of a corporation prior to marriage, the person works full time for the corporation, and the value of the corporation increases significantly. A portion of the increase in value of the person's stock may be community property to the extent the increase is attributable to his or her insufficiently rewarded hard work during the marriage, and a portion will be separate property to the extent the increase is the result of the natural increase or earnings of the original stock. The method of valuation cannot be predicted with certainty.

One question which often arises in community property states is the power to manage and control the community property. Until 1975, California law provided that the husband had the management and control over the community property. Under a revision of the community property laws, both spouses now have management power and control over community property. (Similar changes have occurred in the laws of other community property states.) This has implications in connection with the management and control over a corporation. California law provides that a spouse who is operating or managing a business or an interest in a business that is community personal property has the sole management and control of the business or interest. Thus, if an individual owns all the stock in a manufacturing corporation and that individual is also the manager of the business, or a substantial participant in the management of the business, the individual's spouse will not be able to exercise equal control in regard to the management of that business. This allows people to choose business associates and manage a business without regard to the effect of community property laws.

QUESTIONS AND ANSWERS

Question — Why do stockholders often finance business needs by lending money to their corporations rather than by increasing their equity (stock) interest?

Answer — One of the key advantages of operating a business in the corporate form is that many different types of ownership interests in corporations can be created. The interests of any particular investor can be met by creating a security that fits his special needs and desires. This factor facilitates the acquisition of capital. Suppose that in order to acquire working capital and capital for long-term planning the corporation issued bonds. These are written obligations to repay a definite sum of money on a definite date, usually at least 10, and more often 29 or more, years from the date the bond was issued.

Bonds are a favored means of raising corporate capital. One reason for this is that a corporation will obtain a deduction for the interest paid on the indebtedness, but no deduction is allowed for dividends paid on either preferred or common stock. As long as a corporation can earn money at a higher rate (with the cash raised by issuing the bond) than it costs the corporation (in interest

necessary to "service the debt"), it usually makes sense for the corporation to borrow money. This is known as "leverage."

Issuance of the bonds generally creates no tax liability to either the corporation or the bondholder. This is because the corporation has merely borrowed money and agreed to return it. Conversely, the bondholders have merely loaned money. When the bond "matures," the principal becomes payable and the bondholders are entitled to a tax-free return of their capital investment. In contrast, the return of equity is a taxable dividend, unless the return can qualify as a stock redemption (which is not a dividend).

A distribution by a corporation with respect to its stock is considered a return on the shareholders' investment and is taxable as a dividend to the extent of corporate earnings and profits — unless the distribution can qualify as a "sale" or "exchange," in which case only the gain in excess of basis is taxable.

Any money bondholders receive in the form of interest, and any money they receive at the maturity of their bonds (after 1987) in excess of their capital investment will be taxed at ordinary income rates. Receiving money in excess of capital investment can occur when bonds are purchased at a discount but are paid off at face value. (When bonds are *issued* at a discount by the issuing corporation, a bondholder must include a ratable portion of the discount in income each year as the bond matures. For example, if a bond with a par value of $1,000 was issued for $800 and is payable in 10 years, the $200 discount would be included in the taxpayer's income at the rate of $20 a year.)

Another reason bonds are often favored over an increase in equity is that the accumulation of earnings and profits within the corporation to pay debt obligations can be justified more readily than accumulating income to redeem stock. This helps avoid an additional tax on an unreasonable income accumulation.

Question — What is "thin capitalization"?

Answer — Because the interest paid on corporate indebtedness is deductible, the cost of borrowing money through long-term corporate debt is substantially reduced. However, some shareholders attempt to overdo it — they contribute almost no equity investment and characterize almost their entire contribution as debt owed to them by the corporation. This is known as "thin capitalization," because the capital investment is "thin" in relation to the debt, but the "debt" is really disguised stock.

Once the form of the "debt" is disregarded by the IRS and the substance is treated appropriately, corporate deductions for "interest" payments to shareholders are disallowed. Second, receipt of "interest" payments by shareholder-creditors are reclassified and treated as dividends. Third, when the corporation pays off its "debt" to the shareholders, that payment may be taxed as dividend. This means that instead of treating the amount received as a tax-free repayment of a debt, the shareholder-creditor must report some or all of the distribution as income. Finally, money that the corporation purportedly was accumulating to pay off the "debt" is now subject to the accumulated earnings tax (which is discussed below). Also, a debt that is reclassified as stock could cause a termination of a Subchapter S election, because a Subchapter S corporation is allowed to have only one class of stock.

To determine if a security should be classified as debt rather than equity, the courts usually examine a number of factors such as: Was there an intention by shareholders to enforce payment of the debt? Was there a debt instrument and did it give the shareholders management or voting rights (like stock)? What was the ratio of debt to equity? A general rule of thumb, subject to variation depending upon the industry, is that if the amount of debt exceeds shareholders' equity by more than four to one, the corporation is thinly capitalized. Basically, the court would examine all the factors relevant to determining if a "loan" by shareholders was in reality more like an ownership interest (stock) than a debtor-creditor relationship.[8]

Keep in mind that, while bonds are a tax-favored means of obtaining corporate funds, frequently a corporation does not want to become obligated to make fixed payments for interest and debt amortization. To avoid a cash flow problem, therefore, corporations often finance long-term operations or investments by common stock, which entail no obligation to pay dividends or preferred stock on which dividend payments can frequently be avoided.

Question — How is a corporation taxed?

Answer — A corporation is taxed as an entity separate from its shareholders. A 15 percent rate is applied to the first $50,000 of corporate taxable income, a 25 percent rate applies to the next $25,000, a 34 percent rate is levied on the next $25,000, 39 percent on the next $235,000, then 34 percent on any additional taxable income.

The 39 percent tax on income between $100,000 and $335,000 includes a 5 percent add-on tax that is designed to phase out the graduated rates. Corporations with taxable income of $335,000 or more, in effect pay tax at a flat 34 percent rate on all taxable income.

For example, a corporation with $100,000 of taxable income would pay a tax of $22,250 ($50,000 x 15%, plus 25% of $25,000, plus 34% of $25,000). A corporation with $500,000 of taxable income would pay a tax of $170,000 (34% of $500,000). Corporations, like individuals, are liable for a number of other state and local taxes as well. The corporation would report its federal income tax on IRS Form 1120.

Graphically, the return might look like the illustration at Figure 17.2.

Gross income includes such items as profit from sales and receipts from services. It also includes gains on sales or exchanges, income from rent, royalties, interest, and dividends.

A corporation is entitled to two types of deductions; ordinary deductions and special deductions. Ordinary deductions include compensation of officers and salaries, bonuses, rent payments, charitable contributions, repair expenses, interest paid on indebtedness, casualty losses, deductions for depreciation and amortization of research and experimental costs, advertising, and corporate contributions to pension and profit-sharing plans. A corporation also receives a carryover deduction for a net operating loss.

"Special" deductions include a "dividends received" deduction. Prior law allowed a corporation that owned less than 80 percent of the stock of another corporation to deduct 80 percent of the dividends received. Under current law, there are now three rules:

(1) If the recipient corporation owns less than 20 percent of the voting power and value of stock of the issuing corporation, the 80 percent dividends received deduction is reduced to 70 percent of the amount of the dividend.

(2) If the recipient corporation holds 20 percent or more (up to 79 percent) of the stock of the issuing corporation, the 80 percent dividends received deduction remains at 80 percent.

(3) If the recipient corporation owns 80 percent or more of the stock of the issuing corporation, a 100 percent deduction may apply to dividends received.

The bottom line is that a closely held corporation that holds the stock of a publicly held corporation will likely

Figure 17.2

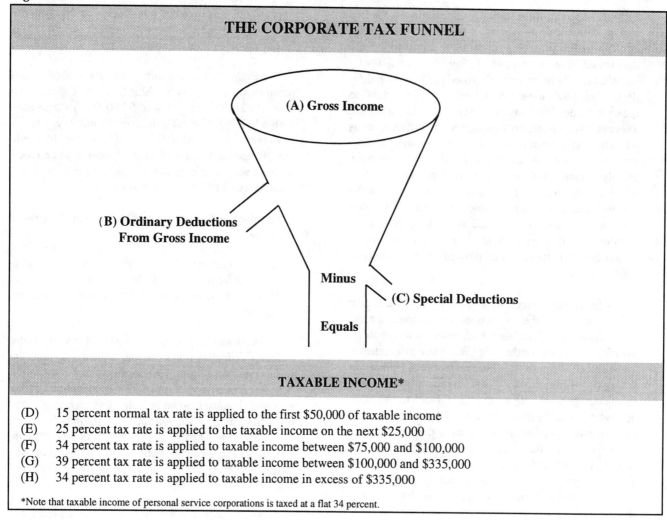

THE CORPORATE TAX FUNNEL

(A) Gross Income

(B) Ordinary Deductions
From Gross Income

Minus

(C) Special Deductions

Equals

TAXABLE INCOME*

(D) 15 percent normal tax rate is applied to the first $50,000 of taxable income
(E) 25 percent tax rate is applied to the taxable income on the next $25,000
(F) 34 percent tax rate is applied to taxable income between $75,000 and $100,000
(G) 39 percent tax rate is applied to taxable income between $100,000 and $335,000
(H) 34 percent tax rate is applied to taxable income in excess of $335,000

*Note that taxable income of personal service corporations is taxed at a flat 34 percent.

be entitled to deduct 70 percent of every dollar it receives in the form of dividends on the stock it holds. It therefore will pay a top tax of 39 percent on 30 percent of each dividend dollar, an effective rate of only 11.7 percent.

A corporation may also elect to amortize its organizational cost over five or more years. This would also be considered a special deduction.

Taxable income is what is left after taking ordinary and special deductions. It is the amount to which the various percentage tax rates are applied. Certain credits are then directly applied against this tax, such as corporate overpayments of tax in previous years, payments for estimated taxes (paid on a quarterly basis), and credit on certain foreign taxes paid. Prior to 1986, an investment credit was also allowed.

Question — Many business and estate planning tools are corporate fringe benefits that are deductible to the extent

reasonable (as well as ordinary and necessary). What is meant by "reasonable"?

Answer — A corporation is entitled to a deduction for salaries or any other compensation for personal services, but only if the services are actually rendered and the amount paid as compensation for those services is considered "reasonable." Reasonable means only that amount which would ordinarily be paid for similar services by other corporations under similar circumstances.

This reasonableness test is imposed most frequently on closely held corporations because of the large degree of coincidence of executive and shareholder interest. It is designed to prevent the shareholders from draining off corporate profits in the disguise of tax-deductible salaries. Corporate profits are usually paid out in the form of dividends that are taxable to the shareholders, but nondeductible by the corporation. The portion of the salary considered unreasonable is usually classified as a disguised dividend and, to that extent, the corporation's deduction is disallowed. However, even though that amount may not be deducted by the corporation, it is still taxable as ordinary income to the shareholder-recipient subject to a maximum rate of 31 percent.[9]

Reasonableness is a question of determining the amount that would ordinarily be paid for like services by like enterprises under similar circumstances. Generally, where an executive employee does not own or have options to purchase stock, arm's length bargaining as to the amount of salary is assumed. One element that could be considered in determining reasonableness is the fact that a given individual was not adequately compensated in prior years. Thus, if high compensation in the current year can be attributed to services rendered in prior years, the total current salary might be considered reasonable.

However, the amount of cash compensation is not the only relevant factor. Corporate contributions to pension and profit-sharing plans are considered business expenses and are allowed as deductions as long as the total amount of all forms of compensation paid on behalf of an individual does not exceed a reasonable total.

Some of the other indirect forms of compensation may be: premiums for life insurance; hospitalization; medical care; and salary continuation plans. Costs of these plans, although generally deductible by the corporation, often do not result in taxable income to the individual. Because the corporation is a separate and distinct tax entity, and because working shareholders would be considered salaried employees, they would be eligible for these forms of indirect compensations. This is true even if they are not only employees, but also officers, directors, and shareholders of the corporation.

An employee may exclude from gross income the following fringe benefits: (1) a "no-additional-cost service" (e.g., free stand-by flights to airline employees); (2) "qualified employee discounts" (e.g., discounts on the selling price of qualified property or services of the employer); (3) certain working condition fringes (e.g., employee parking and athletic facilities); and (4) "de minimis" fringes such as typing of personal letters by the company secretary or the personal use of company copying machines.

In order for the "no-additional-cost services" and the "qualified employee discounts" to be excluded from income of officers, owners and highly compensated employees, they must be provided to employees on a nondiscriminatory basis.

Question — What is the accumulated earnings tax?

Answer — One of the easiest and most common means of financing growth is to accumulate earnings and plow them back into the corporation to purchase new machinery, buildings, and other necessary capital assets. These "plowed-back" earnings and profits begin to add up very quickly. Because the corporate tax rate may be lower than the rate of tax upon the incomes of individual shareholders, they may attempt to use the corporation as a vehicle for reducing taxes by having the corporation retain earnings rather than make taxable distributions in the form of nondeductible dividends.

If a corporation reasonably allows earnings to accumulate in order to fund current or anticipated needs or projects that the corporation has planned, there should not be a problem. However, once earnings are allowed to accumulate beyond the reasonable needs of the business, those earnings may be subject to an additional tax, the accumulated earnings tax.[10]

The accumulated earnings tax is imposed on every corporation that is formed or used for the purpose of avoiding personal income tax with respect to its shareholders by permitting earnings and profits to accumulate instead of being distributed. The purpose of the tax is to discourage the use of a corporation as an accumulation vehicle to shelter its individual stockholders from taxation at personal income tax rates. As a regulative device, the accumulated earnings tax was designed to force the distribution of retained earnings at the point where they no longer serve a legitimate business purpose. Without such a tax on improper accumulations, stockholders could arrange to have dividends paid in years when their incomes were low or they could indefinitely accumulate earnings and profits inside the corporation until the corporation was liquidated.

The Code allows an accumulated earnings credit of $250,000 ($150,000 in the case of personal service corporations) that will be presumed to be for the reasonable business needs of the corporation. A controlled group of corporations is allowed one accumulated earnings credit, not one per corporation. Thus, if a corporation begins to accumulate amounts in excess of $250,000, it should be prepared to show a bona fide business reason for not distributing these earnings in the form of dividends.

The accumulated earnings tax is designed to tax only earnings retained beyond the reasonable needs of the business. The question then becomes: "What reasonable needs would a corporation have for accumulating profits?" The regulations state that working capital needs and capital for building expansion or for the replacement of plant or equipment are among the needs that would allow a business to properly accumulate earnings. In addition to these needs, a sinking fund to retire corporate bonds at maturity has often been found to be a reasonable need to accumulate cash. In other cases, funds set aside to acquire minority interests or quarreling stockholders' interests were also deemed to be retained for reasonable business needs. The Code says that the term "reasonable needs of the business" includes the Section 303 redemption needs of the business (see Chapter 31), although specific protection from the tax (within limits) is provided only in the corporation tax year in which the stockholder dies and in subsequent years.[11] The reasonableness of accumulations in years prior to a year in which the shareholder dies is to be determined solely upon the facts and circumstances existing at the times the accumulations occur.[12]

The accumulated earnings tax rate is 28 percent on all "accumulated taxable income."

The tax, if applicable, is imposed only on "accumulated taxable income"; an amount that is derived from the taxable income of the corporation for the particular year in question. Thus, the tax does not apply to all of the accumulated earnings and profits of the corporation, but only to the accumulated taxable income of the year or years as to which the tax is asserted.

This tax on a corporation's accumulated taxable income is payable in addition to the regular tax payable by the firm. "Accumulated taxable income" basically means the corporation's taxable income for the year in question with certain adjustments (such as a reduction for federal income taxes paid) minus the sum of (a) distributions from current earnings and profits that the shareholders have reported as ordinary income (dividends paid), (b) amounts from earnings and profits that the shareholders have reported as dividends even though no actual distribution was made (disguised dividends), and (c) the accumulated earnings credit.

In determining whether or not the current year's accumulated taxable income has been retained for the reasonable needs of the business, the availability of prior years' accumulated earnings must also be considered. If past years' accumulations are sufficient to meet current needs (i.e., this year's business needs) there is no justification for accumulating current earnings.

Question — Will corporate-owned cash value life insurance purchased for key person, split dollar, or deferred compensation financing cause an accumulated earnings tax problem?

Answer — That depends on whether or not the insurance answers a valid corporate business need. There must also be a close correlation between the type of policy and amount of death benefit and the alleged corporate need. Generally, hedging against the loss of a key employee's service because of unexpected death is considered to be a reasonable business need.

Key person life insurance is insurance that is owned by the corporation insuring the life of a key employee. The purpose of such a policy is to provide a fund at the employee's death which will compensate the corporation for the financial loss resulting from the unavailability of the employee to render services to the corporation. Often, key person insurance death proceeds are also used to help in finding and compensating a suitable replacement. Therefore, the purchase of life insurance and the earnings used to pay policy premiums should not, per se, be subject to the penalty tax. The point is that it is not the amount, but the purpose of the accumulation, that is important.

The same question often arises as to the effect of a split dollar plan. If a corporation attempts to prevent taxation of income to shareholders by accumulating its earnings rather than distributing them, the existence or nonexistence of a split dollar policy will not, by itself, deter the imposition of the tax penalty provided by the law. Conversely, the existence of a split dollar policy will not, per se, incur the accumulations tax penalty if the corporation is not, in fact, accumulating earnings beyond the reasonable needs of the business.

This section of the code exists to deter tax evasion and not to prevent a business from operating in a normal businesslike manner. The same principle applies in cases where the corporation has obligated itself to make pre-retirement death benefits to a key executive under a deferred compensation agreement. An accumulation of corporate earnings to meet obligations under such an agreement is generally considered a reasonable business need (just as the funds accumulated to retire an outstanding corporate bond would be considered reasonable).

A third area where this question often arises is the use of accumulated earnings to provide surplus cash for the redemption of stock. In this case, if the redemption is to be utilized to shift partial or complete control to the remaining shareholders without depleting their personal funds (as for example, where, by shareholder agreement, the corporation will retire shares on the death of a shareholder), it is doubtful that accumulations to reach this result would be found to be a reasonable need. However, if a business purpose can be found, such as an accumulation to purchase the shares of a dissenting minority, then the accumulation may be found to be reasonable. The primary purpose must be a corporate, rather than an individual, benefit from the stock redemption.

Question — What is the personal holding company tax?

Answer — Code section 541 imposes a tax on companies classified as personal holding companies. The tax applies to undistributed personal holding company income and is designed to discourage the use of corporations as "incorporated pocketbooks" wherein income from securities, real property, or personal talents is taxed at corporate rates rather than individual rates.

To be classified as a personal holding company, the corporation must meet both of the following tests: (1) more than 50% of the value of its stock is owned by five or fewer individuals, and (2) at least 60% of its "adjusted ordinary gross income" is "personal holding company income." Personal holding company income consists of (1) passive income, such as rents, royalties, dividends, and interest, and (2) income from personal service contracts under which the corporation is to furnish personal services but the corporation does not have the right to select the individual who will perform the services, and the individual selected by the client owns directly or indirectly 25% or more of the stock in the corporation.

For more on personal holding companies, see Chapter 25.

Question — What problems may a "personal service corporation" with only one significant customer face from the Internal Revenue Service where the primary purpose of incorporating was to obtain tax benefits?

Answer — Code section 269A specifically authorizes the IRS to reallocate between an employee-owner of a "personal service corporation" (defined as a corporation whose principal activity is the performance of personal services, with such services substantially performed by employee-owners) and the "personal service corporation" all income, deductions, credits, exclusions and other allowances to the extent necessary to prevent tax avoidance or evasion or to reflect clearly the income of the "personal service corporation" or any of its employee-owners. The authority to reallocate applies only in the event that substantially all of the services of the "personal service corporation" are performed for or on behalf of one other corporation, partnership or other entity and the "personal service corporation" was formed for the principal purpose of avoiding or evading federal income tax by reducing the income of the employee-owner or by securing for him a significant tax benefit not otherwise available. The

typical corporation affected by this law is a corporate partner in a partnership of personal service corporations.[13]

The potential impact of Section 269A has been greatly reduced by the parity created between corporate and Keogh plans, because the tax benefits of a corporate qualified plan are now available to non-corporate entities.

Question — What is the corporate AMT and how does it affect corporate owned life insurance?

Answer — The corporate AMT (alternative minimum tax) is the excess, if any, of a tentative minimum tax over the regular corporate income tax. Life insurance proceeds and inside buildup on a life insurance contract are among the tax "preferences" added to a corporation's ordinary taxable income to determine its alternative minimum taxable income (AMTI) and, therefore, its alternative minimum tax.

To determine a corporation's alternative minimum tax, the corporation must first compute a "tentative alternative minimum taxable income" (TAMTI) equal to its regular taxable income plus certain disallowed deductions. The corporation must then compute its "adjusted current earnings" (ACE). The ACE adjustment is designed to approximate the corporation's pre-tax net book income as measured for financial accounting purposes and is calculated by beginning with AMTI, adding earnings and profits income items (including life insurance proceeds and inside buildup on a life insurance contract), subtracting certain deductible items, and recalculating certain depreciation deductions. The corporation then increases or decreases its TAMTI by 75% of the amount by which ACE exceeds or falls short of TAMTI to arrive at the final alternative minimum taxable income. The tax itself is a flat 20% of AMTI. A corporation receives a $40,000 exemption that is reduced by 25% of the amount by which AMTI exceeds $150,000 (thus phasing out completely at $310,000).

The AMT can be considered a prepayment of the corporation's regular tax because a credit is allowed that reduces the regular tax of the corporation in future years. This credit is equal to the amount by which the regular tax exceeds the current year's AMT.

For example, a calendar year corporation has ACE of $400 in 1992, $300 in 1993, and $200 in 1994. Unadjusted AMTI is $300 for each of those years. In 1992, ACE exceeds unadjusted AMTI by $100, 75 percent of which ($75) must be included as an additional item of

AMTI. In 1994, unadjusted AMTI exceeds ACE by $100, creating a potential negative adjustment to AMTI of $75. As the aggregate increases to AMTI for prior years equals $75 (the amount added to alternative minimum tax in 1992) and there are no aggregated reductions, the full amount of the potential negative adjustment will reduce AMTI for 1994.

Aside from affecting a corporation's ACE adjustment, corporate-owned life insurance is taxed as follows:

- The premiums are not tax deductible.

- The annual premium reduces earnings and profits to the extent the premium exceeds the annual increase in the cash surrender value of the policy. If the increase exceeds the premium, then that difference will increase earnings and profits.

- The insurance proceeds are income tax free (for regular corporate purposes).

- Upon receipt of the policy proceeds, earnings and profits are increased by the excess of the amount received over the cash surrender value of the policy at the close of the immediately preceding taxable year.

There are several ways of dealing with the AMT. The easiest is merely to make up the difference through additional life insurance coverage. The additional premium can be partially funded with the extra income the corporation should have (assuming its tax bracket dropped from pre-TRA '86 levels). The following calculation shows how to determine the approximate amount of additional life insurance necessary to compensate the corporation for the effect of the AMT:

| Step 1: | State the face amount before the AMT tax: | $1,000,000 |
| Step 2: | Divide the face amount by .85: | $1,176,471 |

This amount, $1,176,471, is (roughly) the before-AMT amount necessary for the corporation to net $1,000,000 after the AMT. Conservative planners will round up this amount.

Another alternative to the purchase of more life insurance is an S corporation election. Had the same business elected S status with no taxable income, there would be no tax at either the corporate or individual level.

ASRS, Sec. 43.

Footnote References

Incorporation

1. Reg. §301.7701-2(a).
2. Reg. §301.7701-2(d).
3. Reg. §301.7701-2(e)(2).
4. Reg. §301.7701-2(c).
5. Reg. §301.7701-2(b).
6. IRC Sec. 351.
7. IRC Sec. 368(c); Reg. §1.351-1(a)(1).
8. IRC Sec. 385.
9. IRC Secs. 1, 61.
10. IRC Secs. 531, 532.
11. IRC Secs. 537(a)(2), 537(b)(1).
12. Reg. §1.537-1(e)(3).
13. IRC Sec. 269A.

Chapter 18

INDIVIDUAL RETIREMENT PLANS (and SEPs)

WHAT IS IT?

Any individual who is not participating in a qualified private or governmental pension plan, profit-sharing plan, HR-10 plan, or tax deferred annuity can set up an individual retirement account (IRA) and take a deduction from gross income equal to the lesser of: (1) $2,000 or (2) 100 percent of compensation includable in his gross income.[1]

If an individual is actively participating in a qualified plan or tax sheltered annuity, a maximum annual contribution of $2,000 can be made to an IRA. A tax deduction for this contribution to an IRA is allowed for single filers with adjusted gross income not in excess of $35,000. The deduction is phased out for single filers with incomes of between $25,000 and $35,000.[2] Tax-deferred compounding of nondeductible IRA contributions is still permitted.[3]

An individual who has earnings and who files a joint return with a non-wage-earning spouse can contribute up to the lesser of $2,250 or 100 percent of compensation for the tax year—reduced in either case by the contributions made for the tax year by him or on his behalf to his own individual retirement plan (other than employer contributions to a simplified employee pension plan)—if he establishes separate IRAs (or IRA subaccounts) for himself and his non-wage-earning spouse. Contributions do not have to be allocated equally to each IRA or IRA subaccount, but at least $250 (and no more than $2,000) must be contributed for the nonworking spouse to take advantage of the $2,250 deduction. A deduction for the full amount contributed is permissible if the individual is not actively participating in a qualified plan or tax sheltered annuity. An individual may contribute up to the same limits even if the spouse does work if the spouse elects to be treated as having no compensation for the year. If that is the case, the amount contributed is fully deductible only if neither the individual or his spouse actively participate in an employer's plan.

Where one or both spouses actively participate in a qualified plan or tax sheltered annuity, a tax deduction is allowed for joint filers with adjusted gross income not in excess of $50,000. The deductions are phased out between $40,000 and $50,000 of joint income.[4]

The Internal Revenue Code also allows certain individuals receiving certain distributions from a qualified plan (includ-ing pension, profit-sharing, stock bonus, or annuity plans) or a tax deferred annuity to "roll over" the distribution within 60 days to an IRA without incurring income tax on the distribution. This tax-free rollover treatment is available to individuals who receive most types of distributions from a qualified plan or tax deferred annuity. Legislation enacted in 1992 broadened the definition of which types of distributions from these plans are eligible for rollover treatment.[5] These rules are effective for distributions made after 1992[6] whereas distributions made prior to this date were subject to generally more stringent rules. Distributions of accumulated deductible employee contributions which were made to such qualified plans or tax deferred annuities may also be rolled over tax free to an IRA (or in some cases even to another qualified employer plan—if such plan permits). No rollover is permitted for benefits attributable to nondeductible employee contributions made by the individual to the qualified plan.

Any part of the taxable portion of a distribution received after 1992, from a qualified retirement plan or a tax sheltered annuity, other than a required minimum distribution, can be rolled over without incurring income tax to an IRA or to another qualified plan or tax sheltered annuity.[7] There is an exception to this general rule allowing rollover treatment. No tax-free rollover is permitted if the distribution is part of a series of substantially equal payments made over the life expectancy of the plan participant or the joint life expectancies of the participant and his or her beneficiary or over a period of ten or more years.[8]

Further, any qualified retirement or annuity plan must allow its participants to elect to have any distribution that is eligible for rollover treatment handled by means of a direct rollover, i.e., a trustee-to-trustee transfer. If this method is not elected, but rather the funds are distributed to the individual participant a mandatory income tax withholding of 20 percent must be made. The participant cannot elect out of withholding from such a distribution. This mandatory 20 percent withholding applies even if the participant receiving the distribution rolls the funds over within 60 days.[9]

Distributions received prior to 1993 were eligible for "roll over" within 60 days to an IRA without incurring income tax on the distribution if the rollover was either a qualified total distribution or a qualifying partial distribution.[10]

Individuals who receive a distribution which includes property can make a bona fide sale of the property and roll over, within the usual sixty day period, all or part of the proceeds to an IRA. It is not necessary to roll over the actual property received.

The spouse of a deceased IRA holder may be able to roll over a distribution received after the deceased spouse's death to an IRA. This is discussed in the question and answer section of this chapter. Simplified employee pensions (SEPs) are also discussed below in the question and answer section.

WHEN IS THE USE OF SUCH A DEVICE INDICATED?

1. When the married client or spouse is covered under a qualified plan and does not make in excess of $50,000. This deduction is phased out for incomes of between $40,000 to $50,000. Even if the contribution is not tax deductible under the above limits, the earnings will accumulate income tax-free. Additionally, the client should be receiving an income which is not needed by the family to maintain its current standard of living, and which could be put aside for retirement.

2. An IRA is indicated where neither the client nor spouse is covered under a qualified plan, but both work. If the client and spouse are both working, each can have his or her own IRA and contribute up to the maximum based on his or her respective income assuming both otherwise qualify.

3. An IRA is also indicated where the client is not covered under a plan, has earned income, is married, and his or her spouse has no income from employment.

4. An IRA may also be indicated where an individual has received a distribution from a qualified plan or tax deferred annuity and seeks to avoid current taxation on all or a part of the distribution.

5. The client may be an employer who does not have any type of qualified retirement plan and would like to establish a plan covering only himself.

6. Where an individual who files a single return is an active participant in a qualified plan, has an adjusted gross income not in excess of $35,000, and wants to make additional tax deductible voluntary contributions to an IRA. This deduction is phased out for such individuals with incomes of between $25,000 and $35,000.

WHAT ARE THE REQUIREMENTS?

1. An individual can set aside retirement savings in a variable premium annuity contract, a regular fixed rate annu-ity contract, or a trusteed or custodial account with a bank, savings and loan, or credit union. Also, it is possible to split total contributions into two IRAs. For example, a part of the permissible contribution could go into a variable premium annuity contract and the balance could be placed into a trusteed bank account.[11]

2. Three parties can make deposits to an IRA. These are the employee, the employee's employer, or the employee's union.

3. Annual contributions must be made in cash. Contributions of other property are not permissible (except in the case of "rollovers").[12]

4. The plan must be established and the contribution made within the taxable year for which a deduction is allowed or before the due date (not including extensions) for filing the individual's tax returns for that taxable year. For most taxpayers, the contribution must, therefore, be made by April 15th.

5. The plan must begin to pay a participant's benefit by the April 1st following the calendar year in which the participant reaches age $70\frac{1}{2}$.

6. If a participant dies *after* distributions have begun, any remaining portion of the participant's interest must be distributed at least as rapidly as under the method of distribution being used as of the date of the participant's death. If the participant dies *before* distributions have begun, the entire remaining interest must be distributed within 5 years to the participant's beneficiaries. If the participant's benefit is payable over the life expectancy of the participant's designated beneficiary or a period certain that does not extend beyond the life expectancy of that beneficiary, and distributions begin within one year of the participant's death, then the 5-year rule does not apply. If the beneficiary is the participant's spouse, the first distribution can be deferred until December 31 of the year in which the employee would have reached age $70\frac{1}{2}$.

HOW IT IS DONE — AN EXAMPLE

The IRA should be relatively easy to establish. Banks and insurance companies provide prototype plans. The IRS also provides prototype trusteed and custodial plans. Once an IRA is established all that need be done is to make contributions. If an employee's earned income is $6,000, the maximum allowable IRA contribution is $2,000 (the lower of $2,000 or 100 percent of includable compensation). If the employee's income were $1,000 the maximum IRA contribution would be

$1,000. If his income is $2,250 or greater, he is married, and his spouse has no earned income, then he can contribute an amount up to a maximum of $2,250 (if the couple files jointly) to an IRA for himself and his spouse. However, the contribution for either spouse cannot be more than $2,000.

Tax savings could be substantial. For example, a $2,000 contribution by an individual in a 15 percent bracket would save $300 a year in taxes. A partner in a partnership who did not care to include any other employees in the plan could establish an IRA for himself without having to cover other employees. If the partner's tax bracket were 28 percent, a $2,000 annual IRA contribution would save $560 a year in taxes.

WHAT ARE THE TAX IMPLICATIONS?

1. Money set aside in an IRA is currently deductible from gross income up to the limits specified.[13]

2. The earnings of the IRA account, between the time they are deposited and the time they are received accumulate tax free.[14]

3. An individual must be at least 59½ years old (unless disabled or unless payments are spread over his life expectancy) to receive an IRA payment without tax penalty. The nondeductible penalty tax on a "premature distribution" is 10 percent of the amount of the distribution which is includable in income. Under some circumstances, the total value of the assets of the account may be deemed to be distributed.[15] (An example of this would be where an individual borrows against his IRA.) So, if your client received (or is deemed to have received) a total distribution at age 53 and his account is worth $5,000 at that time, he must pay a $500 nondeductible tax in addition to the regular income tax on the $5,000 distribution.

    Voluntary deductible employee contributions to an employer plan or government plan if distributed (for purposes other than making a rollover) before age 59½ or disability will also be subject to the 10 percent penalty tax.

4. Upon distribution of the funds accumulated in an IRA account, the client will be taxed at ordinary income tax rates.[16] Lump sum distribution tax treatment is not available for distributions from IRAs. It is also not available for distributions of voluntary employee contributions made to an employer or government plan.

    An additional penalty tax of 15% is imposed if aggregate "retirement" distributions to an individual in a calendar year exceed the greater of (1) $150,000, or (2) $112,500 as adjusted for inflation ($150,000 in 1995). This tax is in addition to any regular income taxes due and applies only to the excess portion of the distribution. All qualified plans and individual retirement plans are aggregated for this additional tax.[17]

5. For estates of decedents dying after 1982 and before 1985, the $100,000 federal estate tax exclusion applicable to a qualified corporate retirement plan is also available for a death benefit payable from an IRA. The Tax Reform Act of 1984 totally eliminated the estate tax exclusion for estates of decedents dying after 1984, unless the participant was receiving benefits prior to January 1, 1985, and had made an irrevocable election as to the form of benefits prior to July 18, 1984. TRA '86 liberalized this exclusion so that benefits from a participant who separated from service before January 1, 1985, for which the form of payment had been elected is exempt up to $100,000 (regardless of whether or not he was in pay status), as long as the election is not later changed.

    If an individual dies with an "excess retirement accumulation" he will pay an additional 15% federal estate tax. An "excess retirement accumulation" means the excess (if any) of (A) the value of the individual's interests in qualified plans and individual retirement plans as of the date of death (or alternate valuation date) over (B) the present value of an annual annuity of $112,500, as adjusted by cost of living ($150,000 in 1995), or $150,000, if that is greater, payable over a term certain equal to the individual's life expectancy immediately before his death.[18] For additional information on this tax, see Chapter 28.

IMPLICATIONS AND ISSUES IN COMMUNITY PROPERTY STATES

The division of community property interests in qualified plan benefits is becoming an increasingly important factor in divorce proceedings in community property states. In many situations the spouses' respective retirement benefits are their largest assets.

IRAs will undoubtedly be the subject of controversy in many divorce proceedings. To some extent, however, the division of an interest in an IRA should be less difficult than dividing an interest in a qualified corporate plan. All benefits in an IRA must be nonforfeitable. Thus, the problems of valuing nonvested benefits will not be present.

In many cases, each spouse will have his or her own IRA. If the contributions to each IRA were similar, each spouse could agree to keep his own IRA in a divorce settlement. If only one spouse has an IRA or one IRA contains substantially more assets than the other spouse's IRA or spouses with equal IRAs or IRA subaccounts cannot agree to divide their IRA interests equally, significant problems could arise. A spouse may find he or she is obligated to divide an interest in his or her IRA with the other spouse. The obligated spouse may not have sufficient assets outside of the IRA to provide the other spouse with the value of his or her interest. Thus, the obligated spouse may seek a distribution from the IRA to provide funds to settle with his or her spouse. If, however, the spouse with the IRA is under age 59½ and not disabled, the spouse will incur a 10 percent "premature distribution" tax as well as be subject to ordinary income tax on the distribution he or she received (or is deemed to receive). To avoid this undesirable result, the spouses could agree to divide the assets of the IRA after the spouse with the IRA attains age 59½. If an agreement cannot be reached, the spouse with the IRA may be able to persuade a court to postpone division of the IRA until he or she attains age 59½.

An exception provided by the Employee Retirement Income Security Act of 1974 (ERISA) could eliminate the undesirable consequences described above. ERISA provides that the transfer of an individual's interest in an IRA to his or her former spouse under a divorce decree or under a written instrument in connection with the divorce is not a taxable distribution. Thereafter, the IRA will be treated as that of the other spouse. This exception appears to apply only to the transfer of the spouse's entire interest in an IRA. Transfers of partial interests may cause the "premature distribution" tax and ordinary income tax to be imposed.

Tax consequences above should be considered when dividing community property IRA or qualified plan interests. Courts have taken varying approaches to consideration of tax aspects in division of retirement benefits. Some are unwilling to consider tax consequences when dividing retirement benefits. Others, however, have held that tax considerations should be taken into account when dividing retirement benefits in divorce proceedings.

QUESTIONS AND ANSWERS

Question — What does it mean to be an "active participant" in a qualified plan for purposes of the IRA contribution limitations?

Answer — The rules vary depending on whether the plan is a defined benefit pension plan or a defined contribution plan.

1. Defined Benefit Pension Plan. An individual is an active participant as long as he is not excluded under the plan's eligibility provisions. Active participation exists even when the individual declines participation, fails to make mandatory contributions or fails to perform the minimum service required to accrue a benefit. The plan being in frozen status does not necessarily mean active participation does not exist.

2. Defined Contribution Plan. An individual is an active participant if either employer contributions, employee contributions, or forfeitures are added to the individual's account.[19]

Question — Can a client borrow from his IRA account?

Answer — No. Borrowing will create a forfeiture of the IRA's tax qualification. Your client will be deemed to have received all the assets in his or her account and must pay ordinary income tax on the amount.[20] In addition, if the client is neither disabled nor 59½ years old at that time, there will also be a 10 percent nondeductible "premature distribution" tax.

Question — How long can an individual wait before beginning to receive distributions from an IRA?

Answer — Distributions do not have to be made until April 1 following the calendar year in which a client reaches age 70½ (of course, payments can begin as early as age 59½ without penalty).[21]

Question — If an individual chooses a particular investment vehicle for his IRA, but later changes his mind, is a shift to another type of investment allowed?

Answer — Yes. It is possible to liquidate an IRA investment and reinvest the proceeds within 60 days in another investment on a tax-free basis. For example, if your client originally purchased mutual funds but later wanted to split his investment between mutual funds and a flexible premium annuity, the change can be made without incurring adverse income tax consequences. This tax-free reinvestment of funds can occur only once each year.

Question — Can an IRA invest in gold coins or stamps?

Answer — If an IRA or any individually directed account under qualified Keogh or corporate retirement plans acquires collectibles, the cost of such collectibles shall be regarded as a current taxable distribution to the plan participant. A collectible is defined as any work of art, any rug or antique, any metal or gem, any stamp or coin, any alcoholic beverage, or any other tangible personal property specified by the IRS. However, an exception to this rule is permitted for IRA investments in gold or silver coins issued by the United States or any coins minted by a state.[22]

Question — A partner owning more than 10 percent of the partnership's capital was a participant in his partnership HR-10 plan. He left the partnership and received the distribution of his retirement plan monies. Can he use a "rollover" IRA? Secondly, assuming he can establish a "rollover" IRA, several years later when he is employed by a corporation which has a retirement plan, can he make a contribution from the "rollover" IRA into the corporate retirement plan?

Answer — The partner can roll over the distribution into a "rollover" IRA, and he may roll over those monies from the "rollover" IRA into another qualified plan.[23] There are no longer any restrictions on rollovers by more-than-five percent owners.

A distribution of voluntary employee contributions which were deductible at the time of contribution may be rolled over to an IRA or to a qualified plan if the plan permits.

Note that distributions received after 1992 are subject to a mandatory 20% income tax withholding unless a direct rollover is used.

Question — Assume an individual established an IRA. He takes distribution prior to age 59^1/$_2$. What are the consequences?

Answer — An individual who receives a distribution from an IRA prior to age 59^1/$_2$ and is not disabled at the time of distribution will generally be subject to a tax of 10 percent of the amount of such distribution which is includable in income, in addition to being required to include the taxable amount of the distribution in income for that taxable year. A third exception to the imposition of the premature distribution penalty is if the distribution from the IRA is one of a series of periodic payments made over the life or life expectancy of the individual.

Question — What is a SEP?

Answer — SEPs are alternatives to qualified plans and permit employers to set up a simplified retirement program funded by contributions to each employee's IRA. A SEP is part HR-10, part employer-sponsored IRA, and part employee-established IRA. (Actually, it's a grown-up IRA account or annuity—no bond purchase plans are permitted.)

Question — How much can be contributed annually to a SEP?

Answer — The dollar limit on contributions to SEPs is $30,000. A SEP is a type of IRA to which an employer can contribute on an employee's behalf. The employee excludes the contribution from gross income up to

(a) $30,000 or

(b) 15 percent of compensation (before the SEP contribution), but

(c) only the first $150,000 of compensation may be counted. (This cap is indexed for inflation ($150,000 in 1995).)

Employee elective deferrals may be made to certain SEPs in any amount up to $7,000, as adjusted for inflation ($9,240 in 1995).[24] Employees are permitted to either elect to have the contribution made to the SEP or can currently receive the contribution in cash. The elective deferrals are considered wages for Social Security tax purposes.

Question — What are the requirements for a SEP?

Answer — The essential requirements are

1. The employer (can be a corporation, partnership, or sole proprietorship) must make a contribution to the plan for each employee age 21 or older who has worked for the employer during at least 3 of the last 5 years. An employer need not contribute on behalf of any employee for a calendar year in which the employee's compensation was less than $300, as adjusted for inflation ($400 in 1995).[25] In the case of elective deferral SEPs, the employer must have had 25 or fewer eligible employees during the prior taxable year, and at least 50 percent must have elected to contribute to the SEP.[26]

2. The employer's contribution cannot discriminate in favor of employees who are "highly compensated." It is possible to exclude nonparticipating union employees with respect to whom there is good faith bargaining on retirement benefits and nonresident aliens in considering whether or not contributions are discriminatory in favor of any member of the prohibited class. A special nondiscrimination test is applicable to salary reduction SEPs. The deferral percentage for each highly compensated eligible employee cannot exceed the average deferral percentage for all other non-highly compensated eligible employees by more than 125 percent.

Employer contributions may be made for an employee who has reached age 70½, unlike the situation with an IRA.

3. A limited disparity between the contribution percentages applicable to compensation above and below the social security wage base is permitted. (This is also referred to as "integration.") An elective deferral SEP may not be integrated. Integration is not permitted for a year in which the employer also maintains an integrated pension, profit sharing, or stock bonus plan or tax deferred annuity.

4. The employee must own the IRA account or annuity. That means 100 percent immediate vesting for all employees. The employer cannot tie any strings on the employee's right to keep or withdraw money contributed to the SEP.

5. The SEP has to be in writing. It must spell out

    (a) what an employee has to do to "get a piece of the action" and

    (b) how the "pie is to be sliced," i.e., the manner in which the amount allocated is to be computed.

Question — Can a person participating in some other employer sponsored plan also be covered by a SEP? Can a person covered by a SEP take a deduction for an IRA contribution?

Answer — Participants in simplified employee pension plans are permitted to participate in other employer qualified plans. Any contribution by an employer to a SEP must be aggregated with other contributions by that employer to other qualified plans for purposes of the overall limits on contributions or benefits. A participant can take a deduction for an IRA contribution, under the limits discussed above. If a joint filer is covered by a SEP and does not make in excess of $50,000 he is allowed to make a deductible contribution to an IRA (reduced for income between $40,000 and $50,000). An individual filer who is covered by a SEP and does not make in excess of $35,000 is similarly allowed to make deductible contributions to an IRA (reduced for incomes between $25,000 and $35,000).

Question — How long does an employer have to make a contribution to a SEP (and deduct it)?

Answer — In general, the employer must make contributions within 3½ months after the close of the calendar year in order to take the deduction for its tax years in which the calendar year ends. If the employer elects, it may use its taxable year instead of the calendar year. In fact, the plan itself need not be established until such dates.

Question — What is a model SEP? What is a non-model SEP?

Answer — To establish a SEP, there must be a written agreement. IRS has issued Form 5305 — SEP, Simplified Employee Pension — Individual Retirement Accounts Contribution Agreement for those employers wishing to have a pre-approved IRS agreement. Plans using the IRS form are called model SEPs, while plans using other agreements are called non-model SEPs. Employers who have previously established a defined benefit plan cannot use a model SEP, but, rather they must use a non-model SEP.

Question — May a divorced spouse make and deduct contributions to a spousal IRA?

Answer — A divorced or legally separated person can make an IRA contribution from taxable alimony or separation payments he or she receives during the year.

Question — May an alternate payee roll over a distribution to an IRA or a qualified plan if made pursuant to a Qualified Domestic Relations Order?

Answer — If an alternate payee who is the spouse or former spouse of the participant receives a distribution by reason of a Qualified Domestic Relations Order, the rollover rules apply to the alternate payee as if the alternate payee were the participant.[27] Thus, the alternate payee has 60 days in which to roll over any portion of an eligible rollover distribution without the distribution becoming includable in income.[28] A distribution may not be rolled over to another qualified plan. Generally, such a rollover must be handled as a direct rollover to avoid a mandatory income tax withholding rate of 20%.[29]

Question — Are there special rules for "inherited" IRAs acquired by someone other than a surviving spouse?

Answer — Yes. Inherited IRAs acquired by someone other than a surviving spouse cannot be "rolled over" tax-free and cannot receive tax-free rollovers from other qualified plans or IRAs. No income tax deduction is allowed for amounts contributed to an inherited IRA.

Question — May a contribution be made to an IRA even though it is not deductible?

Answer — Yes. Designated nondeductible contributions may be made on behalf of an individual to an IRA even though he participates in a qualified pension or profit sharing plan. These contributions are intended to provide a tax incentive for retirement savings, and the tax on the earnings on the nondeductible contributions is deferred until withdrawn. The nondeductible limit is the excess of:

(a) The lesser of $2,000 ($2,250 in the case of a spousal IRA) or 100% of compensation over

(b) the amount allowable as a deduction for IRA contributions by active participants.[30]

Question — Can an individual deduct contributions to an IRA if his compensation exceeds $100,000?

Answer — It depends. As long as the individual or his spouse is not an "active participant" for a taxable year in a tax-qualified plan, he or she may contribute and deduct the full $2,000 IRA contribution irrespective of his or her income.

An individual is considered an "active participant" for a taxable year if either the individual or the individual's spouse (with whom the individual files a joint return) is covered by (1) a qualified pension, profit sharing or stock bonus plan, (2) a qualified annuity plan, (3) a tax sheltered annuity plan, (4) a simplified employee pension plan, (5) a government sponsored plan, or (6) an employee-only contributory plan exempt from tax under Code section 501(c)(18).[31]

Question — When may a surviving spouse roll over a distribution received from a qualified plan or IRA of a deceased spouse?

Answer — A surviving spouse can roll over all or part of a distribution from a qualified plan or IRA of the deceased spouse.[32] If this is done, the IRA of the deceased spouse is treated as if the surviving spouse was the original participant. Thus, the rules pertaining to rollovers discussed in this chapter are applicable.

It should be noted, however, that there may be no subsequent rollover back into another qualified plan. Since it is possible the surviving spouse already has an IRA, or will create one after the rollover, it is a good idea not to commingle the funds from the rollover with the separate IRA funds of the surviving spouse.

Where the deceased spouse's IRA or qualified plan benefit is transferred to a trust in which the surviving spouse is a beneficiary, there is no right to roll over the distribution unless the spouse has a right to remove the IRA account from the trust and exercises that right shortly after the spouse's death. There is some authority in private letter rulings for the proposition that if a distribution from an IRA comes to the spouse through a trust where the trustee has little discretion as to how to direct the distribution, the surviving spouse may roll over the distribution into his own IRA.

ASRS, Sec. 62.

Footnote References

Individual Retirement Plan (IRA)

1. IRC Sec. 219(b). Technically, the initials IRA have a more limited connotation but will be used here to denote any type of individual retirement savings plan.
2. IRC Sec. 219(g).
3. IRC Sec. 408(o).
4. IRC Sec. 219(g).
5. Unemployment Compensation Amendments of 1992, P.L. 102-318, Secs. 521, 522.
6. Unemployment Compensation Amendments of 1992, P.L. 102-318, Sec. 521(e).
7. IRC Sec. 402(c)(4).
8. IRC Secs. 402(c)(4)(A) and 402(c)(4)(B).
9. IRC Sec. 3405(c).
10. IRC Sec. 402(a)(5), as in effect for distributions received prior to January 1, 1993.
11. IRC Secs. 408(a); 408(b).
12. IRC Sec. 408(a)(1).
13. IRC Sec. 219(a).
14. IRC Sec. 408(e)(1).
15. IRC Secs. 72(t); 408(e)(2).
16. IRC Sec. 408(d).
17. IRC Sec. 4980A(a).
18. IRC Sec. 4980A(d).
19. Notice 87-16, 1987-1 CB 446.
20. IRC Sec. 408(e).
21. IRC Secs. 408(a)(6); 408(b)(3).
22. IRC Sec. 408(m).
23. IRC Sec. 408(d)(3)(A).
24. IRC Sec. 402(g).
25. IRC Sec. 408(k)(6).
26. Announcement 80-112, 1980-36 IRB 35; Prop. Reg. §1.408-7(d)(1). IRC Sec. 408(k)(6).
27. IRC Sec. 402(e)(1).
28. IRC Sec. 402(c)(1).
29. IRC Sec. 3405(c)(1).
30. IRC Sec. 408(o)(2)(A).
31. IRC Sec. 219(g).
32. IRC Sec. 402(c)(9).

Chapter 19

INSTALLMENT SALES AND SCINS

WHAT IS IT?

The installment sale is a device for spreading out the taxable gain and thereby deferring the income tax on gain from the sale of property. The key ingredient in an installment sale is that at least one payment will be received by the seller after the taxable year in which the sale occurs.

The self-cancelling installment note, or SCIN, is a variation of the installment sale. When it is used, the note contains a provision under which the balance of any payments due at date of death are automatically cancelled, with language such as the following:

"Unless sooner paid, all sums due hereunder, whether principal or interest, shall be deemed cancelled and extinguished as though paid upon the death of (Seller)."

WHEN IS THE USE OF SUCH A DEVICE INDICATED?

1. An installment sale is indicated when a taxpayer wants to sell property to another individual who may not have enough capital to purchase the property outright. The installment sale provides a way, for example, for employees with minimal capital to buy out a business owner who, in return for allowing a long-term payout, may receive a higher price for his business. This device is often used to create a market for a business where none previously existed.

2. An installment sale is indicated where an individual in a high income tax bracket holds substantially appreciated real estate or securities, other than marketable securities. In certain cases, all or a portion of the tax on a sale of such property can be spread over the period of installments.[1]

   One of the big advantages of the installment sale with respect to certain property is that the taxable gain is prorated over the payment period. This means that the seller will pay the tax due only as actual payments from the sale are received. The seller may be able to shift most of the profit from a high income (high tax) year to a year or years in which he or she is in a lower bracket.

3. The installment sale permits more flexibility than the private annuity, an alternative. The agreement can be made to begin or end whenever the parties involved desire. This eliminates the need to follow a rigid schedule of payments such as is found in a private annuity.

4. An installment sale can be an effective estate freezing device where the sale is between family members and involves rapidly appreciating closely held stock, real estate, or other assets. Used in this manner, the installment sale may serve to freeze the size of an estate subsequent to the sale and thus stabilize the value of the seller's estate for federal estate tax purposes and shift future appreciation to a younger generation. An installment sale to a grandchild for its full fair market value, for example, will avoid the generation-skipping transfer tax.

WHAT ARE THE REQUIREMENTS?

1. A seller of property can defer as much or as little as desired and payments can be set to fit the seller's business or financial needs. The amount of payment received in the year of the sale is irrelevant. A sale for $1,000,000 can qualify even if $500,000 is paid in the year of the sale and the remaining $500,000 (plus interest on the unpaid balance) is paid over the next 5 years.

2. No payment has to be made in the year of the sale. The only requirement is that at least one payment must be made in a taxable year after the year of sale.[2] This means the owner of property can contract to have payments made at the time when it is most advantageous or least disadvantageous. For example, the parties could agree that the entire purchase price for payment of a $1,000,000 parcel of land will be paid 5 years after the sale.

3. No minimum sale price is required.

4. Installment sale treatment is automatic unless the taxpayer elects not to have installment treatment apply.[3]

5. A sale can be made on an installment basis even though the selling price is contingent.[4]

6. Installment reporting is not available for sales of marketable securities.[5]

HOW IT IS DONE — AN EXAMPLE

An individual would like to sell property she now owns. Her accountant has explained that a high tax on the inherent gain in the property could consume a substantial portion of her profit. If she receives all of the sale proceeds in the year of sale, the result is that her entire profit will be taxed in one year. So she would like to find a way to reduce or minimize the impact of taxes or defer those taxes.

The installment sale is a possible solution to that problem. By taking advantage of the installment sale provisions of the Internal Revenue Code, she may be able to save a great deal of money.[6] Under an installment sale, the title to the property passes immediately from the seller to the buyer. But the distinguishing feature of an installment sale is that the seller does *not* receive a lump sum payment outright. Instead, the seller typically receives the sale price in installments spread out over two or more tax years (although a lump sum payment in a later year will qualify for installment reporting).

Example. If Mrs. Murphey sold land which cost her $50,000 and received $100,000, she would have a $50,000 gain reportable all in the year of the sale. But if she sells it for $100,000 and agrees to accept $10,000 a year for 10 years (plus appropriate interest on the unpaid balance), she will not have to report the $50,000 gain in the year of the sale. Instead, since her ratio of gross profit ($50,000) to contract price ($100,000) is 50 percent, she will report $5,000, 50% of each $10,000 payment she receives, as capital gain. (Interest has been ignored here for simplicity.)

To compute the payment, use a hand held financial calculator or computer program. You need to tell the calculator or computer the

(1) interest rate (for semiannual divide annual rate by 2),

(2) number of periods (for semiannual multiply years by 2),

(3) amount to be repaid.

The result will be the annual (or other payment period) payment necessary. For example, to compute the semiannual payment where property worth $100,000 is sold over a 10 year period and the interest rate is 9%, input 4.5 (the annual interest rate divided by 2) and press the i (interest) button, input 20 (two payments a year for 10 years) and press the *N* (number of periods) button, and input the present value of the loan, $100,000. Then press the PV (present value) button. Then press PMT to compute the $7,687.61 outlay.

The rule used to compute the annual gain above is:

Income is realized on each annual payment received in the same proportion the gross profit (selling price less seller's adjusted basis) bears to the total contract price (amount to be received by the seller).

If the sale results in a loss, the installment method may not be used. The loss deduction must be taken in the tax year of the sale.[7]

More technically, for income tax purposes, the installments must be broken into three parts: (a) a return of capital, (b) profit, and (c) interest income.

Interest is segregated from principal payments and taxed as ordinary income. The profit percentage (basically the gain, or difference between the sale price and adjusted basis, ex-

Figure 19.1

Taxation of Seller Under Installment Sale	
A. Recovery of basis (cost element)	Tax free
B. Gain element	Capital gain or ordinary income
C. Interest income	Ordinary income

Computing Tax Free, Gain, and Interest Elements of an Installment Payment		
STEP 1	Segregate interest from payment principal	
STEP 2	Compute portion of principal payment which is gain	$\dfrac{\text{Total gain}}{\text{Sales price}}$ x Principal payment
STEP 3	Compute portion of principal payment which is a return of capital	Principal payment - gain (Step 2)

pressed as a percentage of the total contract price, exclusive of interest) is applied to each installment payment of principal in order to determine the amount of each payment that is gain. The balance is considered a tax-free return of the seller's basis. (See Figure 19.1.)

What if the agreement does not specify an interest charge—or the amount is unreasonably low? This often occurs in intrafamily transactions. These types of sales will be taxed according to what is known as the "unstated interest" rule. Under this rule, the Internal Revenue Service is allowed to "impute" interest (a legal fiction in which all the parties to the transaction are treated as if interest at a statutory rate was paid, compounded semiannually) unless the parties have agreed to at least a "safe harbor" rate of return on the unpaid balance.[8] In other words, a portion of the deferred payments will be treated as interest to both the buyer and seller. For all tax purposes, from the buyer's perspective, that part of a payment which is considered interest does not increase the basis of the property received. However, the buyer may be allowed an interest deduction.

The following rules should be considered: Interest will not be deductible if it is considered "personal." Generally, this means the interest deduction will be denied unless the debt was properly allocable to:

(1) investment purposes (if the property or stock to be purchased is investment property, the interest deduction will generally be allowed only to the extent of the buyer's investment income);

(2) the conduct of a trade or business (other than the trade or business of performing services as an employee), in which case the interest would be deductible without limit;

(3) part of the computation of income or loss from a passive investment activity;

(4) estate or generation-skipping transfer taxes in installments under Code sections 6166 or 6161 (there is no limit on the amount of interest deduction in this case); or

(5) a debt secured by property which at the time the interest is paid or accrued is a qualified residence (this is called "qualified residence interest" and is generally deductible only if the residence in question is the taxpayer's principal residence or a second residence). This deduction is limited to interest on a maximum of $1,000,000 of "acquisition indebtedness" and up to $100,000 of "home equity indebtedness."

Imputed interest is considered only for purposes of the income tax. It does not directly affect the terms of the sale. The imputed interest rules are extremely difficult and will not be discussed at length. The following rules of thumb should be helpful in planning the interest rates that should be built into an installment sale:

(1) There will be no imputed interest problem unless the installment sale contract (a) does not state *any* interest on the unpaid balance, or (b) the specified interest rate is less than the "applicable federal rate" (AFR), except as noted below.

(2) Certain sales of family land to family members require only that the interest rate assumed by the parties be 6 percent, compounded semiannually, or greater if the transaction is for $500,000 or less. The AFR is applied to amounts over $500,000.

(3) If the selling price is under $3,523,600 in 1995 ($3,433,500 in 1994), interest will be imputed at the lower of (a) 9 percent, compounded semiannually, or (b) the applicable federal rate. The selling price under which either rate applies is adjusted annually for inflation.[9]

WHAT ARE THE TAX IMPLICATIONS OF THE INSTALLMENT SALE?

1. Many of the income tax ramifications have been mentioned above. Note also that depreciation recapture as well as any investment tax credit recapture is reportable in full in the year of the sale, even if no proceeds from the sale are received in that year.

   Stock or securities which are traded on an established securities market do not qualify for installment treatment; all payments to be received are treated as received in the year of disposition.

   In addition, installment treatment is generally not allowed for sales of depreciable property to a controlled entity, such as a more than 50% owned partnership or corporation, or trust benefiting the seller or the seller's spouse. All payments to be received are treated as received in the year of disposition.

2. An installment sale will remove the property in question from the transferor-seller's estate, but the present value of any installments due at the seller's death must be included.[10] For instance, if at the date the seller died 10 annual payments remained on an installment sale, and each payment (made at the end of the year) to the estate or its heirs is $12,000, at a 10 percent discount assump-

tion, $73,735.20 would be includable in the seller's gross estate. However, the installment sale is still a valuable estate planning tool since it removes the future appreciation on the property from the transferor-seller's estate without any gift tax implications. For instance, at a 10 percent growth rate, property worth $500,000 when sold in exchange for 10 annual payments would be worth $1,296,871 when the payout was complete.

Additionally, a great deal of the cash proceeds of the sale may be removed from the seller's estate, gift tax free, by maximizing the use of the annual exclusion. After receiving payments, the seller could then give back—at his or her whim—all or a portion of the amounts paid.

3. For federal gift tax purposes, there is a split of authority in the courts as to whether the interest rate charged on the family installment sale must be equal to the prevailing market rate, the applicable federal rate, the special rates applicable to sales of farm land under $500,000, or the 9% rate specified in the case of sales under $3,523,600 (in 1995) that are charged for *income* tax purposes. (See the related discussion in Chapter 20.) The Tax Court has held in two separate cases that if a rate lower than the prevailing market rate is used, there will be a taxable gift measured by the difference between the fair market value of the property sold and the discounted present value of the installment note that is based on the lower interest rate used for sales of land (6%).[11] However, in one of these cases on appeal, the Court of Appeals for the Seventh Circuit reversed the Tax Court decision and held that the use of rates specified for income tax purposes would also control for gift tax purposes.[12] Conversely, in the other case on appeal, the Court of Appeals for the Eighth Circuit sustained the Tax Court's position on the issue and held that the income tax rate does not control for gift tax purposes.[13] The Supreme Court has refused to review the Eighth Circuit Court's decision.

It should be noted that the sales in both of the above cases arose before the adoption of applicable federal rates of interest, and it would seem that these federal rates should eliminate the gift tax problem. However, the law is unclear on what would happen if the federal rates were lower than prevailing market rates.

4. If the seller should die, the remaining payments are "income in respect of a decedent." (See the Questions and Answers, below.) As a result, the estate, or other testamentary beneficiary of the installments due would report the payments in the same way that the decedent would have reported them had he lived.[14] In other words, the allocation of the payments (return of capital, gain, or interest) is not affected by reporting on the installment basis.

There is no step-up in basis at death; however, the testamentary beneficiary of the installments would be entitled to an offsetting income tax deduction to the extent of the estate tax attributable to the installment sale balance which was taxed in the estate.[15]

5. It is important to note the effect of an installment sale on the property's basis for purposes of computing gains and losses and in order to compute the depreciation deduction available to the transferee-buyer. In the case of an installment sale, the transferee-buyer has a new income tax basis for the property, its fair market value at the date of the sale (i.e., the purchase price).[16] The transferee's basis is stepped-up, not carried over, for depreciation purposes.

One result of this stepped-up basis is that (subject to the "second disposition" rules discussed below) a lower bracket family member purchasing the property can sell the property transferred and reinvest the sale proceeds in more liquid or higher yielding assets and probably pay much less in tax on the sale than the transferor-seller would otherwise have had to pay.

An increased basis is of particular advantage in the case of high value, low basis property such as highly appreciated real estate. For example, if the transferor-seller bought undeveloped nonincome-producing land 10 years ago for $10,000 and it is now worth $100,000, he could sell it to his son for its $100,000 fair market value. After holding the land for at least 2 years (see below), the son could then sell it and purchase mutual funds or other income-producing securities with the proceeds of the sale. If the son received $105,000 for the land, his gain would be only the difference between his $100,000 cost and the amount realized on the sale, $105,000 (i.e., his total gain would be $5,000). He does not have to pay tax on the $90,000 gain his father would have been subject to had he sold the land. The advantage is compounded if the son is in a lower tax bracket than his father.

The overall tax savings is even more dramatic if the father is in a relatively high income tax bracket at the time of the sale but is about to retire. Future payments from son to father spread out the profit and defer taxes. Since the father will probably be in a lower tax bracket after retirement, less of his profits will be lost in the form of taxes.

6. Special rules apply to installment sales to related parties. For example, certain "second dispositions" (resales) by a related party purchaser trigger recognition of gain *by the initial seller*. In essence, this rule, stated in more detail below, provides that the original seller's gain on an installment sale will be accelerated if a trustee or other

purchaser related to the seller resells the asset within two years of the installment sale.

7. Generally, interest paid by the purchaser on the unpaid balance will be deductible in full only if the debt is properly allocable to investment purposes (and then only to the extent of investment income) or to business purposes.

Special Rules for Disposition of Property Between Related Parties

Technically, there are three "related party" rules, one applicable to second dispositions of installment sale property by a related purchaser, a second which applies only to installment sales of depreciable property between "closely related" entities, and a third applicable to forgiveness or cancellation of installment debt between related parties.

"Second disposition" rule: The rule for "second dispositions" of installment sale property is as follows: If a related party (defined below) disposes of the property he has purchased in an installment sale (in other words if a "second disposition" occurs) before the initial seller (the person who made the "first disposition") has received all the payments he is due under the installment sale, then the amount realized on the second disposition is treated as received—at the time of the second disposition—by the initial seller. For instance, if a mother sells her daughter appreciated land and the daughter immediately resells the land, the mother must report gain.

The term "related party" for purposes of this rule, includes brothers and sisters, spouses, ancestors, and lineal descendants, as well as most related entities.

Fortunately, the gain reportable is limited. Gain, based on her profit percentage, is reportable by the mother only to the extent the daughter receives more in the second disposition than she has already paid her mother. So the initial seller's gain would be accelerated only to the extent additional cash or other property flows into the related group because of the "second disposition."

Although there are no regulations that illustrate mathematically how the second disposition rules apply, it should be as follows:

1. When the related person disposes of the property (the second disposition) before the person making the first disposition receives all payments due from that sale, the first seller is treated as having received the amount actually received by the second (related) seller—at the time of the second disposition. For example, assume Herb Cheezman bought land for $500,000 and sold it to his son Stephen for $600,000. Assume also that Stephen agreed to pay $60,000 a year for 10 years. (For simplicity, interest is ignored.) In the second year Stephen sells the land to a third party for $1,000,000. Herb is treated as having received $1,000,000 in the second year.

2. There is a limit, however, on the amount Herb must report.

The person making the first disposition (Herb) reports only the amount by which the *lesser of*

A	*(1)*	the total amount realized with respect to the second disposition by the close of the tax year, (in this example it is $1,000,000)	
or	*(2)*	the total contract price for the first disposition (in our example, $600,000)	$600,000

exceeds the total of

B	*(1)*	the sum of payments actually received with respect to the first disposition (Herb received $60,000 X 2 years, or $120,000)	
plus	*(2)*	the aggregate sum *treated* (under the related party — second disposition rules) as received with respect to the first disposition for prior taxable years (here $0)	<u>120,000</u>

So, in this example, Herb would report gain of $480,000

Of course, Stephen would be required to recognize his gain on the sale (i.e., the second disposition)—$1,000,000 (amount realized) minus $600,000 (Stephen's cost basis), or $400,000.

3. Where a second disposition results in recognition of gain to the first seller (Herb), subsequent payments actually received by the first seller from the related purchaser (Stephen) will be tax free until they have equalled the amount realized as a result of the second disposition.

There are limited exceptions to the "second disposition" rule. If the second disposition occurs more than 2 years after the date of the first sale, the rule will not apply (unless the sale was of stock or securities). So, if Stephen waited 2 years and one month before he sold the land, Herb would not realize any gain as a result of Stephen's disposition. Stephen, of course, would have to report gain based on the difference between the amount he realizes on the sale (assume $1,000,000) and his basis (cost) of $600,000. Note that there is *no* 2-year exception for sales of stock or securities. Thus, if Herb sold his son Stephen *stock* instead of land, the time period for the "second disposition" rule is unlimited, and Herb will recognize gain on any subsequent disposition by Stephen, to the extent that Herb has not received all payments due on the sale. (Installment reporting is unavailable for sales of publicly traded stock or securities occurring after 1986.)

This rule also will not apply if the second disposition results from the death of either party or from an involuntary conversion.

Rule for sales of depreciable property: A sale of depreciable property between related entities may not be reported on the installment method, unless it can be shown that avoidance of income tax was not a principal purpose. This rule, unlike the other two "related party" rules, applies only to related entities, such as a corporation and an individual who owns more than 50% of its outstanding stock.

In addition to this rule, there is a special rule for *all* installment sales of depreciable property, regardless of whether the buyer and seller are related. Generally, that rule (described below) requires recapture of certain depreciation deductions claimed by the seller.

Rule for cancellation of debt: If an installment sale between related parties is cancelled or payment is forgiven, the *seller* must recognize gain to the extent that the fair market value on the date of cancellation (or the face amount, if less) exceeds the seller's basis in the obligation. "Related party" has the same meaning for purposes of this rule as for the "second disposition" rule.

Special Depreciable Property Rule

Installment reporting of taxable income does not apply to any personal or real property depreciation recapture. Recapture of these deductions (so-called Section 1245 and 1250 depreciation recapture), up to the amount of the seller's gain, must be reported by the seller in the year of the sale even if any other gain is reported on the installment basis as payments are received.

Since depreciation recapture must be reported in the year the property is sold, that amount can be added to the seller's basis. It therefore has the effect of reducing the reportable income that must be realized each year.

For instance, Charles Plotnick sells tangible personal property to Nick Martin for $70,000, to be paid in 3 installments. Interest is paid on the unpaid balance at current rates. Assume this is 9%. Assume the property originally cost $90,000. It has an adjusted basis of $50,000 at the time of the sale because he has taken depreciation deductions totalling $40,000.

Charles must "recapture" his depreciation up to the amount of his gain (the $20,000 difference between the sale price of $70,000 and his adjusted basis of $50,000). Since he includes the $20,000 of recaptured deductions as income in the year of the sale, he can increase his basis by $20,000 (from $50,000 to $70,000). Since he now has a 100 percent basis, he will realize no gain as payments are received.

Payments, exclusive of interest, should be $23,333 which is tax free as a recovery of basis. But what if he sold the property for $110,000? The gain would be $60,000 (the $110,000 amount realized minus his adjusted basis of $50,000). The entire $40,000 he previously deducted as depreciation must now be recaptured. Since he must report $40,000, he can add that amount to his $50,000 basis. It now totals $90,000.

Each payment, exclusive of interest, is $36,667 ($110,000 ÷ 3). Of this, $30,000 will be a tax-free recovery of basis, and the $3,667 balance will be gain.

Note, however, that installment treatment is not allowed for sales of depreciable property to a controlled entity, such as a more than 50% owned partnership or corporation, or trust benefiting the seller or the seller's spouse. All payments to be received are treated as received in the year of disposition.

WHAT ARE THE TAX IMPLICATIONS OF THE SCIN?

All of the tax rules applicable to the installment sale apply to the self-cancelling installment note. However, there are additional factors to consider.

The Tax Court has held that in the case of installment sales from decedent to his children, with a provision that in the event decedent died before payments were completed, the balance would be cancelled, the installment sale results in realization of taxable gain reported in the decedent's final return.[17] This decision was based on Code section 453B, which provides that where an installment note is cancelled or becomes unenforceable, this is treated as a taxable disposition of the note. On appeal, the 8th Circuit reversed the Tax Court decision, but only by holding that the gain would be fully taxable to the decedent's estate as income in respect of a decedent, not as income on the decedent's final income tax return.[18]

Note that for gift tax purposes, the actual value of the SCIN received by the seller is not equal to its face value, since the risk of death is a factor that clearly affects the value of the note. If this is not considered, the transaction will be treated as a bargain sale, with gift tax consequences to the seller. If the selling price is increased to include consideration of the risk of death, the seller will have to report gain in excess of the actual gain that would have been realized had the property been sold at fair market value. An alternative is to use a higher interest rate.[19]

What are the estate tax consequences of the SCIN? The Tax Court has held that since the balance of the note is cancelled at the death of the seller, there is nothing to include in his or her estate.[20] The IRS agrees, at least in part.

HOW LIFE INSURANCE CAN ENHANCE THIS PLANNING TOOL

Where an individual (or business) transfers property to someone else in return for installment payments, the seller will often purchase insurance on the life (or lives) of the transferee(s) to protect against the potential cessation of payments at the death of the transferee(s). The seller should consider owning, paying premiums on, and being the beneficiary of the policy (the agreed-upon amount of payments made by the purchaser of the property could be increased to provide enough cash to make premium payments).

After the installment sale agreement is signed, the transferee-buyer receives title to the property. This means that the asset itself, as well as any appreciation from the date of the transfer, will be included in the transferee's estate. To provide the liquidity necessary to pay taxes and other death expenses, life insurance is often purchased on the transferee's life by the transferee's spouse, adult children, or on behalf of the transferee's spouse and children by the trustee of an irrevocable trust. The spouse, adult child, or trustee would be the owner, premium payer, and beneficiary of the policy proceeds. In intrafamily transfers, the transferor-seller often will make a gift to the policyholder of enough cash to pay premiums on the insured's life.

A third use of life insurance to improve the benefits of an installment sale is to assure the transferee's family enough cash at his or her death to make the promised installment payments. (Since the property will be in the transferee's estate after the sale, its inclusion could generate substantial estate and inheritance tax problems. This, in turn, creates a need for cash to pay increased death costs and drains the estate of cash to make installment payments.)

If the transferee's spouse, for example, purchases the appropriate amount of insurance on his life, there will be no need to sell or liquidate the transferred asset (perhaps closely held corporate stock) in order to make the agreed upon installment payments. The insurance proceeds can be used to pay death costs, make installment payments, or both.

IMPLICATIONS AND ISSUES IN COMMUNITY PROPERTY STATES

Installment sales by married individuals in community property states often involve real property. In such situations, it is important to ascertain whether the interest in real property is community property. Both spouses should join in any conveyance of community real property. If one spouse does not join in the conveyance of community real property, he or she may be able to void the sale for a specified period (one year from the date of recording of the deed in California). This statute of limitations applies only to land standing in the name of the transferor spouse alone. If the land stands in the name of both spouses, an attempt by either spouse to transfer complete title would be void with respect to the interest of the other spouse. Certain sales made to parties, in good faith, who are not aware of the marriage relationship may be incontestable, but such controversies should be avoided.

A purchaser of personal property should also ascertain whether any community property rights are involved. California does not require the written consent of each spouse in connection with the sale of community personal property if the property is sold for "valuable consideration." Exception: Neither spouse can sell, convey, or encumber the furniture, furnishings, or fittings of the home or wearing apparel of the other spouse or minor children without the written consent of the other spouse.

Problems could arise as a result of recent cases regarding joint property rights of non-marital partners. Some courts have found implied agreements between non-married individuals to treat their property similarly to community property. Caution should be exercised if you are purchasing property from an individual involved in such a relationship. It may be advisable to ask the partner, who may have a claim, to convey his or her interest in the property, if any.

Another possibility to consider is the separate sale of each spouse's interest. One spouse could sell his or her interest outright and recognize all of his or her capital gain immediately, while the other spouse could sell his or her interest on the installment method and spread out his or her capital gain. This can reduce capital gain taxes while effectively allowing a greater amount of the sale price to be received in the year of the sale.

QUESTIONS AND ANSWERS

Question — How can the related party rules be avoided?

Answer — For property other than marketable securities, the related purchaser could hold the property for at least a 2-year period after the sale (to the extent that the special depreciable property rule does not apply). The installment obligation could be structured so that no payments need to be made until after the 2-year holding period has lapsed. If the related party was going to sell the property to raise cash to make installment payments, as an alternative the related party could use the property as collateral for a loan to provide funds needed to make installment payments. (The loan must be bona fide, and the debtor must continue to bear the economic risk of loss.)

A private annuity could be used—instead of an installment sale—to avoid all three related party rules. Since the installment sale rules do not deal with private annuity arrangements, the transferee should be free to dispose of the transferred property at any time without accelerating the recognition of gain to the transferor.

In any installment sale to a related party, the risk of illiquidity of the initial seller in the event of a second disposition by the new owner should be considered. How can this potential problem be overcome? Perhaps the seller might insist on an acceleration clause. This would give the seller the right to demand additional cash payments if the property subject to the installment sale is disposed of before the 2-year waiting period has been met.

It probably would not be advisable to impose formal restrictions on the related purchaser's ability to dispose of the property. Likewise, it probably is not wise to give the seller a legal right to insist that the purchaser must lend him funds to pay a tax imposed on a second disposition. Such contractual restrictions or requirements could be viewed by the IRS as evidence that the entire transaction lacked economic substance.

Question — What type of security can the seller of property under an installment sale require without being taxed on his entire gain in the year of the sale?

Answer — A third party can guarantee payment in the event the buyer defaults. For example, a standby letter of credit

that is used as security for a deferred payment sale will not be treated as a payment received on the installment obligation.[21]

But third party notes or other third party obligations that are transferable or marketable prior to default by the installment buyer will be treated as payments to the seller (and therefore taxable in the year received).[22]

Typically, the IRS and the courts will deem funds placed in an escrow account to secure the interest of the seller to be constructively received—and therefore currently taxable in the year of the sale. However, this result is not certain. No presumption of tax avoidance arises merely because the seller requested an installment payout or merely because the buyer was at all times willing to pay the entire purchase price in a lump sum.

The seller is more likely to be successful in avoiding current taxation of escrowed funds if (1) the arrangement serves a legitimate business purpose, and (2) the seller continues to look to the contractual obligation of the buyer for payment. An example would be where the escrow arrangement was negotiated in a manner which provided that payments from the escrow account were contingent on the seller's continued adherence to his agreement not to compete. This type of agreement would probably not result in constructive receipt by the seller even if he could control the investment of the money in the escrow account.

Question — What are the income and estate tax implications when the holder of an installment obligation dies?

Answer — The right to receive payments under the obligation is treated as income in respect of a decedent. Thus, payments on the installment obligation are taxable income to the person or entity that receives those payments, as they are received. Payments are taxed in the same manner as they would have been taxed had the seller lived and received payment himself.

For estate tax purposes, the present value of the installment obligation is also includable in the decedent's gross estate. But to reduce the harshness of double taxation, a deduction from income is allowed to the recipient based on the federal estate taxes paid by the decedent's estate attributable to the inclusion of the installment obligation. This is called the Section 691 (income in respect of a decedent) deduction.

Question — Is there a problem in arranging an installment sale of property with an existing mortgage upon it?

Answer — Yes. Where property subject to an existing mortgage is sold and the purchaser assumes or takes subject to that mortgage, any debt in excess of the seller's tax basis (cost) will be considered a payment received by the seller in the year of the sale. Any mortgage encumbering the property will be treated as assumed or taken subject to, even though title to the property does not pass in the year of sale and even though the seller remains responsible for payment of the mortgage (as in a "wrap-around" mortgage).[23]

Question — Does the "second disposition" rule mean there are no advantages to a transfer of property (which is not within the special depreciable property rule) from an individual to an irrevocable trust established for his family in return for installment payments?

Answer — Many advantages still exist, including the following:

(1) Taxation on the gain can be spread over a larger number of years (assuming the trust does not dispose of the property within 2 years, and assuming the trust does not benefit the seller or the seller's spouse if the property is depreciable to the trust). This could lower the applicable total rate.

(2) The family of the seller is more secure from the claims of his creditors.

(3) No gift tax is incurred on the transfer if the property is sold to the trust at its fair market value.

(4) The trust may have little or no gain on the resale of the asset since it takes as its basis the full purchase price it agreed to pay. (Of course, the property may appreciate or decline in value during the 2 years it must be held in order to avoid accelerating the initial seller's gain.)

(5) None of the assets of the trust or income will be includable in the original owner's estate if the trust is irrevocable and he maintains no control. (The present value of future payments remaining on the note would, however, be includable if he died within the installment period. This, in turn, could cause a serious lack of liquidity.)

To obtain this favorable treatment, it is important that

(a) the trustee be completely independent and that the grantor maintain no control over the trustee's actions,

(b) there be no prearrangement between the parties requiring the trustee to resell the property,

(c) the original owner not have a stake in the resale by the trust (i.e., the amount he receives cannot be dependent on the amount the trustee receives),

(d) there be a motive—other than tax savings—for the arrangement, and

(e) the "2-year holding rule" be met.

Question — Must there be any down payment in the year of sale to qualify for the installment method of reporting?

Answer — No. There is no requirement that there be any payment in the year of sale. The only requirement of this type is that at least one payment be made in the taxable year after the year in which the property was sold.

Question — Will a bequest of an installment obligation to the obligor avoid tax recognition of the untaxed gain?

Answer — The installment obligation rules cannot be circumvented by cancelling the obligation during the seller's lifetime. Likewise, when an installment seller dies holding an installment obligation, the gain is not forgiven. Instead, gain is reportable by the seller's estate—or the recipient of the obligation—as payments are made. The amount of gain and character of income realized is the same as the deceased seller would have reported had he or she lived. (Note that death itself does not trigger an acceleration of gain; tax is due only if payments are actually or constructively received or if the obligation is sold.)

Under prior law, it had been argued that if an installment obligation was bequeathed to the purchaser of the property, the interests of the obligor and the obligee "merged." Under this theory, there would be no gain realized because the estate would never realize the unpaid balance.

Current tax law accelerates the unrealized gain when the seller makes a bequest of the obligation to the buyer or his estate cancels the debt. Gain or loss will be recognized to the extent the fair market value of the obligation exceeds the obligation holder's basis. (Where the decedent-seller and the purchaser are related, the fair market value of the obligation cannot be less than its face amount.)

If a person forgives an installment obligation in his will, the cancellation is treated as a transfer of the obligation by the decedent's estate. The estate will report the accelerated gain. If a trust or some party other than the decedent held the obligation, the cancellation will be treated as a transfer by that person immediately after the decedent's death.

An installment obligation that becomes unenforceable at the seller's death is treated as if it were cancelled in favor of the obligor.

Question — What is the tax effect where the seller cancels a buyer's obligation to make installments?

Answer — If a seller cancels a buyer's installment obligation (or it becomes unenforceable), the cancellation will be treated as a "disposition" of the obligation. This means the seller must report gain (or loss). The gain (or loss) is measured by the difference between the fair market value of the obligation at the time of its disposition and its basis.

Note that if the seller and buyer are considered "related persons," the fair market value of the obligation will be considered as not less than the face value. For instance, mom sells her summer home in Avalon to her daughter in an installment sale. Mom's basis in the home was $10,000. Her daughter will pay the purchase price, $50,000, in five equal annual $10,000 installments. (Interest is ignored for simplicity.) If mom immediately cancels the daughter's obligation, mom must report gain. Her gain is the difference between the value of what is owed to her, $50,000, and her $10,000 basis. She is also liable for any gift tax on the gift.

A solution would seem to be for mom to forgive, at her whim, and on a year by year basis, all or a portion of each $10,000 payment as it is paid. Her daughter should write a check for the full $10,000 to her. Then, without a prearranged or legally binding plan, she can write her daughter—and son-in-law and each of her grandchildren—checks of $10,000 or under, all of which would be gift tax free (and she could double the amount of each check if her husband joined in on a "split" gift). Mom will recognize gain of $8,000 each of the 5 years, rather than $40,000 in the year of sale.

Question — How is gain computed under the installment sale rules where the sale price is not fixed or determinable?

Answer — Often, the price at which property will change hands depends on some contingency. For example, Susan Harmon may sell her stock in the SH Corporation, a closely held business, to her son Mark in return for installment payments. But rather than selling at a specific dollar price, the amount may be set as a percentage of the gross profits of the business for each of the next 10 years. The parties may—or may not—put a maximum dollar amount on the selling price.

Installment sale treatment is available even when the actual price cannot be determined with precision. If there is a stated maximum selling price, the seller (in this example Susan) can recover basis by means of a "gross profit ratio."[24] This ratio is multiplied by the installment payment (exclusive of interest) to determine the portion of the payment which is gain.

$$\frac{\text{gross profit (realized or to be realized)}}{\substack{\text{total contract price (assume this is} \\ \text{maximum selling price)}}} \quad \text{X} \quad \substack{\text{installment} \\ \text{payment}}$$

(The maximum selling price is defined as the largest price which could be paid assuming all contingencies, formulas, etc., operate in the seller's favor.) The seller then reports income on a pro rata basis (and recovers his basis over the scheduled payment period in equal annual increments) with respect to each installment payment.

Later, if it is found that the contingency will not be met (and therefore the seller will not actually receive the "maximum" selling price) a recomputation of the seller's income is allowed. The seller may report reduced income (not only in the adjustment year, but in all subsequent years). If as a result of the recomputation, the seller does not recover his or her entire income tax basis for the property sold, the amount of basis will be deductible as a loss.[25]

If the sale price is indefinite and no maximum selling price can be determined—but the obligation is payable over a fixed period of time, the seller's basis would be recoverable ratably over that fixed period.[26]

If neither selling price nor payment period can be ascertained with certainty in advance, the arrangement will be closely scrutinized to determine whether there has been a sale or whether the payments, in economic effect, are merely in the nature of rent or royalty income. If it is determined that there has been a sale, the seller's basis will be recovered over 15 years commencing with the date of sale. Any basis not recovered in that time may be carried forward to succeeding years until recovered in full.

Generally, if in any year payments received are less than the basis allocated to that year, the excess basis must be reallocated over the balance of the 15-year period. (A period other than 15 years may be used or required where it is shown that a substantial and inappropriate deferral or acceleration of the recovery of the seller's basis would otherwise result.)[27]

The effect of the contingency sale price rules allowing installment reporting is that taxpayers have little justification for treating transactions as "open." (In open transactions, a taxpayer can recover his entire cost before reporting any gain—rather than reporting gain ratably.) This "cost recovery" method is available only in rare and extraordinary cases involving sales for a contingent price where it is impossible to value a purchaser's obligation to pay a contingent price.

Special rules apply with respect to contingent installment payments for sales of depreciable property to a controlled entity, such as a more than 50% owned partnership or corporation. The rules are:

1. Seller's basis is recovered ratably in annual increments if (a) the installment sale is to a controlled entity and (b) it is impossible to reasonably ascertain the fair market value.

2. All noncontingent payments plus the fair market value of contingent payments must be reported in the year of the sale. For instance, assume Tom Miller sells depreciable property to a corporation he controls for no down payment and 10 percent of the net profits from the business for the next 10 years. Assume the fair market value of the promise can be reasonably ascertained to be $200,000. Tom would have to include $200,000 in income in the year of the sale ($0 noncontingent payments plus $200,000 fair market value of contingent payments).[28]

3. The purchaser of the property may not increase his basis in the property by any amount before such time as the seller includes such amount in income.

Question — How soon does a taxpayer have to elect to report payments in installments?

Answer — No election is necessary. Installment sale treatment is automatic for qualifying sales unless an election is made specifying installment sale treatment is not to apply. Although the temporary regulations are not specific as to how such an election is to be made, reporting the entire gain in gross income for the taxable year in which the sale occurs (on or before the due date for filing the tax return—including extensions) will operate as an election that installment sale reporting is not to apply.[29] Once a valid election out of the installment method has been made, it may not be revoked except under very limited circumstances. The Service has provided guidance in the form of a Revenue Ruling concerning when it will grant permission to make a late election out of the installment method.[30]

Question — When might it be a good idea to forego the installment method of reporting a gain, even though a sale was made on the installment basis?

Answer — If a taxpayer has unrelated losses, he might wish to offset those losses with the gain from the installment sale. He may have unusually low income or high deductions for the year. Thus, he or she would report the full gain in the year of sale even though the sale was an installment sale.

Question — When is interest payable on the unpaid balance of an installment sale deductible by the buyer?

Answer — Interest is deductible only in the period in which that interest is properly allocable. Regardless of how the parties have formed the agreement, the IRS will treat the interest as "constant" (whether the taxpayer is on the cash or accrual method). The Service allocates the interest over the term of the contract. The net effect is that the parties must determine the effective interest on a compound interest basis and use that effective rate to compute the amount of any allowable interest deduction.

This rule limits both the interest deduction and the interest income to the amount of interest that accrues economically. The compounding period used in determining the effective rate of interest will probably be the same as that called for in the parties' agreement.

Question — When will a taxpayer be subject to the interest surcharge for installment sales in excess of $150,000?

Answer — There is a special interest surcharge imposed on certain installment obligations in which the sale price exceeds $150,000 and the aggregate deferred payments for such sales during the taxable year exceeds $5,000,000. There are three exceptions to the application of the surcharge: (1) property used or produced in the trade or business of farming, (2) timeshares and residential lots, and (3) personal use property.[31]

Footnote References

Installment Sales and SCINS

1. IRC Sec. 453.
2. IRC Sec. 453(b).
3. IRC Sec. 453(d).
4. IRC Sec. 453(j); Reg. §15.453-1(c).
5. IRC Sec. 453(k)(2).
6. IRC Sec. 453.
7. Rev. Rul. 70-430, 1970-2 CB 51.

8. IRC Sec. 483.

9. IRC Sec. 1274A; Rev. Rul. 95-10, 1995-5 IRB 37; Rev. Rul. 94-19, 1994-1 CB 216.

10. IRC Sec. 2033; Reg. §20.2033-1.

11. *Ballard v. Comm.,* TC Memo 1987-128; *Krabbenhoft v. Comm.,* 94 TC 887 (1990).

12. *Ballard v. Comm.,* 854 F.2d 185 (7th Cir. 1988).

13. *Krabbenhoft v. Comm.,* 939 F.2d 529 (8th Cir. 1991), *cert. denied,* 502 U.S. 1072 (1991).

14. Reg. §1.691(a)-3.

15. Reg. §1.691(c)-1.

16. IRC Sec. 1012.

17. *Estate of Frane v. Comm.,* 98 TC 341 (1992).

18. *Estate of Frane v. Comm.,* 998 F.2d 567 (8th Cir. 1993).

19. GCM 39503 (5-7-86).

20. *Estate of Moss v. Comm.,* 74 TC 1279 (1980), *acq. in result,* 1981-1 CB 2.

21. Temp. Reg. §15A.453-1(b)(3).

22. Temp. Reg. §15A.453-1(e).

23. Temp. Reg. §15A.453-1(b)(3)(ii).

24. Temp. Reg. §15A.453-1(c)(2).

25. Reg. §15A.453-1(c)(2), Example (5).

26. Temp. Reg. §15A.453-1(c)(3).

27. Temp. Reg. §15A.453-1(c)(4).

28. IRC Sec. 453(g)(1).

29. Temp. Reg. §15A.453-1(d)(3).

30. Rev. Rul. 90-46, 1990-1 CB 107.

31. IRC Sec. 453A(b)(3).

Chapter 20

INTEREST-FREE AND BELOW MARKET RATE LOANS

WHAT IS IT?

An interest-free or below market rate loan involves the lending of money to a party who is required either to pay no interest or to pay a rate of interest less than that which is currently being charged in the marketplace.

Most interest-free (or below market rate) loans are made by a corporation to a nonshareholder employee or from a parent to a child or other family member.

The economic advantage of an interest-free (or below market rate) loan lies in the borrower's ability to use either the funds or the interest from the funds.

There are few, if any, tax advantages to an interest-free or below market rate loan, due to the denial of all personal (consumer) interest deductions, and limitation of investment interest deductions to investment income. There are, however, still many remaining economic and other reasons why interest-free and below market rate loans are viable planning techniques.

WHEN IS THE USE OF SUCH A DEVICE INDICATED?

1. To reduce the estate of the lender to the extent the loan limits future growth in the value of assets and shifts economic wealth to the borrower.

2. As a corporate fringe benefit to enable an employee to purchase a home, provide for a child's college education, purchase stock of the employer-corporation, or to pay medical bills.

3. Transfers of income through interest-free or below market rate loans can be used to support parents, provide support for children in school, or to help them purchase a home or business.

WHAT ARE THE REQUIREMENTS?

1. The transaction must constitute a bona fide debt (preferably in writing).

2. If the parties maintain books or records of account, the debt should be entered.

3. There should be a provision in the debt instrument (assuming a no-interest loan is desired) expressly precluding interest, or, in the case of a below market rate loan, stating the interest to be charged.

In order to assure that a loan from a corporation to its employee is not construed as compensation income, the loan must conform to the following factors:

1. The arrangement must constitute a bona fide debt (preferably a written note containing a reasonable repayment schedule or a note payable on demand).

2. A demonstrated intent to repay must be evidenced by an agreement between the parties. This is especially important where the loan is to a majority shareholder-employee. Otherwise, the IRS could claim that the "loan" is in fact a disguised dividend.

3. The amount of the loan must be reasonable in relation to the salary of the employee.

It is advisable to avoid situations where the corporation borrows money to make interest-free loans to shareholders. The IRS is likely to treat such transactions as if the real loan was made between the lender and the shareholder. Following that reasoning, interest actually paid by the corporation to the lender could be treated as if the corporation paid a dividend to the shareholder who then paid interest to the lender. This attack is especially likely if the shareholder personally guaranteed the loan to the corporation.[1]

HOW IT IS DONE — EXAMPLES

Example 1. Your client, Maxine Grayboyes, is a key singer in the industrial productions corporation called, "Off Broad Street." To enable her daughter to purchase a new home, Maxine advances to her daughter, interest-free, $150,000.

Example 2. Terry Halpern is the owner of "Show Time," a magazine devoted to promoting show business and informing people who work for television, radio, theatre groups, and other entertainment vehicles about new and current events. In order to promote a more favorable press image for herself Farrah Fawcelips lent Terry $4,000,000 at 8 percent interest for 8 years. The best deal Terry could have gotten from a local bank would have been 12 percent.

While interest income will be imputed to the lender in each of these cases (see TAX IMPLICATIONS, below), the nontax advantages of the lender making the funds available to the borrower may be significant.

Example 3. Rich Marino is the President and one-third shareholder of the Bumpy Road Paving Company, Incorporated. Substantial interest-free loans were made by the corporation to him and his brothers, Larry and Tony, who are also shareholders. In order to make these loans, the Bumpy Road Paving Company had to carry interest-bearing obligations to third parties. In other words, suppliers to Bumpy Road Paving extended substantial amounts of credit. Rick, Larry, and Tony personally guaranteed these obligations. In this situation, the substance of the transaction is that Bumpy Road Paving is acting as the agent of the three individual taxpayers. It is as if Bumpy Road Paving, on behalf of Rick, Larry, and Tony, obtained loans and then paid interest to the creditors on behalf of the three shareholders. In essence every time the Bumpy Road Paving Company paid interest, those payments (to the extent allocable to its interest-free loans to the shareholders) actually discharged the personal obligations of the shareholders. To the extent that these actual payments were in fact made, the taxpayers are deemed to have received dividend income and made an interest payment.[2]

WHAT ARE THE TAX IMPLICATIONS?

1. Loans with no interest or a below market rate of interest generally are recharacterized for tax purposes as loans bearing a market rate of interest accompanied by a payment or payments of interest from the lender to the borrower. These phantom payments (the difference between what should have been charged and what in fact was charged for the use of the money lent) are then subject to the general rules for interest deductions. Additionally, the phantom payment from the lender will be characterized as *compensation* from a business to an employee, as a *dividend* from the corporation to its shareholder, or as a *gift* from the shareholders of the corporation to the borrower or from a parent to a child. Such a gift may also be subject to the gift tax.

    Personal interest is not deductible; thus, interest-free or below market loans will often result in taxable income to the borrower to the extent of the excess between what they should be paying and what the borrower in fact pays.

Still, the interest-free or below market loan is appealing, not as a tax shifting device, but as an economically viable tool for accomplishing personal and business objectives.

2. Unless the transaction between a corporation and an employee (or an employee-shareholder) is a bona fide loan, the entire loan may be treated as additional salary or as a disguised dividend.

3. For a more detailed discussion of personal loans and tax issues, see QUESTIONS AND ANSWERS, below.

IMPLICATIONS AND ISSUES IN COMMUNITY PROPERTY STATES

As discussed in Chapter 15, relating to gifts (which should be reviewed in conjunction with this section), some states impose gift taxes on interspousal gifts. The following are some of the potential problem areas which might arise:

If the money lent is the separate property of one spouse (e.g., that spouse having inherited the funds) a gift can occur between the lending spouses if the demand note is made in favor of both spouses. The amount of the gift would be one-half of the value of the note (presumably the face amount of the note).

A similar gift may be found if the money lent is community property and the demand note received in exchange for the funds names only one spouse. It may be possible to show successfully that the named spouse was holding the note as trustee for the community and a gift avoided, but it creates the opportunity for the taxing authorities to claim that a gift was made and thus creates exposure to either gift tax, legal expense, or both, in dealing with the problem created.

Another unintended gift could occur if the money were lent to one spouse and then used to purchase assets in the names of both spouses.

An accidental gift may also result from the repayment of the loan. If the loan is to one spouse and is used to make investments in the name of that spouse, the liability belongs entirely to that spouse. The use of community funds or the separate property of the non-borrowing spouse to repay the loan provides the basis for a taxable gift to be recognized.

If the note is called by the lender and the borrower does not have the funds to repay and his spouse or the community does, then a gift can be avoided by the borrower giving to the spouse (or the community) a note for the amount of funds used to repay his obligation.

These problems can be avoided by careful attention to the source of funds for loans and the manner in which investments or repayments are made.

QUESTIONS AND ANSWERS

Question — How can a loan to a key employee be structured in order to tie that employee into the business?

Answer — By making the loan callable upon separation from service or payable in the event of the employee's preretirement death, the corporation can protect its interest. The employee could protect his own estate by purchasing life insurance in the amount of the loan.

Question — How is "foregone interest" calculated?

Answer — Tax law creates a fiction; for income and gift tax purposes the tax law treats interest-free and below market loans as if a specified level of interest was charged and paid—even if it was not. In other words, interest is imputed on interest-free loans and on other below market rate loans. The amount subjected to gift and income taxation in most cases is the difference between (a) the "applicable federal rate" and (b) the interest actually payable (if any) under the agreement between the parties. This difference is the "foregone interest."[3]

Under this legal fiction, the borrower is treated as paying the foregone interest to the lender and therefore may take an income tax deduction for the "payment" (but only to the extent the borrower is deemed to have investment income if the interest is considered investment interest; no deduction is allowed for personal interest). The lender will be treated as having received the foregone interest and therefore must report the income "received."

Question — What are the implications of a loan that is treated as a gift?

Answer — If a loan is considered a gift, the lender is treated as if he or she made a gift to the borrower in the amount of the "foregone interest." (See the discussion of term and demand loans below.)

Question — What are the implications if a loan is not a gift?

Answer — The tax characterization of a loan which is not a gift depends on the relationship between the parties. In any case, the IRS will treat the lender as having made a transfer to the borrower in the amount of the "foregone interest."

The Service will generally treat foregone interest as a dividend when the borrower is solely a shareholder (nondeductible by the corporation, taxable as ordinary income to the shareholder, as interest paid by the shareholder, and taxable to the corporation as interest income).

If the borrower is solely an employee, the lender will have interest income to the extent of the foregone interest and a corresponding deduction for compensation paid (if reasonable). The borrower will have compensation income, but a deduction for the foregone interest may be denied or limited (see paragraph 1 under "WHAT ARE THE TAX IMPLICATIONS," above).

Question — How will shareholder-employees be treated?

Answer — The foregone interest will generally be treated as a dividend.

Question — How do you compute the amount subject to taxation?

Answer — That depends on two factors: (1) Is the gift tax or is the income tax involved (or both)? (2) Is the loan a demand loan or is it a term loan (including loans with indefinite maturities)?

Demand loans are loans payable in full at any time on the demand of the lender. The amount subject to (both gift and income) tax is the "foregone interest." This foregone interest is measured by the applicable statutory rate specified during each calendar year the loan remains outstanding. This means that from year to year the rate will change. It also means that the interest income is reportable one year at a time.

A term loan is defined as any loan which is not a demand loan. The treatment of these loans depends on whether the loan is a "gift loan" or not. A gift loan is a below market loan where the lender intends to make a gift to the borrower in the amount of the foregone interest.

How much interest is foregone in the case of a term loan? Essentially, the present value of the interest that should have been charged, minus the amount from the present value of the interest that was in fact charged is the foregone interest amount. The difference is the taxable amount. In calculating present values, the statutory discount rate applicable at the time the loan is made must be used.

Where the term loan is not a gift loan (for example, where it is "compensation-related," that is, a loan between an employer and an employee or between an independent contractor and the person for whom he performs services), the taxable amount is the present value of the foregone interest for the entire term of the loan. The borrower is deemed to be paying that interest while the lender is deemed to be receiving the interest and is therefore taxed on it. Taxation in the case of a nongift term loan is at a level rate for each year of the loan.[4] (Withholding is not required by an employer on the deemed payment made to an employee arising from a demand or term loan.)

Where the term loan is a gift loan, the amount subject to taxation is determined in the same way as a nongift loan. But for gift tax purposes, the entire present value of foregone interest is subject to gift tax in the year of the loan. For income tax purposes, each year's foregone interest is taxed on a year by year basis.

If the loan is a term loan, the statutory interest rate affixed to the foregone interest amount will be the applicable federal rate in effect as of the day the loan was made. With respect to a demand loan, the interest rate will change each year as the applicable federal rates change.

Question — Are there transactions that will be treated as interest-free or below market rate loans even though they appear to be something else?

Answer — Yes. Congress was concerned with all transactions that in effect were tax avoidance or significant tax-shifting schemes. Therefore, many situations which do not look like loans will invoke the below market rules. For example, assume a local country club requires its members to pay a refundable, non-interest-bearing deposit as part of their membership fee. In essence, the member is paying part of the fee with the income that the club earns on the deposit. The IRS could easily apply the rules described above.

Question — What are the exceptions and limitations to the interest-free and below market rate loan rules?

Answer — There are a number of important exceptions:

(1) A loan made from one individual to another is exempt from both gift and income tax rules if the outstanding balance on the total of all loans made to that person from the lender does not exceed $10,000. Think of this as the "$10,000 and under de minimus rule."[5]

This protection will not apply if the loan is a gift loan and the loan proceeds are used in connection with income producing property. Furthermore, for term loans that are not gift loans, once the outstanding balance exceeds $10,000, the exception no longer applies, even if the outstanding balance is later reduced below $10,000.[6] Finally, if the loan is a "compensation-related" loan or a "corporate-shareholder" loan (any loan between a corporation and any shareholder), the protection will not apply if federal tax avoidance is a principal purpose for the loan.

(2) The second exception to the general rules governing interest-free and below market rate loans is the "$100,000 and under" rule. This rule provides that where gift loans are made directly between individuals and the outstanding balances due on the aggregate of the loans made to that person by the lender do not exceed $100,000, the law limits the amount of the "foregone" interest.

The limit is the lower of (a) the statutory rate or (b) the borrower's net investment income for the year. If the borrower does not earn more than $1,000 in the year, the law treats the parties as if there were no foregone interest.

The $100,000 and under rule applies only if federal tax avoidance is not a principal purpose of the loan.[7]

ASRS: Sec. 53, ¶20.3(a); Sec. 55, ¶57.5(b); Sec. 63, ¶150.

Footnote References

Interest-Free and Below Market Rate Loans

1. *Creel v. Comm.*, 72 TC 1173 (1979).
2. *Creel*, 72 TC 1173 (1979). For other cases on interest-free loans see *Saunders v. U.S.*, 294 F. Supp. 1276, 1282, (D. Hawaii 1968), *rev'd on other grounds*, 450 F.2d 1047 (9th Cir. 1971); *Joseph Lupowitz Sons, Inc. v. Comm.*, 497 F.2d 862 (3rd Cir. 1974); *Claude J. Lisle et al. v. Comm.*, TC Memo 1976-140; *Albert Suttle v. Comm.*, TC Memo 1978-393; *Zager v. Comm.*, 72 TC 1009 (1979), *aff'd*, 649 F.2d 1137 (5th Cir. 1981); *William G. Martin v. Comm.*, TC Memo 1979-469; *C.F. Williams*, TC Memo 1978-306; *Dolese v. U.S.*, 79-2 USTC ¶9540 (10th Cir. 1979).
3. IRC Sec. 7872(e).
4. IRC Secs. 7872(b)(2), 1272(a)(1).
5. IRC Sec. 7872(c); Prop. Reg. §1.7872-8(b)(3).
6. IRC Secs. 7872(f)(10).
7. IRC Sec. 7872(d)(1).

The Tools and Techniques of Estate Planning

Chapter 21

LIFE INSURANCE

WHAT IS IT?

Life insurance is a contract under which for a stipulated consideration (a premium), one party (the insurer) agrees to pay the other (the insured), or his or her beneficiary, a defined amount upon the occurrence of death or some other specified event. In essence, life insurance is a contract under which economic protection is provided against the risk of cessation of income due to the insured's death. This definition of life insurance includes accidental death benefits under health insurance policies, whole life, endowment, universal, variable, and term life insurance policies. It encompasses both personally-owned and business-owned policies and includes group coverage as well as individually purchased plans.

WHEN IS THE USE OF SUCH A DEVICE INDICATED?

1. Life insurance is an important estate planning tool to provide cash for the payment of estate and inheritance taxes, debts, administrative costs, and other estate expenses.

2. Life insurance will provide an income for family expenses.

3. Life insurance can be used for special needs such as the payment of college expenses, mortgage balances, or other large capital needs.

4. Life insurance is often used as a credit-building tool; lending institutions and other creditors often use life insurance on a debtor's life as security.

5. Life insurance provides a way to pay federal estate taxes at a "discount." For example, if an individual purchases a $100,000 policy and dies within the first year of a contract (after having paid $1,500 in premiums), $100,000 worth of taxes can be paid at a cost of only $1,500. The difference can be roughly thought of as a discount. Furthermore, properly arranged life insurance owned by a third party who is also named beneficiary can be used to pay estate settlement costs with no probate cost, no inheritance or other state death taxes, no income taxes, no transfer fees, and no federal estate taxes.

6. Life insurance can be used as the "funding" mechanism for business continuation agreements.

7. Life insurance can be used by a corporation to finance certain corporate obligations such as nonqualified deferred compensation or salary continuation, as well as be used as key person insurance to indemnify the corporation for the lost services of a key person.

8. Life insurance can be used to fund a charitable gift. (See Chapter 3.)

WHAT ARE THE VARIOUS TYPES OF LIFE INSURANCE?

Term Insurance

Under this type of insurance the insured must die before the term expires for which benefits are to be paid. If the insured survives to the expiration of the "term," the insurance protection terminates. Initially, the cash outlay for insurance protection is relatively low so that the policyowner receives the maximum short term protection for the minimum cash outlay.

There are basically five types of term insurance:

a. *Annual renewable term.* This type of policy is renewable each year (regardless of the insured's physical condition) at an increasing premium.

b. *Convertible term.* This type of policy may be exchanged without evidence of insurability, i.e., without the insured proving that he is physically and otherwise in a standard class of risks, for a whole life, universal life, or endowment type of policy.

c. *Decreasing term.* A familiar kind of decreasing term is often called "mortgage" insurance. The death benefit decreases over the specified period of time, but the premium generally remains level.

d. *Level term.* Here the death benefit remains the same for the entire term of the policy. Generally the premium also remains level. Common term periods are 5, 10, and 15 years.

e.   *Re-entry term.* This type of policy provides a guaranteed term premium for an initial premium but allows the insured to requalify or re-enter after the initial period, if his or her health remains good. Re-entry can occur typically after a five or ten year period. If the insured does not requalify, the rates remain at the guaranteed rates which are much higher than the re-entry rates.

Whole Life Insurance

The major characteristics of whole life insurance are: (a) the premium for a whole life insurance contract remains level throughout the life of the contract; and (b) because of the "reserve" the insurance company needs to maintain a level premium when the insured reaches older ages, "cash value" builds up within the contract (this cash value increases annually and can be borrowed by the policyowner or taken as surrender proceeds).

There are basically two types of whole life insurance. The first type is known as straight life, while the second is known as limited payment life. The difference is basically that under a limited payment life policy, premiums are "compressed," i.e., they are payable over a shorter period of time. For example, if a male age 35 purchased a $100,000 straight life policy, the "face amount" (death benefit) would be $100,000. If he purchased a $100,000 20-payment life policy at the same age, the death benefit would be the same and the protection would be provided for as long as the policyowner wanted to keep the policy in force, i.e., it could be kept in force for the insured's life. But because premiums would be compressed into a much smaller period of time (20 annual payments), they would be considerably higher under the limited payment type of plan.

Two other varieties of whole life are: (a) modified life and (b) preferred risk life. A modified life insurance policy typically provides a given amount of insurance at unusually low premium rates for an initial period (e.g., five years) after issue and then the premium is correspondingly higher for the remainder of the premium period. Modified plans generally have a lower initial cash value than a corresponding face amount of typical straight life would have.

Preferred risk is a type of policy which generally requires that the insured be in above average health. Preferred risk plans are often sold only to professionals or others in low risk occupations or to nonsmokers. Generally, preferred risk policies are sold only in higher amounts (such as $100,000 or greater) and the premiums under such a plan are slightly lower per $1,000 of protection than with standard policies.

Riders, such as waiver of premium (waives premium if insured is disabled for a period of at least six months) and accidental death and dismemberment (doubles the death benefit if death is by accidental means), may be added to the basic contract.

Endowment Insurance

The primary characteristic of endowment insurance is that such a plan pays the face amount (e.g., $100,000) at the sooner of the time of "endowment" (the maturity of the contract, e.g., age 65) or at the insured's death. Endowment policies are basically purchased as a means of forced savings since the protection element is relatively minimal. Various types of endowment policies are often found in pension plans, or personal savings programs. Since the cash value builds up tax free under an endowment policy, such plans are often utilized by individuals in high income tax brackets.

Universal Life Insurance

A universal life policy is interest sensitive life insurance in which the investment, expense, and mortality elements are separately and specifically defined. A contract owner selects a death benefit level. The death benefit may be one that increases over time, coinciding with the increased cash value of the policy (death benefit option II), or, alternatively, the death benefit can remain level regardless of the underlying value changes (death benefit option I). From the premium that is paid, the insurer then deducts a "load" for contractually defined expenses. The remaining premium is then credited toward the contract owner's cash values. Mortality charges are deducted. Interest earned on the remaining cash is then credited at rates based on current investment earnings. (Specific design features will vary from company to company depending on marketing policies and product objectives.) Under this configuration, increased interest rates result in higher cash value levels while increased expense loads and increased mortality charges result in lower cash values. Typically, there is a minimum contractual guarantee as to the interest credited, such as 4 or 4.5%. Mortality costs also have a guarantee through a maximum premium charge for the "pure" cost of the death benefit; however, most companies charge rates lower than the contractually allowed maximum.

There is no such thing as a predetermined "standard" universal life plan; each contract owner selects the level of premium and death benefit desired as well as the length of premium paying period. Significant flexibility in premium payments is possible. Usually a stated minimum premium must be paid the first policy year. But after that the contract owner can vary the amount, the payment date, or frequency of subsequent premiums. (Depending on the amount of the initial premium, additional premiums or premium increases may be limited to stated minimum or maximum levels.) "Stop and go" features allow the discontinuance as well as subsequent resumption of premium payments at any time. As long as there is enough cash value to pay the expense (loading) charges and mortality costs, the policy will remain in force. If the cash value falls below that level, the policy will terminate.

Gross premiums are reduced by specified expense charges (as well as mortality costs) to determine the universal life policy's cash value. Expense loads run between 5 and 10 percent of the gross premium and are charged year after year. Additionally, because of greater first year acquisition costs, an extra first year expense may be levied. (This may be factored into the policy as a "per policy" amount, an amount per $1,000 of death benefits, or as a percentage of first year mortality charges.) Some companies may spread out the additional first year expenses by increasing the annual percentage of gross premium charges on some minimum amount of cumulative premium and set a lower percentage charge on premiums in excess of that stated minimum amount. Alternatively, rather than increasing expense charges, many insurers are recovering expense and surrender costs through "surrender charges." Upon surrender, the contract owner would receive an amount reduced by a surrender charge, a percentage of the cash (or accumulated) value. Generally, the longer the policy is held the less is taken out. Most surrender charges are applicable for 15 years or less.

Similar to traditional policies, riders such as waiver of premium or accidental death and dismemberment may be added to the basic contract.

Also similar to traditional life insurance, loans can be taken against cash values subject to an interest charge. Unlike most traditional whole life policies is the ability to make partial withdrawals of cash values while the insured is alive. Since withdrawals are not loans, no interest charges are incurred.

Variable Life Insurance

A variable life insurance policy resembles a traditional whole life policy with two major distinctions. Both the death benefit payable upon death and the surrender value payable during life are not guaranteed, but can increase or decrease depending upon investment performance of the assets underlying the policy. The death benefit, however, generally, cannot decrease below the initial face amount of the policy, as long as all premiums have been paid. With variable life, you trade the cash surrender value guarantee for the potential of investment growth by directing the overall strategy of your policy's investment program.

The policyowner may allocate the premium, after certain deductions are made, to a particular sub-account held by the insurance company. Among the types of sub-accounts which may be offered are a money market type account, a growth stock account, a bond account, a balanced fund account, and a real estate account. And, depending on the insurance company, the choices may be changed several times a year. The death benefit typically, will be adjusted once a year, whereas, the cash value will be adjusted on a daily basis. Premiums are fixed and always remain the same. Since both the surrender value and death benefit can vary, the product is known as variable life.

Among the charges which are deducted from the premium before any investment is made in a sub-account are administrative and sales expenses, any state premium taxes as well as the cost for the mortality element.

Variable life enjoys the same favorable income tax treatment as other insurance policies. Earnings from the investments are currently income tax deferred. In other words, there is no tax on the internal buildup of cash values until such values are realized by way of surrender, and then only if the surrender value exceeds the policyholder's cost basis, unless the policy is classified as a modified endowment contract. (See question below.) Death benefits, regardless of growth, pass income tax free.

Should a policyholder wish to have access to his cash values and not surrender the policy, he can borrow up to a designated percentage of the cash value (e.g., 90%). Interest, typically, is charged on such loans.

Similar to traditional policies, riders such as waiver of premium or accidental death and dismemberment may be added to the basic contract.

Unlike any other type of insurance, the sale of a variable life insurance product must be accompanied by or preceded by a prospectus approved by the Securities and Exchange Commission.

Variable Universal Life Insurance

Variable universal life is a combination of universal life insurance and variable life insurance. It is like universal life with flexible premiums, adjustable death benefits, policy loan, and partial withdrawal privileges. However, unlike universal life and like variable life, the owner of the life contract and not the insurer decides where the premiums are invested. The alternative accounts where the premiums can be invested are similar to those in the variable life product described above.

Variable universal life is a product subject to the rules of the Securities and Exchange Commission and, therefore, requires a prospectus be given to a prospective client before a sale can be made.

Survivorship Life Insurance

Survivorship life insurance, sometimes called joint and survivor life or second to die life, is a type of life insurance policy which insures two or more people. The policy may be either a whole life, term, universal or variable type of policy. The death benefit under a survivorship policy is not realized until the last of two or more insured individuals dies. At that time the full death benefit is payable to the named beneficiary. Although there are several variations of this type of insurance, some of the policies that are of the whole life variety insure two individuals and provide for an increase in cash values upon the "first death," and, if the policies are participating (dividend paying), also provide for increased dividends. Depending upon the company, the premiums may continue until the survivor's subsequent death or, through a special option, the policy may be paid up at the "first death" and no further premiums would be required.

The policy can insure any two insureds as long as there is an insurable interest. Its use is typically confined to husband-wife, parent-child, or two related business people, such as business owners or key employees. The policy can be considered a very effective tool, relieving the federal estate tax burden of those couples who will be subject to such tax and have elected to take maximum advantage of the marital deduction, so that although there will not be any federal estate tax due upon the first spouse's death, there will be tax due at the survivor's death.

The policy may be owned by any party that could own any of the other traditional types of life insurance policy, including an irrevocable trust. There is no requirement that there be joint owners, despite the fact that there are two individuals insured.

First to Die Life Insurance

First to die insurance is a life insurance policy which insures two or more people. The policy may be a whole life, term, universal, or variable life type of policy. The death benefit is realized when the first of any of the insureds dies at which time the death benefit is payable to the named beneficiary. Some policies, through a rider, allow the survivor to continue coverage if he or she desires after the first insured dies.

The policy can be used in either business or personal planning, where there is a need for coverage only until the death of one of the two insured parties. Using a single first to die policy to insure multiple parties usually costs less in premiums than the purchase of two separate policies.

Single Premium Whole Life Insurance

Single premium whole life insurance is a type of limited pay life insurance policy. Unlike traditional whole life policies, however, where premiums are due generally until age 90 or 100, a single premium whole life policy, as the name implies, requires only one premium.

The policyholder purchases a paid-up policy with just one payment rather than paying premiums year after year. For example, a $25,000 single premium might buy a 55-year-old man $75,000 worth of insurance coverage.

Single premium life offers some of the traditional tax advantages that regular whole life policies afford:

a. The money contributed to the policy builds up tax free through policy cash values.

b. The policyholder can borrow those cash values from the policy. Such a loan may trigger income tax consequences if the policy is classified as a modified endowment contract as it typically would be.

c. The proceeds from the policy (the face value, as distinct from the cash surrender value) at the death of the insured go to the beneficiaries completely income tax free and without probate.

d. One of the main characteristics of this type of insurance is that the policy develops immediate cash values. Interest is generally credited based upon some type of "new money" approach, and may be tied into short or long term investments of the particular insurance company. The values that the policy develops can be availed of either through a surrender of the policy or through a policy loan. Some companies allow the policyholder to borrow these values at no interest cost or at a nominal interest cost to the policyholder. For example, if a policyholder borrows $10,000, the insurance company might charge him 8% interest, but that is not his true cost. The company would credit his cash value account with the 8% interest he paid or 7% or 6% depending upon the company. Thus, the true interest cost to borrow would be anywhere from 0% to 2%. The policyholder need never pay back the loan. However, if the contract is classified as a modified endowment contract, borrowing from the policy will likely result in income tax consequences. Outstanding loans will reduce the death benefit, and interest on the loan is generally not income tax deductible.

WHAT ARE THE VARIOUS FEATURES OF A LIFE INSURANCE POLICY

The professional should be familiar with the particular life insurance policy's ownership provisions, dividend provisions, and various additional benefits such as the accidental death benefit, disability waiver of premium, and guaranteed insurability which is often called insurance of insurability.

The basic ownership rights are the right to name and change the beneficiary, the right to cash in a policy, the right to receive dividends, the right to borrow against policy cash values or to make partial withdrawals, and the right to dispose of some or all of the policy ownership rights mentioned above. An unconditional sale or gift of all ownership rights in a life insurance policy is known as an "absolute" assignment. When a policy is pledged as collateral for a loan, the assignment is known as a "collateral" assignment.

Dividend provisions are particularly important in small and medium estates. Basically, a dividend is a refund of part of the premiums which the insured has paid to a life insurance company and is the result of the insured's participation in the business fortunes of the policy class to which he or she belongs. The size of the dividend is based on the relative amount of favorable mortality, interest, and "loading" (business cost) experience of the insurance company.

The policyowner can:

1. take dividends in the form of cash;

2. use dividends to reduce premiums;

3. buy paid-up additional insurance (each dividend buys a small single premium policy in addition to the basic plan; no physical examination is required; and this additional insurance is purchased without sales charges or other costs);

4. leave the dividend with the company to earn (taxable) interest;

5. purchase one-year term insurance equal to the cash value of the policy;

6. use dividends to "vanish the premiums" on the policy at an earlier than expected date;

7. use some combination of the above dividend options.

A number of additional benefits can be added (usually by a "rider") to a life insurance policy. For example, an accidental death benefit, for a small extra premium, will be paid in addition to the basic death benefit if death occurs in an accident before a specified age. (Typically, the basic death benefit is doubled.)

A second additional benefit which can be added is known as "disability waiver of premium." Under this useful benefit, premiums are waived (taken over by the insurance company) after the insured is totally disabled for a period of six months. Generally, most companies will refund any premiums paid during the first six months of disability. Cash values on a whole life policy will continue to grow.

A third additional benefit that can be added and may be advisable when the insured is young is known as "guaranteed insurability" or "insurance of insurability." This benefit allows the insured to purchase additional life insurance at certain specified future dates without evidence of insurability. On the option date, the insured can exercise all, part, or none of the option to purchase additional insurance; but the options are non-cumulative. The rates for the new insurance are those applicable for the age in the year during which the option is exercised. In other words, if an insured waits until he is 35 to exercise an option, he pays the most favorable rates for males age 35.

WHAT ARE THE TAX IMPLICATIONS?

Taxation of Death Benefits

1. Generally, proceeds payable by reason of the insured's death are exempt from income tax.[1] Such death benefit payments are, therefore, excludable from the gross income of the beneficiary. For the possible effect of the alternative minimum tax on proceeds received by a regular C corporation, see Chapter 1.

2. Where death proceeds are held by the insurance company and the beneficiary receives only the interest (this is known as an "interest only" option), the principal amount, when received, is exempt from income taxes. However, the annual interest earnings are taxable at ordinary income rates to the beneficiary.[2]

3. When the beneficiary chooses to receive death proceeds under a life income or under another settlement option under which payments will be made in installments, the annual interest produced by the death proceeds is taxable to the beneficiary. The balance is recoverable income tax free.[3]

4. As mentioned, generally insurance proceeds paid by reason of the insured's death are excludable from the recipient's gross income. However, where, prior to death a policy or an interest in a policy had been sold or otherwise transferred for valuable consideration, the death proceeds will be exempt only to the extent of (1) the consideration paid by the transferee and (2) the net premiums paid by the transferee after the transfer. The balance of the death proceeds is taxed at ordinary income rates. This is known as the "transfer for value" rule.[4]

For example, Rod Ross purchases a $25,000 policy on his own life. He pays four $500 annual premiums. Then he sells the policy to his son for $2,000. His son now owns a $25,000 policy on Rod's life for which he paid $2,000. Assume that Rod's son pays six additional $500 annual premiums ($3,000) and then Rod dies. At the time of Rod's death, his son would have paid a total of $5,000 for the policy ($2,000 for the policy itself plus $3,000 in premiums). When he receives the $25,000 of proceeds, only his cost, $5,000, will be excludable from income. The remaining $20,000 will be entirely subject to income tax.

The "transfer for value" rule does not apply if the sale or transfer is to (a) the insured, (b) a partner of the insured, (c) a partnership in which the insured is a partner, (d) a corporation in which the insured is a stockholder or officer, or (e) if the transferee's basis is determined in whole or in part by the transferor's basis; slightly oversimplified, if the transfer does not result in a tax basis change. For example, where a policy owned by a partnership is transferred along with other assets to a newly-formed corporation as part of a tax free incorporation or where one corporation transfers a policy to another corporation pursuant to a tax free merger or reorganization, the policy does not become subject to the transfer for value rule.[5]

Transfers between spouses made after July 18, 1984 (or December 31, 1983, if the spouses elect) or incident to a divorce, even if for value, come within an exception to the transfer for value rule.[6]

5. The proceeds of a life insurance policy are generally subject to the federal estate tax. Life insurance on the life of a decedent will be includable in the decedent's gross estate (1) if the proceeds are payable to or for the benefit of his or her estate or, (2) if, at the time of death, the insured possessed any incidents of ownership in the policy (such as the right to change the beneficiary, the right to surrender the policy, or the right to obtain a policy loan);[7] or (3) where the policy is transferred by the decedent within three years of his death.[8] Also, the fair market value of a policy (generally the sum of the cash value plus unearned premiums) owned on another person's life is includable in the owner's gross estate.[9]

6. Gifts of life insurance policies or gifts of premium payments may be subject to the federal gift tax. The value of the gift is based on the fair market value of the insurance policy at the time of the gift or in the case of premium payments, the cash amount of the premiums.[10] The gift tax value of a policy can generally be obtained from the insurance company and is measured differently depending upon the type of policy, i.e., term, whole life, etc.

Taxation of Premiums and Dividends

1. Premiums for personally owned life insurance are not deductible for income tax purposes. They are considered nondeductible personal expenses unless (a) premiums constitute alimony payments, under certain circumstances[11] or (b) premiums are paid on a policy irrevocably assigned to a charity and the insured does not reserve the right to surrender the policy for cash.[12]

2. Life insurance companies generally allow a discount if the premiums are paid one or more years in advance of the due date. The yearly interest increment earned on these pre-paid premiums is currently taxable to the policyowner.[13]

3. Dividends paid on participating policies are not taxable income.[14] This is consistent with the definition discussed above, i.e., life insurance policy dividends are generally considered to be a partial return of premiums. However, if dividends are left on deposit with the insurance company and accumulate interest, any interest on the accumulated dividends is taxable to the policyowner at ordinary income rates.[15] Dividends which are used to purchase paid-up additional insurance or one-year term insurance create no income tax liability. They are considered as if they were dividends paid in cash (a return of capital) and then used to buy single premium insurance. Dividends which exceed cost basis in the contract will constitute taxable income.

Taxation of Living Benefits

1. Where the policyowner receives a lump sum cash settlement in excess of the cost of the contract, the difference is considered ordinary income and is taxable in the year the contract matures or is surrendered.[16] The "cost" of the contract is measured by the total premiums paid (excluding premiums paid for accidental death benefits or waiver

of premium).[17] The dividend option selected will affect the actual cost or total premiums. For example, if dividends are accumulated or applied to purchase paid-up additional insurance, then the cost of the contract would be the gross premiums paid by the policyowner. However, if dividends are not accumulated or not used to purchase paid-up additional insurance, then the net premiums (gross premiums less dividends received in cash or applied to reduce policy premiums) paid determine the cost of the contract.

2. Often, rather than taking a lump sum, a policyowner will choose to take living benefits of a policy under a "settlement option." Proceeds placed under settlement options (other than the interest option) are taxed under the "annuity rules" of Section 72 of the Internal Revenue Code. Basically, these rules are designed so that the annuitant will not be taxed on the portion of the annuity income which is considered to be a return of premium payments.

The portion of the annuity income which is considered to be gain is taxable; therefore, each payment is divided into two parts: (1) a nontaxable return of cost, and (2) taxable income.

To determine which portion of each payment is excludable from gross income and which portion is taxable income, an exclusion ratio or percentage is found. The exclusion ratio is the ratio that the total investment in the contract bears to the total expected return; to find the percentage of each annual payment that is income tax free, divide the investment in the contract (cost) by the expected return.[18] The expected return is the annual payment multiplied by the recipient's life expectancy. (See Table V at Figure 21.1 for multiples representing life expectancy.) The exclusion ratio is then multiplied by each year's total annuity payments to yield the tax-free portion of total payments received during the year. The balance of the payments is taxable as ordinary income.

3. Provided the policy is not classified as a modified endowment contract, only cash distributions and not policy loans can cause current income taxation to the recipient. Where a policyholder reduces the death benefit of a universal life policy, either by switching from an Option II death benefit (increasing death benefit) to an Option I death benefit (level death benefit), or by making a partial surrender, which reduces the face amount of the policy, a new calculation of the policy for the definitional test of life insurance must occur. If the policy has too much cash (after the death benefit reduction), above the maximum allowable under the definitional rules of Code section 7702, the excess must be "forced out" as a distribution.

If the force-out of the cash occurs in years 1 through 5, the policy (after the reduction in the face amount) must meet the guideline premium limitation/cash value corridor test to avoid the forced out distribution from being currently taxed as income to the extent there is a built-in gain in the policy at that time. If the policy after the reduction in face amount meets this test, the cash distributed would be considered a return of basis under the FIFO taxation rules (first in, first out). Only if the amount received exceeded the policyholder's basis would the gain be taxable to the recipient.

If the distribution occurs in policy years 6 through 15, the policy after reduction must meet the corridor percentage limits of Code section 7702. To the extent the cash value exceeds the required amount under this test and is forced out, it is taxable as income to the policyholder to the extent there is a gain in the policy.

For years after the 15th year, the policyholder is taxed on a FIFO basis (no income tax until basis is exceeded).

Provided the policy is not a modified endowment contract, in any year that a cash withdrawal is made and the definitional tests are still met after the withdrawal, any cash withdrawn is taxable only to the extent the amount received in that year and in all previous years exceeds the premiums paid into the contract, i.e., to the extent there is a gain in the contract.[19]

4. How are distributions such as cash withdrawals or policy loans taxable to the recipient if the policy is classified as a modified endowment contract? If a policy falls into this category by failing a test called the seven pay test, distributions from the policy will be taxed less favorably than if the seven pay test is met.

A policy fails the seven pay test if the cumulative amount paid at any time during the first seven years of the contract exceeds the net level premiums that would have been paid during the first seven years if the contract provided for paid-up future benefits. If a material change in the policy's benefits occurs, a new seven year period for testing must begin.

Distributions, including policy loans, from modified endowment contracts are taxed as income first and recovery of basis second, much like distributions from annuity contracts are taxed. Additionally, a penalty tax of 10 percent applies to distribution amounts included in income unless the taxpayer has become disabled, or reached age 59 1/2 or the distribution is part of a series of substantially equal payments made over the taxpayer's life.

Figure 21.1

Table V — Ordinary Life Annuities One Life — Expected Return Multiples					
Age	Multiple	Age	Multiple	Age	Multiple
5	76.6	42	40.6	79	10.0
6	75.6	43	39.6	80	9.5
7	74.7	44	38.7	81	8.9
8	73.7	45	37.7	82	8.4
9	72.7	46	36.8	83	7.9
10	71.7	47	35.9	84	7.4
11	70.7	48	34.9	85	6.9
12	69.7	49	34.0	86	6.5
13	68.8	50	33.1	87	6.1
14	67.8	51	32.2	88	5.7
15	66.8	52	31.3	89	5.3
16	65.8	53	30.4	90	5.0
17	64.8	54	29.5	91	4.7
18	63.9	55	28.6	92	4.4
19	62.9	56	27.7	93	4.1
20	61.9	57	26.8	94	3.9
21	60.9	58	25.9	95	3.7
22	59.9	59	25.0	96	3.4
23	59.0	60	24.2	97	3.2
24	58.0	61	23.3	98	3.0
25	57.0	62	22.5	99	2.8
26	56.0	63	21.6	100	2.7
27	55.1	64	20.8	101	2.5
28	54.1	65	20.0	102	2.3
29	53.1	66	19.2	103	2.1
30	52.2	67	18.4	104	1.9
31	51.2	68	17.6	105	1.8
32	50.2	69	16.8	106	1.6
33	49.3	70	16.0	107	1.4
34	48.3	71	15.3	108	1.3
35	47.3	72	14.6	109	1.1
36	46.4	73	13.9	110	1.0
37	45.4	74	13.2	111	.9
38	44.4	75	12.5	112	.8
39	43.5	76	11.9	113	.7
40	42.5	77	11.2	114	.6
41	41.5	78	10.6	115	.5

With some exceptions, life insurance policies issued on or before June 21, 1988 are grandfathered and not required to comply with the seven pay test.

ISSUES AND IMPLICATIONS IN COMMUNITY PROPERTY STATES

Where community property funds are used to purchase an insurance policy and there has been no agreement otherwise affecting the ownership of the policy, the policy will be owned by the community—and therefore belongs one-half to each spouse.

Thus, if a policy on the husband is community property and the beneficiary is someone other than the spouse, a transfer subject to gift tax will occur when the insured dies and the proceeds are payable to that third person. The amount of the gift will be the wife's one-half interest in the proceeds.

The Tools and Techniques of Estate Planning

For this reason, careful estate planners note the ownership and beneficiary designations of insurance policies to be able to consider any gift tax problems that may exist. Even payment to a trust of which the surviving spouse is the income beneficiary can result in a gift if the surviving spouse does not have a power under the trust to determine to whom the remainder interest is payable at his or her death. The amount of the gift would be the actuarial value (per IRS regulations in cases of normal health circumstances of the life tenant) of the remainder interest at the time of the transfer to trust, in the surviving spouse's half of the insurance proceeds.

The main problem in *acquiring* an insurance policy as the separate property of the non-insured spouse is the presumption in most community property states that property acquired during marriage is community property unless proven otherwise. This means that sufficient documentation of the separate property status of the policy must exist so as to overcome the community property presumption. The first step to indicate that an insurance policy is the separate property of one spouse is to name that spouse as owner of the policy. However, more evidence is usually necessary to overcome the presumption, and this requirement varies from state to state.

After the initial acquisition of a new policy as the separate property of one of the spouses or after the conversion of an existing policy into the separate policy of one spouse, the question arises as to what must be done in the future to retain the separate property status of the policy. The answer is dependent upon two different theories found in community property states that deal with the classification of interests in life insurance policies. These theories are known as the "premium tracing" doctrine and the "inception of title" doctrine.

At least two community property states, California and Washington, follow the "premium tracing" doctrine, which states that the classification of the policy as separate or community property depends on the proportion of premium payments made from separate or community funds. Under this doctrine, the classification of the policy is not constant. Therefore, if the policy is initially acquired as separate property, but 10 percent of the premiums are paid with community funds, absent any documentation taken to ensure the separate status of the policy, 10 percent of the proceeds would be community property. Therefore, each spouse would be treated as owning one-half of the 10 percent.

Under the "inception of title" doctrine, which is followed in at least two community property states, Louisiana and Texas, the policy's ownership does not vary depending on whether premiums are paid with separate or community funds. However, where community funds are used to pay premiums, in the absence of documentation to the contrary, the non-owner spouse will have a right of reimbursement to the extent of one-half of the community funds used to pay the premiums. This right of reimbursement may cause that portion of the proceeds to be includable in the insured spouse's estate.

Therefore, when an insured in a community property state wants to transfer his or her ownership in life insurance policies to his or her spouse, in addition to the transfer by written notification to the insurance company, it is wise to also sign a written waiver waiving any further community interest in the policy.

To effect such a waiver of interest, presently and for the future, it is usually best to use the form of "Community Property Waiver" provided by the insuring company. If no such form is available, you may consider using the type of form illustrated at Figure 21.2. It is recommended that such a written waiver contain the following minimum information: (1) a clear identification of the life insurance policy(ies) involved; (2) a statement indicating the parties' intent that the policy(ies) be held as separate property of one spouse; (3) a clear relinquishment by the other spouse of any community property interest in the policy; (4) and a statement that the payment of any future premiums with community funds shall be treated as a gift of the non-owner-spouse's community interest in those funds to the owner-spouse.

In most cases, even though the insured may be shown on the policy as "Owner" or otherwise indicated as owning the policy, the policy will be considered as community property of the two spouses in the absence of any evidence that there was an agreement between the spouses that it would be his separate property.

A prenuptial agreement can be effective in most states to overcome presumptions of community property and to provide that future premium payments from community property funds will not vest in the community any ownership in the policies on the life of the insured. In view of the increasing frequency of divorce and remarriage, the use of such "prenuptial" agreements is encouraged by most estate planners to avoid subsequent confusion and possible lawsuits related to the ownership of insurance policies.

One type of insurance policy which remains the separate property of the insured, in spite of having premiums paid with community property earnings, is National Service Life Insurance and Servicemen's Group Life Insurance. These policies, made available by the federal government for persons in the service, have been determined to be incapable of transfer of ownership away from the insured on the basis of federal policy. In some cases, however, the courts of California in divorce and dissolution cases, have frustrated the announced

Figure 21.2

WAIVER OF COMMUNITY PROPERTY RIGHTS

The undersigned hereby declares that __he intends to transfer to h_____ spouse, _____, certain policies of life insurance, and that upon said transfer, all rights, privileges and incidents of ownership under any policies so transferred shall be the separate property of said spouse and the undersigned hereby waives any and all community property interest to which __he may, but for this waiver, hereafter be entitled under the community property laws of California or any other state, province or country.

The undersigned consents to the use of community property funds h_____self and h_____ spouse for the payment of any or all premiums and does further agree and declare that any future premium payments on the policies made with community funds shall constitute a gift from the undersigned to h_____ said spouse to the extent of h_____ interest in the community funds so applied.

Any interest the undersigned may have, now or in the future, as a designated payee of the policies is not affected by this waiver.

This instrument is executed in consideration of natural love and affection and shall be binding upon my heirs, executors, administrators and assigns, and is executed with the intent and knowledge that any interested parties may hence forth act in reliance thereon.

Dated _____

_____
Signature

WITNESSED BY:

_____

---

federal intent by awarding community property of equal value to the non-insured spouse. However, the federal policy prevents the transfer of such NSLI policies for purposes of planning for reduction of federal estate taxes. However, only one-half of the proceeds is includable in the insured's gross estate for federal estate tax purposes where the premiums have been paid with community property.

QUESTIONS AND ANSWERS

Question — What is "split dollar" life insurance, how does it work, and what are its advantages?

Answer — Split dollar life insurance is an arrangement, typically between an employer and an employee (it can also be used between relatives such as a father and son or grandfather and grandson), under which the cash values,

death benefits, and cost (premiums) may be split between the parties.

Under the classical arrangement, the employer pays that part of the annual premium which equals the current year's increase in the cash surrender value of the policy. The employee pays the balance, if any, of the premium. Under another version of split dollar, known as an "employer pay all" plan, the corporation pays the entire premium and the employee pays no portion of the premium. This provides an incentive to key employees, a way by which an employer can reward key individuals on a selective basis, and a means to provide stockholder-employees with substantial insurance at a minimal outlay.

In the event of the insured employee's death the corporation typically gets back the cash value or premiums paid by the corporation as a death benefit and the insured employee's beneficiary receives the balance of the proceeds. The result of the arrangement is for the employer to have an increasing death benefit and for the employee's beneficiary to have a decreasing death benefit. To maintain the insured-employee's death benefit on a level basis, dividends can be used to purchase an amount of term insurance equal to the cash surrender value of the contract; or, if a universal life policy is used, the death benefit can be increasing.

Furthermore, intrafamily split dollar would enable a son-in-law to purchase insurance on his life that he otherwise might not be able to afford. This way, a father can provide additional financial security for his daughter.

Split dollar can also be used between a corporation and its employee-stockholders. The corporation could split the premium dollars in such a way that the employee-stockholders could be able to afford sizable policies on each others' lives.

Split dollar thus provides an attractive incentive plan. It can be entirely selective. No Internal Revenue Service approval is necessary and although there is some income tax cost to the employee (a so-called P.S. 58 cost which measures the current economic benefit an employee receives when his employer puts up all or a substantial portion of the premium) that cost is relatively low.[20] (See Figure 21.3.) The split dollar arrangement used creatively can solve a number of estate and business planning problems.

A split dollar plan of insurance can be established as either a collateral assignment type or as an endorsement type arrangement. The income tax results are the same under either type of plan. The collateral assignment method involves either the insured or a third party as the original owner of the contract. The owner then collaterally assigns the policy to the corporation to secure the corporation's interest in the policy.

The endorsement method involves the corporation as the owner of the contract and accordingly it has all policy rights including the right to borrow against the policy. Under this method, the employer endorses out or gives to the insured the right to designate the beneficiary of the pure term insurance protection.

It is possible that a split dollar plan can be arranged so that the death benefit passing to the beneficiary of a majority shareholder will be estate tax free. If the shareholder's spouse—or an irrevocable trust for the benefit of his beneficiaries or any third party—purchases a policy on his life, and then enters into a split dollar agreement with the corporation that prohibits the corporation from taking any action with respect to the policy that might endanger the policyowner's interest, the death benefit can be excludable. Chances of success in keeping the net amount at risk out of a controlling shareholder's estate are significantly increased if the corporation has no rights to policy values except at the insured's death. The corporation's right at that time should be limited to a recovery of the death proceeds equal to its contributions. The collateral assignment method of split dollar should be used to further evidence the limitation of the corporation's rights.[21]

Question — What is a "key person" life insurance policy and how is it taxed?

Answer — A key person life insurance policy is a policy owned by a business which insures the life of a particularly valuable employee for the benefit of a business. It is a good estate planning tool because it provides protection to offset financial loss to a business occurring by reason of the premature death of a valuable employee. Therefore, an employer might want to insure a key person and thereby stabilize and maximize the value of the business interest. Even more common is the situation where the business owner is the key to the success of the business. If the business is to be continued, it should consider insuring the business owner's life.

The business should be the premium payor, owner, and beneficiary of the policy. Proceeds, when received, could be used to offset reduced profits and help pay for replacement of the key individual.

Premiums are not deductible by the corporation or other business entity, but proceeds, when received, will be free of income tax with the possible exception of a corporate level alternative minimum tax.[22]

For federal estate tax purposes, if the insured is a stockholder, the death proceeds will be considered in determining the value of the decedent's stock interest.[23] Even, where the insured is the controlling stockholder, as long as the corporation is the beneficiary, or the proceeds are paid for the benefit of the corporation (for example, to a corporate creditor), the insurance proceeds will not be separately taxable (as insurance) in the insured's estate.[24] So if the business owner controls only 60 percent of the business, only 60 percent of the insurance—enhanced value of the corporate stock—will be includable in his estate for federal estate tax purposes. Note that if the death proceeds are payable to a personal beneficiary of an

Figure 21.3

"P.S. No. 58" RATES

The following rates are used in computing the "cost" of pure life insurance protection that is taxable to the employee.

One Year Term Premiums for $1,000 of Life Insurance Protection					
Age	Premium	Age	Premium	Age	Premium
15	$ 1.27	37	$ 3.63	59	$ 19.08
16	1.38	38	3.87	60	20.73
17	1.48	39	4.14	61	22.53
18	1.52	40	4.42	62	24.50
19	1.56	41	4.73	63	26.63
20	1.61	42	5.07	64	28.98
21	1.67	43	5.44	65	31.51
22	1.73	44	5.85	66	34.28
23	1.79	45	6.30	67	37.31
24	1.86	46	6.78	68	40.59
25	1.93	47	7.32	69	44.17
26	2.02	48	7.89	70	48.06
27	2.11	49	8.53	71	52.29
28	2.20	50	9.22	72	56.89
29	2.31	51	9.97	73	61.89
30	2.43	52	10.79	74	67.33
31	2.57	53	11.69	75	73.23
32	2.70	54	12.67	76	79.63
33	2.86	55	13.74	77	86.57
34	3.02	56	14.91	78	94.09
35	3.21	57	16.18	79	102.23
36	3.41	58	17.56	80	111.04
				81	120.57

The rate at insured's attained age is applied to the excess of the amount payable at death over the cash value of the policy at the end of the year.

insured controlling shareholder (one who owns more than 50 percent of the corporation's stock), the proceeds will be fully includable as life insurance in his estate.

Question — How is group life insurance taxed and how can it be used for estate planning purposes?

Answer — Group life insurance is a life insurance benefit provided by an employer for the benefit of its employees and is one of the most effective tools the stockholder-employee of a closely held corporation has for planning his or her personal estate. Likewise, it is extremely useful in planning the estate of an executive or other common law employee. The primary objective of group life insurance is to provide financial security for the employee's family.

Generally, the premium payor is the business, although many plans are contributory, where the employee pays a portion of the premium. The insured or a third party is given a certificate evidencing the insurance. The beneficiary can be anyone (including a trust) designated by the covered employee.

For estate tax purposes, the proceeds of a group life insurance policy are includable in the gross estate of the employee. However, these proceeds can usually be removed from the insured's estate with little or no gift tax cost by an absolute assignment of all incidents of ownership. If a policy is assigned within three years of the insured's death, the entire proceeds will be includable in the gross estate.[25]

The annual gift where a policy has been assigned by the employee to a third party is apparently equal to the lesser of premium payments made by the employer or the value measured by the government Table I, below. However, the higher of premiums paid or the Table I rates is used for key employees in a discriminatory plan.[26]

Group life insurance premiums paid by the corporation are fully deductible as business expenses, subject to the limitation that they are reasonable compensation after considering all other compensation paid that employee.[27] Furthermore, employer-paid premiums are not considered taxable income to the covered employees to the extent the death benefit does not exceed $50,000 (this amount may be lower in some states).[28] The exception to this rule is that if a plan discriminates in favor of key employees, those employees must include in income the cost of their full coverage, including the first $50,000 of coverage. The cost of the coverage is the higher of the actual cost or the Table I rates shown below. The cost of any coverage which exceeds $50,000 of protection is taxable income to the employee. The value of this additional income is measured by the government table shown below.[29] If the employee contributes toward the cost of the insurance, his contribution can be used to offset his tax liability. When the proceeds of group life insurance are received by the insured employee's family, they are not subject to income taxation.[30]

**Uniform Premiums for $1,000 of
Group Term Life Insurance Protection
(Table I — Regulation Sec. 1.79-3)**

5-Year Age Bracket	Cost — per $1,000 of Protection per Month
Under 30	$ .08
30-34	.09
35-39	.11
40-44	.17
45-49	.29
50-54	.48
55-59	.75
60-64	1.17
65-69	2.10
70 and over	3.76

Question — What is a salary increase or "selective" pension plan?

Answer — A salary increase pension plan (some call this a "Section 162" plan) is an excellent way to: (1) provide benefits where group insurance is either unavailable or inadequate; (2) supplement the benefits of a qualified corporate pension or profit-sharing plan; (3) reward and hold key personnel; (4) provide estate liquidity for corporate executives; and (5) replace part or all of group term life insurance in excess of $50,000.

The corporation pays the premiums on a whole life, universal life, or variable life type policy insuring the selected employee. That employee is named as owner of the policy and designates his own personal beneficiary.

For estate tax purposes, since the policy is owned by the employee who has the right to name the beneficiary, the proceeds will be includable in the employee's gross estate.

The business is able to deduct premiums paid under a "salary increase" pension plan since such premiums are considered additional compensation. The employee must report as ordinary income the amount of premiums paid by the employer under such a plan. When the death proceeds are paid to the insured's personal beneficiary, under this type of plan, they are not subject to income tax.

Advantages of a salary increase plan using life insurance include:

1. Internal Revenue Service approval is not required.

2. The plan is simple and may be established by the mere signing of an application, acceptance by the insurer of evidence of insurability, and payment of the appropriate premium.

3. The employer is free to choose the employees to include in such a plan.

4. No minimum or maximum number of lives must be covered.

5. The employer can decide how much coverage to provide.

6. The cost of the plan is deductible by the employer.

7. The employee owns and has all rights to the insurance policy.

8. Dividends can be used to reduce the premium outlay or to offset the tax cost of the plan.

9. Cash values of the policy may be used without disqualifying the plan or incurring any tax penalties, provided that the policy is not classified as a modified endowment contract. (Interest will be charged on any such loans.)

10. The plan may be discontinued at any time.

Question — Can a person achieve estate tax reduction by giving away the ownership of a policy on his life?

Answer — To the extent that one transfers away all of the incidents of ownership and the policy is not payable directly or indirectly to his estate, then the policy will not be included in his estate for federal estate tax purposes, providing that he survives three years past the date of transfer.

Although a gift of insurance made more than three years before death can be effective in reducing the insured's estate for estate tax purposes, it also reduces the ownership rights of an insured during his lifetime, as many insureds have found upon dissolution of a marriage.

Transfer of insurance is subject to gift tax, and therefore one must also consider the value of the policy when making a gift.

Question — Can interest which is paid on funds borrowed to purchase or carry a life insurance contract be deducted on an individual's income tax return?

Answer — The general rule is that a deduction is not allowed for interest paid on indebtedness incurred to purchase or carry life insurance if such insurance is purchased pursuant to a plan which contemplates the systematic direct or indirect borrowing of part or all of the increase in the cash surrender value of such contract. There are four exceptions to this general rule:

1. *Trade or business exception*—If the indebtedness is incurred in connection with the taxpayer's trade or business, the interest deduction will not be denied.

2. *$100 a year exception*—The interest deduction will be allowed if the interest on the loan is less than $100 a year.

3. *The seven-year exception*—An interest deduction will be allowed in spite of the general rule where at least four of the annual premiums due during the first seven years of the contract are paid by means other than direct or indirect borrowing. Therefore, if a policyholder pays *any* four full years' premiums out of the first seven years' premiums due, the interest deduction on policy loans, including interest on loans made during the first seven years, will be allowed.

4. *The unforeseen event exception*—An interest deduction will be allowed if the indebtedness is incurred as the result of an unforeseen substantial loss of income or unforeseen substantial increase in the taxpayer's financial obligations.[31]

However, even if a personally owned policy comes within one of the four just mentioned exceptions to the

general rule, none of the interest has been allowed as a deduction of personal interest since 1990.

For insurance loans on policies owned by a taxpayer (corporation or other entity) carrying on any trade or business, a deduction will not be allowed for interest on any indebtedness with respect to one or more life insurance policies covering the life of any individual who is an officer, employee, or an individual financially interested in any trade or business carried on by the taxpayer, to the extent the loans aggregate more than $50,000 per insured. However, for a policy owned by such a taxpayer purchased on or before June 20, 1986, if the policy otherwise qualifies for an income tax deduction by coming within one of the four exceptions, interest will continue to be fully tax deductible.[32]

Question — What are the reasons life insurance is often purchased by the trustee of a pension and/or profit-sharing plan?

Answer — Among others, the premium (including any additional rating charge) becomes deductible (as part of the corporation's contribution). The dividend structure of a policy within a pension or profit-sharing plan is generally more favorable than dividends paid on policies owned outside the plan. The death benefit in excess of policy cash value is income tax free, is, generally, exempt from the claims of creditors, and is not subject to the 15 percent tax on excess accumulations from qualified plans and IRAs. With some of the newer type policies, such as universal or variable life, favorable returns can also be achieved.

Question — If an individual exchanges one life insurance policy for another life insurance policy (e.g., whole life to universal life) are there income tax consequences?

Answer — The Code provides that an exchange of one life insurance policy for another life insurance policy, whether with the same company or a different company, is a nontaxable exchange if the policies are on the same life insured. If no cash or other property is received on the exchange, gain is not recognized. If there is an outstanding loan on the original policy which is not paid off, the amount of any loan assumed by the other party is treated as money received on the exchange and will be taxable to the extent the original policy is in a taxable gain position unless the new policy is subject to the same indebtedness.[33]

Question — Is the interest earned on a prepaid premium deposit account taxable as ordinary income to the policyholder?

Answer — Yes. The increase in value of a prepaid deposit account is taxable as income in the year it is applied to the payment of premiums or is made available for withdrawal, whichever occurs first. The amount of income is reportable to the IRS by the insurance company. Any amount so reportable will increase the basis of the contract.[34]

Question — How can you determine the financial strength of a life insurance company?

Answer — In addition to looking at the annual financial reports of each company, there are a number of independent rating services that rate the insurance companies. These ratings can be obtained from the particular rating services. Among the companies who provide ratings are: (1) A.M. Best Company; (2) Standard & Poor's Corporation; (3) Moody's Investors Services; (4) Duff & Phelps Credit Rating Company; and (5) Weiss Research.

Rating services look at the underlying essentials of companies, such as surplus, mortality experience, investments, and expenses. They then assign a letter rating to the company. The top two ratings assigned by the above-mentioned rating services are: A.M. Best Company — A++ and A+; Standard & Poor's — AAA and AA+; Moody's Investors Services — Aaa and Aa1; Duff & Phelps — AAA and AA+; and Weiss Research — A+ and A.

Footnote References

Life Insurance

1. IRC Sec. 101(a).
2. IRC Sec. 101(c).
3. IRC Sec. 101(d)(1)(A), Regs. §1.101-4(a)(1)(i).
4. IRC Sec. 101(a)(2).
5. IRC Sec. 101(a)(2).
6. IRC Sec. 1041.
7. IRC Sec. 2042.
8. IRC Sec. 2035.
9. IRC Sec. 2033.
10. Regs. §25.2512-6.
11. *Lemuel Alexander Carmichael*, 14 TC 1356 (1950), *Est. of Boies C. Hart*, 11 TC 16 (1948).
12. See *Eppa Hunton, IV*, 1 TC 821 (1943); *Ernest Behrend* 23 BTA 1037 (1931), acq. X-2 CB 5.
13. Rev. Rul. 65-199, 1965-2 CB 20.
14. IRC Sec. 72(e)(1)(B); Reg. §1.72-11(b)(1).
15. Reg. §1.61-7(d).
16. IRC Sec. 72(e); Reg. §1.72-11(d).
17. IRC Sec. 72(e)(1)(B).
18. See Reg. §1.72-4.
19. IRC Secs. 7702(e) and (f).
20. Rev. Rul. 64-328, 1964-2 CB 11. If the particular insurer publishes rates for individual, initial issue, one-year term policies which are lower than the PS 58 rates, these rates may be used in place of the PS 58 rates.
21. Rev. Rul. 82-145, 1982-2 CB 213; Rev. Rul. 76-274, 1976-2 CB 278.
22. IRC Sec. 101.
23. Reg. §20.2031-2(f).
24. Reg. §20.2042-1(c)(6).
25. Rev. Rul. 69-54, 1969-1 CB 221 as modified by Rev. Rul. 72-307, 1972-1 CB 307. IRC Sec. 2035.
26. See Rev. Rul. 84-147, 1984-2 CB 201.
27. IRC Sec. 162(a); Reg. §1.264-1.
28. IRC Sec. 79.
29. Reg. §1.79-3.
30. IRC Sec. 101.
31. IRC Sec. 264.
32. IRC Sec. 264.
33. IRS Sec. 1035(a).
34. See Rev. Rul. 65-199, 1965-2 CB 20, and Rev. Rul. 66-120, 1966-1 CB 14.

Chapter 22

LIMITED LIABILITY COMPANIES

WHAT IS IT?

The limited liability company (LLC) is a relatively new form of business organization which is intended to obtain for investors, called members, the same advantages of limited liability as in the corporate form of business, while at the same time avoiding corporation income tax rules. As of this writing, forty-seven states and the District of Columbia have adopted LLC statutes.

As noted above, the LLC is used to obtain the advantages of limited liability for investors and participants (i.e., they cannot be liable for debts of the entity beyond their investment), while being classified as a partnership for federal income tax purposes. The result is avoidance of corporate double tax on income, and in many situations, avoidance of any tax on liquidation. The impact of double taxation of income of normal ("C") corporations is discussed in connection with the S corporation in Chapter 29.

Another significant reason for the use of the LLC is that any losses incurred by the entity will passthrough and be deductible by the members under the partnership rules, provided the LLC is classified as a partnership for income tax purposes. No such passthrough is permitted in the case of a C corporation.

It is helpful to compare the LLC to the S Corporation. Both are formed to avoid double taxation and permit the passthrough of losses to shareholders. However, as discussed in Chapter 29, the use of the S corporation is severely restricted. The number of shareholders is limited. Only individuals, estates, and certain trusts qualify as shareholders. The passthrough of losses to shareholders is generally limited to the income tax basis of their stock plus any loans they have made to the corporation. In the case of partnerships and LLCs, any debt of the entity is also considered in determining how much loss partners or members may deduct. Only voting and nonvoting common stock may be issued in an S corporation, while there are no limitations on classes of memberships in an LLC.

From the estate planning standpoint, a major advantage of either the partnership, or an LLC classified as a partnership, over a C or S corporation is that upon the death of a partner or member, the partnership or LLC may elect to adjust the basis of its assets to fair market value to the extent of the decedent's interest.[1]

The LLC may also be considered an alternate to the family limited partnership, discussed in Chapter 11. The transfer of family business, real estate, or other investments to a family partnership has become a major estate planning technique. It would appear the LLC would function just as well, with the advantage that no family member has to function as a "general" partner and assume liability for debts of the entity. However, as covered in the Questions and Answers section below, there are problems with the use of an LLC in this situation.

In most jurisdictions, the LLC, or its counterpart the limited liability partnership (LLP), may also be used as a form of organization for a professional practice. The advantage is that while a professional will remain liable for his or her own errors or omissions in the practice or business, he or she can avoid liability for the acts of any of the other owners. In an ordinary professional partnership, each partner may be held liable for the errors or omissions of another partner.

WHAT ARE THE REQUIREMENTS?

The content of LLC statutes varies widely. Most statutes borrow heavily from the Uniform Limited Partnership Act (ULPA) discussed in Chapter 11. The intention is to be certain the LLC will be classified as a partnership for federal income tax purposes. Some statutes are drafted to be certain the entity will be classified as a partnership for federal tax purposes, while others permit the entity, by adopting flexible provisions, to be classified either as a partnership or corporation. The former are generally called "bulletproof" statutes; the latter "flexible" statutes.

While it is impossible to generalize on the various statutes, the following will be found, with variations, in all of them:

1. There are articles of organization which set forth the purposes for which the entity is formed, and provides that the entity can generally exercise the same powers as a partnership or corporation.

2. The participants are called members. There generally must be at least two members. Various other entities such as corporations, partnerships, trusts, and estates, can be members.

3. There are provisions for capital contributions similar to partnerships.

4. The key to management is an operating agreement, which governs management of the entity. It also provides that the entity may be managed either by delegation to "Managers," who are elected in somewhat the same manner as a Board of Directors, or retained by all of the members. Unlike partnerships, voting in an LLC is generally in proportion to capital contributions. However, it may be based on profit participation.

5. Allocation of profits and losses and distributions to members are generally covered by the operating agreement. Under most if not all statutes, it is possible to have different classes of members who participate differently in profits, losses, and distributions.

6. Assignment of interests in the LLC generally follows the pattern of the limited partnership, with some unique characteristics. A complete assignment of an interest generally means the assignor is no longer a member. The assignee does not automatically become a member, and is only entitled to receive distributions that would otherwise be made to the member. There may be a provision for admission of an assignee as a member based on a vote of the members or member-managers.

7. The dissolution of the entity, which also has considerable tax consequence, normally will occur upon the unanimous consent of the members, or if the LLC is formed for a fixed term, upon the expiration of that term. However, under most statutes, events such as death, disability, voluntary withdrawal, expulsion, or bankruptcy, of a member results in automatic dissolution, unless the business is continued either by unanimous consent or majority vote of members.

8. Many of the legal requirements can be altered under many state statutes by provisions in the operating agreement or a separate business continuation agreement. However, such alteration could result in the LLC being classified as a corporation for federal income tax purposes, which the members generally want to avoid.

HOW IT IS DONE — AN EXAMPLE

Ten unrelated investors are considering establishing a joint venture to acquire and develop mining property in a western state. This is an extremely risky operation, but if it is successful, there will be large profits. If it is not successful, they would experience large losses. Also, the mining operation may result in considerable liability to its owners, both for debts incurred in the operations, and potential damages to adjacent property or injuries to workers. While some insurance is available to cover these risks, it is not enough.

These investors could form an S corporation, assuming they are all qualified shareholders, and achieve limited liability and direct passthrough of profits and most losses. However, they find the S corporation structure too limiting. Under their proposed agreement, different participants would share in profits and losses unequally, and an S corporation can have only voting and nonvoting stock, with no special allocation of profits and losses. They cannot use a general partnership, because they would all be personally liable for claims and lawsuits. They cannot use a limited partnership, because no participant is willing to assume the liabilities of a general partner.

The LLC would allow all members to achieve limited liability, participate in the venture or delegate management, create different classes of ownership and participation, and a direct passthrough of either profits or losses.

WHAT ARE THE TAX IMPLICATIONS?

Since the key to the use of the LLC is almost always the classification of the entity as a partnership for federal income tax purposes, it must be structured so that it has no more than two of the four corporate characteristics set forth in the Regulations.[2] These are limited liability, centralized management, free transferability of interests, and continuity of life.

Limited Liability. Since one of the purposes of forming an LLC is to achieve limited liability, that corporate characteristic will exist in virtually every situation. It is at least possible, according to the IRS, to structure the LLC so that managing members assume liability for its debts, and avoid this characteristic. However, this seems unrealistic.

Centralized Management. Centralized management refers to delegation of the management functions to managers, who may be members, or under many statutes, do not have to be members. If this is done, the entity has the corporate characteristic of centralized management. However, as discussed below, the IRS will recognize some delegation of management to certain members without finding there is centralized management.

Free Transferability of Interests. Even though interests in LLCs are freely assignable, the corporate characteristic of free transferability of interests is generally lacking, since assignees cannot be admitted as members without the unanimous or majority consent of the other members. An outside agreement or provisions in the operating agreement permitting the admission of new members *without* the consent of existing members will probably result in the LLC having the corporate characteristic of free transferability of interests. The same would probably apply to an agreement where all members agree to vote to admit new members. The IRS will permit some element of free transferability, as discussed below.

Continuity of Life. What all of this means in most situations is that the LLC will have the corporate characteristics of limited liability and centralized management, but lack free transferability of interests. If so, the entity must avoid the fourth characteristic, continuity of life. Limited liability companies generally lack continuity of life because they dissolve on the bankruptcy, death, disability, expulsion, dissolution, or retirement of a member. However, in most states, the LLC may continue in existence upon the unanimous or majority vote of the members. This will not result in continuity of life. Where the entity can continue without the consent of members, it will probably have the corporate characteristic of continuity of life. An outside agreement in which the members agree to continue the business without consent will probably also result in continuity of life.

The IRS has issued a series of both published and private letter rulings and revenue rulings in which it has generally held the LLC lacked at least two corporate characteristics and would be classified as a partnership for federal income tax purposes.[3] It has also issued a revenue procedure which, if followed, will result in the classification of the entity as a partnership.[4] Following is a summary of some of the more important guidelines contained in that revenue procedure:

1. A ruling will not be issued unless the LLC has at least two members. A few state laws permit one member LLCs.

2. In general, if certain members are designated managers by statute or the operating agreement, the LLC lacks the corporate characteristic of continuity of life if the death, insanity, bankruptcy, retirement, resignation or expulsion of any member-manager causes a dissolution of the LLC, *unless* a majority in interest of the remaining members vote to continue the entity.

   This test cannot be met unless the member-managers in the aggregate have at least 1% of each material item of income, loss, deduction, and credit, subject to temporary changes caused by application of Code sections 704(b) or 704(c). It also generally cannot be met unless the member-managers have aggregate capital account balances equal to the lesser of 1% of the total positive capital or $500,000.

   If member-managers are not so designated, then dissolution must occur upon the happening of any of the listed events as to any member, subject to the power of a majority in interest to continue the entity. For purposes of determining a majority in interest, the rules relating to limited partnerships apply.[5]

3. The LLC lacks the corporate characteristic of free transferability of interests if no individual member, or those members who own more than 20% of all interests in the LLC, cannot transfer interests to new members without the consent of a majority in interest of the member-managers. The 1% tests set forth above for member-managers also apply here. If a majority in interest of all members must consent to such a transfer by members described above, the entity lacks free transferability of interests. Note that a power to withhold consent to a transfer does not count if it may not be unreasonable withheld.

4. There is no centralized management if only member-managers manage *unless* the member-managers own in the aggregate less than 20% of the interests in the LLC. Also, the identity of the member-managers cannot be subject to vote, nor can they be removed by the members. Centralized management is lacking if the LLC is managed by all members in their capacity as members.

5. There is no limited liability if one member is liable for all obligations of the entity, based on authority of the controlling statute. However, the assuming members must have an aggregate net worth equal to 10% of the total contributions to the entity. If not, it must be demonstrated that the assuming members have substantial assets that could be reached to satisfy the debts.

   Comment: From the standpoint of the family LLC, no one wants free transferability of interests in any case, and no family member wants unlimited liability. This permits a choice between avoiding continuity of life or centralized management. Although it is possible in most if not all jurisdictions to cover the ruling guidelines in the operating agreement, it will be necessary to change the underlying state statute (i.e., the so-called "default" rule) in order to avoid restriction and valuation issues under Code section 2704(b), discussed in the following sections.

In general, the LLC has the estate planning advantages of the family S corporation, but may not fare so well in comparison to the family limited partnership. Since senior family members generally want to retain control, they would probably want a management agreement vesting management in themselves. Since the entity will dissolve on the death, bankruptcy, etc., of a member, without the unanimous (or possibly majority) consent of the members, it would be possible for dissident family members to force a dissolution. The same will not apply to the limited partnership unless the death or other event relates to the general partners.

COMMUNITY PROPERTY CONSIDERATIONS

In a community property state, the investment in an LLC may be of funds or property which are characterized as community or marital property under state law. If so, the membership interest itself will probably also be classified as community property, even though only one spouse is listed as the member.

Where the membership carries voting or management rights, this classification may be material as to the rights of the spouse of a member to participate in either a vote or management. While state law may vary on this point, some states, such as California, generally restrict the voting or management to the spouse who is designated as the member. If this is not true in your particular jurisdiction, it may be necessary to make the spouses parties to the operating agreement to clear up voting and management rights.

In the event of death of either the member or nonmember spouse, or a divorce, the rights in the membership may be divided to reflect the rights of the spouses under state community property laws. It would appear a nonmember spouse who is assigned an interest in the membership would not have the full rights of a member, but would be treated as an assignee of an interest as described in the foregoing discussion. However, this will again depend on the law of the particular state.

QUESTIONS AND ANSWERS

Question — Will the LLC replace the family limited partnership as an estate planning tool for family business and investments?

Answer — In most family limited partnerships, discussed in Chapter 11, the entity is formed by parents or members of a senior generation who transfer business or investment assets to a partnership in which they retain general partnership interests. They then make gifts of limited partnership interests to children or younger generation members.

One drawback of the family limited partnership is the fact that senior generation members, by acting as general partners, assume personal liability for any debts or obligations of the venture. The LLC could be used in this setting and has the great advantage of allowing the senior family members to avoid personal liability. They may

still retain management of the business or investments by providing in the articles or operating agreement that they will be the managing members. Note that under the tests set forth by the IRS in issuing favorable rulings on classification of the LLC as a partnership for tax purposes, it is possible for senior members to retain a large degree of control.

A major problem with the use of the LLC instead of the family limited partnership is that under state law, the entity will dissolve on the death, withdrawal, etc., of any member for any reason. This would permit transferees to force a dissolution of the entity, unless there is either a unanimous or majority vote, depending on state law, of the remaining members to continue the entity. Many senior family members would not be willing to confer that power on the younger generation. In a family limited partnership, only the withdrawal of the last remaining general partner will trigger a dissolution.

Question — Referring to the preceding question, is there any way of achieving limited liability for the senior family members in the family limited partnership?

Answer — The IRS has issued several rulings, five holding that the general partner in a limited partnership could be a corporation, and in particular, an S corporation. Note that under those rulings, the corporation must have at last a 1% interest in the partnership, and should have some substantial assets. Thus, the senior family members could form a corporation which they control to act as general partner, and will generally be successful in avoiding personal liability. It seems likely they could also use an LLC as the general partner in the family limited partnership.

Question — If the LLC is used as a vehicle for the transfer of family business or investments, what will be the impact on the valuation of transfers of membership interests for federal gift tax purposes.

Answer — As discussed in Chapter 11, one of the reasons for the use of family limited partnerships as a vehicle for gifts is the ability to claim valuation adjustments or discounts to reflect the fact that the transferred limited partnership interests are not marketable, represent minority interests, have no right to participate in control of the entity, and most important, cannot force a dissolution of the entity. In the case of the LLC, the withdrawal of a member for any reason, as noted above, will result in dissolution of the entity. This puts the IRS in the position of arguing that valuation discounts should be reduced or eliminated, since the transferee members are in a position, by withdrawing from the LLC, of realizing the net asset value of their interests in the LLC.

It is possible under many state LLC statutes to modify the right of transferee members to withdraw from the LLC, but this runs the risk of the entity being classified as a corporation for federal tax purposes. A restriction on dissolution may well result in the LLC having the corporate characteristic of continuity of life. If it does, then it may have more than two corporate characteristics, since it will probably also have limited liability and centralized management. It would then be necessary to eliminate centralized management, which means all members could vote. This is probably not an acceptable alternative to senior family members who want to control the entity.

Note that the IRS guidelines discussed above suggest a solution to this problem — the entity dissolves only upon death, withdrawal, etc., of managing members. Assuming the requirements of the guidelines can be met, this would mean that if the senior family members are the only managing members the entity would not dissolve on the withdrawal of a younger generation family member who is not a managing member.

However, there is still a major problem. Under Code section 2704(b), any restriction on the rights of the members to force a liquidation of the LLC which are greater than those imposed by state law will be ignored in valuing their interests. Since the so-called "default" rule under most state LLC statutes is that the entity will dissolve if a membership interest terminates for any reason, that rule can only be modified by a contrary agreement among the members. The IRS will likely characterize this as a restriction which will be ignored for valuation purposes, and will value the transferred interests on the assumption that those members can force a dissolution of the LLC. Only a change in underlying state law will eliminate this problem.

As of this writing, some states have begun to modify their LLC statutes to avoid the so-called "default" rules of Section 2704(b). In particular, Arizona has limited the value of the interest of a family member who withdraws from an LLC, and Colorado has restricted the rights of members who withdraw to receive the full liquidation value of their interests in the LLC.

Question — Will a family LLC be subject to special scrutiny under the same rules applicable to family partnerships?

Answer — If the LLC is classified as a partnership for federal income tax purposes, it will likely be subject to the special restrictions on family partnerships under Code section 704(e). These are discussed in Chapter 11. Basically, the allocation of income to transferee partners will not be recognized for federal income tax purposes if capital is not a material factor in producing the income, substantial capital interests are not transferred, or the managing transferor family members are not adequately compensated for their services. In addition, the regulations under Code section 704(e) provide the allocation of income to transferees will not be recognized if the transferors retain too much control over the transferred interests.

Question — Is the LLC a better alternative for unrelated individuals entering into new ventures or investments?

Answer — Aside from the special problems of family businesses, the LLC will probably be the entity of choice for a variety of new business enterprises, particularly those that involve a degree of risk, or are likely to generate losses.

Like the S corporation, the participating members in the LLC may fully participate in the management and operation of the venture without exposure to personal liability. Examples include real estate, investments in mineral rights, and oil and gas. It should be noted, however, that there is always some possible exposure to liability, as in the case of shareholders in a corporation, if the entity is undercapitalized or used in an abusive manner. However, the entity is not subject to the limitations which apply to S corporations, discussed above.

There are some drawbacks that must be considered. If the business operates in more than one state, the issue will be whether or not it will be recognized as an LLC in a state other than the one in which it was formed. If it is not, the members may be subject to personal liability for debts incurred in the other state. There is a statute which provides for recognition of so-called "foreign" LLCs, but it has not been adopted by all states. There are also unresolved issues on the application of self employment taxes on members of the LLC, although the IRS has now provided some guidance in this area.[6]

Question — Will the LLC become the entity of choice for professional practices?

Answer — In the states that permit its use for professional practices, it has already become the entity of choice. Most of the major accounting firms have already been re-formed as LLCs or LLPs, as have many of the major law firms. What is good for the large professional firms is probably also good for small professional practices.

ASRS, Sec. 42 ¶100.

Footnote References

Limited Liability Companies

1. IRC Secs. 743(b), 754.
2. Reg. §§301.7701-1, 301.7701-2.

3. See, for example, Rev. Rul. 94-51, 1994-32 IRB 11; Rev. Rul. 94-30, 1994-19 IRB 16; Rev. Rul. 93-93, 1993-2 CB 321; Rev. Rul. 93-92, 1993-2 CB 318; Rev. Rul. 93-91, 1993-2 CB 316.
4. Rev. Proc. 95-10, 1995-3 IRB 20.
5. See, for example, Let. Ruls. 9412026, 9411012.
6. Prop. Reg. §1.1402(a)-18.

Chapter 23

MEDICAL EXPENSE REIMBURSEMENT PLAN

WHAT IS IT?

A medical expense reimbursement plan (sometimes abbreviated MERP) is an arrangement provided by an employer (including professional corporations) to reimburse one or more employees for dental expenses, cosmetic surgery, and other medical expenses which are not covered under a medical plan available to all employees. Typically, a medical expense reimbursement plan reimburses employees for medical expenses incurred by the employee, his or her spouse, and dependents.

A MERP is used (1) as a substitute for health insurance, (2) as a supplement to provide payments for medical expenses not covered under the company's health insurance plan (such as dental expenses or cosmetic surgery), or (3) to pay for medical expenses in excess of the limits in the company's health insurance plan.

The objective—from a tax standpoint—of a medical expense reimbursement plan is to provide benefits on a tax-free basis to the employee. A corresponding objective is to make such payments tax deductible by the employer.

WHEN IS THE USE OF SUCH A DEVICE INDICATED?

A medical expense reimbursement plan is particularly useful in the following situations:

1. Where a corporation is closely held and family members are the primary or only employees. The medical expense reimbursement plan makes otherwise nondeductible medical expenses deductible.

2. In a professional corporation where the only employee is a professional in a high income tax bracket or where there are few other employees and they are receiving relatively smaller salaries. The medical expense reimbursement plan makes what might otherwise be nondeductible medical expense payments deductible.

3. Where an employer would like to provide significant (and tax favored) benefits to employees beyond those provided by the basic medical coverage already in force.

WHAT ARE THE REQUIREMENTS?

Aside from "insured" plans (see the last Q&A below), a medical expense reimbursement plan which reimburses an employee for medical expenses incurred for the care of the employee and/or his family must be *non*discriminatory.[1] A plan may be considered discriminatory in either (or both) of two ways. A plan may be considered to discriminate as to: (a) coverage; or (b) operation.[2]

Generally speaking, the penalty for a plan which is considered discriminatory is that all or part of the reimbursements to highly compensated employees will be included in their income.[3] Rank and file employees, however, will be entitled to the income tax exclusion in any event.

As to coverage, a plan must benefit 70 percent or more of all employees. Alternatively, if 70 percent of all employees are eligible to be covered, 80 percent of those individuals must in fact participate in coverage.[4] There is a second alternative: An employer might be able to satisfy nondiscrimination requirements by setting up and covering classes of employees in a manner that does not discriminate in favor of highly compensated employees or their families.[5] Since this is not a definite mathematically determinable test, the IRS will determine on a case by case basis under this alternative whether or not there has been discrimination.

Highly compensated employees—for purposes of discrimination—are defined as (1) the five highest paid officers, (2) shareholders holding more than 10 percent of the outstanding stock of the corporation, and (3) the highest paid 25 percent of all employees.[6]

If a plan discriminates in coverage, a fraction of payments received will be includable.[7] That fraction is:

$$\frac{\text{Amount reimbursed to } \textit{highly compensated} \text{ employees}}{\textit{Total} \text{ amount reimbursed to } \textit{all} \text{ employees}} \times \begin{array}{l}\text{Payment} \\ \text{received by} \\ \text{given highly} \\ \text{compensated} \\ \text{employee}\end{array}$$

Inclusion, in other words, depends on the proportion of total payments that went to highly compensated employees. This percentage will then be multiplied by each highly compensated employee's reimbursement.

For instance, SRL Corporation's plan fails the coverage requirements. The corporation paid out $10,000 in medical reimbursements, $2,500 of which went to highly compensated employees. $2,000 of that went to Ed Staller, a company vice president. Ed must include $500 in income ($2,500/ $10,000) x $2,000 = ¼ x $2,000 = $500).

A plan would be considered *discriminatory in operation* if highly compensated employees have greater benefits than other employees. This means benefit levels cannot be based on a percentage or proportion of compensation. This is known as the "dollar for dollar" discrimination rule. It is applicable to eligible benefits rather than amounts actually paid. (The mere fact that highly compensated employees happen to submit more claims than other employees will not *per se* make the plan discriminatory.)

If the plan discriminates in operation (e.g., a highly compensated employee is eligible for twice the benefit anyone else can get), the recipient highly compensated employee will have to include the entire amount of excess reimbursement actually received in income—whether or not coverage requirements are met. For example, Dayton Coles, president of the State College Coal Company, received a $1,000 reimbursement for dental coverage, a benefit provided only for him and his family. The entire $1,000 is includable in Dayton's income.

HOW IT IS DONE—EXAMPLES

1. Powers, Inc. maintains a self-insured medical expense reimbursement plan covering all of its employees. However, the plan provides limitations on the maximum benefits subject to reimbursement. Those limitations are $5,000 for officers, and $1,000 for all other participants. During a plan year, James Powers, one of the five highest paid officers, received reimbursements in the amount of $3,000. Since the amount of benefits provided for the highly compensated individuals is not provided for all other participants, the plan benefits are deemed discriminatory in operation. Thus, James Powers received an excess reimbursement of $2,000 ($3,000 - $1,000) which constitutes a benefit available to highly compensated individuals, but not to all other participants. This $2,000 will be includable in James Powers' gross income in the tax year in which the medical reimbursement plan year ended. (It is not currently certain but it is the authors' opinion that a member of the prohibited class must also include in income for the year some of the $1,000 as well.[8])

2. Western Industries, Inc. maintains a self-insured medical reimbursement plan for its employees. Benefits subject to

reimbursement under this plan are the same for all plan participants. However, of the 100 employees in the company, only 10 (6 of whom are stockholders) are eligible to participate. Therefore, the plan discriminates as to coverage (eligibility). During the plan year ending in 1995, Jordan Thomas, a highly compensated individual, was hospitalized for surgery, and accrued medical expenses of $4,500 which were reimbursed to him under the plan. During the plan year, the corporation's medical plan paid a total of $50,000 in benefits, $30,000 of which constituted payments to highly compensated individuals. The amount of excess reimbursement, which will be included in the income of Jordan Thomas in 1995, is $2,700. That amount is calculated as follows:

$$\frac{\$30,000}{\$50,000} \quad x \quad \$4,500 \quad = \quad \$2,700$$

IMPLICATIONS AND ISSUES IN COMMUNITY PROPERTY STATES

No significant difference exists with regard to the application of the medical expense reimbursement law in community property states.

QUESTIONS AND ANSWERS

Question — Is a ruling or advance determination letter required?

Answer— No. While no advance rulings are required, as in the case of a qualified pension or profit-sharing plan, it is expected that advance rulings will be available.

Question — If an amount is considered an excess reimbursement and subject to inclusion in the income of the highly compensated individual, *when* is that amount included?

Answer — The amount of the excess reimbursement is included in the income of the highly compensated individual for the taxable year of that individual in which the plan year ends. Thus, if a corporation has a plan year end of June 30, and the highly compensated individual receives an excess reimbursement on November 1, 1995, he will include that amount in his gross income in his 1996 taxable year.

Question — May the benefits be calculated as a percentage of the participant's compensation?

Answer — Generally, no. If a plan covers employees who are highly compensated individuals in addition to rank and file employees, and the type or amount of benefits subject to reimbursement by the plan is in proportion to the employee's compensation, the plan will be deemed to discriminate as to benefits.[9]

Question — What are "Medical Benefits"?

Answer — Generally, the medical expenses which will be considered "medical benefits" subject to this nondiscrimination provision are the same expenses which would result in itemized medical expense deductions from an individual's personal income.

Certain "diagnostic procedures" are not subject to the discriminatory plan rules. Medical diagnostic procedures include routine medical examinations, blood tests and x-rays. They do not, however, include expenses incurred for the treatment, cure or testing of a known illness or disability, or treatment or testing for a physical injury, complaint or specific symptom of bodily malfunction.

Question — If an employer has an insured medical expense reimbursement plan, but that plan has a deductible portion which the employer, pursuant to a plan, agrees to pay, will such payment be subject to the discriminatory medical reimbursement plan rules?

Answer — Yes. The regulations state that the nondiscrimination rules apply to a self-insured portion of an employer's medical plan or arrangement even if the plan is in part written by insurance. Thus, if an employer's medical plan reimburses employees for the deductible amounts under the insured portions, such reimbursement is subject to the medical expense nondiscrimination rules. However, a plan which reimburses employees for premiums paid under an insured plan is not subject to these rules.[10]

Question — Is it possible to exclude any employees under a medical expense reimbursement plan?

Answer — Yes. The "don't have to be covered" class includes (1) employees with less than three years of service; (2) employees under age 25; (3) part-time employees whose customary weekly employment is less than 35 hours; (4) seasonal employees whose customary annual employment is less than nine months; (5) certain union employees who are engaged in collective bargaining units, but only if accident and health benefits were the subject of good-faith bargaining.

Question — The law currently exempts "insured" plans. What is meant by an insured plan?

Answer — Where accident and health insurance benefits are provided by an insurance company, the nondiscrimina-

tion tests do not apply. An insured plan is one in which risk has been shifted to and accepted by an insurer.[11] For example, consider the following:

The Quickbucks Corporation buys from Fastpay Life, a licensed insurance company, a policy which provides an exact reimbursement of 100 percent of an employee's medical expenses. The premium for such a policy is equal to the amount of the expenses reimbursed plus a certain percentage (presumably to provide for the administration costs).

This arrangement appears to be an attempt to avoid the intent of Congress when it excluded insured plans, i.e., Congress felt that underwriting considerations generally preclude or effectively limit abuses in insured plans so the nondiscrimination rules were not necessary with respect to them. The plan purchased by the Quickbucks Corporation is not what Congress meant by an "insured" plan since there is no shifting of the risk to an insurer.

Here's a similar arrangement that also claims to be an insured plan—but probably is *not* what Congress intended:

The Lotsamoney Corporation buys a policy from Livelong Life, a licensed insurance company, which provides for a complete reimbursement of all medical expenses. The premium is level. At the time of the employee's termination of employment, for any reason whatsoever, any amount of premium which has been paid by the employer and has not been used or needed to reimburse an employee is refunded to the employer. (The premium is set high enough so as to likely provide a refund to the employer.)

This second arrangement does shift some risk—but perhaps not enough to be a legitimate plan of insurance. Both arrangements are more like self-insured than insured plans.

Footnote References

Medical Expense Reimbursement Plan

1. IRC Sec. 105(h).
2. IRC Sec. 105(h)(2).
3. IRC Sec. 105(h)(1).
4. IRC Sec. 105(h)(3)(A)(i).
5. IRC Sec. 105(h)(3)(A)(ii).
6. IRC Sec. 105(h)(5).
7. IRC Sec. 105(h)(7)(B).
8. A strict reading of Code section 105(h)(7)(A) indicates that the entire amount paid to or on behalf of a member of the prohibited group would

be fully taxable. In the example above this means that the $1,000 amount available to all employees would not be excludable.

An interpretation of the Senate Finance Committee reports would lead to the conclusion that if there is a benefit that is available to a broad cross-section of employees, but the plan discriminates in some other fashion (whether in providing additional benefits, or in not meeting the coverage tests), then the member of the prohibited class must take into income for the year *some* of the money that he has received under the benefit. For this we have to go to the fraction. In the above example, assume that, while James Powers is the only member of the prohibited group to receive an excess reimbursement during the year, amounts reimbursed to officers (including Powers), *within the $1,000 limit applicable to non-officers*, total $4,000 for the year. Assume further that amounts reimbursed to officers and non-officers alike, within the $1,000 limit, total $10,000 for the year. This means that the percentage received by members of the prohibited class amounts to 40% of the amount received with respect to benefits that are available to the cross-section. In the example, the highly compensated employee received $3,000. Therefore, he receives $2,000 in ordinary income (because that is a benefit not available to the cross-section), plus 40% of the first $1,000 he received (the benefit available to all employees).

What the statute effectively ends up doing is penalizing members of the prohibited class since this was a discriminatory plan, even to some extent with respect to benefits that are available to a broad cross-section of all employees.

9.   Reg. §1.105-11(c)(3)(i).

10. Reg. §1.105-11(b)(2).

11. The Treasury has issued Regulation §1.105-11(b)(1)(ii) for determining what is an insured medical plan. This regulation specifically states that a "plan underwritten by a policy of insurance or a prepaid health care plan *that does not involve the shifting of risk to an unrelated third party* is considered self-insured for purposes of this section" (emphasis added). Thus, a plan which has been underwritten by a policy of insurance which contains no shifting of risk, or merely provides administrative or bookkeeping services, will be considered self-insured under this section.

However, a regular health insurance program, with risk shifted to the insurance company, is not affected.

Chapter 24

NON U.S. PERSONS IN THE ESTATE PLAN

WHAT IS IT?

Special planning opportunities and problems are present where at least some family members are not U.S. citizens. Techniques will depend largely on the following:

(1) The extent to which these individuals have property situated in the U.S.

(2) Whether they are classified as either resident or non-resident aliens.

(3) Whether they were U.S. citizens who have renounced their citizenship through expatriation to other nations.

(4) Whether the spouse of the client is a citizen of the U.S.

Any planning in this area will be contingent on whether or not there is a treaty with the country in question which covers tax issues. The practitioner must always determine if such treaty provisions exist.

WHEN IS THE USE OF SUCH PLANNING INDICATED?

The international or multinational plan will be required in the following situations:

1. Where the client or family member is an alien who is considered to be resident in the U.S. The tests for determining if an alien is a U.S. resident is different for federal income tax law than it is for federal estate tax law. Under the income tax rules, the test is objective, i.e., is the alien physically present in the U.S.?[1] If so, the alien is, subject to a complex set of tests and rules, usually treated as a resident. The federal estate tax regulations defines a U.S. resident as a person who, at the time of his death, is "domiciled" in the U.S. Under these regulations, a non U.S. citizen is not domiciled in the U.S. unless he or she intends to remain here indefinitely.[2] Thus in the case of the estate tax, the test is a subjective test relating to the "intent" of the person. This section will focus on the estate, gift, and generation-skipping transfer tax planning issues.

   If the alien is treated as a resident for estate tax purposes, it follows that the alien's lifetime transfers are subject to gift and estate taxes in essentially the same manner as U.S. citizens resident in the U.S. The basic gift tax law is that the tax applies to all transfers by any individual, whether resident or nonresident.[3] There is an exception for the transfer of intangible property by a nonresident noncitizen.[4]

2. Where the client or family member is not a citizen or resident of the U.S., but is subject to federal estate tax because his or her taxable estate includes property situated in the U.S.[5] This includes any stock issued by a domestic corporation (i.e., a U.S. corporation); any property which was situated in the U.S. when it was transferred by the decedent, but which would be included in his or her estate under IRC §§2035-2038, and debt obligations of U.S. persons or of the U.S., any state or any political subdivision.[6] It does not include life insurance or certain bank deposits and debt obligations.[7]

3. Where a surviving spouse is not a U.S. citizen, regardless of such spouse's domicile, and the issue is the availability of the gift or estate tax marital deduction for transfers of assets to or in trust for the spouse.[8]

4. Where the client is a U.S. citizen not residing in the U.S. The estate and gift taxes are imposed on all U.S. citizens, regardless of where they live.[9] The generation-skipping transfer tax statutes do not specifically cover this, but since the tax is triggered by a taxable transfer for gift or estate tax purposes, the same rule should apply.

WHAT ARE THE REQUIREMENTS?

Subject to the foregoing rules, the goal of estate planning for clients in this category is to minimize the impact of U.S. taxes.

1. To avoid federal income tax, an alien who does not hold a permanent U.S. visa can avoid being physically present in the U.S. for more than 120 days during any three calendar years. This of course will be impossible for most aliens who are actively engaged in business in the U.S., or maintain a home here. If, however, the alien can limit his or her presence in the U.S. to no more than 182 days in any year, U.S. income tax may be avoided if:

a. The alien maintains a principal place of business outside the U.S.

b. An annual declaration is filed with the IRS with information which shows a "closer connection" with a foreign country than the U.S.

2. To avoid federal estate tax, the alien's estate will have to establish the alien's "intent," i.e., that the alien's permanent home is outside the U.S. For example, if the alien has a bigger or better residence in the U.S. than in the alien's home country, this will be difficult. Also, the conduct of business and investment affairs should, to the extent possible, be located outside the U.S. Obviously, the alien should avoid signing documents in which the alien is described as a U.S. resident.

3. Where it appears U.S. residency will be unavoidable for either income or transfer tax purposes, the alien should seek to make gifts of assets to non U.S. persons, such as adult children living in foreign countries, before becoming a U.S. resident. This could be done with irrevocable foreign situs trusts, and limited liability companies (LLCs) discussed in Chapter 22. Many foreign countries recognize LLCs. This may be particularly useful to reduce the size of the alien's taxable estate.

4. Whether or not the alien is deemed a resident under U.S. tax laws, foreign situs trusts may be particularly useful to mitigate tax consequences. It will be essential that such a trust be irrevocable and have an independent trustee. However, the alien could retain some powers over the trust to the extent these powers do not cause the alien to be considered the "owner" of the trust for federal income or estate tax purposes. See in particular the discussion of the Income Taxation of Estates and Trusts in Appendix C.

5. Where the alien can avoid U.S. residency, the use of foreign situs revocable trusts and foreign corporations may be indicated.

6. Where the client is a resident or U.S. citizen, but the client's spouse is not a U.S. citizen, the planner must concentrate on the federal gift and estate tax marital deduction. In general, the gift tax marital deduction is limited to $100,000. The estate tax marital deduction is only available if the bequest ends up in a "qualified domestic trust". This is a trust which meets the requirements for the marital deduction discussed in Chapter 37, but which must include a series of special provisions relating to the trustee and how the trust is administered. If such a trust is used, the decedent's estate can claim the estate tax marital deduction for transfers to it, but most distributions to the surviving spouse, as well as the value of the assets remaining in the trust at the death of the surviving spouse, will be subject to federal estate tax. Moreover, this estate tax is computed by assuming such assets are added to the estate of the predeceased spouse.

7. There are also special rules relating to distributions from foreign situs trusts to U.S. beneficiaries. For example, there is an interest charge if such a trust accumulates income and then distributes the accumulation.[10] If a "U.S. person" contributes property to a foreign situs trust that has at least one U.S. beneficiary, the trust income is taxed to the grantor.[11]

8. The unified credit and state death tax credit are allowed to the estate of U.S. residents even if they are not U.S. citizens.[12]

9. *Foreign Death Tax Credit:* Foreign death taxes are often imposed on property owned by a resident noncitizen where the property is situated outside the U.S. A credit is allowed for estate, inheritance, legacy, or succession taxes paid to a foreign country (or to a U.S. possession). The foreign death tax credit is allowed to the estate of a resident alien. The credit is allowed only for taxes actually paid to the foreign country or U.S. possession.[13]

Basis: The basis in a taxable distribution from a QDT is computed as though the transfer was made by gift rather than by transfer at death. In other words for basis purposes, instead of a step up to its date of death value, the initial basis is carried over and increased (but not above fair market value) by the amount of tax allocable to the growth in the value of the property occurring after the first spouse's death.[51] For example, assume property worth $1,000,000 is placed into a QDT. It grows to $1,300,000 and is paid out to the surviving spouse and taxed at that time as a capital distribution. An upward adjustment is allowed in the recipient's hands to account for the tax paid on the $300,000 of appreciation.

HOW IT IS DONE - AN EXAMPLE

The client is the citizen of a foreign country who is not a resident of the United States. He is considering making a substantial investment in real estate in Hawaii. If he makes this investment directly, he will be subject to federal income tax on all of the income since it is U.S. source income. Further, upon his death, the value of the real property will be subject to U.S. estate tax.

If the real property were held through a foreign corporation, there would be little if any income tax advantage, but this would afford complete protection from federal estate and gift taxes. He may also consider holding the real estate through an irrevocable foreign situs trust, which will also avoid federal estate and gift taxes, but will not avoid federal income tax. However, the trust may be a more flexible arrangement. Further, a combination of the corporation and trust may be considered, with a corporation holding the real estate, and the corporate stock held in the irrevocable trust.

If the property is to be held by a foreign corporation, it is important to be certain the entity will be recognized as a corporation under U.S. law. Some foreign countries have entities which may be nominally be classified as corporations, but which may not be recognized as such in this country. Further, the best procedure to follow is for the alien to transfer the consideration for the purchase of the U.S. real property to the foreign corporation in exchange for stock, then have the corporation purchase the land. There should always be consideration for the transfer of assets to a foreign corporation.

WHAT ARE THE TAX IMPLICATIONS?

As discussed above, where a noncitizen becomes a resident of the U.S. under either the income or estate tax definitions, that person will be subject to taxes in essentially the same manner as a U.S. citizen. The critical first step is to determine whether or not the alien is a resident under either tax. If so, the domestic planning options discussed in this book are generally available.

If the alien is not a resident, then the first step is to avoid U.S. gift and estate taxes by structuring the ownership of assets to avoid direct ownership by the alien of U.S. property or business interests. From the income tax standpoint, nonresident aliens are only taxed on income from sources within the U.S. The U.S. source income rules are detailed and complex (see, in general, IRC §871 and following).

If the nonresident alien does own U.S. situs property, than the federal estate tax will apply under the rules discussed in IRC §§2101 and following and the unified credit available is reduced to $13,000.

There is an excise tax on transfers of certain appreciated property by a U.S. person, including a corporation, partnership, trust or estate, to foreign corporations, estates, trusts, and partnerships.[14] The tax is equal to 35% of the value of the property less its basis and any gain recognized on the transfer. Note that in the case of a transfer to a corporation, this tax only applies if the transfer is paid in surplus or a capital contribution.

Under the Foreign Investment in Real Property Tax Act, various provisions have been added to the law to insure collection of income tax on the transfer of U.S. real property by nonresident aliens, including withholding.[15]

Under proposed regulations, property situated in the U.S. is subject to the generation-skipping transfer tax regardless of the fact the transferor is a nonresident alien. These regulations also seek to extend the tax to transfers of all property to or for the benefit of U.S. persons who are lineal descendants of the transferor, even if the transfer would not be subject to U.S. gift or estate tax. Needless to say, this proposed regulation is highly controversial.

IMPLICATIONS AND ISSUES IN COMMUNITY PROPERTY STATES

Most countries in the world, other than those which follow the British common law system, such as most of the United States, do have community property laws. It is very likely assets acquired by non citizens are community property, and planning should proceed accordingly. In addition, if the alien is resident in a community property state, that state may seek to impose its community property rules on assets or earnings received while domiciled in the state.

QUESTIONS AND ANSWERS

Question — What is a "controlled foreign corporation," and what is its significance?

Answer — A controlled foreign corporation is a foreign corporation in which either more than 50% of the voting stock or more than 50% of the total value of the stock is owned by United States shareholders.[16] The net effect of such status is that any income earned by the corporation will be attributed to and taxed to any shareholders who are U.S. residents.[17] This rule will apply even if the corporate stock is owned through a revocable trust. There are complex rules and exceptions. Note that a similar rule applies to a foreign personal holding company.[18] Personal holding companies are discussed in Chapter 25.

Question — Is the partnership or LLC a viable form of entity for aliens to hold investments or business interests?

Answer — The partnership has the same advantages to aliens as to other taxpayers in avoiding two levels of taxation on its income. However, if the partnership is making U.S. investments, or carrying on a U.S. trade or business, it is subject to stringent withholding requirements. If a nonresident alien owns an interest in a partnership which is carrying on U.S. business, it appears that partnership interest will be subject to U.S. estate tax.

Question — Is an irrevocable foreign trust a viable form of business entity for aliens to hold U.S. investments or business interests?

Answer — Such a trust may be a good planning vehicle, particularly when combined with other entities, such as the foreign corporation or partnership. Again, there are strict withholding requirements on distributions from such trusts. An important advantage of the trust is the potential avoidance of federal estate and gift tax by nonresident aliens. The trust is preferable to any form of direct ownership of U.S. real estate.

Question — A nonresident alien who spends a great deal of time in the U.S. intends to take his daughter, also a nonresident alien, on a shopping trip in this country to purchase expensive jewelry. Is this advisable?

Answer — It would be better for the parent to purchase the jewelry and be the owner, return to the foreign country, and then make a gift of it to his daughter. Otherwise, the transfer is subject to U.S. gift tax.

Question — A decedent is a nonresident alien who was an expatriate from the U.S. four years before her death. Is there any estate tax exposure?

Answer — IRC §2107 specifically provides that if one of the principal purposes of expatriation was to avoid U.S. taxes, and citizenship is lost within 10 years of death, a tax is imposed on the decedent's estate. This would result in inclusion in the decedent's taxable estate of not only property situated in the U.S. as defined in IRC §2104, but also stock in certain foreign corporations.

Question — A nonresident alien wishes to create a trust for the benefit of U.S. citizens. How can the alien avoid U.S. tax on the trust income?

Answer — If the trust is subject to the grantor trust rules under IRC §671-677, the grantor, not the trust or its beneficiaries, will be taxed on the trust income. This also avoids the tax on accumulations discussed above.

Question — What are the requirements of a qualified domestic trust (QDOT)?

Answer —

1. The trust must meet the same requirements for the marital deduction as a trust for the benefit of a citizen spouse (see Chapter 37). Thus, it can be a QTIP trust, a trust over which the surviving spouse has the right to all income and a general power of appointment, or an "estate" trust. In an estate trust, it is not necessary that all of the income be distributed annually to the surviving spouse, so long as all trust distributions must ultimately be made to the spouse or the spouse's estate. Such a trust is often useful where the trust assets are not income producing, such as stock in a closely held corporation.

2. At least one trustee must be an individual who is a U.S. citizen or a domestic corporation. According to proposed regulations, if the value of the trust assets exceeds $2 million, at least one U.S. trustee must be a bank or furnish a bond equal to 65% of the value of the trust. If the trust is worth less than $2 million, either a bond must be furnished or the trust must contain a clause that not more than 35% of its fair market value can be invested in non U.S. real property. Also, an individual U.S. trustee must have a tax home in the U.S. Tangible and intangible U.S. property must be in the U.S. or a U.S. brokerage account.

3. No distribution can be made from the trust unless the trustee who is the U.S. citizen or a domestic corporation has a right under the trust to withhold from the distribution any tax due on the distribution.

4. The executor of decedent's estate must make a QDOT election. If the qualifying trust is a QTIP, both QTIP and QDOT elections must be made.

5. No marital deduction is allowed unless the property is transferred to a QDOT, or a trust reformed to qualify as a QDOT, or is transferred to the QDOT by a surviving spouse, or the surviving spouse becomes a citizen, or there is a treaty. There must be an actual transfer or assignment to a QDOT created by the decedent, executor, or surviving spouse.

6. An estate tax is imposed on QDOT assets on the happening of any of the following events:

    (1) When any distribution other than (a) income to the surviving spouse or (b) a distribution to the surviving spouse on account of hardship is made prior to the surviving spouse's death, and

    (2) When the surviving spouse dies. The entire value of the property in the QDT at that time will be subject to federal estate tax, and

    (3) When the QDT fails to meet any QDT requirement designed to assure that the IRS will collect the estate tax. The estate tax will be imposed as if the surviving spouse died on the date the trust failed the requirement, and

(4) When the QDT pays the tax imposed upon the first of the above triggering events, that tax itself is considered a taxable distribution which sets off yet another tax. In other words the QDT's payment of the estate tax on a distribution is itself a distribution subject to a further estate tax.

7. The estate tax on the QDOT is computed as follows:

Step 1: State the amount involved in the taxable event

Step 2: Add all previous taxable events

Step 3: Compute the federal estate tax on estate of first spouse to die as if total of #1 and #2 above were included in decedent's gross estate.

Step 4: Compute the federal estate tax on estate of first spouse to die as if only amount of previous taxable events were included in decedent's gross estate.

Step 5: Subtract tax computed in step #4 from tax computed in step #3. This is the tax imposed as a result of a current taxable event.

8. If the estate otherwise qualifies, various tax elections are available upon the death of the surviving spouse, such as stock redemptions under IRC §303, valuation elections under IRC §2032 and §2032A, and deferred payment of federal estate tax under IRC §6166. Also, a charitable deduction under IRC §2055 may be available.

Question — What are the planning advantages of gift transfers to a noncitizen spouse?

Answer — Lifetime transfers of up to $100,000 per year to a noncitizen spouse qualify for the gift tax marital deduction. The noncitizen spouse could leverage this gift by purchasing life insurance on the life of the citizen spouse. Such insurance would not be included in the estate of the citizen spouse, and through the use of an irrevocable life insurance trust, discussed in Chapter 36, could be excluded from the estate of the noncitizen spouse in the event such spouse is subject to federal estate tax.

Lifetime gifts to a surviving spouse are particularly useful where such spouse is a U.S. resident subject to federal gift or estate taxes. In this case, gifts of up to $600,000 can be used to take full advantage of the noncitizen spouse's unified credit. Even gifts in excess of that amount, given at the rate of $100,000 per year, can be used to take advantage of the lower estate tax brackets of the noncitizen spouse. This clearly has advantages over the use of a QDOT trust, where the trust assets will eventually be taxed at the probably higher brackets that would be used in computing the tax in the estate of the predeceased spouse.

Question — What is the impact of joint tenancy forms of title holding where one spouse is not a citizen?

Answer — Under IRC §2040(a), the entire value of the joint tenancy property is included in the estate of the spouse who contributed to the joint tenancy. Note that IRC §2040(b), which provides that joint tenancies between husband and wife are deemed owned 50% by each for estate tax purposes, does not apply if the surviving spouse is not a citizen.[19]

Footnote References

1. IRC §7701(b).
2. Reg §20.0-1(b).
3. IRC §2501(a)(1).
4. IRC §2501(a)(2).
5. IRC §2103.
6. IRC §2104.
7. IRC §2105.
8. IRC §2056(d), §2056A, §2523(i).
9. IRC §2001(a), §2501(a).
10. IRC §668.
11. IRC §679.
12. IRC §2010, §2011.
13. IRC §2014.
14. IRC §1491.
15. IRC §897, 1445.
16. IRC §957.
17. IRC §954.
18. IRC §551.
19. IRC §2056(d)(1)(B).

Chapter 25

PERSONAL HOLDING COMPANY

WHAT IS IT?

A personal holding company is a corporation that meets two particular tests (and is not specifically excluded from such status).[1] These two tests are: (1) a stock ownership test; and (2) an income test. Both tests must be met in the same taxable year so that it is possible for a corporation to attain personal holding company status in one year and not in the next.

The stock ownership test works like this: The corporation meets the stock ownership requirements if more than 50 percent in value of its outstanding stock is owned directly or indirectly by or for not more than five individuals at any time during the last half of the taxable year.[2] The second test, the income test, is sometimes referred to as the "60 percent" test. If the stock ownership test has been met and at least 60 percent or more of the corporation's adjusted ordinary gross income is personal holding company income (generally, dividends, interest, rents, or amounts received in return for a certain type of personal services), the corporation will be classified as a personal holding company.[3]

The personal holding company provisions have generally been thought to be odious since there is a tax of 39.6%, separate and in addition to the existing corporate tax on specifically defined undistributed income of personal holding companies.[4] However, personal holding company status can be an estate planning tool if arranged properly.

Care should be exercised in the use of personal holding companies based on the repeal of the *General Utilities* doctrine by the Tax Reform Act of 1986. If assets in the corporation appreciate, generally there will be two taxes created, one at the corporate level (upon a sale of the assets or liquidation of the corporation) and one at the shareholder level (upon a liquidation of the corporation or dividend distribution).

WHEN IS THE USE OF SUCH A DEVICE INDICATED?

1. Where an individual has a large estate consisting of highly appreciated and readily marketable securities and wants to reduce federal estate taxes attributable to those assets.

2. Where an individual would like to reduce the value of his estate through court approved methods for discounts.

3. Where it is desired to achieve gift and estate tax savings for appreciated assets while retaining economic control and flexibility in making economic decisions. However, the planner should give careful consideration to other entities that can achieve the same result without double tax problems. These include, the family partnership, discussed in Chapter 11, the limited liability company, discussed in Chapter 22, and the S corporation, discussed in Chapter 29. In the case of the S corporation, its assets may consist entirely of passive investments, such as marketable securities, without triggering a corporate level tax so long as it has no corporate earnings and profits. About the only time that can occur is if the S corporation had once been a C corporation.

WHAT ARE THE REQUIREMENTS?

A corporation is formed by an individual who owns a substantial amount of appreciated property. He or she transfers a portfolio of common stock of various companies to a newly-formed closely held corporation in return for its stock. This transfer can be accomplished without recognition of any gain. The transfer of assets to a corporation in exchange for its stock will not be a taxable event if the transferor controls 80 percent of the voting power and 80 percent of each class of stock immediately after the transfer.[5]

The individual transferring this stock will have a basis (cost for purposes of determining gain or loss) in the new stock equal to the basis in the property transferred to the corporation.[6] Likewise, the corporation will receive the stock transferred to it with the same basis this property had in the individual's hands.[7]

HOW IT IS DONE — EXAMPLES

Denise Lopez, a wealthy investor, purchased shares of Gro-Quick, a closely held corporation, many years ago. These shares are now worth ten times what she paid for them and are continuing to appreciate rapidly. If Denise retains the stock, the shares will be includable in her estate. If she gives them away, she will incur a sizable gift tax. (The taxable portion of any gifts will be considered adjusted taxable gifts and therefore increase the rate at which the taxable estate will be taxed.) Furthermore, some of her beneficiaries are minor children and she does not want to make outright gifts. However, she does not want to use a trust because of certain administrative problems associated with a trust.

Denise forms a corporation and retains 100 percent of its stock. The stock she transfers to the corporation has a fair market value of one million dollars. The corporation is capitalized as follows: $800,000 (fair market value) of non-voting common stock is issued to Denise. In addition, she receives $200,000 worth of voting common stock. (The breakdown is arbitrary and can be varied according to the particular situation.)

Since one of Denise's main objectives is to maintain control while making gifts to limit future appreciation in value of her estate, she retains the voting stock and begins a gifting program with the non-voting common. She gives, over a period of years, the $800,000 worth of non-voting common to family members. This enables her to continue to direct and control the investment program. Because of the unified transfer credit ($600,000) and the annual exclusions ($10,000 per donee per year) the transfer can be made with little or no gift tax cost. Because the non-voting common stock represents most of the right to the financial growth of the business (80%), substantial future appreciation is removed from Denise's estate. For example, if the underlying assets double in value after the gift of the common stock, 80% of that appreciation is realized in the hands of the donees rather than in Denise's hands.

In the case of family corporations, the use of common and preferred stock in either capitalizing or recapitalizing the entity, followed by a transfer of shares to other family members by gift or sale, may and probably will create a gift tax valuation problem under Code section 2701 or a gift, estate, or generation-skipping transfer tax problem if restrictions on certain classes of stock lapse under Code section 2704. These issues are covered in detail in Chapter 15.

An additional benefit of using a corporation to hold significant assets is the fact that the corporate stock may be worth less than the value of the assets in the corporation. Courts have consistently allowed discounts of 15 percent and more (in one case as much as 55 percent) on the theory that stock of a personal holding company is less attractive to an investor than a similar stock listed on an exchange with ready access to the investing public.

For example, a gift of 100 shares of AT&T is worth more than a gift of shares representing a 10 percent interest in a personal holding company whose only asset is 1,000 shares of AT&T. It is this fact — that an investment in a personal holding company is less desirable than in the underlying shares because the underlying assets can be easily traded in the market while shares in the personal holding company cannot — that is the primary reason for the discount from the net asset value of the underlying shares.[8] Thus, in the example above, Denise's one million dollar portfolio may be valued for estate purposes at considerably less than the one million dollars that the underlying assets are worth. (The value of a gift of less than a controlling interest would be further reduced because of the lack of voting control.)

WHAT ARE THE TAX IMPLICATIONS?

1. As mentioned above, substantial estate and gift tax savings may be possible through "discounts" in the valuation process. (See list of cases in Figure 25.1.)

2. The individual forming the personal holding company can perform bona fide services for it and receive a salary. Assuming the salary paid is reasonable, the individual will be taxed at a maximum rate of 33 percent on compensation and that amount will be fully deductible by the corporation. Any "excess" compensation (compensation deemed unreasonable) would be subject to tax at the corporate level (nondeductible) and then taxed at the individual level. Operating expenses may even generate a net operating loss. (Local and state franchise taxes should be considered.)

3. The taxable income of the corporation can be lowered further by providing a working stockholder and working members of his or her family with various fringe benefits. These include a qualified pension or profit-sharing plan. Furthermore, some medical expenses may be deductible. These expenses must be reasonable in view of the services performed by the employee shareholder.

4. A capital loss of a corporation can be carried back up to three years to offset prior income while individuals are not allowed a carryback of losses.

5. There is, of course, a substantial disadvantage if a personal holding company is not properly handled. As in any corporation, there is the potential for double taxation (the first incident when the corporation sells securities and again when the shareholder receives the proceeds or other property as a dividend or on the liquidation of the corporation). However, the potential for double taxation can be minimized or eliminated by carefully controlling the type of investments and expenses incurred.

Figure 25.1

PERSONAL HOLDING COMPANY CASES INVOLVING ESTATE TAX DISCOUNTS

Case	Company & Holdings	Shs. to be Valued	Total Shares	Discount Allowed
Celia Waterman 20 TCM 281 (1960)	*Maxcell Corp.* (Apt bldgs)	299	571	30.8%
Lida E. Tompkins Est. 20 TCM 1763 (1961)	*H Street Building Corp.* (Gen'l real estate business, building, contracting and construction)	186	650	32.8%
Drybrough v. U.S. 60 TCM 645 (W.D. Ky 1962)	(5 separate real estate holding companies)			35.0%
Harry S. Leyman 40 TC 100 (1963)	*Leyman Corp.* (Real estate, 2 Buick agencies, parking garages)	2,309	9,400	36.7%
Hamm v. Comm. 325 F.2d 934 (8th Cir. 1963)	*United Properties, Inc.* (Commercial real estate and 10 closely held subsidiaries)	263⅓	1,000	27.2%
Gregg Maxcy Est. 28 TCM 783 (1969) Rev'd on appeal, 441 F.2d 192 (5th Cir. 1971)	*Maxcy Securities, Inc.* (Citrus grove, restaurant, mortgages (1) and accounts receivable (2))	164 86	174 174	15.0% 25.0%
Heckscher v. Comm. 63 TC 485 (1975) CCH Dec. 33,023	*Anaheim Realty Co.* (Undeveloped Florida real estate and securities)	2,500	108,675	48.3%
Lloyd R. Smith Est. 9 TCM 907 (1950)	*Smith Investment Co.* (Stock of A O Smith Corp)	408	1,860	22.1%
Bishop Tr. Co. Ltd. v. U.S. 501 USTC #10,764 (DC Hawaii 1950)	*Henry P. Baldwin Ltd.* (Stock listed on Honolulu Exchange)	1,861	15,000	32.8%
Goss v. Fitzpatrick 97 F. Supp. 765 (D.C. Conn. 1951)	*Alden M. Young Co.* (Marketable securities; some real estate)	1,900	13,518	42.9%
Clarence J. Grootematt, Est. 79,049 (P-H)	*Greendale Land Co.* (development and sale of real estate)	40	400	25.0%
Ernest A. Oberting Est. TC Memo 1984-407, 84,407 (P-H)	*Warrior Oil Co.* (percent interest in Indonesian oil contracts)	45	225	65.0%
Estate of Cotchett TC Memo 1974-31, 74,031 (P-H)	*Eddy Investment Co.* (cash and marketable securities)	20,692	103,621	34.0%
Estate of Hayes TC Memo 1973-236, 73,236 (P-H)	*DuQuoin Coca Cola* (farm land, dairy business, soft drink bottling business)	930	5,952	25.0%

The other problem is the imposition of state capital stock or franchise tax on the value of the personal holding company stock or on the net income remaining in the corporation each year.

HOW CAN LIFE INSURANCE ENHANCE THIS TOOL?

It is possible to transfer, in addition to other assets, life insurance policies. Thus, an individual would transfer existing life insurance policies (term, whole life, or endowment) having little present value as compared with their face amounts to the personal holding company in exchange for voting common stock. (Alternatively, the company could purchase insurance on the life of the holder of the voting stock.) By then giving non-voting common stock in the holding company to the donee-family members (alternatively, the corporation could sell those family members stock for cash or other property), most of the eventual appreciation due to the death value of the life insurance can be transferred out of the donor-owner's estate.

Because the decedent's executor will have voting control over the personal holding company by virtue of his ownership of the personal holding company voting common stock, that individual could direct the corporation to make a Section 303 stock redemption, thus providing estate liquidity.

IMPLICATIONS AND ISSUES IN COMMUNITY PROPERTY STATES

The particular form of property ownership between spouses holding an interest in a corporation classified as a personal holding company has no particular bearing on meeting the stock ownership test, by virtue of the family attribution rules. That is, the ownership interest of one's spouse will be attributed back, regardless of whether the spouse's interest is community or separate property.

However, for estate planning purposes, a community property form of ownership is advantageous, as compared to joint tenancy or tenancy in common, because of the "step-up" in the tax basis of both halves of the community property on the death of one spouse.

Of particular importance to estate planners when dealing with a personal holding company is the classification of the income produced by the enterprise, because, in order to meet the "60 percent" test, a significant amount of the income must be classified as personal holding company income (i.e., dividends, interest, rents, etc.).

If the stock ownership is community property, then, absent an agreement to the contrary, the income will also be community property. However, as noted in Chapter 11 on Family Limited Partnerships, in some community property states, if the stock ownership is separate property, this does not necessarily mean that the income produced, or any accretion in value, will also be separate property.

As previously discussed in Chapter 1, if an increase in the value of separate property is attributable to the ability or activity of either spouse, for which the community has not been sufficiently rewarded (e.g., by an appropriate salary), at least a portion of that increase may well be determined to be community property (thereby reducing the gross estate of the original owner-spouse).

In addition, the income produced may be classified as both community and separate property. If one of the spouses invests separate property in a business and conducts that business during marriage, without adequate reward to the community for the spouse's efforts, the resulting profits may be community and separate property in proportion to the amounts attributable to the personal efforts and to capital investment, respectively.

In such circumstance, depending on which spouse dies first, it may be important to be able to show that the profits from, and appreciation in value of, the business are from one (or both) spouse's efforts, rather than merely a natural enhancement in value, in order to spread the increased value between the two estates, and to provide a "step-up" in basis for both halves of the community property at the first death. If the spouse who originally owned the business dies first, then the entire business will receive a "stepped-up" basis regardless of the amount of community property effort.

QUESTIONS AND ANSWERS

Question — How can stock be shifted to children and grandchildren without incurring gift tax costs if the children do not have cash or other property to purchase the stock?

Answer — The parent of a child can lend money directly to his or her children or their custodian or to an irrevocable trust established for their benefit, or guarantee a loan between the child and a third party, such as a bank.[9] The child (or trust) can then purchase stock directly from the corporation for cash. The child could obtain cash to pay back the loan by having the personal holding company declare dividends on the common stock. Even after TRA '86, income shifting from parent to child — and therefore income tax savings — is possible if the child is age 14 or older.

Question — Assuming that personal holding company status is — at some date — considered onerous, how can such classification be avoided?

Answer — As mentioned above, there are two tests — both of which must be met — before a corporation will be classified as a personal holding company. The first requires that five or fewer shareholders own more than 50 percent of the value of the stock at some time during the last six months of the year. This test can be side-stepped by distributing ownership of shares to unrelated parties or by issuing a second class of stock to unrelated parties in order to dilute ownership value.

The second test requires that personal holding company income be greater than or equal to 60 percent of adjusted ordinary gross income. To avoid this test, property that produces personal holding company income, such as rental property, can be transferred out of the corporation (with potential tax consequences). Conversely, by producing income (active as opposed to passive) within the corporation, the 60 percent test can be avoided. Furthermore, expenses related to adjusted ordinary gross income can be deferred into future periods or a depreciation method can be selected to maximize adjusted ordinary gross income. Finally, if there is a potential personal holding company liability, cash dividends can be paid out during the tax year, post year-end dividends can be paid, consent dividend procedures can be used, deficiency dividend procedures can be used and, as a final alternative, the corporation can be liquidated. However, the lack of a capital gains deduction upon a sale or exchange or liquidation makes the liquidation alternative more expensive. In addition, gain from appreciated property that the corporation distributes will be taxed at the corporate level. If the corporation does not have any earnings and profits (or declares a dividend to eliminate any) it can elect S corporation status and avoid any personal holding company tax regardless of the level of passive income. Such an election may bring into play the built-in gain rules.[10]

Question — Is the personal holding company technique a "sure fire" way to obtain an estate or gift tax valuation discount?

Answer — Not every personal holding company will result in an estate or gift tax discount. In *Estate of Lucretia Davis Jephson*,[11] the value of stock in two personal holding companies that were owned by the decedent was not reduced by a lack of marketability discount. The court in the *Jephson* case held that the proper estate tax value was the net asset value of the companies less the cost involved in liquidating them. Note that the result occurred because the decedent owned 100 percent of both companies and therefore had the unqualified right to liquidate them at any time. Note also that all the assets in both companies were cash or marketable securities, and that neither corporation had any significant liabilities. Planners should use this case as a "how not to do it" guideline.

Footnote References

Personal Holding Company

1. Code section 542(c) contains ten types of business entities that are specifically excluded from personal holding company status, such as tax-exempt corporations, banks, and life insurance companies.
2. IRC Sec. 542(a)(2). The ownership test pertains to value and not to the number of outstanding shares. Under constructive ownership rules an individual is deemed to own all the stock directly or indirectly owned by or for his or her brothers and sisters, spouse, ancestors, and lineal descendants. Likewise, stock owned directly or indirectly by or for a corporation, partnership, estate, or trust is considered as being owned proportionately by its shareholders, partners, or beneficiaries. IRC Sec. 544(a).
3. IRC Sec. 542(a)(1). "Adjusted ordinary gross income" is essentially gross income less gains from sales or other dispositions of capital assets and Section 1231 property, and further reduced by depreciation, certain taxes, interest, and rents attributable to income from certain rents and royalties. IRC Section 543(b).
4. IRC Sec. 541.
5. IRC Secs. 351, 368(c); Reg. §1.351-1(b).
6. IRC Sec. 358(a).
7. IRC Sec. 362(a).
8. See chart below which illustrates the percentage discounts allowed in a number of personal holding company cases.
9. TRA '84 severely limited the utility of interest-free loans. See Code section 7872 and Chapter 20 of this book.
10. IRC Sec. 1374.
11. *Est. of Jephson*, 87 TC 297 (1986).

Chapter 26

POWER OF APPOINTMENT

WHAT IS IT?

A power of appointment is a right given in a will, trust, or other instrument by one person (the donor) to another (the donee) allowing the donee to name the recipient (appointee) of the donor's property at some future time. Thus, it is the right to dispose of someone else's property and is, therefore, a way to give someone other than the testator or grantor a right to "complete" the provisions of the latter's will or trust. This authority over the disposition of property can provide substantial flexibility in an estate plan and serve as an important tax-saving tool.

WHEN IS THE USE OF SUCH A DEVICE INDICATED?

1. When an estate owner would like someone other than himself to make decisions concerning his property. A power of appointment is a means of providing for an interested, intelligent and informed person who will likely be living and capable of making a wise choice of (a) who should receive trust property, (b) how much income or principal should be allocated to any given individual, and (c) when principal or income should be paid out. Often, delegation of decision-making through a power of appointment is a way to avoid family conflict or confrontation by placing the decision-making responsibility in the hands of an objective (or outside-the-family) party.

2. When the estate owner does not know what the future needs of his intended beneficiaries will be—or even who or how many beneficiaries he will have. The power of appointment makes it possible to postpone the time of decision as to the ultimate disposition of property until a date when all the relevant facts affecting that decision are known.

3. When the estate owner desires to qualify assets for the marital deduction but would like to provide both asset management through a trust and have some right to designate who will receive the property (a gift over to third parties such as children) if the spouse does not exercise the power. (If the estate owner's primary objective is to be sure children or someone other than the surviving spouse receives the principal, rather than a power of appointment, he should consider a "QTIP" trust, a Qualifying Terminable Interest Property trust which provides the surviving spouse with income for life and then passes principal to the designated remaindermen. This topic is covered in more detail in Chapter 37.)

WHAT ARE THE REQUIREMENTS?

There are no required or "magic" words or phrases for creating a power of appointment. In fact, it is possible to create such a power without even using the word *appoint*. The courts examine whether the words used in the will or trust manifest an intent to create a power. Thus, a power to invade or consume trust corpus is a power of appointment. So, too, is the power to affect the beneficial enjoyment of a trust by altering, amending, revoking or terminating the trust.[1]

A donee might exercise a power by will with specific language such as:

> Under the will of my deceased husband, Alan, I have, as to certain property, a power of appointment by will; I, now, in the exercise of that power, appoint the property subject to such power as follows: (Then the exercise of the power would follow.)

Another way to exercise the power (assuming a specific reference to that power is not required for its exercise) would be for the donee to mention powers as part of a general device or bequest.

> I bequeath and devise all the residue of my property, real and personal, including any property over which I may have a power of appointment, to _____ .

In many states such a general reference to powers of appointment is construed as being sufficient to include that property and in some states the residuary clause need not even refer to powers of appointment to exercise a general power of appointment.

Because of the possibility of confusion and the unintended exercise of a power by the residuary clause in the will of a donee of a power which is exercisable by will, many draftsmen require that the power be exercised by "an instrument other than a will." In this fashion, the donee cannot, intentionally or unintentionally, exercise the power by a will, but instead, must use a separate document.

A *release* of a power is a formal statement that the donee is giving up the power.

A *lapse* is the termination of a power without exercise. Either event may result in inclusion in a donee's estate for federal estate tax purposes, under the same conditions as an exercise; if the donee's property was transferred directly from the donee of a power of appointment to the recipient, would it be includable in the donee's estate? If yes, property subject to the power will be similarly included.

For purposes of trust law, a power of appointment is a "general" one if there are no restrictions on the donee's choice of appointees. Where there are certain restrictions, then the power is termed a "limited" or "special" power.

A separate categorization of powers of appointment exists with regard to federal estate tax. Regardless of whether there are other restrictions on the possible appointees of the power, the power will be termed a "general" power for purposes of federal estate tax law if it can be appointed in favor of any one or more of the group consisting of the holder of the power, his or her estate, creditors or estate's creditors.[2]

The property owner must decide upon a donee. This person can be anyone who has, under local law, the legal capacity to execute the instrument that must be employed to use the power. For example, if the donor specified that the donee must exercise the power by will, the donee must be old enough to execute a valid will. However, the donee need not necessarily have attained that age at the time of creation of the power.

Once a donee has been selected, that person must follow—precisely—the manner of exercising the power of appointment which the donor specified. This means that if the donor provided the donee with a power to be exercised during lifetime, it cannot be exercised by will (since a will takes effect after death). If the donor had not stated how the power is to be exercised, the donee can use any normal method by which the property subject to the power could be transferred. Therefore, real property could be appointed by deed and stock certificates by endorsement.

In some states, a power of appointment will automatically be exercised—regardless of whether or not the donee has referred to the power—by the residuary clause ("all the rest, residue, and remainder I give ...") in the donee's will (unless the donee has stated a contrary intent).[3] In many states, if the donee does not exercise the power, the property subject to appointment does not pass to the donee's intestate successors

(the donee does not technically own the property for property law purposes, even if he holds a general power of appointment under federal tax law); therefore, it will pass according to the donor's desires if they were expressed in a "gift over," also known as a provision in default of appointment.

HOW IT IS DONE — EXAMPLES

Alan Ferry would like to provide his wife with a power of appointment. He might do this by providing in his will language similar to the following:

> Upon the death of my said wife, or, if she shall not survive me, then upon my death, to pay over the principal to such persons (including, but not limited to, my said wife or her estate), and/or corporations, in such estates, interests, and proportions and in such manner, without any restriction or limitation whatsoever, as my said wife may, if she survives me, appoint by making specific reference to this power in and by her last will duly admitted to probate; or, in default of such appointment, then to divide the principal of the trust, as it shall then exist, into as many equal shares as I shall have children then living and deceased children of mine who shall be survived by issue then living.

This provision would give the wife a "general" power of appointment for purposes of the law of trusts. Additionally, it is a general power for estate tax purposes since it is one in which the donee, Alan's wife, has the power to pass on an interest to anyone including herself or her estate, her creditors, or the creditors of her estate. The example illustrates a "testamentary" power, a power exercisable only by will at the donee's death. If Alan's wife predeceases Alan or dies without effectively exercising her power to appoint, the principal goes to the "takers in default" (of exercise), Alan's children.

Suppose Alan wanted to be sure that his property would be kept intact within his family. He could limit the class to whom his wife could appoint by giving her a limited or "special" power. He might use language such as:

> Upon my wife's death, such property shall be distributed to such of my issue and spouses of my issue as she shall appoint by an instrument other than a will making specific reference to this power; and if she shall make no effective appointment, then in equal shares to my children, the issue of any such child who is not then living to take their parent's share, per stirpes. Provided further, that in no event may my wife make any such appointment to herself, her estate, her creditors or the creditors of her estate.

Here, the power is a "special" (or limited) power for trust purposes, and is also not a "general power" for estate tax purposes.

However, if the wife were given the power by her husband to appoint the property to any descendants of the donor's grandfather or the spouses of such descendants, the power would be "special" for trust law purposes, but would be a "general" power for estate tax purposes (since, as a spouse of a descendant of the husband's grandfather, she could include herself within the group of appointees and appoint the property to herself).

For most of our planning purposes, the categorization for estate and gift tax law purposes is more important and we will use that categorization exclusively in the balance of this discussion.

The distinction between a general and a special power has very important tax ramifications which are discussed below.

WHAT ARE THE TAX IMPLICATIONS?

1. The place to start is to classify powers of appointment for federal income, estate, gift and generation-skipping transfer tax consequences in the following categories:

    a. A general power of appointment, which for federal gift, estate, and generation-skipping transfer tax purposes grants the holder the power to appoint the assets to the powerholder, the estate of the powerholder, or creditors either of the powerholder or the powerholder's estate.

        If a power of appointment is "general," the exercise, release, or lapse of the power will be considered a transfer of the property by the powerholder for gift, estate, and generation-skipping transfer tax purposes. If this occurs during life, the result is a taxable gift. If at death, the property is subject to estate tax. Such transfers could also be subject to generation-skipping transfer tax.

        An exception to this rule is a power of appointment which lapses annually, such as the power to appoint $10,000 from a trust each year to any person, which lapses at the end of the year. The lapse of such a power is a taxable gift only to the extent the value of the lapsed transfer exceeds the greater of $5,000 or 5% of the value of the property.

        Another exception to this rule is a power exercisable only with the consent of the creator of the power or a person who has a substantial adverse interest in the

exercise of the power, generally another beneficiary who will lose something if the power is exercised.

    b. A special power to appoint to anyone in the world other than the powerholder, the estate of the powerholder, or creditors either of the powerholder or the powerholder's estate. The exercise, release, or lapse of this power generally has no tax consequences.

    c. A power to appoint property to or for the benefit of the powerholder, but this appointment is limited by so-called "ascertainable standards." These are standards relating to the health, education, support or maintenance of the powerholder. The exercise, lapse, or release of this power has no tax consequences.

    d. For income tax purposes, a power exercisable by the powerholder, acting alone, to vest corpus or income of a trust in the powerholder. This causes the powerholder to be treated as the owner of all or part of the trust for federal income tax purposes.

2. The mere existence of a general power of appointment (as considered for federal estate tax purposes) will cause property subject to it to be includable in a donee's estate. (A power granted in a will is generally considered to be created at the testator's death.[4] A power granted in an inter vivos instrument is considered created on the date the agreement becomes effective, usually the date it is executed.)

3. If a general power is exercised or released by a disposition that, if it were a transfer of property owned by the donee, would be includable in the donee's gross estate under the lifetime transfer rules, the property subject to the power will be includable. For example, where a beneficiary of a trust exercised a power to amend a trust by requiring mandatory payment of trust income to himself during his life instead of discretionary payments as provided by the trust, the trust property was included in his gross estate, being in the nature of a transfer of property with a retained life income interest.[5]

4. A release or lapse of a general power is treated the same as if the donee gave property he could have taken personally (or disposed of to the beneficiary of his choice) to the takers in default. For this reason, a release or lapse of a general power may be subject to gift taxation.[6] A qualified disclaimer of a general power of appointment (perhaps to avoid the tax on generation-skipping transfers) will probably avoid the gift tax problem.

5. Neither the mere existence of a special power of appointment nor the exercise, release, or lapse of such a right will cause inclusion in the donee's gross estate.

6. No gift tax is attracted by the exercise, release, or lapse of a special power of appointment.

ISSUES AND IMPLICATIONS IN COMMUNITY PROPERTY STATES

Since community property excludes property received by inheritance or gift, it would be very unusual for any property received (or given away by permitting a lapse) to be a community property right initially.

However, a community property agreement (some states require it to be in writing) which was all-inclusive, purporting to have both spouses hold as community property all assets they owned, can have the effect, in some states, of creating a gift by transmuting separate property into community property and thus resulting in a gift of one-half of the value from one spouse to the other. If the agreement can be interpreted as including rights of one spouse under a power of appointment, then the right may become community property, resulting in a gift equal to one-half the value of the right at the time of entering into the agreement. Because of the unlimited marital deduction, no federal gift tax would be triggered.

The more common problem encountered is to have the permitted appointee of the property ask to have the property transferred under the exercise of the power titled in the name of his spouse and himself, as community property, thus creating a gift to the other spouse of one-half the value of the property when the other spouse receives his one-half community interest in what was intended to be the sole property of the permitted appointee under the power. As was mentioned above, the unlimited marital deduction would eliminate any gift tax exposure under federal tax law. However, state gift tax law should be examined to see if any state gift tax would be caused by such event.

Where the holder of a "limited" or "special" power has freedom to choose, among the permitted appointees of a power (e.g., where the power includes "the issue of grantor and spouses of such issue"), then the power may be exercised to give each spouse an undivided interest without any gift involvement. The property could, under these circumstances, be appointed to the spouses as community property, joint tenants or tenants in common (each as to one-half), without any gift being recognized.

QUESTIONS AND ANSWERS

Question — How does the rule against perpetuities affect powers?

Answer — The common law rule against perpetuities states the principle that no interest in property is effective unless it *must* vest, if at all, not later than 21 years (plus, if applicable a gestation period) after some life or lives in being at the time an interest is created. In other words, the measuring period under the rule against perpetuities relates back to the creation of the power. (Some states, such as Pennsylvania, use "wait and see" rules. The interest will be valid *unless* it does not *actually* vest within the appropriate period.) In many states, if the donee *could,* in any fashion, make an appointment of the property under the donor's terms beyond the time period permitted by the Rule, the power is void. (The test is whether the power, by its terms, *will* be exercised within the allowable time period allowed by the Rule.)

Question — Is a power to consume, invade, or appropriate property for the benefit of the donee a general power for federal estate tax purposes if it is limited to an ascertainable standard relating to the health, education, support, or maintenance of the donee-decedent?

Answer — No. This makes such provisions extremely useful estate planning techniques for providing financial flexibility without consequent tax burden.[7] The power over income or corpus or both must be reasonably measurable in terms of the donee's needs for health, education, or support (or any combination of these needs). Maintenance and support mean the same thing and are not limited to bare necessities.

Proper wording is essential; if the holder of a power can use property for his "comfort, welfare, or happiness," the power is general and will cause the property interest to be subject to federal taxation.[8]

Question — Is property includable in a beneficiary's estate if an independent trustee has a discretionary right to make distributions to that person?

Answer — Where the donor gives an independent trustee discretionary authority to invade principal to meet a beneficiary's reasonable needs, that power will not cause property to be includable in the beneficiary's estate.[9] This is yet another way to provide additional security without adverse tax effects.

Question — Is property includable in a donee-decedent's estate where there is a requirement that the donee of a general power of appointment must give notice to the trustee before the exercise takes effect?

Answer — Whether or not the notice has been given before death and whether or not the power has actually been exercised, inclusion will result. The mere existence of a general power created after 1942 will cause inclusion of the property subject to the power.

Question — What is a "5 or 5 power"?

Answer — This is another valuable technique used by estate planners to provide flexibility and financial security for a beneficiary with little or no tax consequence. There is a de minimus rule (a rule that says in essence that for administrative reasons the tax law will ignore small amounts) that provides

> "property subject to a general power will be included in a donee-decedent's estate (or considered a taxable gift) only to the extent that the property which could have been appointed by the exercise of the power the donee allowed to lapse exceeds the greater of (a) $5,000 or (b) 5 percent of the total value of the fund subject to the power as measured at the time of the lapse."[10]

Stated another way, to the extent that a lapse of a general power within a calendar year exceeds the greater of (a) $5,000 or (b) 5 percent of the assets subject to the power, the *excess* is treated as a release of a general power and taxed accordingly. The excess may be treated as a gift subject to gift tax or as a transfer which may be subject to estate tax. To make certain that the limits set forth above are not breached, the right of invasion must be made noncumulative.

For example, Brian Gordon was the income beneficiary of a trust with assets of $200,000. The value of the trust remained constant. Brian was also given a noncumulative power (which he did not exercise and which therefore lapsed each year) to withdraw $10,000 of principal a year. On Brian's death, only the $10,000 subject to the power at the time of his death is included in his gross estate. The power that lapsed in prior years can be ignored, since the amount that could be appointed each year did not exceed the greater of $5,000 or 5 percent of the corpus, $200,000.

Jamie Gordon was the income beneficiary of a trust with assets of $80,000. She also had a noncumulative power (which she did not exercise) to withdraw $10,000 of principal a year. At the expiration of each year, Jamie is deemed to have released a general power to the extent of $5,000 (i.e., a $10,000 lapse minus the greater of $5,000 or 5 percent of $80,000 [$4,000]).

Assume that Jamie died in the sixth year of the trust's existence and that the value of the trust assets remained constant at $80,000. Each $5,000 released by Jamie constituted one-sixteenth (5,000/80,000) of the value of the trust assets. Therefore, Jamie's gross estate would include $35,000 on account of this trust. The $35,000 consists of $10,000 on account of the power held by the decedent at the time of her death and $25,000 (i.e., five-sixteenths of the $80,000 value of trust assets equals $25,000) on account of the lapse of the power in each of the five prior years. Each year's lapse is included in the decedent's gross estate to the extent of one-sixteenth of the value of the trust assets because it had the effect of a transfer with a retained life estate.

In addition to the inclusion for estate tax purposes, the failures to exercise the power would result in gifts to the remaindermen of the trust, with the reduction each year by the then value of Jamie's life estate in the lapsed amounts. The relative value of the life estate and remainder interest can be obtained from the government valuation tables in Appendix D.

Question — Is the creation of a special power to appoint trust property to lineal descendants of the transferor or power holder generally a good estate planning technique?

Answer — Most estate planners consider this special power to be an excellent planning technique. Since the appointees are someone other than the powerholder, estate, and creditors, it is a special power, and has no tax consequences to the powerholder. A note of caution, however — if the powerholder has an obligation to support permissible appointees, and the appointment could satisfy that support obligation, it might be classified as a general power. As a result, such a power should not be given to parents permitting them to use it to support their minor children.

One reason such a power is so useful is that it permits someone, generally the surviving spouse to alter the plan of ultimate distribution to take into consideration varying needs of the children and issue. If one adult child is very successful, and another is not, the appointment can be used to alter otherwise equal distributions to them.

An important use of this power is to permit planning for the generation-skipping transfer tax. The powerholder could "skip" generations where the property would otherwise be distributed to children, and shift it to grandchildren. If the property in question is exempt from generation-skipping transfer tax for reasons discussed in Chapter 14, this may be very beneficial.

Question — Can a special (limited) power cause gift tax problems?

Answer — Yes. When an income beneficiary of a trust who also holds a special power of appointment exercises that power during lifetime and in doing so terminates his life interest, there may be a taxable gift. The amount of the gift is the present value of the income interest forfeited by the life tenant-donor. Life income beneficiaries should therefore be careful in exercising a lifetime special power, since the IRS will argue that to the extent the exercise terminates the income interest and that interest goes to someone else, a transfer subject to gift tax has been made.[11]

Question — What is a "hanging power" and is it viable?

Answer — A "hanging power" creates a cumulative power in the beneficiary to appoint any lapsed property in excess of $5,000 per year by will at death.[12] The hanging power thus avoids a lapse of the excess amount by permitting the holder to exercise it in the future. If the trust is not terminated when the beneficiary dies, then he or she is in possession of the power at death. Property subject to that power is therefore includable in the estate for federal estate tax purposes. If the trust terminates before the power holder dies, there is no adverse estate tax result (although there may be gift tax consequences if unused withdrawal powers exceed a 5 or 5 limitation in the year of termination).

Under this hanging power approach, the withdrawal power — up to the 5 or 5 limitation — lapses in any given year. The excess withdrawal power is carried over to future years. In future years the carried-over withdrawals are lapsed to the extent of the 5 or 5 ceiling.

The following illustrates this strategy:

Year	Gift	With-drawal Powers	Lapses
1987	$10,000	$10,000	$5,000
1988	10,000	15,000	5,000
1989	-0-	10,000	5,000
1990	-0-	5,000	-0-
1991	-0-	-0-	-0-

There are a number of unresolved problems in using hanging powers. First, if the gifts continue over a number of years, the total withdrawal potential could be sizable, and a beneficiary might be tempted to make a withdrawal of the total amount available. Second, the cumulative, unused withdrawals are includable in the estate for estate tax purposes. Third, if life insurance is used, premiums are paid throughout the life of the policy, and the cumulative withdrawals may continue to increase. This can be ameliorated using a vanishing premium approach.

A private letter ruling held that the hanging power used by a taxpayer was not valid because it was the type of adjustment clause that was "contrary to public policy."[13] Experts don't totally agree that this spells the end of the hanging power, but suggest caution is advised.

ASRS: Sec. 46; ¶70; Sec.54, ¶44.3(i), Sec. 55, ¶57.5(e); Sec. 58.

Footnote References

Power of Appointment

1. Reg. §20.2041-1(b)(1).
2. IRC Sec. 2041.
3. Casner, *Estate Planning*, 695, Note 16 (3rd ed. 1961, 1977 Supp.).
4. Regs. §§20.2041-1(e), 25.2514-1(e).
5. IRC Sec. 2041(a)(2); Reg. §20.2041-3(d)(1). See also *Est. of Leo M. Gartland*, 34 TC 867 (1960), aff'd 293 F.2d 575 (7th Cir.), cert. den. 368 U.S. 954.
6. IRC Secs. 2514(a), 2514(b).
7. IRC Sec. 2041(b)(1)(A).
8. Regs. §§20.2041-1(c)(2), 25.2514-1(c)(2). See also Rev. Rul. 77-60, 1977-1 CB 282.
9. *Est. of Council*, 65 TC 594 (1975).
10. Regs. §§20.2041-3(d)(3), 25.2514-3(c)(4).
11. *Est. of Ruth B. Regester v. Comm.*, 83 TC 1 (1984).
12. Let. Rul. 8229097.
13. Let. Rul. 8901004.

Chapter 27

PRIVATE ANNUITY

WHAT IS IT?

A private annuity is an arrangement between two parties, neither of whom is an insurance company. The transferor (annuitant) conveys complete ownership of property to a transferee (obligor, the party obligated to make payments to the person who has transferred the property). The transferee, in turn, promises to make periodic payments to the transferor for a period of time. Usually, this period of time is the transferor's life or, in some cases, the transferor's life plus the life of his or her spouse.

There are basically two types of private annuities: (1) the single life annuity under which payments cease at the death of the annuitant; and (2) the joint and last survivor annuity, in which payments continue until the death of the last survivor, e.g., payments continue as long as either the husband or wife is alive. Generally, since payments under this type of arrangement will continue for a longer period of time than payments under a single life annuity, the amount paid each year will be less than that payable under a single life annuity.

WHEN IS THE USE OF SUCH A DEVICE INDICATED?

1. When your client would like to "spread" gains. For example, your client owns low tax basis property. He needs cash and wants to sell a particular asset but wants to avoid "bunching" gains into a single tax year. Generally, such a client will be in a high income tax bracket. A private annuity will enable him to spread his gain (and therefore defer tax) over a number of years. Private annuities have become a more valuable deferral tool since the attractiveness of installment sales has generally declined over the past several years.

2. When your client wishes to retire and shift control of a business to a family member or to a key employee. For example, assume Ed Staller is the sole shareholder of a close corporation. Ed has no heir other than his wife. He has two key employees in the business who are capable of managing it. Ed would like to sell them the business but he is concerned about adequate income upon his retirement. The key employees tell Ed they would like to buy the business but cannot afford to pay Ed in a lump sum. Ed could sell all of his stock to the two key employees and

in return they could promise to pay him an income for his life (and perhaps for his wife's life). The income would be based on the fair market value of the business.

3. When your client desires to remove a sizable asset, such as a business, from his or her estate for estate tax purposes. For example, Abe Marks is the sole shareholder of a closely-held real estate corporation. He has two daughters who are presently working in the business. He could sell the business to his daughters in return for their agreement to pay an annuity for his life only. This will result in a reduction in Abe's estate (and thus save estate taxes) because the value of the business will be removed from his estate for federal estate tax purposes. At Abe's death, annuity payments cease and neither the close corporation stock nor the promised payments will be in his estate.

   The income tax basis received by the daughters for the stock, *after Abe's death*, will be the amount of annuity payments they made to him during his lifetime. Until Abe's death, their basis will be the greater of the amount they paid him or the amount paid plus the present value of all the future payments that will be paid if Abe lives to his life expectancy. Initially, the transferee's basis is equal to the fair market value of the property transferred—assuming no gift is built into the transaction.

4. When your client wishes to obtain a fixed retirement income. For instance, Russ Miller is near retirement age and is a majority shareholder of a close corporation. Presently, his business does not provide pension, profit-sharing, or nonqualified deferred compensation benefits. He would like to retire but depends upon his salary from the business for most of his income. There are key employees present, but they do not have sufficient cash to buy him out. Russ could transfer the business to them in return for their promise to pay him a private annuity. This should yield a higher income than if he sold the business in an installment sale. Furthermore, if the annuity was measured by his lifetime, Russ could be sure he would never outlive the income.

5. When your client owns a large parcel of non-income producing property but is desirous of making it income producing. For example, your client is a widow. Her married son is currently providing $700 a month to

support her. The widow owns real estate which is currently not producing any income, but because of its choice location, is increasing substantially in value. It is expected that the full appreciation in the property will occur over the next 10 years.

A possible solution is for her son to discontinue gifts to his mother and, instead, his mother could transfer the real estate to him in exchange for a monthly lifetime income (say, $750 a month, assuming the present value of the land will support this payment). This will minimize the widow's estate, substantially reduce estate taxes at her death, and, at the same time, give her financial independence. The son becomes the immediate owner of the real estate. The growth in value (and increase in gross estate for tax purposes) will occur in the son's hands and not further increase his mother's estate.

6. When the client's estate is very large and the major or sole heir is a grandchild (or other individual two or more generations below that of the client). Because the private annuity is a sale and not a gift, it will not be subject to the generation-skipping transfer tax.

7. Where the purchaser's objective is to bar others from obtaining the property in question but he cannot afford to pay for the asset in a lump sum outright purchase.

WHAT ARE THE REQUIREMENTS?

1. Any type of property can be used. For example, it is possible to transfer a home, undeveloped real estate, stocks, or a business interest. Preferably, the property transferred will be income producing, rapidly appreciating, and will not be subject to depreciation or investment credit recapture or to indebtedness.

2. It is important to ascertain immediately the ability of the obligor to make annuity payments. If the transferee (the obligor) has substantial independent income, then almost any asset can serve as the property to be sold. But, if the transferee has little or no income, then the property sold should be either income producing or at least should be of a type that the obligor can easily and quickly resell or borrow against.[1]

3. It is extremely important that the obligor's promise be unsecured. If the promise of the obligor is secured, a taxable event will occur immediately on a transfer.[2] This means the annuitant will pay tax on the full amount of the gain. The gain is the difference between the amount realized (the present value of the right to the promised payments) and the transferor's adjusted basis in the property.

4. The transferee (obligor) should be a person not regularly engaged in issuing private annuities.[3] Generally, the obligor would be the natural object of the transferor's (annuitant's) bounty. For example, most private annuities are made between parents and children. The device may also be useful for transfers between employers and trusted key employees.

5. The annuity amount must be determined by measuring the fair market value of the property. We suggest an appraisal by independent court-recognized appraisal experts shortly before the execution of the private annuity.

6. Your client should be in a high estate tax bracket and should be desirous of reducing his or her estate and providing himself or herself with a lifetime income.

7. An agreement with a trust or corporation which has very few assets may be attacked by the IRS as a sham.

8. Payments must be completely contingent on the life (or lives) of the transferor(s).

HOW IT IS DONE — EXAMPLES

George Gargas is 65 years old. He owns farmland with a fair market value of $100,000. His basis is only $10,000. He would like to remove the land from his estate and have his son, Bill, own it. He does not, however, want to pay any gift taxes on the transfer.

A private annuity agreement would be drawn stating that the farmland was sold to Bill in return for Bill's promise to pay his father an income for life. At age 65, the father's life expectancy is 19.5 years (see Appendix D).

Assume the annuity agreement was signed in a month when the federal discount rate was 7.8%. The annual annuity generated by property worth $100,000 is $12,119. This is arrived at by dividing the fair market value of the property transferred by the present value factor for an annuity at the appropriate age (8.2514 — see single life table for 7.8% interest rate in Appendix D).

Out of the $12,119 he receives each year, Bill's father can exclude a portion ($509) from income. Assuming the annuity starting date is after 1986, Bill's father could exclude $509 each year *only* until his basis is recovered.

The exclusion ratio is determined by dividing the father's $10,000 basis in the property by his $236,321 expected return ($12,119 x 19.5 years). The excludable amount is then found by multiplying this exclusion ratio ($10,000/$236,321) by the $12,119 annual payment.

The $11,610 balance of each year's annuity payment ($12,119 minus $509) is taxable ($4,615 at capital gains rates and $6,995 as ordinary income).

As a second example consider Sam Jones, a widower who is 60 years of age, and whose estate includes stock in a closely held family corporation. He proposes to transfer a substantial number of shares to his two children, Junior Jones and Mary Smith, equally. After all discounts, the shares in question have been valued by appraisal at $1 million. Sam's income tax basis for these shares is $500,000. He will receive a life annuity in exchange, as calculated below.

SAM JONES - PRIVATE ANNUITY
PRIVATE ANNUITY

Transfer Date	1/1995
Sec. 7520 Rate	8.6%
Fair Market Value of Property	$1,000,000
Annual Payout	$116,923
Client's Basis	$500,000
Payment Periods in Year	1
Payments made at Beginning or End of Period	End
Age of Annuitant	60
Annuity Factor	8.5526
Payout Frequency Factor	1.0000
Life Expectancy	24.2 Years
Reg. 1.72-5(a)(2) Life Exp. Adj. Factor	-0.5
Adjusted Expectancy	23.7 Years
Tax Free Portion	$21,097
Capital Gain Portion	$21,097
Ordinary Income Portion	$74,730

Courtesy: NumberCruncher software

WHAT ARE THE TAX IMPLICATIONS?

1. For federal estate tax purposes, where the annuity ceases at the death of the transferor, the value of the property sold to the transferee-obligor in return for his promise to pay the annuity is excludable from the annuitant-transferor's estate. This is because property sold by a decedent for full and adequate consideration before death is not taxable in his estate.[4]

   Likewise, the value of the promised payment will be excludable. This is because the selling price in a private annuity arrangement is an income which will expire (in the case of a single life annuity) upon the annuitant's death.

   Note that this is not the case with a joint and survivor annuity. In a joint and last survivor annuity, payments will continue until the death of the last survivor. So if the annuitant's spouse survives, the present value of future payments to her will be includable in the transferor-annuitant's estate (assuming he was sole owner of the property that was transferred in return for the joint and survivor annuity payments).[5] However, because of the unlimited estate tax marital deduction, there would be no federal estate tax.

2. Each annuity payment made by the transferee-obligor to the transferor-annuitant is treated partially as a tax-free return of capital, partially as a capital gain (currently taxed at ordinary rates) and the balance as ordinary income.[6] If the annuity starting date is after 1986, once the transferor-annuitant has recovered his basis, the entire payment will be taxed as ordinary income. The obligor is not allowed a deduction for any payments made to the annuitant.[7]

3. There will be no gift if the annual payments made by the obligor to the annuitant are actuarially determined to be equal to the amount of the property sold. However, if the value of the promise made by the transferee-obligor is less than the value of the property transferred, the difference will constitute a gift by the annuitant-transferor.[8] (If the annuity were a joint and survivor annuity, the value of the survivor annuity would be a gift from the transferor. Since it would be a gift of a future interest, it would not qualify for the gift tax annual exclusion.[9] If the donee were the transferor's spouse, the gift may qualify for the gift tax marital deduction.[10])

   For example, assuming a 7.8% discount rate the government valuation tables indicate an annuity valuation of 8.2514 for a person age 65. If such an individual transfers property with a fair market value of $100,000, a fair exchange would be a life annuity of $12,119 per year ($100,000 divided by 8.2514). But if annuity payments were actually set at, say, $8,000 per year, which has a present value of about $66,011, the difference, $33,989, would constitute a gift from the transferor to the transferee in the year the agreement was signed.

4. The transferee receives a "temporary basis" in the property equal to the value for calculation of the annuity. This provides a means for immediately increasing the basis for depreciation or depletion and can be a very significant benefit. The same basis is available for sale of the property, leaving little, if any, gain to be then taxed.

   However, upon the transferor's death, the basis is adjusted to what the transferee actually paid in annuity payments. If he has retained the property, the only concern for imposition of income tax would be his having depreciated the property below his "adjusted basis". In that event he would realize a gain to the extent of the difference. However, if he had sold the property for a price showing the basis at fair market value and that

Figure 27.1

TAXATION OF SELLER UNDER PRIVATE ANNUITY	
A. Recovery of Basis (cost) Element	Tax Free
B. Gain Element	Capital gain (currently taxed at ordinary rates)
C. Income Element	Ordinary income

**GENERAL FORMULA FOR
COMPUTING ANNUAL PAYMENT — TAX FREE, GAIN AND
ORDINARY INCOME ELEMENTS**

STEP 1.
Compute Annual Payment

$$\frac{\text{F.M.V. of Property Transferred}}{\text{Present Value of Annuity Factor}}$$

STEP 2.
Compute Exclusion Ratio

$$\frac{\text{Seller's Cost Basis}}{\substack{\text{expected return} \\ \text{(annual payment x life expectancy)}}}$$

STEP 3.
Compute Excludible Amount

Exclusion ratio x Annual Annuity

STEP 4.
Compute Gain Element

(until total gain recognized)

$$\frac{\text{Present value of annuity minus property's basis}}{\text{life expectancy of annuitant}}$$

STEP 5.
Compute Ordinary Income Element

Annual Payment
minus sum of   (a) excludible amount and
   (b) gain amount

amount is substantially more than the amount actually paid, the excess will be then immediately taxed to the transferee.

In GCM 39503 the income tax treatment of a private annuity was summarized as follows:

"The income tax treatment afforded unsecured private annuity payments is set forth in Rev. Rul. 69-74, 1969-1 CB 43, which applies the provisions of section 72 to private annuity transactions.

"In Rev. Rul. 69-74, a male taxpayer, aged 74, transferred property (a capital asset) having an adjusted basis of $20,000 and a fair market value of $60,000 to a family member in 1966, in exchange for that member's legally enforceable promise to pay the taxpayer a life annuity of $7,200 per annum, payable

in equal monthly installments of $600. The ruling sets out the following four principles to be applied in determining the tax consequences of such transactions:

"(1) The gain realized on the transaction is determined by comparing the transferor's basis in the property with the present value of the annuity. ...

"(2) The excess of the fair market value of the property transferred over the present value of the annuity acquired constitutes a gift for Federal gift tax purposes where the transaction is not an ordinary business transaction within the meaning of sections 25.2511-1(g)(1) and 25.2512-8 of the Gift Tax Regulations.

"(3) The gain should be reported ratably over the period of years measured by the annuitant's life expectancy and only from that portion of the annual proceeds which is includable in gross income by virtue of the application of section 72 of the 1954 Code. This will enable the annuitant to realize his gain on the same basis that he realizes the return of his capital investment.

"(4) The investment in the contract for purposes of section 72 of the 1954 Code is the transferor's basis in the property transferred. Since the amount of the gain is not taxed in full at the time of the transaction, such amount does not represent a part of the "premiums or other consideration paid" for the annuity contract.

"Rev. Rul. 69-74, 1969-1 CB at 43, 44. Hence Rev. Rul. 69-74 allocates each annuity payment between a capital component, one part of which is treated as a return of basis and the other part as capital gain, and an annuity component, which is treated as ordinary income.

"The first step in determining how to tax the annuitant/transferor is to determine the value of the annuity. This is done by using tables set forth in Treas. Reg. §20.2031-10, which control valuations subsequent to Dec. 31, 1970. As stated above, if the value of the annuity is less then the value of the property transferred, a gift has occurred which will be Taxed as such.

"The next step is to determine the allocation of each payment among capital gain, return of basis, and annuity income. Section 72(b) provides that gross income does not include that part of any amount received as an annuity which bears the same ratio to such amount as the investment in the contract bears to the expected return under the contract. According to Rev. Rul.69-74, the investment in the contract is the transferor's basis in the transferred property. The exclusion ratio, i.e., the amount of each payment deemed a return of investment in the contract and therefore not taxed, is the ratio of the transferor's basis in the transferred   property to the expected return of the contract (life expectancy multiplied by the amount of the annuity). This ratio is applied to each payment received, and that amount is excluded from income.

"The next determination to be made is the capital gain portion of each payment. That is calculated by determining the difference between the annuitant's basis in the transferred property and the value of the annuity, i.e., the annuitant's expected return. Such gain will be recognized ratably over the annuitant/

transferor's life expectancy. The remainder of the payment represents the annuity amount, which is taxed at ordinary income rates for the duration of the annuity.

"If an annuitant dies before the expiration of his or her life expectancy, a ratable portion of gain will have been recognized without a full recovery of basis. On the other hand, if an annuitant lives beyond his or her life expectancy, Rev. Rul. 69-74 provides that the excluded portion forever remains excludable even though the annuitant's basis in the transferred property has been recovered in full. Rev. Rul. 69-74 does provide, however, that once the capital gain portion is recovered in full, it is converted to ordinary income if the seller lives beyond his or her life expectancy.

"Note that secured annuities, unlike unsecured private annuities, bring forth immediate recognition of gain, and thus are not eligible for the treatment provided in Rev. Rul. 69-74."

5. According to GCM 39503, the gift tax consequences of a private annuity arrangement will generally be as follows:

"Rev. Rul. 69-74, 1969-1 CB 43, prescribes the method for calculating whether a gift tax will be imposed in a private annuity situation. The ruling states that `the excess of the fair market value of the property transferred over the present value of the annuity acquired constitutes a gift for Federal gift tax purposes where a transaction is not an ordinary business transaction within the meaning of sections 25.2511-1(g)(1) and 25.2512-8 of the Gift Tax Regulations.' Alternatively, there is a taxable gift by the transferee to the transferor when the fair market value of the property transferred is less than the present value of the annuity. To value the private annuity, the taxpayer is required to use the mortality tables set forth in Treas. Reg. §20.2031-10. See Rev. Rul. 80-80, 1980-1 CB 194."

6. According to GCM 39503, the estate tax consequences of a private annuity arrangement will generally be as follows:

"A private annuity also should not be included in the transferor's gross estate for Federal estate tax purposes. Thus, the estate tax consequences of a private annuity and an installment obligation with a death terminating provision are identical in our opinion."

Thus, care should be exercised in making decisions to sell property recently acquired on a private annuity basis.

HOW CAN LIFE INSURANCE ENHANCE THIS TOOL?

The obligation of the transferee must be unsecured. This means that no specific assets are set aside to protect the transferor in case the transferee defaults. But at the death of the transferee-obligor, the obligation passes to his or her estate. The question then arises as to how to eliminate or minimize the possible hardships on the transferee's family and heirs. (The estate of the transferee will still have to continue promised payments for as long as the transferor-annuitant lives.)

Looking at the same problem from another viewpoint, how do you avoid disrupting the financial security of the transferor-annuitant in case the transferee dies before the transferor? Perhaps the best answer is life insurance. Life insurance can be obtained on the life of the transferee-obligor. It might be owned by and payable to the obligor's spouse (or irrevocable trust for her benefit).

There should be no formal connection between the life insurance and the private annuity; otherwise, the obligation of the transferee might be considered "secured." When the income and estate tax free proceeds are received, the spouse will have cash to (a) continue payments to the transferor, and (b) pay estate taxes caused by the inclusion of the private annuity property in the transferee's estate.[11]

Occasionally, there is a third reason that life insurance may be useful in conjunction with a private annuity. Assume a widow owns a business and has two adult sons and two adult daughters. How can she transfer the business to her sons but at the same time avoid disinheriting her daughters if she does not have considerable other assets?

Life insurance can be used to "equalize" the inheritance. The widow would sell the business to her sons in return for a private annuity. The daughters could be named owners, premium payors, and beneficiaries of a policy (or policies) on their mother's life. Annual gifts by the widow to the daughters could be used to provide premium payments. The widow could obtain the cash to give to her daughters from the private annuity income. When the widow died, each daughter could receive—in the form of tax-free life insurance proceeds—an amount equivalent to what she would have received if the business were divided in four equal shares. (Actually, since the sons are paying their mother for the business, the amount the daughters are to receive might be considerably less than half the value of the business.)

IMPLICATIONS AND ISSUES IN COMMUNITY PROPERTY STATES

In a community property jurisdiction, since the property is owned one-half by each spouse, the practitioner can either arrange a private annuity sale on a joint and survivor annuity basis, or on the basis of a separate annuity contract for each community half of the husband and wife, respectively. If the joint and survivor annuity is used, the total amount payable to the husband and wife is somewhat lower at the beginning than would be the total paid under separate annuities, but that payment remains the same at the death of the first spouse to die. Under the separate annuity approach, at the death of one spouse, the payments to that spouse cease, and the survivor does not have any benefit continuing under the decedent's annuity.

There are implications in community property states also from the standpoint of the purchaser of the property under a private annuity contract. A typical arrangement is to have a private annuity contract between the parents and a child (rather than a child and his spouse). However, it is unlikely that the property acquired by the child will generate sufficient income to make the private annuity payments. If the child uses his earnings to make up the shortfall, the child's spouse could either be acquiring a community property interest in the property purchased, or could be making a gift to the child as each annuity payment is made. Consideration should be given to this aspect before the annuity contract is entered into.

QUESTIONS AND ANSWERS

Question — What are the alternatives to a private annuity?

Answer — One alternative to a private annuity is the installment sale. However, if an annuitant were to die shortly after the sale took place, the death tax results would differ substantially. Since an installment sale is often evidenced by a series of notes, the present value of those notes would be includable in the estate of the seller. But under the private annuity arrangement where payments are to cease on the death of the annuitant, the entire amount of the transferred property could be excluded from the estate of the annuitant at his or her death.

Another disadvantage of an installment sale is that an installment note bearing interest would cause a sizable portion of each payment in the early years to be considered interest to the seller. Where the subject of the sale is publicly traded stock, the installment sale would not defer taxation. The cost of an installment sale is in many cases higher since investment interest is deductible only to the extent of investment income if the asset sold was considered an investment.

Question — What basis does the transferee have in the property he now owns?

Answer — In the case of a private annuity, the transferee-obligor has, as his new tax basis, the fair market value of the property which is the actuarial value of future payments.[12] It is because his basis is the fair market value of the property at the time the agreement is executed that the private annuity is so useful. The new owner can immediately sell the property and reinvest the proceeds in more liquid or higher yielding assets. He does not have to worry about tax on gains which the transferor-annuitant would otherwise have had to face. The basis is "stepped-up," not carried over, for purposes of determining the tax on gain if the property is sold or depreciated. This would enable a fully depreciated property (such as an apartment or office building) to receive a new (fair market value) basis for depreciation by the transferee.[13] (But be aware of potential recapture problems where accelerated depreciation has been used by the transferor.)

Question — What happens to the transferee's basis if the annuitant dies prematurely?

Answer — The transferee may have to readjust his basis or report a gain. If the annuitant dies before the length of his life expectancy according to government tables, the transferee-obligor must make a downward adjustment to his basis for the property. His basis becomes the amount of payments he actually has made. However, if he had sold the property before the annuitant's death, he must report as taxable capital gain the excess of the sales price over the actual annuity payments made.[14]

Question — Can the property that will be the subject of the private annuity be placed in escrow as security for the private annuity?

Answer — A promise to pay a private annuity in return for an appreciated security or other asset does not cause the transferor-annuitant to realize an immediate gain for only one reason—the value of the buyer's promise to pay is deemed to be too contingent to value. In other words, the annuity rules have been allowed in private annuity situations only because of the uncertainty as to whether or not the one agreeing to make payments will be able to make them as agreed when the time for payment actually arrives.

Where there is any type of security that will be activated to protect the transferor in the event of the transferee's default, a completed sale for tax purposes occurs. This makes the entire gain element taxable immediately rather than taxable ratably over the annuity period.

Question — Can the private annuity be used in situations other than between family members?

Answer — Yes. One possible use for a private annuity lies in the stock redemption area. For example, assume a corporation is owned and operated by an elderly widow and her son-in-law. Each owns 50 percent of the corporation's stock. The corporation's financial health is strong. The widow would like to retire but needs the assurance of a steady income. The son-in-law is in a high income tax bracket but is personally "cash poor."

The corporation could purchase the widow's stock in return for the corporation's promise to pay her an income for life. The transaction would give the son-in-law 100 percent ownership of the corporation. No gift tax would be payable assuming the amount of the annual annuity payment was derived from the appropriate government tables and as the result of an arm's length transaction.

If the son-in-law had no primary and unconditional personal obligation to purchase the stock, the use of corporate dollars to effect the redemption will not result in a dividend to him. The widow should receive "sale or exchange" treatment if the redemption completely eliminates her interest (attribution rules do not cause problems in this factual situation but extreme care should be taken before a redemption of stock is affected in any family-owned corporation).

Question — What happens if the annuitant outlives his life expectancy?

Answer — The transferee must continue to make the annuity payments and such payments continue for the life of the annuitant. This is one of the risks involved in a private annuity; the actual amount to be paid by the transferee may exceed the expected return (the annual payments multiplied by the annuitant's life expectancy).

Question — In a previous example in which a 65 year old individual transferred property worth $100,000 in return for an annuity of $12,119 per year, the annuitant's expected return in that example was $236,321. If the individual lived for the full 19.5-year life expectancy, how can it be said that he saved federal estate taxes by transferring property worth $100,000?

Answer — The property transferred is the fair market value of the property on the date of the transfer which in this example occurs 19.5 years prior to the annuitant's death, according to life expectancy tables. Assuming that the fair market value of the property continues to increase at a net rate of 7 percent per year, on the projected date of the annuitant's death in 19.5 years, the fair market value of the property would be $386,970.

The Tools and Techniques of Estate Planning

The entire $236,321 of expected return would not be included in the annuitant's estate since a portion of that amount must be used by the transferor-annuitant to pay tax at ordinary income rates. The annuitant could make sizable gifts to decrease the net amount of cash realized as a result of receiving the annuity payments. In addition, the annuitant will most probably spend the majority of the annuity payments.

Question — If an annuitant lives beyond his life expectancy, what are the tax consequences?

Answer — Where the annuity starting date is after 1986, Code Section 72(b) provides that if an annuitant outlives his life expectancy (and thus has recovered his basis), then the remaining payments will be taxed entirely as ordinary income.

Question — In arranging a private annuity transaction, is it wise to tie the annuity payments to the income generated by the transferred property?

Answer — No. If this is done, the property may be brought back into the transferor's estate at death as a transfer with a retained life estate under Code section 2036.[15]

Question — Can a joint and survivor private annuity be designed?

Answer —Yes. Since the advent of an unlimited estate tax marital deduction between spouses, the joint and survivor annuity has become a more attractive planning technique. It has the advantage of providing security for the surviving spouse with no additional federal estate tax cost at either spouse's death (but may trigger state death taxes since most states do not have an unlimited marital deduction). At the time of the exchange, the gift of the survivor annuity may qualify for the gift tax marital deduction as qualified terminable interest property.[16] A second advantage is that the amount payable by the transferee each year is lower than it would be in a single life private annuity. This makes it easier for a purchaser to meet annual obligations under the private annuity.

For example, assume a client age 65, a spouse age 62, property with a fair market value of $100,000, and a 7.8% interest rate. The annual payment would be only $9,912 for a joint and survivor private annuity. This is $2,207 less than the $12,119 payment for a single life annuity for a 65-year-old client.

Question — Will the use of a trust automatically cause the loss of the tax benefits of the private annuity?

Answer — No. but it is likely that the IRS will treat property for annuity exchanges involving trusts as if the transaction created a grantor trust rather than a sale. Therefore, all the income of the trust would, if the service is successful, be taxed to the seller (grantor, according to the IRS) as owner.

But this harsh result is neither automatic nor certain. The Ninth Circuit Court of Appeals checks to see if annuity payments are tied to the income of the trust, how payments are calculated, and what role the taxpayer takes in trust investment decisions. Case law[17] indicates that client success is most likely where (1) payment is computed by dividing the fair market value of the property by the appropriate annuity factor determined from the government's own tables, (2) the trust is obligated to pay the annuity without regard to the value of the property held in the trust or the income produced by trust assets, and (3) the grantor holds no powers to manage the trust or control the trustee.

The Tax Court has indicated that the annuity may lack substance where the transferor-annuitant retains too much control, the trustee is not independent, and there is a tie-in between the annuity payments and the income produced by the transferred property.[18] In another decision[19], the Tax Court considered the following factors:

1. The relationship between the creation of the trust and the transfer of property to it.

2. The relationship between the income from the property and the annuity payments.

3. The degree of control the annuitant exercises over the property.

4. The nature and extent of the annuitant's continuing interest in the property.

5. The source of the annuity payment.

6. The arm's length nature of the annuity-sale.

Question — May the life expectancy tables used in the IRS regulations always be relied upon in structuring a private annuity transaction?

Answer — The IRS and the courts are indicating that the life expectancy tables may not be used where there is substantial evidence that the annuitant has a very short life expectancy. In general, the courts and the IRS have taken the position the tables must be used unless death is "imminent."[20] However, the courts seemed to limit this to situations where the annuitant was not expected to live over a year.[21] More recently, the IRS has sought a broader rule, and has had success in at least one case.[22]

It appears the IRS is also seeking changes in the mortality tables themselves to reflect this position. They seek to disregard the tables where an individual who is known to have an incurable illness or other deteriorating physical condition is considered terminally ill if there is at least a 50% probability that he will die within one year.[23]

ASRS, Sec. 51.

Footnote References

Private Annuity

1. Where a sale is made to children through a private annuity, they or the trustee representing them should have a source of capital or income — other than solely the income from the transferred property — from which to make required payments, otherwise the IRS could argue that the seller's income is in reality inextricably tied to the success of the enterprise.

2. *Comm. v. Kann*, 174 F.2d 357 (3rd Cir. 1949); *J. Darsie Lloyd v. Comm.*, 33 BTA 905 (1936) acq., 1950-2 CB 3; *Est. of Bell v. Comm.*, 60 TC 469 (1973); *212 Corp. v. Comm.*, 70 TC 788 (1978).

3. Rev. Rul. 62-136, 1962-2 CB 12.

4. IRC Sec. 2033; *Fidelity-Philadelphia Trust Co. v. Smith*, 356 US 274 (1958).

5. IRC Secs. 2039(a), 2039(b).

6. IRC Sec. 72; Rev. Rul. 69-74, 1969-1 CB 43.

7. *F. A. Gillespie & Sons Co. v. Comm.*, 154 F.2d 913 (10th Cir. 1946) (cert. den., reh. den.); *Steinbach Kresge Co. v. Sturgess*, 33 F. Supp. 897 (D.C., N.J., 1940).

8. IRC Sec. 2512(b). To value annuity promise see tables contained in IRS Notice 89-60 and formulas in Notice 89-24. But see also Appendix D.

9. Reg. §25.2503-3(c), Example (2); Rev. Rul. 70-514, 1970-2 CB 198; Let. Rul. 8811017.

10. IRC Sec. 2523(f)(6).

11. IRC Sec. 2033.

12. Rev. Rul. 55-119, 1955-1 CB 352.

13. Rev. Rul. 55-119, 1955-1 CB 352.

14. Rev. Rul. 55-119, 1955-1 CB 352.

15. See *Est. of Cornelia B. Schwartz*, 9 TC 229, acq.; Rev. Rul. 68-183, 1968-1 CB 308.

16. IRC Sec. 2523(f)(6).

17. *LaFarge v. Comm.*, 689 F.2d 845 (9th Cir. 1982), aff'g in part and rev'g in part 73 TC 40 (1979); *Stern v. Comm.*, 84-2 USTC ¶9949 (9th Cir. 1984), rev'g and remanding 77 TC 614 (1981); *Fabric Est. v. Comm.*, 83 TC 932 (1984).

18. See, for example, *Weigl*, 84 TC 1192 (1985).

19. *Stern v. Comm.*, 77 TC 614, rev'd. and remanded 747 F.2d 555 (9th Cir. 1984).

20. Rev. Rul. 80-80, 1980-1 CB 194; *Estate of Nellie H. Jennings* 10 TC 323 (1948).

21. *Estate of Fabric*, 83 TC 932 (1984).

22. *Estate of McLendon*, TC Memo 1993-459; Let. Rul. 9504004.

23. Prop. Reg. §20.7520-3.

Chapter 28

PROFIT-SHARING / 401(k) / PENSION PLAN

WHAT IS IT?

A profit-sharing plan, as its name implies, is a plan for sharing employer profits with employees. A profit-sharing plan need not provide a definite, predetermined formula for determining the amount of profits to be shared. However, there must be a definite formula for allocating these profits to each participant. But absent a definite contribution formula, an employer must make recurring and substantial contributions to a profit-sharing plan.[1]

A pension plan is a retirement plan established and maintained by an employer for the benefit of the employer's employees and their beneficiaries. The primary purpose of a pension plan must be to provide benefits for the employees upon their retirement because of age or disability.

A 401(k) plan, also known as a Cash or Deferred Arrangement (CODA), is actually a feature which is part of a profit-sharing plan, stock bonus plan, and, in some cases which are beyond the scope of this book, a money purchase pension plan. CODAs provide an employee an option to choose whether his employer should pay a certain amount to him in cash or contribute that amount to a qualified profit-sharing or stock bonus plan on his behalf. A plan which contains a 401(k) feature must include the customary provisions required of all defined contribution plans.

WHEN IS THE USE OF SUCH A DEVICE INDICATED?

1. When your client would like to be sure of a steady, adequate, and secure personal retirement income.

2. When your client would like to set aside money for retirement on a tax deductible basis.

3. When your client wants to reward long-service employees and provide for their economic welfare after retirement.

4. When your client would like to put his or her business in a better competitive position for attracting, retaining, and eventually retiring personnel.

5. When your client's corporation is about to run into an accumulated earnings tax problem. The corporation would like to "siphon off" some of its earnings and profits and reduce or eliminate the threat of a penalty tax on unreasonably accumulated earnings.

6. When your client has employees who would like to defer compensation on an elective, pre-tax basis to a qualified retirement plan.

WHAT ARE THE REQUIREMENTS?

1. The plan must be for the exclusive benefit of the corporation's employees.[2]

2. The primary purpose of the plan must be to offer employees a retirement benefit (or, in the case of a profit-sharing plan, provide employees with a share in the company's profits).

3. The plan provisions must set forth, in writing, a description of the plan and details of the plan.[3] Furthermore, details of the plan must be communicated to employees.

4. The plan must be permanent. This means the plan must contain no set termination date.

5. The plan must not discriminate in favor of highly-compensated employees. Plans which are "top heavy," that is, plans which provide more than 60% of aggregate accumulated benefits or account balances for current key employees, must meet stringent vesting, minimum benefit, and other rules.

6. The plan must meet minimum age and service standards, minimum coverage requirements and a minimum participation test.

7. The plan must meet minimum vesting standards and provide that benefits or contributions do not exceed the Section 415 limits.

8. Distributions generally must begin to *all* participants by the April 1 following the year of attaining age 70½. However, (1) employees who are not 5 percent owners and who attained age 70½ before 1988 and (2) participants in governmental or church plans need not begin distributions until April 1 of the year following the year they retire, if that is later.[4]

9. Although 401(k) plans are entitled to favorable tax treatment, they must meet certain special qualification requirements in addition to the regular plan qualification requirements, to get it. The special qualification requirements are as follows:

(a) The plan must permit the employees to elect either to have the employer make a contribution on his behalf or to receive an equivalent amount in cash.

(b) Unlike a typical profit-sharing or stock bonus plan, a 401(k) plan cannot allow employees to receive a distribution of funds held in the plan which are attributable to elective deferrals merely because of the lapse of a fixed number of years or the completion of a specified period of participation.[5]

(c) The employee's rights to benefits derived from elective contributions, as well as from qualified matching and qualified nonelective contributions used to satisfy the ADP test, are nonforfeitable.[6]

(d) The employer cannot condition the availability of any other benefit (except employer matching contributions) on whether an employee elects to make elective contributions under the CODA or to receive cash in lieu thereof.[7]

(e) The plan must meet special nondiscrimination tests with respect to the amount of elective contributions made to the plan each year. See QUESTIONS AND ANSWERS for more details.

(f) Unlike a typical profit-sharing or stock bonus plan, the CODA cannot require, as a condition of participation, that an employee complete more than one year of service for the employer maintaining the plan.

(g) The amount of the elective contributions made to the plan on behalf of a participant cannot exceed $7,000. The $7,000 limitation on elective contributions is adjusted annually based on a cost-of-living index.[8] For 1995 the limit is $9,240.

The requirements for pension and profit-sharing plans listed above are not exhaustive. For example, other requirements include meeting minimum standards on participation, coverage, and funding.[9]

There are two different types of pension plans. The first is known as a fixed or defined benefit plan. Here, definitely determinable retirement benefits are computed using a predetermined benefit formula established when the plan is created. Each employee is promised a specific amount of retirement benefits. The employer's contribution to provide that benefit is based on an actuarial determination of the cost of benefits promised. In other words, contributions are based on benefits and the limits on contributions are based on the benefit they will produce.

A money purchase pension plan, also known as a defined contribution plan, bases the retirement benefit upon an employer's commitment to make an annual contribution. Benefits are directly dependent upon the length of time an employee participates in the plan and the amount of money contributed on his behalf each year (plus interest and appreciation on such funds). In a money purchase pension plan, therefore, the employer is not obligated to provide a specific amount of retirement benefits.

A profit-sharing plan is an arrangement by which an employer shares a portion of corporate profits with employees. Contributions can be made even if there are no profits. It is a type of defined contribution plan. For all defined contribution plans, the limits on annual contributions to the plans are based on a percentage of salary, which directly limits the contributions. There is no limit to the benefits produced by the plan.

The corporation can distribute these payments currently in the form of cash bonuses, or profits can be shared on a deferred basis through contributions to a profit-sharing plan.

In deferred profit-sharing, contributions are made into an irrevocable trust. Funds then accumulate and are distributed to participants, usually as a retirement benefit, at some later date. Under a profit-sharing plan, participants can also receive benefits in the event of a termination other than retirement, such as death, layoff, or disability.

One strong point often related to a plan in which profits are to be shared is that the employer need not make a contribution in years in which no profits are earned. (A substantial amount of contribution flexibility is also possible in a well-designed pension plan.)

A 401(k) plan may stand on its own (e.g., only permit elective contributions) or it may permit other types of employer contributions and/or employee contributions. Under this type of arrangement, an employee can elect to have the employer make an elective contribution on his behalf in the form of a compensation reduction agreement under which the employee elects to reduce cash compensation and to have the employer contribute such amount to the plan on the employee's behalf. In some cases the employer may agree to make a contribution based on the employee's contribution, e.g. 50 cents from the employer for every dollar put in by the employee from his or her compensation.

The following comments will discuss the basic principles of eligibility, vesting, contributions, actuarial assumptions, death benefits, retirement age, and social security integration for plans in general. There are also special rules for "top heavy" plans, see below.

Eligibility

A qualified corporate retirement plan may not use an age or service requirement which would exclude any full-time employee who has attained age 21, or who has completed one year of service, whichever is later.[10] If there is 100 percent immediate vesting, a two-year waiting period is permitted.[11]

A plan must be nondiscriminatory in its coverage of employees. (It is permissible to favor rank and file employees.) A plan will qualify if the plan benefits at least 70% of the nonhighly compensated employees, or a percentage of nonhighly compensated employees which is at least 70% of the percentage of highly compensated employees benefiting under the plan.[12] Alternatively, a plan will qualify if it does not discriminate in favor of highly compensated employees and the average benefit percentage for the nonhighly compensated employees is at least 70% of the average benefit percentage for the highly compensated employees.[13] Additionally, each qualified plan must cover, on each day of the plan year, the lesser of 50 employees or 40% or more of all employees of the employer.[14]

A plan may exclude part-time and seasonal employees, who are those employees who work less than 1,000 hours in a 12-month period.[15] Also, a collective bargaining unit may be excluded if the union prefers not to be covered under a plan and the decision is made as the result of good-faith bargaining.[16]

Vesting

Minimum vesting standards must be met by all plans. Vesting refers to nonforfeitability of benefits by covered employees. The general rule is that the benefits attributable to employee contributions must always be 100 percent vested.[17] Likewise, with respect to a 401(k) plan, an employee's rights to benefits derived from elective contributions, as well as from qualified matching and qualified nonelective contributions used to satisfy the actual deferral percentage (ADP) test, must be 100 percent vested at all times.[18]

Full vesting is required (a) after 5 years or (b) after 7 years under an accelerated graduated vesting schedule.[19]

The following chart shows the required vesting percentages under both methods at various years of service:

Years of Service	(a)	(b)
1	0%	0%
2	0	0
3	0	20
4	0	40
5	100	60
6		80
7		100

A plan must take into account all years of service (generally 1,000 hours in a plan year) completed after the employee attains age 18 for vesting purposes.

Contributions and Benefits

The law imposes certain limitations on contributions and benefits.

Defined Contribution Type Plans

Defined contribution type plans include money purchase pension plans, profit-sharing plans, stock bonus plans, 401(k) plans, ESOPs, thrift plans, and target or assumed benefit plans.

Defined contribution type pension plans have an annual additions limit equal to the lesser of (a) 25 percent of compensation or (b) $30,000. The annual additions dollar limit for contributions to defined contribution plans is $120,000 for 1995.[20]

In the case of a profit-sharing plan, an employer is allowed a maximum deduction equal to 15 percent of the total compensation of plan participants.[21]

Employees are typically not required to contribute their own funds as a condition of plan participation but plans can provide for voluntary contributions. Thrift plans commonly do require employees to contribute and require the employer to make matching contributions.

Defined contribution plans may be integrated with Social Security based on the Social Security tax (excluding hospital premium) for the current year.

Disabled plan participants (other than a disabled employee who is highly compensated) can receive the benefit of an employer contribution to a defined contribution plan based on the annualized compensation of the employee during his last year of employment. All such contributions must be immediately 100 percent vested.[22]

Defined Benefit Plan

A defined benefit plan is a plan which provides a fixed or determinable benefit such as 40 percent of an employee's final three years average salary or one percent times final three years average salary times number of years of plan participation or service with the employer.

The maximum normal retirement benefit for a defined benefit plan, based on Social Security retirement age, is the lesser of (a) 100 percent of the highest three consecutive years of average compensation, or (b) $90,000. The dollar limitation for 1995 is $120,000, as a result of the annual cost-of-living adjustments. There will be greater restrictions on maximum benefits paid before the Social Security age of retirement.[23]

The $90,000 limit was effective for years beginning after December 31, 1982. Prior to TEFRA, the dollar limit had reached $136,425. If benefits were accrued in excess of $90,000 in the case of plans which were in existence on July 1, 1982, they do not have to be reduced and can be maintained as the maximum limit instead of $90,000. However, benefits accrued after December 31, 1982 are subject to the $90,000 limit (limit for 1995 is $120,000).

The above limits are based on the annual payment which, with interest compounded until the retirement date of the employee, will create a fund sufficient to provide the described benefit to the employee for his actuarial life expectancy.

The benefit must be reduced pro-rata if the employee has less than 10 years of plan participation with the employer.[24]

A $10,000 minimum annual benefit may always be provided for an employee who has never been covered by a defined contribution plan maintained by the employer regardless of the rules mentioned above.[25] But this amount must be reduced pro-rata if the employee has served the employer for less than 10 years at retirement.[26]

All the limits above must be actuarially reduced to reflect any post retirement death benefits except in the case of a qualified joint and survivor annuity.[27]

Further reductions must be made in the $120,000 limit where an employee retires before normal retirement age for full Social Security benefits.[28] If retirement benefits are to commence prior to the normal retirement age for full Social Security benefits, the $120,000 limit would be reduced below the previous safe harbor of $75,000 at the rate of approximately 5 percent per year. This reduces age 55 retirement benefits to a new maximum benefit of approximately $52,000.

Benefits beginning after age 65 will be increased actuarially based on an assumption of a five percent interest rate (or if lower the rate specified in the plan).[29]

Furthermore, the $90,000/100 percent limit must be reduced if the normal form of retirement is something other than a nonrefund life annuity.[30] For example, a 15 percent reduction would be required if the normal retirement benefit upon which the $90,000/100 percent limit is based is a life annuity with a cash refund. In 1995, this would drop the maximum indexed limit of $120,000 to $102,000, or 85 percent of the participant's highest three consecutive years of average compensation. In the case of a life annuity with an installment refund, a 10 percent reduction would be required, dropping the maximum benefit to $108,000, or 90 percent. With a 20 year certain life annuity, a 30 percent reduction would be required, bringing the maximum benefit down to $84,000, or 70 percent. Even a 10 year certain life annuity would require a 10 percent reduction.

Be certain to recognize that all of the dollar limits described above will continue to be increased by cost-of-living changes.

Target or Assumed Benefit Plan

A target or assumed benefit plan is a hybrid between a defined contribution and defined benefit plan in which a "target benefit" is established under the plan for each participant, such as 50 percent of an employee's five highest years average salary.

Once the "target benefit" is found, contributions necessary to attain that goal are then actuarially determined based on a conservative interest assumption such as five or six percent and the age of the participant. The plan then becomes a money purchase plan.

The maximum annual addition to the account of a participant in a target benefit plan cannot exceed the lesser of (a) 25 percent of salary or (b) $30,000.[31]

Each participant's account is credited with any investment earnings or gains and losses. This means the actual retirement benefit of a participant under a target benefit plan can be more or less than the actual target itself.

Combination Defined Benefit and Defined Contribution Plans

Often, an employer will cover the same employee with a combination of plans, including a defined benefit pension plan and defined contribution plan, usually a money purchase pension plan. In this case, each plan must first separately meet the general contribution and benefit limitations mentioned above. Furthermore, the contribution and benefit limitations in both plans must be combined and the resulting fraction must not exceed a combination set for the two plans.[32]

The maximum amount which can be contributed under a combination defined benefit pension plan and defined contribution plan is determined as shown below. Both types of payments to the plans are deductible as long as the total of the two "fractions" or percentages does not exceed 1.00 or 100%:

Defined Benefit Plan Fraction	=	Projected Annual Benefit
		the lesser of
		(1) 1.25 x dollar limit, or
		(2) 1.4 x average compensation

Defined Contribution Plan Fraction	=	Sum of Annual Additions
		the sum of the lesser of (for each year of service)
		(1) 1.25 x dollar limit, or
		(2) 1.4 x 25% of compensation

For example, your client, Herb Chase, earns $150,000 per year. Herb's pension benefit at age 65 under a defined benefit plan will be $80,000. Eighty thousand dollars is 66 percent of the maximum amount allowed under the rules discussed above relating to defined benefit plans. (The maximum benefit to which Herb could be entitled would be the lesser of $120,000 per year (the 1995 limit) or 100 percent of his $150,000 salary, with the lesser of these being $120,000.) In addition to the contribution for his benefit to this defined benefit plan, Herb's account also received $10,000 under a defined contribution plan (money purchase or profit-sharing). Herb's computation would be as follows (based on no prior years of service with the employer):

Defined Benefit Plan Fraction	=	$80,000 (Herb's projected annual benefit)
		lesser of
		(1) 1.25 x $120,000 = $150,000
		(2) 1.4 x $150,000 = $210,000
Result:	$\dfrac{\$80,000}{\$150,000}$	= 53%

Defined Contribution Plan Fraction	=	$10,000 (the annual addition to Herb's account)
		lesser of
		(1) 1.25 x $30,000 = $37,500
		(2) 1.4 x $37,500 = $52,500
Result:	$\dfrac{\$10,000}{\$37,500}$	= 27%

Total combined fraction (53% plus 27%) = 80%

Thus Herb's contributions and benefits do not violate the 100 percent combined plan fraction limitation.

If the defined benefit or defined contribution plan which must be combined is top heavy (i.e., 60% of accrued benefits or account balances belong to key employees), the "1.25" in the defined contribution plan and defined benefit plan fractions (regarding dollar limits) will be reduced to "1.0." However, the "1.25" multiplicand can be retained if the following two requirements are met: (1) the plan cannot be "super top heavy" (i.e., the accrued benefits or account balances of key employees cannot exceed 90% of the total benefits for all employees); and (2) the plans must provide additional minimum benefits or contributions for non-key employees (i.e., defined benefit plans must accrue a 3% benefit for each year of service after 1983 and defined contribution plans must have a 4% minimum contribution rate).

The following example shows the possible result where a combination of top heavy plans is involved.

John Smith earns an average salary of $150,000 per year. He is a participant in a defined benefit plan which provides an annual retirement benefit of 60% of salary and a defined contribution plan which provides for an annual contribution of 15% of salary. Both plans are top heavy. John's total combined fraction is determined as follows (based on no prior years of service with the employer):

Defined Benefit Plan Fraction	=	$90,000 (John's projected annual benefit)
		lesser of
		(1) 1.0 x $120,000 = $120,000
		(2) 1.4 x $150,000 = $210,000
Result:	$\dfrac{\$90,000}{\$120,000}$	= .75

Defined Contribution Plan Fraction	=	$22,500 (the annual addition to John's account)
		lesser of
		(1) 1.0 x $30,000 = $30,000
		(2) 1.4 x $37,500 = $52,500
Result:	$\dfrac{\$22,500}{\$30,000}$	= .75

The total combined fraction for John's plans is 1.50, which violates the combined fraction rule, resulting in possible plan disqualification (i.e., loss of tax exempt status). John's problem could be solved by eliminating the defined contribution plan or by reducing the defined benefit plan benefit by two-thirds.

Deduction of Contributions

In a defined benefit pension plan, an employer can contribute and deduct the amount necessary to pay for the benefits promised. Technically stated, the employer may pay and deduct the plan's "normal cost" plus any amount necessary to amortize liability for benefits earned through the past service of employees. Past service (simplified, past service is the cost of financing benefits credited for past services) liability can be amortized over as few as 10 years (but no more than 30 years).[33]

Generally, the deductible contributions referred to above can be made up to the plan's full-funding limitation. The full funding limitation is essentially the amount by which the lesser of (1) 150% of current liability, or (2) the accrued liability under the plan, exceeds the value of the plan's assets.[34]

In a profit-sharing plan an employer can contribute and deduct a maximum of 15 percent of the total compensation of plan participants (without carry-forwards).[35] A $100,000 covered payroll would therefore yield the right to a $15,000 deductible contribution.

Where the employee is utilizing both a pension and profit-sharing plan, the maximum deductible contribution for both plans is the greater of 25 percent of the compensation of covered employees or the contribution required to fund the minimum funding standard. This deduction limitation also applies to combinations of defined benefit and money purchase plans.[36]

Prior to 1987, employees could deduct "qualified voluntary employee contributions" made to the plan up to a maximum of $2,000 per taxable year or, if less, 100% of compensation. The plan had to contain special provisions allowing these contributions.[37] Qualified voluntary employee contributions (made prior to 1987) must be accounted for separately, although separate investment will not be required. No loans to participants or investments in life insurance contracts should be made with plan assets attributable to deductible employee contributions or such action will be considered a distribution.[38]

Since a CODA must be part of a profit-sharing or stock bonus plan, the limitation on the employer's tax-deductible contributions to such a plan is 15% of the participants' total compensation. For purposes of the limitation on annual additions, elective contributions made under a qualified CODA are considered employer contributions.

Actuarial Assumptions

In a defined or fixed benefit pension plan, a conservative estimate should be made as to the rate of return of funds invested in assets other than life insurance. Five to seven percent interest assumptions are typical. Any actual return in excess of the amount assumed must be used to reduce the employer's future contributions.

After challenging the use of rates as low as 5 percent or 6 percent for a number of years, the IRS has backed down on its position that such rates were too conservative. The Tax Court and several circuit courts had sided with the employers in several such cases, noting that Congress intended actuaries to be "afforded a range of latitude in establishing a mix of reasonable assumptions, and that only if such assumptions are 'substantially unreasonable' should they be challenged and changed retroactively."[39]

In a money purchase plan, the investment experience directly affects the amount a participant will have at retirement. Normally, earnings are allocated to the participant's account in proportion to his or her account balance.

In a profit-sharing plan, the investment experience directly affects the amount in a participant's account. Gains and losses must be allocated proportionately to each individual. Typically, such allocations are made in proportion to the account balances of each participant. At retirement a participant may have more or less than was contributed, depending on the investment experience of the plan.

In the event an employee terminates, under a defined benefit plan the portion of a terminated participant's nonvested account is used to reduce future employer contributions.[40] However, in a profit-sharing plan, the funds in a terminated participant's nonvested account (forfeitures) can be allocated among the accounts of remaining participants on the same basis as the following year's contribution, or can be used to reduce future employer contributions, depending upon what provisions have been made in the plan.[41] Generally, forfeitures under all defined contribution plans, including money purchase plans, may also be used to increase participants' account balances.[42]

Mortality is an important actuarial assumption. In a fixed benefit pension plan, if life insurance is included in the plan, the investment account is generally not used to provide the death benefit. Instead, the investment account that would have gone to the deceased employee had he or she lived is used to reduce future employer contributions to the plan. If life insurance is included in the plan, death proceeds generally go to the employee's beneficiary.

In either a money purchase pension plan or a profit-sharing plan, the total funds in a participant's account are paid to a beneficiary as a death benefit. This includes the life insurance proceeds as well as any other investments.

Retirement Age

Generally, plans will make provision for normal, early, and late retirement age. Usually, normal retirement age will be age 65.

Mandatory retirement is generally prohibited. Exceptions exist for certain top executives and for good faith occupational requirements.

Employers are required to accrue additional benefits or pay the actuarial equivalent of normal retirement benefits to employees who choose to work beyond normal retirement age. It is unlawful to eliminate the accrual of further benefit credits to an employee's retirement account after the employee attains normal retirement age.[43]

It is also unlawful to exclude an employee from participation in a pension plan even though his age is within 5 years of the age set for normal retirement. Allowance is made, however, for the extension of the normal retirement date for any such late-age-hired person.[44] Most pension plans state that the normal retirement age of participants over age 55 at the time they enter the plan is 5 years from the date of entering the plan.

Early retirement benefits are generally available under a defined benefit plan at an actuarially reduced amount. In a money purchase plan, the amount of a pension which can be provided with the participant's vested share is what he or she will receive at early retirement. Under a profit-sharing plan, in the case of early retirement, the amount accumulated in a participant's account will be paid generally as a lump sum or as monthly income.

The IRS has challenged the use of retirement ages under age 65 in small defined benefit plans; however, it has backed down on this issue. The Tax Court and several circuit courts had sided with the employers in litigation of some of these cases. (See the discussion above, under "Actuarial Assumptions" with regard to IRS challenges to the use of low interest rates.)

Social Security Integration

Generally speaking, the benefit structure of social security discriminates against the higher-paid employee which usually includes the key shareholders and highly-paid management. Social security benefits replace, relatively speaking, a higher percentage of the lower-paid employee's pre-retirement income. In essence, the business owner is already providing a base pension through contributions to the social security system.

Integration of a retirement plan with social security allows an employer to coordinate the benefits provided by social security with those provided by the employer's retirement plan. Through integration, the two benefits combined produce roughly the same proportionate benefit for higher-paid employees as for lower-paid employees. (The Internal Revenue Code and the IRS currently refer to integration as "permitted disparity.")

For example, in the case of a money purchase or profit-sharing plan, the contribution rate (%) that applies to compensation above the taxable wage base may not exceed the contribution rate (%) that applies to compensation below the taxable wage base by more than the *lesser of* (1) the rate applied to compensation below the wage base or (2) 5.7% points (or, if greater, the rate of social security tax attributable to old-age insurance).[45] Thus, if the plan provides for contributions of 10 percent of pay in excess of the wage base, it would be properly integrated if it provided for contributions of at least 5 percent on pay below the wage base.

It is also possible to integrate a defined benefit pension plan. But here integration is on the basis of benefits rather than contributions.

Top Heavy Plans

Plans which are considered "top heavy" must meet the basic qualification requirements of other qualified plans and, in addition, meet the following requirements: (1) implement one of two alternative rapid vesting schedules; (2) provide minimum nonintegrated contributions or benefits for plan participants who are non-key employees; and (3) reduce the aggregate limit on contributions and benefits for some key employees.[46]

A plan is considered "top heavy" when more than 60 percent of its aggregate accumulated benefits or account balances is provided to key employees. An employee's status and whether or not a plan is top heavy is determined on a year by year basis. The determination is made on the last day of the preceding plan year for existing plans and on the last day of the first plan year for new plans.[47]

"Key employee" is defined as an employee who, at any time during the plan year or any of the 4 preceding plan years, is (1) an officer of the employer having annual compensation greater than 50 percent of the defined benefit dollar limit in effect for any such plan year (50% of $120,000 in 1995); (2) 1 of the 10 employees having annual compensation from the employer of more than the defined contribution dollar limit in effect (currently $30,000) and owning (either personally or applying the constructive ownership provisions of Code section 318) both a more than ½ percent interest and the largest interests in the employer; (3) a 5 percent owner of the employer; or (4) a 1 percent owner of the employer having annual compensation from the employer of more than $150,000.[48]

To be considered an officer for "key employee" purposes, the officer must be an administrative executive who is in regular and continued service. Mere titles do not suffice. In no event may more than fifty employees be considered as officers under the key employee rule.[49] Special rules apply for smaller employers: If the business (or aggregated group of businesses) has fewer than 500 employees, only 10 percent will be considered officers, but if the business has fewer than 30 employees, at least three officers must be counted.

Each additional qualification requirement will be discussed below.

Vesting

A top heavy plan must meet one of two special vesting rules. The first is a three-year 100 percent vesting rule. Under this rule an employee who is at least 21 years old and who has completed at least 3 years of service with the employer (or employers) maintaining the plan must be given a nonforfeitable right to 100% of his accrued benefit derived from employer contributions. The second is a six year graded vesting rule. This provides 20 percent vesting at the end of the second year of service and 20 percent in each succeeding year. Full vesting must be attained by the end of the six year period.[50]

Six-year graded vesting

Years of service	Nonforfeitable percentage
2	20
3	40
4	60
5	80
6 or more	100

Contributions and Benefits

Special limitations on contributions and benefits are imposed where the plan is considered top heavy.[51] Minimum benefits under defined benefit plans must be provided to non-key employees. The benefit accrued during a top heavy year must be at least two percent of average pay for the highest five years for each year of service in which a top heavy plan year ends up to a total of 20 percent of average pay.

In the case of top heavy defined contribution plans, in each year the plan is top heavy, non-key employees must receive minimum contributions of at least three percent of compensation. But if the plan provides the contribution rate of less than three percent for all participants, then instead of the three percent contribution rate, the highest contribution rate percentage on behalf of any key employee can be used (counting only the first $150,000 of compensation, as adjusted for inflation in 1995).

In determining benefits under a top heavy plan, only the first $150,000 of compensation can be counted, as is the case in non-top heavy plans.[52] The $150,000 limit is adjusted annually for inflation, but only in increments of $5,000; thus the limit remains at $150,000 for 1995. Social Security benefits or contributions cannot be counted against the required minimum benefits or contributions.

HOW IT IS DONE — AN EXAMPLE

There are basically three ways an employer places funds into a retirement plan. The first is known as a "fully-insured" plan. Here, the employer places contributions into a funding vehicle of an insurance company, such as a retirement income life insurance contract. The funds usually receive a guarantee as to principal, minimum rate of interest, and annuity purchase rate (the "rate of exchange" at which pension funds can be changed into lifetime payment guarantees). It is the simplest method of investing pension monies.

The second type of investment vehicle is known as the "split funded" plan. Here, the employer places contributions into a trust fund. The trust fund splits contributions into two parts: part of the funds are placed in fixed assets, annuities, and/or life insurance, while the remainder is invested in other investments for diversification. There are principal, interest, and annuity purchase rate guarantees for the funds invested with the insurance company. However, frequently funds invested otherwise have no guarantees of principal or interest, but they may have the advantage of appreciation if invested in equities.

The third type of funding vehicle is known as uninsured. This type of funding implies that the employer contributions are invested solely by investments including equities. Contributions are made by the employer to a trust fund. There are no guarantees as to principal or interest although funds may be applied to buy a guaranteed annuity at normal retirement age. This funding method involves the highest risk because there are no guarantees made by a third party, but in return for the extra risk, this method offers the greatest potential appreciation (or depending upon how the plan is arranged, the lowest possible employer cost).

All three arrangements have advantages and disadvantages. For example, the fully-insured plan guarantees the principal, interest, annuity purchase rates, and expenses. It is the easiest plan to install and administer. The cost and effort of compliance with the Employee Retirement Income Security Act (ERISA) is relatively minimal. A disadvantage is that the growth of dollars in the plan is fixed, and so there is no chance for an equity-type appreciation of funds.

The split funded plan combines guarantees with the possibility of appreciation. The funds invested in insurance contracts obtain guarantees on principal and interest earnings, expense costs, and annuity rates. The side fund is usually invested in growth-oriented securities. Of course, since the side fund is invested in equities, the possibility exists that depreciation in the value of the securities will result in lower benefits for employees (or higher costs for the employer).

The main advantage of a full equity funded approach is that all funds have the possibility of appreciation. If the investment manager is successful, the result will be either reduced cost for the employer or increased benefits for the employees, depending on the type of plan utilized. The disadvantage of this arrangement is that there are no guarantees applied to the funds. Also, if an insurance company is not used, the employer or the plan must pay directly for actuarial, administrative, and investment expenses. The cost of hiring private actuarial and administrative services will be higher for small employers in most cases than if an insurer's services were utilized.

WHAT ARE THE INCOME TAX IMPLICATIONS?

1. Within the limits mentioned above, employer contributions to these plans are fully deductible for income tax purposes.[53]

2. Earnings on plan assets accumulate income tax free.[54]

3. Distributions, when paid out in the form of a lump-sum distribution, are taxable as follows:

   (a) The portion of a taxable distribution attributable to years of participation before 1/1/74 is taxed at capital gains rates. This capital gains treatment was phased-out over a five-year period (1987-1991) for taxpayers who did not attain age 50 before January 1, 1986.

   (b) The portion of a taxable distribution attributable to years of participation after 12/31/73 is taxed at ordinary income rates. However, 5-year income averaging may be available or, if the participant reached age 50 by January 1, 1986, 10-year averaging is available using the 1986 income tax rates.[55] It can therefore be taxed as ordinary income with special income averaging available. The special income averaging provision cannot be used for the portion of a taxable distribution

attributable to deductible employee contributions. Payment of such amounts can be distributed in a different tax year from the balance of the lump sum payment without jeopardizing the special averaging tax treatment given lump sum distributions. See the table in Appendix D for the federal tax consequences of a lump-sum distribution based on 5-year averaging using 1995 federal tax rates and 10-year averaging using the 1986 rates.

Five-year averaging may be elected only if the lump-sum distribution is received after the participant attains age 59½ and the taxpayer elects to treat all such amounts received during the year in the same manner. No more than one election may be made by any taxpayer with respect to any employee.[56]

4. An employee generally does not have to include an employer's contribution in gross income even where rights to the benefits in the plan are fully nonforfeitable. Benefits payable under a qualified retirement plan—including deductible employee contributions and earnings on those contributions—are taxed only when paid to a participant or beneficiary and are not taxed if merely "made available."[57]

However, if life insurance protection is provided under the plan, an employee is considered to have received a distribution each year (a current economic benefit) equal to the portion of the employer's contributions or trust earnings that have been applied during the year to provide pure insurance on the employee's life. This is the so-called "P.S. 58 cost."[58] The employee includes this as income just as if he or she had received a bonus in that amount; however, such costs will be recovered income tax free when benefits are received under the contract. (If life insurance is purchased with deductible employee contributions, the amount spent is treated as a distribution.[59])

When an employee first becomes eligible to receive benefits, those benefits do not have to be paid and immediately rolled over into an IRA to avoid current income taxation. If the plan allows, they can be left in the plan and are not taxed until paid (but if paid to a child or creditor of the employee, they are treated as if paid to the employee).

The plan must place some limits on this deferral of receipt of benefits. It must provide that the entire interest of the participant will be distributed over one of the following permissible periods: (1) the life of the participant; (2) the lives of the participant and his or her "designated beneficiary"; (3) a period not extending beyond the life expectancy of the participant; or (4) a period not extending beyond the life expectancy of the participant and his or her "designated beneficiary."[60] The amount required to be distributed will be greater if the designated beneficiary is not the spouse and is more than 10 years younger than the participant.[61] A designated beneficiary is generally any individual designated by the participant to receive the balance of his or her benefits remaining at the participant's death.

5. An employee who retires and receives periodic payments from the retirement plan is taxed on the receipt of such payments in accordance with the annuity rules. The annuity rules provide for taxation of such payments as ordinary income and an exclusion ratio must be determined. The exclusion ratio is the ratio of the employee's "investment in the contract" (cost) to the employee's "expected return," expressed as follows:

$$\frac{\text{Investment In Contract}}{\text{Expected Return}}$$

The employee's cost or "investment in the contract" is essentially his nondeductible contributions. Where life insurance is included in the plan, it also includes the total of all one year term insurance costs that have been reported as taxable income. The "expected return" is the annual payment the employee will receive multiplied by the employee's life expectancy (see Table V, One Life-Expected Return Multiples in Appendix D). (Adjustments must be made for payouts made over differing time periods or where minimum payout guarantees are present.) Once the fraction is determined, it is multiplied by the annual payment. The product is the amount not subject to taxation. The balance of each payment is taxable as ordinary income.[62] A simplified safe harbor method for taxing annuity payments (see IRS Pub. No. 575) is available for individuals whose annuity starting date is after July 1, 1986.[63]

Distributions of deductible employee contributions are generally taxed under a pro-rata recovery rule.[64]

6. Distributions before the participant attains age 59½ are subject to a 10 percent penalty tax with certain exceptions (death, divorce, disability, payments made over the participant's life starting from separation from service, and medical expenses).[65]

7. A 15% tax is imposed on the amount of any "excess distributions" made to any individual during any calendar year. The individual with respect to whom the excess distributions are made is liable for the tax.[66]

The term "excess distributions" means the aggregate amount of all retirement plan distributions (including IRA distributions) made with respect to any individual during any calendar year to the extent such amount exceeds $150,000. If the retirement distributions of an individual include a lump-sum distribution for which special income tax treatment (as in paragraph 3, above) is elected, the term "excess distributions" is applied separately with regard to the lump-sum distribution, and the $150,000 limitation is multiplied by 5 for a separate limitation of $750,000.

If the accrued benefit of all retirement plans of an employee exceeded $562,500 as of August 1, 1986, the employee could have elected on Form 5329, filed with his 1987 or 1988 income tax return, to have the amount accrued as of August 1, 1986 excluded for purposes of determining the amount of excess distributions tax imposed on his distributions.[67] If the employee elected to "grandfather" the August 1, 1986 balance, the annual limitation is $150,000 (as adjusted for inflation for 1995).

The 15% excess distributions tax cannot be avoided by just not making any large distributions from the plan — see the explanation of the 15% penalty estate tax on "excess accumulations," described below under WHAT ARE THE ESTATE TAX IMPLICATIONS?

8. A beneficiary receiving death benefits from a qualified retirement plan is taxed on the amount received for income tax purposes under either the lump sum or annuity rules. However, voluntary employee contributions which were deductible are not allowed the relief granted lump-sum distributions and are includable in ordinary income.[68] In computing the amount of taxable income the beneficiary must report as a result of the distribution, if the distribution is made in a lump sum and if any portion of the distribution consists of life insurance proceeds for which the employee paid the insurance costs or reported this P.S. 58 cost as taxable income on his return, then the difference between the face amount of the insurance contract and the insurance contract cash value (this difference is called the "pure insurance") passes to the beneficiary free of income tax.[69] Thus, the beneficiary treats only the cash value portion of any death benefit plus any other cash distributions from the plan as income subject to tax.

If, on the other hand, the employee did not pay the insurance cost of the life insurance contract or did not report the cost of such insurance as taxable income, the portion of the insurance proceeds consisting of pure insurance (as defined above) will be considered taxable income to the beneficiary.

9. If the plan participant suffers permanent loss or loss of use of a member or function of the body, or permanent disfigurement, it may be possible for him or her to receive benefits under a qualified plan free of income tax under Code section 105(c). In order for the payment to qualify, the plan must provide 100 percent vesting of benefits if the participant ceases employment due to total and permanent disability, and must also include statutory language from Section 105(c) to establish the dual purpose of the plan (i.e., a retirement plan and an "accident and health" plan).

Code section 105 applies to amounts received under "Accident and Health Plans." A minority of courts have found that a qualified plan can serve a dual function of providing retirement benefits and disability benefits. To the extent benefits are provided due to the participant's disability, they may be income tax free if the requirements of Section 105(c) are satisfied.

Section 105(c)(2) requires that the disability payment be computed by taking the nature of the injury into account in determining the benefit without regard to the period the employee is absent from work. This requirement may be difficult to satisfy in most pension plan contexts. However, a provision giving the committee discretion to determine disability benefits with reference to the nature of the injury may enable the disabled participant to overcome this hurdle.

WHAT ARE THE ESTATE TAX IMPLICATIONS?

Currently there is only a very limited exclusion from the federal estate tax for retirement plan distributions payable at an employee's death.[70] The entire amount attributable to employer contributions is includable in the gross estate of an employee who dies on or after January 1, 1985. The Tax Reform Act of 1984 contained a provision which permitted individuals who were both in pay status and had made an irrevocable election as to the form of benefit distribution to continue to have the benefit of the estate tax exclusion (the unlimited exclusion for participants in pay status prior to January 1, 1983, or the $100,000 exclusion for participants in pay status prior to January 1, 1985). TRA '86 somewhat liberalized the grandfathering provisions by providing that the participant no longer needs to be in pay status as of the applicable date. The participant needs only to have separated from service prior to the applicable date and not to have made any change in the form of benefit to be paid prior to death.

There is a second tier estate tax with regard to the estates of decedents dying after December 31, 1986. The tax is equal to 15% of the decedent's "excess retirement accumulations," and is added to the first tier estate tax.[71] None of the unified credit can be used to offset this increase in tax. Further, no deductions can reduce the tax. This tax "penalty for successful investing" may be disruptive to those estate plans which,

Figure 28.1

SIMPLIFIED EXCESS RETIREMENT ACCUMULATIONS WORKSHEET ©1988, The American College	
Step 1. State total accumulation payable.	$3,000,000
Step 2. State annual protected amount ($150,000 or $112,000 indexed).	$ 150,000
Step 3. State assumed age at death.	55
Step 4. Find discount factor from Table S (see App. D) at 10% interest.	$ 8.2550
Step 5. Multiply step 2 by step 4 to arrive at total protected amount.	$1,238,250
Step 6. Subtract protected amount (step 5) from step 1 to find amount subject to tax (assumes no grandfathering).	$1,761,750
Step 7. Multiply step 6 by .15 to find excess accumulations tax.	$ 264,263

Figure 28.2

PENSION BENEFITS TABLE — 1995*					
Age	**Annuity Factor**	**$150,000**	**Age**	**Annuity Factor**	**$150,000**
41	9.2465	1,386,975	71	6.2564	938,460
42	9.1959	1,379,385	72	6.1009	915,135
43	9.1424	1,371,360	73	5.9425	891,375
44	9.0859	1,362,885	74	5.7805	867,075
45	9.0264	1,353,960	75	5.6144	842,160
46	8.9637	1,344,555	76	5.4437	816,555
47	8.8978	1,334,670	77	5.2689	790,335
48	8.8287	1,324,305	78	5.0906	763,590
49	8.7567	1,313,505	79	4.9103	736,545
50	8.6818	1,302,270	80	4.7295	709,425
51	8.6037	1,290,555	81	4.5501	682,515
52	8.5220	1,278,300	82	4.3730	655,950
53	8.4365	1,265,475	83	4.1993	629,895
54	8.3476	1,252,140	84	4.0287	604,305
55	8.2550	1,238,250	85	3.8608	579,120
56	8.1586	1,223,790	86	3.6970	554,550
57	8.0581	1,208,715	87	3.5398	530,970
58	7.9536	1,193,040	88	3.3883	508,245
59	7.8449	1,176,735	89	3.3299	499,485
60	7.7326	1,159,890	90	3.0929	463,935
61	7.6169	1,142,535	91	2.9496	442,440
62	7.4980	1,124,700	92	2.8136	422,040
63	7.3760	1,106,400	93	2.6865	402,975
64	7.2507	1,087,605	94	2.5697	385,455
65	7.1213	1,068,195	95	2.4638	369,570
66	6.9876	1,048,140	96	2.3697	355,455
67	6.8492	1,027,380	97	2.2840	342,600
68	6.7063	1,005,945	98	2.2069	331,035
69	6.5595	983,925	99	2.1356	320,340
70	6.4093	961,395			

***Assuming 10% interest rate. See "Working With the IRS Valuation Tables" in Appendix D.**

regardless of the size of the estate, contemplated no estate tax to be due at the death of the first spouse to die.

A surviving spouse who is the beneficiary of all (a de minimis exception is provided) of the decedent spouse's aggregate retirement plans may elect to have the excise tax on excess retirement accumulations not apply at the decedent spouse's death. If the election is made, the decedent spouse's aggregate retirement plans will be treated as those of the surviving spouse for purposes of the excise tax on excess retirement distributions and excess retirement accumulations in relation to the surviving spouse.

The term "excess retirement accumulation" means the excess (if any) of —

(1) the value of the deceased employee's interests in all qualified employer plans and IRAs as of the date of death (or alternate valuation date, if elected), over

(2) the present value of a single life annuity with annual payments equal to the greater of $112,500 (indexed at the same time and in the same manner as the dollar limitation on annual benefits under a defined benefit pension plan, $150,000 for 1995) or $150,000. The $150,000 amount is not available if an election has been made to grandfather accrued benefits accumulated in the plan as of August 1, 1986.

The present value of a single life annuity with annual payments equal to the greater of $112,500 (indexed to $150,000 for 1995) or $150,000 is determined using the interest rate and mortality assumptions prescribed by the Treasury as in effect on the date of death and as if the decedent had not died (see Appendix D for valuation tables). The worksheet at Figure 28.1 shows the steps in calculating the amount of the tax, illustrating a total accumulation of $3 million for a decedent age 55 at death for a participant who did not elect to "grandfather" his August 1, 1986 balance of retirement funds and an interest rate of 10 percent. The table at Figure 28.2 shows the application of the annuity factor at decedent ages from 41 through 99 to the nontaxed amounts, thus facilitating the computation illustrated in the worksheet.

If an election was made to grandfather accrued benefits accumulated in the plan as of August 1, 1986, the present value of a single life annuity with annual payments equal to $112,500 (indexed to $150,000 for 1995) is reduced by the present value of the unrecovered grandfather amount (if any) remaining as of the date of death. In other words, if benefits were grandfathered, the amount protected from the excise tax is equal to the greater of (1) the grandfathered amount or (2) the present value of the $112,500 indexed annuity.

Note that excess retirement accumulation does not include life insurance proceeds in excess of cash surrender value.

The credit for estate tax paid on previous transfers does not apply to the excise tax on excess retirement accumulations. Also, no income tax deduction is allowed with respect to income in respect of a decedent for the excise tax on excess retirement accumulations. However, the excise tax on excess retirement accumulations is deductible from the gross estate (for purposes of the first tier tax).

State inheritance tax laws covering distributions from qualified pension and profit-sharing plans vary widely. In Pennsylvania, for example, death benefits are excludable from inheritance taxes as long as such amounts are not available to pay death taxes and other estate expenses; i.e., payments will be state death tax free if payable to a named beneficiary other than the decedent-employee's estate. On the other hand, New Jersey, a neighboring state, taxes retirement plan death benefits payable to any beneficiary other than the deceased employee's spouse, regardless of the manner in which benefits are paid.

IMPLICATIONS AND ISSUES IN COMMUNITY PROPERTY STATES

Many community property implications and issues have been discussed in previous chapters. Some additional tax implications should also be mentioned.

The special 5-year averaging method for the ordinary income portion of a lump-sum distribution can cause a significant reduction in taxes which would otherwise be payable. It would appear to be even more beneficial to treat a lump-sum distribution to a married spouse as two equal portions to each spouse (assuming the benefits are community property). The combined taxes on two $25,000 distributions, using the 5-year averaging method, would be significantly less than the tax on a single $50,000 distribution. To avoid this result, community property laws are disregarded when using the 5-year averaging method.[72] The tax is computed as if only the employee spouse is entitled to the benefit. The spouses can choose to treat the $50,000 distribution (assuming it is community property) as being received in equal portions by each for tax purposes, but they cannot elect the 5-year averaging method.

The same rule, disregarding community property laws, applies to the 15 percent taxes on excess distributions from and excess accumulations in qualified retirement plans. This also provides a result which avoids any benefit from living in a community property state.

Generally, for purposes of divorce, the community property laws are recognized; however, there will be a substantial difference in rights in the event of the prior death of the nonparticipant spouse. Under the Retirement Equity Act of 1984, if the participant spouse is married, the required form of distribution on the death of either spouse is in the form of a survivor annuity for the surviving spouse. Where the participant spouse is the first to die, this means the surviving spouse will receive the required annuity regardless of the community nature of the qualified plan benefit.

Further, where the nonparticipant spouse is the first to die, one court[73] has held that his or her community interest in a pension plan in effect passes to the surviving participant spouse regardless of any direction of the deceased spouse, or any contrary provisions in the will of the deceased spouse. In effect, the required survivor rights supersede state community property laws.

Note that the survivor annuity rule does not apply to distributions from IRAs and Simplified Employee Pensions, discussed in chapter 18, and that the survivor annuity may be waived, as discussed at the end of this chapter.

QUESTIONS AND ANSWERS

Question — Who is a fiduciary and what are the fiduciary responsibility rules established by ERISA (also known as the Pension Reform Act of 1974)?

Answer — A fiduciary is a person who (a) exercises any discretionary authority or discretionary control respecting management of the plan or exercises any authority or control respecting management or disposition of assets; (b) renders investment advice for a fee or other compensation, direct or indirect, with respect to any monies or other property of the plan, or has any authority or responsibility to do so; or (c) has any discretionary authority or discretionary responsibility in the administration of the plan.[74] The term fiduciary also includes persons named by a fiduciary to carry out fiduciary responsibilities (other than trustee responsibilities) under the plan. ERISA established rules governing the conduct of fiduciaries and other persons dealing with the plan. The Labor Department administers certain provisions which pertain to rules and remedies similar to those under traditional trust law governing the conduct of fiduciaries.

Specifically, these fiduciary responsibility rules relate to the structure of plan administration, provide general standards of conduct for fiduciaries, and make certain transactions "prohibited transactions" in which plan fiduciaries may not engage.[75] Other provisions which are enforced by the Treasury Department impose an excise tax on certain persons who violate the prohibited transaction rules.[76]

Basically, ERISA requires each fiduciary of a plan to act with the care, skill, prudence, and diligence under the circumstances then prevailing that a prudent person acting in a like capacity and familiar with such matters would use in conducting an enterprise of like character and with like aims.

Furthermore, ERISA requires that a qualified retirement plan be for the exclusive benefit of the plan's employees and their beneficiaries.[77] Under the "exclusive benefit" umbrella,

(1) the cost of plan assets must not exceed fair market value at the time of purchase;

(2) assets should bring a fair return commensurate with the prevailing rate;

(3) the plan should maintain sufficient liquidity to permit distributions; and

(4) the safeguards and diversity that would be adhered to by a prudent investor must be present.

Question — How does plan termination insurance work?

Answer — ERISA established, within the Department of Labor, a public corporation named the Pension Benefit Guaranty Corporation (PBGC). The PBGC is a federal insurance company which provides mandatory plan termination insurance to protect the benefit rights of workers whose defined benefit pension plans go out of existence. As one of its main duties, the corporation administers plan termination insurance for defined benefit pension plans.

The amount insured is limited to the actuarial value of a benefit as a straight life annuity, payable monthly beginning at age 65, equal to the lesser of: (1) one-twelfth of the average compensation paid the participant during the consecutive five year period of his plan participation during which his compensation was highest; or (2) $750 monthly (adjusted to reflect changes in the social security contribution and wage base — $2556.82 for 1994).[78]

Premiums for PBGC coverage are $19.00 per participant, plus an "additional premium." The "additional premium" is calculated by dividing an amount based on the plan's unfunded vested benefits as of the end of the preceding plan year by the number of plan participants at that time. The additional premium is equal to $9.00 per thousand (or fraction thereof) of the plan's unfunded vested benefits as of the end of the preceding plan year. For plan years beginning before July 1, 1994, the aggregate increase in the premium for a participant due to the additional premium could not exceed $53.00. This cap is phased out for plan years beginning after June 30, 1994.[79]

Question — Can a pension plan make a loan to a participant or plan beneficiary?

Answer — Yes, if the loan is made in accordance with specific provisions in the plan governing such loans, a reasonable charge is made for the use of plan assets, and the loan is adequately secured. Loans must be available to all participants on a reasonably equivalent basis.[80]

Loans to owner employees are "prohibited transactions." Therefore, loans cannot be made from Keogh plans to self-employed individuals or certain partners in partnerships without specific Department of Labor approval.[81] This is one of the main advantages of the use of corporate plans, which do permit such loans.

Limits are imposed on tax-free participant borrowing from qualified plans, from tax sheltered annuities, and from plans (qualified and nonqualified) of federal, state, and local governments and their agencies and instrumentalities.

Certain loan transactions are treated as distributions. Loan transactions include: (1) the direct or indirect receipt of a loan, and (2) the assignment (or agreement to assign) or the pledging (or agreement to pledge) of any portion of an employee's interest in a plan.[82]

Two basic rules and two exceptions apply. The rules and exceptions are as follows:

1. *Loans which are to be repaid within five years* are taxed as distributions only to the extent that the amount of the loan (together with any other outstanding loans the employee has made from plans with the same employer) exceeds the lesser of (a) $50,000 reduced by the highest outstanding loan balance during the prior 12 months, or (b) half of the employee's vested benefits under the employer plans from which he has borrowed (or $10,000, if greater).[83]

2. *Loans which do not have to be repaid within five years* are fully taxable as distributions. Whether or not a loan must be repaid within five years is ascertained as of the date the loan is made.

Some loans of five years or less may be subsequently extended. The loan balance at the time of the extension is considered a distribution at that time.

If repayment under a "five-year-or-less" loan is not made (so at the end of five years the participant still owes the plan money), any remaining amounts due are considered plan distributions.

"More-than-five-year" loans are not converted to "five-year-or-less" loans or in any other way favorably treated merely because they are repaid in five years or less (regardless of the reason for the early repayments).

Exception 1: *Housing loans.* A loan of more than five years made after 1986 is not treated as a distribution to the extent that it is used by the plan participant to purchase the participant's principal residence. "More-than-five-year loans" made before 1987 are not treated as distributions to the extent that they were used to purchase, construct, or substantially rehabilitate a home, apartment, condominium, or mobile home (not used on a transient basis).[84]

Exception 2: *Certain mortgage loans.* Where plan trustees invest a specific percentage or amount of plan assets in residential mortgages or in other types of mortgage investments, such investments are not considered loans as long as the amount lent does not exceed the fair market value of the property the loan was used to pur-

chase. Loans to officers, directors, or owners (or their beneficiaries) are not protected under this exception.

Question — What are the reporting and disclosure requirements of ERISA?

Answer — In general, every plan which is not specifically exempted must file certain reports each year. The annual report for plans with 100 or more participants must include an audited financial statement. Annual Reports of defined benefit plans must contain a certified actuarial report. If the plan terminates, additional special reports are required.

The number of participants covered by a plan has no effect on the reporting and disclosure requirements—an annual report must be filed regardless of how many or how few participants are covered. However, where a plan contains less than 100 participants, a simplified report may be authorized.

Furthermore, certain information must be provided to plan participants and beneficiaries. They must be given a summary of the plan written in a manner understandable by the average participant or beneficiary (Summary Plan Description). Furthermore, beneficiaries and participants can request a status report once a year showing total benefits accrued and nonforfeitable pension benefit rights. Employees who have terminated employment during the plan year must also be given a statement of their deferred vested rights in the plan. Many of these documents become public information and can be inspected.[85]

Failure to meet the reporting and disclosure requirements can result in serious civil and/or criminal penalties, which include fines and imprisonment.

Question — What is a target benefit pension plan?

Answer — It is a retirement plan under which the required contribution is initially based upon an assumed retirement benefit for each participant, but under which the actual retirement benefit received is based upon the market value of the assets in the individual participant's account at the time of retirement.

Question — What is an Age-Weighted Profit-Sharing Plan?

Answer — Under traditional profit-sharing plan arrangements, employer contributions are generally allocated each year to employees either in proportion to relative compensation or in proportion to relative compensation together with integration with Social Security benefits. However, under final regulations, an employer may maintain a qualified profit-sharing plan in which the participant's age is taken into account when allocating the employer's contribution.[86] The result is that significantly larger allocations (as a percentage of pay) are provided to older employees than to younger employees.

An example of the results is as follows:

Employees Age	Compensation	Standard Plan Allocation	Age-Weighted Allocation
25	$ 15,000	$ 860	$ 450
30	22,500	1,290	675
35	30,000	1,700	832
40	60,000	3,400	1,800
45	75,000	4,250	3,054
55	150,000	8,500	13,189
Total	$352,500	$20,000	$20,000

Question — What limitations are imposed on a qualified retirement plan regarding the purchase of ordinary life insurance?

Answer — In a profit-sharing plan, less than 50 percent of the aggregate employer contributions and forfeitures allocated to each participant's account can be used to purchase ordinary life insurance. If insurance may be purchased only with funds that have been accumulated in the plan for two or more years, the 50 percent rule does not apply.[87] In addition to this requirement, a profit-sharing plan must require the trustee at or before retirement either (a) to convert the policies into cash or (b) to distribute the policies to the employee. A money-purchase plan has the same "less than 50 percent" rule with regard to the purchase of ordinary life insurance.

Life insurance is a permissible purchase in a defined benefit pension plan if it meets either of two tests. The first test is essentially the same as the money-purchase plan test. The alternative test is the "100 to 1" test whereby the insurance is permissible if the insurance amount does not exceed 100 times the expected monthly retirement benefit.[88] For example, if the projected monthly benefit is $1,000, the life insurance cannot exceed $100,000.

Question — What is a thrift and savings plan?

Answer — The major characteristic of a thrift and savings plan is that employee-participants must contribute some percentage of compensation to the plan. The employer matches contributions of employees according to some formula. For example, an employer may match each dollar of employee contribution with more or less than $1

of employer contribution. A thrift and savings plan can be tax qualified or can be informal.

A tax qualified thrift and savings plan will result in a current employer deduction for contributions to the plan and, yet, employees will not be currently taxed on employer contributions. Both employer and employee contributions will grow tax-free within the plan. When distributions from a qualified thrift and savings plan are made, they are subject to the same rules applicable to other qualified retirement plans. Typically, a thrift and savings plan will require employees to contribute a percentage of compensation in order to participate. It is important when incorporating thrift and savings features in a plan that such required contributions meet a special nondiscrimination test.[89] All contributions are counted for purposes of the annual additions limitation.

Question — Can a qualified pension or profit-sharing plan provide for voluntary deductible employee contributions?

Answer — No. Prior to 1987, anyone who had earned income, regardless of whether he was an active participant in a qualified plan, could establish an IRA. A voluntary deductible contribution of up to $2,000 could have been made to an employer's plan (if the plan so provided), to an IRA, or as a combination split in any proportion between the two.[90]

Voluntary *nondeductible* employee contributions to qualified pension, profit sharing, or stock bonus plans are allowed, providing they meet a special nondiscrimination test.[91] Also, 100% of employee contributions, whether voluntary or mandatory, will be included in the annual addition for purposes of the dollar limitation. Accordingly, both employer and employee contributions to a defined contribution plan count toward the $30,000/25% limitation.[92]

Question — What is a cash or deferred election and is it subject to current taxation?

Answer — Under a 401(k) plan, an employee can elect to have the employer make an elective contribution to the plan on the employee's behalf or to receive an equivalent amount in cash.

To the extent the employee elects to receive cash, the cash payment will be subject to all payroll taxes currently. If the employee elects to have the employer make an elective contribution, such contributed amount will not be subject to income tax, but it will be subject to social security taxes and the Federal Unemployment Taxes Act

(FUTA).[93] Of course, amounts contributed in excess of the elective deferral limit of $7,000, as indexed for inflation ($9,240 for 1995), are subject to income tax as well.

Question — What special nondiscrimination tests apply to 401(k) plans?

Answer — Qualified 401(k) plans must meet the actual deferral percentage test (ADP), which is designed to limit the extent to which elective contributions made on behalf of highly compensated employees may exceed the elective contributions made on behalf of nonhighly compensated employees.[94]

The amount of elective deferrals to be credited to a participant's account for any plan year must satisfy the following tests.

If the nonhighly compensated group contributes an average of:	The highly compensated group may contribute an average of:
Under 2% of compensation.	2 times the rate of the nonhighly compensated group.
Between 2-8% of compensation.	2% of pay more than the non-highly compensated group.
Over 8% of compensation.	1¼ times the rate of the nonhighly compensated group.

Question — What are excess contributions to a 401(k) plan?

Answer — An excess contribution is the excess of the elective contributions (including qualified nonelective and matching contributions that are treated as elective contributions) made on behalf of highly compensated employees for the plan year over the maximum amount permitted under the ADP test for such plan year.[95]

Question — How do you correct an excess contribution?

Answer — A 401(k) plan will not fail the ADP test for any plan year, and thus will maintain its qualified status if: (1) the amount of excess contributions for such plan year, along with any income attributable thereto, is returned to highly compensated employees within 12 months after the close of the applicable plan year; or (2) the highly compensated employee elects to recharacterize the excess amount contributed as an after-tax voluntary contribution.[96]

Question — What happens if a 401(k) plan fails to correct excess contributions?

Answer — A 10% excise tax is imposed on the employer unless the excess contributions are corrected within 2½ months after the end of the plan year for which they were made.[97] If excess contributions are not corrected before the end of the plan year following the plan year for which the excess contributions were made, the plan will fail to qualify for the plan year for which the excess contributions were made and for all subsequent plan years during which the excess contributions remain in the plan.[98]

Question — Are there certain measures which can be taken to assure compliance with the special nondiscrimination tests for 401(k) plans?

Answer — Yes. The plan may limit the amount subject to deferral and, if necessary, provide for a minimum level of nonelective employer contributions. For example, if a profit-sharing plan provides for nonelective employer contributions of 2% of compensation which is nonforfeitable and subject to appropriate distribution restrictions and eligible employees are limited to deferring an additional 2% of compensation, the nondiscrimination tests will be satisfied in all cases. An alternative would be to make the cash-or-deferred election irrevocable for the entire plan year.

Question — Are there any restrictions on the distribution of elective contributions?

Answer — A 401(k) plan must provide that amounts attributable to elective contributions may not be distributed before the occurrence of one of the following events:

1. The participant's retirement, death, disability, or other termination of service;

2. The termination of the plan without the establishment of a successor defined contribution plan;

3. The sale of the business or subsidiary;

4. The participant's attainment of age 59½, or

5. The participant's financial hardship.[99]

Question — What constitutes "financial hardship" for purposes of permissible distributions?

Answer — For a distribution to be considered as having been made on account of financial hardship it must be made due to an immediate and heavy financial need of the employee and it must be necessary to satisfy that need. The determination of the existence of the immediate and heavy financial need must be made in accordance with

The Tools and Techniques of Estate Planning

nondiscriminatory and objective standards set forth in the plan.

Question — What amounts from the plan may be distributed on account of a financial hardship?

Answer — A distribution that is made due to hardship must be limited to the distributable amount. The "distributable amount" is equal to the employee's total elective contributions as of the date of distribution, reduced by the amount of previous distributions on account of hardship.

Question — What are some examples of permissible hardship distributions?

Answer — A distribution is treated as being made on account of immediate and heavy financial need if it is for:

1. The payment of expenses for medical care that were either previously incurred by, or are necessary for the medical care of, the employee or the employee's spouse or dependents;

2. The costs directly related to the purchase, excluding mortgage payments, of the employee's principal residence;

3. The payment of tuition, related educational fees and room and board for the next 12 months of post-secondary education for the employee, his spouse, children, or dependents; and

4. The payment of amounts necessary to prevent the eviction of the employee from his principal residence or to prevent foreclosure on the mortgage on the employee's principal residence.

The IRS has the authority to expand the above list of expenses found under the regulations, through the issuance of revenue rulings, notices and other documents of general applicability, rather than on an individual basis.[100]

Question — What are examples of distributions which are not treated as necessary to satisfy an immediate and heavy financial need?

Answer — Distributions are not treated as necessary to satisfy an immediate and heavy financial need of an employee:

1. To the extent the amount of the distribution is in excess of the amount required to relieve the financial need. The amount of the immediate and heavy financial need may include amounts necessary to pay federal, state or local income taxes or penalties reasonably anticipated to result from the distribution; and

2. To the extent the need may be relieved from other sources that are reasonably available to the employee, referred to as an "employee resource." For example, a vacation home owned by the employee and his spouse is treated as an employee resource. However, property held in an irrevocable trust for the benefit of the employee's children is not treated as an employee resource.

Question — What are the advantages of life insurance in a qualified retirement plan?

Answer — There are a number of advantages. These include (1) protection against the premature death of a participant, (2) securing the right to use guaranteed annuity rates at a future retirement date, (3) assurance that insurance can be purchased at original age rates when the participant retires or terminates employment, and (4) in a profit-sharing plan providing key person insurance on the lives of corporate officers or valuable employees for the benefit of the trust and its participants.

Question — Can a qualified pension or profit-sharing plan provide any protection from creditors?

Answer — Yes. ERISA provides that a pension, profit-sharing, or HR-10 plan will not be qualified unless it provides that benefits provided under the plan may not be assigned or alienated, voluntarily or involuntarily. An exception to this rule exists for assignments used to secure plan loans to a participant and voluntary and revocable assignments which do not exceed 10 percent of any benefit payment to a participant, unless the assignment is made for purposes of defraying plan administrative costs.[101]

It has generally been accepted in the non-bankruptcy context that the anti-alienation provision protects pension interests from the reach of creditors. The Supreme Court has recently ruled that the anti-alienation provision also protects a debtor's interest in his qualified pension plan from the reach of his creditors in bankruptcy.[102]

In addition, the creation, assignment, or recognition of a right to any benefit payable from a plan under a "qualified domestic relations order" (QDRO) is not treated as a prohibited assignment or alienation under ERISA or the Internal Revenue Code, thus allowing enforcement of state QDROs.[103] All qualified retirement plans are required to provide for the payment of benefits in accordance with the terms of any QDRO.

The term "domestic relations order" means a judgment, decree, or order (including approval of a property settlement agreement) which relates to the provision of child support, alimony payments, or marital property rights to a spouse, former spouse, child or other dependent of a participant, and is made pursuant to state domestic relations law. To be qualified, a domestic relations order must (1) create or recognize the existence of an alternate payee's right to receive all or a portion of the benefits payable with respect to a participant under a plan; (2) clearly specify certain facts (e.g., name and address of participant and alternate payee, amount of benefits to be paid and the number of payments); and (3) not alter the amount or form of benefits under a plan. The term "alternate payee" means any spouse, former spouse, child or other dependent of a participant who is recognized by a domestic relations order as having a right to receive all, or a portion of, a participant's benefits under a plan.[104]

A QDRO can require benefits to be paid to an alternate payee at the participant's earliest retirement age under the plan without regard to whether the participant has separated from service or retired.

Question — When does an employee become subject to tax on benefits accruing in a qualified plan?

Answer — An employee or beneficiary of a qualified plan will not be taxed until benefits are received from the plan. For example, even though a participant in a profit-sharing plan has the unrestricted right to make withdrawals of employer or deductible employee contributions, or the earnings on nondeductible employee contributions, there will be no current tax based on constructive receipt. This increases the appeal of making voluntary contributions to qualified plans even when such contributions are nondeductible.

Question — Are there any restrictions on pension or profit-sharing plan investments in "collectibles"?

Answer — Yes. Investment in "collectibles" by an individually directed account under a qualified plan is treated as a current taxable distribution. Collectibles are defined as (1) art, (2) rugs or antiques, (3) metals or gems, (4) stamps or coins, (5) alcoholic beverages, or (6) any other tangible personal property designated as a "collectible" by the Secretary of the Treasury.[105]

Question — Is a qualified plan required to provide a participant's surviving spouse survivor benefits?

Answer — Yes. A participant's surviving spouse must be provided "automatic survivor benefits."[106] Defined benefit plans and defined contribution plans are required to provide automatic survivor benefits (1) in the form of a "qualified joint and survivor annuity," to a vested participant who receives a plan distribution for reasons other than the participant's death (i.e., termination of employment, retirement or disability); and (2) in the form of a "qualified pre-retirement survivor annuity" to a vested participant who dies before reaching the "annuity starting date" under the plan and who has a surviving spouse.

For automatic survivor coverage purposes, a vested participant means a participant who has a nonforfeitable right to any portion of the accrued benefit or account balance, whether or not the participant is still employed by the employer. The term "annuity starting date" means the first day of the first period for which an amount is payable as an annuity (or, in the case of a non-annuity benefit, the first day on which all events have occurred entitling the participant to the benefit).[107]

The automatic survivor coverage rules do not apply to a profit sharing or stock bonus plan if (a) the plan provides that the participant's vested account balance will be paid to his or her surviving spouse (or to a designated beneficiary if there is no surviving spouse or if the surviving spouse gives the proper consent); (b) the participant does not elect payment of benefits in the form of a life annuity; and (c) with respect to the participant, the plan is not a transferee of a plan required to provide automatic survivor benefits.[108]

A "qualified joint and survivor annuity" is an annuity for the life of the participant with a survivor annuity for the life of the spouse that is not less than 50 percent (and not greater than 100 percent) of the amount that is payable during the joint lives of the participant and spouse, and that is the actuarial equivalent of a single life annuity for the life of the participant.[109]

A "qualified pre-retirement survivor annuity" is an annuity for the life of the surviving spouse of the participant with payments to the surviving spouse which are not less than the payments that would have been made under the qualified joint and survivor annuity (or the actuarial equivalent thereof), under the rules set forth in Code section 417(c).

A qualified joint and survivor annuity and a qualified pre-retirement survivor annuity need not be provided by a plan unless the participant and the surviving spouse have been married throughout the one-year period ending on the earlier of the participant's retirement, disability or the date of the participant's death.[110]

A plan participant may elect not to receive the qualified joint and survivor annuity and/or the qualified pre-retirement survivor annuity at any time during an applicable election period and to receive benefits in another form offered under the plan. The participant is permitted to revoke any such election during the applicable election period. The applicable election period, in the case of a qualified joint and survivor annuity, is the 90 day period ending on the annuity starting date. The applicable election, in the case of a qualified pre-retirement survivor annuity, is a period beginning on the first day of the plan year in which the participant attains age 35 and ending on the date of the participant's death. If the participant separates from service, the applicable election period begins not later than the date of separation.[111]

An election by the participant not to take survivor coverage is effective only if the participant's spouse consents in writing, the consent is witnessed by a plan representative or a notary public, and the spouse's consent acknowledges the effect of the election. Spousal consent is not required if it is established (to the satisfaction of a plan representative) that there is no spouse or that the spouse cannot be located.[112]

Question — Will a plan participant on a one-year leave of absence from work due to a maternity/paternity reason incur a "break-in-service" and therefore cease to participate in the plan?

Answer — No. An employee who is on a leave of absence for maternity/paternity reasons will not incur a one-year break-in-service for purposes of participation or vesting in the year in which a break would otherwise occur.[113] Maternity/paternity reasons include pregnancy, childbirth, adoption or child caring immediately after childbirth or adoption.

Question — What additional taxes may affect a qualified plan or its participants?

Answer — Generally, there are four other taxes affecting retirement plans (which have not been discussed elsewhere). The taxes are as follows:

1. A 20% nondeductible excise tax is imposed on the amount of any "employer reversion" from a qualified plan if (1) a significant amount of the reversion is used to fund benefits in a replacement plan, (2) a significant amount is used to increased the benefits of participants under the terminating plan, or (3) the employer is in bankruptcy. Otherwise, the tax is 50%.[114] Liability for this tax rests on the employer. An "employer reversion" is the amount of cash and the fair market value of other property received (directly or indirectly) by an employer from a qualified plan. Certain mistaken excess payments may be excluded.

2. There is a 50% nondeductible excise tax for the failure to make a minimum required distribution from the plan. The tax is equal to 50% of the amount by which the minimum required distribution exceeds the actual amount distributed during the taxable year. The tax is imposed on the payee. A "waiver" is allowed for "reasonable error" if steps are being taken to pay out the balance due.[115]

3. An additional penalty tax applies in cases where there is an underpayment of tax due to an overstatement of pension liabilities. The amount of the penalty depends on the amount of the overstatement: 20% for overstatements of 200% or more but less than 400% of the correct amount of liabilities and 40% for overstatements of 400% or more.[116]

4. There is a 50% excise tax on prohibited allocations of employer securities acquired in a transaction involving the tax-deferred sale to an ESOP.[117]

Question — Where a beneficiary designation for a pension plan names the surviving spouse as primary beneficiary, but with an alternate gift to a Family Trust in the event of the death of the surviving spouse before the passage of a reasonable time following the participant's death (e.g., 90 days), or in the event of a disclaimer by the surviving spouse, are there any concerns over restrictions created by the Retirement Equity Act of 1984?

Answer — REA '84 generally provides that all benefits from pension and profit sharing plans, with some exceptions, must be in the form of annuities. If the participant has died, then the general provision under REA '84 is that there be an annuity for the lifetime of the survivor as to at least one-half of the property. Whether the transfer can be made to a trust in lieu of the surviving spouse is something being questioned by a number of practitioners today. Indeed, *The REA Book* says that the requirements of the Act cannot be met by naming an irrevocable trust as sole beneficiary even though the surviving spouse is the sole beneficiary of the trust and the benefits payable under the trust meet the survivor annuity benefit requirements of the Act.[118]

If the surviving spouse dies, then it may be that REA '84 no longer applies, and any normal transfer can be made and property can go to a trust outright as opposed to being in an annuity form.

The Tools and Techniques of Estate Planning

On the other hand, the Act seems to lay out clearly the rule that any transfer outside the normal REA '84 rules must be done only on the basis of a written exception being made by the participant and a particular form of written waiver by the surviving spouse of any annuity rights. There have been suggestions that payments by pension plans administrators to trusts without such a formal written request and written waiver might cause the trust to be disqualified.

This is an area of the law in which a pension law expert should be consulted on beneficiary designations involving large amounts.

The beneficiary designation form reproduced at Figure 28.3 (3 pages) at the end of this chapter is used by Ralph Gano Miller in his California practice and contains language designed to overcome the problems inherent in the law as it presently reads.

Question — What are the gift and estate tax consequences of joint and survivor annuities and survivor annuities to a spouse under REA '84?

Answer — These annuity payments automatically qualify for the gift and estate tax marital deduction so long as no payments can be made to anyone other than a spouse until the death of the surviving spouse. This is true even though there could be payments or distributions to another person after the death of both spouses.

Note that in the case of the estate tax marital deduction, the executor of the estate of the first spouse to die can elect out of the marital deduction.

Question — Can a life insurance trust be created within a qualified retirement plan?

Answer — Many commentators believe it can, although there is no authority on this point. The plan would provide for the creation of a separate trust, which is in effect an irrevocable life insurance trust. As discussed in Chapter 36, it is structured so that the insured has no control over the trust, and the policy proceeds cannot be distributed to the insured or his or her estate. The premiums are paid through the plan.

This technique has not been tested, and may run into problems where there is a surviving spouse, because of the survivor annuity rules. Also, some issues have been raised as to whether there could be a problem with a prohibited transaction. Finally, it must be remembered that the growth and income from investments in qualified plans is tax free until retirement, and since the inside build-up of value in life insurance policies is generally also tax free, it may be better to maintain insurance outside of qualified plans.

Question — If a distribution from a qualified plan is made to a surviving spouse on the death of the participant, can he or she roll this over into an individual retirement account (IRA)?

Answer — A spousal rollover is permitted as to all or part of such a distribution, and the distribution will not be subject to income tax to the extent it is rolled over. Spousal rollovers are discussed in chapter 18.

ASRS, Sec. 59.

Footnote References

Profit-Sharing/Pension Plan

1. Reg. 1.401-1(b)(2).
2. IRC Sec. 401(a).
3. ERISA Sec. 402(a)(1).
4. IRC Sec. 401(a)(9).
5. IRC Sec. 401(k)(2)(B)(ii).
6. IRC Secs. 401(k)(2)(C), 401(k)(3)(D).
7. IRC Sec. 401(k)(4)(A).
8. IRC Secs. 401(a)(30), 402(g).
9. See, e.g., IRC Sec. 401(a).
10. IRC Sec. 410(a)(1).
11. IRC Sec. 410(a)(1)(B).
12. IRC Sec. 410(b)(1).
13. IRC Sec. 410(b)(2).
14. IRC Sec. 401(a)(26).
15. IRC Secs. 410(a)(1)(A), 410(a)(3)(A).
16. IRC Sec. 410(b)(3)(A).
17. IRC Sec. 411(a)(1).
18. IRC Secs. 401(k)(2)(C), 401(k)(3)(D).
19. IRC Sec. 411(a)(2).
20. IRC Secs. 415(c)(1), 415(d)(1).
21. IRC Sec. 404(a)(3)(A).
22. IRC Sec. 415(c)(3)(C).
23. IRC Secs. 415(b)(1), 415(d)(1).
24. IRC Sec. 415(b)(5)(A).
25. IRC Sec. 415(b)(4).
26. IRC Sec. 415(b)(5)(B).
27. IRC Sec. 415(b)(2)(B).
28. IRC Sec. 415(b)(2)(C).
29. IRC Sec. 415(b)(2)(D).
30. IRC Sec. 415(b)(2)(B).
31. IRC Sec. 415(c)(1).
32. IRC Sec. 415(e).
33. IRC Sec. 404(a)(1).

34. IRC Sec. 412(c)(7).
35. IRC Sec. 404(a)(3). Pre-1987 unused contribution carryforwards are still available.
36. IRC Sec. 404(a)(7).
37. IRC Sec. 219(e), as amended by TRA '86, Sec. 1101(b).
38. IRC Sec. 72(o)(3).
39. See *Vinson & Elkins v. Comm.*, 93-2 USTC 50,632 (5th Cir. 1993); *Rhoades, McKee & Boer v. U.S.*, 93-2 USTC 50,425 (W.D.MI 1993); *Wachtell, Lipton, Rosen & Katz v. Comm.*, TC Memo 1992-392, aff'd 94-1 USTC 50,272 (2d Cir. 1994).
40. Reg. 1.401-7.
41. Reg. 1.401-4(a)(1)(iii).
42. IRC Sec. 401(a)(8).
43. IRC Secs. 411(b)(1)(H), 411(b)(2).
44. IRC Sec. 411(a)(8).
45. IRC Sec. 401(l).
46. IRC Sec. 416.
47. IRC Sec. 416(g).
48. IRC Sec. 416(i)(1).
49. Reg. 1.416-1, T-13.
50. IRC Sec. 416(b).
51. IRC Sec. 416(c).
52. IRC Sec. 401(a)(17).
53. IRC Secs. 404(a)(1), 404(a)(3).
54. IRC Sec. 501(a).
55. IRC Sec. 402(d)(1).
56. IRC Sec. 402(d)(4)(b).
57. IRC Sec. 402(a).
58. Reg. 1.72-16(b).
59. IRC Sec. 72(o)(3).
60. IRC Sec. 401(a)(9)(A); Prop. Reg. 1.401(a)(9)-1.
61. Prop. Reg. 1.401(a)(9)-2.
62. IRC Sec. 72(b).
63. Notice 88-118, 1988-2 CB 450.
64. IRC Sec. 72(e)(8).
65. IRC Sec. 72(t).
66. IRC Sec. 4980A.
67. IRC Sec. 4980A(f).
68. IRC Sec. 402(d)(4)(A).
69. Reg. 1.72-16(c).
70. IRC Sec. 2039.
71. IRC Sec. 4980A(d).
72. IRC Sec. 402(d)(4)(G).
73. *Ablamis v. Roper*, 937 F.2d 1450 (9th Cir. 1991).
74. ERISA Sec. 3(21)(A).
75. ERISA Sec. 406(a)(1)(D).
76. IRC Sec. 4975(a).
77. ERISA Sec. 404(a)(1).
78. ERISA Sec. 4022(b)(3); PBGC Reg. 2621. App. A.
79. ERISA Sec. 4006, as amended by URAA '94.
80. ERISA Sec. 408(b)(1); Labor Reg. 2550.408(b)-1.
81. IRC Sec. 4975(d); ERISA Sec. 408(d).
82. IRC Sec. 72(p)(1).
83. IRC Sec. 72(p)(2)(A).
84. IRC Sec. 72(p)(2)(B).
85. ERISA Secs. 101-105.
86. See Reg. 1.401(a)(4)-2(b)(4).
87. See Rev. Rul. 61-164, 1961-2 CB 99; Rev. Rul. 66-143, 1966-1 CB 79.
88. See, e.g., Rev. Rul. 60-83, 1960-1 CB 157.
89. IRC Sec. 401(m).
90. IRC Sec. 219(e), as amended by TRA '86, Sec. 1101(b).
91. IRC Sec. 401(m).
92. IRC Sec. 415(c)(2)(B).
93. IRC Secs. 402(g), 3121(v).
94. IRC Sec. 401(k)(3).
95. IRC Sec. 401(k)(8)(B).
96. IRC Sec. 401(k)(8)(A).
97. IRC Sec. 4979.
98. IRC Sec. 401(k)(8).
99. IRC Sec. 401(k)(2)(B).
100. Reg. 1.401(k)-1(d)(2)(iv).
101. ERISA Sec. 206(d).
102. *Patterson v. Shumate*, 112 S.Ct. 2242 (1992).
103. IRC Sec. 401(a)(13(B).
104. IRC Sec. 414(p).
105. IRC Sec. 408(m).
106. IRC Secs. 401(a)(11), 417.
107. IRC Sec. 417(f)(2).
108. IRC Sec. 401(a)(11)(B).
109. IRC Sec. 417(b).
110. IRC Sec. 417(d).
111. IRC Sec. 417(a)(6).
112. IRC Sec. 417(a)(2).
113. IRC Secs. 410(a)(5)(E), 411(a)(6)(E).
114. IRC Sec. 4980.
115. IRC Sec. 4974.
116. IRC Sec. 6662(f).
117. IRC Sec. 4979A.
118. Wilf, et al., *The REA Book* (REA Publishing Company: Philadelphia, 1987), Qs I.54 and I.55. Q. I.67 also addresses the question of the surviving spouse's disclaimer of annuity benefits required under REA, pointing out that such a disclaimer may be a prohibited assignment or alienation, in which event payment pursuant to the disclaimer could subject the plan administrator to fiduciary liability and could endanger the qualified status of the plan.

Figure 28.3

DESIGNATION OF BENEFICIARY FOR

_____

_____

_____   _____
Employee's Name   Employee's Soc. Security No.

1. I hereby designate the following, in the order of priority indicated, as the beneficiary to whom (or to which) any such benefit shall be distributed at the death of the participant:

   A. To _____, my spouse, or if my spouse is not then living, or if my spouse disclaims such benefit (as provided in Paragraph 6 below), then in accordance with Paragraph B below.

   B. To the Trustees of the _____, dated _____, hereinafter called the "Family Trust", to be held, managed, administered and distributed according to the terms and provisions thereof.

2. If at the time of death, none of the above beneficiaries survive me or are in existence, then this Plan and Trust share shall be distributed as then provided in the Plan and Trust Agreement.

3. I reserve the right to revoke or change the designation or any of them shown above, but such revocation or change shall be in writing directed to the Committee, and no such revocation or change shall be effective unless and until received by the Committee.

4. Rights of the designated beneficiaries shall be subject to the terms and conditions of the Plan and Trust Agreement and all rules and regulations formulated thereunder.

5. Payment of any credits or funds in the Trust Account to the beneficiary or beneficiaries designated herein shall be a full and complete release and discharge of the Trustee, the Committee and the Employer to the extent of such payment.

6. Disclaimer may be by any method which is effective under the laws of the State of California or by written transfer of the right to receive the death benefit, provided that such transfer meets the requirements of Section 2518(c)(3) of the Internal Revenue Code as is from time to time amended.

7. Any voluntary contribution account benefits shall be distributed according to the terms of this direction and shall be treated as completely separate benefits for the purposes of disclaimer.

8. This beneficiary designation shall not be construed in any way as a revocation of any election I have made pursuant to Section 242(b)(2) of the Internal Revenue Code.

Dated _____

                                                     _____
                                                              Participant

[See Spousal Consent Over]

Figure 28.3 continued

TO BE EXECUTED IN THE PRESENCE OF A NOTARY PUBLIC

SPOUSE'S CONSENT TO BENEFICIARY DESIGNATION

CAVEAT: THIS BENEFICIARY DESIGNATION MAY NO LONGER BE VALID ONCE THE PARTICIPANT HAS REACHED HIS OR HER "ANNUITY STARTING DATE" as defined in Section 417 of the Internal Revenue Code if the participant elects a distribution in a form other than a qualified joint and survivor annuity unless the participant's spouse at that time properly completes the consent form shown on page 3 hereto.

I, the spouse of the above-named participant, hereby consent to the above Beneficiary Designation, which names an individual(s) or entity other than myself as primary beneficiary of the benefits payable to the participant in the event of his or her death under the Plan. I hereby waive any rights I may have under federal or state law to receive benefits under the Plan in the form of a qualified pre-retirement survivor annuity and acknowledge that I am not to be the direct recipient of any benefits the Plan provides to a participant's "primary beneficiary" (a spouse may be the indirect beneficiary of such benefits in certain circumstances — such as designation of a family trust as primary beneficiary). I further acknowledge that I am familiar with the financial and legal consequences of my consent to my spouse's election to waive a qualified pre-retirement survivor annuity form of benefit.

By my signature below, I am also consenting to any change by my spouse in designation of beneficiary following the date of this consent.

Dated: _____   _____
                                                                    Spouse's Signature

THE SPOUSE'S SIGNATURE MUST BE WITNESSED BY A NOTARY PUBLIC!

STATE OF CALIFORNIA   )
                                                    : ss.
COUNTY OF SAN DIEGO   )

On this _____ day of _____, 19_____, before me, a Notary Public in and for said County and State, personally appeared _____, personally known to me or proved to me on the basis of satisfactory evidence to be the person described in and whose name is subscribed to the foregoing instrument, and executed such instrument before me.

WITNESS my hand and official seal.

_____
Notary Public

The Plan Committee hereby accepts the foregoing beneficiary designation.

Dated _____   By _____

Figure 28.3 continued

SPOUSE'S CONSENT TO BENEFICIARY DESIGNATION

(REQUIRED TO BE COMPLETED IN THE NINETY (90) DAY PERIOD PRIOR TO EITHER (1) THE BEGINNING OF RECEIPT OF ANNUITY PAYMENTS; OR (2) IN THE CASE OF NON-ANNUITY BENEFITS, THE FIRST DAY ON WHICH ALL EVENTS HAVE OCCURRED WHICH ENTITLE THE PARTICIPANT TO RECEIVE BENEFITS)

I, the spouse of the above named participant, hereby consent to the above Beneficiary Designation, which names an individual(s) or entity other than myself as primary beneficiary of the benefits payable to the participant in the event of his or her death following his or her election to waive the Qualified Joint and Survivor Annuity form of distribution under the Plan.

I understand that by consenting to my spouse's election to receive benefits in a form other than a Qualified Joint and Survivor Annuity, I am waiving my right to receive a survivor annuity under the Plan and am hereby consent to payment of any death benefits provided by the Plan to the beneficiary designated above by my spouse. I further represent that I have received as much financial information from the Plan and my spouse as I deemed necessary to consent to my spouse's designation of such beneficiary.

By my signature below, I am also consenting to any change by my spouse in designation of beneficiary following the date of this consent.

Dated _____   Name: _____

                                          Address: _____

                                                        _____

                                                        _____

THE SPOUSE'S SIGNATURE MUST BE WITNESSED BY A NOTARY PUBLIC!

STATE OF CALIFORNIA   )

                            : ss.

COUNTY OF SAN DIEGO)

On this _____ day of _____, 19_____, before me, a Notary Public in and for said County and State, personally appeared _____, personally known to me or proved to me on the basis of satisfactory evidence to be the person described in and whose name is subscribed to the foregoing instrument, and executed such instrument before me.

WITNESS my hand and official seal.

_____
                                    Notary Public

Chapter 29

S CORPORATION

WHAT IS IT?

An "S" corporation is a corporation that has made an election to have its income, deductions, capital gains and losses, charitable contributions, and credits passed through to its shareholders. To a great extent an S corporation is treated for tax purposes similarly to a partnership.

WHEN IS THE USE OF SUCH A DEVICE INDICATED?

1. When your client (currently a sole proprietor or partnership) is entering a new, high risk business, and would like the legal protection against creditors offered by corporate status, but wants to be able to personally deduct losses of the business enterprise if the venture fails. (This same goal can be achieved to a limited degree through the use of Section 1244 stock in a normal corporation.)

   An "S" election enables corporate losses to be passed through the corporation and deducted on the tax returns of the individual shareholders (but only to the extent of the adjusted basis of their stock in the corporation and loans made to the corporation).[1] Thus, losses of an S corporation may be used to offset income earned outside of the business.

2. Where the business, although not inherently risky, has a period of loss during the first years of starting up, the client may elect S corporation status for the early loss years. When the business begins to make a profit, the election may be terminated and future profits taxed to the corporation. The method and other effects of the termination should be carefully planned.

3. When the stockholder(s) would like to take out all corporate income without the normal double taxation on corporate earnings and such payments could not be justified as reasonable compensation. In other words, when S corporation status has been elected, generally there is no tax at the corporate level; typically, income earned by the S corporation is taxed only once, to the individual shareholders, regardless of the amount of income or the services performed, if any, by the shareholders.

Double taxation has always been a problem when income is earned and then accumulated in a regular ("C") corporation. Double taxation under current law is even more onerous than in the past. There are four reasons:

a. Corporate tax rates will often exceed individual rates. This is particularly true in the case of professional service corporations, which are taxed at a flat rate of 35% on every dollar of taxable income. No "run up the brackets" is allowed to these corporations.

b. Distributions of the cash proceeds of a sale of appreciated property (assets with a fair market value in excess of their tax basis) of a regular (C) corporation upon its liquidation, or even distributions of the appreciated property itself, will trigger tax both at the corporate and shareholder levels. (Under prior law, the "built-in gains" in corporate assets usually escaped taxation on the corporate level when the assets were sold or distributed in a liquidation or Section 303 distribution even if the corporation had not made an S election. This is no longer true following the repeal of the *General Utilities* doctrine.)

c. Corporate gains on capital assets may not be eligible for a lower capital gains rate. They are taxed at a maximum rate of 28%; thus, the "lower" rate is only available to those taxpayers in the 31% to 39.6% brackets.

d. The net proceeds of the gain already taxed at the corporate level are again taxed when distributed to shareholders who no longer can take a long term capital gains deduction.

The simplified (it ignores the time value of money) example at Figure 29.1 illustrates one reason so many corporations make S elections.

The double taxation problem suffered by regular corporations' shareholders year after year can be alleviated, or in some cases even eliminated, by an increase in shareholders' salaries (thus reducing corporate taxable income).

But this ploy will not work with the potentially huge tax at the time a corporation is liquidated. First, the tax may be many times the normal "doubletax." Second, it is difficult to justify proportionately large salaries in the year the corporation is going out of business. With the loss of the ability to income average, the ultimate tax on a final liquidation could absorb the work product of years of hard work.

4. When the nontax benefits of incorporation are desired, but the individual shareholders are in lower tax brackets than the corporation and they would like the advantage of the tax savings that can be obtained by having the income earned by the corporation taxed directly to them as individuals.

5. Where it is desired to spread income among a number of family members, an S corporation is a useful device. By giving stock, the tax on corporate earnings may be shifted to a large number of relatively low tax bracket individuals and taxed at their brackets rather than at the client's bracket (provided they are age 14 or over).

6. When avoidance of the AMT (alternative minimum tax) is desirable.

7. When avoidance of the accumulated earnings tax is desirable.

WHAT ARE THE REQUIREMENTS?

1. The corporation must be a domestic corporation. This means it must be created or organized in the U.S. or one of its states.

2. It must have no more than 35 shareholders.

3. Shareholders must be individuals, estates, or a specific type of trust. Nonresident aliens may not be shareholders.

4. The corporation can have only one class of stock. That means each share must confer equal rights to distribution and liquidation proceeds. However, it is possible to provide for differences in voting rights among shares of common stock. For instance, there can safely be a "Class A" and a "Class B" voting stock with different terms or powers, so long as both classes confer equal rights to distribution and liquidation proceeds. Similarly, bona fide buy-sell agreements, agreements restricting transferability of shares, and redemption agreements will not be held to constitute a second class of stock so long as they are not entered into to circumvent the one-class-of-stock requirements and do not establish a purchase price that is significantly in excess of or below the fair market value of the stock.

Figure 29.1

NON S CORPORATIONS UNDER PRIOR AND CURRENT LAW			
		Prior Law	Current Law
Input:	Income Earned and Accumulated	$50,000	$50,000
Input:	Corporate Tax	$8,250	7,500
	Amount Retained by Corporation	$41,750	$42,500
Input:	Tax Rate on Shareholders Upon Distribution of Assets	0.20	0.31
	Tax Payable by Shareholders	$8,350	$13,175
	Total Tax	$16,600	$20,675
Input:	Personal Tax Rate	0.50	0.31
	Probable Tax if S Corporation	$25,000	$15,500
Prior Law	Advantage of C Corporation Status	$8,400	
Curr Law	Advantage of S Corporation Status		$5,175
	Shift in Advantage	$13,575	

A "straight debt instrument" is not considered, for these purposes, a second class of stock. A "straight debt instrument" means a written unconditional promise to pay on demand or on a specified date a sum certain in money so long as: (a) the interest rate (and payment dates) are not contingent on the corporate profits, the discretion of the corporation, or other similar factors, (b) the instrument is not convertible into stock, *and* (c) the creditor is a person, estate or trust eligible to hold S corporation stock. This favorable treatment is not lost merely because the interest rate is dependent upon the prime rate (or a similar factor not related to the debtor corporation).

5. The S corporation cannot be a member of an affiliated group or have an active subsidiary.

HOW IT IS DONE — AN EXAMPLE

There are five equal shareholders of the ABC Corporation, which is currently earning profits of $50,000. The federal corporate tax on $50,000 is $7,500, 15 percent of the first $50,000 of earnings. This means the amount which could be distributed to the S corporation's shareholders is $42,500 ($50,000-$7,500). Each stockholder's share is $8,500 ($42,500 ÷ 5). Of course, this amount is further reduced by personal taxes. Assuming each owner has outside income and is in approximately a 31 percent tax bracket, individual taxes will be about $2,635. The aggregate income tax on all five indi-

viduals' income will be $13,175. In total, the taxes paid are $20,675 ($7,500 of corporate tax plus $13,175 of personal taxes). (The example has been simplified for illustrative purposes.)

Now assume the corporation has elected "S" status. The election, of course, does not change corporate profits, which are still $50,000. However, the $50,000 is now passed directly through to the shareholders (the character of the income also is passed through) and there is no corporate tax to pay. The net profits subject to distribution are $50,000. Dividing that figure by five, each shareholder's share is $10,000. Personal taxes are therefore increased to $3,100 each. The aggregate tax payable is $15,500.

Taxes Before S Election $20,675	Taxes After S Election $15,500

The S election saves $5,175 annually.

WHAT ARE THE TAX IMPLICATIONS?

1. S corporations and their shareholders are taxed under essentially the same rules that apply to partnerships and their partners. Generally, the S corporation does not pay federal income tax. Its income (or loss) is passed through directly to its shareholders and therefore avoids the double tax on corporate earnings.

Figure 29.2

TAX PAYABLE BY ENTITY OR SOLE SHAREHOLDER
C CORPORATION v. S CORPORATION

The chart below compares the tax payable by an entity owned by a sole shareholder who operates as a "C" corporation with the tax the same individual would pay in 1995 if the corporation had elected S corporation status. It is assumed the shareholder files jointly and that the S corporation income is exactly equal to his or her taxable income and does not take earnings and profits out of the C corportion (which would increase the total tax payable and swing the advantage to the S election much more quickly than is apparent in the chart).

Taxable Income	Tax as a C Corporation	Tax as an S Corporation
$ 25,000	$ 3,750	$ 3,750
50,000	7,500	8,930
100,000	22,250	23,103
150,000	41,750	38,923
200,000	61,250	56,923
500,000	170,000	173,689
750,000	255,000	272,689
1,000,000	340,000	371,689
2,000,000	680,000	767,689

2. Essentially, taxable income of an S corporation is computed as follows:

Any income that could affect the individual tax liability of a shareholder is passed directly through the corporation to the shareholders. Likewise, any loss, deduction, or credit that could affect the liability of a shareholder is passed through just as if the entity were a partnership. Even tax exempt income such as municipal bond interest or life insurance proceeds is passed through as tax exempt income.

Shareholders must report or deduct all these "separately treated" items in proportion to their shareholdings. In other words, a 10 percent shareholder would be required to report 10 percent of the corporation's income, but would be entitled to 10 percent of any corporate earned deductions or credits.

Typical separately treated items include (1) gains and losses from corporate sales or exchanges of capital assets, and (2) charitable contributions (the corporation's contributions are passed through to shareholders who add them to their own personal contributions in determining the charitable contribution deduction on their own personal returns).

3. Tax exempt interest received by an S corporation retains its tax exempt character and increases the shareholders' basis. If the interest is subsequently distributed, it is not taxable but reduces the shareholders' basis.

4. Amounts passed through as credits are passed through on a per-share per-day basis and are claimed by the shareholders on their personal returns.

5. Allowances for depletion with respect to oil and gas wells are separately computed for each shareholder. Each shareholder must keep records of his basis in each well, and adjust the basis for any depletion taken.

6. Net operating loss is deductible by a shareholder as an ordinary loss in computing adjusted gross income. If it exceeds the shareholder's other income, it can be carried back for three years and then carried forward for up to 15 years. The amount of loss that can be passed through in a given year is limited to the sum of (a) the basis of the shareholder's S corporation stock and (b) the basis of loans he has made to the corporation. However, losses in excess of this sum can be carried forward indefinitely and will be allowed in any subsequent year in which the shareholder has adequate basis in his stock or in debt the corporation owes him.

The corporation's remaining (the nonseparately computed) income, if any, is taxable to the shareholders. Each shareholder reports on Schedule E of his Form 1040 his pro rata share. Likewise, each shareholder must report his pro rata share of corporate preference items.

All this income must be reported by a shareholder in his taxable year in which, or with which, the corporation's tax year ends. (S corporations must use a calendar year for tax accounting purposes, so the tax year of an S corporation ends on December 31, unless a business reason is established for a fiscal year period.) In the case of a deceased shareholder, pro rata shares of income attributable to the portion of the corporation's tax year prior to his death are reportable on the final return. Income earned in the balance of the year is reported on the estate's income tax return or on the return of the beneficiary who received the stock.

The pro rata shares are determined on a day by day per-share basis. This per-share per-day method of prorating income liability also applies where S corporation stock is sold or given away.

There are two circumstances where an S corporation may pay tax at the maximum corporate rate, currently 34% (35% if corporate income exceeds $10,000,000). Neither will apply unless the corporation at sometime in the past was taxed as a regular (C) corporation.

The first situation is where the S corporation has any earnings and profits derived while it was a C corporation and now has passive investment income, which includes such items as rents, royalties, dividends and interest. The tax is based on the passive income for the year in excess of 25% of its gross receipts.

The second situation occurs where a corporation converts from a C to an S corporation and had appreciated assets at the time of the conversion. The so-called "built in" gain on such assets will be taxed at the corporate level if they are sold within 10 years.

IMPLICATIONS AND ISSUES IN COMMUNITY PROPERTY STATES

A husband and wife, shareholders of community property stock in an S corporation, both must give their consent to the corporation's election to have its earnings taxed to the shareholders. If retention of the S corporation election is desirable, in a situation where an individual is purchasing shares with community property funds, a contract should be entered into with both that individual and his spouse whereby they would agree not to refuse to consent to the election.

The same concern discussed in Chapter 11, dealing with earnings from a separate property investment, should also be considered.

As noted, husband and wife holding stock as community property are counted as only one shareholder. Additionally, community property stock, because half is owned by each spouse, can be more easily given within the scope of the $10,000 annual exclusion without the necessity of filing a gift tax return.

QUESTIONS AND ANSWERS

Question — Under what circumstances can the S election be terminated?

Answer — An election of an S corporation will terminate under any of the following circumstances:

(a) Shareholders holding more than 50 percent of the corporation's stock consent to revoke the election. There is no official form; the corporation files a statement with the IRS revoking the election. The termination is effective for the entire taxable year if the revocation is filed on or before the 15th day of the third month of the taxable year; otherwise, the revocation is effective on the first day of the following taxable year. The entrance of a new stockholder cannot revoke an election unless that person owns more than 50 percent of the corporation's stock and that person revokes the election; if no revocation occurs, new shareholders are bound by the same rules that apply to other shareholders.

(b) The corporation fails to satisfy any of the four qualification requirements discussed above under the heading "What Are the Requirements?" The termination is effective on the day the disqualifying event occurs. For instance, the election ends if the limit on the number of shareholders is exceeded or shares are transferred to an ineligible party. Therefore, a transfer of even one share of S corporation stock to a partnership, corporation, nonresident alien, or nonqualifying trust terminates an election. Likewise, if a second class of stock is issued the election would terminate.

(c) Certain passive income exceeds 25 percent of the corporation's gross receipts for three consecutive tax years and the corporation has accumulated earnings and profits from its days as a "C" (regular) corporation at the end of each such year. This would not be a problem with a newly formed S corporation.

Question — If an S election is terminated, how soon may a new election be made?

Answer — Once terminated, an S election cannot be made again for five years unless the Commissioner of Internal Revenue consents.[2] The IRS may waive the effect of an inadvertent termination for any period if the corporation (a) corrects the event that created the termination and (b) agrees, together with all its shareholders, to be treated as if the election had been in effect for that period. (The IRS has been told in the congressional committee report to "be reasonable" in granting waivers to avoid inflicting undue hardship on S corporations where the corporation's election has been inadvertently terminated and no tax avoidance results from allowing continued S corporation treatment. For instance, if the election was terminated by the corporation's inadvertent violation of the "one class of stock" requirement but no tax avoidance resulted, the IRS should treat the election as if it never terminated.)

Question — When must an election to be taxed as an S corporation be made by an existing C corporation?

Answer — An "S" election may be made (a) at any time during the entire taxable year prior to the election year, or (b) on or before the 15th day of the 3rd month of the election year. Elections made after that date are treated as made for the next tax year. For instance, for an election to be effective in 1996, a corporation must file the election sometime between January 1, 1995 and March 15, 1996.

An effective election presupposes both that all eligibility requirements are met and that the proper consent from shareholders has been obtained. It is possible to obtain an extension of time to file in certain cases even if a shareholder fails to consent in time.

All shareholders on the day the election is made must consent (on IRS Form 2553 or on a separate consent document). Minors can sign the consent even without legal or natural guardians (or such individuals may consent on behalf of a minor who is unable to act). A decedent's personal representative (executor or administrator) signs on behalf of an estate holding S corporation stock.

Question — How is life insurance owned by an S corporation taxed?

Answer — Key person life insurance premiums are nondeductible. Death proceeds are received income tax free by the corporation and are not subject to either an accumulated earnings tax or an alternative minimum tax. When the proceeds are distributed to the corporation's shareholders, they will be treated in the same manner as any other distributions of separately treated items, i.e., it retains its character as tax free income. If a policy is surrendered during the insured's lifetime or the policy matures, any gain is taxable directly to the corporation's shareholders.

Most advisors recommend that insurance that is indicated be owned on a personal basis. This is because shareholders in an S corporation are currently taxed on corporate income used to purchase nondeductible items such as corporate life insurance, even if there is no actual distribution of cash to pay that tax. For instance, if a corporation pays a $10,000 premium, shareholders of an S corporation are taxed on $10,000 even though they do not received it.

The corporation should pay a deductible bonus to each shareholder, which, after tax, would be sufficient to pay premiums on the appropriate amounts of insurance.

Question — Can an S corporation set up a nonqualified deferred compensation plan?

Answer — An S corporation can establish a deferred compensation plan. But the tax advantage enjoyed by a conventional corporation is not available. This is because shareholders are taxed directly and immediately on the current taxable income of the corporation, whether or not that income is distributed. Because premiums are not deductible, the outlay for life insurance that is used to finance the corporation's obligation under the deferred compensation plan is immediately taxable to the individual shareholders. A corporation with a $50,000 gross income, $30,000 of deductible expenses, and which pays $5,000 in key person insurance premiums has only $15,000 available for distribution. Yet shareholders are taxed as if they had received $20,000.

Question — How are S corporations treated for fringe benefit purposes?

Answer — S corporations generally will be treated as partnerships for purposes of plan eligibility and taxation of "employee fringe benefits." All shareholders owning more than 2 percent of the stock will be considered partners.

The result is that most shareholder-employees would not be "employees" for purposes of favorable Section 79 group term, medical reimbursement, or other coverage. This results generally in taxation of the more-than-2% shareholder-employees.

Question — Is an outright gift the best way to shift income to a minor child age 14 or older through an S corporation?

Answer — An outright gift of S corporation stock to a minor makes it impossible to exercise any rights with the stock unless a court-appointed guardian is obtained. This is usually expensive, inconvenient, and typically involves a great deal of administrative inflexibility.

An alternative to an outright gift to a minor is a gift to a custodian under the appropriate Uniform Gifts to Minors Act (UGMA). Unfortunately, this device has its limitations.

First, once the minor reaches age 21 (18 in some states), the shares must be distributed. Many clients feel that this age is an inappropriate time to distribute large amounts of money or securities. Most individuals are unwilling to allow a donee-child to obtain unlimited ownership and control at that time.

A second possible problem is that if the minor dies prior to the age at which the shares must be distributed under applicable local law, the likelihood is great that the shares will be returned to the donor through the operation of state intestacy statutes.

The third potential problem is that the custodian may die or become unable to act. Under the Uniform Gifts to Minors Act it is possible that the custodian could name a successor. (Such a successor may be named by the donor when the UGMA account is established or the custodian may name his or her own successor.) Lacking advance preparations, court proceedings may have to be instituted in order to name a successor custodian; a procedure would entail costs and delays.

A grantor trust, one in which the grantor is treated as if he owned trust property for income tax purposes, is eligible to own stock in an S corporation. A grantor trust can hold S corporation stock regardless of whether it is revocable. In fact such a trust can continue as an S corporation shareholder even after the death of the grantor (but only for a limited period of up to 2 years, and even that period is allowed only if the entire corpus of the grantor trust is includable in the grantor's estate. If the entire corpus of the grantor trust is not includable in the gross estate of the grantor, a grantor trust may hold S corporation stock safely for only 60 days.)

The disadvantage of the grantor trust as a receptacle for S corporation stock is obvious: although the stock will not be in the grantor's estate if the trust is irrevocable, its income will be taxed to the grantor (and therefore the ability to shift the tax on income is lost).

Current law enables a modification of a simple trust to be eligible to hold S corporation stock. This modified conventional trust is called the QSST, the Qualified Subchapter S Trust.

Specifically, a QSST is defined in the Internal Revenue Code as one that:

1. owns stock in one or more S corporations (and may hold other types of assets)

2. actually distributes all of its income to one individual (who must be a United States resident or United States citizen)

3. has trust terms requiring that

    (a) there can be only one beneficiary at any given time

    (b) if corpus is distributed during the term of the trust, it can be distributed only to the individual who is at that time the current income beneficiary

    (c) if an income beneficiary dies, the income interest itself will end at that death or upon the earlier termination of the trust

    (d) if the trust ends before the income beneficiary dies, all the assets of the trust must be distributed to that income beneficiary

4. requires an election to be made by the income beneficiary (or the income beneficiary's legal representative) to have the QSST qualify as such. (Once that election is made, it is irrevocable and can be revoked only if the IRS consents.) That election must be made by each income beneficiary as he or she becomes one. Separate elections must be made if the stock of more than one S corporation is held in the trust.

If the requirements described above are met, the income beneficiary of a QSST (which can be set up during the grantor's lifetime or by will) is treated as the owner of the stock. The consequence is that any income, as well as any gains or losses, passes directly from the S corporation to the minor beneficiary.

What are the advantages of a QSST? A gift of S corporation stock can be made to a minor through the trust without incurring the disadvantages of outright

ownership. This enables an individual to split income among family members while at the same time eliminating the gift from inclusion in his gross estate. So both income shifting and wealth transfers are possible through the QSST.

Unlike a custodianship, a QSST can continue beyond age 18 (or 21) and can last as long as the grantor directed it to last. This means that if the minor dies before the trust terminates, the trust can continue for the lives of a number of successive income beneficiaries and does not have to force trust assets into the estate of the deceased income beneficiary.

Question — What is a Section 678 trust?

Answer — The QSST is not the only alternative to outright and UGMA gifts. "A nongrantor-owner trust" is an eligible S corporation stock shareholder. The criterion for favorable tax treatment under this type of trust (Section 678 governs, and therefore these nongrantor-owner trusts have come to be called "Section 678 trusts") is that the beneficiary must have unrestricted power "exercisable solely by himself to vest the corpus or the income therefrom in himself." In other words, the beneficiary will be taxed on the income from the S corporation held by the trust if he has the right to take both income and corpus whenever he wants. There must be no restrictions on the beneficiary's right to exercise a withdrawal power.

A Section 678 trust can be created by a parent or grandparent who transfers S corporation stock to it for the benefit of a minor. The minor would be given an unrestricted power to withdraw income or corpus for his own benefit.

Question — How are gifts to QSSTs and Section 678 trusts taxed for gift tax purposes?

Answer — From a gift standpoint, a contribution to either trust will be considered a complete gift. Such gifts can qualify for the gift tax annual exclusion either by meeting the requirements of Section 2503(c) or by including a Crummey withdrawal power.

Question — Will the property in a QSST or Section 678 trust be includable in the estate of a beneficiary?

Answer — In the case of a QSST beneficiary, if the beneficiary is given only income rights, assets remaining in the trust at the time of the beneficiary's death will not be includable in his or her estate.

Just the opposite applies in the case of a Section 678 trust. Inclusion is a certainty because, by definition, the beneficiary must be given a general power of appointment (the power of withdrawal) over all or a portion of the trust. Property subject to that power at the time of the beneficiary's death will be includable in his or her estate.

Question — How can a client transfer ownership of a business through an S corporation and at the same time shift income?

Answer — An S corporation is an ideal vehicle to shift both wealth and income to other family members. For instance, assume a doctor, as a sideline, establishes a laboratory or dispensary. He could incorporate the business as an S corporation and give all the shares of the newly formed business to his children (all of whom are 14 or older).

The business would pay no income taxes at the corporate level. The children would pay income taxes on their share of the company's profits (which would otherwise have been taxed to their higher bracket father).

The best type of business for wealth and income shifting purposes is one in which the client performs no services (or the services are only incidental). If the client performs significant services or services that generate all the corporation's income, the IRS is likely to attribute earnings to the client and tax him accordingly. For instance, if the doctor, as a sideline, gives medical lectures for a fee, the S corporation will not be able to shift the tax on income it receives as compensation for his lectures to his children.

Conversely, if income from a passive investment (such as S corporation income from a laboratory run by a person unrelated to the doctor) is channeled to an age 14 or older child, income (and therefore tax) can be shifted without challenge.

It is important to follow formalities. For instance, stock-owning children or their guardians should be invited to shareholder meetings.

Question — How have recent tax law changes affected the popularity of S corporations?

Answer — Recent tax law changes have significantly increased the number of S elections for eligible corporations. Reasons an S election is more valuable than ever include:

1. The relative rate structure makes the maximum corporate income tax rates (39 percent) higher than the maximum individual income tax rate (31 percent).

The passthrough nature of S corporation taxation provides that business income will be taxed at the lower individual rates.

2. The corporate-level exclusion on gains for distributions of property at liquidation was repealed. Therefore, the liquidation of a regular (C) corporation will often result in gain at the corporate level and then again at the shareholder level. This will seldom occur in an S corporation liquidation.

3. A flat tax rate of 35 percent is imposed on all taxable income of personal service C corporations. But corporations electing S corporation treatment are generally not subject to any tax at the corporate level, and their shareholders — even professional shareholders — remain entitled to the "run through the brackets" starting with rates as low as 15 percent.

Although the S election is not available for all businesses and is, likewise, not appropriate for every circumstance, a substantial number of closely held corporations can benefit from these tax advantages.

Question — What are the disadvantages of S corporation status?

Answer — Among the drawbacks to S corporation status are that an S corporation:

(1) cannot accumulate earnings and profits for capital needs at lower corporate brackets;

(2) is limited in its ability to use carryovers (such as, net operating losses or investment tax credits);

(3) is restricted in the fringe benefits it can offer its shareholder-employees (although the tax law doesn't prohibit the S corporation from offering the benefit, because the shareholder-employee is taxable and the benefit may be nondeductible by the corporation, the cost of many fringes is prohibitive);

(4) is not appropriate as a holding vehicle for certain real estate or other investments.

Additionally, shareholders of an S corporation are prohibited from borrowing from their retirement plans (and will likely have to pay back all loans from such plans before an S election becomes effective).

Question — What is the impact of state law on the decision to elect S corporation treatment?

Answer — A decision to elect S corporation status must consider state tax laws:

(1) Some states do not recognize the S corporation's status for state income tax purposes. There are a number of jurisdictions that do not currently allow corporate income to be passed through directly to shareholders as it is under federal law. This means the corporation will have to pay tax at the corporate level.

(2) States tax "passed-through" income at their own rates. Therefore, the reduction of federal tax rates on individuals has not, in many cases, been carried through at the state level.

(3) If the federal income tax base of individuals is used at the state level for computing the state income tax and itemized deductions of a shareholder, an S election may increase the shareholder's state taxable income.

(4) Nonresident shareholders of S corporations typically must pay income tax to the state where the S corporation does business. But if the S corporation is "doing business" in several states, the multiple tax preparations and payments could be burdensome.

(5) Some states require both a federal and a separate state S corporation election. This increases costs and administrative burdens as well as the possibility for unintentional loss of S corporation status. The IRS may not recognize for federal purposes a corporation which was not recognized as such for state purposes.

Question — How does the corporate alternative minimum tax (AMT) affect corporations that have elected S corporation status?

Answer — A tough corporate alternative minimum tax applies to "C" (regular) corporations. Generally, this tax does not apply to S corporations. This means an S election may result in significant tax saving.

Question — Do the passive loss rules affect S corporations?

Answer — If a shareholder does not materially participate in the business, losses from the business would be considered "passive." They can therefore be used only to offset passive income of the shareholder. Likewise, income received by such a shareholder from the business should be considered "passive" and should therefore offset any passive losses from other investments of the shareholder.

Question — Will the pro-rata allocation of income to shareholders in a family S corporation always be allowed for federal income tax purposes?

Answer — Not necessarily. Following rules based on those applicable to family partnerships, discussed in Chapter 11, the allocation of S corporation income to family members may be disregarded if the income is not derived from capital, the transferor family members are not adequately compensated for their services, or the transferor family members retain too much control over the transferred stock.[3]

ASRS, Sec. 43; 53, ¶22.5; 59, ¶490.4(b).

Footnote References

S Corporation

1. IRC Sec. 1366(d), Reg. §1.1363-1.
2. Reg. §1.1362-5(a).
3. IRC Sec. 1366(e).

Chapter 30

SALE (GIFT) — LEASEBACK

WHAT IS IT?

A sale-leaseback involves one party selling property (or in the case of a gift-leaseback, giving property) to another party and then leasing back the same property. This type of transaction is usually intended to secure one or more of a number of income and/or estate tax advantages.

WHEN IS THE USE OF SUCH A DEVICE INDICATED?

1. When your client's problem is cash flow; his corporation is "rich" in assets, but is "poor" in cash. The sale of a selected corporate asset and the immediate leaseback of that asset can generate cash without a loss of the use of that asset.

2. When your client earns a large amount of income and is, therefore, in a high income tax bracket. He wants to divert highly taxed income to a member of his family in a lower tax bracket. The hoped-for result is the netting of more after-tax income within the family unit.

3. When your client owns property that is rapidly appreciating and would like to save estate taxes on that future growth.

4. When your client would like to find an alternative to financing business property through a mortgage. Sale-leasebacks have been called "off balance sheet" financing because the lease obligation will often appear as a footnote on the balance sheet rather than as a liability. This should have the effect of increasing his credit standing and ability to borrow money.

WHAT ARE THE REQUIREMENTS?

1. The transaction must have validity to avoid litigation and conflict with the Internal Revenue Service. There must actually be a completed and irrevocable sale (or gift) and a legally enforceable lease agreement.

2. In the case of a sale, the transaction must represent a necessary business operation and not one designed solely and merely to shift income tax responsibility.

3. The terms of the transaction, and especially the amount of the lease payment, must be arrived at in an arm's length, bona fide manner. Any rent or lease amount should be reasonable.

4. If a trustee is involved, the trustee should, in fact, be independent from the grantor of the trust. When the term of the trust is over, trust corpus should not return to the grantor.

5. Under the kiddie tax rules (see chapter 15), to successfully shift taxation to the bracket of a child, that child must be age 14 or over.

The following factors should be considered: (a) Are the lease provisions, especially payments, strictly observed? (b) Does the lessee pay the entire amount of the promised rent? (c) Is the rent reasonable? (d) Was the sale price equivalent to the fair market value of the property?[1]

A positive answer to these questions is necessary for a successful shift of income tax burdens and the attainment of a rental deduction by the lessee.

If a trust is used, these questions should be asked: (a) Is the trust temporary? (b) Will the property revert to the grantor at the end of a given period (reversionary interest trust)? (c) Is the trust or trustee controlled by the grantor?[2]

A positive answer to any of these questions will result in taxation of income to the grantor.

The danger factors noted above are particularly important where the transactions are between related parties such as (1) a corporation and its stockholders; (2) husbands and wives; (3) parents and children; (4) grantors using relatives as trustees to create benefits for dependents; (5) affiliated corporations with common stockholders; and (6) taxpayers and foundations created by them.

HOW IT IS DONE — EXAMPLES

Your client, Dennis Raihall, is the president of the Son Ray Corporation. He explains to you that the business is in need of cash. It is on the verge of a break-through in its production process that could double corporate earnings, but it needs money to pay for expensive retooling.

The corporation has a number of valuable assets. One of these assets is selected and sold to the LeClair Corporation. The LeClair Corporation pays Son Ray Corporation the fair market value of the asset and now owns it. Since Son Ray Corporation still needs the asset in its business, it arranges to lease it back from the LeClair Corporation for a reasonable rental price. (It is important that the shareholders of the two corporations are not the same individuals.)

There are a number of types of assets the Son Ray Corporation could have sold: trucks, cars, machinery, equipment, fixtures, office buildings, apartment houses, and other types of real property. Furthermore, professional equipment such as computers, X-ray machines, etc., are all possibilities. (CAVEAT: Beware of depreciation and investment credit recapture on the sale. Note that gain is both realized and recognized on the corporate level if an appreciated asset is sold.[3]) It is important to make certain that the proposed sale-leaseback is not prohibited by a loan agreement with the firm's bank.

The after-tax proceeds of the sale will give the Son Ray Corporation additional cash and increase its working capital. Assets continue in operation just as they did before the sale. The basic difference is that instead of Son Ray carrying that particular item on its books as an asset, it now leases the property and pays rent for its use. Son Ray will now have the use of a large sum of cash, the after tax proceeds of the sale, which can be used to generate additional profits.

Suppose that Son Ray Corporation owned a factory it built more than 10 years ago at a cost of $200,000. The market value of the property is currently $250,000 (land $50,000, building, $200,000). The Son Ray Corporation has decided not to mortgage the property because the rate of interest it would have to pay is very high, it would not be able to write off payments of principal, and it feels that it could obtain more cash through a sale. Another reason it chose not to mortgage the property was that such a debt would adversely affect its credit standing and ability to borrow additional funds.

The property could be sold for $250,000 and leased back for 10 years with additional options at an annual rental of $30,000. Only the profit on the sale (net proceeds less adjusted basis) would be subject to tax. If an accelerated method of depreciation had been used, deductions taken in prior years may have to be recaptured and reported as additional income received on the sale. Son Ray Corporation now has the balance of the after tax sale proceeds to develop the process that may double overall corporate earnings.

Another way the leaseback arrangement is often utilized is in intrafamily transfers. For example, your client, Mary Jo Kopeznsky, a highly compensated physician, complains about the high income tax burden she faces every year. She wants you to show her how to maximize her family income by minimizing her overall tax burden.

She could transfer (as a gift) business property she owns (such as expensive medical equipment or a professional office building she owns and shares with a number of other professionals) to an irrevocable inter vivos trust established for her 14 year old daughter. The trustee could be a bank or other independent fiduciary. The trust, at a reasonable rental, leases the building back to Doctor Kopeznsky. This means the doctor does not have to move out of her building or lose the use of her equipment. Her daughter is immediately benefited. It is extremely important that there be no preconceived agreement with the trustee as to the amount of rental to be paid or the terms of the lease.

The trust could either distribute the rental income each year to the doctor's daughter or accumulate it for later distribution to her. For example, when her daughter reaches age 18 (and in many states is no longer a minor), trust income or principal might be distributed each year and paid outright and unconditionally to the daughter. If the daughter chose to, she could use the money to pay for her own college education. If, under the applicable state law a parent is not obligated to provide a college education for an adult child, none of the income will be taxable to the high tax bracket mother, even if it is paid directly to the daughter's college.

WHAT ARE THE TAX IMPLICATIONS?

1. In the case of a sale and leaseback, the corporation that sells an asset must pay tax on any gain realized just as in the case of any other sale. Likewise, just as any partnership or corporation that rents property is allowed to take a tax deduction for the cost of the rental, when a sale-leaseback occurs, the fair rental paid by the seller for the use of its previously owned property is completely deductible as an ordinary and necessary business expense.[4]

2. In the case of a gift-leaseback, proper care will enable the donor to receive a double benefit. First, the donor will obtain a business tax deduction for payments of rent. Then, when the rental income is paid to the trust (assuming it is a nongrantor trust), it will generally be taxed to the trust (as long as it is accumulated) or to the donor's child or other trust beneficiary.[5] Ordinarily, the tax bracket of the beneficiary or the trust will be lower than the donor's. The tax savings can provide an excellent means of establishing a college education fund. When income is paid to

a minor below age 14, the child will be taxed, but at the parent's top bracket, to the extent the payment exceeds $1,300 (as indexed for 1995). Therefore, a recipient child must be 14 or older for the income shift to work.

3. By making an irrevocable gift of an asset (except life insurance transferred by the insured within three years of death), future growth is removed from the client's estate at no additional estate tax cost.

4. There may be gift tax implications if there is an outright gift or if the sales price is less than the property's fair market value.

5. Cost recovery and interest deductions may offset a significant portion of the income from the lease. The lessee will be able to completely deduct the lease payments as an ordinary and necessary business expense. In the case of a sale-leaseback, the lessee would have to report interest income. If the lessee-user acquires the property and subsequently disposes of it, he will be subject to the recapture rules relating to cost recovery deductions, just as if he had been the owner of the property all along.

6. Where the property is sold to family members, and the installment payments are closely geared to the rental paid by the seller under the leaseback, the IRS will contend, and the courts will probably agree, that this is really a transfer with a retained life estate under Code section 2036(a). This will certainly be the case where the lease is in effect for life. See *Est. of Maxwell*,[6] where a mother sold the property to a son on an installment sale, then forgave the payments on the sales price except the interest on the installment note, which was almost exactly the same as the rent she paid. She was in her 80s and had cancer when she sold the property. Although the property here was a personal residence, the same rationale could extend to business assets.

IMPLICATIONS AND ISSUES IN COMMUNITY PROPERTY STATES

With respect to the sale-leaseback, two aspects are present. Initially, if the sale price is later found to be less than what was the then fair market value, the amount of the gift (undervaluation) is spread between both spouses if the asset was community property. However, some states' gift taxes have a much lower threshold than federal gift taxes, as to current cash tax payments, and consideration may be given to filing, in the year of the sale-leaseback, a gift tax return based on some other gift, thus possibly starting any statute of limitation periods to begin to run as to any subsequent imposition of a gift tax deficiency, including interest and penalties.

The second concern is making sure that valid legal title has passed. The California statutory scheme, for example, grants the right to the management and control of community property to either spouse, with certain exceptions. With respect to the lease, mortgage or transfer of real property, both spouses must join in executing the conveying instrument, and practitioners should obtain both signatures for any transfer (including the gift) of any asset.

QUESTIONS AND ANSWERS

Question — In the case of a gift-leaseback, what are the basic prerequisites?

Answer — Where a donor transfers an office building or other income producing assets to a trust for a child and then leases it back:

(1) The donor cannot retain substantially the same control over the property as he or she did before the gift was made.

(2) The leaseback must be in writing and must provide for a reasonable rental (get an appraisal).

(3) The leaseback, as distinguished from the gift in trust, must have a bona fide business purpose.[7]

(4) The trust must have an independent trustee unrelated to the grantor.[8]

Question — What does the Internal Revenue Service look at in the case of sale-leaseback between related parties?

Answer — Basically, the Internal Revenue Service is trying to determine whether the transaction is genuine or merely structured as a sale. If the transaction is, in reality, a disguised loan, at best only part of the "rental" payments will be deductible because they will be considered payments of interest and principal. Only the interest portion can be taken as a tax deduction.[9] Assuming the interest is considered "investment interest," it will be deductible, but only to the extent the taxpayer has investment income. Interest will be deductible without limit if it is considered "business interest." The characterization will be determined case by case, based on the facts and circumstances.

Alternatively, if the transaction is considered a sale, the seller-lessee has to pay a tax on any gain realized. If the property is leased for business purposes, he will be able to deduct his payment under the lease as rent.

The buyer-lessor also would be concerned with the distinction. In the case of a bona fide sale, the buyer-lessor may take depreciation or cost recovery deductions to the extent of the portion of the purchase price which is allocable to buildings or improvements and be entitled to a deduction for all expenses relating to the maintenance and operation of the property.[10] However, if the Internal Revenue Service treats the transaction as a loan, the buyer will not be entitled to these deductions. This is because the buyer will be considered as a mere mortgagee rather than as owner of the property.

If the transaction is considered a sale, the next question is whether or not the sale price is equal to the fair market value of the property. If the sale price is less than the fair market value of the property transferred, the difference may be considered a gift. This may result in a gift tax being imposed on the seller-lessee.

Question — How can the transaction be structured to minimize an Internal Revenue Service challenge that the arrangement is in reality a loan?

Answer — If possible, the transaction should be structured so that it falls within the following safe harbor: (1) the lessor must be a corporation other than a Subchapter S corporation, (2) the lessor must have a minimum "at risk" investment of 10% of the adjusted basis of the property at all times, (3) the term of the lease, including extensions, must not exceed certain limits, (4) the property must be leased within three months of its acquisition or, in the case of a sale-leaseback, it must be purchased by the lessor within three months of the lessee's acquisition for a price not in excess of the adjusted basis of the property in the hands of the lessee.

If the safe harbor test cannot be utilized, then the transaction should have economic reality. In this regard, all the significant burdens and benefits of ownership should be transferred to the new owner. The parties should assume their obligations as lessee and lessor, respectively. The sale price of the property should be fair and reasonable in light of current market conditions and sales of comparable properties. Financial arrangements must be reasonable. The IRS has indicated it will litigate two party gift and leaseback cases (i.e., the lessee is the donor, or an S corporation or partnership).

The transaction should not force a "buy-back." If there is a compulsory repurchase option, the seller is in virtually the same position he would have been in had he mortgaged the property rather than selling it and leasing it back. If a buy-back provision is included, the terms must be arranged and the amount of the purchase price computed as a result of arm's length bargaining.

The buyer must receive the benefit of any appreciation in value. A final factor generally examined is the application of rent toward the repurchase price. The rental price paid by the lessee should be realistic. It should closely approximate rentals for comparable property and comparable facilities. If part of the rent is to be applied to a repurchase price, the Internal Revenue Service might claim that such payments are in reality disguised payments of interest rather than payments for the use of the property.[11]

Question — What is the primary economic disadvantage to funding through a sale-leaseback rather than a mortgage?

Answer — The primary drawback is the loss of the residual value of the property at the termination of the lease. This drawback can be minimized through a repurchase option or option(s) to renew the lease over the expected life of the property.

Question — What terms should be specified in the lease that may help sustain an equal bargaining position between the donor and the trustee?

Answer —

A. Set rent at current market rates (obtain at least one outside appraisal expert's opinion).

B. Provide for a single year lease term that must be renegotiated each year.

C. Place the property on the open market for lease (the higher the rental the grantor actually pays, the greater the overall tax shift). Note, however, that to the extent rents are deemed "excessive," they might be disallowed as deductions.

D. Provide that lease payments are made "as a condition to the continued use or possession of the premises."

E. Trustee should establish—and strictly enforce—a payment schedule. (Where payments were made randomly, in different amounts, at the client's convenience, and not according to a schedule determined by the trustee, it was held that the grantor failed to relinquish total control over trust property.)

Question — In what situations will the grantor be taxed on trust income?

Answer — The grantor will be taxed on trust income:

1. if he or his spouse has retained a reversionary interest;

2. if he or his spouse retains power to control beneficial enjoyment;

3. if he or his spouse retains certain administrative powers;

4. if he or his spouse retains the power to revoke the trust;

5. if the income is used to pay support and maintenance to a person whom the grantor or his spouse is legally obligated to support;

6. if the income can be distributed or accumulated to the grantor or his spouse without the approval of an adverse party.

Note that avoiding these situations does not per se assure a rental deduction. These situations concern only the issue of "Is there a valid trust?" and "To whom is the income taxable?" Although the two issues are concurrently operative, they are treated by the IRS as mutually exclusive.

One possible solution is to have someone other than the client or his spouse fund the trust. For instance, the client's parents could put cash into an irrevocable trust for the client's children. The trust could use that cash to purchase assets owned solely by the client in his own name. The trust could then lease the assets to the client's corporation.

Question — What are the best types of property to use in a gift-leaseback?

Answer — The best types of property are *tangible* assets used in the client's trade, business, or profession, such as: land, depreciated buildings (beware of recapture), office equipment (such as computers, word processors, photocopiers), library, trucks and machinery, and other tangibles and office accoutrements needed in business.

Question — Will *cash* work in a gift-leaseback?

Answer — A client *could* fund the trust with cash. The trustee could then acquire new equipment and lease it to the grantor or the grantor's corporation or purchase equipment from the grantor and then lease it back. (Note that some authorities feel the "transfer of cash" method is more vulnerable to IRS attack than the "transfer of property" method where the cash is used to buy property already owned by the grantor.)

Question — Is geographical location of the taxpayer a consideration in planning a transfer and leaseback arrangement?

Answer — It is with respect to your client's chances of prevailing in litigation with the IRS. The chart at Figure 30.1, "Your Odds in the Circuits," lets you see at a glance where the outlook is favorable, unfavorable, or chancy.

ASRS, Sec. 51.

Footnote References

Sale (Gift)—Leaseback

1. See Rev. Rul. 55-540, 1955-2 CB 39; Rev. Proc. 75-21, 1975-1 CB 715, as modified by Rev. Proc. 79-48, 1979-2 CB 529; *Est. of Franklin*, 64 TC 752 (1975); *Narver v. Comm.*, 76 TC 53 (1980); *Hager v. Comm.*, 76 TC 759 (1981).

2. See *Oakes v. Comm.*, 44 TC 524 (1965); *Audano v. U.S.*, 428 F.2d 251 (5th Cir., 1970).

3. IRC Secs. 1245, 1250.

4. IRC Sec. 162. Can a sale-leaseback result in a deductible loss? Yes, says the Tax Court, if there is a bona fide sale and not an exchange of like-kind property. But, in the favorable case of *Leslie, Co. v. Comm.*, 64 TC 247 (1975), the IRS has non-acquiesced. Nonacq. 1978-47 IRB 5.

5. IRC Secs. 641, 652, 662.

6. 3 F.3d 591 (2nd Cir. 1993), aff'g 98 TC 584 (1992).

7. *Van Zandt v. Comm.*, 341 F.2d 440 (5th Cir. 1965) aff'g. 40 TC 824, cert. den. 382 U.S. 814.

8. *Oakes v. Comm.*, 44 TC 524 (1965).

9. See Rev. Rul. 55-540, 1955-2 CB 39. In *Servousek v. Comm.*, TC Memo 1977-105, the Tax Court allowed a rent deduction on a gift-leaseback of a medical building. In that case a taxpayer (1) gave up all beneficial control over the property; (2) paid a reasonable rent; (3) had a business purpose for the lease (he needed the building for his practice); and (4) retained no equity in the property during the lease period. See also *Lerner v. Comm.*, 71 TC 290 (1978), acq. in result 1984-1 CB 1. *May v. Comm.*, 76 TC 7 (1981).

   For an example of how *not* to arrange a gift-leaseback, see *Frank Lyon Co. v. U.S.*, 38 AFTR 2d 76-5019 (8th Cir. 1976); *Hilton v. Comm.*, 74 TC 305 (1980).

10. IRC Secs. 167, 168, 162; Reg. §1.162-4.

11. See Rev. Rul. 55-540, 1955-2 CB 39; Rev. Proc. 75-21, 1975-1 CB 715, as modified by Rev. Proc. 79-48, 1979-2 CB 529. See also AOD 1984-037.

Figure 30.1

YOUR ODDS IN THE CIRCUITS

Second, Eighth and Ninth Circuits	Third and Seventh Circuits	Fourth Circuit
New York, Vermont, Connecticut, North Dakota, South Dakota, Nebraska, Minnesota, Iowa, Missouri, Arkansas/Montana, Washington, Oregon, Idaho, Nevada, California, Arizona, Alaska, Hawaii, and Guam	Pennsylvania, New Jersey, Delaware and the Virgin Islands/Wisconsin, Illinois, and Indiana	West Virginia, Virginia, Maryland, North Carolina, South Carolina
Courts should side with the taxpayer if 1. Taxpayer doesn't maintain control over property (satisfied by independent trust. 2. Rental payments are reasonable and terms of rent reduced to writing. 3. Leaseback has a business purpose.	Courts will side with taxpayer if Eighth and Ninth Circuit tests are met.	Courts are tougher here than in Eighth, Ninth, Third and Seventh Circuits, and deduction still possible where grantor gives up control and title to property is placed in valid irrevocable trust.
See *Quinlivan v. Comm'r.*, 599 F.2d 269 (C8th Cir. 1979); *Brooke v. Comm'r.*, 468 F.2d 1155 (9th Cir. 1972); *Rosenfeld v. Comm'r.*, 83-1 USTC ¶9341 (2nd Cir. 1983).	See *Brown v. Comm'r.*, 180 F.2d 926 (3rd Cir. 1950); see also *S. Kemp v. Comm'r.*, 168 F.2d 598 (7th Cir. 1948).	See *Perry v. U.S.*, 520 F.2d 235 (4th Cir. 1975), cert. den.

Fifth Circuit	Circuits That Have Not Ruled on Gift Leasebacks
Mississippi, Louisiana, Texas	All others
Taxpayers have consistently failed in attempts to obtain rental deductions. (This court looks at the purpose of the arrangement as well as the arrangement itself and this Circuit has demanded that the taxpayer show a business reason for *both* the leaseback and the gift itself.) But this court has not held that all intra-family trust leasebacks are economic nullities nor has it held that "economic reality" was unattainable with trust leasebacks. It appears that the Fifth Circuit is placing undue weight on the origin of the trustee's title in the property a factor which is not otherwise considered relevant in cases dealing with rental payment deductability.	Taxpayers likely to face litigation but likelihood of success is highest if 1. independent trustee used 2. arm's length lease signed after negotiation with trustee 3. duration of trust exceeds length of lease
See *Van Zandt v. Comm'r.*, 341 F.2d 440 (5th Cir. 1965), cert. den. See also *Butler*, 65 T.C. 327 (1975).	Although there are cases on gift leasebacks in these circuits (cited below), none of these met all the tests set forth by the Tax Court, so it is not known how an Appeals Court in one of these circuits would react to a properly structured arrangement. See *Duffy v. U.S.*, 487 F.2d 282 (6th Cir. 1973).

SECTION 303 STOCK REDEMPTION

WHAT IS IT?

Code section 303 allows a corporation to make a distribution in redemption of a portion of the stock of a decedent that will not be taxed as a dividend. A Section 303 partial redemption can provide cash and/or other property from the corporation without resulting in dividend treatment and provides cash for the decedent shareholder's executor to use to pay death taxes and other expenses.

WHEN IS THE USE OF SUCH A DEVICE INDICATED?

1. When there is a desire to keep control of a close or family corporation within the decedent-shareholder's family after death.

2. When the corporation's stock is a major estate asset and a forced sale or liquidation of the business in order to pay death taxes and other costs is a threat.

3. Where a tax-favored withdrawal of funds from the corporation at the death of the stockholder would be useful.

4. When a redemption of Section 306 stock is desirable.

WHAT ARE THE REQUIREMENTS?

1. The redeemed stock must be included in the decedent's gross estate for federal estate tax purposes.[1]

2. The value for federal estate tax purposes of all stock of the corporation that is included in determining the value of the decedent's gross estate must be *more than* 35 percent of the excess of (1) the value of the gross estate over (2) the sum allowable as a deduction under Code sections 2053 (estate expenses, indebtedness, and taxes) and 2054 (losses).[2]

3. Only an amount equal to the total of (a) all estate, inheritance, legacy, and succession taxes (including generation-skipping transfer taxes) and interest thereon imposed by reason of decedent's death, and (b) funeral and administration expenses (whether or not claimed as a deduction on the federal estate tax return) can be redeemed and receive favorable income tax treatment (i.e., avoid dividend treatment). Any excess will be taxed under the rules of Code section 302.[3] This means any balance may be taxed as a dividend to the "seller," the executor or heir from whom the stock is being redeemed, or the balance may qualify for favorable tax treatment (no realization of taxable gain) if within the purview of Code section 302.

4. A redemption under Section 303 will qualify for favorable tax treatment only to the extent that the interest of a shareholder whose stock is redeemed is reduced either directly or indirectly through a binding obligation to contribute toward the payment of the decedent's administration expenses and death taxes.

In a hypothetical situation, assume the gross estate is $1,250,000; administrative and funeral costs are $250,000, and there are no other deductible expenses. To qualify for a Section 303 redemption, the value of the stock in question must *exceed* $350,000 (i.e., must be more than 35% of ($1,250,000 — $250,000)).

HOW IT IS DONE — EXAMPLES

The Section 303 stock redemption is relatively simple: The corporation redeems stock from the party who receives it at the death of the decedent-stockholder in question. Usually, the recipient of the stock will be the decedent-shareholder's personal representative, that is, the decedent's executor or administrator. Sometimes the seller will be a direct heir, surviving spouse, or trustee of an irrevocable trust created by the decedent. The redemption is protected under Section 303, however, only if it is from a stockholder who is obligated to pay death taxes, funeral, or administration expenses or whose share of the decedent's estate is reduced by these expenses.

Stock may not be redeemed from any stockholder who acquired his stock by purchase or gift (if the donor was not the decedent).[4] For example, if a father wills stock to his son and his son later sells or gives the stock to his brother, the brother's stock is not eligible for a Section 303 stock redemption in the father's estate. Also, Section 303 is not applicable where stock is redeemed from a stockholder who has acquired the stock

Figure 31.1

DETERMINATION OF WHETHER ESTATE QUALIFIES FOR SECTION 303 STOCK REDEMPTION		
FEDERAL ESTATE TAX VALUE OF CORPORATE STOCK IN GROSS ESTATE	(1)	$600,000
GROSS ESTATE LESS ALLOWABLE DEDUCTIONS	(2)	$1,000,000
35% OF GROSS ESTATE LESS ALLOWABLE DEDUCTIONS	(3)	$350,000
QUALIFIES IF (1) IS GREATER THAN (3)		

REDEMPTION UNDER SECTION 303 PROTECTED TO EXTENT OF	
FUNERAL AND ADMINISTRATION EXPENSES	$47,000
FEDERAL ESTATE AND GENERATION-SKIPPING TAXES	$119,800
STATE DEATH TAXES	$33,200
GENERATION SKIPPING TRANSFER TAXES	$0
INTEREST COLLECTED AS PART OF ABOVE TAXES	$0
MAXIMUM ALLOWABLE SECTION 303 REDEMPTION	$200,000

Courtesy of NumberCruncher Software.

from the executor in satisfaction of a specific monetary bequest.[5]

Without adequate prior planning, there may be insufficient funds in the corporation to effect a Section 303 redemption. Generally speaking, cash will be needed if the main purpose of a Section 303 redemption is to provide liquidity. A method of funding that will guarantee the necessary cash on the insured's death is the purchase of life insurance on the stockholder by the corporation.

The life insurance used to fund the Section 303 redemption should be a typical key person policy. The corporation should be the applicant, owner, premium payor, and beneficiary. (In the case of an uninsurable stockholder, a sinking fund can be established by using fixed or variable annuities, mutual funds, or other securities.)

For example, assume Aaron, a widower who dies in 1993, owns 75 percent of a corporation. His son Joshua owns the remaining 25 percent. Aaron's stock is valued at $600,000. His gross estate less allowable deductions under Code sec-tions 2053 and 2054 is $1,000,000. Assume he has minimal estate liquidity. The family corporation is in the 34 percent federal income tax bracket. Aaron is in the 28 percent income tax bracket. The corporation would purchase $200,000 of life insurance on Aaron's life. (This assumes Aaron's estate and inheritance taxes and other death related expenses will approximate $200,000.)

Step 1: At Aaron's death, his stock will pass to his estate. *Step 2:* The corporation then receives the insurance proceeds on Aaron's life. *Step 3:* The corporation uses the life insurance proceeds to pay Aaron's estate for stock qualifying for the Section 303 redemption. *Step 4:* The estate transfers $200,000 worth of stock to the corporation. *Step 5:* Aaron's estate uses the cash to pay federal and state death taxes and administrative and funeral expenses.

WHAT ARE THE TAX IMPLICATIONS?

1. The amount paid to the estate should not be treated as a dividend distribution. Instead, it will be treated as the "exchange price" for the stock and will generally result in

no gain being recognized at all by the estate if the basis for the stock has been "stepped up" by reason of being included in the shareholder's estate, unless the stock was a gift to the decedent within one year of his death and the property passes from the donee-decedent back to the donor or the donor's spouse.[6] However, to the extent the price paid to the estate exceeds the estate's basis, it will pay a tax on any such gain. Although the stock sold is a capital asset, since passage of the 1986 Tax Reform Act, there will not be any deduction from income for any part of the gain, and it will, therefore, be taxed at ordinary income tax rates.

Under the step-up-in-basis rules, a Section 303 redemption typically results in no adverse income tax consequences to the shareholder from whom the corporation made the redemption (generally the executor of the estate).

The favorable treatment occurs because the basis of the stock in the executor's hands (say $10 a share) is "stepped up" to the stock's fair market value for federal estate tax purposes (say $26 a share) and the $26 a share price paid to the executor by the corporation to redeem the stock is generally equal to the stock's basis, i.e., the $26 a share fair market value for federal estate tax purposes. Thus, the amount realized on the "sale" is exactly equal to the seller's basis and there is no taxable gain for income tax purposes. In some cases the value per share paid by the corporation is greater than the value of the stock per share for federal estate tax purposes; when that happens, a capital gain results.

2. The insurance premiums paid on the life of the insured stockholder are not income tax deductible by the corporation.[7]

3. When the proceeds of the key person life insurance are paid to the corporation at the death of the stockholder, they will be received free of federal income taxes (with the possible exception of any corporate level alternative minimum tax).[8]

4. Section 303 redemptions are specifically exempt from attribution (constructive ownership) problems, which helps to make redemptions from family corporations possible without the threat of dividend treatment.

IMPLICATIONS AND ISSUES IN COMMUNITY PROPERTY STATES

In order to qualify (aggregate) an ownership interest in two or more corporations for purposes of meeting the "more than 35 percent of adjusted gross estate" test, there must be at least 20 percent in value of each corporation included in the decedent's estate. In determining the 20 percent stock ownership by decedent, the surviving spouse's half of stock constituting community property may be included by treating it as if it had been included in determining the value of the gross estate of the decedent.

QUESTIONS AND ANSWERS

Question — Is cash the only property that may be distributed by the corporation?

Answer — No. If the need for liquidity exists, cash is generally the most practical type of property, but Section 303 does not require that the corporation make its purchase of the decedent's stock in cash. The corporation can distribute property "in kind." For instance, the corporation might distribute income-producing assets such as rental property (e.g., an apartment house, office building, or parking lot) in return for the stock it receives. Unfortunately, the corporation would recognize gain on the distribution of the appreciated property, and could also have taxable income in the event of recapture of depreciation,[9] liability in excess of basis,[10] and the excess of the fair market value distributed over the adjusted basis.[11]

The corporation can also issue notes to pay for the stock. The redemption rules will be met when the notes are delivered, not when they are actually paid. However, the notes should have a fairly short maturity (5 years or less).

Stock of the corporation making the distribution does not qualify as "property."[12]

Question — Do the funds received in the redemption have to be used to pay estate settlement costs?

Answer — No, the funds received in the redemption do not have to be used directly to pay estate settlement costs. Often, an estate will already have sufficient cash. The estate's settlement costs (exclusive of debts) only serve as a measure of the amount which can be redeemed. As long as the requirements for Section 303 are met, the corporation can redeem the permitted number of shares regardless of whether or not the executor actually needs the cash for liquidity purposes. Similarly, money or property received by the seller does not actually have to be used to pay estate settlement costs.

Question — Is an agreement necessary for Section 303 redemptions?

Answer — Generally, an agreement is unnecessary in the case where the executor will acquire the controlling interest in the corporation. However, an agreement would be advantageous to a minority stockholder. This would provide assurance that his estate will benefit by a Section 303 redemption. (Quite often, however, a complete redemption is preferable to a partial redemption. This is particularly true in the case of the death of a minority shareholder because of the relatively weak voting control position the survivors of such a shareholder will have.) Specific permission should be granted by the stockholder in his will allowing his or her executor to effect the redemption.

Question — Can a Section 303 stock redemption be effected without a majority stockholder's losing control?

Answer — It is possible to effect a 303 stock redemption without losing corporate control or diluting stock interest. Where there is a nonvoting class of stock outstanding, it is permissible for the corporation to redeem only the nonvoting stock.[13]

Generally, only one class of stock (common) is outstanding. There are two or perhaps three ways to accomplish the 303 redemption without creating voting or control problems. Recapitalization is the first method. If a corporation has only one class of stock outstanding, a shareholder may exchange a portion of his or her voting common stock for nonvoting preferred stock of equal value. The new preferred stock is then redeemed under Section 303. This creates no adverse effect on the voting control of the corporation.

A second method of overcoming voting and control problems is the issuance of a preferred stock dividend prior to the death of a decedent-stockholder. A preferred stock dividend is declared on the common stock. This entails no recapitalization and, normally, the dividend is tax free. Then the preferred stock is redeemed pursuant to Section 303.

A third possible means of taking money out of a closely held corporation through section 303 without a relative loss of control was suggested by a ruling that allowed the company to issue a stock dividend of nonvoting stock and to redeem the newly issued stock from the estate without creating a taxable distribution. The approval for such a stock dividend followed by a redemption should be obtained from corporate shareholders.[14]

Question — How is it possible to improve the chances of meeting Section 303 tests?

Answer — Lifetime gifts of personal insurance or other property (except the stock in question) to the surviving shareholder's family may reduce the gross estate of the stockholder (but only to the extent such gifts are not made within three years of the stockholder's death). Gifts of assets within 3 years of death are brought back into the gross estate for purposes of Code section 303 and its tests.

A sale by the stockholder to the corporation of a personally owned life insurance policy on the stockholder's life or a contribution to the capital of the corporation should make qualification for a 303 redemption easier. This is because the stockholder's gross estate may not be significantly changed. The value of his business interest relative to his personal estate should be increased. (This may also make it easier to qualify for an installment payout of estate taxes attributable to the business.) Another technique to accomplish the same result is the purchase by the corporation of new key person insurance coverage.

Question — Can a Section 303 redemption be effected at any time?

Answer — The proceeds must be received after the decedent's death and no later than: (1) three years and 90 days from the due date of the federal estate tax return; or (2) 60 days after a tax court decision in a contest of estate tax liability has become final; or (3) the time permitted for the payment of estate tax installments where the executor has elected and the estate qualifies for a deferred payment of estate taxes attributable to the business under Section 6166 (up to 15 years).

However, where a distribution is made more than four years after the decedent's death, the amount of protected distribution is limited to the lesser of: (a) the amount of taxes, funeral, and administrative expenses remaining unpaid at that time, or (b) the taxes and expenses that are actually paid within one year of the Section 303 payment to the stockholder.

Question — If there is more than one class of stock outstanding, can the aggregate value of all classes be taken into account in meeting the "more than 35 percent test"?

Answer — Yes, all classes of stock can be added together in meeting the "more than 35 percent" test regardless of which class of stock is being redeemed.[15]

Question — May stock of two or more corporations be aggregated for purposes of meeting the "more than 35 percent of adjusted gross estate" tests?

Answer — Only if 20 percent or more in value of the outstanding stock of *each* corporation is included in the decedent's gross estate.[16]

288

Question — Are the constructive ownership (attribution) rules a problem?

Answer — No, to the extent that stock is redeemed under Section 303, these rules can be ignored.

Question — Assume the executor needs cash quickly and before an IRS audit a Section 303 redemption takes place. At the audit of the estate tax return: (a) the IRS increases the valuation on the stock; (b) the IRS decreases the valuation; or (c) for some other reason the redemption does not qualify under Section 303. How can dividend treatment be avoided?

Answer — Arrange for the first contingency by providing that the purchase price and the number of shares redeemed will be adjusted so that the corporation will pay no more, and no less, than the value of the stock is finally determined for federal estate tax purposes. Alternatively, a contingency agreement that voids the purchase and sale could be arranged in the event that the "more than 35 percent" test is not met.

Question — Can the corporation redeem stock other than that held by the executor at the time of the stockholder's death?

Answer — Yes, subject to the limitations discussed directly above; if for any reason stock was included in the decedent-stockholder's gross estate, it can be redeemed even if it is in the hands of someone other than the estate's executor at the time of the redemption.[17] For example, if a mother purchased stock with her own funds and held it jointly with her daughter when she died, the entire value of the stock would be in the mother's estate but the daughter would become the owner of the stock. A 303 redemption would be permissible to the extent the daughter's interest had to bear a portion of her mother's estate's taxes and estate settlement costs. The corporation could purchase (redeem) the stock directly from the daughter.

Likewise (subject to the limitation discussed above regarding an obligation for taxes and expenses), where the stock transferred is considered included in the decedent's estate because of a transfer with a retained life estate, a transfer taking effect at death or a revocable transfer,[18] the corporation could purchase the stock under Section 303 from the new owner. The same result occurs where the stock is placed into a revocable trust. Because the stock would be included in the decedent-stockholder's estate, a redemption from the trustee would be allowed (again, assuming the share of the estate going into the trust bears a direct or indirect burden to pay death taxes or administration costs or is reduced by such amounts).

Question — Will life insurance owned by the corporation to fund the Section 303 redemption cause or aggravate an accumulated earnings tax problem?

Answer — In general, if in any tax year the corporation's taxable income is retained for the purpose of paying insurance premiums (or for any other purpose) in excess of the amount of the $250,000 accumulated earnings credit ($150,000 in the case of personal service corporations), the corporation should be prepared to show that such excess retentions are necessary to meet reasonable needs of the business; such excess retentions that are beyond reasonable business needs may attract the tax. Where an uncommitted key individual life insurance policy (of the appropriate amount and type) is used to shift the risk of the loss of a key person's services, it will generally not cause or aggravate an accumulated earnings tax problem.

Likewise, even though death proceeds do increase earnings and profits (to the extent they exceed premiums paid), they should not, per se, cause or aggravate an accumulated earnings tax problem. Term, whole life, or a similar low cash value policy should be used. Furthermore, the redemption should be effected, wherever possible, in the same fiscal year that death occurs.

Note: The Code provides that "the reasonable needs of the business" include the "Section 303 redemption needs of the business." However, the Internal Revenue Service's position is that this provision applies only to amounts accumulated in the year of death and thereafter.

Many authorities suggest that a third party — such as an irrevocable trust — own the life insurance. At the shareholder's death, the proceeds would be paid to the policyowner who could then make a fully secured loan to the corporation. The corporation could then redeem the stock under Code Section 303. The advantage of this technique is that the insurance proceeds don't "swell" the value of the corporation for estate tax purposes.

Question — If closely held stock is left to a specific legatee under the terms of a deceased stockholder's will, and there is a provision in the will that states that estate and inheritance taxes will be paid out of the residue of the estate, can there be a Section 303 redemption?

Answer — No. There cannot be a Section 303 redemption because the specific legatee will not bear any portion of paying the taxes. The redemption will qualify under Section 303 only to the extent that the interest of the redeemed shareholder is reduced directly or through a binding obligation to contribute to the payment of death taxes or funeral or administration costs.

Question — Can stock of a S corporation qualify for Section 303?

Answer — Yes. Stock of any corporation, including an S corporation, may qualify under Section 303.[19] In addition, any class of stock, common, preferred, voting or non-voting may be redeemed if otherwise qualifying for a Section 303 redemption.

Question — If the executor elects to take an income tax deduction on the estate's income tax return for funeral and administration expenses, rather than deduct such expenses on the estate tax return, does this have any impact on the amount qualifying for redemption under IRC Section 303?

Answer — No. The fact that the executor deducts funeral and administrative expenses on the income tax return of the estate will not reduce the amount of stock that can be redeemed.

ASRS, Sec. 43.

Footnote References

Section 303 Stock Redemption

1. IRC Sec. 303(a).
2. IRC Sec. 303(b)(2)(A).
3. IRC Sec. 303(a).
4. Reg. §1.303-2(f).
5. Reg. §1.303-2(f).
6. Reg. §1.303-1; IRC Sec. 1014(e).
7. IRC Sec. 264(a)(1).
8. IRC Sec. 101(a)(1).
9. IRC Secs. 1245, 1250.
10. IRC Sec. 311(b)(2).
11. IRC Sec. 311(b)(1)(B).
12. Rev. Rul. 65-289, 1965-2 CB 86; IRC Secs. 303(a), 317.
13. Reg. §1.303-2(c)(1).
14. Rev. Rul. 87-132, 1987-2 CB 82.
15. Reg. §1.303-2(c)(1).
16. IRC Sec. 303(b)(2)(B).
17. Reg. §1.303-1.
18. IRC Secs. 2036-2038.
19. Let. Rul. 9009041.

Chapter 32

SPLIT INTEREST PURCHASE OF PROPERTY (Split)

WHAT IS IT?

A "Split" is an arrangement under which two parties agree to purchase an asset. One party (usually a parent) purchases a life estate (the right to receive the income from the property or the right to use, possess, and enjoy the property itself for as long as the life tenant lives). The second party (usually a son or daughter or grandchild of the life tenant) purchases a remainder interest (the right to the property, whatever it is worth, when the first party's interest terminates. If the first party purchased a life interest, by definition his interest terminates when he dies). Each party to the Split pays the actuarial value of the interest purchased.

The adoption of Code section 2702 has considerably reduced and limited the attractiveness of Splits.

WHEN IS THE USE OF SUCH A DEVICE INDICATED?

1. When a client would like to improve current income. If a Split is used to purchase income producing investment property, the client's income is enhanced by the return provided on the remainderman's investment.

2. When it is important to keep property within a family, but the client wants to enjoy it or needs to use it or receive its income for life, a Split may be strong protection against a will contest or an election against the will. Split property passes by contract and should not be part of the probate estate. So generally a disgruntled heir would have no right to property purchased through a Split. Likewise, a Split offers protection against the claims of a client's creditors and, because it does not pass through probate, it affords the parties privacy.

3. When it is desirable to avoid ancillary administration, the Split is useful since at the termination of the first party's interest, the remainderman automatically by contract becomes full and complete owner of the property. This means the cost of multiple probates is avoided.

4. Splits are indicated where federal gift and estate taxes are not a major consideration or will be of relatively minor importance in the overall plan. In some limited circum-

stances, there may still be some transfer tax advantages using a Split.

WHAT ARE THE REQUIREMENTS?

Ownership of the property is bifurcated into two parts: a "term" interest, which may be either the right to receive stipulated payments from the property for a term of years, or life, or in a very limited situation, the right to use the property for that period. The second part is the "remainder" interest, which will pass to the other joint owner when the term expires.

Both the term holder and the remainder holder pay their proportionate part of the purchase price for the property based on government valuation tables setting an actuarial value for the term interest and the remainder interest. It is essential that the purchaser of the term interest furnish no part of the consideration for the purchase of the remainder interest.

Since the term holder and remainder holder are co-owners of the property, it cannot be sold without the consent of both parties. Since under most circumstances the term holder is limited to a fixed dollar payment from the property, he or she will apparently have no other rights in it. In the limited situations where the term holder can retain full possession and enjoyment of the property for the term, he should have all of the legal rights of a joint tenant in the property.

HOW IT IS DONE—AN EXAMPLE

Your client is an about-to-be-separated 50 year old who wishes to invest in a painting or in some unimproved real estate. He has a daughter whom he wants to receive the painting or unimproved real estate at his death. He has used none of his annual exclusion or unified credit. He wants to begin to shift wealth to his daughter who is a financially successful women's clothing designer. If he purchases the painting or unimproved real estate in his own name, he knows that it could be lost in litigation with his wife. He expects the painting or unimproved real estate to appreciate considerably each year.

The 50 year old father purchases a life estate (or term interest) in the painting or unimproved real estate. The father must pay an amount equal to the present value of what the painting or unimproved real estate could be rented for over the father's lifetime (or term interest). The daughter pays the balance. The daughter receives the appreciated property when the father dies (or at the end of the term interest). Comparable rental values may be extremely difficult to obtain; failure to do so could lead to adverse gift tax results.

Alternatively, the father could purchase property with his daughter and retain an annuity or unitrust interest in the property for life (or for a term). The daughter would receive the hopefully appreciated property when the father dies (or at the end of the term interest). The father would pay the actuarial value of his annuity or unitrust interest and the daughter would pay the actuarial value of her remainder interest based upon government valuation tables.

WHAT ARE THE TAX IMPLICATIONS?

Section 2702

For federal gift tax purposes, joint purchases of property are treated as transfers to a trust under the provisions of Code section 2702 (discussed in more detail in Chapter 35), and the person or persons who acquire terms interests in the property in a transaction or series of transaction shall be treated as having acquired the entire property and then having transferred the other interests to the other persons in exchange for any consideration received.[1] Any term interest in property, such as a life estate or term of years, but not co-ownership, such as tenancy in common or joint tenancy, is treated as held in trust under Section 2702.[2] A leasehold is not a term interest if for full and adequate consideration where a good faith attempt is made to determine fair rental value.[3]

In the case of a joint purchase, the amount considered transferred by an individual for this purpose shall not exceed the actual consideration furnished by that person for the property.[4]

As a result of the limitations imposed on the joint purchase under Section 2702, the technique will have disastrous gift tax consequences if the term holder purchases an income interest in the property. Under Section 2702, that income interest is valued at zero for federal gift tax purposes. The term holder will be treated as if he made a gift to the remainderman, equal to the fair market value of the property less the actual consideration paid by the remainderman for the remainder interest. However, the amount of the gift is limited to the actual consideration paid by the term holder.

Retained Annuity or Unitrust Interests

The unfortunate results just described can be avoided if, instead of retaining the income for the term, the term holder retains a fixed annuity payment or a percentage payments based on the annual valuation of the property under the same conditions described in Chapter 35 for GRATs and GRUTs. If the consideration paid by the term holder is exactly equal to the actuarial value of the annuity or unitrust payments, there would be no taxable gift of the remainder, since the value of the annuity or unitrust payments would be subtracted in arriving at the taxable gift, as would the consideration paid by the remainderman.

The Tangible Property Exception

Section 2702 does preserve the traditional form of Split in certain limited circumstances. The nonexercise of rights under a term interest in tangible property, such as a painting or unimproved real property, which does not have a substantial effect on the value of the remainder interest is not valued at zero, but at the amount a third party would pay for the term interest (e.g., the right to possess the painting for life).[5] This means that it is possible to arrange for the split purchase of a work of art, or unimproved real estate, with the term holder acquiring the right to use the property for the term, or life, and the remainder to someone else.

However the valuation of a term interest in tangible property is valued under a willing buyer-willing seller test, not under actuarial tables.[6] This means that to avoid a taxable gift, the term holder would have to prove that what he paid for the term interest in the tangible property is the same as what an unrelated person would pay for the same interest in an arm's length transaction. The difficulties of proving this are tremendous. Comparable sales or rentals are given greater weight in valuation than appraisals in most cases.

The tangible property exception rule applies to property for which no allowance for depreciation or depletion would be allowable, and as to which the failure to exercise any rights with respect to the property will not affect its value. There is a de minimis rule for depreciation of certain improvements.

A conversion of the term interest into some other property right (other than a qualified annuity trust) is treated as a gift transfer of the retained term interest determined at the date of original transfer. Any alteration or improvement of the property which so alters its character that it would not qualify under this rule is treated as a conversion of the property under this rule. If the property is converted, it is possible to switch to a qualified annuity trust described in Chapter 35.

Planning Implications

While the pros and cons of grantor retained interest transfers generally apply here, there is an important difference. Section 2702 is a gift tax provision, and should not apply in determining whether or not the joint purchase has estate tax consequences. If the term holder pays full and adequate consideration for the term interest, whether it be in the form of an annuity or unitrust payment, or the use of qualified tangible property, then the death of the term holder should have no federal estate tax consequences. Unlike a GRIT, GRAT, or GRUT, the term can be for the life of the term holder. The retained interest should not result in inclusion of the value of the property in the term holder's estate because the term holder did not "transfer" the remainder interest, and Code section 2036(a), which applies to transfers in which the transferor retains income or other interests for life, should not be applicable (but see "QUESTIONS AND ANSWERS," below). The joint acquisition of income producing property could be a very useful technique for certain clients.

ISSUES AND IMPLICATIONS IN COMMUNITY PROPERTY STATES

The situation here is analogous to the transfer of community property to a grantor retained annuity trust or unitrust discussed in Chapter 35. If community funds are used to purchase the term interest, presumably the retained interest will either be paid jointly to the transferors or each will receive half of the required payment for the term.

QUESTIONS AND ANSWERS

Question — Can a personal residence trust and joint purchase be combined?

Answer — The personal residence trust and qualified personal residence trust, or QPRT, are discussed in Chapter 35. Many commentators have suggested that a personal residence could be acquired through a joint purchase, and then placed in a personal residence trust.

Under a typical scenario, parent and children would locate residential property which parent wishes to occupy as a personal residence for a term of years. Parent would purchase the term interest in the property, paying full fair market value based upon the actuarial value of a term interest, and the children would purchase the remainder interest, also paying full fair market value but based upon the actuarial value of a remainder interest. Under the joint purchase rule of Code section 2702, the effect would be a gift from parent to children, since the term interest would be valued at zero for federal gift tax purposes.

However, if the residence is committed to a personal residence trust, it can be argued that under the statutory exception described above, the full value of the term interest would be an offset for federal gift tax purposes, and the result is no taxable gift. Further, if the parent dies during the term, it can also be argued that there was no retained interest in the residence which would result in its inclusion in the parent's taxable estate under Code section 2036(a), arguing that that section cannot apply since the parent paid "full and adequate consideration" for the value of the term interest. However, it appears the IRS will take the position that the residence is included in the estate of the parent.

In Letter Ruling 9412036, the parties unsuccessfully attempted to create a split-purchase grantor retained unitrust that would provide one parent a unitrust for life followed by a unitrust for the other parent for life. In purchasing property to be held in trust, the parents would pay the part of the purchase price equal to their actuarial interests in the trust. There would also a right of first refusal should any of the interest holders seek to sell their interests. The trust failed to contain required provisions relating to commutation of interests and adjustments for incorrect valuations, so it did not qualify under Code section 2702.

However, the ruling went even further and held that the property would be includable in a parent's estate under either Code section 2036 or 2039. Under Section 2036, the amount includable would be equal to the lesser of (1) the original value of the parent's transferred share of property held in the trust reduced by the original value of the income interest attributable to transfers to the trust by others, or (2) an amount which would yield the unitrust payment at the parent's death. Under Section 2039, a parent's estate would include that portion of the date of death value of the property that is proportionate to the decedent's share of all trust contributions.

Question — Should the split-purchase technique be completely abandoned?

Answer — In the right situations, the joint or split purchase may still be very useful. Unlike the GRAT or GRUT, the gift in this case is limited to what the term holder pays for the life or term interest, not the entire value of the property. Therefore, even if the term holder retains an income interest valued at zero under the statute, the gift will still be limited to the actuarial value of the income interest (assuming that is what the term holder pays for the term interest), not 100% of the value of the property, as in the case of a GRIT.

If the term holder pays full fair market value for the income interest, annuity interest, or unitrust interest, there should be nothing to include in the term holder's estate at death under Code section 2036(a), since the term holder never transferred an interest for federal estate tax purposes. However, as noted above, the IRS will apparently take the opposite position on this issue.

Footnote References

Split Interest Purchase of Property

1. IRC Sec. 2702(c)(2).
2. Reg. §25.2702-4(a).
3. Reg. §25.2702-4(b).
4. Reg. §25.2702-4(c).
5. IRC Sec. 2702(c)(4).
6. Reg. §25.2702-2(c).

Chapter 33

SURVIVOR'S INCOME BENEFIT PLAN

WHAT IS IT?

A Survivor's Income Benefit (S.I.B.) (often called a Death Benefit Only, "D.B.O.") is an agreement between a corporation and an employee. The corporation agrees that if the employee dies before retirement it will pay a specified amount (or an amount determinable by a specified formula) to the spouse of the employee or another designated class of beneficiary such as children. Typically, the amount may be a multiple of salary such as 2, 3 or 5 times the average base pay in the 3 years preceding death.[1]

A Survivor's Income Benefit Plan should not provide for (or be linked in any way with a plan that provides) retirement benefits of any kind.

WHEN IS THE USE OF SUCH A DEVICE INDICATED?

1. When additional income is desired for the family of an individual in a high estate tax bracket.

2. When an employer would like to provide a selected employee or employees with an impressive fringe benefit over and above qualified retirement plan security.

3. When a client presently covered under a split dollar arrangement is experiencing rapidly-increasing PS 58 costs (usually between age 60 and 65—see Figure 21.3 in chapter 21). The split dollar plan could be converted into a survivor's income benefit so that the security could be continued without the income tax burden.

4. When a corporation would like to provide an immediate death benefit for the family of a young employee which could later be coupled (by changing the S.I.B. to a nonqualified deferred compensation plan) with a retirement benefit.

HOW IT IS DONE — AN EXAMPLE

Nina Wasserman is a 35-year-old senior executive of Ship Shape Model Corporation (S.S.M.). In order to encourage her to give her ultimate effort for S.S.M., the corporation makes a legally binding promise to her that, "If Nina should die while

an executive of S.S.M., S.S.M. will pay her children, Ross and Michelle, a death benefit equal to 3 times the average annual base compensation she received for the 3 years prior to her death—up to a maximum of $500,000. The payments will be made in equal annual installments over a 10-year period." In this example, assume payments would be $50,000 a year. Assume also that S.S.M. is in a 40 percent combined federal and state corporate tax bracket.

S.S.M. could finance its obligation by purchasing a $500,000 life insurance policy on Nina's life. The policy would be owned by and payable to S.S.M. At Nina's death, S.S.M. could use the cash proceeds to purchase $500,000 of tax-free municipal bonds. Assuming the bonds earned 8 percent, the net income from the bonds would be $40,000 a year. This means corporate cash inflow would be $40,000. Outflow, after the corporation's $20,000 tax deduction (40% of $50,000) would be $30,000 ($50,000 - $20,000). Its net positive inflow each year is therefore $10,000. In 10 years the corporation will add $100,000 to its surplus. At the end of the payout period, S.S.M. has the $500,000 of bonds, and it has accumulated $10,000 a year for 10 years. At 8 percent this $10,000 annual amount would grow to $156,455 by the end of the 10th year. This will probably be enough to reimburse the business for its costs, the use of its money, and any administrative expenses it may have incurred.

WHAT ARE THE TAX IMPLICATIONS?

The Employer's Tax Position

1. Premiums the corporation pays on the life insurance policy covering the insured-employee are not deductible.

2. Proceeds received by the corporation at the employee's death are income tax free. Proceeds may be subject to the corporate alternative minimum tax (AMT) as an adjustment for adjusted current earnings. But, at worst, this possible tax on proceeds will generally not exceed 15 percent with respect to the adjustment for adjusted current earnings. Generally the full amount of AMT liability may be carried forward as a credit.

3. Payments made by the corporation to the designated beneficiaries are deductible if—and to the extent—such

payments represent reasonable compensation for services the employee rendered and the plan serves a valid business (as opposed to a shareholder) purpose.

The Employee's Tax Position

1. If the plan is properly drafted, under most circumstances none of the death benefit of an S.I.B. plan will be includable in the covered employee's estate (see the Q&A section below).

2. Payment of premiums by the corporate employer will not be income to the employee.

3. The IRS, reversing an earlier position, now agrees with the Tax Court that when the taxpayer and his employer enter into a D.B.O. plan, there is no taxable gift to the beneficiary, either at the time the plan is entered into, or the death of the employee.[2]

The Beneficiary's Tax Position

Payments received from the corporation by beneficiaries will be treated the same as salary; i.e., each payment will be taxed as deferred salary. Up to $5,000 of the death benefit paid to beneficiaries can be excludable from their gross income (see Chapter 8).

IMPLICATIONS AND ISSUES IN COMMUNITY PROPERTY STATES

In community property states, it may be necessary to determine whether the employee's spouse has any community property interest in the survivor's income benefit. This becomes important upon the divorce of the employee and the spouse. As previously stated, if a survivor's income benefit plan is properly drafted, none of the death benefits should be includable in the employee's estate for federal estate tax purposes, although state laws may vary on this issue. This is because courts have consistently found that the decedent had no interest in the payments at the time of his death.

This may also be the case upon a divorce after an employee has entered into a survivor's income benefit plan. As of the date of the divorce, the employee would have no interest which could be includable in his estate, and thus there may not be any interest which can be divided in a divorce proceeding.

However, many courts and the IRS generally find that the promise of the employer to pay a death benefit to a specified beneficiary in return for the employee's promise to continue working is a transfer by the employee of a property right. Community property states typically provide that a spouse may not make a gift of community personal property or dispose of community personal property without a valuable consideration, unless he or she obtains the written consent of the other spouse. The employee's employment, by its very nature in a community property state, is generating a community property interest in the spouse through salary and other employment benefits.

In a divorce proceeding, although an employee may be performing some services in return for the employer's promise to pay a stated amount to a named beneficiary at the time of the divorce proceeding, it does not follow that there are current property interests which can be divided equally between the spouses. The employee has no current right to any benefit, nor is there any assurance that he will ever have a named beneficiary receive a benefit. The survivor's income benefit is subject to many contingencies, among them the employee's continuing to work for the employer. Assuming the employee's spouse is the beneficiary of the survivor's income benefit plan, the spouse has obtained a benefit during the term of the marriage; i.e., if the employee were to die during the marriage, the spouse would receive the survivor's income benefit.

If the employee's spouse contends that there is an interest which can be valued and divided upon a divorce, the question of whether any value can be attributed to the survivor's income benefit may be solved differently in the various community property states. California, for example, has found that a non-vested benefit from a pension plan is not a mere expectancy, but is a contingent property right. Although we are not familiar with any case actually valuing a survivor's income benefit under this theory, it may be possible that California courts would attempt to value the survivor's income benefit and divide that value in the divorce proceedings. The value would probably be very low because of the substantial discounts for the many contingencies involved in this type of an arrangement.

As one can imagine, severe problems of valuation and the proportion of benefits to pay to a former spouse could arise in the event the employee were to remarry and continue working for the same employer. What portion of the survivor's income benefit is attributable to the employee's employment while married to his first spouse and what portion is attributable to the portion of his employment while married to his second spouse? With vexing problems like this, coupled with the employee's lack of right to a benefit prior to his death, it is likely that a court will put little or no value on the survivor's income benefit plan in the event of a divorce.

In most instances, the employee's spouse will be his or her beneficiary under the survivor's income benefit plan. In this instance, upon his or her death, there will be no controversy over the community property issue, unless he or she had previous marriages. In the event of a divorce, the community property issue may arise, even though the spouse is designated as the beneficiary, but the result is quite uncertain.

QUESTIONS AND ANSWERS

Question — What circumstances would cause death benefits to be includable in the employee's estate?

Answer — The promise of the employer to pay a death benefit to the specified beneficiary in return for the employee's promise to continue working has been considered to constitute a transfer by the employee of a property right.

If the agreement gives the employee the right to change the beneficiary, that retention of the power to designate who will enjoy the "transfer" will cause estate tax inclusion.[3]

If the beneficiary's right to receive the death benefit is conditioned on surviving the employee and the employee retained a right to direct the disposition of the property (for example, where the death benefit is payable to the employee's spouse, but if the spouse does not survive the employee, the death benefit is payable to the employee's estate), that reversionary interest may cause inclusion.[4]

If the beneficiary is a revocable trust established by the employee, the right to alter, amend, or revoke the transfer by changing the terms of the trust would cause inclusion.[5] Another problem relates to an employee who is also a controlling (more than 50 percent) shareholder. Does such an individual, by virtue of his or her voting power, have the right to alter, amend, revoke, or terminate the agreement? The Tax Court has held that the answer is "yes."[6]

If the employee already has post-retirement benefits, such as a nonqualified deferred compensation agreement that pays a retirement benefit, the IRS could claim that the pre-retirement survivor's death benefit and the post-retirement deferred salary plans should be considered as one plan. This would cause the present value of the death benefit to be treated for estate tax purposes as if it were a joint and survivor annuity; the present value of the death benefit would be includable in the deceased employee's estate.[7]

If the death benefit is payable to a trust over which the employee had a general power of appointment, the IRS might argue that he had a power of appointment over the death proceeds.[8]

If the death benefit is funded with life insurance on the employee's life and the employee owned the policy or had veto rights over any change in the beneficiary, the IRS would probably attempt to include the policy proceeds because of the employee's incidents of ownership.[9]

Question — If proceeds are payable to the employee's spouse, will they qualify for the unlimited marital deduction?

Answer — Yes. If for any reason the IRS successfully maintains that the S.I.B. generated a taxable transfer (either during life or at death), there should be no adverse gift or estate tax consequence if the spouse of the employee is named outright beneficiary. It is also possible that the employer could pay S.I.B. payments to a "QTIP" (Qualified Terminable Interest Property) trust established by the employee (see Chapter 36). This would secure the marital deduction—if one were needed—and in any case assure that the principal would pass upon the surviving spouse's death to the party designated by the decedent.

However, if the S.I.B. were not included in the employee's estate for tax purposes, the payment could not result in a marital deduction.

Question — Is a D.B.O. "funded" for ERISA purposes?

Answer — Although the *Dependahl* case[10] stated that D.B.O.s did not qualify for various exemptions from ERISA, at first impression it appeared that the court improperly interpreted both facts and ERISA law in its desire to assist employees who seemed to have been terminated for malicious and unjustifiable reasons.

It now appears that the company involved in this case sent a letter each year to the executives covered by its D.B.O. plan. Those letters advised the participants of the annual status of "their" insurance policies. The obvious implication is that the participants could look to the policies for their families' security under the D.B.O. plan. This fact was not contained in the Court's opinion and may well have been the key reason the Court reached the conclusion the plan was "funded" for ERISA purposes.

The Department of Labor issued an Advisory Opinion subsequent to the *Dependahl* case which states that life insurance is not considered a "plan asset" if:

1. it is owned by and payable to the corporation;

2. it is under total control of the corporation;

3. it is subject to the claims of the corporation's creditors;

4. no participant has a preferred claim against the policies;

5. the policies are not formally tied to the plan; and

6. there will be no representation to any participant or beneficiary that the policies would be used solely to provide plan benefits or represent security for the payment of benefits or that plan benefits would be limited by the amount of the insurance proceeds received by the corporation.

In light of *Dependahl* and the Department of Labor Advisory Opinion, the use of the phrase "to fund" (or "to informally fund") should be avoided in discussing the use of life insurance policies to support the plan in any documentation associated with the plan (i.e., corporate resolutions, plan document, SEC annual report disclosure statements).

Part of the corporate resolution authorizing the plan and the purchase of the supporting policies might better read as follows:

> RESOLVED: that in order for the X-ON Corporation to support its financial obligations under the Death Benefit Only plan and to insure itself against all other financial losses which would be incurred in the event of a pre- or postretirement death of *(Name of Executive)*, the vice-president of the Corporation is hereby authorized to enter into a contract of *(Description of Life Insurance Contract)* life insurance with the _____ Life Insurance Company for coverage of $___ insuring the life of *(Name of Key Executive)*.

Question — Is a voluntary D.B.O. plan the answer to the estate tax question?

Answer — If a death benefit is not made under a contract or plan but is purely voluntary on the employer's part, it will not be includable in the employee's estate.[11] An employer could adopt a program that is something less than a legally binding commitment giving rise to "hopes and expectancies, not enforceable obligations with respect to a death benefit."

Voluntary benefits are not includable in the employee's estate because neither the employee nor the employee's beneficiary possessed any right to compel the employer to pay the benefit, and therefore there was no transfer.

The problem here is a practical one. The benefit provides no peace of mind—nor financial security in an economic sense—except to the extent the employee can rely on the willingness and ability of the employer to pay a substantial sum of money after the employee's death.

Question — What is the formula for a successful D.B.O. plan?

Answer — An employer may offer a plan under which benefits are payable only to "eligible beneficiaries." This class would be determined by the employer and might include spouses and/or children of employees. No benefit would be payable if the employee is not survived by an eligible beneficiary. The employee would have no right to select or change the beneficiary.

ASRS, Sec. 64.

Footnote References

Survivor's Income Benefit Plan

1. Some insurance carriers offer a coverage known as group survivors' income benefit insurance, commonly written as a supplement to group life insurance. Under this coverage, the employee has no choice of beneficiary, benefits are paid only if there is a survivor who qualifies, and a lump-sum payment of the commuted value of benefits is not available.

2. See *Est. of Anthony DiMarco*, 87 TC 653 (1986). acq. 1990-2 CB 1.

3. IRC Sec. 2036; Rev. Rul. 76-304, 1976-2 CB 269.

4. IRC Sec. 2037; *Est. of Fried v. Comm.*, 54 TC 805 (1970), aff'd., 445 F.2d 979 (2nd Cir. 1971), cert. den., 404 US 1016 (1972); Rev. Rul. 78-15, 1978-1 CB 289.

5. IRC Sec. 2038.

6. *Est. of Levin*, 90 TC 723 (1988).

7. IRC Sec. 2039; *Est. of Fusz v. Comm.*, 46 TC 214 (1966), acq. 1967-2 CB 2.

8. IRC Sec. 2041.

9. IRC Sec. 2042.

10. *Dependahl v. Falstaff Brewing Corp.*, 491 F. Supp. 1188 (E.D. Mo. 1980), aff'd in part, 653 F.2d 1208 (8th Cir.), cert. den.; Dept. of Labor Advisory Opinion 81-11A. See also *Belka v. Rowe Furniture Corp.*, 571 F. Supp. 1249 (D. Md. 1983), where the court found a plan to be exempt from ERISA funding requirements where less than 5 percent of total employees were participants, and where participants' compensation averaged $55,000.

11. *Edith L. Courtney v. U.S.*, 84-2 USTC ¶13,580 (N.D. Ohio, 1984).

Chapter 34

TRUST — DEFECTIVE

WHAT IS IT?

A "defective" trust is an irrevocable trust with the following characteristics:

1.   Transfers of property to the trust are completed gifts for federal gift tax purposes.

2.   The trust assets will not be included in the taxable estate of the grantor or grantors.

3.   The income of the trust is taxed to the grantor, who is treated as the "owner" of the trust for federal income tax purposes.

A defective trust is created by intentionally violating one or more of the grantor trust rules found in Code sections 671-677. Under Section 671, trust income or deductions will be attributed to the grantor of the trust if he or she is treated as the owner of the trust under the provisions of Code sections 672-677. These rules are discussed in the section on Income Taxation of Trusts and Estates in Appendix C.

WHEN IS THE USE OF SUCH A DEVICE INDICATED?

The use of a defective trust is indicated when the grantor wishes to continue to be taxed on the trust income for income tax purposes, but wants to remove the trust corpus from his estate for estate tax purposes. By paying the income tax on the income which will pass to the beneficiaries, the grantor is making a tax-free gift. However, it is possible the IRS will challenge this conclusion. In a private letter ruling,[1] the IRS held that if the trust does not contain a clause directing the trustee to reimburse the grantor for any income tax the grantor pays on trust income not distributed to the grantor, the payment of the income tax by the grantor is a taxable gift! Note the following language:

> "If there were not a reimbursement provision, an additional gift to a remainderperson would occur when the grantor paid tax on any income that would otherwise be payable from the corpus of the trust."

Taxing income to the grantor rather than the trust will almost always result in a substantial income tax savings because of the compressed tax rates applied to trusts. Consider the following income tax rates for estates and trusts in 1995:

Taxable income not over $1,550	15%
Over $1,550 to not over $3,700	$232.50 + 28% of excess
Over $3,700 to not over $5,600	$834.50 + 31% of excess
Over $5,600 to not over $7,650	$1,423.50 + 36% of excess
Over $7,650	$2,161.50 + 39.6% of excess

A defective trust is a "grantor" trust which can hold S corporation stock.[2] In this case, it is particularly important that the grantor be treated as the owner of both the income and corpus of the entire trust.

This concept can be used to make a grantor retained annuity trust (GRAT), a grantor retained unitrust (GRUT), or a qualified personal residence trust (QPERT) into a grantor trust. See Chapter 35. One reason for the grantor trust's popularity in this situation is that the grantor can buy back the trust assets at fair market value without recognition of gain or loss.[3]

In the case of a personal residence trust, if the grantor is treated as the owner and the residence is sold, the benefits of Code section 121 (the $125,000 gain exclusion for taxpayers over 55) and Code section 1034 (rollover to a new residence) may be applied to exclude or defer gain from the sale of the residence. Note the trust must be defective as to both income and corpus.

Where a GRAT or GRUT is involved, it is possible that the trust may not generate sufficient income or cash flow to make the annuity or unitrust payments. The GRAT or GRUT distribution may be "in kind," (i.e., of the trust assets) without any income tax consequences to the trust.

A defective trust may facilitate the transfer of installment notes to the trust without accelerating the gain.[4] This technique may be used to set up an income tax deduction for transfers to charitable lead trusts.[5]

WHAT ARE THE REQUIREMENTS?

The trust is irrevocable. Either the grantor or a trustee which is not adverse retains certain powers. The grantor can retain the power in a nonfiduciary capacity to remove trust assets from the trust and substitute other assets of equal value.

This apparently has no adverse estate tax consequences to the grantor. Note the IRS has refused to rule on this in all cases, because it is a question of fact whether or not the grantor is acting in a nonfiduciary capacity.

A nonadverse party, acting in a fiduciary capacity, can be granted certain powers. One of these, which triggers the grantor trust rules of Code section 674, is to add beneficiaries other than afterborn children, so long as the grantor does not control this decision. In one private ruling[6], a trust provided that the trustee could, in its discretion, add as beneficiaries persons who were lineal descendants of the parents of the grantor. This brought the trust under the provisions of Code section 674, making it a grantor trust, eligible to hold S corporation stock.

HOW IT IS DONE — AN EXAMPLE

Francis Osborne owns all of the stock in a corporation which is electing to be taxed under Subchapter S of the Internal Revenue Code. He would like to make a gift of several shares of nonvoting common stock in trust for his children, but he also wants to retain a substantial part of the income stream from that stock for a period of years. You have explained to him the possible use of a grantor retained annuity trust (GRAT) for a term of years. However, a GRAT is not a qualified shareholder in an S corporation, since there is no guarantee that all of the trust income would be paid to the grantor. The annuity could be more or less than that amount.

You propose that the trust contain a provision that Francis has the power, at any time during the term of the trust, to remove the trust assets and substitute other assets of equal value. Under Code section 675(4), if this power is exercisable in a nonfiduciary capacity, the trust will be classified as a grantor trust. Since S corporation stock can be held in a grantor trust, the S election will not be lost. Further, if the grantor does elect to swap trust assets, or repurchase assets from the trust at fair market value, such a swap or purchase will have no income tax consequences to either the trust or to Francis.

WHAT ARE THE TAX IMPLICATIONS?

The following is a summary of the income tax rules pertaining to grantor trusts:

1. Code section 672 contains important definitions relating to adverse and nonadverse parties, and related and subordinate parties. Under the remaining sections, whether the grantor is treated as the owner of the trust may depend on whether certain powers are conferred on persons fitting these categories.

2. Code section 673 imposes the grantor trust rules where the grantor retains a reversionary interest in the trust, that is, a right to some future benefits.

3. Code section 674 covers the retention of control over the enjoyment of the trust by the grantor or certain other persons. It is one of the most complex provisions of the Internal Revenue Code.

4. Code section 675 treats the grantor as the owner of the trust if he or she retains certain administrative powers over it. It is the provision most used in defective trust planning.

5. Code section 676 provides that the grantor is treated as the owner of the trust if he or she can revoke it.

6. Code section 677 imposes the grantor trust rules where the grantor or grantor's spouse retains beneficial enjoyment of the trust, or its income is used to pay premiums on life insurance on the grantor or the grantor's spouse.

Note that the grantor could be the owner of only a portion of the trust, all or part of the trust income, or all or part of the trust corpus. Also note that as a general rule the grantor trust provisions apply if certain powers are retained by the spouse of the grantor.

Many grantor retained powers which cause the grantor to be treated as the owner for income tax purposes will also cause the trust to be included in the grantor's taxable estate, WHICH SHOULD BE AVOIDED. For example, the trust will be included in the grantor's taxable estate if:

1. The grantor retains a reversionary interest that is valued at more than 5% of the trust corpus.[7] Even where the reversionary interest is valued at over 5% of the value of the trust, determined at date of death, Code section 2037 will not apply if beneficiaries could have received distribution of trust assets without surviving the grantor.

2. The grantor personally retains control over the enjoyment of the trust.[8]

3. The grantor retains certain administrative powers, such as the power to vote stock transferred to the trust.[9]

4. The grantor retains the income.[10]

However, many powers can be granted to a nonadverse party other than the grantor (including a spouse, but that is *not* recommended) which will cause the grantor to be treated as the owner of the trust for income tax purposes. A nonadverse party is someone other than an adverse party, defined in the Code as a person with a substantial interest in the trust that would be adversely affected by the exercise or non-exercise of the power.[11]

There are special rules for related or subordinate parties who are presumed subservient to the wishes of the grantor. Related or subordinate parties are the grantor's spouse, mother, father, issue, brother, sister, an employee of the grantor, an employee of a corporation where the stock of the grantor and the trust is significant from the standpoint of voting control, or a subordinate employee of a corporation in which the grantor is an executive.[12]

Under Code section 674(c), certain powers granted to an independent trustee who is nonadverse do not trigger these rules; an independent trustee consists of a trustee or trustees, none of whom are the grantor or grantor's spouse, and no more than half of whom are related or subordinate and subservient to the grantor.

In creating defective trusts, the following are powers most frequently granted to a trustee who is someone other than the grantor but is a nonadverse party:

1. Powers to control beneficial enjoyment of the trust under Code section 674(a), but note the exceptions for certain powers under Section 674(b), and exception for powers of an independent trustee under Section 674(c).

2. Certain administrative powers under Code section 675, including the power to deal with the trust for less than full consideration, the power to borrow from the trust under certain circumstances, the power, in a nonfiduciary capacity, to vote or control investments where the trust includes stock where voting control held by the grantor and trust is significant, and the power to remove assets and substitute assets of equal value. Note that if the grantor retains the power in a nonfiduciary capacity to remove assets and replace them with assets of equal value, he or she is treated as the owner for income tax purposes, but should not be for gift or estate tax purposes.

3. The power to revoke the trust in favor of the grantor under Code section 676 or to distribute income to the grantor under Code section 677. However, since this may subject the trust to the grantor's creditors, it is not recommended.

4. The power to apply income to the payment of premiums on life insurance on the grantor or grantor's spouse under Section 677(a)(3).

IMPLICATIONS AND ISSUES IN COMMUNITY PROPERTY STATES

Where assets transferred to defective trusts are community assets, the planner should be aware of the fact the "grantor" of such a trust will be each spouse as to his or her community interest. For example, if a nonadverse trustee is used, be certain that person is nonadverse as to both spouses. If the grantor retains the power to remove and replace assets, consider the fact that if only one spouse has that power, the grantor trust rule might not apply to the other spouse as to his or her community interest.

In general, the grantor trust rules apply to powers retained by either spouse, and this may not be a serious problem. However, it would be wise to consider this aspect, and also the potential impact of a divorce on the defective trust plan.

QUESTIONS AND ANSWERS

Question — Will the IRS attack the use of the defective trust?

Answer — Based on the private letter ruling cited in the discussion above, it appears the IRS will attack the use of the defective trust, probably arguing that the payment of the income tax by the grantor on trust income distributed to the other beneficiaries is an additional gift to the trust beneficiaries. However, at least one court has held that the payment of income tax on the income of an irrevocable trust is not a gift.[13]

Question — Can the defective trust be used in connection with irrevocable life insurance trusts where trust income is to be used to pay insurance premiums?

Answer — Under Code section 677, the use or possible use of trust income to pay life insurance premiums will cause the grantor trust rules to apply to the trust. This would enable the client to transfer income-producing property to the irrevocable life insurance trust, which then acquires the life insurance, using the income from the property to pay the premiums. Since the payment of the premiums is not deductible, the effect is that the income will be taxed to the grantor. If properly planned, this will remove both the life insurance proceeds and the income-producing property from the grantor's estate. Note the IRS will not presently rule on the income tax consequences of this technique.

Question — Can the defective trust concept be used to shift the income taxation of trust income to beneficiaries?

Answer — If trust beneficiaries are given a general power of appointment over a trust, they will be taxed on its income under Code section 678 whether or not they exercise that power. The beneficiaries may well be in a lower income tax bracket than the trust. This could also be considered where the beneficiaries are minors. However, if they are under 14, consideration must be given to the imposition of the "kiddie tax," under which the income would be taxed at the rates of the parent.

Footnote References

Trust — Defective

1. Let. Rul. 9444033.
2. IRC Sec. 1361(c)(2)(A)(i).
3. Let. Ruls. 9118017, 9230021, 9239015; *Rothstein*, 735 F.2d 704 (2nd Cir. 1984); Rev. Rul. 85-13, 1985-1 CB 184.
4. Rev. Rul. 74-613, 1974-2 CB 153.
5. IRC Sec. 170(f)(2)(B).
6. Let. Rul. 9301020.
7. IRC Secs. 673, 2037(a)(2).
8. IRC Secs. 674, 2036, 2038.
9. IRC Secs. 675, 2036(b).
10. IRC Secs. 677, 2036(a).
11. IRC Sec. 672.
12. IRC Sec. 672(c).
13. *Hogle v. Comm.*, 165 F.2d 352 (10th Cir. 1947).

Chapter 35

TRUST — GRANTOR RETAINED INTERESTS
(GRAT, GRUT, QPRT)

WHAT IS IT?

A grantor retained trust, as its name implies, is an irrevocable trust into which the grantor places assets and retains an interest for a fixed period of years. Principal, at the end of the specified period of years, will pass to a noncharitable beneficiary, such as a child or grandchild of the grantor.

In a grantor retained annuity trust (GRAT), the grantor retains a right to payment of a fixed amount for a fixed period of years. In a grantor retained unitrust (GRUT), the grantor retains a right to payment of a fixed percentage of the value of the trust property (determined annually) for a fixed period of years.

A grantor retained income trust (GRIT), which was commonly used for income property before the adoption of Code section 2702, is now limited to transfers of a personal residence or certain tangible property, such as a painting, in situations where the grantor retains the use of the property during the term of the trust. In the case of the personal residence GRIT, the trust will usually be a qualified personal residence trust (QPRT).

In all of these types of trusts, the grantor is essentially making a current gift of the right to trust assets to the remainderman at a specified date in the future. If the grantor survives the term selected, significant tax as well as other transfer cost reductions may be realized with the GRAT and GRUT. However, with respect to most GRITs, a grantor will now be treated as making a gift of the entire property transferred to trust (rather than a gift of the discounted value of the remainder). A GRIT holding a personal residence (such as a QPRT) is a notable exception to this rule.

WHEN IS THE USE OF SUCH A DEVICE INDICATED?

1. A GRAT, GRUT, or QPRT is particularly useful where the client is single and has a substantial estate upon which federal estate taxes are certain to be paid. Wealthy widows or widowers or divorced individuals can use such a trust as a "marital deduction substitute."

2. A married couple with an estate in excess of the couple's combined unified credit equivalent can use a GRAT, GRUT, or QPRT to eliminate or reduce taxes on the death of the second spouse to die. The larger and more rapidly appreciating these estates are, the more effective such a trust would be.

3. A GRAT, GRUT, or QPRT is effective where income producing property is located in more than one state and unification and probate savings are desired. The GRAT, GRUT, or QPRT would serve to transfer ownership in a manner that would avoid ancillary administration.

4. A GRAT, GRUT, or QPRT will protect assets from a will contest, public scrutiny, or an election against the will if the grantor survives the trust term.

5. A GRIT is a useful technique when a client wants to purchase certain tangible assets such as a work of art, retain the right to display it in his or her own home, but be sure it will pass to a specified person immediately and without probate at death. (However, if the grantor is unable to establish the value of the retained interest through comparable rentals, the gift of the transferred remainder will be valued at 100 percent of the transferred property).

6. A GRAT, GRUT, or QPRT can serve as an alternative to (or be used in conjunction with) a recapitalization or other freezing technique that has the added advantages of gift tax leverage and possible estate tax savings.

7. When the client is young enough to have a high probability of outliving the trust term that is needed to obtain a low present value gift to the remainderman.

8. When the client has assets so substantial that a significant portion can be committed to a remainderman without compromising his own personal financial security.

9. When the client has a high risk-taking propensity and strong incentive to achieve gift and estate tax savings (rather than taking a safer but more costly approach of making an immediate gift).

The Tools and Techniques of Estate Planning

WHAT ARE THE REQUIREMENTS?

1. An irrevocable trust must be established. A GRAT or GRUT must provide that the grantor retains the right to annuity or unitrust payments for a specified number of years (there is no limit to how few or how many years). Payment of the greater of an annuity or unitrust amount is permissible. As you will note below, the longer the specified term of the trust, the greater the value of the retained interest and therefore the lower the taxable gift the grantor is making to the ultimate beneficiaries.

2. Evidence should be obtained of the value of the assets placed in the GRAT or GRUT. It is recommended that one or more qualified appraisers value the property shortly before it is placed into trust.

3. The grantor should be given a mandatory annuity or unitrust interest. The trust should specifically provide that the trustee has no discretion to withhold payments from the grantor (or possession of the trust property from the remaindermen). Payments should be made annually or more frequently.

4. The grantor should be given only the annuity or unitrust interest (or possibly a noncontingent reversion). The trustee should generally be specifically prohibited from making distributions in excess of the annuity or unitrust amounts. While a GRAT or GRUT can provide for payment of income in excess of the annuity or unitrust amount to the grantor, the value of the gift of a remainder interest is not reduced by the value of such an excess income provision.

5. If the trust provides an income interest, the trustee should be prohibited from making discretionary allocations of receipts and disbursements. The trust should provide that the trustee must follow state law "principal and interest" allocation rules.

6. If the trust provides an income interest, the grantor should be authorized to compel the trustee to make any nonproductive property productive by investment in income-producing assets.

7. If the asset placed into the GRIT is a home in which the grantor resides, a written lease should be entered into after the specified term expires. That lease should require the grantor to pay a fair market rental to the remainderman. Terms of the lease should be strictly enforced by the remainderman.[1]

8. While it is not a requirement, the trustee should generally be someone other than the grantor or the grantor's spouse, especially after the grantor's retained interest has ended. Retention of an interest as a trustee could lead to additional income tax (but see Chapter 34 on Defective Trusts) or estate tax exposure.

HOW IT IS DONE — AN EXAMPLE

Assume a widow in a 50% estate tax bracket. Assume the discount rate is 10.6 percent. She places her $200,000 personal residence into an irrevocable trust. The trust provides that she will live in the personal residence for a 10 year term. At the end of that time, the personal residence will pass to her children.

The present value of her right to live in the personal residence for 10 years is $126,974 (.634869 x $200,000). (See Appendix D for valuation tables.) Since the entire value of the personal residence placed in trust is $200,000 and the income interest retained by the grantor is $126,974, the value of the future interest gift being made at that point to the remainderman is the difference, $73,026. This entire amount of $73,026 is a taxable gift, since the gift tax annual exclusion is allowed only for gifts of a present interest. Of course, $600,000 can be sheltered by the unified credit equivalent, which means that the widow will pay no gift tax. Assuming the unified credit has already been used and a 50% gift tax bracket, the tax would be $36,513.

If the $200,000 property appreciates at an after-tax rate of 5%, the property will be worth $325,779 by the end of the 10 year term.

Should the widow die before the term expires, the trust assets would be included in her estate at their date of death value. So there would be no federal death tax savings.

But if the widow survived the 10 year period (no matter by how short a period of time), none of the trust assets would be in her estate. At a 50% estate tax bracket, the savings would be approximately $126,376 [50% x ($325,779 - $73,026)]. Furthermore, since the property would not pass through probate, probate costs on $325,779 would be avoided.

GRATs and GRUTs can provide similar gift, estate, and generation-skipping transfer tax discounts. A married couple could each establish GRATs and GRUTs (or split gifts — see Chapter 15) so as to utilize both spouse's unified credits and marginal gift and estate tax brackets.

WHAT ARE THE TAX IMPLICATIONS?

1. If the grantor outlives the specified term, none of the trust's assets should be included in the grantor's estate. This is because the grantor has retained no interest in trust assets at death. Code Section 2036 (retained life estates) applies only if the grantor retained the right to possess or enjoy the property or the income it produces (a) for life, or (b) for a period not ascertainable without reference to the grantor's death, or (c) for any period which does not, in fact, end before the grantor's death.

2. The gift to the remainderman is a gift of a future interest. It therefore cannot qualify for the annual gift tax exclusion.

3. If the grantor lives beyond the specified term, there should be no further transfer tax since the gift was complete upon the funding of the trust.

4. The taxable portion of post-'76 gifts is considered an "adjusted taxable gift." Since the entire present value of the gift to the remainderman is taxable, that amount is considered an adjusted taxable gift. This will push up the rate at which the other assets in the grantor's estate, if any, will be taxed.

    But a rapidly growing asset will have been transferred at an extremely low transfer tax cost. This results in a significant "leveraging of the unified credit."

    Perhaps more importantly, 100% of post-gift appreciation in the property's value escapes estate, gift, and generation-skipping transfer tax. This makes a GRAT, GRUT, or QPRT an excellent "estate freezing" device with respect to post-transfer appreciation.

5. At the grantor's death beyond the specified term of years, no step-up in basis will be allowed. The remainderman would therefore have a carryover basis in the property. In other words, the remainderman would carry over a portion of the grantor's basis.

    Basis is fractionalized.[2] The grantor takes a percentage equal to his original present value interest percentage. In the example above, the grantor would take about 63% of the basis. The remainderman would therefore receive about 37% of the basis. So if the widow's original basis in the example above was $100,000, the donee's basis would be $36,513 (.365131 x $1,000,000).

    This would obviously result in a substantial gain if the remainderman disposes of the property. But the income tax rate on the gain will probably be well below the federal estate tax and GST tax rates that could have been imposed had the property been included in the widow's estate at her death. Furthermore, the potential for significant tax deferral exists; if the $200,000 personal residence had been retained by the widow, an estate tax would have been due on it 9 months after her death. But if a QPRT is used, tax (probably at a much lower rate) could be deferred for much longer. In fact, tax would be imposed only if and when the remainderman disposes of the property.

6. If the grantor dies before the specified term expires, the date of death value of the property will be includable in the grantor's gross estate.[3] [It is possible, although uncertain, that the value of a GRAT or GRUT included in the grantor's estate could be less than 100 percent of the value of the property in the trust.] If there is an estate tax inclusion, (a) there would be no adjusted taxable gift[4], and (b) the unified credit utilized in making the gift would be restored to the estate. Note that if the spouse of the grantor "split the gift," the unified credit of the nongrantor spouse would not be restored. This could be solved if both spouses in fact are grantors. In other words, have each spouse create a separate GRAT or GRUT.

    It is appropriate for a beneficiary to purchase insurance on the life of the grantor and carry that life insurance during the period of time in which the death of the grantor would cause estate tax inclusion. The insurance proceeds, received estate tax free, could then be used to purchase assets from the grantor's estate and thereby provide estate liquidity.

7. If appreciated property is transferred to a GRAT, GRUT or QPRT, the tax on any gain will eventually be paid by (a) the grantor, or (b) the trust, or (c) the beneficiaries. Having taxes paid by the grantor may not, however, be a disadvantage, since the purpose of the trust is to "defund" the grantor's estate and shift as much wealth as possible to the remainderman with minimal gift taxes. If the trustee sells appreciated property within 2 years of its transfer to the trust, the gain is taxable at the grantor's marginal income tax rates.

8. GRITs, GRATs, and GRUTS are generally subject to Code section 2702.

Section 2702

In valuing a transfer in trust to or for the benefit of a member of the transferor's family, Section 2702(a) provides that all retained interests in trusts that are not "qualified interests" are valued at zero.[5] The amount of any gift is then determined by subtracting from the value of the property the value of the retained interest. The valuation of retained interests in trust under Section 2702 specifically does not apply to incomplete gifts (determined without regard to whether there is consideration); personal residence trusts (see heading below); charitable remainder trusts and pooled income funds; and charitable lead trusts (if the only interest other than the remainder or a qualified annuity or unitrust interest is the charitable lead interest).

Section 2702 also does not apply to assignment of remainder interests in trusts if the only retained interest is distribution of income in the sole discretion of an independent trustee, as defined in Code section 674(c), and certain property settlement agreements.[6]

The following definitions apply under Section 2702:[7]

1. A member of the family includes the spouse of an individual, and the ancestor, lineal descendant, or sibling of an individual or the individual's spouse, or the spouse of any such person.

2. An applicable family member includes the spouse of an individual, and the ancestor of an individual or the individual's spouse, or the spouse of any such person.

3. A transfer in trust includes a transfer to a new trust or an interest in an existing trust, but not a transfer resulting from exercise of a special power of appointment; exercise, release, or lapse of a power of appointment that would not constitute a taxable gift (e.g., lapse of "Crummey" power which does not exceed "5 or 5" limitation); or a disclaimer.

4. A retained interest is one held by the same individual both before and after the transfer to the trust, or a carved out term interest.

Qualified interests are valued under Code section 7520 (i.e., at approximately 120% of the applicable federal midterm interest rate under Code section 1274(d)(1) for the month into which the valuation falls).

A qualified interest is:

1. a qualified annuity interest,

2. a qualified unitrust, or

3. a qualified remainder interest.[8]

Qualified Annuity Interests (GRATs)

A qualified annuity interest is an irrevocable right to receive a fixed amount at least annually, payable to or for the benefit of the holder of the term interest (i.e., the transferor or an applicable family member).[9] A withdrawal right, whether or not cumulative, does not qualify.[10]

The annuity payment can be the greater (but not the lesser) of a fixed dollar amount or a fixed percentage of the initial *or* annual value of the trust, and will be valued at the greater of the two values.[11] Income in excess of the fixed amount can be distributable to the transferor, but is not considered in valuing the retained interest.[12] Subsequent contributions are prohibited. If the annuity is based on a percentage of the value of the trust, there must be a provision to adjust for incorrect valuation similar to the rules of Reg. §1.664-2(a)(1)(iii).[13] Payment can be made after the close of the taxable year of the trust if made by the filing date for the trust income tax returns, determined without regard to extensions. The annuity can be based on a fixed dollar amount or percentage of the value of the trust, and cannot vary except to the extent the amount (or percentage) in any year does not exceed 120% of the amount (or percentage) from the preceding year.[14]

Qualified Unitrust Interests (GRUTs)

A qualified unitrust interest is an irrevocable right to an annual payment of a fixed percentage of the net fair market value of the trust assets, to be determined annually.[15] Rules similar to those applicable to annuity trusts also apply here. Combinations of annuity and unitrust payments are not permitted. However, the trust may permit payment of the greater of an annuity or unitrust amount, to be valued at the higher value.[16]

As to both annuity and unitrust transfers, any payments to other persons are prohibited; the term of the trust must be stated either as a period of years or a fixed term, or the shorter of the two; successive term interests for the same individual are permitted; and there must be no provision for commutation of any interest.[17] The transferor can retain a reversionary interest in either the GRAT or GRUT, contingent upon death during the trust term, but the reversion is valued at zero.

Qualified Remainder Interests

A qualified remainder interest is the right to receive all or a fractional share of the trust on termination of all or a fractional share of the trust, and includes a reversion.[18] It must be non-contingent, i.e., payable to the beneficiary or the beneficiary's estate in all events. All other payments must be annuity or unitrust payments, with no provision for distributions of income in excess of the annuity or unitrust amount. The right to receive a pecuniary amount or the original value of the corpus does not qualify.

The retention of a remainder interest is a relatively rare estate planning technique, since any increase in the value of the transferred property is included in the transferor's's taxable estate, and unless the remainder (reversion) is valued at less than 5% of the value of the transferred property, the grantor will be taxed on the income in any case.[19]

Personal Residence Trusts

A grantor retained income trust can still be utilized effectively where the transferor transfers an interest in a personal residence to a trust and the transferor retains the right to use the property for residential purposes for a term of years. Section 2702 carves out an exception for a personal residence trust. The regulations require such a trust to be limited to holding a single residence, or a fractional interest in a residence — in no case can the term holder hold interests in trust in more than two residences.[20]

The residence may not be occupied by any person other than the grantor, a spouse or dependent; must be available at all times for such use; and cannot be sold or used for any other purposes. The property must be either the principal residence (as defined in Code section 1034) or another residence as described in Code section 280A(d)(1), without regard to Code section 280A(d)(2) (i.e., use as a residence for personal purposes for a number of days that exceeds the greater of 14 days or 10% of the number of days it is rented.)

The residence may include appurtenant structures and adjacent land reasonably appropriate for residence purposes, may be subject to a mortgage, but does not include any personal property, such as furnishings. Residential use includes activities describe in Code section 280A(c)(1) or (4) (i.e., limited use for business or day care if only secondary); and is not used to provide transient lodging and substantial services (i.e., a hotel or bread and breakfast).

Interests owned by spouses in a residence, including community interests, can be transferred to the same trust so long as only the spouses hold the term interest. If there is an involuntary conversion, such as destruction of the residence by fire, or its condemnation, the trust can hold the proceeds of such a conversion, such as insurance proceeds or a condemnation award, so long as there is a qualified replacement under Code section 1033. However, both the proceeds of the involuntary conversion and any income from those proceeds must be invested in a new residence within two years of when the proceeds were received.

Qualified Personal Residence Trust (QPRTs)

Recognizing the lack of statutory guidance for the implementation of the personal residence trust, the regulations carve out a safe harbor called a qualified personal residence trust.[21] The terms are not as restrictive as the personal residence trust, but do contain provisions substantially the same as applicable to personal residence trusts. However, while the regulations seem to require that no assets other than an interest in a personal residence (or the proceeds of an involuntary conversion) can ever be held in a personal residence trust, and the interest in the residence cannot be sold during the term of the trust, the qualified personal residence trust permits both under limited circumstances. It is conceivable this trust could have income. If it does, it must be distributed to the term holder; no distributions can be made to any other person.

The qualified personal residence trust must prohibit the holding of any property other than the personal residence, and contain the following provisions:

1. No distributions to other persons are permitted.

2. Cash can be held for the initial purchase of the residence within three months, or purchase of a replacement residence within three months of the date the cash is added to the trust.

3. Cash can also be held for up to six months for payment of trust expenses, including mortgage payments, and for improvements.

4. If the property is sold or insurance proceeds are received, a two year replacement period is permitted. Excess cash must be distributed at least quarterly or at the termination of the trust to the term holder.

5. If the property is no longer used as a personal residence, the trust must terminate and its assets distributed to the term holder, unless converted into a qualified annuity trust.

In the case of a qualified personal residence trust, it is possible to sell a residence, reinvest only part of the proceeds in a new residence, and convert the rest to an annuity. The governing instrument must prohibit the commutation (prepayment) of the term interest.

Subsequent Transfers of Retained Interests

A reduction of taxable gifts or adjusted taxable gifts is permitted if the individual subsequently transfers an interest in a trust which was valued under Section 2702. The amount of the reduction is the lesser of the increase in taxable gifts resulting from the application of Section 2702, or the increase in the transferor's subsequent taxable gifts, or taxable estate, which results from the subsequent transfer.[22] The rule applies to testamentary transfers only if a term interest in the trust is included in the transferor's taxable estate solely by reason of the operation of Code section 2033 or a remainder interest is included in the transferor's taxable estate, and such interest was valued under Section 2702. Where spouses have split gifts, the adjustment is allocated one-half to each spouse, but one spouse may assign this adjustment to the other.

IMPLICATIONS AND ISSUES IN COMMUNITY PROPERTY STATES

If husband and wife transfer community property to a GRAT or GRUT, each may reserve the right to the payment for the trust term as to his or her respective community interest. It would apparently be possible for them to retain a joint payment for the term. If either dies during the term, the value of his or her community interest in the trust would be included in his or her taxable estate, either in whole or in part. If either or both spouses survive the term, his or her community interest in the trust should not be included in his or her estate. Note that in the case of the personal residence trust and qualified personal residence trust, the spouses can transfer community interests in one or two personal residences to the trust and retain the right to live in the residence for its term.

QUESTIONS AND ANSWERS

Question — What makes a GRAT, GRUT, and QPRT work so well?

Answer — GRATs, GRUTs, and QPRTs are based on two basic principles: gift taxes are based on the value of the gift to the donee and a gift (and therefore the gift tax) must be "discounted" by the cost of waiting. The longer the donee must wait, the lower the gift tax value of the asset placed in trust and therefore the lower the cost of the gift. With discount rates that fluctuate from month to month, there can be wide swings in gift tax cost. For instance, if the discount rate is 11.2 percent, the taxable gift in the example above would be $69,180 (.345901 x $200,000). At a 9.6 percent rate it would be $79,970 (.399848 x $200,000). (See Appendix D for valuation tables.)

The second principle that makes a GRAT, GRUT, and QPRT work is that the federal estate tax doesn't reach a property interest unless the decedent owned it when he died or unless he held a "string," a property right strong enough to cause it to be pulled back into his estate. In a GRAT, GRUT, or QPRT, once the grantor lives longer

than the specified term, he neither owns the property in the trust nor holds any property interest. It therefore escapes estate taxation.

Question — What are the downside risks, costs, or disadvantages of a GRAT, GRUT, and QPRT?

Answer — GRATs, GRUTs, and QPRTs are the closest thing to a "no lose" situation; it is a "what have we got to lose?" technique.

If the client doesn't use a GRAT, GRUT, or QPRT and purchases property in his sole name, the property and any growth on the property will be in his estate.

If the client who sets up a GRAT, GRUT, or QPRT dies during the specified term, the result is that the property plus any appreciation will be includable in his estate (the same result as if the client had done nothing).

There are, of course, costs involved in a GRAT, GRUT, or QPRT. These include:

(a) Attorney fees and the other transaction costs, such as appraisal fees and property titling costs of establishing the trust.

(b) Forfeiture of the ability to shift income during the specified income term (and the eventual estate tax on the consequent addition to the grantor's estate of property purchased by the after-tax net on that income). But, looking at it another way, the grantor has — before and after the trust — the same income and therefore the same income tax, but with a potential of substantial estate tax savings.

(c) Lost opportunity cost. The GRAT, GRUT, or QPRT is an irrevocable trust. So, once assets are placed into the trust, the grantor is precluded from taking other planning measures. If the grantor has used up a sizeable part of or his or her unified credit to offset the gift of the remainder interest in the GRAT, GRUT, or QPRT, then he or she is not in a position to make large gifts of other assets which may substantially appreciate in value. If the grantor dies during the term, the gamble will have been lost.

(d) If the grantor does die during the specified trust term, his executor may be liable for tax on the includable assets — but the property itself might not be available to pay that tax. (Solutions to this issue are discussed further below.)

Question — Assume a husband makes a large transfer to a GRAT, GRUT, or QPRT. To reduce the potential gift tax on the value of the remainderman's interest, his wife consents to "split" the gift and use her unified credit to reduce or eliminate the gift tax. If the husband dies before the specified term expires, will the wife's unified credit be restored?

Answer — No. Although the husband's unified credit is restored if he dies within the specified income term, his wife's unified credit is not restored. A potential solution to this inequity is for the husband to make a gift to his wife. She then could make her own actual contribution to the GRAT, GRUT, and QPRT. (Obviously, the IRS could consider this a step transaction, but this logic presumes that the gift to the wife (assuming the facts indicate it was an outright and unconditional gift) was per se a transfer to an agent of the husband. This presumption is at odds with the trend of constitutional and even tax law, i.e., recognition of a female as an independent person and the trend of antipathy to sexual bias.)

Question — What are the best assets to place into a GRAT or GRUT?

Answer — Aside from cash, assets which possess substantial appreciation potential are the very best assets to place into a GRAT or GRUT.

Question — What happens if the IRS — many years after the GRAT, GRUT, or QPRT is funded — claims that the true value of the property at the time it was placed into the trust was significantly greater than what the grantor claimed?

Answer — If the IRS successfully argues that the gift value of the remainder was understated, (a) additional gift taxes (plus interest) may be due, or (b) more of the client's unified credit may have to be utilized, and (c) if the grantor's death occurred after the specified term of years, the adjusted taxable gift component would be greater than reported. In summary, proper valuation is important but not critical.

Note that the statute of limitations barring the IRS from revaluing a gift (and therefore increasing the rate of tax on gifts the grantor makes in future years) doesn't apply if the grantor didn't pay a gift tax because of the unified credit.[23] Likewise, the IRS claims that if the unified credit prevented liability for a gift tax, it is not barred from revaluing the gift — even after the normal statute of limitations expires — for purposes of increasing the amount of adjusted taxable gifts for estate tax purposes.

In fact, the Service has gone so far as to say that even if a gift tax was paid and the statute of limitations had

run,[24] that it still had the right to revalue post-1976 taxable gifts.

The key to avoiding the entire valuation issue is to begin (before funding the trust) with strong authoritative evidence that the value claimed by the grantor at the time of transaction was in fact sound. This extra effort may be most important if the GRAT, GRUT, or QPRT in fact achieves its major objective — to avoid estate taxation on rapidly appreciating property. Why? Because (a) if the grantor does survive the specified term, and (b) if the property has in fact appreciated substantially, there will be an "adjusted taxable gift." The IRS will argue "if the property at death was worth $ X, how could it have been worth $ Y only a few years later?" Obviously the IRS would argue, "The adjusted taxable gift the grantor made had to be much larger than he claimed." Absent strong evidence to the contrary, the estate would be at a disadvantage and probably would end up paying a much higher rate on the assets actually in the grantor's taxable estate.

Question — Is there an "escape mechanism" that could redirect the remainder interest if the grantor dies during the term? For instance, is there a way to provide that if the grantor's estate has to include GRAT, GRUT, or QPRT assets, funds in the trust return to the grantor's estate rather than going to the remainderman?

Answer — A reversion to the grantor (or better yet to a revocable trust he established during his lifetime to avoid probate), conditioned on his death within the specified term, would create the funds to pay the estate tax. However, the value of a contingent reversion will no longer result in a reduction in the value of the taxable gift to the remainderman in the case of a GRAT or GRUT subject to Code section 2702.

Question — Is there a cutoff age after which the GRAT, GRUT, or QPRT no longer is mathematically logical?

Answer — Since the GRAT, GRUT, and QPRT are "little to lose — a lot to gain" tools, even clients in their 80s may want to use a such a trust. For instance, assuming a discount rate of 10.6 percent, the value of the income interest retained in a five year QPRT is .395739 of the principal. Some clients, especially those who are in very good health, may want to gamble with a GRAT, GRUT, or QPRT. For example, if the 80-year-old client opted for a ten year term, the value of the income interest jumps to .634869 of the funds placed in the QPRT (and therefore the taxable gift to the remainderman drops accordingly). (See Appendix D for valuation tables.)

For clients with a slightly lower risk taking propensity, consider staggered terms. For instance, an 80-year-old client could transfer some property into a five year GRAT or GRUT and some property into a ten year GRAT or GRUT.

Question — Are there problems with using closely held stock with a GRAT or GRUT?

Answer — The major problem with using a GRAT or GRUT which holds closely held stock is caused by the interplay of Code sections 2036(b) and 2035. If voting control is retained over the stock placed into the GRAT or GRUT, it is obvious that the death of the grantor while that right is retained will cause estate tax inclusion of all of the trust's assets.

Question — Are there special provisions that should be inserted into a GRAT, GRUT, QPRT?

Answer — It is extremely important to document the "completeness" of the transfer at the date the trust is funded. Specifically, the trust must provide that the donor has given up all dominion and control over the property.

The grantor must specifically give up any power to revoke the gift of the remainder. The trust should also forbid the grantor to change any beneficial interests in the remainder. Therefore, the grantor can retain no power of appointment (other than possibly a power contingent on the grantor dying during the trust term).

The grantor should generally not be named as trustee (especially after the grantor's retained interest ends). An unrelated, independent trustee should be selected.

The trust should specifically deny the grantor any control over the manner or time in which the beneficiaries will enjoy the trust corpus (otherwise, that corpus will be pulled back into the grantor's estate).

Question — How should clients be advised who are concerned that if they transfer their personal residence into a trust for a term, and still want to live there at the end of the term, they will be unable to do so?

Answer — This is a concern to many clients, and there are planning ideas to help. For example, if the grantor is also the trustee, he or she could simply buy the residence back just before the end of the term. The purchase should be at fair market value. Note that gain or loss can be avoided in this situation if the trust is structured as a "grantor" trust in which the grantor is treated as the owner for income tax purposes (see discussion of defective trusts in Chapter 34).

The biggest difficulty with this solution is that the grantor will have to have other resources to purchase the residence.

In one private letter ruling[25], a personal residence trust created by a husband and wife as to their one-half interests in the residence qualified even though it had both lease and purchase provisions. The trust had a 30 year term. If either grantor died during the term, his or her undivided one-half interest in the residence would be distributed to the survivor. If both died during the term, the trust would terminate and be distributed to children. The grantors will enter into an agreement with the remaindermen permitting them to lease the residence or purchase it at the end of the term at fair market (or rental) value. Note the ruling specifically relates only to qualification of the trust under Code section 2702, not to any estate tax issues.

Question — Can the QPRT be effectively used for a vacation home?

Answer — Possibly the most popular use of the QPRT is for the so-called second or vacation home. Under the facts of one ruling[26], grantor and spouse jointly own two vacation homes which could be successfully transferred to a QPRT. They intend to retitle them so that each spouse owns one property, then each will transfer his or her vacation home to a QPRT until the death of that grantor or a term of ten years. Income, if any, will be distributed to each grantor, and each will have the right to live in his or her residence. If the residences are sold, an annuity will be paid during the remainder of the term. If a grantor survives, the property will remain in trust until the surviving grantor dies. However, income will be accumulated until the death of the surviving spouse and then distributed to children. There is a reversion if the grantor dies during the trust term.

Question — Can stock in an S corporation be placed into a GRAT or GRUT?

Answer — S corporation stock may be an excellent candidate for transfer into a retained interest trust. The income attributable to the stock will pass to the trust and be the basis for the annuity or unitrust payment to the grantor during the term.

Unfortunately, a GRAT or GRUT cannot qualify to hold S stock since not all of the trust income is payable to the beneficiary. See Chapter 29. However, since any trust as to which the grantor is treated as the owner for income

310

tax purposes can hold S stock, the solution has been to make the GRAT or GRUT "defective" for income tax purposes (i.e., taxable under the grantor trust rules). See Chapter 34. There are many examples of this technique in private letter rulings[27].

Question — Assume a grantor age 60 established a GRAT for a term of 15 years, but with a provision that should she die before the end of the term, it will terminate at her death. The value of the property placed in the trust is $500,000, the annuity payout rate is 6%, and the assumed interest rate is 9%. What is the amount of the gift? What would the amount be if the gift was for a 15 year term certain?

Answer — See Figure 35.1 and 35.2.

Footnote References

Trust—Grantor Retained Interests (GRAT, GRUT, QPRT)

1.   *Est. of Barlow v. Comm.*, 66 TC 333 (1970).
2.   *Hunter v. Comm.*, 44 TC 109 (1965); Rev. Rul. 77-413, 1977-2 CB 298; Reg. §1.61-6(a).
3.   IRC Sec. 2036(a)(1); *Est. of Fry v. Comm.*, 9 TC 503 (1947).
4.   IRC Sec. 2001(b).
5.   Reg. §25.2702-1(b).
6.   Reg. §25.2702-1(c).
7.   Reg. §25.2702-2(a).
8.   IRC Sec. 2702(b).
9.   Reg. §25.2702-3(b).
10. Reg. §25.2702-3(b)(1) and (c)(1).
11. Reg. §25.2702-3(d).

Figure 35.1

GRAT FOR SHORTER OF LIFE OR 15 YEARS	
GRANTOR RETAINED ANNUITY TRUST - SHORTER OF TERM OR LIFE	
Transfer Date	2/1992
Table Rate	9.0%
Age to Nearest Birthday	60
Term of Trust	15
Principal	$500,000
Rate of Annuity	6.000%
Payment Period	1
Payments made at Beginning or End of Period	End
Annuity Factor	7.2027
Payout Frequency Factor	1.0000
Amount of Payment Per Period	$30,000
Total Annual Payments	$30,000
Value of Annuity Interest Retained by Grantor	$216,081
Taxable Gift (PV of Remainder Interest)	$283,919

Figure 35.2

GRAT FOR 15 YEARS TERM CERTAIN	
GRANTOR RETAINED ANNUITY TRUST - TERM	
Transfer Date	2/1992
Table Rate	9.0%
Term of Trust	15
Principal	$500,000
Rate of Annuity	6.000%
Payment Period	1
Payments made at Beginning or End of Period	End
Annuity Factor	8.0607
Payout Frequency Factor	1.0000
Amount of Payment Per Period	$30,000
Total Annual Payments	$30,000
Value of Annuity Interest Retained by Grantor	$241,821
Taxable Gift (PV of Remainder Interest)	$258,179

12. Reg. §25.2702-3(b)(iii).
13. Reg. §25.2702-3(b)(2).
14. Reg. §25.2702-3(b)(1)(ii).
15. Reg. §25.2702-3(c).
16. Reg. §25.2702-3(d).
17. Reg. §25.2702-3(d)(2) to (4).
18. Reg. 25.2702-3(f).
19. IRC Sec. 673

20. Reg. §25.2702-5(a) and (b)(1)
21. Reg. §25.2702-5(c).
22. Reg. §25.2702-6(a)
23. Rev. Rul. 84-11, 1984-1 CB 201.
24. IRC Sec. 2504(c).
25. Let. Rul. 9425028.
26. Let. Rul. 9441039.
27. Let. Ruls. 9416009, 9444033.

Chapter 36

TRUST — IRREVOCABLE LIFE INSURANCE

WHAT IS IT?

An irrevocable life insurance trust is, as the name implies, a vehicle for holding life insurance policies. The primary goal of such a trust is to shift the ownership of the policies from the insured's generation to a lower generation in order to remove the policy proceeds from taxation at the death of the insured and/or his spouse. In that way, the family can have a fund of cash which can be used to loan money to or purchase assets from a decedent's estate, thereby creating liquidity in the estate for payment of death taxes, without the funds causing additional death taxes at the death of the insured.

This result can be achieved by giving policies or cash to purchase policies outright to the children or successor generation, as well as by gifts into trust. However, the benefit of using a trust is that a trustee can be chosen who understands the goal of providing liquidity for payment of taxes, and in that way there is more certainty that the proceeds will be used for the intended purpose.

Where the life insurance continues to require payment of premiums after the gift, a typical irrevocable life insurance trust plan will call for the insured to make annual gifts to the trust to cover the premium payments. In order to make those gifts qualify as a "present interest gift" and therefore come within the $10,000 per donor per donee annual exclusion from gift tax, the trust often will have a "Crummey" withdrawal power in the beneficiaries (usually the children).

With a Crummey withdrawal power, each time a contribution is made to the trust, the beneficiary has a temporary right to demand withdrawal from the trust. If the demand right is not exercised, the annual transfer for that year remains in the trust for management by the trustee. If the demand is made, the trustee must deliver the funds to the beneficiary. However, the beneficiary generally will recognize that such a withdrawal may affect the grantor's decision as to future transfers to that trust and the beneficiary may therefore not make a demand. Once the withdrawal right lapses, the Trustee is then free to use the monies which were contributed to pay the premiums on the life insurance policies.

The name "Crummey trust" comes from the name of a party to a lawsuit, *Crummey v. Comm.*, 397 F.2d 82 (9th Cir. 1968).

WHEN IS THE USE OF SUCH A DEVICE INDICATED?

A life insurance trust can be used to good advantage whenever an individual (or a couple) faces a death tax in his or her generation, and wishes to provide liquidity for payment of those taxes with existing life insurance, or insurance to be purchased, without subjecting the proceeds themselves to depletion by death taxes.

In addition, gifts of life insurance generally are valued for gift tax purposes at the "interpolated terminal reserve value," which is usually close to the cash surrender value for a reasonably healthy individual. The face value of the policy is often many times greater than this gift tax value. In such cases, making gifts of life insurance policies is a way to "leverage" the donor's annual gift tax exclusions, unified credit and/or generation-skipping exclusion, by making gifts of policies which have a low current "gift value" in relation to their value at the insured's death.

Specifically, a trust is indicated where the donor does not have confidence that the recipients of the gifts will cooperate in retaining the policies or their proceeds and making them available to the donor's estate for payment of taxes, or where the gifts are made to minor or other beneficiaries, who do not have the capacity or judgment to manage the policies/proceeds.

Where the insured's spouse is an owner or co-owner of the policy, this type of trust is indicated only where the spouse feels comfortable with giving up the use and benefit of the proceeds, since the donor cannot retain any income or other rights over the policies or proceeds and still have the property not taxed at the donor's death.

WHAT ARE THE REQUIREMENTS?

Requirements for Life Insurance Gift Trust

1. The donor(s) must create a trust vehicle to receive the insurance gift (or to receive cash with which to purchase a new policy) which has terms which will achieve the donor's goals both with respect to the availability of funds with which to pay taxes as well as appropriate terms

for managing the assets for the beneficiaries both before and after the insured's death.

2. The donor(s) must then actually transfer the policy to the trust by signing an irrevocable assignment of the policy to the trustee of the trust, or by making a cash gift to the trust to enable the trustee to purchase a new policy.

3. The insured or proposed insured must be in reasonable health in order to avoid the policy being valued at a much greater value for gift tax purposes.

Requirements for Crummey Withdrawal Power

4. Each time a contribution is made to a Crummey trust, the beneficiary must have a right to demand withdrawal of an amount equal to the value of the gift. Frequently, the withdrawal right may be dependent upon the donor also specifying that the withdrawal right will apply to the gift, e.g., "This gift is made subject to the right of withdrawal provided in...." This permits one trust to be able to receive both annual exclusion "Crummey gifts" as well as other gifts that the donor can be assured will not be removed by the beneficiary.

    However, in order for the annual exclusion to be permitted, the withdrawal right cannot be illusory. Implicit in every Crummey trust is the notion that the beneficiary will not exercise the right to withdraw and the gifts to the trust will remain in the trust until termination. However, the right to withdraw must be real and legally possible.

    The exclusion is allowed under a number of circumstances that may be surprising. An example is a gift in trust in which the beneficiary given the right to withdraw (through his guardian) is an infant.

5. For an adult beneficiary to have an effective demand right, he must have effective notice of the demand right.[1] The IRS rulings have emphasized the importance of giving effective notice of the annual trust contributions that are subject to withdrawal, at least to adult beneficiaries. In several cases the IRS has implied that notice may be necessary even for minor beneficiaries.[2] Although this notice is typically made in writing to have evidence that the requirement was met, it seems that even oral notice is adequate.

    With regard to the frequency of notice, it is most common to give notice of each transfer that is subject to the withdrawal power. However, a "once only" notice may be sufficient. Such a notice alerts the beneficiary that the trust has received a gift that gives rise to the withdrawal power. The notice typically states that later contributions may be made that will give rise to additional withdrawal rights. Such a "once only" notice may be sufficient if the original notice states that an annual notice would be given if requested by the beneficiary, thereby putting the burden on the beneficiary to inquire about future annual contributions.[3]

6. In order for the demand right to be effective, an adequate amount of time must be allowed for the exercise of the power of withdrawal, especially if the exercise of the power would require a step such as appointing a guardian for a minor beneficiary. The IRS has not drawn a clear line between reasonable and unreasonable time limits. However, the IRS has disapproved a three-day period as not a sufficient duration,[4] but Crummey withdrawal periods of as little as thirty days after an addition to the trust have been deemed effective.[5]

7. An important feature of a Crummey trust is that it allows the grantor to make gifts that qualify for the annual exclusion from gift tax under IRC §2503. In order to qualify for the annual exclusion, a gift must be one of a "present interest." (A beneficiary must receive the immediate, unfettered, and ascertainable right to use, possess, or enjoy the money or other property placed into the trust for that year.) A "future interest" does not qualify. When a trust has no provisions for a current withdrawal of the gift, at least a portion of each gift is a future interest. It is the right of the beneficiary to withdraw the transferred asset that meets the requirement to make the gift eligible for the annual exclusion.

8. The beneficiary of a Crummey trust must be able to actually receive property if he exercises a demand right. The gift will be eligible for the annual exclusion only to the extent the trust has assets sufficient to satisfy the beneficiary's demand rights.[6]

9. Where a beneficiary is a minor, and is therefore unable to make an effective withdrawal, he will be deemed to have a present interest in the gift if a guardian can make a legally effective demand on his behalf.

10. The IRS has taken the position that the annual exclusion is available only where the beneficiary is a "primary" beneficiary with a substantial interest in the trust other than the withdrawal power. However, the Tax Court has held that invasion powers held by grandchildren were eligible for the annual exclusion where a trust was created for children and the only other interests held by the grandchildren were contingent on the death of their parents before the trust was distributed.[7]

HOW IS IT DONE?

Harry and Donna Bradley would like to make gifts that will qualify for the annual exclusion to each of their two children and four grandchildren. Their annual exclusion amount for gifts to these donees would be $120,000 per year. (The husband and wife can give $10,000 apiece to each of the six individuals.) However, the Bradleys would prefer not to make outright gifts, especially not to the grandchildren.

The Bradleys would instead prefer to have a trust that would continue until their youngest child reaches the age of 35. At that time the trust would be distributed equally to the children and grandchildren. They decide that the trust will not make any distributions of current income.

An irrevocable life insurance trust would meet all the Bradleys' requirements. The trust they create can have all the desired terms plus Crummey powers of withdrawal in all of the children and grandchildren. Separate shares are required if the trust is to be exempt from generation-skipping tax.

ISSUES AND IMPLICATIONS IN COMMUNITY PROPERTY STATES

1. A couple owning community property can give $20,000 per recipient without any need for gift splitting because each spouse owns half the community property.

2. Because of the nature of community property (the fact that each spouse owns a one-half interest in each community asset), it is unusual in a community property state for a Crummey irrevocable insurance trust that benefits the surviving spouse as to the entire trust to be created.

    In a separate property jurisdiction, the typical terms of such a trust might provide that at the death of the insured spouse (e.g., the husband) the proceeds of an insurance policy (purchased with funds given by the husband) will benefit the wife in the form of a life interest in the proceeds. After her death, the proceeds would be available to be lent to her estate (or to purchase assets from her estate) to provide funds to pay estate taxes then due.

    In a community property state, on the other hand, the wife usually is the grantor as to one-half the gifts used to pay the insurance premium, and it would not be appropriate to give the wife a life interest in the entire policy proceeds, for that would be a transfer with a retained interest, includable in the wife's estate as to the one-half purchased with her share of the community property gift.

However, careful drafting can provide her with a life estate in the one-half of the proceeds produced by the husband's share of the community property gifts used to pay the premium. Further, even in a community property state, one spouse may have separate property already, or a "split" of community property can be achieved to produce separate property. With a trust funded by such separate property gifts, the other spouse can have a life estate in all of the policy proceeds without making them subject to estate tax in her estate.

WHAT ARE THE GIFT TAX AND ESTATE TAX IMPLICATIONS?

1. The gift of a life insurance policy is subject to gift tax, usually based on the policy's "interpolated terminal reserve value," usually close to the cash surrender value. However, where the insured is currently uninsurable or is even just in poor health, the policy may have a much greater value.

2. For the grantor/donor, a Crummey withdrawal power is an effective way to make a gift that qualifies for the annual exclusion from gift tax while avoiding the early distribution requirements of other forms of gifts that permit the donor to take advantage of the $10,000 per donee per year exclusion from gift tax. The Crummey withdrawal power can make both cash gifts and gifts of the policies themselves subject to the annual exclusion.

3. However, a second gift tax aspect arises when the beneficiary permits a lapse of his power to remove from the trust the contribution made by the grantor. This lapse of the withdrawal right was not often a problem when annual gifts from each donor were limited to $3,000, since IRC §2514(e) excludes from gift tax gifts that result from lapse of a power to withdraw assets from the trust up to the greater each year of $5,000 or 5% of the trust corpus. If each of two grantors gave $2,500 for a total of $5,000, the *de minimis* protection of IRC §2514(e) kept the lapse of the beneficiary's power from being a gift subject to gift tax.

    However, §2514(e) no longer provided sufficient protection when the annual exclusion amount was increased to $10,000 in 1981, at which time gifts in excess of $5,000 began to be made to Crummey trusts. Unless the trust was quite large, even the 5% aspect of this so-called "five or five" rule did not give enough protection, and the lapse of the withdrawal power to the extent it exceeded the greater of $5,000 or 5% of trust corpus caused a taxable gift by the power holder to the remaindermen of the trust. Since the (possibly unknown) remaindermen did not have a power to withdraw the gift from the trust, the beneficiary made a future interest gift, which did not qualify for the annual exclusion.

4. This taxable gift by the Crummey trust beneficiary has two negative aspects. One is that the beneficiary had made a transfer subject to gift tax and would use up some of his unified transfer credit or have an actual gift tax to pay.

   The other negative aspect is that, since the beneficiary usually had some continuing right in the trust (e.g., a life estate), the property subject to the lapsed power would be included in his estate for estate tax purposes as a transfer in which an interest had been retained.[8]

   The gift tax problem resulting from the lapse of a power relating to trust property in excess of $5,000 or 5% of the trust corpus can be resolved through good tax planning. By reserving in the beneficiary a power that keeps the lapse from being a completed gift (e.g., the power to direct where the trust property will go upon lapse of the withdrawal power), no gift tax is due. However, the estate tax problem is not avoided and the technically incomplete gift is included in the beneficiary's taxable estate. Since most Crummey trusts are intended to be paid out during the beneficiary's lifetime, this is not a great problem for most people.

5. Many trusts will direct the trustee to keep separate those portions of the property over which a withdrawal right has lapsed that are within the "five and five" rule from those portions that exceed the "five and five" limit. The portion within the "five and five" rule can avoid estate tax at the death of the beneficiary. (See Questions and Answers concerning the generation-skipping transfer tax.) The other portion (amounts in excess of the "five and five" limit) will be subject to estate tax at the death of the beneficiary who retains the power of appointment over the gift (in order to avoid the gift tax upon lapse). Careful record keeping is important if a portion of the trust is intended to pass free of both estate tax and generation-skipping transfer tax at the death of the beneficiary.

6. Regardless of how much of the gift is within or in excess of the "five and five" rule, the portion of the trust over which the beneficiary has a right of withdrawal at his death (e.g., the amount subject to the Crummey withdrawal where the withdrawal period had not lapsed) is included in his estate for estate tax purposes. This is because the beneficiary had the power to appoint (or transfer out) the property to himself and thus had a "general power of appointment" as described in IRC §2041. If the beneficiary lives past the point at which the removal power terminates, then the property that was subject to the withdrawal power can no longer be taken out and thus may escape taxation in the beneficiary's estate.

7. The primary goal of the life insurance trust is to remove the life insurance from the donor's taxable estate for death tax purposes. However, where the donor makes a gift of a life insurance policy and then dies within three years of making the gift, the value of the proceeds will be brought back into the donor's estate.[9] However, if an irrevocable life insurance trust purchases a new policy, the insured/donor never holds any incidents of ownership in the policy and the proceeds are not payable to the insured's estate, the insurance proceeds are not included in the insured's estate even if the insured dies within three years of the purchase by the trust.[10] For this reason, it is often better to structure the life insurance trust so that only cash gifts are made to the trust, and those cash gifts are used to purchase the desired insurance on the donor(s).

QUESTIONS AND ANSWERS

Question — Is there a way to avoid the three-year rule and still give an insurance policy?

Answer — No, there is really no way that is effective. Some people have given money to the trust and then let the trust purchase the policy from the insured. This triggers the "transfer for value" rule. Policy proceeds will then be taxed as ordinary income to the extent that they exceed the purchase price of the policy.

Question — How does one avoid the three-year rule and still give an insurance gift?

Answer — Where the donor is still insurable, it may well be that buying a new policy can actually be advantageous since the newer policies give a generally higher effective rate of return (with some unique exceptions). If this is the case, then the donor can give money to the trust and then let the trustee buy the policy. As long as the trustee is not required to purchase insurance with the funds contributed by the grantor and there is no other basis for saying that the grantor's gift of cash was really a gift of an insurance policy, the transfers within three-years of death rule can be avoided.

Question — If a person wants to cash in an insurance policy and buy a new one, are there any income tax aspects to the transaction?

Answer — Yes, to the extent that the insurance policy sale results in receiving more dollars than had been paid in net premiums, the "cashing in" of the policy can result in taxable income.

Question — The generation-skipping tax applies to current gifts to grandchildren. Is it possible to draft a Crummey trust which will be able to avoid such a tax?

Answer — Yes, if separate shares are created. The annual exclusion is available for gift tax purposes, with respect to all power holders who have a beneficial interest in the trust. However, a nontaxable gift which is a direct skip to a trust for the benefit of an individual has an inclusion ratio of zero (i.e., it is not subject to generation-skipping transfer tax) only if (1) during the life of such individual no portion of the trust corpus or income may be distributed to or for the benefit of any other person, and (2) the trust would be included in such individual's estate if such individual were to die before the trust terminated. A Crummey power can be used in conjunction with each such separate share to create an annual exclusion for generation-skipping transfer tax purposes.

Question — What is the maximum number of annual exclusion gifts I can make with a Crummey withdrawal power?

Answer — This is an area in which there has been a great deal of speculation. Some Crummey trusts have included withdrawal powers for individuals who have no beneficial interest in the trust other than the right to withdraw. Theoretically an annual exclusion would be available for each individual with a withdrawal power.

However, the IRS has disallowed a number of exclusions where the beneficiaries' interests included only the withdrawal power. The IRS indicated that annual exclusions will be allowed only for gifts to beneficiaries who hold other beneficial interests in the trust or who have actually exercised their powers. However, the IRS was unsuccessful in disallowing annual exclusions for persons with contingent interests in a trust.

In light of this rule, it would be prudent to include withdrawal powers only for individuals who have a beneficial interest in the trust. The number of annual exclusions available should therefore be limited to the persons who have some rights in the trust other than merely a power to withdraw.

Question — If a beneficiary of a Crummey trust does not exercise the withdrawal power, he is considered to have made a gift to the remaindermen of the trust. Since part of this gift may be taxable, how do we know what is subject to gift tax and what is not?

Answer — For those older trusts in which only gifts of $5,000 or less to the trust were envisioned, there is often no continuing power in the beneficiary to affect the disposition of the gifts after they come into the trust. In this circumstance, any amounts subject to the Crummey withdrawal power in excess of $5,000 will be subject to a taxable gift upon lapse of the power. The exception to this is that if the total trust principal at the time of the gift is in excess of $100,000, then the alternate exception of 5% of the trust corpus under IRC §2514(e) would apply and that is the amount that would not be subject to gift tax.

Question — What should be done with an older trust which relies only on the "five and five" power to avoid a gift by the beneficiary because of the lapse of the withdrawal and as to which the donors now wish to make larger gifts?

Answer — Many practitioners are looking for ways to abandon such older trusts. Some wise practitioners included a provision for some third person to have a power to "kick out" assets. Many persons are arranging to have such a power exercised so that they may start out fresh with a new trust with more effective terms.

In some other cases, some grantors are buying from the trusts insurance policies on their lives (particularly when they cannot get new coverage) and making gifts of those policies to new Crummey trusts.

Question — How should the beneficiaries be notified of the annual withdrawal right?

Answer — The basic requirement is that actual notice must be made in a timely manner. In order to show compliance it may be best to give written notice to all beneficiaries (and to the natural guardian of any minor) at least 30 days before the end of the withdrawal period (which is typically December 31).

Question — Is it sufficient if the beneficiaries are just given notice at the time the trust is created?

Answer — It appears that a "once only" notice may be adequate as long as it indicates that later contributions will give rise to additional withdrawal rights in future years. Such notice should put the burden on the beneficiary to inquire about any future annual contributions.

Question — Can a donee of a Crummey Trust have multiple demand rights no one of which exceeds the greater of $5,000 or 5% of principal and avoid the gift tax problems and estate tax problems when such powers lapse?

Answer — No. A donee is allowed only a single $5,000 or 5% limitation for lapsed withdrawal rights during a calendar year. Thus, where a donor made a $5,000 gift to each of two Crummey Trusts, the donee was required to aggregate the two gifts (as if they were made to the same trust) for purposes at the $5,000 or 5% limitation.[11]

Question — If a grantor of a Crummey Trust retains the right to replace the trustee with someone other than himself, will such a right cause the trust to be includable in his estate for estate tax purposes?

Answer — IRS takes the position that a grantor's retention of the power to remove a trustee without cause and replace him with another trustee is tantamount to the grantor's retention of the trustee's powers, even though the grantor could not name himself as trustee.[12] Therefore, if the trustee had powers or ownership rights over the trust property which if held by the grantor would cause the property to be includable in the grantor's estate, the trust property will be includable in the grantor's estate.

Questions — Is it possible to use a Crummey trust to benefit my children and avoid both gift tax now and generation-skipping tax at my children's deaths?

Answer — Generally, no. In order to obtain both the annual exclusion for gift tax purposes and a zero inclusion ratio for generation-skipping transfer tax purposes, separate trusts (or shares of trusts) must be used. Such separate trusts must benefit only one individual, and consequently, could not benefit both children and grandchildren.

Question — Would it ever be better to have a life insurance trust without a Crummey withdrawal power?

Answer — Yes. Gifts subject to the Crummey power cannot pass through the donees' generation without incurring either an estate tax or a generation-skipping tax as indicated above. However, gifts of life insurance or cash to purchase or maintain insurance can pass tax free through the next generations if the donors make the gifts utilizing their unified transfer credits (or make the gifts subject to gift tax if their unified transfer credits have been used up), and allocate some of their generation-skipping exemptions to the gifts. Each donor has up to $1,000,000 of generation-skipping exemption which can be allocated either to transfers to grandchildren or to trusts which may ultimately pass to grandchildren (e.g., a trust benefiting a child which passes to grandchildren at the child's death).

In the same way that gifts of life insurance can effectively "leverage" the benefits of the donor's unified credit, such gifts can "leverage" the benefits of the generation-skipping exemption because the donor need allocate only enough exemption to cover the "gift" value of the policy as opposed to the face value of the policy.

Question — Can the donor be the trustee of the Crummey trust?

Answer — It is possible in certain very restricted circumstances to have the donor act as trustee. However, this requires a severe restriction of powers of the trustee and it is far better to have both no opportunity for the IRS to attack the transfer as being one that is included in the donor's estate and also to avoid subjecting property to management under very restricted circumstances. The more flexibility that can be given to a competent trustee, the better the trustee can manage the property.

Footnote References

Trust — Crummey

1. Rev. Rul. 81-7, 1981-1 CB 474; Let. Ruls. 7946007, 7947066.
2. Let. Rul. 8019038.
3. Malcolm A. Moore, *22nd Ann. Philip E. Heckerling Inst. on Est. Plan.*, "Tax Consequences and Uses of 'Crummey' Withdrawal Powers: An Update," Paragraph II B 4d (iii).
4. Rev. Rul. 81-7, 1981-1 CB 474.
5. Let. Ruls. 8103074, 8006048, 8004172.
6. Let. Rul. 8103074.
7. TAMs 8727003, 914008; *Est. of Maria Cristofani v. Comm.*, 97 TC 74 (1991), acq. in result 1992-2 CB 1.
8. IRC Sec. 2036.
9. IRC Sec. 2035.
10. *Est. of Joseph Leder v. Comm.*, 90-1 USTC ¶60,001 (10th Cir. 1989); *Est. of Eddie L. Headrick v. Comm.*, 90-2 USTC ¶60,049 (6th Cir. 1990); *Est. of Frank M. Perry, Sr. v. Comm.*, 91-1 USTC ¶60,064 (5th Cir. 1991); AOD 1991-012.
11. Rev. Rul. 85-88, 1985-2 CB 201.
12. TAM 8922003.

Chapter 37

TRUST — MARITAL DEDUCTION AND BYPASS

WHAT IS IT?

The marital/non-marital trust (also commonly referred to as the "A-B trust" or more currently sometimes the "A-B-Q" trust) is an arrangement designed to give the surviving spouse full use of the family's economic wealth, while at the same time minimizing, to the extent possible, the total federal estate tax payable at the deaths of both spouses.

Married couples can usually eliminate federal estate taxes entirely at the death of the first spouse to die through a carefully considered plan capitalizing on the marital deduction coupled with the unified credit. The term "federal estate tax" as used in this chapter means the tax imposed by Chapter 11 of the Internal Revenue Code, and does not deal with the 15% estate tax on "unreasonable accumulations" in retirement plans as discussed in Chapter 28 of this book. If it is desired to achieve the avoidance of federal estate tax at the first death, the great majority of all pre-1982 estate plans must be revised. All previously unplanned estates must still be brought within this planning concept, usually using a trust arrangement to avoid "overqualification" of the estate for the marital deduction because of "underutilization" of the unified credit in the estate of the first spouse to die. The unified credit is equal to $192,800, which is the amount of gift or estate tax due on a transfer of $600,000 of property during lifetime or at death.

Current Planning Techniques

The "no-tax-on-transfers-between-spouses" marital deduction should have triggered a review and a change in most plans and must be considered in dealing with unplanned estates.

Some couples may prefer to have some tax paid at the death of the first spouse to die (since some of the taxed portion will be taxed at the lowest federal estate tax rates (effectively 37%) instead of being shifted to the surviving spouse's estate and added "on top" of the assets the survivor already owns). However, the desire to pay an "up front" tax will be the exception. Further, the surviving spouse may use up the additional assets received or give them away. The majority of "younger" couples may well decide to accept some possible penalty in estate tax rate in order to avoid tax altogether at the death of the first spouse to die. This is obviously an important decision which the estate planner must review at length with the husband and wife.

If the decision is made to avoid tax altogether at the death of the first spouse to die, then the decision must be made as to how much of the estate should be subject to the surviving spouse's power to say where it goes at the survivor's death.

The marital deduction can also be obtained by putting qualifying property into a qualified terminable interest property (QTIP) trust, a trust which provides for all of the income to go to the survivor and which is not subject to any contingencies (e.g., remarriage) or powers in anyone else to defeat the survivor's right to the income. The executor may elect to have all or a portion of such a qualifying trust be subject to the marital deduction. The assets in the QTIP trust or portion of it elected to pass tax free under the marital deduction will be included in the survivor's taxable estate.

For separate property estates where it is desired that *all* of the marital deduction property or *none* of it should be subject to the survivor's power of disposition at death, it will be satisfactory to have only one marital deduction or "A" Trust, since the same rules will pertain to all of the property.

However, for many estates, it may be desirable to limit the spouse's ability to divert all of the marital trust assets (to a new spouse or friend and away from the children) but to provide for such a power as to a portion of the estate. Particularly for community property, where the survivor already owns half, it may be very helpful to obtain the marital deduction for all of the estate in excess of the exemption (with the exempt portion going to the bypass (or "B") trust to avoid tax at the survivor's death), but to still provide that some of the deducted property will ultimately go to the children (or to the brothers or sisters of the first spouse to die if there are no children).

These "deducted" assets can be set aside for the ultimate use of the children by putting a portion of the assets into a trust (perhaps called Trust "Q") which will provide income to the survivor but go to the children at the survivor's death. The rest of the assets deducted as a marital deduction would go to the "A" or marital trust, which will be controllable by the survivor as to its disposition.

Thus, we may often provide a formula which will put into the "B" or family trust the amount of the effective exemption

The Tools and Techniques of Estate Planning

($600,000) at the death of the first spouse. Even though this trust can provide for income to the survivor (and if desirable, can even give to the survivor some limited power of disposition to other people and/or the power to take out each year the greater of $5,000 or 5% of the trust principal), property in this trust will generally escape taxation at the survivor's death. Obviously, the formula to achieve this is very important.

If it is decided to have a zero estate tax at the first death, and if it is desired that the spouse have disposition powers over all or none of the other assets, all of the other assets can go to the marital or "A" trust.

However, if it is desired that the survivor have a power of disposition over only a portion of the assets, then the portion subject to the power can go into the typical marital or "A" trust, and the balance can go into a QTIP trust. Both trusts will qualify for the marital deduction and be included in the survivor's estate at death. Either or both of these trusts can provide for invasion of principal for the benefit of the survivor, but only the "A" trust will be subject to a power of disposition at the survivor's death.

Often the revocable A-B or A-B-Q trust takes the form of a life insurance trust coupled with a "pourover will." Here a revocable ("I can tear it up and forget about it") insurance trust is created during the grantor's lifetime. The trustee is named as the beneficiary of life insurance policies issued on the grantor's life. The grantor's will contains a provision to the effect that the grantor's residuary estate, what is left after payments of debts, expenses, taxes and specific bequests, is to be "poured over" into the living trust. (Think of a funnel. Life insurance passes outside of the funnel directly to the "pool of assets" at the bottom while noncontractual [probate] assets pass through the grantor's will into the top of the funnel and flow down to join the life insurance.)

The trust instrument provides that upon receiving the insurance proceeds from the insurance company and the residuary estate property from the pourover will provisions, the total principal will then be divided into two or three parts: a portion will go to the marital or "A" trust, a portion to the family or "B" trust, and if appropriate, a portion will go to the QTIP trust, which latter will qualify for the marital deduction but be distributed at the survivor's death as provided in the trust instrument (e.g. to the children).

The use of the trust can provide flexibility while achieving the long term goals of the family and minimizing death taxes.

Whether to use a revocable trust to also hold non-insurance assets is usually a question of whether or not the other assets should be subjected to the costs, delays and publicity which usually accompany probate.

WHEN IS THE USE OF SUCH A DEVICE INDICATED?

1. When it is the desire of the spouses that the survivor have full economic benefit of the family's wealth and that the aggregate death taxes payable at the deaths of both spouses be reduced. Where an individual leaves all of his property to his spouse, his estate may be "overqualified" for the marital deduction, as discussed below. Too much property may pass to the surviving spouse and thus be needlessly taxed at the surviving spouse's death. The reason for this result is that the surviving spouse has "ownership" of all of the family wealth and therefore it is taxable for federal estate tax purposes at his death. If the surviving spouse merely had the "benefit" of all of the family wealth (i.e., an A-B or A-B-Q trust arrangement), only the portion that qualified for the marital deduction at the death of the first spouse to die (or which was already owned by the surviving spouse) would be subject to federal estate taxes at the survivor's subsequent death.

   In order to maximize the utility of this technique, the A-B or A-B-Q trust device can be designed to pass to the A trust or to the A and Q trusts together exactly enough property to reduce the federal estate tax in the estate of the first spouse to die to the lowest desired amount—even to zero. Any additional property subject to tax at the decedent's death and passing to the trust would automatically pass into the B (family or nonmarital) trust (portion) and escape death taxation at the death of the second spouse to die.

2. The overqualification problem referred to above results in passing more to the surviving spouse in property interests qualifying for the marital deduction than is necessary to keep the federal estate tax at the decedent's death to the minimum. Overqualification results in wasting (in whole or in part) the decedent's unified credit. For couples with estates over $600,000 (the amount of estate that can have its tax "paid for" by the unified credit), wasting the unified credit of the first to die will likely result in a larger-than-necessary estate tax falling on the surviving spouse's estate at her later death. (An example later in the chapter illustrates the point.) A properly designed A-B or A-B-Q trust could eliminate or minimize this problem.

3. Where the couple plan to set up "generation-skipping trusts"(see Chapter 14) for the children, the $1,000,000 exclusion from generation-skipping transfer tax of the first spouse to die can be lost if the property passes outright to the surviving spouse, or in any form of marital deduction trust other than a qualified terminable interest property trust (QTIP trust).

4. Favorable state inheritance tax treatment may be obtained. Rather than giving property outright to a spouse, if property is placed in a "marital trust," even if the spouse has a general power of appointment over the assets in that trust, the laws of some states exclude such property for state death tax purposes from the estate of the holder of the power of appointment. For example, in Pennsylvania, even though a surviving spouse could reduce the property in a marital trust subject to a general power of appointment to his own possession, it will not be subject to state inheritance tax at the death of such spouse. Thus, from a death-tax viewpoint, in some states it is preferable to leave a surviving spouse's assets in trust coupled with a general power of appointment over such assets, rather than leave the same amount outright, all other things being equal.

However, a majority of states provide for tax-free interspousal transfers but their laws parallel the federal estate tax rules to tax to the surviving spouse's estate the assets in the marital trust which avoided taxation at the first spouse's death.

5. When management of trust property is needed for the benefit of the surviving spouse or other trust beneficiaries.

6. Where it is desired to avoid probate. In addition to the tax reductions and management benefits described above, a person's estate can avoid the expense and delay of probate by transferring the title of the person's assets to a revocable inter vivos trust during the person's lifetime, which trust would also contain the death tax minimization provisions. Since the property is already transferred before the person's death, there is no need for the Court to take charge and transfer the title and therefore no probate proceedings are required.

7. Where one of the spouses is a non-U.S. citizen. (See "Non-U.S. Persons in the Estate Plan," Chapter 24.)

8. Where the first spouse to die wants to be certain that his or her assets, while benefiting the survivor spouse, will eventually benefit the children (or some other beneficiary) and not the husband, wife, or friend of the surviving spouse.

9. Where it is desirable to defer until the first spouse's death the decision of whether to pay some estate tax at that time in order to lower estate tax payments at the survivor's death.

WHAT ARE THE REQUIREMENTS?

Property which passes outright to the surviving spouse can qualify for the federal estate tax marital deduction. It is also possible to qualify certain types of trusts for the marital deduction. There are three types of trusts which will qualify for the marital deduction—the "power of appointment" trust, the "estate" trust, and the QTIP trust.

1. Power of Appointment Trust—Requirements

   (a) The surviving spouse must be entitled to all of the income produced by the assets of the trust (note that the law states "all of the income" not "all of the net income").

   (b) The income produced by the trust must be payable at least annually.

   (c) The surviving spouse must be given a general power of appointment (during lifetime, at death, or both) exercisable in favor of the spouse or the spouse's estate, or the creditors of the spouse or the spouse's estate.

   (d) The power must be exercisable by the surviving spouse in all events.

   (e) No person may have any power to appoint any part of the trust assets to any person other than the surviving spouse.[1]

   An estate owner can give property in trust subject to a power of appointment but require that—to exercise the power—the donee's will (or a different instrument) must make specific reference to such power. This is important because in some states a residuary clause will exercise a general power of appointment automatically unless there is a specific stated intention not to exercise it. In other words, absent the requirement that the donee of a power must specifically refer to it, in certain states the donee is deemed to have exercised the power in favor of his residuary legatee.

   The trust property will qualify for the marital deduction if the spouse is given the power to appoint by at death (i.e., a testamentary power of appointment). The spouse does not have to be given the power to withdraw the principal during lifetime (i.e., an inter vivos power of appointment).[2]

   A trust should provide that the spouse has the right to demand that the trust be made income-producing.[3]

2. Estate Trust—Requirements

(a) The trust must provide for income to the surviving spouse for life (payable to her or accumulated for her benefit).

(b) The remainder of the trust (both principal and any accumulated income) must be payable to the surviving spouse's estate at her death.

An estate trust falls outside the terminable interest rules because no interest passes to anyone other than the spouse and her estate.[4] This will enable the trustee to accumulate income or invest in non-income-producing property. However, accumulations will be taxed as part of the surviving spouse's estate at his death along with the original corpus. In addition, for federal income tax purposes the accumulations will be subject to the throwback rule.

The estate marital trust is indicated where (a) there is a need or desire to invest in non-income-producing property, (b) the survivor will not need trust assets or income during his lifetime, and (c) the property placed into the trust is not likely to appreciate substantially in value.

3. QTIP (Qualified Terminable Interest Property) Trust—Requirements

(a) The same requirements regarding "all income to the surviving spouse and payable at least annually" apply here as they do in the power of appointment trust. Thus, the survivor must receive all of the current beneficial interest in the trust.

(b) However, this trust need not have any power in the surviving spouse to appoint or control the disposition of the property.

(c) There must be no power to shift any of the trust property to anyone other than the spouse during the spouse's lifetime.

(d) The spouse must have the power to require the trustee to make the assets produce income.

With this type of trust, the trustor can be certain that, at the death of the survivor, the property will go to the children or wherever the trustor decides (and not to the survivor's new spouse, which may be the case with the power of appointment trust or the estate trust).

4. Other General Requirements

Assets in the marital trust must pass to or be held for the benefit of the decedent's surviving spouse—the person who is married to the decedent at his death.[5] Although this requirement appears simple to determine, it has been the cause of extensive litigation because of the increasing frequency of divorce and persons living together without formal marriage that is now prevalent in our society.

Furthermore, the decedent's spouse must survive the decedent. In the event of a common accident (such as a plane crash) when it is impossible to ascertain who dies first, the Uniform Simultaneous Death Act (the law in most states) would raise a presumption that neither spouse survived the other and therefore, would defeat the marital deduction. The application of such act can be overcome by inserting into the documents creating the marital trust a survivorship clause which creates a presumption that for purposes of the marital deduction, the spouse is deemed to survive if it is not possible to establish the order of deaths.[6]

HOW IT IS DONE — AN EXAMPLE

Although there are a number of ways to accomplish the same objective, the life insurance trust/pourover will combination is one of the most popular. In this arrangement an individual establishes a trust during lifetime and names the trust as beneficiary of his insurance policies. When the grantor dies, the insurance maintained on his life is paid directly to the trust. The grantor's other assets pass through probate and are "poured over" by will into the trust. The one pourover trust is then split into two or three parts and different trusts are created; the "A" or appointment trust, a "B" or family (also called nonmarital or bypass) trust, and, in some cases, the "Q" or QTIP trust. Since the insurance is held in a trust which is controlled by the insured grantor, it is included in the insured's estate for estate tax purposes.

A — The Survivor's Property Trust or Power of Appointment Trust

The A trust, or power of appointment trust, used to be the primary vehicle for receiving the marital deduction assets before the advent of the QTIP trust, and is still used by some practitioners for that purpose. Where the QTIP trust is used for the marital deduction instead, Trust A often will hold the surviving spouse's property, particularly in community property states, in order to provide unified management of the assets under the umbrella of the estate planning trust.

Trust A would provide that all income from the trust be paid to the surviving spouse during his lifetime. Where Trust A is used as a marital deduction trust, the pourover trust in many cases would contain a funding formula to ensure that the power of appointment trust, together with any QTIP trust, would receive just enough property to reduce the federal estate tax at the death of the grantor to zero.

The formula for trust division, in some cases such as very elderly couples with relatively large estates, may be drafted so as to pay some estate tax at the first death with the property being taxed in relatively low tax brackets. If the clients wish to permit payment of some estate taxes at the first death, this is generally better arranged by having the marital deduction property pass to a QTIP trust, since a QTIP trust allows the decision as to the amount of tax to pay to be deferred until the death of the first spouse to die. At that time, the planner and the family can better assess whether the surviving spouse's financial security may be impaired by early payment of death taxes.

The surviving spouse will usually be given the right to designate by will or other written instrument who will receive the corpus of the marital trust and such appointment may be made to anyone he or she chooses, including his estate. The surviving spouse may also be given the right to withdraw any part of the corpus of the appointment trust during lifetime. At the surviving spouse's death, if the surviving spouse fails to exercise his power of appointment, the remaining corpus in the appointment trust will pass to the next takers under the trust.

B — The Bypass Trust

The second trust, the "B" or bypass nonmarital (family) trust is designed to receive property that is not allocated to the power of appointment trust, the estate trust, or the QTIP trust. An amount equal to the unified credit equivalent (usually $600,000 if no taxable gifts have been made) is placed in this trust. The Trustee may be directed to distribute the net income of this trust to the surviving spouse during his lifetime, or the income may be accumulated or directed to other persons in order to reduce the overall income tax effect on the family. Since the life estate terminates at the death of the surviving spouse, the surviving spouse did not create the life estate, and the surviving spouse has no "general" power of appointment over the trust property, there will be no transfer of property that is includable in the estate of the surviving spouse which is subject to the federal estate tax at death.[7] Thus, this trust "bypasses" the survivor's taxable estate and is therefore often called a CEBT, Credit Equivalent Bypass Trust.

The surviving spouse can be given a "limited" or "special" power of appointment under this family trust. For example, a surviving spouse might be given the right to appoint, at his death, all or any part of the assets in the family trust to a limited class of beneficiaries,[8] such as the children of the grantor. This means that the surviving spouse can distribute the assets in this trust only to the specified children, but can do so in any proportion he or she desires. Such a power of appointment will not be classified as a "general" power and will not subject the corpus of the trust to federal estate taxes at the death of the holder so long as the power cannot be exercised in favor of the holder of the power, his estate, his creditors, or the creditors of his estate.

The bypass trust can also provide a noncumulative right of withdrawal. Typically, this provision states that if the A and Q trusts are depleted, the surviving spouse is given the right to make limited withdrawals from the bypass or family trust. Usually, the surviving spouse is provided with a "noncumulative" (use it or lose it) right to withdraw each year the greater of (a) 5 percent of the corpus of the trust or (b) $5,000.[9] Such a power will not cause the entire corpus of the family trust to be includable in the surviving spouse's estate (although the amount subject to withdrawal in the year of the surviving spouse's death will be included in the surviving spouse's estate).

At the death of the surviving spouse, the family or bypass trust can continue to function for the benefit of the grantor's family, generally his children. The most common dispositive provision requires that the corpus of this trust be divided into separate equal trust funds for the benefit of the grantor's children, who will receive the net income currently and will have the right to demand distributions from principal at stated ages.

Often, rather than having all of the income from the family or bypass trust pass to the surviving spouse for life, a greater degree of flexibility may be obtained by utilizing a "spraying" or "sprinkle" clause. This provision authorizes the trustees (other than a trustee who is a beneficiary), at their discretion, to spray or sprinkle the net income of the bypass trust among the surviving spouse and the grantor's children or other issue (and sometimes spouses of issue) in any way the trustees determine. The trustees can thus apportion the trust's income among the beneficiaries having the greatest need.

Alternatively, since for federal income tax purposes the trust is a separate taxable entity, the trustees could be given the right to apportion the net income of the trust among the trust and the beneficiaries after giving consideration to their relative income tax brackets. Net income generated by the trust is determined substantially in accordance with the same rules applicable to individuals, with certain important differences. Although the taxable income of the trust is subject to the federal income tax, in arriving at taxable income the trust receives a deduction for distributions made or required to be made to beneficiaries during its taxable year to the extent such distributions do not exceed "distributable net income" as that term is defined in the Code.[10] By deflecting income to beneficiaries with little or no personal income, the overall income tax for the family can be reduced. However, unearned income of a child under age 14 in excess of $1,300 (indexed amount for 1995) per year will be taxed at the parent's highest marginal rate (the "kiddie tax").

In addition to income tax savings, the estate tax at the survivor's death may be reduced by use of an "accumulation" provision. Instead of the nonmarital income being paid to the surviving spouse, it may be accumulated in the nonmarital trust and pass, free of estate tax, at the survivor's death. Meanwhile, the survivor has been permitted to invade the appointment trust (or the QTIP trust, if one exists) and consume some of the principal of those trusts (instead of using the income which has been accumulated in the nonmarital trust) and thus the appointment trust, and any QTIP trust which would be taxed at the survivor's death, would be reduced and the estate tax lowered. However, allowing large amounts of income to accumulate in the trust may result in adverse income taxation since the top federal income tax rate of 39.6%, which applies to individuals at incomes above $250,000, kicks in at the $7,500 income level for trusts (amounts shown prior to indexing for inflation).

The "sprinkle," "spray," or "accumulation" clauses should be avoided where the bypass trust will be a recipient of stock in an S corporation. Only certain types of trusts are permitted to own S corporation stock, and a major requirement of such trusts is that the trust benefit only a single individual, and that such individual receive all the income from the trust on an annual basis.[11]

Another alternative, becoming more common in this era of divorce and remarriage, is to use the B trust as a means of benefitting persons other than the present spouse (e.g., children of a prior marriage). The trust can arrange for continued management of the trust assets for nonspousal beneficiaries, with delayed distribution, or provide for outright distribution.

Where the grantor has planned to take advantage of generation-skipping, the B trust would continue to exist during the lives of children (usually giving them some "nongeneral" powers of appointment as well as income rights) so that the property in the trust can qualify as an "exempt" trust and avoid taxation at the death of the children or grandchildren. If generation-skipping is planned, a federal estate tax return should be filed and an election made to allocate to the B trust some of the grantor's $1,000,000 exemption from the generation-skipping transfer tax. See Chapter 14 regarding generation-skipping transfers.

Q — The QTIP Trust

When it is desired that an amount of estate in excess of the effective exemption amount (which exempt amount goes to the "bypass" or family trust) should produce a marital deduction at the death of the first spouse to die but should not be subject to a general power of appointment in the surviving spouse, a QTIP trust may be created.

By providing the opportunity for a marital deduction, placing assets in this trust can result in zero estate tax at the death of the first spouse to die to the extent that the trustee or executor elects to take the marital deduction.

All of the income of this trust must be paid, at least annually, to the surviving spouse. No provision for invasions of the trust can be made for anyone other than the surviving spouse or the marital deduction will be lost. Likewise, it would be lost if there were any condition (e.g., remarriage) or power in anyone else which could prevent the surviving spouse from receiving all the trust income for life. Additionally, the surviving spouse should be given a power to require the trustee to make all of the trust assets income producing.

The principal of this trust may usually be invaded for the benefit of the surviving spouse but the trust terms may provide for first using up all or part of the marital or appointment trust before invading this trust.

To the extent that the trustee has elected to take a marital deduction at the first spouse's death for assets going into that trust (usually 100%), the QTIP (Q) trust will be included in the estate of the surviving spouse.[12] Thus, the marital deduction has merely deferred the tax on any assets in this trust which are not used up for the benefit of the surviving spouse.

Any assets remaining in this trust at the survivor's death will be distributed as the grantor decided, often subject to a nongeneral power in the surviving spouse as to the method of distribution among the issue of the marriage.

If generation-skipping is planned and if some of the grantor-decedent's $1,000,000 exemption from the generation-skipping transfer (GST) tax is still available, provisions are usually made for the QTIP trust to be divided into two trusts: trust Q-E, which will contain property to which will be allocated some of the GST exemption; and trust Q-N, which will not be exempt from the GST tax and which therefore will often have different terms than trust Q-E. Use of this GST split-trust planning to allocate some of the $1,000,000 GST exemption to part of the QTIP is accomplished by what is sometimes referred to as a "reverse QTIP election," discussed later in this chapter.

HOW DO THE MECHANICS OF THE A-B OR A-B-Q TRUST PLAN WORK?

First, an inter vivos (living) trust instrument can be drafted creating the different trusts to be used—(the A or appointment trust, the B or bypass (family) trust and, when desired, the Q, QTIP trust.) Although the trust will come into being during the grantor's lifetime, it will not become operative until it is funded (until assets are placed into the trust) at the grantor's death (or prior to death if it is desired to use this living trust to avoid probate of the trust assets).

The trust is revocable because the grantor possesses the power to alter, amend, or revoke the trust until his death. Most states allow a grantor to name the trustee as beneficiary of his life insurance proceeds and obviates the need to transfer any other property to the trust during his lifetime.[13] But, if insurance is for some reason unavailable, many states recognize a trust funded with a nominal corpus such as $100, or even less.

Either as a means of shifting assets (through probate) to the trust, or as a backup provision to put into the trust any assets unintentionally not placed in the revocable trust during lifetime, the grantor will provide in his will that his probate property, after payment of settlement costs and any specific bequests or devises, will be added (poured over) to the trust. Where liquid assets may be insufficient to pay death costs and administration expenses, a useful provision in the inter vivos trust is to permit the trustee to make cash available to the estate executor through loans or the purchase of estate assets.

Alternatively, this same marital deduction arrangement can be created in a testamentary trust (i.e., one contained in the decedent's will and which will require the assets to be subject to probate).

The essential provision in the A-B or A-B-Q trust is known as the marital deduction formula. All property included in the decedent's probate estate or made payable to the inter vivos trust will be divided in accordance with the formula clause in the trust agreement. Such a clause might provide that the power of appointment, estate, and/or QTIP trust is to be funded in an amount equal to the amount necessary to maximize the marital deduction; or an amount required to reduce the federal estate tax payable to zero, or any other specified portion of the estate. The division of the marital deduction assets between the power of appointment "A" trust and the "Q" trust could be whatever the grantor desires (e.g., half of the separate property going to the "A" trust, and the other half going to the "Q" trust). In any event the funding clause would also provide that the amount of any such marital portion should be reduced by any property includable in the estate which passes directly to the surviving spouse as a result of the grantor's death (e.g., a specific gift of personal effects, life insurance or jointly owned property).

The net balance of the trust corpus, after allocation of the marital deduction amount and after settlement costs are paid, is then allocated to the family ("B") trust.[14] Thus, the A-B/A-B-Q trust is really two or three trusts in one, administered under one trust agreement by the same trustees.

In some multi-marriage situations, the grantor-decedent may be unwilling to defer benefit (above the $600,000 bypass trust level) to children of a prior marriage or other persons until after the death of the present spouse. In that event, the formula may provide for paying some estate tax at the grantor-decedent's death so that assets may pass to these other beneficiaries at that time. Insurance on the grantor-decedent may be an appropriate way to insure that cash is available to pay the required tax when it is due.

Why is the A-B/A-B-Q trust arrangement such an important estate planning tool? To fully appreciate the implications and tax savings potential, it is necessary to examine a typical estate.

A common and often unfortunate arrangement is one where the testator leaves all of his property to his spouse (either by will, by jointly owning all assets with the spouse, or a combination of the two) and therefore overqualifies for the marital deduction and wastes the Unified Credit available at the death of the first spouse to die. As a result, when the settlement of both estates is considered, federal estate taxes may be higher than if other arrangements were made.

Example: Philip Martin dies in 1996 and leaves his entire estate of $1,300,000 to his wife, Kaye, if living, otherwise to their son, Michael. Philip's primary objectives are to retain control of the estate during his lifetime, to provide an adequate income for his wife after his death, and to minimize his estate settlement costs. Assuming Kaye dies in 2004, and that she does not consume any of the principal of the estate, and further assuming that the value of the estate increases at the average rate of 7 percent a year, Figure 37.1 shows how much is paid in federal estate tax in each estate and how much after tax goes to Michael at Kaye's death.

A Typical Pre-1981 A-B Trust

Prior to 1981, the typical trust to avoid additional taxes over the death of a husband and wife was to pass to the surviving wife outright or in trust an amount equal to the then marital deduction (the greater of one-half of the separate property or $250,000). This essentially resulted in equalizing the estates taxable at each death (assuming the couple's assets

Figure 37.1

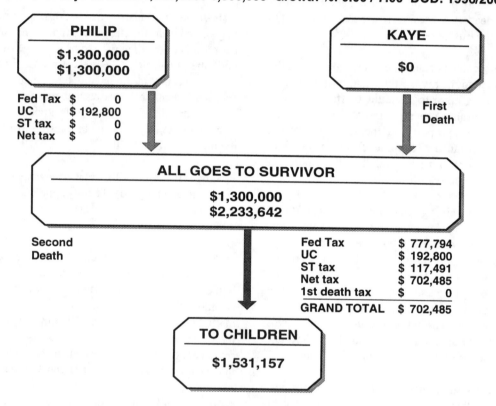

Example 1. Philip's Entire Estate Passes to Kaye

Note: The values in the chart below are shown net of debts, and funeral and administration expenses have been ignored. Also, it is assumed that upon Philip's death there has not been any depletion of property, and any possible credit for federal estate taxes on prior transfers has not been taken into account. The state death tax credit is assumed to equal the state death tax paid at the second death, and thus is not shown either as a debit or credit as the second death.

Estate today / at death 1,300,000 / 1,300,000 Growth %: 0.00 / 7.00 DOD: 1996/2004

PHILIP	KAYE
$1,300,000	$0
$1,300,000	

Fed Tax	$ 0		First
UC	$ 192,800		Death
ST tax	$ 0		
Net tax	$ 0		

ALL GOES TO SURVIVOR

$1,300,000
$2,233,642

Second
Death

Fed Tax	$ 777,794
UC	$ 192,800
ST tax	$ 117,491
Net tax	$ 702,485
1st death tax	$ 0
GRAND TOTAL	$ 702,485

TO CHILDREN

$1,531,157

Flowchart created by the ViewPlan, Inc. VISTA program.

Observation: Since the marital deduction is taken on the whole $1,300,000 of adjusted gross estate at Philip's death, his unified credit of $192,800 is wasted. At Kaye's death, the total net property of $1,300,000, plus the effect of inflation, is subject to federal estate taxation. Thus, the marital deduction portion passes tax free in Philip's estate, but is taxed in Kaye's estate. The Unified Credit which was wasted at Philip's death results in the equivalent amount of property ($600,000 as of 1987), plus inflation on that sum, being needlessly taxed at Kaye's death. This is a principal factor in diminishing the estate going to Michael, their only child.

were acquired from the husband's earnings), at least for larger estates. The concept of equalizing the estates is still probably the most economical method of minimizing the taxes over the deaths of both husband and wife where the estates of the husband and wife will be over the available equivalent exemptions. In other cases, however, the tax burden will be greater.

If Philip had a trust designed to equalize the estates (e.g., by giving to Kaye under the marital deduction one-half of his assets), Figure 37.2 shows how much would be paid in federal estate tax in each estate and how much would pass to Michael

on Kaye's death (same assumptions as stated in the previous example).

A Typical Post-1981 A-B or A-B-Q Trust to Reduce the Tax at the First Death to Zero

If Philip had wished to be certain that no federal tax were paid at his death, regardless of the size of his estate, he could have provided for an amount of marital deduction to go to Kaye which would exactly equal the amount of deduction

Figure 37.2

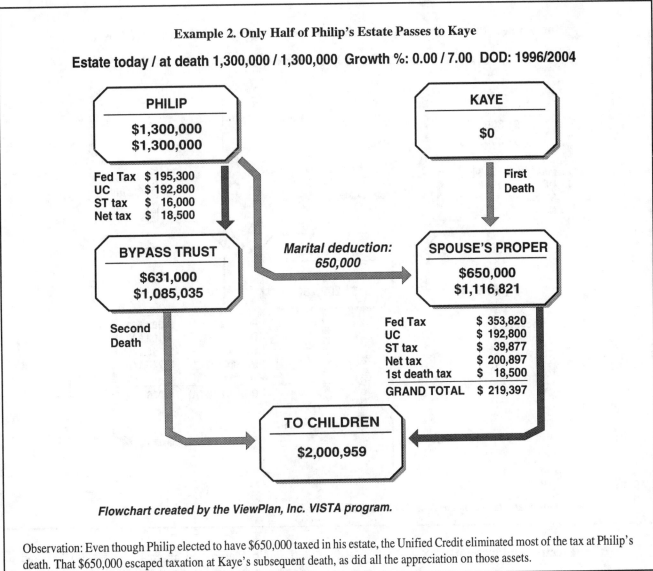

Example 2. Only Half of Philip's Estate Passes to Kaye

Estate today / at death 1,300,000 / 1,300,000 Growth %: 0.00 / 7.00 DOD: 1996/2004

PHILIP

$1,300,000
$1,300,000

Fed Tax $ 195,300
UC $ 192,800
ST tax $ 16,000
Net tax $ 18,500

KAYE

$0

First
Death

BYPASS TRUST

$631,000
$1,085,035

Marital deduction:
650,000

SPOUSE'S PROPER

$650,000
$1,116,821

Fed Tax $ 353,820
UC $ 192,800
ST tax $ 39,877
Net tax $ 200,897
1st death tax $ 18,500
GRAND TOTAL $ 219,397

Second
Death

TO CHILDREN

$2,000,959

Flowchart created by the ViewPlan, Inc. VISTA program.

Observation: Even though Philip elected to have $650,000 taxed in his estate, the Unified Credit eliminated most of the tax at Philip's death. That $650,000 escaped taxation at Kaye's subsequent death, as did all the appreciation on those assets.

needed to reduce his federal estate tax to zero. This is called the "zero tax marital deduction." In that event, Figure 37.3 shows the amount of federal tax that would be paid in each estate and how much would pass to Michael upon Kaye's death.

Comparison of Plans

Savings in federal estate taxes generally occur at the survivor's death. The federal estate tax payable in Philip's estate is the same in his overqualified arrangement (example 1) as it is in the Post-1981 A-B (or A-B-Q) trust arrangement (example 3)—in both cases it is $-0-. Actually, the savings in federal estate taxes occur in Kaye's estate. The trust arrangement accomplishes this because the equivalent exemption amount at Philip's death is never

taxed in either estate. The savings afforded by example 2 (equalizing the estates) over the Post-1981 A-B trust example comes from the fact that having some of the property taxed in Philip's estate means that it is taxed at lower brackets, and all the increase in value after Philip's death on the taxed property is removed from Kaye's estate. However, the amount paid in taxes is gone, and is not available to provide benefit to the survivor (or growth for the estate). The taxable amounts for each plan are illustrated in Figure 37.4.

Although it is not apparent from Figure 37.4, the second arrangement is "optimum" for the first spouse's death (zero estate tax then, regardless of the size of the estate), but it theoretically results in more overall tax if the spouse does not use up some of the estate or give some of it away during her lifetime.

The Tools and Techniques of Estate Planning

Figure 37.3

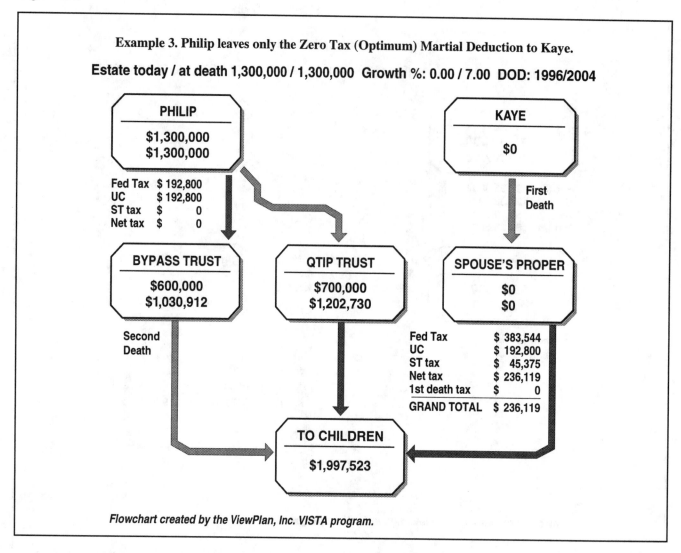

Example 3. Philip leaves only the Zero Tax (Optimum) Martial Deduction to Kaye.

Estate today / at death 1,300,000 / 1,300,000 Growth %: 0.00 / 7.00 DOD: 1996/2004

PHILIP
$1,300,000
$1,300,000

Fed Tax $ 192,800
UC $ 192,800
ST tax $ 0
Net tax $ 0

KAYE
$0

First Death

BYPASS TRUST
$600,000
$1,030,912

Second Death

QTIP TRUST
$700,000
$1,202,730

SPOUSE'S PROPER
$0
$0

Fed Tax $ 383,544
UC $ 192,800
ST tax $ 45,375
Net tax $ 236,119
1st death tax $ 0
GRAND TOTAL $ 236,119

TO CHILDREN
$1,997,523

Flowchart created by the ViewPlan, Inc. VISTA program.

Electing to Pay Some Tax

As can be seen from the comparison in Figure 37.4, there can be some tax saving by paying tax early, where property is increasing in value. For example, if an asset now worth $100,000 is projected to be worth $500,000 at the second death, it is usually much more economical to pay the tax based on the current $100,000 value than on the $500,000 it will be worth later.

The drawback to the "old A-B" arrangement (Figure 37.2) is that the tax is *forced* to be paid at the first death. However, if a QTIP trust is used, the executor will have a right to elect how much of the property over the amount sheltered by the unified credit will be subject to tax—none of it, all of it, or any amount in between! Thus, the QTIP allows you to keep your options open, and decide at death how much, if any, tax to pay. If the loss of the funds used to pay the taxes will not impair the surviving spouse's security, substantial saving could be realized by paying some tax early.

If Philip Martin had an estate of $2,500,000, and an insurance policy on his life of $300,000, his executor might elect to use that available cash to pay some tax at his death. Figure 37.5 shows a comparison of the results where no tax is paid, where all the tax is paid (no marital deduction is taken), and where the executor uses the $300,000 of cash to pay the tax.

Observation: Although many practitioners have abandoned the concept of insuring each spouse in favor of having "survivor insurance," which pays only at the death of the survivor, Figure 37.5 shows the benefits of having some cash available at the first death. Thus, insurance on each spouse's life is still a viable consideration.

However, the best estate tax results are obtained by placing in a separate irrevocable trust created during lifetime any insurance acquired to pay estate taxes. Insurance proceeds in a properly structured irrevocable life insurance trust will not

The Tools and Techniques of Estate Planning

Figure 37.4

Comparison of Results
For: PHILIP and KAYE MARTIN

	All To Spouse	Opt Marital	Var Marital
Estate At Death of PHILIP			
Taxable estate after marital deduction	0	600,000	650,000
Federal tax	0	192,800	195,300
Less unified credit & gift tax paid	192,800	192,800	192,800
State tax	0	0	16,000
Plus out-of-pocket gift tax paid	0	0	0
Total Tax	0	0	18,500
Estate At Death of KAYE			
Taxable estate	2,233,642	1,202,730	1,116,821
Federal tax	777,794	383,544	353,820
Less unified credit & gift tax paid	192,800	192,800	192,800
State tax	117,491	45,375	39,877
Plus out-of-pocket gift tax paid	0	0	0
Total Tax	702,485	236,119	200,897
Total Taxes (both spouses)	702,485	236,119	219,397
SAVINGS IN TAXES	0	466,366	483,088
Total Estate Passing To Heirs	1,531,157	1,997,523	2,000,959
INCREASE IN BENEFIT	0	466,366	469,802

Created by the ViewPlan, Inc. VISTA program.

be subject to estate tax at the death of either spouse (see Chapter 36).

Another reason for paying tax early may be to preserve the $1,000,000 generation-skipping exemption of the first spouse to die. In a typical optimum marital deduction arrangement where only $600,000 goes to the bypass trust, the executor will almost certainly allocate $600,000 of the decedent's generation-skipping exemption to that trust. The amounts passing under the marital deduction generally "belong" to the surviving spouse for generation-skipping purposes and the remaining $400,000 of the decedent's exemption could be lost.

It is possible to override this loss of the $400,000 of exemption by using a QTIP trust, but in many cases this can be done only by a complex arrangement of having two or three separate QTIP trusts. This could saddle the trustee (who is often the surviving spouse) with an accounting nightmare and additional income tax returns that would continue throughout his remaining life.

What may be a better arrangement for a spouse who has his full unified credit available is to simply provide that $1,259,600

goes to credit shelter or bypass trusts. This will result in $259,600 of tax being due at the decedent's death, leaving the full $1,000,000 remaining, to which the generation-skipping exemption may be allocated. Although this may require the creation of a separate trust to hold the $259,600 to be used in payment of the tax, that trust will disappear after the taxes are paid, leaving only the bypass and one QTIP trust for the trustee to administer during the surviving spouse's lifetime. An easy way to provide liquidity for payment of that $259,600 tax is by life insurance.

If only one spouse has significant assets, an insurance policy on that spouse is appropriate. However, where both spouses have significant property, as in a community property state, a "first-to-die" policy may result in lower premium payments than a policy on each spouse.

IMPACT OF THE REVERSE QTIP ELECTION

The generation-skipping transfer (GST) tax, discussed in Chapter 14, is having an increasing impact on the design of the

Figure 37.5

Comparison of Results
For: PHILIP and KAYE MARTIN

	Opt Marital	Elected Tax
Estate At Death of PHILIP		
Taxable estate after marital deduction	600,000	2,500,000
Federal tax	192,800	887,000
Less unified credit & gift tax paid	192,800	192,800
State tax	0	138,800
Plus out-of-pocket gift tax paid	0	0
Total Tax	0	833,000
Estate At Death of KAYE		
Taxable estate	3,264,554	0
Federal tax	1,229,708	0
Less unified credit & gift tax paid	192,800	192,800
State tax	206,597	0
Plus out-of-pocket gift tax paid	0	0
Total Tax	1,243,505	0
Total Taxes (both spouses)	1,243,505	833,000
SAVINGS IN TAXES	0	410,505
Total Estate Passing To Heirs	3,051,961	2,864,216
INCREASE IN BENEFIT	187,745	0

Created by the ViewPlan, Inc. VISTA program.

QTIP trust in new estate plans. The plan must be designed in such a way as to obtain the maximum use of the $1 million GST exemption which is available to all clients. As illustrated in this chapter, the amount allocated to the Bypass trust in the usual estate plan will usually not exceed $600,000, designed to offset the unified credit. If the GST exemption is first allocated to the Bypass trust, that leaves $400,000 available. Congress has provided that the exemption can be allocated to a QTIP trust, on the basis of what is called the "reverse QTIP election." Under that election, even though a marital deduction is claimed for a QTIP trust, the estate can elect to treat the trust, solely for GST purposes, as if it is still part of the decedent's taxable estate. In that case, the GST exemption can be allocated to it and shelter it from any future GST tax, as discussed in Chapter 14.

However, the law provides that the reverse QTIP election can only be made as to a "separate" QTIP trust. This means that if the total amount to be allocated to the QTIP trust for marital deduction purposes exceeds the GST exemption available, it will be necessary to create two QTIP trusts, one to offset the remaining GST exemption, and the other to take advantage of the remaining marital deduction.

For example, assume the total value of the decedent's taxable estate is $2,000,000, and $600,000 will be allocated to a Bypass trust; $1,400,000 to a QTIP trust. If the executor chooses to allocate $600,000 of the exemption to the Bypass trust, and $400,000 to the QTIP, it will be necessary to split the one QTIP trust into two trusts, one in the amount of $400,000, and one in the amount of $1,000,000. According to private rulings, these trusts may have identical terms.

To implement this planning, most wills and trusts now contain specific provisions for dividing one QTIP trust into two shares, frequently based on a formula to reflect the amount of GST exemption the executor elects to allocate to the QTIP.

AB TRUST VERSUS ABQ TRUST

In some cases, pre-1982 trusts were amended to take advantage of the new optimum marital deduction (no tax due at first spouse's death) by merely changing the provisions allocating assets between trusts A and B so as to reflect the unlimited marital deduction and the unified credit. The result

Figure 37.6

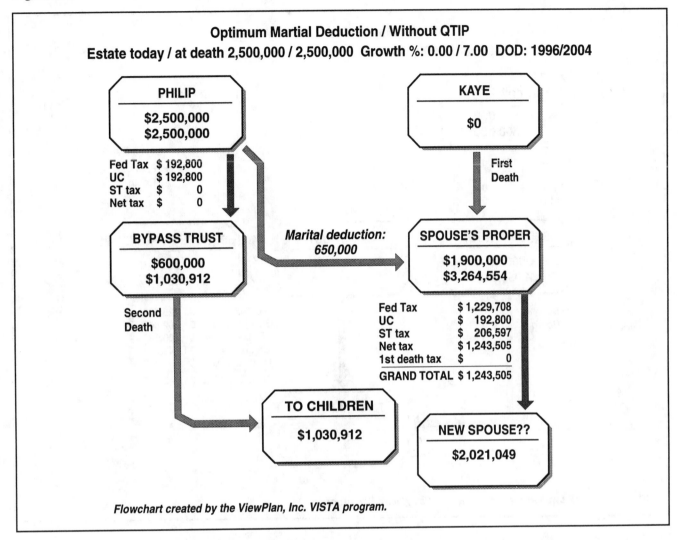

Optimum Martial Deduction / Without QTIP

Estate today / at death 2,500,000 / 2,500,000 Growth %: 0.00 / 7.00 DOD: 1996/2004

PHILIP
$2,500,000
$2,500,000

KAYE
$0

Fed Tax $ 192,800
UC $ 192,800
ST tax $ 0
Net tax $ 0

First
Death

BYPASS TRUST
$600,000
$1,030,912

Marital deduction:
650,000

SPOUSE'S PROPER
$1,900,000
$3,264,554

Second
Death

Fed Tax $ 1,229,708
UC $ 192,800
ST tax $ 206,597
Net tax $ 1,243,505
1st death tax $ 0
GRAND TOTAL $ 1,243,505

TO CHILDREN
$1,030,912

NEW SPOUSE??
$2,021,049

Flowchart created by the ViewPlan, Inc. VISTA program.

under this AB trust arrangement is that the estate of the first to die will often pass $600,000 to trust B and the remainder to trust A, subject to the surviving spouse's right to say where it goes at his or her death.

Figure 37.6 shows the results of this for Philip Martin's $2,500,000 estate with only $1,030,912 required to be paid to Michael at Kaye's death and $2,021,049 available for Kaye to shift at her death to Butch, her new husband, a result that Philip may not desire.

Figure 37.7 shows how, instead, by employing an ABQ trust arrangement, Philip can still provide for zero estate tax at his death, provide for Kaye during her lifetime, and still preserve the remaining estate ($3,051,961) for Michael at Kaye's estate.

WHAT ARE THE TAX IMPLICATIONS?

1. For a typical revocable intervivos trust, no gift tax is payable upon creation of the trust since the grantor, at all times, has retained the right to terminate the trust.[15]

2. After death, the assets which qualify for the marital deduction (the assets actually going into the power of appointment, estate, and/or "Q" trust) are includable in the decedent's gross estate for federal estate tax purposes, but since they qualify for the marital deduction, they are not subject to estate tax.[16] In many situations the assets of these trusts will be minimal since the available credit will reduce the marital deduction amount and property passing outside the will may be sufficient to satisfy the marital deduction remaining. For example, if the decedent's adjusted gross estate is $900,000, the optimum marital

Figure 37.7

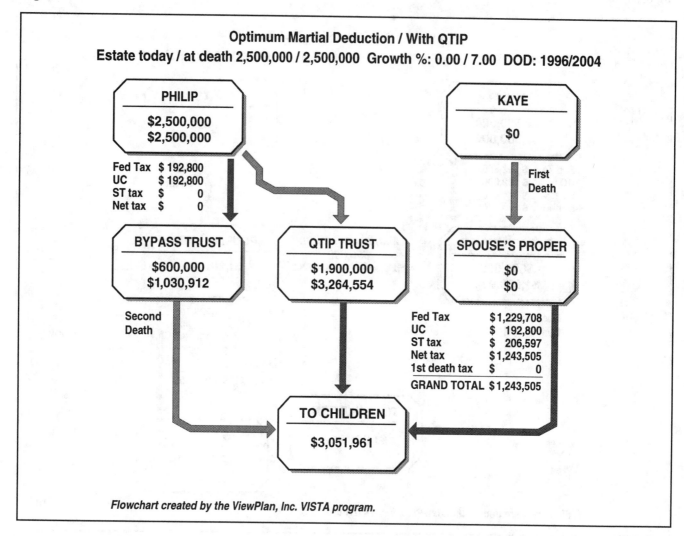

Optimum Martial Deduction / With QTIP

Estate today / at death 2,500,000 / 2,500,000 Growth %: 0.00 / 7.00 DOD: 1996/2004

PHILIP

$2,500,000
$2,500,000

Fed Tax $ 192,800
UC $ 192,800
ST tax $ 0
Net tax $ 0

KAYE

$0

First
Death

BYPASS TRUST

$600,000
$1,030,912

Second
Death

QTIP TRUST

$1,900,000
$3,264,554

SPOUSE'S PROPER

$0
$0

Fed Tax $1,229,708
UC $ 192,800
ST tax $ 206,597
Net tax $1,243,505
1st death tax $ 0
GRAND TOTAL $1,243,505

TO CHILDREN

$3,051,961

Flowchart created by the ViewPlan, Inc. VISTA program.

deduction is $300,000 ($900,000 less the effective exemption of $600,000 = $300,000). If the decedent left $350,000 worth of life insurance proceeds to his wife, she would already have received more than the maximum allowable marital deduction. It is important to remember that the marital deduction portion, which is established by formula, can be given outright to the surviving spouse instead of in trust.

3. Assets which are not used to fund the marital deduction trusts (A and Q) are, by formula, placed into the family or bypass trust. The value of these assets is includable in the grantor's estate for federal estate tax purposes, but the available unified credit will actually result in zero tax. Further, since the surviving spouse receives no more than the income (and perhaps certain limited powers of appointment) from the bypass trust and did not transfer the property to the trust, at the surviving spouse's death these assets will not be taxed again.[17]

4. During the grantor's lifetime, income produced by any of the assets transferred to a revocable inter vivos trust will be taxed to the grantor since no irrevocable gift had been made and the grantor remained the owner of trust assets and income for both estate and income tax purposes. At the grantor's death, the income produced by trust assets will be taxable to the trust or to the income beneficiary depending on whether the income is accumulated by the trust or paid out to the income beneficiary.[18] Except for certain allowances made for accumulation of income for children under age 21, accumulated income is taxable to the income beneficiary in the year of distribution. However, the beneficiary will receive a credit for taxes paid by the trust when a distribution from the trust is made. This is known as the "throwback" rule.[19]

5. In California and certain other states which have placed limits on real property tax increases, certain transfers of the real property will cause the loss of such limits. However, transfers to revocable trusts where the owner-

The Tools and Techniques of Estate Planning

grantor still has the beneficial ownership and control of the property will not cause a problem. It is at the owner-grantor's death, when the trust becomes irrevocable, that the property tax laws may cause an increase in property tax, a circumstance that must be anticipated and which sometimes can be avoided.

IMPLICATIONS AND ISSUES IN COMMUNITY PROPERTY STATES

Where the draftsman is dealing with community property, it should be noted that one-half of the property already belongs to the surviving spouse, and will not be subject to the "pour over" provisions of the will of the first spouse to die, unless the first spouse specifically indicates his desire to effect distribution of both halves of the community, *and* the surviving spouse acquiesces freely in that distribution.

To the extent the surviving spouse elects to retain his community half of the property outside the trust, then a problem of split ownership and management arises, with the survivor owning one-half of the assets, and the trustee of the trust owning the other half. If the surviving spouse does allow his half of the community property to pass to the trust, it would typically go into the "A" or power of appointment trust, so the survivor retains control over how the assets are distributed during lifetime or at death.

The marital deduction rules apply to community property as well as separate property states, so community property state couples may also elect to defer the payment of any federal estate tax until the survivor's death.

Where a marital deduction is used, it will reduce the tax at the first spouse's death, but it may increase the tax at the second death if the surviving spouse does not use up the marital deduction portion during his lifetime, and result in somewhat higher overall taxes for both estates. However, most couples would prefer to minimize the tax at the first spouse's death in order to leave more assets available for the survivor's support, and take the risk of having slightly higher overall taxes.

In both community and common law states, holding property in joint tenancy (tenancy by the entirety) with right of survivorship between spouses will result in the property going outright to the surviving spouse, regardless of the provisions of the decedent's will. The marital deduction provisions may be drafted to reduce the marital deduction by the value of the assets passing outside the trust and thus still result in the optimum marital deduction amount passing to the spouse, so long as the assets passing outside the will do not exceed the optimum marital deduction amount. However, holding large amounts of property in joint tenancy can defeat the trust planning to a very significant degree since such holdings can be more than the optimum marital deduction and reduce the first to die spouse's estate to under $600,000 (thus resulting in a portion of the unified credit being wasted).

In many instances, a couple living in a community property state may have separate property as well as community property, and both kinds of property must be considered in determining the amount which will be optimum for the marital deduction.

The laws in Louisiana are unique and particular care should be taken to obtain counsel knowledgeable in Louisiana law and general tax law if a couple settle in or has community property located in Louisiana.

In any event, it is very important for persons who have an estate plan drafted with only separate property in mind to have the plan reviewed and most probably redrafted upon becoming a resident of a community property state.

QUESTIONS AND ANSWERS

Question — What are the disadvantages of an A-B/A-B-Q trust?

Answer — First, if the trust is an inter vivos trust and is currently "funded" (properties placed in the trust during the lifetime of the grantor), then trustee's fees must be paid. This fee can often be minimized or avoided if the grantor serves as his own trustee, which is permissible in some jurisdictions, or reserves the right and obligation to administer trust assets during lifetime—unless disabled.

Second, after the death of the grantor the surviving spouse cannot have full control of the assets which have been placed in the nonmarital trust(s). However, it is permissible to give the surviving spouse the right to invade principal at his own discretion to the extent of a noncumulative right to withdraw up to 5 percent of the corpus or $5,000 annually, whichever is greater.[20] If the surviving spouse is the trustee and if such spouse needs funds for his support, education, or maintenance, in addition to the income of the nonmarital trust and $5,000 or 5 percent of the trust's capital, then the trustee can be authorized to invade principal for such purposes. This use of an ascertainable standard would prevent him from being taxed on the trust property.[21]

Furthermore, the trustee (assuming the trustee was an independent party) may be given a power in its sole and absolute discretion to distribute principal to the surviving spouse for any reason satisfactory to the trustee. However, here the surviving spouse has no right to demand a distribution of principal. A further power that can be given to the surviving spouse is the right to appoint during lifetime or at death to and among a specified class of individuals (but this class must exclude the spouse, his estate, his creditors, and the creditors of his estate).[22] For example, the grantor could state that his spouse has the right to appoint by will to and among the grantor's issue, parents, or siblings. However, where the surviving spouse has a right to income from the trust property for life and a power of appointment over trust property during life, exercise of the power of appointment during life will result in a taxable gift of the spouse's life estate in any property appointed to someone else.

Question — What functions does the trustee have in the A-B/A-B-Q trust?

Answer — The trustee will hold the assets placed in the trust during the lifetime of the grantor(s) and will serve as the recipient of life insurance payable to it as well as property "poured over" from the decedent's will. The trustee will be the legal owner of the corpus assets of both trusts and manage the trusts in accordance with the provisions of the trust agreement. The trust agreement can be either extremely flexible or severely restrictive, depending on the objectives of the grantor.

The trustee's primary duties are twofold: (1) to manage and invest the trust corpus in such a manner as to generate income for the beneficiaries; and (2) to preserve the corpus. In many instances a corporate fiduciary may be indicated, either as sole or cotrustee if the estate is sizable or if conflicts in interest are likely to arise between individual trustees.

Question — What are the different ways to write provisions that qualify for the maximum or optimum marital deduction?

Answer — The first is for the testator to leave a specific dollar amount bequest; however, this technique is not recommended since it is impossible, in most cases, to arrive at a dollar amount that will exactly equal the desired marital deduction at the time of the grantor's death with any degree of accuracy.

The second way is use of a funding formula which is geared to the marital deduction provisions of the Internal Revenue Code. Either a pecuniary formula bequest or a fractional share bequest is the formula clause to use. A pecuniary formula bequest is used where the testator wants his widow to receive a fixed dollar amount (a general legacy). An example of such a clause follows:

"If my wife, Deborah, survives me, I give, devise, and bequeath to my trustees (in trust "A" or trust "Q") an amount exactly sufficient—and no larger—to reduce the federal estate tax due at my death to the lowest possible amount, after taking into consideration all other property passing to my wife or which has passed to my wife and which qualifies for the marital deduction and after allowance of all applicable credits except the credit for property received by me from a transferor who died within two years after my death."[23]

Under this clause the property qualifying for the marital deduction is paid to the marital ("A" and/or "Q") trusts. The remainder of the property after satisfying the marital deduction is bequeathed to the family trust.

Instead of a fixed amount, the testator may want to give his widow a fractional share of the estate. Here, the sum which goes to the widow may fluctuate after the decedent's death and, in essence, she receives a share in the residue. In this case, the clause (the fractional share bequest) should read somewhat as follows:

"If my wife, Deborah, survives me, I give, devise, and bequeath to my trustees (in trust A or trust Q) the following fractional share of my residuary estate (before such estate is diminished by the payment therefrom of estate, inheritance, or death taxes):

(a) The numerator of the fraction shall be exactly sufficient—and no larger—to reduce to the lowest possible amount the federal estate tax due at my death, after taking into consideration all other property passing to my wife or which has passed to my wife and which qualifies for the marital deduction and after allowance of all applicable credits except the credit for property received by me from a transferor who died within two years after my death.

(b) The denominator of the fraction shall be the value of my residuary estate, before it is diminished by the payment therefrom of estate, inheritance, or death taxes."

IT IS IMPORTANT TO NOTE THAT MANY OTHER PROVISIONS ARE REQUIRED, IN ADDITION TO THE FUNDING FORMULA, IN ORDER TO OBTAIN THE MARITAL DEDUCTION.

Question — Which type of funding formula is preferable?

Answer — This depends upon the circumstances. The most important thing to look at is the type of assets the grantor owns.

If there is a probability of a substantial increase in value during the period of settlement of the trust or estate, then the pecuniary formula clause may have some benefit if it gives the residual amount (after the marital deduction) to the bypass trust. Under these circumstances, any increase in the size of the estate can be shifted to the bypass trust and thus reduce taxation at the survivor's death.

If there is a possibility that the estate may drop in value, then it may be wise to use a pecuniary formula clause that specifies the exact amount to go to the bypass trust and lets the residue go to the marital deduction trust.

In any use of a pecuniary formula clause, it is possible to recognize an income tax where assets that have increased in value since the date of death are used to satisfy distribution to a trust. In these circumstances a gain can be recognized and taxed.

A fractional share clause avoids the problem of any recognition of income tax gain upon transfer of assets to a trust to fund a bequest. Additionally, it shifts any increase or decrease proportionately to both the marital deduction trust and the bypass trust.

However, with the fractional share clause, the executor cannot pick and choose the assets to be placed in the bypass trust, and thus there may be less opportunity for post-mortem planning.

Question — What are some of the advantages of an estate trust over a power of appointment trust?

Answer — Under the estate trust, it is not necessary that all of the income be paid out to the surviving spouse. Instead, some of the income can be accumulated and kept in the trust. Where there is concern for use of income and a great deal of income available, an estate trust may provide more protection for the survivor.

Additionally, the estate trust may in some cases make it easier to retain assets that are not producing income for the trust.

Question — What are the advantages of having the marital deduction pass to a QTIP trust?

Answer — Many advantages exist. One important one is giving the trustee the power to determine how much of the trust is to be taxed at the death of the first spouse to die. Under the QTIP provisions, it is possible to arrange to have additional estate tax, so that there will be a tax to pay that is larger than the unified credit. This may be helpful

in having the tax paid early and therefore having this additional property out of the way of inflation for the survivor's lifetime.

A second important benefit of a QTIP trust is that the trustor can be certain that, at the death of the survivor, the property will go where the trustor wanted the property to go and not merely to the survivor's new friend or new spouse (as is the case under the power of appointment trust where the surviving spouse must be given a power to appoint the property at the survivor's death).

Where it is desirable to give the surviving spouse some control over the disposition of assets, e.g., among the mutual issue of the decedent and survivor, the QTIP trust permits the modification of the disposition by the survivor if the trustor wants that to happen.

Last, the QTIP trust is the only optimum marital arrangement by which the grantor's full $1,000,000 exemption from the generation-skipping transfer tax can be preserved for the next generation, with the property still benefiting the surviving spouse during the survivor's lifetime and still have no estate tax due at the grantor's death.

Question — Can an A-B/A-B-Q trust be set up in an individual's will?

Answer — Yes. This is called a testamentary (as contrasted to an inter vivos) trust. Rather than have a separate trust instrument and a separate will, the two are combined into the will document. The provisions of the testamentary trust are generally the same as the inter vivos trust provisions.

Question — Are there any drawbacks to setting up the A-B/A-B-Q trust in the will rather than as an inter vivos document?

Answer — Use of a testamentary trust will *require* a probate at the grantor's death. Often there is a delay in probating a will. If the trust were part of the will, it would not function until the will was probated. Thus, if life insurance were payable to a testamentary trust, there could be a delay in getting funds into that trust.

Some states for inheritance tax purposes will tax insurance payable to a testamentary trust as opposed to proceeds payable to an inter vivos trust. This will unnecessarily cause additional costs to the estate.

ASRS, Sec. 51, ¶280.

Footnote References

Trusts—Marital Deduction

1. Reg. §20.2056(b)-5.
2. Reg. §20.2056(b)-5(a)(4).
3. Reg. §20.2056(b)-5(f)(4).
4. *Comm. v. Ellis*, 252 F.2d 109 (3rd Cir. 1958), rev'g in part, 26 TC 694.
5. Reg. §20.2056(a)-1.
6. For special rules which apply when one spouse is a non-U.S. citizen see, Chapter 24.
7. Rev. Rul. 66-86, 1966-1 CB 216.
8. Reg. §20.2041-1(c).
9. IRC Sec. 2041(b)(2); Reg. §20.2041-3(d)(3).
10. IRC Secs. 651, 661.
11. Additional requirements must be met in order for a trust to qualify as a "Qualified Subchapter S Trust," as outlined in IRC Section 1361(d).
12. IRC Sec. 2044. The property in the trust includable in the surviving spouse's estate under section 2044 is considered property acquired from a decedent, and thus in the hands of the one to whom the property passes from the surviving spouse has a basis equal to the fair market value of the property at the date of the surviving spouse's death or alternate valuation date (see the discussion of basis in Appendix C). IRC Secs. 1014(b)(10), 2044(c).
13. It is extremely important to check the applicable state law to be sure that merely naming a trust as life insurance beneficiary will serve as adequate corpus.
14. See Rev. Proc. 64-19, 1964-1 CB 682.
15. Regs. §§25.2511-2(b), 25.2511-2(c).
16. IRC Sec. 2056.
17. *Est. of Milner v. Comm.*, 6 TC 874 (1946).
18. IRC Secs. 641, 652, 662.
19. IRC Secs. 665-669.
20. IRC Sec. 2041(b)(2); Reg. §20.2041-3(d)(3).
21. Reg. §20.2041-1(c)(2).
22. Reg. §20.2041-1(c)(1).
23. Certain additional provisions must be added to this "funding" formula in order to guarantee the marital deduction. See, e.g., Rev. Proc. 64-19, 1964-1 CB 682.

Chapter 38

TRUST — REVOCABLE

WHAT IS IT?

An *inter vivos* (living) trust is a relationship, created during the lifetime of the grantor (the person establishing the trust), in which one party (the trustee) holds property for the benefit of another (the beneficiary).

It can be established for a limited period of time, last until the occurrence or nonoccurrence of a specific event, or it can continue after the death of the grantor.

A revocable living trust is one created by the grantor during lifetime in which during his lifetime the grantor retains the right to revoke the trust, change its terms, or regain possession of the property in the trust.

A revocable trust becomes irrevocable when the grantor, during his lifetime, relinquishes title to property placed in the trust and gives up all right to revoke, amend, alter, or terminate the trust, or when the grantor dies.

WHEN IS THE USE OF SUCH A DEVICE INDICATED?

1. Where the grantor wishes someone else to accept management responsibility.

2. Where the grantor wishes to assure continuity of management and income flow of a business or other assets in the event of death or disability.

3. Where the grantor wishes to secure investment advice.

4. Where the grantor wishes to protect against his own legal incompetency or physical incapacity, or the incompetency or incapacity (physical, mental, or legal) of beneficiaries.

5. Where the grantor desires privacy in the handling and administration of his assets during lifetime and at death.

6. Where the grantor wishes to minimize estate administration costs and delay at death.

7. Where the client would like to see the trust (and the trustee) in operation.

8. Where the client wishes to avoid ancillary administration of assets situated in other states by placing title in the trustee.

9. Where the client would like to reduce the potential for an election against, or a contest of, the will.

10. Where the client would like to select the state law under which the provisions of the dispositive document will be governed.

WHAT ARE THE REQUIREMENTS?

1. In order for a trust to exist, there must be trust property (also known as trust principal, *res* or corpus).

2. There must be the following parties, although in some jurisdictions it is possible for the same individual to hold all these positions:

    (a) a "grantor," sometimes referred to as a "settlor," or "trustor"—any person who transfers property to and dictates the terms of a trust;

    (b) a trustee—a party to whom property is transferred by the grantor, who receives legal title to the property placed in the trust, and who generally manages and distributes income according to the terms of a formal written agreement (called a trust instrument) between the grantor and the trustee;

    (c) a beneficiary—a party for whose benefit the trust is created and who will receive the direct or indirect benefit of the use of income from and/or principal of the trust property, as follows:

       (1) income beneficiary—the beneficiary who receives income, generally for life or for a fixed period of years or until the occurrence or nonoccurrence of a particular event;

       (2) remainderman—the ultimate beneficiary of trust property, who can also be for the specified period of time the income beneficiary.

3. The grantor and trustee must be legally competent.

HOW IT IS DONE — AN EXAMPLE

Russ Miller, a successful real estate broker, feels that if his wife survives him, she will be able to handle the assets in his estate and properly manage them. However, he is afraid that if his spouse predeceases him, his children will be unable to properly manage the assets left to them. His estate is not subject to significant estate taxes.

Russ makes his life insurance proceeds and/or other assets payable to his wife, if she survives him. However, if Russ's wife predeceases him, those assets are payable to a trust Russ set up during life. This type of *inter vivos* trust is revocable since Russ can always revoke the trust and repossess the property or change the terms of the trust. Often, such a trust is designed as a "contingent," or "step up," or "stand by" trust, since it will take effect only in the event of the contingency that the grantor's wife predeceases him.

Under different circumstances or to meet different objectives, an irrevocable living trust would be indicated. For example, if Russ were in a high income tax bracket, as well as a high estate tax bracket, he might consider transferring assets to an irrevocable trust for the benefit of his wife or children. The trust could accumulate income during Russ's life or distribute that income to, or use it for the benefit of, his children (but not for Russ's own benefit). At Russ's death, the trust could provide income to his wife for life and at her death, provide income and eventually principal for his children.

WHAT ARE THE TAX IMPLICATIONS?

1. For federal income tax purposes, all income is taxed to the grantor at the grantor's tax rate, since he is considered owner of the trust corpus.[1]

2. No gift tax is generated by establishing or funding a revocable trust since the gift is not completed until the trust becomes irrevocable.[2]

3. Since the grantor has not irrevocably disposed of any assets, the entire trust corpus will be included in the grantor's estate for federal estate tax purposes.[3]

ISSUES AND IMPLICATIONS IN COMMUNITY PROPERTY STATES

In dealing with community property, the inter vivos trust would have two grantors, the husband and the wife. For a revocable trust, where the grantors intend to retain the beneficial ownership of the property, care must be taken to ensure that accidental gifts under state gift tax law are not made by giving either spouse ownership rights over the other spouse's half of the property. The unlimited gift tax marital deduction eliminates a federal gift tax problem on interspousal gifts. Thus, if the trust is revoked, the property should be clearly indicated as being returned to the husband and wife, as co-owners, and not to one spouse or the other.

Is the character of community property altered by transfer to a revocable trust? If the transfer is simply by husband and wife to trustee, and each retains a right to revoke, and the instrument specifically provides that the character of the property remains community in the trust and also if it is withdrawn from the trust, and state law recognizes the ability of the parties to achieve the intended result, the character of the property will remain unchanged. This means that, upon the death of the first spouse, the decedent's one-half and the surviving spouse's one-half interest in the trust will receive a new basis equal to fair market value at death or the alternate valuation date, and only the decedent's one-half of the property in the trust will be included in his estate. There will be no gift at the time the trust is created and there will be no gift upon the death of the first spouse unless, at that time, the trust becomes irrevocable. This is avoided by language that divides the trust into two trusts upon death of one of the donors; the trust in which the decedent's one-half is placed becomes irrevocable and the other remains revocable. This is the kind of a revocable trust most frequently used as an effective planning device.

Much care must be taken in determining the source and nature of title holding of property before taking the position that it is community property, as one may when the property is transferred to a trust which indicates that it is held as community property. Taxable gifts under state law may result if the property is the separate property of either spouse or is joint tenancy real property originally acquired with the separate property of one spouse. Although the unlimited marital deduction for federal gift tax purposes reduces the gift tax risks,[4] there still may be state gift tax implications. In addition, it could well inspire litigation in the event of a dissolution if there was not a clear intent between the parties that a gift take place.

Where insurance has been purchased with community property (and therefore belongs one-half to each spouse), care must be taken that the terms of a trust, becoming irrevocable at the death of the insured, do not result in a taxable gift by the surviving spouse of all or part of the survivor's half interest in the insurance proceeds. Such gifts are usually to the remaindermen of the trust and not subject to the marital deduction.

As noted in the discussion of "flower bonds," such bonds may be used to pay estate tax at par only to the extent they are owned by the decedent. Where a community property couple has placed some or all of their assets in a revocable trust to avoid probate, it is difficult to arrange that bonds be purchased as the separate property of the ill or older spouse unless the trust provides for the holding of the separate property of such grantor-spouse. For such circumstances, many community property estate planners now draft such trusts so as to have specific provisions for the holding of the separate property of each spouse, as well as community property, even though the spouses may only have community property at the time of the creation of the estate plan.

Great care must be taken in the drafting of the provisions regarding the division of property at the death of one community property owning spouse so as to avoid unintended gifts by the surviving spouse. At times, such trusts may be intended to benefit the survivor more if he agrees to have his property also be managed and distributed according to the terms of the trust. Such "election" provisions may also result in gifts by the surviving spouse and, if used, should be drafted carefully by an experienced estate planner.

The marital deduction rules make it important that all pre-1982 inter vivos trusts be examined carefully and revisions considered to take advantage of the very important provisions which make it possible to have completely tax-free interspousal transfers. Chapter 37, on the Marital Deduction, reviews this in more detail.

Community property and separate property states generally have similar rules as to how long property can be held in trust and as to other trust law matters. However, property rights are different as to separate and community property, and estate plans involving trusts must be reviewed and probably revised when one moves from a separate property state to a community property state and vice versa.

QUESTIONS AND ANSWERS

Question — Why, if there can be no federal income or estate tax savings, are revocable trusts so appealing?

Answer — Some of the popularity of revocable trusts is pure hype and misunderstanding. Books have been written (and authors have grown rich) preying on the public's ignorance of the true costs of the probate system and its safeguards. Avoiding probate also means avoiding court supervision of the person you've named to manage, invest, and distribute your wealth to those you love. That may not be so advantageous since no one is officially looking over the trustee's shoulder to protect the assets and income of the client's beneficiaries. The actual costs of probate are much lower than these merchants of "panic and panacea" would have the public believe. The wildly

exaggerated administrator's or executor's fees described in their books are cut to zero if a family member is involved and agrees to serve with no fee. (Most executors waive all fees because it is in their best interest taxwise to do so. Outside administrators charge fees, but so would an outside trustee. Attorneys' fees are negotiable. Ethical attorneys charge by the hour (and document their time) or charge a flat fee that is not dependent on the size of the probate estate. These simplistic "buy this book and your problem is solved" books rarely discuss the fact that federal and state death tax returns must be filed and death tax paid and the cash to pay the costs of filing those returns and paying those taxes must be available, even if a revocable trust has been used. More importantly, these books and the uninformed newspaper columnists or radio commentators who highlight them and tout them to their readers or listeners mislead the public into thinking that no further planning or thought is necessary.

Furthermore, there are up front costs involved in setting up a revocable trust, funding it, and operating it. Because of the multiplicity of contingencies which must be considered, only a skilled attorney should draft the trust. The attorney must be paid. (Legal fees to create the revocable trust arrangement and the necessary pour-over will which accompanies it will often be greater than the legal fees to prepare a normal will and testamentary trust). The title to real estate must be changed. The conveyancer must be paid. Tax returns must be filed on trust income and a federal estate tax return and state inheritance tax returns must be prepared. The CPA or attorney who prepares those forms must be paid (fees for preparing the income tax return will be deductible, if at all, only to the extent they exceed 2 percent of the grantor's adjusted gross income). The trustee must make decisions, safeguard, invest, and distribute trust income and principal. The trustee must be paid (or a family member serving for no fee must himself pay the cost in terms of time). Additional fees may be incurred when the client dies for the handling of the postmortem income of the trust.

Perhaps the greatest cost of simplistic avoidance of probate through consumer form book trusts is the loss of the opportunity to gain real tax savings, creditor proof assets, avoid will contests, and achieve overall objectives through more certain means.

Yet, the revocable living trust is a highly useful estate and financial planning tool if used as part of an overall plan and if drafted and maintained by knowledgeable planners who in fact do what they are supposed to do. Many times, the nontax advantages of a revocable trust coupled with the built in flexibility far outweigh the tax savings potential of an irrevocable trust or outright gift.

Question — What is a "Pour-over Trust?"

Answer — As its name implies, a pour-over trust is one into which assets can be "poured" or funneled from the client's will, life insurance, pension or profit sharing plan, or other employee benefit plan. This type of revocable trust is set up by the client during life and serves as a receptacle for any asset the client would like to pour into it. This unification is particularly useful if the client owns property in more than one state since it may save heirs a great deal of aggravation in addition to the cost savings inherent in avoiding multiple probates. Cash from an IRA, HR-10, ESOP, pension, profit sharing plan, or from some other trust (or someone else's estate) may serve as the funding vehicles. Almost all states have laws regarding the validity of pour-overs to trusts established during the client's lifetime.

Question — What is a "Contingent Trust?"

Answer — A contingent trust (also known as a step up or standby trust) is one which takes over to manage and invest assets if and when the client is no longer able to do so. A contingent trust is triggered upon the occurrence of one or more specified contingencies such as the client's physical, mental, or emotional incapacity. It may also be triggered by the client upon an extended trip. Such a trust works well when co-ordinated with a durable power of attorney (see Chapter 6) and can help avoid the need for cumbersome and expensive probate proceedings. The client could appoint himself as trustee. The trust would provide that the grantor (client) would be succeeded by a corporate fiduciary and/or another person if the grantor becomes incompetent. Typically, this would be the same trustee designated to serve upon the client's death.

Incapacity could be defined in a number of ways — as broadly or as narrowly as the client desires. Quite often, the step up trustee takes over (a) upon the decision of a third party such as a child or friend, or (b) upon the trustee's decision that incapacity has occurred but only after a determination of incompetency by one or more specified doctors, or (c) upon a decision solely by the trustee that the grantor is incompetent, or (d) upon a judicial proceeding of incompetency, or (e) upon the determination of an independent arbitrator.

Question — When is a revocable trust funded?

Answer — Funding of a revocable trust can occur at the establishment of the trust or at any later date although most states require at least a token funding at the creation of the trust. The holder of a durable power of attorney may be authorized to make transfers of assets or shift the title

to property to a previously established revocable trust. In some cases, courts have allowed such transfers even where not specifically authorized by the terms of the durable power although specific authorization is, of course, preferable. This court assistance is most likely where the dispositive terms of the revocable trust track closely with the terms of the client's will.

Question — What provisions should a trust contain if it is designed to provide property management during the grantor's incompetency?

Answer — The trust should (1) provide for income distribution to or for the grantor's benefit, (2) authorize that trust assets could be distributed to others to implement or continue a gifting program (within the limits of the annual gift tax exclusion), (3) specify that any pledges already made to a qualified charity be satisfied, (4) state that the management of a business interest be delegated to certain family members.

Question — When does a revocable trust become irrevocable?

Answer — A revocable trust becomes irrevocable upon the death of the grantor client. Generally, a grantor lacks the power to revoke a trust during incompetency. It is possible to specify that as soon as the client is deemed to be incompetent the trust becomes irrevocable. This would block a person acting under a durable power of attorney from changing the plan of disposition in the revocable trust. Note that the irrevocability of a trust may trigger adverse gift tax implications. A taxable gift is made when a client parts with dominion and control over property. But immediate gift taxation can be blocked. The client could retain a life income in the trust's assets and delay taxation on the gift of the remainder interest (the portion going at his death to the ultimate beneficiaries of the trust) by the reservation of a testamentary power of appointment over that remainder interest. This should work even if the grantor is mentally incompetent since it is assumed that he may regain competency at any time before death.

Question — What happens to the assets in a revocable trust when a client dies?

Answer — Assuming a trust is funded at the time of a client's death, assets can be paid directly and immediately to the named beneficiaries and the trust can be terminated. Alternatively, the trust can be continued. The trust, which is now irrevocable, can serve as a receptacle to receive assets poured over into it. It can then continue to exist until its purpose or term has been completed. A third possibility is that the assets in the trust can be consolidated with another trust.

Assets in the trust at the grantor's death are subject to federal estate tax which will be based, not on the value of the assets when contributed to the trust, but on the value as of the date of death. Planners should consider an immediate payout to the designated remaindermen upon a grantor's incompetency so that the trust assets will have been consumed or transferred long (more than three years) prior to the grantor's death. To escape estate taxation the grantor must also give up the lifetime rights to trust income. This tax saving maneuver, of course, must be balanced with the client's need for continuing income during lifetime.

Question — What is the easiest way to shift joint property into a revocable trust?

Answer — It may make sense to have a husband and wife each establish revocable trusts. Each would be trustee of his or her trust. The trust instrument would authorize the trustees to take and hold the title to trust property in their individual names without disclosing their fiduciary capacity. By a separate recorded document the client and spouse declare that whatever is registered in their names as jointly held property (whether already held or acquired at some point in the future) shall belong one half each to their revocable trusts as tenants in common.

This joint declaration "magic wand" to convert true joint ownership into revocable trust ownership was conceived by Frederick R. Keydel of Joslyn, Keydel, Wallace, and Joslyn of Detroit Michigan and described in an article in Probate and Property, American Bar Association, Vol. 2. No. 7, pp. 13-17. It enables spouses to simply and instantly convert all of their jointly owned property into trust owned property — one half in each trust — without the need to disturb record titles, reissue stock certificates, or change bank and broker account records. The declaration of trust makes the property trust owned while appearing to be jointly held. The unlimited marital deduction eliminates federal gift taxes. The joint declaration can specify which jointly held property is to become trust owned or can specify proportions of ownership other than 50-50.

Benefits of this "magic wand" technique include:

(1) To outsiders, the property appears to be held in the "normal" manner

(2) There will be no change in the income tax reporting of income from the two trusts

(3) No 1041 forms need be filed

(4) Sales, transfers, loans, and other transactions can be carried out by the clients under a durable joint property power of appointment. Under such a power, each joint titleholder authorizes the other to sign all joint property documents in his behalf in connection with any and all joint property transactions.

Question — What factors should be considered in selecting a trustee?

Answer — A trustee should possess business judgment (even if there is no business), honesty, and integrity. The trustee must be able and willing to exercise a high degree of care over trust property and avoid (however tempting) investments or acts which are likely to result in losses.

A trustee must have legal capacity to contract. This precludes the appointment of a minor or incompetent adult. Geographical considerations contraindicate an individual who lives a considerable distance from the client or his heirs.

The type and size of assets to be placed into the trust, as well as the client's goals, are important considerations in selecting a trustee. Obviously, if the client's primary asset is a business, the trustee will have much more responsibility and must have higher and broader competence than if the trust's assets consisted mainly of cash.

Investment skill is necessary. Under the "prudent man" rule, a trustee will be liable to the beneficiary for losses unless he exercises the same care and skill that a person of ordinary prudence would exercise in dealing with his own property. But the Uniform Probate Code, now in effect in some form in most states, raises this standard for professional trustees by providing: "If the trustee has greater skill than that of a man of ordinary prudence, he is under a duty to exercise such skill."

Because a trustee must examine and review the trust periodically, administrative and legal skills and knowledge are important. Accounting must be made to the client and eventually to the other beneficiaries. All parties must be advised accurately on the tax and other legal effects. Provisions in the trust must, from time to time, be interpreted.

Question — Does a family member, close friend, or business associate make a good trustee?

Answer — There are significant advantages and disadvantages to naming a family member or business associate as trustee. A nonprofessional trustee is indicated where the minimum fee charged by local professional fiduciaries is higher than it's feasible to pay.

Is it appropriate for a family member, a close friend, or a business associate to serve as trustee? The obvious advantage is that such a person may have a working knowledge of the client, the family, and the finances and business. But selection of a person as trustee must also consider conflicts of interest and ethical problems. For instance, how will a trustee who is also a beneficiary react when faced with a choice that favors him at the expense of other beneficiaries or that favors other beneficiaries at his expense? Will the trustee favor other beneficiaries at his own expense? Will the fees charged by a family member or business associate as trustee be understood and accepted without resentment or will it cause conflict? Will the trustee's "hard choices" be injurious to family relationships? Is the trustee likely to show favoritism or be easily persuaded?

Can an untrained individual deal with the legal, tax, and investment functions of being a trustee? Even though a trustee is legally entitled to hire agents to serve as investment counselors, accountants, and attorneys to assist on special problems, the trustee remains responsible for the ultimate decisions. Would an untrained individual know whom to call? Would the trustee know if the advice he is receiving is both legally and practically correct? Does the trustee understand that he is personally liable for unpaid federal estate taxes if a distribution is made to beneficiaries before the estate tax liability is fully paid (even if the trust provides for immediate distributions from the trust on the grantor's death)? If a distribution is made that can't be recovered, the trustee will be personally liable to the extent remaining trust assets are insufficient to pay the estate's estate tax liability.

Question — When is a corporate trustee indicated?

Answer — A corporate fiduciary (with or without individuals as co-trustees) is clearly indicated where it is likely that the trust will span more than one generation. Corporate fiduciaries are also indicated where the amount placed into the trust is large and/or will require skillful and constant attention. If there is likelihood of family conflict, corporate fiduciaries can make decisions on a more objective disinterested basis than family members.

Question — What role does state law play in the choice of trustee?

Answer — A trust will be invalid if it does not meet state law requirements. Planners should be aware of two potential

problems: (1) the Doctrine of Merger and (2) The Passive Trust theory.

When the same person is both trustee and beneficiary, the trust ceases to exist as a separate entity. Legal title to the property (held by the trustee) merges with the equitable (beneficial) title (held by the beneficiary). The result is that if the sole beneficiary of the trust is also the sole trustee, the beneficiary becomes the owner of the total rights in the trust assets. This is known as a "fee simple" or "fee simple absolute." The trust, as such, ceases to exist.

A second potential problem occurs in the case of a so-called "passive trust." This is a trust that gives the trustee no meaningful duties to perform and gives the beneficiary unfettered enjoyment and management control of assets. The result is a merger of the legal title and the equitable title; the trust ceases to exist. Either through operation of law or through judicial action, where the trustee's duties are purely ministerial and all significant authority and decision making are placed in the hands of the beneficiary, the beneficiary receives total title to the property that was in the trust.

Question _ What is the effect of a revocable trust on creditors?

Answer — The ability of a revocable trust to protect assets from the claims of the client's creditors will depend on state law and the provisions of the trust document. As a general rule, if the grantor has retained the right to trust assets or the right to alter, amend, revoke, or terminate the trust, there will be little if any protection from the claims of creditors. In the typical revocable living trust the client retains too many rights over the trust assets to put those assets beyond the reach of creditors.

Question — Are there advantages to making the trust the beneficiary of qualified plan benefits?

Answer — First, naming a revocable trust as beneficiary of qualified pension or profit sharing plan or IRA or HR-10 payments helps to unify the administration of the estate and achieve the client's objectives. Second, a trust serves as a means of deferring the distribution of assets to beneficiaries who may not be ready or able to handle large sums of money. Third, a trust enables the sprinkling of capital and the spraying of income to those beneficiaries who need or deserve it the most or who are in the lowest tax brackets. Fourth, payment of qualified plan benefits to a trustee makes it possible for the trustee to make certain advantageous tax elections on behalf of the estate.

Question — Can a revocable trust safely hold the stock of an S corporation?

Answer — To be eligible to elect the "pass through" taxation similar to a partnership, a corporation must meet stringent requirements. The only trusts which qualify as eligible shareholders of S corporations are:

1. Voting trusts

2. A trust receiving stock under a will (but only for the first 60 days after the stock is transferred to the trust)

3. Section 678 trusts (See Chapter 29)

4. Grantor trusts (which includes revocable living trusts over which the grantor has retained all powers or to whom income is taxable under Code Sections 671-677)

5. QSST (Qualified Subchapter S Trust). The requirements of a QSST are: (a) The trust must own stock in one or more S corporations, (b) the trust may have only one income beneficiary at a time, (c) the trust must distribute to (and only to) that income beneficiary all income annually or more frequently, (d) principal may be paid out but only to the income beneficiary, (e) the beneficiary must be a U.S. citizen or resident, (f) the income beneficiary must receive income for life or receive the entire amount of principal upon the termination of the trust, and (g) the beneficiary must "elect" QSST status.

If any other type of trust owns stock in an S corporation, the S election is automatically nullified. The result is that the corporation would be taxed as a regular corporation and the pass through of income or deductions would be denied.

Question — Are there situations in which a revocable living trust is contra-indicated?

Answer — Yes. A revocable living trust may not make sense if there is no specific reason to set it up other than to save probate and administration costs — and the certain immediately payable present value cost of drafting the trust and maintaining it will exceed the future possible savings. A revocable living trust is not indicated where the client is not likely to follow through with the retitling of property and the other prerequisites and operating procedures to assure the continued validity of the trust and to assure it will be legally recognized when the client dies. Stock in a professional corporation can not be transferred to a revocable trust because of the prohibition against ownership by anyone other than a professional. If Section 1244 stock is held by a revocable living trust, it may not qualify for ordinary loss treatment. The deduction allowed to estates for the amount of income permanently set aside for charitable purposes is not allowed to trusts. A living trust is not necessary if the client's estate is modest, the mortgage paid off, and there is no reason to keep probate proceedings private, and the executor of the estate is a family member who will probably waive executor's fees. Finally, a revocable trust is not indicated if a less complex less expensive durable power of attorney can satisfy the need. For instance, a broadly drawn durable power of attorney will enable the holder to do many of the same ministerial tasks (such as preparing and filing tax returns) as the trustee of a trust.

Question — Are there disadvantages in putting investment real estate in a revocable trust?

Answer — There may be several. The impact on real property taxes must be considered. Some states have provisions for reassessment of real property for property tax purposes if it is transferred. If highly appreciated property is transferred to a revocable trust, this could result in a costly reassessment. Some states, such as California, exempt property transferred to a revocable trust from reassessment. Also, it should be determine whether or not the transfer will accelerate the payment of any mortgage or deed of trust on the property under so-called "acceleration" provisions in the note or mortgage. Again, many transactions are exempt.

Finally, great care should be taken to determine if the real property is presently generating losses or will be expected to do so after the death of the owner. Under Code section 469, losses from various activities, including some rental real estate activities, are characterized as passive losses, not deductible except under limited circumstances. However, Section 469(i) allows deduction for losses of up to $25,000 per year if the owner is actively participating in the management of the property. Section 469(i)(4) permits continued deduction of such losses for two years after the death of the owner by the owner's estate. It is generally assumed the use of the term "estate" could not be extended to cover revocable trusts. The safer course is to allow such property to pass through an estate, which after two years could distribute it to the trust under pour-over provisions discussed above.

Question — What is an "administrative" trust?

Answer — Practitioners generally use this term to refer to the revocable trust immediately after the death of the grantor where it is to be further divided into separate trusts, such as the Marital Deduction and Bypass trusts discussed in Chapter 37. Since the actual funding of such separate trusts may take months or even years, most practitioners believe the revocable trust continues to be a separate trust entity for a period commencing with the death of the grantor and ending on the date any separate trusts are finally funded. Unfortunately, many living trust documents fail to indicate what to do with that trust during the interim period, which could have important tax consequences.

Question — If the grantor of a revocable trust is contemplating making gifts from the trust assets, is it better for the grantor to direct the trustee to make the gifts directly, or for the grantor to remove the assets from the trust and make the gifts directly?

Answer — The grantor should remove the assets from the trust and make the gifts directly. If the gifts are made directly by the trustee, and the grantor dies within 3 years of the gifts, there is a good chance the value of the gifts will be brought back into the grantor's taxable estate, even those gifts that would fall within the $10,000 annual gift tax exclusion discussed in Chapter 15.

The reason for this result is that Code section 2035(d)(2) mandates that any gifts made within three years of death from any property over which the grantor has a power of revocation, as defined in Code secton 2038, those gift will be included in the grantor's estate. The Tax Court has essentially agreed with this result, unless it is deemed the trustee first transferred the assets to the grantor, who then made the gifts directly[5].

Question — Will the use of revocable trusts present any problems if the grantor or husband and wife grantors are seeking public assistance for medical care?

Answer — The requirements for federal and state assistance for medical care, generally called "Medicaid," are discussed in Chapter 7. As noted in that chapter, the use of revocable trusts could have an adverse effect on the eligibility of the grantors for such assistance.

ASRS, Sec. 48.

Footnote References

Trusts—Inter Vivos

1. IRC Sec. 671.
2. *Burnet v. Guggenheim*, 288 U.S. 280 (1933).
3. IRC Sec. 2038.
4. IRC Sec. 2523.
5. *Est. of Jalkut*, 96 TC 675 (1991).

Chapter 39

TRUST — SECTION 2503(b) AND 2503(c)

WHAT IS IT?

A Section 2503(c) trust is a gift tax tool that enables a grantor to make a gift to a minor in trust and still obtain the annual gift tax exclusion. The use of this irrevocable funded trust for gifts to minors eliminates many of the following practical objections to outright gifts:

1. Brokers are reluctant to deal in securities owned by minors since minors may disaffirm either a purchase of stock that subsequently falls in value or a sale of stock that later rises in value.

2. Property titled in a minor's name is, to a large extent, "frozen." It is difficult to sell or exchange that property since a minor's signature on a real estate deed gives the buyer no assurance of permanent title.

3. Guardianship must be used to avoid many of the objections of an outright transfer to a minor, but a guardian must generally post bond and account periodically to a local Orphans' (sometimes called Surrogate's or Probate) Court.

Another gift tax tool that enables a grantor to make a gift to a minor in trust and still obtain the annual gift tax exclusion is the 2503(b) trust, discussed in the question and answer section of this chapter.

WHEN IS THE USE OF SUCH A DEVICE INDICATED?

When your client wishes to make a gift to minor children and:

1. When the grantor's income tax bracket is high and the donee's income tax bracket is relatively low. Significant income shifting, and therefore income tax saving, is still possible, once the child reaches age 14.

2. When the grantor owns an asset which is likely to appreciate substantially over a period of time but does not want the appreciation includable in his gross estate.

3. When use of the gift tax annual exclusion is necessary or desirable.

WHAT ARE THE REQUIREMENTS?

1. A gift to a minor through a Section 2503(c) trust will not be considered a gift of a future interest (so the gift will qualify for the annual gift tax exclusion) if the income and principal may be expended by or on behalf of the beneficiary at any time prior to the time the beneficiary reaches age 21. (Regardless of when a person becomes an adult under state law, the "magic" age is still 21 for Section 2503(c) purposes.)

2. Unexpended income and principal must be payable to the beneficiary when that individual reaches age 21.

3. If the child dies before age 21, trust corpus must go to the minor's estate or appointee under his will.[1]

4. Even if the minor is legally unable to exercise a power or to execute a will because he or she is under legal age, this fact will not cause the transfer to fail to satisfy the above conditions. Furthermore, it is permissible to provide that the trust will continue beyond the donee's 21st birthday, as long as anytime after reaching age 21, the donee can obtain the property in the trust at if he wishes. Thus, the trust property does not have to be forced on a trust beneficiary upon reaching age 21.[2]

HOW IT IS DONE — AN EXAMPLE

Jeff Mandell transfers stock in his closely held corporation to three trusts for his three minor boys. Assuming the trusts qualify under Section 2503(c), the irrevocable transfer of stock annually to the trusts will be considered gifts of a present interest. This will allow Jeff to obtain the $10,000 annual exclusion and therefore minimize or eliminate any gift taxes.

Gifts, to the extent they qualify for the annual exclusion (without taking gift splitting into account), reduce the value of Jeff's estate and the income from any dividends paid on the stock is taxed currently either to the trust, if accumulated, or to the children, if distributed. Such a trust is often used to start children on a life insurance program by providing the trust with sufficient cash each year to pay premiums for the insurance on the boys' lives. Alternatively, trust income could be used to purchase nonnecessaries or be accumulated and used to help provide nonnecessaries when the children reach college age.

WHAT ARE THE TAX IMPLICATIONS?

1. If the income of the trust is distributed each year, it is taxable to the recipient.[3] To the extent income is accumulated, it will be taxed to the trust.[4] Eventually, when a distribution of income accumulated in a prior year is made, the beneficiary will pay tax on the distribution as though the income had been distributed annually; however, the beneficiary will receive credit for any taxes paid by the trust.[5] (This is the so called "throwback" rule.)

   The throwback rule is not applicable to accumulations due to sales of capital assets or to accumulations for beneficiaries made during the years they were under age 21, since Section 2503(c) requires that the property and any accumulated income pass to the donee at age 21.

2. Gifts to the trust constitute a present interest. Therefore, the annual gift tax exclusion of $10,000 applies as long as the conditions mentioned above are met.

3. Appreciation on property from the date it is placed in trust will be removed from the grantor's gross estate. (However, the entire value of the 2503(c) trust will be includable in the grantor's estate if the grantor is the trustee at the time of his death.)

   Generally, the gross estate of a decedent does not include the value of transfers, other than transfers of life insurance, made by a decedent within three years of his death.[6]

   To the extent the transfers exceed or otherwise do not qualify for the annual gift tax exclusion, they may not result in estate tax savings. This is because the taxable portion of any gift is added back in the estate tax computation as an "adjusted taxable gift" at the date of gift value (less a credit for any gift tax paid on the transfer). Nevertheless, a benefit from the gift may result because the property brought back into the computation as an adjusted taxable gift is valued as of the date of the gift. Post-transfer appreciation is excluded.

   For instance, if a single individual gives his brother $210,000 worth of stock, $200,000 would, after the donor's death, be considered an adjusted taxable gift in his estate ($10,000 qualifies for the gift tax annual exclusion). That would be true even though the stock had appreciated in value to $300,000 by the time of the donor's death. The appreciation in value, $100,000 ($300,000-$200,000) would never enter the estate tax computation.

   Transfers made within three years of death of interests in property otherwise included in the gross estate under Sections 2036, 2037, 2038 or 2042 are included in the gross estate at their date of death values. An unfavorable aspect of the law is that a transfer of insurance by the insured within three years of death continues to be includable in the gross estate.

IMPLICATIONS AND ISSUES IN COMMUNITY PROPERTY STATES

Where community property is the subject of a gift into a 2503(c) trust, each spouse is considered as being the grantor of one-half, by reason of the community ownership. For that reason, it is important that neither spouse be named as the trustee or successor trustee of the trust in order to avoid the problem of having the trust property included in the grantors' estates (see second question and answer below). In some states, if one spouse transfers community real or personal property to a trust for the benefit of a third party, such spouse must obtain the written consent of the nondonor spouse prior to such transfer or the gift could be entirely set aside.

QUESTIONS AND ANSWERS

Question — If it is likely that the grantor will make only one gift and that gift will be a relatively modest amount of marketable securities and there is little likelihood that further gifts will be made in subsequent years, should a Section 2503(c) trust be used?

Answer — No. Generally, the complexities and expenses of creating such a trust contra-indicate its use for small gifts or "single shot" gifts. In this type of situation, the use of the Uniform Gifts to Minors Act (UGMA) or the Uniform Transfers to Minors Act (UTMA) might be a more appealing alternative. However, where it seems likely that additional gifts will be made in future years, and a substantial amount of valuable property will ultimately be transferred to the minor, additional flexibility is called for and indicates the use of a trust.

The type of property in question may affect which device will be used. For example, the Internal Revenue Service has held that stock in an S corporation may be held by a custodian under the Uniform Gifts to Minors Act.[7] However, if a gift of stock in an S corporation is made to a Section 2503(c) trust, the corporation's election may be automatically terminated, since generally a

346

trust may not be a shareholder of an S corporation.[8] The law does allow a trustee to be an S corporation shareholder, but only if (a) the grantor is treated for income tax purposes as the owner of trust property (a so-called "grantor trust"), or (b) the trust was created primarily to vote stock (a so-called "voting trust"), or (c) the trust receives the stock under a will (a so-called "testamentary trust" and it holds S corporation stock only up to a maximum of 60 days after the stock is transferred to the trust), or (d) a "Section 678" trust (see last question and answer).

One reason a trust is often used instead of the Uniform Gifts to Minors Act is custodianship: the U.G.M.A. provides that only one person may be custodian and specifies how a successor custodian may be named. But if a trust is created, the grantor may designate a line of succession of trustees and may provide for two or even more trustees to act together.

Question — Are there any adverse tax consequences if the donor acts as the trustee of a Section 2503(c) trust?

Answer — Yes. If the donor acts as trustee and dies in that capacity before the child has reached age 21, the assets in the trust may be includable in his estate (the same result occurs if the donor appoints himself as custodian under the Uniform Gifts to Minors Act or the Uniform Transfers to Minors Act and dies while serving in that capacity before the custodianship ends). The same result occurs where the grantor dies while serving as successor trustee or custodian.

For example, where the husband is appointed successor trustee upon the death of his wife, the corpus is taxed in the grantor-trustee's estate because of the trustee's power to "alter, amend, revoke or terminate" the trust. Even if the only power retained is the ability to advance principal to the beneficiaries from time to time in the discretion of the trustee, the grantor, as trustee, has the power to accelerate the termination date. In essence, this is the power to terminate the trust and, therefore, adverse estate tax consequences occur if the grantor is the trustee or one of the trustees (or the custodian in case of a Uniform Gifts to Minors Act or Uniform Transfers to Minors Act).[9]

Question — If a father places dividend-bearing securities into a 2503(c) trust for his minor son using an independent bank as trustee, what types of expenditures of income would cause the income to be taxed to the father?

Answer — If the income is or may be used to pay premiums on a life insurance policy on the life of either the grantor or the grantor's spouse, or if it is used for the support of a minor whom the grantor is legally obligated to support, then such income will be taxed to the grantor (father).[10] Note that the use of capital to pay premiums would not cause the grantor to be subject to income tax on trust income.

Question — In addition to giving the donee the continuing right to compel distribution upon reaching 21 is there any other arrangement which can avoid a mandatory distribution of principal and income to the donee child at age 21?

Answer — Yes. The donee can be given a right during a *limited period* of time to compel immediate distribution of the trust corpus by giving written notice to the trustee which, if not exercised, will permit the trust to continue by its own terms.

Question — What is a 2503(b) trust?

Answer — A 2503(b) trust is one which requires a mandatory distribution of income to the trust beneficiary on an annual or more frequent basis. All or portions of gifts to such trusts will qualify as gifts of a present interest and thus are eligible for the annual gift tax exclusion. For example, arbitrarily assuming a 10.6 percent discount rate, if the trust provides income for life to the donee to be distributed at least annually and if the donee is age eleven, then based on government valuation tables (see Appendix D) the amount of the gift which will be considered as a present interest if $10,000 was put into a 2503(b) trust would be $9,885.80 (the actuarial value of an 11 year old's right to income on $10,000 paid annually for life).

In some respects a 2503(b) trust is more flexible than either a 2503(c) trust or a custodianship account since a 2503(b) trust does not require distribution of principal and unexpended income at age 21 or sooner. Furthermore, a 2503(b) trust can last for the lifetime of the beneficiary or for any lesser period of time. Also, unlike the case with a 2503(c) trust or a custodianship, under a 2503(b) trust, the principal does not ever have to be paid over to the income beneficiary. Trust principal can go to a donee specified by the grantor of the trust or can go to a person specified by the income beneficiary.

As income is earned by a 2503(b) trust, it must be distributed to the trust beneficiary. However, it can be deposited in a custodial account and used for the benefit of the minor or left to accumulate in the custodial account until the minor reaches majority. At that time, the accumulated income will be turned over to the beneficiary. Each year, as it is earned, the income of the trust will be taxed to the minor except to the extent it has been used to discharge a support or other legal obligation of a grantor-parent.

If the minor is under age 14, income will be taxed to the minor, but (with respect to unearned income in excess of $1,300, as indexed for 1995) at the parents' top bracket. If the minor is 14 or older, all income (earned and unearned) is taxed to the minor at the minor's bracket.

For gift tax purposes, the entire amount placed into such a trust is treated as a gift. The gift is divided into two portions: an income portion and a principal (remainder) portion. The income portion will qualify for the $10,000 annual exclusion while the balance is considered a future interest gift and will not qualify for the exclusion.[11] To protect the annual exclusion for the income portion, the trust instrument should specifically deny the power of the trustee to invest in non-income producing property.

Question — Is it possible to make a gift into a trust which can retain the property for a child past age 21 and still have the entire gift qualify for the annual exclusion?

Answer — Yes; based on the *Crummey*[12] case, if the donee has an immediate, unfettered, and ascertainable legal right at the time the gift is made to take out the amount put in, then the gift will be considered a present interest gift and qualify for the annual gift tax exclusion.

Ordinarily, failing to exercise a power to take property out of a trust (where the trust goes on under some circumstances to someone else) is a gift by the donee to the extent of the value which goes to someone else. However, there is a specific exception[13] which ignores the gift consequence to the donee where the power is to appoint (i.e., to give) to oneself no more than the greater of $5,000 or 5 percent of the trust corpus. To come within this rule, this type of trust gives the beneficiary the right to remove only this "5 or 5" amount each year (on a non-cumulative basis). However, the $5,000 limit is less than the amount of the annual exclusion.

There may be other persons (e.g. grandparents, uncles, aunts, etc.) who would like to make gifts to the trust. It is most probable that Crummey trusts can deal with these large gift potentials, and still not have a gift when the donee does not exercise his power by giving the donee a power to appoint the trust at his death to anyone other than himself (or his estate, creditors or estate creditors). This will bring the non-appointment trust assets into the donee's taxable estate, but that is not usually an unacceptable condition.

Note that gifts to grandchildren may be subject to generation-skipping transfer tax. See Chapter 14.

Question — Is a 2503(c) trust a good receptacle for holding stock in an S corporation?

Answer — A 2503(c) trust is not an eligible shareholder of S corporation stock. A qualified subchapter S trust (QSST) or a Section 678 trust is a better vehicle for this purpose.

A QSST is defined in the Internal Revenue Code as one that:

1. owns stock in one or more S corporations (and may hold other types of assets)

2. actually distributes all of its income to one individual (who must be a United States resident or United States citizen)

3. has trust terms requiring that

    (a) there can be only one beneficiary at any given time

    (b) if corpus is distributed during the term of the trust, it can be distributed only to the individual who is at that time the current income beneficiary

    (c) if an income beneficiary dies, the income interest itself will end at that death or upon the earlier termination of the trust

    (d) if the trust ends before the income beneficiary dies, all the assets of the trust must be distributed to that income beneficiary

4. requires an election to be made by the income beneficiary (or the income beneficiary's legal representative) to have the QSST qualify as such. (Once that election is made, it is irrevocable and can be revoked only if the IRS consents.) That election must be made by each income beneficiary as he or she becomes one. Separate elections must be made if the stock of more than one S corporation is held in the trust.

If the requirements described above are met, the income beneficiary of a QSST (which can be set up during the grantor's lifetime or by will) is treated as the owner of the stock. The consequence is that any income, as well as any gains or losses, passes directly from the S corporation to the minor beneficiary.

What are the advantages of a QSST? A gift of S corporation stock can be made to a minor through the trust without incurring the disadvantages of outright ownership. This enables an individual to split income among family members while at the same time eliminating the gift from inclusion in his gross estate. So both income shifting and wealth transfers are possible through the QSST.

Unlike a custodianship, a QSST can continue beyond age 18 (or 21) and can last as long as the grantor directed it to last. This means that if the minor dies before the trust terminates, the trust can continue for the lives of a number of successive income beneficiaries and does not have to force trust assets into the estate of the deceased income beneficiary.

The Nongrantor-Owner (Section 678) Trust

The QSST is not the only alternative to outright and UGMA or UTMA gifts. A "nongrantor-owner trust" can be an eligible S corporation stock shareholder. The criterion for favorable tax treatment under this type of trust (Section 678 governs, and therefore these nongrantor-owner trusts have come to be called "Section 678 trusts") is that the beneficiary must have unrestricted power "exercisable solely by himself to vest the corpus or the income therefrom in himself." In other words, the beneficiary will be taxed on the income from the S corporation held by the trust if he has the right to take both income and corpus whenever he wants. There must be no restrictions on the beneficiary's right to exercise a withdrawal power.

A Section 678 trust can be created by a parent or grandparent who transfers S corporation stock to it for the benefit of a minor. The minor would be given an unrestricted power to withdraw income or corpus for his own benefit.

How are gifts to QSSTs and Section 678 trusts taxed for gift tax purposes? The answer is that from a gift standpoint, a contribution to either trust will be considered a complete gift. Such gifts can qualify for the annual present-interest gift tax exclusion either by meeting the requirements of Section 2503(c) or by including a Crummey withdrawal power.

Estate Tax Implications

Will the property in a QSST or Section 678 trust be includable in the estate of a beneficiary? The answer in the case of a QSST beneficiary is that if the beneficiary is given only income rights, assets remaining in the trust at the time of the beneficiary's death will not be includable in his estate.

Just the opposite applies in the case of a Section 678 trust. Inclusion is a certainty since, by definition, the beneficiary must be given a general power of appointment (the power of withdrawal) over all or a portion of the trust. Property subject to that power at the time of the beneficiary's death will be includable in his estate.

The QSST and the Section 678 trust offer two ways to shift both business-generated income and wealth to minors at minimal gift tax cost.

Question — What are the disadvantages of a 2503(c) trust?

Answer — There are four "costs":

1. Expenses entailed in drafting ($500-$2,000).

2. Expenses involved in filing tax returns and estimated quarterly payments (cost depends on complexity of returns and time entailed).

3. A section 2503(c) trust can have only one beneficiary; this means money can't be transferred from the fund of a child who "goes astray" to the fund of a child who "has seen the light."

4. The 2503(c) trust is irrevocable; the grantor must relinquish total control to obtain tax savings.

ASRS, Sec. 51, ¶230.2(d).

Footnote References

Trust—Section 2503(b) and 2503(c)

1. Reg. §25.2503-4.
2. Rev. Rul. 74-43, 1974-1 CB 285.
3. IRC Secs. 652, 662.
4. IRC Sec. 641; Reg. §1.641(a)-2.
5. IRC Sec. 668; Regs. §§1.668(a)-1A to 1.668(b)-4A.
6. IRC Sec. 2035.
7. TIR No. 113, Nov. 26, 1958.
8. Regs. §§1.1371-1(a), 1.1371-1(d).
9. IRC Sec. 2038; Rev. Rul. 59-357, 1959-2 CB 212; Rev. Rul. 70-348, 1970-2 CB 193.
10. IRC Sec. 677.
11. *Herr v. Comm.*, 35 TC 732 (1961), aff'd. 303 F.2d 780 (3rd Cir. 1962), acq. 1968-2 CB 2. See also *Pettus v. Comm.*, 54 TC 112 (1970); *Est. of David H. Levine v. Comm.*, 526 F.2d 717 (2nd Cir. 1976), rev'g. 63 TC 136.
12. *Crummey v. Comm.*, 397 F.2d 82 (9th Cir. 1968). See Chapter 36 on Crummey trusts.
13. IRC Sec. 2514.

Chapter 40

TRUST — TAX BASIS REVOCABLE

WHAT IS IT?

Basically, the tax basis revocable trust is a revocable living trust discussed in Chapter 38. However, this form of the revocable trust is structured to achieve a step up in the income tax basis of property owned by either spouse on the death of either spouse. This is accomplished by using a general power of appointment in tandem with a marital deduction so that all of the property owned by the spouses will pass through the taxable estate of the first spouse to die. The tax basis revocable trust is a fairly recent development and there is little authority regarding use of the technique to obtain a step up in basis.

WHEN IS THE USE OF SUCH A DEVICE INDICATED?

This device may be considered in a variety of scenarios where one or both spouses own appreciated property. It is probably most advantageous where the combined estates of both spouses will be less than the available exemption equivalent provided by the unified credit (generally, a total of $1,200,000). It will also be most advantageous where one spouse owns considerably more appreciated property than the other.

WHAT ARE THE REQUIREMENTS?

This technique starts with the establishment of either one revocable trust by both spouses, or separate revocable trusts by each spouse. In one such trust that was the subject of a private letter ruling,[1] husband and wife created a joint revocable trust. Under its terms, the wife was given a general power of appointment over the assets transferred to the trust by the husband. She died without exercising that power. For federal estate tax purposes, the fact she had that power at the date of her death resulted in inclusion of the husband's property in her taxable estate.[2] Since that was true, its income tax basis would be adjusted to fair market value at the date of her death.[3]

Since the wife in this example did not exercise her general power of appointment over the property of the husband, he can still revoke the trust. As a result, the estate of the wife can claim a federal estate tax marital deduction for the value of the property passing to the husband as the surviving spouse.[4] In other words, the husband ends up with the same property he had before, but with a brand new income tax basis.

However, the IRS held that the property in question did not receive a new income tax basis at the death of the wife. It held that the provisions of Code section 1014(e) would be applicable. Under that section, if property is transferred from one spouse to another within one year of the death of the transferee spouse, and at the death of that spouse is distributed to the transferor spouse, there is no basis adjustment. Under the facts of the ruling, the property had been transferred to the trust within one year of her death.

An obvious drawback to this arrangement, in addition to the possible rejection of it by the IRS, is that the donee spouse may in fact exercise his or her power of appointment. This technique should be considered only in the case of very stable marriages.

The proponents of the technique seek to minimize this disadvantage by using one or two revocable trusts in which the general power of appointment is limited to appointment of the assets by the nonowner spouse to the creditors of the nonowner spouse. Further, the general power of appointment may be limited to a testamentary power, i.e., a power only exercisable by a will or other document at death. Further, the impact of the power may be further limited by restricting it to only certain assets, generally the ones which either have or which are most likely to appreciate in value.

HOW IT IS DONE - AN EXAMPLE

James and Martha Edwards, husband and wife, who live in a state which does not recognize community property law, create a joint revocable trust in 1995. Under its terms, either spouse can revoke the trust while alive. If it is revoked, any assets contributed to the trust by either spouse will be returned to that spouse. Upon the death of either spouse, the deceased spouse has the power to direct the payment of any of his or her debts and taxes from assets contributed to the trust by the surviving spouse.

Assume the only contributions to the trust are separate assets of James worth $500,000, with an income tax basis of $100,000. Martha dies more than one year after the transfer. Since she has a general power of appointment over the trust, i.e., a power to appoint to her creditors, the property in the trust will be included in her taxable estate and presumably its income tax basis will be adjusted to its fair market value, $500,000.

Will the property also be included in the taxable estate of James on his subsequent death? That depends on the terms of the trust. If he can still revoke the trust, it will. If he cannot revoke the trust, but the assets are transferred to a trust which qualifies as a QTIP trust (see Chapter 37), it will be if the estate of Martha elected the marital deduction.

Assuming in this case James has no other substantial assets, there may be little estate tax risk on his subsequent death. If there is, it can be solved by a qualified disclaimer by James (assuming he can disclaim, see below), or in the case of the QTIP trust, by making no QTIP election or a partial QTIP election when Martha dies.

WHAT ARE THE TAX IMPLICATIONS?

This device is entirely tax motivated. As discussed above, it requires that the revocable trust or trusts grant the spouse who does not own the property a power of appointment over it which will qualify as a general power of appointment for federal estate tax purposes. It assumes this power will not be exercised and that since the surviving spouse, who is really the owner of the property, has a power to revoke the trust, the estate of the nonowner spouse will obtain a full marital deduction for the property.

What if the owner spouse is the first to die? Since he or she has a power to revoke the trust, all of the property is included in his or her taxable estate.[5] As a result, it will obtain a new income tax basis. If the surviving nonowner spouse has a general power of appointment over the property, it should qualify for the marital deduction.[6] The problem is that in that case it will all also be taxed in the estate of the surviving nonowner spouse. As a result, this technique requires the use of qualified disclaimers, discussed in Chapter 5.

The disclaimer should be available on the death of either spouse. For example, assume the nonowner spouse dies first, and does not exercise his or her general power of appointment. The owner spouse can revoke the trust, therefore the trust assets will all become part of his or her estate. The owner spouse may be able to disclaim enough of the property to assure the use of the available unified credit of the nonowner spouse, currently as much as $600,000. That part of the property could then pass either directly to children or other family members, or to a trust for the benefit of the family. If this is effective, that part of the property will not be included

in the estate of the owner spouse and will not be subject to estate taxation.

Insofar as the authors are aware, the IRS has not ruled on whether or not the disclaimer would be effective in the foregoing situation. In effect, the owner is disclaiming an interest in property he or she already owns, not generally permitted under the disclaimer rules. However, since the IRS has conceded, in at least one private ruling, that the property passes first through the taxable estate of the nonowner spouse, the surviving owner spouse should have a disclaimer power.

The other use of the disclaimer here is in the event the owner spouse is the first to die. Since the surviving nonowner spouse has a general power of appointment over the trust, it would all pass through his or her taxable estate. The surviving nonowner spouse may disclaim a sufficient part of the property to take advantage of the available unified credit of the predeceased spouse, avoiding estate taxation to that extent. Again, the disclaimed property could pass to children, other family members, or in trust.

IMPLICATIONS AND ISSUES IN COMMUNITY PROPERTY STATES

Under applicable provisions of the Internal Revenue Code,[7] upon the death or either spouse, all of the community property owned by the spouses receives a new income tax basis equal to fair market value on the death of either spouse. Therefore, to the extent the property is community in nature, the tax basis revocable trust is not necessary. In fact, the tax basis revocable trust is often recommended as a way to achieve the same tax basis that would result if the property were community property.

Where either spouse owns separate property in a community property state, the tax basis revocable trust may be proposed as method of obtaining the income tax basis adjustment on the death of either spouse. Depending on state law, that result could also be obtained by converting the separate property to community property, which of course confers equal ownership on both spouses.

QUESTIONS AND ANSWERS

Question — Are the intended tax results of the tax basis revocable trust assured?

Answer — The only ruling on the tax consequences of this device, described above, denied the stepped up basis in trust assets on the death of the nonowner spouse. The rationale for that ruling is a statutory provision that only applies where property is transferred from one spouse to the other, the donee spouse dies, and the property is retransferred to the donor. That will not be the usual planning situation.

Also, as noted above, there may be some question as to the availability of a disclaimer by the owner spouse following the death of the nonowner spouse, on the theory that one cannot disclaim property he or she already owns. However, since that property passes first through the estate of another person, the disclaimer should be available. It should be noted the IRS now concedes that where an individual places property in joint tenancy with another person, either joint tenant could have partitioned the property at will while both tenants were alive, and the other person is the first to die, the transferor can disclaim the survivorship interest in the transferee's half of the joint tenancy.

Question — What are the advantages and disadvantages of joint trusts or separate trusts?

Answer — The joint trust is most commonly used for smaller estates where the federal estate tax is not a major factor, or where only one spouse is contributing property to the trust. Where the federal estate tax and/or contributions by both spouses are involved, many practitioners prefer the use of separate trusts.

In this scenario, each spouse contributes property to a separate trust, and retains the power to revoke it during his or her lifetime, as well as income and other benefits. After the death of the first spouse, the surviving spouse is the beneficiary of both trusts for life, and they are both structured to qualify as QTIP trusts. As in the case of the joint trust, the deceased spouse has a power to appoint appreciated assets in the survivor's trust to creditors to create a general power of appointment. Also, the surviving spouse may have a power of revocation over the trusts. The use of disclaimers and QTIP election described above will apply here.

Footnote References

Trust — Tax Basis Revocable

1. Let. Rul. 9308002.
2. IRC Sec. 2041(a)(2).
3. IRC Sec. 1014(a).
4. IRC Sec. 2056.
5. IRC Secs. 2036, 2038.
6. IRC Sec. 2056(b).
7. IRC Sec. 1014(b)(6).

Chapter 41

UNIFORM GIFTS/TRANSFERS TO MINORS ACTS

WHAT IS IT?

The revised Uniform Gifts to Minors Act (UGMA) provides that an adult, while he or she is alive, may make a gift of certain types of property, such as securities, money, or a life insurance (or annuity) contract to a minor by (depending upon the property) registering the property in the name of or delivering it to the donor (except in the case of unregistered securities) or another adult person or trust company as custodian for the minor.

Many states have amended their Acts to expand the types of property that can be the subject of a custodial gift to include real property, personal property and intangibles, and a few states permit transfers to custodians from other sources, such as trusts and estates, as well as lifetime gifts.

Following the expansive approach taken by these states, the National Conference of Commissioners on Uniform State Laws in 1983 approved the Uniform Transfers to Minors Act (UTMA). The UTMA allows any kind of property, real or personal, tangible or intangible, to be made the subject of a custodial gift, and in addition permits transfers from trusts, estates, guardianships, and from other third parties indebted to a minor who does not have a conservator. At this writing over four-fifths of the states have replaced their UGMA with the UTMA. Most of the rest will no doubt soon fall in line.

Under both the UGMA and the UTMA, the minor acquires both legal and equitable title to the subject matter of the gift.

Custodial gifts avoid many of the problems and expenses of other methods of transferring property to a minor such as outright gifts, trusts, or guardianship arrangements.

WHEN IS THE USE OF SUCH A DEVICE INDICATED?

1. When a parent would like to gift money or property for a child's benefit without giving it to him or her outright and without having to set up a trust.

2. When a parent would like to shift some of the income tax burden from his or her high tax bracket to a minor child's lower bracket.

3. When the $10,000 annual gift tax exclusion is desired.

4. When a parent would like to reduce his or her potential estate tax burden by shifting future appreciation in the value of an asset to a child.

5. Where the donor does not object to the donee's receiving the property outright upon reaching the age specified in the relevant statute — generally 18 or 21, depending on state law and often on the nature of the transaction creating the custodianship. (In several states, the age for termination of at least certain custodianships can, within limits, be changed.)

WHAT ARE THE REQUIREMENTS?

1. Property must be transferred to a custodian who holds it as custodian for the minor under the relevant state's Gifts or Transfers to Minors Act.[1]

2. If there are two or more children to whom a parent wishes to make gifts, a custodian must be appointed for each child.[2]

3. Once made, a custodial gift is irrevocable.[3]

4. The property must be distributed to the child when he or she reaches the age specified in the relevant statute — generally 18 or 21.[4] (In several states, the age for termination of at least certain custodianships can, within limits, be changed. In New York, for example, the age of termination under the act is 18, but in at least certain circumstances the donor may provide that the custodianship will last until the beneficiary reaches age 21.[5])

HOW IT IS DONE — AN EXAMPLE

Tony Arcangelo transfers his 10 shares of IBM stock to Mrs. Arcangelo as custodian for their son, Fred, by having the stock registered as follows: "Ginny Arcangelo as custodian for Fred Arcangelo under the *Pennsylvania* Uniform Transfers to Minors Act." Such a gift is a present interest gift and would qualify for the $10,000 annual gift tax exclusion. The future appreciation in the value of the stock as well as the original gifted value of the stock would be out of Mr. Arcangelo's estate. Any dividend income would be taxed to Fred. (However, see tax implications below.)

WHAT ARE THE TAX IMPLICATIONS?

1. Income from any custodial property will be taxed to the minor whether distributed or not, except to the extent it is used to discharge a legal obligation of some other person (for example, a parent's obligation to support a child). Where income produced by a custodial gift relieves an individual such as a parent of a legal obligation, the income is taxed to that person.[6]

   If the minor is under age 14, all unearned income in excess of $1,300, although it will be taxed to the minor, will be taxed at the parents' tax bracket. The first $650 of a child's unearned income will bear no tax because of the child's standard deduction. The next $650 will be taxed to the child at the child's tax bracket and any excess will be taxed to the child at the parents' bracket. For children 14 and over, all unearned income will be taxed to them at their appropriate bracket.

2. The gift is one of a present interest and qualifies for the $10,000 annual gift tax exclusion.[7] The exclusion will be allowed even if state law has lowered the age of majority to 18 and custodial property will be distributed to the donee at that age.[8] It seems, though, that extending the custodianship beyond the donee's age 21 (which some states permit) will disqualify the gift for the annual exclusion.[9] Note that there is a growing trend in state divorce courts to assume that a financially well off parent has a legal duty to send children to college, even if they are, under state law, adults. We suggest that custodial income be accumulated until the child reaches college age. Income can then be paid out, semester by semester, in a series of unconditional checks. The child should deposit those checks in his own account and use the funds as needed.

3. The value of property transferred will generally be included in the estate of a deceased minor-donee. So if the donee dies, assets in the custodial account will be includable in his or her estate.

4. Custodial property will be included in the estate of the donor if the donor appoints himself or herself as custodian and dies while serving in that capacity.[10] Likewise, if the donor becomes successor custodian and then dies, the value of the property transferred will be includable in the donor's estate.[11]

5. State gift taxes must be considered. Most states do not have gift taxes, although nearly all have some form of estate or inheritance tax. Some of the handful of states with gift taxes have annual exclusions less than the federal $10,000 exclusion.

IMPLICATIONS AND ISSUES IN COMMUNITY PROPERTY STATES

Where community property is the subject of a gift under the Uniform Gifts to Minors Act, each spouse is considered to be the donor as to one-half the value of the property given. Thus, in the example given above, if the Arcangelos lived in a community property state, Mrs. Arcangelo would not be a good choice for custodian, since if she were to die, one-half of the gift made to Fred from their community property would be included in her estate on the basis of the rules relating to revocable trusts.

The same problems as discussed in chapter 39 may arise if one spouse gives community property without the written consent of the nondonor spouse.

Typically, in community property states, a brother or sister of the parents may be a good choice for custodian.

QUESTIONS AND ANSWERS

Question — What types of property can be transferred to a custodian for the benefit of a minor?

Answer — In most states that retain the UGMA, at least money, securities (for example, stocks, bonds, evidence of indebtedness, certificate of interest or participation in an oil, gas or mining title or lease), certain life or endowment insurance policies, and certain annuity contracts may be the subject of a custodial gift.[12] The general intention of the UTMA is to allow custodial transfers of any interest in any kind of property.[13] Since the laws of different states vary, it is important to check your own state's laws.

There is a caveat with respect to gifts of insurance. Gifts of insurance are still included in the decedent's gross estate at their date of death value, regardless of the value of the policy, if the policy is transferred by the insured within three years of his death.

Question — Who may be a custodian?

Answer — Generally, the original custodian may be (depending on the transaction) the donor, an adult (generally age

18 or 21) other than the donor, a trust company, or a bank with trust powers.[14] Sometimes, the list of eligible individuals is limited to an adult member of the minor's family, and the minor's guardian. Since eligibility to serve as custodian is so dependent upon the nature of the transaction creating the custodial property, and because the states' laws vary, it is important to check your state's statute.

Question — What use may be made of custodial property?

Answer — Under the UGMA, the custodian may use the custodial property for the support, maintenance, education, and benefit of the minor to the extent that the custodian in his or her discretion deems suitable and proper.[15]

Under Section 14 of the UTMA, custodial property may be expended for the use and benefit of the minor, a more expansive use of custodial property than under the UGMA.

Question — May there be one custodial account for two or more minors?

Answer — No, a separate custodial account must be established for each beneficiary. Only one custodian can be appointed for each account.[16] However, any number of separate gifts may be made.

Question — Who receives the custodial property if a minor dies?

Answer — Custodial property passes to the administrator or executor of the minor's estate.[17]

Question — Where a life insurance policy on a minor's life is placed in a custodianship account, may the custodian be the beneficiary?

Answer — Under the UGMA, no. The beneficiary may be, depending upon the state, the minor, a member of the minor's family, or the minor's estate.[18] The situation under the UTMA is less clear. Generally a custodian can pay premiums on a custodial life insurance policy on the life of the minor only if the minor or the minor's estate is the sole beneficiary.[19] But some UTMA states let the custodian pay premiums on a custodial policy on the life of the minor even if the custodian is the beneficiary.[20] Otherwise the matter is unclear. Consult your state's statute.

Question — If a custodian dies before the minor is legally an adult, how is a successor custodian appointed?

Answer — Generally, if a custodian has designated a successor, that designee becomes the custodian. The revised UGMA seems to say that if the custodian has not picked a successor, the minor's guardian will be appointed; if there is no guardian and the minor is at least 14, the minor can pick the successor — but if the minor does not pick the successor, the court (upon petition) will designate a successor; if there is no guardian and the minor is not yet 14, the court (upon petition) will choose the successor. Under the UTMA, if the custodian has not picked a successor, the minor can pick the successor if the minor is at least 14; if the minor does not pick a successor or is less than 14, the minor's guardian will be appointed; if there is no guardian, the court (upon petition) will select a successor.[21] But the relevant state law must be checked.

Question — Must the custodian under the Uniform Gifts to Minors Act file an income tax return?

Answer — No fiduciary return is required by the custodian. This factor, as well as the fact that no trust agreement is required, makes the custodianship perhaps the least expensive and administratively the simplest method of transferring property to a minor.

Question — If an individual (an adult) purchases a life insurance policy on his or her own life, can he or she name the custodian of a minor as beneficiary?

Answer — Yes. Under the UTMA, the owner of a life insurance policy or annuity contract can name the custodian of a minor as beneficiary.[22] Some states' versions of the UGMA permit designating the custodian as beneficiary on at least some insurance policies and annuity contracts.[23] This provides a means for a child to be beneficiary without appointing a guardian or creating a trust for the minor. State laws must be checked.

Question — Under either the UGMA or UTMA can a custodian invest a minor's funds in life insurance?

Answer — Virtually all states that have a version of the UGMA or of the UTMA allow a donor to make custodial gifts of life insurance. However, not all states with versions of the UGMA specifically authorize the custodian to invest a minor's funds in life insurance. Particular state statutes must be checked.

Under the UTMA, the custodian can invest a minor's funds in life insurance. The custodian may invest in life insurance or endowment policies on

(1) The life of the minor so long as the minor or the minor's estate is the sole beneficiary

(2) The life of another person in whom the minor has an insurable interest so long as the minor, the minor's estate, or the custodian is the irrevocable beneficiary[24]

State laws must be checked.

ASRS, Sec. 48.

Footnote References

Uniform Gifts/Transfers to Minors Acts

1. E.g., 20 Pa. Cons. Stat. Ann. Sec. 5309. (Pennsylvania Uniform Transfers to Minors Act.)
2. E.g., 20 Pa. Cons. Stat. Ann. Sec. 5310.
3. E.g., 20 Pa. Cons. Stat. Ann. Sec. 5311(b).
4. E.g., 20 Pa. Cons. Stat. Ann. Sec. 5320.
5. N.Y. Est. Powers & Trusts Law Secs. 7-4.4(d), 7-4.9(d), 7-4.11.
6. Rev. Rul. 59-357, 1959-2 CB 212 (taxation of income on property transferred under statutes patterned after the Uniform Gifts to Minors Act or that act's predecessor, the Model Act Concerning Gifts of Securities to Minors); Rev. Rul. 56-484, 1956-2 CB 23 (taxation of income on property transferred under statutes patterned after the Model Act Concerning Gifts of Securities to Minors); *see also Joseph Anastasio v. Comm.*, 67 TC 814 (1977) (taxation of income on property transferred under New York Uniform Gifts to Minors Act), *aff'd without published opinion*, 573 F.2d 1287 (2d Cir. 1978).
7. Rev. Rul. 59-357, 1959-2 CB 212 (transfer of property under statutes patterned after the Uniform Gifts to Minors Act or that act's predecessor, the Model Act Concerning Gifts of Securities to Minors); Rev. Rul. 56-86, 1956-1 CB 449 (transfer of property under Colorado statute patterned after the Model Act Concerning Gifts of Securities to Minors).
8. Rev. Rul. 73-287, 1973-2 CB 321.
9. See, e.g., *id.* (gifts terminating at age 18 qualify for the annual exclusion because Code section 2503(c) requires that property pass to the donee by at least age 21).
10. Rev. Rul. 59-357, 1959-2 CB 212 (property transferred under statutes patterned after the Uniform Gifts to Minors Act or that act's predecessor, the Model Act Concerning Gifts of Securities to Minors); Rev. Rul. 57-366, 1957-2 CB 618 (property transferred under statutes patterned after the Model Act Concerning Gifts of Securities to Minors).
11. E.g., Rev. Rul. 70-348, 1970-2 CB 193 (property transferred under statute patterned after Uniform Gifts to Minors Act).
12. E.g., N.Y. Est. Powers & Trust Law Secs. 7-4.1(n) and 7-4.2(a)
13. See, e.g., the Prefatory Note to the UTMA, 8B U.L.A. 497, 499 (West 1993); UTMA Sec. 1(6) and the comment thereto, 8B U.L.A. 497, 507-508 (West 1993).
14. E.g., 20 Pa. Cons. Stat. Ann. Sec. 5309.
15. E.g., N.Y. Est. Powers & Trust Law Sec. 7-4.4(b).
16. E.g., 20 Pa. Cons. Stat. Ann. Sec. 5310.
17. E.g., 20 Pa. Cons. Stat. Ann. Sec. 5320.
18. E.g., Conn. Gen. Stat. Ann. Sec. 45a-549(j); Mich. Comp. Laws Ann. Sec. 554.454(10).
19. UTMA Sec. 12(c), 8B U.L.A. 497, 536 (West 1993).
20. See, e.g., N.C. Gen. Stat. Sec. 33A-12(c).
21. See UGMA (1966) Sec. 7, 8A U.L.A. 367, 404-405 (West 1993); UTMA Sec. 18, 8B U.L.A. 497, 548-549 (West 1993).
22. See UTMA Secs. 3, 9(a)(4), 8B U.L.A. 497, 515, 525 (West 1993).
23. See, e.g., Del. Code Ann., tit. 12, Secs. 4501(8), 4501(12), 4501(13), 4502(a)(5).
24. UTMA Sec. 12(c), 8B U.L.A. 497, 536 (West 1993).

Chapter 42

VALUATION PLANNING

WHAT IS IT?

Valuation planning describes any technique used to affect the valuation of property or business interests for gift, estate, or generation-skipping transfer tax purposes. Since the basis for valuation of assets for these purposes is fair market value, which is defined in regulations as what a willing buyer would pay a willing seller, it may be possible to undertake planning moves which can actually reduce the value of the property, and thus reduce federal transfer taxes.

WHAT ARE THE REQUIREMENTS

The client transfers interests in property to other family members, thus reducing the value of the interests in the same property retained by the client. In fact, since the transferred interests represent less than 100 percent ownership of the property, even the transferred interests have a lower value. By fractionalizing the ownership of the property or business interests through transfers to family members, the client reduces the value of the property or business interests for gift and estate tax purposes.

HOW IT IS DONE — AN EXAMPLE

Client owns 100 percent of the stock in a closely held corporation, which is engaged in real estate development. He transfers 10 percent interests to each of his children, either outright or in trust. Since the transferred interests are minority interests, the value of the stock for gift tax purposes may be reduced. Further, since the client now owns 70 percent rather than 100 percent of the business, the value of his interest may also be reduced, since he is no longer able to sell the entire business unless his children agree.

WHAT ARE THE TAX IMPLICATIONS?

Introduction

Valuing property for federal gift, estate, and generation-skipping transfer tax purposes is a most complex and often uncertain process. Frequently the taxpayer's valuation has differed widely from the value established by the Internal Revenue Service. Courts will then be asked to resolve the valuation question.

Thus, value is a variable upon which reasonable minds can and will continue to differ. But value is not determined by a mere flip of the coin. The use of careful and thorough appraisals by qualified experts, documentation of sales of similar property recently sold, and well drawn arm's length restrictive agreements (such as a buy-sell arrangement) have proved effective tools in substantiating favorable values.

General Valuation Rules

The Internal Revenue Code says very little about how to value items includable in the gross estate for federal estate tax purposes. Although the Code speaks of the "value" of the gross estate, there is no place in the Code where the word "value" is defined.

The general rule: "Value" is "fair market value," "the price at which the property would change hands between a willing buyer and a willing seller, neither being under any compulsion to buy or to sell and both having reasonable knowledge of relevant facts." Thus, the value a particular person would place on property may vary greatly from the measure of worth placed on that same item by the Government. In fact, it is neither necessary that there be an established market for an item, nor that there be the "willing buyer and seller" spoken of in the Regulations. In the absence of an actual sale, the value is based on a hypothetical sale.

Generally, when an organized market does in fact exist, the market price will prevail. The ignorance of a material fact by the buying public or its inability to properly assess the significance of certain events does not form a basis for reducing the price indicated on the organized market. The contrary result applies in the absence of an established market. A purchase or sale is not regarded as determinative of value in situations in which one of the parties was ignorant of a material fact.

The following external factors have had varying effects on the probative value of sales: (a) the frequency of sales (the courts tend to disregard isolated or sporadic sales); (b) the relationship between the buyer and the seller (it is unusual for sales between parents and children or employers and employees to be given great weight in the light of their almost definitional unequal bargaining positions); (c) offers to purchase or sell (offers as opposed to options present little evidence of value).

Not only should all the factors affecting value be considered, but there should be sound reasoning for the relative weight given to each one.

Determining Value

The Internal Revenue Service would likely consider all the facts and circumstances which a hypothetical buyer and seller would consider. The derived price at which the property would have changed hands between parties "X" and "Y" thus determines the Service's valuation. By this rule, a forced sale—or a sale outside of regular business channels—would not be determinative of the value.[1] Thus, generally, the Service's position is that the price at which the item or a comparable item would have been sold at retail is determinative.

Value is basically a question of fact in those situations where there is an established market for identical property. But valuation problems become essentially problems of evidential proof (and often, opinion) where:

1. There are different markets for the same property, such as in the case of a property with both wholesale and retail markets.

2. The appraisal of the worth must be made on the basis of comparison with somewhat similar property (which properties should be selected?; how comparable is it?). What is derived is at best an opinion based upon fact.

3. The property in question is unique, such as a patent or copyright. Here, the data must be analyzed (is the examiner capable of making an adequate analysis?), and an opinion must be formulated as to how much the potential anticipated benefits are worth.

Since in practice valuation problems are frequently viewed by the Service and the courts as problems of negotiation and compromise, the appraiser's object should be to derive a fair and sound value which, if litigated, would be sustained by the court. Evidence and proof secured in the form of expert advice through appraisal, promptly after death, would likely have a greater probative value than evidence obtained at a later date. (As to the valuation of specific types of property, one must turn to the regulations, rulings and court decisions.)

Date Assets are Valued

Generally, federal estate taxes are based either on the fair market value of the transferred property as of the date the decedent died or the value of the property six months after the date of the decedent's death (alternate valuation date).[2] Once selected for valuation purposes — date of death or alternate valuation — such date applies to all assets in the estate.

If the alternate valuation date is selected and if the property is distributed, sold, exchanged, or otherwise disposed of within six months of the decedent's death, it will be valued as of that date, not the six month date.[3] Certain types of property diminish in value as time goes on; for example, the present value of an annuity reduces each time a payment is made. Any such property interest or estate whose value is affected by the mere passing of time is valued as of the date the decedent died.[4]

Valuation of Real Property

Because of the uniqueness of land, the value of any real property as of a given date may be subject to widely differing opinions. Absent a market for such property, the greater of (a) the highest price available or (b) the salvage value will control. Where there is a market for real property, the basic factors that affect valuation are:

1. The nature and condition of the property, its physical qualities and defects, and the adequacy or inadequacy of its improvements.

2. The size, shape, and location of the property.

3. The actual and potential use of the property and how the trends of development and economic conditions (such as population growth) affect it.

4. How suitable the property is for its actual or intended use.

5. Zoning restrictions.

6. Size, age, and condition of the buildings (degree of deterioration and obsolescence).

7. The market value of other properties in the area in which the property is located.

8. The value of net income received from the property. Rentals are often capitalized and then adjusted for depreciation. (See discussion of capitalization of income, below.) The same principle can be applied to gross rents. This method, however, must be adjusted to account for operating costs.

9. The value accepted by state probate courts for purposes of state death taxes, if based on appraisals made by qualified real estate experts.

10. Prices at which comparable property in the same area was sold at a time near the applicable valuation date (providing it was an arm's length transaction for the best price obtainable). Usually more than one "comparable property" sale will be used, especially where the property to be valued is a personal residence or undeveloped acreage.

11. How much, taking depreciation into account, would it cost to duplicate the property? The cost or value of land would have to be separated from the total value. The cost of reproducing the building, using present cost figures, would have to be estimated, and then the loss in value due to depreciation would have to be subtracted from the total of the other two figures.

12. Unusual facts.

In the event of a sale of real property within a reasonable period of time after the decedent's death, in such a manner as to insure the highest possible price, the amount received will usually be accepted as its value. Unaccepted offers to purchase the property will also be considered. What of a sale at auction? Usually, this price will be accepted only if it appears that there was no other method that would have obtained a higher price.

Land does not have to produce income or have an active market to attain substantial value. Where lands are in or adjacent to a settled community, owners frequently hold such lands in anticipation of realizing their true value from future sales. For example, a home at the edge of an expanding shopping center might be worth far more to the shopping center developer than it would to a potential buyer in the residential market.

Special Valuation of Certain Farm and Business Real Property

An executor may elect to value qualifying real property on the basis of its actual "special" use rather than its "highest and best" use. This rule, especially useful where the price of farmland is artificially increased by, or has not kept up with, the price per acre of encroaching housing developments, enables the executor to value the farmland at its value for farming purposes. The maximum reduction of the decedent's gross estate under this provision is $750,000.

The following are the qualification requirements:

1. On the date of the decedent's death, the property must be involved in a "qualified use." That term is defined by Code section 2032A(b)(2) as use as a farm for farming purposes or in a trade or business other than farming.

2. The value of the qualified property (less debts or unpaid mortgages) in the decedent's estate must equal at least 50% of the decedent's gross estate (less debts or unpaid mortgages).

3. At least 25% of the gross estate (less debts and unpaid mortgages on all property in the gross estate) must be qualified farm or closely held business real property.

4. Such property must pass to a "qualified heir." This term is defined at section 2032A(e) to include the decedent's immediate family plus his ancestors or lineal descendants, his spouse or the spouse of a descendant, or a lineal descendant of a grandparent.

5. The real property must have been owned by the decedent or a member of his family and used as a farm or in a closely held business for an aggregate of five years or more of the eight year period ending on the date of the decedent's death. During this period the decedent or a member of his family must have been a material participant in the operation of the farm or other business.

If the above conditions are met, the property qualifies for the special valuation rule.

Then if the executor elects to apply section 2032A, the value for a farm is determined as follows:

A. Average annual gross cash rental for comparable land.

B. Average annual state and local real estate taxes for such comparable land.

C. Average annual effective interest rate for all new Farm Credit Bank Loans.

Formula: $\dfrac{A\text{-}B}{C}$ = value for section 2032A purposes.

This formula provides that the income that is to be capitalized is the average annual gross cash rental income (for five years prior to the decedent's death) less the average annual state and local real estate taxes (for the same five year period) for that comparable land.

"Comparable land" is (1) land used for farming purposes and (2) must also be located in the same vicinity as the farmland to be valued. If there is no comparable land, or if the executor chooses to have the farm valued in the manner of a qualifying closely-held business, other factors are applied.

Figure 42.1

Determination of Whether Estate Qualifies for Current Use
Valuation of Farm Real Estate or Business Real Estate
(Husband's)(Wifes's) Estate When (He)(She) Dies (First)(Second)

Less

(1) Gross estate (Form 102, line 1)* .... $_____

(2) Unpaid mortgages or indebtedness on property
included in estate at gross value
(Fact Finder, pp. 4, 5, 6, 20) .... $_____

Equals

(3) Adjusted value of gross estate .... $_____

(4) 50% of adjusted value of gross estate .... $_____

(5) 25% of adjusted value of gross estate .... $_____

(6) Value of real and personal property of
farm or closely held business
(Fact Finder, pp. 4 & 5) .... $_____

Less

(7) Unpaid mortgages or indebtedness on farm
or closely held business real or personal
property included in estate at gross value
(Fact Finder, pp. 4, 5, 6, 20) .... $_____

Equals

(8) Adjusted value of real and personal property
of farm or closely held business .... $_____

(9) Qualified real property (Form 101) .... $_____

Less

(10) Unpaid mortgages or indebtedness on qualified
real property included in estate at gross value
(Fact Finder, pp. 4, 5, 20) .... $_____

Equals

(11) Adjusted value of qualified real property .... $_____

REAL PROPERTY OF FARM OR CLOSELY HELD BUSINESS QUALIFIES FOR CURRENT-USE VALUATION IF LINE 8 EQUALS OR EXCEEDS LINE 4 **AND** LINE 11 EQUALS OR EXCEEDS LINE 5.

This also assumes that (a) the decedent was a U.S. citizen or resident, (b) the real property passes to a qualified heir, and (c) for 5 out of the last 8 years before the decedent's death, the real property was used in the farm or closely held business, and the decedent or a family member materially participated in the farm or business operation.

*The full highest and best-use value and not the current-use value is used in determining the value of the gross estate for the 50% and 25% tests.

© 1983 by The American College as part of Advanced Estate Planning I and II courses.

FORM 108B

Figure 42.2

Special Use (2032A) Valuation

Input: **Capitalization Rate** 0.0920

	Years Prior To Death		Gross Rent Comparable Land		Real Estate Taxes	Capitalized Value
Input:	1995	Input:	$120,000	Input:	$5,000	$1,250,000
	1994		$90,000		$4,500	$929,349
	1993		$80,000		$4,000	$826,087
	1992		$70,000		$3,500	$722,826
	1991		$60,000		$3,000	$619,565
	Totals		$420,000		$20,000	
	Five Yr. Average		$84,000		$4,000	

Special (Current) Use Value $869,565

Source: NumberCruncher Software

The executor may not use cash rentals from the farm to be valued. The rentals used from comparable farmland must have been the result of arm's length bargaining.

The capitalization rate, the average annual effective interest rate on new Farm Credit Bank loans, is the average billing rate charged on new agricultural loans to farmers in the farm credit district in which the qualified property is located. These amounts are published by the IRS according to the Farm Credit Bank district in which property is located. A reproduction of the relevant parts of the latest ruling on this topic follows.

In order to determine the special use value of a farm under the formula method the average annual effective interest rates on new Farm Credit Bank loans to be used for estates of decedents dying in 1995 are as follows:

Federal Credit Bank District in Which Property is Located	Interest Rates Year of Death '95
Baltimore	8.93%
Columbia	9.20%
Omaha	8.63%
Sacramento	9.87%
St. Paul	9.03%
Spokane	8.97%
Springfield	8.90%
Texas	9.28%
Wichita	8.79%

These are the states within each Farm Credit Bank district:

District	States
Baltimore	Delaware, District of Columbia, Maryland, Pennsylvania, Virginia, West Virginia.
Columbia	Florida, Georgia, North Carolina, South Carolina.
Omaha	Iowa, Nebraska, South Dakota, Wyoming.
Sacramento	Arizona, California, Hawaii, Nevada, Utah.
St. Paul	Arkansas, Illinois, Indiana, Kentucky, Michigan, Minnesota, Missouri, North Dakota, Ohio, Tennessee, Wisconsin.
Spokane	Alaska, Idaho, Montana, Oregon, Washington.
Springfield	Connecticut, Maine, Massachusetts, New Hampshire, New Jersey, New York, Rhode Island, Vermont.
Texas	Alabama, Louisiana, Mississippi, Texas.
Wichita	Colorado, Kansas, New Mexico, Oklahoma.

The following example assumes a capitalization rate of 9.2%.

$$\frac{A-B}{C} = \text{value for section 2032A purposes.}$$

$$\frac{\$84,000 - \$4,000}{9.20\%} = \$869,565$$

If there is no comparable land, or if the executor elects to have the farm valued in the manner of a qualifying closely held business, then the following factors shall apply.

1. The capitalization of income that the property can be expected to yield for farming or closely held business purposes over a reasonable period of time under prudent management using traditional cropping patterns for the area, taking into account soil capacity, terrain configuration and other factors.

2. The capitalization of the fair rental value of the land for farmland or closely held business purposes.

3. Assessed land values in a state which provides a differential or use value assessment law for farmland or real estate owned by a closely held business.

4. Comparable sales of other farms or closely held business land in the same geographical area far enough removed from a metropolitan or resort area so that nonagricultural use is not a significant factor in the sales price.

5. Any other factor which fairly values the farm or closely held business value of the property.

If a farm or a closely held business qualified for the special valuation rules and its value so determined is used for federal estate tax purposes, then an additional estate tax will be imposed if within 10 years after the decedent's death and before the death of the qualified heir, the qualified heir who receives such property disposes of any interest in that property, other than to a qualified family member, or ceases to use that property in the manner in which it was used to qualify for this special tax treatment.

Generally, the additional tax imposed shall be the excess of the tax that would have been imposed on the property if it was valued at its best use over the tax imposed because the property was valued at its "qualified use" value.

If the additional tax is imposed, it is due six months after the date of the disposition of the property or the cessation of its use as a farm or as part of the closely held business. The qualified heir who received such property is personally liable for the additional tax imposed.

Valuation of Life Insurance

Proceeds of life insurance on the life of the decedent receivable by or for the benefit of his estate will be taxed in the insured decedent's estate.[5] In addition, where the decedent held incidents of ownership, such ownership will invoke taxation.[6] The amount includable is the amount receivable by the beneficiary. This includes dividends and premium refunds. In determining how much is includable, no distinction is made between an ordinary life policy, a term policy, group insurance, or an accidental death benefit.

If a settlement option is elected, the amount that would have been payable as a lump sum is the amount includable. If the policy did not provide for a lump sum payment, the amount includable is the commuted amount used by the insurance company to compute the settlement option payments.

The value of an unmatured policy owned by a decedent on the life of another is included in the policy owner's gross estate where he predeceases the insured.

1. If a new policy is involved, the gross premium paid would be the value.

2. If the policy is paid-up or a single premium policy, its value is its replacement cost, that is, the single premium which that company would have charged for a comparable contract of equal face value on the life of a person who was the insured's age (at the time the decedent-policyholder died).

3. If the policy is an established whole life policy, the value is found by adding any unearned portion of the last premium to the interpolated terminal reserve.

4. If the policy is a term policy, the value is the unused premium.

Valuation of U.S. Government Bonds

Series E bonds are valued at their redemption price (market value) as of the date of death since they are neither negotiable nor transferable and the only definitely ascertainable value is the amount at which the Treasury will redeem them.

Certain U.S. Treasury Bonds (so-called "flower bonds") owned by a decedent at the date of death and forming part of his gross estate, may be redeemed at par value if used to pay federal estate taxes. These bonds are valued at the higher of the market price or par value.[7]

Even if such bonds are not used to pay estate taxes, the courts have often held that where the bonds could have been used for the payment of estate taxes, to that extent they will be valued at the higher of the market or par value.[8] Where the bonds could not be applied to pay the estate tax, their value is market (the mean quoted selling price).

Valuation of Household and Personal Effects

The general rule for valuing household property and personal effects such as watches, rings, etc., is: the "willing buyer-willing seller" rule. A room by room itemization is typical, especially where household goods include articles of artistic or intrinsic value such as jewelry, furs, silverware, paintings, engravings, antiques, books, statuary, oriental rugs, coin or stamp collections.

In other than community property states, "household goods" and like personalty acquired by and used by husband and wife during marriage are generally presumed to be the property of the husband. Therefore, in the absence of sufficient evidence to rebut this presumption, household goods and personal effects would be includable in the husband's estate.

Valuation of Annuities, Life Estates, Terms for Years, Remainders and Reversions

Commercial annuities (annuities under contracts issued by companies regularly engaged in their sale) are valued by reference to the price at which the company issues comparable contracts. A retirement income policy, from the point in time that there is no longer an insurance element, is treated as a contract for the payment of an annuity.

Where the annuity is noncommercial, such as a private annuity, the present value of future payments determines its fair market value. Likewise, for gift and estate tax purposes, the fair market value of life estates, terms for years, remainders, and reversions is their present value.

An annuity is defined as a systematic liquidation of principal and interest. Payments might be made for the life of the annuitant (life annuity) or over a period of years (term certain).

A life estate is a disposition of property in which the primary beneficiary receives distributions of only income. Payments might be made for the life of the recipient or could be based on the life of a third party but the income beneficiary of a life estate receives no right to enjoy the principal. In other words, a life estate is the right of a person for his life, or for the life of another person, to receive the income from or the use of certain property. An example would be, "I give my home to my wife for life." The wife's interest would be a life estate. At her death, the property would go to some other party, called a "remainderman," or revert to the grantor.

In the case of a term certain arrangement, the present value of income for a given number of years is found in a like manner.

A remainder (the beneficiary gets the principal after a third party has enjoyed the income for life, or for a given period of time) is actuarially equivalent to a "reversion." An example of a remainder would be "to my son John, for life, remainder to Mary." Instead of coming back to the grantor (a reversion) the property "remains" away from the grantor and goes instead to Mary. Mary is said to have a remainder interest. An example of a reversion is where the principal (after a given beneficiary has enjoyed an income for life or for a given period) "reverts" to the grantor. If the grantor dies before the person enjoying the lifetime interest, his right to "will" that reversion to his heirs, who will some day receive the principal, is valued under the same rules as annuities, remainders, and life estates.

Annuities, life estates, reversions, remainders, and terms for years are valued according to a discount rate which changes monthly.

The first step in valuing an annuity based on a life (or on the joint lives of two or more people), a life estate, or a reversion or remainder based on a life (or joint lives) is to convert one of the unknowns (the length of the lifetime involved) to a known (life expectancy). This is done by means of a mortality table, which, based on a study of the longevities of a large number of people over a selected period of time, indicates the expectancy of life (in years) for a mythical individual who represents the average experience at each age of life.

The second step is to determine a proper discount interest rate (the second unknown that should be attributed to the interest being valued). When that interest rate is determined, a valuation table can be constructed which converts the two factors to be applied, life expectancy and the rate of interest, into one factor to be applied to the amount of the periodic payment, to determine the present worth or value of the property interest.

The valuation tables in Appendix D (Tables B and S) are used to do term and life computations. A more detailed explanation for use for the tables can be found there.

Valuation must be based on an interest rate (rounded to the nearest $2/10$ths of one percent) equal to 120 percent of the federal midterm rate in effect for the month in which the valuation date falls.

Two qualifications need to be added to this explanation of the law respecting valuation. First, these valuation provisions do not apply to interests valued with respect to qualified plans (including tax sheltered annuities and IRAs) or in other situations specified in Treasury regulations. Second, if an income, estate, or gift tax charitable contribution is allowable for any part of the property transferred, the taxpayer may elect to use the discount rate for either of the two months preceding the month in which the valuation date falls. However, if a transfer of more than one interest in the same property is made with respect to which the taxpayer could use the same interest rate, such interest rate is to be used with respect to each such interest.[9]

Valuation of Listed Stocks

Where a stock has an established market and quotations are available to value the stock as of the date in question, the fair market value per share on the applicable valuation date governs for both gift and estate tax purposes.

The FMV is based on selling prices when there is a market for the stock or bond. This would be the mean between the highest and lowest quoted selling price on the valuation date. If there were no sales on the valuation date, but there were sales on dates within a reasonable period both before and after the valuation date, the FMV is determined by taking a weighted average of the means between the highest and lowest sales on the nearest date before and the nearest date after the valuation. The average is then weighted inversely by the respective number of trading days between the selling date and the valuation date.

Where there is a large block of stock which could not be marketed in an orderly manner, the block might depress the market because it could not be converted to cash as readily as could a few shares. Therefore, selling prices and bid and asked prices may not reflect fair market value. Sometimes it may be necessary to value this type of stock as if it were closely held and not actively traded. If this can be established, a reasonable modification of the normal basis for determining FMV can be made. In some cases, a "blockage" discount is determined by the effect that block would have had on the market if it were sold over a reasonable period of time and in a prudent manner.[10] A similar situation occurs where sales at or near the date of death are few or of a sporadic nature and may not indicate a fair market value.[11]

The converse of the "blockage" situation above is where the block of stock to be valued represents a control-ling interest (either actual or effective) in a going business. Here, the price of normally traded shares may have little relation to the true value of the controlling lot. The large block could have the effect of increasing value because of its element of control.

Valuation of Corporate Bonds

The valuation of bonds is similar to that of listed common stock. The means of the selling prices on or near the applicable valuation date, or, if there were no sales, the means of bona fide asked prices weighted inversely to the number of trading days from the valuation date will determine the fair market value of the bonds.

In the absence of sales or bid and asked prices, the value must be determined by:

(1) Ascertaining the soundness of the security.

(2) Comparing the interest yield on the bond in question to yields on similar bonds.

(3) Examining the date of maturity.

(4) Comparing prices for listed bonds of corporations engaged in similar types of business.

(5) Checking the extent to which the bond is secured.

(6) Weighing all other relevant factors including the opinion of experts, the good will of the business, the industry's economic outlook, the company's position in the industry and its management.

Valuation of Interests in Closely Held Corporations

There are at least seven situations in which the estate planner must value a business or professional practice. Valuation plays a critical role when a planner needs to

• plan for a client's estate liquidity

• establish a price for buy-sell purposes (should a buy-out be necessitated by death, disability or other health problems, retirement, or lifetime termination of relationship (e.g., sale of an interest in the business or practice to a third party)

• properly recognize the business's or practice's worth in a client's prenuptial or postnuptial agreement

- apportion assets in a marital dissolution

- ascertain the worth of the business or practice as loan collateral

- perform a "fiscal checkup" to test the financial health of a client's business or practice, detect adverse financial trends, or uncover opportunities (for instance, a doctor might find that patients are getting older and the business or practice should try to attract younger people or can profitably move into a new area of specialty)

- prepare an estate tax valuation

In the settlement of many estates, the valuation of closely held corporate stock can be a most difficult, time-consuming, and costly problem, especially when a confrontation arises between the Executor and the Internal Revenue Service. But careful use of a properly drafted restrictive business agreement can help alleviate and control the problem.

What exactly is "closely held stock"? Various criteria have been used to define such stock. Some of these are: (a) the number of stockholders; (b) restrictions imposed on a shareholder's ability to transfer the stock; (c) absence of exchange listing or regular quotation in the "over-the-counter" market; (d) an irregular, limited history of sales or exchanges.

For general purposes, however, stock can be considered "closely held" where there is some question as to whether its value can be found solely by reference to an established market. The problem of valuing closely held stock is compounded because, by definition, such stock is seldom traded.

The relevant Internal Revenue Code Sections and Regulations[12] are of little help. They are so vague and general that their application to a specific valuation question is of minimal planning value.

Valuing Stock and Partnership Interests for Estate Planning Purposes

Basic factors to consider. The fair market value of a closely held corporation or partnership is determined in the same manner as stock in a professional practice. Reg. §20.2031-3; Rev. Rul. 80-202, 1980-2 CB 363. In determining the value of a closely held business, Rev. Rul. 59-60, 1959-1 CB 237, the master guideline for valuing all businesses, requires that eight factors must be considered:

- *Nature of the business and the history of the enterprise from its inception.* This factor measures the risk, stability, depth of management of the business, and the diversity of its operations. With respect to the valuation of a professional practice, the appraiser should review the stability of the practice's financial history, its growth patterns, changes in ownership, market share, marketing approach, and "product" breakdown. For example, is this a law practice that does 70 percent negligence and personal injury work, 20 percent financial and estate planning, and 10 percent real estate? Significant events should be emphasized and events not likely to recur should be eliminated.

- *Economic outlook in general and for the specific industry in particular.* Here, the appraiser must evaluate the "industry" outlook and the position of the practitioner with reference to his competition. The appraiser should consider the cyclical nature of the practitioner's business, the direction of the national economy, and any unique elements in the professional's practice position.

- *Book value of the stock and the financial condition of the business.* The appraiser here must consider the asset value of the professional's practice. Note that the professional's statements are historical-cost based; they should be adjusted to reflect fair market value. Depreciation as recorded under generally accepted accounting principles need not bear any relationship to economic depreciation and the true net value of the assets under consideration.

- *Earnings capacity of the company.* The earnings of a professional practice have been held by many valuation authorities to be the essence of its fair market value, since "everyone knows that the value of shares in a ... company depends chiefly on what it will earn." (Judge Learned Hand in *Borg v. Int'l Silver*, 11 F.2d 147 (1925).) What is at issue is earnings *capacity*, future income potential, not net income. Adjustments should be made for salaries, travel, and entertainment expenses, nonrecurring items, and potential legal and tax liabilities. In a corporate setting, note that loans to shareholders may represent disguised dividends; loans from shareholders may represent equity rather than debt.

- *Dividend paying capacity.* The emphasis again is on *capacity*, not actual payout. With the professional corporation, the appraiser should focus on cash flow projections and relate dividend capacity to earnings capacity, with due consideration for the need to reinvest in the professional's practice.

- *Goodwill or intangible values.* Goodwill has been extensively discussed above. In its simplest form, goodwill is the excess earnings of the practice over the normal return on tangible assets. Note that the normal return should be the "fair rate of return" earned by comparable practitioners. Tangible assets should be valued at their fair market value rather than at historically based book value.

- *Sales of the stock and the size of the block to be valued.* Here, recent sales are most important. Has the interest in the practice been sold to insiders? What percentage of the practice has been sold? Have there been any recent events since the sale that would affect significantly the value of the practice?

- *The market price of stock of corporations engaged in the same or a similar line of business having their stock traded in a free and open market.* This factor is extremely difficult to apply to professional practices. Few professional practices exist as public corporations. Those that do rarely are comparable to closely held professional practices. A publicly held practice by definition has a value premium for marketability.

The following discussion summarizes four often-used approaches to business valuation: (1) book value, (2) comparable company, (3) capitalization of income, and (4) going concern value.

(1) Book Value

Book value (essentially assets minus liabilities) is a particularly good place to begin the process of valuing a closely held corporation in each of the following situations:

1. Where the business in question is primarily an asset holding company—such as an investment company.

2. Where the company is in the real estate development business and assets are the major profit making factor.

3. Where one person is the sole or major driving force since such businesses are typically worth only their liquidation value upon the death, disability, or termination of employment of such a person.

4. Where the liquidation of the corporation is in process or imminent at the valuation date. The impact of sacrifice sales and capital gains taxation must often be considered since the true value of a liquidating business is only the amount available to shareholders after all expenses and taxes.

5. Where the business is highly competitive but only marginally profitable. Past profits thus become an unreliable tool to measure potential future earnings.

6. Where the assets or the business itself is relatively new.

7. Where some form of merger is likely to occur with another firm.

8. Where the business is experiencing large deficits.

Book value must be adjusted since the assets of most businesses are usually carried on the company's books at historical cost rather than fair market value.

Adjustments are recommended in the following cases:

1. When assets are valued at cost. For instance, the primary assets of a closely held investment company consist of marketable securities. These are typically carried on the company's books at cost. Likewise, land is an asset most companies will carry at cost but which may be worth considerably more on the open market. The result is a book value which bears little or no relationship to the true present worth of the business.

2. When assets have been depreciated at a rate in excess of their true decline in economic value. A good example is the operating company (one which produces or sells products or services to the public) that has purchased machinery or equipment originally costing $1,000,000 but which, on the company's books, has been depreciated down to $300,000. The equipment may be worth a lot more or a lot less than either its cost or the $300,000 figure at which it is presently carried.

3. When items such as potential lawsuits or unfavorable long-term leases have not been shown in the footnotes of the firm's balance sheet.

4. When one or more assets with significant economic value have been completely "written off"—thus reflecting a book value far below the price which they should realistically bring.

5. When the business has carried assets such as franchises and goodwill on the books at a nominal cost.

6. When the business experiences difficulty in collecting its accounts receivable.

7. When the firm's inventory includes goods that are either obsolete or for some other reason are not readily marketable.

8. Where the working capital or liquidity position of the business is poor (low current assets relative to current liabilities).

9. Where the firm is burdened with a substantial amount of long-term indebtedness.

10. Where the retained earnings are high only because they have been accumulated over a long period of time. Such a business may have poor current earnings and the outlook for increased earnings in the future may be dim.

After the adjustments described above have been made, the value of any other class of stock with a priority as to dividends, voting rights, or preference to assets in the event of a sale or liquidation must be subtracted. For example, the owner of common stock can't realize the value of the assets until owners of preferred stock have been satisfied.

Once the adjusted book value has been determined for the entire business, it is then necessary to divide the book value by the number of shares outstanding to determine the value per share.

Book value should rarely be used as the only means of valuing a closely-held business. It should be used in conjunction with or as a means of testing the relevancy of the capitalization of earnings and other methods. (Be sure not to "double count" an asset when combining two or more methods).

Book value should not be used when capital plays a minor role in profit making or where you are valuing the stock of a party who does not have the voting power to force liquidation, since in that case book values have little relevance.

Book Value Calculation

Input:	"Adjusted" Asset Value of	
	Common Stock	$500,000
Input:	Total Adjusted Liabilities	$100,000
Input:	Par Value of Preferred Stock	$50,000
	Total Deductions	$150,000
	Adjusted Book Value of Entire	
	Business	$350,000
Input:	Number of Common Shares	
	Outstanding	1,000
	Value Per Share of Common Stock	$350.00

(2) Valuation By Reference To Comparable (Traded Securities) Companies

A business can sometimes be valued by reference to the value of a comparable company if the stock of that second company is listed, and actively traded, on a securities exchange or on the over-the-counter (OTC) market.

The price per share of the publicly traded stock is divided by its earnings per share. The resulting ratio is then applied to the earnings per share of the business to be valued in order to arrive at the market value per share.

Comparable traded securities research should start with federal government publications such as the *Standard Industrial Classification* manual (which categorizes industries), the *S.E.C. Directory of Companies Required to File Annual Reports* (which, as its name implies, lists companies which must file reports under various S.E.C. acts), the U.S. Department of Commerce, *Census of Business* (which is a compilation of statistics and ratios on various businesses), Dun & Bradstreet's *Dun's Review* (which gives key operating and financial ratios), Moody's *Investors Service and Manual* (which provides a detailed description of many publicly held corporations), and Standard & Poor's *Corporation Records* (which provides financial and operating ratios for many corporations).

Be sure to check trade magazines for the industry in question. Many associations also provide detailed information for members of their industry.

In searching for comparable companies, look for similarities in product line, service, size, marketing and geographic area, growth, profitability, overhead, and competitive position. Examine balance sheets and income statements (use the ratios template) to compare ratios and trends. Seldom, if ever, will a perfect match be found and many adjustments may have to be made even after a "close fit" is found.

This technique has a number of shortcomings: first, it is difficult to use. Second, an enormous expenditure of time and effort is required to compile accurate and adequate information concerning the business to be valued, the comparable business or businesses, and then to analyze and evaluate the data.

The larger the closely-held business, the more likely this approach will be appropriate since the size, corporate capital structure, earnings, liabilities, rate of growth, and diversification are more likely to be comparable to a publicly traded company.

Value Per Share of Closely Held Stock

Input: Per Share Market Price of Similar
        Publicly Traded Company $45.00

Input: Earnings Per Share of Similar
        Publicly Traded Company $4.50

Input: Earnings Per Share of Business
        to be Valued $14.00

        Computed Price/Earnings Ratio 10.00

        Equivalent Capitalization Rate 0.10

        Value Per Share of Closely
        Held Business $140.00

(3) Capitalization of Income

No formula exists that applies to all assets and that will be accepted by both the IRS and the courts. Converting the projected flow of income from a business or asset into its present value, i.e., "capitalizing the income," provides a

simple, reasonably accurate, and commonly accepted way of estimating fair market value.

The concept of income capitalization is simple: determine what amount of income is realistic and proper under the circumstances and then apply a capitalization rate that meets the same criterion. In essence the capitalization rate is the desired rate of return; the rate of return an investor would be willing to accept for the given level of risk. A high risk investment would equate to a high capitalization rate (which in turn results in a lower value). The asset or business is then presumed to be worth the result when adjusted earnings are divided by the capitalization rate.

The graph at Figure 42.3 illustrates the valuation of a business generating adjusted earnings of $100,000 a year using ten different capitalization rates.

Transforming theory into practice is often complex and frustrating. The brief comments below, pertaining to "adjust-

Figure 42.3

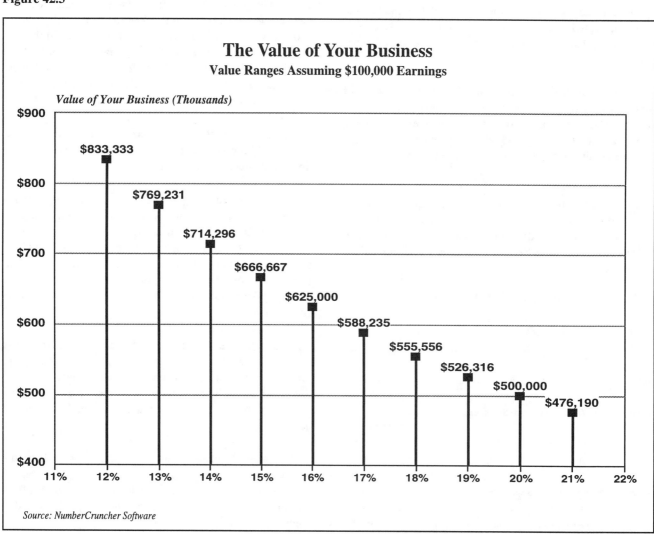

The Value of Your Business
Value Ranges Assuming $100,000 Earnings

Value of Your Business (Thousands)

Source: NumberCruncher Software

ing" the earnings and selecting the appropriate rate of return may help:

(A) Adjustments to income (in the case of a business, use five year average after-tax profits):

(1) Add back excessive salaries

(2) Reduce earnings if salaries were too low

(3) Add back bonuses paid to stockholder-employees

(4) Add back excessive rents paid to shareholders

(5) Reduce earnings where rents paid to shareholders were below what was reasonable in the market

(6) Eliminate nonrecurring income or expense items

(7) Adjust for excessive depreciation

(8) Adjust earnings for major changes in accounting procedures, widely fluctuating or cyclical profits, or abnormally inflated (or deflated) earnings.

(9) If there has been a strong upward or downward earnings trend, "weight the average" to obtain a more realistic appraisal of the company's prospects.

(B) Determine the capitalization rate (this is the amount that is divided into adjusted earnings). The result is the same as multiplying the reciprocal of the rate, (the result of dividing the number one by 5). In other words, you obtain the same result by multiplying $100,000 of income by 5 as you do if you divide the income by .20.

In deciding on a capitalization rate, consider the following:

(1) A smaller capitalization rate will result in a higher value. A higher capitalization rate results in a lower value. You can check this by examining the value of a business with an adjusted after tax income of $50,000 a year capitalized at 6 percent (that is, divided by .06), $833,333 and comparing the result with one capitalized at 15 percent (i.e. divided by .15), $333,333.

(2) Stable businesses with large capital asset bases and established goodwill should be less risky investments and you should use a lower capitalization rate than if you were valuing a small business with little capital, financial history, or management depth.

Assign a high capitalization rate to a personal business that depends on the presence of only one or two key people. An investor purchasing this type of business would want a high rate of return as a reward for that risk. (Another way to say the same thing is that such an investor would not make the investment unless a rapid return of capital through a high income stream was expected.)

Comparison Chart

"MULTIPLIER" (MULTIPLY THIS TIMES EARNINGS)		OR	CAPITALIZATION RATE (DIVIDE THIS INTO EARNINGS)
LOW	28.6	=	3.5 %
RISK	25	=	4 %
	20	=	5 %
	16.67	=	6 %
	14.29	=	7 %
	12.5	=	8 %
	11.11	=	9 %
	10	=	10 %
	9.09	=	11 %
	8.33	=	12 %
	7.69	=	13 %
	7.14	=	14 %
	6.67	=	15 %
	6.25	=	16 %
	5.88	=	17 %
	5.56	=	18 %
	5.26	=	19 %
	5	=	20 %
	4	=	25 %
HIGH	3.33	=	30 %
RISK	2.86	=	35 %

It is important to note that there are no "correct" or "official" rates. Even the IRS uses different rates at different times and under different circumstances. It is for this reason that the capitalization of income template provides ten automatic options (which you can change to provide an infinite number of variations).

(4) Valuation of a Business As a "Going Concern"

A closely-held business should (and often does) produce an income in excess of the amount that could be expected from the mere employment of the capital its shareholders have invested. That additional amount of income is derived from an intangible value in the business, a value in excess of the total value of the tangible assets.

By capitalizing this "earnings attributable to intangibles," i.e., by dividing the additional profits generated by the firm's goodwill, by an appropriate rate, it is possible to estimate goodwill value. If this amount is then added to book (net tangible asset) value, the total business value can be found.

Some of the elements that may comprise a firm's goodwill include:

(1) Location of the business

(2) Reputation of the business

(3) Public recognition of the company's name

(4) Lists of customers and prospects owned by the business

(5) Management effectiveness and depth

(6) Sales, operations, and accounting skills

(7) Employee morale

(8) Position of the business relative to competitors

(9) Other factors that generate income in excess of that amount which could be expected after multiplying the value of tangible assets by a reasonable rate of return.

Note that goodwill does not include the portion of profits attributable to the corporation's ownership of patents, copyrights, formulas, or trademarks, even though they are intangible, since these are all specifically identifiable.

Goodwill, as in the case with other valuation formulas and procedures, should be used only as a guideline and not as the sole determinate of value. Goodwill has minimal relevance to the valuation of most investment companies since they usually do not have large amounts of intangibles. Officially the IRS does not give strong credibility to goodwill (although the service still insists that goodwill must be taken into account in the valuation process).

Going Concern Value

Input:	Average Annual Earnings	$100,000
Input:	Average Annual Asset Value	$500,000
Input:	Estimated Capitalization Rate	0.200
Input:	Rate of Return on Tangible Assets	0.16

Option	Return On Tangible Assets	Earn From Tangible Assets	Earn From Intangible Assets	Goodwill Value	Total Business Value
1	0.160	$80,000	$20,000	$100,000	$600,000
2	0.170	$85,000	$15,000	$75,000	$575,000
3	0.180	$90,000	$10,000	$50,000	$550,000
4	0.190	$95,000	$5,000	$25,000	$525,000
5	0.200	$100,000	$0	$0	$500,000

A reduction in value is often allowed because the shares being valued represent a "minority" interest in the business. Courts tend to aggregate the lack of marketability inherent in a closely held corporation with the minority interest principle although the "minority interest" discount arises because such shares have no power to force dividends, compel liquidation, or to control corporate policy. This in turn limits the potential market for such stock to the remaining (and usually controlling) shareholders and reduces the price at which such shares would be purchased.

Conversely, where the shares in question represent a "controlling" interest, the IRS will generally attempt to increase the stock's value. "The size of the block of stock itself is a relevant factor to be considered. Although it is true that a minority interest in an unlisted corporation's stock is more difficult to sell than a similar block of listed stock, it is equally true that control of a corporation, either actual or in effect, representing as it does an added element of value, may justify a higher value for a specific block of stock."

Discount For Loss of Key Employee

Both the IRS and the courts have long recognized that the loss of a manager, scientist, salesperson, or other key individual will almost always have a serious effect on the earning power and sometimes on the very stability of a business. Although the principle applies in publicly-held businesses, it is particularly true in a closely-held corporation where profits are dependent on the ability, initiative, judgment, or business connections of a single person or small group of owner-employees. A discount in valuation may therefore be appropriate. (This same concept may also be used in determining the amount of key employee insurance a corporation should own.)

There is no universally recognized and accepted formula for computing the economic effect of the loss of a key person. One used in several court cases utilizes a discount approach: a percentage discount is taken from the going-concern value of the business.

Some authorities feel that if the business will survive the death of the key employee, and in time a competent successor can be found, a discount factor of from fifteen to twenty percent should be used. Where the business is likely to fail, or be placed in serious jeopardy upon the death (or disability) of the key employee, a discount of from twenty to forty-five percent is more appropriate. The exact discount factor should be arrived at through consultation with the officers of the company and the firm's accounting and legal advisers.

Some questions that should be answered in the process of determining the factor (or range of factors) to be used include:

(1) How long will it take for a new person to reach the efficiency of the key individual?

(2) How much will it cost to locate and situate a replacement? Will the new employee demand more salary? How much will it cost to train the new person?

(3) What mistakes is a replacement likely to make during the "break in" period and how much are those mistakes likely to cost the company?

(4) What proportion of the firm's current net profits are attributable to the key employee?

(5) Is the employee engaged in any projects which, if left unfinished at death or disability, would prove costly to the business? How costly? Would a potentially profitable project have to be abandoned or would a productive department have to be closed?

(6) Would the employee's death result in the loss of clientele or personnel attracted to the business because of his personality, social contacts, or unique skills, talents, or managerial ability?

(7) What effect would the key employee's death have on the firm's credit standing?

(8) What proportion of the firm's actual loss is it willing to self insure, if any?

Key Employee Valuation

Input: Fair Market Value of Business
        with Key Employee $750,000
Input: Discount Percent (%) without
        Employee ....

Discount Percent	Value W/O Key Employee	Value of Key Employee
0.16	$630,000	$120,000
0.17	$622,500	$127,500
0.18	$615,000	$135,000
0.19	$607,500	$142,500
0.20	$600,000	$150,000
0.21	$592,500	$157,500
0.22	$585,000	$165,000
0.23	$577,500	$172,500
0.24	$570,000	$180,000

There are a number of ways—other than the approach used in the template—to value a key person's contribution to a corporation's profits. One way is to measure the number of working years remaining to the executive (say 10). Estimate the annual loss of earnings attributable to that person (say $30,000 per year). Then discount (see present value templates) the value of that annual loss (for example, at ten percent). This will result in the present value of the key person's services, about $113,000.

Alternatively, the goodwill template could be adjusted to measure the goodwill produced through the efforts of the management team and this total would then further be apportioned (perhaps by relative salaries) among the key employees.

For instance, assume a firm had an average annual asset value of $450,000 and an average annual earnings after taxes of $75,000. If ten percent were thought to be a fair rate return on tangibles, then $45,000 ($450,000 x .10) of the $75,000 would be attributable to tangibles. The remaining $30,000 would be attributable to goodwill. Assume sixty percent of this, $18,000, could reasonably be allocated to management. If it takes five years to replace the entire management team, then $18,000 should be multiplied by five, or a total of $90,000. If the executive in question drew eighty percent of the total salaries of the management team, then that person's worth would approximate $72,000 ($90,000 x .80).

Most shareholders of closely held corporations restrict the marketability of co-shareholder's stock through "purchase options" or mandatory buy-sell agreements. If the terms of such agreement definitely fix the values of the shares in question, it is not necessary to examine either book value or earnings. The price fixed in the restrictive agreement will serve as the shares' market value, but to "peg" the value of such stock for federal estate tax purposes:

1. The agreement as to per share value must be made at arm's length and must have been fair and adequate at the time the agreement was executed.

2. The agreement must be binding during the lifetime of the stockholder; that is, he must be obligated to offer the stock to the corporation or other shareholders (a "first offer" commitment) at the specified offer price before offering it to an outsider if he wishes to dispose of his stock during his lifetime.

3. The agreement must be "binding" at death—his executor must be legally obligated to sell the shares to the corporation at the price fixed by the agreement. Furthermore, the price stated in the agreement must either be fixed, (e.g., fixed dollar price or book value on the repurchase date) or determinable according to the formula.

The Treasury believes that taxpayers in general tend to keep values low and therefore restrictions which tend to limit the value of family owned closely held stock will be closely scrutinized to determine whether the agreement is a bona fide arm's length business arrangement and not just a device to pass the decedent's shares for less than adequate consideration. See discussion of Section 2703 in Chapter 1.

Valuing a Professional Practice

This section explains why estate planners must be able to value professional practices and discusses

- how a professional practice differs from a typical business, and why these differences are important

- considerations in valuing goodwill

- how to value a professional's stock for buy-sell purposes

- a shortcut approach to valuing a professional practice

- how to use the "prior transactions," "capitalization of billings," and "excess earnings" valuation methods

- rough rules of thumb

A Complex Task

Valuation of a manufacturing business is difficult enough; the valuation of a professional practice, with its many intangible factors, is more complex still. Productivity, goodwill, and the multitude of other factors that affect a professional practice are difficult to quantify. Rules of thumb may differ widely from one appraiser to another and from one group of professionals to another. Some variables may have greater weight for some buyers than for others. For example, a young doctor seeking to purchase a practice may wish to buy one for about the same costs he'd incur if starting from scratch. Conversely, many hospitals purchase the practices of retiring staff physicians to help insure that the practice will continue to fill hospital beds. The hospital might pay more for the practice if the doctor typically referred patients to it, or if the practice might otherwise be sold to a competing hospital.

The questions asked and the methods used differ depending on the purpose of the valuation and the type of practice in question. For instance, valuations for divorce, one of the most common reasons a professional practice is valued, will emphasize the practitioner's age and health, experience, length of practice, financial success, skills, and reputation. The value of the goodwill these factors might generate could be more important to the divorce court than the factors leading to strong marketability

which would be important for estate tax purposes. Factors established by statute and case law, which tend to vary widely from state to state, must also be taken into account. For example, some states give more weight than others to minority interests or lack of marketability discounts with reference to professional corporations.

Why a Professional Practice is Different

A professional practice differs from other businesses mainly because of:

Expertise. The expertise — or, more important, the *perceived* expertise — of the professionals involved is of paramount importance in determining the fees that can be charged and the income that can be earned from the practice. The education, training, and experience a professional brings to his practice, and the "consumer's" dependence on the delivery of the practitioner's services, are extremely important economic factors which must be considered in determining value. For example, a patient needing brain surgery typically does not shop for a bargain price.

Entry barriers. Higher education, licensing, and certification requirements all serve to slow or limit entrants into professional practice. If, for any reason, licensing or certification is lost, the practitioner can no longer practice. If a professional dies or is permanently disabled, his family members cannot continue to operate the practice unless they are duly licensed and certified in the same profession.

Professional goodwill. Reputation and recommendations are the life blood of the professional practice. Although some professionals obtain significant business from "walk-in" traffic due to location or advertisement, most depend mainly on referrals from peers and the recommendation of present clients to bring in new business. This is particularly true with respect to specialists. For this reason, trust, respect, and "liking" of the practitioner — by peers as well as patients or clients — are crucial to the success of the practice.

Nontransferability. Substitution may be difficult or impossible. Professional skills are to some extent unique and not interchangeable. Consider the relationship between psychiatrist and patient: If the psychiatrist is ill for three weeks and unable to work, an attorney-spouse can't "run the store."

Continuing education. In most professions, information becomes outdated, and the professional must engage in continuous education. This may be through formal course work or by keeping up with professional journals and magazines.

Why The Differences Are Important

Most businesses have as part of their value an asset called "goodwill." This can be defined as the quantified expectation of future profits from some source other than mere dollars at work. For instance, if a firm enjoys $80,000 of earnings on a $60,000 capital investment which can reasonably be expected to return 20% ($12,000) at a given risk level, then $68,000 of income ($80,000-$12,000) is attributable to something other than capital. This business-oriented goodwill is an asset of the business that generates value over and above the entity's net asset value.

In a professional practice there are two types of goodwill: business-oriented (stemming from the entity) *and* professional (originating from the individual).

Business-oriented goodwill is attributable to the elements of a professional practice that are similar to those of a regular business: location, operating systems, staff, and patient or client base. Business-oriented goodwill can have significant transferable value, value that can be sold to another licensed practitioner.

Professional goodwill, on the other hand, depends on the unique characteristics of the particular practitioner. At the professional's death, disability, or retirement, that portion of the practice income attributable to professional goodwill will generally leave with the individual. Much of this personal goodwill, however, can be transferred in a sale to another practitioner by creating a well-organized transition in which the departing professional lends credibility to the entering professional.

Valuing Business-Oriented Goodwill and Future Income Flow

Although many sources are available to provide information for valuing a practice's transferable business-oriented goodwill and its likely future earnings, the most accurate source will typically be the firm's own CPA. The CPA should examine ten factors.

Projected earnings. Projected earnings are normally an extension of past earnings. Financial statements and tax returns (specifically income statements, balance sheets, and cash flow statements) should be examined and adjusted to determine:

- *The level of gross income.* Net income figures may be misleading, since principals may be taking profits in the form of perquisites and benefits as well as salaries. The CPA should determine how salaries compare to the "norm" for services performed. Are they too high? Alter-

natively, if they are lower than comparable payments to similar professionals, does this indicate cash flow or earnings problems?

- *Earnings trend.* At least five years should be reviewed. Measure each year's amount as a percent of a "base" year. A business "trending up" indicates the likely presence of growing goodwill. However, the CPA must also consider whether there are unusual or nonrecurring factors that artificially inflate or deflate income. Large pension contributions, malpractice claims, fees or court costs, and salary structures should be studied particularly carefully. The inability of one or more professionals to work during the period examined would obviously have a strong impact on earnings. Did the professional, out of choice, work 40 hours a week or only 20?

Competition. An increased demand for established practices is typically reflected in an increase in prices. This has occurred in a number of professions due, in large part, to the increase in the number of newly licensed professionals — e.g., dentistry. An appraiser must also consider the number of other practitioners in the area, how thoroughly their practices saturate the market, and the price trend for services similar to those being valued.

Size of patient or client base. The greater the number of satisfied current patients or clients, the greater the likelihood that a large number of referrals will be made to the practice. More emphasis should be given to this factor when selling the entire practice than when valuing the practice for purposes of appointing assets in a divorce or legal separation. The distribution of the client base should also be evaluated. Consider whether the clients are repeaters, recent additions, referrals from prior clients, young or old, etc. How many patients or clients are seen each day?

Payment sources. How the professional is paid greatly influences both the level and the stability of the practice's income. Measure how likely the practice is to be paid for services rendered, and how soon. Government programs typically pay less per procedure than the usual fee, so the source of payment may also indicate how much will be paid. Questions that should be asked by an appraiser include:

- Is the practice dependent on any particular group of patients or clients for a significant portion of its income?

- What percentage of patients pay bills through private insurance, Medicare, Medicaid, other sources?

- What is the aging of the professional's accounts receivable? Are monthly bills paid in 30, 60, 90 days, etc.? (This is a good indication of the financing needs and efficiency of the practice's collection procedures.)

Practitioner's workload. Income figures alone do not tell how many hours it took to generate a given level of profit. A practice that took 40 hours of work to generate a given amount of earnings is worth more than one that took 70 hours to develop the same earnings. Factors that must be considered in this area include:

- Is the practice a "personal" type or "mass production" type? How much time spent with the patient or client was due merely to the practitioner's work style?

- Does the practitioner spend time on administrative or other problems which could be handled more efficiently and at lower cost by an office manager or other staff?

Fee structure. A great deal can be ascertained by examining the practice's fee structure. A professional who has been consistently and *successfully* charging above-average fees probably has developed significant professional goodwill. If fees are average or below average, perhaps there is an uncovered problem or a potential to increase revenues. An appraiser should ascertain:

- How do this practitioner's fees compare with fees charged in the community by other practitioners of similar reputation and skill?

- When was the last time fees were raised?

- How often have fees been raised in the last five years, and for what reasons?

- Was there measurable resistance to the last increase in fees (a significant drop-off in then current or prospective patients or clients)? Would there be a sizable loss of patients or clients if a fee increase was instituted? How large an increase would the market bear?

- Is billing computerized and how well is the system working?

Staff strength. Second only to the principal(s) in importance to the value of a professional practice is the quality and depth of the staff. Staff includes nonowner professionals (who may or may not carry clientele away if they leave), paraprofessionals, and clerical employees. Questions that should be asked by an appraiser in this area are:

- How long have the various individuals been with the practice; would they be likely to stay if the owner-professional(s) were to die or the practice were sold?

What patients or clients (or essential skills) would nonowners take with them if they left? What costs would be involved in recruiting replacements and training them?

- What duties do the nonowners in the practice perform? What percentage of the total practice can be performed without the owner-professional?

- How well are nonowners compensated compared to similar employees in similar practices?

- Are there enforceable employment contracts, covenants not to compete, or special fringe benefits that would tie key employees to the practice even if new ownership takes over?

Location of the practice. In general, practices located in economically vibrant and growing communities are more valuable than those in unattractive and depressed areas, but this is not always true. For example, a dentist may have a higher volume of business in an area where preventive tooth care has not been stressed; a criminal attorney may have more potential business in the inner city than in a suburb.

Ironically, a practice producing a high income isn't necessarily more valuable in a community where there is a shortage of professionals; it would be relatively easy for a new practitioner to take advantage of the demand. Conversely, in a community saturated by and long-settled with professionals, start-up time and expense would be high for a new practitioner; so the value of an established practice with a full appointment book and a well-trained staff would therefore be higher.

Physical and mental health of the professional. Particularly in marital distribution situations, the professional's health is a dominant valuation factor. Significant professional goodwill may exist if the professional is in good health and can repeat or improve upon his past earnings record. But what if past earnings were generated by years of 80-hour weeks which are no longer feasible? A surgeon who has a blood-pressure problem, or worse yet, an alcohol or other drug problem, may not be capable of sustaining the workload that "built the business."

Age of the professional. Age is another factor that should be given great weight in a valuation for divorce or separation purposes. Age, aside from its tangential relationship to health, can be used to indicate how long a past flow of earnings can reasonably be projected into the future. Although it is logical to project the earnings of a young practitioner for a longer time than a practitioner only a few years from retirement, an appraiser must consider that the earnings of a younger practitioner are lower and less certain.

Shortcut approach to buy-sell valuations. Since nonprofessionals cannot generally hold stock in a professional corporation and since most states require that such stock be bought back by the corporation or its surviving shareholders within a relatively short period of time after the transfer of interest, it is essential that a fully funded buy-sell agreement be utilized to protect the interests of all parties. Quite often the parties to such an agreement are unwilling to hire an independent appraiser to value their stock according to the appropriate sophisticated methods. For this reason, a quick and relatively inexpensive method of determining value is often desired, such as the "one times annual net income" formula all too often used for solo private practices.

Although there is no universal rule or perfect formula for arriving at a price, the simplified worksheet shown in Figure 42.4 provides a quick way to "guesstimate" the worth of a physician's practice; it can be easily modified to apply to other professional practices.

Warning: Remember that the guidelines in the worksheet are only that; they will vary depending on the circumstances. Be sure to review the list of assumptions accompanying the worksheet. Note that a solo practice is almost always worth less than one where two or more professionals work together. This is why many practitioners bring in one or more associates well before they retire and negotiate a buyout that will effect a long and smooth transition period. This worksheet should be considered only a starting place for a full valuation.

Valuation Methods

Prior transactions method. Perhaps the most reliable method of valuing a practice, when it is available, is to ascertain the price it sold for in a previous transaction. This assumes, of course, that there was a recent sale or exchange and that it was at arm's length. Consideration should also be given to the magnitude of prior transactions — e.g., the purchase of greater than 50% of a practice creates a control premium, whereas the purchase of less than a 50% interest should involve a minority discount.

Capitalization of billings method. A practice can be valued by dividing the net income by the cost of capital. For example, using this formula, if the practice produced an adjusted net income after the owner's salary of $100,000, and it was assumed that capital should be "costed" at 20% (i.e., a buyer with a similar risk opportunity would demand a 20% return on his investment), the practice would be worth $500,000 ($100,000 divided by 20%).

Another traditional way of arriving at a practice value is by using a multiple of gross billings. The formula for determining the multiple to use is: net income percentage divided by capitalization rate equals percentage of billing factor. For example, assume the firm in our prior example billed $500,000 during the year. Since its adjusted net income was $100,000, its net income percentage on billings was 20% ($100,000 ÷ by $500,000). Given the 20% capitalization rate, its value is $500,000, or 100% of billings (20% ÷ 20% = 1 or 100%). If the same firm billed only $400,000 but still netted $100,000 (a percentage of billing factor of 25%), it would be worth *more* than 100% of the billings. Using the formula, we get a 125% multiple: 25% ÷ by 20% = 1.25 or 125%. Thus, the practice's value, on these facts, would still be $500,000 (i.e., $400,000 x 125%).

Excess earnings method. This is another simple, widely-used — and often court-blessed — method of quantifying the value of intangible assets. Essentially, earnings (pretax, *including* the professional owner's salary and fringe benefits) are adjusted as discussed above. Then the earnings in excess of that which is earned by similar professionals in similar types of practices are computed and that excess is "capitalized" (divided by a percentage to arrive at the capital it would take to produce it annually). The result is the estimated value of the goodwill in the practice. This would be added to the fair market value of tangible assets to arrive at a total value.

For example, assume Doctor Know's average compensation for the last five years — after appropriate adjustments and weighting for its upward trend — was $180,000, but that similar physicians earned only $120,000 during the same period. This indicated that the difference, about $60,000 a year, is due to something other than return on tangible assets.

Excess earnings for most professional practices are capitalized at rates between 20% and 100%. The wide variation is a result of varying risk levels and differing ages of the professionals in question; the median capitalization rate is 33 $1/3$%. Here are the goodwill values of Doctor Know's practice at various capitalization rates:

Rate	Adjusted Excess	Value
20%	$60,000	$300,000
25%	$60,000	$240,000
33%	$60,000	$180,000
50%	$60,000	$120,000
100%	$60,000	$ 60,000

This brings up the question asked at the beginning of the discussion on valuations of businesses: what is meant by a "capitalization rate" and how does the appraiser know what capitalization rate to use? The capitalization rate is the projected cost of capital. But there is no fixed and certain answer to the question of "What is the right rate to use?" A good

Figure 42.4

Worksheet for Valuing a Physician's Practice
WORKSHEET ASSUMPTIONS

ACCOUNTS RECEIVABLE. Sellers sometimes exclude accounts receivable from the sale of the practice to keep the sales price down or to simplify the process; the selling professional collects the revenue from the receivables and the buyer doesn't have to worry about the collectibility or the trouble of collection. Conversely, the purchaser may want a practice with accounts receivable to maintain contact with the patients or clients (similar to purchasing a customer list).

Bills outstanding for more than one year are considered uncollectible; those that have been turned over to collection agencies are not considered as part of accounts receivable. Accounts receivable within 30 days of billing are considered worth between 80% and 90% of their face value. Between 30 and 60 days, the value drops to between 50% and 80%; while in most practices, accounts receivable are worth little after 60 days, *unless* a government agency or private insurer will pay the claim.

Practice point. It is important to view accounts receivable in perspective. Has the professional been "cleaning out" his accounts receivable and living off previous work he's now collecting for? Has he imposed fee increases which create the impression of a constant level of patient volume which is in reality decreasing? Has the professional done a good job of collecting and reporting accounts receivable? In many cases, poor bookkeeping or collection procedures understate the true value of the practice. For instance, a practice may be building its patient volume but, because of inefficiencies or poor pricing of services, hasn't generated a representative cash flow.

BUILDINGS/LAND. The fair market value of the real estate owned by the practice must be used rather than the book value.

EQUIPMENT/FURNISHINGS. A potential purchaser views equipment as capital that will have to be replaced. Equipment depreciates rapidly, partially due to wear and partially to obsolescence caused by the introduction of more effective or efficient (less labor intensive) or easier to use technology.

Some appraisal experts suggest that each item be priced between original cost and present book value. This worksheet suggests that equipment less than five years old be listed at 40% of its cost and older equipment at about 20% of cost. Where appropriate, use an actual fair market value appraisal; for example, certain furniture-say, an antique desk-may have value in excess of its original cost.

DRUGS/SUPPLIES. Most physicians have at least a two-month supply of drugs and other supplies. Divide the annual supply cost by six. Unused disposables are typically worth their cost less 10% to 20%, although a buyer may not choose to use what is currently in inventory, further reducing the practice value.

GOODWILL. Various methods of determining goodwill are discussed throughout this reading. The worksheet rule of thumb-25% of annual gross-can be used as an alternative to another commonly used guideline, $3 to $5 per record of regularly seen patients. Note that these are "quick guess" guidelines; they should not substitute for appropriate financial analysis and evaluation.

Value of Accounts Receivable

	Age	Percent of Face Value	Example	Your Figure
Input:	0-30 days	80-90%	$ 20,000	$_____
Input:	31-60 days	50-60%	50,000	_____
Input:	61 days or more	0 unless insurance	5,000	_____

Buildings and Land

			Example	
Input:	Market value of building and land		1,000,000	_____

Equipment and Furnishings

	Age	Percent of Face Value	Example	
Input:	Less than 5 years	40% of cost	$ 30,000	_____
Input:	5 years or more	20% of cost	4,000	_____
Input:	Drugs, supplies (last 2 month's bills)		12,000	_____
Input:	Cash and market value of invested securities		10,000	_____
Input:	Goodwill (25% of annual gross)		200,000	_____
	Total estimate of practice assets		$1,331,000	$_____

Liabilities

			Example	
Input:	Balance owed on equipment and furnishings		$ 5,000	_____
Input:	Salaries, bonuses, severance pay due		60,000	_____
Input:	Taxes due		40,000	_____
Input:	Accounts payable		23,000	_____
Input:	Insurance premiums due		70,000	_____
Input:	Mortgage balance		80,000	_____
Input:	Other liabilities		3,000	_____
	Total estimate of practice liabilities		$ 281,000	_____
	Total estimate of practice assets		$1,331,000	_____
	Total estimate of practice liabilities		281,000	_____
	Estimate of value practice		$1,050,000	_____

appraiser will consider such things as (1) how many more productive years the professional has, (2) where on the income-producing cycle the professional was as of the valuation date (highest income-producing years for most professionals occur between ages 45 and 55), and (3) changes in the profession, the economy, and in government regulation. For instance, skyrocketing malpractice costs are rapidly changing the practicing environment, causing many professionals to drastically change the way they work.

Most appraisers working with professional corporations will be conservative and use relatively high capitalization rates, 50% to 100% (meaning a low multiplier). *Reason:* It is more difficult to maintain "excess earnings" than earnings produced by passive income investments and, further, total earnings have been used as a base. If pretax earnings after reduction for owner's compensation and benefits is used as the base, a 20% or 40% capitalization rate (and thus a higher multiple) would be more appropriate. The table below sets out various capitalization rates and their related multipliers for determining value using the excess earnings method.

Capitalization Rate/Value

Capitalization Rate	Value (multiply adjusted excess by this rate)
3.5%	28.57/1
4.0%	25.00/1
5.0%	20.00/1
6.0%	16.67/1
7.0%	14.29/1
8.0%	12.50/1
9.0%	11.11/1
10.0%	10.00/1
11.0%	9.09/1
12.0%	8.33/1
13.0%	7.69/1
14.0%	7.14/1
15.0%	6.67/1
16.0%	6.25/1
17.0%	5.88/1
18.0%	5.56/1
19.0%	5.26/1
20.0%	5.00/1
25.0%	4.00/1
30.0%	3.33/1

Caveat: As is the case with any valuation method, the excess earnings concept has its limitations. Goodwill can be understated, because even a practice without excess earnings may have considerable worth as a going concern. On the other hand, goodwill can be overstated, because the excess earnings method does not consider whether or not the practice is marketable. Third, many subjective judgments are required (such as the appropriate weight to give the trend of earnings, the adjustments to make to earnings, and the capitalization rate to use).

Rough Rules of Thumb for Valuations

Almost all tax practitioners and financial planners use rules of thumb (often called SWAGs, scientific wild asset guesses) that they've developed as the byproduct of practical experience. SWAGs lie between calculations and pure conjecture and serve as starting places in the valuation process, later to be abandoned or modified. They can also be used where more precise methods are deemed impractical. The following rough rules of thumb are suggested for valuing various professions:

- *Medical:* Net asset value plus 20% to 40% of annual revenue for goodwill (referral practices would be worth less, continuing client base practices worth more).

- *Veterinary:* Net asset value plus 60% to 90% of annual revenue for goodwill.

- *Legal:* Because client's files can't be sold (lawyers are ethically precluded from selling their law practices), personal goodwill typically does not enter into the valuation process. Therefore, net asset value is often the major value determinant. In the case of distribution upon divorce, if there is a buy-sell agreement, the price set in the agreement is usually considered merely an indication of value and is certainly rebuttable. Remember that work-in-progress fees are not reflected in the records of a law firm. So, even if the firm's accounting records are accurate and nonfraudulent, a firm that takes no retainers and sends no bills but has many contingent fee arrangements, can easily be undervalued. Conversely, fees contingent on events that may not occur must be discounted.

- *Accounting:* Net asset value plus a goodwill payment of from 80% to 130% of annual revenue (paid out over time). Another common method uses 20% of projected fees for five years, discounted for both attrition and the time value of money. According to the CPA Handbook, a third commonly used formula is 40% of gross receipts for the prior three years and a percentage of average annual fees as follows: 100% for clients served over four years, 75% for clients served from three to four years, 50% for clients served from two to three years, and 25% for clients served from one to two years.

- *Dental:* Net asset value plus 30% to 40% of annual revenues for goodwill.

- *Engineering/Architecture:* Net asset value plus 25% to 50% of annual revenues for goodwill (firms with few continuing clients would, of course, have little if any goodwill).

Data Needed in the Valuation Process

Valuation experts should review each of the following:

- Last five years' profit and loss statements and balance sheets (certified financial statements by an independent CPA firm are preferable). Five years is a common time frame because it (1) minimizes the possibility of "valuation planning," (2) covers a complete business cycle, (3) examines good as well as bad times, (4) permits discounting or elimination of "aberration years," and (5) illustrates the stability and trend of profits. Graphs are particularly useful in identifying and illustrating aberration years or the direction and velocity of a profit trend.

- Last five years' federal income tax returns.

- Any business leases.

- Last five years' fee schedules.

- Brochures on the firm.

- Articles of incorporation and by-laws, and minutes of board of directors' meetings for the last five years.

- Last five years' appointment books.

- State employment research data (particularly information from state professional licensing department).

- Demographic and practice economics information available from state or county professional societies (such as the state or local medical or bar association).

- Studies published in professional journals such as the American Medical Association's "Socioeconomic Characteristics of Medical Practice" (published annually), or by the American Bar Association, or in private publications such as "Medical Economics," or, for the legal profession, "Corporate Law Department Surveys and Survey of Law Form Economics" (Altman-Weil Management Consultants, Inc., published annually) and "Compensation of Attorneys" (Steven Langer and Associates).

PLANNING FOR VALUATION DISCOUNTS IN CLOSELY HELD AND FAMILY BUSINESSES

Various other circumstances have substantial impact on the valuation of business, including restrictive agreements, such as cross purchase or redemption plans, and partnership liquidation agreements. Code Section 2703 (see Chapter 1) will have a substantial impact on the use of such agreements in many closely held businesses.

Lower valuation for the business interest may result where it does not fully participate in the future growth of the business, i.e., preferred stock and "frozen" partnership interests (see Chapter 13), and long-term installment sales (see Chapter 19).

A failure to undertake proper valuation planning for the family business will leave the estate at the mercy of the IRS, and may make it impossible to retain the enterprise. To be really effective, any plan must contain the following elements:

1. A present transfer of interests in the business from family members in the older generation to those in younger generations, either by sale, gift or both.

2. A shift of all or part of the future growth of the enterprise to the younger generation.

3. The owners of the family business should seriously consider taking full use of their unified credit and even their $1 million GST tax exemption during life through transfers of interests in family businesses.

For a good example, see TAM 9131006, where decedent created a family partnership to engage in real estate operations and transferred mostly limited partnership interests to 4 children and 14 grandchildren, with one general partnership interest to a son, all covered by the $10,000 annual exclusion. No gift tax returns were filed, and all income was allocated to the decedent for a management fee. Held — no gift or estate tax consequences, profits were to be allocated proportionately to the partners, and all limited partnership interests were transferable, subject to a right of first refusal.

On the other hand, retention of value in the estates of the older generation may facilitate stock redemptions, particularly under Code section 303 (Chapter 31); deferred payment of tax under Code section 6166 (Chapter 10), and special use valuation for real property under Code section 2032A.

Regardless of the difficulties, the conclusion is inescapable that lifetime transfers of interests in family business enterprises are almost essential to planning for succession.

The two most common discounts available for family and closely held businesses are the discounts for lack of marketability and for a minority interest. Similarly, an additional discount may be appropriate to reflect those instances in which a limited partner cannot withdraw from the partnership and is locked in to his investment (i.e., a "lock-in" discount). Also, other discounts may be applied to reflect built in capital gains or key management personnel.

MINORITY INTEREST DISCOUNTS

The cases have been liberal in permitting substantial discounts in value based on the fact that the decedent's interest in the business is a fractional or minority interest.[13] In some instances, value may be increased to reflect a control premium.

The minority interest discount principle refers to the fact that the owner of less than a majority interest in an enterprise cannot by himself control day-to-day or long range managerial decisions, impact future earnings, control efforts for growth potential, establish executive compensation, or get at the corporate assets through liquidation. Because the owner of a minority interest lacks these benefits of control over the business an acquiror of a minority interest will pay less for that interest, on a pro-rata basis, than if he or she were acquiring a controlling interest in the business. In instances where the owner lacks the ability to exercise control over the operations of the enterprise, the owner's interest may be worth significantly less than its "liquidation" value.

For many years, the Service was uncomfortable with the idea that minority interests owned among family members could be valued at a discount even though the collective ownership of the individual family members gave the family control of the corporation. In 1981, the Service issued Revenue Ruling 81-253, 1981-2 CB 187, which stated that no minority interest discount would be allowed for intrafamily transfers of shares of stock in a corporation controlled by the family in the absence of discord among the family members (the concept is commonly referred to as the "family attribution" principle.) However, after experiencing a long line of cases in which the family attribution principle was rejected,[14] the Service announced its abandonment of the family attribution principle in Revenue Ruling 93-12, 1993-1 CB 202. The new position of the Service is that it no longer will seek to deny minority interest discounts solely because an entity is controlled by related persons.

In determining the size of the minority interest discount to be applied, each case must take into consideration all relevant facts and circumstances.[15] The amount of discount applied in other cases is not normally a determinant as to the proper discount to be applied in a given case.[16] The reference to prior cases and articles discussing discounts is appropriate for demonstrating the existence of a discount, but will not be given any weight for proving the magnitude of discount in a specific case.

A crucial factor in establishing the minority interest discount is the bundle of rights which are possessed by the owner of the corporate or partnership interest. Such rights will be set forth by both a combination of applicable state law, corporate articles and bylaws, partnership agreement, or other rights and restrictions agreed to by the parties.[17] An appraiser who conducts an examination of ownership rights must disregard any provision which constitutes an "applicable restriction" under Section 2704(b) and the attorney may have a duty to inform the appraiser of those rights which fall within this definition. Thus, restrictive provisions which are drafted into an agreement should be carefully considered before being implemented.

While the courts, Service and taxpayers all agree that a minority interest is worth less than a controlling interest on a pro-rata basis, the issue now is not whether a minority interest discount is allowable, but rather the amount of the minority interest discount.

The primary source of data utilized by business appraisers to determine discounts for minority interests in operating entities comes from acquisitions of controlling interests in the public marketplace. This data is utilized because the applicable minority interest discount can be calculated as the inverse of the control premium paid by an investor who acquires various rights which are otherwise unavailable to the minority interest. A number of comprehensive sources which accumulate such information are readily available to the public. Two well-known sources of control premium data are *Mergerstat Review*, published by Merrill Lynch and *The Industrywide Control Premium Study*, published by Houlihan Lokey Howard & Zukin, Inc.

In determining minority interest discounts for privately-held real estate concerns, a different source of empirical data is often utilized. With the decision in *Estate of Edgar A. Berg v. Commissioner*,[18] the Tax Court has specified that a permissible approach for determining minority interest discounts for interests in real estate companies is the "REIT Approach." This approach involves an analysis of publicly traded real estate entities (including real estate investment trusts or "REITS") that report the aggregate appraised values of their real estate holdings.

Advanced estate planners and appraisers are quick to point out that the use of REIT data may be inapplicable for valuing smaller less diverse corporations and partnerships. They argue that the relatively larger size of the typical publicly traded REIT makes such an entity incomparable for discount purposes. This observation is supported by the recent trend of many REITs in 1994 to trade at premiums rather than discounts.

A better means of gauging the discount for family limited partnerships and corporations which are of relatively small capitalization (under $25,000,000) may be achieved by making comparison to smaller privately owned limited partnerships traded on the "secondary" market. These entities typically have partnership agreements which contain similar restrictions to those found in family limited partnerships and usually maintain a less diverse asset base that the typical REIT. Discounts for such entities generally are higher than found in REITs. Data on the trading of such interests is now available through a number of sources.[19]

LACK OF MARKETABILITY DISCOUNTS

The lack of marketability principle is well documented and is based on the fact that stock in a closely-held business enterprise is less attractive and more difficult to sell than publicly traded stock.[20] Lack of marketability discounts relate to the inherent lack of flexibility in getting in and out of investments with no ready market. Where an active trading market does not exist, then other factors may be used as valuation benchmarks, and the lack of marketability discount becomes operative and applicable.

One 1987 study commented on a noticeable trend in the Tax Court over the past years to steadily increase the amount of discounts allowed for lack of marketability. As stated in the study:

> Some fourteen cases were reviewed from 1969 through 1984. For the four cases (1969-1976), lack of marketability discounts allowed by the Tax Courts ran at a mean of 18.35 percent, with a range of from 15 percent to 25 percent. From 1974 to about 1979, the mean rose to 24 percent on the five cases, ranging from 10 percent to 35 percent. From 1979 on through 1984, the mean nonmarketability discount was about 29 percent (28.7 percent) and the range of five cases was from 10 percent to 50 percent.[21]

Since 1984, the Tax Court's allowance of discounts has declined, on average, from prior years, as shown by a review of sixteen cases during 1985 through 1992 in which the Tax Court allowed a specific discount for lack of marketability. These cases indicate the allowance of discounts ranging from 10 to 36 percent with a mean discount of 21 percent.[22]

The Service issued Revenue Ruling 77-287, 1977-2 CB 319, in order to provide information and guidance to taxpayers, Service personnel, and others concerned with the valuation, for federal tax purposes, of securities that cannot be immediately resold because they are restricted from resale pursuant to federal securities laws. In valuing restricted securities, Revenue Ruling 77-287 states that the following documents and facts should be reviewed:

1. A copy of any declaration of trust, trust agreement, and any other agreements relating to the shares of restricted stock;

2. A copy of any document showing any offers to buy or sell or indications of interest in buying or selling the restricted shares;

3. The latest prospectus of the company;

4. Annual reports of the company for 3 to 5 years preceding the valuation date;

5. The trading prices and trading volumes of the related class of traded securities one month preceding the valuation date;

6. The relationship of the parties to the agreements concerning the restricted stock, such as whether they are members of the immediately family or perhaps whether they are officers or directors of the company; and

7. Whether the interest being valued represents a majority or minority ownership.

The following table summarizes some of the published studies on lack of marketability discounts as applied to restricted stock interests.

Study	Mean Discount
SEC Institutional Investor Study (1966-1969)[23]	24%
FMV Opinions, Inc. Study (1979-1992)[24]	23%
Houlihan Advisors Study (1980-1991)[25]	24%
Gelman Study (1968-1970)[26]	33%
Trout Study (1968-1972)[27]	33%
Maroney Study[28]	36%
Maher Study (1969-1973)[29]	35%
Standard Research Consultants Study (1978-1982)[30]	45%
Willamette Management Associates Study (1981-1984)[31]	42%-74%
Robert W. Baird & Company Study (1980-1981)[32]	60%
Robert W. Baird & Company Study (1985-1986)	43%

The above restricted stock studies cover a wide period of time (1966 through 1992) and a large number of transactions. The average and median discounts found in each study are consistent with the range of average discounts falling in the 25% to 45% range.

LOCK-IN DISCOUNT

For partnerships, consideration should always be given as to whether the interest can be liquidated through the enforcement of withdrawal rights. In some states, if the partnership agreement does not provide a time for when capital will be returned, a limited partner is given the right to withdraw from the partnership no sooner than six months after giving notice to the general partner. In other states, applicable state law prohibits the return of capital to a limited partner except upon the occurrence of certain events specified in the partnership agreement (e.g., upon expiration of the partnership term). California recently amended its limited partnership act to remove withdrawal rights unless specified in the partnership agreement.

If the partnership agreement or state law does not confer upon the limited partner any right to withdraw capital, then the interest may remain in the partnership until expiration of the partnership term (often 35-50 years in length). In such case, the limited partner is "locked-in" to maintaining his investment in the partnership and a lock-in discount is appropriate.

In determining whether a lock-in discount is applicable, Section 2704(b) must be reviewed. Under this section, a lock-in discount may not exist for federal tax purposes if it constitutes an "applicable restriction" under state law (see discussion below). In such case, the limited partner may be locked in to the partnership under the partnership agreement but prevented by section 2704(b) from considering the effect of the withdrawal restriction if such restriction is more stringent that applicable state law.

OTHER DISCOUNTS

In valuing interests in corporations which hold investment assets (e.g., real property, marketable securities, coins, etc.) consideration should be given as to whether there are potential capital gains which will be taxed at the corporate level. Although the courts have stated that such a discount is not allowed unless there is a plan to liquidate the asset and incur the tax, the existence of potential capital gains is a factor which most likely will increase the lack of marketability discount.

CHAPTER 14

Effective October 8, 1990, Chapter 14 of the Code must be considered in valuing interests in corporations and partnerships. Chapter 14 presents valuation rules for determining the value of interests in corporations and partnerships which are controlled by family members (generally where more than 50% of value is held by the family). The application of these statutes can result in a gift even though no wealth is actually transferred to other family members (e.g. Section 2701's use of the subtraction method for valuing applicable retained interests) and cause certain restrictive provisions in an agree-ment to be disregarded for transfer tax purposes (e.g., Section 2704(b)'s disregard of "applicable restrictions").

Section 2701 applies to valuation of corporate and partnership interests designed for estate freeze purposes. In instances where there are capital interests which have a preference as to income distributions, the valuation of transfers (including recapitalizations) among family members may produce a gift tax. In instances in which there are no preferences as to capital ownership, Section 2701 generally does not apply.

Section 2702 applies to interests in trusts (e.g., GRITs, GRATs and GRUTs, split interest purchases) and does not require consideration in valuing a closely held business.

Section 2703 applies to "any option, agreement, or other right to acquire or use the property at a price less than the fair market value of the property (without regard to such option, agreement or right) or any restriction on the right to sell or use such property." Thus, a right or restriction contained in a partnership agreement, articles of incorporation, corporate bylaws, shareholders' agreement, or any other agreement will fall subject to Section 2703. Similarly, a right or restriction may be implicit in the capital structure of an entity.[33] Such rights and restrictions will have no effect for valuation purposes unless the following three conditions exist: (1) there is a bona fide business purpose, (2) the agreement is not a testamentary device to transfer property to members of the decedent's family for less than full and adequate consideration in money or money's worth, and (3) the terms are comparable to similar arrangements entered into by persons in arm's length transactions.

Section 2704 applies to lapsed voting and liquidation rights in a corporation or partnership if the individual holding such right immediately before the lapse and members of such individual's family hold, both before and after the lapse, control of the entity. If lapsed voting or liquidation rights exist, then the amount of the transfer is determined by the value of the interest before the lapse minus the value after the lapse.

A voting right means a right to vote with respect to any matter of the entity. In the case of a partnership, the right of the general partner to participate in partnership management is a voting right.[34] A liquidation right is defined as a right or ability to compel the entity to acquire all or a portion of the holder's equity interest in the entity, including by reason of aggregate voting power, whether or not its exercise would result in the complete liquidation of the entity.[35] A lapse of a voting right occurs at the time a presently exercisable voting right is restricted or eliminated, while a lapse of a liquidation right occurs at the time a presently exercisable liquidation right is restricted or eliminated. However, a transfer of an interest which results in a lapse of a liquidation right is not subject to §2704 if the rights with respect to the transferred interest are not restricted or eliminated.

Additionally, Section 2704 allows for the value of property to be determined without consideration of any "applicable restrictions." An applicable restriction is defined as any restriction

1. which effectively limits the ability of the corporation or partnership to liquidate.

2. with respect to which either of the following applies

    a. The restriction lapses, in whole or in part, after the transfer [of an interest in the corporation or partnership to (or for the benefit of) a member of the transferor's family], or

    b. The transferor or any member of the transferor's family, either alone or collectively, has the right after such transfer to remove, in whole or in part, the restriction.

Excepted from the definition of applicable restrictions are any commercially reasonable restriction which arises as part of any financing by the corporation or partnership with a person who is not related to the transferor or transferee, or a member of the family of either, or any restriction imposed, or required to be imposed, by any federal or state law. An example of an applicable restriction is where a partnership agreement requires unanimous vote to liquidate where state law imposes a less stringent requirement (e.g., unanimous consent of the general partners and a majority of limited partners).

As discussed above, a lock-in discount may be negated by section 2704(b) if the lock-in discount is created by an applicable restriction.

FRACTIONAL INTEREST DISCOUNTS

The courts have long recognized that the value of a fractional interest in real property may be less than the pro-rata value of the same real property if held as a full fee simple.[36] Among the factors cited by the courts in justifying the application of a discount to the pro-rata value of a fractional interest in real property are the following:

1. The owner of a fractional interest will have greater difficulty in finding a ready market for the sale of the interest due to the fact that a buyer of the interest will have to share ownership with another;

2. The owner of a fractional interest cannot sell the fee interest in the property or lease the property without the consent of the holder of the remaining interest(s);

3. The owner of a fractional interest by himself generally cannot obtain a loan from normal sources of credit secured by only a partial interest in the real property;

4. The owner of a fractional interest may not have the right to exclusive use of the property so as to put it to its highest and best use;

5. An action by an owner of a fractional interest to partition real property does not guaranty that the partitioning co-owner will receive property whose utility is equal to that of the entire parcel from which the partition took place;

6. The cost of bringing an action to partition real property is often substantial and a fee interest in a portion of the property received may be worth less than the proportionate share of the whole property or the sales proceeds (if the property may not be fairly partitioned) may not equal the property's fair market value; and

7. The existence of an undivided fractional interest is a legal matter affecting title to real property and often cannot be solved without obtaining legal counsel and commencing legal proceedings at significant cost.

For these reasons, many courts have allowed a discount to the proportionate value of real property in order to arrive at the value a willing purchaser would be willing to pay for an undivided fractional interest in real property.[37] If the taxpayer asserts that a discount from the proportionate value of the entire property is warranted, the taxpayer must prove that a willing buyer would purchase the property and a willing seller would sell the property at a price which is less than its proportionate value. Generally, the taxpayer may satisfy this burden by using expert opinion testimony of competent and experienced real estate brokers or appraisers, backed by records of actual sales of fractional interests in the same or similar property.[38]

The IRS valuation manual acknowledges the allowance by courts of decreases in value for partial ownership. The Guide states that the extent of ownership rights in each case is to be determined under state law. Although the IRS Valuation Manual states that the fractional interest discount is generally based on the cost of dividing the land (e.g., survey costs, court costs, legal fees, etc.) the following other factors must be considered:

1. Size of the fractional interest.

2. Number of owners.

3. Size of tract and likelihood of partition.

4. Use of land.

5. Access to financing.

Whereas co-owners are free to contract with one another and impose restrictions upon their ownership rights, one means of negating the IRS' "cost of partition" argument is through the use of a Co-Ownership Agreement in which each co-owner agrees to waive his right to partition the subject property. Such waivers serve a legitimate business purpose of keeping the property in the immediate family for future generations.[39] It should be kept in mind that a Co-Ownership Agreement is likely to invoke the requirements of section 2703 and will not have any effect for federal tax purposes unless the three requirements for the safe harbor are met.

The restricted stock studies indicate that investors will typically discount a security which cannot be quickly sold by a range of 25% to 45%. However, the business entities involved in the above restricted stock studies are more risky than an ownership interest in real property. Consequently, an ownership interest in real property is likely to demand a lower discount typically ranging from five percent to twenty percent.

USING FRACTIONAL INTERESTS WITH FAMILY PARTNERSHIPS

Another advanced planning technique is to reduce asset values by applying multiple discounts. This concept is referred to as "double discounting" and permits the use of fractional interests with a family limited partnership to gain the benefits of all four discounts (i.e., fractional interest discount, minority interest discount, lack of marketability discount and lock-in discount).

Under this planning, the family limited partnership will own less than one hundred percent of the real property. Usually, the remaining interest in the property will be owned outside the partnership by children or grandchildren. Ownership of such undivided interests in the form of a generation-skipping trust is often desirable since the income from the fractional interest can be distributed to the child or grandchild and used to pay expenses of education or other expenses (e.g.,

music lessons, art, dance, travel to Europe) which are not legal obligations of the parents. The use of a Co-Ownership Agreement to waive the right to partition or cause a forced sale should be included in this planning in order to prevent the child or grandchild from attempting to liquidate its fractional interest.

AVOIDING PITFALLS

In planning for discounted asset values, watch out for the problem created by *Estate of Smith*, 94 TC 872 (1990), holding that for purposes of computing adjusted taxable gifts on the federal estate return, the value of all lifetime gifts may be reconsidered, even if a gift tax return was filed and the statute of limitations has run. While additional gift tax cannot be collected, this could force the taxable estate into a higher bracket and alter marital deduction gifts. Thus in *Estate of Lenheim*, TC Memo 1990-403, this rule was used to revalue gifts of decedent's stock in a family corporation to his sons over a period of 4 years, even though the statute of limitations had expired on the gifts.

Also, do no overlook *Estate of Murphy*, TC Memo 1990-472, where 18 days before death decedent transferred less than 1% to each of two children to bring her percentage below 50%, and her estate claimed a minority discount. The Tax Court allowed a discount for lack of marketability, but rejected the minority discount, noting that cases which permitted that discount, like *Estate of Bright*, arose before unification of the transfer tax, suggesting that minority discounts may no longer be available.

Note that the cases indicate that courts are closely examining the approach used by experts in valuing business interests, and the qualifications of the appraisers. In *Estate of Campbell*, TC Memo 1991-615, the court emphasized the importance of evaluating both earnings and net asset values in arriving at the actual value, and allowed a substantial discount. In *Estate of Berg*, TC Memo 1991-279, a 60% discount in the value of closely held stock was claimed to represent both minority and lack of marketability discounts. The appraisal was by petitioner's CPA, Mr. Whalen, an experienced practitioner who had served on the faculty of several universities and had testified as an expert witness in several cases on lack of marketability and minority discounts, but as the court noted, with no formal education as an appraiser. The court said: "we find the appraisal by Whalen, who is not a certified appraiser, unpersuasive for two reasons. First, he relies on *Estate of Andrews v. Commissioner*, supra, which does not support petitioner's position. The only other support for Whalen's appraisal is two articles by H. Calvin Coolidge." Although the underpayment penalty which was assessed was later reversed by the Eighth Circuit, this case is a good example of why a formal appraisal should always be commissioned.

CONTROL AND THE SWING VOTE ISSUE

It is well established that if the business interest being valued is a controlling interest, then a premium must be added to the valuation to reflect control. Recently, the IRS has applied this concept to situations where the transfers to individual family members were of minority interests, but they could collectively exercise control over the business entity. A donor owned 100% of the stock in a family corporation. He transferred 30% to each of 3 children, and 5% to his spouse. The gifts were valued at net asset value less a 25% discount for minority interest and lack of marketability.

In Letter Ruling 9436005, the IRS held that even though each gift is valued separately under Revenue Ruling 93-12, 1993-1 CB 202, since the blocks were transferred simultaneously, each had a "swing vote" characteristic, meaning that the owner of any 30% block could join with the owner of any other 30% block to exercise control, and that characteristic affected the value of the gift, citing *Estate of Winkler*, TC Memo 1989-231. The IRS pointed out that had the gifts been sequential, the first 30% would not have the swing vote characteristic, but the second would. Further, the transfer of the second 30% would increase the value of the first 30%, and would be an indirect gift. The same would occur on the transfer of the third 30% block.

COSTS OF LIQUIDATION AS A VALUATION FACTOR

Where valuation of interests in corporations is based on the value of the underlying assets of the corporation, should that value be discounted for a hypothetical income tax that would be incurred if the corporation were liquidated to reach the assets? The IRS steadfastly denies such a discount is available.

THE PARTITION THEORY

The IRS has also ruled that when valuing undivided interests in property, rather than permitting discounts, the property should be valued under the "partition" theory. Under that theory, the value of the property in question is reduced by the hypothetical costs of a legal action to partition it. For example, in the case of an undivided one half interest in a farm, the valuation would start with 100% of the value of the farm, then subtract the legal costs of partitioning it into two farms of equal value, and dividing the result by two.

In what appears to be a blow to the IRS theory of valuation of undivided interests in property based on the cost of partition rather than fractional discounts, the Tax court has held a fractional interest discount is appropriate for a decedent's interest in a farm. In *Estate of Cervin*, TC Memo 1994-550, the court held the farm could not be easily partitioned and a homestead could not be easily sold. In finding higher discounts, the court did not really reject the partition theory, other than with respect to homestead property. It concluded that a partition would involve substantial costs and fees, and the ability of the co-owners to agree on relative values. In other words, it used a discount rather than hypothetical costs of partition. It also rejected reliance by the estate's experts on case decisions and articles, indicating that it is up to the court, not the appraiser, to evaluate the significance of such authorities!

CONCLUSION

The valuation of a professional practice is an art, not a science. Many variables must be considered and evaluated. The quality of evaluation will be, in part, a function of the appraiser's skill in applying experienced judgment and subjectivity to the objective facts that are gathered.

References

Valuing Small Business and Professional Practices, Dow Jones-Irwin, Homewood, Illinois, 1986, is an excellent text in the business valuation area. Other helpful references are:

Advanced Sales Reference Service, The National Underwriter Company, Cincinnati, Ohio.

Estate Valuation Handbook, Wiley Law Publications, New York, 1983.

"New Warnings on Stock Valuation," *CLU Journal,* May 1985, 60.

"Present Value Analysis in Estate Planning after ERTA," *CLU Journal,* May 1985, 52.

The Professional Handbook of Business Valuation, Addison-Wesley Publishing Co., Reading, Massachusetts.

Footnote References

Valuation Planning.

1.   Regs. §§20.2031-1(b); 25.2512-1.
2.   IRC Secs. 2031(a); 2032(a)(2).
3.   IRC Sec. 2032(a)(1).
4.   IRC Sec. 2032(a)(3).
5.   IRC Sec. 2042(1).

6. IRC Sec. 2042(2).

7. Rev. Rul. 69-489, 1969-2 CB 172.

8. *Bankers Trust Co. v. U.S.*, 284 F.2d 537 (2nd Cir. 1960), cert. denied.

9. IRC Sec. 7520.

10. See *Est. of David Smith*, 57 TC 650 (1972), acq. 1974-2 CB 4.

11. Reg. §20.2031-2(e).

12. IRC Secs. 2031, 2512. Regs. §§20.2031-1(b), 2(b), 2(f) and 25.2512-2.

13. See, e.g., *Gallun v. Comm.*, 33 TCM 1316 (1974); *Kirkpatrick v. Comm.*, 34 TCM 1490 (1975); *Est. of Thalheimer v. Comm.*, 33 TCM 877 (1974); *Northern Trust Co.*, 87 TC 349 (1986).

14. See, e.g., *Est. of Bright v. U.S.*, 81-2 USTC ¶13,436 (5th Cir. 1981) (community property interest in stock of one spouse not attributed to other spouse to produce a control premium); *Propstra v. U.S.*, 82-2 USTC ¶13,475 (9th Cir. 1982) (fractional interest discount allowed for decedent's community property interest in real property); *Est. of Lee*, 69 TC 860 (1978), nonacq. 1980-1 CB 2 (fractional interest discount allowed for community stock ownership); and *Est. of Andrews*, 79 TC 938 (1982) (discounts permitted for stock in corporation owned by siblings).

15. *Northern Trust Co. v. Comm.*, 87 TC 349, 384 (1986); See also Reg. §20.2031-2(f).

16. *LeFrak v. Comm.*, 66 TCM 1297, 1308 (1993).

17. See Hall and Polacek, "Strategies for Obtaining the Largest Valuation Discounts," *Estate Planning*, January-February 1994, pp. 38, 42.

18. 61 TCM 2949, 2958 (1991).

19. The Partnership Spectrum published by Partnership Profiles, Inc. of Dallas, Texas publishes limited partnership trading data for many partnerships on a bi-monthly basis.

20. *Central Trust Co. v. U.S.*, 62-2 USTC ¶12,092; *Messing v. Comm.*, 48 TC 502 (1967), acq. 1968-1 CB 2.

21. See *Est. of Mark Gallo v. Comm.*, 50 TCM 470 (1985) (lack of marketability discount of 36 percent); *Est. of Charles B. Gillet*, 50 TCM 636 (1985) (lack of marketability discount of 15 percent allowed); *Northern Trust Co.*, 987 TC 297 (1986) (discount for lack of marketability of 25 percent allowed); *Est. of Stirton Oman*, 53 TCM 52 (1987) (20 percent discount for lack of marketability allowed from appraised value); *William O. Adair*, 54 TCM 705 (1987) (15 and 30 percent marketability discount granted on two separate blocks of stock); *Est. of Bertha B. Mosher*, 54 TCM 1578 (1987) (discount of 10 percent for lack of marketability); *Thomas E. Reilly v. Comm.*, 88-2 USTC ¶13,782 (1988) (30% discount for lack of marketability permitted); *Est. of Clara S. Roeder Winkler*, 57 TCM 373 (1989) (25% lack of marketability discount for nonvoting stock); *Est. of Edwin Wallace Neff*, 57 TCM 669 (1989) (10% discount for lack of marketability due to history of repurchases by corporation); *Est. of Ruben Rodriguez*, 56 TCM 1033 (1989) (10% discount for lack of marketability allowed, 35% discount for lack of marketability not proven by taxpayer); *Est. of Albert L. Dougherty*, 59 TCM 772 (1990) (25% discount for lack of marketability allowed to 100% interest in privately-held corporation); *Est. of Edgar A. Berg*, 61 TCM 2949 (1991) (10% discount for lack of marketability allowed after taxpayer could not rebut evidence offered by Service's expert); *John R. Moore v. Comm.*, 62 TCM 1128 (1991) (25% discount for lack of marketability applied to limited partnership gifts.

22. See fn. 17 at page 41 (citing Moore, "Valuation Revisited", 126 *Trusts and Estates* 40 (Feb. 1987)).

23. The 1971 Institutional Investor Study ("SEC Study") on restricted securities performed by the Securities & Exchange Commission (SEC) which was published in March 1971 (in eight volumes) analyzed the characteristics of (1) the restricted securities' purchasers and issuers, (2) the size of the transactions in dollars and shares, (3) the marketability discounts on different trading markets, and (4) the resale provisions.

24. Unpublished.

25. See Garlick, Houlihan Valuation Advisors, Valuation Report, Fall 1993, pp. 1-2.

26. Milton Gelman, "An Economist-Financial Analyst's Approach to Valuing Stock of a Closely-Held Company," *Journal of Taxation*, June 1972, pp. 353-4. This study analyzed the prices paid for interests in four closed-end investment companies who specialized in the investing of restricted securities. The study compared 89 transactions occurring during 1968 through 1970. The average and median discounts were approximately thirty-three percent (33%). Approximately sixty percent of the purchases occurred at trades of over thirty percent.

27. This study analyzed sixty sales of letter stocks to mutual funds during 1968 through 1972. The average discount was 33.45%. Similar to the SEC Study, companies listed on national exchanges generally had lower discounts than did companies traded over-the-counter. See Robert K. Trout, "Estimation of the Discount Associated with the Transfer of Restricted Securities," *Taxes*, June 1977, pp. 381-5

28. This study analyzed restricted stock sales for investment companies. For 146 transactions, the average discount was 35.6% and the median was 33.0%. See Robert E. Maroney, "Most Courts Overvalue Closely-held Stocks," *Taxes*, March 1973, pp. 144-54, 151, 154.

29. J. Michael Maher's study was published in 1976 and found an average marketability discount of 35.43% for transactions during 1969 through 1973. This study was similar to the Maroney study. See J. Michael Maher, "Discounts for Lack of Marketability for Closely-held Business Interest," *Taxes*, Sept. 1976.

30. In 1983, Standard Research Consultants compared letter stock sales to the SEC Study. In twenty-eight private placements of restricted stock during 1978 through 1982, the study found discounts between 7% to 91% with a median of 45%. See "Revenue Ruling 77-287 Revisited," SRC Quarterly Reports, Spring 1983, pp.1-3.

31. This study reviewed letter stock sales during the period 1981 through 1984 and found a median discount of 31.2% for thirty-three transactions. See Shannon Pratt, *Valuing a Business*, 2nd Edition, 1989, p. 247. Also, Willamette Management Associates performed five studies on the prices of private company sales shortly before public offerings during the period 1975 through 1985. On average, higher discounts were found than in the studies of restricted stocks. The median discounts during this period fell within a range of 50% to 80% with an average of 42% to 74%. See Shannon Pratt, *Valuing a Business*, 2nd Ed., 1989, pp. 250-55.

32. Two studies were conducted by this company. The first study reviewed initial public offerings during January 1980 through June 1981 and found discounts on average of 60% with a 66% median. The second study reviewed offerings during January 1985 through June 1986 and

found discounts on average of 43% with the same median. See John D. Emory, "The Value of Marketability as Illustrated in Initial Public Offerings of Common Stock — January 1980 through June 1981," *Business Valuation News*, Sept. 1985, pp. 21-24; "The Value of Marketability as Illustrated in Initial Public Offerings of Common Stock — January 1985 through June 1986," *Business Valuation Review*, Dec. 1986, pp. 12-14.

33. Reg. 25.2703-(3).

34. Reg. §25.2704-1(a)(2)(iv).

35. Reg. §25.2704-1(a)(2)(v).

36. See *Est. of George W. Youle*, 56 TCM 1594; *Est. of Evelyn L. Wildman*, 58 TCM 1006; *Est. of Louis D. Whitehead*, 33 TCM 253 (1974); *Nancy M. Mooneyham v. Comm.*, 61 TCM 2445 (1991).

37. See *Est. of Ila Jean Anderson v. Comm.*, 56 TCM 78 (1988) (discount of 20% allowed to value of undivided one-half community property interest); *Nancy N. Mooneyham v. Comm.*, 61 TCM 2445 (1991) (discount of 15% percent allowed to undivided one-half interest in real property owned as tenants-in-common by brother and sister); *Est. of Evelyn L. Wildman v. Comm.*, 58 TCM 1006 (1989) (discount of 15% allowed to value of undivided one-fifth interest in real property owned as tenants-in-common); *Est. of Harriet L. Feuchter v. Comm.*, 63 TCM 2104 (1992) (partnership owning undivided one-half interest in three tracts of land allowed 15% discount); *Est. of John Baggett v. Comm.*, 62 TCM 333 (1991) (decedent's undivided twenty-five percent interest in real property discounted 35% to reflect fractional interest); *Est. of Eleanor O. Pillsbury v. Comm.*, 64 TCM 284 (1992) (15 percent discount applied to undivided 77 percent and 23 percent fractional interests held in trust).

38. *Stewart* 31 BTA 201 (1934).

39. See Polacek and Lehn, "Tax Court Allows Sizable Fractional Interest Discount," *Trusts & Estates*, Sept. 1994, pp. 29, 37.

Chapter 43

WILLS

WHAT IS A WILL?

A will is the legal expression of declaration of an individual's wishes as to the disposition of his property after death. Revocable during the individual's lifetime, a will is not operative until death and is applicable to the situation which exists at death.

WHEN IS THE USE OF SUCH A DEVICE INDICATED?

1. The most important reason for creating a will is to provide the testator ("testatrix" is the feminine form; either form means the one who makes or executes the "will and testament") with an opportunity to control the passing of his property and thereby to avoid "intestacy." Without a will the decedent's assets will pass by the laws of intestate succession of the state in which the decedent resides or in which his property is located.

    The principle of the intestate succession laws is to distribute the decedent's property as the government believes the decedent would have wanted had a will been executed.

    Typically, the rules for distribution of separate property are as follows:

    A. Should the decedent die intestate with a spouse but no children, the spouse takes the entire estate.

    B. If a spouse and children survive, each takes some portion of the estate.

    C. If only the decedent's children survive, they take the entire estate.

    D. If no spouse or children survive, the estate goes to the decedent's parents, and if they do not survive, then to decedent's siblings or their heirs.

    E. The next level of intestate takers are the decedent's grandparents and their heirs (the aunts, uncles, and cousins of decedent).

    F. If none of the decedent's heirs survive, the next takers are the issue of decedent's pre-deceased spouse.

    G. If none of the above survive, the estate goes to the next of kin.

    H. The state is the final taker.

    While the rules above are typical, the laws in a particular state may have some variation. The above rules generally apply in the nine community property states (California, Arizona, Nevada, New Mexico, Washington, Louisiana, Idaho, Texas, and Wisconsin) as to separate property; but if the property is held as community property, even where there are children, all community property goes to the surviving spouse in the absence of a will.

    Louisiana has unique rules which limit what a spouse may do with property, in some circumstances forcing the transfer of property to a certain person (usually the surviving spouse) regardless of the terms of the will.

    Be certain to remember that real property in a particular state is subject to the rules of that state. Therefore, for example, a will dealing with oil interests or other interests in land located in Louisiana is subject to the laws of Louisiana, even though the testator is a resident of New Jersey.

2. As described above, without a valid will the decedent's property goes to his relatives as provided by statute. By making a will, a person can pass property in a different manner than that provided by statute. With a will, property generally can be left to one or more relatives, of any degree, or friends or charities to the exclusion of others.

    However, many states have laws which require the spouse and/or children to take some share of the estate. Property can be willed to non-relatives such as friends or charities, subject to rules in certain states that require some rights to pass to the spouse or children.

3. In a will, the testator can name the "personal representative" of the estate. A person or institution can be named to act as executor ("executrix" is the feminine form) and

be appointed to carry out the directions in the will and to dispose of the property according to the testamentary provisions.

The named personal representative may often be a relative or close friend. But, if the estate is large or complicated, the testator should consider appointing either a professional or an institution accustomed to dealing with assets and with the sometimes complicated rules of probate. If the testator feels it wise to name a person who has no experience in probating a will but who may be well acquainted with the testator's personal affairs, an alternative is to suggest that the executor hire a specified attorney to assist with the probate.

The will may provide that the executor need not be bonded, which can save money for the estate, but which gives up some protection. If there is no valid will or if no executor is named or if the named executor for any reason fails to qualify or ceases to act, the court will appoint an "administrator" ("administratrix" is the feminine form) to administer the estate.

4. A will can set out the terms of a trust in which the named trustee can manage assets on behalf of the beneficiaries for many years after the death of the testator. This may be especially appropriate in order to manage assets for the benefit of the testator's minor children. Such a trust is referred to as a "testamentary" trust since it is created through the decedent's last will and testament and comes into being at the probate of the will.

The terms of a testamentary trust are very important. Sometimes people have such trusts terminate when a child reaches age 18 or 21. Such an early distribution, at a time before the child has had the experience of handling large sums of money, often results in the child's not going to college and also losing all of the inheritance.

5. When there are minor children, the will can nominate a guardian of both the "person" and the "estate" of each child. State laws generally require a court to give significant weight to such a nomination by a parent who has custody of a child. Without such a provision, the court names the guardian upon the death of the parent(s) based on available information and often depending on who volunteers.

6. A will allows the testator to make alternative provisions in case some of the heirs predecease him. For instance, if a child dies, the testator may want to leave that share to the child's siblings, or perhaps to the child's issue.

7. Some types of property are not affected by the provisions in a will. Assets held in joint tenancy or tenancy by the entirety pass by right of survivorship to the remaining joint tenant(s). Policies of life insurance, IRAs, and certain other assets pass by contract to the person(s) named in beneficiary designations.

8. Even where an individual has a living trust which holds most of his assets in order to avoid probate, it is still very important to have a will which will "pour over" into the previously established trust any assets which were not already transferred to the trust.

9. A will can also be important in order to name an executor where a personal representative is needed to make elections for generation-skipping, QTIP, or other purposes.

10. The majority of states provide that if a spouse or child is not named in a will, such a person is deemed to be a "pretermitted heir." Regardless of what the will says, such person will take the share of the estate that would be given to that person under the state's rules of intestacy. Thus, it is wise to mention all such persons in the will so that they cannot claim to be pretermitted heirs left out of the will only because they were overlooked by the testator.

11. A will affords the testator the opportunity to minimize estate taxes and other transfer costs and provide who is to bear the burden of such costs.

WHAT ARE THE REQUIREMENTS?

1. The general rule is that any person 18 or more years of age who is of sound mind may make a will.[1] While this is the general rule, a few states have a different minimum age requirement.

2. The law ordinarily requires less mental capacity to make a will than to make a contract. An individual can make a will even if he is sick, elderly, weak, or of low mental capacity. In general, most states require that the testator know (1) the nature and extent of his property and (2) the natural objects of his bounty.

3. Except where a "holographic will" (one written entirely in the testator's handwriting) or an oral ("nuncupative") will is allowed, wills must meet certain legal requirements. Typically, an attested will must be in writing, signed by the testator (or in the testator's name by some other person in the testator's presence and at his direction), and must be witnessed by at least two persons.[2] Some states still require three witnesses while at least one, Pennsylvania, requires no witnesses at the time the will is signed.

4. Approximately half of the states recognize a holographic or handwritten will.[3] A will which is not effective under other provisions may be effective as a holographic will, whether or not witnessed, if it is dated and the signature and the material provisions are in the handwriting of the testator.[4] In some states, having printed or typed material on the holographic will can invalidate it.

5. Less than half of the states recognize oral (nuncupative) wills. This is a will declared or dictated by the testator during the last illness, before a sufficient number of witnesses, and later reduced to writing. In some states such wills are valid only under certain circumstances. For instance, they may be valid only to transfer a limited amount of personal property.[5]

HOW ARE THE TERMS OF A WILL DECIDED?

John Lee is preparing for his retirement and has decided to "get his affairs in order." He knows that without a will, his spouse and his children will each receive a portion of his estate. Since John's wife is a wealthy woman in her own right, as the recipient of the estate of her parents, John would rather leave his assets to the children. The children are not experienced in dealing with assets and his wife deals well with assets.

John has three children. The youngest has been estranged from the family for many years. John makes a will leaving all of his assets in a trust for the benefit of his two other children, one-half to each. He names his eldest child as executor of the estate and the second child as the successor executor. John's wife was named as the trustee of the trust for the two older children.

John realizes that certain of his assets, his life insurance and his IRA account, will not pass by his will. He has named his two eldest children as equal beneficiaries of those assets. To avoid his wife and estranged child taking intestate shares as pretermitted heirs, his will names them but leaves nothing to them.

John has made his decisions on the basis of need and degree of positive feelings he has for each beneficiary. His exclusion of his wife does not indicate a lack of feeling for her (a fact he may wish to communicate in the will) but a recognition that she does not need his assets for her security and also that adding more to her estate would increase the share which would ultimately be paid in death taxes.

By leaving the funds for the two older children in trust with his wife as trustee, he has provided good management to protect the trust assets for the children. The trust terms also provide John's wife with latitude as to the distribution of the assets as between the children and how and when they will receive the assets. Thus, John has not deprived his wife of some continuing parental control.

Although some people would "always leave things equally to the children," John has recognized the estrangement of the one child and has made the difficult but perhaps logical decision to leave the assets to the children who are still close to the family. In making such decisions, there is simply no "right way" that can always be applied to distributing assets; the decisions must be made on the basis of what is important to each testator and the circumstances of the persons and organizations he wishes to benefit.

HOW IS A WILL CHANGED OR REVOKED?

A will may be changed by writing a separate document which is not intended to be a new will but which is meant to change a provision of an existing will. Such a document is called a "codicil."

A new will, to the extent that it does not state that it is revoking all prior wills, may often merely change the terms of an existing will. In other words, the unrevoked prior will(s) remain valid to the extent not inconsistent with a later will. For this reason, it is good practice to make clear in a will that it is intended to revoke all prior wills, if that is the testator's goal.

Generally, a codicil must follow the same rules as a will in order to be valid.

Revocation of a will also may occur by destroying a will or defacing it with the intent to revoke. Sometimes the issue of the testator's intent (e.g., if the will is burned together with other papers or trash, was there an intention to revoke the will?) will result in expensive litigation. A specific statement of revocation in a new will (or writing "Revoked" across an old will and signing and dating that revocation) often may achieve the testator's goals more effectively.

Certain circumstances will cause the revocation of a will without any action on the part of the testator. Examples of this include revocation by marriage and revocation by divorce. Particular state law must be checked.

WHAT ARE THE DEATH TAX IMPLICATIONS?

At death, federal estate taxes are imposed on property which is transferred to the beneficiaries. However, each U.S. resident has a unified credit which eliminates the tax on the first $600,000 in estate assets.

While many states have abolished their state death taxes (except for a "credit estate tax," i.e., an estate tax sufficient to absorb the credit allowed against the federal estate tax for state death taxes actually paid) the majority do still have death taxes. Such a state death tax may be due even though there is no federal estate tax to pay.

If the decedent's assets are valued in excess of $600,000, federal estate tax will be owed unless a deduction can be taken. The most common deductions are the marital deduction (discussed in Chapter 37, Trust-Marital Deduction and By-pass) and the charitable deduction (discussed in Chapter 2, Charitable Contribution).

Other deductions generally available include the following:

A. Debts of the decedent;

B. Administration expenses;

C. Casualty losses to estate assets; and

D. Funeral expenses.

If a married individual wishes to minimize taxes at his death, he should be certain to have a will that provides for all assets in excess of $600,000 to pass to his spouse or to a trust for the benefit of the spouse, so a marital deduction can be taken for those assets. The taxable estate will thus be reduced to the value which can be "sheltered" by the decedent's unified credit.

However, if all of the assets are left to a spouse, there will be a 100% marital deduction and no assets will be available to take advantage of the unified credit (which is a "use it or lose it" benefit). The result will be that all of the assets will be taxed at the death of the surviving spouse and the unified credit of the first-to-die spouse will be wasted. This is reviewed in more detail in Chapter 37, relating to the marital deduction.

Generally, unless the will provides otherwise, estate taxes are apportioned among all beneficiaries of the estate (although in a few states death taxes are paid from the residue).[6] Alternatively, the testator may want to provide that taxes should be paid from the residue (assets not specifically disposed of elsewhere in the will) so that the recipients of specific gifts will not be responsible for the tax on the gift(s) they receive.

For example, if the will provides for taxes to be paid from the residue, Susie, the distributee of the decedent's Rolls Royce, will not have to make an out of pocket payment for her share of estate taxes, providing that there are sufficient assets in the estate residue to pay such taxes.

WHAT ARE THE INCOME TAX IMPLICATIONS?

For income tax purposes a probate estate is a separate taxable entity. A Federal fiduciary income tax return (Form 1041), and often a state income tax return, must be filed annually during the period of administration if sufficient income ($600 or more for the federal return) is received during a 12 month period.

No income tax is recognized solely as the result of a death. As a matter of fact there may be a tax benefit at death, since most of the assets in the decedent's gross estate receive a new income tax basis equal to the fair market value of each asset at the time of the decedent's death. Assuming the asset increased in value or is worth more than its basis in the decedent's hands during lifetime, it receives a "step-up" in basis. The taxable gain inherent in the asset disappears. Thus, an asset could be sold immediately after death and there would be no income tax to pay. For example, assume, 20 years before his death, a client purchased stock for $20 a share. If it was valued in his estate at $80 a share, that $80 would become the new basis for purposes of determining gain if his beneficiary sold it.

One exception to this rule is that type of asset which would have been subject to income tax if the decedent had received it. Unpaid fees due to a doctor or lawyer who reports his income on a cash basis, or notes resulting from the sale of property reported on the installment method would be examples of these. These assets are generally termed "income in respect of decedent" and they retain whatever income tax basis the testator had in them.

ISSUES AND IMPLICATIONS IN COMMUNITY PROPERTY STATES

Assets held as community property are owned equally by the spouses. At death, each spouse has testamentary power of distribution over his or her half of the community assets. Thus there is no certainty that the survivor will receive the decedent's one-half share of the community assets, but the absence of a will generally will produce that result.[7]

In common law (non-community property) states, the surviving spouse may sometimes be protected against disinheritance through laws of forced shares, dower, or curtesy.

In a community property state, the will of the deceased spouse may affect the survivor's half of the community property. For example, the decedent's will may purport to give all of the community property assets (the shares of both husband and wife) to a trust for the benefit of the surviving spouse and the children. If so, the survivor must elect whether to take under the will (thus assenting to the decedent's disposition of the survivor's one-half community property interest) or to take his or her one-half of the community property outright (denying the decedent's power to dispose of the survivor's community property interest) which will often require the survivor to give up rights conditionally given by the will in the decedent's share of community property assets.

QUESTIONS AND ANSWERS

Question — All of my client's assets are held in joint tenancy or in a manner in which a beneficiary is designated (e.g., IRAs). Does my client need a will?

Answer — While the assets currently owned by the client will pass to the survivors or beneficiaries without probate, at some time the client may acquire additional assets which are titled in another manner. Also, the named joint tenant(s) or beneficiary/ies might predecease the client. A will is always valuable to prevent against intestacy.

Question — Is it difficult to change a will as circumstances change?

Answer — A will can be amended or revoked at any time during the lifetime of the testator. It is possible to revoke a will in full and to create a new will, or to revoke only a portion of the will and add new provisions by means of a codicil. The will itself can provide for changing circumstances by making provisions for successor beneficiaries and/or executors in the event of the death of any named beneficiaries and/or executors.

Question — When should a will be updated?

Answer — Generally, a will should be reviewed at more or less regular intervals. Most specifically a will should be reviewed:

(1) When there are significant changes in the value of property that is intended to be distributed.

(2) Where the testator has moved from one state to another.

(3) Where there have been changes in family circumstances such as births, deaths, marriages, divorces.

(4) Where the personal representative, guardian or trustee can no longer serve as originally expected.

(5) Where federal or state tax laws change.

(6) Where changes in business ventures occur.

(7) Where disposition or other objectives change.

This list is not all encompassing but is representative of some of the major changes to cause a will review and possible change.

Question — Can the imposition of estate taxes at death be avoided by having assets pass outside the will?

Answer — The gross estate includes all assets owned by the decedent at death. This includes assets held in the decedent's name, assets transferred to a revocable trust by the decedent, the decedent's interest in joint tenancy assets, proceeds of life insurance from policies owned by the decedent, and the value of most retirement plans (IRAs, for example). Even assets outside the United States are subject to federal estate tax for a U.S. citizen. Unless a will employs tax avoidance devices such as the marital or charitable deductions, the will really has no effect on the amount of estate tax that is owed.

However, some state death taxes are inheritance taxes, which vary the amount of deduction and tax rate based upon the relationship of the recipient to the testator. To the extent that the will provides a different distribution of property than would an intestacy, the amount of inheritance tax to be paid may be changed. The other form of death tax, called an estate tax, is a tax based in general on the total value of the assets in the estate, rather than how much is inherited by each person and the relationship of that person to the testator. Two areas where even estate taxes are affected by who is the recipient of a bequest or devise include gifts made to spouses (which may result in a marital deduction) and transfers to charities (which may qualify for a charitable deduction).

Question — Does a client with a modest estate need a will?

Answer — There are many reasons almost every adult should have a will. Even though an estate is modest, it can be important to name a guardian for both the person and the estate of the client's children. A client may have very strong feelings that a close friend is the best person to care for the children and if those wishes are not expressed, the children may end up in the custody of relatives or others who would not have been chosen to deal with the children and/or their assets. In some cases a client may wish to leave the personal custody of a child to one person and leave the management of the child's assets to another.

Question — Suppose a client planned to avoid probate by putting assets in a revocable intervivos trust (a "living trust"). Can the client change the disposition of assets in the trust by changing his will?

Answer — As long as the client has actually placed the assets in the intervivos trust, his will will not have any effect on these assets unless the trust provides for amendment or exercise of a power of appointment to be made by a will. When a living trust is used, generally the will is only a "pour-over will" which directs to the trust any assets not already placed in the trust. The revocable trust can be changed by a written amendment in the form set out in the trust for such changes.

In order to avoid the question of whether the trust terms are to be changed or a power of appointment exercised inadvertently by a will, the majority of planners provide that changes in a trust can be made only by an instrument in writing other than a will.

Question — Can probate be avoided through an intervivos trust?

Answer — Yes, but only if the title of assets has been transferred from your client's name to that of the trustee of the trust. Failure to make the transfers will leave assets subject to a will and subject to the costs and delays of going through a probate in order to get into the trust.

Question — Is it expensive to have assets subject to probate?

Answer — Probate fees vary from state to state. In some states, they can be as high as a flat 5% of all probate property — plus additional fees for "extraordinary work" (preparing tax returns, some sales of property, fighting will contests, etc.). Both the executor and the attorney for the estate are entitled to a fee for their services.

Question — Assume a trust is desired to protect a client's children. Will it cost more to use a testamentary trust included as part of his will or more if an "intervivos trust" is used as a separate instrument?

Answer — There are at least three cost aspects to consider. One is the cost of going through probate, which is required for a testamentary trust but which can be avoided if assets are transferred before death to an intervivos trust. A different aspect is that many states require regular accounting to be made to the court by testamentary trusts, giving possibly better supervision but resulting in added attorney fees and court costs for each accounting. Lastly, the legal fees for drafting an intervivos trust may be greater since its use requires two documents (the trust and a "pour-over" will) and often some documentation to transfer title of assets.

Question — Is there any benefit to having property go through probate as opposed to having assets transferred to an intervivos trust prior to death?

Answer — Going through probate involves stricter supervision of the management and disposition of assets. To the extent that a client is concerned that the trustee who administers the trust may not carry out the trust terms in exactly the manner desired, the probate procedure may have some substantial benefit.

Another benefit of probate is that it has a "cut-off period" for creditors. As part of the probate process, a notice of the death is given to all creditors.[8] After notice, creditors have a specified period of time in which to file their claims and those creditors who do not make their claims within that time are thereafter cut off. With an intervivos trust, generally these claims are not cut off. For example, suppose a doctor were to die and a malpractice claim developed ten months after his death. That claim might well be cut off by a proper probate, but it would not be cut off with regard to any assets held in an intervivos trust at his death. Those assets have not gone through the "cleansing action" of probate. Some states, such as California, are considering a similar termination of creditors' rights for assets held in intervivos trusts.

Question — Under what circumstances can a will be challenged or contested when offered for probate?

Answer — A will can be contested by an interested or aggrieved party on many different grounds. Among the most common causes for contesting are:

(1) The testator lacked sufficient mental capacity.

(2) The testator was unduly influenced at the time the will was drafted.

(3) The will was not executed according to the statutory formalities.

(4) The will offered for probate has been revoked.

(5) The will offered for probate was a forgery.

Question — What things should an estate planner examine in reviewing a will?

Answer — See "How to Review a Will: A Checklist for the Estate and Financial Planner" in Appendix B.

Footnote References

Wills

1. Uniform Probate Code §2-501.
2. Uniform Probate Code §2-502.
3. Dan E. McConaughey, *Wills*, 18 (1984).
4. Uniform Probate Code §2-503.
5. Dan E. McConaughey, *Wills*, 22 (1984).
6. Uniform Probate Code §3-916.
7. Robert J. Lynn, *Introduction to Estate Planning*, 2nd Ed., 23 (1978).
8. Notice is usually given by publication. However, the United States Supreme Court has struck down as unconstitutional an Oklahoma statute that bars claims presented more than two months after notice by publication. The Court held that such notice does not necessarily satisfy the requirement of due process, that if a creditor's identity is known or reasonably ascertainable, the creditor must receive actual notice. *Tulsa Professional Collection Services, Inc. v. Pope*, No. 86-1961, 4-19-88, rev'g and remanding 733 P.2d 396.

THE FIRST INTERVIEW

Often, in order to encourage cooperation and full disclosure of pertinent data, it is necessary or helpful to explain to a client what estate planning is, who should be concerned with estate planning, how the federal estate tax laws work, and the mistakes that are commonly made because of a lack of proper planning. Ralph Miller, in his California law practice, to help his clients prepare for the interview, gives them an "Optional Checklist for Discussion." This extensive checklist is reproduced elsewhere in Appendix A. Finally, the delicate subject of anatomical gifts is discussed from the perspective of the estate planner.

WHAT IS ESTATE PLANNING?

A. The process of planning the accumulation, conservation, and distribution of an estate in the manner which most efficiently and effectively accomplishes your personal tax and nontax objectives. Every estate is planned — either by you or by the state and federal governments.

B. "Controlled estate planning" is a systematic process for uncovering problems and providing solutions in clients' L.I.V.E.S.:

1. <u>L</u>ack of liquidity

2. <u>I</u>mproper disposition of assets

3. <u>I</u>nflation (need to diversify and "inflation-proof" portfolio)

4. <u>I</u>nadequate income or capital at retirement/death/disability

5. <u>V</u>alue — need to stabilize and maximize value of business and other assets

6. <u>E</u>xcessive transfer costs

7. <u>S</u>pecial problems

WHO NEEDS ESTATE PLANNING?

More sophisticated planning than a simple will is indicated for:

1. Individuals with estates exceeding the unified credit equivalent.

    Currently $600,000.

2. Individuals in income tax brackets in excess of 15 percent.

3. People with:

    a. Children who are minors.

    b. Children (or spouses or other dependents) who are exceptionally artistic or intellectually gifted.

    c. Children (or spouses or other dependents) who are retarded, emotionally disturbed, or physically handicapped.

    d. Spouses (or children or other dependents) who can't or don't want to handle money, securities or a business.

    e. Closely held business interests.

    f. Property in more than one state.

    g. Charitable objectives.

    h. Special property such as fine art, a coin, gun, or stamp collection.

    i. Pets.

WHAT ARE THE TOOLS OF PROPERTY TRANSFER?

A. Lifetime transfers by gift or sale; gifts may be outright or in trust

B. Transfers at death
1. Will
2. Intestacy
3. Operation of law

C. Methods of transfer
1. Will — key vehicle of testamentary transfer
    a. Definition: Legal declaration of what a person wants done with his property or estate upon his death
    b. What a will can and should do
        (1) Distribute property according to your wishes
        (2) Make gifts of specific property to whomever you wish, including friends, charity, or devoted employee
        (3) Name executor of choice and direct that executor serve without bond
        (4) Nominate guardian of minors and incompetents
        (5) Designate source for payment of taxes
        (6) Use marital deduction most effectively
        (7) Denote appropriate procedure for disposition of estate in the event of a common disaster
    c. Limitations on disposition by will or trust
        (1) Extent to which you can disinherit spouse
        (2) Duration of trust
        (3) Prohibitions on appointment of minor or incompetent as executor
    d. Validity of will
        (1) Execution
            (a) Signing
            (b) Witnessing
    e. Revocation of will
        (1) By declaration in later will
        (2) Codicil
        (3) Execution of later will wholly inconsistent with former will
        (4) Intentional destruction of will
        (5) Operation of law
    f. Grounds to contest will in your state
        (1) Improper execution
        (2) Lack of testamentary capacity
        (3) Undue influence in making will
        (4) Fraud
        (5) Forgery
        (6) Revocation by testator or operation of law
    g. Taking "against the will" (Right of election)
2. Intestate succession as a means of transferring property
    a. Who can inherit
    b. Statutory scheme
    c. Family allowances
    d. Problems inherent in allowing state law to control dispositive scheme

3. Operation of law as a means of transferring property
   a. Contracts
      (1) Insurance
      (2) Antenuptial and postnuptial agreements
   b. Jointly held property
4. Disclaimers
   a. Defined — unqualified refusal to accept bequest or gift
   b. Must be in writing and received by transferor, his legal representative or holder of legal title to property
   c. Refusal received within 9 months of date when transfer creating the interest was made or, if later, day the person reaches 21 years of age
   d. The disclaimant never accepted the interest or any of its benefits
   e. Without direction by disclaimant, interest then passes to spouse of the decedent or person other than disclaimant.
   f. Disclaimed interest in property is undivided portion of the interest
   g. A power over property may be disclaimed under above rules

D. Estate administration — What it is and how it works
   1. Probate process
      a. Definition of probate — the process of proving:
         (1) the last will
         (2) the testator's intention
      b. What is probate versus nonprobate property
      c. Steps in settling an estate
         (1) Proving the will
            (a) Determine existence of will
               (i) Examine safe deposit boxes
               (ii) Search valuable papers
            (b) Deposit original will for probate
            (c) Locate witnesses to attest to validity of signature
            (d) Self-proving (notarized) wills
            (e) Appointment of executor — grant of Letters Testamentary
         (2) When there is no will
            (a) Petition court for appointment of administrator of estate
            (b) Grant of Letters of Administration
            (c) Necessity to post bond
         (3) Basic duties of personal representative (executor or administrator)
            (a) Assemble property of estate
            (b) Safeguarding and interim management of property
            (c) Advertise estate in legal and nonlegal newspapers
            (d) Locate and communicate with beneficiaries
            (e) Pay debts and expenses of estate
            (f) Make interim distributions to beneficiaries where indicated
            (g) Prepare inventory of estate
            (h) File and pay state inheritance or estate tax
            (i) File Federal estate tax return if necessary

      (j) Make final accounting

      (k) Distribution of net estate

      (l) Closing of estate and discharge of personal representative

E. How property can be owned
1. Distinction between "real" and "personal" property
2. Kinds of personal property
    a. Tangible
    b. Intangible
3. Undivided interest in property
    a. Tenancies in common
    b. Joint tenancies with right of survivorship
      (1) Advantages
      (2) Disadvantages
      (3) Federal taxation of jointly held property with right of survivorship
    c. Tenancies by the entirety
    d. Community property interests
    e. Other property interests
      (1) Distinction between legal and equitable ownership
      (2) Distinction between present and future rights
      (3) Distinction between vested and contingent remainders

F. Trusts
1. Definition of trust — legal fiduciary arrangement with respect to property
2. Five necessary elements
    a. Creator
    b. Trust property or res
    c. Trustee
    d. Beneficiaries
    e. Terms of trust or trust instrument
3. Types of trusts
    a. Intervivos
      (1) Revocable
      (2) Irrevocable
    b. Testamentary
4. Duration of trusts: rule against perpetuities

G. Fiduciaries
1. Types of fiduciaries
    a. Personal representative
      (1) Executor
      (2) Administrator
    b. Trustee
    c. Guardian

2. Fiduciary duties and responsibilities — duty to:
   a. Give undivided loyalty to the beneficiary
   b. Not delegate responsibilities to others which trustee can perform
   c. Keep accounts and to furnish information to beneficiaries (make full disclosure)
   d. Maintain and preserve trust property
   e. Make trust productive
   f. Pay income to beneficiaries when the trust instrument so provides
   g. Keep trust property separate (not commingle assets unless so instructed by trust instrument)
   h. Deal impartially with beneficiaries when more than one exists
   i. Communicate with other trustees and to act in concert with other trustees
   j. Not to self-deal or profit at beneficiaries' expense
   k. Enforce claims of trust, compromise and defend claims against trust

3. Powers of a trustee — Trustees' powers are limited by
   a. the terms of the trust,
   b. the law of the state in which the trust is being administered, and
   c. those necessary or appropriate powers that are not expressly forbidden by the terms of the trust.

The trustee may be given absolute discretion to make decisions and exercise judgments without leave of court as long as the act is not illegal.

The Tools and Techniques of Estate Planning

HOW DO THE FEDERAL ESTATE TAX LAWS WORK?
AN OVERVIEW

A. **Your gross estate — all property owned at your death and transferred by reason of your death (with special exceptions and limitations) is subject to tax. This includes:**

1. Property owned at death.
2. Property passing under state laws to your surviving spouse (or children).
3. Certain gifts made within 3 years of your death.
4. Gifts where you have retained certain rights or interests.
5. Gifts which don't take effect until your death.
6. Gifts which you can revoke, alter, amend or terminate.
7. Annuities.
8. Jointly owned property — except to the extent your survivor can prove contribution. (Only 50 percent of the estate tax value of jointly held property owned solely by husband and wife is includable.)
9. Property over which you possess certain powers.
10. Life insurance you own or which is payable to or for the benefit of your estate.
11. Marital deduction property in which you have a qualifying income interest.

B. **Deductions — your gross estate may be reduced by:**

1. Funeral expenses.
2. Administrative costs.
3. Debts and mortgages.
4. Certain taxes payable at your death.
5. Certain losses.
6. A "marital deduction" for property passing to your surviving spouse in a qualifying way.
7. A charitable deduction.

C. **After allowable deductions are taken, certain taxable gifts made during your lifetime are added back and estate tax rates are applied. Gift taxes which would have been paid if rates in effect at your death had been in effect at time of gifts, on the gifts added back, reduce the tax otherwise payable.**

D. **Then the following credits reduce the estate tax:**

1. Unified credit.
2. State death tax credit.
3. Foreign death taxes.
4. Estate tax on prior transfers.

E. **A 15 percent additional estate tax is imposed on an "excess retirement accumulation" in qualified pension and profit sharing plans (including HR-10 plans), tax-sheltered annuities, and IRAs.**

F. **The remaining amount is the net estate tax — generally payable in cash within nine months from the date of your death.**

The worksheet on the following page may be useful in understanding the operation of the federal estate tax law.

FEDERAL ESTATE TAX LAW
HOW IT WORKS

G. The Computation

(1) Start with: **Gross Estate** $_____

Subtract:
(a) Funeral expenses $_____
(b) Administrative expenses _____
(c) Debts _____
(d) Taxes _____
(e) Losses _____

(2) Result: **Adjusted Gross Estate** $_____

Subtract:
(a) Marital Deduction $_____
(b) Charitable Deduction _____

(3) Result: **Taxable Estate** $_____

(4) Add: **Adjusted Taxable Gifts** $_____
(Taxable portion of Post '76 gifts)

(5) Result: **Tentative Tax Base** $_____

(6) Compute: **Tentative Tax** $_____

(7) Subtract: Gift taxes which would have
been payable on gifts made after
1976 if tax rate schedule in effect
at decedent's death had been
applicable $_____

(8) Result: **Tax Payable Before
Reduction for Credits** $_____

(9) Subtract:
(a) Unified Credit $_____
(b) State Death Tax Credit _____
(c) Credit for Foreign Death Taxes _____
(d) Credit for Tax on Prior Transfers _____

(10) Add: **15% Excess Accumulations Tax** $_____

(11) Result: **Net Federal Estate Tax Payable** $_____

THE TEN MOST COMMON ESTATE PLANNING MISTAKES

(And How To Avoid Them)

by Stephan R. Leimberg
Copyright 1990 by Stephan R. Leimberg

This entire commentary is devoted to the types of problems that can cost you and your family tens of thousands of dollars and unbelievable heartache. Since only a fool learns from his own mistakes, this commentary is dedicated to the wise man (and woman) who can profit from the lessons so many have expensively learned the hard way.

Here are ten areas of common (and serious) mistakes that can be easily solved with the assistance of a financial services professional. Have you made one or more of these mistakes? If you haven't checked, how do you know?

Mistake 1: Improper Use of Jointly-Held Property

If used excessively or used by the wrong parties (especially by unmarried individuals) the otherwise "poor man's will" becomes a poor will for an otherwise good man or woman. In short, jointly held property can become a nightmare of unexpected tax and nontax problems including:

A. When property is titled jointly there is the potential for both federal and state gift tax.

B. There is the possibility of double federal estate taxation; if the joint ownership is between individuals other than spouses, the entire property will be taxed in the estate of the first spouse to die — except to the extent the survivor can prove contribution to the property. Then, whatever the survivor receives and does not consume or give away will be included (and taxed a second time) in the survivor's gross estate.

C. Once jointly owned property with right of survivorship has passed to the survivor, the provisions of the decedent's will are ineffective. This means the property is left outright to the survivor who is then without the benefit of management protection or investment advice.

D. The surviving spouse can give away or at death leave the formerly jointly owned property to anyone she wants regardless of the desires of the deceased spouse. In other words, holding property jointly equates to a total loss of control since the surviving spouse can ignore the decedent's wishes as to the ultimate dispo-

sition of the property. This loss of control can be especially horrendous when the joint owners are not related.

E. Since the jointly held property passes directly to the survivor (who then could possibly squander, gamble, give away, or lose the property to creditors), the decedent's executor could be faced with a lack of adequate cash to pay estate taxes and other settlement expenses.

F. A well drawn estate plan is designed to avoid double taxation — often by passing at least a portion of the estate into a CEBT (Credit Equivalent Bypass Trust). In this manner up to $600,000 can be sheltered from federal estate tax at both the first decedent's death and then again (since the surviving spouse has only an income interest) escape estate tax at the death of the surviving spouse. But holding property in joint tenancy thwarts that objective. Instead of going to a bypass trust to avoid a second tax, the property goes directly to the survivor and will be taxed at the survivor's death. So the credit of the first spouse to die is wasted.

Mistake 2: Improperly Arranged Life Insurance

A. The proceeds of life insurance are often payable to a beneficiary at the wrong time (before that person is emotionally or physically or legally capable of handling it) or in the wrong manner (outright instead of being paid over a period of years or paid into trust).

B. There is inadequate insurance on the life of the key person in a family (the "breadwinner") or the key person in a corporation (the "rainmaker").

C. Often, no contingent (backup) beneficiary has been named. The "Rule of Two" should be applied here: In any dispositive document there should be — for every name in the document — at least two backups.

D. The proceeds of the policy are includable in the gross estate of the insured because the policy was purchased by the insured and then transferred within three years of the insured's death. The solution is to have the ultimate beneficiary, acting without direction from the insured and using her (or its) own money, purchase and own the insurance from its inception. That party should also be named beneficiary.

E. When the policyowner of a policy on the life of another names a third party as beneficiary, at the death of the insured, the proceeds are treated as a gift to the beneficiary from the policy owner. For example, if a wife purchases a policy on her husband's life but names her children as beneficiaries, at the husband's death she is making a gift in the amount of the proceeds to the children.

F. If a corporation names someone other than itself (or its creditor) as the beneficiary of insurance on the life of a key employee, when the proceeds are paid, the IRS will argue that the proceeds are not income tax free and should be treated as either dividends if paid to or on behalf of a shareholder or compensation if paid to an employee who is not a shareholder (assuming the premiums were never reported as income or there was no split dollar agreement or no "P.S. 58" income reported). Worse yet, if the insured owned more than 50 percent of the corporation's stock, he is deemed to have incidents of ownership (that means federal estate tax inclusion of the proceeds) in the policy on his life. So, for example, the same $1,000,000 proceeds could be taxed as a dividend for income tax purposes ($280,000 income tax) and also be taxed as an asset in the estate for estate tax purposes ($550,000 maximum tax).

G. Whenever life insurance is paid to the insured's estate, it is needlessly subjected to the claims of the insured's creditors and in many states unnecessarily subjected to state inheritance tax costs. Probate costs are increased without reason and the proceeds are then subjected to the potential for an attack on the will or an election against the will.

H. If a life insurance policy — or any interest in a life insurance policy — is transferred for any kind of valuable consideration in money or money's worth, the proceeds may lose their income tax free status. For example, if a child buys the $1,000,000 term insurance policy owned on her father's life from his corporation or business partner, when she receives the proceeds, the entire $1,000,000 will be subject to ordinary income tax ($280,000).

I. Where a husband is required by a divorce decree or separation agreement to purchase or maintain insurance on his life, he will receive no income tax deduction for premium payments if he owns the policy — even if his ex-wife is named as irrevocable beneficiary. No alimony deduction is allowed on the cash values in a policy the husband is required to transfer to his ex-wife under a divorce decree. The safest way to assure a deduction is for the husband to increase his tax deductible alimony and for the ex-wife to purchase new insurance on his life which she owns and on which she is the beneficiary. It is extremely important for each spouse recently divorced to immediately review his or her own life, health and disability insurance situation.

Mistake 3: Lack of Liquidity

A. Most people don't have the slightest idea of how much it will cost to settle their estates or how quickly the taxes and other expenses must be paid. Worse yet, they don't realize that a forced (fire) sale of their most precious assets, highest income producing property, or loss of control of their family business will result from an insufficiency of cash. (If you haven't checked, how do you know your executor will have enough cash to avoid a forced sale?)

B. Liquidity demands have increased significantly in the last few years and should be revisited by those who have not done a "what if ..." hypothetical probate. Among the expenses that demand cash from the estate's executor are:

1. Federal Estate Taxes

2. State Death Taxes

3. Federal Income Taxes (including taxes on pension distributions)

4. State Income Taxes (including taxes on pension distributions)

5. Probate and Administration Costs

6. Payment of Maturing Debts

7. Maintenance and Welfare of Family

8. Payment of Specific Cash Bequests

9. Funds to Continue Operation of Family Business, Meet Payroll and Inventory Costs, Recruit Replacement Personnel, and Pay for Mistakes While New Management is Learning the Business

10. Generation-Skipping Transfer Tax (55%)

11. Excise Tax on Excess Pension Accumulations (15%)

Most larger estates will be subjected to almost all of these taxes and costs.

The Tools and Techniques of Estate Planning

Mistake 4: Choice of the Wrong Executor

A. Naming the wrong people to administer the estate can be disastrous. The person who administers the estate must — with dispatch — often without compensation, with great personal financial risk, and without conflict of interest:

1. Collect all assets

2. Pay all obligations

3. Distribute the remaining assets to beneficiaries

Although this three step process seems simple, in reality these tasks are highly complex, time consuming, and in some cases technically demanding. Is the named executor capable?

B. Selection of a beneficiary as an executor can result in a conflict of interest. That person may be forced to choose between his interest and that of the other beneficiaries. This problem can be solved by adding an independent third party such as a bank trust department to serve alone or together with a family member.

C. Selection of a business associate may result in a conflict of interest. If the executor's job is to decide whether or not to sell the business interest or the task is to obtain the highest possible sales price, the executor will be responsible for the course of action that will best serve the beneficiaries' interests. Yet that may be diametrically opposed to his own. He may be selling himself out of a job or demanding a higher price for the business than he is willing to pay.

D. Sometimes the selected executor has neither the time nor the inclination to devote to the sometimes long and drawn out process of estate administration. Does the executor even live in the state of the testator?

E. The appointment of executors who do not know or get along well with the family members they are to serve sometimes results in chaos.

Mistake 5: Will Errors

A. One of the greatest mistakes is dying without a valid will. This results in "intestacy" which is another way of saying that the state will force its own will upon the heirs it chooses.

B. Too many wills have not been updated. A will should be reviewed at least:

1. At the birth, adoption, or death of a child

2. Upon the marriage, divorce, or separation of anyone named in the will

3. Upon every major tax law change

4. Upon a move of the testator to a new state

5. On a significant change in income or wealth of either the testator or a beneficiary

6. On any major change in the needs, circumstances, or objectives of the testator or the beneficiaries

Mistake 6: Leaving Everything to Your Spouse

A. Many people feel that there will be no federal estate tax because of the unlimited estate tax marital deduction and so they leave their entire estates to their spouses. But upon the death of the surviving spouse, everything that he or she received (assuming it has not been consumed or given away) is then piled on top of the assets that spouse owns. It is then that the "second death wallop" occurs with federal estate tax starting at a minimum of 37 percent on taxable amounts in excess of $600,000 and reaching up to a confiscatory maximum of 55 percent. The solution can be simple: The establishment of a CEBT (credit equivalent bypass trust). Up to $600,000 of assets can be left to a trust that provides income to the surviving spouse as well as other financial security but will not be taxed in her estate no matter when she dies or no matter how large trust funds grow. The balance of the estate can go in trust or outright to the surviving spouse. If that amount together with the surviving spouse's own assets doesn't exceed $600,000, this portion will also pass estate tax free when the surviving spouse dies.

B. Some individuals leave huge amounts outright to a surviving spouse, amounts that they themselves have never managed (few people have ever managed huge amounts at one time let alone managed spouses at any time). Often the survivor doesn't have the slightest training or experience in handling and investing a large stock portfolio, real estate holdings, or running a family business.

Mistake 7: Improper Disposition of Assets

A. An improper disposition of assets occurs whenever the wrong asset goes to the wrong person in the wrong manner or at the wrong time. Leaving an entire estate to surviving spouse or leaving a large or complex estate outright to a spouse unprepared or unwilling to handle it is a good example. Leaving a sizeable estate outright to a teenager is another.

B. "Equal but inequitable" distributions are common. If an estate is divided equally among four children who have drastically different income or capital needs, an equal distribution can be very unfair. Consider, for example, four children, the oldest of which is a brilliant and financially successful medical doctor and the youngest of which has serious learning disabilities and is still in junior high school. Think of a family with a physically handicapped child and three healthy children with no physical problems. Obviously, their needs and circumstances are not the same. Should each child receive an equal share? The proper solution may be a "sprinkle" provision in a trust that empowers the trustee to provide extra income or principal to a child that needs more in a given year.

C. Obvious examples of improper dispositions include the gift of a high powered sports car to a child, or to a senior citizen who no longer drives. "That can't happen in my estate," many people would be tempted to say. But upon the death of a primary beneficiary at the same time or soon after the testator, quite often there is no secondary beneficiary, or the second beneficiary who is named shouldn't receive the asset in the same manner as the primary beneficiary. The solution is to consider a trust or custodial arrangements and to provide in the will or other dispositive instruments for young children and legally incompetent people. Consider also the importance of a well considered "common disaster" or "simultaneous death" provision so that the asset avoids needless second probates and double inheritance taxes and goes to the right person in the right manner.

Mistake 8: Failure to Stabilize and Maximize Value

A. Many business owners have not stabilized the value of their businesses in the event of the disability or death of key personnel. What economic "shock absorbers" have been put in place to cushion the blow caused if a key employee was lured away by competition at the wrong time? Who will pay for the fixed expenses of the practice or business if the key employee is not there to generate income? Key employee life and disability insurance coupled with good business overhead coverage will certainly help.

B. Buy-sell agreements are essential to a business that is to survive the death of one of its owners. Yet many businesses have no such agreement. Or the agreement isn't in writing. Or the price (or price setting mechanism) doesn't reflect the current value of the business. Or the agreement isn't properly funded. So there is no guarantee that the heirs will receive the price they are entitled to — or no assurance that the surviving owners will have the cash they need to buy out the heirs (especially the dissident ones who want to tell them how to run their company).

C. Wills, trusts, life insurance contracts, HR-10 (Keogh) plans, IRAs, tax deferred annuities, without "backup" beneficiaries mean that money that could otherwise pass outside of the probate estate may instead be subjected unnecessarily to such costs and risks. The value of all those instruments and wealth transfer tools can be enhanced at no cost by merely naming secondary beneficiaries.

Mistake 9: Lack of Adequate Records

A. It can drive your executor crazy — and cost thousands of dollars of expenses — if estate and financial documents are hard to find. Take out a safe deposit box. Tell your executor where it is and make sure your executor has or can get the key and has access to it. Put all your important documents in that box. Each year, put an updated list of the names and phone numbers of advisors your family can count on in the box. Check with your attorney on the rules that apply at death: some safe deposit boxes are "frozen" (the state requires that the bank seal the box from entry until the inheritance tax examiner can inventory the contents) and there can be lengthy delays in getting to the papers in the box.

B. It is possible for an executor to obtain new copies of old income tax returns from the IRS — but why put the executor to the trouble and expense? Be sure to keep tax returns and records at least six years.

C. Many survivors have never been told what the decedent's goals were, what assets they can rely on for income or capital needs, or how best to utilize the available resources. Most widows or surviving children never had a meaningful discussion with the decedent about their financial security if...

Mistake 10: Lack of a "Master Strategy" Game Plan

A. Do it yourself estate and financial planning is the closest thing to do it yourself brain surgery. Few people can do it successfully. Yet, even do it yourself planning — from taking courses or reading books or listening to radio shows on the subject — is preferable to no planning. Actually, an intelligent layman can learn and do quite a bit if the time is taken at least once a year to quantify in dollar terms financial needs and objectives ("here's what we must have and here's what we'd like to have"), current financial status (here's where we are), and a game plan for getting to the goal in the most efficient and effective way. Using the right team of CPA, attorney, life insurance agent, trust officer, and other financial services professionals to conduct an annual "Financial Firedrill" to help formulate and execute that plan can make all the difference.

The Bottom Line

A key principle in estate planning is that *you can't eliminate the big mistakes in your estate plan until you've identified them.* Every family (and single person) — every year — should stage a "financial firedrill." Become informed. Edu-cate yourself now. Educate your survivors — before they are the survivors! Teach them how to handle money and make decisions. Show them, by example, how to read the bottom line on where their financial security stands.

A "financial firedrill" means that, with the assistance of competent financial services professionals, you annually measure your needs. Establish an order of priorities and then develop and put into effect plans to make certain that you are on target to meet your financial security needs.

RALPH GANO MILLER   CLIENT_____
MILLER, EWALD, MONSON, HOSHAW & SCHECHTER,
A Professional Law Corporation,

OPTIONAL CHECKLIST FOR DISCUSSION

As an option in preparing for our meeting, you may wish to review the following, which covers many of the specific areas of potential benefit and some of the areas of unique problems that relate to various circumstances in which clients find themselves. By reviewing the list and checking off those items which relate to your circumstances, we will be able to focus more clearly on your particular concerns at our estate planning conference. This will also provide you an opportunity to consider beforehand the matters which will come under discussion.

Please do not delay your meeting because of the fact that you have not had a chance to review the checklist, since there will be an opportunity in our discussions to cover any area in which you have an interest.

Checklist Index

CHECKLISTS FOR VARIOUS CIRCUMSTANCES

Please do recognize that the comments in this checklist are necessarily incomplete and that many important areas of potential benefit and detriment have not been covered. Therefore, you should not take any actions on the basis of the material in these lists without consultation with one of the attorneys in our office or with some other attorney.

[Some editing of the checklist has been done for this book.]

Copyright 1990
Ralph Gano Miller
1132o9004

1.   HOW TO USE THE CHECKLISTS

To save you time, you will probably wish to review only those aspects of the checklist which actually relate to your circumstances, since some aspects are redundant. Using the list of topics below, check the ones which relate to your circumstances, or to areas in which you might be interested (such as incorporating a business which presently might be held as a sole proprietorship).

In every case, you will wish to review either Checklist A or B (depending on your marital status). In addition, as an example, if you have an incorporated business or professional practice, you may wish to review the following additional areas:

Owners of Private Corporations
Professionals

Once you have determined the topics you wish to review, you can then turn to the appropriate page for each topic as shown below and check off the individual items of interest which are listed under that topic. Please also use the check-off boxes at the bottom of each page of the checklists to indicate those pages which you wish to review at our conference.

In reviewing specific areas of potential benefit or problems, please note that those which relate to non-tax matters (N), estate, gift or generation-skipping tax (E) or income or payroll tax (I) are indicated by the letter next to the check-off box to provide an easier means of identifying those areas which are of special interest to you.

The references to chapters after the heading of each item are to chapters of the [10th edition of *The Tools and Techniques of Estate Planning*].

Checklist Index

CHECKLISTS FOR VARIOUS CIRCUMSTANCES

A. ALL HUSBANDS AND WIVES WITH SOME ESTATE

AREAS OF POSSIBLE BENEFIT

[ ]N*   (1)   <u>Avoidance of Probate</u>: Use of a trust to both avoid the cost of probate and to eliminate the very substantial delays and restrictions of probate can be a benefit to even a very small estate. Although this course of planning is usually very beneficial, it may not apply to the extent that there are many potential liabilities of the decedent (e.g., a physician or engineer or attorney with no malpractice coverage or coverage which may be inadequate) which might be "scraped off" through the probate creditors-claim process. For some professionals or businesses, the unavailability of adequate malpractice coverage is probably the only strong argument for not avoiding probate. However, even for these persons, an intervivos trust will provide a means of keeping "safe from creditors" assets such as insurance and retirement plan proceeds from being mixed with other assets in a probate estate. For most estates, avoidance of probate (and conservatorship) is a major benefit to consider.

[ ]N   (2)   <u>Providing Assistance with Asset Management</u>: Use of a trust may also provide financial planning assistance to a child or a spouse who is not experienced in handling funds and also delays distribution of trust principal until the beneficiary gains more experience in managing assets. Gifts outright to a child (which usually will be held by a court appointed guardian), being distributed at age 18 or 21 may also destroy planning for college. This problem may be avoided by a trust to provide for education and living expenses and distribution of the proceeds at later dates (e.g., one-third each at ages 25, 30 and 35).

[ ]N   (3)   <u>Broad Durable Power of Attorney</u>: Like most states, California now permits one to give to another person a power of attorney which will be valid even if the person giving it becomes incompetent. This can aid greatly in the proper use of funds and avoid a conservatorship of the estate in some situations for a period of time. However, some people are unwilling to invest someone else with a power to deal broadly with their assets.

[ ]N   (4)   <u>Limited Durable Power of Attorney</u>: Some people prefer to give someone else only the power to transfer to a trust created by the grantor of the power property owned by the grantor. With this power, if the grantor is in a coma or otherwise unable to act, the holder of the power can shift the ownership of the grantor's assets to a revocable trust (previously created by the grantor) in order to avoid their being subject to probate at the grantor's death.

[ ]N   (5)   <u>Health Care Power of Attorney</u>: California now also allows one to designate a person who will have the power to make health care decisions, often permitting the avoidance of a conservatorship of the person. This document also allows one to indicate their wishes as to being placed in a rest home (as opposed to staying in their own home). It also provides a means of giving instructions as to any donation of body parts after death.

[ ]N   (6)   <u>"Pull the Plug" Directive</u>: Those persons who want to do so now may have a directive created, strictly adhering to state requirements, which may direct a physician to not sustain their life when there is no reasonable expectation that they may regain the use of their faculties.

[ ]N   (7)   <u>Clarification of Property Rights Through Property Agreement</u>: The actual ownership of property acquired before and during marriage is usually of importance, and often can be difficult to trace for either estate or income tax purposes or for marital rights purposes. A brief agreement can set forth and even change the form of title of their assets. This can be particularly important for people living in a community property state in order to receive a new stepped-up income tax basis (at one spouse's death) on both halves of property which they considered community property but which was titled as joint tenancy property.

[ ]N   (8)   <u>Provision of Liquidity Through Insurance</u> (Chapter 21): Where liquidity is important, it can be provided by life insurance, something which has become a "better buy" item in recent years.

---

*   The letters N, I or E after each check-off box indicates whether the specific item is more related to non-tax matters (N), income or payroll tax (I) or estate gift or generation-skipping tax (E).

ALL HUSBANDS AND WIVES WITH SOME ESTATE

[ ]E (9) <u>Full Use of Unified Transfer Credit</u> (Appendix C): Since every citizen or resident has the Unified Transfer Credit available to offset either gift tax during his or her lifetime or estate tax at death (see also Chapter 15), most estate planning for married couples since 1981 has been focused on the maximum use of the credit at the death of the first spouse to die so that, at the death of the second spouse, certain assets that have been already taxed and set aside (nearly always in a trust) will not be subject to tax again at the survivor's death.

[ ]E (10) <u>Measured Use of The Marital Deduction</u> (Chapter 37): Property left to a surviving spouse or to a marital deduction trust that qualifies for the [marital deduction will not be] subject to tax at the death of the first spouse. A great bulk of estate planning for spouses now calls for a measured amount of property to be taxed so as to result in a tax equal to the remaining Unified Transfer Credit, with the balance of the property subject to the marital deduction and thus, deferred as to estate tax until survivor's death. The property that has been taxed (with the tax offset by the Unified Transfer Credit) can escape taxation at the death of the surviving spouse.

Most estate plans executed before 1982 did not contain provisions which meet the criteria of the present law.

With proper planning, the surviving spouse may now have all of the assets available without any reduction for taxes to be paid to the Federal government (i.e., having a zero net estate tax to pay) and thus have a more financially secure position for the remainder of her or his life. However this approach can result in more overall estate taxes for the spousal unit than might be the case if some estate tax were paid at the first spouse's death. Use of the Qualified Terminable Interest Property (QTIP) concept of obtaining the marital deduction can be flexible so as to permit payment of none, some or all of the estate tax due at the first death, to be decided after the first spouse's death.

[ ]E (11) <u>Use of Annual Gift Tax Exclusion</u> (Chapter 15): Outright gifts and other gifts qualifying as "present interests" with values up to $10,000 can be made to each person in the world each year without creating any taxable gifts.

Where financial security permits, a program of annual gifts of $10,000-or-less can greatly reduce the amount of tax to be paid at the death of anyone. Currently, such gifts may be made even a few minutes before death and thus may also be a part of death-bed tax planning.

[ ]E (12) <u>Taxable Gifts of Appreciating Property</u> (Chapter 15): Where financial security permits, gifts made now of property which is expected to increase in value can be good planning even though a gift tax results.

Use of the Unified Transfer Credit to offset such gift tax will essentially reduce the amount of credit left available for offsetting estate tax at death. However, gifting an asset now which is worth $100,000 is much better than having that same asset included in one's estate if it is then expected to be worth $500,000.

If the gift is community property, it is divided between the two spouses. Where the property given is separate property, the availability of "gift splitting" (Chapter 15) permits the same result.

[ ]E (13) <u>Sales to Next Generation of Appreciating Property</u>: Future appreciation in a property may be avoided by a sale of the entire property to the persons who would otherwise inherit it. The potential estate tax benefits here must be weighed against the income taxes paid by the seller which would have never been paid if the property were retained until death.

[ ]E (14) <u>Gifts of Insurance</u>: A transfer of insurance, either outright or through the use of non-revocable trusts, may be an example of a gift with a high potential for appreciation since, for gift tax purposes, the gift is measured only by the value of the property at the time of the gift (usually the "interpolated terminal reserve value," approximately the same as the cash surrender value of the policy). Regardless of the gift value, the entire face amount of the policy will be paid over to the donee(s) at the insured's death. Besides being extremely effective in transferring values without significant transfer tax, such planning can often be done without any significant impairment of the financial security of the donor(s).

[ ]E (15) <u>Private Annuities</u> (Chapter 27): (The 1988 Technical Corrections Act created a floating rate at 120% of the mid-term Applicable Federal Rate [for valuing such annuities].)

ALL HUSBANDS AND WIVES WITH SOME ESTATE - Cont.

[ ]E   (16)   <u>Sales of Remainder Interests in Property</u>: [Generally, no longer feasible due to Code section 2702.]

[ ]E   (17)   <u>Split Interest Purchases of Property</u> [(Chapter 32): Generally, less feasible than previously due to Code section 2702.]

[ ]E   (18)   <u>Freezing Values of Assets</u> (Chapter 13): Partnership "freezes" and corporate arrangements with different classes of stock can in many circumstances shift the increase in value from one generation to the next [but such transactions are now generally subject to Code section 2701.]

[ ]E/N   (19)   <u>Use of Generation-Skipping Trusts</u> (Chapter 14): Although changes in tax law in 1976 (modified by the Tax Reform Act of 1986) added the generation-skipping tax to the Internal Revenue Code, thus restricting what had been almost an open field for delaying tax through successive generations, it still left some very significant areas of benefit which should be considered. The 1986 TRA Amendments substantially enhanced those areas of benefit.

Up to $1,000,000 per donor ($2,000,000 for a married couple with proper planning) can now benefit the children and go to their children (the grandchildren of the donors) without any tax at the death of each child or his spouse or anyone else in his generation. All larger estates should consider the possible use of this planning technique, including its use in relation to property that may be inherited by the client.

Apart from the estate tax benefits, this type of trust can also provide lifetime financial assistance and a measure of security to a child who is not "money wise."

[ ]E/N   (20)   [Deleted]

[ ]I   (21)   <u>Grantor Retained Income Trusts (GRITs)</u> (Chapter 35): Another technique used to reduce the transfer tax impact of a gift involves creating a trust which retains for the donor the right to the income from the gifted property for a certain number of years. [Generally, grantor retained annuity trusts (GRATs) and grantor retained unitrusts (GRUTs) will now be used instead of GRITs due to Code section 2702.]

[ ]I/E   (22)   <u>Charitable Remainder Trusts</u> (Chapter 2): In circumstances where one has an asset with a very low income tax basis and not producing income satisfactorily (or if another reason exists to dispose of it), it is possible to avoid tax on the gain on sale by creating a trust which will ultimately go to a charity, transferring the asset to the trust and having the trust sell it. The original owner(s) may retain an income stream from the newly invested sales proceeds, which have not been reduced by any income taxes. Insurance on the donor(s) may often be a basis for replacing the value of the assets which otherwise would have gone to the children of the donor(s).

POTENTIAL PROBLEMS

[ ]N   (1)   <u>Possible Estate Liabilities</u>: To the extent that the decedent has a large amount of potential liabilities (e.g., an anesthesiologist or civil engineer or tax shelter attorney who has neglected to carry professional liability insurance or a businessman who has found himself saddled with large debts), probate may be of some benefit in that most states provide a creditors claim period which cuts off liabilities to those creditors that do not file their claims in the proper way within that period.

Differences in state laws affect this, but there are some circumstances where most of the assets, if not all of the assets, should be subjected to probate in order to "cleanse" them of potential liabilities of the decedent. The availability of adequate professional or business liability insurance is a factor to be considered in determining whether to have assets (other than insurance or retirement fund benefits) be probated.

[ ]N   (2)   <u>Diversion of Assets to Replacement Spouse</u>: Children are often unintentionally deprived of security and benefits where assets are held in joint tenancy with a surviving spouse or left outright to a surviving spouse and that surviving spouse remarries. Without a trust to protect the children, there is no way to be certain that the children will receive any

ALL HUSBANDS AND WIVES WITH SOME ESTATE - Cont.

benefits, particularly if the survivor remarries and is subject to pressure to prove his or her love and devotion to a new spouse by joint tenancy ownership or a new will.

[ ]N   (3)   <u>Distributions to Children at Early Ages</u>: An estate built with great care and effort may be wasted, with little or no real benefit to the next generation, by leaving the property outright to a child who has no experience or ability in managing the assets. Early distributions also usually have a very adverse effect on educational planning.

[ ]N   (4)   <u>Loss of Mental Capacity</u>: If no trust has been created to hold the assets and provide a successor trustee to manage the assets, or where no one has been given a broad durable power of attorney, incapacity may cause serious disruption of a business and also disrupt payment of normal expenses of living. In this circumstance, a relatively cumbersome and expensive court conservatorship of the estate is the only way to provide some management for the assets.

[ ]N   (5)   <u>Spouse's and Children's Ignorance of Estate Affairs</u>: Failure to provide information as to the existence and/or location of assets may seriously disrupt the process of garnering the estate assets and properly managing them.

[ ]N   (6)   <u>Lack of Liquidity</u>: Although liquidity may not be required with current planning techniques at the first spouse's death for estate tax, it may well be required for other purposes, particularly if the decedent was in business or farming. Further, for larger estates, at the death of the second spouse, there may be a need to either have cash liquidity or liquidate many of the estate assets at a loss in order to pay death taxes.

Although it is now possible to have a zero estate tax liability at the death of the first-to-die spouse, there are circumstances where it may be beneficial to have funds available at the first death to pay estate taxes on assets at that time and avoid the increase in value which may take place during the lifetime of the surviving spouse. Where other liquidity may not be available, insurance on one or both of the spouses (or the survivor of them) may be the best answer.

[ ]E   (7)   <u>Having an Estate Plan Which Does Not Qualify For the [Unlimited] Marital Deduction</u> (Chapter 37): Many pre-1982 estate plans now result in payment of substantial federal estate tax at the death of the first spouse to die. The "totally tax-free transfer to a surviving spouse" simply doesn't happen under many pre-1982 estate plans, including some plans which use trusts to reduce estate taxes.

[ ]E   (8)   <u>Loss of Unified Transfer Credit (UTC)</u>: (Chapter 37): The most frequently encountered estate "problem" for married couples is that of the first spouse to die leaving all assets outright to a surviving spouse.

The Economic Recovery Tax Act of 1981 (ERTA) provided for a deduction for estate tax purposes as to any assets left to a surviving spouse. Thus, the decedent leaving all assets to a surviving spouse has no tax to pay (since all the tax will be deferred until the survivor's death) and thus, loses the advantage of the unified transfer credit to reduce the overall estate and gift taxes on the estates of the two spouses. This is true regardless of whether the decedent had separate property or community property. See Chapter 37 for a description of the use of a trust to create sufficient tax and take advantage of the UTC so that the property in that trust, taxed at the first spouse's death and segregated until the survivor's death, can avoid tax at the survivor's death.

[ ]E/N   (9)   <u>New Generation-Skipping Laws</u>: The Tax Reform Act of 1986 abolished the prior generation-skipping laws and instituted new rules for deaths and gifts after September 25, 1985. Many trusts which were drafted with the prior rules in mind do not now meet the requirements of the new law and should be reviewed. Also, direct gifts to grandchildren can now trigger not only death taxes but also generation-skipping taxes, and should be reevaluated.

[ ]E   (10)   <u>State Inheritance Taxes</u>: Not all state laws follow the current federal tax rules allowing a total marital deduction for gifts to surviving spouses. Planning must also consider the applicable laws of the state since such inheritance taxes can be significant.

California, Florida, Nevada and a number of other states have no inheritance or other death tax which would cause a higher overall death tax. Some states do have a "pick-up" tax which takes advantage of the federal credit for state death taxes and lets them share some of the federal estate tax.

ALL HUSBANDS AND WIVES WITH SOME ESTATE - Cont.

[ ]E   (11)   <u>Gifts with Retained Interests</u> (Appendix C): Where the donor retains an interest in a property (either technically as by retaining a life estate in property deeded to someone else or practically as by continuing to live in and make use of a house given to someone else), the property will be brought back into the donor's estate for estate tax purposes. Proper planning, e.g. paying full market rent on the residence given away but continuing to be used, can avoid and adverse results in some situations.

[ ]E   (12)   <u>Custodianship Gifts</u> (Chapter 41): A typical example of a retained right is the donor who makes a gift to a child and appoints himself or herself as the custodian of the gift until the child reaches maturity. Such gifts will be brought back into the taxable estate of the donor if he or she is the custodian of the gift.

[ ]E   (13)   <u>State Gift Taxes</u>: As with inheritance taxes, state gift tax laws often differ from federal laws, and many states have lower or no amounts of gifts which are excluded from gift tax and there may well be no marital deduction available for certain gifts in certain states. State gift taxes can be very substantial. As with inheritance taxes, a number of states (California, Florida, Nevada and several others) have no gift taxes which cause any additional tax to be paid.

[ ]E   (14)   <u>Accidental Gifts</u>: Although planned giving can be a most effective way of reducing transfer taxes, care should be taken to not create unintended taxable gifts.

          Except as between husband and wife, nearly every creation of a co-ownership with any other person (e.g., putting a stock or piece of real property in joint tenancy with someone) creates a taxable gift. Obtaining competent tax advice is the only way to avoid such gifts.

          The Tax Act of 1984 focused on interest-free loans or below-market-rate loans and created new and dangerous areas of potential unintended taxable gifts (Chapter 20).

[ ]E   (15)   <u>Insurance Gifts Within Three Years of Death</u> (Chapter 21): Tax law changes in 1981 abolished the Three-Year Contemplation Of Death Rule with regard to most gifts but not with regard to insurance and certain other gifts. Thus, either direct or indirect gifts of insurance within that period can result in the taxability of the insurance proceeds in the donor's estate. Community property rules may often present unique problems in identifying the donor of insurance (Chapter 21).

[ ]E   (16)   <u>Lack of a Qualifying Marriage</u>: The increasing frequency of absence of a formal marriage makes this a very real danger for couples who in other times would have married. Depending on state law, either a formal or a common law marriage can qualify for the marital deduction, but there must be a "marriage." Documentation for a marriage or a divorce in foreign countries must be examined by a competent attorney. California and several other states do not recognize "common law" marriages (those based on people living together).

[ ]E/I   (17)   <u>Failure to be Aware of Law Changes</u>: Although laws sometimes change in regard to wills and trusts, the changes are much more frequent with regard to estate, gift and income taxes. Ignorance of such changes can have very adverse effects on an estate plan. Estate plans should be reviewed regularly with competent counsel.

[ ]E/I   (18)   <u>Property Tax Reassessment at Death</u>: Where state law (e.g., Proposition 13 in California) has prevented valuation increases for property tax purposes, death can lift the barrier to such increases in valuation and also to tax increases. Some exceptions to such increases often do exist and estate planning must be done with property tax matters in mind.

[ ]E/I   (19)   <u>Retirement Plan Beneficiary Designation Forms</u>: Where benefits built up in a qualified retirement plan are planned to be transmitted at death, this is accomplished not by one's will or trust but by using a beneficiary designation form created for such a purpose. In those circumstances where there is a gift to anyone other than the surviving spouse of a participant (perhaps a gift over to a trust in the event the spouse does not survive or disclaims the gift), great care must be taken to see that the laws created by the Retirement Equity Act of 1984 are not violated. This law generally restricts all transfers of benefit from a qualified plan other than in the form of annuity payments. Further, any spouse of at least one year has an immediate right to half of the value in the plan to be left to her or him in the form of an annuity. Beneficiary designation forms must be carefully reviewed to spot any violations of this law.

ALL HUSBANDS AND WIVES WITH SOME ESTATE - Cont.

[ ]E/I (20) <u>Possible Retirement Plan Control By Will</u>: A California court has surprisingly said that regardless of retirement plan rules and possible preemption of state law by federal law, an interest in a retirement plan may be controlled by one's will. Many other states follow California law. Therefore, until this matter is resolved, it may be necessary to have one's will reference and confirm the effect of plan beneficiary designation forms. Otherwise, planning for proper direction of such plan proceeds may be frustrated.

ALL HUSBANDS AND WIVES WITH SOME ESTATE - Cont.

B. SINGLE PERSONS

AREAS OF POSSIBLE BENEFIT

(1)   Implications for the Single Client: With the exception of a marital deduction, all the potential benefits described in the checklist for "Husbands and Wives" are available to a single person. This group includes persons who have never married, those who have had an annulment or divorce and also survivors of marriage, both with and without children. However, the marital deduction is available only to the extent that there is an existing spouse who receives a lifetime gift or assets transmitted at death.

With the possible exception of the annuity (discussed below), there are few unique estate planning benefits available for a single person, although income taxation rules may from time to time give some advantage to a single person as compared to one who is married.

[ ]N   (2)   Use of Annuities: For those persons who truly have no financial responsibility for anyone else, the purchase of commercial annuities may have some application in increasing the cash available each month during the person's lifetime. However, the need for protection of purchasing power from inflation often argues against putting the majority of one's assets into such investments. Certain annuities provide some degree of protection from inflation.

[ ]I   (3)   Use of Charitable Remainder Trusts (Chapter 2): Where the single person has no need for concern over leaving assets to children or other persons, consideration should be given to obtaining a current income tax deduction by giving to a charity the right to use property after the single person's death. Although the flexibility of sale and/or consumption of the asset is lost, the income is retained and income tax lessened because of the deduction. Gain on sale of assets placed in the trust can escape taxation if placed in such a Trust.

POTENTIAL PROBLEMS

(1)   Implications for the Single Client: All the potential problems with regard to the above "All Husbands and Wives With Some Estate" apply to the single person. The exception is that there is no accidental loss of unified credit by leaving all the assets to a surviving spouse since the marital deduction does not apply to a single person.

[ ]N   (2)   Difficulty in Finding Conservator of Person or Estate: For those single persons who have no children, it is often much more difficult to find someone in whom they have enough confidence to make decisions regarding their person and all their assets when the single person is no longer able to make such decisions well.

[ ]N   (3)   The Lee Marvin Syndrome: Unmarried persons who have a live-in companion but no written agreement as to ownership of property or rights to income have a substantial exposure to lawsuits that may drastically reduce assets that would otherwise go to the beneficiaries of their estate plan. A written property agreement can solve this problem.

[ ]N   (4)   Heirs' Lack of Knowledge of Estate: Assets of a single person are frequently never all found since the executor, often an unrelated person and often a corporate fiduciary, may never have been given information as to the existence or location of assets.

[ ]N   (5)   Single Parent Finding Guardian For Children: Failure to direct some thought and effort toward the often difficult question of finding a suitable guardian for the children of a single parent often results in not only not finding a suitable guardian but also often causes the single parent to delay having a will or trust drafted.

[ ]E   (6)   No Easy Way to Defer Estate Taxes (Chapter 37): Without a valid surviving spouse, estate taxes must be faced and the single person's estate must be prepared to bear the brunt of such taxes.

SINGLE PERSONS

C. PERSONS WITH POTENTIAL INHERITANCE

AREAS OF POSSIBLE BENEFIT

[ ]N   (1)   Avoidance of Probate And/Or Conservatorships for Parents: Probate of a parent's estate and particularly that of the surviving parent, puts the burden of such delays and costs directly on the client. Use of an intervivos trust will permit the avoidance of such a probate. It also permits the avoidance of what may be an expensive and cumbersome conservatorship (or guardianship) proceeding where the parent is not managing assets well. A trust which is contained in one's will does not avoid probate at the death of the owner of the property.

[ ]E   (2)   Generation-skipping Trust (Chapter 14): Where the client has an expectation of an inheritance, there should be a discussion of the possibility of receiving such inheritance in the form of a trust which typically gives the client as trustee the control over and all the benefits from the assets to be inherited, but also permits the avoidance of the additional generation-skipping tax on up to []$1,000,000 per donor[] of the property for estate tax purposes.

POTENTIAL PROBLEMS

[ ]N   (1)   Reduction of Parental Control Over Children: Direct gifts to clients' children from the clients' parents may often interfere significantly with parental control, particularly as to education of the client's children. Use of a trust may avoid this problem and still provide the benefit the grandparents desire.

[ ]N   (2)   Dissipation of Estate by Parent's New Spouse: Where the parent leaves all assets to a new spouse with the intent that she or he will leave it to the children of the prior marriage, the children often never receive any of the assets. Use of a trust by the parent to control the assets would avoid this problem. Often such a trust can be best created before the death of either parent.

[ ]E   (3)   Loss of Generation-Skipping Exemption: There is an exception from generation-skipping tax of $1,000,000 per donor, or $2,000,000 for a couple. However, without proper planning, the exemption of both parents and particularly that of the first parent to die can be lost. This is a very important aspect if generation-skipping for an inheritance is planned.

[ ]E   (4)   Accidental Application of Generation-Skipping Tax: Planning in which the parent of the client plans to benefit both the client and the client's children may often unwittingly cause application of the generation-skipping tax, resulting in the effective inclusion in the client's estate of assets which will really go on to benefit the next generation. Under some circumstances, the Unified Transfer Credit of the child will be unavailable to pay some of the tax and the 55% generation-skipping tax may apply[].

PERSONS WITH POTENTIAL INHERITANCE

D. PERSONS MOVING FROM OTHER STATES OR COUNTRIES

AREAS OF POSSIBLE BENEFIT

[ ]E (1) <u>Gifts to Permit Both Spouses to Use Unified Transfer Credit</u>: Where one spouse has more property (because of state laws or inheritance) than the other spouse, gifts to the spouse with the smaller estate should be considered in order to be certain that such spouse has sufficient estate to take advantage of the full amount of the Unified Transfer Credit ($600,000 of estate) and/or generation skipping exclusions ($1,000,000 of estate). Where the spouse with the larger amount of assets is unwilling to make outright gifts to the other spouse, consideration may be given to having the other spouse purchase and continue to own life insurance on his or her life in an amount which will take advantage of the opportunity to pass assets tax free because of the Unified Transfer Credit.

If the gift is of real property or some other asset that may be subject to laws of another state, care must be taken to determine if that state imposes gift taxes on transfers between spouses.

[ ]E (2) <u>Change of Residence to Avoid State Death Taxes or Even U.S. Estate Taxes</u>: Since many states (e.g., Florida, Nevada, California, etc.) now have no additional death taxes beyond what the federal estate tax would be, changing one's residence to one of those states may avoid significant death taxes. For those persons willing to give up U.S. citizenship, death taxes may be reduced substantially on property outside the country.

[ ]E (3) <u>Possibility of Non-Residents Making Gifts Before Becoming Residents</u>: In some circumstances, non-residents (e.g., an exile from San Salvador temporarily living in the U.S. but who is as yet not a U.S. resident) may be able to make gifts without being subject to U.S. gift taxes. In some such cases, planning may include gifts to family members made before becoming a resident of the U.S.

[ ]I (4) <u>Ownership Change to Community Property</u> (Appendix C, How Basis is Determined): Where one spouse has separate property (e.g., acquired through earnings in a separate property state or from inheritance) that has increased in value, consideration should be given to changing that property to community property. If the property is left as separate property and the non-owning spouse dies, the property will retain its present income tax basis. If the property is changed to community property, in a properly conceived estate plan, it is possible that the death of either spouse will provide the survivor with a new and increased income tax basis for the property equal to the fair market value of the property at the time of the death of the first spouse to die.

POTENTIAL PROBLEMS

[ ]N (1) <u>Ancillary Probate</u>: If a person retains ownership of real property in another state, there will probably have to be two probates, one for the state of residence and another for the state in which the retained real property is located. Use of a trust to hold such out-of-state property can usually avoid this costly and cumbersome circumstance.

[ ]N (2) <u>State Law Differences for Execution and Administration of Wills and Trusts</u>: A will drafted in one state may simply not be valid to transfer real property or certain other assets located in another state since the formalities required of such a document and the rules for inheritance, qualification of executors, etc., are controlled by the law of each state. The will must be examined by an attorney in the state in which the clients are currently residents.

[ ]X (3) <u>Surviving Spouse's Rights Differ From State to State</u>: State laws also differ as to what rights the spouses have in property acquired during marriage (e.g., community property spouses each having a half interest in earnings during the marriage), rights in separate property at the death of a spouse, and also intestacy rules (which operate in the absence of a valid will). All of these differences may be magnified in comparing the laws of different countries.

[ ]N (4) <u>Real Property in Other States Usually Subject to that State's Laws</u>: Even though the residence of the owners was considered in drafting their wills, laws of the location of the property will usually apply — including the aspect of the validity of the form of the will, rights of surviving spouses and the rules of intestacy.

PERSONS MOVING FROM OTHER STATES OR COUNTRIES

[ ]N (5) <u>Foreign Residents</u>: For those persons who have previously lived in or who are currently residents of or perhaps even have property in other countries, there must be an examination of the law of the other country to see if a will must be drafted in accordance with its laws in order to be effective as to assets in that country.

[ ]E (6) <u>Accidental Gifts Prior to 1982</u> (Chapter 15): Transfers of ownership between husband and wife prior to 1982 may very well have resulted in taxable gifts for federal estate tax purposes and for a state's gift tax purposes even though no gift was intended. Putting separate property (e.g., which was inherited or which was earned in a separate property state) of one spouse into co-ownership with the other in many cases resulted in taxable gift, and ERTA did not wipe out such prior gift tax liabilities. Such transfers should be reviewed to determine if any gift tax liability exists or if any steps should be taken to currently record the circumstances which argued against the transaction having been considered a gift.

[ ]E (7) <u>Possibility of Two State Death Taxes Applying</u>: By having indicia of residence (e.g., drivers license, lodge membership, income tax filings, etc.) in two or more states, it is possible to be subject to state death tax in each state.

[ ]E (8) <u>Different U.S. Estate and Gift Tax Rules for Non-Residents</u>: Foreign citizens who are not U.S. residents do not have all of the estate tax benefits of U.S. citizens in relation to federal estate and gift tax and also often with regard to state gift and death taxes. Such non-citizens with significant assets must have their estate plans prepared by an attorney who is aware of the impact of such differences on estate planning.

[ ]E (9) <u>Special Trust Required to Obtain Marital Deduction For Transfer To Non-Citizens</u>: A recent law change took away the benefit of the marital deduction for transfers to spouses who are not U.S. citizens unless the transferred property is held in a special form of trust. Such qualifying trusts must have a trustee that is a citizen of or a corporation created in the United States. This rule will now invalidate any prior estate plan involving non-citizens which is not amended to comply with these new rules.

PERSONS MOVING FROM OTHER STATES OR COUNTRIES - Cont.

E. OWNERS OF PRIVATE CORPORATIONS

AREAS OF POSSIBLE BENEFIT

[ ]N   (1)   <u>Shield Against Corporate Liabilities</u> (Chapter 17): Wherever the business activity has some potential financial dangers, a business operated through a properly organized and operated corporation with sufficient capital may protect the other assets of a client.

[ ]N   (2)   <u>Pooling of Capital for Business</u> (Chapter 17): Issuance of shares to various persons permits the pooling of capital and thus raising of more funds than would otherwise be available to any individual proprietor for the capital needs of a business activity.

[ ]N   (3)   <u>Maintaining Value of Business — Buy and Sell Agreement</u> (Chapter 1): Often the most important aspect of estate planning is preserving the values built up in the private corporation, and executing a proper buy and sell agreement may be an effective way of doing this in many situations which involve private corporations.

[ ]N   (4)   <u>Capitalization to Permit Retention of Control</u>: In circumstances where gifts of stock to family members are contemplated, consideration might be given early to issuance of both voting and non-voting stock.

[ ]N   (5)   <u>Use of a Voting Trust to Permit Retention of Control</u>: Where issuance of non-voting stock is not practical, the possibility of maintaining control is feasible in some circumstances by the use of a voting trust.

[ ]E   (6)   <u>Early Gifts of Stock Within Family</u>: Where it is likely the corporation will appreciate in value, gifts of stock at an early stage of the corporation's growth may permit the transfer of a much larger part of the future value without there being any significant gift tax consequences. [The effect of Code section 2701 on such transfers must be considered (Chapter 13).]

[ ]E   (7)   <u>Capitalization to Permit Easier Corporate Freeze — A Lost Planning Tool</u>: When an increase in the value of a corporation is a very significant possibility, consideration was previously given early to issuance of both preferred stock (which can be recovered by the corporation at stated prices) and common stock (to be given to the next generation) which will not have such restrictions, and thus will have the major potential for increase in value. [The effect of Code section 2701 on such transfers must be considered (Chapter 13).]

[ ]E   (8)   <u>Corporation or Partnership May Qualify More Assets for Estate Tax Deferral</u> (Chapter 10): All of the "business assets" in a going business corporation may qualify at a client's death to meet the minimum percentage limits in order to achieve deferral of the related estate tax over a period of as long as 14 years and with some of the tax bearing interest at a very low rate. Although the 1984 Tax Act eliminated the value of "passive assets" in considering the value to be ascribed to a business for this purpose, holding assets in a corporation or partnership may still result in a larger amount qualifying for deferral of tax than if such assets were owned by an individual proprietor.

[ ]I   (9)   <u>Retaining Rights at Original Incorporation of Business</u> (Chapter 17): As opposed to putting all the assets of a business into the corporation in exchange for stock, when forming a corporation consideration should be given to taking back a note in place of some of the stock so that some money or other assets can be later drawn out of the corporation against such note without recognition of income tax.

[ ]I   (10)   <u>Fringe Benefit Planning</u>: The following are some of the most typically used fringe benefit planning techniques:

        (a)   group term life insurance (Chapter 21)
        (b)   medical reimbursement plans (Chapter 22)
        (c)   disability insurance deductibility
        (d)   cafeteria plans
        (e)   split-dollar insurance coverage (Chapter 21)

OWNERS OF PRIVATE CORPORATIONS

(f) education costs
(g) financial counseling
(h) prepaid group legal services
(i) dependent care assistance
(j) auto and travel costs

[ ]I   (11) <u>Use of High Profile Qualified Retirement Plans</u> (Chapters 9, 16 & 28): Pension and profit sharing plans, both for corporations and for individual proprietors and partners, now are recognized by tax experts as probably the most effective tax shelter for those persons in a business or profession.

[ ]I   (12) <u>Use of Dividends Received Deduction</u>: When investment of corporate funds is considered, the deduction afforded corporations of 80% (70% in some circumstances) of any dividends received should be taken into consideration.

[ ]I   (13) <u>Use of Corporation's Initial Low Income Tax Rate</u> (Chapter 17): Tax rates as low as 15% for income tax purposes makes the corporation a very useful tool for building capital for some businesses or professions. However, the Budget Reconciliation Act of 1987 ordained that all "personal service corporations" (e.g., most of those to practice law, medicine, or consulting using shareholders as employees) do not have the advantage of the lower corporate tax rate after 1987. Thus, all income of such corporations will be taxed at the [35%] rate.

[ ]I   (14) <u>Electing Subchapter "S" Status</u> (Chapter 29): Where circumstances warrant, the corporation may be shifted to being taxed like a partnership through election into "S" status, thus having the income taxed at the share-holder's own individual rate. The ability to make this election is subject to a number of important rules. [Relative tax brackets of corporations and shareholders should be considered.]

Since stock of "S" corporations cannot be held for a significant period of time in most trusts without revocation of the "S" election, the existence of a possible future addition of such a corporation in one's estate must be brought to the attention of the estate planner. It is possible to draft trusts which can continue to hold "S" corporation stock without revocation of the "S" election.

[ ]I   (15) <u>Shifting Income to Low Tax Bracket Family Members</u> (Chapter 29): The Subchapter "S" election described above also permits the shifting of income to other family members by giving them ownership of stock. [Relative tax brackets of each should be considered.] Income of children under age 14 is generally taxed at the parent's marginal tax rate.

[ ]I   (16) <u>Using an ESOP to Defer or Avoid Gain on Sale</u> (Chapter 9): The 1984 Tax Reduction Act (TRA) rules now permit deferral of gain on a sale of the corporation stock in certain circumstances by the use of an Employee Stock Ownership Plan as the buyer and the reinvestment of sale proceeds in domestic stock on the open market. This is a [new and] potentially important benefit for many clients.

[ ]I   (17) <u>Using an ESOP to Redeem Stock With Pre-Tax Dollars</u> (Chapter 9): The installation of an ESOP can provide the means in some circumstances to redeem stock by making deductible cash contributions to a qualified plan to build up a fund for the purchase. In some circumstances this can also provide for acquisition of the stock in conjunction with a bank loan and the repayment of that loan with tax deductible funds contributed to the ESOP.

[ ]E   (18) [Deleted]

[ ]I   (19) <u>Non-Cash Deductions Through Use of ESOP</u> (Chapter 9): Where taxable income may be high and cash resources low, the installation of the ESOP can provide for cash-free deductions by having the corporation issue stock to the ESOP. However, this planning also shifts some stock ownership to the employees of the corporation.

[ ]I   (20) <u>Lifetime Stock Redemptions to Remove Cash</u>: Where some shareholders are not related, it may be possible to redeem stock of certain shareholders with the recognition of gain as a sale instead of dividend treatment. This will be of significant benefit if and when preferential treatment is reinstated for long-term capital gains.

OWNERS OF PRIVATE CORPORATIONS - Cont.

[ ]I   (21)   <u>Avoiding Tax on Underlying Gains</u>: Even though the corporation may contain assets (e.g., unrecognized receivables, appreciated inventory, fixed assets which have been depreciated, etc.), that would normally produce income to the corporation when sold, under many circumstances all of the assets may be sold together through a sale of the corporation's stock, and thus a gain avoided at the corporation's level until the asset is sold or converted to cash. The selling shareholder, however, recognizes the gain which may exist with regard to his stock. However, item (29) below regarding the loss of the General Utilities Doctrine should be reviewed.

[ ]I   (22)   <u>Stock Redemption at Death to Pay Death Taxes</u> (Chapter 31): Special rules permit redemption of stock under Section 303 in an amount equal to the total of both federal and state death taxes without having the redemption treated as a dividend.

[ ]I   (23)   <u>Total Stock Redemption at Death of Community Property Shareholder</u> (Appendix C - Basis): By holding property in community property form, the death of one spouse gives the surviving spouse an income tax basis in both halves of the stock equal to the then fair market value. The corporation can then be liquidated and no gain is recognized at the shareholder level.

         However, after 1988 the 1986 Tax Reform Act now requires corporations which have not elected Subchapter S status under certain specific rules to recognize any gain inherent in the assets upon liquidation (e.g., a building worth $100,000 with a cost basis to the corporation of only $30,000), as noted also in item (29) below.

[ ]I   (24)   <u>Shifting of Income Between Tax Years</u> (Chapter 17): By having a fiscal year of the corporation that overlaps the owner-employee's usual December 31st taxable year (e.g., having a January 31st year end for the corporation), it is possible to shift income from one year to the next. Holding back salary payments during the year and making them in January of the succeeding year may shift income from one taxable year of the owner-employee to his next taxable year, without creating any taxable income for the corporation. Generally, this is now possible only for non-Subchapter S corporations which are not personal service corporations.

[ ]I   (25)   <u>$50,000 Borrowable From Qualified Retirement Plan</u> (Chapter 28): Under the restrictions imposed by the Tax Equity and Fiscal Responsibility Act (TEFRA), the amount of money that can be borrowed by a participant from a corporate qualified plan is [generally] limited to $50,000. However, that is much better than the circumstance of Keogh plans, for individual proprietors and partners, which do not permit any borrowing.

[ ]I   (26)   <u>Full Deduction for California Income Tax Purposes of Plan Contributions</u>: Several states restrict the deduction allowed for contributions allowed to non-corporate retirement plans (Keogh plans). Some states, like California, have recently conformed to federal law and now permit a full deduction. However, this can be an important reason for using a corporation in those states which have income tax rules which restrict such deductions.

[ ]I   (27)   <u>$5,000 Death Benefits</u>: Up to $5,000 may be received by corporate employees including owner-employees under a valid written contract as a death benefit. This amount is free of income tax to the recipient but deductible to the corporation.

[ ]I   (28)   <u>Rollover of Qualified Plan Account to IRA on Retirement or Death of Spouse</u> (Chapter 18): Recognition of income tax can be avoided by a "terminating" qualified retirement plan participant or spouse of a deceased participant by transferring — under certain conditions — the plan proceeds to an Individual Retirement Account.

[ ]I   (29)   <u>Loss of the General Utilities Doctrine</u>: After 1988 liquidation of corporations other than subchapter S corporations will result in recognizing a tax at the corporate level on the excess of value of any assets over the corporation's income tax basis in them. E.g., a real property owned by the corporation with a corporate tax basis (cost less depreciation) of $20,000 but which is worth $100,000 at time of liquidation, will result in a corporate tax on the $80,000 difference. Even some subchapter S corporations can recognize all or part of this corporate gain upon liquidation under the "built in gain" rules.

OWNERS OF PRIVATE CORPORATIONS - Cont.

Prior to 1989, the General Utilities court case had crystallized the rule that no corporate tax was recognized upon many liquidations. TRA '86 legislated a reversal of this doctrine. Now a taxable gain can be recognized at both the corporate and shareholder levels upon liquidation of a corporation.

POTENTIAL PROBLEMS

[ ]N   (1)   <u>Wrong Choice of Form of Buy-and-Sell Agreement</u> (Chapter 1): Whether you use a stock redemption agreement or a cross purchase agreement depends on several factors which should be reviewed with a competent advisor to avoid loss of potential benefits.

[ ]N   (2)   <u>Buy-In Problems Created by High Stock Values</u>: Where future shareholders may not have much capital and where the corporation has accumulated a great deal of fair market value, many qualified prospective co-shareholders may be preempted from buying into the corporation. An example of this might be a large medical radiology group that over the years has accumulated in the operating corporation a very large amount of value related to accounts receivable and to the radiology equipment used in the practice. For a bright young doctor, it may simply cost too much to consider buying into such a corporation.

[ ]N   (3)   <u>Cash Problems in Redeeming Shares</u>: The same problem as described above of accumulating too much in the way of asset values in a corporation may make the redemption of shares a very difficult problem.

[ ]N   (4)   <u>Piercing of Corporate Veil by Creditors</u> (Chapter 17): Inadequate capitalization or failure to follow corporate procedures may result in a corporation failing to provide a shield for shareholders as to any liability for corporate debts.

[ ]N   (5)   <u>Securities Law Problems</u> (Chapter 17): Failure to observe legal requirements in creating a corporation may cause adverse civil results and even criminal penalties. The incorporation should be done by an experienced and competent attorney.

[ ]E   (6)   <u>Corporate Owned Insurance on Life of Majority Shareholder</u> (Chapter 21): Ownership by the corporation of insurance on the majority shareholder may result in that insurance being included in the taxable estate of the client-shareholder.

[ ]E   (7)   <u>Stock Valuation Problems</u> (Chapter 42): The various methods approved by the courts for valuation of corporations should be reviewed with a competent tax attorney in determining the value which estate tax authorities will place on the corporate stock. The client may be unpleasantly surprised to learn of the high value which will be assigned to a corporate ownership.

[ ]E   (8)   <u>Loss of Estate Tax Exclusion of Pension and Profit-Sharing Benefits</u> (Chapter 28): For deaths after 1984, except for some unusual circumstances, the exclusion previously available for values in qualified corporate retirement plans (as well as those of partnerships and individual proprietors) is no longer allowed. Many estate plans require important revisions because of this change in the law.

[ ]I   (9)   <u>Double Taxation of Dividends</u>: (Chapter 17): Where a corporation accumulates earnings, it pays income tax on them (unless it has elected to be taxed under Subchapter S). However, when the dividends are paid to the shareholder, the corporation receives no deduction or offset against taxable income but the shareholder is subject to income tax on the dividends received. For this reason, very few large dividends are paid to shareholders of privately owned non-subchapter S corporations.

[ ]I   (10)   <u>Real Property Owned by Corporation</u>: In many planning circumstances where the business activity itself is in a corporation, the ownership of the building in which the business is carried on is maintained outside the corporation. Failure to do this may cause recognition of gain at both corporate and individual levels, in those circumstances where either the business or the real property are to be sold separately or where non-subchapter S corporations (and even some "S" corporations) liquidate after 1988.

OWNERS OF PRIVATE CORPORATIONS - Cont.

[ ]I (11) <u>Corporation Ignored as Sham by Taxing Authorities</u> (Chapter 17): Failure to observe the requirements for corporate meetings, salary arrangements, separation of ownership as between shareholder and corporation, etc., may result in all the corporate income being taxed to the individual shareholders.

[ ]I (12) <u>Possible Dividend Treatment for Payments or Benefits to Shareholder</u> (Chapter 17): Certain salary payments and other payments to or for the benefit of shareholders (e.g., personal use of a corporate auto) may be challenged by the IRS and denied as deductions to the corporation on the basis that they are "dividends."

[ ]I (13) <u>Special IRS Scrutiny For Corporate Partners</u> (Chapter 17): The 1982 TEFRA rules gave IRS a new tool to use against those corporations which are partners of a partnership, e.g., medical or legal "incorporated partnerships." Corporations in this situation should review IRC Code Section 269A with competent tax counsel to see if changes in the form of business or practice should be considered.

[ ]I (14) <u>Limitation on Accumulation of Corporate Earnings</u> (Chapter 17): Accumulation of corporate earnings beyond $250,000 ($150,000 for service corporations in many professional areas) may result in an additional tax [equal to 39.6%]. Avoidance of such tax on such accumulations requires a showing that the earnings are required to be retained for the "reasonable needs of the business."

[ ]I (15) <u>Extra Tax on "Incorporated Pocketbooks"</u> (Chapter 17): Where 60% of the corporate income is from rents, royalties, dividends, interest and certain personal service income (with some very significant exceptions), a large extra income tax may apply.

[ ]I (16) <u>No More No/Low Interest Loans From Corporation</u> (Chapter 20): The 1984 Tax Act rules now cause a recognition of income, as a dividend, where a corporate owner has a loan from his corporation at no interest or at a rate lower than market. Since it is a dividend, the corporation gets no deduction.

[ ]I (17) <u>[Payroll Taxes]</u>: Income received as salary by a shareholder-employee is subject to social security tax paid by both the corporation and the employee. [There is currently a special income tax deduction of 50% of the self-employment tax.] Payment of rent or dividends are not subject to this tax or to any state payroll taxes.

[ ]I (18) <u>Possible Second Tax on Liquidations</u>: Under the 1986 Tax Reform Act for C-type corporation liquidations after 1988, the corporation will be taxed to the extent that any assets have a value in excess of the corporation's basis in them (e.g., a building with $100,000 which has a tax basis of only $30,000). Certain Subchapter S corporations can avoid this corporate level of tax, which is in addition to the tax on the shareholder to the extent that the net proceeds from the liquidation exceed his or her basis in the corporate stock.

OWNERS OF PRIVATE CORPORATIONS - Cont.

F.   INDIVIDUAL PROPRIETORS

AREAS OF POSSIBLE BENEFIT

[ ]N   (1)   No Corporate Creation or Operation Costs: The individual proprietorship is the simplest form of doing business and avoids legal fees for incorporation as well as those for subsequent annual meetings, etc.

[ ]I   (2)   Only One Level of Income Taxation: By avoiding the corporation, one avoids the taxation of income at the corporate level and its subsequent second taxation where the payment to the shareholder is deemed to be a dividend, as opposed to being an expense deductible to the corporation (e.g., salary). One also avoids the corporate tax (which is in addition to the shareholder tax) on appreciation at the time of the sale of the business (followed by a liquidation).

[ ]I   (3)   Assets Removable From Business Without Tax: Unlike the corporation or certain partnership circumstances, the individual proprietorship allows the taxpayer to remove assets or add assets without the recognition of any gain for income tax purposes.

[ ]I   (4)   Avoidance of Social Security Tax for Family Employees: Payments of salary to spouses or children permits shifting of income from an individual proprietor to other persons in the family without payment of social security taxes. This is becoming more important as social security taxes are increasing.

[ ]I   (5)   [Payroll Taxes: There is currently a special income tax deduction of 50% of the self-employment tax.]

[ ]I   (6)   Ability to Produce Losses Which Can Offset Salary or Other Taxable Income: Where the business is actively pursued by the owner (and thus is not a "passive" activity) and produces a tax loss, the amount of the loss can be used to reduce the amount of ordinary taxable income. However, if the taxpayer does not materially participate in an active business or the activity is considered passive, then any loss will be considered a passive loss and can only offset passive income. Passive income does not include portfolio income (e.g., interest, dividends). The 1986 Tax Reform Act defers the deduction from losses from "passive" activities. Tax shelters were the target of this legislation. "Material participation" by the individual is now required in order to have the loss be currently applied to offset other income of the individual.

POTENTIAL PROBLEMS

[ ]N   (1)   Lack of Shield Against Liabilities (Chapter 17): Unlike a corporation, the individual proprietor is liable for all debts of the business.

[ ]N   (2)   No Ability to Borrow From Keogh Plan (Chapter 16): Unlike a corporate plan, the individual proprietor cannot borrow from his Keogh plan.

[ ]N   (3)   More Difficult to Give Some of Business and Retain Control: Unlike a corporate circumstance, it is very difficult to give interests in the individual proprietorship without having to deal with the possibility of some control shifting to the donee.

[ ]I   (4)   All Inherent Gain in Assets Recognized on Sale of Business: Sale of an individual proprietorship will result in the recognition of gain taxed as ordinary income with regard to sale of accounts receivable, inventory and other assets which have a value in excess of income tax basis. This problem should not be [as] significant after 1987 when the tax rates for ordinary income and capital gain are [substantially] equalized. If capital gain treatment is restored, then this will again be an important factor.

[ ]I   (5)   Lack of Corporate Fringe Benefits: The various corporate fringe benefits described above for corporations generally do not apply to an individual proprietorship.

INDIVIDUAL PROPRIETORS

[ ]I   (6)   <u>Low Keogh Plan Deduction Limit For Some State Income Taxes</u>: Some states permit only a small income tax deduction for contributions to Keogh plans. Recently, some states, e.g., California, now permit the full deduction for such contributions.

[ ]I   (7)   <u>All Income Taxable at Individual Rates</u>: None of the income developed by an individual proprietorship will be taxed at the often lower corporate rates or on the tax return of other family members.[]

[ ]I   (8)   <u>No Use of ESOP Available</u>: Unlike the corporation, the sale of an individual proprietorship may not have the gain deferred by sale to an ESOP and investment in corporate common stock.

[ ]I   (9)   <u>No Shifting of Income Between Tax Years</u>: All of the income earned in a taxable year will be subject to tax in that year as opposed to the circumstances of a corporation with a fiscal year different from that of its shareholder-employee.

[ ]I   (10)   <u>All Business Earnings Subject to Self-Employment Tax</u>: Unlike the corporation, where retained income may be subject only to income tax and not social security tax, earnings of an individual proprietor business are generally subject to both income tax and self-employment tax.

[ ]N   (11)   <u>No Pooling of Capital For Business Purposes</u> (Chapter 17): Since no other persons may be involved in the proprietorship, the individual may supply only his own or borrowed funds.

[ ]N   (12)   <u>Difficult to Create Market-At-Death For Business</u> (Chapter 1): Although buy-and-sell agreements may, under unusual circumstances, be created for individual proprietorships, the lack of a partner or other shareholders as a potential ready buyer is a disadvantage in creating a market for the business.

[ ]E   (13)   <u>Fewer Assets May Qualify For Estate Tax Deferral</u> (Chapter 10): In determining whether or not an estate meets the percentage requirements necessary to qualify for deferral of a portion of the estate tax, only those assets of an individual proprietorship which can be shown to relate directly to the business may be included in determining such percentages.

[ ]I   (14)   <u>No Shifting of Income to Children</u>: Unlike a partnership or a Subchapter "S" corporation, the individual proprietorship income cannot be shifted to other persons but children can be hired as employees and paid a deductible salary if they perform needed tasks. Under the 1986 TRA, income in excess of $1,000 [$1,300 in 1995] shifted to children under age 14 will be taxed at their parents' top marginal rate.

[ ]I   (15)   <u>No Operation of Individual Proprietorship In a Trust</u>: Unlike almost all other assets, there is a significant danger in holding and operating an individual proprietor business in a trust. The danger is that IRS may be able to tax the entire trust as if it were a corporation, a very bad result! Therefore, any business operated in trusts, including revocable intervivos family planning trusts, should be operated through a corporation or a partnership, which type of entity can be operated through the trust without this danger.

INDIVIDUAL PROPRIETORS - Cont.

G. PARTNERS [and Members of LLCs]

AREAS OF POSSIBLE BENEFIT

[ ]N   (1)   <u>Pooling of Capital for Business</u>: Like a corporation, the assets of more than one person may be combined to meet the capital needs of the business.

[ ]N   (2)   <u>Market For Business — Buy-and-Sell Agreement</u> (Chapter 1): The existence of partners [or members] often creates a market for business interests which does not exist for an individual proprietorship.

[ ]N   (3)   <u>[]Protection From Liability Available Through Limited Partnerships and LLCs</u>: Although the general partner(s) will always be liable for all debts and other liabilities of the partnership, a limited partnership may be created which will limit both the liability and control of a limited partner. [In the case of a LLC, all members will be isolated from personal liability.]

[ ]E   (4)   <u>Reduced Value of Certain Partnerships [and LLCs] For Estate Tax Purposes</u> (Chapter 11): The family partnership was a vehicle often used for attempting to "freeze" the value of real property and other assets including business interests [but such transactions are now generally subject to Code section 2701 (Chapter 13).]

However, certain partnerships [and LLCs] which have restrictions on withdrawal of assets after death of a partner [or member] can still be a very effective vehicle for reducing value of a partner's [or member's] interest in a partnership [or LLC] [but see discussion of Code sections 2701 and 2704 (Chapter 13) and 2703 (Chapter 1)].

[ ]I   (5)   <u>Some Removal of Assets From Business or Even Liquidation Without Tax</u>: Unlike a corporation, under proper circumstances, assets may sometimes be removed from a partnership [or LLC] or the partnership [or LLC] may be liquidated without the recognition of any gain for income tax purposes. Gain may be recognized without competent advice.

[ ]I   (6)   <u>Only One Level of Income Tax</u>: Like an individual proprietorship, there is no double taxation of income (at both the corporate and an individual level). This benefit is really often a detriment where lower corporate income tax rates might otherwise apply (e.g., the 15% corporate rate for the first $50,000 of income each year for corporations which are not "personal service corporations").

[ ]I   (7)   <u>Some Shifting of Income to Other Family Members</u> (Chapter 11): By observing the relevant rules, some income may be shifted to other family members by giving interests in the ownership of the partnership [or LLC].

[ ]I   (8)   <u>Special Allocations of Income Between Partners [or Members] May be Possible</u> (Chapter 11): With a partnership [or LLC] agreement drafted by an attorney with experience in dealing with such "special allocations," it may be possible to allocate income and even income tax deductions among the partners [or members] in such a way as to optimize income tax planning.

[ ]I   (9)   <u>Losses May Be Available to Offset Personal Income</u>: Like an individual proprietorship, losses from active general partnerships flow through to the taxpayer and may offset personal income, e.g., salary, interest, etc. However, losses from passive activities and activities in which the partner does not materially participate can only offset passive income. Passive income does not include portfolio income (e.g., interest, dividends).

POTENTIAL PROBLEMS

(1-10)   The numbered items listed for the potential problems of individual proprietors also apply to partnerships [and LLCs]:

[ ]N   (11)   <u>Possible Liability For Actions of Partners</u>: Certain actions of a partner in relation to a general partnership may result in liability for all the other partners.

PARTNERS

[ ]I   (12)   <u>Tax Due on Certain Removals of Assets From Business</u>: Certain assets, e.g., accounts receivable which have not been taken into income or highly appreciated inventory, may result in the recognition of income if withdrawn from the partnership [or LLC] under some circumstances.

[ ]I   (13)   <u>Greater Tax Shelter Audit Potential</u>: Because the partnership has been used so frequently for tax shelters, the IRS now seems to view all partnerships with more suspicion.

[ ]I   (14)   <u>Disposition of Certain Partnership [or LLC] Interests May Trigger Recognition of Gain</u>: Where the income tax basis of the partner [or member] has been significantly reduced (as by depreciation expense), it may become impossible to even give away a partnership [or LLC] interest without the recognition of a large amount of gain.

[ ]I   (15)   <u>Accidental Loss of Right to Partnership [or LLC] Deductions</u>: In attempting to deal with certain sophisticated tax shelter partnerships, the 1984 Tax Act imposed rules on all partnerships [or LLCs] which may cause a partner's [or member's] share of expense to be capitalized as opposed to being available to offset income.

[ ]I   (16)   <u>Limited Partnerships Targeted by 1986 Tax Reform Act</u>: TRA'86 disallowed current deduction of all "passive losses." [If the limited partner does not materially participate, losses from the limited partnership generally] cannot be taken currently but must be deferred until there is "passive income" (which excludes dividends, interest and certain other income) against which the passive loss can be offset.

[ ]I   (17)   <u>Inactive General Partners Not Allowed Current Partnership Loss Deductions</u>: In focusing on "passive income" as a likely way to deal with tax shelters, TRA'86 requires that there be "material participation" in the activity in order for even a general partner to currently deduct the loss from the partnership. A lower standard of "active participation" is required for real estate rental activity.

[ ]I   [(18)   <u>Avoiding Corporate Classification</u>: In structuring both limited partnerships and LLCs, care must be taken to avoid at least two of the four corporate characteristics — limited liability, free transferability of interest, continuity of life, and centralized management.]

PARTNERS - Cont.

H. BUSINESS PERSONS IN GENERAL

AREAS OF POSSIBLE BENEFIT

[ ]N   (1)   Creating and Maintaining Market For Business (Chapter 1): Whether the business is in a corporate, partnership or individual proprietorship form, planning can be done to create a market for the business whether that may be by creating a buy-and-sell agreement or whether it is accumulating information on other prospective purchasers of the business.

[ ]E   (2)   Sharing of Name Goodwill Within Family (Chapter 15): It may be possible to bestow benefits onto family members by permitting the use of a business name without the actual recognition of a gift or the application of a gift tax.

[ ]E   (3)   Personal Financial Guarantees For Family Members (Chapter 15): Like the use of a family name, personal financial guarantees may currently permit the bestowing of real benefits on a family member or other person without the actual recognition of a gift or the application of a gift tax [but beware of continuing expansion of the *Dickman* deemed gift theory].

[ ]E   (4)   Special Use (Low) Valuation For Estate Tax (Chapter 42): Unlike investments in cash, securities or investment real property, certain assets involved in a business (such as real property used for business) or farming may be subject to special rules which will permit use of lower values for estate tax purposes.

[ ]E   (5)   Deferral and Installment Payments For Estate Tax (Chapter 10): Again, unlike investments in cash, securities or investment real property, investment of the assets in an active business may permit the payment of related estate tax over a period as long as 14 years and at a very low interest rate for a portion of the tax.

POTENTIAL PROBLEMS

[ ]N   (1)   Heirs Ignorant of Market For Business (Chapter 1): Preservation of estate values argues strongly for communicating to spouse and heirs any plans for the business and especially potential markets for the sale of the business.

[ ]N   (2)   Lack of Instruction to Heirs as to Disposition or Continuation of Business: Often only the family member active in the business knows whether it should be continued or sold upon his death. Failure to communicate to other family members on this point may result in a tragically wrong decision as to the disposition or continuation of the business.

[ ]N   (3)   Lack of Successor Management (Chapter 1): Existence of a buy-and-sell agreement may provide for some successor management that otherwise would not be available for the business. The universal dislike for thinking of one's own death often results in no planning in this important area for maintenance of the value of the business.

[ ]N   (4)   Lack of Cash Reserves at Owner's Death (Chapter 21): Failure to provide for cash availability (e.g., through insurance) at the death of the person on whom the business depends often results in the complete collapse of the business.

BUSINESS PERSONS IN GENERAL

I. RANCHER OR FARMER

AREAS OF POSSIBLE BENEFIT

[ ]E   (1)   <u>Special Use (Low) Valuation For Estate Tax</u> (Chapter 42): Ranches and farms actually worked by the client are subject to very favorable rules for valuation as farm land rather than their value for use as shopping centers, subdivisions, etc.

[ ]E   (2)   <u>Deferral and Installment Payments For Estate Tax</u> (Chapter 10): Ranchers and farmers are particularly favored in the application of rules for the deferral of tax and payment (at low interest rates to some degree) over a period as long as 14 years.

[ ]I   (3)   <u>No Income Recognized Until Sale of Product</u>: Special cash basis rules for farmers permit the reaping of crops without the recognition of the income until the time the crops are actually sold and value received by the seller.

[ ]I   (4)   <u>Some Greater Flexibility For Cash Deduction</u>: Although the 1984 Tax Reduction Act placed some restrictions on the deductibility of farm payments, the farmer generally has more flexibility in this regard than the average business man.

[ ]I   (5)   <u>Avoidance of Income Tax at Death on Some Products</u>: Certain crops and livestock may receive a new income tax basis at death so as to prevent any recognition of gain upon their being sold.

POTENTIAL PROBLEMS

[ ]N   (1)   <u>Liquidity Problems of Land Ownership</u> (Chapter 21): Typically, a farmer or rancher has the greatest need for estate tax liquidity (often in the form of insurance) since so much of the total value of the farm is in the form of land that may not be readily saleable without destroying the farm as a viable unit.

[ ]N   (2)   <u>Loss of Political Power</u>: Because efficiency of operation and a number of other factors have drastically reduced the number of farmers in relation to the rest of the nation, the formerly very impressive political power of the American farmer or rancher has deteriorated greatly. This fact, combined with increasing free world trade in agriculture, has resulted in reductions in income received from certain areas of farming.

[ ]E   (3)   <u>Loss of Special Use Valuation and of Deferral of Estate Tax</u> (Chapters 10, 42): Changing the farm operation to a cash rent basis can cause loss of these particularly important estate tax benefits.

RANCHER OR FARMER

J. PROFESSIONALS

General Comment: Usually the term "professional" is applied to those persons who have met certain educational goals and who usually perform services for others, e.g., Architects, Dentists, Doctors, Engineers, Lawyers, etc.

Although many of these people work for large companies as employees, a large proportion work essentially for themselves, as individual proprietors, partners and in corporate form. Thus, the professional should review the appropriate checklists for Individual Proprietorships, Partners [or LLCs], or Owners of Private Corporations, or perhaps that of the Corporate Executive where the category may be appropriate (usually thought of as applying to highly paid employees of large corporations).

Over the years, many professionals have incorporated for income tax benefit reasons. The 1982 TEFRA rules were designed in part to remove incentives for such incorporations. However, there are many benefits of incorporation still available and the professional who is not yet incorporated should review the possible benefits and detriments listed in the checklist for Owners of Private Corporations to determine if his estate might be improved by incorporating.

Below are listed some specific areas of possible benefit or problems which generally apply to professionals, regardless of the form in which they practice their profession:

AREAS OF POSSIBLE BENEFIT

[ ]N   (1)   Cost Savings Available From Professional Groups: Frequently, membership in professional groups may provide medical or insurance coverage at lower rates than are generally available.

[ ]N   (2)   Market For Business/Practice Enhanced by Professional Group: Some groups provide special services for retirees or estates of deceased members in finding a purchaser for the practice or business. Although professional goodwill may often die with a practitioner, in many cases such services can be very beneficial.

POTENTIAL PROBLEMS

[ ]N   (1)   Licensing Limitation on Marketability of Business or Practice: Most states limit the practice of many professions only to those persons who are licensed by the state. Upon the death of someone practicing one of these professions, there is only the limited market of state licensees to whom the practice or business may be transferred. Such restrictions on marketability obviously will reduce the value that will be received from such a sale.

[ ]N   (2)   Licensing Restrictions on Transfers to Family Members: The same license restrictions typically often prevent shifting the value of the business or profession to the next generation over a period of years.

[ ]N   (3)   Personal Liability Even Where Corporate Form Used: Except for those professionals who perform work for the benefit of large corporations as opposed to benefiting the public, there is always some personal exposure of a professional who performs services for another person or entity. Although a sufficiently capitalized and properly operated corporation can shield the owner-employee from liability caused by the acts of other persons, each individual is still liable for his or her own acts regardless of the fact that the business may be carried on in a corporate form.

[ ]I   (4)   No Low Corporate Tax Rates: For most professionals who use the corporate form, after 1987 there will be the corporate disadvantage that income left in the corporation cannot be taxed at only 15% or 25% rates for lower levels of income. These lower corporate tax rates will not be available to such corporations.

PROFESSIONALS

K. CORPORATE EXECUTIVES

AREAS OF POSSIBLE BENEFIT

[ ]N   (1)   Sick Pay - Disability Pay: Executives working for large corporations whose welfare and profitability does not depend solely on their efforts have a very real benefit in the contract provisions usually available for continuation of pay regardless of whether they may be sick or disabled. Agreements to spread compensation over future years often produce income tax benefits for the employee. Typically, this is available in and feasible for large corporations where the lack of current deductibility for such future payments is not the significant problem that it is for the smaller, private corporations.

[ ]I   (2)   Income Tax Benefits Allowed to All Corporate Employees (Chapter 17): The various possible benefits described in the Owners of Private Corporations check-list are all available to the extent that the corporation is willing to tailor its decisions to benefit the corporate executive. Often the cost of including other employees of a large corporation may limit flexibility in benefits available to executives but they may still be very substantial.

[ ]I   (3)   "Non-Qualified" Deferred Compensation (Chapter 4): The stability and good financial position of many large corporations permit many executives to enter, reasonably worry-free, into agreements which defer some portion of their compensation to future years (usually after a planned retirement date) when income tax can be expected to have less impact. Additionally, many such arrangements provide the equivalent of accumulation of "effective interest" (in the form of increase of the compensation based on how long it is deferred) which is not taxed until it is received.

[ ]I   (4)   Incentive Stock Options: The 1981 ERTA provisions created a new type of "Incentive Stock Option" which is better than previously available options, and may both defer taxation and shift such benefits from ordinary income rates to capital gain rates. Strict rules must be adhered to in issuing such options. After 1987, and unless and until the law changes, capital gains and ordinary income are [substantially] taxed at the same rates.

[ ]I   (5)   Regular and Restricted Stock Options: Although they may not qualify for the special tax benefits afforded incentive stock options, options to buy stock of a very successful business may be very valuable. By having certain restrictions on such options, in some instances the amount of gain recognized may be substantially reduced without a proportionate reduction in real value to the corporate employee.

[ ]I   (6)   "Phantom Stock" Plans: Contracts can provide both current income based upon the equivalent of ownership of stock and also future payment for equity which would be equal to the amount which stock might have appreciated.

[ ]I   (7)   Education: Any company employee can receive tax-free, under many circumstances, education which is related to the business and designed to improve existing skills or to qualify a person for an existing job even though these expenses are all paid for and deducted by the employer company. This fringe benefit was threatened in 1989 but it was continued for a theoretically limited time.

[ ]I   (8)   Professional and Business Club Dues: Like education, if these are really related to the business, they may be received tax-free by an individual and can be deducted by the corporation. However, a greater scrutiny is being directed at such benefits.

[ ]I   (9)   Death Benefits Over the $5,000 Limit: In addition to the $5,000 of death benefits allowed tax-free to all employees, some large companies also have practices of making greater payments which may be considered gifts to the employees. However, the IRS frequently does not quietly accept the concept of seeing a deductible expense result in no taxable income to the employee.

[ ]I   (10)   Expense Accounts: Like the private corporation, travel and entertainment expenses paid for by the employee may be reimbursed to the executive tax-free ([50%] not deductible by the corporation in some cases), to the extent that it may be shown that they are required for a company to carry out its business. More strict substantiation of such expenses has been required in recent years.

CORPORATE EXECUTIVES

[ ]I (11) Company Lodging: A long line of cases show that there may be a reasonable deduction for the corporation to provide an employee with tax-free lodging where it is in the best interests of the company that he live on the corporate premises or close to such premises. Each case must be examined on its own merits.

[ ]I (12) Additional Executive "Perks" and Benefits: Many other additional executive perquisites are frequently offered, including housing aid, company cars, country club dues, tickets for various performances, sabbatical leaves, and similar niceties. In 1981, the IRS was given an 18-month delay in its advice on regulating and possibly taxing such fringe benefits. The deadline passed for 1984 with some decisions made but without the great crackdown that IRS envisioned. However, new laws were passed as part of the 1984 Tax Act which restricted greatly the possibility of receiving significant benefits without the recognition of income. Some benefits may well end up as a basis for income recognition by the recipients.

POTENTIAL PROBLEMS

[ ]N (1) Possibility of Being Lulled into a False Sense of Security and High Spending Habits: Since most of us prefer to ignore unpleasant things, many executives who have relied upon retirement based on time spent with the employer have not felt it necessary to put aside funds for retirement and often find that a change in corporate structure may cut off their plans for relying on corporate funding for retirement.

[ ]N (2) Non-Diversification of Assets Through Investment in Company Stock: Often executives show their loyalty and find some job leverage by investing all of their available funds in stock of the employer corporations. This may be increased by the existence of an employer "stock savings plan" which invests in stock of the employer. Employees of companies like Sears have done well with such circumstances, but many others would have done much better to diversify their asset holdings.

[ ]N (3) Directing Available Cash Into Tax Shelters With Little/No Real Value: Where the executive feels frustrated that all of his earnings are taxable as ordinary income and that he has no "tax benefits," he often succumbs to the thought of reducing current income tax by putting his or her cash into "tax shelters." With the exception of certain investments in real property and occasionally oil programs on a diversified basis, most such "investments" do not produce real assets which provide security for retirement or for the family in the event of death of the executive.

Further, under the 1986 Tax Reform Act, most tax shelters will not be effective in providing current deductions against salary income. An exception is "actively" managed real property producing losses up to $25,000. Even this exemption is phased out as the taxpayer's adjusted gross income increases from $100,000 to $150,000, at which level no rental property losses are allowed regardless of how actively the properties are managed by the taxpayer.

[ ]E (4) Forced Migrancy Can Cause Asset Title Problems: Company mandated moves between separate property and community property states can cause accidental gifts between spouses (not taxable if made after 1981 for federal tax purposes) and confusion with title which should be reviewed with competent tax counsel.

[ ]I (5) Loss of Deduction For Unreimbursed Travel and Entertainment Expenses: The 1984 Tax Act now requires a substantiation of all such expenses. For the executive who plans to deduct on his own return such expenses which are not reimbursed by his employer, if he has a tax return preparer do his return, the preparer will require a written certificate from the executive that adequate records exist. Further, the 1986 TRA permits such deductions only when they, together with other "miscellaneous" deductions, exceed 2% of adjusted gross income.

[ ]I (6) Recognition of Income From "Perks" and Discounts: The 1984 Tax Act also restricted greatly the scope of benefits which can be received tax free by the employee. Those benefits which create no additional cost for the employer, like filling empty airline seats with employees or their relatives, may continue to be tax-free (in a more scrutinized form), but those which actually cost the employer are now subjected to rules which reduce benefits usually afforded tax free to executives.

[ ]I (7) New "Golden Parachute" Excise Tax: The 1984 Tax Act also focused on payments or property transfers that are contingent on a change in ownership or control of a corporation or its assets and, for large payments (over [] certain salary limits), a 20% excise tax is imposed on the recipient - in addition to income tax!

CORPORATE EXECUTIVES - Cont.

L. PERSONS PLANNING FOR RETIREMENT

AREAS OF POSSIBLE BENEFIT

[ ]N/I   (1)   <u>Build Up of Assets in Qualified Plan</u> (Chapter 28): Using the income-tax-free provisions of a qualified retirement plan permits a much more rapid build up of assets to provide financial security for retirement than would the same amount paid out as additional current salary.

[ ]N   (2)   <u>Receipt of Social Security Payments Before Actual Retirement</u>: Although the relatively vague social security (SS) eligibility rules may sometimes prevent it, some persons upon reaching age 62 or 65 have shifted their earnings to future years (e.g., to age 70 when earnings do not inhibit SS payments) by deferred compensation arrangements with employers or by shifting income to a corporation or pension plan in order to be able to draw the social security benefits for which they paid over past years.

[ ]I   (3)   <u>Stretching Qualified Plan Benefits Over Retirement Period</u> (Chapter 28): Where the plan rules permit, electing to receive plan benefits over a period of time may often provide a larger total retirement benefit by postponing the recognition of income tax until payments are received, and thus permitting a large amount of such benefits still in the plan to continue tax-free production of income for future payments to the retired employee. Generally payment from such plans must start on April 1 of the year after the participant reaches age 70 $\frac{1}{2}$.

[ ]I   (4)   <u>Qualifying for "Lump Sum Averaging" for Qualified Plan Payments</u> (Chapter 28): Some plans may require a "lump sum" distribution of plan assets. Meeting certain requirements can permit the availability of certain rules of income taxation which, for smaller and medium size plan benefits which are paid out as "lump sums," can result in lower income taxes than otherwise would result. Very strict rules must be observed.

[ ]I   (5)   <u>Use of Deferred Compensation Program to Reduce Income Taxes</u>: Where the employer makes it feasible and one's financial stability and budget permits, shifting some current compensation to future years after retirement may both reduce income tax overall and also, under some circumstances, permit an employee who does not retire at 65 to begin to receive Social Security (SS) payments. Local SS offices are looking more closely at such arrangements, however.

[ ]I   (6)   <u>Use of Corporation to Receive Income Produced After Retirement</u>: Many employers, particularly those with significant pension benefits, may permit an employee to "retire" and to stay on as a consultant without significant employee benefits. Using a corporation to provide such consulting services may often reduce income tax and sometimes make social security payments currently available. Social Security offices now actively seek to restrict such practices.

[ ]I   (7)   <u>Use of Sale of Residence Rules</u>: Where retirement plans may call for sale of the taxpayer's residence, care should be taken to come within the rules which permit a taxpayer who has reached age 55 to postpone the recognition of gain on up to $125,000 of sale proceeds.

POTENTIAL PROBLEMS

[ ]N   (1)   <u>Loss of Insurance or Medical Benefits Previously Provided by Employment</u>: Failure to review company insurance programs may result in loss of life insurance or medical coverage which might have been assumed before retirement by the employee at lower group rates not usually available to individuals.

[ ]N   (2)   <u>Failure to Create Estate For Retirement</u>: Although this problem may not be solvable in some circumstances, it can be avoided in many circumstances with good planning and will power.

[ ]N   (3)   <u>Stagnation of Physical and Mental Abilities</u>: Studies consistently show that continued mental abilities and physical capacities can be maintained where activity is continued as opposed to cessation of physical and mental effort upon retirement. Planning for continued activity in an area where one has the opportunity to find satisfaction will not only improve financial circumstances but also lead to a longer and fuller life.

PERSONS PLANNING FOR RETIREMENT

[ ]I   (4)   <u>Failure to Qualify Lump Sum Retirement Plan Benefit for "Lump Sum Averaging"</u>: Failure to follow strict rules (e.g., permitting only one "averaging" after age 59 ½) can cause retirement benefit payments to be taxed at regular ordinary income tax rates.

[ ]I   (5)   <u>Requiring Sale of Company Stock Held in Retirement Plan</u>: Lack of good tax advice can lose a tax benefit to those persons who are retiring from employment which included a qualified retirement plan which, in the retiree's account, contained stock contributed by the employer or purchased by the plan. Correct treatment will permit the acquisition of such stock and taxation only at the price at which it was acquired by the plan. Sale of the stock by the plan before distribution will result in loss of the benefit.

[ ]I   (6)   <u>New Penalty Excise Tax on "Excess Distributions"</u>: After 1986, annual payments from retirement plans in excess of $150,000 ($112,580 [$150,000 as indexed for 1995] if "grandfathering" is elected) are subject to a new excise tax of 15%. Amounts held in plans as of 8/1/86 (if at least $562,500) can be elected to be exempt from such new tax but any taxpayer making such election to "grandfather" these amounts will have to use the lower annual limit of 112,500 [$150,000 as indexed for 1995] on non-exempt payments. A lump sum total of five times the annual amount is also exempted from this new excise tax. Distributions from IRA, Keogh plans and corporate plans are lumped together for these calculations.

[ ]E   (7)   <u>New Penalty Estate Tax on "Excess Accumulations"</u>: For deaths after 1986, an accompanying new estate tax (not subject to any credits or deductions other than a modified marital deduction) will be applied to all plan accumulations which are in excess of the amount needed to fund for the participant's lifetime, payments equal to the new annual limit ($150,000/$112,580 [$150,000 as indexed for 1995]). This tax, at a 15% rate, is intended to prevent people from avoiding the new penalty excise tax on distributions by permitting funds to build up in retirement plans. Estates of married persons with large amounts in retirement plans previously could have a zero estate tax to pay at the first spousal death. This new penalty estate tax now can cause an estate tax to be payable at the death of the first spouse to die.

PERSONS PLANNING FOR RETIREMENT - Cont.

M. PERSONS PLANNING FOR MARRIAGE

AREAS OF POSSIBLE BENEFIT

[ ]N   (1)   <u>Entering Into Premarital Agreement Clarifying Title Holding</u>: Hindsight clearly shows the advantage to both parties of facing the question of property rights and laying out in a clear agreement any understandings with regard to change of ownership of property. Listing the property belonging to each person at the beginning of the marriage has much merit and little real detriment.

[ ]N   (2)   <u>Entering Into Premarital Agreement Clarifying Ownership of Earnings and Retirement Plan Rights</u>: Not only should the separate property or community property rights of each party in the earnings of either party be clarified before the marriage but, particularly where there may be retirement plans, the separate property aspects of such retirement rights generated before the marriage should be clarified. The increasing importance of private retirement plan rights to many people argues for maintaining them as separate property until it is certain that the new marriage will be a stable one.

[ ]N   (3)   <u>Executing New Will After or In Contemplation of Marriage</u>: By executing a will which recognizes either an impending marriage or one that has just occurred, the new spouse will not be in the position of being a "pretermitted heir" and thus the testamentary scheme will not be disrupted by the laws of intestacy which favor such "pretermitted heirs."

[ ]N   (4)   <u>Use of Trust to Avoid Probate as to Prenuptial Agreement Assets</u>: Where a spouse-to-be has been given certain rights, e.g., life estate, in specific assets in place of other marital rights, it may serve both purposes of avoiding probate and that of avoiding future creditors of the donor by placing that asset or set of assets into an irrevocable trust.

[ ]E   (5)   <u>Ability to Defer Estate Tax With Marital Deduction</u> (Chapter 37): The existence of a formal marriage permits the deferral of estate tax by an arrangement which benefits the new spouse at least during her or his life- time. The "Q-Tip" trust will permit the assets to avoid taxation at the death of the owning spouse as long as the income is paid to the new spouse. At the new spouse's death, the assets can thereafter go to the children of the prior marriage or to anyone else. This may often permit a business, which could not currently provide the funds for estate tax without causing its collapse, to mature and be in a position where cash reserves may be developed for payment of estate tax at the death of the second spouse and thus preserving the asset for the children of the first marriage.

Obviously, for the presently single person who wants to provide a benefit for a "live-in partner," marriage can provide a totally estate tax-free transition at his death.

[ ]E   (6)   <u>The Ability to Make Tax-Free Gifts by Deferral Until Marriage</u>: Gifts in large amounts which would produce a gift tax if given to a "friend" or "live-in partner" can be transferred totally free of gift tax if given to a person with whom there has been a formal marriage.

[ ]E   (7)   <u>Creating Estate Tax Deductible Liability in Place of Marital Right of Spouse</u>: In some states, the amount that would be automatically given under state laws to a spouse would not result in any deduction for estate tax purposes. Many such rights can be replaced with a clear liability which, when reduced to a proper contract, may result in a deductible liability for the estate of the deceased spouse.

POTENTIAL PROBLEMS

[ ]N   (1)   <u>Ineffective Termination of Prior Marriages</u>: In order for the marital deduction to be available, there must be a real marriage. The failure to properly terminate a prior marriage will prevent the next marriage from being effective.

[ ]N   (2)   <u>Lack of New Estate Plan</u>: Failure to execute a will or trust which recognizes the new marriage may give the new spouse rights, as a pretermitted heir, which divert assets from the children of a prior marriage. E.g., in California, half of the separate property of a wife will go to her new husband as a pretermitted heir if he is not recognized in her will, and thus the child of the wife from a former marriage will receive only half of the assets of the mother.

PERSONS PLANNING FOR MARRIAGE

[ ]N (3) <u>Failure to Recognize the Possible Automatic Payments "to Spouse"</u>: Many company death benefits, salary continuation rights and pension benefits may be paid automatically "to the spouse of the employee" where there has been a failure to properly designate the employee's intended objects of his bounty, e.g., his mother or his children from a former marriage.

[ ]E (4) <u>Making Significant Gifts Before Marriage</u> (Chapter 15): Since the marital deduction does not apply to gifts made other than to spouses, gifts made before marriage are only subject to the $10,000 exclusion, with the excess being subject to gift tax.

[ ]N (5) <u>Failure to Deal With Rights in Retirement Plans</u>: Where either or both of the spouses have rights that have been built up in retirement plans, failure to deal with such rights by a written agreement may have a very bad result in the event of a divorce or a death.

[ ]E (6) <u>Automatic Right of New Spouse to Half of Retirement Plan Benefits</u>: Now, upon one year of marriage, the participant's spouse receives the equivalent of the right to half of the pension benefits. Without a specific manner of written approval of the new spouse, the participant cannot direct all of his plan benefit to the children of his prior marriage or to anyone else! Without the prescribed form of written approval from the new spouse, existing designation of persons other than the spouse are invalid as to the spouse's half! This is very important for persons about to marry.

PERSONS PLANNING FOR MARRIAGE - Cont.

N. PERSONS PLANNING FOR SEPARATION OR DIVORCE

POSSIBLE AREAS OF BENEFIT

[ ]N   (1)   Use of Alimony and/or Child Support Trust to Insure Payment: Putting assets into a separate non-revocable trust, at the time of the divorce, may insure actual payment of such amounts as compared to the possible results of leaving the assets in the hands of the other spouse.

[ ]N   (2)   Use of Insurance Trust to Insure Premium Payment: Life insurance may be a most important asset in many instances, and both the ability of the other spouse to cancel the policy and the failure of the other spouse to make premium payments can be avoided by placing into an nonrevocable trust both the policy and assets which will produce income to make the premium payments.

[ ]I   (3)   Avoiding Income Tax and Changing Beneficiary Designation on Division of Pension Plan Benefits: Proper planning and a tolerant employer can result in the division of retirement benefits upon divorce without the often premature recognition of income tax caused by the actual distribution of such assets.

    Now, under current law, a properly drafted Qualified Domestic Relations Order (QDRO) can provide for such segregation and the ability of the divorced spouse who was not a plan participant to have a new and changed provision for beneficiary arrangements in the even of death prior to distribution of the assets from the qualified retirement plan.

[ ]I   (4)   Arranging Deductibility of Some Legal Costs: Certain aspects of a divorce, e.g., advice in regard to taxation, may be deductible. Identifying these amounts and limiting other areas of cost may result in significant income tax savings.

[ ]I   (5)   Qualifying Alimony For Deductibility: The 1984 Tax Act set some new requirements for deductibility of alimony which should be reviewed and observed in arranging alimony payments so that the desired deductibility can be provided. Where there is only a single income earner, such deductibility can result in an overall larger amount available to both persons after income taxes.

[ ]I   (6)   Providing For Children as Income Tax Exemptions: The existing rules for this area were modified by the 1984 Tax Act so as to provide a definite means of shifting such exemptions in the manner the parties desire. Such rules must be observed closely in the child support agreement and they may even be drafted in such a way as to help enforce child support payments.

[ ]I   (7)   Contribution to IRA Based on Alimony Receipt: Under the rules of the 1984 Tax Act, amounts received which qualify for alimony may now be the basis for a deductible payment into an IRA.

POTENTIAL PROBLEMS

[ ]N   (1)   Failure to Change Estate Plan: Although divorce may effectively revoke a will as to spousal benefits, divorce does not necessarily change the effect of a will or trust in some circumstances, and estate plans should be reviewed and perhaps revised in contemplation of or promptly after any divorce or separation in order to carry out the intentions of the client.

[ ]N   (2)   Loss of Medical Plan Coverage: Where one spouse's employment provides medical plan benefits for both spouses and possibly for children, most divorce or legal separation circumstances will terminate such protection for the non-employed family members where the employee works for a small company. However, under the Consolidated Omnibus Budget Reconciliation Act (COBRA), employers of 20 or more employees must provide, at 2% over cost, coverage for dependents of terminated employees where there has been a separation or divorce.

[ ]N   (3)   Loss of Life Insurance Coverage: As with the employer provided medical plan coverage described above, divorce or legal separation often destroys possible life insurance protection previously afforded.

PERSONS PLANNING FOR SEPARATION OR DIVORCE

[ ]I   (4)   <u>Recognition of Income Tax on Retirement Plan Division</u>: Division of retirement plan rights, which result in distribution of the assets to the participant or the spouse, will result in current income tax, a circumstance that may well be avoided by seeking an arrangement for division of the retirement benefits or other available means of preventing receipt and current income tax recognition. The 1984 Retirement Equity Act addressed a portion of this problem, but actions which are not founded on good tax advice can still result in the unnecessary recognition of gain. A properly drawn Qualified Domestic Relations Order (QDRO) can shift benefits to a non-participant spouse without forcing recognition of income tax. Even where assets are distributed from a qualified plan to the spouse of the participant, income tax may be deferred by reinvesting such distribution in an Individual Retirement Account within 60 days of its receipt.

PERSONS PLANNING FOR SEPARATION OR DIVORCE - Cont.

ANATOMICAL GIFTS

Why Talk About It?

Perhaps one of the most emotionally charged issues which should be discussed between a planner and a client is the making of anatomical gifts.

One way or another, the issue must be faced. If a client wants to make a gift he should know how to do it. Conversely, if a client is strongly against a gift of one or more organs, as estate planners we have a duty to protect them against the violation of their desires by others after they die.

What Is It?

The Uniform Anatomical Gifts Act (UAGA) has been enacted in every state. The purpose of this Act is to encourage various types of organ donations and to avoid inconsistency among the various jurisdictions.

The UAGA provides that any person over 18 may donate his entire body or any one or more of its parts. The donee can be any hospital, physician, medical or dental school, or various organ banks or storage facilities. Organ gifts can be made for education, research, therapy, or transplants. These gifts become effective at death and can be made by will.

How Does It Work?

There are two ways a gift can be made under the UAGA. One is that the donor can designate a specific individual to receive the gift. For instance, the person might specify that one of his eyes be given to a blind sister. A hierarchy of donees can be established and various body parts can be specified to go to specific donees.

A second way the UAGA works is to allow persons other than the decedent to have the power to make the gift. In other words, various family members can donate a person's body or organs. If there is no actual knowledge that the decedent does not want to make an anatomical gift, his spouse, adult children, parents and siblings can make a donation. The UAGA establishes a priority system of relatives starting with the deceased's spouse and moving down from closest to furthest relatives who can make, or refuse to allow, anatomical gifts. The gifts can be made by these third parties unless (1) there is actual knowledge that the decedent would not want to make an anatomical gift, or (2) unless someone in the same or higher

"class" opposes the gift. Donations can be authorized by third parties either before or after an individual's death.

Because of the possibility that an ill-intentioned relative would use anatomical gifts to obtain postmortem revenge, a person's intention regarding such gifts should be clearly specified one way or the other.

What Are the Requirements?

The UAGA requires that gifts must be made in writing by the donor and attested to by at least two witnesses. The donor must be of sound mind at the time of the writing (although there is no procedure for proving legal capacity in a manner similar to that used in probate). When gifts are made by family members, a written document is not a legal requirement and a telegram or tape recording may satisfy statutory formalities.

Many states provide for the making of anatomical gifts through a donation or a taped telephone conversation noted on a driver's license. But most authorities feel that because of the wide variety and the potential for problems with regard to revoking gifts made in such a way, it is better to either make or object to an anatomical gift through a document other than a driver's license.

When Is the Client Dead?

The Uniform Anatomical Gifts Act does not provide for a specific definition of death. Most states define death as a "total and irreversible loss of brain function" and require the opinion of at least two physicians. The UAGA forbids the physician who certifies death to participate in any organ removal or transplant procedures.

What Must the Estate Planner Do to Meet a Client's Wishes?

Regardless of the estate planner's personal feelings about anatomical gifts, the client's wishes should be honored. Likewise, regardless of the wishes of family members, the client's desires regarding anatomical gifts should be met if possible. Estate planners should explain to clients that a traditional funeral service is possible in most cases (check with local clergy) even if an entire body is left for medical research. This will alleviate a great deal of the tension regarding anatomical gifts. You might also point out that the anatomical gift is a "postself" device, a way to continue to have meaning beyond the event of your physical death.

Documents meeting the requirements of the Uniform Anatomical Gifts Act should be prepared separate and apart from the will. A codicil to the decedent's will would be useful to state the client's intentions regarding anatomical gifts in a way that does not disclose the other provisions of the will. If at all possible the client should designate a specific donee such as a family member or medical institution (and there should be "backup" donees in case the primaries can't or won't accept the gift for any reason).

What Should the Estate Planner Do Where a Client Feels Strongly about Not Making an Anatomical Donation?

If a client does not want a gift of his body parts to be made, such desires should be clearly and strongly expressed. Prepare a "nonconsent" document and if the client feels quite strongly about not wishing to make an anatomical gift, consider providing in the will that any bequests made to an individual who consents to an anatomical gift will be void.

The discussion of anatomical gifts is one more facet of the uncomfortable—but highly important—nontax aspects of estate planning. It's part of the process by which the estate planner learns not only to face facts but to face a face.

STATEMENT REGARDING ANATOMICAL GIFTS*

© 1982, Real Property, Probate and
Trust Law Section
American Bar Association

I, _____ of _____, _____
make the following statement regarding anatomical gifts which I have checked and initialled:

SPECIFIC GIFTS

ENTIRE BODY

☐ I give my entire body, for purposes of anatomical study to _____.
If, for any reason, _____, does not accept this gift, I give my
body to _____, for purposes of anatomical study.

GIFTS TO INDIVIDUALS

☐ I give my _____ to _____, if needed by him or her for purposes
       (part or parts)
of transplantation or therapy.

☐ I give my _____ to _____, if needed by him or her for purposes
       (part or parts)
of transplantation or therapy.

GIFTS TO INSTITUTIONS AND PHYSICIANS

☐ I give my _____ to _____,
       (part or parts)   (name of hospital, bank, storage facility, or physician)
for purposes of research, advancement of science, therapy, or transplantation.

☐ I give my _____ to _____,
       (part or parts)   (name of hospital, bank, storage facility, or physician)
for purposes of research, advancement of science, therapy, or transplantation.

PROSTHETIC DEVICES

☐ I give my _____ to _____ for critical
      (type of prosthetic device)   (name of hospital)
evaluation, study, and research.

INTENTION

☐ If any anatomical gift cannot be effectuated because of the donee's non-existence,
inability, or unwillingness to accept it, I request that one of the authorized persons
make anatomical donations in a manner consistent with my desires expressed in this
statement.

☐ I express my desire not to make anatomical gifts under any circumstances. It is my wish
that no part be used for transplantation, therapy, study, or research. I request that
my personal representative and next of kin respect my wishes.

THIS STATEMENT INCORPORATES ALL OF THE PROVISIONS ON THE REVERSE OF IT.

Signed this ____ day of _____, 19 ____ at _____.

*Printed with permission of the Real Property, Probate, and
Trust Law Section of the American Bar Association. Copies of
this form can be obtained from the Order Fulfillment Department of the American Bar Association, 750 N. Lake Shore
Drive, Chicago, Illinois 60611, at a cost of $4.00 per pad (100
forms) or $3.50 per pad for orders of 10 pads or more.

_____

_____   _____
       Witness   Witness

Appendix A

DATA GATHERING AND ANALYSIS

There is no question that the most important skill of an estate planner is the ability to understand who his client is, where that client stands in relation to the objectives (realized or subconscious) he may have, and what things have to be done to move the client closer to the realization of these goals. Knowledge of the client, the objects of the client's bounty, the client's property, and the relation of each to the others is essential to the estate planner in utilizing this skill.

An ability to gather accurate, comprehensive, and useful information is most efficiently developed through the use of a data gathering system. Each question in the pages that follow is designed to help the attorney, the CPA, the trust officer or life underwriter obtain comprehensive and useful information in a logical, orderly manner.

The reason for some questions will be apparent, the justification for others will be less obvious but equally important. Not every question should be asked of every client or prospective client. Nor are the forms and questions meant to be used "as is" in every case. They are meant only as a starting place, to be adapted to suit each professional's needs and method of operation. Some will use only a few pages, others will ask almost every question and use almost every page. It is important to recognize that the data gathering and worksheet forms in TOOLS AND TECHNIQUES must be used carefully and selectively, and modified to both the needs of the planner and the circumstances of the client.

FORMS

Sample Information Request Letter

Many estate planners and conservationists prefer to obtain as much knowledge as possible about a potential client before their initial interview. This saves the time of all concerned. If handled properly, pre-interview data gathering helps prepare both the client and the estate planner for the interview and involves the client in the planning process.

The sample information request letter reiterates the "when and where" of the first meeting. A controllable atmosphere, such as the professional's office, is usually a much better location for data gathering than a client's home or office.

The client is asked to complete as much of the data gathering form as possible in advance of the first meeting and mail it back to the planner. Note that these are simple "non-threatening" questions, but are necessary for a multiplicity of reasons.

Data Gathering Forms

Page 448 — The Cover Page

There is a reason for every page and every line of the data gathering forms. A client notes immediately that his file is considered personal and confidential. The client also notes that it will probably take a number of interviews to complete the initial process and then the case will be reviewed at specified times. The use of the forms indicates to the client that the planner has an organized, systematic and professional approach to estate planning.

Pages 449-450 — Family Information

Here, the client is asked to print or type information about family members. Note that Question 7 is designed to list not only the names and addresses of children but also their spouse's names, as well as the names and ages of any grandchildren.

Supplementary pages may have to be added where the client or his children have large families. It may also be helpful, where grandchildren are no longer living with their parents, to list their addresses and, if appropriate, the names of their spouses. Whenever possible, obtain social security and telephone numbers.

Often a client will be providing financial support for individuals outside his immediate family. Their names and relationship, as well as their addresses, are essential if the client wishes to provide for them either during or after his death. Likewise, clients will often want to provide financial assistance to a charitable organization. Formal names, addresses, and other vital information about such charities should be stated on this page (or on attached supplementary pages).

Page 451

A simple stick diagram of the client's family, his parent's family, and spouse's parent's family is an invaluable tool when Seniors, Juniors, and third and fourth generation children have the same names. Such a diagram also helps to

The Tools and Techniques of Estate Planning

445

understand who's who if your client has been divorced, remarried, and has children by both marriages.

Pages 452-453 — Advisors

Here, a client is forced to think about who has been, or has to be, selected to care for both the person and the property of children (or grandchildren) who are minors. A client must also select an individual or corporate fiduciary (or more than one of each or combination of both) to serve as a personal representative after his death. Alternates for both primary guardian(s) and executor(s) are essential as backups in the event the primary is ineligible, incapacitated, or for any other reason fails to qualify or ceases to act.

It is important that each member of the estate planning team locate other members of the team and inform them of progress and problems in planning the client's estate. Cooperation between the members of the team will assure the client of the best possible coordination of planning.

Page 454 — Checklist of Documents

This list outlines the key documents that are of use to the estate planner. In various situations special documents such as contracts, leases, or other agreements should be added. But generally, those shown will provide adequate information for the first interview.

Pages 455-462 — Alternative Form for Community Property Residents

An alternative data gathering form which will be particularly useful to residents of community property states can be found beginning on page 403. Community property planners (and common law planners who have had clients move to or from community property states) should notice a number of questions in the forms pertaining to "changes of state of residence during marriage." Problems of the peripatetic client are becoming more acute every day. The final page of the alternative forms dealing with inheritance tax information will be particularly useful in community property states.

SAMPLE INFORMATION REQUEST LETTER

Dr. Allen A. Murphy
6061 Kathleen Drive
Bala Cynwood, PA   19010

Dear Dr. Murphy:

I'm looking forward to meeting with you and your wife on Wednesday, June 16, at 2 p.m. in my office.

As I promised on the phone, I have enclosed the first several pages of a comprehensive data form we'll be using in creating an estate conservation plan. Please complete as much as you can and mail it to me in the enclosed envelope.

Also enclosed you will find a list of documents we will need. I would appreciate if you would send me photocopies of the documents in advance of our meeting or, if you prefer, you can bring them with you on Wednesday. (We can probably save a great deal of time if I can study these papers in advance of our meeting.)

Please feel free to call me if you have any questions.

Sincerely yours,

Charles McClu

CMcC/dl
Enc.

PERSONAL AND CONFIDENTIAL FILE

of

Dr. Allen A. Murphy

Initial Interview: 9/11/82

Interviewer: Charles McClu

**Dates of
subsequent
interviews or
review:**

PLEASE COMPLETE (print or type) AND RETURN IN THE ENCLOSED ENVELOPE:

			Birthdate	Soc. Sec. No.
1.	Full name	Dr. Allen Albert Murphy	9/11/30	158-43-0865
2.	Nicknames	Al		
3.	Spouse's name	Stephanie Louise Murphy	1/1/33	158-20-3621
4.	Nicknames	Stephie		
5.	Home address:	6061 Kathleen Drive Bala Cynwood PA 19010	Home phone:	EI 3-5424
6.	Business address:	2700 Bryn Mawr Ave. Hill Hill PA 19101	Bus. phone:	La 5-9500

7.

	Children (and Spouses)	Address	Phone	Birthdate
a.	Kathleen	same as above	see above	7/6/62
b.	Christopher	"	"	9/1/64
c.	Charles	"	"	11/15/66
d.	Lawrence	"	"	6/2/70

Names and Ages of Grandchildren

a.   b.   c.   d.

8. Parent's Names   Address   Age   Phone Number

Yours: a. _Deceased_   _____ ___   _____

          b. _Deceased_   _____ ___   _____

Your
Spouse's: a. _William Lamont_   _872 W. Overbrook St._   67   _Lo 6-1276_

          b. _Mary Lamont_   _same as above_   66   _Lo 6-1276_

9. Dependants (other than children)/Relationship

William Lamont | Father-   _see above_   67   "
                   in-law

Mary Lamont | mother-   _see above_   66   "
                   in-law

10. Beneficiaries (other than those listed above):

_____ _____ ___   _____

_____ _____ ___   _____

_____ _____ ___   _____

11. Please sketch a family tree showing any brothers and sisters:

Advisors

12. Guardians for children   primary: Address   Phone Number

George and Jessica Walters   767 Fawnhill Road   El 3-5353
(Guardian of Person)   Radnor
                                 PA   19008

Sam Cohen (close friend)   868 Knox Drive   El 3-5126
(Guardian of Property)   Radnor
                                 PA   19008

13. Guardians for children   alternate:

Robert and Louise Lamont   121 Peyton Place   609-522-8707
(Guardian of Person)   N. Wildwood
                                 N. J.   19808

Stephen and Evelyn Toll   222 Fayette Lane   609-522-7604
(Guardian of Property)   Wildwood
                                 N. J.   19807

14. Executors   primary:

Allen (Stephie's will)

Stephie (Allen's will)

15. Executors   alternate:

Sam Cohen   see above

Sam Cohen   see above

16. Accountant:

Frank Vallei, CPA   #1 Bala Avenue   Mo 4-3874
                           Bala Cynwood
                           PA   19010

	Address	Phone Number

17. Attorney — personal:

Robert P. Krauss   1401 Walnut Street   Lo 8-5700
Philadelphia
PA 19102

Attorney — business:

Robert P. Krauss   see above   "

18. Banker/Trust Officer:

Allen Gart (Vice Pres. and Senior Trust Officer)   Girand Trust Co.   Lo 8-4858
Girand Plaza
Philadelphia, PA 19101

19. Insurance advisor:

20. Investment advisor broker:

Donald Rahill / Bob Eclair   Newbuilder & Co.   Lo 7-6000
121 Rothschild Bldg.
Philadelphia, PA 19010

21. Other information not listed above:

Allen's doctor - Dr. Alton Blake

CHECKLIST OF DOCUMENTS TO BRING TO INTERVIEW

Present Wills _____

Personal Income Tax Returns: Last 3 Years (federal and state) _____

Business Tax Returns: Last 3 Years (include P&L and balance sheets) _____

Life/Health/Disability Insurance Policies _____

Employee Benefit Plan Descriptions (Pension, Profit Sharing, Group Insurance, etc.) _____

Business Buy-Sell Agreements and Employment Contracts _____

Pre or Post-Nuptial Agreements and Divorce Decrees/Property Settlements _____

Trust Documents — created by you or by others for your (or your family's) benefit _____

Gift Tax Returns _____

Homeowner's Policy and Personal Property Floaters _____

Deeds to Real Estate _____

Other documents to bring _____ _____

_____ _____

_____ _____

RALPH GANO MILLER   Client _____

INFORMATION AND DOCUMENTS

FOR ESTATE PLANNING

<u>PLEASE BRING WITH YOU COPIES OF:</u>

Present Wills, if any

Deeds to real property (for title purposes) and any information regarding title to property, cost and present fair market value.

Manner of title holding of any stock (how the ownership appears on the certificates) and value of each stock.

Last three years' income tax returns.

Any available financial statements.

Copies of any gift tax returns filed.

If you feel appropriate, photos or a snapshot of yourself and spouse.

<u>IF IN BUSINESS:</u>

Any partnership agreements.

Any corporate minute books.

Any buy-and-sell agreements.

Last three years' income tax returns (partnership or corporation).

<u>FILLING OUT INFORMATION SHEETS</u>

It is most helpful (as well as cost-saving for you) if you can fill out the attached forms and bring them with you when you come in. However, please do not delay your appointment for lack of answers to the questions, since we can often assist you with troublesome items at the conference.

The Tools and Techniques of Estate Planning   455

RALPH GANO MILLER   Page 1

CONFIDENTIAL DATA FOR

_____

FAMILY INFORMATION

Full Legal Name	Relation	Birthdate	H&W - Birthplace Children-Addresses
_____	Husband	__/__/__	_____
_____	Wife	__/__/__	_____
_____	Child Phone _____	__/__/__ Add.	_____ _____
_____	Child Phone_____	__/__/__ Add.	_____ _____
_____	Child Phone _____	__/__/__ Add.	_____ _____
_____	Child Phone _____	__/__/__ Add.	_____ _____
_____	Child Phone _____	__/__/__ Add.	_____ _____

Other Dependents (Describe)_____

Adopted Children? ( ) Yes ( ) No   Who?_____

Marriage Date _____ Where _____

Previous marriages for either spouse? Yes ( ) No ( ) <u>If Yes, list on back
dates of Marriage term and full name of prior spouse(s) and nature of termination,
(e.g. divorce, death)</u>.

Residence Address _____ Years there___ Phone_____

Previous Residence Address_____Years there _____

Any changes of State of residence during marriage? ( ) Yes ( ) No. <u>If Yes,
give dates on back</u> -- Year you came to California _____

Husband's Parents, brothers and sisters	Age	Name and age of spouse (for bro. or sis.)	City and State of residence	Health	Estimated Net Worth
*(F) _____	__	_____	_____	____	_____
*(M) _____	__	_____	_____	____	_____
*( ) _____	__	_____	_____	____	_____
*( ) _____	__	_____	_____	____	_____
*( ) _____	__	_____	_____	____	_____

Wife's Parents, etc.

*(F) _____	__	_____	_____	____	_____
*(M) _____	__	_____	_____	____	_____
*( ) _____	__	_____	_____	____	_____
*( ) _____	__	_____	_____	____	_____
*( ) _____	__	_____	_____	____	_____

*(F) - Father; (M)-Mother, (B)-Brother, (S)-Sister

MISCELLANEOUS INFORMATION

Husband's Occupation _____

Husband's Employer _____

Address _____ Phone _____

Number of Years _____ Title _____ Dept. _____

Husband's Previous Occupation _____

Wife's Occupation _____

Wife's Employer _____

Address _____ Phone _____

Husband's Social Security Number _____ Wife's _____

Employer ID Number (for corporation or partnership, if any) _____

If you own your own business, do you have information on prospective purchasers
in the event of your death or on other aspects of disposition of the business? If
yes, who knows the location of this information?

_____

Has Social Security status been reviewed lately: ( ) Yes ( ) No.

Armed Service: Branch _____ Serial No. _____

   Current Status _____ Disability _____

Husband and wife both U.S. Citizens? ( ) Yes ( ) No. If not, describe:

_____

Life Insurance Agent _____

Casualty Insurance Agent _____

Accountant _____

Investment Advisor _____

Personal Physician _____

Business Associates _____

_____

Safe Deposit Box No. _____ Location _____

   In whose names? _____

Is there a homestead filed on your home? ( ) Yes ( ) No

PLANNING INFORMATION

Do you have a pre or post-nuptial agreement? ( ) Yes ( ) No. If so, bring in.

Have either of you created a living trust?   ( ) Yes ( ) No If yes:

    Who created?   ( ) Husband   ( ) Wife   ( ) Both

    Who is the Trustee? _____

    Who are the beneficiaries?_____

Have you ever made a gift under the Uniform Gift to Minors Act? ( ) Yes ( ) No

    If Yes, Who is the custodian?_____

    Who are the donees? _____

    What was given? _____

Have either of you ever made gifts in excess of $10,000 to any person (including
your spouse) in any one year? If so, describe_____

_____

Are you or any member of your immediate family beneficiaries of a trust?

    ( ) Yes ( ) No. If so, who? _____

Do either of you expect to receive gifts or inheritances? ( ) Yes ( ) No.

    If so, Who? _____ How much? _____

    From Whom? _____

Describe any health problems or special needs of individual family members:

_____

_____

What is your estimate of the emotional maturity of your children? _____

_____

_____

Compare, in terms of your own priorities, the importance of adequate funds in order to do the following (indicate ranking by first, second, etc.):

    Enjoy a comfortable retirement   _____
    Take care of selves and family dur-
    ing a period of long term disability   _____
    Provide College educations for all children   _____
    Take care of your family in the event of your
    death   _____
    Any others that are important to you (specify)   _____

    _____   _____
    _____   _____
    _____   _____

PLANNING INFORMATION - CONTINUED

If your children are minors (under age 18), please indicate your first and second choices of guardian for the children if something should happen to the two of you:

```
First Choice        _____
Relationship        _____
Address             _____
City, State         _____
                    _____

Second Choice       _____
Relationship        _____
Address             _____
City, State         _____
                    _____
```

Which Bank or other corporate fiduciary might you wish to name as Executor or Trustee under your documents (recognizing that such institution may well be named only in an alternate capacity) _____

If your immediate family (e.g. spouse, children, grandchildren, etc.) were all to be deceased, to whom would you wish your property to pass (for example, you might want to have it go one-half to the heirs of each of you, or to a charity or charities, etc.): _____

_____

For older clients, would you want to designate a conservator of your person and estate in the event of your inability to manage your property? If so, who?

_____

Do you have any preference as to funeral and/or burial arrangements, or wish to place a limit on costs? If so, please fill out the following:

```
Religious Services, if any _____
```

Disposition of Body (e.g. specify burial or cremation, any preference for undertaking arrangements, particularly if you have made any such arrangements, and with whom) _____

_____

_____

```
Location of Interment _____

Limitation on Overall Cost (e.g. not to exceed $_____) _____
```
_____

RALPH GANO MILLER

SUPPLEMENTAL SCHEDULE "I"

LIFE INSURANCE

Company	Policy #	Issue Date	Owner*	Type**	Primary Beneficiary	Secondary Beneficiary, if any	Amount of Premium	Cash Value	Amount of Loan	Face Amount
On Life of Husband:										
On Life of Wife:										

*Unless otherwise indicated, insurance is usually owned by the insured; ownership by a spouse or someone else may sometimes reduce death taxes and therefore your agent may have arranged for an ownership other than by the insured

** e.g. Whole Life, Term, Endowment, Annuity, etc.

HEALTH INSURANCE

MEDICAL EXPENSE

MEDICAL EXPENSE POLICY NUMBERS											
NAME OF INSURANCE COMPANY OR SERVICE TYPE PLAN											
INSURED											
OWNER OF POLICY											
TYPE OF CONTINUANCE OR RENEWAL PROVISION											
TERMINATION DATE FOR CHILD COVERAGE											
BASIC HOSPITAL											
ROOM RATE											
NO. OF DAYS											
HOSPITAL EXTRAS											
OTHER BENEFITS											
SURGICAL											
MAXIMUM											
TYPE OF SCHEDULE											
MAJOR MEDICAL											
DEDUCTIBLE											
COINSURANCE											
INSIDE LIMITS											
OVERALL MAXIMUM											

DISABILITY INCOME

DISABILITY INCOME POLICY NUMBERS											
NAME OF INSURANCE COMPANY											
INSURED											
OWNER OF POLICY											
TYPE OF CONTINUANCE OR RENEWAL PROVISION											
DEFINITION OF DISABILITY											
MONTHLY DISABILITY INCOME											
ACCIDENT											
SICKNESS											
PARTIAL DISABILITY											
ACCIDENT											
SICKNESS											
WAITING PERIOD											
ACCIDENT											
SICKNESS											
BENEFIT PERIOD											
ACCIDENT											
SICKNESS											
SUPPLEMENTARY BENEFITS											

Appendix A
Data Gathering and Analysis

RALPH GANO MILLER

INHERITANCE TAX INFORMATION

1.   Did either of you own any real or personal property at date of marriage? If Yes, list below and attach real property tax bill for year of marriage, if available.

General Description of each asset   Approximate market value at mar.

_____
_____
_____

2.   Husband's occupation at date of marriage _____
        Husband's net worth at date of marriage _____
        Wife's occupation at date of marriage _____
        Wife's net worth at date of marriage _____

3.   If either of you have received any real or personal property after date of marriage by gift, bequest, devise or joint tenancy survivorship, list:

General Description of Each Asset	Full name and relation- ship of person rec'd from	Date rec'd	Approx. value on date rec'd
_____	_____	_____	_____
_____	_____	_____	_____

If California Inheritance Tax determination was made, Name of Estate _____
_____ Court Case No. (if any) _____ County _____

If Received by Gift, State of residence of donor*s) at date of gift: _____
_____

4.   Have any assets listed under 1 or 3 been transferred to anyone else (including spouse)? If Yes, for any such assets sold, give:

Asset	Date of Sale	Proceeds Received	Subsequent disp. of proceeds
_____	_____	_____	_____
_____	_____	_____	_____

For any such assets transferred without full consideration, give:

Asset	Date of Transfer	Names & addresses of persons transferred to	Consideration if any
_____	_____	_____	_____
_____	_____	_____	_____

5.   States in which you have resided after marriage, including California   Combined net worth upon taking up residence in each state (all assets, including cash)

_____
_____

6.   Does net worth at date of last arrival in California include any separate property of either of you? If Yes, state source and value:

_____
_____

7.   Trace subsequent disposition of combined net worth of spouses after last arrival in California _____

_____
_____
_____
_____

8.   Did either of you receive damages or a settlement for personal injury after September 11, 1957? If Yes, show dates, amounts received and subsequent disposition: _____

9.   Have you ever obtained a legal separation (separate maintenance) or an interlocutory divorce? If Yes, attach copy of decree and any property settlement agreement _____ Date of reconciliation _____

10.   Give on attachment any additional information bearing upon the separate or community status of your property.

The Tools and Techniques of Estate Planning

ANNUAL REVIEW CHECKLIST

Below you will find a number of questions. A positive answer to any of them may indicate a need to review your estate plan. Check the appropriate boxes and return to me.

Specific Bequests

☐ I would like to make specific bequests to individuals not presently included in my plans — or delete the names of one or more persons (or charities) currently named.

☐ I would like to change the amounts of some of the bequests I have made.

Changes in Valuation

☐ The value of my estate has changed more than 20 percent in the last two years.

Special Provisions for Children

☐ My health (my spouse's or children's health) has deteriorated substantially in the last year.

Newly Born or Adopted Children

☐ A child (grandchild) has been born (or adopted) since our last review.

Handicapped or Incompetent Children

☐ A child (grandchild or other dependent) has become handicapped or seriously injured since our last review.

Status of Family Marriages

☐ A member of the family has become divorced or separated since our last review.

Cancellation of Loans to
Children and Equalization of Inheritance

☐ I would like to discharge an obligation owed to me by cancelling the loan in my will.

☐ I would like to provide a clause to equalize any gifts made in the past (or to be made in the future) to certain children (grandchildren).

Life Insurance

☐ I have added (or dropped) more than $50,000 of life insurance since our last review.

☐ I have (or would like to) changed a beneficiary designation on an existing policy.

☐ I feel I may need more life insurance but I don't know how much to purchase or what type to consider.

Gifts to Minors

☐ I would like to make substantial gifts to minor children (grandchildren).

Gifts to Charities

☐ I would like to add (delete) one or more charitable beneficiaries.

☐ I would like to change the amount of my bequest to certain charities.

Business Interests

☐ I have entered into a stock (partnership) buy-sell agreement since our last review.

☐ My business situation has changed significantly since our last review.

Guardian, Executors and Trustees

☐ I would like to name a particular person as advisor to my executor and trustees.

☐ I would like to reconsider the designation of the guardians, executors, and trustees I have named.

Other

☐ I would like to review my estate plans for the following reasons.

☐ I'd like to know how the latest tax law affects my estate plan.

CHECKLIST OF INFORMATION TO KEEP IN SAFE DEPOSIT BOX

The following information or materials should be kept in your safe deposit box:

☐ (1) Birth certificates

☐ (2) Marriage certificates (including artifacts or documentation from any prior marriages or divorces)

☐ (3) Your will (and spouse's will) and trust agreements

☐ (4) Listing of life insurance policies or certificates

☐ (5) Your Social Security numbers

☐ (6) Military discharge papers

☐ (7) Bonds, stocks, and other securities

☐ (8) Real estate deeds

☐ (9) Business (Buy-Sell) Agreement

☐ (10) Automobile titles and insurance policies

☐ (11) Property insurance policies

☐ (12) Additional:

LIST numbers of all checking and savings accounts including bank addresses and location of safe deposit boxes:

_____   _____   _____

_____   _____   _____

LIST name, address, and phone number of fire and life insurance agent:

_____   _____   _____

LIST name, address, and phone number of accountant:

_____   _____   _____

LIST name, address, and phone number of (current or past) employer. State date when you retired if applicable. Include employee benefits booklets:

_____   _____   _____

_____   _____   _____

LIST all debts owed to *and* owed by you:

_____   _____   _____

_____   _____   _____

LIST the names, addresses, telephone numbers and birth dates of your children and other beneficiaries (including charitable beneficiaries):

_____   _____   _____

_____   _____   _____

_____   _____   _____

SELECTION OF EXECUTOR, TRUSTEE, AND ATTORNEY

Note: The pages appearing below, "How to Select an Executor, Trustee, and Attorney," by Stephan R. Leimberg and Charles K. Plotnick, are reproduced with the publisher's permission from THE HANDBOOK OF ESTATE PLANNING, edited by D. Larry Crumbley (Dow-Jones-Irwin, Inc.: Homewood, IL 60430), copyright 1988 by Dow Jones-Irwin.

2

How to Select an Executor, Trustee, and Attorney

Stephan R. Leimberg, Esq.
Professor of Taxation and Estate Planning,
The American College

Charles K. Plotnick, Esq.
Practicing Attorney

═══════════════════

INTRODUCTION

Selecting the people to carry out the provisions of an estate plan is one of the most important and difficult tasks involved in the estate planning process. This chapter concerns three of the most essential parties in the estate planning process: the executor, the trustee, and the attorney. It will establish practical guidelines in the selection process from the point of view of the person who ultimately must make those choices, the client.

It is impossible to make a proper selection of any member of the estate planning team without understanding—in general terms—what it is that the individual should be doing and how that person interacts with others who have important roles to fulfill. For this reason, you'll find a brief discussion of the duties of the executor, trustee, and estate's attorney before the attributes and selection criteria of each are covered.

The authors are grateful for the significant assistance of Lawrence Brody, Esq., of Bryan, Cave, McPheeters and McRoberts in St. Louis, Missouri.

PART I—SELECTING AN EXECUTOR

DUTIES OF THE EXECUTOR

An executor is the person (and/or institution) named in a valid will to serve as the personal representative of a testator when his or her will is being probated. Technically, this person is referred to as the "executor" if male and "executrix" if female but is commonly referred to as the executor or personal representative regardless of gender.

When death occurs, the executor must locate and probate the decedent's will (prove that it was the decedent's will and that it in fact was his or her last will). The executor must then collect the decedent's property; pay debts, taxes, and expenses; and distribute any remaining assets to the beneficiaries specified in the decedent's will.

An executor's responsibilities typically last from nine months to two or three years. In rare instances (such as when there is a contest of a will or the estate remains open for tax or other reasons) the executor's duties continue for a period of years.

ATTRIBUTES OF A GOOD EXECUTOR

When choosing an executor, the major attributes to consider are:

1. Sensitivity.
2. Competence.
3. An understanding of the needs and appreciation of the circumstances of the beneficiaries.
4. Knowledge of the nature, value, and extent of the decedent's assets.
5. Experience in the administration of estates.
6. Business and investment experience.
7. Familiarity with the decedent's business.
8. Ability to serve.
9. Willingness to serve.
10. Geographic proximity to the estate's beneficiaries and the estate's assets.
11. Lack of any conflict of interest.
12. Integrity and loyalty.

Sensitivity. Although the intangible attribute of "caring" both about the people involved and the performance of one's duties cannot be accurately or objectively measured, this single quality is perhaps the most important of all the factors in the selection process. It is always possible

Appendix B
Selection of Executor, Trustee, and Attorney

for the personal representative, if lacking knowledge in certain areas, to learn more about the subject or hire others with expertise.

The highest preference should be given to the identification of an individual who is willing and able to give concerned personal attention and extra effort to the psychological as well as financial needs and individual circumstances of the beneficiaries. Often this individual will be the beneficiary with the largest share of the estate and almost always will be a close relative or friend of the decedent.

Competence. Competence encompasses both the legal ability to serve and the intellectual and emotional capacity to serve effectively.

Legal capacity entails U.S. citizenship and the satisfaction of state law requirements such as (*a*) age (21 or 18 in most states), (*b*) mental competency (generally, the same required to be a testator or in some states a higher capacity, the ability to contract), and (*c*) domicile (some states require that the executor be a domiciliary of the state in which the will is probated while others allow executors from other states but may require that an out-of-state executor post a bond).

Intellectual capacity in a general sense does not require that the executor be completely aware of all the decedent's personal affairs or the intricacy of the decedent's business. What is necessary is that the person selected has the ability to analyze the situation as quickly as possible under the circumstances, determine what facets of the estate administration can be handled within the bounds of the executor's personal knowledge and capabilities, and then secure the appropriate professional assistance in those areas in which the executor knows he or she lacks experience. In other words, the executor must have the ability to organize both facts and people and understand and follow through with what must be done.

Emotional capacity involves the ability to make a multitude of important decisions. Often these decisions (e.g., the selection of and negotiations with the estate's attorney and tax elections) must be made within a relatively short time span and yet may have tremendous financial significance to the estate and its beneficiaries. An intelligent individual capable of making quick, well-considered decisions will more than make up for an initial lack of experience.

An understanding of the needs and circumstances of the beneficiaries. Personal knowledge of the beneficiaries, their ages, health conditions, income requirements, strengths, weaknesses, and eccentricities is extremely helpful to an executor. One child, for instance, may need immediate and continuing medical care, while another may be a highly successful surgeon. An elderly parent may need cash to meet the daily necessities of life or be so wealthy that a delay in the distribution of assets from a deceased child may have no adverse effect.

Knowledge of the nature, value, and extent of the decedent's assets. If an executor is familiar with the specific assets that comprise the estate, that information can be of great use in performing each of the most essential of his or her duties. For example, if one of the principal assets of the estate is a business in which the executor was active in the management, the advantage to the estate of that experience and continuity could be quickly translated into dollars.

Many individuals invest in or amass collectibles for pleasure. An executor with expertise in this area would know how to safeguard, transport, insure, have appraised, and sell such items far more readily than an executor with no particular knowledge of the subject matter. This is particularly true with respect to large collections of art, precious gems, stamps, coins, and many other similar items.

One of the most troublesome responsibilities of an executor is also one that must be started early in the estate administration process—the discovery and assembly of all the decedent's assets. An executor who is privy to the extent of the estate and knows the location of all of the assets or the names of those persons who can help in this key part of the estate's probate will have a great advantage. This should simplify the tasks and enable the executor to realize a great deal more from those assets. Prior familiarity is of considerable benefit if the decedent's assets were varied and located in different states or overseas.

Experience at administering an estate. Although death is a common occurrence, few individuals have experience in being executors. Obviously, if an individual has probated at least one or two estates, he or she is an ideal candidate. Note that this criterion emphasizes one of the major strengths of a corporate fiduciary vis-à-vis an individual. Few if any individuals have probated as many estates as a bank or trust company specializing in estate planning and administration. In ultra large or highly complex estates this consideration should be given high priority.

Business and investment experience and familiarity with the testator's investments and business. Intelligence and emotional maturity may not be enough to successfully handle the administration of an estate. The brightest spouse or most intelligent child may lack the business or investment experience to handle a large corporation or a sizable stock and bond portfolio. The experience-tested executor clearly will have an edge in a case where significant business or investment decisions will have to be made.

Professional executors such as banks and trust companies are in the business of collecting, managing, and investing securities. They typically have separate departments to handle, analyze, and evaluate securities, supervise and sell real estate, and run businesses. To a lesser degree, professional advisors and associates (even friendly competitors in rare cases) who knew the operation of the decedent's business can provide invaluable service to the estate.

Obviously, a buy-sell agreement can incredibly simplify the task of an executor where a business interest comprises the bulk of an individual's estate. But where there is no such agreement, the executor must—at least temporarily—assume whatever role the decedent had in the business.

Depending on the circumstances and nature of the business, it could be either continued or terminated. But without knowledge of the details of the business or expertise in the specific area involved, the executor or administrator would obviously be working under a considerable handicap. Even a professional executor such as a bank or trust company may not have the requisite expertise if the decedent's business was in a specialized or personalized area in which particular or unique knowledge was necessary to survive in the marketplace.

Clearly, the executor who has an in-depth understanding of the inner workings of the decedent's business or profession has a tremendous edge over the neophyte. But although there is no substitute for experience, intelligent individuals who have the ability to obtain the necessary information and experience as well as the time and inclination to administer the estate can usually do a credible and often an outstanding job, if they are willing to put time and effort into the performance of their duties.

Consider also that individuals or banks with strong investment or business expertise can be named as coexecutors or can be hired on an hourly or annual retainer basis by the estate's executor. Certainly, any executor without extensive investment knowledge should secure the services of skilled advisors and investment personnel where appropriate. An executor who does nothing—to the detriment of the estate's beneficiaries—is just as liable to surcharge as the executor who makes a mistake of commission. So it is essential for a nonprofessional executor to secure competent advice when dealing with an estate largely composed of securities.

Ability and willingness to serve. It is extremely important in selecting a personal representative to consider the ability of the chosen person (or persons) to serve. The duties and responsibilities of an executor can amount to considerable time and effort, ranging from dozens of hours to hundreds and even thousands of hours. The decedent's heirs suffer the consequences if the designated executor is unable or unwilling to perform the necessary tasks.

Most laymen are under the impression that to name someone the executor of an estate is to bestow upon them a great honor. To the extent the term *executor* carries with it the ultimate in trust, this impression is justified. But with that honor, the personal representative must accept an awesome measure of responsibility and potential liability.

An executor is considered a *fiduciary*. This means a potential lawsuit by beneficiaries for breach of confidentiality, conflicts of interest, failure to exercise due care or diligence or prudence, failure to properly preserve or protect estate assets, failure to file timely and proper tax returns or maintain adequate records, and the breach of the duty to make all major discretionary decisions personally and not to delegate such decisions. This responsibility and potential personal liability may drastically reduce the willingness of the nominee to accept the position. (For this reason, no one can be forced to accept the position of executor. And for that reason every will should provide at least one, and preferably more than one, backup executor in case the one named fails to qualify or ceases to act.)

Geographic proximity to the estate's assets and beneficiaries. Testators should consider, when selecting an executor, the physical distance the executor may have to travel and the time the executor may have to spend away from home. For example, New York state law may allow a son who lives in California to be the executor of his father's estate—but will the son be able to take the time away from his own job (not to mention his family) to serve properly? What expenses will be incurred out of the son's pocket or what nonreimbursable income will be lost by the son because he must be handling an estate on the opposite end of the continent? Quite often, the executor's fee or the size of the estate will be insufficient to economically justify the executor's expenditure of time. In such instances it may be preferable to appoint a local executor—perhaps a bank or a trust company—and to have the distant relative serve as an unofficial advisor to the executor or as a coexecutor.

Lack of a conflict of interest. An otherwise logical choice of a particular individual or individuals may fail to consider potential conflicts of interest. For example, an older child may well be qualified to manage her father's affairs. But will a conflict arise between the personal interest of that older child and a surviving parent or younger siblings? Such problems can easily occur when the executor makes decisions on where to take certain deductions or other tax-oriented elections.

The problem of a potential conflict of interest is particularly acute where a business associate is named as executor. It is imperative to consider in advance of such a nomination the effect that the associate's handling of the business ("to sell or not to sell," and if so, to whom and at what price?) will have on the testator's personal heirs. What if the most likely purchaser is the associate himself? How can the heirs be assured they have received a fair price for the business interest? Or how can they know the right decision was to sell rather than to retain the business? How do they know he did not pay himself an exorbitant salary (as well as an exorbitant executor's fee)? It is inevitable that doubt will linger when a partner or coshareholder is named as executor, regardless of how careful that person is to make decisions impartially and in the best interest of the beneficiaries.

Another area in which a conflict of interest can easily occur is where a client names the attorney who drafted the will as executor. In our opinion an attorney who unilaterally names himself or his law partner as attorney—without the knowledge or express direction of the client—has committed a breach of ethics and has clearly acted improperly.

If the attorney who drew the will is named as executor, then technically, he or she is not an employee or agent of the beneficiaries. That means they have no power to fire him as executor if he doesn't answer phone calls or if letters requesting information about the estate go unanswered. It will be difficult for beneficiaries to challenge his actions or lack of actions. If that person hires himself or his business partner as the estate's attorney, beneficiaries have little right to question the legality. Who, aside from the court upon final audit of the estate, can question the fee that such an executor pays himself as attorney? The appointment of attorney as executor reduces the checks and balances desirable in the probate of an estate and—aside from the other issues of competency, ability, and willingness to take the time away from the practice of law to do a proper job—creates inevitable conflict of interest.

There are, of course, exceptions to the general rule that the attorney who draws the will should not be named as the estate's executor. For instance, if the attorney is a close relative of the testator or the natural object of his bounty, it is proper and in most cases appropriate for that attorney to be named as executor. If the attorney is the one individual most familiar with the decedent's assets, family, and business, then the attorney may be a logical choice, but in this case it may be best to name the attorney as coexecutor with a family member.

The very possibility of a conflict of interest may put the potential executor in an uncomfortable and even dangerous situation. In many cases such an individual will injure his own interest in the attempt to bend over backwards to avoid the appearance of impropriety. Nevertheless, he will always be conscious of the likelihood of secondguessing by beneficiaries if they feel the apportionment of profits or proceeds was inadequate. Such an individual should, in many cases, properly and promptly refuse to serve as executor.

One possible solution to a potential conflict of interest is to name a business associate as an advisor or as coexecutor with a bank and to name some third coexecutor so there could not be a tie vote. In fact, wherever there is any potential for a conflict of interest a professional fiduciary should be considered. Impartiality is one of the major strengths of having a bank or trust company serve as executor.

Integrity and loyalty. These are among the duties owed by a fiduciary to the beneficiaries of the estate. But it is as essential that the testator have absolute trust in the honesty and loyalty of the executor for reasons that go beyond the obvious legal or ethical implications; an important part of the estate planning process is the peace of mind an individual obtains in knowing that his or her affairs are in order and that the financial security he has paid for during his lifetime will serve those he loves and wants to benefit in the years beyond his lifetime. For these reasons, it is essential that the testator have absolute trust that his will will be carried out as he intended to the best of the executor's ability.

Fees. Although fees are not among the listed attributes of a good executor, they are an important consideration in the selection process. The amount of fee a personal representative is entitled to may be determined by (1) the statutory law of the state where the estate is probated, or (2) local county rules or customs governing what the personal representative is entitled to charge for services rendered to the estate, or (3) in the case of professional executors such as banks or trust companies, an advertised fixed and scheduled fee (for a large estate the scheduled fee may possibly be lowered by negotiation, in which an attorney specializing in estate administration can be invaluable), or (4) provisions in the will or in separate contractual agreements between the testator and the nominated executor.

An executor is entitled to reasonable compensation for services rendered. Fees should not be determined solely on the basis of the monetary amount of the decedent's probate assets but should take into account the nature of the executor's tasks, the time spent, the complexity of the problems and decisions that have to be made, the professional background and competence of the executor, and the ultimate results and benefits obtained for the heirs.

There are valid tax and nontax reasons why an executor who is a relative or friend of the testator may or may not accept a fee. Although the selection process should encompass the likely course of action the executor will take in this regard, it is important that this factor not override or take the place of the other selection criteria.

In many cases testators expect that family members named as executors will charge no fees but that professional fiduciaries will. Although in many situations this assumption will be correct, this selection criterion should be tempered by considering the mistakes the nonprofessional may make that the professional would not and the opportunities the nonprofessional may miss that the professional would not.

Summary. The choice of executor(s) and backups (there should always be at least one and preferably two backups) is complicated by a combination of family, personal, tax, and nontax considerations both tangible and intangible. All of these must be considered and balanced, for the executor's tasks and responsibilities are often complex and their successful and prompt completion is always—from the heirs' viewpoint—crucial.

PART II—SELECTING A TRUSTEE

DUTIES OF THE TRUSTEE

A trustee is the person (and/or institution) named in a trust agreement to carry out the objectives and follow the terms of the trust. A trustee can be an individual (professional or nonprofessional) or a corporate fiduciary. It is also possible and common to appoint both individual and corporate trustees for reasons that will be discussed below.

It is useful in enumerating the duties and listing the attributes of a good trustee to consider the typical objectives that a trust is designed to accomplish. These goals include the following actions:

1. Reduce or eliminate income or estate or generation-skipping transfer taxes at the federal or state level.
2. Reduce or eliminate probate costs.
3. Provide a vehicle that will serve as a receptacle for both probate and nonprobate assets and facilitate attainment of other estate planning objectives through unified administration.
4. Provide for minor children in a manner more flexible and custom-tailored to the grantor's desires than the Uniform Gifts or Uniform Transfers to Minors Acts allow.
5. Provide for recipients who are legally of majority age but who lack the emotional or intellectual maturity or physical capacity or technical training to handle large sums of money or an investment portfolio or a family business.
6. Provide for individuals who have the capacity to handle large sums of money or an investment portfolio or a family business but choose not to make the necessary investment decisions or deal with the constant problems or devote the degree of attention required.
7. Postpone full ownership of trust assets until the beneficiaries of the trust have attained ages specified by the grantor or until events specified by the grantor have occurred.
8. Enable the investment of an asset that does not lend itself to fragmentation. This often occurs where the grantor desires to spread the beneficial ownership among a number of individuals. Life insurance policies and real estate are just two examples of assets that are difficult to split up or are worth substantially more if held together.

9. Limit the parties who can obtain the assets and achieve particular dispositive objectives. For instance, where family control of a business or a specific asset is important, the grantor will want to limit the class of beneficiaries and prevent recipients from disposing of property to persons outside the family. A common example is the desire to protect assets from the consequence of an unsuccessful marriage.

The duties of the trustee may therefore include the satisfaction of a number of tax and nontax objectives that include but are not limited to the investment, management, and protection of trust assets and compliance with the dispositive intentions of the grantor.

To a great extent the selection process and decision criteria for selecting a trustee will follow the same pattern as in choosing an executor; premium will be placed on many of the same attributes. But there are several significant distinctions.

Unlike the role of the executor, which is typically concluded within a year or two, the trustee's responsibilities commonly last for at least one generation and often last beyond two or three generations. This fact should have a significant effect on the choice of trustee or on the decision to name both cotrustees and successor trustees (or to provide a mechanism for their appointment by a resigning trustee or by the beneficiaries).

A second distinguishing factor is that the choice of trustee, unlike the selection of the executor, is tax sensitive. In other words, there will be situations in which tax consequences will vary widely (results ranging from success to tax disaster) according to whether the grantor, the grantor's spouse, the beneficiaries, the grantor's business associates, the grantor's professional advisors, or a totally independent third party is named as trustee.

The decision is further complicated by a multiplicity of personal, family, business, investment, and nontax considerations—which must all be weighed by the grantor and the attorney drafting the trust. Quite often, a trade-off between flexibility and tax-saving objectives will be required. And even with the aid of skilled counsel, some compromise may be necessary.

ATTRIBUTES OF A GOOD TRUSTEE

When selecting a trustee, the major attributes to consider are:

1. Availability.
2. Impartiality and lack of conflict of interest.
3. Financial security.
4. Investment sophistication, policy, and track record.
5. Business sophistication.

6. Accounting and tax-planning expertise.
7. Recordkeeping and reporting ability.
8. Knowledge of and sensitivity to beneficiaries and their circumstances.
9. Fees.
10. Tax-neutral impact.
11. Decision-making abilities.
12. Competence.
13. Standard to which trustee will be held.
14. Integrity.
15. Flexibility to meet changing circumstances.
16. Willingness to serve throughout the term of the trust.
17. Experience as a trustee.
18. Neutral state law impact.

Availability. This criterion has two aspects, permanency and proximity. Corporate trustees are often considered because they possess one attribute that individuals (even individuals who are professional trustees) do not possess—perpetual existence, at least in the sense that a bank (or its successor) is likely to be in business during the entire term of the trust even if it lasts for generations, whereas individuals, even professional trustees, may with unpredictable frequency retire or make a career change or die or become disabled. Although banks may take holidays, they never take vacations. So to some extent it can be said that corporate fiduciaries have an availability advantage over individuals.

This perpetual-existence theory must be considered in perspective; only change lasts forever. The real issue is whether the trustee will be able to serve effectively long enough. The briefly considered answer to this question would still seem to give unparalleled advantage to a bank, especially when the possible senility or emotional instability or physical disability of an individual trustee is considered. It is particularly difficult to protect beneficiaries against these human frailties, since there is no automatic retirement mechanism for superannuated or mildly incompetent trustees.

But consider that with change in personnel at senior management, professional, and clerical levels, even if the same legal entity is involved, both the personalities and the principles on which money is managed and invested may have changed so drastically as to constitute a new entity for all practical purposes. Surely, in the time span of a trust running for two or more generations, turnover in most banks will effect a drastic if not revolutionary change in people dealing with and policies affecting trust beneficiaries. The bank that was so friendly and competent (perhaps because its senior management gave great priority to trust business in the years in which the trust was established) may be cold and less than satisfactory to a second generation of beneficiaries.

Availability must also be considered in geographic terms. An individual trustee is likely—over a long period of time—to move from the city in which the trust or its beneficiary is located. Of course, although banks generally remain and in fact are becoming regional in scope, since beneficiaries often move (or perhaps did not live in the same city or state or country as the grantor to begin with), dealing with the bank selected by the grantor may no longer be convenient. Consider provisions giving beneficiaries the power to change from one corporate fiduciary to another. (See discussion below of removal and replacement of trustees.)

Impartiality and absence of a conflict of interest. How will the trustee react when faced with a choice that favors him at the expense of other beneficiaries—or favors others at his expense? What are the intra-family implications of those choices? For instance, will he alienate one family member by (even properly) denying a distribution, or ingratiate himself to another by being liberal in his policy of making distributions? Can he say no to one child and yes to another without causing a never-ending family feud? A trustee who is also a family member may be forced by conscience or by duty to make choices injurious to the harmony of family relationships.

Will the trustee (such as the grantor's spouse) be subject to the influence of one or more children (or a second spouse or lover) to make distributions that may not be in the best interest of other beneficiaries? Is the family member-trustee easily persuaded or likely to show favoritism? The remarriage of a spouse or child who is named as trustee may result in less than impartial decisions—especially where the trustee has been given discretionary powers over trust income or principal—even if the new spouse is not included in the class of possible recipients.

A child/trustee may take on the role of a parent to his or her remaining parent or siblings. This may be positive, but it also may result in an attempt to control the lives of family members through the family finances as if that person were a parent rather than a child.

An independent professional trustee is not subject to such problems. Since the choice between no and yes may be one of the most important duties of a trustee, this ability of a professional trustee to be objective and impartial should be given high preference in the decision-making process.

Conflict of interest can occur even where there is no issue of impartiality. For example, assume the grantor names his attorney as trustee. The attorney/trustee would most likely be objective and impartial as between the conflicting interests of family members. But consider these questions:

Once the grantor has died, who will negotiate with the attorney to ensure that fees are reasonable?

Appendix B
Selection of Executor, Trustee, and Attorney

Who could fire the attorney (or trustee) if services were not performed properly or in a timely manner?

Can the attorney remain impartial as a trustee if he represents the business of one of the beneficiaries?

Is it appropriate for an accountant serving as trustee to continue in the dual capacity if he also represents a business owned by the trust?

What if there is an argument between the attorney/trustee and the grantor (or the trust's beneficiaries) that is entirely personal or is on the attorney/client level and has nothing to do with the relationship he has as a trustee?

Is it possible for an attorney/trustee to fairly represent the beneficiaries, the grantor, or cotrustees in a trust-related situation?

Will the attorney or accountant be willing to allocate appropriate time to the trust or will that person concentrate on obtaining and servicing professional clients (especially if the fees for serving as trustee are substantially lower than that charged in the professional's practice)?

Conflict of interest problems would plague a business associate or partner who was named trustee. For instance, if the trust held stock in one or more businesses in which the trustee was an officer or shareholder, his salary, or his stock interest would be affected by his actions taken as a trustee. What if the trustee was the art dealer for the trust of an artist who trusted him and had the highest degree of respect for the dealer's integrity, judgment, and marketing expertise? Assume the trust's assets consisted mainly of the artist's paintings. The dealer/trustee would be bound to obtain the highest price possible when selling trust assets. But as a dealer, he would want to pay the lowest possible price. Would it be appropriate to continue as trustee under those circumstances? It is risky to name anyone who is likely to buy or lease assets from or sell or lease assets to the trust or have any other dealings with trust property.

Some of these impartiality and conflict-of-interest problems can be overcome or minimized if anticipated in advance. But in most cases, if such problems can occur, they will. Often, the problem is not that an unethical transaction has occurred or an improper decision has been made. Rather, it is that the parties are uncomfortable merely because the beneficiaries know it could happen and the trustee knows the beneficiaries may distrust, second-guess, or sue him merely because they suspect a conflict of interest could have occurred or might occur.

Financial security. This refers to the security of the funds entrusted to the trustee and the "depth of the trustee's pockets" in the event of a successful malfeasance or misfeasance suit by beneficiaries. A nonprofessional trustee will not have an internal audit staff to review the acts of the person administering the trust. This lack of a system of checks and balances is one of the major shortcomings of an individual nonprofessional trustee. Conversely, banks and trust companies are audited both internally and (usually by the state) externally. All investments made by a corporate fiduciary must be approved by a trust investment committee, and the portfolio, which is typically diversified, is reviewed frequently.

If sued, will the fiduciary be available to answer for and be able to pay damages for a wrongful act? The answer is likely to be "no" with respect to an individual trustee but "yes" with respect to a corporate fiduciary. For example, in the event of an embezzlement or some other impropriety or breach of trust, the odds of a recovery from a bank or trust company are significantly higher than from an individual trustee merely because of the relative sizes of the fiduciary's own assets. Banks serving as trustees are required to meet minimum amounts of capitalization requirements.

An individual trustee can acquire physical security for trust assets by hiring safe deposit and other facilities. Banks and trust companies have such protection on site but of course build charges for their use into their fees.

Investment sophistication, track record, and investment policy. The trustee's ability to successfully invest and reinvest trust funds is one of the more important attributes to consider in the selection process. In this regard, many professional and even nonprofessional individuals have proved more astute or competent than their corporate counterparts. In some cases the grantor's opinion of a spouse or child as "financially inept" has proved to be an incorrect perception.

But the highly computerized and experienced investment departments of banks and professional individual fiduciaries do have an advantage over anyone who is not a professional investor. A further advantage of the professional trustee is that trust assets can be invested in a bank's common trust funds, which increases the safety of trust investments through diversity.

The ultimate decision in this category should not be made until the various track records are compared. The performance of commercial trust departments has varied considerably from bank to bank and from the investment returns of other investment managers.

Investment policy is an important consideration in the selection process. Corporate fiduciaries tend to be conservative. This may be either attractive or a drawback depending on how aggressive the grantor's own style or personal objectives are.

The investment decisions of an ultraconservative trustee may not be suited to the beneficiaries' risk-taking propensities or their growth and income objectives. But this in turn may be more in keeping with the grantor's long-range goals of restraining the lifestyle of income and principal recipients.

So the ultimate decision is not between professional and nonprofessional or between individual and corporate fiduciary; it must be made on the basis of the type of investment policy the grantor of the trust desires and the particular trustee that will come closest to matching that policy.

Business sophistication. Where one or more businesses are held in the trust, it is extremely important that the trustee have expertise in running that type of business. Even if the trustee should and will sell it, knowing when and how best to dispose of it is a very important skill. If the business is large or large relative to other trust assets, or if it is a specialized or personal service type of business, this may mean that a family member, business associate, professional advisor, or even a former competitor may have to be considered in spite of impartiality issues or potential conflicts of interest.

Typically, corporate fiduciaries do not continue businesses left in trust. The business is quickly sold and the proceeds are reinvested. In most cases that will be the appropriate course of action, since few banks have enough of the right type of personnel to continue the success of a growing business, and a failing business should usually be liquidated as quickly as possible. Nonprofessional individual fiduciaries rarely have the time to run a business even if they have the expertise and experience.

Accounting and tax planning expertise. Corporate fiduciaries have a definite advantage over nonprofessional individual trustees when considering the myriad accounting procedures, tax compliance, and tax planning opportunities that must be handled by a trustee. The level of sophistication, expertise, and experience that should be applied over the lifetime of any trust is one that few nonprofessionals can provide. This means that most family members will simply be incapable of fully understanding all of the problems that must be avoided and the availability and implications of the tax and property law elections that must be weighed. Even knowledgeable attorneys and accountants do not have the requisite practical day-to-day experience unless they practice solely in this field.

It is possible and in many cases appropriate for a trustee to hire agents for advice and assistance. Most trustees will communicate regularly with outside attorneys and accountants. But planning policy and decisions must be made by the trustee; these are among the duties that cannot be delegated. Thus, the trustee must have a working knowledge of the accounting laws and both federal and state tax laws (income, estate, gift, and generation-skipping). Will an untrained trustee know whom to call or if the advice received is both legally correct and practical? Will a nonprofessional understand the interplay between tax, trust, and property law well enough to interpret provisions in the trust and adequately inform beneficiaries about the tax and other legal effects of various choices?

Recordkeeping and reporting ability.   A trust is a long-term arrangement under which accountings must be made periodically over many years to a number of parties that may include the grantor, the beneficiaries, the appropriate federal and state taxing authorities, and the supervising court. This requires regular statements of the receipts, disbursements, and assets of the trust in an intelligible form, and careful long-term record storage.

Knowledge of and sensitivity to beneficiaries and their circumstances.   In some cases an understanding of the family involved and their special needs or desires and how they relate to the grantor's objectives should properly take priority over many of the other objectives on this list. If the financial encouragement of a handicapped child, for example, is not provided through the trust, the trust may fail in its purpose regardless of how much tax it saves or how closely the trustee meets both the letter of the law and the terms of the trust itself. *Sensitivity* here is therefore used interchangeably with *flexibility*. If flexibility in dealings with trust beneficiaries and a high degree of personal sensitivity are primary considerations, a nonprofessional trustee is indicated.

Fees.   Corporate and other professional fiduciaries charge a fee for their services. Usually, this fee is based on a percentage of the income and principal of the trust. A distribution fee equal to a percentage of the principal disbursed from the trust is also often charged (upon termination or otherwise). Although this fee is typically set according to a standard schedule of fees, it may be possible to negotiate the fee in the case of a trust with a large amount of assets. This may be an amount agreed on or may be a flat hourly charge. Where trust assets consist solely of unfunded life insurance trusts, unimproved real estate, or closely held stock, the nonprofessional may be the best choice for a trustee. Likewise, trusts with assets of less than $200,000 in value are often discouraged from using corporate fiduciaries because of the fees.

Many individuals name their spouses or relatives or close friends or even trust beneficiaries because they will serve as a personal favor or as an accommodation and will not charge a fee to act as a trustee. This may be an economic necessity where the value of trust assets is small and payment of the minimum fees to the corporate fiduciary would significantly reduce the income and principal of the trust. But in most cases, the fee saved by using a nonprofessional amounts to a false economy.

There is a further aspect with respect to fees and the selection of a trustee; in selecting a relative who is also a beneficiary, will the fees charged be understood by and acceptable to other beneficiaries, or will such fees—even if reasonable for the services performed—be resented and cause conflict?

Tax-neutral impact. A revocable trust has a neutral impact on taxes at both federal and state levels. As long as the grantor has reserved the right to revoke the trust at any time, in most situations he will be treated as if he had not established a trust and had remained as the outright owner of the property in the trust. So with respect to a revocable trust, it does not matter for tax purposes who is selected as trustee. For example, the grantor will be taxed on the income of a revocable trust whether he names himself, his spouse, a beneficiary, a friend, a business associate, a professional whom he employs, or an independent corporate or other professional fiduciary.

But if one of the major reasons for establishing an irrevocable trust is to save taxes (federal and state income, estate, or generation-skipping transfer), the identity of the trustee is a very tax-sensitive decision: Inclusion of the trust's assets in income (or in the gross estate or in the generation-skipping tax base) will result if the wrong party is selected as trustee. The potential for adverse tax results increases significantly when the trustee is given discretionary powers over the income or principal of the trust if the trustee or a cotrustee is the grantor, his or her spouse, a family member (or some combination of them), or if one or more of these people becomes a trustee under a successor provision in the trust.

Consequently, the adverse tax consequences can be avoided very simply by providing that these individuals may not become a trustee or by specifying that if such a person is a trustee, he or she may not participate in a decision that will result in the to-be-avoided tax result. For example, a surviving spouse/trustee would be prohibited from exercising a broad discretionary power over principal in her own favor if the objective of the trust was to prevent inclusion of assets in her estate. But it is obvious that favorable tax results are obtained at the cost of a loss of flexibility.

The following commentary summarizes the major income and estate tax consequences of powers held by various parties. It emphasizes that before naming the grantor or anyone with an interest in the trust as trustee, consideration must be given to these implications.

I.   Powers to affect beneficial enjoyment.
    A.   Power to distribute income to the grantor or the grantor's spouse.
        1.   Grantor as trustee.
            a.   Grantor taxed on the income of the trust since the grantor will be treated as the owner of trust assets.
            b.   Assets in the trust includable in the grantor's gross estate.
        2.   Nonadverse party as trustee.
            a.   Grantor taxed on the income of the trust.

       b. Assets in the trust not includable in the grantor's gross estate.

  3. Adverse party as trustee.

       a. Grantor not taxed on trust income.

       b. Assets in the trust not includable in grantor's gross estate.

B. Power to distribute income to beneficiaries other than the grantor or the grantor's spouse without the restriction of an ascertainable standard.

  1. Grantor as trustee.

       a. Grantor taxed on the income of the trust since the grantor will be treated as the owner of the trust.

       b. Assets in the trust includable in the gross estate of the grantor if the power can be exercised by the grantor alone or with any other party (adverse or not).

  2. Nonadverse party as trustee.

       a. Grantor taxed on the income of the trust since the grantor will be treated as the owner of the trust (unless the power is limited to withholding distributions temporarily during legal disability).

       b. Assets in the trust not includable in the estate of the grantor unless the grantor has retained the right to substitute himself as trustee.

  3. Independent party as trustee.

       a. Grantor not taxed on the income of the trust.

       b. Assets in the trust will generally not be includable in the grantor's gross estate unless the grantor can substitute himself as beneficiary.

C. Power—subject to an ascertainable standard—to distribute income to beneficiaries other than the grantor or the grantor's spouse.

  1. Grantor as trustee.

       a. Grantor taxed on the income of the trust since the grantor will be taxed as the owner of the trust (unless the power can be exercised only with the consent of an adverse party).

       b. Assets in the trust will generally not be includable in the grantor's gross estate since the power can only be exercised pursuant to ascertainable standards.

  2. Person other than the grantor (or the grantor's spouse) as trustee.
   a. Grantor not taxed on the income of the trust.
   b. Assets in the trust will generally not be includable in the grantor's estate unless the grantor can substitute himself as trustee.

D. Power—subject to an ascertainable standard—to distribute principal to a beneficiary or class of beneficiaries.
  1. Grantor as trustee.
   a. Grantor not taxed on the income of the trust.
   b. Assets in the trust will generally not be included in the grantor's estate because exercise of the power is limited by an ascertainable standard.
  2. Person other than grantor as trustee.
   a. Assets in the trust will generally not be included in the grantor's estate because exercise of the power is limited by an ascertainable standard.

E. Power to distribute principal to a current income beneficiary.
  1. Grantor as trustee.
   a. Grantor not taxable on the income of the trust.
   b. Assets in the trust will be includable in the grantor's gross estate unless the power is limited by an ascertainable standard.
  2. Person other than grantor as trustee.
   a. Grantor not taxable on the income of the trust.
   b. Assets in the trust will not be includable in the grantor's gross estate unless the grantor can substitute himself as trustee.

F. Power to distribute or accumulate income for a current income beneficiary.
  1. Grantor as trustee.
   a. Income of the trust not taxable to the grantor.
   b. Assets in the trust will be includable in the grantor's estate unless the power can be exercised only pursuant to an ascertainable standard.
  2. Person other than grantor as trustee.
   a. Income of the trust not taxable to the grantor.
   b. Assets in the trust will not be includable in the grantor's estate unless the power can be

exercised without an ascertainable standard and the grantor can substitute himself as the trustee.

G. Power to make mandatory distributions of income or principal to specified beneficiaries other than the grantor or the grantor's spouse.
  1. Grantor as trustee.
     a. Income of the trust not taxable to the grantor unless trust income is used to discharge his legal obligations.
     b. Assets in the trust will not be included in the grantor's gross estate because the grantor has retained no power to affect beneficial enjoyment of trust property.
  2. Person other than grantor as trustee.
     a. Income of the trust not taxable to the grantor unless trust income is used to discharge his legal obligations.
     b. Assets in the trust not includable in the grantor's gross estate.

II. Administrative powers.
  A. Power to allocate receipts between principal and income.
     1. Grantor as trustee.
        a. Grantor not taxable on the income of the trust.
        b. Assets of the trust will not be includable in the grantor's estate unless the power can be exercised by the grantor in a nonfiduciary capacity either alone or in conjunction with another person.
     2. Person other than grantor as trustee.
        a. Grantor not taxable on the income of the trust.
        b. Assets of the trust will not be includable in the grantor's estate.
  B. Power to use trust income to pay premiums on insurance insuring the life of the grantor or the grantor's spouse.
     1. Grantor as trustee.
        a. Grantor is taxable on the income of the trust to extent the income is or may be used for the payment of life insurance premiums without the consent of an adverse party.
        b. Assets of the trust will not be includable in the grantor's gross estate assuming the trust both owns and is beneficiary of the policy proceeds.
     2. Nonadverse party as trustee.
        a. Grantor will be taxed on the income of the trust.

       b. Assets of the trust will not be includable in the gross estate of the grantor.

   3. Adverse party as trustee.

       a. Grantor will not be taxed on income of the trust.

       b. Assets of the trust will not be includable in the gross estate of the grantor.

C. Power to purchase, exchange, or otherwise deal with trust assets for less than adequate consideration.

   1. Grantor as trustee.

       a. Grantor will be taxed on income of the trust if he or a nonadverse party (or both) can exercise the power without the consent of an adverse party.

       b. Assets of the trust will be includable in the gross estate of the grantor.

   2. Nonadverse party as trustee.

       a. Grantor will be taxable on trust income if the nonadverse party can exercise the power without the consent of an adverse party.

       b. Assets in the trust will not be includable in the estate of the grantor unless the grantor can substitute himself as trustee.

   3. Adverse party as trustee.

       a. Grantor not taxed on the income of the trust.

       b. Assets in the trust will not be includable in the estate of the grantor unless the grantor can substitute himself as trustee.

D. Power to borrow trust income or principal without adequate interest or adequate security.

   1. Grantor as trustee.

       a. Grantor taxed on trust income if trust property can be loaned to grantor without adequate interest or security (income will not be taxed to grantor if approval of adverse party needed).

       b. Assets in trust will be includable in grantor's gross estate.

   2. Person other than grantor as trustee.

       a. Grantor not taxed on trust income if person other than grantor is trustee and that person has the power to make loans to anyone.

       b. Assets will not be included in grantor's gross estate unless he can substitute himself as trustee.

E. Power to vote the securities of a controlled corporation.

   1. Grantor as trustee.

    a. Grantor taxed on income of trust if (1) power can be exercised in a nonfiduciary capacity and (2) the stockholdings of the grantor and the trust are significant from the viewpoint of control.

    b. Assets in the trust must be included in the grantor's gross estate.

  2. Person other than grantor as trustee.

    a. Grantor taxed on trust income if power to vote securities held by person with nonadverse interest in a nonfiduciary capacity without consent of person in fiduciary capacity, assuming stockholdings of grantor and trust are significant from the viewpoint of control.

    b. Assets in the trust will not be included in the grantor's estate unless he has retained the power to substitute himself as trustee.

F. Power to reacquire trust principal by substituting property of equal value.

  1. Grantor as trustee.

    a. Grantor will be taxed on trust income if the power can be exercised by anyone in a nonfiduciary capacity without the consent of a person in a fiduciary capacity.

    b. Assets in the trust will be includable in the gross estate of the grantor.

  2. Persons other than the grantor as trustee.

    a. Grantor will be taxed on trust income if the power can be exercised by anyone in a nonfiduciary capacity without the consent of a person in a fiduciary capacity.

    b. Assets in the trust will not be includable in the grantor's gross estate unless he can substitute himself as trustee.

III. Powers over principal.

  A. Power to revoke the trust and revest the principal in the grantor or in grantor's spouse.

    1. Grantor as trustee.

      a. Grantor taxed on trust income unless power can be exercised only with consent of adverse party.

      b. Assets in trust includable in grantor's gross estate if power exercisable only by grantor alone or with any person whether or not adverse (unless the power can be exercised only with consent of all persons with a vested or contingent interest in the estate).

2. Nonadverse party as trustee.
   a. Grantor taxed on trust income unless power can be exercised only with consent of adverse party.
   b. Assets in trust not includable in grantor's estate unless power is exercisable by trustee and grantor can substitute himself as trustee.
3. Adverse party as trustee.
   a. Grantor not taxed on trust income.
   b. Assets in trust not includable in grantor's gross estate.

B. Power to terminate trust and distribute principal to beneficiaries.
1. Grantor as trustee.
   a. Grantor not taxed on trust income if principal can be paid out only to income beneficiaries in same proportion as they currently receive income, or if principal can be paid out only with the approval of an adverse party.
   b. Assets in the trust are includable in the grantor's gross estate if the grantor can exercise the power alone or with any other person whether or not adverse.
2. Adverse party as trustee.
   a. Grantor not taxed on trust income.
   b. Assets in trust not includable unless power exercisable by trustee and grantor can substitute himself as trustee.
3. Nonadverse party as trustee.
   a. Grantor taxed on trust income unless approval of adverse party required or unless payment must be made to current income beneficiaries in proportion to income receipts.
   b. Assets in trust not includable unless power exercisable by trustee and grantor can substitute himself as trustee.
4. Independent Trustee.
   a. Grantor not taxed on trust income if half or more of trustees are independent.
   b. Assets in trust not includable unless power exercisable by trustee and grantor can substitute himself as trustee.

IV. Powers to discharge legal obligations.
  A. Power to discharge support obligation.
    1. Grantor as trustee.
      a. Grantor not taxable on trust income merely because of the existence of the power unless he has the power in a nonfiduciary capacity or the power is to support his or her spouse. But the grantor will be taxed on the income to the extent it in fact is used to discharge the grantor's support obligation.
      b. Assets in the trust will be includable in the grantor's estate if trust income may be used to discharge the grantor's legal obligation.
    2. Persons other than grantor as trustee.
      a. Grantor not taxable on income unless it is in fact used to discharge the grantor's legal obligation.
      b. Assets in the trust will not be included unless the grantor could substitute himself for the trustee.

Decision-making ability. The trustee selected must be able to make many decisions, some of great significance, over an extended period of time. This entails the need for emotional maturity and wisdom as well as knowledge.

Competence. A trustee must have the legal capacity to contract. This precludes the appointment of a minor or an incompetent adult. In many states a nonresident individual can act as a trustee (although as a practical matter, geographical considerations often contraindicate selecting a person who lives a considerable distance from the beneficiaries of the trust). Some states bar nonresident corporations from serving as trustees.

Skill to which trustees will be held. A trustee will be held to a high degree of skill and care. Under the "prudent man" rule, a trustee must use the same degree of care and skill that a person of ordinary prudence would exercise in dealing with his own property.

The Uniform Probate Code, adopted by many states, places a higher standard on professional trustees by providing that if the trustee has greater skill than that of a man of ordinary prudence, he is under a duty to exercise such skill.

Integrity. Honesty and loyalty are the watchwords of trusts. Vast sums of money and other assets are entrusted to fiduciaries who must exercise a high degree of care over trust property and act consistently on behalf of trust beneficiaries.

Flexibility to meet changing circumstances. Change in tax law and in the circumstances and goals of each of the beneficiaries is the only certainty. Since a trust is a mechanism specifically designed to meet that change, the trustee must be willing and able to change as well.

Willingness to serve throughout the term of the trust. An individual trustee could easily lose interest through the long years and even generations a trust may last. Corporate fiduciaries are more likely than individuals to continue for the full term.

Experience as a trustee. This is the most rare of all characteristics. Obviously, past experience in administering a trust is invaluable. Through experience, the fiduciary is more likely to appreciate the broad and complex multiplicity of laws involved, know who to call on for assistance, avoid many mistakes, and more efficiently administer and execute the terms of the trust.

Neutral state law impact. State trust laws must be considered in selecting a trustee. If state law trust requirements are not met, the trust will be invalid and provide none of any intended tax benefits. This is because federal law's recognition of a trust as a separate tax entity presupposes validity of the trust under state law.

When a beneficiary is named as trustee, the Doctrine of Merger must be considered. This doctrine holds that the trust as a separate entity ceases to exist when the legal title to the property held by the trustee is identical to the beneficial interest held by the beneficiary. For instance, if the grantor's son is both the sole trustee and the sole beneficiary, the trust will cease to exist.

COTRUSTEES

After considering each of the desirable characteristics of a good trustee, it will become obvious to most grantors that it is impossible to select a trustee that has all of the advantages and none of the disadvantages. Many grantors therefore attempt to obtain the strengths of both the corporate and the nonprofessional trustee by naming a cotrustee. Often, one or more family members and a corporate fiduciary are selected.

Combining the positive aspects of more than one trustee has a cost; certain drawbacks or issues must be considered. For instance, if two trustees are selected, what is the procedure if they do not agree on a given issue? If three or more are selected, will the majority rule? What responsibility does a dissenting trustee have for an action (or nonaction) taken by the majority?

REMOVAL AND SUCCESSION OF TRUSTEES

As part of the selection process itself, a grantor should think about the removal of current trustees and the appointment of successor trustees (typically, at least two should be named). The trust instrument itself should consider issues such as the following:

Who, if anyone, should be given the power to remove trustees?

Should such a power be given to the grantor, the beneficiaries, the trustee(s), or an outside party?

How narrow or broad should a removal power be (i.e., under what circumstances should someone be able to remove a trustee)?

How often may a removal power be exercised?

How will succession be determined?

What restrictions will be placed on the successor trustee?

What are the various tax consequences of allowing the grantor or the beneficiaries to remove a trustee and without restriction appoint a new one?

Summary. The selection of a trustee is a most difficult one because of the longevity of most trusts, the complexity of the tax and other laws with which the trustee must comply, and the sensitivity a trustee must have to both the grantor's objectives and the beneficiary's needs and desires. For these reasons, one or more cotrustees (almost always professionals) is indicated where the terms of the trust are complex or the estate is large.

PART III—SELECTING AN ATTORNEY

DUTIES OF THE ATTORNEY

The duties of the attorney will depend on the client's stage in the estate planning cycle—accumulation, conservation, or distribution. In actuality it is sometimes difficult to know where one stage ends and another begins. Clearly, the attorney must be aware in each stage of the implications of what is done at that stage for the other two stages—and of the consequences to the client and his beneficiaries. For instance, it may be easier and less expensive in the planning stage of the cycle to draft a simple will than a series of more complex trusts. But the client's family may have fared better in the later stages had the attorney done a more extensive estate plan.

An estate planning attorney must gather data regarding the client and his family or other potential beneficiaries and their circumstances; the client's sources of wealth, income, liabilities, and expenses; and the client's financial goals and fears. The attorney must then assemble this data and relate each of these objective facts and subjective feelings to each other and be able to ascertain the client's current position and the extent of his weaknesses in the following areas:

1. Liquidity: Will the client during his lifetime and his executor at his death be able to pay taxes and other expenses without the need for a forced sale?
2. Disposition of assets: Are they going to the right person at the right time in the right manner?
3. Adequacy of capital and income: Does the client have enough capital and income in the event of death or disability, or at retirement, or for special family needs such as the care of a retarded or physically handicapped child, or for charitable bequests?
4. Stability and maximization of value: Has the client first put a floor under and then maximized the value of the assets he currently owns? For instance, the value of a business without adequate liability or fire insurance coverage has not been stabilized; the value of a partnership without a fully funded buy-sell plan has not been maximized.
5. Excessive transfer costs: Is the client paying too much in income taxes, or will the client's estate pay an unnecessary amount of estate or other death taxes or transfer costs?
6. Special needs: Does the client have special needs or desires that must be met, such as making gifts to a charity, supporting a poor relative, or protecting a spendthrift spouse?

An estate planning attorney must not only understand these problems and their solutions but also be able to communicate them to the client in a manner that will allow the client to make informed decisions.

Often the attorney must organize the entire estate planning team. Always the attorney should work with the client and the client's other professional advisors in establishing an order of priorities and responsibilities and make sure each aspect of the plan is completed in a timely manner.

Only the attorney can draft the appropriate documents. These range in complexity and length from a simple durable power of attorney, which may run four or five pages, to the recapitalization of the client's business and the complete restructuring of the nature of the client's estate plan, which may take hundreds of drafted pages.

ATTRIBUTES OF A GOOD ATTORNEY

Many of the same attributes important in the selection of an executor or trustee are also of key importance in the search for an attorney. For example, an attorney with business experience who is also familiar with the client's business can be invaluable. The major attributes that should be considered in the selection of an estate planning (or administration) attorney are competence, compassion, clarity, and affordability.

Competence.   The level of competence necessary depends to a great extent on the nature and extent of the client's wealth and the complexity of the client's situation. Most general practitioners are competent to draft a power of attorney or simple will. This may be all that is necessary in smaller estates where all the parties involved including the beneficiaries are self-sufficient adults and there are no unusual assets, objectives, or problems.

But once the estate reaches the size at which federal estate taxes may be imposed, or if the client or any of the client's beneficiaries are under a legal, physical, mental, or emotional disability, or if there is any unusual fact pattern, it is best to find an attorney who specializes in estate planning and administration. The question is How do you find an attorney in the estate planning field, and then how do you ascertain his or her competence? Some of the ways to locate attorneys practicing in the estate planning field are discussed below.

1. Call the county or city estate planning council. Ask for a copy of the membership directory. This should contain lists of not only attorneys but also CPAs, CLUs, trust officers, and other key members of the estate planning team. This list, of course, does not ensure any specific level of competence, but most estate planning councils require peer nomination for entrance, and membership fees help eliminate those who do not spend substantial time in the practice of estate planning. More important, estate planning councils make continuing education and in-depth seminars available to their members. The best attorneys active in the estate planning and administration field tend to be members of an estate planning council.

2. Many states now certify attorneys in selective areas of practice. Texas, for example, examines an attorney through a rigorous additional state bar–administered examination in the estate planning area. Attorneys who have earned the right to specialize in estate planning through certification will usually signify that in their telephone book listings and on their business cards and stationery.

3. Trust officers are excellent sources for finding attorneys active in estate planning. Visit three or four banks with large trust offices. Ask for the two or three most competent attorneys. If the same name is mentioned favorably by more than one trust officer, he or she might be a good choice. CLUs, ChFCs, CFPs, and CPAs are also excellent sources for the names of competent attorneys who specialize in estate planning.

4. Attorneys who specialize in estate planning often lecture at business meetings or adult education courses. After attending one or two sessions, a person should find it easy to tell if the attorney can communicate complex legal matters effectively.

5. Practicing attorneys who teach estate planning in law schools, in the tax masters' programs at business schools, and especially those who

have taught the American College's estate planning courses for several years are excellent candidates.

6. Some attorneys write in professional journals such as *Taxation for Accountants, the Practical Lawyer, Estate Planning Magazine, The CLU Journal, Trusts and Estates Magazine,* or the *Journal of Accountancy.* Some write regular newspaper columns or do radio talk shows on estate planning.

7. Attorneys with an LLM (masters) in taxation generally have higher than average expertise in the estate planning area.

8. Friends and business associates may be able to provide referrals.

9. Bar association referral services and local law schools with tax masters programs are also good sources of estate planning attorneys.

Compassion. The single most important distinction between a truly good estate planning attorney and the average practitioner is not a superior knowledge of the tax law, nor is it the sense of combativeness that makes winners out of litigation attorneys: it is an attitude of being counselor rather than advocate. The estate planning attorney will be keenly sensitive to the importance of a client's business, for instance, not only as figures on a ledger sheet but also as a personification of the client and as part of a goal-striving behavior. Such an attorney will be extremely conscious of the circumstances, needs, hopes, and fears of the client and of his intended beneficiaries.

Clarity. An estate planning attorney must be able to communicate. Often, the attorney will captain the estate planning team. This means he or she must be able to request information from other professionals, explain to them what each member of the estate planning team is doing and what remains to be done. The attorney must also be able to communicate clearly with nonprofessionals, such as the client or the client's family, the nature and extent of problems the client may not have known existed.

Clarity encompasses not only transferring information but also the urgency of deciding and then acting. The estate planning attorney must be able to convey the importance of the client's doing certain things (such as signing a will, obtaining adequate amounts of life or disability insurance, or establishing a buy-sell agreement) now!

Affordability. Malpractice premiums for estate planning and administration attorneys are among the highest in the profession. This is indicative of the complexity of the practice and of the potential for making expensive mistakes. The point is, selecting the right attorney is a cost-saving factor. The lowest fee may be far from the least expensive.

Clients should demand a written and signed statement of the attorney's hourly fee or an estimate of the overall cost for planning or administering the estate—before allowing work to begin.

There is one more important consideration involving the relationship of an attorney to the estate of a deceased person. In most cases the attorney who drafted a will or trust or other estate planning document should be employed to help execute it. That attorney will probably know the client and his intentions better than anyone else. But if the personal representative of a deceased person is not satisfied with the deceased person's attorney or if the decedent gave no indication of his or her choice of attorney for the estate, the personal representative should, in practically every instance, make his or her own independent selection of an attorney qualified in the area of administering the decedent's estate.

Since the executor has the full responsibility if something goes wrong, the executor has the right and responsibility to personally select the estate's attorney—regardless of which attorney drew the decedent's will. In fact, a number of states protect that right with specific legislation.

Summary. The selection of an attorney who specializes in estate planning should focus primarily on identifying someone who has competence, compassion, the ability to communicate clearly with other professionals and with clients, and who is willing to work at a price that is in line with a client's means.

HOW TO REVIEW A WILL:
A CHECKLIST FOR THE ESTATE AND FINANCIAL PLANNER

by Stephan R. Leimberg
Copyright 1988 by Stephan R. Leimberg

Note: A version of this article under the title "How To Review a Will" has appeared in the magazine *Financial Planning* in two parts, April and May, 1988.

INTRODUCTION

A will is the legal document that specifies how a person wants to dispose of the real and personal property he owns in his own name at the time of his death. Most mentally competent adults have the legal capacity to draw a will. But few persons are knowledgeable enough to do so properly. Only an attorney should draft a will and even most attorneys should not attempt to draw their own.

Despite this, every member of the estate planning team, including the financial planner, should know how to review a will.

First, it is necessary to coordinate the will properly with other dispositive documents such as employee benefit plans. For example, if the will is not synchronized with an executive's pension, group insurance, and 401(k) plan, there is no way to minimize overall death taxes and provide for a smooth and efficient estate administration.

Second, it is impossible to know if there will be appropriate liquidity unless the will and its various dispositive schemes are examined.

Third, wills become outdated, tax laws change (for instance, a marital deduction provision in a will drafted before September 13, 1981, may not qualify for the unlimited marital deduction), and the circumstances, needs, and desires of the parties are always in flux. The attorney who drafted the will may have died and it may have been many years since the will was revised or reviewed.

Every professional in the estate planning team must therefore be able to examine a will and spot — in general terms at least — what's wrong.

"What's wrong" with a given will is more often a question of what has been omitted or what has changed than what has been improperly drafted. "What's wrong" is even more often

the failure of the draftsman to match the facts of the case or the circumstances or desires of the parties with the documents. "What's wrong" may be something the accountant, for instance, knows that no other professional knows. "What's wrong" may be that the will has not been updated for years and no longer addresses the current circumstances or client goals or latest tax law.

The following is a (by no means complete) checklist designed to give each member of the estate planning team the tools needed to examine a will:

INTRODUCTORY CLAUSE

Start with the introductory ("exordium") clause which should be the first paragraph in the will. The purpose of this preamble is to

(1) identify the testator, the person disposing of property at death;

(2) establish domicile, the county that will have legal jurisdiction for purposes of determining the validity of the will and interpreting will provisions, for purposes of state inheritance taxation (technically, what is said in a will about the testator's domicile is not dispositive but is evidence which will usually be considered even if subordinated to proof of facts to the contrary);

(3) declare that the document in question is intended to dispose of the testator's property at death and no matter how many wills have been written in the past, this is meant to be the last will; and

(4) revoke all prior wills. This is designed to nullify old and forgotten wills — and "codicils" (legally effective modifications of existing wills).

An example of this introductory clause is:

I, Edward Grieg, a resident of and domiciled in the city of Bryn Mawr in Montgomery County, Pennsylvania, declare this to be my last will. I revoke all wills and codicils made prior to this will.

Planners should check:

(1) Is the spelling of the client's name correct? Has the client's full name been used?

(2) Is the client "A/K/A" ("also known as"), i.e., is there some other name by which the client is known and should that name be listed?

(3) Is the domicile correct? For tax or other planning purposes, would it make sense to begin to document a different domicile? Will the will meet all the statutory requirements of the stated domicile? If the client spends a great deal of time in more than one residence, could the address mentioned in the will trigger a "double domicile" problem (e.g., where more than one state claims the decedent was a domiciliary of the state and therefore has the right to impose an inheritance tax)?

(4) Is there a reason prior wills and codicils should not be revoked? Instead of a new will, should the present document be a codicil making a small change but otherwise ratifying an existing will? For instance, if there is a potential for an attack on this will on the grounds of mental incompetency, fraud, or undue influence, a prior will providing a similar disposition will help prove the mental capacity of the testator and may discourage would-be contestants from attacking the current will. Conversely, if a beneficiary has been deleted, a new will should be drawn rather than a codicil to avoid the mention of the eliminated beneficiary.

After the introductory clause, the will can take either of two directions. It can (1) describe the steps that take place in administering the testator's estate (such as payment of debts and taxes and then payment of legacies) or it can (2) dispose of legacies first and describe obligations later. We will take the former approach in formulating this checklist.

DEBTS CLAUSE

The next clause usually pertains to the payment of debts, expenses, and costs. The purposes of this clause are:

(1) To state the source from which each debt will be paid. (This is an extremely important point because of the death tax implications. For instance, if a surviving spouse rather than some other beneficiary must pay debts, to that extent the marital deduction will be decreased and taxes may be increased. Furthermore, if the burden falls on the wrong person(s), the testator's goals may not be met.)

(2) To establish as debts items which might not otherwise be considered the testator's obligations.

An example of the payment of debts clause is:

I direct all of my debts (including any expenses of my last illness) and my funeral expenses be paid.

Planners should check:

(1) Does the testator have any rights to property held in the trust of another person (a so-called "power of appointment") and, if so, what effect does the debts clause have on that property? Does it expose that property to the claims of creditors?

(2) Will the beneficiaries receive more or less than the client intended when the will was drawn because of the operation of this provision? Has the size of the debt changed since the will was drawn? What will be the federal and state death tax impact of the clause?

(3) What is the effect of the Equal Rights Amendment in the state of domicile? In some states the will of a married woman should contain a direction to pay debts and taxes. Otherwise, the burden of her funeral and medical expenses will be placed on her surviving husband — thus barring a deduction for payment of those expenses by her estate.

(4) Did the will provide detailed funeral arrangements? Most authorities feel this is inadvisable since the will may not be found or may not be accessible in sufficient time after the testator's death. Should such provisions be placed in a "Letter of Instructions," an informal and nonlegal list of requests, suggestions, and recommendations that should not be placed in the will?

(5) Does the client intend that "payment of debts" include the mortgage on property left to a specific individual? In some states, absent an express direction to the contrary, when specific property is left to an individual (a "specific bequest"), any debt on that property will not be paid off. In other states, such a clause will require the executor to satisfy the mortgage. Does the named beneficiary of a life insurance policy that has been pledged as the collateral for a loan have the right to have the loan paid off because of the "pay my [just] debts" clause? The planner must check state law. In at least one state the answer depends on who the lender is. The result, absent specific direction to the contrary, is one way if the lender is the insurance company (the beneficiary takes only the net proceeds) and another (the beneficiary is entitled to have the estate pay off the debt out of other estate assets) if the creditor is an independent lending institution.

TAX CLAUSE

The clause pertaining to the payment of death taxes can either be stated next or appear after the provisions disposing of property.

The purpose of the tax clause is to establish the source for the payment of the federal estate tax, the state inheritance and estate tax, and any federal or state generation-skipping transfer tax.

This is an example of a tax clause:

I direct that all inheritance, estate, transfer, succession, legacy and other death taxes upon property required to be included in my taxable estate whether or not passing under this Will [except (1) transfer taxes levied pursuant to the provisions of Chapter 13 of the Internal Revenue Code of 1986, relating to "generation-skipping transfers," or any similar state law, and (2) taxes on property held in trust under the Will (or any revocable trust) of my spouse], and any interest and penalties thereon, shall be charged against and paid from my residuary estate passing under Article *FOURTH* of Part I of this my Will.

Planners should check:

(1) State "apportionment" statutes. If there is no tax clause in the will or if it does not adequately address the payment of a particular death tax, state law will allocate the burden of taxes among the beneficiaries. Many states require beneficiaries to pay a share of estate taxes unless the will provides otherwise. The result is often an inappropriate or unintended reduction of the shares of certain beneficiaries or adverse tax consequences. (For example, there may be a spiraling reduction of the estate tax marital deduction. The deduction is allowed only for the net amount passing to the surviving spouse. If that amount is reduced by an estate tax burden, the tax increases — further reducing the amount passing to the spouse, etc.) An "anti-apportionment" tax clause may be the solution. For instance, suppose you wanted a child to receive $100,000 of your client's $2,000,000 estate free and clear. Without special provision, that child would be forced to pay his share of taxes, or 1/20 of the total federal and state death taxes. With a special tax clause, the child will receive the entire $100,000.

(2) Does the client expect or want property passing outside the probate estate to pay its share of tax if it in fact generates tax? For instance, assume $1,000,000 of pension proceeds (or life insurance) is payable to the client's two oldest children and $1,000,000 of cash is payable to the client's two youngest children. Who is to pay the tax on the $2,000,000? What if the $1,000,000 of pension proceeds (or life insurance) is state inheritance tax exempt but the cash is not? Unless the will provides to the contrary, estate taxes must be paid by recipients of property passing outside the will. The will should specify who pays taxes on both probate and nonprobate property.

(3) Assume a sizable amount of property will pass through a revocable living trust. Is the tax clause in that instrument coordinated with the tax clause in the will or are they incompatible? What if assets under the will are to "pour over" into a previously funded trust which itself will generate significant estate taxes. Is there (should there be) a will provision calling upon the trust to help the estate pay taxes? Does the trust have a provision recognizing and empowering a "call" on its assets to pay the probate estate's taxes?

(4) Who is to pay the tax on a generation-skipping transfer? Absent a contrary direction, the taxes will probably be payable from the assets of the fund subject to the tax. Some draftsmen specifically provide that such taxes are not to be imposed on the "skip person's" estate.

(5) Assume the facts indicate that very large taxable gifts have been made by the client. The taxable portion of these gifts — to the extent not included in the client's gross estate — will be considered "adjusted taxable gifts." They will increase the rate of federal estate tax payable on the taxable estate remaining. Will an unexpectedly high burden be placed on the assets remaining because of these prior gifts and should the tax clause take such gifts into account in apportioning the tax burden?

(6) Should certain beneficiaries be insulated from tax for either tax reasons or to accomplish the dispositive goals of the client or better meet the needs of the beneficiaries? For example, should a child to whom property has been given be exempted by the will from paying the estate tax on that property?

TANGIBLE PERSONAL PROPERTY CLAUSE

A clause pertaining to the disposition of tangible personal property is often next. The purposes of this clause are:

(1) to provide for who will receive personal property and the terms under which they will receive it; and

(2) to make special dispositions among the persons and the organizations of the testator's choice.

An example of the tangible personal property dispositive clause is:

> I give to my daughter, Eva Grieg, all of my clothing, household furnishings, jewelry, automobiles, books, pictures, and all other articles of tangible personal property owned by me at the date of my death. If my daughter, Eva Grieg, does not survive me, I give the property mentioned above in equal shares to my grandchildren, Gretta and Gail Grieg or the survivor who is alive at the date of my death.

or

> I give the Philadelphia Museum of Art my painting of "Helga" by Andrew Wyeth.

Planners should check:

(1) Does (or should) the client make specific bequests of all "intimate" items such as a watch or ring? Absent such provisions, if personal property has been left to several individuals, the result is often needless expense in determining who gets what or reducing the estate to cash (not to mention the potential for bitter intrafamily fights). If specific bequests have been made, has each item been described in enough detail so that there will be no confusion as to which diamond ring the testator meant? (Use the same description as is found in the insurance policy covering the loss or theft of the item).

(2) Has provision been made in case the item specifically left to a beneficiary is not owned by the decedent at death? For instance, what if one ring is sold and the proceeds are used to purchase a second. Does the named beneficiary receive the second ring?

(3) If the item specifically bequeathed has been lost, stolen, etc. and the loss has been covered by insurance, would the client want the named beneficiary to receive the insurance? In many states the bequest of an item of personal property does not — absent specific direction to the contrary — also pass the insurance covering the item.

(4) Does the client intend to pass — under the category of personal property — cash in a safe deposit box, travelers' checks, and cash found in his home or on his person? Does the client know that cash on deposit is typically not considered tangible personal property?

(5) If the client has property in many different places, consider allowing the executor — at the expense of the estate — to take possession of the property "as and where is" (a provision which will permit the beneficiary to receive the property free of delivery costs and protect the fiduciary and beneficiaries during administration from the risk that specific assets will be lost).

(6) The phrase "personal effects" may not encompass items of household use or even a car. Consider specific mention of items of tangible personal property.

(7) Is there a "catchall" phrase that passes the residue of tangible personalty? The phrase, "all other tangible personal property" should dispose of any residual property.

(8) Should the will confirm that certain property such as household furnishings, silverware, etc. belongs to someone else?

(9) Does this clause dispose of property by referring to an instrument outside the will? This "incorporation by reference" is not recommended since it often leads to litigation.

(10) The use of the term "contents" should be avoided. Personal property should not be described by its location.

General checkup of legacies:

(1) Has property been left outright to a minor who is legally incapable of handling it or to a person under a physical, mental, or emotional handicap who does not have the physical or intellectual capacity?

(2) Are all beneficiaries named alive? Are there "backup" beneficiaries (at least two) for each beneficiary? Are they the beneficiaries the client currently desires?

(3) Are any of the gifts conditioned on events or circumstances which are impossible, "against public policy," or in violation of the Constitution? For example, a bequest would be invalidated by the courts if it were made on the condition that the recipient first divorce her spouse.

(4) Are there gifts to "my issue" (which would unintentionally disinherit an adopted person)?

(5) Do gifts to charities meet state law requirements? Has the charity's full legal (corporate) name and address been stated? (The popular name is often different from the full legal name). Have you checked the IRS's "Cumulative List of Organizations" or obtained assurances from the charity itself to make sure the gift to the charity will qualify for a tax deduction? Has the client named a backup charity? Check to be sure the will specifies that taxes are to be paid from the portion of the residue not passing to charity. Otherwise, what should be a tax-free bequest must bear its portion of the total taxes. That reduces the charity's share and therefore increases taxes. This in turn creates a new cycle of problems.

(6) If someone is intentionally omitted, have you checked state law to see if such an omission is permissible? Are there defamatory statements in the will concerning an heir? (At the probate of the will, such statements may become libelous and expose the client's estate to an action for damages.)

(7) Does the will make so many specific bequests of cash that the residuary estate doesn't have enough left to pay estate taxes? Keep in mind that the IRS can attach the assets of any beneficiary for the unpaid estate tax. Check to be sure the executor will have a sufficient reserve of funds for paying estate tax and all the bequests to residuary beneficiaries.

(8) Note that a tangible personal property clause should nearly always be used where the residue of the estate will be paid to a trust. Few clients want trusts involved in handling personal effects such as jewelry, or household furniture, antiques, or cars.

DEVISES OF REAL ESTATE CLAUSE

The next clause pertains to "devises," testamentary grants of real property. The purposes of the devises clause are:

(1) to specify which real estate is to be disposed of under the will and to dispose of that real estate, and

(2) to handle the problems where the property has been sold or destroyed prior to the testator's death.

An example of a devise is:

I leave my residence located at 207 Rawles Run Lane, Bryn Mawr, Pa. to my daughter, Larrissa Grieg. If, at the time of my death, I am no longer using the property at 207 Rawles Run Lane as my residence, then this devise is to be void and of no effect; however, if I own any other real estate which I am using as my residence at that time, then, in such an event, I devise such other real estate to my daughter, Larrissa Grieg. If my daughter, Larrissa Grieg, does not survive me, this devise shall lapse and such real estate shall become part of my residuary estate.

SPECIFIC BEQUESTS OF INTANGIBLES AND CASH

After disposing of tangible personal property and real estate, the will may then cover specific gifts of intangibles (property where the item itself is evidence of value) such as gifts of cash or accounts receivable. An example of a gift of an intangible asset is:

I give 100 shares of Rohm and Haas stock to my niece, Danielle Green.

or

I give the sum of Five Thousand ($5,000) dollars to my sister, Sara Black, if she survives me.

Planners should check:

(1) Has provision been made in the event the primary beneficiary does not survive the decedent?

(2) Does the will spell out what gift, if any, is made if the decedent does not possess, at the time of death, the stock mentioned in the will? What if the stock had been sold but new stock was purchased with the proceeds?

RESIDUARY CLAUSE

The next clause is called the "residuary clause." The purposes of the residuary clause are to:

(1) transfer all assets not disposed of up to this point,

(2) (in some cases) provide a mechanism for "pouring over" assets from the will to a previously established (inter vivos) trust (if a pourover is made, it is important to review the trust as carefully as the will itself), and

(3) provide for an alternative disposition in case the primary beneficiary has died or the trust to which probate assets (assets passing under a valid will or by intestacy) were to be poured over was for some reason invalid, previously revoked, or never came into existence.

An example of a residuary clause is:

All the rest, residue, and remainder of the property which I own at the date of my death, real and personal, tangible or intangible, regardless of where it is situated, I leave to my daughter, Larrissa Grieg. But if Larrissa Grieg does not survive me, then I leave the said property in equal shares to my grandchildren, Ronald Reimus and Reginald Reimus or to the survivor of them.

Planners should check:

(1) Has a spouse been disinherited? If so, is the client aware of the "elective rights" (rights to a portion of the probate estate and perhaps certain other property owned by the decedent at death regardless of what the will provides) the surviving spouse has even if the will is valid? (It may be

possible to control the surviving spouse to some degree by inserting a provision at least as attractive as the spouse's intestate share or by a provision reducing or eliminating the share of a person in whom the spouse is interested if he exercises his right of election. An alternative is a pre- or post-nuptial agreement).

(2) Has the client, inadvertently, exercised a "power of appointment" (a right to direct the disposition of property in a trust established by someone else)? In some states, a residuary clause automatically exercises a general power of appointment unless the trust requires that it must be specifically referred to in order to make a valid exercise or unless the will itself states that no exercise is intended.

(3) Is there a disposition to a young adult, minor, or a person legally, mentally, or emotionally incompetent that should be made in trust? Is there provision for the executor to retain the property during the minority of such a person or to use income or principal for that person's benefit? Has the right person been named as the custodian of a child's property and are there backups in case that person is unwilling or unable to serve?

(4) Is there a default provision in case a trust into which the residue was to have poured is for any reason revoked or never came into existence?

(5) If a child dies, will that child's share pass to the parties desired by the client?

(6) Does the will address the possibility of the birth of a child to the client (it's never too late)?

(7) Has the client, in lieu of leaving his residuary estate outright to his spouse, created a marital deduction formula disposition through a so-called formula clause?

Marital deduction formula clauses are very important to review and analyze. They are often found in the wills of clients who own assets of at least $600,000. Such clauses typically divide the client's estate into two parts, one "marital" and the other "nonmarital." The marital portion passes property to the client's surviving spouse as part of the marital deduction and may contain an outright or trust disposition. The nonmarital portion is designed to set aside property exempted from federal estate tax by reason of the client's available unified credit and passes property to persons other than the surviving spouse (or to a credit equivalent "bypass trust" for the benefit of the surviving spouse that will not be included in the spouse's estate on his death).

The language used in the formula typically takes the form of a fixed sum (a "pecuniary marital deduction") or a fraction of the client's residuary estate (a "fractional share marital deduction"). The formula clause (especially if it is a pecuniary one) will also have to contain a provision for funding the marital deduction when assets are distributed to it.

If the marital deduction clause directs that the property is to be held in trust, the surviving spouse must be entitled to all of the trust's net income in each year and no other person may be interested in the income or principal during the survivor's lifetime.

Any planner who regularly reviews client wills should familiarize himself with marital deduction requirements, or, at least, direct inquiries to persons who have expertise in this area.

POWERS CLAUSE

The next clause is often one pertaining to the powers of the executor (and trustee if the will establishes a "testamentary trust," a trust created at the testator's death under the will). The purposes of the powers clause are to:

(1) give the executor (and trustee) specific power and authority over and above those provided by state law to enable the executor to conserve and manage the property, and

(2) limit, where desired and appropriate, the executor's power and authority (for instance, the client may not want the executor to make certain investments), and

(3) provide authority to continue a business (or handle other property with special management or investment problems) and the special flexibility necessary to accomplish that objective, and

(4) protect the executor against suit by other beneficiaries by specifying the powers necessary to accomplish the executor's role.

An (abbreviated) example of a powers clause is:

I authorize my executor (as well as any substitute executor) in his, her, or its discretion, with respect to all property, real and personal, in addition to the powers conferred by law, to:

1. retain assets

2. purchase investments

3. hold cash

4. vote and grant proxies

5. sell, exchange, or dispose of

6. distribute in cash or in kind

7. delegate to agents

8. assign or compromise claims

9. borrow funds

10. lease, manage, develop real estate

11. abandon property

12. make certain tax elections

13. receive and use employee benefits

Planners should check:

(1) Are there any assets or problems in this case which require special powers to fulfill the desires of the client or provide the executor with sufficient flexibility? (Beware of "boilerplate" clauses). Are there powers that should be added?

(2) Will any power adversely affect the estate tax marital deduction? For instance, a marital deduction trust, under Code section 2056(b)(5) or (b)(7), must provide that the surviving spouse receive all income at least annually. Consider the impact of a power allowing the trustee under a testamentary trust to retain nonincome producing property. Unless the will/trust also contains a provision allowing the surviving spouse to demand that the trust assets be sold or made income producing, the marital deduction may be lost. Will such a power thwart other objectives of the testator? For instance, what if the unproductive property was stock in a family corporation? A sale of such stock would raise income but could cause the loss of family control of the corporation.

The draftsman might consider including a "savings clause" that would nullify any power, duty, or discretionary authority that might jeopardize the marital deduction.

(3) Will any of the powers granted cause a conflict of interest? For instance, if the executor is a bank, discretionary authority to invest in its own securities or common trust funds will cause a conflict that must be specifically "forgiven" by the will (assuming the client wants to do so).

(4) Is there specific authority for the executor to make distribution "in kind" (as opposed to selling estate assets and making the distribution in cash?) In some states absent specified power to do so, the executor may have no choice: the distribution must be made in cash.

APPOINTMENT OF FIDUCIARIES CLAUSE

The appointment of the executor, trustee of any testamentary trust, and guardian of any minor child, often comes toward the end of the will.

The purposes of the fiduciary appointment clause are:

(1) to name the individual(s) or corporate fiduciary or combinations of individual(s) and fiduciaries who will administer the testator's estate and any trust which the will creates;

(2) to give the executor the appropriate power to act on behalf of the estate and carry out the terms of the will;

(3) to specify if and how the executor is to be compensated;

(4) state whether or not the executor is to post bond;

(5) to specify the authority of and decision making process for co-executors; and

(6) to name guardian(s) and successor guardian(s) of any minor child of the testator.

An example of the appointment clause is:

I appoint my nephew, Farnsworth Dowlrimple III, as the executor under this will. If for any reason he fails to qualify or ceases to act, I appoint the Left Bank and Trust of Overflow, Pa. as my executor. I confer upon my executor all the powers enumerated in clause _____ above. No executor shall be required to furnish any bond or other security in any jurisdiction. I direct that my nephew, Farnsworth, shall receive no compensation for his services as Executor and that the Left Bank and Trust of Overflow, Pa. be entitled to be compensated for its services as executor in accordance with its regularly adopted schedule of compensation in effect and applicable at the time of the performance of such services.

Planners should check:

(1) Does the client trust the individual who is currently named as executor and backup executor? Is that indi-

vidual or corporate fiduciary legally qualified to act as executor? (Has the attorney who drew the will been named as executor? Typically, absent special circumstances, this raises a number of ethical questions and raises the spectre of a conflict of interest.)

(2) Should the executor's bond be waived?

(3) Is the executor named willing to serve? (How recently has the client checked?)

(4) Is the guardian for minors willing to act? Is he able to act? Is that person suitable?

(5) Is a prolonged estate (or trust) administration anticipated? If so, consider giving executors (trustees) the power to appoint successors by filing an instrument with the probate or other appropriate court.

TESTATOR'S SIGNING CLAUSE

The next to the last clause in a will is typically the testator's signing or "testimonium" provision. The purposes of the testimonium clause are

(1) to establish that the document is intended to be the testator's last will,

(2) to meet statutory requirements that require the testator's signature at the logical conclusion of the will, and

(3) to state the date on which the will was signed.

An example of a testimonium clause is:

In witness of the above, I subscribe my name, this 11th day of September, 1988 at Bryn Mawr, Pennsylvania to this, my last will, which consists of 13 pages (each of which I have initialed at the bottom).

Planners should check:

(1) Is the will signed by the testator at its logical end? Is each page numbered? Is the page count correct?

(2) Are there duplicate or triplicate signed wills in existence? If the testator was given a signed duplicate which is not found at his death, it is possible that a presumption will arise that the testator destroyed it with the intention of revoking it. The potential for litigation is therefore increased significantly. The better practice is for only one original to be executed.

ATTESTATION CLAUSE

The final clause in a will is the "attestation" provision. The purposes of the attestation (often called the witness) clause are to:

(1) witness the testator's signing,

(2) comply with statutory requirements,

(3) underline the testamentary character of the document, and

(4) comply with state law requirements in cases where the testator signed by a mark (such as an "X") or where, at the testator's direction and on his behalf, the will was signed by someone else (as would be the case where the testator was physically incapable of signing but mentally competent).

An example of an attestation clause is:

This will was signed by Edward Grieg, the testator, and declared to be his last will in our presence. We, at his request and in his presence and in the presence of each other, state that we witnessed his signing and declaration and at his request we have signed our names as witnesses this 11th day of September, 1988.

Planners should check:

(1) Are there three witnesses to the testator's signing? Although most states require less, three witness will comply with the most stringent probate requirements of any state and as a practical matter provide stronger evidence of the competence and testamentary intent of the testator.

(2) Were any of the witnesses beneficiaries under the will? This is inadvisable for at least two reasons: First, the witnesses may become incompetent to testify as to the execution or validity of the will. Second, witnesses who are also beneficiaries may be prevented from receiving bequests under the will.

(3) Are the addresses of the witnesses stated? Although addresses may not be legally required, they make it easier to locate and identify witnesses when needed.

(4) Is the will "self proving"? I.e., in some states a notarized affidavit attached to the will signed by the witnesses (and in some states, the testator, also) which describes the circumstances of the execution of the will may permit the will to be admitted to probate without the requirement that the witnesses be found or appear before the court in the probate proceeding.

OTHER CLAUSES

There are, of course, many other clauses which should be considered in reviewing a will. Some additional points for the planner to check are:

(1) Is the federal estate tax marital deduction important? If so, consider that the Uniform Simultaneous Death Act, which applies in most states, presumes that the testator survives in the event of a simultaneous death involving the testator and a beneficiary. This would cause a loss of the estate tax marital deduction unless the will superseded state law by providing a "common disaster" clause. This provision makes the presumption that the testator's spouse is deemed to have survived.

(2) Does the will consider the possibility that one or more beneficiaries will disclaim? The will should state who will receive property if the named beneficiary renounces his interest. The transfer is then treated as if the decedent had left property directly to the ultimate recipient.

(3) Have the provisions in the will been coordinated with other dispositive instruments? For instance, is the will coordinated with all trusts, with employee benefit plans, buy-sell agreements, and life insurance beneficiary designations?

(4) Are the problems of minors, incompetents, and other beneficiaries with special needs or circumstances properly addressed in the will? In other words, is the right asset going to the right person at the right time and in the right manner?

Has the client considered the financial burden that may be placed on the guardians of minor children, and have appropriate financial provisions been made so that they can afford to raise both the client's children and their own? (Some may want to set up a special life insurance funded trust that, if necessary, can provide to the guardians needed dollars, but, if not, will go to the client's children later in life.)

(5) Is the client's spouse's will coordinated with the client's will?

(6) Is there a "spendthrift clause" to provide protection against the claims of creditors?

SUMMARY

Although only an attorney should draft a will, every member of the estate planning team should make it a practice to review a client's will on a regular basis. The nonattorney's role in the will review process should be thought of not as a replacement for or as a means of "second guessing" the attorney, but rather as a source of additional strength in the planning process. The estate planner can provide in that regard a valuable resource to ascertain how the client's total dispositive plan can most effectively and efficiently meet the current needs, circumstances, and goals of both the client and the client's beneficiaries.

DEATH-SENSITIZATION FOR THE ESTATE PLANNER

It is no wonder that CLUs, CPAs, trust officers, and attorneys involved in the estate planning process spend so much time in tax planning and relatively minimal effort on "people" planning; pitifully little formal thought has been given — in or out of the classroom — to the human factor in the estate planning process. It is fascinating that the subject of life — and death — appears so seldom in the curriculum of estate planning courses given in law schools, in insurance training classes, or in estate planning seminars and workshops.

Isn't it ironic that death, the very reason for the estate planner's existence, the "biological center of the personal service involved," is hardly ever discussed in texts on estate planning?

This commentary pertains to the psychological rather than the tax aspects of death, and is meant to serve as a compilation of some of the things the estate planner — both as a professional member of a human services team and as a person — should know about death and dying. Although the thoughts and words below have been synthesized from the works of a number of scholars, a special debt is owed to Dr. Elizabeth Kubler-Ross (On Death and Dying) and Thomas L. Shaffer (Death, Property, and Lawyers). The former is a psychiatrist and social scientist of extraordinary skill and sensitivity, whose books are based on the results of hundreds of actual interviews with dying patients and their families; the latter is the dean of Notre Dame Law School, who has written the most comprehensive text available to the estate planning professional on the subject of death. One text that is not cited but should be read by every member of the estate planning team is Widow, by Lynn Caine. It is a frank, intimate, and shocking account of death from a widow's point of view.

WHY SHOULD THE ESTATE PLANNER THINK ABOUT DEATH AND DYING?

Reduction of Client's Anxiety

Many professionals, even those highly learned in the law, associate estate planning merely with dispositive and tax goals. A young attorney specializing in estate planning was introduced to a well-known and highly respected probate judge by one of the attorney's clients. The client spoke admiringly of the young man's talents as an estate planner and when the judge asked, "Young man, are you really that good?"

the attorney quipped, "I guess I must be — it seems that once I draw a will, my clients seem to live forever." The judge retorted, "Well then how do you know what you are doing will work?" Although the judge's retort was clever, perhaps he missed the point. A client does not have to die for the estate planning process to be successful. Estate planning can and should be an end in itself.

One of the most important goals of the estate planning process is the reduction of fear and anxiety about death. That, in fact, is what the estate planning experience (from the client's viewpoint) should be about, a personal reconciliation to death.

Properly handled, the estate planning experience can be one of great psychological satisfaction. In fact, that peace of mind is the only payoff the client himself receives from making a will. After all, will the client, by making a will, avoid family fights? Will the client, by a complex scheme of wills and trusts, save taxes? Just what is it the client wants out of the estate planning process?

Estate planning, in its broadest sense, presents an opportunity for a significant, growing, healthy encounter with one's own death. "Death is resented, perhaps, because the event itself cannot be controlled. Yet through planning, even though he cannot abolish death, the client can frustrate it by removing the worst consequences of its surprise."

Melville, in *Moby Dick*, wrote about the constructive nature and therapeutic effect on death anxiety of the will-making process:

> It may seem strange that of all men sailors should be tinkering at their last wills and testaments.... After the ceremony was concluded upon the present occasion, I felt all the easier; a stone was rolled away from my heart. Besides, all the days I should now live would be as good as the days that Lazarus lived.... I survived myself....

Free Client's Energy to Life-Related Matters

A second reason that the planning experience is an end unto itself is the relationship between death and life. Worrying about death and its consequences is emotionally expensive. Society's taboos regarding death generate delusions that in turn siphon off energy from the task of living. If the client spends energy maintaining the denial of mortality, that much less strength is available to be used in meaningful living.

An individual's values in life are affected strongly by the way he has (or has not) dealt with death and dying. Philosophers, psychiatrists, and religious scholars stress that death should be dealt with before it is imminent, because only by giving meaning to death can one give meaning to life. They explain that a human's mortality is a good thing, that only by the limited scope of one's time can existence be dramatic and intense. What is important is how (rather than how long) we live and that we maximize the creative possibilities of life.

How can an openness (between the professional and a client) about death enhance the client's ability to live well? By helping the client come to terms with death, and by helping him create an atmosphere in which he would be willing to die, it is easier for the client to learn to see his life in relationship with others in a clearer perspective and to make his lifetime interpersonal relationships more meaningful. In other words, we can show our client that rather than repress his fears of death he should "use as an antidote for death an extensive love of life." Estate planning, then, is to reduce our client's anxiety about death and free his emotional energies for life-oriented activities.

As practitioners in people-serving professions, our efforts have consequences beyond property distribution, beyond tax savings, and even beyond the financial security of our client's survivors. What we do affects not only those who survive the client, but also the client himself. A great deal of our efforts must be directed toward the psychological satisfaction of our client.

Additional Psychological Factors Encouraging Testamentary Process

What other factors concern an individual enough for him to pay money to have a will and trust drawn? Why does he purchase life insurance and reduce his current spendable income to pay premiums? Why does he make inter vivos gifts?

Basically, there are four additional reasons. One is that structuring the future and providing support for survivors is a moral imperative. (Just as it would be immoral to neglect predeath support duties, so would it be immoral to neglect postdeath obligations.)

A second powerful impetus is guilt. Many clients feel that money or other property will somehow make up for neglect. They attempt to pay back a wife or children in property for the time they were too busy at the office to take with their family.

Security devices such as wills, trusts, and life insurance provide a client with a means of doing something to stabilize

the future of his family and rob death of its ability to threaten him with his own hungry children.

Perhaps the most powerful reason for the testamentary process is the step it enables a person to take toward immortality. Some have called this the concept of "postself." Essentially, it recognizes that individuals engage in cognitive and emotional maneuverings in the present so they can survive, continue to live, and have a measure of impact and influence after the event of their physical deaths.

The Estate Planner's Responsibility by Definition or Default

Why must the estate planner (in addition to other human services teams) be involved with the subjects of death and dying? Possibly the responsibility is his by definition — or perhaps the burden rests upon him by default. Social taboos have caused the dismissal of the subject of death from the public mind. This in turn shifts the weight to those of us who are forced by our relationship with the client to deal with their feelings about death and dying. Regardless of the reason, as advisors we must recognize that our clients — even those in the prime of life — have thoughts and reactions to death; and an essential part of the estate planning process relates to a healthy resolution of those feelings.

Resolution of Professional's Own Anxieties Necessary to His Utility

It is impossible for the estate planner to help his client until his own feelings and anxieties about death are first resolved. Not until the professional knows and can deal with his own fears and thoughts concerning death can he properly construct policies and priorities based on the needs and desires of his client — rather than his own defenses.

There are many thoughts embedded in the minds and hearts of clients that beg to be shared with another human being. But we often close off the openness necessary to the flow of such information because we are unwilling to talk directly about death. A discussion of death — even the very word — is kept to a bare minimum or surrounded with euphemisms by the attorney or trust officer in the will-making process or the insurance agent in the sales interview.

The feelings of the professional, however, do not go unnoticed or without effect. His values and attitudes are communicated (both verbally and nonverbally) to a client regardless of whether the estate planner intends such message or not. His annoyance, impatience, lack of interest, or personal anxiety affects his clients more than he realizes. Our method of handling our own feelings sometimes conveys that we cannot, do not want to, and are unwilling to listen to those of others.

Rewards of Openness to the Estate Planner and Client

Substantial rewards are available to both the estate planner and his client who are willing to talk about death and dying long before it happens. A healthy and strong individual is less frightened and better able to deal with the interpersonal and financial implications of death "when it is still miles away than when it is right in front of the door." It is also easier for the client's family to discuss such matters in times of relative health and well-being. Appropriate arrangements for children and others are more rationally made while the head of the household is still functioning. (The value of such predeath conversations seems obvious — yet we often postpone such talks to serve our own defenses rather than the best interests of the client and his family.)

The rewards to the estate planner are abundant. If we are strong enough to examine our own reactions more closely and take an honest look at ourselves, our own growth and maturity is nurtured. When we learn to listen, we reduce the powerlessness (and often frustration and anger) of those toward whom we profess to offer human caring.

WHY THE WORD "DEATH" IS UNSPOKEN

When the topic of death is raised — or when the professional must deal with a dying client — his concerns about his own mortality are raised toward consciousness. His childhood feeling about separation and death are reawakened. Talking about one's own death is even more sensitive and more terrible. Because it is an unknown, death is associated with a bad act, a frightening happening. We deny death by discussing it — if at all — in euphemistic language. Much of this extends from the societal taboo concerning the recognition of man's mortality.

The problem, of course, is not uniquely reserved to the estate planner. The medical profession offers a good example of the reluctance of other professionals to meet the problem. For instance, the physician often prefers not telling a patient he has cancer. And unless the patient is persistent, the doctor might disregard the patient's questions. Even those questions intuitively perceived as a "real wish to know" are often ignored: "No one wants to know he is dying." Professionals have difficulty stating a diagnosis to a patient. They tend to use a staccato, impersonal, medical textbook style.

THE ESTATE PLANNING INTERVIEW — AN OPPORTUNITY TO TOUCH, TO FEEL, TO HELP

Coming to Grips with Life and Death

The estate planning interview is perhaps the first time in a client's life when he will be confronted with his property, his beloved ones, his mortality, and the relationship of each to the others. The impact of death must be discussed and met head on. He must recognize and internalize the possibility of unexpected sudden death and, in some cases, eventuality of rapidly approaching certain death. He must come face to face with the effects of the orphaning of his children, the potential for family strife, the problems inherent in projects left unfinished, and the psychological and financial burdens of liabilities outstanding. Additionally, the estate planning interview is an opportunity to come to grips with and eliminate the uncertainty involved in the mysterious machinery of probate.

The Process of Human Counseling

This reduction in tension and anxiety does not just happen: it must be part of a carefully thought out process on the part of the estate planner. The hoped-for result will not occur if the experts, the CPA, the CFP, the CLU, the ChFC, the attorney, or the trust officer, think of the estate planning interview as a mental tug-of-war involving on the one side the estate planner, who knows or makes up the rules, and on the other the client, who becomes willing to accept those rules by dependence on the estate planner. This psychology can only result in an arrangement that the client will probably not understand or even want. How could he if he has not "bought into" the ultimate plan?

What must the professional do to involve the client and turn what might otherwise be a cold, impersonal gathering of data into an opportunity for human counseling? It is not so difficult a task for the estate planner to identify issues or face problems. What the estate planner needs to learn is how to face a face.

Listen to the client. Study not only what the client (and his family) says, but also what he does not say. Try to understand what the client's body language (the shrug of a shoulder, the positioning of the hands, the apparent physical tension on the face, the lifting of the eyebrows, or the fleeting frown) really means. Summarize what you have been told and reflect accurately on what you have seen, felt, and heard.

Be sensitive to the client's world. Accept his feelings and try to understand them. Communicate honestly — and humanly. Be open, involved, and willing to enter the client's world. The professional must want to be personally helpful. To do this he must be tuned in not only to the client's feelings but also to his own.

The Tools and Techniques of Estate Planning

Objectives of the Estate Planning Interview

The goal of the estate planner should be to help his client come to his own realizations and conclusions. To accomplish this, he must find out how the client feels about life and death — and the values and relationships that death will affect or destroy. So he must search for feelings and attitudes as well as information. The failure of an estate planner is more often a failure of perception than a restricted range of information, an incomplete understanding of "people facts" rather than "fact facts."

More specifically, the estate planner must understand his client's system of needs, his modes of expressing or revealing himself, his ideas about life, and his feelings and practices relating to his family and his career. There must also be an appreciation of the client's feelings about property, security, health, and perhaps most importantly, an ability to contemplate all of these things in relation to each other.

The Role of Property in the Testamentary Process

It is extremely important that the estate planner have an understanding of the roles of property in the testamentary process: "Our clients' thoughts and emotions are deeper, more puzzling realities than taxation or legal rhetoric." Clients are people, complex, and worthy of behavioral examination.

At its simplest level, a client's thoughts about his property could be considered mere statements on a ledger. But on higher levels, property is both an expression and an extension of a client himself, a part of the way he defines himself. (This is clearly seen when a person is stripped of his possessions. He is attacked at the deepest layers of his personality; there is less man left since something of himself has been taken away from him. The first day of basic training in the army, incarceration as a prisoner of war, and even routine hospital check-ins serve as examples of the loss of identity that is coupled with the loss that comes when clothing and other material possessions are taken away.)

The items on a person's desk, perhaps mementos of difficult business careers, are not significant for their economic values but are important because — like other property — they are an idiom of the owner's personality.

If we accept the premise that property represents and immortalizes a person, then when a person makes a gift (inter vivos or testamentary) he is really giving part of himself. He is giving his own nature and substance, since the property he gives is not inert but has the life and personification of the giver. His attitude toward giving, therefore, expresses the relationships between the people he loves and the things — the wealth and objects — he owns.

Property is used in the exercise of power, love, guilt, remorse, hope, and resignation. A person's needs, feelings, thoughts, and actions grow and attach in different manners to different kinds of properties. A home, for example, represents a protective attachment to a person's family. A business may represent the continuation or perhaps completion of a personal project (goal-striving behavior).

The estate planner should incorporate the role of personification of property in the estate planning process. He should understand that clients — in drawing wills — are interested as much in values and identifications in their property as they are in taxes. They are interested in the people they love.

WHAT IS DEATH AND WHAT DOES IT MEAN?

Death — Multifaceted Meanings and Effects

In the most general sense, death is the continuing and constantly accelerating process that begins the moment we are born. Perhaps that definition should set the stage for how we live: "We can realize that we might die at any moment and yet live as though we were never going to die."

Death attaches to each individual's soul, psyche, relationships, and property — but does so in different ways for different people. The meanings of the word "death" fluctuate, therefore, from person to person:

> To some, death is the bringer of financial distress: With the extreme treatment and costs of hospitalization, financial burdens are added. Little luxuries at first and necessities later on may not be afforded any more. The immense sums that such treatment and hospitalization cost in recent years have forced many patients to sell the only possessions they had; they were unable to keep a house which they built for their old age, unable to send a child through college, and unable, perhaps, to make many dreams come true.

Death to many conjures up images of loss of dignity and independence. Guilt, anxiety, and fear color perceptions of dying. Death is frightening because it is uncertain, because it will sever important relationships (especially relationships that involve mutual obligations), and because it will cause experience to cease.

Social scientists, physicians, and philosophers have looked upon death as part of life. They have asked, if one is not able to die, is he really able to live?: "We die as we have lived. Death belongs to life as birth does. The walk is in the raising of the foot as in the laying of it down." Others have said that "death is an important interface — part of a larger process which is somehow related to what it is to be human."

Dying — How It Colors Perceptions of Death

We know much more about dying than we do about death. As estate planners, we are sometimes confronted with a client who has been told he has a limited time to live or who may even be on his deathbed. What are the feelings some of these people might experience? Some have said that dying is partially reliving the past, partially preoccupation with the illness, and partially just going on living. And death? Some say it is very much like rest: "In the end a dying man needs to die like a sleepy man needs to sleep."

Do dying and death represent failure? To many, they do. To others, the thoughts of dying and death generate fear of losing time, physical decay, the cessation of thought, and irreversibility, and the loss of pleasure. Still others view the process of dying as a deprivation, a threat, a punishment, and a devouring of their persons.

People who are dying experience a tremendous range of problems — from the purely practical (such as transportation to and from the hospital) to the deeply internal emotional experience, such as dealing with intense sadness, anger, and guilt. Perhaps worst of all is the loneliness: "He was ...interrupted, left dangling, perhaps to die alone.... It was the isolation, the exclusion we had forced upon him. We could not be with him — we could not even hear him." The vast change in life-styles makes dying alien and lonely, mechanical and dehumanizing.

Interaction between the Estate Planner and the Dying Client

There are a number of tools and techniques in use where members of the estate planning team are aware that death is impending:

Unlike the normal estate planning situation, however, deathbed estate planning by definition usually precludes detailed research and requires immediate decisions. The estate planner is likely to propose technically sound recommendations which may be personally unacceptable to the client and his family. They may not even be willing to listen to recommendations. Sometimes, the client or his family will make requests which are technically unsound or even illegal. These must, of course, be delicately rejected.

How much can be accomplished depends on a number of variables. Three of the most important are the client's state of mind, the emotional involvement of near relatives, and the relationship between the estate planner and the client.

If the client is physically, mentally, and emotionally able to assist, his cooperation can vastly increase the effectiveness of predeath planning. But, as will be further explained below, some persons lose all interest when they learn death is near. Often the client has been kept ignorant of the gravity of his situation by a well-intentioned physician or family member. This at least complicates, if not totally frustrates, the estate planner's ability to render meaningful service.

Family members are sometimes more emotionally crippled by the impending loss they will suffer than is the client himself. His spouse, children, or other close relatives may be incapable of making logical decisions or taking pragmatic action. The special taboos against mentioning a will or "getting things in order" have kept even estate planning specialists from being of much help when faced with their own dying parents.

A close relationship between the estate planner and the client gives the advisor perspective and insight into the client's personal objectives and his family's potential problems. Even more important, the advisor's role must be to provide emotional ballast, to objectively help his client and his client's family arrange a list of priorities and implementation procedures.

THE DYING CLIENT — EXPRESSIONS OF GRIEF

It is important for the estate planner to understand how grief is expressed by both the dying client and his survivors. How these individuals come to terms with impending death and move through the various stages of grief is thought to be strongly influenced by a person's basic personality. The leading authority feels there are essentially five stages through which a persons goes: denial, anger, bargaining, depression, and acceptance. (These stages can occur in any order at any time.)

Denial is a temporary defense. In the young there is the typical "It can't happen to me" reaction. Denial serves as a healthy way of dealing with the uncomfortable and painful fact of impending death.

An expression of anger, which can be directed without reason at doctors, friends, relatives, or estate planning advisors, is thought to vary in intensity with the dying client's early life experiences. It is yet another means of expressing powerful emotional trauma.

Bargaining ("Let me live one more year and I'll be good to my children, donate money to my religious organization, etc.") is an attempt on an emotional level to postpone what is inevitable on the intellectual and physical levels.

Depression is a reaction that is a common response to the actual loss of health or use of part of the body. It is a preparatory measure to the impending loss of life.

Acceptance is often (but not always) the final stage. At this point the dying client is void of feelings and expresses an increased desire and need for sleep. The dying person's family often needs more help, support, and understanding than the client.

Another authority suggests that the stages of grief are

(1) shock

(2) disorganization

(3) expression of volatile emotions

(4) guilt

(5) feelings of loss and loneliness

(6) periods of relief and reestablishment

Feelings expressed by a dying professor included panic (he was terrified that he had lost control of his fate, decisions were made without his knowledge or consent, and he gradually found himself passively accepting the decisions), anger (he felt dehumanized, an object instead of a person), the need to talk (he wanted to share his feelings and vent his frustrations), and deep depressions (he had feelings of guilt and inadequacy as a husband and father).

WHAT THE ESTATE PLANNER CAN DO FOR THE DYING CLIENT

Although the estate planning process should give all clients a feeling of control, a sense of usefulness, and the satisfaction of completing unfinished business, this goal is particularly important in the case of a client who has been told — because of a particular medical condition such as cancer or a failing heart — that he or she has only a limited time to live.

The Importance of Providing the Client with Control

What should occur in the estate planning process is a series of experiences that result in change through (the client's)

choice. The professional can increase the client's dignity by empowering him with as much control as possible. But it is not enough to give the dying client a voice; he must also be given a listener. Only then can he be an active participant in decision making. Psychiatrists have found that hopelessness and depression are precipitated when individuals cannot (or perceive they cannot) act on their environment. Any actions the estate planner can take to bring the dying client into the problem-solving process will help relieve the client's feelings of helplessness and increase the quality of his remaining life.

A word of warning, however, is in order. Even for the healthy client, "the testamentary experience is death-confronting, novel, and taboo-defying." For the dying client, such experience could possibly be overwhelming. Obviously, a great deal of discretion must be exercised by all the parties involved.

Helping the Client to Feel Useful by Encouraging the Completion of Unfinished Business

By presenting the estate planning process as an unfinished project, the client is given a developmental task with which he is involved. He is given value and a meaningful tie to life. This final stage — even though quite possibly limited in terms of absolute time — may be relatively as important as all previous tasks in life.

Family, as well as members of the estate planning team, must interface with the dying person and his environment. They must help the client maintain his autonomy and dignity by encouraging him to participate — and thus help him to face death in his own way. This conceptualization allows family members to help the dying person complete his unfinished business in a meaningful way that will benefit all concerned.

"Death ceases to be an absurd and intolerable scandal only when a person knows he has given meaning to his life." So the estate planner confronted with someone dying must do what he can do to give that person the sense of pride, a feeling of worth, and a knowledge he has resolved much of his unfinished business.

Development of a Support System of Advisors

The dying person and his survivors need large doses of supportive intervention which can best be accomplished by knowing his previous history of reactions to stress.

The nature of the client's response to grief will be largely determined by the quality of his lifetime personal relationships, and the use he makes of the defense mechanisms such as denial or anger and the retraction of his ego. Start where the client is — let him face impending death, denial, or acceptance, whichever he selects. Do not force him to behave according to your preconceptions or hustle him along a preplanned course.

In dealing with the dying client (or his family) proceed at the rate determined by the client's receptivity. Sense where the client is emotionally:

> Set your pace at the rate at which they are able to understand. Do the correct thing financially even if it may provoke angry confrontations at some subsequent date.... The widow will generally be more rational and receptive to good advice in approximately six to nine months after the death. Do not make brisk unexplained conclusions or assertions. Do not be provoked into anger. Be deliberate, correct, and extremely open and proper. Diplomacy, patience, genuineness, and warmness are essential. Take the time to be empathetic, to listen attentively, to have unconditional positive regard.... If you find yourself becoming very angry or acting abruptly, it is best to consider why this is so and excuse yourself from the ongoing exchange until you have better composure.

Strengthen the coping mechanisms whether they be made of denial or acceptance. Reduce anxiety and fear. Help the family to understand the feelings of the dying individual and help the family with their feelings.

Perhaps the most meaningful service is the opportunity the estate planner has to allow his client to share his feelings before death and to work through those feelings, rational or irrational.

The dying need reassurance they will not be left alone. If we, as estate planners, have the courage not to desert them, they offer us a gift in return — help in completing our own unfinished business.

EFFECT OF DEATH ON THE SURVIVORS

A breadwinner's death results in drastic changes in the life of the family. These include loss of security and an end to the survivors' dependence on the decedent. Survivors will be required to take over many of the decedent's roles and tasks, accept a strange new schedule, and shoulder what are sometimes actually (and are almost always perceived as) harsh and awesome new responsibilities. Especially for widows, this often means a sudden involvement in business and financial affairs.

In every substantial estate, the widow (if there is one) has major roles to perform. Yet in most situations she lacks even a modicum of previous exposure or training to function efficiently in handling legal, business, probate or taxation problems. Quite often she has never balanced a checkbook, let alone handled an $800,000 estate. She has not been shown how to do things which will be her certain responsibility. Nor has she been taught to avoid acts which she should not even attempt.

Ironically, at the very time the widow is first involved in these matters, she is in the worst possible frame of mind. She is depressed, unhappy and insecure, and her entire social life has changed. After the few days when her friends, relatives and close family are there to comfort her, they will return to their normal lives. The widow is left — alone and lonely. Confronting her with strange and complex legal duties is like throwing her into a pitch-black room. She loses all sense of direction, does not know where the light switch is and is afraid to move because all sorts of risks and impediments are there in the darkness.

How does the widow feel? One widow said, "I feel like one of those spiraled shells washed up on the beach. Poke a straw through the twisting tunnels inside and nothing is there — no flesh, no life. Whatever lived there has dried up and gone!"

And, although the male pronoun is commonly used to designate the breadwinner/decedent, it is quite often the *man* who survives. Studies show that a widower faces even more serious emotional problems than many widows do. Men seldom have a support system to hold them up — and *keep* them up.

The word "widow" is appropriate — it comes from Sanskrit and it means "empty." The shock of that emptiness is always immediately felt. Another widow said, "It took me some time to grasp the meaning of what happened. The word 'death' didn't mean anything to me. All I thought of was that it would be impossible for Marty to be here one day and gone the next. It was as if the earth had just opened up and swallowed him. My shock turned to panic; I felt lost. I didn't want to see or talk to anyone. The thought of going to bed frightened me because I would always wake up in the middle of the night trying to stifle a scream. I couldn't believe Marty was dead."

Years ago, we had the benefit of a socially accepted collection of rites and ceremonies to help survivors make the transition. In some societies, these rites were performed for weeks or even months after an individual's death. But today, we do not often have elaborate wakes, mourning clothes or annual remembrances. Many of society's rules, rites and ceremonies of the past are gone. And so survivors are not really sure how to cope with death — they have to make their own decisions at to what to do and how to react. This uncertainty produces anxiety.

Survivors experience guilt for what they did or did not do in life to or for the deceased, or simply embarrassment for having lived while the deceased died. Survivors may feel guilty because the death of the deceased has relieved them from heavy, emotionally and financially draining burdens. ("If he'd die already, the financial nightmare would end.")

At the same time, the bereaved may feel anger at being deserted and left to face life's problems. A young daughter, speaking of her father who had just died, told us, "I felt as though he didn't have the right to die. I wasn't ready for him to die."

Perhaps the most difficult of all emotions that survivors must overcome is a deep sense of loneliness and resentment at being left alone. There are 10 million widows in our country — one out of every 6 women over age 21. A study of over 1,700 widows showed that loneliness is the single most serious problem of widowhood. One of those widows said, "It's funny, but it's love and companionship that you miss. You don't get someone out of your system so easily after 26 years ...Being lonesome is a big void that can't be filled."

The second most serious problem of widowhood is the financial pressure of raising children without a father.

So besides their emotional problems, families are likely to have financial problems, or at least concern as to how they will pay current bills and continue to get along after the breadwinner's death. One widow said, "After my husband died, there was the emotional shock. The pain was so deep — so consuming — it seemed unendurable. But I learned to live with it. The economic shock was something else. It didn't strike as fast or hit as furious. It's the sort of thing you don't even notice at first. But after a while, the shock of your economic plight begins to creep into your consciousness like some black, oozing reality that you can't believe or escape. It's true ... money can't compensate two children for the loss of their father; money can't reach out in the night and caress you; money can't come home at night with a briefcase, a twinkle and a hug; but money can give you some peace of mind." And so survivors must be concerned, among other things, with the need for money — because, to the extent the decedent did not provide it, his survivors have the problem of raising it — or doing without it. This in turn creates incredible psychological pressures.

Bereavement is not a commonplace occurrence in our lifetimes. The whirlwind shock of sudden change is a crisis with which many family members feel particularly unable to cope. Quite often a real, and almost always a perceived, imbalance exists between the difficulty and importance of the problems and the resources available to deal with them. Obviously, professional psychiatric and psychological help may be required.

Survivors must release their ties with the deceased. They must adjust to their new environment and form new relationships. The family must allow mourning to occur, relinquish the memory of the deceased as a force in family affairs and activities, and realign themselves in terms of readjusting responsibilities and needs.

It is particularly important that all (both children and adults) who are touched by the death of the decedent be given an opportunity to adequately work out their feelings about the event. You can expect problems to occur when a person of any age is unable to express grief or tries to hold back natural responses. Symptoms of the morbid and abnormal reactions which tend to occur when there is an unnatural delay include:

- exhausting overactivity

- symptoms similar to those manifested in the last illness of the deceased, or the outbreak of other psychosomatic illnesses such as asthma or colitis (this is a combination of normal mourning and the "It should have been me" feeling)

- furious (and usually unreasonable) hostility toward specific persons (often including the estate's executor)

- agitated and acute depression (sometimes leading to suicidal thoughts)

- extreme and prolonged difficulty in sleeping

- preoccupation with the image of the deceased (you may find dozens of pictures of the deceased suddenly appear throughout the house)

- difficulty in continuing normal social interaction and a withdrawal of interest in the outside world

ABOUT THE WILL AND PROBATE — WHAT THEY MEAN TO THE SURVIVORS

The will and the probate process itself fulfill important functions in the process of emotional repair known as mourning. The will is the last communication of the deceased. It has unique emotional meanings because in it the decedent states many of his feelings about the bereaved. Of course, the decedent's thoughts are usually not implicit in the words used. But in terms of *who* receives property, *how* that property is to be received, and *when* it will be received, the testator has expressed approval (or disapproval), gratitude (or revenge), and confidence (or a lack of confidence). Likewise, the terms of a will may emphasize that the testator recognized one child's need or another child's deservingness. Or the testator may have favored a blood relative over someone who is loved but is not related (or vice versa).

It is important to recognize that what the testator meant to say when his will was written may not be how it is taken by the beneficiaries. A devoted but less needy son who gets less than a proportionate part of his father's estate may resent the injustice of being left less than his less worthy brother.

CHOICE OF EXECUTOR — WHAT IT MEANS

A person is selected as an executor because of the testator's trust and confidence in that person. They may have had a close or very deep emotional relationship.

A bereaved executor, in performing his or her duties, facilitates the process of coming to terms with the testator's death. By carrying out the wishes of the deceased the executor is retaining and strengthening his or her relationship with the deceased, but at the same time, while going through the stages of the probate process, the executor is gradually "letting go."

Of course, the opposite is true in some situations. For instance, assume a widow had always been dependent on her husband for every decision. If the couple's son or a bank is named as executor, the sense of helplessness precipitated by the loss of her husband is increased by the lack of control she continues to experience. Her helplessness may generate fear and distrust. The result may be that every move the executor makes may be questioned or viewed with suspicion.

WHAT CAN — AND SHOULD — THE EXECUTOR DO?

One of the positive results of the estate planning process is to give survivors a feeling of control, a sense of usefulness and the satisfaction of completing the decedent's (and their own) unfinished business. Increase the family members' dignity by empowering them with as much control as possible. Keep in mind that it is not enough to give survivors a voice; one must also give them a listener. Only then can they be active participants in the decision-making process. Hopelessness

and depression are precipitated and exacerbated when individuals cannot (or perceive they cannot) act on their environment.

Any steps taken to bring all family members into the decision-making process will relieve their feelings of helplessness. The death of a loved one will be experienced as less absurd, and may become more tolerable, if the family knows that the life of the deceased had meaning.

Accumulating an estate, buying life insurance, preparing the will and trust are all like buying a car, filling it with gas, and expecting that a wife or child who has never been in a car can get in and drive that vehicle in heavy traffic. We cannot, of course, make survivors into mechanics, but we can help them learn where the steering wheel is, how to make the car go, how to put on the brakes and how to read road signs. The more that can be done to explain what comes next and how the family can take the wheel, the better off they will be.

SUMMARY

As a member of the estate planning team, you must be extremely conscious of the trauma of the bereaved. Understanding the five stages of grief experienced by a dying person (denial, anger, bargaining, depression and acceptance) will help you understand what survivors experience. Every person will react to death differently than others. How the bereaved react is largely dependent on their relationship with the deceased, their emotional and financial dependence, the energy and time they have devoted to the deceased, and how many other important relationships they may have.

Death often results in drastic life-style changes. These are coupled with various physical symptoms of grief that can be normally anticipated, as well as abnormal reactions that occur when the mourning process is delayed or repressed.

Probate is an important part of the "letting go" process; it is also a means of completing the unfinished business of the deceased and at the same time a beginning of the family's taking control.

If the estate planner can serve as a neutral outsider who is not himself emotionally overinvolved, he can be of great assistance in listening to the client's family's concerns, their wishes, and needs.

Any steps an estate planner takes to bring the survivors into the probate process and give them control will help relieve their feelings of helplessness and help them readjust.

PROBATE — A PRIMER FOR THE COULD-BE EXECUTOR

Copyright 1990 by Charles K. Plotnick and Stephen R. Leimberg

Any adult could be an executor. But few of us would want to be if we knew the awesome, complex, and time-consuming responsibilities and potential liabilities the task entails.

GENERAL ROLE OF AN EXECUTOR

When a person dies, the law requires that his property must be collected. After debts, taxes, and expenses are paid, the remaining assets are distributed to whoever is entitled to that property. That distribution is determined by the person's will or the intestate laws of the state. It is the executor's or administrator's responsibility to collect the assets, to pay the death taxes, debts, and expenses of the decedent (the person who died), and to make the appropriate distribution of any remaining assets. The entire process by which these tasks are accomplished (with the guidance and supervision of the court system) is called "probate." The court that oversees the process is called the probate or orphans' or surrogates' court.

DISTINCTION BETWEEN EXECUTOR AND ADMINISTRATOR

An "executor" is the person appointed in the will of the decedent. If the decedent left no will, or if the will is invalid for some reason, then either the surviving spouse of the decedent, or one or more of the persons entitled to his or her estate, may be appointed as the "personal representative." That person is called the "administrator" of the estate.

It is this person who will "probate" the decedent's will; i.e., the will will be accepted as the decedent's, and as the decedent's *last* will. (Probate is used here in its most narrow sense.)

FUNERAL ARRANGEMENTS

Typically, the funeral will take place before the executor has been appointed. So the executor's only legal duty with respect to the funeral will be to pay the bill if it is reasonable.

APPOINTMENT OF THE PERSONAL REPRESENTATIVE

Even before the appointment of a personal representative of a decedent's estate, a determination has to be made as to where the deceased person was domiciled. A person's domicile is his permanent and principal home, the place to which

he always intends to return. The difference between domicile and residence is that your residence is where you happen to be living. Domicile requires not only your presence, but also an intention to make it your permanent home.

The will must then be recorded in the office of the local register of wills of the county in which the decedent was domiciled. The register of wills will issue either "letters of administration" to the administrator or "letters testamentary" to the executor. These "letters" are proof of the legal authority of the personal representative to collect and deal with the assets of the decedent's estate. (To make things simpler, the register of wills gives the executor "short certificates," brief documents evidencing the fact that you are the executor or administrator of the decedent's estate.)

The executor or administrator is now the person who actually has title to the decedent's property and who acts on behalf of the estate.

EMPLOYMENT OF THE ATTORNEY FOR THE ESTATE

An executor is entitled to use any qualified attorney he or she would like. The term "qualified attorney" is stressed because of the complexity of handling an estate. Generally, an executor may use any attorney he feels is competent — even if the decedent named a different attorney in his will.

For both state law and federal tax purposes, the executor or administrator must keep informed as to exactly how the estate is being administered. He can't just close his eyes and shift all the responsibility to the attorney. In one case, a court held an administratrix responsible for the actions of her attorney where she had surrendered all her duties to the attorney and exercised no effective supervision whatsoever over his activities. The court felt that she did not exercise that degree of care, prudence, circumspection, and foresight that a prudent person would employ in matters of her own.

COLLECTING THE ASSETS

After the executor is appointed, the first thing he should do is to get together with the members of the decedent's family, assuming that they are the decedent's beneficiaries, and make sure that he has a clear understanding of the size and nature of the decedent's estate. The second step, if the size, nature, and complexity of the estate warrant, is to hire competent counsel. Once appropriate counsel has been employed the executor should take specific steps to safeguard and collect the decedent's assets as quickly as possible.

It is extremely important that the executor take every possible measure to make certain that he has a complete inventory of all of the decedent's assets. In this regard, he should review the decedent's past income tax returns and cancelled checks to determine if there are any purchases, accounts, securities, or other assets of which the executor is not otherwise aware.

Prior income tax returns, for example, might list interest from bank accounts or dividends from securities of which the executor has no knowledge. From this information, the executor can trace the present location of the assets and determine whether those assets were still owned by the decedent at the time of his death. In addition, the executor must try to collect all outstanding claims that the decedent had against others at his death. In one case, a court even held the executor responsible for failing to make a claim that the estate was the beneficiary of — and therefore entitled to — monies from another state.

The executor should advertise the fact that he has been appointed executor so that creditors or other persons who might have an interest in the decedent's estate will have public notice of his death and thus have time to present any claims against the estate to the executor. The public notice also gives creditors warning that claims must be made before a certain date. If notice of one's appointment as executor is advertised, and the prescribed period of time elapses from the first date of publication, then the executor files his final account with the court. Only after that time elapses and the executor has accounted for what came into the estate, what went out, and what he paid to the beneficiaries can the executor be discharged of all responsibility for handling the estate. Since the "final account" will also be advertised, claims of creditors following the filing of the final account will not be allowed. The executor is then discharged from personal liability.

There is no special order in which the executor must collect the decedent's assets, but it is usually logical to file the appropriate claim form to collect the decedent's life insurance as soon as possible. There are also forms for collecting social security and veterans' administration benefits. Sometimes unpaid salary, as well as other fringe benefits, must be collected. Arrange to have the decedent's safe-deposit box opened and make a list of its contents.

It is important for the executor to open an estate checking account and a savings account. The executor can then take all the liquid assets and pass them through the checking account and savings account, if appropriate, in order to have an accurate accounting of the assets collected and bills paid.

The executor should give notice of the decedent's death to the banks where the decedent had his accounts. He should obtain from the banks letters giving the exact values of the accounts on the date of death, the dates that the accounts were opened, and the exact names on the accounts.

All securities in the decedent's name should be assembled, and the executor should maintain close contact with the decedent's broker to be certain that he has an accurate record of all the securities that the decedent owned, or had an interest in, at the time of his death. There are certain forms the executor must obtain to transfer title to stocks or bonds. The executor must also determine the value of the securities on the decedent's date of death according to the valuation method prescribed by the Internal Revenue Service.

If the decedent held real estate in his own name, the executor must be certain that the property is protected, that appropriate amounts of insurance are obtained or maintained, and that adequate safeguards are instituted to maintain the security of the property. If it is decided that the property should be sold, the executor is responsible for making sure that the sale is conducted properly and a fair price is received. Even if the executor makes a completely innocent mistake, it could cost him money. For example, one executor mistakenly obligated an estate to two real estate commissions. As a result, the court held that the executor was personally responsible for the amount of the overpayment.

It is also necessary for the executor to have court approval for the sale of real estate unless that power is specifically given to him in the will. In another case, the court found that even where the will gave the executor all the powers set forth in the general statutes of the state, which included the power to sell any property of the decedent without court approval, the executor still did not have the right to sell real estate without court approval.

As assets are collected, they should also be valued. This means an appraisal must be made of the real property and of any personal property that the decedent owned, such as jewelry, clothing, automobiles, and household furniture and effects. And, of course, a value has to be placed on any business interest of the decedent. In one recent case, the court felt that because the executor erred in calculating the value of the decedent's shares in a corporation, and thereby obtained a sales price below the value of the shares, the executor should be surcharged.

HANDLING THE BUSINESS

Where the executor finds a business among the decedent's assets, particular attention must be given to the books of the business. He should examine prior tax returns and take whatever action is necessary to ensure that the business is being run as efficiently as possible. A determination will have to be made as to whether the business should be continued or liquidated. In this regard, the executor can be guided by the decedent's instructions in his will, by the wishes of the family, or by whatever professional guidance the executor can obtain. If the decedent had any business agreements, such as a buy-sell agreement with a surviving partner, or with a surviving shareholder if the business is incorporated, or with the corporation itself, then the executor must comply with the provisions of the agreement.

Very serious problems can arise in trying to conserve the value of a decedent's business or real estate. If the decedent's business was a sole proprietorship, then it terminates on his death. A partnership also terminates, in effect, unless the proper predeath agreements have been made, such as buy-sell agreements that would enable the surviving partner or partners to continue the business. If the business is closed for any period of time following the decedent's death, its value as a going concern is greatly diminished. An interruption of the normal flow of business will result in the loss of customers and a large drop in the value for which the business might be sold. If the assets of the business are perishable, or have a time value, then the executor faces the problem of taking immediate action or having these business assets dissipated.

Unfortunately, the executor can be held personally responsible for negligence in the management of a decedent's business. In fact, the results in most cases where businesses are continued without court authorization are generally unfavorable to the personal representatives. The court in one such case held that the personal representative did not have the unqualified right to perpetuate a decedent's enterprise without approval of the court, and that any loss to the estate suffered by continuation of the business fell upon the representative.

INVESTING AND PROTECTING THE ASSETS

The executor should take steps to ascertain that the assets are properly invested, so that there will be no possibility of the executor's being held responsible for dissipating the assets or allowing their value to decrease unreasonably. In investing these assets, an executor is required to exercise the same degree of judgment that a reasonable person would exercise in the management of his own estate. In one case, the executrix held an estate balance of approximately $6,000 in a noninterest-bearing checking account for 3 years because of the need for ready cash and liquidity of funds. The court, however, felt that it would have been more prudent to invest the money and not permit it to remain idle. The executrix was consequently charged for failing to invest the funds.

Protection of assets is another responsibility of an executor, who must make certain that silverware, jewelry, and art objects are protected and insured, so that he will not be held responsible in the event of loss by theft, fire, or other unforeseen calamity.

The executor must try to obtain a fair price if he sells the assets. For example, the executor of the estate of a prominent painter sold paintings to an art dealer, and the dealer later resold the paintings at prices ranging from six to ten times what the dealer paid the estate for them. The court held the executor responsible for the loss to the estate.

What does an executor do when property is not in the decedent's name alone, but the decedent owns it jointly with his wife, or another family member, or even a business associate? Whenever property is held in joint names, the applicable state law will determine whether the decedent's interest in the property will be included as part of his estate to be administered by the executor or whether, in fact, the property will pass directly to the remaining joint owner or owners. For example, in most states, property owned jointly by husband and wife is owned as a joint tenancy with the right of survivorship (sometimes know as "tenancy by the entirety"). The right of survivorship means that upon the death of one of these joint owners the survivor owns all property rights to the exclusion of the executor.

However, property is sometimes owned by several persons "in common." In this situation, each person has an undivided right to a certain percentage of the property. Where the decedent owned a tenancy in common, the executor will represent the decedent's interests in his or her proportionate share of the property. In some cases, questions can be raised as to what exactly the decedent's interest is, and these cases require extreme caution on the part of the executor. There is also the problem of the responsibility for the taxes due on the decedent's interest in his share of the jointly held property.

PAYMENT OF TAXES, DEBTS, AND EXPENSES

A decedent's assets must often be converted into cash in order to pay expenses, debts, and taxes. Since no two decedents own exactly the same property, no two estates will be handled in an identical manner. There is very little demand for some of the personal property that people own. Therefore it is hard to realize cash from many of these assets. Of course, assets such as the proceeds of life insurance, certificates of deposits, and Treasury bills may be available to take care of the estate's liabilities. Listed securities can also be quickly converted to cash, but the market value at the time that funds are needed might preclude their sale at that time. Assets such as real estate and business interests are not readily convertible into cash, and it might take months, or even years in the case of business interests, to realize cash from these assets. Therefore the executor has to analyze the assets of the estate after they have been assembled, determine what amounts of cash will be needed to cover the debts, expenses, and taxes of the estate, and then develop a plan to make the necessary funds available when required.

Typical debts that the decedent might have outstanding at his death include outstanding loans, credit card balances, and day-to-day bills such as household bills, telephone, electric, gasoline, department store charges, and past taxes.

Common expenses are the costs of administering the estate. These include probate costs, legal fees, executor's or administrator's fees, fees for appraisers, costs included in selling real estate and personal property, costs arising on account of the decedent's last illness, and the costs involved in winding up the executor's business.

Numerous categories of taxes must be paid in the process of settling an estate. In many estates the executor must pay two categories of death taxes — state inheritance and estate taxes, and the federal estate tax. In addition, the executor is also responsible for the payment of unpaid income taxes, both federal and state, and any state personal property and real estate taxes that might be due on the personal and real property in the decedent's name.

State death taxes are typically paid by the executor out of the estate's assets. (Technically, with respect to an inheritance tax, the person receiving the property is taxed on his right to receive such assets. An estate tax taxes the right to transfer property.) The amount of any inheritance tax, which is on the transfer itself, usually depends on the relationship of the beneficiary or receiver of the property to the decedent. For example, in Pennsylvania property left to children, grandchildren, parents, or anyone in the family line is taxed to the recipient at the rate of 6 percent, while property left to all other beneficiaries is taxed at 15 percent. There are exceptions for certain types of property held jointly by husband and wife for which no tax is due. There are also specific exemptions, such as for the proceeds of life insurance paid to a named beneficiary, for charitable bequests, and for real estate located outside of the taxing state.

Where a decedent owns real estate located in a state different from that of his domicile at the time of death, the state in which the real estate is located has the right to tax the property. This often leads to problems, especially in those cases where two states are trying to tax the same property.

A federal estate tax return must be filed if the decedent's net assets exceed a specified amount at the time of his or her death. This amount was $275,000 in 1983, $325,000 in 1984, $400,000 in 1985, $500,000 in 1986, and $600,000 in 1987 and subsequent years. (It is important to remember that the decedent's estate for federal estate tax purposes may be different from the decedent's estate for state death tax purposes.) The federal estate tax is a graduated tax. Maximum estate tax rates are currently 55 percent (but estates over $10,000,000 may pay an additional 5 percent surtax). There is also a unified credit that can be applied to the tax payable. The credit, which reduces the tax otherwise payable dollar for dollar, was $79,300 for 1983, $96,300 for 1984, $121,800 for 1985, $155,800 for 1986, and $192,800 for 1987 and subsequent years.

Tax returns must, of course, accompany tax payments. The federal estate tax return is a long and highly complex form, requiring a great deal of time both in assembling the necessary information and in preparing the return. There are important questions that must be answered by the executor as well as available options that can result in considerable tax savings to the estate, and with which the executor must be familiar. Before listing the assets on the return, the executor must first decide on the value of the assets at the time of death. For cash or listed securities, the value of the asset is fixed. However, in determining the value of a business interest or of real estate, it is first necessary to have the properties in question appraised. Appropriate parallels should then be drawn between similar assets, so that a valuation can be arrived at that will keep taxes to a minimum, but will also be acceptable to the government as a fair representation of the market value of the properties as of the date of the decedent's death.

The executor has the choice of using the value of property as of the date of death or selecting the alternate valuation date value. This simply means valuing the assets in the estate at a date 6 months following the decedent's death. Alternate valuation would be advantageous in the event that the value of the property had fallen during that period, and this is a very important decision on the part of the executor.

There are also certain types of closely held business property and farm property that may qualify for specific tax advantages because of the nature of the property. The executor should be aware of these special elections as well as other important valuation rules and should use them to the best advantage of the estate and its beneficiaries.

Another very important tax-saving device is the marital deduction. Under prior law the estate of a decedent received a deduction for any property left to the decedent's spouse in a qualified manner in an amount equal to the greater of one-half of the decedent's adjusted gross estate or $250,000. Under current law, it is now possible to transfer an unlimited amount of money and/or property to a surviving spouse who is a U.S. citizen, outright or in trust, and not pay any federal estate tax. It is even possible to provide that the surviving spouse will receive only the income from that property, with the remainder passing at death to some third party, such as the couple's children. (Under prior law, this would have caused a loss of the marital deduction.) Prompt action on the part of the executor, though is essential if this enhanced flexibility is to be secured. Still other choices and elections must be made by executors to fully maximize the almost unlimited tax-saving potential of current law.

Federal estate taxes are due 9 months from the date of death. There are serious penalties if the return is not filed promptly or if an extension is not requested within a specified time period. In certain circumstances, there are options available to an executor that will extend the time period for the payment of all or a portion of the federal estate tax. If the estate qualifies, no payment of the tax is required for 4 years (although interest at an extremely favorable rate is payable during this time). The executor can then pay the tax due (plus interest) in up to ten annual installments. This can stretch out the payments for up to 14 years.

The executor is responsible for knowing all of these dates and taking advantage of all options and elections. Courts have held that where the untimely filing of federal estate tax returns resulted in a loss to the estate, the executor was personally responsible. There are many cases where beneficiaries have attempted to surcharge executors for their failure to take advantage of tax saving and expense-saving opportunities.

In many cases there are other taxes to be paid and other forms to be filed. For example, income taxes have to be paid on the income that the decedent earned prior to his death. Tax also has to be paid on the income generated from the assets in the estate. Options are available to the executor in regard to the timing of the estate's income tax return, and the executor should make this determination after a thorough review of the entire tax picture of the decedent, the estate, and the beneficiaries.

There is also a federal (and in some cases a state) gift tax, the returns for which would have been filed by the decedent in most cases. The executor should review any transfers made by the decedent prior to his death and make a determination as to whether any gift taxes are due. If so, the appropriate gift tax returns should be filed. Thus an executor has to be aware of the recent changes in the gift tax laws as well as the changes in the state and income tax provisions.

DISTRIBUTING REMAINING ASSETS

Once an executor has assembled the decedent's assets and paid appropriate debts, expenses, and taxes, he must distribute any remaining assets according to the decedent's will or under state intestacy laws. In the case of a very small estate where the spouse might be the executor and sole beneficiary, distribution can be accomplished by turning the property over to the beneficiary and accepting a "receipt and release" to the executor of any liability to the beneficiary. However, while this is certainly the most expedient and inexpensive way of concluding an estate, the executor may remain liable for any unpaid debts and for outstanding taxes and may be responsible for any number of other problems that might arise.

If the executor wishes to be formally discharged from his duties, responsibilities, and liabilities, then it is necessary to prepare a final account of administration. Unpaid creditors and beneficiaries are given notice of the filing of the account. In the event that there are charitable gifts in the will, the notice must be sent to the attorney general or other appropriate official appointed to protect the interests of the charities. On the date of the audit, those persons having any objections appear and are given the right to a further hearing, if necessary, to present their position to the court. When the court is satisfied that all of the procedures in handling the estate have been complied with, then the account is approved, a formal schedule of distribution is presented and approved, and the executor distributes the assets to the beneficiaries and is discharged from his responsibilities. When trusts have been established in the decedent's will, assets are transferred from the executor to the trusts so that these trusts can be immediately implemented if assets have not already been so transferred.

Complications in making distribution often occur because the people mentioned in the decedent's will are not all available to take distribution, or assets that are supposed to pass to named beneficiaries are not in the decedent's estate at the time of his death, or are there in different form. For example, if a decedent leaves his estate equally to his two brothers, and subsequent to the writing of the will but prior to his death the two brothers die, with one leaving two children and the other survived solely by his wife, how should the executor distribute the proceeds? The answer would depend upon an interpretation of the decedent's will, or the law of the state of domicile, or perhaps a combination of both.

Further complications arise when a decedent has bequeathed specific assets that are no longer in his estate at the time of his death. For example, bequests of "all my money in my savings account at XYZ Bank to my brother" and "all of my stock certificates to my sister" would be complicated if, before his death, the decedent had closed out his bank account and used part of the funds to purchase securities and part to purchase an automobile. In any event, if the executor made distribution in any contested situation without court approval, the executor could be held personally responsible if it was later determined that the distribution was improper.

Of course, the executor must make distribution promptly, unlike the tardy executrix who one court felt unreasonably and intentionally withheld distribution of the funds to her sisters, under the will of their mother, and was charged with interest at the legal rate during the period of the delay.

SUMMARY

Being an executor is a serious business. In addition to having to understand incredibly complex state and federal tax laws, the executor must also be accountable to the decedent's family, his beneficiaries if they are not members of his family, his creditors, his business associates, various branches of government for the myriad of taxes for which the executor is responsible, and finally to the court for the proper performance of his duties. It is for these reasons that the use of a corporate fiduciary should be considered (as sole or coexecutor) by every estate owner.

CHECKLIST OF EXECUTOR'S PRIMARY DUTIES

1. Probate of will.
2. Advertise Grant of Letters.
3. Inventory of safe deposit box.
4. Claim for life insurance benefits — obtain Form 712 from insurance company
   a. Consider mode of payment.
5. Claim for pension and profit-sharing benefits.
   a. Consider mode of payment.
   b. Obtain copies of plan, IRS approval and beneficiary designation.
6. Apply for lump sum Social Security benefits and V.A. benefits.
7. File Form 56 — Notice of Fiduciary Relationship.
8. Open estate checking and savings accounts.
9. Write to banks for date of death value.
10. Value securities.
11. Appraisal of real property and personal property.
12. Obtain 3 years of U.S. individual income tax returns and 3 years of cancelled checks.
13. Obtain 5 years financials on business interest plus all relevant agreements.
14. Obtain copies of all U.S. gift tax returns filed by decedent.
15. Obtain evidence of all debts of decedent and costs of administering estate.
16. Were any of decedent's medical expenses unpaid at death?
17. Has the estate received after death income taxable under Section 691 of the IRC?
18. Prepayment of state inheritance tax — check state law to determine if permissible and advantages and if so, the applicable deadlines.
19. Consider requesting prompt assessment of decedent's U.S. income taxes.
20. File personal property tax returns — due February 15 of each year estate in administration.
21. File final U.S. and state individual tax return (IRS Form 1040) — due April 15 of the year after the year in which death occurs and gift tax returns — due by time estate tax return due.
22. Is the estate subject to ancillary administration?
23. Are administration expenses and losses to be claimed as an income or estate tax deduction?
24. Obtain alternate valuation date values for federal estate tax return.
25. Payment of U.S. estate tax with flower bonds — must be tendered to Federal Reserve with Form within 9 months of death.
26. Consider election of extension of time to pay U.S. estate or generation-skipping transfer tax (Sections 6161 or 6166) — must be filed on or before due date of U.S. estate tax returns including extensions.
27. Consider election to defer payment of inheritance tax on remainder interests — where permitted, determine deadline for election.
28. Consider election for special valuation of farm or business real estate under IRC Section 2032A — must be made with timely filed U.S. estate tax return.
29. Elect (or do not elect) to qualify certain terminable interest property for marital deduction.
30. Ascertain if credit for tax on prior transfers is allowable.
31. File inheritance and federal estate tax return — federal due within 9 months of death — extensions may be requested — check local state law for due date and possible extensions.
32. File inventory — check local state law for requirements and due date.
33. Consider requesting prompt assessment of U.S. estate tax return.
34. Apply for U.S. I.D. number if estate will file U.S. income tax returns.
35. File U.S. Fiduciary Income Tax Return (Form 1041) — choice of fiscal year.
36. Consider redemption under IRC Section 303.
37. Apply for tax waivers.
38. File account or prepare informal family agreement.
39. Prepare audit notices and statement of proposed distribution.
40. File schedule of distribution if applicable.

CHOOSING AN ENTITY — A CHECKLIST OF ISSUES TO CONSIDER

PROPRIETORSHIP

(1) One person owner

(2) Few employees

(3) Relatively low income

(4) Relatively low start up costs

(5) No double tax on business earnings

(6) Not possible to "time" or "split" income

(7) Administration of estate difficult

(8) Valuation freezing techniques not available

(9) Should not be operated as part of a trust

(10) No shield against personal liability

(11) Income reportable on owner's individual income tax return

(12) Not possible to borrow from available type of retirement plan (Keogh plan)

(13) Funds in Keogh plan generally not safe from creditors

(14) Generally may avoid franchise tax imposed by many states on operating as a corporation

(15) Self employment (payroll) tax now equal to total of employer and employee federal payroll tax

PARTNERSHIP & LLC

(1) Sharing of net profits

(2) Presence of loss sharing

(3) Pass through of losses

(4) Avoidance of double taxation on profits

(5) Relatively low start up costs

(6) Relatively economical operation costs

(7) Taxable years must match those of partners or members

(8) No restrictions on who can invest or number of investors

(9) Easy to convert to another form of entity

(10) No accumulated earnings tax

(11) No personal holding company tax

(12) Unlimited personal liability unless limited partnership or LLC used to protect limited partners or members

(13) Subject to "at risk" limitations

(14) Losses not deductible in excess of basis

(15) Interest deduction limits at personal level

(16) Equity received for services creates income

(17) On contribution of encumbered property, generally, only liabilities assumed by other partners or members in excess of contributing partner's basis is taxable

(18) Income splitting — wealth shifting potential

(19) IRS can reallocate income if member of family renders services without reasonable compensation

(20) Partners who render services are treated as employees for certain fringe benefit purposes but tax law typically precludes nontaxable fringe benefits for most partners or members

(21) Separate income tax return required

(22) Not possible to borrow from available type of retirement plan (Keogh plan)

(23) Funds in Keogh plan generally not safe from creditors of partner

(24) Franchise tax imposed on partnerships or LLCs by some states

Appendix B
Choosing an Entity—A Checklist of Issues To Consider

CORPORATIONS — "C"

(1) Limited liability to creditors if capital is adequate and corporate amenities observed   _____

(2) Shareholder-employees can exclude certain fringe benefits from income   _____

(3) Income taxed at corporate level subject to tax again at shareholder level on payment of dividend or on liquidation   _____

(4) Reasonableness of compensation an issue   _____

(5) Accumulated earnings and alternative minimum tax liability   _____

(6) Losses trapped at corporate level   _____

(7) Passive loss rules avoided at corporate level and deductions at corporate rates   _____

(8) Flexibility in terms of numbers of shareholders   _____

(9) Can have more than one class of stock   _____

(10) Stock can be used as compensation   _____

(11) Ability to form subsidiaries   _____

(12) Must be adequately capitalized   _____

(13) Decision making centralized through management structure   _____

(14) Possible to retain earnings without tax at personal level but taxed at corporate level   _____

(15) Dividends received exclusion   _____

(16) Low federal income tax rate on first $75,000 of income   _____

(17) 35 percent flat rate on certain professional service corporations   _____

(18) Subject to double taxation upon liquidation   _____

(19) Separate income tax returns required   _____

(20) Franchise tax imposed by many states   _____

(21) Non-calendar fiscal year end may be chosen by regular corporations, permitting some shift of income from one year to next by timing of salaries — not for personal service corporations in many circumstances   _____

(22) Possible for employees to borrow up to $50,000 from their accounts in corporate retirement plans   _____

(23) Employees' funds in corporate retirement plans generally safe from creditors   _____

CORPORATION — "S" — DIFFERENCES FROM "C" CORPORATION

(1) Restrictions on who can hold stock   _____

(2) Limits on number of investors   _____

(3) Only one class of stock (common) allowed   _____

(4) No subsidiaries possible   _____

(5) Some states do not recognize pass through of income or losses   _____

(6) Limited liability as with "C" corporation   _____

(7) Decision making centralized through management structure   _____

(8) Pass through of income, losses, and credits   _____

(9) Difficult to do estate planning since certain trusts cannot own S stock   _____

(10) Limits on type of business an S corporation can be   _____

(11) Potential for accidental or nonvoluntary termination of S election   _____

(12) Limits on employee benefits for owners   _____

Appendix C

COMPUTING THE FEDERAL ESTATE TAX

The federal estate tax is a tax on the transfer of property when a person dies. It is measured by the value of the property rights that are shifted from the decedent to others; that is, it is a tax on the right to transfer property or an interest in property, rather than a tax on the right to receive property — the basic characteristic of an inheritance tax.

It is important to recognize that the estate tax is not limited to property actually transferred by the decedent at death. To thwart tax avoidance schemes, the tax is levied on certain lifetime transfers that in essence are tantamount to testamentary dispositions and on transfers over which the decedent retained certain interests or powers.

GENERAL

Basically, the federal estate tax is computed in six stages:

(1) The *gross estate* is the total of all property in which the decedent had an interest and that is required to be included in the estate.

(2) The *adjusted gross estate* is determined by subtracting allowable funeral and administration expenses (as well as certain debts, taxes, and losses) from the gross estate. The calculation of the adjusted gross estate is primarily for the purpose of determining whether or not Section 303 redemption and/or 6166 installment payout tests can be met.

(3) The *taxable estate* is determined by subtracting from the adjusted gross estate any allowable marital deduction or charitable deduction.

(4) The *federal estate tax payable before credits* is determined as follows: (a) the *tentative tax base* is calculated by adding to the taxable estate any "adjusted taxable gifts" (essentially, this means the taxable portion of post-1976 gifts that were not already included in the decedent's gross estate); (b) the "unified rate schedule" (applicable to both estate and gift taxes) is then applied to determine the tentative tax; (c) the aggregate amount of gift tax which would have been payable with respect to gifts made by the decedent after 1976 if the tax rate schedule (IRC Sec. 2001 (c)) as in effect at the decedent's death had been applicable at the time of such gift is then subtracted from the tentative tax to arrive at the estate tax payable before credits.

(5) To determine *net federal estate tax*, the estate tax payable before credits is reduced, dollar-for-dollar, by subtracting the amount of any allowable:

(a) unified credit

(b) state death tax credit

(c) credit for foreign death taxes

(d) credit for tax paid on prior transfers

(6) Any tax imposed on "excess accumulations" is added to the tax as above computed. The tax is 15 percent of the excess of a participant's interest in all qualified plans and IRAs at death over the present value of an annuity for a term certain with annual payments equal to the limitation on excess distributions (generally $150,000) and payable for a period equal to the life expectancy of the participant immediately before death.

The resulting federal estate tax is imposed on the decedent's estate and is usually payable by the decedent's executor on the date the return is due, i.e., within nine months of the decedent's death.

Each stage mentioned above will now be examined in more detail. The form at Figure C-1.1 may be useful in following the flow of dollars from the gross estate to the net federal estate tax payable. References to the applicable line of such form will be made throughout the text. Section references in the headings are to Code sections.

ASCERTAINING THE GROSS ESTATE (LINE 1)

The total of the value of the following (as of the appropriate valuation date) equals the gross estate for federal estate tax purposes:

(1) property owned outright;

Appendix C
Computing the Federal Estate Tax

Figure C1.1

minus	*STAGE 1*	(1) Gross Estate	_____
		(2) Funeral and administration expenses (estimated as _____ % of _____)	_____
		(3) Debts and taxes	_____
		(4) Losses	_____
		Total deductions	_____
equals			
	STAGE 2	(5) Adjusted gross estate	_____
minus			
		(6) Marital deduction	_____
		(7) Charitable deduction	_____
		Total deductions	_____
equals			
	STAGE 3	(8) Taxable estate	_____
plus			
		(9) Adjusted taxable gifts (post-1976 lifetime taxable transfers not included in gross estate)	_____
equals			
		(10) Tentative tax base (total of taxable estate and adjusted taxable gift)	_____
compute			
		(11) Tentative Tax	_____
minus			
		(12) Gift taxes which would have been payable on post-1976 gifts	_____
equals			
	STAGE 4	(13) Estate tax payable before credits	_____
minus			
		(14) Tax credits	
		(a) Unified credit _____	
		(b) State death tax credit _____	
		(c) Credit for foreign death taxes _____	
		(d) Credit for tax on prior transfers _____	
		Total reduction _____	
equals			
	STAGE 5	(15) Net federal estate tax payable	_____
plus			
	STAGE 6	(16) 15% tax on excess accumulations from qualified plans and IRAs	_____
equals			
		(17) TOTAL FEDERAL ESTATE TAX	$_____

© 1990 Stephan R. Leimberg

The Tools and Techniques of Estate Planning

(2) certain property transferred gratuitously within three years of death and gift taxes paid on all gifts made within three years of death;

(3) certain lifetime transfers where the decedent retained the income or control over the income from the property transferred;

(4) certain gratuitous lifetime transfers where the transferee's possession or enjoyment of the property is conditioned on surviving the decedent;

(5) gratuitous lifetime transfers over which the decedent retained the right to alter, amend, or revoke the gift;

(6) annuities or similar arrangements purchased by the decedent and payable for life to both the annuitant and to a specified survivor (joint and survivor annuities);

(7) certain jointly held property where another party will obtain the decedent's interest at death by survivorship;

(8) general powers of appointment (a power so large that it approaches actual ownership of the property subject to the power);

(9) life insurance in which the decedent possessed incidents of ownership (economic benefits in the policy) or which was payable to or for the benefit of the decedent's estate.

(10) QTIP in the estate of the surviving spouse.

(1) Property Owned Outright (§2033)

All property owned by an individual at the time of death valued on the applicable valuation date is includable in the computation of the gross estate. This section of the tax law causes property to be includable if (a) it was beneficially owned by the decedent at the time of his death and (b) it was transferred at death by the decedent's will or by state intestacy laws. But because the tax is levied on the transmission of property at death, the measure of that inclusion is the extent to which the property interest passes from the decedent to an heir, legatee, or devisee. Regardless of how much the decedent owned during lifetime, property interests are includable only to the extent such rights are passed on to some other party at the estate owner's death.

All types of property owned by a decedent outright at death, whether real or personal property (both tangible and intangible) are includable. This means that intangible personal property such as stocks, bonds, mortgages, notes, and other amounts payable to the decedent are includable in the gross estate, as well as tangible personal property such as a decedent's jewelry and other personal effects.

However, decedent must possess more than the bare legal title to property before it can be includable in the estate. For example, if under state law the decedent was the trustee of property or was a "strawman" owner and had no beneficial interest in the property, no part of such property would be includable in the estate. So if the president of a corporation signed as owner of a life insurance policy on his life but all premiums were paid by the corporation, the policy was carried and treated as a corporate asset on its books, and the corporation was named beneficiary, the proceeds should not be includable as insurance in his estate (he would be considered a mere nominal owner).

Furthermore, the decedent's gross estate will include the value of his share of certain property held in concert with others. For instance, if an individual holds property as a tenant in common with another person, the decedent's share will be includable as property owned at death. Similarly, the value of the decedent's share of community property will be included in his estate.

It is important to note that no inclusion is required for property in which the decedent's interest was obtained from someone else and was limited to lifetime enjoyment; i.e., an interest that terminated at the decedent's death and that the decedent had no right to transmit at death will not be included. So if Brett gives Eric the right to live in Brett's home in Miami for as long as Eric lives (and nothing more), the value of that home will not be includable in Eric's estate. On the other hand, if Brett had given Eric's wife, Pat, the house in Miami for her lifetime and the remainder to Eric, and Eric dies before Pat, Eric's gross estate will include the value of his remainder interest, since it does not terminate at his death. An interest will be includable even if it is limited, contingent, or extremely remote as long as it does not end when the decedent dies. (Of course, the contingency or remoteness of the interest will affect its valuation.)

The right to future income earned but not received prior to a decedent's death is a property interest that will be includable in the decedent's estate. Future income rights include bonuses, rents, dividends, interest payments and the decedent's share of any post-death partnership profits earned but not yet paid at death. The right of a life insurance agent to receive renewal commissions is a prime example of entitlement to future income. Such rights, as of the date of death or the alternate valuation date, whichever is applicable, are generally considered property owned outright and must be included in the decedent's gross estate. The income tax term for such right is "income in respect of a decedent" and a special income tax deduction to the extent of the estate tax attributable to the "income in respect to a decedent" is allowed under IRC Section 691.

(2) Certain Property Transferred Gratuitously Within Three Years of Death (§2035)

The general rule is that gifts (transfers for less than full and adequate consideration in money or money's worth) made within 3 years of death are not, with certain exceptions, includable regardless of the size of the gift or the manner in which it is made. There are two major classes of exemptions:

The first class of exceptions to that general rule is a transfer of an interest in property which is included in the value of the gross estate under Code section 2036 (transfer with retained life estate), 2037 (transfer taking effect at death), 2038 (revocable transfer), 2042 (life insurance) or would have been included under any of such sections if such interest had been retained by the decedent. For example, inclusion is still required to the extent the transfer by the insured within 3 years of death was "with respect to a life insurance policy."

When testing to see if a decedent's estate qualifies for a Code section 303 stock redemption, a Code section 6166 installment payout of estate tax, or special use valuation under Code section 2032A (the second class of exceptions), property given away within 3 years of death may be brought back into the gross estate. Even though, for purposes of computing the estate tax, a transfer within 3 years of death would not be brought back, it would be "brought back" in to see if the decedent's estate would qualify under the 303 (or 6166 or 2032A) tests. In qualifying for the section 6166 election, the "more than 35% of adjusted gross estate" requirement (see chapter 8) is met only if the estate meets such requirement both with and without application of the three-year inclusion rule of Code section 2035.

(3) Gratuitous Lifetime Transfers Where the Decedent Retained the Income or Control over the Income (§2036)

If an estate owner, during lifetime, transferred property as a gift, the value of that property will be includable in the donor's gross estate if the donor retained, for the donor's life (or for a period incapable of being determined without referring to the date of the donor's death or for a period that does not in fact end before the donor's death):

(a) a life estate;

(b) the possession, enjoyment, or right to income from the property; or

(c) the right to specify who will possess or enjoy either the property itself or the income it produces.

For example, Carolyn transfers stock in Texas Electric Company to a trust. She provides that the income from the trust is payable to herself for life and that the corpus will then pass to her daughter. The Texas Electric Company stock would be includable in Carolyn's estate, since she has retained a life estate.

The rationale for including this type of lifetime transfer is that the right to enjoy or control property or designate who will receive the property or its income is characteristic of ownership. Therefore, a transfer subject to this type of retained right is—to an important degree—essentially an incomplete disposition. Since the donee's possession or enjoyment of the property cannot begin until the decedent dies and "transfers" the retained interest, the donor will continue to be treated as owning the property.

(4) Gratuitous Lifetime Transfers Conditioned On Surviving the Decedent (§2037)

Property must be included in a decedent's gross estate if the lifetime gift the decedent made is contingent on the donee's surviving the decedent. If the donee can obtain possession or enjoyment through ownership only by being alive at the time the donor dies, and the donor retained a significant (more than 5% chance) right to regain the property personally (either while living or through the right to dispose of it by will or intestacy at death), the value of the property transferred (not the value of the interest retained) will be includable. This is often called the "But if...back to..." Code section. Why? Because it will not be operative unless the transferring document provides wording to the effect of: *"But if* the donee does not survive the donor, the property comes *back to* the donor."

The right to regain the property is called a "reversionary interest." To cause inclusion, the actuarial value of the transferor's reversionary interest must be significant. Stated more precisely, the right to regain the property (or the right to dispose of it) must be worth actuarially more than 5 percent of the property's value.

For example, during his lifetime, Stuart transferred property to his wife, Mona, for her lifetime. Upon Mona's death, the property was to return to Stuart if he was living. If he was not living, the property was to go to Stuart's daughter, Ellen. Stuart dies before Mona. Stuart's daughter can obtain the possession or enjoyment of the property only if she survives Stuart. If she is not alive at the time Stuart dies, neither she nor her heirs will receive any interest in the property. Stuart retained a reversionary interest under the original transfer. If

Stuart's reversion is worth more than five percent (5%) of the value of the property he placed in trust, the value of the remainder interest will be includable in Stuart's estate. Such a transfer is includable because it is considered to be, in substance, a substitute for disposing of the property by will.

(5) Gratuitous Lifetime Transfers in Which the Decedent Retained the Right to Alter, Amend, or Revoke the Gift (§2038)

If the decedent made a transfer of property during lifetime but retained a power (alone or together with others) to alter, amend, revoke, or terminate the gift, the value of property subject to that power (not the entire value of the transfer of property) will be included in the gross estate.

The courts have interpreted this provision broadly and the mere power retained by the donor to vary the timing of when a beneficiary will receive an interest (even if the beneficiary cannot forfeit the interest) will cause inclusion. Furthermore, if the donor has retained any of such forbidden powers, inclusion is required even if the donor holds those powers in his capacity as trustee and cannot regain the property or personally benefit from it in any way. (The capacity in which the power is held is irrelevant.) The provision is so broad that the mere retention and possession of such power is all that is required; the donor-decedent does not have to have the physical or mental capacity to use it.

(6) Annuities or Similar Arrangements Purchased by the Decedent and Payable for Life to Both the Annuitant and Specified Survivor (§2039)

If there is an annuity (or similar payment) payable as a result of the recipient's surviving the decedent and if the payment is made under a contract that also provided the decedent with a payment (or a right to a payment) for life (or for a period which did not in fact end before death or for a period which cannot be ascertained without referring to death), the value of that income right is includable in the decedent's gross estate. The value of the survivorship interest in a commercial annuity is the amount that the same insurance company would charge for a single annuity on the survivor at the time of the first annuitant's death. The value of a survivorship private annuity is determined using government valuation tables. For example, Steve purchased a private annuity that would pay him $20,000 a year for life and upon his death would pay his wife, Jayne, $10,000 a year for as long as she lives. If Steve died before Jayne, the present value of future annuity payments to Jayne would be includable in his gross estate. Using the government valuation tables reproduced in Appendix D (Table S), if Jayne were age 55 when Steve died and a 10.6 percent discount rate was applicable, the annuity would have a present value at that time of $78,999.

This inclusion provision applies not only to commercial joint and survivor annuities but also to certain other types of payments made under a contract or agreement to the survivor(s) of the decedent.

The general rule stated above is subject to three qualifications. First, contracts (such as a life annuity) that provide payments to the decedent and end at death are not subject to this provision since they are not capable of "death time" transmission; i.e., there is no transferable interest.

Second, to the extent the survivor or anyone other than the decedent furnished part of the original purchase price, that portion of the survivor's annuity will not be included in the decedent's gross estate. So if the survivor paid one-third of the initial premium, only two-thirds of the value of survivor's income interest would be includable. If the decedent's employer furnished all or part of the purchase price, that contribution is treated as if it were made by the decedent.

Where the death proceeds of a life insurance policy are taken under a settlement option, they are considered life insurance proceeds rather than an annuity and are not taxed according to annuity rules.

(7) Jointly Held Property Where Another Party Will Obtain the Decedent's Interest at Decedent's Death by Survivorship (§2040)

There are two rules that affect the estate taxation of property held jointly with the right of survivorship. The first is the "50-50 rule." It provides that only 50 percent of certain property titled and held jointly by the decedent and spouse with rights of survivorship, or as tenants by the entirety, will be includable in the decedent's estate—regardless of the size of his contribution (in fact, even if contribution of more than half can be proven by the survivor, this rule must be used).

For example, if Stan and his wife, Shelley, purchase 100 shares of AT&T for $50,000 and hold the property as joint tenants with rights of survivorship, even if the entire contribution was made by Stan from his salary, only 50% will be included in his estate. If the stock is worth $120,000 at that time, $60,000 will be included in his estate.

This 50-50 rule applies to both real and personal property regardless of how it was acquired or when it was purchased.

But it can be used only in the case of a joint tenancy between spouses (and only between spouses) or a tenancy by the entirety (and if joint interest was created after 1976).

The "percentage-of-contribution rule" (also known as the "consideration-furnished rule") is the second rule that affects the estate taxation of property held jointly with the right of survivorship and is used where the 50-50 rule does not apply. Essentially, this provision measures the estate tax includability of jointly held property with survivorship rights by referring to the portion of the purchase price attributable to the decedent's contribution.

Actually, the rule is that jointly held property is includable in the estate of the first joint owner to die, except to the extent the survivor can prove contribution (out of funds other than those acquired by gift from the decedent). So if the survivor can prove contribution of one-third of the original purchase price, only two-thirds of the value of the jointly held property will be includable in the decedent's estate. If the survivor can prove contribution of two-thirds of the original purchase price, only one-third would be includable in the decedent's estate.

Assume Stan and his son Bill purchased 200 shares of stock for $100,000. Bill contributes $60,000. At Bill's death, 60 percent of the value of the stock at that time is includable in Bill's estate. If the stock has an estate tax value of $120,000, $72,000 (.60 x $120,000) would be includable.

(8) General Powers of Appointment (§2041)

When a power of appointment (the right to say who is to receive property in trust) is so extensive that it approaches actual ownership of the affected property, property subject to the power will be includable in the gross estate of the person who holds the power. Such property will be includable in a decedent's gross estate regardless of whether the power could be exercised at death or only during lifetime.

Inclusion of property over which a decedent held a general power of appointment will be required in certain circumstances even if the power is "released" (formally given up) or in some cases if the power is allowed to "lapse" (fails through the lack of use).

Likewise, the lifetime exercise or release of a general power is often treated as if the decedent made a lifetime transfer of the property subject to the power. So if the exercise (or release) is made within three years of the decedent's death, it will (to the extent that a gift tax return was required to be filed) be brought back into the computation of the gross estate.

(9) Life Insurance in Which the Decedent Possessed Incidents of Ownership or Which Was Payable to or for the Benefit of the Decedent's Estate (§2042)

If a decedent dies possessing any incidents of ownership in a life insurance policy on his life, regardless of the identity of the beneficiary, the proceeds will be includable in the decedent's gross estate. The term "incidents of ownership" refers to the right to benefit from the policy (or decide who is to enjoy the benefit) in an economic sense. For example, if an insured had the right to name a policy beneficiary, surrender a policy, or borrow its cash value, the insured would be enjoying the economic benefits of a policy.

Almost any meaningful ownership attribute in the policy held by the decedent will cause the entire proceeds to be includable in the gross estate. This is true regardless of how the decedent obtained the ownership rights or whether the use of such powers could directly or indirectly benefit the decedent. Mere possession of the ownership right at death (not the capacity to utilize the power) is all that is required to cause inclusion.

A decedent's gross estate will also include the proceeds of any policy payable to his executor or for the benefit of the decedent's estate—whether or not the decedent had retained any incidents of ownership in the policy at death. Therefore naming the insured's estate or executor either the direct or indirect beneficiary (such as naming a trustee beneficiary and requiring the use of trust assets to satisfy estate obligations) will cause inclusion of the proceeds—even if the insured possessed none of the incidents of ownership in the policy.

Corporate owned life insurance is includable in a decedent's estate if he owned more than 50 percent of the corporation's stock at his death, but only to the extent it is payable to a party other than the corporation or its creditors. Assume Chuck Heikenen owned 60 percent of the CH Corporation. The corporation owned a $1,000,000 policy on Chuck's life. If the $1,000,000 were payable to the corporation, it would push up the value per share of the stock included in Chuck's estate. But if the $1,000,000 were payable to Chuck's brother, the entire $1,000,000 would be includable. (The IRS would probably also claim that the distribution constituted either a dividend or deferred compensation and apply income tax to the distribution as well.)

(10) Assets Which Have Qualified for QTIP (Qualified Terminable Interest Property) Treatment and Must Be Included in the Surviving Spouse's Estate (§2044)

If a marital deduction (either gift or estate tax) was allowed for the transfer of property in which the decedent had a qualifying income for life, such property must be included in the decedent's gross estate. For instance, if $1,000,000 deduction was allowed at Sam's death to his estate for property left to his wife, Sadie, at Sadie's death the value of such property at the time of her death will be included in her estate.

So if an election to have qualified terminable interest property qualify for the estate tax marital deduction (or the gift tax marital deduction) is made, the value of that property in the estate of the first spouse to die (or for gift tax purposes) will be included in the estate of the surviving spouse — unless that spouse made a lifetime transfer of his "qualifying income interest for life" (which would have resulted in a gift subject to gift tax).

The Date Assets Are Valued. Generally, federal estate taxes are based on the fair market value of the transferred property as of (a) the date the decedent died, or (b) an "alternate valuation date," six months after the date of the decedent's death. (This optional valuation date is designed to alleviate hardship where there is a sudden and sharp decline in the value of the estate's assets). The executor can choose either date but must value all assets using the chosen date. The election must be made at the time a timely return is filed. Generally this means within nine months of the decedent's death but could be longer if the time to file is extended by the IRS.

If property is distributed, sold, exchanged or otherwise disposed of within six months after the decedent's death and the alternate valuation date is elected, the asset disposed of will be valued as of the disposition date. Certain types of property diminish in value as time goes on; for example, the present value of an annuity reduces each time a payment is made. Any such property interest (where the value is affected by the mere passing of time) is valued as of the date the decedent died (even if the alternate valuation date is selected). An adjustment to the value of such asset is then made for any difference in value due to factors other than the mere lapse of time.

The alternate valuation election is available only in those situations in which such an election will result in a reduction of the federal gross estate size *and* in a reduction of federal estate tax liability. In other words, both the total property value in the gross estate and the federal estate tax liability must be reduced below the date of death values in order for the alternate valuation date to be elected.

This provision prevents a "no cost" step-up in basis and thwarts the executor who might intentionally value property high in order to obtain a higher income tax basis, while knowing there would be no additional estate tax to pay because of the unlimited marital deduction or because the unified credit would absorb any estate tax otherwise payable.

DETERMINING THE ADJUSTED GROSS ESTATE (LINE 5)

Once the gross estate is calculated, certain deductions are allowed in arriving at the adjusted gross estate.

Deductions allowed fall into three categories:

(1) funeral and administrative expenses;

(2) debts (including certain taxes); and

(3) casualty and theft losses.

Funeral expenses, subject to certain limitations, are deductible (see line 2). Such expenses would include interment, burial lot or vault, grave marker, perpetual care of the grave site, and transportation of the person bringing the body to the place of burial. Deductions are generally limited to a "reasonable" amount.

Administrative expenses encompass those costs of administering property that are includable in the decedent's gross estate. Essentially this means the expenses incurred in the collection and preservation of probate assets, in the payment of estate debts, and in the distributing of probate assets to estate beneficiaries. Such expenses include court costs, accounting fees, appraisers' fees, brokerage costs, executors' commissions, and attorneys' fees. These vary widely from location to location and depend on the size of the estate and the complexity of the administration problems involved.

Deductions cannot exceed the amount allowed by the laws of the jurisdiction under which the estate is being administered.

Certain administration costs may be deducted from either the federal estate tax return (Form 706) or from the estate's income tax return (Form 1041). The estate's executor has the option of electing either one (but not both).

Generally, the executor will elect to deduct attorneys' fees and executors' commissions from the return in which the tax rates are higher. This will result in an overall tax saving, but note that a deduction on the income tax return, as opposed to the estate tax return, or vice versa, may result in favoring one beneficiary or group of beneficiaries over another.

Bona fide debts, including mortgages and other liens, that were (a) personal obligations of the decedent at the time of death (together with any interest accrued to the date of death), and (b) founded on adequate and full consideration in money or money's worth are deductible (line 3). Mortgages are deductible if the decedent was personally liable and the full value of the property was includable in the estate. But if the decedent had no personal liability for the payment of the underlying debt and the creditor would look only to encumbered property for payment, the mortgage would result in a reduction in the value of the property subject to the mortgage.

In the case of community property, only those claims and expenses that were the decedent's personal obligations are deductible in full. This means an allocation of claims and expenses must be made. Since only one-half of the total community property is includable, only half of any obligation attributable to community property is deductible.

Certain taxes unpaid at the time of the decedent's death are considered debts. Three common deductible taxes are:

(1) income taxes unpaid but reportable for some tax period prior to the decedent's death;

(2) gift taxes that were not paid on gifts the decedent made sometime prior to death; and

(3) property taxes that accrued but remained unpaid at the time of the decedent's death.

The 15 percent excess accumulations tax is a deductible debt and serves to reduce the federal estate tax payable.

Casualty and theft losses incurred by the estate are deductible if the loss arose from fire, storm, shipwreck (or other casualty), or theft (line 4).

To be deductible, the loss must have occurred during the time the estate was in the process of settlement and before it was closed. Such deductions are limited in two respects: the deduction is reduced (1) to the extent that insurance or any other compensation is available to offset the loss, and (2) to the extent that a loss is reflected in the alternate valuation (an executor can elect to value assets in the estate either on the date of death or at the alternate date).

At the executor's option, losses may be deducted from either the estate tax return or the estate's income tax return. Typically, they will be taken on the return which produces the highest deduction.

DETERMINATION OF TAXABLE ESTATE (LINE 8)

The adjusted gross estate may be reduced by (1) a marital deduction, and (2) a charitable deduction.

A marital deduction (line 6) is allowed for property that (a) is included in the decedent's gross estate, and (b) passes at the decedent's death to a surviving spouse, (c) "in a qualifying manner" (in a manner that gives the surviving spouse control and enjoyment essentially tantamount to outright ownership or that meets the requirements of qualified terminable interest property (QTIP), as defined below).

The maximum amount allowable as a marital deduction for federal estate tax purposes is the net value of the property passing to the surviving spouse in a qualifying manner. Otherwise, there is no limit to the marital deduction. An individual could conceivably transfer his entire estate to his spouse estate tax free.

Under prior law most "terminable interests" (where the surviving spouse's interest would cease upon the occurrence or nonoccurrence of a particular event and the children or some other party would receive the marital property) would not qualify for the marital deduction.

Most terminable interests can qualify for the marital deduction if the executor makes the appropriate QTIP election in a timely manner. A qualifying terminable interest is one which (a) passes from the decedent, (b) gives the surviving spouse a lifetime income payable at least annually, and (c) the decedent's executor makes an irrevocable election on his estate tax return.

The election is really the price of qualifying what under prior law would not have qualified. For instance, an individual can now provide, "income to my wife for life. At her death the principal goes to my children." The election would obligate the wife's estate to pay the appropriate estate tax on the interest as if she were the ultimate recipient instead of the children. In other words, the value of the principal is included in the estate of the life tenant. (Her executor is, however, entitled to recover from the person who receives the principal the share of estate taxes generated in her estate by the inclusion of that property—unless in her will she chooses to exonerate that individual.)

A charitable deduction (line 7) is allowed for the fair market value of any type of gift to a "qualified charity" at a decedent's death. The deduction is limited to the net value of the property includable in the gross estate that is transferred to the charity. In other words, a decedent could conceivably leave his entire estate to charity and receive a deduction for the entire amount.

ESTATE TAX PAYABLE BEFORE CREDITS (LINE 13)

Once the taxable estate (Line 8) is found, adjusted taxable gifts are added to arrive at the tentative tax base. Adjusted taxable gifts are defined as the taxable portion of all post-1976 gifts. A gift is taxable to the extent it exceeds any allowable (a) annual gift tax exclusion, (b) gift tax marital deduction (similar to the estate tax marital deduction but for lifetime gifts to a spouse), (c) gift tax charitable deduction. Gifts that for any reason have already been includable in a decedent's gross estate (i.e., a gift with a retained life estate) are not considered adjusted taxable gifts.

Adding adjusted taxable gifts to the taxable estate makes the estate tax computation part of a unified transfer tax calculation. The process uses a cumulative approach, with "death time" dispositions merely being the last in a series of gratuitous transfers. The net effect of adding in adjusted taxable gifts is to subject the taxable estate at death to rates that are higher than if the computation did not consider lifetime gifts.

When adjusted taxable gifts (line 9) are combined with the taxable estate, the result is the "tentative tax base," the amount upon which the tax rates are based.

At this point, the "tentative tax" (line 11) is computed by applying the appropriate rates (see the Unified Rate Schedule for Estate and Gift Taxes, reproduced in Appendix D) to the tentative tax base. These rates are "progressive." The tax on a tentative tax base of $1,000 is $180. On $100,000, the tax is $23,800. On $1 million, the tentative tax is $345,800.

The advantage of the unified credit and graduated rates is lost to estates in excess of $10,000,000. This is accomplished in the following manner: The gift and estate tax liability for taxable transfers in excess of $10,000,000 is increased by imposing an additional 5 percent add-on tax on the excess of (a) the taxable transfer over (b) $10,000,000.

This 5 percent add-on tax ends when cumulative transfers reach $21,040,000. At that point, the 55 percent rate becomes applicable to additional amounts. So a taxable estate of $3,000,000 or more is taxed at 55 percent on any amount in excess of $3,000,000 plus a 5 percent add-on tax for the taxable estate exceeding $10,000,000 but not exceeding $21,040,000.

For example, assume an individual who died in 1995 has a taxable estate of $25,000,000. The tentative tax would be $13,390,800. This is $1,290,800 on the first $3,000,000 plus a 55 percent tax rate applied to the next $22,000,000, a tax of $12,100,000. This is further increased by a 5 percent add-on tax on $11,040,000 ($21,040,000 - $10,000,000). The total tentative tax would therefore be $13,942,800. (Note that if the flat 55 percent rate were applied to the entire $25,000,000 estate, the tax would total $13,750,000. If the $192,800 credit, which is phased out by operation of the five percent add-on tax, is then added, the result is $13,942,800.)

(The five percent rate adjustment does not affect the maximum federal estate tax rate for purposes of computing the generation skipping transfer tax (GST tax). That remains at 55 percent for generation skipping transfers.)

Since the taxable portion of gifts made after 1976 have already been added back in as adjusted taxable gifts, the gift tax generated (or that would have been generated) by such gifts is subtracted at this point (line 12).

DETERMINING THE NET FEDERAL ESTATE TAX PAYABLE

Certain tax credits are allowed as a dollar-for-dollar reduction of the estate tax. These credits (line 14) are (a) the unified credit, (b) the state death tax credit, (c) the credit for foreign death taxes, and (d) the credit for taxes on prior transfers.

A unified credit is allowed against the estate tax otherwise payable. The term "unified credit" was adopted because that credit is used as an offset against gift as well as estate taxes. However, to the extent the unified credit has been used against gift taxes, the credit available against the estate tax is, in effect, lowered. No refund is available if the credit exceeds the estate tax.

Note that the required computation process has the effect of reducing the credit by requiring the "add back" of adjusted taxable gifts. In other words, although the $192,800 unified credit in the example below does not appear to be reduced by $1,800 (the tax on a $10,000 gift which was not paid only because the decedent used $1,800 of credit), the effect is the same because of the adding back of the $10,000 worth of adjusted taxable gifts. Stated another way, adding back $10,000 of adjusted taxable gifts "restores" the $1,800 of unified credit.

For example, assume a widow died in 1995 with a $900,000 taxable estate. In 1977 she made only one taxable gift of $10,000 (after utilizing the annual exclusion). The widow paid no gift tax because $1,800 of her unified credit was applied to offset the $1,800 gift tax liability. These facts resulted in the following estate tax liability (ignoring other tax credits):

Taxable Estate		$900,000
Adjusted taxable gifts		10,000
Total		$910,000
Tax on $910,000		310,700
Less:	gift taxes paid on	
	lifetime transfers	-0-
Less:	unified credit	192,800
Tax due		$117,900

The second credit allowed against the estate tax is for any death taxes paid to a state because of property includable in the decedent's gross estate. This includes estate, inheritance, legacy, or succession taxes. The maximum credit allowable is the lower of (a) the death tax actually paid to the state, or (b) the ceiling amount provided in the maximum credit table reproduced in Appendix D. Note that the IRS table used to calculate the state death tax credit is based on the taxable estate (line 8) rather than the tentative tax base (line 11).

A credit for foreign death taxes, the third credit available, is intended to prevent double taxation. It is allowed for death taxes paid to a foreign country or a United States possession on property that is (a) included in the decedent's gross estate, and (b) situated (and subject to tax) in that country or possession. The credit is available only to United States citizens or resident aliens.

Finally, where a prior decedent (the transferor) transferred property (which was taxed at death) to the decedent and the property is includable in the present decedent's estate, a credit will be allowed for all or part of the estate tax paid by the transferor's estate on the transferred property. The present decedent must have received the property prior to death. The transferor must have died within ten years before or two years after the present decedent.

As long as the property was includable in the transferor's estate and passed from the transferor to the present decedent, the method of transfer is irrelevant; it can be by will, by intestacy, by election against the will, by lifetime gift, as life insurance proceeds, or as joint property with right of survivorship.

Interestingly enough, the law arbitrarily assumes that property that was in the transferor's estate and that was transferred to the present decedent is subject to double taxation (and is therefore entitled to the credit). There is no requirement that the property actually be in existence at the present decedent's death or if in existence subject to federal estate tax at that time.

The credit is the lower of:

(1) the federal estate tax attributable to the transferred property in the transferor's estate, or

(2) the federal estate tax attributable to the transferred property in the estate of the present decedent.

The credit is reduced by 20 percent increments every two years, and at the end of ten years after the transferor's death no credit is allowable. For example, between years two and four only 80 percent of the credit is allowable.

EXCISE TAX ON EXCESS RETIREMENT ACCUMULATIONS

After the net federal estate tax (line 15) has been determined, the excise tax on any "excess retirement accumulation" must be computed. The tax is equal to 15 percent of the individual's "excess retirement accumulation." This is defined as the excess of

1. The decedent's interest in all qualified retirement plans and IRAs

over

2. The present value of an annuity for a term certain, with annual payments equal to the limitation on distributions in effect for the year in which death occurs, and payable for a term certain equal to the individual's actuarial life expectancy immediately before his death.

For instance, assume a 65 year old who had $3,000,000 in his pension when he died and a maximum permissible retirement payout of $150,000 a year. Multiplying $150,000 by the annuity factor for a decedent 65 years old as of date of death and arbitrarily assuming a 10.6 percent discount rate (6.8598 —see valuation tables in Appendix D), the maximum present value in this hypothetical is determined to be $1,028,970. The "excess" ($3,000,000 - $1,028,970) would be $1,971,030. The 15% tax imposed on that amount would be $295,654. This tax is deductible as a debt in computing the federal estate tax.

EXAMPLES

Examples of the estate tax computation process utilizing some of the Advanced Estate Planning Course I forms prepared by The American College and used in its Advanced Estate Planning courses can be found at Figures C-1.2 through C-1.6. These are:

Example

(1) Estate tax computation — No lifetime gifts

(2) Estate tax computation — Life gift, no gift tax

(3) Comparison to Example 2 — Same facts except no lifetime gift

(4) Estate tax computation — Lifetime gift, gift tax

(5) Comparison to Example 4 — Same facts except no lifetime gift

PAYMENT OF THE ESTATE TAX

As mentioned above, the estate tax is due at the time the return is to be filed nine months after the decedent's death. A return must be filed if the gross estate exceeds $600,000, the "exemption equivalent" provided by the unified credit. The $600,000 threshold amount is lowered by the total of any adjusted taxable gifts (which have not been included in the gross estate). Therefore, in some estates filing will be required even if the taxable estate is far less than the exemption equivalent.

The "reasonable cause" extension. As stated previously, the tax is due 9 months from the date of the decedent's death.

But an executor or administrator can request that the IRS grant an extension of time for paying the tax—up to 12 months from the date fixed for the payment—if there is reasonable cause. Furthermore, the IRS could, at its discretion, upon the executor's showing of reasonable cause, grant a series of extensions which—in total—could run as long as 10 years from the due date of the original return. There is no definition of reasonable cause in the Internal Revenue Code or Regulations. However, the Regulations give illustrative examples of situations where reasonable cause will be found:

(a) a substantial portion of the estate consists of rights to receive future payments such as annuities, accounts receivable, or renewal commissions and the estate cannot borrow against these assets without incurring substantial loss;

(b) the gross estate is unascertainable at the time the tax is normally due because the estate has a claim to substantial assets that cannot be collected without litigation; or

(c) an estate does not have sufficient funds to pay claims against the estate (including estate taxes when due) and at the same time provide a reasonable allowance during the period of administration for decedent's surviving spouse and dependent children because the executor, despite reasonable efforts, cannot convert assets in his possession into cash.

The "up to 14-year closely held business interest" extension: Under IRC Section 6166, an executor may elect to pay estate tax attributable to a closely held business in 14 annual installments if the interest in the closely held business exceeds 35 percent of the adjusted gross estate. This extension is explained in detail in chapter 8.

Appendix C
Computing the Federal Estate Tax

Figure C1.2

Example 1

Herb Stevens, recently divorced, died in 1995. His gross estate is $940,000. Funeral and administrative costs total $25,000. Debts and taxes total $15,000. He made no taxable gifts during his lifetime. The estate tax liability would be computed as follows:

Determination of Cash Requirements			Herb Stevens
	(1)	Gross Estate	$940,000
Minus			
	(2)	Funeral and Administration Expenses	25,000
		(Estimated as _____% of _____)	
	(3)	Debts and Taxes	15,000
	(4)	Losses	0
		Total Deductions	40,000
Equals			
	(5)	Adjusted Gross Estate	$900,000
Minus			
	(6)	Marital Deduction	0
	(7)	Charitable Deduction	0
		Total Deductions	0 0
Equals			
	(8)	Taxable Estate	$900,000
Plus			
	(9)	Adjusted Taxable Gifts (Post '76 Lifetime Taxable Transfers not included in Gross Estate)	0
Equals			
	(10)	Tentative Tax Base (Total of Taxable Estate and Adjusted Taxable Gifts)	$900,000
Compute			
	(11)	Tentative Tax	306,800
Minus			
	(12)	Gift Taxes Payable on Post '76 Gifts	0
Equals			
	(13)	Tax Payable Before Credits	$306,800
Minus			
	(14)	Tax Credits	State death tax payable
		(a) Unified Credit	192,800
		(b) State death tax credit	27,600 27,600
		(c) Credit for tax on prior transfers	0
		(d) Credit for foreign death taxes	0
		Total Reduction	220,400
Equals			
	(15)	Net Federal Estate Tax Payable	$86,400
Plus			
	(16)	Tax on Excess Accumulations from Qualified Plans and IRAs	0
Plus			
	(17)	Total Cash Bequests	0
Equals			
	(18)	Total Cash Requirements (sum of 2, 3, State Death Tax Payable; 15, 16, and 17)	$154,000

Appendix C
Computing the Federal Estate Tax

Figure C1.3

Example 2

Mary Joe Murphey, a single woman, has a gross estate of $1,000,000 at the time of her death in 1995. Assume funeral and administrative expenses are $60,000 and debts and taxes total $40,000. She made no gifts prior to 1977 but made a $100,000 taxable gift (she gave $110,000, $100,000 of which was taxable) to her niece in December of 1977. Her gift tax liability was $23,800 on the gift but this was entirely offset by the gift tax credit. Her estate would be computed as follows:

Determination of Cash Requirements			Mary Jo Murphey — Gift of $100,000
	(1) Gross Estate		$1,000,000
Minus			
	(2) Funeral and Administration Expenses	60,000	
	(Estimated as _____ % of _____)		
	(3) Debts and Taxes	40,000	
	(4) Losses	0	
	Total Deductions	100,000	
Equals			
	(5) Adjusted Gross Estate		$900,000
Minus			
	(6) Marital Deduction	0	
	(7) Charitable Deduction	0	
	Total Deductions	0	0
Equals			
	(8) Taxable Estate		$900,000
Plus			
	(9) Adjusted Taxable Gifts (Post '76 Lifetime Taxable Transfers not included in Gross Estate)		$100,000
Equals			
	(10) Tentative Tax Base (Total of Taxable Estate and Adjusted Taxable Gifts)		$1,000,000
Compute			
	(11) Tentative Tax	345,800	
Minus			
	(12) Gift Taxes Payable on Post '76 Gifts	0	
Equals			
	(13) Tax Payable Before Credits		$345,800
Minus			
	(14) Tax Credits		
	(a) Unified Credit	192,800	State
	(b) State death tax credit	27,600	Death
	(c) Credit for tax on prior transfers	———	Tax
	(d) Credit for foreign death taxes	———	Payable 27,600
	Total Reduction	220,400	
Equals			
	(15) Net Federal Estate Tax Payable		$125,400
Plus			
	(16) Tax on Excess Accumulations from Qualified Plans and IRAs		0
Plus			
	(17) Total Cash Bequests		0
Equals			
	(18) Total Cash Requirements (sum of 2, 3, State Death Tax Payable; 15, 16, and 17)		$253,000

Appendix C
Computing the Federal Estate Tax

Figure C1.4

Example 3

If no gift had been made, Mary Jo's Federal estate tax liability is slightly less than it would have been if she gave away the $100,000. (Because her taxable estate is higher, the credit for state death taxes is increased, which in turn lowers the Federal estate tax liability. But to total liability need ($253,000 including funeral and administration expense, Federal and state taxes, and the Federal gift tax) is the same, because of the increase in state death taxes):

		Determination of Cash Requirements			Mary Jo Murphey — No Gift
	(1)	Gross Estate			$1,100,000
Minus					
	(2)	Funeral and Administration Expenses		60,000	
		(Estimated as _____% of _____)			
	(3)	Debts and Taxes		40,000	
	(4)	Losses		0	
		Total Deductions		100,000	
Equals					
	(5)	Adjusted Gross Estate			$1,000,000
Minus					
	(6)	Marital Deduction		0	
	(7)	Charitable Deduction		0	
		Total Deductions		0	0
Equals					
	(8)	Taxable Estate			$1,000,000
Plus					
	(9)	Adjusted Taxable Gifts (Post '76 Lifetime Taxable Transfers not included in Gross Estate)			0
Equals					
	(10)	Tentative Tax Base (Total of Taxable Estate and Adjusted Taxable Gifts)			$1,000,000
Compute					
	(11)	Tentative Tax		345,800	
Minus					
	(12)	Gift Taxes Payable on Post '76 Gifts		0	
Equals					
	(13)	Tax Payable Before Credits			$345,800
Minus				State	
	(14)	Tax Credits		Death	
		(a) Unified Credit	192,800	Tax	
		(b) State death tax credit	33,200	Payable	33,200
		(c) Credit for tax on prior transfers			
		(d) Credit for foreign death taxes			
		Total Reduction	226,000		
Equals					
	(15)	Net Federal Estate Tax Payable			$119,800
Plus					
	(16)	Tax on Excess Accumulations from Qualified Plans and IRAs			0
Plus					
	(17)	Total Cash Bequests			0
Equals					
	(18)	Total Cash Requirements (sum of 2, 3, State Death Tax Payable; 15, 16, and 17)			$253,000

Tax savings can be realized by making a gift large enough — even after credits — to generate a gift tax. The savings results from being able to exclude the gift tax paid from the estate tax calculation (assuming the donor lives more than three years after the gift is made, since the tax on a gift made within 3 years of death is brought back into the gross estate — even if the gift itself is not brought back into the computation).

The Tools and Techniques of Estate Planning

Appendix C
Computing the Federal Estate Tax

Figure C1.5

Example 4

Bob Hopkins, a single individual, owned property worth $2,300,000 (before the gift). He gave a taxable gift of $1,000,000 (the annual exclusion is ignored), to his friend, Flicka. The gift tax was $345,800. Bob made the gift in December 1977 and took a credit of $30,000, so the tax actually paid was $315,800. Assuming funeral and administrative costs of $100,000 and debts and taxes of $150,000, the computation of estate tax liability if he died in 1995 would be:

Determination of Cash Requirements   Bob Hopkins

	(1)	Gross Estate			$984,200
Minus					
	(2)	Funeral and Administration Expenses		100,000	
		(Estimated as _____ % of _____)			
	(3)	Debts and Taxes		150,000	
	(4)	Losses		0	
		Total Deductions		250,000	
Equals					
	(5)	Adjusted Gross Estate			$734,200
Minus					
	(6)	Marital Deduction		0	
	(7)	Charitable Deduction		0	
		Total Deductions		0	0
Equals					
	(8)	Taxable Estate			$734,200
Plus					
	(9)	Adjusted Taxable Gifts (Post '76 Lifetime Taxable Transfers not included in Gross Estate)			$1,000,000
Equals					
	(10)	Tentative Tax Base (Total of Taxable Estate and Adjusted Taxable Gifts)			$1,734,200
Compute					
	(11)	Tentative Tax		661,190	
Minus					
	(12)	Gift Taxes Payable on Post '76 Gifts		315,800	
Equals					
	(13)	Tax Payable Before Credits			$345,390
Minus					
	(14)	Tax Credits		State Death Tax Payable	
		(a) Unified Credit	192,800		
		(b) State death tax credit	19,642	19,642	
		(c) Credit for tax on prior transfers			
		(d) Credit for foreign death taxes			
		Total Reduction	212,442		
Equals					
	(15)	Net Federal Estate Tax Payable			$132,948
Plus					
	(16)	Tax on Excess Accumulations from Qualified Plans and IRAs			0
Plus					
	(17)	Total Cash Bequests			0
Equals					
	(18)	Total Cash Requirements (sum of 2, 3, State Death Tax Payable; 15, 16, and 17)			$402,590

Appendix C
Computing the Federal Estate Tax

Figure C1.6

Example 5

But if Bob had retained the $1,000,000, the computation would have resulted in an increased liability (funeral, administrative expenses, debts, and taxes are assumed to remain the same for illustrative purposes):

Determination of Cash Requirements			Bob Hopkins
	(1) Gross Estate		$2,300,000
Minus			
	(2) Funeral and Administration Expenses (Estimated as _____% of _____)	100,000	
	(3) Debts and Taxes	150,000	
	(4) Losses	0	
	Total Deductions	250,000	
Equals			
	(5) Adjusted Gross Estate		$2,050,000
Minus			
	(6) Marital Deduction	0	
	(7) Charitable Deduction	0	
	Total Deductions	0	0
Equals			
	(8) Taxable Estate		$2,050,000
Plus			
	(9) Adjusted Taxable Gifts (Post '76 Lifetime Taxable Transfers not included in Gross Estate)		0
Equals			
	(10) Tentative Tax Base (Total of Taxable Estate and Adjusted Taxable Gifts)		$2,050,000
Compute			
	(11) Tentative Tax	805,300	
Minus			
	(12) Gift Taxes Payable on Post '76 Gifts	0	
Equals			
	(13) Tax Payable Before Credits		$805,300
Minus			
	(14) Tax Credits		State Death Tax Payable
	(a) Unified Credit	192,800	
	(b) State death tax credit	103,200	103,200
	(c) Credit for tax on prior transfers		
	(d) Credit for foreign death taxes		
	Total Reduction	296,000	
Equals			
	(15) Net Federal Estate Tax Payable		$509,300
Plus			
	(16) Tax on Excess Accumulations from Qualified Plans and IRAs		0
Plus			
	(17) Total Cash Bequests		0
Equals			
	(18) Total Cash Requirements (sum of 2, 3, State Death Tax Payable; 15, 16, and 17)		$862,500

Two reasons for the increased liability are (1) the $315,800 gift tax would not be removed from the gross estate and (2) $1,315,800 more property is subject to state death taxes. This is an important reason for lifetime gifts in states with no state gift tax. The difference would be even more dramatic if the estate had grown at 10 percent or more each year.

The Tools and Techniques of Estate Planning

FORMS FOR ANALYZING ASSETS AND FOR DETERMINING FEDERAL ESTATE TAX, CASH NEEDS, AND CAPITAL AND INCOME AMOUNTS

(These forms were used by the late Herbert Levy in his private practice.)

The form titled "Analysis of Assets" (following page) is used to analyze the assets of the husband and the wife. It has the flexibility to indicate that in the estate of the second to die you can include any assets which the second to die would expect to receive from the estate of the first to die. Thus, for example, if real estate is owned jointly and would all be included in the estate of the first to die, the value of that real estate would be set forth in the column marked "Joint" across from the line titled "Real Estate" and that same amount would appear in the column marked "Probate" for the analysis of the assets in the estate of the second to die at the line marked "Real Estate". The space on the form for "notes" would cross-reference the fact that it is the same property.

The Analysis of Assets form can also be used in a manner which would merely show the assets owned by each of the two people outright before either dies and the interest that each has in jointly held property to the extent that the interest would be taxable in that person's estate if that person dies first.

The columns marked "Probate" and "Joint" specifically categorize the property. The columns marked "Life Insurance" and "Other" have specific purposes. The life insurance column is to clearly set forth and segregate life insurance which would be includable in an estate (but not in the probate estate) and the column marked "Other" would be used for property being taxed but which is not subject to probate nor is jointly held property, such as power of appointment property or Section 2035 property which has been added back because a gift of life insurance was made within three years of death.

The columns are all totalled and the totals carried over to a form which shows the federal estate tax computation. The first two columns on the federal estate tax computation would be the computation for a person dying first followed by the spouse dying second. The next two columns would be a reverse computation, that is, the spouse who is deemed to die second would now die first and the spouse who was deemed to die first would now die second. This gives you, on one piece of paper before any planning suggestions are made, the federal estate tax consequences, regardless of the order of deaths. The total cash needs of the estate are set forth on a separate page specifically for that purpose. This schedules out not only the federal estate tax but also the state death taxes, administration expenses, liabilities and cash bequests which all are a drain on estate liquidity.

The summary page is designed to show the total passing for the next generation under a present plan or alternate plans. The total assets of the second to die should not include any assets that were included in the estate of the first to die. Thus, for example, jointly held property would be eliminated from the line called "Total Assets of the Second to Die". Without such an elimination, we would be duplicating certain property, and the results would be fallacious.

The balance of the form attempts to show how much money would be available on an annual income basis to the surviving spouse after computing productive assets available to that survivor from various sources.

ANALYSIS OF ASSETS

_____ DIES FIRST

DESCRIPTION	PROBATE	JOINT	LIFE INS.	OTHER
REAL ESTATE				
STOCKS & BONDS (PUBLIC)				
STOCKS & BONDS (PRIVATE)				
MORTGAGES, NOTES & CASH				
INSURANCE — DECEDENT OWNED				
MISCELLANEOUS PROPERTY				
SECTION 2035 PROPERTY & GIFT TAX				
SECTION 2036-2038 PROPERTY				
POWER OF APPOINTMENT PROPERTY				
ANNUITIES — SECTION 2039				
INHERITANCES NOT YET RECEIVED				
TOTAL				

NOTES:

_____ DIES SECOND

DESCRIPTION	PROBATE	JOINT	LIFE INS.	OTHER
REAL ESTATE				
STOCKS & BONDS (PUBLIC)				
STOCKS & BONDS (PRIVATE)				
MORTGAGES, NOTES & CASH				
INSURANCE — DECEDENT OWNED				
MISCELLANEOUS PROPERTY				
SECTION 2035 PROPERTY & GIFT TAX				
SECTION 2036-2038 PROPERTY				
POWER OF APPOINTMENT PROPERTY				
ANNUITIES — SECTION 2039				
INHERITANCES NOT YET RECEIVED				
TOTAL				

NOTES:

CLIENT: _____   DATE: _____   FILE NO: _____

FEDERAL GROSS ESTATE:

PROBATE PROPERTY

JOINT PROPERTY

LIFE INSURANCE

OTHER PROPERTY

TOTAL FED. GROSS ESTATE

LESS: ADM. EXP. (%)

DEBTS

ADJUSTED GROSS ESTATE

LESS: MARITAL DED. (M.D.)

CHARITABLE CONTR.

PLUS: ADJ. POST 1976 GIFTS

FEDERAL ESTATE TAX BASE

TAX ON ESTATE TAX BASE

LESS: UNIFIED CREDIT

STATE DEATH TAX CR.

OTHER CREDITS

GIFT TAX PD. CR.

FEDERAL ESTATE TAX

15% EXCESS ACCUMULATED TAX

NOTES:

CASH NEEDS OF ESTATE

FEDERAL ESTATE TAXES _____

STATE DEATH TAXES _____

DEBTS & ADMIN. EXP. _____

CASH BEQUESTS _____

TOTAL CASH NEEDS OF ESTATE _____

LESS: PROBATE PROPERTY (_____)

SURPLUS (DEFICIT) _____

The Tools and Techniques of Estate Planning

CLIENT: _____ DATE _____ FILE NO. _____

SUMMARY

TOTAL ASSETS OF 1st TO DIE   _____ _____ _____

TOTAL ASSETS OF 2nd TO DIE   _____ _____ _____

CASH NEEDS OF 1st TO DIE   (_____) (_____) (_____)

CASH NEEDS OF 2nd TO DIE   (_____) (_____) (_____)

BALANCE AFTER 2nd TO DIE   _____ _____ _____

ADD LIFETIME GIFTS   _____ _____ _____

TOTAL TO NEXT GENERATION   _____ _____ _____

SURPLUS PROBATE ASSETS AFTER FIRST TO DIE   _____ _____ _____

ADD: ASSETS OF SURVIVOR   _____ _____ _____

    M.D. ASSETS TO OR FOR SURVIVOR   _____ _____ _____

    NON. M.D. ASSETS FOR SURVIVOR   _____ _____ _____

    NON TAXED ASSETS TO OR FOR SURVIVOR   _____ _____ _____

LESS: NON-PRODUCTIVE ASSETS   (_____) (_____) (_____)

TOTAL PRODUCTIVE ASSETS AFTER FIRST SPOUSE DIES   ════════ ════════ ════════

INVESTMENT RETURN AT _____ %   _____ _____ _____

ADD: QUAL. RETIREMENT PLAN PAYMENT   _____ _____ _____

    DEFERRED COMPENSATION   _____ _____ _____

    TAXABLE ANNUITY PAYMENT   _____ _____ _____

    SOCIAL SECURITY PAYMENT   _____ _____ _____

TOTAL PROJECTED ANNUAL INCOME TO
    SURVIVING SPOUSE   ════════ ════════ ════════

NOTES:

Appendix C
Forms for Analyzing Assets

This form allows for inclusion of an inflation factor in estimating estate costs where the second spouse to die is assumed to survive 10 years.

RALPH GANO MILLER, APLC

Net Value of
Estate Assets

SPH $_____

SPW $_____

CP $_____

Tot. $_____

Type of Plan:

( ) Simple Wills (all to surviving spouse)

( ) A B Trust to equalize estates and avoid "double tax"

( ) Optimum Martial Deduction (A-B or A-B-C Trust)

Death H in 19 ____ , W 10 yrs later

****

Death of Husband (H)

1. H's Adjusted Gross Estate (AGE) $_____

   Less Marital Deduction (MD) _____

   Taxable Estate $_____

   Federal Tax on Base Rate _____ = _____

   Marg Rate _____ @ ____ % _____

   Total Tentative Tax _____

2. State Death Tax Credit:

   Base Rate _____ = _____

   Marg. Rate _____ @ ____ _____

   Total _____ − _____

3. Unified Credit − _____

4. Total Tax $_____

Death of Wife (W)

1. Wife's adjusted gross estate $_____

   Plus Husband's MD _____

   Less Tax at H's death _____

   Wife's total AGE _____

   Increased by inflation

   @ ____/yr for 10 yrs =

   W's new AGE _____

2. W's New AGE $_____

   Federal Tax on Base Rate _____ = _____

   Marg Rate _____ @ ____ % _____

   Total Tentative Tax _____

3. State Death Tax Credit:

   Base Rate _____ = _____

   Marg. Rate _____ @ ____ _____

   Total _____ − _____

3. Unified Credit − 192,800

4. Total Tax $_____

TOTAL TAX OVER BOTH DEATHS:

Tax at H's death $_____

Tax at W's death _____

TOTAL _____

The Tools and Techniques of Estate Planning

COMPUTING THE FEDERAL GIFT TAX

This chapter will present an overview of the federal gift tax law and basic planning considerations in the following order:

1. Purpose, Nature, and Scope of Gift Tax Law

2. Advantages of Lifetime Gifts

3. Technical Definition of a Gift

4. Gratuitous Transfers That Are Not Gifts

5. Exempt Gifts

6. Requirements for a Completed Gift

7. Valuation of Property for Gift Tax Purposes

8. Computing the Tax on Gifts

9. Reporting of Gifts and Payment of the Tax

10. Relationship of the Gift Tax System to the Income Tax System

11. Determination of the Basis of Gift Property

12. Relationship of the Gift Tax System to the Estate Tax System

13. Factors to Consider in Selecting Appropriate Subject of a Gift

(1)
PURPOSE, NATURE, AND SCOPE OF GIFT TAX LAW

Purpose

If an individual could give away his entire estate during lifetime without the imposition of any tax, a rational person would arrange affairs so that at death nothing would be subject to the federal estate tax. Likewise, if a person could, freely and without tax cost, give income-producing securities or other property to members of his family, the burden of income taxes could be shifted back and forth at will to lower brackets, and income taxes would be saved.

The federal gift tax was designed to discourage taxpayers from making such inter vivos (lifetime) transfers and, to the extent that this objective was not met, to compensate the government for the loss of estate and income tax revenues.

Nature

The gift tax is an excise tax, a tax levied not directly on the subject of the gift itself or on the right to receive the property, but rather on the right of an individual to transfer money or other property to another. (The tax is imposed only on transfers by individuals, but certain transfers involving corporations are treated as indirect transfers by corporate stockholders.)

The gift tax is based on the value of the property transferred.

The gift tax is computed on a progressive schedule based on cumulative lifetime gifts. In other words, the tax rates are applied to total lifetime taxable gifts (all gifts less the exclusions and deductions described in Section 8) rather than only to taxable gifts made in the current calendar year.

Scope

The regulations summarize the comprehensive scope of the gift tax law by stating that "all transactions whereby property or interests are gratuitously passed or conferred upon another, regardless of the means or device employed; constitute gifts subject to tax." Almost any transfer or shifting of property or an interest in property can subject the donor (the person transferring the property or shifting the interest) to potential gift tax liability to the extent that the transfer is not supported by adequate and full consideration in money or money's worth, i.e., to the extent that the transfer is gratuitous.

Direct and indirect gifts, gifts made outright and gifts in trust (of both real and personal property) can be the subject of a taxable gift. The gift tax is imposed on the shifting of property rights, regardless of whether the property is tangible or intangible. It can be applied even if the property transferred (such as a municipal bond) is exempt from federal income or other taxes.

The broad definition includes transfers of life insurance, partnership interests, royalty rights, and gifts of checks or notes of third parties. Even the forgiving of a note or cancellation of a debt may constitute a gift.

Almost any party can be the donee (recipient) of a gift subject to tax. The donee can be an individual, partnership, corporation, foundation, trust, or other "person." (A gift to a corporation is typically considered a gift to the other shareholders in proportion to their proprietary interest. Similarly, a gift to a trust is usually considered to be a gift to the beneficiary[ies] in proportion to their interest.)

In fact, a gift can be subject to the tax (assuming the gift is complete) even if the identity of the donee is not known at the date of the transfer and cannot be ascertained.

(2)
ADVANTAGES OF LIFETIME GIFTS

Nontax-Oriented Advantages

Individuals give property away during their lifetimes for many reasons. Although a detailed discussion of the nontax motivations for lifetime giving is beyond the scope of this article, some of the reasons include (a) privacy that would be impossible to obtain through a testamentary gift, (b) potential reduction of probate and administrative costs, (c) protection from the claims of creditors, (d) the vicarious enjoyment of seeing the donee use and enjoy the gift, (e) the corresponding opportunity for the donor to see how well or how poorly the donee manages the business or other property, and (f) provision for the education, support, and financial well-being of the donee.

Tax-Oriented Advantages

The unification of the estate and gift tax systems attempted to impose the same tax burden on transfers made during life as at death. The disparity of treatment between lifetime and "deathtime" transfers was minimized through the adoption of a single unified estate and gift tax rate schedule. Both lifetime and "deathtime" gifts are subject to the same rate schedule and are taxed cumulatively, so that gifts made during lifetime push up the rate at which gifts made at death will be taxed.

Although at first glance it seemed that unification eliminated the advantage of inter vivos gifts, there are still some significant advantages.

First, an individual can give up to $10,000 gift tax free every year to each of an unlimited number of donees. This means that a person desiring to make $10,000 gifts to each of his four children and four grandchildren could give a total of $80,000 each year without gift tax liability. (This $10,000 annual gift tax exclusion is described in greater detail in Section 8.)

Since an individual's spouse can also give such gifts, up to $20,000 per year of money or other property, multiplied by an unlimited number of donees, can be transferred gift tax free. In the example above, the donor and spouse together could give up to $160,000 annually on a gift tax-free basis. In fact, one spouse can make the entire gift if the other spouse consents; the transaction can then be treated as if both spouses made gifts. This is known as "gift splitting." Split-gift provisions are also covered in Section 8.

Gift tax free transfers can translate into significant federal estate tax savings. Consider the estate tax savings potential if the amount given to the donees over the life expectancy of the donor is invested (in life insurance, annuities, mutual funds, etc.). Figure C3.1 illustrates the potential estate or generation-skipping transfer tax savings possible if a 40-year-old donor split gifts to five donees over his life expectancy.

Figure C3.1

ESTATE TAX OR GST TAX ADVANTAGE OF THE GIFT TAX ANNUAL EXCLUSION	
INPUT: DONOR'S AGE	40
INPUT: DONEES' ANNUAL AFTER-TAX RETURN ON GIFTS	0.060
INPUT: AMOUNT OF UNUSED ANNUAL EXCLUSION	$20,000
INPUT: NUMBER OF DONEES X	5
	$100,000
DONOR'S LIFE EXPECTANCY (YEARS) X	42.5
TOTAL AMOUNT OF GIFTS	$4,250,000
INPUT: DONOR'S PROJECTED ESTATE TAX OR GST TAX BRACKET X	0.55
POTENTIAL ESTATE TAX OR GST TAX SAVINGS	$2,337,500
PROJECTED VALUE OF GIFTS AT LIFE EXPECTANCY	$18,164,489
POTENTIAL ESTATE TAX OR GST TAX SAVINGS IF ANNUAL GIFTS INVESTED BY DONEES AT COMPOUND INTEREST	$9,990,469

Courtesy of NumberCruncher Software.

Appendix C
Computing the Federal Gift Tax

A second tax incentive for making an inter vivos as opposed to testamentary ("deathtime") gift is that if a gift is made more than 3 years prior to a decedent's death, the amount of any gift tax paid on the transfer is not brought back into the computation of the gross estate. In the case of a sizable gift, avoidance of the "gross up rule" can result in meaningful tax savings. ("Gross up rule" means that all gift tax payable on taxable gifts made within 3 years of death are included in calculating the value of the gross estate even if the gift itself is not added back.) For example, if an individual makes a $1 million taxable gift, the $345,000 gift tax payable on that transfer will not be brought back into the estate tax computation if the gift was made more than 3 years before the donor's death.

Third, any appreciation accruing between the time of the gift and the date of the donor's death escapes estate taxation. This may result in a considerable estate tax (as well as probate and inheritance tax) saving. If a father gives his daughter stock worth $100,000 and it grows to $600,000 by the date of the father's death, only the $100,000 value of the stock at the time of the gift enters into the estate tax computation. The $500,000 of appreciation does not enter into the computation of an "adjusted taxable gift" and thus does not push up the decedent's marginal estate tax bracket.

An excellent way of making use of this advantage is a gift of life insurance to an adult beneficiary or to an irrevocable trust for adult or minor beneficiaries more than 3 years prior to the insured's death. A $1,000,000 death benefit could be removed from a donor's estate at the cost of only the gift tax on the value of the policy at the time of the transfer (in the case of a whole life policy, usually roughly equivalent to the policy cash value plus unearned premiums at the date of the gift). If the insured lives for more than 3 years after the transfer and the premiums are present interest gifts of $10,000 a year or less, there would be no estate tax inclusion and none of the "appreciation" (the difference between the death benefit payable and the adjusted taxable gift if any at the time the policy was transferred) would be in the insured's estate.

Fourth, there are often strong income tax incentives for making an inter vivos gift. This advantage derives from moving taxable income from a high-bracket donor to a lower-bracket age 14 or over donee. For example, shifting $10,000 of annual income through the transfer of income-producing securities, real estate, or other property results in an immediate and annually recurring $2,000 savings if the property is given by a 40 percent bracket parent to a child in a 20 percent state and federal combined income tax bracket. The year-in year-out income tax savings may far exceed the estate tax savings, as Figure C3.2 illustrates.

Fifth, gifts of the proper type of assets more than 3 years prior to death may enable a decedent's estate to meet the mathematical tests for a Section 303 stock redemption, a Section 6166 installment payout of taxes, and the Section 2032A special-use valuation of farms and certain other business real property.

Sixth, no gift taxes have to be paid until the transferor makes *taxable* gifts in excess of the unified credit exemption equivalent of $600,000. Only taxable gifts in excess of a donor's unused exemption equivalent will cause a loss of income and/or capital because of gift taxes paid.

Figure C3.2

INCOME SHIFTING — CHILD 14 OR OVER		
INPUT: AMOUNT OF INVESTMENT		$100,000
INPUT: RATE OF RETURN ON INVESTMENT		0.100
INPUT: YEARS INVESTMENT LASTS		4
INPUT: PARENT'S COMBINED (FEDERAL AND STATE) TAX BRACKET		0.40
INPUT: CHILD'S COMBINED (FEDERAL AND STATE) TAX BRACKET		0.20
	PARENT	**CHILD**
INTEREST INCOME	$10,000	$10,000
TAX	$4,000	$2,000
AFTER-TAX INCOME	$6,000	$8,000
ANNUAL ADVANTAGE		$2,000
TOTAL SAVINGS OVER 4 YEARS		$10,210
TOTAL SAVINGS OVER 9 YEARS		$29,875
TOTAL SAVINGS OVER 14 YEARS		$61,545

The Tools and Techniques of Estate Planning

(3)
TECHNICAL DEFINITION OF A GIFT

Elements of a Gift

Under common law, a gift is defined simply as a voluntary transfer without any consideration. But for tax law purposes, neither the Code nor the Regulations specifically define what is meant by the term "gift." However, the regulations dealing with the valuation of gifts provide that

> Value of property transferred
>   minus
> Consideration received
>   equals
> Gift

in cases where property is transferred for less than adequate and full consideration in money or money's worth.

Note that this definition focuses on whether the property was transferred for adequate and full consideration in money or the equivalent of money, rather than turning on whether the transferor intended to make a gift. This is because Congress did not want to force the IRS to have to prove something as intangible and subjective as the state of mind of the transferor. This does not negate the importance of donative intent, but, instead of probing the transferor's actual state of mind, an examination is made of the objective facts of the transfer and the circumstances in which it was made.

Certain factors are examined by courts to determine if there was an "intent" to make a gift:

(1) Was the donor competent to make a gift?

(2) Was the donee capable of accepting the gift?

(3) Was there a clear and unmistakable intention on the part of the donor to absolutely, irrevocably, and currently divest himself of dominion and control over the gift property?

Assuming that these three objective criteria are met, three other elements must be present. There must be

(1) an irrevocable transfer of the present legal title to the donee so that the donor no longer had dominion and control over the property in question;

(2) a delivery to the donee of the subject matter of the gift (or the most effective way to command dominion and control of the gift); and

(3) acceptance of the gift by the donee.

Although all these requirements must be met before a gift is subject to tax, the essence of these tests can be distilled into the following factors (state law is examined to determine the presence or absence of these elements):

(1) There must be an "intention" by the donor to make a gift.

(2) The donor must deliver the subject matter of the gift.

(3) The donee must accept the gift.

Adequate and Full Consideration in Money or Money's Worth Defined

Sufficiency of Consideration Test

Since the measure of a gift is the difference between the value of the property transferred and the consideration received by the transferor, a $100,000 building that is transferred from a mother to her daughter for $100,000 in cash clearly does not constitute a gift. However, the mere fact that consideration has been given does not pull a transaction out of the gift tax orbit; to be exempt from the tax the consideration received by the transferor must be equal in value to the property transferred. This is known as the "sufficiency of consideration test." If the daughter in the example above had paid $60,000, the excess value of the building, $40,000, would not be removed from the scope of the gift tax. To escape the gift tax, there must be "adequate and full consideration" equal in value to the property transferred.

Effect of Moral, Past, or Nonbeneficial Consideration

Consideration is not "in money or money's worth" when the consideration is moral consideration, past consideration, or consideration in the form of a detriment to the transferee that does not benefit the transferor. The classic example is the case where a man transferred $100,000 to a widow when she promised to marry him. (Upon remarriage she would forfeit a $100,000 interest in a trust established for her by her deceased husband; the $100,000 from her fiance was to compensate her for the loss.) The Supreme Court held that the widow's promise to marry her fiance was not sufficient consideration because it was incapable of being valued in money or money's worth. Nor was her forfeiture of $100,000 in the trust sufficient consideration, since, although the widow did in fact give up something of value, the benefit of that value did not go to the transferor, her fiance.

*Consideration in Marital Rights and
Support Rights Situations*

Two issues often arise in connection with the consideration question: (1) Does the relinquishment of marital rights constitute consideration in money or money's worth? (2) Does the relinquishment of support rights constitute consideration in money or money's worth?

The Code is specific in the case of certain property settlements. It provides that transfers of property or property interests made under the terms of a written agreement between spouses in settlement of marital or property rights are deemed to be for an adequate and full consideration. Such transfers are therefore exempt from the gift tax, whether or not the agreement is supported by a divorce decree, if the spouses enter into a final decree of divorce within 2 years after entering the agreement. So, for example, if a husband agrees to give his wife $10,000 as a lump-sum settlement on divorce in exchange for her release of all marital rights she may have in his estate, the $10,000 transfer is not subject to the gift tax if the stated requirements above are met. But even in a case where the 2-year requirement was not met, a taxpayer has successfully argued that the transfer was not made voluntarily and was therefore not a gift.

A spouse's relinquishment of the right to support constitutes consideration that can be measured in money or money's worth. Likewise, a transfer in satisfaction of the transferor's minor children's right to support is made for money's worth. (But most transfers to (or for the benefit of) adult children are generally treated as gifts unless, for some reason, state law requires the transferor to support that child.)

Transfers Pursuant to Compromises or Court Orders

Consideration is an important factor where a transfer is made pursuant to compromises of bona fide disputes or court orders. Such transfers are not considered taxable gifts because they are deemed to be made for adequate and full consideration. For example, if a mother and daughter are in litigation and the daughter is claiming a large sum of money, a compromise payment by the mother to the daughter is not a gift. However, in an intrafamily situation in which the court is not convinced that a bona fide arm's length adversary proceeding was present, the gift tax will be imposed. For example, in a case where a widow "settled" with a son who threatened to "break" his father's will, the gift tax was levied.

Likewise, the gift tax can be applied even in the case of a transfer made pursuant to (or approved by) a court decree if there is not an adversary proceeding. For instance, if an incompetent's property was transferred to his mother, the transfer would be a gift even though it was approved by court

decree (assuming the incompetent had no legal duty to care for the parent).

Types of Gifts

Direct Gifts

Cash or tangible personal property is the subject of most transfers that can be reached by the gift tax law. Generally, delivery of the property itself effectuates the gift. In the case of corporate stock, a gift occurs when endorsed certificates are delivered to the donee or his agent or the change in ownership is delivered to the corporation or its transfer agent. Real property is typically given by the delivery of an executed deed.

If a person purchases a U.S. savings bond but has the bond registered in someone else's name and delivers the bond to that person, a gift has been made. If the bonds are titled jointly between the purchaser and another, no gift occurs until the other person has cashed in the bond or has the bond reissued in his name only. See Section 6, "Requirements for a Completed Gift."

Income that will be earned in the future can constitute a gift presently subject to tax. For example, an author can give his right to future royalties to his daughter. Such a gift is valued according to its present value; i.e., the gift is not considered to be a series of year-by-year gifts valued as the income is paid, but rather a single gift valued on the date the right to future income is assigned. Current valuation will be made even if, for some reason, the payments are reduced substantially or even if they cease. No adjustment is required or allowed if the actual income paid to the donee is more or less than the valuation.

Forgiving a debt constitutes a gift in nonbusiness situations. For example, if a father lends his son $100,000 and later cancels the note, the forgiveness constitutes a $100,000 gift. However, if the father lends the son $100,000 and the initial agreement is that the loan is repayable immediately upon the father's demand, no gift is made.

Some forgiveness of indebtedness, however, constitutes income to the benefited party. If a creditor tore up a debtor's note in return for services rendered by the debtor, the result would be the same as if the creditor compensated the debtor for the services rendered and then the debtor used the cash to satisfy the debt. The debtor realizes income and does not receive a gift.

Payments in excess of one's obligations can be gifts. Clearly a person does not make a gift when he pays his bills. Therefore when a person pays bills or purchases food or clothing for his wife or minor children, he is not making gifts.

Courts have allowed considerable latitude in this area. But if a father gives his minor daughter a $50,000 ring, the IRS may claim the transfer goes beyond his obligation of support. Payments made in behalf of adult children are often considered gifts. For example, if a father pays his adult son's living expenses and mortgage payments, or gives an adult child a monthly allowance, the transfer is a gift subject to tax.

In another situation, the taxpayer, pursuant to an agreement incorporated in a divorce decree, created two trusts for the support of his minor children. He put a substantial amount of money in the trusts, which provided that after the children reached 21 they were to receive the corpus. The court measured the economic value of the father's support obligation and held that the excess of the trust corpus over that value was a taxable gift. Only the portion of the transfer required to support the children during their minority was not subject to the gift tax.

Indirect Gifts

Indirect gifts, such as the payment of someone else's expenses, are subject to the gift tax. For instance, if a person makes payments on an adult son's car or pays premiums on a life insurance policy his wife owns on his life, such payments are gifts.

The shifting of property rights alone can trigger gift tax consequences. In one case an employee gave up his vested rights to employer contributions in a profit-sharing plan. He was deemed to have made a gift to the remaining participants in the plan. Similarly, an employee who has a vested right to an annuity is making a gift if he irrevocably chooses to take a lesser annuity coupled with an agreement that payments will be continued to his designated beneficiary. No gift occurs until the time the employee's selection of the survivor annuity becomes irrevocable.

Third-party transfers may be the medium for a taxable gift. For example, if a father gives his son $100,000 in consideration of his son's promise to provide a lifetime income to the father's sister, the father has made an indirect gift to his sister. Furthermore, if the cost of providing a lifetime annuity for the sister is less than $100,000, the father also has made a gift to his son.

The creation of a family partnership may involve an indirect gift. The mere creation or existence of a family partnership (which is often useful in shifting and spreading income among family members and in reducing estate taxes) does not, per se, mean a gift has been made. But if the value of the services of some family member partners is nil or minimal and earnings are primarily due to assets other than those contributed by the partners in question, the creation of the partnership (or the contribution by another partner of assets) may constitute a gift.

At the other extreme, in cases where new partners are to contribute valuable services in exchange for their share of the partnership's earnings and where the business does not contain a significant amount of capital assets, the formation of a family partnership does not constitute a gift.

Transfers by and to corporations are often forms of indirect gifts. Technically, the gift tax is not imposed upon corporations. But transfers by or to a corporation are often considered to be made by or to corporate stockholders. The regulations state that if a corporation makes a transfer to an individual for inadequate consideration, the difference between the value of the money or other property transferred and the consideration paid is a gift to the transferee from the corporation's stockholders. For example, a gratuitous transfer of property by a family-owned corporation to the father of the shareholders of a corporation could be treated as a gift from the children to their father.

Generally, a transfer to a corporation for inadequate consideration is a gift from the transferor to the corporation's other shareholders. For example, a transfer of $120,000 by a father to a corporation owned equally by him and his three children is treated as a gift of $30,000 from the father to each of the three children. (The amount of such a gift is computed after subtracting the percentage of the gift equal to the percentage of the transferor's ownership.)

A double danger lies in corporate gifts. The IRS may argue that (1) in reality the corporation made a distribution taxable as a dividend to its stockholders and (2) that the shareholders in turn made a gift to the recipient of the transfer. Since any distribution from a corporation to a shareholder generally constitutes a dividend to the extent of corporate earnings and profits, the IRS could claim that a transfer was first a constructive dividend to the shareholders and then a constructive gift by them to the donee. For example, if a family-owned corporation sold property with a fair market value of $450,000 for $350,000 to the son of its shareholders, the transaction could be considered a $100,000 constructive dividend to the shareholder-parents, followed by a $100,000 constructive gift by them to their son.

Life insurance or life insurance premiums can be the subject of an indirect gift in three types of situations: (1) the purchase of a policy for another person's benefit, (2) the assignment of an existing policy, and (3) payment of premiums. (The first two of these three situations are discussed directly below. Premium payments are discussed in Section 7.)

If an insured purchases a policy on his life and

(1) names a beneficiary(ies) other than his estate, and

(2) does not retain the right to regain the policy or the proceeds or revest the economic benefits of the policy (i.e., retains no reversionary interest in himself or his estate); and

(3) does not retain the power to change the beneficiaries or their proportionate interests (i.e., makes the beneficiary designation irrevocable)

he has made a gift measurable by the cost of the policy. All three of these requirements must be met, however, before the insured will be deemed to have made a taxable gift.

If an insured makes an absolute assignment of a policy or in some other way relinquishes all his rights and powers in a previously issued policy, a gift is made. It is measurable by the replacement cost (in the case of a whole life policy generally equal to the interpolated terminal reserve plus unearned premium at the date of the gift).

This can lead to an insidious tax trap. Assume a wife owns a policy on the life of her husband. She names her children as revocable beneficiaries. At the death of the husband, the IRS could argue that the wife has made a constructive gift to the children. In this example the gift is equal to the entire amount of the death proceeds. It is as if the wife received the proceeds to which she was entitled and then gave that money to her children.

An extension of this reasoning, which was actually (and successfully) applied by the IRS, is a case where the owner of policies on the life of her husband placed the policies in trust for the benefit of her children. Because she reserved the right to revoke the trust at anytime before her husband died, she had not made a completed gift until his death. It was not until his death that she relinquished all her powers over the policy. When the husband died the trust became irrevocable, and therefore the gift became complete. The value of the gift was the full value of the death proceeds rather than the replacement value of the policy when it was placed in trust.

(4)
GRATUITOUS TRANSFERS THAT ARE NOT GIFTS

A number of common situations do not attract the gift tax because they do not involve gifts in the tax sense. These situations fall into three basic categories: (A) where property or an interest in property has not been transferred, (B) certain transfers in the ordinary course of business, and (C) sham gifts.

The Requirement That Property or an Interest in Property Be Transferred

(1) Gratuitous Services Rendered

The gift tax is imposed only on the transfer of "property" or "an interest in property." Although the term "property" is given the broadest possible meaning, it does not include services that are rendered gratuitously. Regardless of how valuable the services one person renders for the benefit of another person, those services do not constitute the transfer of property rights and do not, therefore, fall within the scope of the gift tax.

Difficult questions often arise in this area. For example, if an executor performs the multiplicity of services required in the course of the administration of a large and complex estate, the services are clearly of economic benefit to the estate's beneficiaries. Yet since services are just that, they do not constitute a transfer of property rights. If the executor formally waives the fee (within 6 months of appointment as executor) or fails to claim the fees or commissions by the time of filing and indicates through action (or inaction) that he intends to serve without charge, no property has been transferred.

Conversely, once fees are taken (or if the fees are deducted on an estate, inheritance, or income tax return), the executor has received taxable income. If he then chooses not to (or neglects to) actually receive that money and it goes to the estate's beneficiaries, he is making an indirect (and possibly taxable) gift to those individuals.

(2) Interest-Free Loans

Does the right to use property (such as money) at no charge constitute a gift of property? Yes, the Code treats interest-free and below market rate loans as taxable gifts. It imposes a gift tax on the value of the right to use the borrowed money, the so-called "foregone interest" (see Chapter 20), generally the going rate of interest the money could earn in the given situation. (By this reasoning, giving someone the use of real estate or other property, such as a vacation home or car, at little or no rent would seem to be a gift, but the IRS has been focusing on property interest transfers rather than permitted-use cases.)

(3) Disclaimers (Renunciations)

Generally, a potential donee is deemed to have accepted a valuable gift unless he expressly refuses it. But in some cases an intended donee may decide (for whatever reason) that he does not want or does not need the gift. If he disclaims the right to the gift (refuses to take it), it will usually go to someone else as the result of that renunciation.

By disclaiming, the intended transferee is in effect making a transfer to the new recipient subject to the gift tax unless the disclaimer meets certain rules.

A disclaimer that meets those rules is called a "qualified disclaimer" and is treated for gift tax purposes as if the property interest went directly from the original transferor to the person who receives it because of the disclaimer. In other words, the disclaimant is treated as if he made no transfer of property or an interest in property to the person to whom the interest passes because of the disclaimer. This makes the qualified disclaimer an important estate-planning tool.

There are a number of requirements for a qualified disclaimer of gifted property:

(1) The refusal must be in writing.

(2) The writing must be received by the transferor, his legal representative, or the holder of the legal title to the property no later than 9 months after the later of (a) the date on which the transfer creating the interest is made or (b) the date the person disclaiming is 21.

(3) The person disclaiming must not have accepted the interest or any of its benefits.

(4) Because of the refusal, someone other than the person disclaiming receives the property interest. The person making the disclaimer cannot in any way influence who is to be the recipient of the disclaimer.

(4) Promise to Make a Gift

Although income that will be earned in the future can be the subject of a gift, the promise to make a gift in the future is not taxable even if the promise is enforceable. This is because a mere promise to make a transfer in the future is not itself a transfer. The IRS agrees, as long as the gift cannot be valued. But if the promise is enforceable under state law, the IRS will attempt to subject it to the gift tax when it becomes capable of valuation.

Transfers in the Ordinary Course of Business

(1) Compensation for Personal Services

Situations often arise in business settings that purport to be gifts from corporate employers to individuals. The IRS often claims that such transfers are, in fact, compensation for personal services rather than gifts. The IRS argues that the property transfers constitute income to the transferee rather than a gift by the transferor. In these cases the focus changes to the effect on the transferee: Has the transferee received taxable income or has he received a tax-free gift?

A payment may be taken out of the normal gift tax rules (and thus be considered taxable income to the recipient) by the Regulations, which state that "the gift tax is *not* applicable to...ordinary business transactions." An ordinary business transaction, defined as a sale, exchange, or other transfer of property (a transaction which is bona fide, at arm's length, and free from donative intent) made in the ordinary course of business, will be considered as if made for an adequate and full consideration in money or money's worth.

A situation will be considered an ordinary business transaction and not be classified as a tax-free gift to the recipient if it is "free from donative intent." This means that donative intent becomes quite important. The taxpayer-recipient, of course, would like to have the transaction considered an income tax-free gift. The IRS would reap larger revenues if the transfer were considered compensation and therefore were taxable income.

When will a payment be considered a tax-free gift to the recipient (the donor must still pay any gift taxes) rather than taxable income? A gift is deemed to have been made if the donor's dominant reason for making the transfer was detached and disinterested generosity (for example where an employer makes flood relief payments to his employees because of a feeling of affection, charity, or similar impulses) rather than consideration for past, present, or future services of the recipient employees.

A transfer is not a gift if the primary impetus for the payment is (a) the constraining force of any legal or moral duty or (b) anticipated benefit of an economic nature.

Among the factors typically studied in examining the donor's intent are

(1) the length and value of the employee's services

(2) the manner in which the employer determined the amount of the reputed gift

(3) the way the employer treated the payments in corporate books and on tax returns, i.e., was the payment deducted as a business expense? (The corporation's characterization of payment is often persuasive where the corporation makes a payment or series of pay-

ments to the widow of a deceased employee. The employer generally prefers to have such payments taxed as compensation to the employee's survivors so that the corporation can deduct payments as compensation for past services of the employee.)

In one case, a business friend gave the taxpayer a car after the taxpayer had furnished him with the names of potential customers. The car was not a gift but was intended as payment for past services as well as an inducement for the taxpayer to supply additional names in the future. In another case, however, the employer had made a payment of $20,000 to a retiring executive when he resigned. After examining the employer's esteem and kindliness, and the appreciation of the retiring officer, the court stated that the transfer was a non(income) taxable gift. Another court, in a similar case, came to the same conclusion when it found payments were made "from generosity or charity rather than from the incentive of anticipated economic benefit."

This type of issue, gift or compensation, is settled on a case-by-case basis after an analysis of the circumstances evidencing motive or intent. Usually the intrafamily transfer will be considered a gift even if the recipient rendered past services. Transfers to persons outside the family will usually be considered compensation.

(2) Bad Bargains

A bad bargain is another "ordinary course of business" situation; a sale, exchange, or other property transfer made in the ordinary course of business is treated as if it were made in return for adequate and full consideration in money or money's worth. This assumes the transaction is (a) bona fide, (b) at arm's length, and (c) not donative in intent.

There are a number of court-decided examples of "bad bargains" that have not resulted in gift tax treatment. In one case, certain senior executive shareholders sold stock to junior executives at less than fair market value pursuant to a plan arranged to give the younger executives a larger stake in business profits. The court noted that the transfers were for less than adequate consideration but stated that "the pertinent inquiry for gift tax purposes is whether the transaction is a genuine business transaction, as distinguished, for example, from the marital or family type of transaction." Bad bargains, sales for less than adequate money's worth, are made every day in the business world for one reason or another; but no one would think for a minute that any gift is involved, even in the broadest sense of the term "gift."

Another example of a "no-gift" situation would be where a group of businessmen convey real estate to an unrelated business corporation with the expectation of doing business with that corporation sometime in the future.

But the "ordinary course of business" exception has its limits; no protection from the gift tax law would be afforded where the transferor's motive was to pass on the family fortune to the following generation. In one case a father transferred property to his children at a price below the fair market value. In return he received noninterest-bearing notes rather than cash, and in the children's behalf he continued to make certain payments with respect to the property. The court found these actions showed that in reality he was not dealing with his children at arm's length. It is possible that the same result could occur if the father employed the son at a wage of $50,000 a year but the son rendered services worth only $20,000 a year. The IRS could claim that the $30,000 difference constituted a gift.

Sham Gifts

It is often advantageous for income or estate tax purposes to characterize a transaction as a gift. The taxpayer's goal is to shift the burden of income taxes from a high- to a relatively lower-bracket age 14 or older relative. But if the transfer has no real economic significance other than the hoped-for tax savings, it will be disregarded for tax purposes; i.e., if the transaction does not have meaning apart from its tax sense, it will not be considered a gift by the IRS or by the courts and will therefore not shift the incidence of taxation. For example, a well-known golfer contracted with a motion picture company to make a series of pictures depicting his form and golf style. In return the golfer was to receive a lump sum of $120,000 plus a 50 percent royalty on the earnings of the picture. But before any pictures were made he sold his father the right to his services for $1. The father, in turn, transferred the rights to the contract to a trust for his son's three children. The court held that the entire series of transactions had no tax effect and that the income was completely taxable to the golfer.

Assignments of income

Assignment of income questions are among the most common and also confusing in the tax law because they often involve inconsistent property, gift, and income tax results. For example, a person could agree to give his son one-half of every dollar he earned in the following year. The agreement might be effective for property law purposes, and the son could have an enforceable legal right to half his father's income. Gift tax law might also recognize the transfer of a property right, and the present value of a father's future income could be subject to the gift tax. Yet for income tax purposes the father would remain liable for taxes on the entire earnings.

A general agent for a life insurance company assigned renewal commissions to his wife. The wife had a property law right to the commissions. The present worth of the renewals the wife would receive was treated as a gift. Yet, the general agent was subject to income tax on the commissions as they were paid. In a similar case a doctor transferred the right to accounts receivable from his practice to a trust for his daughter. Again, the court held that as the trustee received payments from the doctor's patients, those sums were taxable to the doctor even though he had made an irrevocable and taxable gift to the trust.

Gifts of income from property meet a similar fate. For example, if a person assigns the right to next year's rent from a building to her daughter or next year's dividends from specified stock to her grandson, the transfers will be effective for property law purposes and will generate gift taxes. But the income will be taxable to the donor for income tax purposes.

Gifts of property, however, produce a more satisfactory result to the donors; if the tree (property) is given away, the fruit (income) it bears will be taxable to the tree's new owner. Thus if the donor in the examples above had given the building and the stock, gifts equal to the value of those properties would be made; and the income produced by those assets would be taxed to her daughter and grandson respectively. Likewise, if stock that cost the donor $1,000 is transferred to a donee at a time when it is worth $2,500 and is later sold by the donee for $3,000, the donee takes the donor's cost ($1,000) as his basis, and is taxed on the gain ($2,000).

(5)
EXEMPT GIFTS

A few types of gratuitous transfers are statutorily exempted from the gift tax. A qualified disclaimer, described above, is a good example. Certain transfers of property between spouses in divorce and separation situations are further examples.

Tuition paid to an educational institution for the education or training of an individual is exempt from the gift tax regardless of the amount paid or the relationship of the parties; no family ties must exist for this unlimited exclusion to apply. This means parents, grandparents, or even friends can pay private school or college tuition for an individual without fear of incurring a gift tax.

Still another exempt transfer is the payment of medical care. A donor, any donor, can pay for the medical care of a donee without making a gift. This allows children or other relatives or friends to pay the medical expenses of needy individuals (or anyone else) without worrying about incurring a gift tax.

(6)
REQUIREMENTS FOR A COMPLETED GIFT

A completed transfer is necessary before the gift tax can be applied. The phrase "completed transfer" implies that the subject of the gift has been put beyond the donor's recall, i.e., that he has irrevocably parted with dominion and control over the gift. There would be no completed gift if the donor had the power to change the disposition of the gift and thus alter the identity of the donee(s) or amount of the gift. More technically stated, if the donor can (alone or in conjunction with a party who does not have a substantial amount to lose by the revocation) revoke the gift, it is not complete.

Parting with dominion and control is a good test of completeness, but in a number of cases it is difficult to ascertain just when that event occurs. Some of the more common problem areas are (a) incomplete delivery situations, (b) cancellation of notes, and (c) incomplete transfers to trusts.

When Delivery is Complete

Incomplete delivery situations involve transfers where certain technical details have been omitted or a stage in the process has been left uncompleted. For example, no gift is made at the moment the donor gives the donee a personal check or note; the transfer of a personal check is not complete and taxable until it is paid (or certified or accepted) by the drawee or it is negotiated for value to a third person. For instance, if a check is mailed in December, received in late December, but not cashed until January of the following year, no gift is made until that later year. This is because typically the maker of a check is under no legal obligation to honor the check until it is cashed (presented for payment or negotiated to a third person for value). Likewise, a gift of a negotiable note is not complete until it is paid.

An individual on his deathbed will sometimes make a gift *causa mortis* (in anticipation of his imminent death) and then quite unexpectedly recover. Assuming that the facts indicate (1) the transfer was made in anticipation of death from a specific illness and that (2) the gift was contingent on the occurrence of the donor's death, neither the original conveyance nor the return of the property to the donor is subject to the gift tax if the transferor recovers and the transferee returns the property. A gift *causa mortis* is therefore incomplete as long as the donor is alive but becomes complete at the donor's death.

A gift of stock is completed on the date the stock was transferred or the date endorsed certificates are delivered to the donee (or his agent) or to the corporation (or its transfer agent).

Transfer of U.S. government bonds is governed by federal rather than state law. Even if state law requirements for a valid gift are met, for tax purposes no completed gift has been made until the registration is changed in accordance with federal regulations. For example, if a grandmother purchases a U.S. savings bond that is registered as payable to her and to her two children as co-owners, no gift is made to the grandchildren until one of them surrenders the bond for cash.

The creation of a joint bank account (checking or savings) constitutes a common example of an incomplete transfer. Typically, the person making a deposit can withdraw all of the funds or any portion of them. Therefore, the donor has retained a power to revoke the gift and it is not complete. When the donee makes a withdrawal of funds from the account (and thereby eliminates the donor's dominion and control), a gift of the funds occurs.

A similar situation occurs in the case of a joint brokerage account; the creation and contribution to a joint brokerage account held in "street name" is not a gift until the joint owner makes a withdrawal for his personal benefit. At that time, the donee acquires indefeasible rights and the donor parts irrevocably with the funds. Conversely, if a person calls her broker and says, "Buy 100 shares of Texas Oil and Gas and title them in joint names, mine and my husband's, with rights of survivorship," the purchase constitutes a gift to her husband. He has acquired rights that he did not have before to a portion of the stock. (No gift tax would be due in this case due to the unlimited gift tax marital deduction described below.)

Totten trusts (bank savings accounts where the donor makes a deposit for the donee (Joanne Q. Donor in trust for James P. Donee) and retains possession of the savings book) are typically revocable transfers. Here again, because the donor can recover the entire amount deposited, no gift occurs until the donee makes a withdrawal of funds.

Some property cannot conveniently be delivered to the intended donee; farm property is a good example. Where it would be difficult or impossible to make physical delivery of the gift, a gift will usually be considered completed where the delivery is as complete as possible. In one case, a father owned cattle he wished to give his minor children. The court held that the gift was complete when he branded the livestock with each child's initials even though he kept the cattle with others he owned. The court held that the father was acting as the natural guardian of the children and had done everything necessary to make a completed gift.

Real estate is transferred by executing a deed in favor of the donee. But if the donor retains the deed, does not record it, makes no attempt to inform the donee of the transfer, and continues to treat the property as his own, no transfer occurs.

Cancellation of Notes

In many cases, a transfer of property will be made and then the transferor will take back installment notes from the transferee. The transaction will be treated as a sale for income tax purposes. However, if the transferor forgives the notes, the forgiveness would be a gift.

Cancellation of notes is a frequently used technique for two reasons. First, it provides a simple means of giving gifts to a number of donees of property which is not readily divisible. Second, by forgiving the notes over a period of years, the donor could maximize the use of the $10,000 annual exclusion and unified credit discussed below in Section 8. A good example is a situation where the donor deeds real estate to her sons and takes back notes payable serially on an annual basis. Each son is required to pay his mother $10,000 per year. But when the notes become due, the donor marks the note "cancelled by gift." The gift would occur in the year each note was cancelled, as long as there is no preestablished and predetermined plan for the donor to forgive notes on a systematic basis in future years.

Note that although the annual exclusion would eliminate the gift tax consequences, in this example there is an income tax liability since the donor is actually selling the real estate to her sons. The difference between the donor's basis (cost plus or minus appropriate adjustments) and the amount she'll realize on the sale is taxable (under the installment sales rules since the notes are payable over more than one tax year).

Incomplete Gifts in Trust

Donors will sometimes transfer property to a trust but retain the right to revoke the transfer. When property is transferred to such a revocable trust, that transfer is not a completed gift. Only when the donor relinquishes all his retained control over the transferred property (i.e., when the trust becomes irrevocable) is a completed gift made.

Tax liability is measured by the value at the moment the gift becomes complete rather than at the time of the transfer. This can have harsh tax consequences. For example, if the donor retains the power to alter the interests of the trust beneficiaries, even if he cannot exercise any powers for his own benefit, the transfer is not complete.

Assume, for instance, that the donor transfers stock to a trust for his two children and three grandchildren. The income of the trust is payable to the donor's children for as long as they live. Then the remainder is payable to his grandchildren or their estates. If the donor retains the power to vary the amount of income his children will receive or reach into corpus to enhance their security, the gift is incomplete. But the gift will be complete when the donor relinquishes control. If that happens when the stock has substantially increased in value, as is often the case, the gift tax payable by the donor may also substantially increase.

GRATs (grantor retained annuity trusts) and GRUTS (grantor retained unitrusts) are based on the fact that gift tax liability is measured by the property's value at the moment the gift becomes complete. By making a gift to an irrevocable nonreversionary trust, but reserving an annuity or unitrust interest for a specified period of years, an individual reduces the value of the gift.

When the property is ultimately transferred, many years after the grantor contributed the property to the trust, it may have appreciated significantly. In essence this "leverages" the annual exclusion and the unified credit, since the date of transfer value is typically much greater than the value of trust assets at the inception of the trust.

(7)
VALUATION OF PROPERTY FOR GIFT TAX PURPOSES

Valuation is the first step in the gift tax computation process. Only after the property is valued can the applicable annual exclusion and various deductions be applied in arriving at the amount of the taxable gift and the ultimate gift tax. (See Chapter 42 regarding "Valuation Planning.")

The value of the property on the date the gift becomes complete is the amount of the gift. Value, for gift tax purposes, is defined as "the price at which the property would change hands between a willing buyer and a willing seller, neither being under any compulsion to buy or to sell, and both having reasonable knowledge of relevant facts."

Although the provisions of the gift tax law on valuation parallels the estate tax law in many respects, there is one major difference: property transferred during lifetime is valued for gift tax purposes on the date the gift is made. No alternate valuation is allowed.

There are certain valuation problems unique to the gift tax law. These include problems associated with (1) indebtedness with respect to transferred property, (2) restrictions on the use or disposition of property, (3) transfers of large blocks of stock, (4) valuation of mutual fund shares, and (5) valuation of life insurance and annuity contracts.

Indebtedness with Respect to Transferred Property

Generally, when the subject of a gift is encumbered or otherwise subject to an obligation, only the net value of the gift, the value of the property less the amount of the obligation, is subject to the gift tax. Under this rule, which assumes the donor is *not* personally liable for the debt, the amount of the gift is the donor's equity in the property.

However, if the donor is personally liable for the indebtedness which is secured by a mortgage on the gift property, a different result occurs. In this case the amount of the gift may be the entire value of the property, unreduced by the debt. The reason for the difference is that where a solvent donor makes a gift subject to a debt and the creditor proceeds against the pledged property, the donee is, in effect, paying the donor's personal debt. In some cases this makes the donee a creditor of the donor. If the donee can then collect from the donor the amount he has paid to the donor's creditor, the donee has received the entire value of the gift rather than merely the equity.

For example, assume the donor transfers a $100,000 building subject to a $40,000 mortgage on which he is personally liable. If the donor's creditors collect the $40,000 by proceeding against the pledged building and the donee is subrogated to that creditor's rights against the donor-debtor (i.e., the donee now stands in the shoes of the creditor), the donee can collect an additional $40,000 from the donor.

A third possibility is that the donor-debtor is personally liable for the indebtedness secured by a mortgage on the gifted property, but the donee has no right to step into the creditor's shoes and recover the debt from the donor. In this case the amount of the gift is merely the amount of the donor's equity in the property. In the example above, that amount would be $60,000 ($100,000 fair market value minus $40,000 of indebtedness).

Where the donee has no right to proceed against the donor and recover the debt, actual facts must determine the result. If the donor in fact pays off the liability after transferring the mortgaged property to the donee, he is making an additional gift. But if the donee pays off the liability (or if the mortgagee forecloses), the gift was only the donor's equity.

Among the obligations that could be imposed upon a donee is a requirement that the donee pay the gift tax. This is called a "net gift." The donor has primary liability to pay the gift tax, and the donee is only secondarily liable. The donor could expressly or by implication require the donee to pay the donor's gift tax liability. If the donee is required to pay the gift tax imposed on the transfer (or if the tax is payable out of the transferred property), the value of the donated property must be reduced by the amount of the gift tax. But the gift tax computation is based on the value of the property transferred. Obviously, the two figures, the net amount transferred and the tax payable on the transfer, are interdependent. Fortunately, there is a revenue ruling formula for making the computation.

An example of a net gift and the formula are illustrated in the NumberCruncher printout below:

TRUE TAX ON A NET GIFT

INPUT:	YEAR OF GIFT	1995
INPUT:	TAXABLE GIFT	$1,000,000
	GIFT TAX ON GIFT	$345,800
	UNIFIED CREDIT	– $192,800
	TENTATIVE TAX	$153,000
TRUE TAX ON NET GIFT EQUALS:		
	TENTATIVE TAX	
	(1.00 + RATE OF TAX)	$110,072

It is important to note that, for income tax purposes, there are net gift cases which state that the donor must recognize gain where the donee pays the tax or where payment is made from the gifted property. Gain is realized by the donor for income tax purposes to the extent the gift tax paid by the donee exceeds the donor's basis for the property. It is as if the donor sold the property for an amount equal to the gift tax, realized a gain, and then gave the remaining value of the gift property to the donee.

Restrictions on the Use or Disposition of Property

Value is affected by restrictions placed on the donee's use or ability to dispose of the property received. The general rule is that most restrictive agreements do not fix the value of such property but often have a persuasive effect on price. For example, a donor gives stock to his daughter subject to an agreement between the corporation and its shareholders. Under that agreement, the corporation is entitled to purchase those shares at their book value, $30 per share, upon the retirement or death of the stockholder.

Does the existence of a restrictive agreement fix the value of the shares at book value? After all, in the example, no buyer would pay more than $30 a share while the restriction is operative. But if the stock has "use values" other than sale values (for example, if the stock paid dividends of $10 a year) it may have a fair market value in excess of $30. On one hand, the corporation's option right to purchase the stock at $30 a share limits the fair market value, but on the other hand "use values," such as the right to receive dividends, increase the fair market value.

How much the use values increase the fair market value is largely dependent on how much time is likely to pass before the corporation has an opportunity to exercise its option and on the probability of the corporation's exercising its option at that time.

In the example above, a court would probably state that the existence of a restrictive agreement would not fix the purchase price, since the circumstances requiring purchase (retirement or death) do not exist at the date of the gift. But the existence of the agreement itself is likely to have a depressing effect on the market value of the stock and result in a discounted gift tax value. (However, see discussion of Code section 2703 in Chapter 1 and Code section 2704 in Chapter 13 regarding restrictions which may be disregarded when valuing property.)

Transfers of Large Blocks of Stock

Another principle that applies to some degree to both lifetime and "deathtime" gifts is the so-called blockage rule. The blockage rule is not based on forced sale value. Instead, it attempts to value gifts of large blocks of stock based on the price the property would bring if the stock was liquidated in a reasonable time in some way outside the usual marketing channels. The marketability (and therefore the value) of a massive number of shares of stock may have a lower value than the current per share market value of the same stock because of the depressive effect if the block is dumped on the market all at once. The utility of blockage evaluation is diminished and may be inapplicable when a large block is divided among a number of donees or when gifts are spread over a number of tax years.

Valuation of Mutual Fund Shares

Mutual fund shares are valued at their net asset value, the price of the fund net of any "load" charge.

Valuation of Life Insurance and Annuity Contracts

When a life insurance policy is the subject of a gift, the value is the policy's replacement value: the cost of similar or comparable policies issued by the same company.

If the policy is transferred immediately (within the first year) after its purchase, the gift is equal in value to the gross premium paid to the insurer.

If the policy is paid up at the time it is assigned (or is a single-premium policy), the amount of the gift is the amount of premium the issuing company would charge for the same type of single-premium policy of equal face amount on the insured's life, based on the insured's age at the transfer date. (Impaired health of the insured is not considered by the Regulations, but it is possible that the IRS would argue that the adverse health of the insured at the time of the gift may affect evaluation.)

If the policy is in a premium-paying stage at the time it is transferred, the value of the gift is generally equal to (a) the interpolated terminal reserve plus (b) unearned premiums on the date of the gift.

Except in the early years of most contracts, the interpolated terminal reserve is roughly equivalent to the policy's cash value. In special conditions, such as where the interpolated terminal reserve does not approximate the policy's true value (for example, if the insured donor was terminally ill and had only 1 or 2 months to live), the value of a premium-paying policy may be more than the sum of the interpolated terminal reserve plus unearned premiums as of the date of the gift. (Unearned premiums are defined as the proportionate part of the last premium paid that is attributable to the remainder of the period for which the premium was paid.)

Mr. Martin owned an ordinary life policy on his partner's life to fund a cross-purchase agreement. The policy was 9 years and 4 months old at the time of Mr. Martin's death. The gross annual premium was $2,800, and Mr. Martin died four months after the most recent "premium due" date. Assuming no accrued dividends or policy loans, the policy would be valued as follows:

Terminal reserve at end of 10th year	$14,601
Terminal reserve at end of 9th year	12,965
Increase (10th year)	$ 1,636
Portion of year between death of Mr. Martin and last preceding premium due date is $^4/_{12}$ ($^1/_3$) of a year.	
$^1/_3$ of increase in reserve ($^1/_3$ of $1,636)	$ 545
+	
Terminal reserve — end of 9th year	12,965
=	
Interpolated terminal reserve at date of Martin's death	13,510
+	
$^2/_3$ of gross premium	1,874
Total value of insurance policy	$15,384

The interpolated reserve method will be allowed as long as the contract is not an unusual contract and this method does not develop an amount that varies greatly from the true value of the contract.

Premiums paid by (or on behalf of) the donor after the transfers are also gifts. Therefore, when an owner of a life insurance policy irrevocably assigns that policy to another person or a trust, each premium he pays subsequent to the transfer is considered a gift to the new policy owner (or the beneficial owner[s] of the trust's assets).

Usually the premium payor and the donor are the same. However, the IRS has stated that if an employee assigns his group life insurance policy to an irrevocable trust he had established for his family, a cash premium paid by the employer is deemed to be a gift of the amount of the premium. The deemed gift is from the employee to the beneficiaries of the trust. But (in a rather poorly considered and not widely accepted ruling) the assignment of the group term coverage itself was held not to be a taxable gift because the coverage had no ascertainable value.

A "split-dollared policy" is often assigned to a trust. If an insured-employee assigns the right to name the beneficiary of the proceeds in excess of the cash surrender value of a life insurance policy under an employer-pay-all plan to an irrevocable trust, a gift is made annually; the yearly tax liability of the employee is the greater of (a) the "P.S. 58" cost of the insurance coverage or (b) the difference between the net premium and the annual increase in cash surrender values.

(8)
COMPUTING THE TAX ON GIFTS

Gift tax rates are applied to a net figure, "taxable gifts." Before the tax on a transfer is computed, certain reductions are allowed. These reductions may include

(1) "gift splitting"

(2) an annual exclusion

(3) a marital deduction

(4) a charitable deduction

Gift Splitting

The tax law permits a married donor, with the consent of the nondonor spouse, to elect to treat a gift to a third party as though each spouse has made half of the gift. The election must be made on the applicable gift tax return of the donor spouse.

Gift splitting is an artificial mechanism: even if one spouse makes the entire gift, the single transfer is treated for tax computation purposes as though each spouse made only one-half of the gift. This means that the rate of tax that each will pay is separately calculated by reference to his own particular prior gifts.

Furthermore, if a nondonor spouse has agreed to treat half of the donor spouse's gift as if made by the nondonor spouse, it will have a direct effect on the future gift tax and estate tax that spouse will eventually have to pay if the gift exceeds the annual exclusion. Even though such spouse did not *actually* make half the gift, it will, nevertheless, to the extent it exceeds the $10,000 annual exclusion, become an "adjusted taxable gift" to be added to all other gifts deemed to have been made for purposes of calculating the future gift tax bracket and to be added to the taxable estate at the nondonor spouse's death.

Gift splitting, which applies only to gifts by a married donor to a third party and only with respect to noncommunity property, was introduced into the tax law to equate the tax treatment of common-law taxpayers with that of community-property residents. When one spouse earns a dollar in a community-property state, fifty cents is deemed to be owned by the other spouse automatically and immediately. Therefore, if the couple gave that dollar to their daughter, each spouse would be treated as having given only fifty cents.

Gift splitting places the common-law resident in the same relative position. For example, if a married individual in a common-law state gives his son a gift worth $20,000 and the requisite gift splitting election is made, for purposes of the gift tax computation that individual is considered to have given only $10,000. His spouse is treated as if she gave the other $10,000, even if, in fact, none of the gift was her property.

If the spouses elect to "split" gifts to third parties, all gifts made by either spouse during that reporting period must be split.

The privilege of gift splitting is available only with regard to gifts made while the couple is married. Therefore, gifts the couple makes before they are married may not be split even if they are later married during the same calendar year. Likewise, gifts made after the spouses are legally divorced or one spouse dies may not be split. But gifts made before one spouse dies may be split even if that spouse dies before signing the appropriate consent or election; the deceased spouse's executor can make the appropriate election or consent.

The Annual Exclusion

Purpose of the Exclusion

A *de minimis* rule is one that is instituted primarily to avoid the bother of administrative record keeping. The annual gift tax exclusion is a classic example of such a rule. It was instituted to eliminate the need for a taxpayer to keep an account of or report numerous small gifts. Congress intended that the amount of the annual exclusion be set large enough so that no reporting would be required in the case of wedding gifts or other occasional gifts of relatively small amounts.

Effect of Gift Splitting Coupled with Exclusion

Generally, the annual exclusion allows the donor to make, tax free, up to $10,000 worth of gifts (other than "future-interest gifts" as they are defined below) to any number of persons each year. Since an exclusion of up to $10,000 is allowed per donee per year, the total maximum excludable amount is determined by multiplying the number of persons to whom gifts are made by $10,000. For example, if an unmarried individual makes cash gifts this year of $2,000, $8,000, and $16,000 to his brother, father, and son, respectively, the $2,000 gift would be fully excludable, the entire $8,000 gift to his father would be excludable, and $10,000 of the $16,000 gift to his son would be excludable.

If the same individual is married and his spouse consents to splitting the gift, each spouse is deemed to have made one-half of the gift. This means that both spouses can maximize the use of their annual exclusions. Assuming the nondonor spouse made no gifts, the computation at Figure C3.3 shows that none of the $26,000 of gifts would be subject to tax.

Figure C3.3

Donee	Amount of Gift to Donee	Treated as if Donor Gave	Exclusion	Subject to Tax	Treated as if Nondonor Spouse Gave	Exclusion	Subject to Tax
Brother	$ 2,000	$ 1,000	$ 1,000	—	$ 1,000	$ 1,000	—
Father	$ 8,000	$ 4,000	$ 4,000	—	$ 4,000	$ 4,000	—
Son	$16,000	$ 8,000	$ 8,000	—	$ 8,000	$ 8,000	—
Totals	$26,000	$13,000	$13,000	—	$13,000	$13,000	—

Appendix C
Computing the Federal Gift Tax

Present versus Future Interest

An annual exclusion is allowed only for "present-interest gifts" and is denied to "gifts of future interests." A present interest is one in which the donee's possession or enjoyment begins at the time the gift is made. A future interest refers to any interest or estate in which the donee's possession or enjoyment will not commence until some period of time after the gift is made. More technically, "future interest" is a legal term, and includes reversions, remainders, and other interests or estates, whether vested or contingent, and whether or not supported by a particular interest or estate, which are limited to commence in use, possession, or enjoyment at some future date or time."

An easy way to distinguish between a present interest (which qualifies for the gift tax annual exclusion) and a future interest (which does not qualify for the gift tax exclusion) is to ascertain:

> At the moment of the gift, did the donee have an immediate, unfettered, and actuarially ascertainable legal right to use, possess, or enjoy the property in question?

If the answer is "Yes," the gift is a present interest. If the answer is "No," the gift is a future interest gift.

Clearly, the outright and unrestricted gift of property to a donee (even a minor) that passes legal and equitable title qualifies as a present-interest gift.

A single gift can be split into two parts: one a present interest that qualifies for the annual exclusion and the other a future interest that does not. For example, a widowed donor creates a trust this year and places income-producing property in the trust. The income is payable annually to the donor's son for life. At the son's death, the remainder is payable to the donor's grandson. The gift to the son of the right to receive income annually for life is a present-interest gift since he has unrestricted right to its immediate use, possession, or enjoyment. Arbitrarily assuming a 10% discount rate, if the son is 30 years old at the time of the gift and $100,000 is placed into the trust, the present value of that gift would be worth $96,329 ($100,000 times .96329, which is the present value of the stream of income produced by $100,000 of capital and payable annually for the life of a 30-year-old, according to tables in government regulations — see valuation tables in Appendix D). Of the $96,329, $10,000 would be excludable.

If the donor was married and the appropriate election and consent were filed, each spouse could claim a $10,000 exclusion even though only the donor placed property in the trust. No exclusion is allowed with respect to the ultimate gift of the

corpus to the grandson, since his possession or enjoyment may not commence for some time in the future.

Assume the donor and his spouse had provided that their son was to receive income for 10 years and then the principal was to pass to another beneficiary, a grandson. Arbitrarily assuming a 10% discount rate, if the donor had placed only $1,000 in the trust, the exclusion for the gift of the income interest would be $614.46 ($1,000 times .614457, the income interest valuation factor from Table B in Appendix D). Gift splitting with a spouse would not increase the amount of the exclusion. Each spouse would be allowed a $307.23 exclusion.

No exclusion would be allowed for the gift of the future interest (remainder) that passes to the grandson at the end of 10 years, even though he has an interest that cannot be forfeited. This is because he does not have the right to immediate possession or enjoyment; any delay (no matter how unlikely or how short) in the absolute and immediate right of use, possession or enjoyment, is fatal to the gift tax exclusion.

Note that if the trustee in either situation above had been given the power or discretion to accumulate the income, rather than distribute it, the donor's son would not have received the unfettered and immediate use of the income, and it would be impossible to ascertain the present value of the income interest. For example, assume the trustee is directed to pay the net income to the son for as long as he lives, but is authorized to withhold payments of income during any period he deems advisable and add such payments to corpus. In this case, even the income interest would be a gift of a future interest. No annual exclusion would be allowed.

Where a trustee is required by the trust agreement to accumulate income for a time (or until the occurrence of a specified event), the income interest is a future interest.

The number and amount (or availability) of exclusions depends on the identity of the donee(s), the type of asset involved, and restrictions, if any, placed on the asset.

Summary of Rules for Ascertaining the Amount and Availability of the Gift Tax Annual Exclusion

These rules regarding the annual exclusion can be summarized as follows:

(1) A gift in trust is a gift to a trust's beneficiaries and not to the trust in determining the number of annual exclusions to which a donor is entitled.

The Tools and Techniques of Estate Planning

(2) The value of an income interest in a trust qualifies for the exclusion if the trustee is required to distribute trust income at least annually even if the value of the remainder interest does not qualify.

(3) The gift of an interest that is contingent upon survivorship is a gift of a future interest. (If a gift in trust is made with income going to the grantor's son for life, then income to the grantor's daughter for life, the gift to the son will qualify but the daughter's interest will not.)

(4) A gift is one of a future interest if enjoyment depends on the exercise of a trustee's discretion. (The nature of the interest must be present as of the date of the gift and is not, for example, determined by what the trustee may subsequently do or not do in the exercise of a discretionary power.)

(5) A gift must have an ascertainable value to qualify for the exclusion. (The exclusion will be denied if the donor or anyone else can divert the income from the beneficiary.)

Identity of Donees

When a gift is made in trust, the beneficiaries of the trust (and not the trust itself) are considered the donees. For instance, if there are three life income beneficiaries, up to three annual exclusions could be obtained. Conversely, if five trusts were established for the same beneficiary, only one exclusion is allowed. (Technically, the actuarial value of each gift in trust to that beneficiary would be totaled. That per donee total is then added to direct gifts the donor made to that beneficiary to ascertain whether and to what extent an annual exclusion remains and is allowable for the present transfer.)

A transfer to a corporation is treated as a gift to its shareholders. However, the gift is one of a future interest.

Transfers to two or more persons as joint tenants with right of survivorship, tenants by the entireties, or tenants in common are considered multiple gifts. Each tenant is deemed to receive an amount equal to the actuarial value of his interest in the tenancy. If, for example, one person has a one-half interest in a tenancy in common, a cash gift of $6,000 to the tenancy would be treated as a $3,000 gift to that person. This would be added to other gifts made directly by the same donor to determine how much of the exclusion will be allowed. In all probability, gifts to partnerships should follow the same rules: a gift to a partnership should be treated as if made to each partner in proportion to his partnership interest.

Note that a joint gift, in which neither party can sever his interest without the other's consent, will be considered a future interest gift and not qualify for the annual exclusion. For instance, if Herb gives Diana and Laura joint ownership in a policy on his life, Herb has made a future interest gift to each daughter.

Gifts to Minors

Outright gifts to minors pose no particular qualification problem. The IRS states in a revenue ruling that "an unqualified and unrestricted gift to a minor, with or without the appointment of a guardian, is a gift of a present interest." But there are, of course, practical problems involved, especially with larger gifts. Although minors can buy, sell, and deal with some limited types of property, such as U.S. savings bonds, gifts of other types of property create difficulties. For example, some states do not give minors the legal capacity to purchase their own property, care for it, or sell or transfer it. Some states forbid the registration of securities in a minor's name, and a broker may be reluctant to deal in securities titled in a minor's name. In many states a minor has the legal ability to disaffirm a sale of stock sold at a low price that later rises in value. Furthermore, a buyer receives no assurance of permanent title when a minor signs a real estate deed.

Legal guardianship of the minor is not a viable answer in many situations. Since guardianship laws are rigid, a guardian must generally post bond, and periodic and expensive court accounting is often required. Most importantly, a parent may not want to give a legal minor control over a large amount of cash or other property.

To minimize these and other practical problems involved with most large gifts to minors, such transfers are generally made in trust or under some type of guardianship or custodian arrangement. An incredible amount of litigation developed over whether such gifts qualified for the annual exclusion. Code section 2503 provides clear and precise methods of qualifying gifts to minors for the exclusion. There are three basic means of qualifying "cared-for gifts" to minors under Section 2503: (1) a Section 2503(b) trust, (2) a Section 2503(c) trust, or (3) the Uniform Gifts to Minors Act (or the Uniform Transfers to Minors Act).

Section 2503(b) Trust. To obtain an annual exclusion for gifts to a trust, an individual can establish a trust which requires that income *must* be distributed at least annually to or for use of the minor beneficiary. The trust agreement would state how income is to be used and would give the trustee no discretion as to its use. The minor would receive possession of the trust principal whenever the trust agreement specifies. A distribution does not have to be made by age 21; corpus may

Figure C3.4

Factor	Trust	UGMA	UTMA
Type of property	Donor can make gifts of almost any type of property	Type of property must be permitted by appropriate statute. Gift of real estate may not be permitted	Donor can make gifts of almost any type of property
Dispositive provisions	Donor can provide for disposition of trust assets if donee dies without having made disposition	Disposition must follow statutory guideline	Disposition must follow statutory guideline
Investment powers	Trustee may be given broad virtually unlimited investment powers	Custodian limited to investment powers specified by statute	Custodian limited to investment powers specified by statute
Time of distribution of assets	Trust can continue automatically even after beneficiary reaches age 21. Trustee can make distribution between state law age of majority and age 21	Custodial assets must be paid to beneficiary upon reaching statutory age	Custodial assets must be paid to beneficiary upon reaching statutory age

be held for as long as the beneficiary lives or for any shorter period of time. In fact, the principal can actually bypass the income beneficiary and go directly to the individuals whom the grantor, or even the named beneficiary, has specified. The trust agreement can also control the dispositive scheme if the minor dies before receiving trust corpus. Trust assets do not have to be paid to the minor's estate or appointees.

Mandatory payment of income to (or in behalf of) beneficiaries seems onerous, especially while the beneficiary is a minor. But such income could be deposited in a custodial account and used for the minor's benefit or left to accumulate in a custodial account until the minor reaches majority (at which time the unexpended amount would be turned over to the beneficiary).

Although the entire amount of property placed in a 2503(b) trust would be considered a gift, for exclusion purposes it would be split into two parts: income and principal. The value of the income, measured by multiplying the amount of the gift by a factor that considers both the duration over which the income interest will be paid and the discounted worth of $1 payable over the appropriate number of years, would be eligible for the annual exclusion. The balance of the gift would not qualify for the annual exclusion.

For example, assume a donor places $10,000 into a Section 2503(b) trust that is required to pay his 10-year-old daughter

all income until she reaches age 25. Assume a 10 percent discount rate. The present value of the income the daughter would receive over those 15 years is $7,606.08 ($10,000 x .760608). If the income were payable for her entire life, the present value would jump to almost $9,880.

It is important to note that, according to at least one revenue ruling, the annual exclusion would be denied for a 2503(b) trust that permits principal to be invested in nonincome-producing securities, nonincome-producing real estate, or life insurance policies (since they do not produce taxable income).

Section 2503(c) Trust. The Section 2503(b) trust described above has the advantage of not requiring distribution of principal at the minor's reaching age 21, but it does require a current (annual) distribution of income. The Section 2503(c) trust requires the distribution of income and principal when the minor reaches 21. But it does not require the trustee to distribute income currently.

Certain requirements make it possible for a donor to obtain the exclusion by a gift to a minor under Section 2503(c): the trust must provide (1) the income and principal may be expended by or on behalf of the beneficiary and (2) to the extent not so expended income and principal will pass to the beneficiary at 21 or (3) if the beneficiary dies prior to that time, income and principal will go to the beneficiary's estate or appointees under a general power of appointment. (The annual exclusion will not be lost merely because local law prevents a minor from exercising a general power of appointment.)

A substantial amount of flexibility can be built into the 2503(c) trust. Income that has been accumulated as well as any principal in the trust can be paid over to the donee when he reaches age 21. This may be indicated if the sums involved are not substantial. But the donor may want the trust to continue to age 25 or some other age. It is possible to provide continued management of the trust assets and at the same time avoid forfeiting the annual exclusion by giving the donee, at age 21, a right for a limited but reasonable period to require immediate distribution by giving written notice to the trustee. If the beneficiary fails to give written notice, the trust can continue automatically for whatever period the donor provided when he established the trust. Some states have lowered the age of majority from 21 to age 18 or some in between age. A trust can provide that the distribution can be made between the age of majority and age 21 without jeopardizing the Section 2503(c) exclusion. (The rule is that age 21 is the maximum rather than the minimum age at which the right to trust assets must be made.)

A 2503(c) trust has a number of advantages over the type of custodianship found in the Uniform Gifts to Minors Act or Uniform Transfers to Minors Act arrangements, as shown in Figure C3.4.

Uniform Gifts (Transfers) to Minors Act. The Uniform Gifts to Minors Act or the Uniform Transfers to Minors Act (reference to either Act herein is simply to the Uniform Act— see chapter 41 for background) provides an alternative to the Section 2503(c) trust. The Uniform Act is frequently utilized for smaller gifts because of its simplicity and because it offers the benefits of management, income and estate tax shifting, and the investment characteristics of a trust with little or none of the setup costs.

The Uniform Act is also indicated over a trust if the gift consists of stock in an S corporation. That's because, generally speaking, a trust (other than a voting or "grantor" trust) cannot hold S corporation stock without causing a loss of the election privilege. The result might be double taxation of corporate profits and forfeiture of the privilege of passing through profits (and losses) to shareholders. (See the discussion of QSSTs and Section 687 Trusts in Chapter 29.)

The original Uniform Gifts to Minors Act was approved in 1956 and provided for gifts of money and securities to minors. In 1966, the Uniform Act was revised to accommodate gifts of life insurance policies and annuity contracts. Over the years between 1956 and 1984, all states adopted one or other of the

Uniform Acts or variations thereof. Most states from time to time added to the kinds of property that could be given under the Act. In 1983, the National Conference of Commissioners on Uniform State Laws, concerned about the lack of uniformity among the states with respect to the Uniform Gifts to Minors Act, yielded to the expansive approach taken by most of the states and approved the Uniform Transfers to Minors Act.

The 1983 Act accommodates gifts, lifetime and testamentary, of any interest in property. At this writing, about eighty percent of the states have replaced their Uniform Gifts to Minors Act with the Uniform Transfers to Minors Act. For up to date highlights of state UGMA and UTMA provisions, see the *Advanced Sales Reference Service* (published by the National Underwriter Company) at ¶550 of section 48.

By way of example, in Pennsylvania, a state which has a variation of the Uniform Transfers to Minors Act, a custodianship gift may be made as follows:

§5309. Manner of creating custodial property and effecting transfer

(a) **Creation of custodial property.**—Custodial property is created and a transfer is made whenever:

(1) An uncertificated security or a certificated security in registered form is either:

(i) registered in the name of the transferor, an adult other than the transferor or a trust company, followed in substance by the words: "as custodian for (name of minor) under the Pennsylvania Uniform Transfers to Minors Act"; or

(ii) delivered if in certificated form, or any document necessary for the transfer of an uncertificated security is delivered, together with any necessary endorsement to an adult other than the transferor or to a trust company as custodian, accompanied by an instrument in substantially the form set forth in subsection (b).

(2) Money is paid or delivered to a broker or financial institution for credit to an account in the name of the transferor, an adult other than the transferor or a trust company, followed in substance by the words: "as custodian for (name of minor) under the Pennsylvania Uniform Transfers to Minors Act."

(3) The ownership of a life or endowment insurance policy or annuity contract is either:

(i) registered with the issuer in the name of the transferor, an adult other than the transferor or a trust company followed in substance by the words: "as custodian for (name of minor) under the Pennsylvania Uniform Transfers to Minors Act"; or

(ii) assigned in a writing delivered to an adult other than the transferor or to a trust company whose name in the assignment is followed in substance by the words: "as custodian for (name of minor) under the Pennsylvania Uniform Transfers to Minors Act."

(4) An irrevocable exercise of a power of appointment or an irrevocable present right to future payment under a contract is the subject of a written notification delivered to the payor, issuer or other obligor that the right is transferred to the transferor, an adult other than the transferor or a trust company, whose name in the notification is followed in substance by the words: "as custodian for (name of minor) under the Pennsylvania Uniform Transfers to Minors Act."

(5) An interest in real property is recorded in the name of the transferor, an adult other than the transferor or a trust company, followed in substance by the words: "as custodian for (name of minor) under the Pennsylvania Uniform Transfers to Minors Act."

(6) A certificate of title issued by a state or the Federal Government which evidences title to tangible personal property is either:

(i) issued in the name of the transferor, an adult other than the transferor or a trust company, followed in substance by the words: "as custodian for (name of minor) under the Pennsylvania Uniform Transfers to Minors Act"; or

(ii) delivered to an adult other than the transferor or to a trust company, endorsed to that person followed in substance by the words: "as custodian for (name of minor) under the Pennsylvania Uniform Transfers to Minors Act."

(7) An interest in any property not described in paragraphs (1) through (6) is transferred to an adult other than the transferor or to a trust company by a written instrument in substantially the form set forth in subsection (b).

(b) Form.—An instrument in the following form satisfies the requirements of subsection (a)(1)(ii) and (7):

TRANSFER UNDER THE PENNSYLVANIA

UNIFORM TRANSFERS TO MINORS ACT

I, (name of transferor or name and representative capacity if a fiduciary), hereby transfer to (name of custodian), as custodian for (name of minor) under the Pennsylvania Uniform Transfers to Minors Act, the following: (insert a description of the custodial property sufficient to identify it).
Dated:_____

_____
(Signature)

(name of custodian) acknowledges receipt of the property described above as custodian for the minor named above under the Pennsylvania Uniform Transfers to Minors Act.
Dated:_____

_____
(Signature of custodian)

The Effect of Type of Asset

The type of asset given and restrictions placed on that asset may prevent the donor from obtaining the annual exclusion.

An outright "no strings attached" gift of life insurance will qualify for the annual exclusion. Life insurance (and annuity policies) are subject to the same basic test as any other type of property in ascertaining whether the interest created is "present or future," even though the ultimate obligation under a life insurance policy, payment of the death benefit, is to be discharged in the future. A policy does not have to have cash value at the time of the gift to make the transfer one of a present interest. But the annual exclusion would be lost if the donor prevented the donee from surrendering the policy or borrow-ing its cash value or limited the donee's right to policy cash values in any way.

When a life insurance policy is transferred or otherwise assigned to a trust, will the transfer of policy cash values constitute a present interest? The answer depends on the terms of the trust. Generally, the gift will be one of a future interest, since beneficiaries are not usually given an immediate right to possession or enjoyment of the policy values or other items constituting trust corpus. For example, a trust will typically provide no payments to beneficiaries unless they survive the insured. Furthermore, there is generally no actuarially sound method of making an allocation between the value of a present interest and future interest. Unless the given beneficiary's present interest can be ascertained, no exclusion is allowed. (A related attack used by the IRS is that insurance is nonincome-producing property. This concept is discussed further below.)

Premium payments will usually be considered present- or future-interest gifts depending on the classification of the policy itself; if the assignment of the policy was considered a present interest, premiums paid by the donor after the transfer will qualify for the annual exclusion. For instance, if a person makes an absolute assignment of a policy on his life to his daughter but continues to pay premiums, premiums paid subsequent to the transfer would be present-interest gifts. Conversely, if the gift of the policy was a future interest, premium payments made by the donor after the transfer may also be considered future-interest gifts.

A gift in trust of a life insurance policy or of premiums can be made a present interest by inserting a "Crummey" power (named after the major case in this area). A Crummey power gives the named individual(s) an immediate, unfettered, and actuarially ascertainable right; in short, the absolute right to withdraw a specified amount or portion of the assets contributed to the trust. This withdrawal right (essentially, a general power of appointment over a specified amount or portion of each year's contribution to the trust) makes the gift in trust of a life insurance policy or of premiums qualify for the gift tax annual exclusion.

Clearly, an outright gift of nonincome-producing property will qualify for the gift tax exclusion. Will the same property qualify if placed in a trust? The IRS uses three arguments to disallow annual exclusions:

(1) the right to income (which is the only current right given to a life beneficiary) from a gift of nonincome-producing property is a future interest since its worth is contingent upon the trustee's converting it to income-producing property;

(2) it is impossible to ascertain the value of an income interest in property that is not income-producing at the time of the gift; and

(3) if a gift tax exclusion *is* allowable, the exclusion must be limited to the actual income produced by the property (or expected to be produced) multiplied by the number of years over which the income beneficiary is expected to receive the income, discounted to its present value.

Nondividend-paying stock is a good example of property that may not qualify for the gift tax exclusion when it is placed into a trust. The IRS has been successful in a number of cases in disallowing an exclusion for gifts in trust of stock in closely held corporations paying no dividends. Gifts in trust of life insurance policies pose the same problem: a mother assigns policies on her life to a trust created to provide financial protection for her daughter. Upon the mother's death, the policy proceeds will be reinvested and the daughter will receive the net income of the trust for life. Will the mother be allowed the exclusion for the present value of her daughter's income interest? The regulations answer in the negative since the daughter will not receive income payments until her mother dies.

But even these last two types of property can qualify for the annual exclusion if the beneficiary is given the power to require the trustee to make assets in the trust income-producing. Consider, however, the potential adverse implications of that power if the beneficiary chooses to exercise it.

Gift Tax Marital Deduction

An individual who transfers property to a spouse is allowed an unlimited deduction (subject to certain conditions) known as the gift tax marital deduction.

The purpose of the gift tax marital deduction is currently to enable spouses to be treated as an economic unit.

Requirements to Qualify for Gift Tax Marital Deduction

For a gift to qualify for the gift tax marital deduction, the following conditions must be satisfied: (1) The donor's spouse must be a United States citizen at the time the gift is made. (2) The recipient of the gift must be the spouse of the donor at the time the gift is made. (3) The property transferred to the donee-spouse must not be the type of terminable interest that will disqualify the gift for the marital deduction.

Most of the qualifications above are self-explanatory. The terminable interest rule for marital deduction gifts is similar to the rule employed for estate tax purposes. Essentially, the effect of these rules is that generally no marital deduction will be allowed where (a) the donee-spouse's interest in the transferred property will terminate upon the lapse of time or at the occurrence or failure of a specified contingency (b) where the donee-spouse's interest will then pass to another person who received his interest in the property from the donor-spouse and (c) who did not pay the donor full and adequate consideration for that interest.

The exception is for a gift of "QTIP" assets. (In the past a gift or bequest of a terminable interest in property, one which could end for example at a spouse's death and therefore escape taxation, would not have been eligible for the gift (or estate) tax marital deduction.)

Current law now provides that if a donor spouse gives a donee spouse a "qualifying income interest for life," it will qualify for a gift (or estate) tax marital deduction. To qualify,

(1) the surviving spouse must be entitled to all the income from the property (and it must be payable annually or more frequently), and

(2) no person can have a power to appoint any part of the property to any person other than the surviving spouse, and

(3) the property must be taxable at the donee-spouse's death (in the case of a bequest the first decedent's executor makes an irrevocable election that the property remaining at the surviving spouse's death is taxable in her estate).

Also, a life estate with power of appointment in the donee spouse qualifies for the marital deduction.

Gift Tax Charitable Deduction

A donor making a transfer of property to a qualified charity may receive a charitable deduction equal to the value of the gift (to the extent not already excluded by the annual exclusion). The net effect of the charitable deduction, together with the annual exclusion, is to avoid gift tax liability on gifts to qualified charities. There is no limit on the amount that can be passed, gift tax free, to a qualified charity.

The gift tax deduction is allowed for all gifts made during the calendar year by U.S. citizens or residents if the gift is to a qualified charity. A qualified charity is defined as (a) the

Appendix C
Computing the Federal Gift Tax

United States, a state, territory, or any political subdivision or the District of Columbia if the gift is to be used exclusively for public purposes; (b) certain religious, scientific, or charitable organizations; (c) certain fraternal societies, orders, or associations; (d) certain veterans' associations, organizations, or societies.

Technically the charitable deduction is limited. A charitable deduction is allowed only to the extent that each gift exceeds the annual exclusion. For example, during the calendar year a single client makes total gifts of $51,000: $26,000 to his daughter and $25,000 to The American College. After taking annual exclusions, gifts qualifying for the charitable deduction would amount to $15,000 (the $25,000 gift to The American College less the $10,000 annual exclusion). Therefore the client's charitable deduction would be limited to $15,000. The reason for the rule is this: If the annual exclusion were already deducted, the allowance of a charitable deduction equal to the total amount of the gift would result in an extra $10,000 exclusion. The operation of these rules is illustrated below.

In certain cases a donor will transfer a remainder interest to a qualified charity. A personal beneficiary will be given all or part of the income interest in the transferred property, and the charity will receive the remainder at the termination of the income interest. Where a charitable remainder is given to a qualified charity, a gift tax deduction is allowable for the present value of that remainder interest only if at least one of the following conditions is satisfied:

(1) the transferred property was either a personal residence or a farm; or

(2) the transfer was made to a charitable remainder annuity trust; or

(3) the transfer was made to a charitable remainder unitrust; or

(4) the transfer was made to a pooled income fund.

The terms "charitable remainder annuity trust," "charitable remainder unitrust," and "pooled income fund" are defined in essentially the same manner as they are for estate and income tax purposes.

Calculating Gift Tax Payable

The process of computing the gift tax payable begins with ascertaining the amount of taxable gifts in the current reporting calendar year. In order to find the amount of taxable gifts, it is first necessary to value all gifts made. If appropriate, the gift is then "split," annual exclusions and marital and charitable deductions are applied. An example and computation format will illustrate the process.

Assume a single donor in the last month of 1995 makes certain outright gifts: $160,000 to his son, $125,000 to his daughter, $8,000 to his grandson, and $25,000 to The College For Financial Planning (a total of $318,000).

Computing Taxable Gifts

Step 1	*List* total gifts for year		$318,000
Step 2	*Subtract* one-half of gift deemed to be made by donor's spouse (split gifts)	$ 0	
	Gifts deemed to be made by donor		$318,000
Step 3	*Subtract* annual exclusion(s)	$ 38,000	
	Gifts after subtracting exclusion(s)		$280,000
Step 4	*Subtract* marital deduction	$ 0	
Step 5	*Subtract* charitable deduction	$ 15,000	
	Taxable gifts		$265,000

Note that, although there were four donees, the annual exclusion was $38,000 and did not total four times $10,000, or $40,000. This is because the annual exclusion is the lower of (a) $10,000 or (b) the actual net value of the property transferred. In this example the gift to the grandson was only $8,000, which limits the annual exclusion for that gift to $8,000.

A slight change in the fact pattern above will illustrate the computation where the donor is married and his spouse consented to split their gifts to third parties. In this case, only half the gifts made by the donor would be taxable to the donor (half the gifts made by the donor's spouse to third parties would also be included in computing the donor's total gifts).

A separate (and essentially identical) computation is made for the donor's spouse. That computation would show (a) the other half of the husband's gifts to third parties plus (b) half of the wife's actual gifts to third parties (since all gifts must be split if any gifts are split).

Computing Taxable Gifts

Step 1	*List* total gifts for year		$318,000
Step 2	*Subtract* one-half of gift deemed to be made by donor's spouse (split gifts)	$159,000	
	Gifts deemed to be made by donor		$159,000
Step 3	*Subtract* annual exclusion(s)	$ 34,000	
	Gifts after subtracting exclusion(s)		$125,000
Step 4	*Subtract* marital deduction	$ 0	
Step 5	*Subtract* charitable deduction	$ 2,500	
	Taxable gifts		$122,500

(The calculation on the wife's return would parallel this return)

The Tools and Techniques of Estate Planning

Note that in this example the annual exclusions were computed *after* the split and each donor's exclusions would be:

(a)	Gift to son	$10,000
(b)	Gift to daughter	10,000
(c)	Gift to grandson	4,000
(d)	Gift to The College for Financial Planning	10,000
		$34,000

The charitable deduction for each spouse would be $2,500 [{$25,000 divided by 2} less $10,000].

If the married donor in the fact pattern directly above had also made an outright gift of $200,000 to his wife, the computation would be as follows:

Computing Taxable Gifts

Step 1	*List* total gifts for year		$518,000
Step 2	*Subtract* one-half of gift deemed to be made by donor's spouse (split gifts)	$159,000	
	Gifts deemed to be made by donor		$359,000
Step 3	*Subtract* annual exclusion(s)	$ 44,000	
	Gifts after subtracting exclusion(s)		$315,000
Step 4	*Subtract* marital deduction	$190,000	
Step 5	*Subtract* charitable deduction	$ 2,500	
	Taxable gifts		$122,500

When the total value of taxable gifts for the reporting period is found, the actual tax payable is computed using the following method:

Computing Gift Tax Payable

Step 1	Compute gift tax on all *taxable* gifts regardless of when made (use unified rate schedule)	$_____
Step 2	Compute gift tax on all *taxable* gifts made prior to the present year's gift(s) (use unified rate schedule)	$_____
Step 3	Subtract Step 2 result from Step 1 result	$_____
Step 4	Enter gift tax credit remaining	$_____
Step 5	Subtract Step 4 result from Step 3 result to obtain *gift tax payable*	$_____

For instance, a widow gives $1,400,000 to her daughter and $100,000 to The College for Financial Planning in 1995. Both transfers are present-interest gifts. If she had made no previous taxable gifts in the current or prior years or quarters, the computation would be as follows:

Computing Taxable Gifts

Step 1	*List* total gifts for year		$1,500,000
Step 2	*Subtract* one-half of gift deemed to be made by donor's spouse (split gifts)	$ 0	
	Gifts deemed to be made by donor		$1,500,000
Step 3	*Subtract* annual exclusion(s)	$ 20,000	
	Gifts after subtracting exclusion(s)		$1,480,000
Step 4	*Subtract* marital deduction	$ 0	
Step 5	*Subtract* charitable deduction	$ 90,000	
	Taxable gifts		$1,390,000

To find the gift tax payable on this amount, the procedure would be as follows:

Computing Gift Taxable Payable

Step 1	Compute gift tax on all *taxable* gifts regardless of when made ($1,390,000)	$508,500
Step 2	Compute gift tax on all *taxable* gifts made prior to the present gift(s)	$ 0
Step 3	Subtract Step 2 result from Step 1 result	$508,500
Step 4	Enter gift tax (unified) credit remaining (1995)	$192,800
Step 5	Subtract Step 4 result from Step 3 result to obtain *gift tax payable*	$315,700

The Step 1 entry, $508,500, is found by using the unified rate schedule for estate and gift taxes. Note that the unified rate table is used regardless of when the gifts were made.

If the donor in the example above had made $100,000 of additional taxable gifts in 1984 (a total of $1,490,000), the computation would be as follows:

Computing Gift Taxable Payable

Step 1	Compute gift tax on all *taxable* gifts regardless of when made ($1,490,000)	$551,500
Step 2	Compute gift tax on all *taxable* gifts made prior to the present gift(s)	$ 23,800
Step 3	Subtract Step 2 result from Step 1 result	$527,700
Step 4	Enter gift tax credit remaining (1995)	$169,000
Step 5	Subtract Step 4 result from Step 3 result to obtain *gift tax payable*	$358,700

This illustrates the cumulative nature of the gift tax (the $100,000 prior taxable gifts pushed the present $1,390,000 of taxable gifts into a higher bracket) and the progressive rate structure.

Credits

A unified credit can be applied against the tax on gifts made either during lifetime or at death or part can be applied against each. The gift tax credit, which provides a dollar-for-dollar reduction of the tax otherwise payable, is as follows:

Donors Making Gifts in	Receive a Credit of
1982	$ 62,800
1983	79,300
1984	96,300
1985	121,800
1986	155,800
1987 and later years	192,800

In the example directly above since the taxable gifts in prior years used up part of the available credit, to that extent they are not available to reduce the tax liability for the present gifts.

Note also that the utility of both graduated rates and the unified credit is lost where ultra-large gifts have been made (see Unified Rate Schedule for Estate and Gift Taxes in Appendix D).

(9)
REPORTING OF GIFTS AND PAYMENT OF THE TAX

Future-Interest Gifts

A gift tax return is required for a gift of a future interest regardless of the amount of the gift. For example, if an individual transfers $100,000 to an irrevocable trust payable to the grantor's wife for life and then to the grantor's son, a gift tax return would be required regardless of the value of the son's remainder interest.

The term "future interest" is defined the same as for annual exclusion purposes: a gift in which the donee does not have the unrestricted right to the immediate use, possession, or enjoyment of the property or the income from the property.

Present-Interest Gifts

No gift tax return is due (if no future interest gifts are made) until present-interest gifts made to one individual exceed $10,000. At that point, a return must be filed on an annual basis when a gift to one person in one year exceeds $10,000 even if no gift tax would be due (e.g., if gift splitting provisions eliminated the tax). For example, if a married woman gave $15,000 to her son and split the gift, the transfer would be tax free. However, a gift tax return would be required because it exceeded the annual exclusion limit (and because the gift was split). A return must be filed where a couple elects to split gifts.

A gift tax return must be filed and the gift tax due, if any, on reported gifts must be paid by April 15 of the year following the year in which the taxable gifts were made. When an extension is granted for income tax return filing, that automatically extends the time limit for gift tax return filing.

Gifts to Charities

No return must be filed and no reporting is required for charitable contributions of $10,000 or less in value unless a noncharitable gift is also made. In that case, the charitable transfer must be reported at the same time the noncharitable gift is noted on a gift tax return. If the value of the charitable transfer exceeds $10,000, the general rule is that the transfer must be reported on a gift tax return for that year.

If a split-interest gift is made to a charity (where there are charitable and noncharitable donees of the same gift), the donor will not be able to claim a charitable deduction for the entire value of the transfer. In this case the donor must file and report the transfer subject to the filing requirements discussed above. For example, if an individual establishes a charitable remainder trust with payments to his daughter for life and the remainder payable to charity at her death, a gift tax return would have to be filed.

Liability for Payment — Net Gift

The donor of the gift is primarily liable for the gift tax. However, if the donor for any reason fails to pay the tax when it falls due, the donee becomes liable to the extent of the value of the gift. This liability begins as soon as the donor fails to pay the tax when due.

If a donor makes a gift and the donee decides, voluntarily, to pay the gift tax out of the property just received, the gift tax value of the gift is the entire fair market value of the property. In other words, if the donee is not obligated by the terms of the gift to pay the gift tax but chooses to pay it anyway, he must pay a tax based on the full fair market value of the property received based on the donor's gift tax bracket.

Conversely, if the terms of the gift obligate the donee to pay the gift tax, the value of the gift (and therefore the amount of the gift tax liability) is reduced. If a gift is made subject to an express or implied condition at the time of transfer that the gift tax is to be paid by the donee or out of the property transferred, the donor is receiving consideration (taxable as income) in the amount of the gift tax to be paid by the donee.

The value of the "net gift' is measured by the fair market value of the property passing from the donor less the amount of any gift tax paid by the donee. In computing the donee's gift tax liability, you must use the donor's unified credit.

The formula used to compute the donee's tax is:

tentative tax $\div$ (1.00 + donor's gift tax bracket)

For instance, assume a retired, 66 year old, single donor living almost entirely from the income of $4,000,000 worth of tax-free municipal bonds who made no prior gifts made a gift of property worth $1,010,000. The gift was made to his niece on the condition that she pay the federal gift taxes. As the NumberCruncher printout below illustrates, the tentative tax on a taxable gift of $1,000,000 ($1,010,000 - $10,000 annual exclusion) is $153,000. But the gift tax actually payable is $110,072.

True Tax on a Net Gift

Input:	Year of Gift	1995
Input:	Taxable Gift	$1,000,000
	Gift Tax on Gift	$345,800
	Unified Credit	- $192,800
	Tentative Tax	$153,000
True Tax on Net Gift Equals:		
	Tentative Tax ÷ (1.00 + Rate of Tax)	$110,072

Note that the formula is not applicable if the gift is split between the donor and spouse, each of whom is in a different gift tax bracket because either or both have made prior taxable gifts. Quite often, however, you can determine the correct tax bracket by inspection and adjusting for the bracket differential by computing the tentative tax in the correct lower bracket. In other situations you'll have to make trial computations using first the bracket indicated by the tentative taxable gift and then later using the next lower bracket.

Time Tax Is Due

Generally, the gift tax must be paid at the same time the return is filed. However, reasonable extensions of time for payment of the tax can be granted by the IRS, but only upon a showing of "undue hardship." This means more than inconvenience. It must appear that the party liable to pay the tax will suffer a "substantial financial loss" unless an extension is granted. (A forced sale of property at a sacrifice price would be an example of a substantial financial loss.)

(10)
RELATIONSHIP OF THE GIFT TAX SYSTEM TO THE INCOME TAX SYSTEM

When the gift tax law was written, one of the principal purposes was to complement the income tax law by discouraging taxpayers from making gifts to reduce their taxable incomes. It is true that to some extent the gift tax does supplement the income tax system and there is some overlap. However, it is important to note that the tax treatment accorded a given transaction when the two taxes are applied will not necessarily be consistent.

A lack of consistency between the gift and income tax systems forces the practitioner to examine four different issues:

(1) Is the transfer one upon which the gift tax will be imposed?

(2) Will the transfer constitute a taxable exchange subject to the income tax?

(3) If the transfer was made in trust, will the income from the transferred property be taxable to the donor, or will the incidence of taxation be shifted to the recipient of the property (the trust or its beneficiaries)?

(4) If the income is taxable to the beneficiary, will it be taxable at the parent's rate or at the beneficiary's tax bracket (as it would be if (a) the income were earned income no matter what the beneficiary's age, or (b) the beneficiary were age 14 or older no matter whether the income was earned or unearned)?

In summary, the treatment of a transaction for gift tax purposes is not necessarily consistent with the income tax consequences. Therefore it is important not to place undue reliance upon the provisions and interpretations of the income tax law when determining probable results or potential interpretations of the gift tax system (or vice versa).

(11)
DETERMINATION OF THE BASIS OF GIFT PROPERTY

When property is transferred from a donor to a donee and the donee later disposes of the property through a sale or other taxable disposition, gain depends on the donee's basis. In return, the donee's basis is "carried over" from the donor; i.e., the donor's cost basis for the gift property immediately prior to the gift becomes the donee's cost basis for that property.

For example, if an individual has paid $10 a share for stock and transfers it when it is worth $20, and the donee sells it when it is worth $30, the donee's cost basis for that property is the donor's $10 cost. The gain, therefore, is the difference between the amount realized by the donee, $30, and the donee's adjusted basis, $10.

An addition to basis is allowed for a portion of any gift tax paid on the transfer from the donor to the donee. The basis addition is for that portion of the tax attributable to the "appreciation" in the gift property (the excess of the property's gift tax value over the donor's adjusted basis determined immediately before the gift). This increase in basis may be added to the donee's carryover basis for the property.

Stated as a formula, the basis of gifted property is the donor's basis increased as follows:

$$\frac{\text{NET APPRECIATION IN VALUE OF GIFT}}{\text{AMOUNT OF GIFT}} \quad X \quad \text{GIFT TAX PAID}$$

This means the basis carried over from the donor is increased by only the gift tax on the net appreciation in the value of the gift. For example, an individual bought stock worth $40,000 and gave it to his daughter when it was worth $100,000. If the donor paid $18,000 in gift taxes at the time of the gift, the daughter's basis would be

a. Donor's basis $40,000
plus
b. Gift tax on "net appreciation in value" (here, the difference between the $100,000 value of the gift at the time of transfer and the donor's cost, $40,000)

$$\frac{\$60,000}{\$100,000} \quad X \quad \$18,000 \quad = \quad \underline{10,800}$$

equals
c. Daughter's basis $50,800

However, for purpose of determining loss, if the basis of the gifted property is lower than the fair market value of the property at the time of the gift, the basis is equal to such fair market value.

(12)
RELATIONSHIP OF THE GIFT TAX SYSTEM TO THE ESTATE TAX SYSTEM

We are operating under a unified estate and gift tax system. The unification correlates the estate and gift tax laws in three essential ways:

(1) Lifetime gifts and testamentary transfers are taxed by using the same tax rates (so-called unified tax rates), rather than separate and different rates.

(2) There is a single unified tax credit that can be applied to lifetime and "deathtime" gifts. The unified tax credit replaces what was previously a specific estate tax exemption and a specific gift tax exemption.

(3) The estate tax imposed at death is found by adding the taxable portion of gifts made during lifetime (after 1976) to the taxable estate (any gift tax paid on post-1976 transfers can be subtracted to arrive at the estate tax liability) to arrive at the tentative tax base.

For these reasons, there are many correlations between the two tax systems. Like the income tax law, however, the gift tax law is not always consistent with the estate tax law.

When a gift is made, certain issues must be considered. In spite of the lifetime transfer, will the transferred property be included among the other assets in the donor's gross estate upon his death? Will the property a donor transfers during lifetime be subjected first to a gift tax and later included in the donor's gross estate? For example, if a donor gives a policy of insurance on his life to his son, the transfer would be considered a taxable gift and if the donor dies within 3 years after making the gift, the transferred property would be includable in his gross estate.

Likewise, if the donor transfers property but retains a life interest, both gift and estate taxes will be payable. Although the gift tax paid may generally be subtracted in arriving at the estate tax liability, because of the "time value" of money (i.e., the donor's loss of the use of gift taxes paid), the net result is less favorable than a mere washout (i.e., it is in essence a prepayment of the death tax).

(13)
FACTORS TO CONSIDER IN SELECTING APPROPRIATE SUBJECT OF A GIFT

Gift tax strategy must be part of a well-planned and carefully coordinated estate-planning effort. This in turn requires careful consideration as to the type of property to give. There are a number of strategies and factors that must be examined in selecting the types of property that are appropriate for gifts.

Some of the general considerations in planning gift tax property include:

(1) Is the property likely to appreciate in value? Other things being equal, planners generally try to pick property that will appreciate substantially in value from the time of the transfer. The removal from the donor's estate of the appreciation in the property (as well as the income from the property) should save a meaningful amount of estate taxes.

The best type of property will have a low gift tax value and a high estate tax value. Life insurance, for example, is property with a low present value but a high appreciation potential. If held until the date the insured dies, its appreciation in value is guaranteed.

(2) Is the donee in a lower income tax bracket than the donor? Income splitting between the donor and a donee age 14 or older can be obtained by transferring high income-producing property to a family member in a lower bracket. High income-producing property is best for this purpose. High-dividend participating

preferred stock in a closely held business or stock in a successful S corporation is a good example of high income-producing property.

Conversely, if the donor is in a lower bracket than the donee (for instance, if the parent who is retired makes a gift to a financially successful middle-aged child), the use of low-yield growth-type property may be indicated. Typically, gifts to children under age 14 should emphasize growth.

(3) Is the property subject to indebtedness? A gift of property subject to indebtedness that is greater than its cost to the donor may result in a taxable gain. A gift of such property causes the donor to realize capital gain on the excess of the debt over basis. For example, the gift of a building that cost the donor $10,000, appreciated to $100,000, and was mortgaged to $70,000 would result in an income tax gain to the donor on the difference between the debt outstanding at the time of the transfer and the donor's basis (assume $70,000 and the donor's basis, $10,000). In this example, the gain would be $60,000. It would be realized at the time the gift became complete.

(4) Is the gift property's cost basis above, below, or approximately the same as the property's fair market value? Income tax law forbids the recognition of a capital loss if the subject matter of the gift has a cost basis above the property's present fair market value. Neither the donor nor the donee can recognize a capital loss with respect to such property. Furthermore, if the gift property's cost basis is above present fair market value, there will be no gift tax addition to basis because that addition depends on appreciation at the time of the transfer. Since there is no appreciation, no gift tax addition would be allowed.

Conversely, if the donor's cost basis for income tax purposes is very low relative to the fair market value of the property, it might be advantageous to retain the property until death because of the "stepped-up basis" at death rules. (This is especially true if inclusion of the property will generate little or no gift tax because it will pass to a surviving spouse and qualify for a marital deduction or if the asset owner is "sheltered" by the unified credit.) The result of the stepped-up basis provision is that a portion of the future capital gain would be avoided in the event the property is later sold by the estate or heir. But if the property should be sold, it may pay to transfer it first to a low-bracket age 14 or over family member by gift; that individual could then sell it and realize a lower tax. For instance, on a $10,000 gain, a father in a 28% bracket would pay $2,800 in tax. If, instead, he gave the stock to his college age daughter, who was in a 15% bracket, she'd pay (slightly less than) $1,500 in tax, a $1,300 ($2,800-$1,500) saving.

A third possibility is that the donor's cost basis is approximately the same or only slightly below fair market value. Again, the rules providing for a gift tax addition to basis are of little help. The addition to basis is limited to gift tax allocable to appreciation in the property at the time of the gift. One further factor that should be considered is the likelihood that the donee will want or need to sell the property in the foreseeable future. If this is not likely, the income tax basis (except for depreciable property) will be relatively meaningless.

INCOME TAXATION OF TRUSTS AND ESTATES

GENERAL SCHEME OF TAXATION

Trusts and estates are treated in the tax law as separate taxpayers that are required to file annual federal income tax returns. The problem that Congress faced in taxing the income of trusts or estates was whether to tax such entities in a manner similar to corporations or partnerships or to tax them as some hybrid entity.

If a trust or estate were taxed like a corporation there would be a double taxation—the trust or estate would be taxed on its income for the year, and the beneficiaries would be taxed a second time on the distribution received. Beneficiaries would be treated like shareholders who receive taxable dividends, even though the corporation's taxable income includes the same distribution. The double taxation, especially for small estates or trusts, would make this approach highly unfavorable to taxpayers.

If a trust or estate were taxed as a partnership, the trust or federal estate tax return would merely be informational. All income of the trust or estate would be taxed to the individual beneficiaries, just as partners in a partnership must report their proportionate share of the taxable income of the partnership on their own individual returns. This method would be particularly harsh in cases where the trustee has discretion to either accumulate or distribute income and chose to accumulate it, or in an estate where an executor has no duty to distribute income until the termination of the estate. If this approach had been adopted, a beneficiary could be paying tax on amounts not yet received.

Congress adopted a hybrid approach for estates and trusts known as the "sharing" concept. The general rule is that the trust or estate will pay income tax on the amount it retains. Beneficiaries will pay the tax on the income of the trust or estate actually distributed to them. The mechanics of obtaining this result are obtained through the utilization of the distributable net income (DNI) concept. Thus income is taxed only once.

The concept of DNI is utilized to achieve three main results. First, it ensures that the trust or estate receives a deduction for amounts distributed and provides a limit for that deduction. For example, assume that a trust earns $10,000 in income and distributes $6,000 of that income to the sole beneficiary. The trust would be taxed on the amount it retains,

$4,000, and would have a special deduction of $6,000 for the amounts distributed.

Second, DNI limits the portion of distributions that is taxable to beneficiaries. If the trust in the above example distributed $12,000 to the beneficiary, the trust would be allowed to deduct $10,000, and the trust would have no tax liability. The beneficiary would be taxed on only $10,000 of the $12,000 he received.

The first $10,000 is deemed to have come from income. The balance, $2,000, is considered a tax-free distribution of trust corpus. In this case, for tax purposes, the characterization of the $12,000 and its breakdown into income and corpus are not left to the trustee. The Code, under the "income first" rule, ignores the trustee's classification of a distribution as "income" or "corpus"; instead, it deems all amounts distributed to be income to the extent of DNI. For example, assume the trust had interest income of $10,000 that a trustee decided to accumulate. In the same year the trustee decided to distribute $10,000 of corpus to one of the beneficiaries. If the trustee made the distribution, the beneficiary would be deemed to have received $10,000 in income, even though in actuality the trustee might have been distributing an amount from corpus.

The third function of DNI is to ensure that the character of distributions to a beneficiary remains the same as in the hands of a trust or estate. Tax-exempt interest received by a trust and distributed to a beneficiary retains its character as tax-exempt and is exempt from ordinary income taxation to the beneficiary or heirs. Likewise, what enters the trust or estate as ordinary income remains ordinary income when received by beneficiaries or heirs. This is known as the "conduit" theory.

INCOME TAXATION OF TRUSTS

A trust is a tax-paying entity. The taxable income of a trust is computed in basically the same manner as that of an individual. The tax on the taxable income is imposed at the special rates applicable only to trusts (and estates). These rates are even higher than those for single (unmarried) individuals.

In computing tax liability, multiple trusts are treated as one trust and their incomes are aggregated if the trusts have substantially the same grantor or grantors and substantially the same primary beneficiary or beneficiaries and if a principal purpose for the existence of the trusts is the avoidance of federal income tax.

Generally, for tax purposes trusts are treated as separate entities from the grantor, the trustee, and the beneficiary. The basic question in the income taxation of trusts is, "Who will be taxed on trust income—the trust, the beneficiary, or the grantor?" Generally, the burden of taxation falls on either the trust itself or the beneficiary. But it is possible for the income of the trust to be taxed to the grantor. For this reason, trusts are categorized for income tax purposes as either a "simple" trust or a "complex" trust. Either type of trust may also be a "grantor" trust.

A "simple" trust is one in which the trust agreement requires that all trust income be distributed currently to the beneficiaries. A simple trust may not make distributions from amounts other than current income. Principal may not be distributed and no charitable gifts can be made by this type of trust; otherwise, it will be deemed a complex trust for that taxable year.

A simple trust is treated as a separate tax entity. As such, it has the same deductions an individual has, subject to certain exceptions. It also has a special deduction for income that is distributable to its beneficiaries. The net result is that a simple trust does not pay tax on income it pays out. The beneficiary of a simple trust will report the income that he receives or that is receivable by him. In other words, a simple trust acts like a funnel—a true and complete conduit for passing the trust income from the grantor to the beneficiaries.

A second type of trust is known as the "complex" trust. A complex trust is any trust which is not a simple trust, that is, a complex trust is one in which the trustee either must—or may— accumulate income. The trustee of a complex trust—unlike the trustee of a simple trust—can also distribute corpus (principal). He can also make gifts to charities.

A complex trust—like a simple trust—is a separate tax entity. It is allowed a special deduction for actual distributions of income but pays tax on any income it does not distribute. Generally, the same rules that govern complex trusts apply also to the income taxation of a decedent's estate.

A trust is not allowed a standard deduction. Further, the personal exemption is limited to $300 for a simple trust and $100 for a complex trust. (If a trust is required to distribute its income to a beneficiary, it will not lose the $300 exemption even if it distributes corpus or makes a charitable contribution in a given year and thus is considered complex for all other purposes.)

The power of a trustee of a complex trust to accumulate income allows a potential tax abuse. The trustee could accumulate income and pay the income tax in years when the trust had a lower tax bracket than the beneficiary. Accumulated income could be distributed in later years without any tax consequence to the beneficiary. Although the income tax rate compression brought about by the Tax Reform Act of 1986 limits this advantage, there are rules in place to eliminate the possibility of tax abuse of such income-shifting. These "throwback rules" provide that distributions by a trust of previously accumulated income are taxed substantially the same as if they were distributed when earned (i.e., "thrown back" to the year earned). However, income accumulated prior to the beneficiary's birth or before attaining age 21 is not subject to this throwback rule.

In some cases the trust itself is disregarded as a taxable entity. A grantor trust, for example, is either a simple or complex trust in which the trust is disregarded by the Code as a taxable entity. Generally, in the case of either a simple or a complex trust, the trust or its beneficiary will be taxable on the income of the trust. However, in some cases the grantor is taxed on the trust income whether or not the grantor actually receives the income.

Code Sections 671 to 677 discussed below are known as the "grantor-trust" rules. An understanding of these rules is essential for the tax planner.

Sec. 671—Substantial Owner Rules

When the grantor of a trust is treated as the owner of a portion of the trust corpus for income tax purposes, those items of income, deductions, and credits that are attributable to that portion of the trust are deemed to be those of the grantor. Accordingly, the grantor of the trust is deemed the recipient of trust income and is allowed a deduction to the extent there are trust expenses and/or credits. Note, however, that the grantor is owner only for income tax purposes under this rule. The estate tax exclusion must be tested under estate tax rules. (This applies to all the Code sections covered below.)

Sec. 673—Reversionary Interest Rules

For income tax purposes (subject to a limited exemption for reversionary interests taking effect on the death of a minor lineal descendant under age 21) the grantor is treated as the owner of that portion of a trust in which the grantor or the grantor's spouse has a reversionary interest in either the corpus or the income: if, as of the date of inception of that trust or at the time of an addition to that trust, the value of the reversionary interest exceeds 5 percent of the value of the property in which the reversion is retained. Arbitrarily assuming a 10 percent interest rate, the value of the reversionary interest exceeds 5 percent of the value of a term trust if the trust runs approximately 32 years.

Sec. 674—Beneficial Interest Rules

In general, where a grantor of a trust, a nonadverse party, or both can control the beneficial enjoyment of a trust, the grantor is taxed as the owner of the trust for income tax purposes. Where the grantor or nonadverse party needs consent of an adverse party to change the beneficiary's enjoyment of the trust, the grantor is not deemed the owner of the trust corpus, and the income earned from such a trust is not attributable to the grantor.

Sec. 675—Administrative Powers Rules

The retention by the grantor of certain administrative powers can result in the grantor's being deemed the owner of the corpus of the trust for income tax purposes. Powers exercisable by the grantor, or even a nonadverse party, that would cause the income to be attributable to the grantor are:

1. a power that enables the grantor to purchase, exchange, or otherwise deal with or dispose of the corpus or income of the trust for less than adequate consideration in money or money's worth;

2. a power that allows the grantor to borrow trust corpus or income without adequate interest or security;

3. a power of administration exercisable in a nonfiduciary capacity by any person without the approval or consent of any person in a fiduciary capacity. Powers of administration are such powers as the power to vote stock of a corporation in which the grantor or the trust has a significant voting interest, the power to control investment of the trust funds, and the power to reacquire the trust corpus by substituting other property of an equivalent value.

Sec. 676—Power to Revoke Rules

The grantor is treated for income tax purposes as the owner of any portion of a trust if he can revoke the trust either acting alone or with a nonadverse party (unless the power is as remote as that permitted under the Section 673 reversionary interest rules).

Sec. 677—Income for Benefit of Grantor Rules

The grantor of a trust is treated as the owner of the trust for income tax purposes if the income of the trust is or may—at the discretion of the grantor or a nonadverse party, or both—be distributed to the grantor, held or accumulated for future distribution to the grantor, or applied to the payment of premiums on life insurance policies on the life of the grantor or the grantor's spouse.

In addition, the income from property transferred in trust is taxable to the grantor of the trust where the income is distributed to the grantor's spouse, held or applied for future distribution to the grantor's spouse, or applied to the payment of premiums on life insurance policies on the life of the grantor's spouse.

Sec. 678—"Person Other than Grantor" Rules

Finally, if a person other than the grantor has the power, exercisable solely by himself, to vest the corpus or income therefrom in himself, such a person is treated as the owner of the corpus so that trust income will be taxable to that individual (unless the trust income is otherwise taxable to the grantor).

When appreciated property is given to a trust and sold by the trustee within 2 years, a tax is imposed on the trust equal to that which the grantor would have paid if the gain had been included in his income for the year the sale occurred.

INCOME TAXATION OF ESTATES

Decedent's Final Return

An executor or administrator has the duty to file two different types of income tax returns for a decedent. He must file a decedent's last life return and an estate's income tax return.

A decedent-taxpayer's tax year ends with the date of his death. For example, if "X" dies on March 30, an income tax return must be filed for the short year of January 1 to March 30. The return must be filed on the regular due date, April 15th, of the following year. The amount of income and deductible expenses that must be reported depends on the deceased taxpayer's regular method of accounting.

For cash-basis taxpayers, only income actually or constructively received must be reported. Deductions can be taken only for expenses actually paid. If the decedent was on the accrual method, the return will show all income and deductions accrued through the date of death.

Income in Respect of a Decedent (Section 691 Income)

Since this is the final income tax return for the individual, if he was a cash-basis taxpayer, income which he earned but had not received by the date of his death would not be included in his final return, because he did not actually or constructively receive the item by the date of death. For example, an insurance agent's renewal commissions paid after death cannot be included in his last life return, assuming the deceased agent was a cash-basis taxpayer.

Income which the decedent would have included in gross income if he had lived and had received it does not escape taxation. Thus, income in respect of a decedent is actually broader than the cash basis example above. For example, installment payments received after a decedent's death are taxed to the recipient of the payments. In other words, the estate or the beneficiary who receives income in respect of a decedent will pay tax upon it in the same manner that it would have been taxed to the decedent. If it would have been ordinary income to the decedent (had he lived), it will be ordinary income to the estate or beneficiary. What would have been return of capital to the decedent remains tax free when recovered by the estate or beneficiary.

The estate or beneficiary that includes an item of income in respect of a decedent is entitled to a deduction on the same income tax return for the amount of additional federal estate tax attributable to inclusion of that item in the decedent's federal estate tax return.

Taxation of the Estate

As a taxable entity, an estate must pay tax on its income. If the income of the estate consists of dividends from stock and interest from bonds, these items will comprise the gross income of the estate. Likewise, if there is rental income, royalty income, income from the sale or exchange of property, or income from a business carried on by the executor or administrator, then the income of the estate will include those items as well.

Because an estate is considered a separate tax entity, it has not only income but also deductions. An estate may deduct reasonable amounts paid for administration costs including executor's fees, legal fees in connection with the administration of the estate, and expenses of preparing the income tax return of the estate. If the estate manages a business, it will be entitled to deduct ordinary and necessary business expenses.

Some of these expenses, such as administration expenses, may be taken on either the income tax return of the estate or as deductions from the gross estate to obtain the net estate for federal estate tax purposes. However, the same expense generally may not be taken as a deduction from both the estate income tax return and the estate tax return. In these cases, the executor would have to weigh the relative advantages and take the deduction where it would be most advantageous.

An estate is also entitled to a deduction for amounts of income distributed. An estate may take a $600 personal exemption. As previously mentioned, to the extent that the estate retains income, it will be taxed, and to the extent that the beneficiaries receive income, they are taxed. Estates, in contrast to trusts, are not subject to taxation under the "throwback rules" discussed previously.

The estate may have income and DNI available to distribute to beneficiaries. The only beneficiaries who will not pay income tax on distributions of income from estates are those who receive specific bequests under the will in three installments or less. For example, assume that the will of the decedent, Leslie Little, states "$5,000 to my favorite nephew, Al, and all the rest, residue, and remainder to my cousin, Jeffrey Little." During the first year of the administration of the estate, assets held by the executor generate $16,000 of income. The executor distributes $5,000 to Al and $11,000 to Jeffrey. Since Al's $5,000 was a specific bequest, he is not taxed. This amount is considered a distribution of estate corpus. In this case, Jeffrey would be taxed on the $11,000 he received, and the estate would be taxed on the remaining $5,000 of income.

On the other hand, if Leslie's will stated that the $5,000 bequest to Al was to be paid in five equal annual installments, and in the first year he received $1,000, he would be taxed on the $1,000 only if the payment is made out of income. Beneficiaries will be taxed also on any specific bequests that are required to be paid out of income.

As previously mentioned the "income first" rule requires that all distributions are deemed to be paid out of income first, even if the executor, administrator, or trustee in fact distributes principal in the form of cash or property. For example, assume in the previous example that the distribution to Jeffrey consisted solely of stock. Jeffrey would still be deemed to receive income.

CONCLUSION

The estate planner must attain a degree of familiarity with the income taxation of estates and trusts to properly service clients. Only through a working knowledge of the income tax ramifications of various trust arrangements will a member of the estate planning team be able to perform properly.

HOW BASIS IS DETERMINED

WHAT BASIS IS AND WHY IT IS IMPORTANT

Basis is the starting point in any computation used to determine how much gain (or loss) is incurred upon a sale of property. Gain, for example, is found by the following formula:

Amount realized - Adjusted basis = Gain

Therefore, the higher the basis, the lower the reportable gain on a sale of an asset.

Basis is also the key factor in determining the allowable depreciation deduction that may be taken on buildings and other business or investment assets that wear out over time. Again, a high basis is advantageous since depreciation, the recovery of capital over a given useful life through annual deductions or amortization, the recovery of cost in equal annual increments, depends directly on how much capital— that is, how much investment—the taxpayer has in the property.

Basis, therefore, is generally what a person or other taxpayer "paid" for property. For instance, if property is acquired through a purchase, usually the basis of that asset is its cost. In a loose sense, basis can be thought of as the actual or constructive cost of property for tax purposes (although technically the term, basis, has broader implications).

BASIS AT DEATH

Assets owned by a decedent receive a new federal income tax basis equal to the property's fair market value for federal estate tax purposes.[1] When the fair market value of the asset is higher than the pre-death basis, the old basis is "stepped-up" to the fair market value. Thus, if a father bought a farm for $5,000 and it was valued at $50,000 for federal estate tax purposes when he died and left it to his son, the son (or the father's estate) might have to pay an estate tax, but the son could then sell the farm for its $50,000 value without having to pay any income tax. This is because the $5,000 basis is "stepped up" to $50,000. Using the formula above, when the new adjusted basis of $50,000 is subtracted from the amount realized on the sale, $50,000, there is no gain. This concept is particularly important in buy-sell agreements where stock is purchased at a shareholder's death at a pre-arranged price or under a pre-arranged formula.

NO STEP-UP IN BASIS WHERE DECEDENT HAD ACQUIRED PROPERTY BY GIFT WITHIN A YEAR OF DEATH IF PROPERTY IS LEFT TO DONOR OR DONOR'S SPOUSE

Under prior law, some owners of appreciated property transferred that property to a dying individual and had then received a step-up in basis when the property was left to them under the decedent's will or by intestacy.

Current law contains a provision intended to prevent the avoidance of income taxes on appreciated property by such transfers to dying donees. The law currently provides that if (a) the decedent had received appreciated property by gift during the one-year period ending on the date of death and (b) that property was acquired from the decedent by (or passes from the decedent to) the donor of that property (or to the donor's spouse), the basis of that property in the donor's hands (or in the hands of the donor's spouse) is the adjusted basis of the property in the hands of the decedent immediately before death. In short, the old trick would not work any more.

For example, assume a daughter transferred property with a $10,000 cost and $100,000 fair market value to her mother within one year of the mother's death. Assume the mother left the property to her daughter. The mother's basis would not be stepped up. Rather, it would remain the same as it was in the mother's hands just before she died. In most cases, this means that the daughter will receive the same basis (with adjustments for any gift taxes she paid upon the gift to the mother) as she had before she made the gift.

There is a solution: If the donee-decedent lives for more than one year after receiving the gift, or if the gift is left to anyone other than the donor or the donor's spouse, the property will receive a stepped-up basis. So the property could be left to grandchildren in this example and it would receive a $100,000 basis.

EFFECT OF STEP-UP BASIS RULES ON STOCK REDEMPTIONS AND CROSS PURCHASE AGREEMENTS

As noted in the chapter on Section 303 Stock Redemptions, there are specific rules as to the non-recognition of income tax gain upon the redemption of stock to pay death taxes in certain situations.

Stock includable in the decedent's estate receives a new basis equal to its value at death (or the alternate valuation date if elected). This is usually close to the redemption value, particularly if the stock redemption is promptly carried out. Typically, no or little gain is recognized by the estate or other seller of the stock upon the redemption.

OVERALL EFFECT

The step-up in basis rule has an effect on all tax planning that relates to the sale of assets after death or assets which might be held until death.

There is an incentive for the owner of property with a very low income tax basis, in relation to its market value, to hold the property until death so that the estate can sell it without any income tax on the appreciation in value.

However, inflation is becoming a greater factor in planning, and the wise estate planner will take into consideration the probable future increase in value, with possible concurrent increase in death taxes (consider the implications of both the unified credit and the unlimited marital deduction), and balance this against a current sale. This is particularly appropriate to consider where the sale would be to a person who would eventually receive the property upon the owner's death.

POSSIBLE FUTURE TAX ON APPRECIATION

Informal discussion with Treasury Department officials and a review of the Department's consistent efforts to tax property which has appreciated and is held at death leads to the conclusion that there may be future efforts to tax such appreciation.

Therefore, clients should be urged to keep accurate records with regard to the cost of assets, including such items as purchase price, improvements, depreciation, etc.

IMPLICATIONS AND ISSUES IN COMMUNITY PROPERTY STATES

Stepped-up basis focuses attention on the manner of holding title to property between spouses.

If property is held by spouses in a community property state as the separate property of one spouse, it will all be included in the spouse's estate and receives a new basis at death. The entire property can go to the surviving spouse under the marital deduction rules and will not be subject to tax. Thus, the entire property gets a new stepped-up basis even though it may escape estate tax entirely.

If the property is held as community property, only one-half of the property is included in the estate of the first spouse to die but, equalizing the basis with the separate property arrangement, both halves receive a new income tax basis.[2]

However, this step-up in basis does not occur if the property is held in joint-tenancy or tenancy-in-common.

Take the example of a husband and wife purchasing property using funds earned while residents of a community property state. They want to hold the property in some form of co-ownership. The cost of the property was $1,000 and, at the date-of-death of the first spouse to die, the value is $10,000.

The couple has three different ways to take the property in co-ownership:

1. As joint-tenancy (or tenants by the entirety);

2. As tenants in common; or

3. As community property.

Note the significant difference in income tax basis in Situation II, Figure C-6.1.

Thus, with the reinstatement of the stepped-up basis rule, where property has been paid for with community property earnings or if the contribution to the acquisition was otherwise equal, it again affords a significant advantage as to federal income tax to hold such property in community property as opposed to either joint-tenancy (known as tenancy by the entirety in some states as applied to spouses) or tenancy-in-common.

As to state income tax, one must look to the basis rules of the particular community property state to determine the basis of property for that state's income tax. For example, California now follows the federal rule - the income tax basis of community property will adjust to fair market value on the

Figure C-6.1

Situation I — Property sold for $10,000 prior to death of either spouse					
Plan:	**#1** **Tenants by Entirety**		**#2** **Tenants in Common**		**#3** **Community Property**
Sales price of property		$10,000		$10,000	$10,000
Tax basis of spouses:					
Husband's half	$500		$500		$500
Wife's half	500		500		500
Total Basis		$1,000		$1,000	$1,000
		$9,000		$9,000	$9,000

Situation II — Property sold for $10,000 after death of husband					
Plan:					
Sales price of property		$10,000		$10,000	$10,000
Tax basis of spouses:					
Husband's half	$5,000		$5,000		$5,000
Wife's half	500		500		5,000
Total Basis		5,500		5,500	10,000
Taxable gain on sale		$4,500		$4,500	$-0-

death of either spouse, but only a decedent's one-half interest in joint tenancy property will be so adjusted.

Federal income tax is generally much more important than state income tax for most returns and therefore the double step-up in federal income tax basis of property held as community property will continue to be a very important tax planning consideration.

QUESTIONS AND ANSWERS

Question — Does property receive a new income tax basis equal to fair market value when it is given away during one's lifetime?

Answer — No. In general, the donee retains the donor's basis, increased by the amount of gift tax (or a part thereof) paid with respect to the gift. (See "Computing the Federal Gift Tax," section (11), this appendix.) However, if such basis is greater than the fair market value of the property at the time of the gift, then for purposes of determining loss, upon the donee's sale of the property, the basis is such fair market value.[3] If the property is given in trust, the donee's basis is the donor's basis increased or decreased by any gain or loss the donor recognized on the transfer under the

law applicable in the year of the transfer.[4] Where property is transferred between spouses, or between former spouses if the transfer is incident to the divorce, the transferee's basis is the same as the transferor's basis.[5]

Property which is given away, but for some reason is brought back into the donor's estate for death tax purposes will receive a new basis equal to the fair market value at the time of death. Thus, having a gift brought back into the estate may be good for the donee (who gets a new basis) but bad for the estate (which has to pay death taxes on a larger estate).

Question — If a property is sold with the seller taking back a note and the installment basis of recognizing gain is elected, does the note receive a new basis if the seller dies owning the note?

Answer — No. The gain which is inherent in the note will still be recognized.[7] Thus, a sale of the property before death will result in the gain being recognized, either during the seller's lifetime or after his death.

Question — If, instead of selling an asset such as stock, the shareholder enters into a buy-sell agreement, does the stock receive a stepped-up basis?

Answer — Yes. In general, the stock receives a new basis if it is still held by the shareholder at death as long as there is not a binding executed contract that did not depend on death.

However, entering into a contract of sale that calls for payment of a purchase price and the delivery of an asset upon completion of the payment will generally be treated as if the stock were sold and a note taken back. Gain will still be recognized to the extent there is any payment yet to be made on the purchase of the asset.

Question — If an attorney (or other taxpayer) reporting on the cash basis for income tax purposes dies with clients owing money for services rendered, do these debts receive a stepped-up basis?

Answer — No. Such amounts, which would have been income to the decedent if he had lived, are termed "income in respect of a decedent"[8] and do not receive a stepped-up basis at death. They will be taxed to the taxpayer's estate as income, just as they would have been if he had received them during his lifetime.

Question — Does the person's estate which receives such "income in respect of a decedent" receive any deductions for the estate tax paid on such amounts included in the estate?

Answer — Yes. There is an income-tax deduction for a portion of the estate tax paid on such amounts of "income in respect of a decedent".[9]

Question — If an estate is so small that no estate tax is payable or if no tax is payable because of the unlimited estate tax marital deduction, does the property still receive a stepped-up basis?

Answer — Yes. Regardless of the size of the estate or whether or not a federal estate tax is payable, a stepped-up (or stepped-down if the property has decreased in value below the original cost) basis will apply. Payment of estate tax is not a condition for receiving a new income tax basis.

Question — If a Personal Representative elects to use the alternate valuation date (six months after death) for valuing property for estate tax purposes, does that affect the stepped-up basis rule?

Answer — Yes. If the alternate valuation date is elected for federal estate tax purposes,[10] the fair market value of the property on that six-months-after-death date will be the new income tax basis of the property.[11]

Question — How is basis adjusted in a generation-skipping transfer?

Answer — Very similarly to the basis adjustment allowed when a gift tax is paid on a transfer. The transferee's basis is increased—but not beyond the fair market value of the property transferred—by an amount equal to that portion of the GST tax imposed on the transfer generated by the potential gain in the property immediately prior to the transfer.

Basis Adjustments for Taxable Distributions or Direct Skips

Fair market value of transferred property	$1,000,000
Adjusted basis of transferred property immediately before GS transfer	$600,000
GST tax imposed on transfer	$500,000
Increase in transferee's basis	$200,000
Transferee's new BASIS	$800,000

If the GST tax is imposed because of a taxable termination that occurs at the same time as, and as the result of, an individual's death, the property's basis is stepped up similar to the normal step-up in basis of property at death (with certain limitations).

Footnote References

How Basis is Determined

1. IRC Sec. 1014
2. IRC Sec. 1014(b)(6)
3. IRC Sec. 1015(a), (d)
4. IRC Sec. 1015(b)
5. IRC Sec. 1015(e)
6. IRC Sec. 1014(b)(2), (3), (9)
7. IRC Sec. 691(a)(4)
8. IRC Sec. 1014(c) and IRC Sec. 691
9. IRC Sec. 691(c)
10. IRC Sec. 2032
11. IRC Sec. 1014(a)(2)

POST MORTEM TAX ELECTIONS CHECKLIST

Part A: Income Tax Elections

Section 1: Decedent's Final Returns(s)

I. Were medical expenses of the decedent paid after death?

   A. Medical expenses incurred before death and paid by the estate during the year beginning the year after the date of death may be accrued and deducted on the decedent's income tax return for the year in which the expense was incurred. IRC Secs. 213(a), 213(c).

   B. In the alternative, the medical expense can be deducted as a debt of the decedent for federal estate tax purposes under Code section 2053(b).

II. Did the decedent own any U.S. Savings bonds?

   A. If the decedent had not elected to accrue and report as income interest on Series E and EE Savings bonds, the personal representative may elect to do so on the final return. IRC Sec. 454(a); Rev. Rul. 68-145, 1968-1 CB 203.

   B. If this election is not made, the accrued interest is income in respect of a decedent, and a decedent's estate could elect to accrue it on the estate's income tax return.

III. Did the decedent transfer any property before death which may be replaced under the involuntary conversion rules, or make an installment sale?

   A. If property of the decedent was involuntarily converted, i.e., it was destroyed by natural disaster, condemned, etc., the estate or successor to the decedent may be able to replace it and avoid any taxation of gain to decedent for income tax purposes under Code section Sec. 1033.

   B. The right to roll over the gain on a sale of a personal residence under Code section 1034 will probably not be available, nor will the exclusion of $125,000 of the gain from income if the decedent was more than 55 under Code section 121 unless the sale was consummated prior to death. See Rev. Rul. 82-1, 1982-1 CB 26.

C. If a decedent made an installment sale, the estate can elect out of installment reporting. IRC Sec. 453, Let. Rul. 8545052.

IV. Filing a joint return — A joint return may be filed for decedent and surviving spouse for the year of death, unless the spouse remarries before the end of the year. IRC Sec. 6013(a)(2).

Section 2: Decedent's Estate and Trusts (Appendix C, Income Taxation of Estates and Trusts)

I. Should the estate elect a fiscal year?

II. Should the executor waive commissions?

   A. If the executor or administrator of the estate intends to waive commissions, this should be done before undertaking any duties. Rev. Rul. 64-225, 1964-2 CB 15.

   B. However, it may still be possible to waive them later if no fee was deducted for any tax purpose or claimed in any probate accounting. Rev. Rul. 66-167, 1966-1 CB 20.

III. Where should administrative expenses and casualty losses be deducted?

   A. These may be claimed either as estate tax deductions under Code sections 2053 or 2054 or income tax deductions under Code section 642.

   B. If claimed as income tax deductions, a waiver of the right to claim them as estate tax deductions must be filed. IRC Sec. 642(g); Reg. §§1.642(g)-1, 1.642(g)-2.

Section 3: Partnerships in which Decedent Had Interests (Chapter 11)

I. Should the partnership elect to adjust the income tax basis of partnership assets?

   A. If an appropriate election is made under Code sections 754 and 743(b), the basis of a deceased partner's interest in partnership assets will be adjusted to date of death or estate tax value.

B. Even if the election is not made, if within two years after death partnership assets are distributed "in kind" to the successor of a deceased partner, the distributee may adjust basis in the same manner as provided in Code section 743(b).

Section 4: Closely Held Corporations in which Decedent Had Interests (Chapters 17, 29)

I. Should the estate make or continue an S election?

II. What are considerations in planning distributions from estates to trusts and other beneficiaries?

A. Where the executor has discretion as to funding of trusts with specific trust assets, no funding with S corporation stock should be undertaken until a determination is made as to whether the trust is a qualifying shareholder.

B. Make certain any distributee trust is a qualified trust.

Part B: Estate Tax Elections

Section 1: Alternate Valuation Elections

I. Should the estate elect to value assets at the alternate valuation date, which is:

A. Six months after the date or death, or

B. The date the asset is "disposed of" by the estate. IRC Sec. 2032.

C. However, the election is only available if it reduces the actual size of the gross estate and the estate tax liability are reduced by the election. IRC Sec. 2032(c).

Section 2: Special Use Valuation Elections (Chapter 42)

I. Did the decedent own land used in farming or closely held business?

II. Will the family continue the use of the property and materially participate in its operation?

Section 3: Marital Deduction Elections

I. Did the decedent employ a trust which qualifies as a QTIP?

A. QTIP elections (Chapter 37)

II. Is the surviving spouse a noncitizen?

A. Establishing qualified domestic trusts (Chapter 34)

Section 4: Payment and Deferred Payment of Federal Estate Tax (Chapter 10)

I. Did the decedent own an interest in a closely held business?

II. What is its value in relation to the total estate?

III. Is the closely held business interest in a corporation?

A. Code section 303 stock redemptions (Chapter 31)

Part C: Employee Benefits
(Chapters 8,9,16,18,28)

I. Is a spousal rollover available?

II. Should lump sum distributions and averaging be considered?

III. Will the 15% excise tax apply?

Part D: Disclaimers (Chapter 5)

I. Should any beneficiaries of the estate consider refusing to accept their inheritance?

Part E: Generation-Skipping Elections
(Chapter 14)

I. How should the $1 million generation-skipping transfer tax exemption be allocated?

II. Should a reverse QTIP election be made?

INCOME TAX RATE SCHEDULES

	Taxable Years Beginning in 1995
STANDARD DEDUCTION:	
Married, filing jointly	$6,550
Married, filing separately	3,275
Head of Household	5,750
Single	3,900
PERSONAL EXEMPTION*:	$2,500

SCHEDULE X — SINGLE INDIVIDUALS

Taxable Years Beginning in 1995

Taxable Income			Tax on Lower Amount	Tax Rate on Excess
$ -0-	to	$ 23,350	$ -0-	15%
23,350	to	56,550	3,503	28%
56,550	to	117,950	12,799	31%
117,950	to	256,500	31,833	36%
256,500	to	......	81,711	39.6%

SCHEDULE Y-1 — JOINT RETURNS AND SURVIVNG SPOUSES

Taxable Years Beginning in 1995

Taxable Income			Tax on Lower Amount	Tax Rate on Excess
$ -0-	to	$39,000	$ -0-	15%
39,000	to	94,250	5,850	28%
94,250	to	143,600	21,320	31%
143,600	to	256,500	36,619	36%
256,500	to	......	77,263	39.6%

SCHEDULE Y-2 — MARRIED FILING SEPARATELY

Taxable Years Beginning in 1995

Taxable Income			Tax on Lower Amount	Tax Rate on Excess
$ -0-	to	$19,500	$ -0-	15%
19,500	to	47,125	2,925	28%
47,125	to	71,800	10,660	31%
71,800	to	128,250	18,309	36%
128,250	to	....	38,631	39.6%

SCHEDULE Z — HEAD OF HOUSEHOLD

Taxable Years Beginning in 1995

Taxable Income			Tax on Lower Amount	Tax Rate on Excess
$ -0-	to	$31,250	$ -0-	15%
31,250	to	80,750	4,688	28%
80,750	to	130,800	18,548	31%
130,800	to	256,500	34,063	36%
256,500	to	......	79,315	39.6%

*Subject to phase out at higher levels of taxable income.

TAX RATE SCHEDULE FOR ESTATES AND TRUSTS

Taxable Years Beginning in 1995

Taxable Income			Tax on Lower Amount	Tax Rate on Excess
$ -0-	to	$1,550	$ -0-	15%
1,550	to	3,700	233	28%
3,700	to	5,600	835	31%
5,600	to	7,650	1,424	36%
7,650	to	......	2,162	39.6%

TAX RATE SCHEDULE FOR CORPORATIONS‡

Taxable Years Beginning in 1993 and Later ‡‡

Taxable Income			Tax on Lower Amount	Tax Rate on Excess
$ -0-	to	$ 50,000	$ -0-	15%
50,000	to	75,000	7,500	25%
75,000	to	100,000	13,750	34%
100,000	to	335,000	22,250	39% *
335,000	to	10,000,000	113,900	34%
10,000,000	to	15,000,000	3,400,000	35%
15,000,000	to	18,333,333	5,150,000	38% **
18,333,333	to	......	......	35%

‡ Personal Service Corporations are taxed at a flat rate of 35%.

‡‡ Corporations with taxable income over $10,000,000 that had a fiscal year that began in 1992 and ended in 1993 were required to use a blended rate. See Ann. 93-133, 1993-32 IRB 12.

* A 5% surtax is imposed on income above $100,000 until the benefit of the 15 and 25% tax rates has been canceled. Thus, taxable income from $100,000 to $335,000 is taxed at the rate of 39%.

** Corporations with taxable income over $15,000,000 are subject to an additional tax of the lesser of 3% of the excess over $15,000,000 or $100,000. Thus, taxable income exceeding $18,333,333 is taxed at 35%. See Ann. 93-133, 1993-32 IRB 12.

LUMP SUM DISTRIBUTIONS

Net Lump Sum Taxable Amount	10 Yr. Averaging*		5 Yr. Averaging**	
	Tax	Effective Tax Rate	Tax 1995	Effective Tax Rate
$ 10,000	$ 550	.06	$ 750	.08
20,000	1,100	.06	1,500	.08
30,000	2,521	.08	3,300	.11
40,000	4,187	.10	6,415	.16
50,000	5,874	.12	9,845	.19
75,000	10,305	.14	18,518	.24
100,000	14,471	.14	26,269	.26
150,000	24,570	.16	43,371	.29
200,000	36,922	.18	61,371	.30
250,000	50,770	.20	79,371	.31
300,000	66,330	.22	98,937	.33
500,000	143,682	.29	178,137	.35
1,000,000	382,210	.38	376,137	.37
2,000,000	882,210	.44	772,137	.38
3,000,000	1,382,210	.46	1,168,137	.39
4,000,000	1,882,210	.47	1,564,137	.39
5,000,000	2,382,210	.48	1,960,137	.39

* Amount of tax and effective tax rates rounded.

** The 5-year averaging table takes into account the minimum distribution allowance.

Income averaging for lump sum distributions is discussed in more detail in Chapter 28.

The Tools and Techniques of Estate Planning

UNIFIED RATE SCHEDULE FOR ESTATE AND GIFT TAXES
(IRC Sec. 2001(c))

If the amount with respect to which the tentative tax to be computed is:	*The tentative tax is:*
Not over $10,000	18% of such amount.
Over $10,000 but not over $20,000	$1,800 plus 20% of the excess of such amount over $10,000.
Over $20,000 but not over $40,000	$3,800 plus 22% of the excess of such amount over $20,000.
Over $40,000 but not over $60,000	$8,200 plus 24% of the excess of such amount over $40,000.
Over $60,000 but not over $80,000	$13,000 plus 26% of the excess of such amount over $60,000.
Over $80,000 but not over $100,000	$18,200 plus 28% of the excess of such amount over $80,000.
Over $100,000 but not over $150,000	$23,800 plus 30% of the excess of such amount over $100,000.
Over $150,000 but not over $250,000	$38,800 plus 32% of the excess of such amount over $150,000.
Over $250,000 but not over $500,000	$70,800 plus 34% of the excess of such amount over $250,000.
Over $500,000 but not over $750,000	$155,800 plus 37% of the excess of such amount over $500,000.
Over $750,000 but not over $1,000,000	$248,300 plus 39% of the excess of such amount over $750,000.
Over $1,000,000 but not over $1,250,000	$345,800 plus 41% of the excess of such amount over $1,000,000.
Over $1,250,000 but not over $1,500,000	$448,300 plus 43% of the excess of such amount over $1,250,000.
Over $1,500,000 but not over $2,000,000	$555,800 plus 45% of the excess of such amount over $1,500,000.
Over $2,000,000 but not over $2,500,000	$780,800 plus 49% of the excess of such amount over $2,000,000.
Over $2,500,000 but not over $3,000,000	$1,025,800 plus 53% of the excess of such amount over $2,500,000.
Over $3,000,000	$1,290,800 plus 55% of the excess over $3,000,000.

*In the case of decedents dying and gifts made after 1987, the tentative tax as determined above is increased by an amount equal to 5 percent of so much of the amount with respect to which the tentative tax is computed as exceeds $10,000,000 but does not exceed $21,040,000.

UNIFIED GIFT AND ESTATE TAX RATE SCHEDULE IN THE CASE OF DECEDENTS DYING AND GIFTS MADE AFTER 1983			
(A)	(B)	(C)	(D)
Amount subject to tentative tax		Tax on amount in Column A*	Tax rate on excess over amounts in Column A
exceeding	but not exceeding		Percent
$ —	$10,000	$ —	18
10,000	20,000	1,800	20
20,000	40,000	3,800	22
40,000	60,000	8,200	24
60,000	80,000	13,000	26
80,000	100,000	18,200	28
100,000	150,000	23,800	30
150,000	250,000	38,800	32
250,000	500,000	70,800	34
500,000	750,000	155,800	37
750,000	1,000,000	248,300	39
1,000,000	1,250,000	345,800	41
1,250,000	1,500,000	448,300	43
1,500,000	2,000,000	555,800	45
2,000,000	2,500,000	780,800	49
2,500,000	3,000,000	1,025,800	53
3,000,000	10,000,000	1,290,800	55
10,000,000	21,040,000	5,140,800	60
21,080,000	—	11,764,800	55

*Before credits. Includes 5 percent add-on tax.

TRANSFERS MADE AFTER 1987

The advantage of the unified credit and graduated rates is lost to estates (or for taxable gifts) in excess of $10,000,000. This is accomplished in the following manner: the gift and estate tax liability for taxable transfers in excess of $10,000,000 is increased by imposing an additional 5 percent tax on the excess of

(a) The taxable transfer

over

(b) 10,000,000

This 5 percent add-on tax ends when cumulative transfers reach $21,040,000. At that point the 55 percent rate becomes applicable to additional amounts. So a taxable estate of $3,000,000 or more is taxed to 55 percent on any amount in excess of $3,000,000 plus a 5 percent add-on tax for the taxable estate exceeding $10,000,000 but not exceeding $21,040,000.

For example, assume an individual who dies in 1995 has a taxable estate of $25,000,000. The tentative tax would be $13,390,800. This is further increased by a 5 percent add-on tax on $11,040,000 ($21,040,000 - $10,000,000), $552,000. The total tentative tax would therefore be $13,750,000. If the $192,800 credit that is phased out by operation of the 5 percent add-on tax is then added, the result is $13,942,800.)

MAXIMUM CREDIT TABLE FOR STATE DEATH TAXES

The amount of any state death taxes paid may be subtracted from the federal estate tax as determined under the preceding table, provided, however, that the maximum to be subtracted may not exceed the maximum determined under the following table:*

If the taxable estate is:	The maximum tax credit shall be:
Not over $150,000	8/10ths of 1% of the amount by which the taxable estate exceeds $100,000.
Over $150,000 but not over $200,000	$400 plus 1.6% of the excess over $150,000.
Over $200,000 but not over $300,000	$1,200 plus 2.4% of the excess over $200,000.
Over $300,000 but not over $500,000	$3,600 plus 3.2% of the excess over $300,000.
Over $500,000 but not over $700,000	$10,000 plus 4% of the excess over $500,000.
Over $700,000 but not over $900,000	$18,000 plus 4.8% of the excess over $700,000.
Over $900,000 but not over $1,100,000	$27,600 plus 5.6% of the excess over $900,000.
Over $1,100,000 but not over $1,600,000	$38,800 plus 6.4% of the excess over $1,100,000.
Over $1,600,000 but not over $2,100,000	$70,800 plus 7.2% of the excess over $1,600,000.
Over $2,100,000 but not over $2,600,000	$106,800 plus 8% of the excess over $2,100,000.
Over $2,600,000 but not over $3,100,000	$146,800 plus 8.8% of the excess over $2,600,000.
Over $3,100,000 but not over $3,600,000	$190,800 plus 9.6% of the excess over $3,100,000.
Over $3,600,000 but not over $4,100,000	$238,800 plus 10.4% of the excess over $3,600,000.
Over $4,100,000 but not over $5,100,000	$290,800 plus 11.2% of the excess over $4,100,000.
Over $5,100,000 but not over $6,100,000	$402,800 plus 12% of the excess over $5,100,000.
Over $6,100,000 but not over $7,100,000	$522,800 plus 12.8% of the excess over $6,100,000.
Over $7,100,000 but not over $8,100,000	$650,800 plus 13.6% of the excess over $7,100,000.
Over $8,100,000 but not over $9,100,000	$786,800 plus 14.4% of the excess over $8,100,000.
Over $9,100,000 but not over $10,100,000	$930,800 plus 15.2% of the excess over $9,100,000.
Over $10,100,000	$1,082,800 plus 16% of the excess over $10,100,000.

* This table resembles the table contained in IRC Section 2011(b), but it is not the same. The table in the Code is based on the *adjusted taxable estate*, defined as the taxable estate reduced by $60,000. This table is a modification of that table and can be used directly from the *taxable estate*.

WORKING WITH THE IRS VALUATION TABLES

by
Stephan R. Leimberg and Robert J. Doyle

It is essential that an estate planner understand how to work with the IRS *Actuarial Values* Alpha (IRS Pub. 1457) and Beta (IRS Pub. 1458) volumes[1] if the planner uses any tool or technique involving annuities, life estates, remainders, and terms of years. A portion of these actuarial/valuation tables are reproduced at the end of this article.

Specifically, an estate planner must understand the impact of mortality and discounting assumptions and how to compute present values if a suggestion to a client or tax computation pertains to:

(1) valuing property for federal estate, gift, and generation-skipping transfer tax purposes (Code sections 2031, 2512, and 2624);

(2) valuing charitable contributions for income, gift, and estate tax purposes (Code sections 170, 641, 664, 2522, and 2055);

(3) valuing amounts qualifying for the federal estate and gift tax marital deduction (Code sections 2056 and 2523); and

(4) valuing the annuity amount protected from the 15 percent excise tax for excess retirement accumulations.

Note that the rules explained below do not apply for purposes of (a) the pension and profit sharing rules provided in Code sections 401 to 409 and (b) "any other provision" specified by the IRS.[2]

THE VALUATION PROCESS

The Computational Rules. To make these time value of money computations, a discount (interest) rate (rounded to the nearest $2/10$ths of one percent) based on the 120% applicable federal midterm rate (120% of AFMR) (computed from the average market yield of U.S. obligations) must be used for the month of the valuation is to be made.

Once the discount rate is set, it does not change. This rate can be found each month in a revenue ruling released by the IRS. Look for Table 5 in the ruling which shows the rate under Code section 7520 for the coming month. The rate can also be found in each issue of *Taxline*, a monthly newsletter published by the National Underwriter Company.

Finding the discount rate is relatively simple; working with the number to compute the deduction for a charitable remainder trust or to make any other valuation is a much more difficult matter. Computer software can make the task easier.

"Date stamping" all illustrations involving time value of money sensitive concepts is recommended since the positive or negative results of a given concept can vary significantly from month to month. The importance of timely implementation of suggestions can not be over-emphasized.

An important qualification in the application of these rules in charitable situations should be kept in mind: if an income, estate, or gift tax charitable contribution is allowable for any part of the property transferred, the taxpayer may elect to use either the month of transfer discount rate or the discount rate for either of the two months preceding the month in which the valuation date falls. In essence this provides an incredible three month choice not available in other circumstances. In fact if the client waits until toward the end of the month when the following month's discount rate is published, the client can choose among four month's discount rates.

DOING THE COMPUTATIONS:

For gift, estate, and generation-skipping transfer tax valuation purposes, the fair market value of remainder interests,[3] terms for years,[4] annuities,[5] and life estates[6] is the present value of future payments.

Remainders and Reversions

The following example illustrates how the values of remainders and reversions are computed under the rules:

Assume a client makes a transfer of $100,000 to an irrevocable trust. The income interest lasts for a term of 10 years. What is the gift tax value of that gift? Assume that the discount rate is 9.8 percent. The present value of the gift can be determined directly by this process:

(1) Start with *Actuarial Values Alpha Volume* (portions of the valuation tables are reproduced following this discussion of working with the tables)

(2) Go to Table B (Which shows the present worth of an annuity, an income interest, and a remainder interest for a term certain)

(3) Find the appropriate interest rate (9.8%) subtable of Table B

(4) Go down column (1) under "Years" to "10," and then across to the right under column (4), "Remainder." The six-decimal-place factor is 0.392624.

(5) Multiplying 0.392624 by $100,000 produces a present value of $39,262.40.[7]

Income Interests

Using the same example as above, with the same assumptions, the value of the ten-year term certain income interest would be determined as follows:

(1) Go to the 9.8 percent subtable of Table B

(2) Go down column (1) to the appropriate number of years (10 in this case) and across to column (3), "Income Interest." The factor in this case is 0.607376. (Alternatively, subtract the remainder factor (0.392624) — found either by formula or from IRS Table B — from 1.000000.)

The right to a stream of income from a trust that will certainly last for ten years is worth roughly 61 cents for every dollar placed into the trust if money is presumed to be worth 9.8 percent per year. If $100,000 were placed into a trust lasting ten years, the present value of the income stream would be $60,737.60. Together with the $39,262.40 remainder, the two would be worth 100 percent of the original $100,000.

Annuities

Another example may be used to illustrate how term annuities are valued. Assume a client makes a gift of an annuity interest for a ten-year term. Assume again that the discount interest rate is 9.8 percent. The valuation factor is found once again in the 9.8 percent subtable of Table B in the same manner as above under Column (2), "Annuity."[8] The factor is 6.1977. To compute the present value of the annuity from the factor, multiply the annuity payable annually by the factor.

For instance, if the annuity payable was $10,000 a year (payable at the end of each year), the present value of payments to be made for ten years is $61,977 ($10,000 x 6.1977). This procedure can be used to compute term certain valuation

factors for charitable lead and remainder annuity trusts for terms of years.

Because the annuity factors from Table B are based on the assumption annuity payments will be made once a year at the end of the year, these factors must be adjusted when payments are more frequently and/or at the beginning of each payment period.[9]

Life Estates and Annuities for Life

Tables S and R(2) in ALPHA provides practitioners with annuity, life estate, and remainder interest valuation factors for single and joint lives, respectively, based on a wide range of rates and ages between 0 and 109. (Portions of these valuation tables are reproduced following this discussion of working with the tables.) At 9.8 percent, for example, the value of a single life estate is found by this process:

(1) Find the 9.8 percent page in Table S.

(2) Look below "Age" (col. 1) to the appropriate age, for example, 60

(3) Follow the row to the right until finding the factor under "Life Estate" (col. 3). With these assumptions, as Table 3 shows, the life estate factor would be 0.76842.

The value of the life annuity factor can be found by looking under "Annuity" (col. 2) or it may be computed directly by dividing the life estate factor by the discount rate. Here it would be 0.76842/0.098 = 7.8410.

SUMMARY AND SUGGESTIONS

Almost every time value of money or longevity sensitive estate and financial planning tool or technique has, to some extent, been affected by the monthly changing valuation rules. Illustrating the numerical advantages of a given concept is now more difficult because present and future monetary values will vary (sometimes considerably) from month to month and the certainty of accomplishing stated objectives has become less certain than ever.

Planners should "date stamp" all written proposals and suggestions to clients and impress upon them the importance of timely (but carefully planned) implementation of suggested tools and techniques. To avoid malpractice situations, planners should base illustrations on ranges of rates rather than making projections dependent on just one discount rate.

More attention must be paid by planners to the trend of interest rates and the impact of that trend on tools and techniques. Timing is essential since starting a tool or technique in one month rather than another may result in significant tax savings (or costs). The "wait and see" approach (waiting until the IRS publishes the 120% of AFMR figure) and selecting the optimum month for making a gift can, by itself, result in substantial valuation differences.

FOOTNOTES

1. These two IRS volumes are available for a fee by writing to the Superintendent of Documents, United States Government Printing Office, Washington, DC, 20404.

2. IRC Sec. 7520(b). See "IRS Actuarial Valuation Tables — The New Look," Tax Management Memorandum, Vol. 30, No. 7, March 27, 1989. The authors feel the IRS authority to exempt particular situations from the new valuation system is meant to extend to situations where "the valuation depends upon interest rate assumptions which are plan specific."

    With respect to a charitable remainder unitrust, although the stipulated percentage payout is the principal factor involved in calculating the client's deduction, the computation must also take into account the impact of the frequency of payout (monthly, quarterly, semiannually, etc.), and the number of months between the valuation date and the first required payout. These unitrust factors and an explanation of their use can be found in *Actuarial Values Beta Volume* (IRS Pub. 1458).

3. A remainder is the right to use, possess, and enjoy property when the prior owner's interest ends. A remainder interest is valued by subtracting the present value of any prior interest from the fair market value of the property.

    A reversion, which has the same monetary value as a remainder interest, is a future right the transferor of property has retained to use, possess, or enjoy the property in question. It is the fixed right to future possession that was never given away or sold.

4. An income interest for a term of years is a right — limited to a specific period of time — to the income from property or the right to use nonincome producing property. It is not dependent on some outside measurement such as the life of one or more persons.

5. An annuity is a systematic liquidation of principal and interest over a period of time. The length of the annuity can be set to last for a fixed number of years regardless of events. Alternatively, payments can take the form of a "life annuity" measured by the span of one or more lives. For instance, the payments can last for the life of a client or the joint lives of the client and his or her spouse.

6. A life estate is the right to use, possess, and enjoy property or the income it produces for the life of a specified person. That measuring life (using age based on the individual's nearest birthday) can be the life of the holder of the life interest or may be measured by the life of some other person (an estate per autre vie). A life estate can also be payable for more than one life (for instance, the life estate can last for the joint lives of the client and his or her spouse). The life income beneficiary receives no right to enjoy principal.

7. Remainder factors for a term certain may be computed directly without the use of the ALPHA Table B. In the text example the remainder factor is computed in the following manner:

    Step 1: Add 1 to the applicable interest rate (9.8 percent). Result: 1.098

    Step 2: Increase the result of Step 1 to the exponential power of the number of years in the term (10). Result: 2.546967

    Step 3: Divide the result of Step 2 into the number 1 to arrive at the remainder factor. Result: 0.392624. (IRS Notice 89-24 indicates that valuation factors for term interests must be computed to 6 decimal places.)

    Step 4: The result of Step 3 is then multiplied by the value of the principal placed into the trust to arrive at the gift or estate or GST tax value of the remainder interest. So if $100,000 were placed into the trust, the remainder (or reversion) would have a value of $39,264.40, as indicated in the text.

8. Alternatively, the term annuity factor may be computed directly by dividing the applicable discount rate (9.8% in this case) into the "income factor." In this example, dividing 9.8 percent into 0.607376 results in an annuity factor of 6.1977.

    Although valuation factors for incomes and remainders for terms of years must be rounded to 6 decimal places according to Notice 89-24, valuation factors for annuities for terms of years are still rounded to 4 decimal places. Valuation factors for life estates and remainders that are based on life expectancy are rounded to 5 decimal places and for life annuities are rounded to 4 decimal places.

    Practitioners doing these computations by hand must take into account the sometimes significant differences these rounding conventions can make.

9. Certain adjustments must be made to the annuity factor if an annuity is paid more frequently than annually and/or is paid at the beginning rather than the end of each period. For instance, if payments are made weekly, monthly, quarterly, or semiannually, enjoyment of the annuity is to some extent accelerated as compared with annual payments that are assumed to be paid at the end of the year.

    The adjusted value is computed by multiplying the normal end-of-year factor by a second factor which converts the weekly, monthly, quarterly, or semiannual payments into amounts that are actuarially equivalent to a single payment at the end of the year. Likewise, if payments are based on a life expectancy but are payable at the beginning of weekly, monthly, quarterly, semiannual, or annual periods, certain adjustments must be made.

    Frequency adjustment factors are given in Table K (reproduced at the end of this article) of ALPHA for various interest rates and payment frequencies.

    The adjustment factors are applied in the following manner. The annual annuity factor, once found, is multiplied by the appropriate frequency adjustment factor. For example, the value of an 10-year term annuity of $5,000 paid at the end of each semiannual period (20 payments) would be derived by multiplying the $10,000 total annual payment by the annual factor of 6.1977 (computed on the basis of a 9.8 percent discount rate) and by 1.0239 (from table K) to derive a value of $63,458.25 as compared to $61,977 when the payments are made at annual intervals.

    If an annuity is based on life expectancy and payments are made at the beginning of an interval, rather than the end, the value is determined by computing the value with payments that are made at the end of the interval plus one interval's payment. For example, a monthly annuity of $5,000 payable at the beginning of each month for the life of a 60 year old would be valued as follows if the discount rate were 9.8 percent. The single life annuity factor from Table S(9.8) of ALPHA is 7.8410. The total annual payment, $60,000, is multiplied by 7.8410 and by the monthly periodic adjustment factor from Table K, 1.0442. The result is $491,254.33. Finally this value must be adjusted for the fact that payments are at the beginning rather than the end of each month. To make this final adjustment, simply add one monthly payment, $5,000, to $491,254.33 to derive the value of the annuity, $496,254.33.

Actuarial Values Alpha Volume does not provide a table of adjustment factors for term annuities with payments that are made at the beginning of annual, semiannual, quarterly, monthly, or weekly intervals. Annuity Adjustment Factors Table B, reproduced from the *Advanced Sales Reference Service*, can be used where term annuity payments are made at the beginning of an interval. Simply multiply the total annual payment by the product of (1) the annual annuity factor multiplied by (2) the factor from the Annuity Adjustment Factors Table B.

VALUATION TABLES

TABLE 80CNSMT

Age x	l(x)	Age x	l(x)	Age x	l(x)
(1)	(2)	(1)	(2)	(1)	(2)
0	100000	37	95492	74	59279
1	98740	38	95317	75	56799
2	98648	39	95129	76	54239
3	98584	40	94926	77	51599
4	98535	41	94706	78	48878
5	98495	42	94465	79	46071
6	98459	43	94201	80	43180
7	98426	44	93913	81	40208
8	98396	45	93599	82	37172
9	98370	46	93256	83	34095
10	98347	47	92882	84	31012
11	98328	48	92472	85	27960
12	98309	49	92021	86	24961
13	98285	50	91526	87	22038
14	98248	51	90986	88	19235
15	98196	52	90402	89	16598
16	98129	53	89771	90	14154
17	98047	54	89087	91	11908
18	97953	55	88348	92	9863
19	97851	56	87551	93	8032
20	97741	57	86695	94	6424
21	97623	58	85776	95	5043
22	97499	59	84789	96	3884
23	97370	60	83726	97	2939
24	97240	61	82581	98	2185
25	97110	62	81348	99	1598
26	96982	63	80024	100	1150
27	96856	64	78609	101	815
28	96730	65	77107	102	570
29	96604	66	75520	103	393
30	96477	67	73846	104	267
31	96350	68	72082	105	179
32	96220	69	70218	106	119
33	96088	70	68248	107	78
34	95951	71	66165	108	51
35	95808	72	63972	109	33
36	95655	73	61673	110	0

Appendix D
Valuation Tables

TABLE K
ADJUSTMENT FACTORS FOR ANNUITIES
PAYABLE AT THE END OF EACH INTERVAL

FREQUENCY OF PAYMENTS

INT. RATE	ANNUALLY	SEMI ANNUALLY	QUARTERLY	MONTHLY	WEEKLY
2.2%	1.0000	1.0055	1.0082	1.0100	1.0107
2.4%	1.0000	1.0060	1.0090	1.0110	1.0117
2.6%	1.0000	1.0065	1.0097	1.0119	1.0127
2.8%	1.0000	1.0070	1.0104	1.0128	1.0137
3.0%	1.0000	1.0074	1.0112	1.0137	1.0146
3.2%	1.0000	1.0079	1.0119	1.0146	1.0156
3.4%	1.0000	1.0084	1.0127	1.0155	1.0166
3.6%	1.0000	1.0089	1.0134	1.0164	1.0175
3.8%	1.0000	1.0094	1.0141	1.0173	1.0185
4.0%	1.0000	1.0099	1.0149	1.0182	1.0195
4.2%	1.0000	1.0104	1.0156	1.0191	1.0205
4.4%	1.0000	1.0109	1.0164	1.0200	1.0214
4.6%	1.0000	1.0114	1.0171	1.0209	1.0224
4.8%	1.0000	1.0119	1.0178	1.0218	1.0234
5.0%	1.0000	1.0123	1.0186	1.0227	1.0243
5.2%	1.0000	1.0128	1.0193	1.0236	1.0253
5.4%	1.0000	1.0133	1.0200	1.0245	1.0262
5.6%	1.0000	1.0138	1.0208	1.0254	1.0272
5.8%	1.0000	1.0143	1.0215	1.0263	1.0282
6.0%	1.0000	1.0148	1.0222	1.0272	1.0291
6.2%	1.0000	1.0153	1.0230	1.0281	1.0301
6.4%	1.0000	1.0158	1.0237	1.0290	1.0311
6.6%	1.0000	1.0162	1.0244	1.0299	1.0320
6.8%	1.0000	1.0167	1.0252	1.0308	1.0330
7.0%	1.0000	1.0172	1.0259	1.0317	1.0339
7.2%	1.0000	1.0177	1.0266	1.0326	1.0349
7.4%	1.0000	1.0182	1.0273	1.0335	1.0358
7.6%	1.0000	1.0187	1.0281	1.0344	1.0368
7.8%	1.0000	1.0191	1.0288	1.0353	1.0378
8.0%	1.0000	1.0196	1.0295	1.0362	1.0387
8.2%	1.0000	1.0201	1.0302	1.0370	1.0397
8.4%	1.0000	1.0206	1.0310	1.0379	1.0406
8.6%	1.0000	1.0211	1.0317	1.0388	1.0416
8.8%	1.0000	1.0215	1.0324	1.0397	1.0425
9.0%	1.0000	1.0220	1.0331	1.0406	1.0435
9.2%	1.0000	1.0225	1.0339	1.0415	1.0444
9.4%	1.0000	1.0230	1.0346	1.0424	1.0454
9.6%	1.0000	1.0235	1.0353	1.0433	1.0463
9.8%	1.0000	1.0239	1.0360	1.0442	1.0473
10.0%	1.0000	1.0244	1.0368	1.0450	1.0482
10.2%	1.0000	1.0249	1.0375	1.0459	1.0492
10.4%	1.0000	1.0254	1.0382	1.0468	1.0501
10.6%	1.0000	1.0258	1.0389	1.0477	1.0511
10.8%	1.0000	1.0263	1.0396	1.0486	1.0520
11.0%	1.0000	1.0268	1.0404	1.0495	1.0530
11.2%	1.0000	1.0273	1.0411	1.0503	1.0539
11.4%	1.0000	1.0277	1.0418	1.0512	1.0549
11.6%	1.0000	1.0282	1.0425	1.0521	1.0558
11.8%	1.0000	1.0287	1.0432	1.0530	1.0568
12.0%	1.0000	1.0292	1.0439	1.0539	1.0577
12.2%	1.0000	1.0296	1.0447	1.0548	1.0587
12.4%	1.0000	1.0301	1.0454	1.0556	1.0596
12.6%	1.0000	1.0306	1.0461	1.0565	1.0605
12.8%	1.0000	1.0310	1.0468	1.0574	1.0615
13.0%	1.0000	1.0315	1.0475	1.0583	1.0624
13.2%	1.0000	1.0320	1.0482	1.0591	1.0634
13.4%	1.0000	1.0324	1.0489	1.0600	1.0643
13.6%	1.0000	1.0329	1.0496	1.0609	1.0652
13.8%	1.0000	1.0334	1.0504	1.0618	1.0662
14.0%	1.0000	1.0339	1.0511	1.0626	1.0671

Appendix D
Valuation Tables

ANNUITY ADJUSTMENT FACTORS TABLE B*
(For valuation dates occurring after April 30, 1989)

FREQUENCY OF PAYMENTS

INTEREST RATE**	ANNUALLY	SEMI ANNUALLY	QUARTERLY	MONTHLY	WEEKLY
5.2%	1.0520	1.0388	1.0323	1.0279	1.0263
5.4%	1.0540	1.0403	1.0335	1.0290	1.0273
5.6%	1.0560	1.0418	1.0348	1.0301	1.0283
5.8%	1.0580	1.0433	1.0360	1.0311	1.0293
6.0%	1.0600	1.0448	1.0372	1.0322	1.0303
6.2%	1.0620	1.0463	1.0385	1.0333	1.0313
6.4%	1.0640	1.0478	1.0397	1.0343	1.0323
6.6%	1.0660	1.0492	1.0409	1.0354	1.0333
6.8%	1.0680	1.0507	1.0422	1.0365	1.0343
7.0%	1.0700	1.0522	1.0434	1.0375	1.0353
7.2%	1.0720	1.0537	1.0446	1.0386	1.0363
7.4%	1.0740	1.0552	1.0458	1.0396	1.0373
7.6%	1.0760	1.0567	1.0471	1.0407	1.0383
7.8%	1.0780	1.0581	1.0483	1.0418	1.0393
8.0%	1.0800	1.0596	1.0495	1.0428	1.0403
8.2%	1.0820	1.0611	1.0507	1.0439	1.0413
8.4%	1.0840	1.0626	1.0520	1.0449	1.0422
8.6%	1.0860	1.0641	1.0532	1.0460	1.0432
8.8%	1.0880	1.0655	1.0544	1.0471	1.0442
9.0%	1.0900	1.0670	1.0556	1.0481	1.0452
9.2%	1.0920	1.0685	1.0569	1.0492	1.0462
9.4%	1.0940	1.0700	1.0581	1.0502	1.0472
9.6%	1.0960	1.0715	1.0593	1.0513	1.0482
9.8%	1.0980	1.0729	1.0605	1.0523	1.0492
10.0%	1.1000	1.0744	1.0618	1.0534	1.0502
10.2%	1.1020	1.0759	1.0630	1.0544	1.0512
10.4%	1.1040	1.0774	1.0642	1.0555	1.0521
10.6%	1.1060	1.0788	1.0654	1.0565	1.0531
10.8%	1.1080	1.0803	1.0666	1.0576	1.0541
11.0%	1.1100	1.0818	1.0679	1.0586	1.0551
11.2%	1.1120	1.0833	1.0691	1.0597	1.0561
11.4%	1.1140	1.0847	1.0703	1.0607	1.0571
11.6%	1.1160	1.0862	1.0715	1.0618	1.0581
11.8%	1.1180	1.0877	1.0727	1.0628	1.0590
12.0%	1.1200	1.0892	1.0739	1.0639	1.0600
12.2%	1.1220	1.0906	1.0752	1.0649	1.0610
12.4%	1.1240	1.0921	1.0764	1.0660	1.0620
12.6%	1.1260	1.0936	1.0776	1.0670	1.0630
12.8%	1.1280	1.0950	1.0788	1.0681	1.0639
13.0%	1.1300	1.0965	1.0800	1.0691	1.0649
13.2%	1.1320	1.0980	1.0812	1.0701	1.0659
13.4%	1.1340	1.0994	1.0824	1.0712	1.0669
13.6%	1.1360	1.1009	1.0836	1.0722	1.0679
13.8%	1.1380	1.1024	1.0849	1.0733	1.0688
14.0%	1.1400	1.1039	1.0861	1.0743	1.0698
14.2%	1.1420	1.1053	1.0873	1.0754	1.0708
14.4%	1.1440	1.1068	1.0885	1.0764	1.0718
14.6%	1.1460	1.1083	1.0897	1.0774	1.0727
14.8%	1.1480	1.1097	1.0909	1.0785	1.0737
15.0%	1.1500	1.1112	1.0921	1.0795	1.0747

* For use in calculating the value of a term certain annuity payable at the beginning of each period.

** Use appropriate interest rate for the month in which the valuation date occurs.

Reprinted from the *Advanced Sales Reference Service*

© 1989 The National Underwriter Company

The Tools and Techniques of Estate Planning

Appendix D
Valuation Tables

TABLE B
SHOWING THE PRESENT WORTH OF AN ANNUITY, OF AN
INCOME INTEREST, AND OF A REMAINDER INTEREST
FOR A TERM CERTAIN

INTEREST RATE

	6.6%				6.8%		
(1)	(2)	(3)	(4)	(1)	(2)	(3)	(4)
YEARS	ANNUITY	INCOME INTEREST	REMAINDER	YEARS	ANNUITY	INCOME INTEREST	REMAINDER
1	0.9381	.061914	.938086	1	0.9363	.063670	.936330
2	1.8181	.119994	.880006	2	1.8130	.123287	.876713
3	2.6436	.174479	.825521	3	2.6339	.179108	.820892
4	3.4180	.225590	.774410	4	3.4026	.231374	.768626
5	4.1445	.273536	.726464	5	4.1222	.280313	.719687
6	4.8260	.318514	.681486	6	4.7961	.326136	.673864
7	5.4653	.360708	.639292	7	5.4271	.369041	.630959
8	6.0650	.400289	.599711	8	6.0179	.409214	.590786
9	6.6276	.437419	.562581	9	6.5710	.446830	.553170
10	7.1553	.472250	.527750	10	7.0890	.482050	.517950
11	7.6504	.504925	.495075	11	7.5739	.515028	.484972
12	8.1148	.535577	.464423	12	8.0280	.545907	.454093
13	8.5505	.564331	.435669	13	8.4532	.574819	.425181
14	8.9592	.591305	.408695	14	8.8513	.601891	.398109
15	9.3426	.616609	.383391	15	9.2241	.627238	.372762
16	9.7022	.640346	.359654	16	9.5731	.650972	.349028
17	10.0396	.662614	.337386	17	9.8999	.673195	.326805
18	10.3561	.683502	.316498	18	10.2059	.694003	.305997
19	10.6530	.703098	.296902	19	10.4924	.713486	.286514
20	10.9315	.721480	.278520	20	10.7607	.731728	.268272
21	11.1928	.738724	.261276	21	11.0119	.748809	.251191
22	11.4379	.754901	.245099	22	11.2471	.764803	.235197
23	11.6678	.770076	.229924	23	11.4673	.779778	.220222
24	11.8835	.784311	.215689	24	11.6735	.793799	.206201
25	12.0858	.797666	.202334	25	11.8666	.806928	.193072
26	12.2756	.810193	.189807	26	12.0474	.819221	.180779
27	12.4537	.821944	.178056	27	12.2166	.830731	.169269
28	12.6207	.832969	.167031	28	12.3751	.841509	.158491
29	12.7774	.843310	.156690	29	12.5235	.851600	.148400
30	12.9244	.853011	.146989	30	12.6625	.861049	.138951
31	13.0623	.862112	.137888	31	12.7926	.869896	.130104
32	13.1917	.870649	.129351	32	12.9144	.878180	.121820
33	13.3130	.878658	.121342	33	13.0285	.885936	.114064
34	13.4268	.886170	.113830	34	13.1353	.893198	.106802
35	13.5336	.893218	.106782	35	13.2353	.899999	.100001
36	13.6338	.899829	.100171	36	13.3289	.906366	.093634
37	13.7277	.906031	.093969	37	13.4166	.912327	.087673
38	13.8159	.911849	.088151	38	13.4987	.917910	.082090
39	13.8986	.917307	.082693	39	13.5755	.923136	.076864
40	13.9762	.922427	.077573	40	13.6475	.928030	.071970
41	14.0489	.927230	.072770	41	13.7149	.932613	.067387
42	14.1172	.931735	.068265	42	13.7780	.936903	.063097
43	14.1812	.935962	.064038	43	13.8371	.940921	.059079
44	14.2413	.939926	.060074	44	13.8924	.944682	.055318
45	14.2977	.943646	.056354	45	13.9442	.948204	.051796
46	14.3505	.947135	.052865	46	13.9927	.951502	.048498
47	14.4001	.950408	.049592	47	14.0381	.954590	.045410
48	14.4466	.953478	.046522	48	14.0806	.957481	.042519
49	14.4903	.956359	.043641	49	14.1204	.960188	.039812
50	14.5312	.959061	.040939	50	14.1577	.962723	.037277
51	14.5696	.961595	.038405	51	14.1926	.965097	.034903
52	14.6057	.963973	.036027	52	14.2253	.967319	.032681
53	14.6395	.966204	.033796	53	14.2559	.969400	.030600
54	14.6712	.968296	.031704	54	14.2845	.971348	.028652
55	14.7009	.970259	.029741	55	14.3114	.973172	.026828
56	14.7288	.972100	.027900	56	14.3365	.974881	.025119
57	14.7550	.973828	.026172	57	14.3600	.976480	.023520
58	14.7795	.975448	.024552	58	14.3820	.977977	.022023
59	14.8026	.976968	.023032	59	14.4026	.979380	.020620
60	14.8242	.978394	.021606	60	14.4219	.980693	.019307

Appendix D
Valuation Tables

TABLE B
SHOWING THE PRESENT WORTH OF AN ANNUITY, OF AN INCOME INTEREST, AND OF A REMAINDER INTEREST FOR A TERM CERTAIN

INTEREST RATE

	7.0%				7.2%		
(1)	(2)	(3)	(4)	(1)	(2)	(3)	(4)
YEARS	ANNUITY	INCOME INTEREST	REMAINDER	YEARS	ANNUITY	INCOME INTEREST	REMAINDER
1	0.9346	.065421	.934579	1	0.9328	.067164	.932836
2	1.8080	.126561	.873439	2	1.8030	.129817	.870183
3	2.6243	.183702	.816298	3	2.6148	.188262	.811738
4	3.3872	.237105	.762895	4	3.3720	.242782	.757218
5	4.1002	.287014	.712986	5	4.0783	.293640	.706360
6	4.7665	.333658	.666342	6	4.7373	.341082	.658918
7	5.3893	.377250	.622750	7	5.3519	.385338	.614662
8	5.9713	.417991	.582009	8	5.9253	.426621	.573379
9	6.5152	.456066	.543934	9	6.4602	.465132	.534868
10	7.0236	.491651	.508349	10	6.9591	.501056	.498944
11	7.4987	.524907	.475093	11	7.4245	.534567	.465433
12	7.9427	.555988	.444012	12	7.8587	.565827	.434173
13	8.3577	.585036	.414964	13	8.2637	.594988	.405012
14	8.7455	.612183	.387817	14	8.6415	.622190	.377810
15	9.1079	.637554	.362446	15	8.9940	.647566	.352434
16	9.4466	.661265	.338735	16	9.3227	.671237	.328763
17	9.7632	.683426	.316574	17	9.6294	.693318	.306682
18	10.0591	.704136	.295864	18	9.9155	.713916	.286084
19	10.3356	.723492	.276508	19	10.1824	.733130	.266870
20	10.5940	.741581	.258419	20	10.4313	.751054	.248946
21	10.8355	.758487	.241513	21	10.6635	.767775	.232225
22	11.0612	.774287	.225713	22	10.8802	.783372	.216628
23	11.2722	.789053	.210947	23	11.0822	.797922	.202078
24	11.4693	.802853	.197147	24	11.2708	.811494	.188506
25	11.6536	.815751	.184249	25	11.4466	.824155	.175845
26	11.8258	.827805	.172195	26	11.6106	.835965	.164035
27	11.9867	.839070	.160930	27	11.7636	.846983	.153017
28	12.1371	.849598	.150402	28	11.9064	.857260	.142740
29	12.2777	.859437	.140563	29	12.0395	.866847	.133153
30	12.4090	.868633	.131367	30	12.1638	.875790	.124210
31	12.5318	.877227	.122773	31	12.2796	.884132	.115868
32	12.6466	.885259	.114741	32	12.3877	.891915	.108085
33	12.7538	.892765	.107235	33	12.4885	.899174	.100826
34	12.8540	.899781	.100219	34	12.5826	.905946	.094054
35	12.9477	.906337	.093663	35	12.6703	.912263	.087737
36	13.0352	.912465	.087535	36	12.7522	.918156	.081844
37	13.1170	.918191	.081809	37	12.8285	.923653	.076347
38	13.1935	.923543	.076457	38	12.8997	.928781	.071219
39	13.2649	.928545	.071455	39	12.9662	.933564	.066436
40	13.3317	.933220	.066780	40	13.0281	.938026	.061974
41	13.3941	.937588	.062412	41	13.0860	.942189	.057811
42	13.4524	.941671	.058329	42	13.1399	.946071	.053929
43	13.5070	.945487	.054513	43	13.1902	.949693	.050307
44	13.5579	.949054	.050946	44	13.2371	.953072	.046928
45	13.6055	.952387	.047613	45	13.2809	.956224	.043776
46	13.6500	.955501	.044499	46	13.3217	.959164	.040836
47	13.6916	.958413	.041587	47	13.3598	.961907	.038093
48	13.7305	.961133	.038867	48	13.3954	.964465	.035535
49	13.7668	.963676	.036324	49	13.4285	.966852	.033148
50	13.8007	.966052	.033948	50	13.4594	.969078	.030922
51	13.8325	.968273	.031727	51	13.4883	.971155	.028845
52	13.8621	.970349	.029651	52	13.5152	.973093	.026907
53	13.8898	.972289	.027711	53	13.5403	.974900	.025100
54	13.9157	.974101	.025899	54	13.5637	.976586	.023414
55	13.9399	.975796	.024204	55	13.5855	.978158	.021842
56	13.9626	.977379	.022621	56	13.6059	.979625	.020375
57	13.9837	.978859	.021141	57	13.6249	.980994	.019006
58	14.0035	.980242	.019758	58	13.6426	.982270	.017730
59	14.0219	.981535	.018465	59	13.6592	.983461	.016539
60	14.0392	.982743	.017257	60	13.6746	.984572	.015428

The Tools and Techniques of Estate Planning

Valuation Tables

TABLE B
SHOWING THE PRESENT WORTH OF AN ANNUITY, OF AN
INCOME INTEREST, AND OF A REMAINDER INTEREST
FOR A TERM CERTAIN

INTEREST RATE

	7.4%				7.6%		
(1)	(2)	(3)	(4)	(1)	(2)	(3)	(4)
		INCOME				INCOME	
YEARS	ANNUITY	INTEREST	REMAINDER	YEARS	ANNUITY	INTEREST	REMAINDER
1	0.9311	.068901	.931099	1	0.9294	.070632	.929368
2	1.7980	.133055	.866945	2	1.7931	.136275	.863725
3	2.6053	.192789	.807211	3	2.5958	.197282	.802718
4	3.3568	.248407	.751593	4	3.3418	.253979	.746021
5	4.0567	.300192	.699808	5	4.0352	.306672	.693328
6	4.7082	.348410	.651590	6	4.6795	.355643	.644357
7	5.3149	.393306	.606694	7	5.2784	.401155	.598845
8	5.8798	.435108	.564892	8	5.8349	.443453	.556547
9	6.4058	.474029	.525971	9	6.3521	.482763	.517237
10	6.8955	.510269	.489731	10	6.8328	.519296	.480704
11	7.3515	.544013	.455987	11	7.2796	.553250	.446750
12	7.7761	.575431	.424569	12	7.6948	.584804	.415196
13	8.1714	.604684	.395316	13	8.0807	.614130	.385870
14	8.5395	.631922	.368078	14	8.4393	.641385	.358615
15	8.8822	.657283	.342717	15	8.7726	.666715	.333285
16	9.2013	.680897	.319103	16	9.0823	.690255	.309745
17	9.4984	.702883	.297117	17	9.3702	.712133	.287867
18	9.7751	.723355	.276645	18	9.6377	.732466	.267534
19	10.0327	.742416	.257584	19	9.8863	.751362	.248638
20	10.2725	.760164	.239836	20	10.1174	.768924	.231076
21	10.4958	.776689	.223311	21	10.3322	.785245	.214755
22	10.7037	.792075	.207925	22	10.5318	.800414	.199586
23	10.8973	.806402	.193598	23	10.7173	.814511	.185489
24	11.0776	.819741	.180259	24	10.8896	.827613	.172387
25	11.2454	.832161	.167839	25	11.0499	.839789	.160211
26	11.4017	.843725	.156275	26	11.1987	.851105	.148895
27	11.5472	.854493	.145507	27	11.3371	.861621	.138379
28	11.6827	.864518	.135482	28	11.4657	.871395	.128605
29	11.8088	.873853	.126147	29	11.5853	.880479	.119521
30	11.9263	.882545	.117455	30	11.6963	.888921	.111079
31	12.0356	.890638	.109362	31	11.7996	.896767	.103233
32	12.1375	.898173	.101827	32	11.8955	.904058	.095942
33	12.2323	.905189	.094811	33	11.9847	.910835	.089165
34	12.3206	.911722	.088278	34	12.0675	.917133	.082867
35	12.4028	.917804	.082196	35	12.1446	.922986	.077014
36	12.4793	.923468	.076532	36	12.2161	.928426	.071574
37	12.5505	.928741	.071259	37	12.2826	.933481	.066519
38	12.6169	.933651	.066349	38	12.3445	.938179	.061821
39	12.6787	.938222	.061778	39	12.4019	.942546	.057454
40	12.7362	.942479	.057521	40	12.4553	.946604	.053396
41	12.7898	.946442	.053558	41	12.5049	.950375	.049625
42	12.8396	.950132	.049868	42	12.5511	.953880	.046120
43	12.8861	.953568	.046432	43	12.5939	.957138	.042862
44	12.9293	.956767	.043233	44	12.6338	.960165	.039835
45	12.9695	.959746	.040254	45	12.6708	.962979	.037021
46	13.0070	.962520	.037480	46	12.7052	.965594	.034406
47	13.0419	.965102	.034898	47	12.7372	.968024	.031976
48	13.0744	.967507	.032493	48	12.7669	.970283	.029717
49	13.1047	.969745	.030255	49	12.7945	.972382	.027618
50	13.1328	.971830	.028170	50	12.8202	.974332	.025668
51	13.1591	.973771	.026229	51	12.8440	.976145	.023855
52	13.1835	.975578	.024422	52	12.8662	.977830	.022170
53	13.2062	.977261	.022739	53	12.8868	.979396	.020604
54	13.2274	.978828	.021172	54	12.9059	.980851	.019149
55	13.2471	.980286	.019714	55	12.9237	.982204	.017796
56	13.2655	.981645	.018355	56	12.9403	.983461	.016539
57	13.2826	.982909	.017091	57	12.9556	.984629	.015371
58	13.2985	.984087	.015913	58	12.9699	.985715	.014285
59	13.3133	.985183	.014817	59	12.9832	.986724	.013276
60	13.3271	.986204	.013796	60	12.9955	.987661	.012339

Appendix D
Valuation Tables

TABLE B
SHOWING THE PRESENT WORTH OF AN ANNUITY, OF AN
INCOME INTEREST, AND OF A REMAINDER INTEREST
FOR A TERM CERTAIN

INTEREST RATE

	7.8%				8.0%		
(1)	(2)	(3)	(4)	(1)	(2)	(3)	(4)
YEARS	ANNUITY	INCOME INTEREST	REMAINDER	YEARS	ANNUITY	INCOME INTEREST	REMAINDER
1	0.9276	.072356	.927644	1	0.9259	.074074	.925926
2	1.7882	.139477	.860523	2	1.7833	.142661	.857339
3	2.5864	.201741	.798259	3	2.5771	.206168	.793832
4	3.3269	.259500	.740500	4	3.3121	.264970	.735030
5	4.0138	.313080	.686920	5	3.9927	.319417	.680583
6	4.6511	.362783	.637217	6	4.6229	.369830	.630170
7	5.2422	.408889	.591111	7	5.2064	.416510	.583490
8	5.7905	.451660	.548340	8	5.7466	.459731	.540269
9	6.2992	.491336	.508664	9	6.2469	.499751	.500249
10	6.7710	.528141	.471859	10	6.7101	.536807	.463193
11	7.2088	.562283	.437717	11	7.1390	.571117	.428883
12	7.6148	.593954	.406046	12	7.5361	.602886	.397114
13	7.9915	.623334	.376666	13	7.9038	.632302	.367698
14	8.3409	.650588	.349412	14	8.2442	.659539	.340461
15	8.6650	.675870	.324130	15	8.5595	.684758	.315242
16	8.9657	.699323	.300677	16	8.8514	.708110	.291890
17	9.2446	.721079	.278921	17	9.1216	.729731	.270269
18	9.5033	.741261	.258739	18	9.3719	.749751	.250249
19	9.7434	.759982	.240018	19	9.6036	.768288	.231712
20	9.9660	.777349	.222651	20	9.8181	.785452	.214548
21	10.1726	.793459	.206541	21	10.0168	.801344	.198656
22	10.3641	.808404	.191596	22	10.2007	.816059	.183941
23	10.5419	.822267	.177733	23	10.3711	.829685	.170315
24	10.7068	.835127	.164873	24	10.5288	.842301	.157699
25	10.8597	.847057	.152943	25	10.6748	.853982	.146018
26	11.0016	.858123	.141877	26	10.8100	.864798	.135202
27	11.1332	.868389	.131611	27	10.9352	.874813	.125187
28	11.2553	.877912	.122088	28	11.0511	.884086	.115914
29	11.3685	.886745	.113255	29	11.1584	.892672	.107328
30	11.4736	.894940	.105060	30	11.2578	.900623	.099377
31	11.5710	.902542	.097458	31	11.3498	.907984	.092016
32	11.6615	.909594	.090406	32	11.4350	.914800	.085200
33	11.7453	.916135	.083865	33	11.5139	.921111	.078889
34	11.8231	.922203	.077797	34	11.5869	.926955	.073045
35	11.8953	.927832	.072168	35	11.6546	.932365	.067635
36	11.9622	.933054	.066946	36	11.7172	.937375	.062625
37	12.0243	.937898	.062102	37	11.7752	.942014	.057986
38	12.0819	.942391	.057609	38	11.8289	.946310	.053690
39	12.1354	.946560	.053440	39	11.8786	.950287	.049713
40	12.1850	.950427	.049573	40	11.9246	.953969	.046031
41	12.2309	.954013	.045987	41	11.9672	.957379	.042621
42	12.2736	.957341	.042659	42	12.0067	.960536	.039464
43	12.3132	.960428	.039572	43	12.0432	.963459	.036541
44	12.3499	.963291	.036709	44	12.0771	.966166	.033834
45	12.3839	.965947	.034053	45	12.1084	.968672	.031328
46	12.4155	.968411	.031589	46	12.1374	.970993	.029007
47	12.4448	.970697	.029303	47	12.1643	.973141	.026859
48	12.4720	.972817	.027183	48	12.1891	.975131	.024869
49	12.4972	.974784	.025216	49	12.2122	.976973	.023027
50	12.5206	.976608	.023392	50	12.2335	.978679	.021321
51	12.5423	.978301	.021699	51	12.2532	.980258	.019742
52	12.5624	.979871	.020129	52	12.2715	.981720	.018280
53	12.5811	.981327	.018673	53	12.2884	.983075	.016925
54	12.5984	.982678	.017322	54	12.3041	.984328	.015672
55	12.6145	.983932	.016068	55	12.3186	.985489	.014511
56	12.6294	.985094	.014906	56	12.3321	.986564	.013436
57	12.6432	.986173	.013827	57	12.3445	.987559	.012441
58	12.6561	.987173	.012827	58	12.3560	.988481	.011519
59	12.6680	.988101	.011899	59	12.3667	.989334	.010666
60	12.6790	.988962	.011038	60	12.3766	.990124	.009876

Appendix D
Valuation Tables

TABLE B
SHOWING THE PRESENT WORTH OF AN ANNUITY, OF AN INCOME INTEREST, AND OF A REMAINDER INTEREST FOR A TERM CERTAIN

INTEREST RATE

	8.2%				8.4%		
(1)	(2)	(3)	(4)	(1)	(2)	(3)	(4)
YEARS	ANNUITY	INCOME INTEREST	REMAINDER	YEARS	ANNUITY	INCOME INTEREST	REMAINDER
1	0.9242	.075786	.924214	1	0.9225	.077491	.922509
2	1.7784	.145828	.854172	2	1.7735	.148977	.851023
3	2.5678	.210562	.789438	3	2.5586	.214923	.785077
4	3.2974	.270390	.729610	4	3.2828	.275759	.724241
5	3.9718	.325684	.674316	5	3.9510	.331881	.668119
6	4.5950	.376787	.623213	6	4.5673	.383654	.616346
7	5.1709	.424018	.575982	7	5.1359	.431415	.568585
8	5.7033	.467669	.532331	8	5.6604	.475476	.524524
9	6.1953	.508012	.491988	9	6.1443	.516121	.483879
10	6.6500	.545297	.454703	10	6.5907	.553617	.446383
11	7.0702	.579757	.420243	11	7.0025	.588208	.411792
12	7.4586	.611606	.388394	12	7.3824	.620118	.379882
13	7.8176	.641040	.358960	13	7.7328	.649555	.350445
14	8.1493	.668244	.331756	14	8.0561	.676712	.323288
15	8.4559	.693387	.306613	15	8.3543	.701764	.298236
16	8.7393	.716624	.283376	16	8.6295	.724874	.275126
17	9.0012	.738099	.261901	17	8.8833	.746194	.253806
18	9.2433	.757948	.242052	18	9.1174	.765861	.234139
19	9.4670	.776292	.223708	19	9.3334	.784005	.215995
20	9.6737	.793246	.206754	20	9.5327	.800743	.199257
21	9.8648	.808915	.191085	21	9.7165	.816183	.183817
22	10.0414	.823396	.176604	22	9.8860	.830427	.169573
23	10.2046	.836780	.163220	23	10.0425	.843568	.156432
24	10.3555	.849150	.150850	24	10.1868	.855690	.144310
25	10.4949	.860582	.139418	25	10.3199	.866872	.133128
26	10.6238	.871148	.128852	26	10.4427	.877189	.122811
27	10.7428	.880913	.119087	27	10.5560	.886705	.113295
28	10.8529	.889938	.110062	28	10.6605	.895485	.104515
29	10.9546	.898279	.101721	29	10.7569	.903584	.096416
30	11.0486	.905988	.094012	30	10.8459	.911055	.088945
31	11.1355	.913113	.086887	31	10.9279	.917947	.082053
32	11.2158	.919698	.080302	32	11.0036	.924306	.075694
33	11.2900	.925784	.074216	33	11.0735	.930171	.069829
34	11.3586	.931408	.068592	34	11.1379	.935582	.064418
35	11.4220	.936606	.063394	35	11.1973	.940574	.059426
36	11.4806	.941411	.058589	36	11.2521	.945179	.054821
37	11.5348	.945851	.054149	37	11.3027	.949427	.050573
38	11.5848	.949955	.050045	38	11.3494	.953346	.046654
39	11.6311	.953747	.046253	39	11.3924	.956961	.043039
40	11.6738	.957253	.042747	40	11.4321	.960297	.039703
41	11.7133	.960492	.039508	41	11.4687	.963373	.036627
42	11.7498	.963486	.036514	42	11.5025	.966211	.033789
43	11.7836	.966254	.033746	43	11.5337	.968830	.031170
44	11.8148	.968811	.031189	44	11.5624	.971245	.028755
45	11.8436	.971175	.028825	45	11.5890	.973473	.026527
46	11.8702	.973359	.026641	46	11.6134	.975529	.024471
47	11.8949	.975378	.024622	47	11.6360	.977425	.022575
48	11.9176	.977244	.022756	48	11.6568	.979175	.020825
49	11.9386	.978969	.021031	49	11.6761	.980788	.019212
50	11.9581	.980563	.019437	50	11.6938	.982277	.017723
51	11.9760	.982036	.017964	51	11.7101	.983650	.016350
52	11.9926	.983397	.016603	52	11.7252	.984917	.015083
53	12.0080	.984655	.015345	53	11.7391	.986086	.013914
54	12.0222	.985818	.014182	54	11.7520	.987164	.012836
55	12.0353	.986893	.013107	55	11.7638	.988159	.011841
56	12.0474	.987886	.012114	56	11.7747	.989077	.010923
57	12.0586	.988804	.011196	57	11.7848	.989923	.010077
58	12.0689	.989653	.010347	58	11.7941	.990704	.009296
59	12.0785	.990437	.009563	59	11.8027	.991424	.008576
60	12.0873	.991162	.008838	60	11.8106	.992089	.007911

The Tools and Techniques of Estate Planning

Appendix D
Valuation Tables
TABLE B
SHOWING THE PRESENT WORTH OF AN ANNUITY, OF AN
INCOME INTEREST, AND OF A REMAINDER INTEREST
FOR A TERM CERTAIN

INTEREST RATE

	8.6%				8.8%		
(1)	(2)	(3)	(4)	(1)	(2)	(3)	(4)
YEARS	ANNUITY	INCOME INTEREST	REMAINDER	YEARS	ANNUITY	INCOME INTEREST	REMAINDER
1	0.9208	.079190	.920810	1	0.9191	.080882	.919118
2	1.7687	.152108	.847892	2	1.7639	.155223	.844777
3	2.5494	.219253	.780747	3	2.5403	.223550	.776450
4	3.2684	.281080	.718920	4	3.2540	.286351	.713649
5	3.9304	.338011	.661989	5	3.9099	.344073	.655927
6	4.5399	.390434	.609566	6	4.5128	.397126	.602874
7	5.1012	.438705	.561295	7	5.0669	.445888	.554112
8	5.6181	.483154	.516846	8	5.5762	.490706	.509294
9	6.0940	.524083	.475917	9	6.0443	.531899	.468101
10	6.5322	.561770	.438230	10	6.4745	.569760	.430240
11	6.9357	.596474	.403526	11	6.8700	.604559	.395441
12	7.3073	.628429	.371571	12	7.2334	.636543	.363457
13	7.6495	.657853	.342147	13	7.5675	.665940	.334060
14	7.9645	.684948	.315052	14	7.8745	.692960	.307040
15	8.2546	.709897	.290103	15	8.1567	.717794	.282206
16	8.5217	.732870	.267130	16	8.4161	.740619	.259381
17	8.7677	.754024	.245976	17	8.6545	.761599	.238401
18	8.9942	.773503	.226497	18	8.8736	.780881	.219119
19	9.2028	.791439	.208561	19	9.0750	.798604	.201396
20	9.3948	.807955	.192045	20	9.2602	.814893	.185107
21	9.5717	.823163	.176837	21	9.4303	.829865	.170135
22	9.7345	.837166	.162834	22	9.5867	.843626	.156374
23	9.8844	.850061	.149939	23	9.7304	.856274	.143726
24	10.0225	.861935	.138065	24	9.8625	.867899	.132101
25	10.1496	.872868	.127132	25	9.9839	.878584	.121416
26	10.2667	.882936	.117064	26	10.0955	.888404	.111596
27	10.3745	.892206	.107794	27	10.1981	.897430	.102570
28	10.4737	.900742	.099258	28	10.2923	.905726	.094274
29	10.5651	.908602	.091398	29	10.3790	.913351	.086649
30	10.6493	.915840	.084160	30	10.4586	.920360	.079640
31	10.7268	.922505	.077495	31	10.5318	.926801	.073199
32	10.7982	.928642	.071358	32	10.5991	.932722	.067278
33	10.8639	.934292	.065708	33	10.6609	.938163	.061837
34	10.9244	.939496	.060504	34	10.7178	.943165	.056835
35	10.9801	.944287	.055713	35	10.7700	.947762	.052238
36	11.0314	.948699	.051301	36	10.8180	.951987	.048013
37	11.0786	.952761	.047239	37	10.8622	.955870	.044130
38	11.1221	.956502	.043498	38	10.9027	.959440	.040560
39	11.1622	.959947	.040053	39	10.9400	.962720	.037280
40	11.1991	.963119	.036881	40	10.9743	.965736	.034264
41	11.2330	.966039	.033961	41	11.0058	.968507	.031493
42	11.2643	.968729	.031271	42	11.0347	.971054	.028946
43	11.2931	.971205	.028795	43	11.0613	.973395	.026605
44	11.3196	.973485	.026515	44	11.0858	.975547	.024453
45	11.3440	.975585	.024415	45	11.1082	.977525	.022475
46	11.3665	.977518	.022482	46	11.1289	.979343	.020657
47	11.3872	.979299	.020701	47	11.1479	.981014	.018986
48	11.4063	.980938	.019062	48	11.1653	.982549	.017451
49	11.4238	.982448	.017552	49	11.1814	.983961	.016039
50	11.4400	.983837	.016163	50	11.1961	.985258	.014742
51	11.4549	.985117	.014883	51	11.2097	.986450	.013550
52	11.4686	.986296	.013704	52	11.2221	.987546	.012454
53	11.4812	.987381	.012619	53	11.2336	.988554	.011446
54	11.4928	.988380	.011620	54	11.2441	.989479	.010521
55	11.5035	.989301	.010699	55	11.2538	.990330	.009670
56	11.5133	.990148	.009852	56	11.2626	.991112	.008888
57	11.5224	.990928	.009072	57	11.2708	.991831	.008169
58	11.5308	.991646	.008354	58	11.2783	.992492	.007508
59	11.5385	.992308	.007692	59	11.2852	.993099	.006901
60	11.5455	.992917	.007083	60	11.2916	.993657	.006343

The Tools and Techniques of Estate Planning

TABLE B
SHOWING THE PRESENT WORTH OF AN ANNUITY, OF AN INCOME INTEREST, AND OF A REMAINDER INTEREST FOR A TERM CERTAIN

INTEREST RATE

	9.0%				9.2%		
(1)	(2)	(3)	(4)	(1)	(2)	(3)	(4)
		INCOME				INCOME	
YEARS	ANNUITY	INTEREST	REMAINDER	YEARS	ANNUITY	INTEREST	REMAINDER
1	0.9174	.082569	.917431	1	0.9158	.084249	.915751
2	1.7591	.158320	.841680	2	1.7544	.161400	.838600
3	2.5313	.227817	.772183	3	2.5223	.232052	.767948
4	3.2397	.291575	.708425	4	3.2255	.296750	.703250
5	3.8897	.350069	.649931	5	3.8696	.355999	.644001
6	4.4859	.403733	.596267	6	4.4593	.410255	.589745
7	5.0330	.452966	.547034	7	4.9994	.459941	.540059
8	5.5348	.498134	.501866	8	5.4939	.505440	.494560
9	5.9952	.539572	.460428	9	5.9468	.547106	.452894
10	6.4177	.577589	.422411	10	6.3615	.585262	.414738
11	6.8052	.612467	.387533	11	6.7413	.620203	.379797
12	7.1607	.644465	.355535	12	7.0891	.652201	.347799
13	7.4869	.673821	.326179	13	7.4076	.681503	.318497
14	7.7862	.700754	.299246	14	7.6993	.708336	.291664
15	8.0607	.725462	.274538	15	7.9664	.732908	.267092
16	8.3126	.748130	.251870	16	8.2110	.755411	.244589
17	8.5436	.768927	.231073	17	8.4350	.776017	.223983
18	8.7556	.788006	.211994	18	8.6401	.794887	.205113
19	8.9501	.805510	.194490	19	8.8279	.812168	.187832
20	9.1285	.821569	.178431	20	8.9999	.827993	.172007
21	9.2922	.836302	.163698	21	9.1574	.842484	.157516
22	9.4424	.849818	.150182	22	9.3017	.855755	.144245
23	9.5802	.862219	.137781	23	9.4338	.867907	.132093
24	9.7066	.873595	.126405	24	9.5547	.879036	.120964
25	9.8226	.884032	.115968	25	9.6655	.889227	.110773
26	9.9290	.893607	.106393	26	9.7670	.898559	.101441
27	10.0266	.902392	.097608	27	9.8598	.907106	.092894
28	10.1161	.910452	.089548	28	9.9449	.914932	.085068
29	10.1983	.917845	.082155	29	10.0228	.922099	.077901
30	10.2737	.924629	.075371	30	10.0942	.928662	.071338
31	10.3428	.930852	.069148	31	10.1595	.934672	.065328
32	10.4062	.936562	.063438	32	10.2193	.940176	.059824
33	10.4644	.941800	.058200	33	10.2741	.945216	.054784
34	10.5178	.946605	.053395	34	10.3243	.949832	.050168
35	10.5668	.951014	.048986	35	10.3702	.954058	.045942
36	10.6118	.955059	.044941	36	10.4123	.957929	.042071
37	10.6530	.958769	.041231	37	10.4508	.961473	.038527
38	10.6908	.962174	.037826	38	10.4861	.964719	.035281
39	10.7255	.965297	.034703	39	10.5184	.967691	.032309
40	10.7574	.968162	.031838	40	10.5480	.970413	.029587
41	10.7866	.970791	.029209	41	10.5751	.972906	.027094
42	10.8134	.973203	.026797	42	10.5999	.975189	.024811
43	10.8380	.975416	.024584	43	10.6226	.977279	.022721
44	10.8605	.977445	.022555	44	10.6434	.979193	.020807
45	10.8812	.979308	.020692	45	10.6625	.980946	.019054
46	10.9002	.981016	.018984	46	10.6799	.982551	.017449
47	10.9176	.982584	.017416	47	10.6959	.984022	.015978
48	10.9336	.984022	.015978	48	10.7105	.985368	.014632
49	10.9482	.985341	.014659	49	10.7239	.986600	.013400
50	10.9617	.986551	.013449	50	10.7362	.987729	.012271
51	10.9740	.987662	.012338	51	10.7474	.988763	.011237
52	10.9853	.988681	.011319	52	10.7577	.989710	.010290
53	10.9957	.989615	.010385	53	10.7671	.990577	.009423
54	11.0053	.990473	.009527	54	10.7758	.991371	.008629
55	11.0140	.991259	.008741	55	10.7837	.992098	.007902
56	11.0220	.991981	.008019	56	10.7909	.992763	.007237
57	11.0294	.992643	.007357	57	10.7975	.993373	.006627
58	11.0361	.993251	.006749	58	10.8036	.993931	.006069
59	11.0423	.993808	.006192	59	10.8092	.994443	.005557
60	11.0480	.994319	.005681	60	10.8142	.994911	.005089

The Tools and Techniques of Estate Planning

Appendix D
Valuation Tables

TABLE B

SHOWING THE PRESENT WORTH OF AN ANNUITY, OF AN INCOME INTEREST, AND OF A REMAINDER INTEREST FOR A TERM CERTAIN

INTEREST RATE

(1) YEARS	(2) ANNUITY	(3) INCOME INTEREST	(4) REMAINDER	(1) YEARS	(2) ANNUITY	(3) INCOME INTEREST	(4) REMAINDER
	9.4%				9.6%		
1	0.9141	.085923	.914077	1	0.9124	.087591	.912409
2	1.7496	.164464	.835536	2	1.7449	.167510	.832490
3	2.5134	.236256	.763744	3	2.5045	.240429	.759571
4	3.2115	.301879	.698121	4	3.1975	.306961	.693039
5	3.8496	.361864	.638136	5	3.8298	.367665	.632335
6	4.4329	.416695	.583305	6	4.4068	.423052	.576948
7	4.9661	.466814	.533186	7	4.9332	.473588	.526412
8	5.4535	.512627	.487373	8	5.4135	.519697	.480303
9	5.8990	.554504	.445496	9	5.8517	.561767	.438233
10	6.3062	.592782	.407218	10	6.2516	.600152	.399848
11	6.6784	.627772	.372228	11	6.6164	.635176	.364824
12	7.0187	.659755	.340245	12	6.9493	.667131	.332869
13	7.3297	.688990	.311010	13	7.2530	.696287	.303713
14	7.6140	.715713	.284287	14	7.5301	.722890	.277110
15	7.8738	.740140	.259860	15	7.7829	.747162	.252838
16	8.1114	.762468	.237532	16	8.0136	.769309	.230691
17	8.3285	.782877	.217123	17	8.2241	.789515	.210485
18	8.5269	.801533	.198467	18	8.4162	.807952	.192048
19	8.7084	.818586	.181414	19	8.5914	.824774	.175226
20	8.8742	.834174	.165826	20	8.7513	.840122	.159878
21	9.0258	.848422	.151578	21	8.8971	.854126	.145874
22	9.1643	.861446	.138554	22	9.0302	.866903	.133097
23	9.2910	.873351	.126649	23	9.1517	.878561	.121439
24	9.4067	.884233	.115767	24	9.2625	.889198	.110802
25	9.5126	.894180	.105820	25	9.3636	.898903	.101097
26	9.6093	.903273	.096727	26	9.4558	.907759	.092241
27	9.6977	.911584	.088416	27	9.5400	.915838	.084162
28	9.7785	.919181	.080819	28	9.6168	.923210	.076790
29	9.8524	.926125	.073875	29	9.6868	.929936	.070064
30	9.9199	.932473	.067527	30	9.7508	.936073	.063927
31	9.9816	.938275	.061725	31	9.8091	.941673	.058327
32	10.0381	.943578	.056422	32	9.8623	.946782	.053218
33	10.0896	.948426	.051574	33	9.9109	.951443	.048557
34	10.1368	.952858	.047142	34	9.9552	.955696	.044304
35	10.1799	.956908	.043092	35	9.9956	.959577	.040423
36	10.2193	.960611	.039389	36	10.0325	.963118	.036882
37	10.2553	.963995	.036005	37	10.0661	.966348	.033652
38	10.2882	.967089	.032911	38	10.0968	.969296	.030704
39	10.3183	.969917	.030083	39	10.1248	.971985	.028015
40	10.3458	.972502	.027498	40	10.1504	.974439	.025561
41	10.3709	.974864	.025136	41	10.1737	.976678	.023322
42	10.3939	.977024	.022976	42	10.1950	.978721	.021279
43	10.4149	.978998	.021002	43	10.2144	.980585	.019415
44	10.4341	.980803	.019197	44	10.2321	.982285	.017715
45	10.4516	.982452	.017548	45	10.2483	.983837	.016163
46	10.4677	.983960	.016040	46	10.2630	.985253	.014747
47	10.4823	.985338	.014662	47	10.2765	.986544	.013456
48	10.4957	.986598	.013402	48	10.2888	.987723	.012277
49	10.5080	.987750	.012250	49	10.3000	.988798	.011202
50	10.5192	.988802	.011198	50	10.3102	.989779	.010221
51	10.5294	.989764	.010236	51	10.3195	.990675	.009325
52	10.5388	.990644	.009356	52	10.3280	.991492	.008508
53	10.5473	.991448	.008552	53	10.3358	.992237	.007763
54	10.5551	.992183	.007817	54	10.3429	.992917	.007083
55	10.5623	.992854	.007146	55	10.3493	.993537	.006463
56	10.5688	.993468	.006532	56	10.3552	.994103	.005897
57	10.5748	.994029	.005971	57	10.3606	.994620	.005380
58	10.5802	.994542	.005458	58	10.3655	.995091	.004909
59	10.5852	.995011	.004989	59	10.3700	.995521	.004479
60	10.5898	.995440	.004560	60	10.3741	.995913	.004087

The Tools and Techniques of Estate Planning

Appendix D
Valuation Tables

TABLE B
SHOWING THE PRESENT WORTH OF AN ANNUITY, OF AN INCOME INTEREST, AND OF A REMAINDER INTEREST FOR A TERM CERTAIN

INTEREST RATE

	9.8%				10.0%		
(1)	**(2)**	**(3)**	**(4)**	**(1)**	**(2)**	**(3)**	**(4)**
		INCOME				**INCOME**	
YEARS	**ANNUITY**	**INTEREST**	**REMAINDER**	**YEARS**	**ANNUITY**	**INTEREST**	**REMAINDER**
1	0.9107	.089253	.910747	1	0.9091	.090909	.909091
2	1.7402	.170540	.829460	2	1.7355	.173554	.826446
3	2.4956	.244572	.755428	3	2.4869	.248685	.751315
4	3.1836	.311997	.688003	4	3.1699	.316987	.683013
5	3.8102	.373403	.626597	5	3.7908	.379079	.620921
6	4.3809	.429329	.570671	6	4.3553	.435526	.564474
7	4.9006	.480263	.519737	7	4.8684	.486842	.513158
8	5.3740	.526651	.473349	8	5.3349	.533493	.466507
9	5.8051	.568899	.431101	9	5.7590	.575902	.424098
10	6.1977	.607376	.392624	10	6.1446	.614457	.385543
11	6.5553	.642419	.357581	11	6.4951	.649506	.350494
12	6.8810	.674334	.325666	12	6.8137	.681369	.318631
13	7.1776	.703401	.296599	13	7.1034	.710336	.289664
14	7.4477	.729873	.270127	14	7.3667	.736669	.263331
15	7.6937	.753983	.246017	15	7.6061	.760608	.239392
16	7.9178	.775941	.224059	16	7.8237	.782371	.217629
17	8.1218	.795939	.204061	17	8.0216	.802155	.197845
18	8.3077	.814152	.185848	18	8.2014	.820141	.179859
19	8.4769	.830740	.169260	19	8.3649	.836492	.163508
20	8.6311	.845847	.154153	20	8.5136	.851356	.148644
21	8.7715	.859605	.140395	21	8.6487	.864869	.135131
22	8.8993	.872136	.127864	22	8.7715	.877154	.122846
23	9.0158	.883548	.116452	23	8.8832	.888322	.111678
24	9.1219	.893942	.106058	24	8.9847	.898474	.101526
25	9.2184	.903408	.096592	25	9.0770	.907704	.092296
26	9.3064	.912029	.087971	26	9.1609	.916095	.083905
27	9.3865	.919881	.080119	27	9.2372	.923722	.076278
28	9.4595	.927032	.072968	28	9.3066	.930657	.069343
29	9.5260	.933544	.066456	29	9.3696	.936961	.063039
30	9.5865	.939476	.060524	30	9.4269	.942691	.057309
31	9.6416	.944878	.055122	31	9.4790	.947901	.052099
32	9.6918	.949798	.050202	32	9.5264	.952638	.047362
33	9.7375	.954278	.045722	33	9.5694	.956943	.043057
34	9.7792	.958359	.041641	34	9.6086	.960857	.039143
35	9.8171	.962076	.037924	35	9.6442	.964416	.035584
36	9.8516	.965461	.034539	36	9.6765	.967651	.032349
37	9.8831	.968543	.031457	37	9.7059	.970592	.029408
38	9.9117	.971351	.028649	38	9.7327	.973265	.026735
39	9.9378	.973908	.026092	39	9.7570	.975696	.024304
40	9.9616	.976237	.023763	40	9.7791	.977905	.022095
41	9.9832	.978358	.021642	41	9.7991	.979914	.020086
42	10.0030	.980289	.019711	42	9.8174	.981740	.018260
43	10.0209	.982049	.017951	43	9.8340	.983400	.016600
44	10.0373	.983651	.016349	44	9.8491	.984909	.015091
45	10.0521	.985110	.014890	45	9.8628	.986281	.013719
46	10.0657	.986439	.013561	46	9.8753	.987528	.012472
47	10.0781	.987649	.012351	47	9.8866	.988662	.011338
48	10.0893	.988752	.011248	48	9.8969	.989693	.010307
49	10.0995	.989756	.010244	49	9.9063	.990630	.009370
50	10.1089	.990670	.009330	50	9.9148	.991481	.008519
51	10.1174	.991503	.008497	51	9.9226	.992256	.007744
52	10.1251	.992261	.007739	52	9.9296	.992960	.007040
53	10.1322	.992952	.007048	53	9.9360	.993600	.006400
54	10.1386	.993581	.006419	54	9.9418	.994182	.005818
55	10.1444	.994154	.005846	55	9.9471	.994711	.005289
56	10.1498	.994676	.005324	56	9.9519	.995191	.004809
57	10.1546	.995151	.004849	57	9.9563	.995629	.004371
58	10.1590	.995584	.004416	58	9.9603	.996026	.003974
59	10.1630	.995978	.004022	59	9.9639	.996387	.003613
60	10.1667	.996337	.003663	60	9.9672	.996716	.003284

The Tools and Techniques of Estate Planning

Appendix D
Valuation Table

TABLE S(6.6)
SINGLE LIFE, 6.6 PERCENT, BASED ON LIFE TABLE 80CNSMT
SHOWING THE PRESENT WORTH OF AN ANNUITY, OF A LIFE ESTATE,
AND OF A REMAINDER INTEREST

AGE	ANNUITY	LIFE ESTATE	REMAINDER	AGE	ANNUITY	LIFE ESTATE	REMAINDER
(1)	(2)	(3)	(4)	(1)	(2)	(3)	(4)
0	14.6692	.96817	.03183	55	10.9495	.72266	.27734
1	14.8305	.97881	.02119	56	10.7738	.71107	.28893
2	14.8236	.97836	.02164	57	10.5934	.69916	.30084
3	14.8119	.97759	.02241	58	10.4082	.68694	.31306
4	14.7971	.97661	.02339	59	10.2184	.67442	.32558
5	14.7799	.97547	.02453	60	10.0248	.66164	.33836
6	14.7610	.97422	.02578	61	9.8277	.64863	.35137
7	14.7403	.97286	.02714	62	9.6275	.63542	.36458
8	14.7178	.97137	.02863	63	9.4245	.62201	.37799
9	14.6932	.96975	.03025	64	9.2183	.60841	.39159
10	14.6665	.96799	.03201	65	9.0084	.59455	.40545
11	14.6374	.96607	.03393	66	8.7942	.58042	.41958
12	14.6064	.96402	.03598	67	8.5758	.56601	.43399
13	14.5741	.96189	.03811	68	8.3533	.55132	.44868
14	14.5416	.95975	.04025	69	8.1278	.53643	.46357
15	14.5093	.95762	.04238	70	7.8999	.52139	.47861
16	14.4772	.95549	.04451	71	7.6706	.50626	.49374
17	14.4451	.95338	.04662	72	7.4401	.49104	.50896
18	14.4128	.95125	.04875	73	7.2081	.47574	.52426
19	14.3796	.94905	.05095	74	6.9740	.46028	.53972
20	14.3453	.94679	.05321	75	6.7370	.44464	.55536
21	14.3100	.94446	.05554	76	6.4970	.42880	.57120
22	14.2732	.94203	.05797	77	6.2546	.41280	.58720
23	14.2347	.93949	.06051	78	6.0107	.39671	.60329
24	14.1938	.93679	.06321	79	5.7674	.38065	.61935
25	14.1502	.93391	.06609	80	5.5262	.36473	.63527
26	14.1034	.93082	.06918	81	5.2894	.34910	.65090
27	14.0531	.92750	.07250	82	5.0581	.33384	.66616
28	13.9995	.92397	.07603	83	4.8335	.31901	.68099
29	13.9422	.92019	.07981	84	4.6150	.30459	.69541
30	13.8813	.91617	.08383	85	4.4020	.29053	.70947
31	13.8164	.91188	.08812	86	4.1963	.27695	.72305
32	13.7475	.90733	.09267	87	4.0002	.26401	.73599
33	13.6742	.90250	.09750	88	3.8128	.25164	.74836
34	13.5968	.89739	.10261	89	3.6307	.23963	.76037
35	13.5151	.89200	.10800	90	3.4523	.22785	.77215
36	13.4294	.88634	.11366	91	3.2799	.21648	.78352
37	13.3393	.88039	.11961	92	3.1177	.20577	.79423
38	13.2449	.87416	.12584	93	2.9671	.19583	.80417
39	13.1459	.86763	.13237	94	2.8295	.18675	.81325
40	13.0425	.86080	.13920	95	2.7053	.17855	.82145
41	12.9344	.85367	.14633	96	2.5952	.17128	.82872
42	12.8220	.84625	.15375	97	2.4952	.16468	.83532
43	12.7051	.83854	.16146	98	2.4052	.15874	.84126
44	12.5837	.83052	.16948	99	2.3221	.15326	.84674
45	12.4575	.82220	.17780	100	2.2449	.14816	.85184
46	12.3267	.81356	.18644	101	2.1712	.14330	.85670
47	12.1912	.80462	.19538	102	2.0944	.13823	.86177
48	12.0512	.79538	.20462	103	2.0130	.13286	.86714
49	11.9071	.78587	.21413	104	1.9226	.12689	.87311
50	11.7589	.77609	.22391	105	1.8112	.11954	.88046
51	11.6064	.76602	.23398	106	1.6522	.10905	.89095
52	11.4491	.75564	.24436	107	1.4242	.09400	.90600
53	11.2870	.74495	.25505	108	1.0572	.06978	.93022
54	11.1205	.73396	.26604	109	0.4690	.03096	.96904

Appendix D
Valuation Tables

TABLE S(6.8)
SINGLE LIFE, 6.8 PERCENT, BASED ON LIFE TABLE 80CNSMT
SHOWING THE PRESENT WORTH OF AN ANNUITY, OF A LIFE ESTATE,
AND OF A REMAINDER INTEREST

AGE	ANNUITY	LIFE ESTATE	REMAINDER	AGE	ANNUITY	LIFE ESTATE	REMAINDER
(1)	(2)	(3)	(4)	(1)	(2)	(3)	(4)
0	14.2596	.96965	.03035	55	10.7500	.73100	.26900
1	14.4172	.98037	.01963	56	10.5809	.71950	.28050
2	14.4114	.97998	.02002	57	10.4071	.70768	.29232
3	14.4011	.97927	.02073	58	10.2285	.69554	.30446
4	14.3877	.97837	.02163	59	10.0454	.68309	.31691
5	14.3721	.97731	.02269	60	9.8583	.67037	.32963
6	14.3549	.97613	.02387	61	9.6677	.65741	.34259
7	14.3360	.97485	.02515	62	9.4741	.64424	.35576
8	14.3153	.97344	.02656	63	9.2774	.63087	.36913
9	14.2927	.97190	.02810	64	9.0777	.61728	.38272
10	14.2681	.97023	.02977	65	8.8741	.60344	.39656
11	14.2411	.96840	.03160	66	8.6662	.58930	.41070
12	14.2124	.96644	.03356	67	8.4539	.57487	.42513
13	14.1824	.96440	.03560	68	8.2375	.56015	.43985
14	14.1523	.96236	.03764	69	8.0179	.54522	.45478
15	14.1224	.96032	.03968	70	7.7959	.53012	.46988
16	14.0927	.95830	.04170	71	7.5724	.51492	.48508
17	14.0632	.95630	.04370	72	7.3474	.49962	.50038
18	14.0334	.95427	.04573	73	7.1209	.48422	.51578
19	14.0028	.95219	.04781	74	6.8921	.46866	.53134
20	13.9712	.95004	.04996	75	6.6603	.45290	.54710
21	13.9387	.94783	.05217	76	6.4253	.43692	.56308
22	13.9048	.94553	.05447	77	6.1878	.42077	.57923
23	13.8694	.94312	.05688	78	5.9486	.40451	.59549
24	13.8316	.94055	.05945	79	5.7097	.38826	.61174
25	13.7913	.93781	.06219	80	5.4728	.37215	.62785
26	13.7479	.93485	.06515	81	5.2400	.35632	.64368
27	13.7012	.93168	.06832	82	5.0126	.34086	.65914
28	13.6513	.92829	.07171	83	4.7915	.32582	.67418
29	13.5979	.92466	.07534	84	4.5763	.31119	.68881
30	13.5410	.92079	.07921	85	4.3664	.29692	.70308
31	13.4802	.91665	.08335	86	4.1635	.28312	.71688
32	13.4156	.91226	.08774	87	3.9701	.26997	.73003
33	13.3469	.90759	.09241	88	3.7851	.25739	.74261
34	13.2741	.90264	.09736	89	3.6053	.24516	.75484
35	13.1972	.89741	.10259	90	3.4290	.23317	.76683
36	13.1163	.89191	.10809	91	3.2586	.22158	.77842
37	13.0313	.88613	.11387	92	3.0981	.21067	.78933
38	12.9421	.88006	.11994	93	2.9491	.20054	.79946
39	12.8485	.87370	.12630	94	2.8128	.19127	.80873
40	12.7504	.86703	.13297	95	2.6898	.18291	.81709
41	12.6479	.86006	.13994	96	2.5808	.17549	.82451
42	12.5412	.85280	.14720	97	2.4818	.16876	.83124
43	12.4301	.84525	.15475	98	2.3926	.16270	.83730
44	12.3145	.83739	.16261	99	2.3103	.15710	.84290
45	12.1944	.82922	.17078	100	2.2338	.15190	.84810
46	12.0697	.82074	.17926	101	2.1608	.14694	.85306
47	11.9403	.81194	.18806	102	2.0848	.14177	.85823
48	11.8065	.80284	.19716	103	2.0042	.13629	.86371
49	11.6687	.79347	.20653	104	1.9147	.13020	.86980
50	11.5269	.78383	.21617	105	1.8043	.12269	.87731
51	11.3808	.77390	.22610	106	1.6465	.11196	.88804
52	11.2300	.76364	.23636	107	1.4200	.09656	.90344
53	11.0744	.75306	.24694	108	1.0547	.07172	.92828
54	10.9145	.74218	.25782	109	0.4682	.03184	.96816

The Tools and Techniques of Estate Planning

605

Appendix D
Valuation Tables

TABLE S(7.0)
SINGLE LIFE, 7.0 PERCENT, BASED ON LIFE TABLE 80CNSMT
SHOWING THE PRESENT WORTH OF AN ANNUITY, OF A LIFE ESTATE,
AND OF A REMAINDER INTEREST

AGE	ANNUITY	LIFE ESTATE	REMAINDER	AGE	ANNUITY	LIFE ESTATE	REMAINDER
(1)	(2)	(3)	(4)	(1)	(2)	(3)	(4)
0	13.8711	.97098	.02902	55	10.5567	.73897	.26103
1	14.0251	.98176	.01824	56	10.3940	.72758	.27242
2	14.0204	.98143	.01857	57	10.2264	.71585	.28415
3	14.0112	.98079	.01921	58	10.0541	.70379	.29621
4	13.9992	.97995	.02005	59	9.8773	.69141	.30859
5	13.9851	.97895	.02105	60	9.6966	.67876	.32124
6	13.9693	.97785	.02215	61	9.5123	.66586	.33414
7	13.9520	.97664	.02336	62	9.3248	.65274	.34726
8	13.9330	.97531	.02469	63	9.1344	.63940	.36060
9	13.9122	.97385	.02615	64	8.9407	.62585	.37415
10	13.8894	.97226	.02774	65	8.7431	.61202	.38798
11	13.8644	.97051	.02949	66	8.5413	.59789	.40211
12	13.8377	.96864	.03136	67	8.3350	.58345	.41655
13	13.8098	.96669	.03331	68	8.1244	.56871	.43129
14	13.7819	.96473	.03527	69	7.9107	.55375	.44625
15	13.7542	.96279	.03721	70	7.6943	.53860	.46140
16	13.7267	.96087	.03913	71	7.4763	.52334	.47666
17	13.6994	.95896	.04104	72	7.2568	.50797	.49203
18	13.6719	.95704	.04296	73	7.0356	.49249	.50751
19	13.6437	.95506	.04494	74	6.8119	.47683	.52317
20	13.6146	.95302	.04698	75	6.5851	.46096	.53904
21	13.5846	.95093	.04907	76	6.3550	.44485	.55515
22	13.5534	.94874	.05126	77	6.1222	.42856	.57144
23	13.5207	.94645	.05355	78	5.8876	.41213	.58787
24	13.4858	.94401	.05599	79	5.6531	.39572	.60428
25	13.4485	.94139	.05861	80	5.4203	.37942	.62058
26	13.4082	.93858	.06142	81	5.1915	.36341	.63659
27	13.3648	.93554	.06446	82	4.9678	.34774	.65226
28	13.3183	.93228	.06772	83	4.7501	.33251	.66749
29	13.2685	.92880	.07120	84	4.5382	.31767	.68233
30	13.2154	.92508	.07492	85	4.3313	.30319	.69681
31	13.1584	.92109	.07891	86	4.1313	.28919	.71081
32	13.0979	.91685	.08315	87	3.9404	.27583	.72417
33	13.0333	.91233	.08767	88	3.7578	.26305	.73695
34	12.9648	.90754	.09246	89	3.5803	.25062	.74938
35	12.8923	.90246	.09754	90	3.4060	.23842	.76158
36	12.8160	.89712	.10288	91	3.2375	.22663	.77337
37	12.7357	.89150	.10850	92	3.0787	.21551	.78449
38	12.6513	.88559	.11441	93	2.9313	.20519	.79481
39	12.5626	.87939	.12061	94	2.7964	.19575	.80425
40	12.4697	.87288	.12712	95	2.6746	.18722	.81278
41	12.3724	.86607	.13393	96	2.5666	.17966	.82034
42	12.2710	.85897	.14103	97	2.4685	.17279	.82721
43	12.1654	.85158	.14842	98	2.3801	.16661	.83339
44	12.0553	.84387	.15613	99	2.2986	.16090	.83910
45	11.9408	.83586	.16414	100	2.2229	.15560	.84440
46	11.8218	.82753	.17247	101	2.1506	.15054	.84946
47	11.6982	.81888	.18112	102	2.0753	.14527	.85473
48	11.5704	.80993	.19007	103	1.9954	.13968	.86032
49	11.4386	.80070	.19930	104	1.9068	.13347	.86653
50	11.3027	.79119	.20881	105	1.7974	.12582	.87418
51	11.1627	.78139	.21861	106	1.6409	.11486	.88514
52	11.0181	.77126	.22874	107	1.4158	.09911	.90089
53	10.8687	.76081	.23919	108	1.0522	.07366	.92634
54	10.7149	.75005	.24995	109	0.4673	.03271	.96729

The Tools and Techniques of Estate Planning

Appendix D
Valuation Tables

TABLE S(7.2)

SINGLE LIFE, 7.2 PERCENT, BASED ON LIFE TABLE 80CNSMT
SHOWING THE PRESENT WORTH OF AN ANNUITY, OF A LIFE ESTATE,
AND OF A REMAINDER INTEREST

AGE	ANNUITY	LIFE ESTATE	REMAINDER	AGE	ANNUITY	LIFE ESTATE	REMAINDER
(1)	(2)	(3)	(4)	(1)	(2)	(3)	(4)
0	13.5024	.97217	.02783	55	10.3694	.74659	.25341
1	13.6529	.98301	.01699	56	10.2126	.73531	.26469
2	13.6491	.98273	.01727	57	10.0511	.72368	.27632
3	13.6410	.98215	.01785	58	9.8848	.71171	.28829
4	13.6301	.98137	.01863	59	9.7141	.69941	.30059
5	13.6172	.98044	.01956	60	9.5394	.68683	.31317
6	13.6028	.97940	.02060	61	9.3610	.67399	.32601
7	13.5870	.97826	.02174	62	9.1796	.66093	.33907
8	13.5695	.97700	.02300	63	8.9950	.64764	.35236
9	13.5502	.97562	.02438	64	8.8072	.63412	.36588
10	13.5291	.97410	.02590	65	8.6155	.62032	.37968
11	13.5059	.97243	.02757	66	8.4194	.60620	.39380
12	13.4810	.97064	.02936	67	8.2189	.59176	.40824
13	13.4551	.96877	.03123	68	8.0140	.57701	.42299
14	13.4291	.96689	.03311	69	7.8058	.56202	.43798
15	13.4033	.96504	.03496	70	7.5950	.54684	.45316
16	13.3779	.96321	.03679	71	7.3824	.53153	.46847
17	13.3526	.96139	.03861	72	7.1681	.51610	.48390
18	13.3273	.95956	.04044	73	6.9520	.50054	.49946
19	13.3012	.95769	.04231	74	6.7333	.48480	.51520
20	13.2744	.95576	.04424	75	6.5114	.46882	.53118
21	13.2467	.95377	.04623	76	6.2861	.45260	.54740
22	13.2179	.95169	.04831	77	6.0579	.43617	.56383
23	13.1877	.94952	.05048	78	5.8277	.41960	.58040
24	13.1555	.94719	.05281	79	5.5975	.40302	.59698
25	13.1209	.94470	.05530	80	5.3688	.38655	.61345
26	13.0835	.94201	.05799	81	5.1438	.37035	.62965
27	13.0431	.93910	.06090	82	4.9237	.35450	.64550
28	12.9998	.93598	.06402	83	4.7094	.33908	.66092
29	12.9533	.93264	.06736	84	4.5006	.32405	.67595
30	12.9035	.92905	.07095	85	4.2968	.30937	.69063
31	12.8502	.92521	.07479	86	4.0995	.29516	.70484
32	12.7933	.92112	.07888	87	3.9112	.28161	.71839
33	12.7326	.91675	.08325	88	3.7309	.26863	.73137
34	12.6681	.91210	.08790	89	3.5555	.25600	.74400
35	12.5997	.90718	.09282	90	3.3833	.24360	.75640
36	12.5277	.90200	.09800	91	3.2167	.23160	.76840
37	12.4518	.89653	.10347	92	3.0596	.22029	.77971
38	12.3719	.89078	.10922	93	2.9136	.20978	.79022
39	12.2879	.88473	.11527	94	2.7801	.20017	.79983
40	12.1997	.87838	.12162	95	2.6595	.19148	.80852
41	12.1073	.87173	.12827	96	2.5525	.18378	.81622
42	12.0109	.86478	.13522	97	2.4553	.17678	.82322
43	11.9104	.85755	.14245	98	2.3678	.17048	.82952
44	11.8055	.85000	.15000	99	2.2870	.16466	.83534
45	11.6963	.84213	.15787	100	2.2120	.15926	.84074
46	11.5827	.83396	.16604	101	2.1404	.15411	.84589
47	11.4647	.82546	.17454	102	2.0658	.14874	.85126
48	11.3424	.81665	.18335	103	1.9868	.14305	.85695
49	11.2162	.80756	.19244	104	1.8989	.13672	.86328
50	11.0861	.79820	.20180	105	1.7906	.12892	.87108
51	10.9518	.78853	.21147	106	1.6353	.11774	.88226
52	10.8130	.77853	.22147	107	1.4117	.10164	.89836
53	10.6695	.76820	.23180	108	1.0497	.07558	.92442
54	10.5216	.75756	.24244	109	0.4664	.03358	.96642

Appendix D
Valuation Tables
TABLE S(7.4)
SINGLE LIFE, 7.4 PERCENT, BASED ON LIFE TABLE 80CNSMT
SHOWING THE PRESENT WORTH OF AN ANNUITY, OF A LIFE ESTATE,
AND OF A REMAINDER INTEREST

AGE	ANNUITY	LIFE ESTATE	REMAINDER	AGE	ANNUITY	LIFE ESTATE	REMAINDER
(1)	(2)	(3)	(4)	(1)	(2)	(3)	(4)
0	13.1519	.97324	.02676	55	10.1877	.75389	.24611
1	13.2990	.98413	.01587	56	10.0367	.74272	.25728
2	13.2960	.98391	.01609	57	9.8809	.73119	.26881
3	13.2889	.98338	.01662	58	9.7204	.71931	.28069
4	13.2791	.98265	.01735	59	9.5554	.70710	.29290
5	13.2673	.98178	.01822	60	9.3865	.69460	.30540
6	13.2541	.98081	.01919	61	9.2139	.68183	.31817
7	13.2396	.97973	.02027	62	9.0382	.66883	.33117
8	13.2235	.97854	.02146	63	8.8593	.65559	.34441
9	13.2056	.97722	.02278	64	8.6772	.64211	.35789
10	13.1860	.97577	.02423	65	8.4911	.62834	.37166
11	13.1645	.97417	.02583	66	8.3006	.61424	.38576
12	13.1413	.97245	.02755	67	8.1056	.59981	.40019
13	13.1170	.97066	.02934	68	7.9062	.58506	.41494
14	13.0928	.96887	.03113	69	7.7034	.57005	.42995
15	13.0689	.96710	.03290	70	7.4978	.55484	.44516
16	13.0452	.96534	.03466	71	7.2904	.53949	.46051
17	13.0218	.96362	.03638	72	7.0812	.52401	.47599
18	12.9984	.96188	.03812	73	6.8701	.50839	.49161
19	12.9743	.96010	.03990	74	6.6563	.49256	.50744
20	12.9495	.95827	.04173	75	6.4391	.47649	.52351
21	12.9240	.95638	.04362	76	6.2184	.46016	.53984
22	12.8974	.95441	.04559	77	5.9947	.44361	.55639
23	12.8695	.95234	.04766	78	5.7689	.42690	.57310
24	12.8396	.95013	.04987	79	5.5428	.41017	.58983
25	12.8076	.94776	.05224	80	5.3181	.39354	.60646
26	12.7728	.94519	.05481	81	5.0968	.37717	.62283
27	12.7352	.94241	.05759	82	4.8803	.36114	.63886
28	12.6948	.93941	.06059	83	4.6693	.34553	.65447
29	12.6513	.93620	.06380	84	4.4637	.33031	.66969
30	12.6048	.93275	.06725	85	4.2627	.31544	.68456
31	12.5547	.92905	.07095	86	4.0681	.30104	.69896
32	12.5013	.92509	.07491	87	3.8823	.28729	.71271
33	12.4441	.92087	.07913	88	3.7043	.27412	.72588
34	12.3834	.91637	.08363	89	3.5311	.26130	.73870
35	12.3188	.91159	.08841	90	3.3609	.24871	.75129
36	12.2508	.90656	.09344	91	3.1961	.23651	.76349
37	12.1790	.90124	.09876	92	3.0407	.22501	.77499
38	12.1033	.89564	.10436	93	2.8962	.21432	.78568
39	12.0236	.88975	.11025	94	2.7640	.20453	.79547
40	11.9399	.88356	.11644	95	2.6445	.19569	.80431
41	11.8521	.87706	.12294	96	2.5385	.18785	.81215
42	11.7604	.87027	.12973	97	2.4422	.18073	.81927
43	11.6646	.86318	.13682	98	2.3556	.17431	.82569
44	11.5647	.85579	.14421	99	2.2755	.16839	.83161
45	11.4605	.84808	.15192	100	2.2012	.16289	.83711
46	11.3520	.84005	.15995	101	2.1303	.15764	.84236
47	11.2391	.83170	.16830	102	2.0564	.15218	.84782
48	11.1221	.82304	.17696	103	1.9781	.14638	.85362
49	11.0013	.81409	.18591	104	1.8912	.13995	.86005
50	10.8765	.80486	.19514	105	1.7838	.13200	.86800
51	10.7478	.79534	.20466	106	1.6297	.12060	.87940
52	10.6144	.78547	.21453	107	1.4075	.10416	.89584
53	10.4765	.77526	.22474	108	1.0473	.07750	.92250
54	10.3343	.76474	.23526	109	0.4655	.03445	.96555

Appendix D
Valuation Tables

TABLE S(7.6)
SINGLE LIFE, 7.6 PERCENT, BASED ON LIFE TABLE 80CNSMT
SHOWING THE PRESENT WORTH OF AN ANNUITY, OF A LIFE ESTATE,
AND OF A REMAINDER INTEREST

AGE	ANNUITY	LIFE ESTATE	REMAINDER	AGE	ANNUITY	LIFE ESTATE	REMAINDER
(1)	(2)	(3)	(4)	(1)	(2)	(3)	(4)
0	12.8185	.97421	.02579	55	10.0116	.76088	.23912
1	12.9624	.98514	.01486	56	9.8660	.74981	.25019
2	12.9600	.98496	.01504	57	9.7157	.73839	.26161
3	12.9537	.98448	.01552	58	9.5607	.72661	.27339
4	12.9449	.98381	.01619	59	9.4013	.71450	.28550
5	12.9342	.98300	.01700	60	9.2378	.70208	.29792
6	12.9221	.98208	.01792	61	9.0708	.68938	.31062
7	12.9087	.98106	.01894	62	8.9005	.67644	.32356
8	12.8938	.97993	.02007	63	8.7272	.66326	.33674
9	12.8773	.97867	.02133	64	8.5505	.64984	.35016
10	12.8590	.97729	.02271	65	8.3698	.63610	.36390
11	12.8389	.97576	.02424	66	8.1846	.62203	.37797
12	12.8172	.97411	.02589	67	7.9950	.60762	.39238
13	12.7946	.97239	.02761	68	7.8009	.59287	.40713
14	12.7720	.97067	.02933	69	7.6033	.57785	.42215
15	12.7497	.96897	.03103	70	7.4028	.56262	.43738
16	12.7277	.96730	.03270	71	7.2005	.54724	.45276
17	12.7060	.96566	.03434	72	6.9962	.53171	.46829
18	12.6843	.96401	.03599	73	6.7899	.51603	.48397
19	12.6620	.96231	.03769	74	6.5808	.50014	.49986
20	12.6391	.96057	.03943	75	6.3682	.48399	.51601
21	12.6155	.95878	.04122	76	6.1520	.46755	.53245
22	12.5909	.95691	.04309	77	5.9327	.45088	.54912
23	12.5651	.95495	.04505	78	5.7111	.43404	.56596
24	12.5375	.95285	.04715	79	5.4891	.41717	.58283
25	12.5077	.95059	.04941	80	5.2682	.40039	.59961
26	12.4754	.94813	.05187	81	5.0507	.38385	.61615
27	12.4403	.94546	.05454	82	4.8375	.36765	.63235
28	12.4026	.94260	.05740	83	4.6298	.35187	.64813
29	12.3619	.93951	.06049	84	4.4272	.33647	.66353
30	12.3183	.93619	.06381	85	4.2291	.32141	.67859
31	12.2713	.93262	.06738	86	4.0372	.30682	.69318
32	12.2211	.92880	.07120	87	3.8538	.29289	.70711
33	12.1672	.92471	.07529	88	3.6781	.27954	.72046
34	12.1099	.92036	.07964	89	3.5070	.26653	.73347
35	12.0490	.91572	.08428	90	3.3388	.25375	.74625
36	11.9847	.91083	.08917	91	3.1758	.24136	.75864
37	11.9166	.90567	.09433	92	3.0220	.22967	.77033
38	11.8449	.90022	.09978	93	2.8790	.21880	.78120
39	11.7694	.89447	.10553	94	2.7481	.20885	.79115
40	11.6898	.88843	.11157	95	2.6297	.19986	.80014
41	11.6063	.88208	.11792	96	2.5247	.19188	.80812
42	11.5190	.87544	.12456	97	2.4293	.18463	.81537
43	11.4278	.86851	.13149	98	2.3435	.17810	.82190
44	11.3324	.86127	.13873	99	2.2642	.17208	.82792
45	11.2329	.85370	.14630	100	2.1905	.16648	.83352
46	11.1293	.84582	.15418	101	2.1203	.16114	.83886
47	11.0213	.83762	.16238	102	2.0471	.15558	.84442
48	10.9093	.82910	.17090	103	1.9696	.14969	.85031
49	10.7935	.82030	.17970	104	1.8835	.14314	.85686
50	10.6739	.81121	.18879	105	1.7771	.13506	.86494
51	10.5503	.80182	.19818	106	1.6242	.12344	.87656
52	10.4222	.79209	.20791	107	1.4034	.10666	.89334
53	10.2896	.78201	.21799	108	1.0448	.07940	.92060
54	10.1528	.77161	.22839	109	0.4647	.03532	.96468

The Tools and Techniques of Estate Planning

Appendix D
Valuation Tables

TABLE S(7.8)
SINGLE LIFE, 7.8 PERCENT, BASED ON LIFE TABLE 80CNSMT
SHOWING THE PRESENT WORTH OF AN ANNUITY, OF A LIFE ESTATE,
AND OF A REMAINDER INTEREST

AGE	ANNUITY	LIFE ESTATE	REMAINDER	AGE	ANNUITY	LIFE ESTATE	REMAINDER
(1)	(2)	(3)	(4)	(1)	(2)	(3)	(4)
0	12.5010	.97508	.02492	55	9.8407	.76757	.23243
1	12.6417	.98605	.01395	56	9.7003	.75662	.24338
2	12.6400	.98592	.01408	57	9.5552	.74531	.25469
3	12.6344	.98549	.01451	58	9.4055	.73363	.26637
4	12.6264	.98486	.01514	59	9.2514	.72161	.27839
5	12.6166	.98410	.01590	60	9.0933	.70927	.29073
6	12.6055	.98323	.01677	61	8.9315	.69666	.30334
7	12.5931	.98227	.01773	62	8.7665	.68379	.31621
8	12.5794	.98119	.01881	63	8.5984	.67067	.32933
9	12.5640	.98000	.02000	64	8.4269	.65730	.34270
10	12.5471	.97867	.02133	65	8.2514	.64361	.35639
11	12.5283	.97721	.02279	66	8.0715	.62957	.37043
12	12.5080	.97562	.02438	67	7.8869	.61518	.38482
13	12.4868	.97397	.02603	68	7.6979	.60044	.39956
14	12.4656	.97232	.02768	69	7.5054	.58542	.41458
15	12.4448	.97070	.02930	70	7.3099	.57017	.42983
16	12.4243	.96910	.03090	71	7.1124	.55477	.44523
17	12.4042	.96753	.03247	72	6.9129	.53921	.46079
18	12.3841	.96596	.03404	73	6.7113	.52348	.47652
19	12.3634	.96435	.03565	74	6.5067	.50753	.49247
20	12.3422	.96269	.03731	75	6.2987	.49130	.50870
21	12.3204	.96099	.03901	76	6.0869	.47478	.52522
22	12.2976	.95922	.04078	77	5.8718	.45800	.54200
23	12.2738	.95735	.04265	78	5.6543	.44104	.55896
24	12.2481	.95535	.04465	79	5.4363	.42403	.57597
25	12.2205	.95320	.04680	80	5.2192	.40710	.59290
26	12.1904	.95085	.04915	81	5.0052	.39041	.60959
27	12.1577	.94830	.05170	82	4.7955	.37405	.62595
28	12.1224	.94555	.05445	83	4.5909	.35809	.64191
29	12.0844	.94258	.05742	84	4.3913	.34252	.65748
30	12.0435	.93939	.06061	85	4.1960	.32729	.67271
31	11.9993	.93595	.06405	86	4.0066	.31252	.68748
32	11.9520	.93226	.06774	87	3.8257	.29841	.70159
33	11.9013	.92830	.07170	88	3.6522	.28488	.71512
34	11.8472	.92408	.07592	89	3.4832	.27169	.72831
35	11.7896	.91959	.08041	90	3.3169	.25872	.74128
36	11.7287	.91484	.08516	91	3.1557	.24615	.75385
37	11.6643	.90982	.09018	92	3.0036	.23428	.76572
38	11.5963	.90451	.09549	93	2.8620	.22323	.77677
39	11.5245	.89891	.10109	94	2.7323	.21312	.78688
40	11.4489	.89302	.10698	95	2.6151	.20398	.79602
41	11.3695	.88682	.11318	96	2.5111	.19586	.80414
42	11.2863	.88033	.11967	97	2.4166	.18849	.81151
43	11.1993	.87355	.12645	98	2.3315	.18185	.81815
44	11.1083	.86645	.13355	99	2.2529	.17573	.82427
45	11.0133	.85904	.14096	100	2.1799	.17003	.82997
46	10.9141	.85130	.14870	101	2.1104	.16461	.83539
47	10.8108	.84324	.15676	102	2.0379	.15896	.84104
48	10.7035	.83487	.16513	103	1.9611	.15297	.84703
49	10.5925	.82621	.17379	104	1.8758	.14631	.85369
50	10.4777	.81726	.18274	105	1.7704	.13809	.86191
51	10.3591	.80801	.19199	106	1.6187	.12626	.87374
52	10.2360	.79841	.20159	107	1.3993	.10915	.89085
53	10.1084	.78846	.21154	108	1.0423	.08130	.91870
54	9.9767	.77819	.22181	109	0.4638	.03618	.96382

The Tools and Techniques of Estate Planning

Appendix D
Valuation Tables

TABLE S(8.0)

SINGLE LIFE, 8.0 PERCENT, BASED ON LIFE TABLE 80CNSMT
SHOWING THE PRESENT WORTH OF AN ANNUITY, OF A LIFE ESTATE,
AND OF A REMAINDER INTEREST

AGE	ANNUITY	LIFE ESTATE	REMAINDER	AGE	ANNUITY	LIFE ESTATE	REMAINDER
(1)	(2)	(3)	(4)	(1)	(2)	(3)	(4)
0	12.1984	.97587	.02413	55	9.6749	.77399	.22601
1	12.3360	.98688	.01312	56	9.5394	.76315	.23685
2	12.3348	.98679	.01321	57	9.3994	.75195	.24805
3	12.3299	.98639	.01361	58	9.2547	.74038	.25962
4	12.3227	.98582	.01418	59	9.1056	.72845	.27155
5	12.3137	.98510	.01490	60	8.9526	.71621	.28379
6	12.3035	.98428	.01572	61	8.7959	.70367	.29633
7	12.2921	.98336	.01664	62	8.6360	.69088	.30912
8	12.2793	.98234	.01766	63	8.4729	.67783	.32217
9	12.2650	.98120	.01880	64	8.3064	.66452	.33548
10	12.2492	.97994	.02006	65	8.1360	.65088	.34912
11	12.2316	.97853	.02147	66	7.9610	.63688	.36312
12	12.2126	.97701	.02299	67	7.7814	.62251	.37749
13	12.1927	.97542	.02458	68	7.5974	.60779	.39221
14	12.1729	.97383	.02617	69	7.4097	.59278	.40722
15	12.1534	.97227	.02773	70	7.2190	.57752	.42248
16	12.1343	.97074	.02926	71	7.0263	.56210	.43790
17	12.1156	.96925	.03075	72	6.8314	.54651	.45349
18	12.0969	.96775	.03225	73	6.6343	.53074	.46926
19	12.0778	.96622	.03378	74	6.4342	.51473	.48527
20	12.0581	.96465	.03535	75	6.2305	.49844	.50156
21	12.0379	.96303	.03697	76	6.0229	.48183	.51817
22	12.0168	.96135	.03865	77	5.8120	.46496	.53504
23	11.9947	.95958	.04042	78	5.5986	.44788	.55212
24	11.9709	.95767	.04233	79	5.3844	.43075	.56925
25	11.9452	.95562	.04438	80	5.1710	.41368	.58632
26	11.9172	.95338	.04662	81	4.9605	.39684	.60316
27	11.8867	.95094	.04906	82	4.7541	.38032	.61968
28	11.8537	.94830	.05170	83	4.5526	.36421	.63579
29	11.8180	.94544	.05456	84	4.3559	.34847	.65153
30	11.7796	.94237	.05763	85	4.1633	.33307	.66693
31	11.7381	.93905	.06095	86	3.9766	.31812	.68188
32	11.6936	.93549	.06451	87	3.7980	.30384	.69616
33	11.6458	.93166	.06834	88	3.6267	.29014	.70986
34	11.5947	.92757	.07243	89	3.4597	.27677	.72323
35	11.5402	.92321	.07679	90	3.2953	.26362	.73638
36	11.4825	.91860	.08140	91	3.1359	.25087	.74913
37	11.4214	.91372	.08628	92	2.9853	.23882	.76118
38	11.3569	.90855	.09145	93	2.8451	.22761	.77239
39	11.2887	.90310	.09690	94	2.7167	.21734	.78266
40	11.2168	.89734	.10266	95	2.6006	.20805	.79195
41	11.1411	.89129	.10871	96	2.4976	.19981	.80019
42	11.0618	.88495	.11505	97	2.4039	.19231	.80769
43	10.9789	.87831	.12169	98	2.3196	.18557	.81443
44	10.8920	.87136	.12864	99	2.2417	.17934	.82066
45	10.8011	.86409	.13591	100	2.1694	.17356	.82644
46	10.7063	.85650	.14350	101	2.1005	.16804	.83196
47	10.6073	.84859	.15141	102	2.0288	.16230	.83770
48	10.5045	.84036	.15964	103	1.9527	.15622	.84378
49	10.3980	.83184	.16816	104	1.8682	.14946	.85054
50	10.2879	.82303	.17697	105	1.7638	.14110	.85890
51	10.1739	.81391	.18609	106	1.6132	.12906	.87094
52	10.0556	.80444	.19556	107	1.3952	.11162	.88838
53	9.9328	.79463	.20537	108	1.0399	.08319	.91681
54	9.8060	.78448	.21552	109	0.4630	.03704	.96296

The Tools and Techniques of Estate Planning

Appendix D
Valuation Tables

TABLE S(8.2)
SINGLE LIFE, 8.2 PERCENT, BASED ON LIFE TABLE 80CNSMT
SHOWING THE PRESENT WORTH OF AN ANNUITY, OF A LIFE ESTATE,
AND OF A REMAINDER INTEREST

AGE	ANNUITY	LIFE ESTATE	REMAINDER	AGE	ANNUITY	LIFE ESTATE	REMAINDER
(1)	(2)	(3)	(4)	(1)	(2)	(3)	(4)
0	11.9096	.97659	.02341	55	9.5139	.78014	.21986
1	12.0442	.98763	.01237	56	9.3832	.76942	.23058
2	12.0435	.98757	.01243	57	9.2479	.75833	.24167
3	12.0392	.98722	.01278	58	9.1081	.74686	.25314
4	12.0327	.98668	.01332	59	8.9638	.73503	.26497
5	12.0245	.98600	.01400	60	8.8156	.72288	.27712
6	12.0150	.98523	.01477	61	8.6639	.71044	.28956
7	12.0045	.98437	.01563	62	8.5088	.69772	.30228
8	11.9926	.98340	.01660	63	8.3506	.68475	.31525
9	11.9793	.98230	.01770	64	8.1890	.67149	.32851
10	11.9645	.98109	.01891	65	8.0233	.65791	.34209
11	11.9480	.97974	.02026	66	7.8531	.64396	.35604
12	11.9302	.97827	.02173	67	7.6784	.62963	.37037
13	11.9115	.97674	.02326	68	7.4991	.61492	.38508
14	11.8929	.97522	.02478	69	7.3161	.59992	.40008
15	11.8747	.97372	.02628	70	7.1301	.58467	.41533
16	11.8568	.97226	.02774	71	6.9419	.56924	.43076
17	11.8394	.97083	.02917	72	6.7515	.55362	.44638
18	11.8220	.96941	.03059	73	6.5588	.53782	.46218
19	11.8042	.96795	.03205	74	6.3630	.52177	.47823
20	11.7860	.96645	.03355	75	6.1636	.50541	.49459
21	11.7673	.96491	.03509	76	5.9602	.48873	.51127
22	11.7477	.96331	.03669	77	5.7533	.47177	.52823
23	11.7272	.96163	.03837	78	5.5437	.45459	.54541
24	11.7051	.95982	.04018	79	5.3333	.43733	.56267
25	11.6812	.95786	.04214	80	5.1236	.42013	.57987
26	11.6551	.95572	.04428	81	4.9165	.40315	.59685
27	11.6266	.95338	.04662	82	4.7133	.38649	.61351
28	11.5957	.95085	.04915	83	4.5149	.37022	.62978
29	11.5623	.94811	.05189	84	4.3211	.35433	.64567
30	11.5262	.94515	.05485	85	4.1312	.33875	.66125
31	11.4871	.94195	.05805	86	3.9469	.32364	.67636
32	11.4452	.93851	.06149	87	3.7706	.30919	.69081
33	11.4000	.93480	.06520	88	3.6015	.29532	.70468
34	11.3517	.93084	.06916	89	3.4365	.28179	.71821
35	11.3002	.92661	.07339	90	3.2740	.26847	.73153
36	11.2455	.92213	.07787	91	3.1163	.25553	.74447
37	11.1876	.91738	.08262	92	2.9672	.24331	.75669
38	11.1263	.91235	.08765	93	2.8285	.23193	.76807
39	11.0614	.90704	.09296	94	2.7013	.22151	.77849
40	10.9930	.90142	.09858	95	2.5863	.21208	.78792
41	10.9209	.89551	.10449	96	2.4842	.20370	.79630
42	10.8453	.88931	.11069	97	2.3914	.19609	.80391
43	10.7661	.88282	.11718	98	2.3078	.18924	.81076
44	10.6831	.87601	.12399	99	2.2307	.18291	.81709
45	10.5962	.86889	.13111	100	2.1591	.17704	.82296
46	10.5054	.86144	.13856	101	2.0908	.17145	.82855
47	10.4106	.85367	.14633	102	2.0197	.16562	.83438
48	10.3120	.84558	.15442	103	1.9444	.15944	.84056
49	10.2098	.83720	.16280	104	1.8607	.15257	.84743
50	10.1040	.82853	.17147	105	1.7572	.14409	.85591
51	9.9945	.81955	.18045	106	1.6078	.13184	.86816
52	9.8807	.81021	.18979	107	1.3912	.11408	.88592
53	9.7625	.80053	.19947	108	1.0375	.08507	.91493
54	9.6403	.79050	.20950	109	0.4621	.03789	.96211

The Tools and Techniques of Estate Planning

Appendix D
Valuation Tables

TABLE S(8.4)
SINGLE LIFE, 8.4 PERCENT, BASED ON LIFE TABLE 80CNSMT
SHOWING THE PRESENT WORTH OF AN ANNUITY, OF A LIFE ESTATE,
AND OF A REMAINDER INTEREST

AGE	ANNUITY	LIFE ESTATE	REMAINDER	AGE	ANNUITY	LIFE ESTATE	REMAINDER
(1)	(2)	(3)	(4)	(1)	(2)	(3)	(4)
0	11.6338	.97724	.02276	55	9.3575	.78603	.21397
1	11.7655	.98830	.01170	56	9.2314	.77543	.22457
2	11.7653	.98828	.01172	57	9.1007	.76446	.23554
3	11.7615	.98797	.01203	58	8.9655	.75310	.24690
4	11.7556	.98747	.01253	59	8.8259	.74137	.25863
5	11.7480	.98683	.01317	60	8.6824	.72932	.27068
6	11.7393	.98610	.01390	61	8.5352	.71696	.28304
7	11.7295	.98528	.01472	62	8.3849	.70433	.29567
8	11.7185	.98436	.01564	63	8.2313	.69143	.30857
9	11.7061	.98331	.01669	64	8.0743	.67824	.32176
10	11.6923	.98215	.01785	65	7.9133	.66472	.33528
11	11.6768	.98085	.01915	66	7.7478	.65082	.34918
12	11.6600	.97944	.02056	67	7.5777	.63653	.36347
13	11.6424	.97796	.02204	68	7.4030	.62185	.37815
14	11.6249	.97649	.02351	69	7.2246	.60687	.39313
15	11.6078	.97505	.02495	70	7.0431	.59162	.40838
16	11.5911	.97365	.02635	71	6.8593	.57618	.42382
17	11.5748	.97228	.02772	72	6.6733	.56055	.43945
18	11.5587	.97093	.02907	73	6.4848	.54473	.45527
19	11.5421	.96954	.03046	74	6.2933	.52863	.47137
20	11.5252	.96812	.03188	75	6.0979	.51223	.48777
21	11.5078	.96666	.03334	76	5.8986	.49548	.50452
22	11.4897	.96513	.03487	77	5.6956	.47843	.52157
23	11.4707	.96354	.03646	78	5.4899	.46115	.53885
24	11.4501	.96181	.03819	79	5.2832	.44379	.55621
25	11.4279	.95994	.04006	80	5.0769	.42646	.57354
26	11.4035	.95790	.04210	81	4.8732	.40935	.59065
27	11.3769	.95566	.04434	82	4.6731	.39254	.60746
28	11.3479	.95323	.04677	83	4.4777	.37613	.62387
29	11.3166	.95059	.04941	84	4.2867	.36008	.63992
30	11.2826	.94774	.05226	85	4.0994	.34435	.65565
31	11.2458	.94465	.05535	86	3.9176	.32908	.67092
32	11.2063	.94133	.05867	87	3.7436	.31446	.68554
33	11.1636	.93774	.06226	88	3.5766	.30043	.69957
34	11.1179	.93391	.06609	89	3.4135	.28674	.71326
35	11.0691	.92980	.07020	90	3.2529	.27324	.72676
36	11.0173	.92545	.07455	91	3.0969	.26014	.73986
37	10.9622	.92083	.07917	92	2.9494	.24775	.75225
38	10.9040	.91593	.08407	93	2.8120	.23621	.76379
39	10.8423	.91075	.08925	94	2.6860	.22563	.77437
40	10.7771	.90528	.09472	95	2.5721	.21606	.78394
41	10.7083	.89950	.10050	96	2.4710	.20756	.79244
42	10.6362	.89344	.10656	97	2.3790	.19984	.80016
43	10.5605	.88709	.11291	98	2.2962	.19288	.80712
44	10.4812	.88042	.11958	99	2.2197	.18646	.81354
45	10.3981	.87344	.12656	100	2.1488	.18050	.81950
46	10.3111	.86613	.13387	101	2.0811	.17482	.82518
47	10.2202	.85850	.14150	102	2.0107	.16890	.83110
48	10.1256	.85055	.14945	103	1.9361	.16263	.83737
49	10.0275	.84231	.15769	104	1.8532	.15567	.84433
50	9.9259	.83378	.16622	105	1.7506	.14705	.85295
51	9.8206	.82493	.17507	106	1.6024	.13460	.86540
52	9.7111	.81573	.18427	107	1.3872	.11652	.88348
53	9.5973	.80617	.19383	108	1.0350	.08694	.91306
54	9.4795	.79628	.20372	109	0.4613	.03875	.96125

Appendix D
Valuation Tables
TABLE S(8.6)
SINGLE LIFE, 8.6 PERCENT, BASED ON LIFE TABLE 80CNSMT
SHOWING THE PRESENT WORTH OF AN ANNUITY, OF A LIFE ESTATE,
AND OF A REMAINDER INTEREST

AGE	ANNUITY	LIFE ESTATE	REMAINDER	AGE	ANNUITY	LIFE ESTATE	REMAINDER
(1)	(2)	(3)	(4)	(1)	(2)	(3)	(4)
0	11.3701	.97783	.02217	55	9.2057	.79169	.20831
1	11.4991	.98892	.01108	56	9.0839	.78121	.21879
2	11.4992	.98893	.01107	57	8.9575	.77035	.22965
3	11.4959	.98865	.01135	58	8.8268	.75910	.24090
4	11.4905	.98818	.01182	59	8.6916	.74748	.25252
5	11.4836	.98759	.01241	60	8.5526	.73552	.26448
6	11.4755	.98690	.01310	61	8.4100	.72326	.27674
7	11.4664	.98611	.01389	62	8.2641	.71071	.28929
8	11.4562	.98523	.01477	63	8.1150	.69789	.30211
9	11.4446	.98423	.01577	64	7.9625	.68478	.31522
10	11.4316	.98312	.01688	65	7.8060	.67132	.32868
11	11.4170	.98186	.01814	66	7.6450	.65747	.34253
12	11.4012	.98050	.01950	67	7.4793	.64322	.35678
13	11.3846	.97908	.02092	68	7.3091	.62858	.37142
14	11.3681	.97766	.02234	69	7.1351	.61362	.38638
15	11.3521	.97628	.02372	70	6.9579	.59838	.40162
16	11.3364	.97493	.02507	71	6.7785	.58295	.41705
17	11.3212	.97363	.02637	72	6.5966	.56731	.43269
18	11.3062	.97233	.02767	73	6.4123	.55146	.44854
19	11.2908	.97101	.02899	74	6.2248	.53534	.46466
20	11.2751	.96965	.03035	75	6.0335	.51888	.48112
21	11.2589	.96827	.03173	76	5.8381	.50207	.49793
22	11.2421	.96682	.03318	77	5.6389	.48495	.51505
23	11.2244	.96530	.03470	78	5.4370	.46758	.53242
24	11.2053	.96366	.03634	79	5.2338	.45011	.54989
25	11.1846	.96188	.03812	80	5.0310	.43267	.56733
26	11.1619	.95992	.04008	81	4.8306	.41543	.58457
27	11.1369	.95777	.04223	82	4.6336	.39849	.60151
28	11.1098	.95544	.04456	83	4.4411	.38194	.61806
29	11.0803	.95291	.04709	84	4.2528	.36574	.63426
30	11.0484	.95016	.04984	85	4.0681	.34986	.65014
31	11.0137	.94718	.05282	86	3.8887	.33443	.66557
32	10.9764	.94397	.05603	87	3.7170	.31966	.68034
33	10.9360	.94050	.05950	88	3.5520	.30547	.69453
34	10.8928	.93678	.06322	89	3.3909	.29162	.70838
35	10.8465	.93280	.06720	90	3.2320	.27796	.72204
36	10.7973	.92857	.07143	91	3.0777	.26468	.73532
37	10.7450	.92407	.07593	92	2.9317	.25213	.74787
38	10.6896	.91931	.08069	93	2.7957	.24043	.75957
39	10.6309	.91426	.08574	94	2.6710	.22970	.77030
40	10.5688	.90891	.09109	95	2.5581	.21999	.78001
41	10.5032	.90327	.09673	96	2.4578	.21137	.78863
42	10.4343	.89735	.10265	97	2.3667	.20354	.79646
43	10.3620	.89113	.10887	98	2.2846	.19648	.80352
44	10.2861	.88460	.11540	99	2.2089	.18996	.81004
45	10.2065	.87776	.12224	100	2.1385	.18391	.81609
46	10.1232	.87059	.12941	101	2.0716	.17815	.82185
47	10.0360	.86310	.13690	102	2.0018	.17215	.82785
48	9.9452	.85529	.14471	103	1.9279	.16580	.83420
49	9.8510	.84719	.15281	104	1.8457	.15873	.84127
50	9.7533	.83879	.16121	105	1.7441	.14999	.85001
51	9.6520	.83007	.16993	106	1.5970	.13734	.86266
52	9.5466	.82101	.17899	107	1.3832	.11895	.88105
53	9.4370	.81158	.18842	108	1.0326	.08881	.91119
54	9.3234	.80181	.19819	109	0.4604	.03959	.96041

The Tools and Techniques of Estate Planning

Appendix D
Valuation Tables

TABLE S(8.8)
SINGLE LIFE, 8.8 PERCENT, BASED ON LIFE TABLE 80CNSMT
SHOWING THE PRESENT WORTH OF AN ANNUITY, OF A LIFE ESTATE,
AND OF A REMAINDER INTEREST

AGE	ANNUITY	LIFE ESTATE	REMAINDER	AGE	ANNUITY	LIFE ESTATE	REMAINDER
(1)	(2)	(3)	(4)	(1)	(2)	(3)	(4)
0	11.1178	.97837	.02163	55	9.0582	.79712	.20288
1	11.2441	.98948	.01052	56	8.9405	.78676	.21324
2	11.2446	.98952	.01048	57	8.8183	.77601	.22399
3	11.2417	.98927	.01073	58	8.6918	.76488	.23512
4	11.2368	.98884	.01116	59	8.5609	.75336	.24664
5	11.2304	.98828	.01172	60	8.4262	.74151	.25849
6	11.2230	.98762	.01238	61	8.2879	.72933	.27067
7	11.2145	.98688	.01312	62	8.1463	.71688	.28312
8	11.2050	.98604	.01396	63	8.0016	.70414	.29586
9	11.1941	.98508	.01492	64	7.8534	.69110	.30890
10	11.1819	.98401	.01599	65	7.7012	.67771	.32229
11	11.1682	.98280	.01720	66	7.5445	.66391	.33609
12	11.1532	.98148	.01852	67	7.3831	.64972	.35028
13	11.1376	.98011	.01989	68	7.2172	.63511	.36489
14	11.1220	.97874	.02126	69	7.0475	.62018	.37982
15	11.1069	.97741	.02259	70	6.8745	.60496	.39504
16	11.0922	.97612	.02388	71	6.6992	.58953	.41047
17	11.0780	.97487	.02513	72	6.5215	.57389	.42611
18	11.0640	.97363	.02637	73	6.3412	.55803	.44197
19	11.0496	.97237	.02763	74	6.1577	.54188	.45812
20	11.0350	.97108	.02892	75	5.9703	.52538	.47462
21	11.0200	.96976	.03024	76	5.7786	.50852	.49148
22	11.0043	.96838	.03162	77	5.5833	.49133	.50867
23	10.9879	.96694	.03306	78	5.3849	.47387	.52613
24	10.9702	.96537	.03463	79	5.1853	.45631	.54369
25	10.9509	.96367	.03633	80	4.9858	.43875	.56125
26	10.9296	.96180	.03820	81	4.7886	.42140	.57860
27	10.9062	.95975	.04025	82	4.5947	.40433	.59567
28	10.8808	.95751	.04249	83	4.4050	.38764	.61236
29	10.8531	.95507	.04493	84	4.2194	.37131	.62869
30	10.8230	.95243	.04757	85	4.0373	.35528	.64472
31	10.7903	.94955	.05045	86	3.8602	.33970	.66030
32	10.7550	.94644	.05356	87	3.6907	.32478	.67522
33	10.7169	.94308	.05692	88	3.5277	.31044	.68956
34	10.6759	.93948	.06052	89	3.3685	.29643	.70357
35	10.6320	.93561	.06439	90	3.2115	.28261	.71739
36	10.5853	.93150	.06850	91	3.0588	.26917	.73083
37	10.5356	.92713	.07287	92	2.9143	.25646	.74354
38	10.4828	.92249	.07751	93	2.7796	.24460	.75540
39	10.4269	.91757	.08243	94	2.6560	.23373	.76627
40	10.3676	.91235	.08765	95	2.5442	.22389	.77611
41	10.3050	.90684	.09316	96	2.4449	.21515	.78485
42	10.2392	.90105	.09895	97	2.3546	.20720	.79280
43	10.1701	.89497	.10503	98	2.2732	.20004	.79996
44	10.0974	.88857	.11143	99	2.1981	.19343	.80657
45	10.0212	.88186	.11814	100	2.1284	.18730	.81270
46	9.9413	.87484	.12516	101	2.0621	.18146	.81854
47	9.8577	.86748	.13252	102	1.9930	.17538	.82462
48	9.7705	.85980	.14020	103	1.9197	.16894	.83106
49	9.6800	.85184	.14816	104	1.8384	.16178	.83822
50	9.5860	.84357	.15643	105	1.7376	.15291	.84709
51	9.4885	.83499	.16501	106	1.5917	.14007	.85993
52	9.3870	.82606	.17394	107	1.3792	.12137	.87863
53	9.2813	.81676	.18324	108	1.0302	.09066	.90934
54	9.1718	.80712	.19288	109	0.4596	.04044	.95956

Appendix D
Valuation Tables

TABLE S(9.0)
SINGLE LIFE, 9.0 PERCENT, BASED ON LIFE TABLE 80CNSMT
SHOWING THE PRESENT WORTH OF AN ANNUITY, OF A LIFE ESTATE,
AND OF A REMAINDER INTEREST

AGE	ANNUITY	LIFE ESTATE	REMAINDER	AGE	ANNUITY	LIFE ESTATE	REMAINDER
(1)	(2)	(3)	(4)	(1)	(2)	(3)	(4)
0	10.8762	.97886	.02114	55	8.9148	.80233	.19767
1	11.0000	.99000	.01000	56	8.8011	.79209	.20791
2	11.0007	.99006	.00994	57	8.6829	.78146	.21854
3	10.9982	.98984	.01016	58	8.5604	.77044	.22956
4	10.9938	.98944	.01056	59	8.4337	.75903	.24097
5	10.9879	.98891	.01109	60	8.3031	.74728	.25272
6	10.9810	.98829	.01171	61	8.1689	.73520	.26480
7	10.9731	.98758	.01242	62	8.0315	.72283	.27717
8	10.9642	.98678	.01322	63	7.8909	.71018	.28982
9	10.9540	.98586	.01414	64	7.7469	.69722	.30278
10	10.9425	.98483	.01517	65	7.5988	.68390	.31610
11	10.9296	.98366	.01634	66	7.4463	.67017	.32983
12	10.9154	.98239	.01761	67	7.2891	.65602	.34398
13	10.9006	.98105	.01895	68	7.1273	.64146	.35854
14	10.8859	.97973	.02027	69	6.9618	.62656	.37344
15	10.8717	.97845	.02155	70	6.7929	.61136	.38864
16	10.8579	.97721	.02279	71	6.6216	.59595	.40405
17	10.8446	.97601	.02399	72	6.4479	.58031	.41969
18	10.8315	.97483	.02517	73	6.2715	.56444	.43556
19	10.8181	.97363	.02637	74	6.0918	.54827	.45173
20	10.8044	.97240	.02760	75	5.9082	.53174	.46826
21	10.7904	.97114	.02886	76	5.7203	.51483	.48517
22	10.7759	.96983	.03017	77	5.5286	.49757	.50243
23	10.7606	.96846	.03154	78	5.3338	.48004	.51996
24	10.7441	.96697	.03303	79	5.1376	.46238	.53762
25	10.7261	.96535	.03465	80	4.9414	.44473	.55527
26	10.7062	.96356	.03644	81	4.7473	.42726	.57274
27	10.6843	.96159	.03841	82	4.5563	.41007	.58993
28	10.6604	.95944	.04056	83	4.3695	.39325	.60675
29	10.6343	.95709	.04291	84	4.1865	.37679	.62321
30	10.6060	.95454	.04546	85	4.0068	.36062	.63938
31	10.5751	.95176	.04824	86	3.8321	.34489	.65511
32	10.5418	.94876	.05124	87	3.6647	.32982	.67018
33	10.5057	.94551	.05449	88	3.5038	.31534	.68466
34	10.4668	.94201	.05799	89	3.3464	.30118	.69882
35	10.4251	.93826	.06174	90	3.1911	.28720	.71280
36	10.3807	.93427	.06573	91	3.0401	.27360	.72640
37	10.3335	.93001	.06999	92	2.8970	.26073	.73927
38	10.2832	.92549	.07451	93	2.7637	.24873	.75127
39	10.2299	.92069	.07931	94	2.6413	.23771	.76229
40	10.1734	.91560	.08440	95	2.5304	.22774	.77226
41	10.1136	.91022	.08978	96	2.4320	.21888	.78112
42	10.0506	.90456	.09544	97	2.3425	.21083	.78917
43	9.9845	.89860	.10140	98	2.2619	.20357	.79643
44	9.9149	.89234	.10766	99	2.1875	.19687	.80313
45	9.8419	.88577	.11423	100	2.1184	.19066	.80934
46	9.7652	.87887	.12113	101	2.0527	.18474	.81526
47	9.6850	.87165	.12835	102	1.9842	.17858	.82142
48	9.6012	.86411	.13589	103	1.9116	.17205	.82795
49	9.5142	.85627	.14373	104	1.8310	.16479	.83521
50	9.4238	.84814	.15186	105	1.7312	.15581	.84419
51	9.3299	.83970	.16030	106	1.5864	.14277	.85723
52	9.2321	.83089	.16911	107	1.3752	.12377	.87623
53	9.1302	.82172	.17828	108	1.0278	.09251	.90749
54	9.0245	.81221	.18779	109	0.4587	.04128	.95872

The Tools and Techniques of Estate Planning

TABLE S(9.2)
SINGLE LIFE, 9.2 PERCENT, BASED ON LIFE TABLE 80CNSMT
SHOWING THE PRESENT WORTH OF AN ANNUITY, OF A LIFE ESTATE,
AND OF A REMAINDER INTEREST

AGE	ANNUITY	LIFE ESTATE	REMAINDER	AGE	ANNUITY	LIFE ESTATE	REMAINDER
(1)	(2)	(3)	(4)	(1)	(2)	(3)	(4)
0	10.6447	.97931	.02069	55	8.7754	.80734	.19266
1	10.7660	.99047	.00953	56	8.6655	.79722	.20278
2	10.7669	.99056	.00944	57	8.5512	.78671	.21329
3	10.7648	.99036	.00964	58	8.4326	.77580	.22420
4	10.7607	.98999	.01001	59	8.3097	.76450	.23550
5	10.7553	.98949	.01051	60	8.1831	.75284	.24716
6	10.7489	.98890	.01110	61	8.0529	.74087	.25913
7	10.7416	.98822	.01178	62	7.9195	.72859	.27141
8	10.7332	.98746	.01254	63	7.7829	.71603	.28397
9	10.7236	.98658	.01342	64	7.6429	.70315	.29685
10	10.7128	.98558	.01442	65	7.4989	.68990	.31010
11	10.7006	.98445	.01555	66	7.3503	.67623	.32377
12	10.6872	.98322	.01678	67	7.1972	.66214	.33786
13	10.6732	.98193	.01807	68	7.0394	.64763	.35237
14	10.6593	.98065	.01935	69	6.8779	.63276	.36724
15	10.6458	.97942	.02058	70	6.7130	.61759	.38241
16	10.6328	.97822	.02178	71	6.5456	.60220	.39780
17	10.6204	.97707	.02293	72	6.3757	.58656	.41344
18	10.6081	.97594	.02406	73	6.2032	.57069	.42931
19	10.5956	.97479	.02521	74	6.0272	.55451	.44549
20	10.5828	.97362	.02638	75	5.8473	.53795	.46205
21	10.5698	.97242	.02758	76	5.6630	.52100	.47900
22	10.5563	.97118	.02882	77	5.4748	.50368	.49632
23	10.5421	.96987	.03013	78	5.2835	.48608	.51392
24	10.5267	.96845	.03155	79	5.0906	.46834	.53166
25	10.5098	.96691	.03309	80	4.8977	.45059	.54941
26	10.4912	.96519	.03481	81	4.7066	.43301	.56699
27	10.4707	.96330	.03670	82	4.5186	.41571	.58429
28	10.4482	.96124	.03876	83	4.3345	.39877	.60123
29	10.4237	.95898	.04102	84	4.1541	.38217	.61783
30	10.3970	.95652	.04348	85	3.9768	.36587	.63413
31	10.3678	.95384	.04616	86	3.8044	.35000	.65000
32	10.3363	.95094	.04906	87	3.6391	.33480	.66520
33	10.3020	.94779	.05221	88	3.4801	.32017	.67983
34	10.2652	.94440	.05560	89	3.3246	.30586	.69414
35	10.2256	.94075	.05925	90	3.1710	.29173	.70827
36	10.1834	.93687	.06313	91	3.0215	.27798	.72202
37	10.1384	.93273	.06727	92	2.8800	.26496	.73504
38	10.0905	.92833	.07167	93	2.7479	.25281	.74719
39	10.0396	.92365	.07635	94	2.6266	.24165	.75835
40	9.9856	.91868	.08132	95	2.5168	.23155	.76845
41	9.9285	.91342	.08658	96	2.4193	.22258	.77742
42	9.8683	.90788	.09212	97	2.3306	.21441	.78559
43	9.8050	.90206	.09794	98	2.2507	.20706	.79294
44	9.7383	.89593	.10407	99	2.1769	.20028	.79972
45	9.6683	.88948	.11052	100	2.1085	.19398	.80602
46	9.5947	.88272	.11728	101	2.0433	.18799	.81201
47	9.5176	.87562	.12438	102	1.9755	.18174	.81826
48	9.4371	.86821	.13179	103	1.9036	.17513	.82487
49	9.3534	.86051	.13949	104	1.8238	.16779	.83221
50	9.2664	.85251	.14749	105	1.7248	.15868	.84132
51	9.1760	.84420	.15580	106	1.5811	.14546	.85454
52	9.0817	.83552	.16448	107	1.3713	.12616	.87384
53	8.9834	.82648	.17352	108	1.0255	.09434	.90566
54	8.8814	.81709	.18291	109	0.4579	.04212	.95788

The Tools and Techniques of Estate Planning

Appendix D
Valuation Tables

TABLE S(9.4)
SINGLE LIFE, 9.4 PERCENT, BASED ON LIFE TABLE 80CNSMT
SHOWING THE PRESENT WORTH OF AN ANNUITY, OF A LIFE ESTATE,
AND OF A REMAINDER INTEREST

AGE	ANNUITY	LIFE ESTATE	REMAINDER	AGE	ANNUITY	LIFE ESTATE	REMAINDER
(1)	(2)	(3)	(4)	(1)	(2)	(3)	(4)
0	10.4226	.97973	.02027	55	8.6399	.81215	.18785
1	10.5415	.99090	.00910	56	8.5335	.80215	.19785
2	10.5427	.99101	.00899	57	8.4229	.79176	.20824
3	10.5408	.99084	.00916	58	8.3081	.78096	.21904
4	10.5372	.99049	.00951	59	8.1890	.76977	.23023
5	10.5321	.99002	.00998	60	8.0662	.75822	.24178
6	10.5262	.98946	.01054	61	7.9398	.74634	.25366
7	10.5193	.98882	.01118	62	7.8102	.73416	.26584
8	10.5115	.98808	.01192	63	7.6775	.72168	.27832
9	10.5025	.98724	.01276	64	7.5414	.70889	.29111
10	10.4923	.98628	.01372	65	7.4012	.69571	.30429
11	10.4807	.98519	.01481	66	7.2566	.68212	.31788
12	10.4680	.98399	.01601	67	7.1073	.66809	.33191
13	10.4547	.98274	.01726	68	6.9534	.65362	.34638
14	10.4415	.98150	.01850	69	6.7957	.63880	.36120
15	10.4288	.98031	.01969	70	6.6347	.62366	.37634
16	10.4166	.97916	.02084	71	6.4711	.60829	.39171
17	10.4049	.97806	.02194	72	6.3050	.59267	.40733
18	10.3934	.97698	.02302	73	6.1361	.57679	.42321
19	10.3817	.97588	.02412	74	5.9638	.56060	.43940
20	10.3698	.97476	.02524	75	5.7875	.54402	.45598
21	10.3576	.97362	.02638	76	5.6067	.52703	.47297
22	10.3450	.97243	.02757	77	5.4220	.50967	.49033
23	10.3318	.97119	.02881	78	5.2340	.49200	.50800
24	10.3174	.96984	.03016	79	5.0444	.47418	.52582
25	10.3017	.96836	.03164	80	4.8546	.45634	.54366
26	10.2842	.96672	.03328	81	4.6666	.43866	.56134
27	10.2650	.96491	.03509	82	4.4814	.42125	.57875
28	10.2438	.96292	.03708	83	4.2999	.40419	.59581
29	10.2207	.96075	.03925	84	4.1221	.38747	.61253
30	10.1955	.95838	.04162	85	3.9472	.37104	.62896
31	10.1680	.95579	.04421	86	3.7770	.35504	.64496
32	10.1381	.95298	.04702	87	3.6138	.33969	.66031
33	10.1056	.94993	.05007	88	3.4567	.32493	.67507
34	10.0706	.94664	.05336	89	3.3030	.31048	.68952
35	10.0330	.94310	.05690	90	3.1511	.29621	.70379
36	9.9928	.93932	.06068	91	3.0032	.28230	.71770
37	9.9499	.93530	.06470	92	2.8631	.26913	.73087
38	9.9043	.93101	.06899	93	2.7323	.25683	.74317
39	9.8557	.92644	.07356	94	2.6122	.24554	.75446
40	9.8042	.92159	.07841	95	2.5034	.23532	.76468
41	9.7495	.91645	.08355	96	2.4067	.22623	.77377
42	9.6919	.91104	.08896	97	2.3188	.21797	.78203
43	9.6313	.90534	.09466	98	2.2396	.21052	.78948
44	9.5674	.89933	.10067	99	2.1664	.20365	.79635
45	9.5001	.89301	.10699	100	2.0986	.19727	.80273
46	9.4295	.88638	.11362	101	2.0341	.19120	.80880
47	9.3555	.87941	.12059	102	1.9669	.18488	.81512
48	9.2780	.87213	.12787	103	1.8956	.17819	.82181
49	9.1975	.86456	.13544	104	1.8165	.17076	.82924
50	9.1137	.85669	.14331	105	1.7185	.16154	.83846
51	9.0266	.84850	.15150	106	1.5758	.14813	.85187
52	8.9357	.83996	.16004	107	1.3673	.12853	.87147
53	8.8408	.83104	.16896	108	1.0231	.09617	.90383
54	8.7423	.82178	.17822	109	0.4570	.04296	.95704

Appendix D
Valuation Tables

TABLE S(9.6)
SINGLE LIFE, 9.6 PERCENT, BASED ON LIFE TABLE 80CNSMT
SHOWING THE PRESENT WORTH OF AN ANNUITY, OF A LIFE ESTATE,
AND OF A REMAINDER INTEREST

AGE	ANNUITY	LIFE ESTATE	REMAINDER	AGE	ANNUITY	LIFE ESTATE	REMAINDER
(1)	(2)	(3)	(4)	(1)	(2)	(3)	(4)
0	10.2095	.98011	.01989	55	8.5081	.81678	.18322
1	10.3260	.99129	.00871	56	8.4052	.80690	.19310
2	10.3274	.99143	.00857	57	8.2981	.79662	.20338
3	10.3258	.99128	.00872	58	8.1868	.78593	.21407
4	10.3225	.99096	.00904	59	8.0714	.77485	.22515
5	10.3178	.99051	.00949	60	7.9522	.76341	.23659
6	10.3123	.98998	.01002	61	7.8295	.75163	.24837
7	10.3059	.98936	.01064	62	7.7036	.73955	.26045
8	10.2985	.98866	.01134	63	7.5746	.72716	.27284
9	10.2900	.98784	.01216	64	7.4422	.71445	.28555
10	10.2804	.98692	.01308	65	7.3058	.70135	.29865
11	10.2694	.98586	.01414	66	7.1649	.68783	.31217
12	10.2574	.98471	.01529	67	7.0194	.67386	.32614
13	10.2447	.98349	.01651	68	6.8693	.65945	.34055
14	10.2322	.98229	.01771	69	6.7153	.64467	.35533
15	10.2202	.98114	.01886	70	6.5580	.62957	.37043
16	10.2086	.98003	.01997	71	6.3981	.61422	.38578
17	10.1976	.97897	.02103	72	6.2356	.59862	.40138
18	10.1868	.97793	.02207	73	6.0703	.58275	.41725
19	10.1758	.97688	.02312	74	5.9016	.56655	.43345
20	10.1647	.97581	.02419	75	5.7287	.54996	.45004
21	10.1534	.97473	.02527	76	5.5514	.53294	.46706
22	10.1416	.97360	.02640	77	5.3701	.51553	.48447
23	10.1293	.97241	.02759	78	5.1854	.49780	.50220
24	10.1159	.97112	.02888	79	4.9990	.47991	.52009
25	10.1012	.96971	.03029	80	4.8123	.46198	.53802
26	10.0848	.96814	.03186	81	4.6271	.44421	.55579
27	10.0667	.96640	.03360	82	4.4447	.42669	.57331
28	10.0468	.96450	.03550	83	4.2659	.40953	.59047
29	10.0250	.96240	.03760	84	4.0905	.39269	.60731
30	10.0013	.96012	.03988	85	3.9180	.37613	.62387
31	9.9752	.95762	.04238	86	3.7500	.36000	.64000
32	9.9469	.95490	.04510	87	3.5888	.34452	.65548
33	9.9161	.95194	.04806	88	3.4336	.32963	.67037
34	9.8828	.94875	.05125	89	3.2817	.31505	.68495
35	9.8470	.94531	.05469	90	3.1315	.30062	.69938
36	9.8088	.94164	.05836	91	2.9851	.28657	.71343
37	9.7679	.93772	.06228	92	2.8464	.27326	.72674
38	9.7244	.93354	.06646	93	2.7169	.26082	.73918
39	9.6780	.92908	.07092	94	2.5979	.24939	.75061
40	9.6287	.92435	.07565	95	2.4900	.23904	.76096
41	9.5764	.91933	.08067	96	2.3943	.22985	.77015
42	9.5212	.91404	.08596	97	2.3071	.22148	.77852
43	9.4631	.90846	.09154	98	2.2286	.21394	.78606
44	9.4018	.90257	.09743	99	2.1561	.20698	.79302
45	9.3373	.89638	.10362	100	2.0889	.20053	.79947
46	9.2695	.88987	.11013	101	2.0249	.19439	.80561
47	9.1982	.88303	.11697	102	1.9583	.18800	.81200
48	9.1237	.87588	.12412	103	1.8877	.18122	.81878
49	9.0462	.86843	.13157	104	1.8094	.17370	.82630
50	8.9655	.86069	.13931	105	1.7122	.16437	.83563
51	8.8815	.85263	.14737	106	1.5706	.15078	.84922
52	8.7938	.84421	.15579	107	1.3634	.13089	.86911
53	8.7023	.83542	.16458	108	1.0207	.09799	.90201
54	8.6071	.82628	.17372	109	0.4562	.04380	.95620

The Tools and Techniques of Estate Planning

Appendix D
Valuation Tables

TABLE S(9.8)
SINGLE LIFE, 9.8 PERCENT, BASED ON LIFE TABLE 80CNSMT
SHOWING THE PRESENT WORTH OF AN ANNUITY, OF A LIFE ESTATE,
AND OF A REMAINDER INTEREST

AGE	ANNUITY	LIFE ESTATE	REMAINDER	AGE	ANNUITY	LIFE ESTATE	REMAINDER
(1)	(2)	(3)	(4)	(1)	(2)	(3)	(4)
0	10.0047	.98046	.01954	55	8.3798	.82122	.17878
1	10.1190	.99166	.00834	56	8.2802	.81146	.18854
2	10.1205	.99181	.00819	57	8.1765	.80130	.19870
3	10.1192	.99168	.00832	58	8.0687	.79073	.20927
4	10.1162	.99138	.00862	59	7.9567	.77976	.22024
5	10.1119	.99096	.00904	60	7.8410	.76842	.23158
6	10.1067	.99046	.00954	61	7.7219	.75675	.24325
7	10.1007	.98987	.01013	62	7.5996	.74476	.25524
8	10.0938	.98919	.01081	63	7.4741	.73246	.26754
9	10.0858	.98841	.01159	64	7.3453	.71984	.28016
10	10.0767	.98751	.01249	65	7.2125	.70683	.29317
11	10.0662	.98649	.01351	66	7.0753	.69337	.30663
12	10.0548	.98537	.01463	67	6.9334	.67947	.32053
13	10.0427	.98418	.01582	68	6.7869	.66512	.33488
14	10.0308	.98302	.01698	69	6.6366	.65039	.34961
15	10.0194	.98190	.01810	70	6.4829	.63532	.36468
16	10.0085	.98083	.01917	71	6.3266	.62000	.38000
17	9.9981	.97982	.02018	72	6.1676	.60442	.39558
18	9.9880	.97882	.02118	73	6.0058	.58857	.41143
19	9.9777	.97782	.02218	74	5.8405	.57237	.42763
20	9.9673	.97680	.02320	75	5.6710	.55576	.44424
21	9.9567	.97576	.02424	76	5.4971	.53871	.46129
22	9.9458	.97468	.02532	77	5.3190	.52127	.47873
23	9.9342	.97356	.02644	78	5.1376	.50348	.49652
24	9.9217	.97233	.02767	79	4.9543	.48552	.51448
25	9.9080	.97098	.02902	80	4.7706	.46752	.53248
26	9.8926	.96948	.03052	81	4.5883	.44965	.55035
27	9.8756	.96781	.03219	82	4.4086	.43204	.56796
28	9.8569	.96597	.03403	83	4.2324	.41477	.58523
29	9.8363	.96396	.03604	84	4.0594	.39782	.60218
30	9.8138	.96175	.03825	85	3.8892	.38114	.61886
31	9.7891	.95933	.04067	86	3.7233	.36489	.63511
32	9.7623	.95671	.04329	87	3.5641	.34929	.65071
33	9.7330	.95384	.04616	88	3.4108	.33426	.66574
34	9.7014	.95074	.04926	89	3.2607	.31955	.68045
35	9.6673	.94740	.05260	90	3.1121	.30498	.69502
36	9.6309	.94383	.05617	91	2.9673	.29079	.70921
37	9.5919	.94001	.05999	92	2.8299	.27733	.72267
38	9.5503	.93593	.06407	93	2.7016	.26476	.73524
39	9.5060	.93159	.06841	94	2.5837	.25320	.74680
40	9.4589	.92697	.07303	95	2.4769	.24273	.75727
41	9.4088	.92206	.07794	96	2.3819	.23343	.76657
42	9.3559	.91688	.08312	97	2.2955	.22496	.77504
43	9.3002	.91142	.08858	98	2.2177	.21733	.78267
44	9.2414	.90566	.09434	99	2.1458	.21029	.78971
45	9.1794	.89958	.10042	100	2.0792	.20376	.79624
46	9.1142	.89320	.10680	101	2.0158	.19755	.80245
47	9.0457	.88648	.11352	102	1.9498	.19108	.80892
48	8.9740	.87945	.12055	103	1.8799	.18423	.81577
49	8.8993	.87213	.12787	104	1.8023	.17662	.82338
50	8.8216	.86452	.13548	105	1.7059	.16718	.83282
51	8.7406	.85658	.14342	106	1.5655	.15341	.84659
52	8.6560	.84828	.15172	107	1.3596	.13324	.86676
53	8.5675	.83962	.16038	108	1.0184	.09980	.90020
54	8.4755	.83060	.16940	109	0.4554	.04463	.95537

The Tools and Techniques of Estate Planning

Appendix D
Valuation Tables

TABLE S(10.0)
SINGLE LIFE, 10.0 PERCENT, BASED ON LIFE TABLE 80CNSMT
SHOWING THE PRESENT WORTH OF AN ANNUITY, OF A LIFE ESTATE,
AND OF A REMAINDER INTEREST

AGE	ANNUITY	LIFE ESTATE	REMAINDER	AGE	ANNUITY	LIFE ESTATE	REMAINDER
(1)	(2)	(3)	(4)	(1)	(2)	(3)	(4)
0	9.8078	.98078	.01922	55	8.2550	.82550	.17450
1	9.9199	.99199	.00801	56	8.1586	.81586	.18414
2	9.9216	.99216	.00784	57	8.0581	.80581	.19419
3	9.9205	.99205	.00795	58	7.9536	.79536	.20464
4	9.9178	.99178	.00822	59	7.8449	.78449	.21551
5	9.9138	.99138	.00862	60	7.7326	.77326	.22674
6	9.9090	.99090	.00910	61	7.6169	.76169	.23831
7	9.9034	.99034	.00966	62	7.4980	.74980	.25020
8	9.8969	.98969	.01031	63	7.3760	.73760	.26240
9	9.8893	.98893	.01107	64	7.2507	.72507	.27493
10	9.8806	.98806	.01194	65	7.1213	.71213	.28787
11	9.8707	.98707	.01293	66	6.9876	.69876	.30124
12	9.8598	.98598	.01402	67	6.8492	.68492	.31508
13	9.8483	.98483	.01517	68	6.7063	.67063	.32937
14	9.8370	.98370	.01630	69	6.5595	.65595	.34405
15	9.8262	.98262	.01738	70	6.4093	.64093	.35907
16	9.8158	.98158	.01842	71	6.2564	.62564	.37436
17	9.8060	.98060	.01940	72	6.1009	.61009	.38991
18	9.7965	.97965	.02035	73	5.9425	.59425	.40575
19	9.7869	.97869	.02131	74	5.7805	.57805	.42195
20	9.7771	.97771	.02229	75	5.6144	.56144	.43856
21	9.7672	.97672	.02328	76	5.4437	.54437	.45563
22	9.7570	.97570	.02430	77	5.2689	.52689	.47311
23	9.7462	.97462	.02538	78	5.0906	.50906	.49094
24	9.7345	.97345	.02655	79	4.9103	.49103	.50897
25	9.7216	.97216	.02784	80	4.7295	.47295	.52705
26	9.7072	.97072	.02928	81	4.5501	.45501	.54499
27	9.6912	.96912	.03088	82	4.3730	.43730	.56270
28	9.6736	.96736	.03264	83	4.1993	.41993	.58007
29	9.6542	.96542	.03458	84	4.0287	.40287	.59713
30	9.6329	.96329	.03671	85	3.8608	.38608	.61392
31	9.6095	.96095	.03905	86	3.6970	.36970	.63030
32	9.5840	.95840	.04160	87	3.5398	.35398	.64602
33	9.5562	.95562	.04438	88	3.3883	.33883	.66117
34	9.5262	.95262	.04738	89	3.2399	.32399	.67601
35	9.4937	.94937	.05063	90	3.0929	.30929	.69071
36	9.4589	.94589	.05411	91	2.9496	.29496	.70504
37	9.4217	.94217	.05783	92	2.8136	.28136	.71864
38	9.3820	.93820	.06180	93	2.6865	.26865	.73135
39	9.3396	.93396	.06604	94	2.5697	.25697	.74303
40	9.2945	.92945	.07055	95	2.4638	.24638	.75362
41	9.2465	.92465	.07535	96	2.3697	.23697	.76303
42	9.1959	.91959	.08041	97	2.2840	.22840	.77160
43	9.1424	.91424	.08576	98	2.2069	.22069	.77931
44	9.0859	.90859	.09141	99	2.1356	.21356	.78644
45	9.0264	.90264	.09736	100	2.0696	.20696	.79304
46	8.9637	.89637	.10363	101	2.0068	.20068	.79932
47	8.8978	.88978	.11022	102	1.9414	.19414	.80586
48	8.8287	.88287	.11713	103	1.8721	.18721	.81279
49	8.7567	.87567	.12433	104	1.7952	.17952	.82048
50	8.6818	.86818	.13182	105	1.6997	.16997	.83003
51	8.6037	.86037	.13963	106	1.5603	.15603	.84397
52	8.5220	.85220	.14780	107	1.3557	.13557	.86443
53	8.4365	.84365	.15635	108	1.0160	.10160	.89840
54	8.3476	.83476	.16524	109	0.4545	.04545	.95455

Appendix D
Valuation Tables

TWO-LIFE REMAINDER FACTORS* — 6.6% INTEREST RATE**
(For valuation dates occurring after April 30, 1989)

AGE	5	10	15	20	25	30	35	40	45	50
5	.00853	.00990	.01129	.01265	.01397	.01525	.01650	.01769	.01881	.01986
10	.00990	.01168	.01355	.01540	.01723	.01903	.02078	.02244	.02399	.02542
15	.01129	.01355	.01599	.01848	.02098	.02349	.02595	.02829	.03047	.03248
20	.01265	.01540	.01848	.02170	.02503	.02844	.03181	.03503	.03802	.04073
25	.01397	.01723	.02098	.02503	.02936	.03389	.03846	.04289	.04702	.05075
30	.01525	.01903	.02349	.02844	.03389	.03979	.04593	.05202	.05781	.06309
35	.01650	.02078	.02595	.03181	.03846	.04593	.05398	.06222	.07025	.07776
40	.01769	.02244	.02829	.03503	.04289	.05202	.06222	.07301	.08389	.09435
45	.01881	.02399	.03047	.03802	.04702	.05781	.07025	.08389	.09811	.11221
50	.01986	.02542	.03248	.04073	.05075	.06309	.07776	.09435	.11221	.13053
55	.02083	.02674	.03430	.04314	.05402	.06775	.08450	.10397	.12556	.14841
60	.02170	.02793	.03595	.04526	.05682	.07173	.09034	.11248	.13768	.16510
65	.02247	.02899	.03741	.04708	.05916	.07501	.09519	.11969	.14815	.17989
70	.02310	.02990	.03869	.04864	.06107	.07763	.09910	.12557	.15687	.19247
75	.02359	.03063	.03979	.04995	.06259	.07966	.10209	.13013	.16375	.20257
80	.02394	.03119	.04067	.05101	.06377	.08116	.10428	.13350	.16892	.21028
85	.02416	.03155	.04132	.05179	.06461	.08218	.10575	.13576	.17241	.21557
90	.02430	.03176	.04174	.05232	.06517	.08283	.10666	.13716	.17459	.21890
95	.02438	.03187	.04199	.05265	.06550	.08321	.10718	.13796	.17585	.22085
100	.02443	.03193	.04212	.05283	.06569	.08341	.10746	.13839	.17652	.22189

AGE	55	60	65	70	75	80	85	90	95	100
5	.02083	.02170	.02247	.02310	.02359	.02394	.02416	.02430	.02438	.02443
10	.02674	.02793	.02899	.02990	.03063	.03119	.03155	.03176	.03187	.03193
15	.03430	.03595	.03741	.03869	.03979	.04067	.04132	.04174	.04199	.04212
20	.04314	.04526	.04708	.04864	.04995	.05101	.05179	.05232	.05265	.05283
25	.05402	.05682	.05916	.06107	.06259	.06377	.06461	.06517	.06550	.06569
30	.06775	.07173	.07501	.07763	.07966	.08116	.08218	.08283	.08321	.08341
35	.08450	.09034	.09519	.09910	.10209	.10428	.10575	.10666	.10718	.10746
40	.10397	.11248	.11969	.12557	.13013	.13350	.13576	.13716	.13796	.13839
45	.12556	.13768	.14815	.15687	.16375	.16892	.17241	.17459	.17585	.17652
50	.14841	.16510	.17989	.19247	.20257	.21028	.21557	.21890	.22085	.22189
55	.17145	.19363	.21384	.23143	.24586	.25707	.26484	.26980	.27271	.27427
60	.19363	.22204	.24872	.27263	.29271	.30862	.31985	.32712	.33142	.33374
65	.21384	.24872	.28259	.31394	.34102	.36299	.37878	.38912	.39531	.39867
70	.23143	.27263	.31394	.35357	.38901	.41867	.44049	.45504	.46387	.46868
75	.24586	.29271	.34102	.38901	.43360	.47237	.50179	.52187	.53425	.54104
80	.25707	.30862	.36299	.41867	.47237	.52117	.55975	.58707	.60442	.61404
85	.26484	.31985	.37878	.44049	.50179	.55975	.60745	.64259	.66573	.67873
90	.26980	.32712	.38912	.45504	.52187	.58707	.64259	.68499	.71391	.73038
95	.27271	.33142	.39531	.46387	.53425	.60442	.66573	.71391	.74793	.76759
100	.27427	.33374	.39867	.46868	.54104	.61404	.67873	.73038	.76759	.78931

*The present value of $1.00 due at the death of the survivor of two persons.

**Use appropriate interest rate for the month in which the valuation date occurs.

Reprinted from the *Advanced Sales Reference Service*
©1992 The National Underwriter Company

The Tools and Techniques of Estate Planning

Appendix D
Valuation Tables

TWO-LIFE REMAINDER FACTORS* — 6.8% INTEREST RATE**
(For valuation dates occurring after April 30, 1989)

AGE	5	10	15	20	25	30	35	40	45	50
5	.00749	.00873	.01000	.01125	.01247	.01368	.01486	.01599	.01707	.01808
10	.00873	.01035	.01206	.01377	.01546	.01715	.01879	.02037	.02186	.02325
15	.01000	.01206	.01430	.01659	.01892	.02126	.02358	.02581	.02790	.02985
20	.01125	.01377	.01659	.01956	.02266	.02585	.02903	.03209	.03496	.03758
25	.01247	.01546	.01892	.02266	.02668	.03093	.03525	.03946	.04342	.04702
30	.01368	.01715	.02126	.02585	.03093	.03648	.04229	.04808	.05363	.05873
35	.01486	.01879	.02358	.02903	.03525	.04229	.04991	.05776	.06548	.07273
40	.01599	.02037	.02581	.03209	.03946	.04808	.05776	.06808	.07853	.08865
45	.01707	.02186	.02790	.03496	.04342	.05363	.06548	.07853	.09223	.10589
50	.01808	.02325	.02985	.03758	.04702	.05873	.07273	.08865	.10589	.12366
55	.01903	.02453	.03162	.03993	.05020	.06326	.07928	.09801	.11889	.14110
60	.01988	.02571	.03324	.04200	.05295	.06715	.08500	.10635	.13077	.15748
65	.02063	.02675	.03468	.04380	.05525	.07038	.08978	.11345	.14110	.17208
70	.02126	.02765	.03596	.04536	.05714	.07298	.09365	.11928	.14975	.18456
75	.02175	.02838	.03705	.04666	.05866	.07500	.09663	.12383	.15661	.19464
80	.02210	.02894	.03794	.04773	.05985	.07650	.09883	.12721	.16179	.20237
85	.02233	.02930	.03859	.04851	.06070	.07753	.10030	.12948	.16531	.20770
90	.02247	.02952	.03902	.04905	.06126	.07819	.10122	.13089	.16751	.21107
95	.02255	.02963	.03927	.04938	.06160	.07858	.10176	.13171	.16879	.21305
100	.02259	.02969	.03941	.04956	.06179	.07878	.10204	.13214	.16947	.21410

AGE	55	60	65	70	75	80	85	90	95	100
5	.01903	.01988	.02063	.02126	.02175	.02210	.02233	.02247	.02255	.02259
10	.02453	.02571	.02675	.02765	.02838	.02894	.02930	.02952	.02963	.02969
15	.03162	.03324	.03468	.03596	.03705	.03794	.03859	.03902	.03927	.03941
20	.03993	.04200	.04380	.04536	.04666	.04773	.04851	.04905	.04938	.04956
25	.05020	.05295	.05525	.05714	.05866	.05985	.06070	.06126	.06160	.06179
30	.06326	.06715	.07038	.07298	.07500	.07650	.07753	.07819	.07858	.07878
35	.07928	.08500	.08978	.09365	.09663	.09883	.10030	.10122	.10176	.10204
40	.09801	.10635	.11345	.11928	.12383	.12721	.12948	.13089	.13171	.13214
45	.11889	.13077	.14110	.14975	.15661	.16179	.16531	.16751	.16879	.16947
50	.14110	.15748	.17208	.18456	.19464	.20237	.20770	.21107	.21305	.21410
55	.16361	.18541	.20536	.22284	.23724	.24848	.25632	.26133	.26429	.26587
60	.18541	.21335	.23973	.26349	.28354	.29951	.31084	.31818	.32255	.32491
65	.20536	.23973	.27325	.30443	.33149	.35356	.36948	.37994	.38623	.38964
70	.22284	.26349	.30443	.34389	.37933	.40914	.43115	.44588	.45484	.45973
75	.23724	.28354	.33149	.37933	.42398	.46296	.49265	.51299	.52556	.53247
80	.24848	.29951	.35356	.40914	.46296	.51209	.55105	.57874	.59636	.60615
85	.25632	.31084	.36948	.43115	.49265	.55105	.59928	.63492	.65843	.67167
90	.26133	.31818	.37994	.44588	.51299	.57874	.63492	.67793	.70735	.72412
95	.26429	.32255	.38623	.45484	.52556	.59636	.65843	.70735	.74198	.76200
100	.26587	.32491	.38964	.45973	.53247	.60615	.67167	.72412	.76200	.78413

*The present value of $1.00 due at the death of the survivor of two persons.

**Use appropriate interest rate for the month in which the valuation date occurs.

Reprinted from the *Advanced Sales Reference Service*
©1992 The National Underwriter Company

TWO-LIFE REMAINDER FACTORS* — 7.0% INTEREST RATE**									
(For valuation dates occurring after April 30, 1989)									

AGE	5	10	15	20	25	30	35	40	45	50
5	.00659	.00771	.00887	.01002	.01115	.01228	.01339	.01447	.01551	.01649
10	.00771	.00918	.01074	.01231	.01389	.01546	.01702	.01852	.01995	.02130
15	.00887	.01074	.01280	.01491	.01707	.01926	.02145	.02357	.02558	.02746
20	.01002	.01231	.01491	.01765	.02053	.02351	.02651	.02943	.03218	.03471
25	.01115	.01389	.01707	.02053	.02427	.02825	.03233	.03634	.04013	.04361
30	.01228	.01546	.01926	.02351	.02825	.03346	.03895	.04447	.04979	.05471
35	.01339	.01702	.02145	.02651	.03233	.03895	.04617	.05366	.06106	.06807
40	.01447	.01852	.02357	.02943	.03634	.04447	.05366	.06351	.07356	.08334
45	.01551	.01995	.02558	.03218	.04013	.04979	.06106	.07356	.08674	.09997
50	.01649	.02130	.02746	.03471	.04361	.05471	.06807	.08334	.09997	.11720
55	.01741	.02254	.02919	.03699	.04670	.05911	.07444	.09245	.11264	.13422
60	.01825	.02369	.03078	.03903	.04938	.06291	.08003	.10061	.12427	.15028
65	.01899	.02472	.03220	.04080	.05165	.06609	.08473	.10760	.13445	.16467
70	.01961	.02561	.03347	.04235	.05353	.06867	.08856	.11338	.14302	.17705
75	.02009	.02635	.03456	.04365	.05504	.07068	.09153	.11791	.14986	.18710
80	.02044	.02690	.03546	.04472	.05623	.07219	.09374	.12130	.15505	.19485
85	.02067	.02727	.03611	.04551	.05708	.07322	.09522	.12358	.15859	.20021
90	.02081	.02748	.03654	.04605	.05765	.07388	.09615	.12501	.16082	.20362
95	.02090	.02760	.03680	.04639	.05800	.07428	.09669	.12583	.16212	.20562
100	.02094	.02766	.03694	.04658	.05819	.07449	.09698	.12628	.16281	.20670

AGE	55	60	65	70	75	80	85	90	95	100
5	.01741	.01825	.01899	.01961	.02009	.02044	.02067	.02081	.02090	.02094
10	.02254	.02369	.02472	.02561	.02635	.02690	.02727	.02748	.02760	.02766
15	.02919	.03078	.03220	.03347	.03456	.03546	.03611	.03654	.03680	.03694
20	.03699	.03903	.04080	.04235	.04365	.04472	.04551	.04605	.04639	.04658
25	.04670	.04938	.05165	.05353	.05504	.05623	.05708	.05765	.05800	.05819
30	.05911	.06291	.06609	.06867	.07068	.07219	.07322	.07388	.07428	.07449
35	.07444	.08003	.08473	.08856	.09153	.09374	.09522	.09615	.09669	.09698
40	.09245	.10061	.10760	.11338	.11791	.12130	.12358	.12501	.12583	.12628
45	.11264	.12427	.13445	.14302	.14986	.15505	.15859	.16082	.16212	.16281
50	.13422	.15028	.16467	.17705	.18710	.19485	.20021	.20362	.20562	.20670
55	.15620	.17760	.19729	.21463	.22900	.24027	.24816	.25323	.25623	.25784
60	.17760	.20507	.23113	.25472	.27474	.29076	.30217	.30959	.31403	.31642
65	.19729	.23113	.26429	.29528	.32231	.34445	.36049	.37107	.37744	.38091
70	.21463	.25472	.29528	.33454	.36997	.39990	.42208	.43698	.44607	.45104
75	.22900	.27474	.32231	.36997	.41463	.45381	.48375	.50433	.51709	.52410
80	.24027	.29076	.34445	.39990	.45381	.50321	.54255	.57058	.58847	.59842
85	.24816	.30217	.36049	.42208	.48375	.54255	.59127	.62737	.65126	.66472
90	.25323	.30959	.37107	.43698	.50433	.57058	.62737	.67099	.70089	.71795
95	.25623	.31403	.37744	.44607	.51709	.58847	.65126	.70089	.73610	.75648
100	.25784	.31642	.38091	.45104	.52410	.59842	.66472	.71795	.75648	.77902

*The present value of $1.00 due at the death of the survivor of two persons.

**Use appropriate interest rate for the month in which the valuation date occurs.

Reprinted from the *Advanced Sales Reference Service*
©1992 The National Underwriter Company

Appendix D
Valuation Tables

AGE	5	10	15	20	25	30	35	40	45	50
5	.00580	.00681	.00788	.00893	.00998	.01104	.01209	.01312	.01411	.01506
10	.00681	.00815	.00958	.01103	.01248	.01396	.01543	.01686	.01823	.01953
15	.00788	.00958	.01146	.01341	.01541	.01747	.01953	.02155	.02348	.02529
20	.00893	.01103	.01341	.01594	.01862	.02141	.02424	.02701	.02965	.03209
25	.00998	.01248	.01541	.01862	.02210	.02583	.02968	.03349	.03712	.04047
30	.01104	.01396	.01747	.02141	.02583	.03072	.03590	.04116	.04625	.05100
35	.01209	.01543	.01953	.02424	.02968	.03590	.04274	.04988	.05698	.06374
40	.01312	.01686	.02155	.02701	.03349	.04116	.04988	.05928	.06894	.07839
45	.01411	.01823	.02348	.02965	.03712	.04625	.05698	.06894	.08162	.09443
50	.01506	.01953	.02529	.03209	.04047	.05100	.06374	.07839	.09443	.11114
55	.01595	.02074	.02698	.03431	.04347	.05527	.06993	.08725	.10676	.12772
60	.01677	.02187	.02853	.03630	.04610	.05899	.07539	.09523	.11815	.14346
65	.01750	.02288	.02994	.03805	.04833	.06211	.08002	.10211	.12818	.15765
70	.01812	.02377	.03120	.03958	.05019	.06466	.08381	.10783	.13667	.16991
75	.01860	.02450	.03229	.04088	.05170	.06666	.08677	.11234	.14348	.17993
80	.01895	.02505	.03319	.04196	.05289	.06818	.08898	.11573	.14867	.18770
85	.01918	.02542	.03384	.04276	.05375	.06922	.09047	.11803	.15224	.19309
90	.01932	.02564	.03428	.04331	.05433	.06989	.09141	.11948	.15449	.19653
95	.01941	.02576	.03454	.04365	.05468	.07029	.09195	.12031	.15580	.19856
100	.01946	.02582	.03468	.04383	.05487	.07050	.09224	.12076	.15650	.19965

AGE	55	60	65	70	75	80	85	90	95	100
5	.01595	.01677	.01750	.01812	.01860	.01895	.01918	.01932	.01941	.01946
10	.02074	.02187	.02288	.02377	.02450	.02505	.02542	.02564	.02576	.02582
15	.02698	.02853	.02994	.03120	.03229	.03319	.03384	.03428	.03454	.03468
20	.03431	.03630	.03805	.03958	.04088	.04196	.04276	.04331	.04365	.04383
25	.04347	.04610	.04833	.05019	.05170	.05289	.05375	.05433	.05468	.05487
30	.05527	.05899	.06211	.06466	.06666	.06818	.06922	.06989	.07029	.07050
35	.06993	.07539	.08002	.08381	.08677	.08898	.09047	.09141	.09195	.09224
40	.08725	.09523	.10211	.10783	.11234	.11573	.11803	.11948	.12031	.12076
45	.10676	.11815	.12818	.13667	.14348	.14867	.15224	.15449	.15580	.15650
50	.12772	.14346	.15765	.16991	.17993	.18770	.19309	.19653	.19856	.19965
55	.14918	.17018	.18961	.20680	.22112	.23241	.24036	.24548	.24851	.25015
60	.17018	.19717	.22291	.24632	.26628	.28234	.29383	.30133	.30582	.30825
65	.18961	.22291	.25569	.28647	.31344	.33565	.35180	.36249	.36895	.37247
70	.20680	.24632	.28647	.32551	.36090	.39093	.41328	.42833	.43756	.44260
75	.22112	.26628	.31344	.36090	.40556	.44489	.47507	.49588	.50882	.51594
80	.23241	.28234	.33565	.39093	.44489	.49455	.53423	.56259	.58074	.59084
85	.24036	.29383	.35180	.41328	.47507	.53423	.58341	.61997	.64421	.65789
90	.24548	.30133	.36249	.42833	.49588	.56259	.61997	.66415	.69452	.71186
95	.24851	.30582	.36895	.43756	.50882	.58074	.64421	.69452	.73030	.75103
100	.25015	.30825	.37247	.44260	.51594	.59084	.65789	.71186	.75103	.77396

*The present value of $1.00 due at the death of the survivor of two persons.
**Use appropriate interest rate for the month in which the valuation date occurs.

Reprinted from the *Advanced Sales Reference Service*
©1992 The National Underwriter Company

Appendix D
Valuation Tables

TWO-LIFE REMAINDER FACTORS* — 7.4% INTEREST RATE**
(For valuation dates occurring after April 30, 1989)

AGE	5	10	15	20	25	30	35	40	45	50
5	.00511	.00603	.00700	.00797	.00894	.00993	.01092	.01190	.01286	.01377
10	.00603	.00724	.00855	.00988	.01123	.01261	.01400	.01536	.01668	.01793
15	.00700	.00855	.01028	.01207	.01393	.01585	.01780	.01972	.02157	.02332
20	.00797	.00988	.01207	.01441	.01689	.01951	.02218	.02481	.02734	.02970
25	.00894	.01123	.01393	.01689	.02013	.02363	.02726	.03088	.03436	.03759
30	.00993	.01261	.01585	.01951	.02363	.02821	.03312	.03811	.04299	.04757
35	.01092	.01400	.01780	.02218	.02726	.03312	.03959	.04639	.05320	.05972
40	.01190	.01536	.01972	.02481	.03088	.03811	.04639	.05537	.06464	.07377
45	.01286	.01668	.02157	.02734	.03436	.04299	.05320	.06464	.07685	.08923
50	.01377	.01793	.02332	.02970	.03759	.04757	.05972	.07377	.08923	.10543
55	.01464	.01912	.02496	.03185	.04050	.05171	.06573	.08238	.10123	.12159
60	.01545	.02022	.02649	.03381	.04307	.05535	.07107	.09019	.11239	.13701
65	.01616	.02122	.02788	.03553	.04527	.05842	.07562	.09696	.12226	.15098
70	.01677	.02209	.02913	.03705	.04711	.06095	.07937	.10262	.13066	.16314
75	.01725	.02282	.03021	.03834	.04862	.06294	.08232	.10711	.13744	.17311
80	.01760	.02338	.03111	.03942	.04981	.06445	.08452	.11050	.14264	.18089
85	.01783	.02375	.03177	.04023	.05067	.06550	.08602	.11281	.14622	.18631
90	.01798	.02397	.03221	.04078	.05125	.06617	.08697	.11427	.14849	.18979
95	.01806	.02408	.03248	.04113	.05161	.06658	.08752	.11511	.14982	.19184
100	.01811	.02414	.03262	.04132	.05181	.06680	.08782	.11557	.15054	.19294

AGE	55	60	65	70	75	80	85	90	95	100
5	.01464	.01545	.01616	.01677	.01725	.01760	.01783	.01798	.01806	.01811
10	.01912	.02022	.02122	.02209	.02282	.02338	.02375	.02397	.02408	.02414
15	.02496	.02649	.02788	.02913	.03021	.03111	.03177	.03221	.03248	.03262
20	.03185	.03381	.03553	.03705	.03834	.03942	.04023	.04078	.04113	.04132
25	.04050	.04307	.04527	.04711	.04862	.04981	.05067	.05125	.05161	.05181
30	.05171	.05535	.05842	.06095	.06294	.06445	.06550	.06617	.06658	.06680
35	.06573	.07107	.07562	.07937	.08232	.08452	.08602	.08697	.08752	.08782
40	.08238	.09019	.09696	.10262	.10711	.11050	.11281	.11427	.11511	.11557
45	.10123	.11239	.12226	.13066	.13744	.14264	.14622	.14849	.14982	.15054
50	.12159	.13701	.15098	.16314	.17311	.18089	.18631	.18979	.19184	.19294
55	.14253	.16313	.18228	.19932	.21359	.22490	.23289	.23806	.24113	.24279
60	.16313	.18964	.21504	.23826	.25816	.27425	.28580	.29338	.29793	.30039
65	.18228	.21504	.24743	.27799	.30489	.32715	.34340	.35420	.36074	.36430
70	.19932	.23826	.27799	.31679	.35212	.38223	.40472	.41994	.42928	.43439
75	.21359	.25816	.30489	.35212	.39674	.43621	.46661	.48764	.50075	.50797
80	.22490	.27425	.32715	.38223	.43621	.48610	.52609	.55477	.57316	.58341
85	.23289	.28580	.34340	.40472	.46661	.52609	.57570	.61269	.63729	.65117
90	.23806	.29338	.35420	.41994	.48764	.55477	.61269	.65743	.68825	.70586
95	.24113	.29793	.36074	.42928	.50075	.57316	.63729	.68825	.72458	.74565
100	.24279	.30039	.36430	.43439	.50797	.58341	.65117	.70586	.74565	.76896

*The present value of $1.00 due at the death of the survivor of two persons.

**Use appropriate interest rate for the month in which the valuation date occurs.

Reprinted from the *Advanced Sales Reference Service*
©1992 The National Underwriter Company

The Tools and Techniques of Estate Planning

TWO-LIFE REMAINDER FACTORS* — 7.6% INTEREST RATE**
(For valuation dates occurring after April 30, 1989)

AGE	5	10	15	20	25	30	35	40	45	50
5	.00450	.00534	.00623	.00712	.00802	.00895	.00988	.01081	.01173	.01262
10	.00534	.00644	.00764	.00886	.01012	.01141	.01272	.01401	.01527	.01649
15	.00623	.00764	.00922	.01087	.01260	.01440	.01624	.01806	.01984	.02153
20	.00712	.00886	.01087	.01303	.01534	.01779	.02031	.02281	.02523	.02751
25	.00802	.01012	.01260	.01534	.01835	.02163	.02506	.02850	.03183	.03494
30	.00895	.01141	.01440	.01779	.02163	.02593	.03057	.03532	.03999	.04440
35	.00988	.01272	.01624	.02031	.02506	.03057	.03669	.04317	.04970	.05599
40	.01081	.01401	.01806	.02281	.02850	.03532	.04317	.05174	.06065	.06947
45	.01173	.01527	.01984	.02523	.03183	.03999	.04970	.06065	.07239	.08437
50	.01262	.01649	.02153	.02751	.03494	.04440	.05599	.06947	.08437	.10006
55	.01346	.01764	.02313	.02960	.03777	.04842	.06183	.07783	.09604	.11580
60	.01425	.01872	.02462	.03151	.04028	.05198	.06705	.08547	.10695	.13090
65	.01495	.01970	.02599	.03322	.04244	.05500	.07152	.09212	.11666	.14466
70	.01555	.02057	.02723	.03472	.04427	.05749	.07522	.09772	.12498	.15669
75	.01603	.02129	.02831	.03601	.04576	.05947	.07815	.10218	.13173	.16662
80	.01638	.02185	.02922	.03709	.04696	.06099	.08036	.10558	.13693	.17440
85	.01661	.02222	.02988	.03790	.04783	.06204	.08187	.10790	.14052	.17985
90	.01676	.02244	.03033	.03846	.04841	.06272	.08282	.10936	.14282	.18336
95	.01685	.02256	.03059	.03881	.04878	.06313	.08338	.11022	.14416	.18543
100	.01689	.02262	.03074	.03900	.04898	.06335	.08368	.11068	.14488	.18655

AGE	55	60	65	70	75	80	85	90	95	100
5	.01346	.01425	.01495	.01555	.01603	.01638	.01661	.01676	.01685	.01689
10	.01764	.01872	.01970	.02057	.02129	.02185	.02222	.02244	.02256	.02262
15	.02313	.02462	.02599	.02723	.02831	.02922	.02988	.03033	.03059	.03074
20	.02960	.03151	.03322	.03472	.03601	.03709	.03790	.03846	.03881	.03900
25	.03777	.04028	.04244	.04427	.04576	.04696	.04783	.04841	.04878	.04898
30	.04842	.05198	.05500	.05749	.05947	.06099	.06204	.06272	.06313	.06335
35	.06183	.06705	.07152	.07522	.07815	.08036	.08187	.08282	.08338	.08368
40	.07783	.08547	.09212	.09772	.10218	.10558	.10790	.10936	.11022	.11068
45	.09604	.10695	.11666	.12498	.13173	.13693	.14052	.14282	.14416	.14488
50	.11580	.13090	.14466	.15669	.16662	.17440	.17985	.18336	.18543	.18655
55	.13623	.15642	.17530	.19218	.20639	.21771	.22573	.23095	.23406	.23574
60	.15642	.18245	.20750	.23053	.25035	.26646	.27808	.28572	.29032	.29282
65	.17530	.20750	.23950	.26982	.29664	.31893	.33527	.34617	.35280	.35641
70	.19218	.23053	.26982	.30836	.34361	.37378	.39642	.41177	.42123	.42641
75	.20639	.25035	.29664	.34361	.38817	.42776	.45836	.47959	.49287	.50019
80	.21771	.26646	.31893	.37378	.42776	.47784	.51812	.54710	.56574	.57613
85	.22573	.27808	.33527	.39642	.45836	.51812	.56814	.60554	.63047	.64456
90	.23095	.28572	.34617	.41177	.47959	.54710	.60554	.65080	.68206	.69994
95	.23406	.29032	.35280	.42123	.49287	.56574	.63047	.68206	.71893	.74033
100	.23574	.29282	.35641	.42641	.50019	.57613	.64456	.69994	.74033	.76401

*The present value of $1.00 due at the death of the survivor of two persons.

**Use appropriate interest rate for the month in which the valuation date occurs.

Reprinted from the *Advanced Sales Reference Service*
©1992 The National Underwriter Company

Appendix D
Valuation Tables

TWO-LIFE REMAINDER FACTORS* — 7.8% INTEREST RATE**
(For valuation dates occurring after April 30, 1989)

AGE	5	10	15	20	25	30	35	40	45	50
5	.00397	.00473	.00555	.00637	.00720	.00807	.00895	.00984	.01072	.01157
10	.00473	.00574	.00683	.00796	.00912	.01033	.01156	.01280	.01401	.01518
15	.00555	.00683	.00828	.00981	.01141	.01309	.01482	.01656	.01826	.01990
20	.00637	.00796	.00981	.01180	.01394	.01623	.01861	.02099	.02331	.02550
25	.00720	.00912	.01141	.01394	.01674	.01981	.02305	.02632	.02951	.03251
30	.00807	.01033	.01309	.01623	.01981	.02385	.02823	.03275	.03722	.04148
35	.00895	.01156	.01482	.01861	.02305	.02823	.03403	.04020	.04646	.05253
40	.00984	.01280	.01656	.02099	.02632	.03275	.04020	.04838	.05693	.06544
45	.01072	.01401	.01826	.02331	.02951	.03722	.04646	.05693	.06822	.07981
50	.01157	.01518	.01990	.02550	.03251	.04148	.05253	.06544	.07981	.09500
55	.01239	.01630	.02146	.02754	.03525	.04538	.05819	.07357	.09116	.11033
60	.01316	.01736	.02292	.02941	.03770	.04885	.06329	.08103	.10183	.12512
65	.01386	.01832	.02427	.03109	.03983	.05181	.06768	.08757	.11138	.13866
70	.01445	.01918	.02550	.03258	.04164	.05428	.07134	.09311	.11961	.15057
75	.01492	.01990	.02658	.03386	.04313	.05625	.07425	.09754	.12632	.16045
80	.01528	.02046	.02748	.03494	.04432	.05776	.07646	.10094	.13151	.16822
85	.01551	.02083	.02815	.03576	.04520	.05882	.07797	.10327	.13513	.17369
90	.01566	.02105	.02859	.03632	.04578	.05950	.07893	.10474	.13744	.17723
95	.01574	.02117	.02887	.03668	.04615	.05992	.07950	.10561	.13879	.17933
100	.01579	.02123	.02901	.03687	.04635	.06014	.07980	.10607	.13953	.18046

AGE	55	60	65	70	75	80	85	90	95	100
5	.01239	.01316	.01386	.01445	.01492	.01528	.01551	.01566	.01574	.01579
10	.01630	.01736	.01832	.01918	.01990	.02046	.02083	.02105	.02117	.02123
15	.02146	.02292	.02427	.02550	.02658	.02748	.02815	.02859	.02887	.02901
20	.02754	.02941	.03109	.03258	.03386	.03494	.03576	.03632	.03668	.03687
25	.03525	.03770	.03983	.04164	.04313	.04432	.04520	.04578	.04615	.04635
30	.04538	.04885	.05181	.05428	.05625	.05776	.05882	.05950	.05992	.06014
35	.05819	.06329	.06768	.07134	.07425	.07646	.07797	.07893	.07950	.07980
40	.07357	.08103	.08757	.09311	.09754	.10094	.10327	.10474	.10561	.10607
45	.09116	.10183	.11138	.11961	.12632	.13151	.13513	.13744	.13879	.13953
50	.11033	.12512	.13866	.15057	.16045	.16822	.17369	.17723	.17933	.18046
55	.13025	.15005	.16864	.18536	.19950	.21082	.21888	.22414	.22728	.22899
60	.15005	.17559	.20029	.22311	.24285	.25897	.27064	.27835	.28300	.28553
65	.16864	.20029	.23188	.26195	.28868	.31099	.32742	.33841	.34511	.34876
70	.18536	.22311	.26195	.30022	.33537	.36559	.38835	.40384	.41341	.41866
75	.19950	.24285	.28868	.33537	.37985	.41953	.45031	.47174	.48517	.49259
80	.21082	.25897	.31099	.36559	.41953	.46977	.51033	.53959	.55846	.56899
85	.21888	.27064	.32742	.38835	.45031	.51033	.56073	.59852	.62378	.63806
90	.22414	.27835	.33841	.40384	.47174	.53959	.59852	.64429	.67597	.69411
95	.22728	.28300	.34511	.41341	.48517	.55846	.62378	.67597	.71336	.73508
100	.22899	.28553	.34876	.41866	.49259	.56899	.63806	.69411	.73508	.75912

*The present value of $1.00 due at the death of the survivor of two persons.

**Use appropriate interest rate for the month in which the valuation date occurs.

Reprinted from the *Advanced Sales Reference Service*
©1992 The National Underwriter Company

TWO-LIFE REMAINDER FACTORS* — 8.0% INTEREST RATE**
(For valuation dates occurring after April 30, 1989)

AGE	5	10	15	20	25	30	35	40	45	50
5	.00351	.00420	.00494	.00570	.00648	.00728	.00812	.00896	.00980	.01063
10	.00420	.00511	.00612	.00715	.00823	.00936	.01053	.01170	.01286	.01399
15	.00494	.00612	.00745	.00885	.01034	.01191	.01355	.01520	.01683	.01842
20	.00570	.00715	.00885	.01069	.01268	.01482	.01707	.01933	.02155	.02367
25	.00648	.00823	.01034	.01268	.01529	.01816	.02121	.02432	.02738	.03027
30	.00728	.00936	.01191	.01482	.01816	.02195	.02609	.03039	.03467	.03877
35	.00812	.01053	.01355	.01707	.02121	.02609	.03158	.03745	.04345	.04931
40	.00896	.01170	.01520	.01933	.02432	.03039	.03745	.04526	.05346	.06169
45	.00980	.01286	.01683	.02155	.02738	.03467	.04345	.05346	.06432	.07553
50	.01063	.01399	.01842	.02367	.03027	.03877	.04931	.06169	.07553	.09024
55	.01143	.01508	.01993	.02565	.03293	.04255	.05480	.06958	.08656	.10516
60	.01218	.01612	.02136	.02748	.03532	.04594	.05978	.07687	.09700	.11964
65	.01286	.01707	.02269	.02913	.03741	.04885	.06409	.08330	.10639	.13296
70	.01345	.01792	.02391	.03060	.03920	.05129	.06771	.08876	.11452	.14474
75	.01392	.01864	.02498	.03188	.04068	.05324	.07060	.09317	.12119	.15456
80	.01427	.01919	.02588	.03297	.04188	.05476	.07280	.09656	.12638	.16233
85	.01451	.01956	.02656	.03379	.04276	.05582	.07432	.09890	.13001	.16783
90	.01465	.01979	.02701	.03435	.04335	.05651	.07529	.10039	.13233	.17139
95	.01474	.01991	.02728	.03471	.04372	.05693	.07586	.10126	.13371	.17351
100	.01479	.01997	.02743	.03491	.04393	.05715	.07617	.10173	.13445	.17466

AGE	55	60	65	70	75	80	85	90	95	100
5	.01143	.01218	.01286	.01345	.01392	.01427	.01451	.01465	.01474	.01479
10	.01508	.01612	.01707	.01792	.01864	.01919	.01956	.01979	.01991	.01997
15	.01993	.02136	.02269	.02391	.02498	.02588	.02656	.02701	.02728	.02743
20	.02565	.02748	.02913	.03060	.03188	.03297	.03379	.03435	.03471	.03491
25	.03293	.03532	.03741	.03920	.04068	.04188	.04276	.04335	.04372	.04393
30	.04255	.04594	.04885	.05129	.05324	.05476	.05582	.05651	.05693	.05715
35	.05480	.05978	.06409	.06771	.07060	.07280	.07432	.07529	.07586	.07617
40	.06958	.07687	.08330	.08876	.09317	.09656	.09890	.10039	.10126	.10173
45	.08656	.09700	.10639	.11452	.12119	.12638	.13001	.13233	.13371	.13445
50	.10516	.11964	.13296	.14474	.15456	.16233	.16783	.17139	.17351	.17466
55	.12459	.14398	.16229	.17883	.19290	.20422	.21231	.21761	.22079	.22251
60	.14398	.16904	.19339	.21599	.23564	.25176	.26348	.27125	.27595	.27851
65	.16229	.19339	.22456	.25437	.28099	.30331	.31981	.33089	.33767	.34137
70	.17883	.21599	.25437	.29235	.32738	.35763	.38050	.39613	.40580	.41111
75	.19290	.23564	.28099	.32738	.37176	.41151	.44246	.46407	.47766	.48517
80	.20422	.25176	.30331	.35763	.41151	.46189	.50270	.53223	.55133	.56199
85	.21231	.26348	.31981	.38050	.44246	.50270	.55346	.59162	.61719	.63166
90	.21761	.27125	.33089	.39613	.46407	.53223	.59162	.63787	.66996	.68835
95	.22079	.27595	.33767	.40580	.47766	.55133	.61719	.66996	.70785	.72989
100	.22251	.27851	.34137	.41111	.48517	.56199	.63166	.68835	.72989	.75428

*The present value of $1.00 due at the death of the survivor of two persons.

**Use appropriate interest rate for the month in which the valuation date occurs.

Reprinted from the *Advanced Sales Reference Service*
©1992 The National Underwriter Company

Appendix D
Valuation Tables

TWO-LIFE REMAINDER FACTORS* — 8.2% INTEREST RATE**
(For valuation dates occurring after April 30, 1989)

AGE	5	10	15	20	25	30	35	40	45	50
5	.00311	.00373	.00441	.00511	.00583	.00658	.00737	.00817	.00898	.00978
10	.00373	.00456	.00548	.00644	.00744	.00849	.00959	.01071	.01182	.01292
15	.00441	.00548	.00670	.00800	.00938	.01085	.01239	.01397	.01553	.01706
20	.00511	.00644	.00800	.00969	.01154	.01355	.01566	.01782	.01994	.02199
25	.00583	.00744	.00938	.01154	.01397	.01666	.01954	.02250	.02542	.02820
30	.00658	.00849	.01085	.01355	.01666	.02022	.02413	.02822	.03231	.03626
35	.00737	.00959	.01239	.01566	.01954	.02413	.02932	.03492	.04066	.04631
40	.00817	.01071	.01397	.01782	.02250	.02822	.03492	.04237	.05024	.05818
45	.00898	.01182	.01553	.01994	.02542	.03231	.04066	.05024	.06068	.07151
50	.00978	.01292	.01706	.02199	.02820	.03626	.04631	.05818	.07151	.08576
55	.01056	.01398	.01853	.02391	.03079	.03993	.05164	.06584	.08224	.10028
60	.01129	.01499	.01993	.02570	.03312	.04323	.05650	.07296	.09244	.11444
65	.01196	.01592	.02124	.02732	.03517	.04609	.06073	.07927	.10167	.12755
70	.01254	.01677	.02245	.02878	.03694	.04850	.06431	.08467	.10970	.13919
75	.01301	.01748	.02352	.03006	.03842	.05044	.06717	.08905	.11633	.14896
80	.01336	.01803	.02442	.03114	.03961	.05195	.06937	.09243	.12151	.15672
85	.01359	.01840	.02509	.03196	.04049	.05302	.07090	.09478	.12515	.16223
90	.01374	.01863	.02555	.03254	.04109	.05371	.07187	.09628	.12749	.16582
95	.01383	.01875	.02583	.03290	.04147	.05414	.07245	.09716	.12888	.16796
100	.01388	.01881	.02598	.03310	.04167	.05437	.07276	.09763	.12963	.16912

AGE	55	60	65	70	75	80	85	90	95	100
5	.01056	.01129	.01196	.01254	.01301	.01336	.01359	.01374	.01383	.01388
10	.01398	.01499	.01592	.01677	.01748	.01803	.01840	.01863	.01875	.01881
15	.01853	.01993	.02124	.02245	.02352	.02442	.02509	.02555	.02583	.02598
20	.02391	.02570	.02732	.02878	.03006	.03114	.03196	.03254	.03290	.03310
25	.03079	.03312	.03517	.03694	.03842	.03961	.04049	.04109	.04147	.04167
30	.03993	.04323	.04609	.04850	.05044	.05195	.05302	.05371	.05414	.05437
35	.05164	.05650	.06073	.06431	.06717	.06937	.07090	.07187	.07245	.07276
40	.06584	.07296	.07927	.08467	.08905	.09243	.09478	.09628	.09716	.09763
45	.08224	.09244	.10167	.10970	.11633	.12151	.12515	.12749	.12888	.12963
50	.10028	.11444	.12755	.13919	.14896	.15672	.16223	.16582	.16796	.16912
55	.11921	.13821	.15623	.17260	.18659	.19789	.20602	.21136	.21456	.21631
60	.13821	.16278	.18678	.20915	.22870	.24481	.25658	.26441	.26916	.27175
65	.15623	.18678	.21752	.24706	.27356	.29588	.31245	.32362	.33046	.33420
70	.17260	.20915	.24706	.28474	.31964	.34991	.37288	.38863	.39840	.40378
75	.18659	.22870	.27356	.31964	.36389	.40370	.43480	.45659	.47032	.47792
80	.19789	.24481	.29588	.34991	.40370	.45419	.49523	.52502	.54433	.55513
85	.20602	.25658	.31245	.37288	.43480	.49523	.54632	.58484	.61071	.62537
90	.21136	.26441	.32362	.38863	.45659	.52502	.58484	.63155	.66404	.68268
95	.21456	.26916	.33046	.39840	.47032	.54433	.61071	.66404	.70242	.72476
100	.21631	.27175	.33420	.40378	.47792	.55513	.62537	.68268	.72476	.74950

*The present value of $1.00 due at the death of the survivor of two persons.

**Use appropriate interest rate for the month in which the valuation date occurs.

Reprinted from the *Advanced Sales Reference Service*
©1992 The National Underwriter Company

The Tools and Techniques of Estate Planning

TWO-LIFE REMAINDER FACTORS* — 8.4% INTEREST RATE**
(For valuation dates occurring after April 30, 1989)

AGE	5	10	15	20	25	30	35	40	45	50
5	.00275	.00332	.00394	.00458	.00525	.00596	.00670	.00747	.00824	.00901
10	.00332	.00407	.00492	.00580	.00672	.00771	.00875	.00981	.01088	.01194
15	.00394	.00492	.00604	.00723	.00851	.00989	.01135	.01284	.01434	.01582
20	.00458	.00580	.00723	.00880	.01052	.01239	.01439	.01644	.01847	.02044
25	.00525	.00672	.00851	.01052	.01277	.01530	.01801	.02082	.02362	.02630
30	.00596	.00771	.00989	.01239	.01530	.01863	.02233	.02621	.03014	.03394
35	.00670	.00875	.01135	.01439	.01801	.02233	.02725	.03257	.03808	.04352
40	.00747	.00981	.01284	.01644	.02082	.02621	.03257	.03968	.04724	.05490
45	.00824	.01088	.01434	.01847	.02362	.03014	.03808	.04724	.05727	.06774
50	.00901	.01194	.01582	.02044	.02630	.03394	.04352	.05490	.06774	.08154
55	.00977	.01297	.01725	.02231	.02881	.03750	.04869	.06233	.07816	.09566
60	.01048	.01396	.01862	.02406	.03109	.04072	.05343	.06929	.08813	.10951
65	.01114	.01488	.01991	.02566	.03310	.04352	.05759	.07548	.09720	.12240
70	.01171	.01571	.02111	.02710	.03485	.04590	.06111	.08082	.10514	.13391
75	.01218	.01642	.02217	.02837	.03631	.04783	.06396	.08516	.11172	.14361
80	.01253	.01697	.02307	.02946	.03751	.04934	.06616	.08854	.11690	.15136
85	.01276	.01734	.02375	.03028	.03839	.05041	.06768	.09089	.12054	.15689
90	.01291	.01757	.02421	.03086	.03900	.05111	.06866	.09240	.12290	.16050
95	.01300	.01769	.02449	.03123	.03938	.05153	.06925	.09329	.12430	.16266
100	.01305	.01775	.02464	.03143	.03959	.05176	.06956	.09377	.12505	.16383

AGE	55	60	65	70	75	80	85	90	95	100
5	.00977	.01048	.01114	.01171	.01218	.01253	.01276	.01291	.01300	.01305
10	.01297	.01396	.01488	.01571	.01642	.01697	.01734	.01757	.01769	.01775
15	.01725	.01862	.01991	.02111	.02217	.02307	.02375	.02421	.02449	.02464
20	.02231	.02406	.02566	.02710	.02837	.02946	.03028	.03086	.03123	.03143
25	.02881	.03109	.03310	.03485	.03631	.03751	.03839	.03900	.03938	.03959
30	.03750	.04072	.04352	.04590	.04783	.04934	.05041	.05111	.05153	.05176
35	.04869	.05343	.05759	.06111	.06396	.06616	.06768	.06866	.06925	.06956
40	.06233	.06929	.07548	.08082	.08516	.08854	.09089	.09240	.09329	.09377
45	.07816	.08813	.09720	.10514	.11172	.11690	.12054	.12290	.12430	.12505
50	.09566	.10951	.12240	.13391	.14361	.15136	.15689	.16050	.16266	.16383
55	.11411	.13271	.15044	.16664	.18054	.19183	.19998	.20535	.20859	.21035
60	.13271	.15681	.18044	.20259	.22203	.23813	.24993	.25781	.26261	.26523
65	.15044	.18044	.21076	.24002	.26639	.28870	.30533	.31657	.32348	.32727
70	.16664	.20259	.24002	.27738	.31213	.34241	.36547	.38133	.39120	.39664
75	.18054	.22203	.26639	.31213	.35624	.39608	.42732	.44928	.46315	.47084
80	.19183	.23813	.28870	.34241	.39608	.44667	.48792	.51796	.53747	.54840
85	.19998	.24993	.30533	.36547	.42732	.48792	.53932	.57818	.60434	.61917
90	.20535	.25781	.31657	.38133	.44928	.51796	.57818	.62533	.65821	.67708
95	.20859	.26261	.32348	.39120	.46315	.53747	.60434	.65821	.69706	.71969
100	.21035	.26523	.32727	.39664	.47084	.54840	.61917	.67708	.71969	.74477

*The present value of $1.00 due at the death of the survivor of two persons.

**Use appropriate interest rate for the month in which the valuation date occurs.

Appendix D
Valuation Tables

TWO-LIFE REMAINDER FACTORS* — 8.6% INTEREST RATE**
(For valuation dates occurring after April 30, 1989)

AGE	5	10	15	20	25	30	35	40	45	50
5	.00244	.00296	.00353	.00411	.00473	.00540	.00610	.00683	.00757	.00831
10	.00296	.00364	.00442	.00523	.00609	.00701	.00799	.00900	.01003	.01105
15	.00353	.00442	.00544	.00655	.00773	.00903	.01040	.01182	.01326	.01469
20	.00411	.00523	.00655	.00799	.00959	.01135	.01323	.01518	.01712	.01903
25	.00473	.00609	.00773	.00959	.01169	.01405	.01662	.01929	.02196	.02455
30	.00540	.00701	.00903	.01135	.01405	.01719	.02067	.02437	.02813	.03179
35	.00610	.00799	.01040	.01323	.01662	.02067	.02533	.03040	.03568	.04093
40	.00683	.00900	.01182	.01518	.01929	.02437	.03040	.03719	.04444	.05183
45	.00757	.01003	.01326	.01712	.02196	.02813	.03568	.04444	.05408	.06420
50	.00831	.01105	.01469	.01903	.02455	.03179	.04093	.05183	.06420	.07755
55	.00905	.01205	.01608	.02084	.02698	.03524	.04594	.05905	.07433	.09129
60	.00975	.01302	.01742	.02255	.02920	.03838	.05056	.06583	.08406	.10484
65	.01039	.01392	.01869	.02412	.03118	.04113	.05464	.07192	.09297	.11751
70	.01096	.01474	.01987	.02555	.03291	.04348	.05812	.07718	.10081	.12888
75	.01142	.01544	.02093	.02681	.03436	.04539	.06094	.08149	.10734	.13851
80	.01177	.01599	.02183	.02790	.03556	.04690	.06313	.08486	.11251	.14625
85	.01200	.01637	.02251	.02873	.03644	.04797	.06466	.08722	.11616	.15179
90	.01215	.01659	.02297	.02931	.03705	.04867	.06565	.08873	.11853	.15542
95	.01224	.01672	.02326	.02968	.03743	.04910	.06624	.08963	.11994	.15760
100	.01229	.01678	.02341	.02988	.03764	.04934	.06656	.09012	.12071	.15879

AGE	55	60	65	70	75	80	85	90	95	100
5	.00905	.00975	.01039	.01096	.01142	.01177	.01200	.01215	.01224	.01229
10	.01205	.01302	.01392	.01474	.01544	.01599	.01637	.01659	.01672	.01678
15	.01608	.01742	.01869	.01987	.02093	.02183	.02251	.02297	.02326	.02341
20	.02084	.02255	.02412	.02555	.02681	.02790	.02873	.02931	.02968	.02988
25	.02698	.02920	.03118	.03291	.03436	.03556	.03644	.03705	.03743	.03764
30	.03524	.03838	.04113	.04348	.04539	.04690	.04797	.04867	.04910	.04934
35	.04594	.05056	.05464	.05812	.06094	.06313	.06466	.06565	.06624	.06656
40	.05905	.06583	.07192	.07718	.08149	.08486	.08722	.08873	.08963	.09012
45	.07433	.08406	.09297	.10081	.10734	.11251	.11616	.11853	.11994	.12071
50	.09129	.10484	.11751	.12888	.13851	.14625	.15179	.15542	.15760	.15879
55	.10927	.12747	.14492	.16093	.17474	.18602	.19419	.19959	.20286	.20464
60	.12747	.15110	.17437	.19628	.21560	.23168	.24352	.25145	.25629	.25894
65	.14492	.17437	.20426	.23323	.25946	.28175	.29843	.30975	.31672	.32055
70	.16093	.19628	.23323	.27027	.30486	.33513	.35827	.37423	.38420	.38970
75	.17474	.21560	.25946	.30486	.34881	.38866	.42003	.44214	.45615	.46392
80	.18602	.23168	.28175	.33513	.38866	.43932	.48077	.51103	.53075	.54179
85	.19419	.24352	.29843	.35827	.42003	.48077	.53244	.57163	.59808	.61308
90	.19959	.25145	.30975	.37423	.44214	.51103	.57163	.61921	.65245	.67156
95	.20286	.25629	.31672	.38420	.45615	.53075	.59808	.65245	.69177	.71469
100	.20464	.25894	.32055	.38970	.46392	.54179	.61308	.67156	.71469	.74009

*The present value of $1.00 due at the death of the survivor of two persons.

**Use appropriate interest rate for the month in which the valuation date occurs.

Reprinted from the *Advanced Sales Reference Service*
©1992 The National Underwriter Company

Appendix D
Valuation Tables

TWO-LIFE REMAINDER FACTORS* — 8.8% INTEREST RATE**
(For valuation dates occurring after April 30, 1989)

AGE	5	10	15	20	25	30	35	40	45	50
5	.00217	.00264	.00316	.00370	.00427	.00489	.00556	.00625	.00696	.00768
10	.00264	.00326	.00397	.00472	.00551	.00638	.00730	.00827	.00925	.01024
15	.00316	.00397	.00491	.00593	.00703	.00824	.00954	.01090	.01228	.01365
20	.00370	.00472	.00593	.00727	.00875	.01040	.01217	.01402	.01589	.01772
25	.00427	.00551	.00703	.00875	.01070	.01292	.01534	.01788	.02044	.02293
30	.00489	.00638	.00824	.01040	.01292	.01586	.01916	.02267	.02627	.02980
35	.00556	.00730	.00954	.01217	.01534	.01916	.02356	.02840	.03345	.03851
40	.00625	.00827	.01090	.01402	.01788	.02267	.02840	.03487	.04182	.04896
45	.00696	.00925	.01228	.01589	.02044	.02627	.03345	.04182	.05110	.06087
50	.00768	.01024	.01365	.01772	.02293	.02980	.03851	.04896	.06087	.07380
55	.00839	.01121	.01500	.01949	.02528	.03313	.04337	.05596	.07071	.08716
60	.00908	.01215	.01632	.02116	.02745	.03620	.04787	.06258	.08022	.10041
65	.00971	.01304	.01757	.02270	.02940	.03890	.05187	.06855	.08897	.11285
70	.01027	.01386	.01874	.02412	.03110	.04121	.05531	.07375	.09671	.12409
75	.01073	.01455	.01979	.02537	.03255	.04311	.05811	.07803	.10319	.13365
80	.01107	.01510	.02069	.02645	.03374	.04461	.06029	.08139	.10834	.14137
85	.01131	.01547	.02137	.02729	.03463	.04569	.06183	.08374	.11200	.14692
90	.01146	.01570	.02184	.02787	.03524	.04640	.06282	.08527	.11438	.15057
95	.01155	.01583	.02212	.02825	.03563	.04683	.06341	.08617	.11581	.15277
100	.01160	.01589	.02227	.02845	.03584	.04707	.06373	.08666	.11658	.15397

AGE	55	60	65	70	75	80	85	90	95	100
5	.00839	.00908	.00971	.01027	.01073	.01107	.01131	.01146	.01155	.01160
10	.01121	.01215	.01304	.01386	.01455	.01510	.01547	.01570	.01583	.01589
15	.01500	.01632	.01757	.01874	.01979	.02069	.02137	.02184	.02212	.02227
20	.01949	.02116	.02270	.02412	.02537	.02645	.02729	.02787	.02825	.02845
25	.02528	.02745	.02940	.03110	.03255	.03374	.03463	.03524	.03563	.03584
30	.03313	.03620	.03890	.04121	.04311	.04461	.04569	.04640	.04683	.04707
35	.04337	.04787	.05187	.05531	.05811	.06029	.06183	.06282	.06341	.06373
40	.05596	.06258	.06855	.07375	.07803	.08139	.08374	.08527	.08617	.08666
45	.07071	.08022	.08897	.09671	.10319	.10834	.11200	.11438	.11581	.11658
50	.08716	.10041	.11285	.12409	.13365	.14137	.14692	.15057	.15277	.15397
55	.10467	.12249	.13964	.15547	.16919	.18044	.18863	.19406	.19736	.19916
60	.12249	.14564	.16855	.19022	.20942	.22547	.23734	.24531	.25020	.25287
65	.13964	.16855	.19800	.22669	.25276	.27503	.29175	.30314	.31017	.31403
70	.15547	.19022	.22669	.26338	.29780	.32805	.35126	.36733	.37739	.38294
75	.16919	.20942	.25276	.29780	.34158	.38143	.41291	.43517	.44930	.45715
80	.18044	.22547	.27503	.32805	.38143	.43213	.47376	.50424	.52415	.53531
85	.18863	.23734	.29175	.35126	.41291	.47376	.52570	.56520	.59191	.60709
90	.19406	.24531	.30314	.36733	.43517	.50424	.56520	.61317	.64678	.66611
95	.19736	.25020	.31017	.37739	.44930	.52415	.59191	.64678	.68654	.70974
100	.19916	.25287	.31403	.38294	.45715	.53531	.60709	.66611	.70974	.73547

*The present value of $1.00 due at the death of the survivor of two persons.

**Use appropriate interest rate for the month in which the valuation date occurs.

Reprinted from the *Advanced Sales Reference Service*
©1992 The National Underwriter Company

The Tools and Techniques of Estate Planning

TWO-LIFE REMAINDER FACTORS* — 9.0% INTEREST RATE**
(For valuation dates occurring after April 30, 1989)

AGE	5	10	15	20	25	30	35	40	45	50
5	.00192	.00235	.00283	.00333	.00386	.00444	.00507	.00573	.00641	.00711
10	.00235	.00292	.00357	.00426	.00500	.00581	.00668	.00760	.00854	.00950
15	.00283	.00357	.00444	.00538	.00640	.00754	.00876	.01005	.01137	.01270
20	.00333	.00426	.00538	.00661	.00799	.00953	.01121	.01297	.01476	.01653
25	.00386	.00500	.00640	.00799	.00981	.01189	.01417	.01658	.01903	.02143
30	.00444	.00581	.00754	.00953	.01189	.01465	.01776	.02111	.02455	.02794
35	.00507	.00668	.00876	.01121	.01417	.01776	.02193	.02654	.03138	.03625
40	.00573	.00760	.01005	.01297	.01658	.02111	.02654	.03271	.03939	.04627
45	.00641	.00854	.01137	.01476	.01903	.02455	.03138	.03939	.04830	.05774
50	.00711	.00950	.01270	.01653	.02143	.02794	.03625	.04627	.05774	.07025
55	.00780	.01044	.01402	.01824	.02371	.03118	.04096	.05306	.06730	.08325
60	.00847	.01137	.01530	.01987	.02583	.03417	.04536	.05953	.07659	.09620
65	.00909	.01224	.01653	.02139	.02774	.03681	.04928	.06538	.08517	.10842
70	.00964	.01304	.01769	.02279	.02942	.03910	.05267	.07051	.09282	.11952
75	.01009	.01373	.01874	.02404	.03086	.04098	.05545	.07475	.09925	.12901
80	.01044	.01428	.01964	.02512	.03205	.04248	.05762	.07810	.10438	.13671
85	.01067	.01465	.02032	.02595	.03294	.04355	.05916	.08046	.10805	.14227
90	.01082	.01488	.02078	.02654	.03355	.04427	.06015	.08199	.11044	.14594
95	.01092	.01501	.02107	.02692	.03394	.04470	.06075	.08290	.11188	.14815
100	.01097	.01507	.02123	.02713	.03416	.04494	.06107	.08340	.11265	.14936

AGE	55	60	65	70	75	80	85	90	95	100
5	.00780	.00847	.00909	.00964	.01009	.01044	.01067	.01082	.01092	.01097
10	.01044	.01137	.01224	.01304	.01373	.01428	.01465	.01488	.01501	.01507
15	.01402	.01530	.01653	.01769	.01874	.01964	.02032	.02078	.02107	.02123
20	.01824	.01987	.02139	.02279	.02404	.02512	.02595	.02654	.02692	.02713
25	.02371	.02583	.02774	.02942	.03086	.03205	.03294	.03355	.03394	.03416
30	.03118	.03417	.03681	.03910	.04098	.04248	.04355	.04427	.04470	.04494
35	.04096	.04536	.04928	.05267	.05545	.05762	.05916	.06015	.06075	.06107
40	.05306	.05953	.06538	.07051	.07475	.07810	.08046	.08199	.08290	.08340
45	.06730	.07659	.08517	.09282	.09925	.10438	.10805	.11044	.11188	.11265
50	.08325	.09620	.10842	.11952	.12901	.13671	.14227	.14594	.14815	.14936
55	.10030	.11774	.13461	.15024	.16386	.17509	.18329	.18875	.19208	.19389
60	.11774	.14042	.16297	.18439	.20347	.21949	.23138	.23940	.24432	.24702
65	.13461	.16297	.19199	.22037	.24629	.26852	.28528	.29673	.30382	.30772
70	.15024	.18439	.22037	.25672	.29096	.32117	.34445	.36061	.37075	.37636
75	.16386	.20347	.24629	.29096	.33454	.37438	.40595	.42835	.44261	.45054
80	.17509	.21949	.26852	.32117	.37438	.42511	.46690	.49759	.51768	.52896
85	.18329	.23138	.28528	.34445	.40595	.46690	.51908	.55887	.58585	.60119
90	.18875	.23940	.29673	.36061	.42835	.49759	.55887	.60723	.64119	.66073
95	.19208	.24432	.30382	.37075	.44261	.51768	.58585	.64119	.68139	.70486
100	.19389	.24702	.30772	.37636	.45054	.52896	.60119	.66073	.70486	.73089

*The present value of $1.00 due at the death of the survivor of two persons.

**Use appropriate interest rate for the month in which the valuation date occurs.

Reprinted from the *Advanced Sales Reference Service*
©1992 The National Underwriter Company

TWO-LIFE REMAINDER FACTORS* — 9.2% INTEREST RATE**
(For valuation dates occurring after April 30, 1989)

AGE	5	10	15	20	25	30	35	40	45	50
5	.00171	.00210	.00254	.00300	.00350	.00404	.00463	.00526	.00592	.00659
10	.00210	.00262	.00322	.00385	.00454	.00530	.00612	.00700	.00790	.00882
15	.00254	.00322	.00402	.00488	.00583	.00689	.00805	.00928	.01055	.01183
20	.00300	.00385	.00488	.00603	.00731	.00875	.01033	.01201	.01372	.01542
25	.00350	.00454	.00583	.00731	.00900	.01094	.01310	.01539	.01774	.02005
30	.00404	.00530	.00689	.00875	.01094	.01354	.01648	.01966	.02295	.02623
35	.00463	.00612	.00805	.01033	.01310	.01648	.02043	.02482	.02945	.03415
40	.00526	.00700	.00928	.01201	.01539	.01966	.02482	.03071	.03711	.04375
45	.00592	.00790	.01055	.01372	.01774	.02295	.02945	.03711	.04568	.05480
50	.00659	.00882	.01183	.01542	.02005	.02623	.03415	.04375	.05480	.06691
55	.00726	.00974	.01311	.01709	.02226	.02936	.03871	.05034	.06408	.07955
60	.00791	.01064	.01437	.01868	.02433	.03227	.04300	.05665	.07315	.09220
65	.00852	.01150	.01558	.02017	.02620	.03487	.04685	.06239	.08158	.10421
70	.00906	.01229	.01672	.02156	.02786	.03712	.05019	.06745	.08912	.11516
75	.00951	.01298	.01776	.02280	.02929	.03899	.05294	.07166	.09550	.12458
80	.00985	.01352	.01866	.02387	.03047	.04048	.05511	.07499	.10062	.13225
85	.01009	.01390	.01934	.02471	.03137	.04156	.05664	.07735	.10428	.13782
90	.01024	.01412	.01981	.02531	.03198	.04227	.05764	.07889	.10669	.14150
95	.01034	.01425	.02010	.02569	.03238	.04271	.05825	.07981	.10813	.14374
100	.01039	.01432	.02026	.02590	.03259	.04295	.05857	.08031	.10892	.14496

AGE	55	60	65	70	75	80	85	90	95	100
5	.00726	.00791	.00852	.00906	.00951	.00985	.01009	.01024	.01034	.01039
10	.00974	.01064	.01150	.01229	.01298	.01352	.01390	.01412	.01425	.01432
15	.01311	.01437	.01558	.01672	.01776	.01866	.01934	.01981	.02010	.02026
20	.01709	.01868	.02017	.02156	.02280	.02387	.02471	.02531	.02569	.02590
25	.02226	.02433	.02620	.02786	.02929	.03047	.03137	.03198	.03238	.03259
30	.02936	.03227	.03487	.03712	.03899	.04048	.04156	.04227	.04271	.04295
35	.03871	.04300	.04685	.05019	.05294	.05511	.05664	.05764	.05825	.05857
40	.05034	.05665	.06239	.06745	.07166	.07499	.07735	.07889	.07981	.08031
45	.06408	.07315	.08158	.08912	.09550	.10062	.10428	.10669	.10813	.10892
50	.07955	.09220	.10421	.11516	.12458	.13225	.13782	.14150	.14374	.14496
55	.09615	.11321	.12979	.14523	.15876	.16995	.17816	.18365	.18700	.18883
60	.11321	.13543	.15761	.17879	.19774	.21372	.22562	.23368	.23865	.24137
65	.12979	.15761	.18620	.21428	.24003	.26222	.27901	.29052	.29767	.30160
70	.14523	.17879	.21428	.25028	.28432	.31449	.33782	.35407	.36430	.36995
75	.15876	.19774	.24003	.28432	.32770	.36751	.39917	.42169	.43608	.44408
80	.16995	.21372	.26222	.31449	.36751	.41825	.46018	.49106	.51133	.52272
85	.17816	.22562	.27901	.33782	.39917	.46018	.51258	.55265	.57988	.59538
90	.18365	.23368	.29052	.35407	.42169	.49106	.55265	.60138	.63567	.65543
95	.18700	.23865	.29767	.36430	.43608	.51133	.57988	.63567	.67629	.70003
100	.18883	.24137	.30160	.36995	.44408	.52272	.59538	.65543	.70003	.72637

*The present value of $1.00 due at the death of the survivor of two persons.

**Use appropriate interest rate for the month in which the valuation date occurs.

The Tools and Techniques of Estate Planning

Appendix D
Valuation Tables

TWO-LIFE REMAINDER FACTORS* — 9.4% INTEREST RATE**
(For valuation dates occurring after April 30, 1989)

AGE	5	10	15	20	25	30	35	40	45	50
5	.00153	.00188	.00228	.00271	.00317	.00368	.00424	.00483	.00546	.00611
10	.00188	.00235	.00290	.00349	.00413	.00484	.00562	.00645	.00731	.00820
15	.00228	.00290	.00364	.00444	.00532	.00631	.00741	.00858	.00979	.01103
20	.00271	.00349	.00444	.00549	.00668	.00804	.00953	.01112	.01276	.01441
25	.00317	.00413	.00532	.00668	.00826	.01009	.01212	.01430	.01654	.01877
30	.00368	.00484	.00631	.00804	.01009	.01252	.01530	.01833	.02148	.02463
35	.00424	.00562	.00741	.00953	.01212	.01530	.01904	.02322	.02766	.03219
40	.00483	.00645	.00858	.01112	.01430	.01833	.02322	.02884	.03498	.04139
45	.00546	.00731	.00979	.01276	.01654	.02148	.02766	.03498	.04322	.05203
50	.00611	.00820	.01103	.01441	.01877	.02463	.03219	.04139	.05203	.06375
55	.00676	.00910	.01228	.01602	.02091	.02767	.03661	.04779	.06105	.07604
60	.00740	.00998	.01351	.01758	.02293	.03050	.04079	.05393	.06990	.08840
65	.00800	.01082	.01470	.01905	.02477	.03305	.04456	.05957	.07817	.10019
70	.00853	.01160	.01583	.02041	.02641	.03527	.04785	.06455	.08561	.11100
75	.00898	.01228	.01686	.02165	.02782	.03712	.05058	.06872	.09193	.12034
80	.00932	.01282	.01776	.02272	.02900	.03861	.05274	.07205	.09703	.12799
85	.00955	.01320	.01844	.02356	.02990	.03968	.05428	.07441	.10070	.13356
90	.00971	.01343	.01891	.02416	.03052	.04040	.05528	.07595	.10312	.13727
95	.00980	.01355	.01920	.02454	.03092	.04085	.05589	.07688	.10457	.13952
100	.00985	.01362	.01936	.02475	.03114	.04109	.05622	.07738	.10536	.14074

AGE	55	60	65	70	75	80	85	90	95	100
5	.00676	.00740	.00800	.00853	.00898	.00932	.00955	.00971	.00980	.00985
10	.00910	.00998	.01082	.01160	.01228	.01282	.01320	.01343	.01355	.01362
15	.01228	.01351	.01470	.01583	.01686	.01776	.01844	.01891	.01920	.01936
20	.01602	.01758	.01905	.02041	.02165	.02272	.02356	.02416	.02454	.02475
25	.02091	.02293	.02477	.02641	.02782	.02900	.02990	.03052	.03092	.03114
30	.02767	.03050	.03305	.03527	.03712	.03861	.03968	.04040	.04085	.04109
35	.03661	.04079	.04456	.04785	.05058	.05274	.05428	.05528	.05589	.05622
40	.04779	.05393	.05957	.06455	.06872	.07205	.07441	.07595	.07688	.07738
45	.06105	.06990	.07817	.08561	.09193	.09703	.10070	.10312	.10457	.10536
50	.07604	.08840	.10019	.11100	.12034	.12799	.13356	.13727	.13952	.14074
55	.09220	.10889	.12519	.14044	.15385	.16501	.17323	.17875	.18212	.18397
60	.10889	.13066	.15248	.17341	.19221	.20815	.22007	.22817	.23317	.23592
65	.12519	.15248	.18063	.20840	.23398	.25611	.27293	.28450	.29170	.29567
70	.14044	.17341	.20840	.24404	.27788	.30800	.33137	.34770	.35801	.36371
75	.15385	.19221	.23398	.27788	.32104	.36081	.39254	.41519	.42969	.43776
80	.16501	.20815	.25611	.30800	.36081	.41154	.45360	.48466	.50511	.51660
85	.17323	.22007	.27293	.33137	.39254	.45360	.50620	.54654	.57401	.58966
90	.17875	.22817	.28450	.34770	.41519	.48466	.54654	.59562	.63024	.65020
95	.18212	.23317	.29170	.35801	.42969	.50511	.57401	.63024	.67126	.69526
100	.18397	.23592	.29567	.36371	.43776	.51660	.58966	.65020	.69526	.72189

*The present value of $1.00 due at the death of the survivor of two persons.

**Use appropriate interest rate for the month in which the valuation date occurs.

Reprinted from the *Advanced Sales Reference Service*
©1992 The National Underwriter Company

The Tools and Techniques of Estate Planning

Appendix D
Valuation Tables

TWO-LIFE REMAINDER FACTORS* — 9.6% INTEREST RATE**
(For valuation dates occurring after April 30, 1989)

AGE	5	10	15	20	25	30	35	40	45	50
5	.00136	.00168	.00205	.00244	.00287	.00335	.00388	.00445	.00505	.00568
10	.00168	.00212	.00262	.00316	.00375	.00442	.00516	.00595	.00678	.00764
15	.00205	.00262	.00330	.00404	.00486	.00579	.00682	.00794	.00910	.01030
20	.00244	.00316	.00404	.00501	.00612	.00739	.00880	.01031	.01189	.01347
25	.00287	.00375	.00486	.00612	.00759	.00930	.01122	.01330	.01544	.01758
30	.00335	.00442	.00579	.00739	.00930	.01159	.01422	.01709	.02011	.02314
35	.00388	.00516	.00682	.00880	.01122	.01422	.01776	.02174	.02599	.03036
40	.00445	.00595	.00794	.01031	.01330	.01709	.02174	.02710	.03300	.03918
45	.00505	.00678	.00910	.01189	.01544	.02011	.02599	.03300	.04091	.04943
50	.00568	.00764	.01030	.01347	.01758	.02314	.03036	.03918	.04943	.06076
55	.00631	.00850	.01151	.01504	.01966	.02609	.03464	.04538	.05818	.07271
60	.00693	.00937	.01271	.01656	.02163	.02885	.03872	.05138	.06682	.08479
65	.00752	.01020	.01388	.01800	.02343	.03135	.04241	.05690	.07494	.09637
70	.00805	.01097	.01500	.01935	.02505	.03354	.04565	.06182	.08227	.10704
75	.00848	.01164	.01602	.02058	.02645	.03537	.04836	.06595	.08854	.11630
80	.00882	.01218	.01692	.02165	.02763	.03685	.05051	.06926	.09362	.12392
85	.00906	.01255	.01760	.02249	.02853	.03793	.05204	.07162	.09729	.12949
90	.00921	.01278	.01808	.02309	.02915	.03865	.05305	.07317	.09972	.13321
95	.00931	.01291	.01837	.02348	.02955	.03910	.05366	.07410	.10118	.13548
100	.00936	.01298	.01853	.02369	.02977	.03934	.05400	.07461	.10198	.13671

AGE	55	60	65	70	75	80	85	90	95	100
5	.00631	.00693	.00752	.00805	.00848	.00882	.00906	.00921	.00931	.00936
10	.00850	.00937	.01020	.01097	.01164	.01218	.01255	.01278	.01291	.01298
15	.01151	.01271	.01388	.01500	.01602	.01692	.01760	.01808	.01837	.01853
20	.01504	.01656	.01800	.01935	.02058	.02165	.02249	.02309	.02348	.02369
25	.01966	.02163	.02343	.02505	.02645	.02763	.02853	.02915	.02955	.02977
30	.02609	.02885	.03135	.03354	.03537	.03685	.03793	.03865	.03910	.03934
35	.03464	.03872	.04241	.04565	.04836	.05051	.05204	.05305	.05366	.05400
40	.04538	.05138	.05690	.06182	.06595	.06926	.07162	.07317	.07410	.07461
45	.05818	.06682	.07494	.08227	.08854	.09362	.09729	.09972	.10118	.10198
50	.07271	.08479	.09637	.10704	.11630	.12392	.12949	.13321	.13548	.13671
55	.08845	.10477	.12079	.13584	.14915	.16027	.16850	.17404	.17743	.17929
60	.10477	.12609	.14755	.16823	.18689	.20278	.21471	.22285	.22788	.23065
65	.12079	.14755	.17527	.20273	.22813	.25020	.26704	.27866	.28591	.28992
70	.13584	.16823	.20273	.23801	.27164	.30169	.32509	.34150	.35188	.35764
75	.14915	.18689	.22813	.27164	.31456	.35427	.38607	.40883	.42344	.43158
80	.16027	.20278	.25020	.30169	.35427	.40497	.44715	.47839	.49900	.51059
85	.16850	.21471	.26704	.32509	.38607	.44715	.49994	.54052	.56824	.58403
90	.17404	.22285	.27866	.34150	.40883	.47839	.54052	.58994	.62488	.64504
95	.17743	.22788	.28591	.35188	.42344	.49900	.56824	.62488	.66630	.69054
100	.17929	.23065	.28992	.35764	.43158	.51059	.58403	.64504	.69054	.71746

*The present value of $1.00 due at the death of the survivor of two persons.

**Use appropriate interest rate for the month in which the valuation date occurs.

Reprinted from the *Advanced Sales Reference Service*
©1992 The National Underwriter Company

The Tools and Techniques of Estate Planning

Appendix D
Valuation Tables

TWO-LIFE REMAINDER FACTORS* — 9.8% INTEREST RATE**
(For valuation dates occurring after April 30, 1989)

AGE	5	10	15	20	25	30	35	40	45	50
5	.00122	.00151	.00185	.00221	.00261	.00306	.00356	.00410	.00468	.00528
10	.00151	.00191	.00237	.00287	.00342	.00404	.00474	.00549	.00629	.00712
15	.00185	.00237	.00299	.00368	.00444	.00531	.00629	.00735	.00847	.00963
20	.00221	.00287	.00368	.00458	.00561	.00680	.00813	.00957	.01108	.01261
25	.00261	.00342	.00444	.00561	.00698	.00858	.01040	.01237	.01442	.01649
30	.00306	.00404	.00531	.00680	.00858	.01073	.01322	.01596	.01884	.02176
35	.00356	.00474	.00629	.00813	.01040	.01322	.01657	.02036	.02444	.02864
40	.00410	.00549	.00735	.00957	.01237	.01596	.02036	.02548	.03114	.03710
45	.00468	.00629	.00847	.01108	.01442	.01884	.02444	.03114	.03875	.04698
50	.00528	.00712	.00963	.01261	.01649	.02176	.02864	.03710	.04698	.05795
55	.00589	.00796	.01080	.01413	.01850	.02461	.03280	.04312	.05548	.06956
60	.00650	.00880	.01198	.01562	.02042	.02731	.03677	.04897	.06391	.08136
65	.00708	.00962	.01313	.01703	.02219	.02975	.04039	.05439	.07187	.09273
70	.00760	.01038	.01423	.01837	.02378	.03191	.04359	.05923	.07910	.10325
75	.00803	.01104	.01525	.01958	.02517	.03373	.04626	.06332	.08531	.11243
80	.00837	.01158	.01614	.02065	.02635	.03520	.04840	.06661	.09037	.12002
85	.00861	.01195	.01683	.02149	.02725	.03628	.04994	.06898	.09404	.12559
90	.00876	.01219	.01730	.02210	.02788	.03700	.05095	.07053	.09647	.12932
95	.00886	.01231	.01760	.02248	.02828	.03745	.05157	.07147	.09795	.13161
100	.00891	.01238	.01776	.02270	.02850	.03770	.05190	.07198	.09875	.13285

AGE	55	60	65	70	75	80	85	90	95	100
5	.00589	.00650	.00708	.00760	.00803	.00837	.00861	.00876	.00886	.00891
10	.00796	.00880	.00962	.01038	.01104	.01158	.01195	.01219	.01231	.01238
15	.01080	.01198	.01313	.01423	.01525	.01614	.01683	.01730	.01760	.01776
20	.01413	.01562	.01703	.01837	.01958	.02065	.02149	.02210	.02248	.02270
25	.01850	.02042	.02219	.02378	.02517	.02635	.02725	.02788	.02828	.02850
30	.02461	.02731	.02975	.03191	.03373	.03520	.03628	.03700	.03745	.03770
35	.03280	.03677	.04039	.04359	.04626	.04840	.04994	.05095	.05157	.05190
40	.04312	.04897	.05439	.05923	.06332	.06661	.06898	.07053	.07147	.07198
45	.05548	.06391	.07187	.07910	.08531	.09037	.09404	.09647	.09795	.09875
50	.06956	.08136	.09273	.10325	.11243	.12002	.12559	.12932	.13161	.13285
55	.08488	.10085	.11657	.13144	.14464	.15572	.16394	.16950	.17292	.17479
60	.10085	.12172	.14282	.16324	.18176	.19760	.20954	.21770	.22277	.22556
65	.11657	.14282	.17010	.19725	.22247	.24448	.26133	.27299	.28030	.28433
70	.13144	.16324	.19725	.23216	.26557	.29555	.31898	.33546	.34592	.35172
75	.14464	.18176	.22247	.26557	.30826	.34790	.37975	.40261	.41733	.42554
80	.15572	.19760	.24448	.29555	.34790	.39856	.44083	.47224	.49300	.50470
85	.16394	.20954	.26133	.31898	.37975	.44083	.49379	.53461	.56255	.57849
90	.16950	.21770	.27299	.33546	.40261	.47224	.53461	.58435	.61959	.63994
95	.17292	.22277	.28030	.34592	.41733	.49300	.56255	.61959	.66139	.68589
100	.17479	.22556	.28433	.35172	.42554	.50470	.57849	.63994	.68589	.71308

*The present value of $1.00 due at the death of the survivor of two persons.

**Use appropriate interest rate for the month in which the valuation date occurs.

Reprinted from the *Advanced Sales Reference Service*
©1992 The National Underwriter Company

The Tools and Techniques of Estate Planning

TWO-LIFE REMAINDER FACTORS* — 10.0% INTEREST RATE**
(For valuation dates occurring after April 30, 1989)

AGE	5	10	15	20	25	30	35	40	45	50
5	.00109	.00136	.00167	.00200	.00237	.00279	.00326	.00378	.00434	.00492
10	.00136	.00172	.00214	.00260	.00312	.00370	.00436	.00508	.00585	.00664
15	.00167	.00214	.00272	.00335	.00406	.00488	.00580	.00681	.00789	.00901
20	.00200	.00260	.00335	.00419	.00515	.00626	.00752	.00889	.01033	.01181
25	.00237	.00312	.00406	.00515	.00642	.00793	.00964	.01152	.01348	.01547
30	.00279	.00370	.00488	.00626	.00793	.00994	.01230	.01490	.01767	.02048
35	.00326	.00436	.00580	.00752	.00964	.01230	.01547	.01909	.02300	.02705
40	.00378	.00508	.00681	.00889	.01152	.01490	.01909	.02398	.02941	.03516
45	.00434	.00585	.00789	.01033	.01348	.01767	.02300	.02941	.03672	.04467
50	.00492	.00664	.00901	.01181	.01547	.02048	.02705	.03516	.04467	.05528
55	.00551	.00746	.01015	.01329	.01742	.02324	.03107	.04099	.05292	.06657
60	.00611	.00829	.01130	.01474	.01929	.02586	.03494	.04669	.06115	.07810
65	.00667	.00908	.01243	.01613	.02103	.02826	.03849	.05200	.06896	.08925
70	.00718	.00984	.01352	.01745	.02260	.03039	.04164	.05677	.07609	.09963
75	.00761	.01049	.01453	.01865	.02398	.03219	.04429	.06083	.08224	.10873
80	.00795	.01103	.01542	.01972	.02515	.03365	.04642	.06411	.08728	.11629
85	.00819	.01140	.01610	.02057	.02605	.03473	.04795	.06647	.09094	.12186
90	.00834	.01163	.01658	.02117	.02668	.03546	.04897	.06803	.09338	.12560
95	.00844	.01176	.01688	.02156	.02708	.03591	.04958	.06897	.09487	.12790
100	.00849	.01183	.01704	.02178	.02731	.03616	.04992	.06948	.09568	.12916

AGE	55	60	65	70	75	80	85	90	95	100
5	.00551	.00611	.00667	.00718	.00761	.00795	.00819	.00834	.00844	.00849
10	.00746	.00829	.00908	.00984	.01049	.01103	.01140	.01163	.01176	.01183
15	.01015	.01130	.01243	.01352	.01453	.01542	.01610	.01658	.01688	.01704
20	.01329	.01474	.01613	.01745	.01865	.01972	.02057	.02117	.02156	.02178
25	.01742	.01929	.02103	.02260	.02398	.02515	.02605	.02668	.02708	.02731
30	.02324	.02586	.02826	.03039	.03219	.03365	.03473	.03546	.03591	.03616
35	.03107	.03494	.03849	.04164	.04429	.04642	.04795	.04897	.04958	.04992
40	.04099	.04669	.05200	.05677	.06083	.06411	.06647	.06803	.06897	.06948
45	.05292	.06115	.06896	.07609	.08224	.08728	.09094	.09338	.09487	.09568
50	.06657	.07810	.08925	.09963	.10873	.11629	.12186	.12560	.12790	.12916
55	.08149	.09710	.11255	.12721	.14030	.15134	.15956	.16514	.16858	.17047
60	.09710	.11753	.13828	.15845	.17682	.19260	.20454	.21273	.21784	.22065
65	.11255	.13828	.16513	.19196	.21699	.23893	.25579	.26750	.27485	.27892
70	.12721	.15845	.19196	.22650	.25968	.28958	.31303	.32958	.34011	.34595
75	.14030	.17682	.21699	.25968	.30212	.34168	.37357	.39654	.41135	.41963
80	.15134	.19260	.23893	.28958	.34168	.39228	.43465	.46620	.48712	.49891
85	.15956	.20454	.25579	.31303	.37357	.43465	.48776	.52880	.55696	.57304
90	.16514	.21273	.26750	.32958	.39654	.46620	.52880	.57884	.61437	.63491
95	.16858	.21784	.27485	.34011	.41135	.48712	.55696	.61437	.65655	.68128
100	.17047	.22065	.27892	.34595	.41963	.49891	.57304	.63491	.68128	.70875

*The present value of $1.00 due at the death of the survivor of two persons.

**Use appropriate interest rate for the month in which the valuation date occurs.

Reprinted from the *Advanced Sales Reference Service*
©1992 The National Underwriter Company

1980 COMMISSIONERS STANDARD
ORDINARY MORTALITY TABLE
(Life expectancy, years)

Age	Male	Female	Age	Male	Female	Age	Male	Female	Age	Male	Female
0	70.83	75.83	25	47.84	52.34	50	25.36	29.53	75	8.31	10.32
1	70.13	75.04	26	46.93	51.40	51	24.52	28.67	76	7.84	9.71
2	69.20	74.11	27	46.01	50.46	52	23.70	27.82	77	7.40	9.12
3	68.27	73.17	28	45.09	49.52	53	22.89	26.98	78	6.97	8.55
4	67.34	72.23	29	44.16	48.59	54	22.08	26.14	79	6.57	8.01
5	66.40	71.28	30	43.24	47.65	55	21.29	25.31	80	6.18	7.48
6	65.46	70.34	31	42.31	46.71	56	20.51	24.49	81	5.80	6.98
7	64.52	69.39	32	41.38	45.78	57	19.74	23.67	82	5.44	6.49
8	63.57	68.44	33	40.46	44.84	58	18.99	22.86	83	5.09	6.03
9	62.62	67.48	34	39.54	43.91	59	18.24	22.05	84	4.77	5.57
10	61.66	66.53	35	38.61	42.98	60	17.51	21.25	85	4.46	5.18
11	60.71	65.58	36	37.69	42.05	61	16.79	20.44	86	4.18	4.80
12	59.75	64.62	37	36.78	41.12	62	16.08	19.65	87	3.91	4.43
13	58.80	63.67	38	35.87	40.20	63	15.38	18.86	88	3.66	4.09
14	57.86	62.71	39	34.96	39.28	64	14.70	18.08	89	3.41	3.77
15	56.93	61.76	40	34.05	38.36	65	14.04	17.32	90	3.18	3.45
16	56.00	60.82	41	33.16	37.46	66	13.39	16.57	91	2.94	3.15
17	55.09	59.87	42	32.26	36.55	67	12.76	15.83	92	2.70	2.85
18	54.18	58.93	43	31.38	35.66	68	12.14	15.10	93	2.44	2.55
19	53.27	57.98	44	30.50	34.77	69	11.54	14.38	94	2.17	2.24
20	52.37	57.04	45	29.62	33.88	70	10.96	13.67	95	1.87	1.91
21	51.47	56.10	46	28.76	33.00	71	10.39	12.97	96	1.54	1.56
22	50.57	55.16	47	27.90	32.12	72	9.84	12.26	97	1.20	1.21
23	49.66	54.22	48	27.04	31.25	73	9.30	11.60	98	0.84	0.84
24	48.75	53.28	49	26.20	30.39	74	8.79	10.95	99	0.50	0.50

The Tools and Techniques of Estate Planning

TABLE V
ONE LIFE-EXPECTED RETURN MULTIPLES

Age	Multiples (Life Expectancy)	Age	Multiples (Life Expectancy)	Age	Multiples (Life Expectancy)
5	76.6	42	40.6	79	10.0
6	75.6	43	39.6	80	9.5
7	74.7	44	38.7	81	8.9
8	73.7	45	37.7	82	8.4
9	72.7	46	36.8	83	7.9
10	71.7	47	35.9	84	7.4
11	70.7	48	34.9	85	6.9
12	69.7	49	34.0	86	6.5
13	68.8	50	33.1	87	6.1
14	67.8	51	32.2	88	5.7
15	66.8	52	31.3	89	5.3
16	65.8	53	30.4	90	5.0
17	64.8	54	29.5	91	4.7
18	63.9	55	28.6	92	4.4
19	62.9	56	27.7	93	4.1
20	61.9	57	26.8	94	3.9
21	60.9	58	25.9	95	3.7
22	59.9	59	25.0	96	3.4
23	59.0	60	24.2	97	3.2
24	58.0	61	23.3	98	3.0
25	57.0	62	22.5	99	2.8
26	56.0	63	21.6	100	2.7
27	55.1	64	20.8	101	2.5
28	54.1	65	20.0	102	2.3
29	53.1	66	19.2	103	2.1
30	52.2	67	18.4	104	1.9
31	51.2	68	17.6	105	1.8
32	50.2	69	16.8	106	1.6
33	49.3	70	16.0	107	1.4
34	48.3	71	15.6	108	1.3
35	47.3	72	14.6	109	1.1
36	46.4	73	13.9	110	1.0
37	45.4	74	13.2	111	.9
38	44.4	75	12.5	112	.8
39	43.5	76	11.9	113	.7
40	42.5	77	11.2	114	.6
41	41.5	78	10.6	115	.5

Frequency of Payment Adjustment Table

If the number of whole months from the annuity starting date to the first payment date is	0-1	2	3	4	5	6	7	8	9	10	11	12
And payments under the contract are to be made: Annually	+0.5	+0.4	+0.3	+0.2	+0.1	0	0	-0.1	-0.2	-0.3	-0.4	-0.5
Semiannually	+ .2	+ .1	0	0	- .1	- .2	....	....	....	....	....	....
Quarterly	+ .1	0	- .1	....	....	....	....	....	....	....	....	....

FIGURING COMPOUND INTEREST AND ANNUITY VALUES

The two tables that follow on the next two pages enable the estate planner to make various projections in actual cases. They show the compound interest and annuity functions at interest rates of 5 and 10 percent.

There are three functions which can be used for compound interest computations:

1. Amount of $1 (what a dollar will be worth at some date in the future if the deposit is made immediately).

    For Example, if $1,000 is invested today and grows at a rate of 10 percent per year compounded annually, it will be worth $1,948.72 in 7 years. (Go to Form A on the following page. Find 7th year. Look under "Amount of 1" column. The value is 1.948717 multiplied by $1,000.)

2. Amount of $1 per period (what a series of $1 deposits will be worth at some date in the future if the deposits are made at the end of each period).

    For example, if $1,000 is invested at the end of each year for 10 years and the return has been 10 percent interest compounded annually, the value of the fund is $15,937. (Go to Form A. Find 10 years. Look under the "Amount of 1 per Period" column. The value is 15.937,425. Multiply this by $1,000.)

3. Sinking fund payment (how much you need to deposit at the end of each period to have a given sum of money at a specified point in the future).

    For example, you'll need $100,000 in 5 years to pay off a debt. If you can earn 10 percent compounded annually on your money, you must deposit $16,379.74 each year for 5 years. (Go to Form A. Find 5 years. Look under the "Sinking Fund Payment" column. The value is .1637974808. Multiply that figure by $100,000.)

There are three functions which enable annuity computations:

1. Present worth of $1 (the value of $1 today if it will not be received until some time in the future).

For example, you are owed $1,000 and it will be paid to you in 10 years. Assuming a 5 percent interest rate, the present value of that debt is $613.91. (Go to Form B. Find 10 years. Look under the "Present Worth of 1" column. The value is 0.613,913. Multiply that by $1,000.)

2. Present worth of $1 per period. (How much is a future stream of dollars—payable at the end of each year— worth today?)

    For example, suppose you were to receive $1,000 at the end of each year for the next 20 years. Assuming 10 percent interest, that stream of dollars would be worth $8,513.56 today. (Go to Form A. Find 20 years. Look under the "Present Worth of 1 per Period" column. The value is 8.513,564. Multiply that by $1,000.)

3. Periodic payment to amortize $1. (What mortgage payment must be made each year to pay off a given loan? In other words, you have a dollar now. What annuity do you have to pay each year—given a certain number of years—to pay off the loan?)

    For example, what is the annual payment needed to pay off a $100,000 loan over 10 years if a 10 percent interest rate is payable on the unpaid balance? Assuming payments are made annually at the end of each year and interest is compounded annually, the amount is $16,274.54. (Go to Form A. Find 10 years. Look under the "Periodic Payment to Amortize 1" column. The value is 0.1627453949. Multiply that by $100,000.)

There is one measurement function: total interest (how much interest is paid over a given period of time where a loan is amortized by regular periodic payments).

For example, assume you were going to borrow $100,000 over 10 years at 10 percent interest. The total interest you'd pay on such a loan is $62,745. (Go to Form A. Find 10 years. Look under the "Total Interest" column. The value is 0.627,454. Multiply that by $100,000.)

Figuring Compound Interest and Annuity Values 10 percent

YEAR	Amount of 1 What a single $1 deposit grows to in the future. The deposit is made at the beginning of the first period.	Amount of 1 Per Period What a series of $1 deposits grow to in the future. A deposit is made at the end of each period.	Sinking Fund Payment The amount to be deposited at the end of each period that grows to $1 in the future.	Present Worth of 1 What $1 to be paid in the future is worth today. Value today of a single payment tomorrow.	Present Worth of 1 Per Period What $1 to be paid at the end of each period is worth today. Value today of a series of payments tomorrow.	Periodic Payment to Amortize 1 The mortgage payment to amortize a loan of $1. An annuity certain, payable at the end of each period worth $1 today.	Total Interest The total interest paid over the term on a loan of $1. The loan is amortized by regular periodic payments.
1	1.100 000	1.000 000	1.000 000 0000	0.909 091	0.909 091	1.100 000 0000	0.100 000
2	1.210 000	2.100 000	0.476 190 4762	0.826 446	1.735 537	0.576 190 4762	0.152 381
3	1.331 000	3.310 000	0.302 114 8036	0.751 315	2.486 852	0.402 114 8036	0.206 344
4	1.464 100	4.641 000	0.215 470 8037	0.683 013	3.169 865	0.315 470 8037	0.261 883
5	1.610 510	6.105 100	0.163 797 4808	0.620 921	3.790 787	0.263 797 4808	0.318 987
6	1.771 561	7.715 610	0.129 607 3804	0.564 474	4.355 261	0.229 607 3804	0.377 644
7	1.948 717	9.487 171	0.105 405 4997	0.513 158	4.868 419	0.205 405 4997	0.437 838
8	2.143 589	11.435 888	0.087 444 0176	0.466 507	5.334 926	0.187 444 0176	0.499 552
9	2.357 948	13.579 477	0.073 640 5391	0.424 098	5.759 024	0.173 640 5391	0.562 765
10	2.593 742	15.937 425	0.062 745 3949	0.385 543	6.144 567	0.162 745 3949	0.627 454
11	2.853 117	18.531 167	0.053 963 1420	0.350 494	6.495 061	0.153 963 1420	0.693 595
12	3.138 428	21.384 284	0.046 763 3151	0.318 631	6.813 692	0.146 763 3151	0.761 160
13	3.452 271	24.522 712	0.040 778 5238	0.289 664	7.103 356	0.140 778 5238	0.830 121
14	3.797 498	27.974 983	0.035 746 2232	0.263 331	7.366 687	0.135 746 2232	0.900 447
15	4.177 248	31.772 482	0.031 473 7769	0.239 392	7.606 080	0.131 473 7769	0.972 107
16	4.594 973	35.949 730	0.027 816 6207	0.217 629	7.823 709	0.127 816 6207	1.045 066
17	5.054 470	40.544 703	0.024 664 1344	0.197 845	8.021 553	0.124 664 1344	1.119 290
18	5.559 917	45.599 173	0.021 930 2222	0.179 859	8.201 412	0.121 930 2222	1.194 744
19	6.115 909	51.159 090	0.019 546 8682	0.163 508	8.364 920	0.119 546 8682	1.271 390
20	6.727 500	57.274 999	0.017 459 6248	0.148 644	8.513 564	0.117 459 6248	1.349 192
21	7.400 250	64.002 499	0.015 624 3898	0.135 131	8.648 694	0.115 624 3898	1.428 112
22	8.140 275	71.402 749	0.014 005 0630	0.122 846	8.771 540	0.114 005 0630	1.508 111
23	8.954 302	79.543 024	0.012 571 8127	0.111 678	8.883 218	0.112 571 8127	1.589 152
24	9.849 733	88.497 327	0.011 299 7764	0.101 526	8.984 744	0.111 299 7764	1.671 195
25	10.834 706	98.347 059	0.010 168 0722	0.092 296	9.077 040	0.110 168 0722	1.754 202
26	11.918 177	109.181 765	0.009 159 0386	0.083 905	9.160 945	0.109 159 0386	1.838 135
27	13.109 994	121.099 942	0.008 257 6423	0.076 278	9.237 223	0.108 257 6423	1.922 956
28	14.420 994	134.209 936	0.007 451 0132	0.069 343	9.306 567	0.107 451 0132	2.008 628
29	15.863 093	148.630 930	0.006 728 0747	0.063 039	9.639 606	0.106 728 0747	2.095 114
30	17.449 402	164.494 023	0.006 079 2483	0.057 309	9.426 914	0.106 079 2483	2.182 377

FORM A

The Tools and Techniques of Estate Planning

Figuring Compound Interest and Annuity Values 5 percent

	Amount of 1	Amount of 1 Per Period	Sinking Fund Payment	Present Worth of 1	Present Worth of 1 Per Period	Periodic Payment to Amortize 1	Total Interest
	What a single $1 deposit grows to in the future. The deposit is made at the beginning of the first period.	What a series of $1 deposits grow to in the future. A deposit is made at the end of each period.	The amount to be deposited at the end of each period that grows to $1 in the future.	What $1 to be paid in the future is worth today. Value today of a single payment tomorrow.	What $1 to be paid at the end of each period is worth today. Value today of a series of payments tomorrow.	The mortgage payment to amortize a loan of $1. An annuity certain, payable at the end of each period worth $1 today.	The total interest paid over the term on a loan of $1. The loan is amortized by regular periodic payments.

YEAR							
1	1.050 000	1.000 000	1.000 000 0000	0.952 381	0.952 381	1.050 000 0000	0.050 000
2	1.102 500	2.050 000	0.487 804 8780	0.907 029	1.859 410	0.537 804 8780	0.075 610
3	1.157 625	3.152 500	0.317 208 5646	0.863 838	2.723 248	0.367 208 5646	0.101 626
4	1.215 506	4.310 125	0.232 011 8326	0.822 702	3.545 951	0.282 011 8326	0.128 047
5	1.276 282	5.525 631	0.180 974 7981	0.783 526	4.329 477	0.230 974 7981	0.154 874
6	1.340 096	6.801 913	0.147 017 4681	0.746 215	5.075 692	0.197 017 4681	0.182 105
7	1.407 100	8.142 008	0.122 819 8184	0.710 681	5.786 373	0.172 819 8184	0.209 739
8	1.477 455	9.549 109	0.104 721 8136	0.676 839	6.463 213	0.154 721 8136	0.237 775
9	1.551 328	11.026 564	0.090 690 0800	0.644 609	7.107 822	0.140 690 0800	0.266 211
10	1.628 895	12.577 893	0.079 504 5750	0.613 913	7.721 735	0.129 504 5750	0.295 046
11	1.710 339	14.206 787	0.070 388 8915	0.584 679	8.306 414	0.120 388 8915	0.324 278
12	1.795 856	15.917 127	0.062 825 4100	0.556 837	8.863 252	0.112 825 4100	0.353 905
13	1.885 649	17.712 983	0.056 455 7652	0.530 321	9.393 573	0.106 455 7652	0.383 925
14	1.979 932	19.598 632	0.051 023 9695	0.505 068	9.898 641	0.101 023 9695	0.414 336
15	2.078 928	21.578 564	0.046 342 2876	0.481 017	10.379 658	0.096 342 2876	0.445 134
16	2.182 875	23.657 492	0.042 269 9080	0.458 112	10.837 770	0.092 269 9080	0.476 319
17	2.292 018	25.840 366	0.038 699 1417	0.436 297	11.274 066	0.088 699 1417	0.507 885
18	2.406 619	28.132 385	0.035 546 2223	0.415 521	11.689 587	0.085 546 2223	0.539 832
19	2.526 950	30.539 004	0.032 745 0104	0.395 734	12.085 321	0.082 745 0104	0.572 155
20	2.653 298	33.065 954	0.030 242 5872	0.376 889	12.462 210	0.080 242 5872	0.604 852
21	2.785 963	35.719 252	0.027 996 1071	0.358 942	12.821 153	0.077 996 1071	0.637 918
22	2.925 261	38.505 214	0.025 970 5086	0.341 850	13.163 003	0.075 970 5086	0.671 351
23	3.071 524	41.430 475	0.024 136 8219	0.325 571	13.488 574	0.074 136 8219	0.705 147
24	3.225 100	44.501 999	0.022 470 9008	0.310 068	13.798 642	0.072 470 9008	0.739 302
25	3.386 355	47.727 099	0.020 952 4573	0.295 303	14.093 945	0.070 952 4573	0.773 811
26	3.555 673	51.113 454	0.019 564 3207	0.281 241	14.375 185	0.069 564 3207	0.808 672
27	3.733 456	54.669 126	0.018 291 8599	0.267 848	14.643 034	0.068 291 8599	0.843 880
28	3.920 129	58.402 583	0.017 122 5304	0.255 094	14.898 127	0.067 122 5304	0.879 431
29	4.116 136	62.322 712	0.016 045 5149	0.242 946	15.141 074	0.066 045 5149	0.915 320
30	4.321 942	66.438 848	0.015 051 4351	0.231 377	15.372 451	0.065 051 4351	0.951 543

FORM B

The Tools and Techniques of Estate Planning

Appendix E

THE UNAUTHORIZED PRACTICE OF LAW

It is sometimes difficult to draw the boundaries of professional responsibility in an area as complex and sophisticated as estate planning. Special skills and learning are necessary prerequisites not only to the attorney but also to a CPA, CFP, ChFC, CLU, trust officer, or other individual serving a client in an advisory capacity.

Yet it is clear that regardless of how knowledgeable an advisor is, only the attorney may practice law. The practice of law is regulated and limited for a number of reasons:

First, the public needs and deserves protection against advice by self-styled advisors who have been neither trained nor examined (nor licensed) by recognized educational or governmental authorities.

Second, many non-lawyers who are highly skilled in specific areas such as tax law may lack the broader viewpoint and depth provided by a good law school.

Third, the lawyer-client relationship is one of confidentiality, relative objectivity, and impartiality. Even the most ethical sales person, service provider, or trust officer cannot claim complete objectivity; his job is to sell a given investment, contract, service, or the use of a particular financial institution. This does not imply that the CFP, CLU, ChFC, or trust officer or CPA does not have highly important tasks to perform as a member of the estate planning team. On the contrary, it is often that individual who motivates the client to take action — and follows through to make sure the plan is implemented.

Were this the only responsibility and utility of those members, their positions on the "team" would be secure. But, in reality, each of those individuals can perform a function that serves as a valuable complement to the attorney's task. In fact, the attorney should not be "practicing" life insurance, providing trust services, or replacing the accountant. The very idea of an estate planning team implies that each member serves the client with his own special and essential skills. When any member of the team usurps the province of the other, it is the client who loses. Stated in a more positive manner, the client is best served if the non-attorney and attorney work together to formulate, implement, qualify, and maintain a plan which suits the client's needs and objectives.

Returning to the topic of the unauthorized practice of law, the central issue must be: What is it? Clearly, the preparation of instruments and contracts by which legal rights are secured constitutes an invasion of the attorney's province. So, the non-attorney who drafts a will or a trust for a client is patently guilty of the unauthorized practice of law. But what of the person who reviews a will or trust and advises clients as to the desirability in their circumstances of specific clauses or instruments? Does every discussion of a legal principle constitute unauthorized practice? Is the recognized subject matter expert excused from the proscription against unauthorized practice? What if no fee is charged for the rendering of advice? Does long-time custom and tradition offer a valid reason for practice by non-lawyers?

A working knowledge of the tax law is essential to professionals in the life insurance, trust, and accounting disciplines. Generally, the protection of the public can be achieved without hampering or unduly burdening professionals with impractical and technical restrictions which have no reasonable justification. To say that non-attorneys cannot discuss any pertinent legal principles with a client would be so unrealistic and narrow as to be absurd.

But what can be safely discussed — and what cannot? Essentially, where a statute or legal interpretation has become so well-known and settled that no further legal issue is involved, there should be no problem in suggesting its simple application on a general basis. This is known as the "general-specific" test; no violation arises from the sharing of legal knowledge which is either generally informatory or, if specific, is so obvious as to be common knowledge. It is only when legal rules (which are general in nature) are applied to specific factual situations that the line is crossed. Providing advice involving the application of legal principles to a specific situation is clearly the "practice of law" under the "general-specific" test.

A second criterion is known as the "complexity" theory. This theory states that the non-attorney should not answer "difficult" or "complex" questions of law. One court stated that "practicing as an attorney...is the giving of advice or the rendition of any sort of service...when the giving of such advice or the rendition of such service requires the use of any degree of legal knowledge or skill."

But perhaps the court should have gone beyond the questions of difficulty or complexity of subject matter into the issue of whether legal judgment was exercised by the non-attorney and relied on by the client. When basic legal principles are applied to specific and actual facts or the resolution

The Tools and Techniques of Estate Planning

645

of controversial or uncertain questions of law is required in an actual case, the practice of law is involved.

No safety can be found in an argument that the non-lawyer is both a specialist and an acknowledged expert in the field. The rationale for this seemingly harsh stand is that the interest of the public is not protected by narrow specialization of a person who lacks the broad perspective and orientation of a licensed attorney. That dimension of skill and knowledge comes only from a thorough understanding of legal concepts, processes, and the interaction of all the branches of law. In other words, the rules may have been learned by the non-lawyer but often the full meaning and import of the rule and its components — and the impact of that rule on other seemingly unrelated rules — may not be fully understood by even a highly competent specialist who is not also a licensed attorney.

Charging fees for legal advice seems important only where such fees were charged. Most courts have had little trouble finding violations where clients relied on advice or were provided with legal services regardless of whether or not fees were charged. Likewise, practices of the past provide little defense in the present. Recent decisions indicate that even custom and tradition long acquiesced in by the Bar does not make proscribed activities any less the practice of law.

Almost everyone agrees that the actual drafting of a will or trust or the preparation of the instruments and contracts by which legal rights are secured is the practice of law. The odds are very high that he who drafts such documents is practicing law.

Beyond this point, however, (and in the minds of some, even at this point) things become hazy. Each state has the right to decide — independently from all other states — what is meant by the "unauthorized practice of law."

Review the following fact patterns and ask, "Will this constitute the unauthorized practice of law?"

- The planner reviews a will or trust and advises a client that — in this particular circumstance — that document will (or will not) have specific legal implications or that the instrument in question is "right" or "not right" for them.

- After analyzing client information, the planner decides on the type of trust arrangement the client should have and selects the specific provisions that should be inserted into the plan documents.

- The planner makes "bottom line recommendations" as to which trust provisions would be most suitable to a client's needs.

- The planner drafts amendments to an existing trust.

- The planner does the initial draft of a power of attorney, but submits it for review, approval, and adoption by the client's lawyers.

- The planner gives advice regarding the impact of tax and other laws on an irrevocable trust.

If these actions are the unauthorized practice of law, is the client denied the benefit of receiving advice from accountants, actuaries, CFPs, CLUs, ChFCs, or trust officers who are experts in their fields? Would prohibiting such actions by these experts amount to a questionable restraint on interdisciplinary competition? Is it not only possible, but highly likely, that the non-attorney expert is better suited than the attorney in matters such as product choice and design? Would thwarting the non-attorney from performing these vital roles significantly increase the cost of estate planning? In some states these are still open questions. As a practical matter, practitioners should avoid most problems by working closely with the client's attorney at the earliest opportunity.

This book is not designed to help the non-lawyer eliminate the need for an attorney. To the contrary, it is a text designed for all the members of the estate planning team to help delineate the large number of alternative solutions to general problem areas. Definitive solutions, i.e., the choice of which specific tools or techniques to use in a given case or the decisions as to how they should be used must be considered only by the client, together with his attorney. Likewise, the drafting or adopting of instruments needed to execute the techniques or utilize the tools discussed below is exclusively the province of the lawyer.

Every member of the estate planning team is obligated to be aware of these tools and techniques, to understand their limitations as well as their problem-solving potential, and to be knowledgeable enough to discuss them in general terms with clients and their other advisors.

ETHICS
WHAT THE ESTATE PLANNER MUST KNOW
A Practical Guideline

WHY ETHICS?

Ethics are standards of an aspirational and inspirational nature reflecting commitments to model standards of exemplary professional conduct.[1] Every major profession[2] has adopted some form of "near law," a Code, Canon, or set of guidelines to what the profession expects of its members.[3] This discussion is meant to provide a checklist for the practitioner in the estate planning field.[4] It is not intended to be anything more than what its title implies, a "practical guideline," a self-monitoring device to help estate planners.

Why do professional organizations need such codes of conduct? Why do estate planners need a practical code of ethics?

First, ethics are a means of creating standards by which conduct can be measured both by the member and by the group itself. Second, ethics serve as a way to acknowledge an obligation to society, to the professional group, and to the client. Third, ethics assure the profession will be governed by high standards. Fourth, ethics are a means of examining priorities and building a tradition based on integrity.

A fifth reason for ethics is as a limitation on power. It is the "power of the experts" that ethics are meant to control: the attorney, accountant, trust officer, life insurance agent, and other members of the estate planning team all know things the client does not.[5] This special knowledge gives the professional Kafka-like power over a layman who must put great faith and trust in (and take great risk in the accuracy and appropriateness of) what he is told. The client cannot possibly know the full extent of the problems, possibilities, and consequences without the assistance of the planner.

The preparation of an estate plan vests in the planner enormous power for another reason: the planner is a person in whom the client places a great trust and confidence. It is this potential abuse of power that ethics are designed to prevent or limit.

The premise upon which practical ethics must be based is that power must be exercised in the interest of those for whose benefit it was entrusted rather than abused for the self aggrandizement of the planner. The limitations and restrictions on the planner must not, however, be so great as to be so unenforceable, unrealistic, and impractical as to be counter productive. Practical ethics, therefore, must strike a balance. The questions that follow are designed to help do just that:

HONESTY: Has the planner engaged in any business or professional activity which involved an act (or omission) of a dishonest, deceitful, or fraudulent nature?

Has the planner used his license, degree, or designation to attribute to himself a depth or scope of knowledge, skills, and professional capabilities he does not, in fact, possess?

Has the planner been fair and honest in dealings with the IRS and in fostering confidence in the system?[6]

COMPETENCY: Does the planner have the requisite legal knowledge, practical skill, and has he exercised thoroughness?

Has the planner undertaken a role which entails responsibilities in addition to that inherent to the profession — and if so — is he properly trained and equipped (and willing and otherwise able) to perform them in a competent and efficient manner?[7]

Has the planner done the proper preparation? In other words, is he qualified to perform the services requested and does he know enough to perform any services required beyond those requested?

What has the planner done to understand the specific facts and circumstances of the client, the client's family, other beneficiaries, and their needs and objectives?[8]

Does the planner keep abreast of changing economic and legislative conditions which may affect the client's plan?[9]

REPRESENTATION: Has the planner established the boundaries of his relationship so that the client knows what he will or will not do? Has the planner specified those limits in writing for all parties concerned?

Has the planner — in any way — denied the client the benefit of the knowledge and skill of another professional who could assist in serving the client?[10]

DILIGENCE: Did the planner do what was required in a reasonably prompt manner?

If the planner is responsible for preparing IRS forms, documents, affidavits, or other papers for the client, did he do so in a timely manner?

Did the planner advise a client promptly of any non-compliance, error, or omission having to do with a state or federal tax return or other document the client was required by law to complete?

COMMUNICATION: Did the planner return phone calls or answer letters promptly? Did he keep the client (and other professionals) informed on a regular basis of economic and legal changes that may impact upon the client's plans?[11]

CONFIDENTIALITY: Did the planner keep client information confidential (except to the extent specifically authorized by the client to disclose it)?[12]

FEES: Did the planner charge fees which were reasonable and fair in light of the situation?[13] (Was the fee based on (a) the amount of work performed or the number of hours it took to do the work, (b) the difficulty and judgment involved in the problems that had to be solved, (c) the importance of the problem, and (d) his professional expertise, skill, and standing?)

Did the planner communicate, in writing, the formula by which fees or other charges would be based?

Has the planner billed, only after performing services in a satisfactory manner?

Has the planner refunded any advance fee which has not been fully earned?

CONFLICT OF INTEREST:[14] Did the planner inform the parties he is representing of their respective rights and the pros and cons of the proposed action (or inaction) on each party?

Did the planner draft an instrument giving him or a member of his family an interest in the client's estate (assuming he is not a member of the client's family)?[15]

Has the planner written himself (or his partner) into the will as attorney for the estate and also as executor?

Has the planner used the special knowledge he has to the detriment of the client in any way?[16]

Does the planner represent two parties who have or are likely to have conflicting interests?[17] (This problem is known as "simultaneous representation.") If so, is the planner satisfied that he can perform adequately and did he make full disclosure to, and obtain consent from, the parties?[18]

Has the planner, in any way, allowed the pursuit of financial gain or any other personal benefit to interfere with the exercise of sound professional judgment and skills?[19]

Has the planner made full disclosure of any obvious conflicts of interest in writing to the client?

Has the planner drawn an instrument which exonerates him from liability that may be incurred in another role (such as the attorney who may also serve as executor)?[20]

DISCLOSURE: Has the planner (or his associates, partners, or employer), in any other way, breached his duty of loyalty to the client by failing to disclose information?

Has the planner withheld information from another professional or governmental official that it is important and appropriate for that person to know?

Has the planner misrepresented the benefits, costs, or limitations of any estate planning tool or technique or failed to fully explain the advantages and disadvantages of viable alternatives?[21]

DIRECT CONTACT: Has the planner obtained information directly from the client or was it obtained second or third hand from another party or advisor acting as a conduit?[22]

COURTESY: Has the planner's courtesy extended, not only to the client, but also to the other professionals who seek to serve that person?[23]

PUBLIC REGARD: Has the planner followed the laws applicable to his business and professional activities?[24]

Has the planner done what he can to raise the level of integrity and professionalism and avoided activities which detract from the opinion the public has of his profession?

Has the planner impaired the reputation of another practitioner?

Has the planner competed unfairly?

Has the planner used his degree or designation in less than a responsible or dignified or appropriate manner?

Does the planner avoid associating with those who are not ethical?[25]

Has the planner provided the public with useful and objective information concerning potential problems, possible solutions, and impartial advisory opinions?

Has the planner attempted — in all dealings with the public — to avoid the appearance of impropriety?

MENTORING: Has the planner helped others enter the profession? Has he helped them attain and retain competence?[26]

Has the planner encouraged and assisted others in obtaining higher levels of professional competence?

It is not enough to NOT advocate, sanction, participate in, or carry out an unethical act. Professional ethics require more than merely NOT doing the things you should not do. It forbids condoning the unethical act of another and requires taking positive action to do the things that should be done. For instance, *The Code of Ethics of the International Association for Financial Planning* directs its members to:

"Oppose those who are deficient in moral character or professional competence, whose actions may cause financial harm to their clients."

Ethics are a reminder that the estate planner is more of a counselor than an advocate, more of an advisor than a scholar. Ethics reinforce the importance of the role of all the members of the estate planning team as intermediaries and protectors who look out for the overall best interests of the family unit in recommending a course of action.

Ethics do not demand absolute, unreasoning, and undivided loyalty to a single client nor does it demand saint-like perfection in any other area. But ethics has its (generally quite affordable) price — professional honesty, integrity, and competence compatible with the realities of modern practice. In fact, the increased pride and respect gained from others (and ourselves) is well worth the price. Can any planner afford not to pay it?

FOOTNOTES

1. See *Code of Professional Ethics of the American Institute for Property and Liability Underwriters.*

2. See "For the Long Term — Professional Ethics and The Life Underwriter," *Life Association News*, December 1985, for an excellent discussion on that subject. Dr. Clarence C. Walton, the author of that article, states that among the characteristics of a mature professional are:

   A. Primary commitment to the interest of the client,
   B. Possession of expert knowledge,
   C. Self regulation, and
   D. Awareness of the long term consequences of his or her action

   Dr. Walton provides excellent guidelines for organizations who sincerely wish to promote and enforce a code of ethics.

3. Information on the Code of conduct for your profession should be obtained by writing to the appropriate national organization to which you belong. Attorneys should write to Information Officer, Office of Professional Ethics, American Bar Association, Chicago, Ill., for information on the ABA's Model Rules of Professional Conduct.

4. Attorneys working in this field will find excellent guidance from "Ethical Issues In Estate Practice" printed as part of the ESTATE PRACTICE UPDATE of the Pennsylvania Bar Institute, 104 South Street, Harrisburg, Pa. 17108-1027 (800-932-4637 or 717-233-5774).

5. See "Estate Planners: Where Do Your Ethics Lie?," *Trusts and Estates*.

6. The duties of a professional to the IRS are spelled out in IRS circular 230 which embraces, under a uniform standard, many of the traditional ethical and professional standards common to national professional organizations. See "Regulations Within The IRS," *Trusts and Estates*, April 1990, p. 30.

7. See "Draft Statement of Principles Comes Not A Moment Too Soon," *Trusts and Estates*, December 1988, p. 12. For instance, a competent attorney may serve in other fiduciary roles such as an executor or trustee. One competent to handle the role of attorney may not have the training or skill (or time) to serve as an executor or trustee.

8. *The Code of Ethics of the American Society of CLU and ChFC* states, "A member must make a conscientious effort to ascertain and to understand all relevant circumstances surrounding the client."

9. *The Code of Ethics of The American Society of CLU and ChFC* states, "A member shall continue his education throughout his professional life." Interpretive comment adds, "a member must continue to maintain and to improve his professional abilities. Continuing education includes both the member adding to his knowledge of the practice of his profession; and, the member keeping abreast of changing economic and legislative conditions which may affect the financial plans of the insuring public."

10. For instance, by making an unfair comparison between a person who has a license, degree, or designation, and one who does not.

    In an excellent *Trusts and Estates* article entitled, "ETHICS," the author, Frederic G. Corneel, poses a situation in which an insurance agent suggested to a consumer that he buy a very large amount of life insurance and adopt an estate plan including a revocable insurance trust. At the customer's request, the agent recommends a lawyer. The client tells the lawyer about his estate and the amount of insurance recommended to him. In the lawyer's opinion the amount of insurance is very much in excess of what is needed.

    What should the lawyer do? Corneel answers that the lawyer must, of course, be guided by what he believes to be in the best interest of the client. But then he adds, "The other point for the lawyer to keep in mind is that he may well be mistaken in his evaluation of how much insurance is necessary or that, this may be a question of business, personal, or investment preference which the client is just as capable of making as the lawyer himself.

Corneel then states that "before giving his opinion to the client, however, the lawyer would be well advised to speak first with the insurance agent. The agent may have information or thought to bear on the problem that the lawyer has not considered and that might well affect his view on the matter. This is not only in the lawyer's interest, who by a simple telephone call may be kept from making a fool of himself, but it is in the interest of the client not to become the battlefield of a war among experts unless the war is unavoidable."

11. *The Code of Ethics of the American Society of CLU and ChFC* states, "A member shall render continuing advice and service." It's interpretive comment provides, "Advice and service to be competent must be ongoing as the client's circumstances change and as these changes are made known to the member."

12. *The Code of Ethics of the American Society of CLU and ChFC* states, "A member shall respect the confidential relationship existing between client and member."

13. An excellent guide to the factors which affect attorney's fees in estate administration can be found in "Attorney's Fees in Estate Administration," *The Chase Review*, January 1990 (Chase Private Banking Group, 1211 Avenue of the Americas, New York, New York 10036).

14. *The Code of Ethics of the International Association for Financial Planning* states, "The reliance of the public and the business community on sound financial planning and advice imposes on the financial planning profession an obligation to maintain high standards of technical competence, morality, and integrity. To this end, members of the International Association for Financial Planning, Inc. shall at all times maintain independence of thought and action..." *The Code of Ethics of the American Society* states, "In a conflict of interest situation the interest of the client must be paramount."

15. See "Legal Ramifications of Unethical Estate Planning Practices," *Trusts and Estates*, October 1985, p. 47 for court response to situations in which (a) an attorney made himself legatee or devisee, (b) the attorney named himself or his partner as executor or trustee with powers to confer upon himself many of the benefits of ownership, (c) the attorney contrived to assure himself professional employment (together with a rather generous fee arrangement) representing the fiduciary in connection with the probate of a will or the administration of a trust.

16. *The Code of Ethics of the American Society of CLU and ChFC* states, "A member possessing a specific body of knowledge which is not possessed by the general public has an obligation to use that knowledge for the benefit of the client and to avoid taking advantage of that knowledge to the detriment of the client.

17. It is quite common for a planner to work with several members of the same family. In planning, conflicts of interests may arise over (a) the exercise of tax elections or options, (b) the interpretation of a clause in a will or trust or other document, or (c) the exercise or non-exercise of discretionary authority by a fiduciary. The attorney represents multiple clients when providing advice for both spouses, parent and child, or testator and beneficiary. An excellent discussion of these conflicts can be found in the January 1990 issue of *The Chase Review*. See also "Conflicts of Interest in Estate Planning and Administration," *Trusts and Estates*, June 1984, p. 18.

18. QTIP planning presents inevitable conflicts of interest that demand full disclosure. For instance, "Is a QTIP trust contrary to the wishes or needs of a spouse who wants to obtain greater control of her spouse's property on his death?" "Is a large inter vivos intraspousal gift contrary to the interests of a wealthy spouse if some day in the future divorce occurs?"

The solution to multiple representation is, as mentioned in the body of this discussion, a "plain English" explanation of the meaning and personal impact of the planners' suggestions.

19. *Code of Professional Ethics of The American Institute for Property and Liability Underwriters, Inc.*

20. For instance, instruments should not include exculpatory provisions which would relieve the draftsperson of malpractice or malfeasance liability unless the instrument is reviewed by independent counsel for the instrument's creator.

21. Each professional must ask himself three questions:

A. What are the pros and cons of the viable alternatives?

B. Which alternatives offer the client and client's family or other intended beneficiaries the greatest financial security and the least overall cost?

C. What if the client does nothing?

Then these three issues must be shared with the client's other advisors and with the client.

22. Only through direct relations can a professional be sure that he has all of the relevant facts including an understanding of the client's objectives and fears and can make sure both parties fully understand each other.

23. *The Code of Ethics of the American Society of CLU and ChFC* states, "A member is to accord due courtesy and consideration to those engaged in related professions who are also serving the client."

24. *The Code of Ethics of the American Society of CLU and ChFC* states, "A member has a legal obligation to obey all laws applicable to his business and professional activities. The placement of this Guide within the Code raises this obligation to the level of an ethical obligation."

25. *The Code of Ethics of the International Association for Financial Planning* states, "Avoid association with anyone who does not comply with the spirit of these principles."

26. *The Code of Ethics of the American Society of CLU and ChFC* states, "Encouraging others who might be qualified to enter into a practice is one hallmark of a professional."

MALPRACTICE IN ESTATE PLANNING — HOW TO AVOID IT — AND THE LAWSUIT THAT COMES WITH IT

"You have a malpractice case if there is no reasonable explanation for a terrible result."[1]

More technically stated, when a professional breaches the duty owed to another party and the other party is injured as a result of that breach, there is malpractice.[2]

Errors in estate planning and estate tax constitute the third most common type of legal malpractice.[3]

Reducing the risk of a malpractice suit and enhancing available defenses is the subject of this discussion.

"TARGET OF OPPORTUNITY" — WHY ME?

Those professionals wise enough to know that malpractice is a disease that may attack anyone will not ask the question, "Why Me?" Instead, they will ask, "When?" Malpractice claims are made uncomfortably often against those who — out of ignorance, arrogance, or incompetence — thought it could not happen to them. Suits are also brought against those estate planners with fine reputations who honestly thought they had done everything right. It is a dangerous misconception to think that only those who are clearly sloppy and unethical encounter malpractice claims.[4]

Mere good faith and honest intent will not protect the practitioner who has caused a client loss. It may be true that an estate planner will not be held liable for the failure to foresee the ultimate resolution of a debatable point of law or for an error in judgment if he acts in good faith and in an honest belief that his advice and acts are well founded and in the best interest of his client.[5] But such an estate planner can still be sued and still incur most of the costs of someone who in fact is guilty of malpractice.

Who are likely "targets of opportunity"?

DEEP POCKETS. When clients sue, they sue everyone in sight. But the bulk of the litigation effort is understandably against those from whom recovery is most likely. Your firm's appearance of success is a magnet. Furthermore, "judges and juries alike may be inclined to assess the loss of the poor helpless individual against the large, seemingly impersonal institution that manages billions of dollars every day."[6] This problem is particularly evident where the defendant is a trust, insurance company, or large law firm.

INSURANCE. Certainly one contributing factor is the common knowledge that professionals carry insurance for malpractice. Almost all professionals in the financial services field carry one or more high limit insurance coverages. Some plaintiffs feel they are not suing the professional; they are suing the insurer.

TOUTED EXPERIENCE, SKILL, AND KNOWLEDGE. In general, professionals who obtain or retain clients by holding themselves out as possessing a higher level of skill than other practitioners will be held to that higher level. If an advisor's business card says, "Estate Planner" or "Tax Specialist" or he has an advanced degree or a CFP, CLU, ChFC or otherwise advertises greater expertise or skill than an ordinary practitioner, he is expected to exercise that expertise or skill.[7]

IMPERSONAL. It is far easier to sue a party perceived as a "giant institution guided by computers rather than people" than to sue a long time advisor who has served with warmth, openness, compassion and has provided substantial personal attention in a respectful manner. This public image of banks, insurance companies, large law firms, and other institutions as impersonal money machines can best be changed from the top down by an insistence on courtesy and attention to the client from everyone in the firm.

BIG GUY vs LITTLE GUY. There is a feeling in this country, right or wrong, that the "Big Guys" are using their weight to beat up on the "Little Guys." So when the little guy gets into the judicial system, a jury may feel sympathetic and tend to punish the big guy with an angry vengeance.

FRUSTRATION WITH THE LAW(S). The potential for malpractice increases in proportion to both the complexity, speed of change, and labyrinthine interrelationship of various federal and state corporate, tax, probate, and securities laws — and clients' confusion and frustration. From the estate planner's point of view, the combination is a nightmare. If the planner feels this way, think of how angry clients must be when told that last year's law is now out and all the time, money, and emotional energy must be invested all over again.[8]

SIMPLE LIABILITY vs COMPOUND LIABILITY

One author who both sues and defends members of estate planning teams said, "There are basically two types of malpractice liability: Simple and Compound (may be read "expensive" and "grossly expensive)."[9]

Simple liability is for simple errors in judgment or simple negligence. These mistakes are expensive but are part of the (reducible) costs of doing business. Missing a tax deadline or miscomputing a liquidity need would be examples of simple liability.

Compound liability is for gross breach of fiduciary duty, self-dealing, active concealment, fraud, oppression, and gross negligence. The author stated that "Gross negligence is usually accompanied by a fatal dose of institutional arrogance, an always fatal disease for which there is no known cure."[10] Lack of respect and common courtesy often turn what could otherwise have been a minor incident into a major, expensive legal battle.

TO WHOM IS ONE LIABLE?

This question is not always as easy to answer as it sounds. The simple answer is one is liable to those who employ you. The general rule is that a duty is only to the person with whom contracted, your client.

But one may also be liable to others as well.[11] For example, an insurance agent may have created an agency relationship with the purchaser of a life insurance policy. This would make him or her the agent of the insurance company for some purposes and agent of the client for others.

An advisor is not liable — even for an act of negligence — to someone to whom he owes no duty.[12] The legal term is "privity." But the defense that there is no privity, no duty to an injured party, can easily be forfeited and is currently being eroded in the courts.[13] For instance, if you advise the president of a family-owned corporation improperly about the appropriateness of a stock redemption plan and one is established because of reliance on your advice, unexpected dividend taxes upon the purchase by the corporation of its stock could be claimed by another family member shareholder.

This six-pronged test may be used to determine privity[14]:

1. To what extent is the transaction intended to benefit the third person?

2. Can harm to that third person be foreseen?

3. How likely is it that the third person will suffer real injury?

4. How close is the connection between the advisor's conduct and the injury that the third party could suffer?

5. How "morally wrong" is the advisor's action?

6. Would future harm to this or some other client be served by finding privity here?

At least one state will grant "standing" (the right to sue) to a narrow class of third party beneficiaries where it is clear that the client intended to benefit that party and the client is unable to enforce the contract.[15] Generally, for a third party to collect, written evidence must show that the client's intent was frustrated and the beneficiary's loss was a direct result of the planner's negligence.

WHAT CAN GET THE ADVISOR INTO TROUBLE?

IF ONE SAYS HE KNOWS, HE'D BETTER. Estate planning is too complex to be a sideline. Failure to exercise reasonable care and skill in performing duties for a person induced to rely on an advisor because of his professed skills, knowledge, or experience ("John Jones, Estate Planner") can result in liability for loss incurred.[16] Failure to exercise the degree of expertise which one professes to possess coupled with inducing reliance on that assertion to achieve a sale or sell a service creates a duty to act properly.[17] If one holds himself out as an expert and directly or indirectly promises to provide a product or service to serve a specific purpose or accomplish a particular objective, he assumes the liability for the achievement of that purpose or objective.[18] The skill, knowledge, diligence, and care used must equal or exceed that standard ordinarily exercised by others in the same profession.[19] In short, if one calls himself a professional (or by action or inaction allow others to rely on him as such), he must assume the responsibilities and duties generally associated with such a status — or be held liable for the client's loss.

NOT KNOWING WHO THE CLIENT IS. Interview both spouses (separately if appropriate). If there is marital discord or if this is a second marriage, consider recommending separate counsel. If "the couple" is perceived as the client, both should be treated accordingly. Do not talk down to or ignore the younger, or female, or less wealthy spouse — or to some other member of the family. Develop and maintain good relationships with all the members of the client's family to the extent appropriate.

There are many cases where the planner never or seldom meets the client. For instance, assume a will was prepared for a husband and wife on the instructions of the husband. If the planner never met the wife, how can it be argued that she has been properly represented by counsel or that she understood what she signed? The situation is a "lack of informed consent" case in the making.

When a spouse chooses not to read documentation or does not want to listen to complicated tax law, that same problem exists even though caused by his or her own inaction. The solution is to commit both parties — in the engagement letter — to read documents prepared for them within a specified time and to encourage them to seek independent counsel of their choice should either feel that is appropriate.

IF ONE SAYS HE WILL, HE'D BETTER. An advisor should never create false expectations by making promises he has no intention of keeping or by promising results he does not know he can deliver. He may be held liable to the beneficiaries of an estate if he promises to keep them informed of significant developments and then does not.[20] He has an obligation to substantially finish the task he has begun for a client, decline the appointment, or with the client's consent, accept the employment and associate a lawyer who is competent. He must also prepare adequately for, and give appropriate attention to, the work he has accepted.

OVERNIGHT EXPRESS. Clients often want insurance issued and wills drawn almost overnight — at the very time when they are about to leave on an extended vacation or business trip. This means there is insufficient time to collect, analyze, and act upon complete asset information. Death bed planning is more of the same only worse. One should refuse to be rushed (but be prepared to work quickly).

HOW DOES ONE STAY OUT OF TROUBLE?

HIRING — AND FIRING — THE CLIENT. The advisor should ask why the client has chosen him. It is flattering to think that one has been selected because of one's expertise or reputation, but the reason may be because another practitioner decided not to represent the client. One should obtain as much information about the client's background with other professionals as possible before agreeing to work with the client. The first interview should be considered a primary opportunity to screen and qualify the client. Perhaps the potential client should be discarded if he seems to be a perfectionist, unrealistic, hurried, angry, overly optimistic, overly fee-conscious, or if he wants services one is not positive he can provide cost effectively.[21] One should beware of clients who are wealthy but in constant cash flow difficulty, seem immature, refuse to

accept responsibility for their own actions, or appear constantly ambivalent.[22] These personality types are likely to present a future litigation problem.

Trust your instincts. One should turn down a client who requests something that is not quite right. If a client has outgrown the advisor's capacity, he should either recommend another firm or bring a specialist in to work with the client. If the advisor feels the client cannot be trusted, he should refuse to work with the client.

RISK TAKING PROPENSITY. One of the biggest causes of claims is that the professional misjudges or never considers or does not reevaluate the risk taking propensity of the client and the client's beneficiaries as their circumstances change. The solution is constant communication.

EXPERTISE BOUNDARIES. The advisor should do only those things he is competent (and licensed) to do — and do those things competently. Should a life insurance agent review a will or trust? Should an attorney or accountant judge the adequacy or appropriateness of a client's life insurance portfolio? Should a trust company review documents? Should a financial planner serve as trustee?[23]

Document examination exposure is real. Should one disclaim any liability for review of document viability or efficacy? Incompetent, inconsistent, and informal review is a formula for disaster. If the task is undertaken, it should be done by a person with the appropriate training, expertise, and time to do the job competently and enthusiastically. "You assume an obligation to your client to undertake reasonable research in an effort to ascertain relevant legal principals and to make an informed decision as to a course of action based on an intelligent assessment of the problem."[24]

Furthermore, the estate planner has a duty to either avoid involving a client in "murky" areas of the law if there are viable alternative tools or techniques that are available or to inform the client of the risks and let the client make the decision.[25]

Lack of specialized investment knowledge on the part of the planner or fiduciary often results in investment problems. Numerous trust funds are managed by individuals who adopt a passive and simplistic approach. The need for professional investment management and the complexity of modern portfolio theory is ignored or overlooked and too little time is spent in making investment decisions or addressing overall investment policy and asset allocation.[26]

RESOURCE LIMITS. The advisor should not accept engagements that will require resources beyond what he can cost effectively deliver. For example, if his operation does not have the backup personnel to properly service a high number of clients, he should not agree to do estate conservation for a firm's top 100 executives.

OUTSIDE EXPERTS. An advisor should seek help before it is needed. When appropriate, he should recommend that another professional be used, either in his place or together with him. If the advisor makes a specific recommendation, he may be held liable for the actions of that professional. One way to protect himself is by giving out the names of at least three qualified professionals (make sure the criteria for "qualified" extends beyond mere reputation), or stay involved with the representation.

THE "ENGAGEMENT LETTER"

The engagement letter is the first and primary step in insulating oneself from a successful malpractice suit. An engagement letter should be obtained in every client relationship at the first possible time. The letter spells out the extent and limits of the services to be performed. The following are critical elements of such a letter:

Scope of services and description of work product;

Period of time covered;

Responsibilities undertaken;

Responsibilities the client is expected to assume;

Fee arrangements — amount, terms, and frequency of billing;

Arrangements for update and extension of service;

List of parties represented — and exclusion of those not represented;

Intended use and potential distribution (or restriction) of the advisor's work product[27]; and

Client's acceptance signature and date.

PUT IT (ALL) IN WRITING

Protecting one's self means meticulous record keeping starting at the onset of the relationship. Changes in risk taking propensity or attitude of the client or his family, comments at meetings, phone conversations, and other special instructions should be noted. The advisor's files should clearly reflect and support his recollection of events and should be dictated and transcribed as soon as possible after the occurrence (or preferably contemporaneous with the events). The more complete and organized the files, the more likely the judge, jury, or board of arbitrators will consider the advisor's word persuasive (assuming, of course, the files corroborate what he is now saying).

Whenever possible, quote the client's exact words.[28] This is particularly important whenever a client — or one of his other advisors — decides to pursue an aggressive tax policy or take an investment risk (and doubly important if one has advised against that course of action). For instance, if an attorney tells a client that the business does not need all of the life insurance the agent is suggesting, the agent should attempt to take down as accurately as possible the exact words of the attorney. The attorney should do the same.

Contemporaneous and near verbatim notes should also be taken if the client asks that the advisor not do a service (or anything) he would normally do or if the client asks him to attempt a service that he ordinarily would not do. For instance, if the client asks a trust officer not to review a will and trust that the bank will be handling, the trust officer should memorialize the request (and probably treat the request with suspicion).

Detailed notes are particularly important if the client seems uncooperative or unwilling to provide the information or documents (or access to personally interview a family member) that are necessary to do the job properly.

FEES. Fees should not be set at levels that will require cutting corners or operating at a loss for this engagement. The fee must be large enough to justify internally the time that should be invested in a case — or the case should be turned down. Fees should include the costs that will be incurred to meet high ethical standards and avoid malpractice by implementation of systematic quality control and other appropriate courses of action.

A fee dispute which results in litigation with a client may trigger a malpractice case. The solution is to secure a written agreement as to fees and billing procedures at the onset of the relationship with the client. One should think carefully about the wisdom of suing the client and the likelihood and expense of a malpractice lawsuit by the client. It is wise to communicate the basis or rate of fee or other method of compensation to a new client in writing before or as soon as possible after the relationship begins. The client should be billed periodically and provided detailed information of the services rendered and the time invested.

DATA FORMS. Many times the error or omission of the estate planner is due to an incomplete or incorrect understanding of the facts. The advisor should obtain comprehensive and accurate data by developing a data gathering system. Some planners feel they can gather data without forms or checklists but inevitably forget to ask questions such as, "Are both you and your spouse U.S. citizens?" or "Have you named yourself the custodian of a Uniform Transfers To Minors Account for gifts you made to your children?" One must be sure to confirm with the client the facts gathered — before acting upon them.

The advisor should verify property ownership and dispositive arrangements from the documents themselves. It is astounding how often otherwise competent attorneys draft wills and trusts that do not match the way property is owned. The forms should match the facts. It is necessary to check wills, divorce agreements, retirement and employee benefit brochures rather than rely on the client's memory. Current life insurance policy information should be confirmed by writing to the insurer.

LIMITS OF THE RELATIONSHIP

The client's instructions must be followed — correctly. This entails first truly understanding what those instructions are. Then it requires a written memorandum (preferably signed by the client). Meticulous records of all conversations should be made. If investments are or will be involved in the relationship, an investment policy should document agreed-upon investment objectives, risk parameters, return targets, volatility tolerance, and asset allocation ranges.

A written consent should be obtained for actions outside the scope of the relationship as contained in the engagement letter.

RECORDS AND SYSTEMS

THE RIGHT STUFF. The advisor should keep research documents that indicate decisions were made in a methodical and logical manner and that a deliberate investigation preceded and supported each suggestion. Documents which illustrate the tax law as it existed at the time tax decisions were made should be retained.[29] Memos to the file, prepared contemporaneously with conversations with a client and decision making, are highly useful in establishing the background and intent at the time an action was taken. Controversial decisions should be made only with the informed knowledge and written consent of the client. Any oral advice should also be documented immediately.

The advisor needs to develop and use a presentation system that will prove that regular discussions covering all of the important areas of estate planning with a client took place.[30] A checklist should be incorporated into that system in order to demonstrate that these issues have been discussed with the client and reflect the client's circumstances and objectives.

A retrieval system should be established to locate documents or plans that need updating for specific changes. For example, all estate planning clients should have been contacted to review wills and trusts drawn prior to September 13, 1981 because of the change to the unlimited marital deduction. Yet each year dozens of cases and rulings occur because the documents were never updated. Were the clients ever informed by their advisors of the need for a document review?

TRIGGER SYSTEM. A checklist of follow-up procedures should be developed so time-sensitive responsibilities will be met by the appropriate parties and unreasonable delays in the preparation and implementation of the plan can be avoided. Set deadlines, establish priorities, and specify responsibilities. Create a "tickler file (docketing system) to meet all deadlines, statutes of limitations, and filing and payment deadlines. Set up a centralized system to personally remind the party responsible for action and review at given times or events. Incorporate into the system a series of client reminders (e.g., "It's been three years since your will was reviewed..." or "Major new tax law changes suggest we should review your estate plan as soon as possible.).

QUALITY CONTROL

An advisor is responsible for the errors or omissions of his partners, associates, and employees. Quality control is therefore not a luxury. It is a business necessity.

UNDERSTANDING OF ETHICAL ISSUES. According to a recent article on malpractice written by a Commissioner of the Texas Board of Legal Specialization, almost half the candidates who sat for the certification in Texas in Estate Planning and Probate Law demonstrated "a profound lack of knowledge of ethical problems which often lead to professional liability claims."[31] One should discuss with colleagues the danger when a breach of ethics is coupled with an angry or disgruntled client or family member.

WHO IS THE QUARTERBACK? In any operation larger than a one-person firm it is essential that the activities of the entire staff are co-ordinated by a "quarterback" who accepts responsibility. This person must be sure that all staff members are kept informed and that there is a logical and automatic flow of necessary information, that no tasks have been overlooked, and that no efforts are duplicated. He must also be sure that information received by staff members is properly recorded and relayed to him and to the central file on each client. For instance, consider the law suit potential if the beneficiary of an estate dies within nine months of the original decedent and the same trust company serves as executor of both estates. If significant taxes could be saved by a timely disclaimer but two separate individuals are assigned to the two estates and they do not communicate with each other, the lost opportunity when the timely disclaimer period expires could turn into a lawsuit.

There should also be a quarterback for the estate planning team. All members of that team are negligent if they do not come to an agreement as to who is to do what and when each task is to be done. Liability occurs when essential tasks fall through the cracks.

INDEPENDENT REVIEW. An effective method of quality control is to have final products be reviewed by a well qualified associate before it is shared with a client.

REVIEW OF STAFF COMPETENCE, EXPERIENCE, QUALIFICATION. Estate planning, almost by definition, requires the input of many professionals. Most planners not only must cooperate with other planners outside their offices but must also rely on paralegal and associates within their offices. Few full blown estate plans contain no issues other than federal or estate death taxes and quite often the planner seeks advice from others on his staff. Staff members must be currently competent, and they must be well trained in and conform to standardized office procedures, policies, and proper file management techniques. Appropriate supervision for all levels of staff should be built in. Continuing education should be part of any firm's ongoing business plan.

EXTERNAL COMMUNICATIONS

Almost every authority who speaks and every article that is written on malpractice states that many lawsuits could probably have been avoided by a simple solution: "Communicate, Communicate, Communicate!"[32]

Many, or even most, of the grievance complaints and malpractice actions can be headed off if the advisor will:

MAKE IT CLEAR AND MAKE IT OFTEN. The estate planner should avoid technical jargon. He should not assume lay persons understand what he means by such terms as "a marital trust," a "durable power of attorney," or "a unified credit." He can use word pictures, graphs, flow charts, or diagrams to illustrate his points — and give the clients copies to take home.[33]

He should continually inform clients of all actions he and his staff have taken (or not taken); forward to clients copies of documents sent to other professionals; provide the client with periodic written reports even if a particular report merely explains why no progress has been made since the last report; and confirm in writing all transactions, expenses, fees, income, or other events of importance.

He should inform the client of any changes in the relationship or responsibilities of the parties; make sure reports are understandable; and use graphs, charts, and checklists to show the progress he has made.

He should confirm through a series of scheduled meetings among the client and other advisors objectives, responsibilities, and timetables (see the Action Matrix at the conclusion of this article).

A newsletter is a good way to keep in touch with clients on a regular basis.

The advisor should schedule regular reviews and give special emphasis to contacting clients from whom he has not heard or had contact with in a given period of time; and document his attempt to contact those who do not respond.

He should keep copies of all correspondence and conversations with other members of the estate planning team who are working with the client.

He should study the client's verbal and body language to be sure he is understood and encourage the client to call or write to him after the meeting to ask questions if "he has not made himself understood."

AVOID CASUAL OR INFORMAL ADVICE. The advisor should not give advice at cocktail parties or other social events.[34] Liability can be imposed even though you have not charged a fee for your services if a client relies on information you have provided.

CALLING BACK — PROMPTLY. A careful advisor will return telephone calls promptly. If this is impossible, his secretary or an associate should do so for him so the client does not feel ignored.

AVOIDING "HEEL COOLING." A planner should not keep clients waiting on the phone or in his office. He should be sure he receives messages promptly — and accurately. He should not allow a phone call to interrupt a meeting with a client. It is a good idea to reward staff members for being extra polite. In short, give the client respect and common courtesy.

AVOIDING (OR NEUTRALIZING) PROBLEMS

CONFLICTS WITH EXISTING CLIENTS.[35] The duty of loyalty requires any estate planner to be extremely cautious about serving a client in more than one capacity. For instance, the client of an attorney or CPA may want that person to serve as an executor or trustee — while at the same time desiring that person to continue to provide planning advice and other services to various family members. Can the advice be disinterested and objective? Can the professional ethically charge fees for both services? Can those fees honestly be set at "arms' length"?

Corporate fiduciaries are particularly susceptible. For instance, could the banking side of an institution, as a lender, acquire and share non-public information about a borrower company with the trust department which, as an investor for its trust accounts, is considering making investments in the same company?[36] (Use of non-public information to make investment decisions might subject a corporate fiduciary to a violation of the SEC's Rule 10b-5.[37])

Although there is no legal prohibition against representing more than one client in a single transaction, estate planners should be particularly alert for situations in which there is an obvious or potential difference in their interests. For instance, in establishing a buy-sell agreement, a stock redemption plan may favor younger shareholders with lower percentages of ownership at the expense of older shareholders who own a larger percentage of the company's stock. Likewise, a defined benefit plan typically favors older, long service employees while profit-sharing and defined contribution pension plans usually are to the benefit of younger employees.

Another conflict of interest problem that often occurs where more than one person is represented is the disclosure of confidential information. Can an estate planner freely tell a wife what her husband has disclosed? Can a planner share information from one shareholder with others? The planner needs to inform all parties that information may not be privileged or confidential as to other members of the group unless specific direction is given.

Some conflicts of interest are unavoidable but must be recognized. For instance, consider the family that requests estate planning advice as a unit but who, as individuals, have different needs and desires. What should be done in a marital situation where a husband calls and requests a QTIP trust as opposed to the classic general power of appointment marital trust? What happens when there are children of a prior marriage and the client wants to make lifetime gifts to them? What if a client is ill or infirm in some way and is or becomes dependent on someone else for basic needs? How will the "undue influence issue" be handled? What are the planner's responsibilities and duties when a child, a charitable development officer, or another professional brings the case to him? What if that person also pays his fee?

Any possible conflicts of interest should be disclosed — in writing — to the client as quickly as possible or the planner should withdraw without disclosure if confidential information is involved. Recognition of disclosure and acceptance of its consequent risks should be acknowledged in any instrument signed by the client.

The planner should avoid or treat extremely carefully any financial involvement in a client's business or in a business venture.

CONFLICTS WITH FUTURE CLIENTS. Will acceptance of this client create a conflict for more desirable work with another client in the future?[38]

RED FLAG PROCEDURES. It is important for the planner to train himself and his staff to recognize "red flags." A procedure for identifying problems and quickly dealing with them is essential.

DEALING WITH PROBLEMS. The planner must routinely review and deal with problems promptly. If a problem occurs, he must call or write the client immediately and explain the problem and the potential consequences and alternatives. If a client is angry or dissatisfied, he ought to take immediate action — talk to the client and resolve the problem. He cannot safely assume the problem will go away or that the client will forget it.

THE PROBLEM TEAM. A good idea is to create a "Problem Team" in the firm which meets immediately every time the potential for a dissatisfied client is recognized. That team should not only review the file in the case in point but also any other procedures, activities, omissions, or oversights which may trigger future problems that could develop into litigation.

EARLY ACTIVE REMEDIAL CONCILIATORY EFFORTS. The quicker an attempt is made to resolve the problem to the client's satisfaction, the less likely there will be litigation. Providing a large apology might avoid writing a small check. Writing a small check might avoid defending a large lawsuit. One litigation attorney put it this way: "The good will that can be generated by such an act and accompanying attitudes might be much cheaper and better in the long run than paying expensive attorneys for years of litigation with an uncertain outcome."[39] Sometimes, assigning a new person to speak to the client will serve to quell the objection.

ABOUT YOUR MALPRACTICE INSURANCE

SUFFICIENT LEVELS OF COVERAGE. The first step in evaluating your current insurance is to see if you have enough insurance to cover any likely risk. But this is only a first step.

"CLAIMS MADE" POLICIES. Most malpractice coverage is sold on a "claims made" basis. This means the policy only covers claims which are first asserted and reported to the insurer within the policy year.

"PRIOR ACTS" COVERAGE. The cause of action alleging estate planning malpractice typically does not occur until years after the estate planning documents are signed. If the policy has a "prior acts" coverage, it covers a claim asserted during a policy year in which the negligence giving rise to the claim occurred in some prior year.[40] If a policy lacks or excludes prior acts or limits prior acts coverage, it is likely that there will be a "coverage gap." There will be no coverage under the policy in effect when the alleged negligence occurred because the claim was not made in that policy year. The current policy will not cover the alleged negligence because negligence alleged to have occurred before the present policy year is excluded or omitted from the coverage.

THE "TAIL." A tail is an extended reporting option somewhat related to prior acts coverage. If one purchases a tail, he is permitted (usually at the end of each policy year or earlier if the policy is canceled during the term) to convert "claims made" coverage to "occurrence" coverage for any negligence allegedly committed — but not yet reported — up to the end of that policy year. The extended reporting of claims option available through a tail is expensive. The premium is a multiple of the regular annual premium. Tails should be considered by retiring planners who will no longer keep their full malpractice coverage in force or by attorneys who are forced to switch malpractice insurance carriers because of a cancellation or a refusal of a carrier to renew coverage (typically due to claims made) if the new carrier refuses to provide prior acts coverage. Tails are "cut off" after some period of time unless the tail is unlimited. Under an unlimited tail, the insurer remains liable for negligence occurring before the policy period expires regardless of when the claim is asserted.

THE DEDUCTIBLE. Most estate planners opt for a higher deductible in order to reduce the premium outlay. But one should check to see if the legal costs he would incur in a malpractice suit apply against his share of the deductible. Does the deductible apply "per claim" or "per policy year"? Where there is more than one claim in a given policy year, a per claim deductible becomes a hidden cost: a second deductible must be satisfied in the event of a second claim within a

year. A per year deductible means the deductible amount need be paid only once in a given year regardless of the number of claims. Because when it rains, it pours, a per claim provision might prove quite costly.

SETTLEMENT. Some policies give the insurer the right to limit its exposure through a provision entitled, "Settlement." This means the insurer can force a settlement with the plaintiff (regardless of the insured's wishes) because of the cost. Some settlement provisions state that if one does not wish to settle under specified terms, the insurer will limit its payment to the amount specified in a settlement agreement at which point all other exposure (including defense cost) becomes the insured's obligation. Why might an insured not want to settle — even though economically it might make sense? The psychological cost of admitting wrongdoing or malpractice — coupled with the loss in reputation — are strong reasons why he may want to maintain the right to say, "NO" to a settlement. One should be sure that right does not expose him to a loss of coverage above the limits in the proposed settlement.

DUTY TO DEFEND vs DUTY TO INDEMNIFY. A "duty to defend" policy requires the insurer to appoint defense counsel and pay that attorney's fees as billed. An "indemnification" policy allows the insured to select counsel but he must fund his defense unless he can reach an interim fee agreement.[41] The insured will not be reimbursed for defense costs until the case is concluded. Obviously, interim funding can be a problem.

DEFINITION OF "DAMAGES." The way covered damages is defined is crucial. One may be exposed to fines, penalties, punitive, or even treble, damages. Check with the insurance agent to clarify how broadly or narrowly the policy construes the term "damages."

INNOCENT PARTNER COVERAGE. Does the policy provide coverage for the defalcations of another member of the firm? One is liable for his partner's embezzlement even if he has not benefited by it. The insurer will deny a claim based on your partner's fraud and/or criminal activity unless there is "innocent partner" coverage.

OTHER KEY PROVISIONS. A malpractice policy ideally will provide coverage for the defense costs if it is claimed the insured is guilty of intentional conduct (even though the policy does not indemnify the costs of the intentional conduct). Does the policy cover libel or slander or defense of RICO claims?

INSURER'S STABILITY. It is important to check the financial stability of the insurer and to be sure the insurer has a solid reputation for integrity and responsiveness. It is worth finding out if the insurer itself has been involved in litigation with its own insureds. The lowest premium will not compensate you for the aggravation and other costs of suing the carrier to get it to defend properly a malpractice case.

HANDLING A CLAIM. A detailed discussion of malpractice claims procedures is beyond the scope of this article. However, the following steps will help in the defense of a malpractice suit:

1. Notify the insurer immediately no matter how small the suit is.

2. Once the insured has been notified formally that he is being sued, say as little as necessary to the suing client.

3. Secure all work product immediately.

4. Inform the entire staff of the problem and the action game plan.

5. Do whatever is necessary to assist in the defense of the case.

THE TOTAL COST

The frequency of malpractice actions in the 1990s can be expected to increase many times what it was in the 1980s. No profession in the estate planning team will escape unscathed. There are no conclusive signs of this trend reversing.[42]

DIRECT COSTS. Malpractice premiums are in the highest classification — along with corporate securities work — for a very good reason. The dollars at risk are big.

LOSS OF REPUTATION. The cost of a malpractice suit cannot be measured merely in terms of the court judgment or out-of-court settlement or the cost of attorneys. The cost to a professional's reputation (win or loose) may be staggering. For instance, it would be difficult to attract new partners or new associates if one has been successfully sued for malpractice.

LOSS OF STANDING WITH PEERS. Estate planning is a process based partially on knowledge and largely on trust. A malpractice suit calls into question competence which in turn destroys confidence, not only of current and potentially future clients but also the confidence of other members of the planning team with whom one must deal.

THE PSYCHOLOGICAL TRAUMA. An estate planner who becomes a defendant in a lawsuit must deal with the incredible pressure and emotional trauma of being sued.[43] Often, the planner (and perhaps office associates, partners, and friends) will see the action taken by the client as an attack on his professional ability, integrity, or judgment. This cannot help the practitioner's morale and will probably result in adverse fallout on other projects. This psychological strain is compounded by time; the legal process is typically long and drawn out over a period of years even if the claim is unfounded.

HIDDEN ECONOMIC COSTS. Colleagues from whom the practitioner received referrals and the general public may hear about the lawsuit. This will cause almost certain financial damage. The planner is required to participate in his own defense whether or not he is adequately insured. This, in turn, translates into dozens or sometimes hundreds of unbillable hours gathering facts and records and recreating the facts, giving depositions, briefing defense attorneys, and testifying at trial.

CUT AND RUN? If it appears a matter cannot be resolved by the procedures discussed above, consider "discharging the client." Obviously, this is a last resort but it should not be overlooked in a "heads they win — tails we lose situation."

SUMMARY

Creating and maintaining a successful estate planning practice requires a methodical systematic approach to risk management. Planners are vulnerable to litigation no matter how careful they are. But the risk of a claim and the potential for a successful claim can be substantially reduced through continuing a vigorous and systematized policy of internal and external positive communication, common sense courtesy, quality control, and a strong emphasis on high quality continuing education of every member of the firm.

A planner should check that he has:

• Established and improved client relationships.

• Controlled the management of client relationships.

• Improved office practices.

• Identified problem areas.

• Corrected problems before they occur.

Looking at everything in this discussion positively, the "action suggestions" described here can also be thought of not only as defensive but as the blueprint for a vigorous office organizing and client market building campaign.

FOOTNOTES

1. Attorney Jack Olendar of Washington, D.C. quoted in "Avoiding Malpractice Suits: Some Sound Advice," *Trusts and Estates*, April 1990, p. 18. Another good rule of thumb mentioned in this same well-written article is that "we have a true and grievous malpractice claim" where the facts and results would "surprise and dismay the average trust and estate lawyer."

2. Legal malpractice consists of three elements: (1) a duty, (2) a breach of duty, and (3) resulting damages.

3. "How Estate Planners Can Cope With The Increasing Risk of Malpractice Claims," *Estate Planning*, May 1985.

4. See "Avoiding Malpractice Suits: Some Sound Advice," *Trusts and Estates*, April 1990, p. 12.

5. This is called the "best judgment" or "good faith" defense.

6. "Corporate Fiduciaries Face Special Liability Problems," *Trusts and Estates*, December 1988, p. 29.

7. *Killey Trust*, 457 Pa. 474 (1974). Large corporate planners such as banks and trust companies will likely be held to a higher level of competence than others because of their access to information and expertise.

   On the other hand, the sophistication, education, and expertise of the client is not a defense. See *Blankenheim v. E.F. Hutton and Co. Inc.*, HOO4920 (Calif. Ct. App. 2/15/90), which held that the relationship between a stockbroker and his customer is fiduciary in nature, imposing on the former the duty to act in the highest good faith toward his customer. The court held that the plaintiff's concession that they were experts in the accounting and taxation area and any experience the plaintiff may have acquired following his investment was irrelevant to reliance on the broker's representations at the time of the sale.

8. Consider, for example, that the estate planner must consider the provisions of federal (and perhaps state) securities laws if the client holds more than 10 percent of a covered class of equity securities. Did you know that a malpractice claim might be converted into an unfair trade practice claim in order to gain the advantage of a longer statute of limitations? In one case the attorney drafted a trust that failed to qualify for the marital deduction. This action was barred by a 3 year statute of limitations. So the plaintiff also sued for a violation of the state's Unfair Trade Practice Act which had a much longer statute of limitations and allowed a suit by "any person who purchases or leases goods, services, or property." The estate successfully alleged that the draftsman had engaged in an unfair and deceptive act and practice by holding himself out as an attorney reasonably skilled in the preparation and drafting of last wills and testaments and in his ability to comply with the decedent's wishes and to minimize the tax obligations of her estate.

9. "Protecting the Corporate Fiduciary's Tender Backside," *Trusts and Estates*, February 1988, p. 63.

10. Adjectives which might characterize "institutional arrogance" include unreasonable, unknowledgeable, intransigent, implacable, belligerent, and rude.

11. See "Court Decisions Reinforce the Idea That An Insurance Agent Who Holds Himself Out To Have Great Expertise Will Be Bound To the Exercise of it," *Trusts and Estates*, October 1988, p. 55.

12. See *Bell v. Manning*, 613 S. W.2d 335.

13. *Lucas v. Hamm*, 15 Cal. Rptr. 821 (1961).

14. The California Supreme Court used this test in *Biakanja v. Irving*, 320 P.2d 16 (1958).

    Although there is a trend toward relaxing the requirement of privity, New York and Texas are staunch supporters of the rule. See *Victor v. Goldman*, 344 N.Y.S.2d 672 (1973) and *Dickey v. Jansen*, 731 S.W.2d 581 (1987).

15. Pennsylvania Supreme Court in *Guy v. Liederbach*, 459 A.2d 744 (1983).

16. See *Bogley v. Middletown Tavern, Inc.*, 421 A.2d 444 (1984). Of course, the knee jerk defense is, "The insurance was purchased in an arms' length transaction involving no confidential or fiduciary relationship between the insured and the agent." This tact might work if the agent never professed to be anything other than a salesperson. See *Lazovick v. Sun Life Ins. Co. of America*, 586 F. Supp. 918 (E.D. Pa. 1984).

17. See *Anderson v. Knox*, 297 F.2d 702 (9th Cir. 1961), cert. den., 370 U.S. 915 (1962); *Gediman v. Anheuser Busch, Inc.*, 299 F.2d 537 (2d Cir. 1962).

18. See *Wright Body Works v. Columbus Interstate Insurance*, 210 S.E. 2d 801 (1974).

19. *State Farm Life v. Fort Wayne National Bank*, 474 N.E. 2d 524 (Ind 1985).

20. *Morales v. Field, DeGoff, Huppert and MacGown*, 99 Cal. Appl 3d 307.

21. See "Does This Prospect Mean Trouble?," *Practical Financial Planning*, October/November 1988, p. 23.

22. See "Reducing the Risk of Estate Planning Malpractice," BNA, *Tax Management Estates, Gifts, and Trusts Journal*, March/April 1984, p. 36.

23. See "How Not To Be A Trustee," *Financial Planning*, May 1990, p. 69.

24. *Horne v. Peckham*, 97 Cal. App. 3d 404 (1979).

25. Where there is reasonable doubt among well informed practitioners, there should be no liability. But this assumes a diligent quest for answers was made. Failure to research an issue or fully understand the facts will result in a denial of the "unsettled law" defense. See *Martin v. Burns*, 429 P.2d 660 (1967).

26. See "Steps To Protect The Fiduciary From Liability For Investment Decisions," *Estate Planning*, July/August, 1989, p. 228.

27. In "Taming The Liability Monster," *L&H Perspective*, V. 15, No. 1/ 1989, p. 38, the author states that "A nightmare for the professional is reliance by unknown third parties on their work product." Where might this nightmare be more real than in estate planning where a great deal of it is done specifically for others? (Of course, it is the planner's responsibility to know who those third party beneficiaries are and what circumstances and needs and desires they may have).

28. As one attorney was interviewing a couple, he would pause from time to time to "capsulize" their thoughts into a dictaphone. Before he did, he would remind them each time, "Be sure to stop me if this isn't exactly what you want or if I've misunderstood what you've just said."

29. You may have to prove that, at the time you were making the decision, the available information was much different than it is at the time litigation occurs. See "How To Manage A Growing Tax Practice," *The Practical Accountant*, May 1990, p. 27.

30. See "Avoiding and Handling Malpractice Claims Against Estate Planners," *Estate Planning*, September/October 1989, p. 267.

31. See "Avoiding Malpractice Suits: Some Sound Advice," *Trusts and Estates*, April 1990, p. 12.

32. See "Coping With Administrative Problems: There's More To Life and Death Than Taxes," 21 *U. of Miami Institute on Estate Planning*, Chapter 17 (1987).

33. Some attorneys use commercially written brochures to make their points or to give clients something to take home that will help them understand more complex concepts. A number of highly useful client- oriented brochures are available from Financial Data Corporation, P.O. Box 1332, Bryn Mawr, Pa. 19010 (610-525-6957).

34. See *Newton Estate*, TC Memo 1990-208, for an example of the damage a well intended but offhand remark can do. The executor's reliance on the statement of an attorney as to the filing deadline did not constitute reasonable cause for the filing delay where the attorney admittedly had not been retained to render advice on federal estate tax matters, was not paid any fee for the advice, did not normally practice in that area of the law, and had advised the executor to verify any information with a tax practitioner. The "offhand remark" may not result in a malpractice case for this attorney — but it certainly would not result in a love affair with the client either.

35. Consider an index which includes data on clients and other parties to transactions with which the firm is involved. Include a procedure through which the system automatically updates the files to add the names of new family members, business associates, or others related to the client.

36. "Corporate Fiduciaries Face Special Liability Problems," *Trusts and Estates*, December 1988, p. 29.

37. The classic solution is a corporate policy which restricts or limits the information flow between the banking and the trust departments.

38. Obtain a "Waiver of Conflict" letter with respect to one time consulting arrangements. Obtain advance written consent to future simultaneous adverse representation on any matter not substantially related to the matter undertaken for a new client.

39. "Protecting the Corporate Fiduciary's Tender Backside," *Trusts and Estates*, February 1988, p. 72.

40. See "About Your Malpractice," *Lawyer's Digest*, May 1988, p. 11.

41. "How the Accountant/Financial Planner Can Reduce Exposure to Liability Claims," *The Practical Accountant*, February 1990, p. 15.

42. See "Taming the Liability Monster," *L&H Perspective*, Vol. 15/No. 1, 1989, p. 37.

43. See "Strategies to Avoid Malpractice," *Practical Financial Planning*, April/May 1989, p. 29.

Figure E1.1

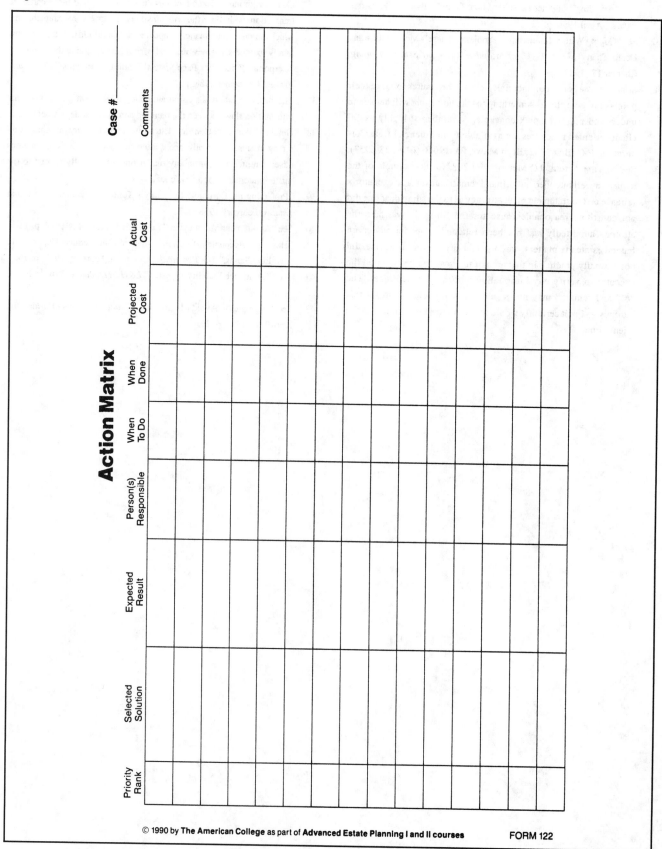

Action Matrix

Case # _____

Priority Rank	Selected Solution	Expected Result	Person(s) Responsible	When To Do	When Done	Projected Cost	Actual Cost	Comments

INDEX

The Tools and Techniques of Estate Planning

G

The Tools and Techniques of Estate Planning

The Tools and Techniques of Estate Planning

The Tools and Techniques of Estate Planning

Complete Your
LEIMBERG
TOOLS & TECHNIQUES
LIBRARY

this handy postage-paid form to order addi-
al copies of *The Tools & Techniques of Estate*
nning or copies of

The Tools & Techniques of Employee Benefit
and Retirement Planning – 4th edition
The Tools & Techniques of Financial
Planning – 4th edition
The Tools & Techniques of Life Insurance
Planning

   or call **1-800-543-0874** and ask for
Operator SE, or **FAX: 1-800-874-1916**

PRICES*
The Tools & Techniques
of Estate Planning
Single copy $42.50
5 copies, ea. 40.40
10 copies, ea. 38.25
25 copies, ea. 36.15

The Tools & Techniques
of Employee Benefit & Retirement Planning
Single copy $37.50
5 copies, ea. 35.60
10 copies, ea. 33.75
25 copies, ea. 31.95

The Tools & Techniques
of Financial Planning
Single copy $37.50
5 copies, ea. 35.60
10 copies, ea. 33.75
25 copies, ea. 31.95

The Tools & Techniques
of Life Insurance Planning
Single copy $37.50
5 copies, ea. 35.60
10 copies, ea. 33.75
25 copies, ea. 31.95

SPECIAL PACKAGE PRICES
Order two different titles for $64.00,
three different titles for $93.00,
or all four titles for $120.00.

PAYMENT INFORMATION
Add shipping & handling charges to all orders as follows. If
our order exceeds total amount listed in chart, call 1-800-543-
874 for shipping & handling charge. Any order of 10 or more
ems or over $250.00 will be billed by actual weight, plus a
andling fee. Unconditional 30 day guarantee.

SHIPPING & HANDLING (Additional)	
ORDER TOTAL	SHIPPING & HANDLING
$20.00 - 39.99	$6.00
40.00 - 59.99	7.00
60.00 - 79.99	9.00
80.00 - 109.99	10.00
110.00 - 149.99	12.00

SALES TAX (Additional)
Sales tax is required for residents of the following
states: CA, DC, FL, GA, IL, NJ, NY, OH, PA.

NATIONAL UNDERWRITER

The National Underwriter Co.   2-SE
Customer Service Dept. #2-SE
505 Gest Street, Cincinnati, OH 45203-1716

Please send me the following:
_____ copies of *The Tools & Techniques of Estate Planning* (#285)
_____ copies of *The Tools & Techniques of Employee Benefit and Retirement Planning* (#271)
_____ copies of *The Tools & Techniques of Financial Planning* (#277)
_____ copies of *The Tools & Techniques of Life Insurance Planning* (#270)

❒ Check enclosed*   ❒ Charge My VISA/MC/AmEx (circle one)   ❒ Bill me

Card #_____ Exp. Date _____
Signature_____
Name_____ Title_____
Company_____
Address_____
City_____ State_____ Zip+4_____
Business Phone (_____)_____

*Make check payable to The National Underwriter Company. Please include the appropriate shipping & handling
and any applicable sales tax.   Offer expires 12/31/96*

NATIONAL UNDERWRITER

The National Underwriter Co.   2-SE
Customer Service Dept. #2-SE
505 Gest Street, Cincinnati, OH 45203-1716

Please send me the following:
_____ copies of *The Tools & Techniques of Estate Planning* (#285)
_____ copies of *The Tools & Techniques of Employee Benefit and Retirement Planning* (#271)
_____ copies of *The Tools & Techniques of Financial Planning* (#277)
_____ copies of *The Tools & Techniques of Life Insurance Planning* (#270)

❒ Check enclosed*   ❒ Charge My VISA/MC/AmEx (circle one)   ❒ Bill me

Card #_____ Exp. Date _____
Signature_____
Name_____ Title_____
Company_____
Address_____
City_____ State_____ Zip+4_____
Business Phone (_____)_____

*Make check payable to The National Underwriter Company. Please include the appropriate shipping & handling
and any applicable sales tax.   Offer expires 12/31/96*

NATIONAL UNDERWRITER

The National Underwriter Co.
Customer Service Dept #2-SD
505 Gest Street, Cincinnati, OH 45203-1716

PROOF OF PURCHASE FOR CONTINUING EDUCATION
The Tools & Techniques of Estate Planning
Stephan R. Leimberg, Jerry A. Kasner, Stephen N. Kandell, Ralph
Gano Miller, Morey S. Rosenbloom, Herbert L. Levy.
©1995 The National Underwriter Company

YOU MUST RETURN THIS PROOF OF PURCHASE WITH YOUR COMPLETED CE EXAM.

BUSINESS REPLY MAIL

FIRST CLASS MAIL   PERMIT NO. 68   CINCINNATI, OH

POSTAGE WILL BE PAID BY ADDRESSEE

The National Underwriter Co.
Customer Service Dept. #2-SE
505 Gest Street
Cincinnati, Ohio 45203-9928

BUSINESS REPLY MAIL

FIRST CLASS MAIL   PERMIT NO. 68   CINCINNATI, OH

POSTAGE WILL BE PAID BY ADDRESSEE

The National Underwriter Co.
Customer Service Dept. #2-SE
505 Gest Street
Cincinnati, Ohio 45203-9928